The Heath Anthology of American Literature

Volume E

Contemporary Period:
1945 to the Present

The Heath Anthology of American Literature

Seventh Edition

Volume E
Contemporary Period:
1945 to the Present

Paul Lauter
Trinity College
General Editor

John Alberti
Northern Kentucky University
Editor, Instructor's Guide

Mary Pat Brady
Cornell University

Kirk Curnutt
Troy University

Daniel Heath Justice
University of British Columbia

James Kyung-Jin Lee
University of California, Irvine

Richard Yarborough
University of California, Los Angeles
Associate General Editor

Wendy Martin
Claremont Graduate University

D. Quentin Miller
Suffolk University

Bethany Schneider
Bryn Mawr College

Ivy T. Schweitzer
Dartmouth College

Sandra A. Zagarell
Oberlin College

WADSWORTH
CENGAGE Learning·

Australia · Brazil · Japan · Korea · Mexico · Singapore · Spain · United Kingdom · United States

WADSWORTH
CENGAGE Learning

The Heath Anthology of American Literature, Seventh Edition
Volume E, *Contemporary Period: 1945 to the Present*

Edited by Paul Lauter, Richard Yarborough, John Alberti, Mary Pat Brady, Kirk Curnutt, Daniel Heath Justice, James Kyung-Jin Lee, Wendy Martin, D. Quentin Miller, Bethany Schneider, Ivy T. Schweitzer, and Sandra A. Zagarell

Editor in Chief: Lyn Uhl
Publisher: Michael Rosenberg
Senior Development Editor: Leslie Taggart
Development Editor: Craig Leonard
Assistant Editor: Erin Bosco
Editorial Assistant: Rebecca Donahue
Media Editor: Janine Tangney
Marketing Brand Manager: Lydia LeStar
Content Project Manager: Rosemary Winfield
Art Director: Marissa Falco
Production Technology Analyst: Jeff Joubert
Print Buyer: Betsy Donaghey
Rights Acquisition Specialist: Jessica Elias
Production Service: Tania Andrabi, Cenveo Publisher Services
Text Designer: Shawn Girsberger
Cover Designer: Tani Hasegawa
Cover Image: Ralph Fasanella, *New York City*, 1950. Oil on canvas, 28 × 60 in. American Folk Art Museum, Gift of Ralph and Eva Fasanella, 1995.8.1
Compositor: Cenveo Publisher Services

For product information and technology assistance, contact us at **Cengage Learning Customer & Sales Support, 1-800-354-9706**.

For permission to use material from this text or product, submit all requests online at **www.cengage.com/permissions**.
Further permissions questions can be emailed to **permissionrequest@cengage.com**.

Library of Congress Control Number: 2012916936

ISBN 13: 978-1-133-31026-6
ISBN 10: 1-133-31026-5

Wadsworth
20 Channel Center Street
Boston, MA 02210
USA

Cengage Learning is a leading provider of customized learning solutions with office locations around the globe, including Singapore, the United Kingdom, Australia, Mexico, Brazil and Japan. Locate your local office at **international.cengage.com/region**.

Cengage Learning products are represented in Canada by Nelson Education, Ltd.

For your course and learning solutions, visit **www.cengage.com**.
Purchase any of our products at your local college store or at our preferred online store **www.cengagebrain.com**.

Instructors: Please visit **login.cengage.com** and log in to access instructor-specific resources.

Printed in the United States of America
4 5 6 7 8 9 10 23 22 21 20 19

CONTENTS

THE 1960s: POSTMODERNISM AND OTHER VIOLENT CHANGES   3011

■

IN FOCUS
Aesthetics and Politics of the 1960s and 1970s—Black, Brown, Yellow, Red   3269

■

THE 1970S: DECADE OF DISILLUSIONMENT   3293

THE 1990s: NEW WORLD DISORDER   3758

PREFACE

The *Heath Anthology of American Literature* represents a remarkable success story. It is not the story of a book, a small board of editors, or even a few publishing houses. It is, rather, the story of the thousands of students and faculty who have in the last quarter century transformed the study of American literature.

LITERATURE AS AN INCLUSIVE CULTURAL FORM

When in 1978 we began the Reconstructing American Literature project (from which the anthology developed), the definition of what constituted American literature was very narrow in terms of the authors covered, the forms of writing included, and the ideas of literary study then dominant. Today's students would hardly recognize the anthologies or the syllabi that characterized the work of critics and teachers back in the 1950s or 1960s. That work would appear as odd today as 1900 baseball uniforms or perhaps Victorian hoop skirts—recognizable but remote from our society or culture.

The *Heath Anthology of American Literature* was part of a movement for cultural change. That movement took as its goal conceiving American literature as an inclusive cultural form, a form of creativity that spoke of and to the lives of all Americans and that spoke with many voices and in many different ways. It has always been our intent and practice to represent the writers who traditionally had constituted American literature. It was and remains our goal to be as inclusive as the limits of these five volumes permit.

A DIVERSE COMMUNITY OF SCHOLARS

Because societies and cultures change, our understanding of the meaning of *inclusive* likewise changes. As readers will see, today's seventh edition of the *Heath Anthology* differs in what we think are interesting and useful ways from the first edition of 1980 or even from the more recent sixth edition. We have updated a large number of headnotes as well as introductions. And we have made certain changes in the literary texts contained in the anthology. Many of these changes are specified below.

Most of the ideas for change originated with teachers and students who have used the anthology. The particular character of the *Heath Anthology* has always depended on the participation in the project of a wide community of scholars and teachers. Unlike other anthologies, the *Heath* includes introductory notes that have been written by scholars who specialize in a particular author. In their diverse yet consistent approaches, these headnotes illustrate for students how writing about literature is not limited to any single standard.

More important, perhaps, these contributing editors, together with readers, consultants, and users of the anthology, have provided guidance to our large and diverse editorial board as we determine the changes that will make the anthology most useful. We hope that a new generation of students and teachers will share with us their ideas about what works in the anthology and what does not, what texts and configurations might be changed, and what more we might provide so that they can make the best use of these books.

BROADENING THE "LITERARY"

What is the "best use"? The answers to that question will, of course, vary enormously depending on the students and teachers involved. One could teach a fairly traditional course using *The Heath Anthology of American Literature*, emphasizing only the writers historically considered significant. There are rich selections in these volumes of writers like Edwards, Franklin, Emerson, Hawthorne, Melville, Thoreau, Whitman, Dickinson, James, Twain, and modernists like Eliot, Fitzgerald, Hemingway, Pound, Stevens, Wharton, and the like. But we have from the beginning of this project striven to include many writers who would not have been part of such a traditional course, like Frederick Douglass, Lydia Maria Child, Frances Harper, Sarah Piatt, Charles W. Chesnutt, Mary Wilkins Freeman, Kate Chopin, José Martí, and Randolph Bourne, just to name a few from earlier times. One of the accomplishments that we are most proud of is the transformative impact of the *Heath Anthology* on the American literary canon. The inclusion of a number of important new (that is, underappreciated) authors in the *Heath* has played an important role in catalyzing a wider and deeper awareness of their significance.

Likewise, these books contain abundant selections of fiction, poetry, drama, and also nonfictional prose, polemical and historical essays, songs, chants, speeches, and the like. Another major goal of the *Heath Anthology* has been to broaden our understanding of what constitutes the "literary." On the one hand, we want to provide students with a large selection of well-known texts whose literary power and cultural relevance had been established by generations of critics and teachers—William Bradford's "Of Plymouth Plantation," Benjamin Franklin's *Autobiography*, poetry by Bradstreet and Dickinson, "Young Goodman Brown," "Self-Reliance," "Civil Disobedience," "Annabel Lee," "Daisy Miller," "The Open Boat," *The Awakening, The Waste Land*, "Hills Like White Elephants," "Sonny's Blues," "Howl."

At the same time, we wish to provide exemplary texts that, because of their forms or subjects, have seldom been taught and often little read. Thus, we include, for example, "sorrow songs" or spirituals, nineteenth-century folk songs and stories, *corridos* and blues lyrics, and poems written on the walls of Angel Island prison by Chinese detainees.

Likewise, we include nonfictional forms such as the spiritual autobiographies of Thomas Shepard and Elizabeth Ashbridge, sketches by Fanny Fern, polemical letters by Angelina and Sarah Grimké, columns by Finley Peter Dunne, José Martí's important "Our America," Randolph Bourne's "Trans-National America," Martin Luther King's "I Have a Dream," and chapters from Gloria Anzaldúa's *Borderlands/La Frontera*. The sixth edition extended this goal by incorporating journal entries from several members of the Lewis and Clark expedition, letters protesting Cherokee removal, "proletarian" folk songs, and graphic narratives by Art Spiegelman, Lynda Barry, and others.

The seventh edition widens the lens still further by including a broader span of written texts by Native American authors from all parts of the country, the work of many more Spanish-language writers of all centuries, including those from the period of the Mexican Revolution, Chinese American immigrants such as novelist and future actor H. T. Tsiang, and essays such as Carlos Bulosan's "The Freedom from Want" that dramatize both the allure and the pitfalls of nationalism. A section of Spoken Word poetry now concludes the anthology. It is our hope that teachers and students will be able to take advantage of what remains, by far, the most inclusive and varied anthology in the field.

LONG AND SHORT WORKS

The *Heath Anthology* has also from its beginning balanced longer complete works with shorter texts by the wide variety of authors included. Thus, this edition includes the full texts of Royall Tyler's "The Contrast," Susanna Rowson's play *Slaves in Algiers; or, A Struggle for Freedom*, Melville's "Benito Cereno" and "Billy Budd," Frederick Douglass's *Narrative*, Abraham Cahan's "The Imported Bridegroom," Kate Chopin's *The Awakening*, Nella Larsen's *Passing*, George C. Wolfe's *The Colored Museum*, and Arthur Miller's *A View From the Bridge*, among many other longer works.

HISTORICAL AND SOCIAL CONTEXTS

It has always been our view that literature, like any art form, must in part be studied in relation to the historical and social contexts from which it develops and to which it speaks. We have therefore systematically included in the volumes important historical texts ranging from the Declaration of Independence to decisive court decisions like those that enabled Indian "removal" or imposed and finally helped end racial segregation. These "In Focus" sections can be read for their own interest, since they are vivid documents in and of themselves. But they can also be read to provide contexts to the more traditionally literary texts that constitute the primary content of the anthology. With the *Heath Anthology*'s unusually wide selection, they provide instructors with broadened opportunities to help students perceive continuity and change in the literary and cultural history of what is now the United States.

Likewise, in this electronic age, we have the following electronic resources for both instructors and students:

- **Heath Anthology Premium Website for Volumes A, B, C, D, and E.** This robust Premium Website includes a wide variety of multimedia resources to help bring to life the works and time periods featured in the *Anthology*. The website can be navigated by volume and centers around thirty of the most commonly taught works for each volume. Each is supported by reading comprehension quizzes, interactive media such as audio or video, Web links, and author biographies. In addition, the Premium Website features materials to help provide historical, social, and political context for these works, such as maps and images. A glossary of literary terms is also provided, in both list form and as interactive flashcards. A variety of eBooks are available as an optional add-on to the Premium Website, including *The Scarlet Letter* and *Adventures of Huckleberry Finn*. Access the Premium Website at www.cengagebrain.com.

- **The Heath Blog.** Available as a link from the Instructor Companion Site and from the Premium Website, the Heath Blog is dedicated to providing tools, information, and pedagogical approaches for instructors and students of American literature and culture. It provides virtual space for conversations about what choices we make when we anthologize texts, how these texts are presented and received in the classroom, and how they resonate with contemporary concerns. All users are encouraged to respond to the blog articles with their own commentary and suggestions. Instructors may access the Instructor Companion Site at www.login.cengage.com, and the Premium Website is available for students via www.cengagebrain.com.

- *Online Instructor's Manual.* The *Online Instructor's Manual*, edited by John Alberti, offers suggestions for approaching texts and authors, model assignments, and useful exam and discussion questions. This helpful resource is available on the Instructor Companion Site, which can be accessed at www.login.cengage.com.

- **Instructor Companion Site.** This password-protected website provides access to both the downloadable Online Instructor's Manual and the Heath Blog.

CHANGES IN THE SEVENTH EDITION

The seventh edition includes 176 new works across the five volumes.

WHAT IS NEW IN VOLUME A, BEGINNINGS TO 1800

Changes to Volume A, Beginnings to 1800, are relatively few but draw on the latest scholarship to update translations and headnotes as well as enrich our offerings from Native and Spanish America. As in the other volumes in the seventh edition, we have added a new "In Focus: Northern New York—Mohegan/Brotherton Tribes" section that highlights the region of Northern New York. Included in this section are writers pulled from other places in the sixth edition, such as Handsome Lake, Samson Occom, and Hendrick Aupaumut, complemented by a new excerpt from Joseph Johnson, son-in-law and close associate of Occom, capped by an introductory headnote that discusses the many interrelations among these figures across tribal affiliation and the larger cultural movements they shaped. We have added Corn Tassel to "Native American Political Texts and Oratory" to continue integrating Native American writing and oratory throughout Volume A.

The selections from Gaspar Perez de Villagrá have been expanded and newly translated and form the hub of a group of hemispheric Spanish American writers recounting the exploration and conquest of North and South America, including new entries by Juan de Oñate, Fray Alonso Gregorio de Escobedo on the conquest of Florida, and Felipe Guaman Poma de Ayala on the conquest of Peru. Excerpts from Gaspar de Villagrá and Fray Alonso Gregorio de Escobedo are reprinted in the original Spanish.

Later in the volume, we have included two new selections from the revolutionary literature of Spanish America—a popular broadside by José Álvarez de Toledo and one of the founding documents of Latin American history, Simón Bolívar's "Letter from Jamaica," which now concludes Volume A.

The selections from New Netherland writer Adriaen van der Donck have been updated with a new translation, and we have added the entirety of Susanna Rowson's popular play *Slaves in Algiers* in the place of excerpts from her novel *Charlotte Temple*.

In the critical sections, we have added significant excerpts from Bartolomé de las Casas on the plight of the Indians, Aníbal Quijano and Immanuel Wallerstein on "Americanity," Trish Loughran on eighteenth-century print culture, and a blog post on "Decolonial Aesthetics" that reinforces the salience of colonial literature and coloniality to the present postmodern moment.

WHAT IS NEW IN VOLUME B, EARLY NINETEENTH CENTURY: 1800–1865

Volume B, Early Nineteenth Century: 1800–1865, has a newly restructured section on Native American literature, with new selections that include excerpts from Black Hawk and Mary Jemison, which frame the opening section as an exploration of complex and often misunderstood Native identities. Other Native writers, like William Appess and Jane Johnston Schoolcraft, are interspersed throughout the volume, working against the notion that Native voices precede other voices. A new "In Focus" section dedicated to the Cherokee nation and the literature surrounding Cherokee removal has been added. This enables instructors to focus on a particular Native nation, gaining a nation-specific focus that helps students understand both the Cherokee context in specific, and the larger imperative to encounter Native writing as nationally specific.

The "Cultures of Spanish America" section has been restructured and greatly expanded, with new works in English and in Spanish (with translations provided) by Victoria Moreno, José María Heredia, José María Tornel, and Vicente Pérez Rosales.

Finally, a new section focusing on "The Caribbean in the Antebellum Imagination," with works by Martin Delany, Lucy Holcombe Pickens, and Miguel Tolón, has been added.

WHAT IS NEW IN VOLUME C, LATE NINETEENTH CENTURY: 1865–1910

Thoroughly reconceived, Volume C, Late Nineteenth Century: 1865–1910, reflects even more vividly the extraordinary writing that flourished as the United States became a modern, diverse nation with an international presence. The overarching concept of this volume is that the literature written between 1865 and 1910 was so plentiful and so diverse that no single set of organizational categories does it justice. We have therefore devised several complementary categories to showcase this variety in a comprehensible manner.

Now book-ending the volume are sections on significant literary trends—"Varieties of Postwar Realism: Prose and Poetry" and literature "On the Cusp of a New Century." Of the other four sections in Volume C, one centers on Siouxian peoples ("Nation within a Nation: Lakotas/Dakotas/Nakotas"); two are organized geographically ("Writing and Place" and "Redefining the South"); and another ("Outside/Inside U.S.A.: Expansion and Immigration") foregrounds the era's cultural and political ferment with writing by or about immigrants and literature created in response to the shifting borders of the nation and to its geopolitical expansion.

All of these sections contain new material in addition to the literature of past editions. Most notably, we now feature four authors new to the *Heath Anthology*—the "Hoosier poet" James Whitcomb Riley, the witty Vermont regionalist Rowland E. Robinson, the Southern plantation tradition writer Thomas Nelson Page, and the proto-modernist poet Sadakichi Hartmann.

There are many new selections by familiar authors, among them Henry James's "The Figure in the Carpet," a section of Zitkala-Sa's "Impressions of an Indian Childhood," Mary E. Wilkins Freeman's "Old Woman Magoun," and Charles W. Chesnutt's "The Doll." We also restored the Frank Norris section.

Still further, we introduce two exciting, little-known Latino narratives—"Memories of California"/"Recuerdos de California" by Carlos F. Galán and "The Tale of a Glove"/"Historia de un guante" by N. Bolet Peraza. These selections are presented in Spanish and in English translations produced for the *Heath Anthology* by contributing editor John Alba Cutler.

In addition, Volume C now offers new or substantially revised headnotes on a number of authors included in earlier editions—Henry James, Sarah Orne Jewett, Mary E. Wilkins Freeman, Frances E. W. Harper, Alice Dunbar-Nelson, and Jack London. Finally, we also present new and revised "In Focus" sections, complete with new and updated introductory essays.

WHAT IS NEW IN VOLUME D, MODERN PERIOD: 1910–1945

Volume D, Modern Period: 1910–1945, continues to demonstrate the diversity of the literary period known as modernism by introducing readers to the array of modernisms that constitute it—the hermetic experiments of Ezra Pound and T. S. Eliot, the more commercial expression of loss and uncertainty in popular efforts by F. Scott Fitzgerald and Edna St. Vincent Millay, the ethnically complex fusion of African American and dominant-culture aesthetics that typify the Harlem Renaissance, and the political activism of the proletarian movement of the 1930s and its internal debates over the social functions of art.

Volume D continues to expand notions of both modernity and modernism by widening the scope of literary experience. Included here for the first time is a section on the literature of the Mexican Revolution, featuring Industrial Workers of the World (IWW) organizer Ricardo Flores Magón's *cri de guerre* "Land and Liberty" and a newly translated excerpt from the Spanish version of Leonor Villegas de Magnon's "La Rebelde," among others. There are two stories from Maria Cristina Mena, and a poem and two novel excerpts of H. T. Tsiang, who captures the despair of New York Chinatown like no other 1930s' writer. The famous "rent party" chapter from Wallace Thurman's *Infants of the Spring* (1932) features thinly veiled portraits of leading Harlem Renaissance writers. Also included are Meridel LeSueur's story "Annunciation" and an excerpt from her posthumously published novel, *The Girl*; Jose Garcia Villa's "Footnote to Youth" (the most famous Filipino short story of the 1930s); and a selection of poetry that expands our notions of modernist experimentation. Mexican American folklorist Jovita Gonzalez's essay "Shades of the Tenth Muses" provides a hallucinatory meditation on canon inclusion.

WHAT IS NEW IN VOLUME E, CONTEMPORARY PERIOD: 1945 TO THE PRESENT

Volume E, Contemporary Period: 1945 to the Present, has been radically restructured to reflect ongoing changes in what is considered contemporary and to make it easier for instructors and students to locate major trends and developments in the contemporary period. We have organized this section by decades, basing their placement on the date of publication rather than by the birth date of authors.

Some of the period's prolific, established authors such as Tennessee Williams, Arthur Miller, Toni Cade Bambara, Ishmael Reed, Sherman Alexie, and John Updike are represented by different works from the ones we included in previous editions.

Although we have had to reduce or cut some selections by authors previously represented in this section in the interest of limiting the volume to a reasonable length, more striking is the list of writers we have added to this volume. New authors to the seventh edition include John Cheever, Mitsuye Yamada, Kurt Vonnegut, Ralph Molina, Luís Valdez, Richard Ford, George C. Wolfe, Ann Beattie, Percival Everett, Martin Espada, Demetria Martinez, T. C. Boyle, Stephen Dunn, Natasha Trethewey, Junot Díaz, Dave Eggers, Jane Trenka, ZZ Packer, Francisco Goldman, and Manuel Munoz.

We have also added substantial new "In Focus" sections of Ojibway writings from the contemporary period, and the volume concludes with a section of "Spoken Word Poetry," which showcases some important new voices and the genre that they have helped to develop but which connects a current trend to the oral traditions that form the origin of American literature in its earliest years.

ACKNOWLEDGMENTS

We want to extend our thanks to all of the contributing editors who devoted their time and scholarship to introductory notes, choices of texts, and teaching materials. For the current edition, they include the following:

Katherine Bassard, Virginia Commonwealth University

Paula Bernat Bennett (Emerita), Southern Illinois University

Renée Bergland, Simmons College

Leah Blatt Glasser, Mount Holyoke College

David Budbill, poet and independent scholar

Raul Bueno, Dartmouth College

Keith Byerman, Indiana State University

Floyd Cheung, Smith College

Jonathan Chua, Ateneo de Manila

Hillary Chute, Harvard University

Michael C. Cohen, University of California, Los Angeles

Raúl Coronado, University of Chicago

Denise Cruz, Indiana University

Suzanne del Gizzo, Chestnut Hill College

Jared Demick, University of Connecticut

Joseph Dewey, University of Pittsburgh, Johnstown

Lyn Di Lorio, The City College of New York

Amy Doherty Mohr, Amerika Institut, Ludwig Maximilians Universität, Munich

Jennifer Emery-Peck, Oberlin College

Armando García, University of Pittsburgh

Caroline Gebhard, Tuskegee University

June Howard, University of Michigan

Caren Irr, Brandeis University

Gene Jarrett, Boston University

Ann Keniston, University of Nevada, Reno

Ryan James Kernan, Rutgers University

Kathy Knapp, University of Connecticut

Sara Kosiba, Troy University

Rodrigo Lazo, University of California, Irvine

Katherine E. Ledford, Appalachian State University

Marissa López, University of California, Los Angeles

Crystal J. Lucky, Villanova University

Manuel Martin-Rodriguez, University of California, Merced

Lauren R. Maxwell, The Citadel

Keith Mitchell, University of Massachusetts, Lowell

Charles Molesworth, City University of New York, Queens

Paula Moya, Stanford University

Viet Nguyen, University of Southern California

Ben V. Olguin, University of Texas, San Antonio

Yolana Padilla, University of Pennsylvania

Josephine Park, University of Pennsylvania

Robert Dale Parker, University of Illinois, Urbana-Champaign

Soojin Pate, Minneapolis Community and Technical College

Elizabeth Petrino, Fairfield University

Peter Reed, University of Mississippi

Domino Renee Perez, University of Texas, Austin

Ana Patricia Rodriguez, University of Maryland, College Park

Ramón Saldívar, Stanford University

James Schiff, University of Cincinnati

Lavina Dhingra, Bates College

E. Thomson Shields, East Carolina University

Susan Shillinglaw, San Jose State University

Amjrit Singh, Ohio University

Scott Slovic, University of Nevada, Reno

James Smethurst, University of Massachusetts, Amherst

Mayumi Takada, Bryn Mawr College

Justine Tally, Universidad de la Laguna

Kara Thompson, College of William and Mary

Lisa Thompson, State University of New York, Albany

Darlene Unrue, University of Nevada, Las Vegas

Joanne van der Woude, Columbia University

Ariana Vigil, University of North Carolina, Chapel Hill

Jennifer Wallach, University of North Texas

Hilary Wyss, Auburn University

Yvonne Yarbro-Bejarano, Stanford University

Thanks to Oberlin College for funding student researchers and to Amanda Shubert and Hillary Smith for the incomparable work they have done in that capacity. We also want to thank student researchers Carson Thomas and Kyle Lewis from Dartmouth College and Brandy Underwood from the University of California, Los Angeles for excellent editorial help.

We especially want to thank those who reviewed this edition:

David Anderson, University of North Texas

Craig Barrette, Brescia University

Robert Bennett, Montana State University

Brett Bodily, North Lake College

Kathryn Brewer-Strayer, Stillman College

Delmar Brewington, Piedmont Technical College

Brad Campbell, California Polytechnic State University

Beth Capo, Illinois College

Charles Cuthbertson, Southern Utah University

Joshua Dickinson, Jefferson Community College

Sharynn Owens Etheridge-Logan, Claflin University

April Gentry, Savannah State University

Wendy Gray, J. Sargeant Reynolds Community College

Deirdre Hall, University of North Carolina, Greensboro

Amy Hankins, Ottawa University

Tena Helton, University of Illinois, Springfield

Tai Houser, Broward College

Melanie Jenkins, Snow College

Bruce Johnson, Providence College

David Jones, University of Wisconsin, Eau Claire

Thomas Long, University of Connecticut

Marit MacArthur, California State University, Bakersfield

Bridget Marshall, University of
　Massachusetts, Lowell
John Miller, Longwood University
Keith Mitchell, University of
　Massachusetts, Lowell
Emmanuel Ngwang, Claflin
　University
Miles Orvell, Temple University
Priscilla Perkins, Roosevelt
　University
Jane Rosecrans, J. Sargeant
　Reynolds Community College
Christopher Schroeder,
　Northeastern Illinois University
Claudia Slate, Florida Southern
　College
Jimmy Smith, Union College

Blythe Tellefsen, Fullerton College
Ruthe Thompson, Southwest
　Minnesota State University
Stephanie Tingley, Youngstown
　State University
Terri Tucker, Southwest Texas
　Junior College
Tondalaya VanLear, Dabney S.
　Lancaster Community College
Trent Watts, Missouri University of
　Science and Technology
Michelle Weisman, College of the
　Ozarks
Eric Wertheimer, Arizona State
　University
Julie Wilhelm, Lamar University

We would like to continue to thank the many scholars who contributed to this as well as to earlier editions of this work. Their names are listed in the *Online Instructor's Manual* that accompanies this anthology.

The Heath Anthology of American Literature

Volume E

Contemporary Period:
1945 to the Present

AN IMAGE GALLERY
1945 TO THE PRESENT

■ **E-READERS.** The Information Age has changed our understanding of literature—not only its place in the cultural landscape, but its medium. The book, the technology that has packaged literature since the Middle Ages, has suddenly changed in the twenty-first century as computer screens have begun to replace it. The e-reader in particular has been a source of excitement for some as books are now cheaper and more readily available than ever before. Critics, though, wonder whether we read too quickly or too superficially in this medium, scrolling and hunting for information as we do on the Internet rather than encountering literature at a slower pace. The way we read literature complements questions about what is considered literature. The excerpts we have included here from graphic narratives by Art Spiegelman (pages 3767–3779), Lynda Barry (pages 3813–3818), Alison Bechdel (pages 4013–4021), and Chris Ware (pages 3794–3799) can help frame that debate.

■ **THE ATOMIC BOMBING OF HIROSHIMA (1945).** On August 6, 1945, the *Enola Gay*, a B-29 bomber, dropped a 9,700-pound uranium bomb on the Japanese city of Hiroshima, which had a population of almost 300,000 civilians and 43,000 soldiers. About 70,000 people probably died immediately. With the effects of radioactive fallout, the five-year death total may have reached or even exceeded 200,000. On August 9, another bomb was dropped on Nagasaki, and one day later Japan surrendered unconditionally, ending World War II. The United States had achieved victory, but at a tremendous cost. The poems by Mitsuye Yamada (pages 2884–2889) about Japanese Americans who were assigned to internment camps in the 1940s demonstrate an immediate cost to the people who were interned, but the anger and anxiety evident in a poem like Allen Ginsberg's "America" (pages 2972–2974) is also directly related to the United States' military dominance based on its detonation of the atomic bomb.

■ **JACKSON POLLOCK, ONE: NUMBER 31, 1950 (c. 1950).** Jackson Pollock (1912–1956) created three wall-size paintings in 1950. In 1947, he began experimenting with the technique of laying a canvas on the floor and dribbling or pouring paint directly onto its surface. Often photographed creating huge paintings, Pollock saw himself as a medium. He commented, "[T]he painting has a life of its own. I try to let it come through." Abstraction and artistic experimentation are illustrated in a number of works from the mid-twentieth century, such as the poems of Charles Olson (pages 2765–2773) and John Ashbery (pages 3065–3070) and the fiction of Thomas Pynchon (pages 3022–3032), John Barth (pages 3146–3163), and Donald Barthelme (pages 3366–3371). (*The Museum of Modern Art/Licensed by SCALA/Art Resource, NY. © 2012 The Pollock-Krasner Foundation/Artists Rights Society (ARS), New York*)

Yale University Art Gallery/Art Resource, NY.

■ **EDWARD HOPPER, WESTERN MOTEL (1957).** Edward Hopper (1882–1967) captures the loneliness and isolation of American life in this image of a woman sitting on a bed next to a motel window. A car waits outside, and beyond is a stark and bleak landscape. Suitcases occupy the bottom left corner of the painting. As with all of Hopper's paintings, the light is rich and beautiful, but the viewer is left with a sense of rootlessness and transience. The woman is caught, momentarily still, but she will soon move outside the frame, into the car, and down the road to, presumably, another lonely motel. The mood of loneliness is pervasive in mid-twentieth-century literature, and perhaps nowhere clearer than in the work of the confessional poets of the early 1960s, particularly Robert Lowell (pages 3014–3020), Sylvia Plath (pages 3052–3057), and Anne Sexton (pages 3048–3051).

One of four different styles of the Jubilee

One of four different styles of the Levittowner

Levittown IN 1957

One of five different styles of the Pennsylvanian

One of four different styles of the Country Clubber

■ **LEVITTOWN IN 1957.** Levittown, Pennsylvania, was the second of the mass-produced planned suburban communities built after World War II by the developer Levitt & Sons. (The first was built on Long Island, New York, from 1947 to 1951, and the third and fourth were built in New Jersey and Puerto Rico.) The Pennsylvania town, built from 1951 to 1957, included churches, schools, swimming pools, and a shopping center. About 70,000 residents lived there, mostly veterans and their families. The houses cost from about $8,000 to $18,000 and were fully equipped and landscaped. Veterans could buy them for no money down (others needed a $90 down payment). Homeowners made a monthly mortgage payment of about $60 to the Veterans Administration or the Federal Housing Administration. The suburbs have been a ubiquitous backdrop for fiction in the second half of the twentieth century. The story "The Enormous Radio" by John Cheever (see pages 2737–2745) is a great example of the way the suburbs can have nightmarish undertones despite (or maybe because of) their surface blandness and uniformity.

Bettmann/CORBIS

■ **MARTIN LUTHER KING, JR., GIVING A SPEECH IN WASHINGTON, D.C., IN 1963.** On August 28, 1963, more than 200,000 people of all races gathered at the Lincoln Memorial to demand equal justice for all citizens under the law. Martin Luther King, Jr. (1929–1968) delivered his "I Have a Dream" speech (see pages 3072–3075) at this gathering. Figures like King and Nelson Mandela, who might be said to be King's counterpart in South Africa, became subjects of poems by Lucille Clifton (pages 3524–3530) and June Jordan (pages 3532–3538) as the poetic and the political merged.

■ **ANDY WARHOL, *SELF-PORTRAIT*, 1983.** A leading figure in the pop art movement of the late 1960s through the early 1980s, Warhol (1928–1987) was famous for taking familiar objects (such as Campbell's soup cans) or people (such as Marilyn Monroe or Elvis Presley) and reproducing their image, often with garish or cartoonish colors. Warhol himself became a celebrity in the age of fleeting fame. Here, his trademark shock of white hair looks like an explosion across the canvas, and his face, rather than basking in the attention of the viewer, is as expressionless as a death mask. Warhol's work provokes viewers to question the costs of fame and commercial success and the relationship between art and the marketplace. Anxiety over such fame can be seen in Art Spiegelman's excerpt from *Maus II* (pages 3769–3779), in which the author, who has become famous writing about his father's experiences in Nazi concentration camps, rejects the media sources that are capitalizing on his fame and even questions whether he can continue to tell his father's story given the societal pressures that surround him.

■ **MALCOLM X.** Malcolm X (born Malcolm Little, 1925–1965) was an important figure in the Nation of Islam, a group that promoted black nationalism in the early 1960s. He was an articulate and persuasive advocate for African American identity, integrity, and independence. In addition to Malcolm X's writings, literature in general was affected by his rise as a public figure and his assassination in 1965, which was a key event in a decade that saw massive shifts in American race relations. The Black Arts Movement, especially the works of Amiri Baraka (pages 3096–3120) included here, was catalyzed by Malcolm X's assassination, and the difference in tone between works that preceded the civil rights movement and those that came after is clear. Toni Morrison's story "Recitatif" (pages 3541–3555) and George C. Wolfe's play *The Colored Museum* (pages 3598–3631), both published in the 1980s, demonstrate the racial tensions that lingered after the dust of the turbulent 1960s had settled.

■ **ALLEN GINSBERG READING "HOWL" IN WASHINGTON SQUARE IN 1966 (pages 2963–2971).** The writing of the Beats (*Beat* meaning "beatific, holy" with connotations of the musical beat as well as fatigue) was intended to be shared with an audience in a performance that united poet and listeners. After a visit to India, Allen Ginsberg (1926–1997) brought back a mantra-like chant that enhanced the delivery of his poetry. He became a kind of prophet, shedding light on America's aberrations in his poetry. The Beat writers included here in addition to Ginsberg—Jack Kerouac, Lawrence Ferlinghetti, Bonnie Frazer, Joyce Johnson, Gary Snyder, and Albert Saijo—ushered in a new aesthetic that emphasized spontaneity, experience, and a spiritual quest that stretched beyond conventional Western thought (see pages 2960–3010).

■ **HUYNH CONG (NICK) UT, *VIETNAM NAPALM, TRANG BANG* (1972).** Ever since Matthew Brady displayed his Civil War photos in his New York gallery, photography has transformed perceptions of war. In the past, paintings depicted fallen heroes and brave generals leading their troops. Photography is much more democratic. The Vietnam War was the most photographed war to that date. Photojournalists flocked to the tiny country, and many soldiers documented personal experiences with their own cameras. This photo by Nick Ut (b. 1951) sheds light on the effects of war on the innocent bystanders who are outside the heroic frames. Our section "In Focus: The U.S. War in Vietnam and Its Aftermath" (pages 3164–3225) showcases more than a half-dozen writers who wrote about the conflict and its lingering tensions.

■ **VIEW OF THE EARTH AS SEEN BY THE *APOLLO 17* CREW TRAVELING TOWARD THE MOON (1972).** This image has been interpreted in many different ways. When it was taken in 1972, Americans saw the earth as part of a larger universe—"the last frontier"—that was just beginning to be explored. From a twenty-first-century perspective, with the earth's resources in peril, we view this globe as a delicate ecosystem that is under attack. The story "Blinded by the Light" (pages 4001–4011) by T. C. Boyle demonstrates the fragility of the earth as well as the recklessness of the humans who inhabit it.

Getty Images

Philip Scalia/Alamy

■ **NUYORICAN POETS CAFÉ.** Founded in 1973, this coffeehouse on Manhattan's Lower East Side was a site of artistic and cultural display for the city's burgeoning population of Hispanic and Latino artists and became a model for a national movement toward ethnic solidarity. Styled after the Beat generation readings of the late 1950s, the Nuyorican Poets Café also set the stage for the poetry "slams," or competitive open-mike readings, that became popular in the 1990s and remain so in the twenty-first century. Early figures from the Nuyorican Poets Café such as Tracie Morris and Saul Stacey Williams are included here, and their legacy is clear in the work of the poets in our concluding "In Focus: Spoken Word Poetry" (pages 4137–4161).

CONTEMPORARY PERIOD: 1945 TO THE PRESENT

When the United States emerged from World War II, it was unquestionably the most powerful nation the world had yet known. Its factories and farms had been crucial to the Allies' military victory. Its technology had produced the atomic bomb, a weapon of unsurpassed force. Unlike many other industrial powers, its cities were untouched by the war's devastation, and its industries quickly converted their enormous productive capacities from making guns and tanks to producing cars and refrigerators. American engineers talked of producing virtually free power through atomic fission. And as Johnny came marching home, Rosie was told to leave riveting to raise babies in the newly built suburbs.

By the mid-1970s, the United States had essentially been defeated by a small Asian nation on the distant battlefield of Vietnam. Its president had resigned after a scandal called Watergate. Its factories, like some of its large cities, were in decay. Its monopoly on weapons of mass destruction had long disappeared into a random world where stateless terrorists could be the enemy. Indeed, the fabric of American society was being shredded in harsh and sometimes violent conflicts over war, human rights, and continuing and deepening poverty. Johnny and Rosie had probably gone separate ways; the house in the suburbs had begun to disintegrate. Far from creating a harmonious chorus singing "one for all, all for one," Americans had issued a cacophony of competing voices, all demanding a large piece of the action.

The closing years of the twentieth century and the first years of the twenty-first are marked by even more staggering cultural changes. The Cold War ended and the Berlin Wall was reduced to rubble, leaving one global superpower standing. Computers, once clunky, inefficient machines the size of houses that could do little for common citizens, became sleek, portable, cheap, and finally indispensable household appliances that connect us to one another. Phones became cordless, then mobile, and finally "smart." The Information Age was suddenly upon us, and technology has become something that Americans (and most of the rest of the world) have embraced: by the middle of the booming 1990s the future had arrived, and now seems to keep reinventing itself every day. The lone superpower also became a target, though, as the terror attacks we call 9/11 shattered America's sense of infallibility. In the first years of the twenty-first century, America initiated two wars as well as a covert "war on terror" that can never end in any conventional sense. Barack Obama was elected president in 2008, a circumstance unimaginable just 50 years earlier when African Americans were still fighting for their basic civil rights.

The literature chosen to represent the last half of the twentieth century and the first years of the twenty-first attempts to show the differences of outlook and attitude as well as the rich spectrum of cultural and aesthetic perspectives. Many of the writers of this period have lived with the fear of the bomb or school shootings; the agony of wars in Vietnam, the Persian Gulf, Iraq, and Afghanistan; the exhilaration and liberation of the March on Washington; the Stonewall Riots and Woodstock; and the uncertainty following the terror attacks of September 11, 2001. Their works sometimes chronicle, sometimes protest, and sometimes ignore these events. Yet like everyone else, writers are in some measure creatures of their time, and since they are often—in Henry James's words—people on whom "nothing is lost," we will find their world and ours inscribed in their books.

"What validates us as human beings validates us as writers," Gloria Anzaldúa affirms as she urges people to express their beliefs and their individuality through the act of writing. The validation of all human experience through writing is more nearly possible now than ever before in American history. Beginning in the mid-1960s, publishers and readers have become increasingly interested in work by immigrants, minorities, women, homosexuals, and political radicals. As large-scale commercial publishing has become more concentrated, with big publishers swallowed by bigger conglomerates, many groups have established smaller independent houses to create more specialized lists. Today, small ("alternative") publishers and academic presses offer alternatives to the commercial concentration on "soon-to-be-major-movie" titles. The Internet has also transformed the nature of publishing, popularizing on-line journals, blogs, and Facebook and Twitter posts that turn spontaneous observations into instant publications, though often insubstantial ones. Aware of the public's appetite for convenient access, publishers now offer e-books that can be downloaded instantly and stored and read on devices so efficient that we can hold libraries in the palms of our hands. The principle of the Information Age is that we are all connected, all the time; and yet, rapidly accelerating technology can have the effect of intensifying isolation or anonymity.

Contemporary American literature is remarkable because it portrays a variety of experiences, but still, many works share the sense of cultural instability that leads to those feelings of anonymity and isolation, or even alienation. "Postmodernism," the name often given to recent cultural developments, has no single agreed-upon definition, but it surely involves the decentering of literary and cultural authority, as well as the dissolution of traditional boundaries like those between "high" and "popular" cultures or between "American" and "other" literatures. Whatever else it may imply, the postmodern era presents little that is stable, unitary, and comforting for readers, offering instead the inevitability of uncertainty, diversity, and change. Whether strictly postmodern or not, today's writers don't shy away from unpleasant or unfamiliar subject matter. Contemporary literature does not wear blinders, and it is not intended for readers who live in an unreal world. Except for some science fiction and science fantasy, much contemporary literature is not escapist. Current writers' artistry consists in shaping literature from their daily milieu, often crowded and chaotic, with paradoxical tensions that threaten to sever self from society. Late in the twentieth century, when Carolyn Forché writes about the brutal dismembering of war (and the military man's delight in the torture that has become a daily event), or Paula Vogel chronicles the life of a young girl molested by her uncle, our attention is drawn to the emotional meaning of that telling. Style supports meaning, as it did during modernism, but with somewhat different effects. Much contemporary writing has stopped pretending that there is a hierarchical order to experience, or that education can give shape to the chaos of twentieth-century life. While modernists believed that knowledge meant control, many postmodernists have accepted an utter lack of order as today's cultural norm. Randomness, surprise, and dysfunction are as valuable as more orderly patterns of experience—and the literature about it—that dominated letters earlier, in the twentieth century. There is sometimes irony or even outrageous humor in this writing, partly as a defense against the possible pain of contemporary existence and partly as an acknowledgement that existence itself is absurdly funny when viewed from a certain perspective.

Another critical difference between modern and postmodern literature involves difference itself. The 1950s are often said to have offered a unified vision of American culture. We then knew, or so the myth has it, what constituted American, indeed "Western," history and culture, and therefore we knew what students should study and critics should criticize. And it is certainly true that curricula and literary texts of the period offer a degree of uniformity unimaginable today. But in fact the seeds of today's diversity had already been sown and were rapidly sprouting, as the liberating "Howl" of Ginsberg's famous 1957 poem released him (and his readers) from the clutches of mechanical, militaristic, capitalistic, boring, heterosexual society. The Civil Rights movement began to change American society and therefore American culture as well. In many respects, the question for ethnic and minority writers, as for ethnic and minority people, had once been how they might fit themselves into mainstream culture rather than how mainstream culture should be forced to accommodate them.

But in the 1950s older definitions of cultural norms based upon race and ethnicity were, after years of attack, falling. In 1954 the Supreme Court agreed that separate education for black and white students produced inherently unequal opportunities for minorities, thus setting aside the legal basis for segregated schools. In 1955, Rosa Parks refused to accept the concept that black people belonged at the back of the bus; her arrest for refusing to give up her seat to a white person and move to the rear set the stage for the Montgomery bus boycott and the prominence of the young black minister Martin Luther King, Jr. These and hundreds of other instances of resistance ultimately pluralized American culture. The question shifted from how an ethnic minority writer might fit *into* mainstream culture to how alternative centers of culture, alternative understandings of its nature and functions, might be established *by* minority writers and *for* minority communities. By the end of the century, Toni Morrison, the first African American recipient of the Nobel Prize in literature, showed just how far such efforts had come.

The developing movements for change spread ideas about, for example, black pride, and thus generated a new consciousness about culture and history among those who had been marginalized. Writers of color, white women, and gay writers responded to the imperative to speak for themselves and for others like themselves who had been silenced in history. But more: to do so, they had to define their own distinctive voices, create their own artistic forms and critical discourses, develop their own institutions for cultural work.

There is another, perhaps more far-reaching consequence of this radical pluralization of American literary traditions. As contemporary United States literature has lost its dominantly Anglo-American, largely male, and mostly heterosexual definition, it has become more accessible and perhaps more interesting to many from outside the United States, those readers who view the new American literature focused on ethnicity, race, and the "subaltern" as a vital part of a global dialogue about the relationship of colonized peoples to their (mainly European) colonizers. Paradoxically, it may be that the very decentering of American literature has made it more integral to international culture while reflecting our true status as a nation of immigrants.

New themes and subjects call for new techniques, and the contemporary period includes literature as technically varied as that in any time before it. Earlier modernism—with its difficult but unforgettable texts such as Faulkner's *The Sound and the Fury*, Toomer's *Cane*, and Eliot's *The Waste Land*—strongly influences some contemporary writers who see formal innovation as a means not only for extending the domain of what is termed "literature" but also for shaking readers free from their conventional assumptions about their world. For some contemporary writers, however, formal innovation is of less consequence than expressing the experiences of communities that had previously been marginalized, and challenging readers with issues like sexual identity. Much recent literature makes use of oral elements, which remain particularly strong in many minority cultures, as well as echoing traditional rituals and tales, from the Beat writers of the 1950s through the Nuyorican Poets' Café writers of the 1970s, to the poets represented in our "Spoken Word" section at the end of this volume. Contemporary authors often blend realistic elements with elliptical or surreal details, rejecting the notion that writing must "represent" a knowable reality lying "behind" the surface of language, suggesting instead that any narrative is a fictional construction subject to deconstruction and reassembly by changing communities of readers.

This anthology aims to give today's readers a *representative* selection of contemporary writing. Space prohibits any attempt at comprehensiveness, but the works that follow show the sheer excellence of the writing of our time, the late twentieth century as well as the nascent twenty-first.

THE LATE 1940S AND 1950S: VICTORY CULTURE

American involvement in World War II ushered in a widespread spirit of optimism that most Americans had not felt for two decades. In 1941 Henry Luce, the publisher of *Time* magazine, wrote, "Throughout the 17th century and the 18th century and the 19th century, this continent teemed with manifold projects and magnificent purposes. Above them all and weaving them all together into the most exciting flag of all the world and of all history was the triumphal purpose of freedom. It is in this spirit that all of us are called, each to his own measure of capacity, and each in the widest horizon of his vision, to create the first great American Century." Following Luce's proclamation, the twentieth century came to be known as the "American Century," largely because of the United States' economic prosperity and its military might. The United States imagined itself as a hardworking, resourceful nation that would sacrifice in times of need and enjoy its prosperity in times of plenty. Part of this cultural optimism came from the transition from the Great Depression that had blighted the nation in the 1930s to the spirit of victory following the Second World War, which ended in 1945. From the American soldiers who landed on the French coast to help end the spread of Nazism and fascism, to the scientists who developed the atomic bomb that would give the United States its enduring title of "superpower," to the women who filled in the factory jobs while the men were fighting overseas, to the children who gathered tin cans to be recycled into bullets and other materials of war, all of America seemed to be involved in the military triumph.

Of course, this version of the story is not without its contradictions or its long-term implications. A culture that appears ebullient and victorious on the surface is invariably masking some form of misery. In 1945, when soldiers were disembarking from ships to reunite with their sweethearts, returning to their affordable suburban homes to eat produce from victory gardens and to make the babies that would produce the largest native-born population explosion in U.S. history, the story of the American Century was also being conceived, but a number of other stories were beginning as well. At home, the United States was certainly enjoying the start of a long period of prosperity, but the jubilant nation was not without its troubles. The atomic bombs that had concluded the war marked the beginning of the Atomic Age, when competition between nuclear powers produced widespread anxiety and advanced the terrifying notion that the planet could be instantly destroyed. Everyone was at risk, and the powerless had not necessarily become powerful just because their nation had. Although African American soldiers following World War II did not face the lynch mobs that attacked some black soldiers returning from World War I, segregation was still the law in the American South in 1945, and the civil rights movement that responded to widespread inequality turned violent over the course of the next two decades, culminating in late-1960s race riots in the Watts section of Los Angeles, in Newark, and in Detroit, to name just the most prominent three. In 1942 President Franklin Roosevelt signed executive order 9066, which resulted in the relocation of over 100,000 Japanese Americans—more than half of them U.S. citizens—to "war relocation" or "internment" camps (described in Mitsuye Yamada's poems in this volume). Discrimination against Asian Americans was thus backed by the power of the executive branch of the government just as discrimination against African Americans in the South was backed by the power of the legislative and judicial branches. The tide of immigration from Europe that rose in the 1920s had abated, but new immigration from Spanish-speaking countries in the Western Hemisphere—especially from Puerto Rico in the years just after the war—radically changed the demographics of the United States and resulted in new forms of discrimination against Spanish-speaking communities struggling to preserve their heritage in a nation that had, once again, forgotten its multicultural nature.

Global politics supposedly became more stable in the aftermath of World War II, but there were also contradictions in that story. In 1946, the year after World War II ended, British Prime Minister Winston Churchill warned of an "iron curtain" descending over eastern Europe. The United States now had a formidable adversary in the collection of nations known as the Soviet Union. Within the next few years this adversary had developed its own atomic bomb and in 1957 launched a satellite into space. Also in 1946 Ho Chi Minh was elected president of North Vietnam. While the United States set up a new agency called the Central Intelligence Agency (CIA) to gather information about what was going on behind the iron curtain, a new enemy was quietly materializing in Southeast Asia. All those babies born in 1946 and over the following few years would find themselves debating, arguing, and protesting over the mandatory draft for the war in Vietnam in the late 1960s. More than 60,000 of them died in that war, and in 1970 on a campus in Ohio, four young antiwar protesters were shot as the National Guard struggled to control a young generation vociferously exercising its right to free speech. As the United States gave birth to a victorious mood in 1946, labor pains might not have been immediately evident, but there were certainly growing pains in its future.

In addition to the wars that have traditionally helped to define history, a number of cultural changes had an undeniable impact on the literature of the third quarter of the twentieth century. One prominent change was the development of the modern American suburb, with a man named William Levitt as its spearhead. Responding to a need for affordable housing in the aftermath of World War II, from 1947 to 1951 he developed Levittown, an instant community halfway between New York City and the defense industry plants on Long Island. After the war, reunited couples needed a place to raise their families, and the demand for these modest houses on curved streets and cul-de-sacs off a main thoroughfare was overwhelming. The houses were essentially identical, but this homogeneity did not seem to bother these middle-class families. The Levittown model produced countless similar communities even into the twenty-first century, but especially in the first few decades after World War II. As a result,

U.S. cities tended to languish from the 1950s through the 1980s, and rural regions steadily decreased as suburbs began to sprawl outward and encroach upon farmland. American culture and the American landscape would never be the same. The American Dream became a cliché in the 1950s, and the image of a married couple in a comfortable, modest home surrounded by a picket fence containing a couple of kids and a dog remains a surprisingly common definition of this dream. It all began in Levittown.

These suburban homes were likely to have two culturally significant accessories: a car and a television. The preponderance of automobiles in the 1950s, churned out in Detroit as a way of keeping the economy growing after the defense industry waned, gave rise to a host of other industries (initially fast-food chains and drive-in theaters, and later malls and strip malls) initially associated with the baby boomers who became old enough to drive in the early 1960s. In conjunction with the interstate highway system, a development initiated by President Eisenhower in the 1950s, the automobile enabled American families to travel throughout their nation easily, increasing the trend toward national isolation by encouraging domestic travel while enabling Americans to enjoy their vaunted sense of freedom. The interstate highway system also replaced the national railway system as the primary means of transporting goods. The economic benefits of this innovation are manifold—trucks can go more places than trains can—but the environmental cost of so many road vehicles has proven great, especially as scientists become aware of the perils of global warming and as social costs rise in the form of inferior public health from poor air quality and the depletion of nonrenewable natural resources.

The impact of television on American culture cannot be overestimated. Television quickly replaced the radio as the main form of family entertainment. Because of its visual and audio content, television was exponentially more appealing than its predecessor—more like life, more like the movies, but easily packaged to fit into the center of everyone's living room. As a way to sell products, television was also unparalleled, and its ubiquity contributed to a consumerist mentality that has dominated American culture ever since. Nightly news broadcasts gradually overtook newspapers as America's primary source of information. In the 1950s, though, television was primarily a form of entertainment in which white families could watch idealized versions of themselves projected in such shows as *The Donna Reed Show*, *The Dick Van Dyke Show*, and *Leave It to Beaver*.

The rise of television and the development of the modern suburb had profound implications for American literary culture during this period. If families were watching more television, it follows that they were reading fewer books. Literature began to affect middle-class culture less than it had had in the previous half century, and writers responded to these cultural changes with innovation (and even despair). Also, the depiction of American culture on television, reflecting the rise of the suburbs, was homogenous in many ways. It was not until the 1970s that members of ethnic or racial minorities were represented with any regularity on television. In the preceding decades, then, authors who wrote about the experiences of these minorities or who sought to record marginal experiences were likely to hunt for small, alternative publishing houses, which proliferated during this period. Rather than cater to mainstream

American taste, which appeared to be growing flat and bland from a steady diet of television, innovative American authors of every ethnic and racial background pursued publishing or performance venues that did not demand that their works be scrubbed clean. During these decades, avant-garde publishing houses appeared; poets could be found performing their poetry in nightclubs and coffeehouses; and the concept of the off-Broadway play began to gain legitimacy in the American theater. The spirit of individualism and rebellion that has always characterized American culture remained alive during the 1940s and 1950s; it was just less apparent.

Arguably the best and most enduring literature of this period is some of the most experimental and iconoclastic, but some mainstream or popular works are also worthy of attention. Grace Metalious's scandalous novel *Peyton Place* (1956) exposed the sexual affairs of a fictional small town in New England. Sloan Wilson's *The Man in the Gray Flannel Suit* (1955), also a popular 1956 film, revealed the simmering discontent under the passive exterior of a typical suburban commuter who had also been in the war. These novels were hugely popular in their day but have not withstood serious critical literary analysis over time. However, one of the most profound works of the decade, Ralph Ellison's *Invisible Man* (1952), achieved critical acclaim as well as popular success, and Ellison became the first African American to win the National Book Award. (See his acceptance speech, published as "Brave Words for a Startling Occasion," in this volume.) Many critics count Ellison's novel among the greatest works of American fiction. The nameless narrator of this novel (usually referred to as "Invisible Man"), an African American who considers himself invisible, endures a series of humiliations that stem from his racial identity. Unconsciously following the Great Migration from the South—the region of his birth—to New York City, Invisible Man gradually becomes aware of his profound marginality in American society, though at the book's conclusion he continues to believe in the validity of American ideals.

Awareness of marginality was a keynote of the literary 1950s. Two other works of fiction fitting this description that achieved popular and critical success during that decade were James Baldwin's *Giovanni's Room* (1956) and Jack Kerouac's *On the Road* (1957). Baldwin, an African American living as an expatriate in Paris in the fifties, gained attention for his bildungsroman *Go Tell It on the Mountain* (1953) and his manifesto, a collection of essays titled *Notes of a Native Son* (1955). Both reflected his experience as a poor black youth, but both were largely devoid of another facet of his identity, his bisexuality. *Giovanni's Room* tackled this subject in a way that had not been broached before this time. Baldwin's publishers were fearful of the explicit homoerotic content of the book, which is ironic considering that the novel scrutinizes the forces that would lead a young man to suppress his homosexual desires in order to conform to the heterosexual lifestyle considered "normal" by his culture. Kerouac's *On the Road* also dabbles in bisexuality, but that is only one of many experiences chronicled in the novel that might be considered "deviant" by conservative Americans. Kerouac's novel, written in a fluid, spontaneous idiom, describes characters who experiment with illegal drugs, who drink excessive amounts of alcohol, who hitchhike, who travel like hoboes on boxcars, who drive at speeds over 100 miles per hour, all in pursuit of some elusive "IT," some quasi-spiritual experience that will give meaning to their lives since they have rejected the values and lifestyles of mainstream Americans. As a central figure of the so-called Beat generation, Kerouac's writings influenced a vast number of young people who were discontented with the suburban lifestyle into which they were born. Kerouac's friend Allen Ginsberg, the other leading figure in the Beat movement, published the long poem "Howl" in 1956. The explicit homosexual content of this poem caused an uproar even greater than Baldwin's novel. Following a performance of the poem at the now famous City Lights bookstore in San Francisco, U.S. customs agents tried to ban the published version of Ginsberg's poem by seizing copies of the book as they arrived in the port. This case of censorship did not hold up in superior court, and "Howl" became a sensation as well as a classic. Baldwin's story "Sonny's Blues," Kerouac's piece "The Vanishing American Hobo," and Ginsberg's "Howl" (as well as other poems) can all be found in this volume.

Poor, marginalized men like Ellison, Baldwin, Kerouac, and Ginsberg struggled to get their experiences and visions into print, but women writers of the 1950s were also revealing a widespread resistance to the cultural expectations that would keep them barefoot, pregnant, and in the kitchen. In 1963 Betty Friedan published *The Feminine Mystique*, a nonfiction work that explored the discontentment that so many middle-class women experienced. In the suburbs, the invention (and near saturation) of labor-reducing items like dishwashers, vacuum cleaners, and washing machines certainly made the domestic sphere a less arduous place to work, but many women were questioning whether their role as "homemakers" could be fulfilling enough. In the 1960s and 1970s this questioning became a full-fledged social/political movement called feminism, but we can see its origins in women's writings of the 1950s. Early poetry by Adrienne Rich, for example, often focused on women who wanted to reject a conventionally gender-stereotyped lifestyle that had been preordained. Rich eventually became a leading figure in the feminist movement.

It could be argued that American drama reached its golden period in the third quarter of the twentieth century. Some of the most enduring and well-respected figures in American drama were active during this period: Arthur Miller and Tennessee Williams. Following in the footsteps of their predecessor Eugene O'Neill, these three writers continued to experiment with the form and content of plays. In line with the confessional school of poetry, the theater of the 1950s tended to focus on the problems of modern-day heroes, contemporary men and women who were, at least in Miller's conception, ordinary individuals with tragic flaws. Miller's influential essay "Tragedy and the Common Man" argued that the strains of classical tragedy could still be heard on the contemporary stage, but that the theater now concerned itself with types that the audience could immediately recognize as their neighbors, or themselves, rather than the "great men" of classical drama. Miller's plays, including *A View from the Bridge* (reprinted here), clearly illustrate his ideas from this essay. Williams's plays, like Miller's, reveal the despair of ordinary characters trapped by the expectations of their culture.

Arthur Miller's prominence in the theater in the 1940s and 1950s indicates another trend in American literature of this period: the rise to prominence of Jewish writers. Especially in the realm of fiction, Jewish voices and the Jewish experience, which had not been as visible in the early twentieth century, began to emerge in the 1950s. The most prominent, critically respected, award-winning writers of this period were, for the first time in American literary history, not from an Anglo/Christian background. Bernard Malamud, Philip Roth, Grace Paley, Norman Mailer, and Nobel laureate Saul Bellow all became active in the years following the end of World War II, and they remain some of the most significant authors of the twentieth century (and Roth continues to gain notoriety in the twenty-first). As *The Heath Anthology of American Literature* shows, American literature has always been more diverse than it appeared to be, but only in the second half of the twentieth century was that diversity recognized, or rewarded, by the mainstream literary establishment.

HISAYE YAMAMOTO
1921–2011

Hisaye Yamamoto once said that she "didn't have any imagination" and that she "just *embroidered* on things that happened, or that people told [her] happened." The statement, though spoken out of modesty, reveals the extent to which personal and historical circumstances formed the grist to her fictional mill. Born in Redondo Beach, California, Yamamoto was a child of Japanese immigrants. She started writing when she was a teenager and contributed regularly to Japanese American newspapers. During World War II she was interned for three years in Poston, Arizona, where she served as a reporter and a columnist for the *Poston Chronicle* (the camp newspaper) and published a serialized mystery. After the war she worked from 1945 to 1948 for the *Los Angeles Tribune*, a black weekly. Soon afterward her short stories began to appear in national journals, and she received a John Hay Whitney Foundation Opportunity Fellowship (1950–1951). She was also encouraged by Yvor Winters to accept a Stanford Writing Fellowship but chose instead to work from 1953 to 1955 as a volunteer at a Catholic Worker rehabilitation farm on Staten Island founded by Dorothy Day. She returned to Los Angeles after marrying Anthony DeSoto.

Yamamoto was one of the first Japanese American writers to gain national recognition after the war, when anti-Japanese sentiment was still rampant. Four of her short stories were listed as "Distinctive Short Stories" in Martha Foley's *Best American Short Stories* collections: "The High-Heeled Shoes" (1948), "The Brown House" (1951), "Yoneko's Earthquake" (1951), and "Epithalamium" (1960). "Yoneko's Earthquake" was also chosen as one of the *Best American Short Stories: 1952*. In 1986 she received from the Before Columbus Foundation the American Book Award for Lifetime Achievement.

Because Yamamoto excelled in depicting Japanese American communal life, it is helpful to see her fiction in historical and social context. Most Japanese immigrants came to America between 1885 and 1924. The first waves of immigrants consisted mainly of single young men who saw North America as a land of opportunity. After establishing themselves in the new country, some returned to Japan to seek wives, while others arranged their marriages by means of an exchange of photographs across the Pacific. Hence a large number of Japanese "picture brides" came to this country after the turn of the century to meet bridegrooms they had never seen in person. By 1930 the American-born Nisei (second generation) already outnumbered the Issei (first generation), and about half of the Japanese American population lived in rural areas in the western United States. Japanese was the language generally spoken at home, so that many Nisei (including Yamamoto) spoke only Japanese until they entered kindergarten.

Despite the preoccupation with survival in America, a number of Issei maintained their interest in Japanese poetry. There were literary groups engaged in the traditional forms of *haiku, tanka,* and *senryu,* as well as numerous magazines devoted to Issei poetry. Nisei, on the other hand, mostly expressed themselves in the English sections of Japanese American newspapers. The vibrant Japanese American literary movement was disrupted by the advent of World War II, when more than 110,000 Japanese Americans were incarcerated under the Japanese Relocation Act of 1942.

The prewar and postwar experiences of many Japanese Americans are reflected in the work of Yamamoto, who persistently explored the relationship between Issei men and women and between immigrant parents and their children. Because of the prevalence of arranged marriages among the Issei, compatibility between couples could hardly be assumed. In "Seventeen Syllables," it is through the naive perceptions of a Nisei daughter—Rosie—that we glimpse the dark nuances of Issei silences. While intergenerational differences are not peculiar to Japanese Americans, the gap between the Issei and the Nisei is widened by language and cultural barriers. Rosie's inability to appreciate her mother's Japanese haiku bespeaks her more general incomprehension of her mother's life story. The child's partial understanding allows Yamamoto to tell the mother's story obliquely.

King-Kok Cheung
University of California, Los Angeles

PRIMARY WORKS

Seventeen Syllables and Other Stories, 1988.

Seventeen Syllables

The first Rosie knew that her mother had taken to writing poems was one evening when she finished one and read it aloud for her daughter's approval. It was about cats, and Rosie pretended to understand it thoroughly and appreciate it no end, partly because she hesitated to disillusion her mother about the quantity and quality of Japanese she had learned in all the years now that she had been going to Japanese school every Saturday (and Wednesday, too, in the summer). Even so, her mother must have been skeptical about the depth of Rosie's understanding, because she explained afterwards about the kind of poem she was trying to write.

See, Rosie, she said, it was a *haiku*, a poem in which she must pack all her meaning into seventeen syllables only, which were divided into three lines of five, seven, and five syllables. In the one she had just read, she had tried to capture the charm of a kitten, as well as comment on the superstition that owning a cat of three colors meant good luck.

"Yes, yes, I understand. How utterly lovely," Rosie said, and her mother, either satisfied or seeing through the deception and resigned, went back to composing.

The truth was that Rosie was lazy; English lay ready on the tongue but Japanese had to be searched for and examined, and even then put forth tentatively (probably to meet with laughter). It was so much easier to say yes, yes, even when one meant no, no. Besides, this was what was in her mind to say: I was looking through one of your magazines from Japan last night, Mother, and towards the back I found some *haiku* in English that delighted me. There was one that made me giggle off and on until I fell asleep—

> It is morning, and lo!
> I lie awake, comme il faut,
> sighing for some dough.

Now, how to reach her mother, how to communicate the melancholy song? Rosie knew formal Japanese by fits and starts, her mother had even less English, no French. It was much more possible to say yes, yes.

It developed that her mother was writing the *haiku* for a daily newspaper, the *Mainichi Shimbun*, that was published in San Francisco. Los Angeles, to be sure, was closer to the farming community in which the Hayashi family lived and several Japanese vernaculars were printed there, but Rosie's parents said they preferred the tone of the northern paper. Once a week, the *Mainichi* would have a section devoted to *haiku*, and her mother became an extravagant contributor, taking for herself the blossoming pen name, Ume Hanazono.

So Rosie and her father lived for awhile with two women, her mother and Ume Hanazono. Her mother (Tome Hayashi by name) kept house, cooked, washed, and, along with her husband and the Carrascos, the Mexican family hired for the harvest, did her ample share of picking tomatoes out in the sweltering fields and boxing them in tidy strata in the cool packing shed. Ume Hanazono, who came to life after the dinner dishes were done, was an earnest, muttering stranger who often neglected speaking when spoken to and stayed busy at the parlor table as late as midnight scribbling with pencil on scratch paper or carefully copying characters on good paper with her fat, pale green Parker.

The new interest had some repercussions on the household routine. Before, Rosie had been accustomed to her parents and herself taking their hot baths early and going to bed almost immediately afterwards, unless her parents challenged each other to a game of flower cards or unless company dropped in. Now if her father wanted to play cards, he had to resort to solitaire (at which he always cheated fearlessly), and if a group of friends came over, it was bound to contain someone who was also writing *haiku*, and the small assemblage would be split in two, her father entertaining the non-literary members and her mother comparing ecstatic notes with the visiting poet.

If they went out, it was more of the same thing. But Ume Hanazono's life span, even for a poet's, was very brief—perhaps three months at most.

One night they went over to see the Hayano family in the neighboring town to the west, an adventure both painful and attractive to Rosie. It was attractive because there were four Hayano girls, all lovely and each one named after a season of the year (Haru, Natsu, Aki, Fuyu), painful because something had been wrong with Mrs. Hayano ever since the birth of her first child. Rosie would sometimes watch Mrs. Hayano, reputed to have been the belle of her native village, making her way about a room, stooped, slowly shuffling, violently trembling (*always* trembling), and she would be reminded that this woman, in this same condition, had carried and given issue to three babies. She would look wonderingly at Mr. Hayano, handsome, tall, and strong, and she would look at her four pretty friends. But it was not a matter she could come to any decision about.

On this visit, however, Mrs. Hayano sat all evening in the rocker, as motionless and unobtrusive as it was possible for her to be, and Rosie found the greater part of the evening practically anaesthetic. Too, Rosie spent most of it in the girls' room, because Haru, the garrulous one, said almost as soon as the bows and other greetings were over, "Oh, you must see my new coat!"

It was a pale plaid of grey, sand, and blue, with an enormous collar, and Rosie, seeing nothing special in it, said, "Gee, how nice."

"Nice?" said Haru, indignantly. "Is that all you can say about it? It's gorgeous! And so cheap, too. Only seventeen-ninety-eight, because it was a sale. The saleslady said it was twenty-five dollars regular."

"Gee," said Rosie. Natsu, who never said much and when she said anything said it shyly, fingered the coat covetously and Haru pulled it away.

"Mine," she said, putting it on. She minced in the aisle between the two large beds and smiled happily. "Let's see how your mother likes it."

She broke into the front room and the adult conversation and went to stand in front of Rosie's mother, while the rest watched from the door. Rosie's mother was properly envious. "May I inherit it when you're through with it?"

Haru, pleased, giggled and said yes, she could, but Natsu reminded gravely from the door, "You promised me, Haru."

Everyone laughed but Natsu, who shamefacedly retreated into the bedroom. Haru came in laughing, taking off the coat. "We were only kidding, Natsu," she said. "Here, you try it on now."

After Natsu buttoned herself into the coat, inspected herself solemnly in the bureau mirror, and reluctantly shed it, Rosie, Aki, and Fuyu got their turns, and Fuyu, who was eight, drowned in it while her sisters and Rosie doubled up in amusement. They all went into the front room later, because Haru's mother quaveringly called to her to fix the tea and rice cakes and open a can of sliced peaches for everybody. Rosie noticed that her mother and Mr. Hayano were talking together at the little table—they were discussing a *haiku* that Mr. Hayano was planning to send to the *Mainichi*, while her father was sitting at one end of the sofa looking through a copy of *Life*, the new picture magazine. Occasionally, her father would comment on a photograph, holding it toward Mrs. Hayano and speaking to her as he always did—loudly, as though he thought someone such as she must surely be at least a trifle deaf also.

The five girls had their refreshments at the kitchen table, and it was while Rosie was showing the sisters her trick of swallowing peach slices without chewing (she chased each slippery crescent down with a swig of tea) that her father brought his empty teacup and untouched saucer to the sink and said, "Come on, Rosie, we're going home now."

"Already?" asked Rosie.

"Work tomorrow," he said.

He sounded irritated, and Rosie, puzzled, gulped one last yellow slice and stood up to go, while the sisters began protesting, as was their wont.

"We have to get up at five-thirty," he told them, going into the front room quickly, so that they did not have their usual chance to hang onto his hands and plead for an extension of time.

Rosie, following, saw that her mother and Mr. Hayano were sipping tea and still talking together, while Mrs. Hayano concentrated, quivering, on raising the handleless Japanese cup to her lips with both her hands and lowering it back to her lap. Her father, saying nothing, went out the door, onto the bright porch, and down the steps. Her mother looked up and asked, "Where is he going?"

"Where is he going?" Rosie said. "He said we were going home now."

"Going home?" Her mother looked with embarrassment at Mr. Hayano and his absorbed wife and then forced a smile. "He must be tired," she said.

Haru was not giving up yet. "May Rosie stay overnight?" she asked, and Natsu, Aki, and Fuyu came to reinforce their sister's plea by helping her make a circle around Rosie's mother. Rosie, for once having no desire to stay, was relieved when her mother, apologizing to the perturbed Mr. and Mrs. Hayano for her father's abruptness at the same time, managed to shake her head no at the quartet, kindly but adamant, so that they broke their circle and let her go.

Rosie's father looked ahead into the windshield as the two joined him. "I'm sorry," her mother said. "You must be tired." Her father, stepping on the starter, said nothing. "You know how I get when it's *haiku*," she continued, "I forget what time it is." He only grunted.

As they rode homeward silently, Rosie, sitting between, felt a rush of hate for both—for her mother for begging, for her father for denying her mother. I wish this old Ford would crash, right now, she thought, then immediately, no, no, I wish my father would laugh, but it was too late: already the vision had passed through her mind of the green pick-up crumpled in the dark against one of the mighty eucalyptus trees they were just riding past, of the three contorted, bleeding bodies, one of them hers.

Rosie ran between two patches of tomatoes, her heart working more rambunctiously than she had ever known it to. How lucky it was that Aunt Taka and Uncle Gimpachi had come tonight, though, how very lucky. Otherwise she might not have really kept her half-promise to meet Jesus Carrasco. Jesus was going to be a senior in September at the same school she went to, and his parents were the ones helping with the tomatoes this year. She and Jesus, who hardly remembered seeing each other at Cleveland High where there were so many other people and two whole grades between them, had become great friends this summer—he always had a joke for her when he periodically drove the loaded pick-up up from the fields to the shed where she was usually sorting while her mother and father did the packing, and they laughed a great deal together over infinitesimal repartee during the afternoon break for chilled watermelon or ice cream in the shade of the shed.

What she enjoyed most was racing him to see which could finish picking a double row first. He, who could work faster, would tease her by slowing down until she thought she would surely pass him this time, then speeding up furiously to leave her several sprawling vines behind. Once he had made her screech hideously by crossing over, while her back was turned, to place atop the tomatoes in her green-stained bucket a truly monstrous, pale green worm (it had looked more like an infant snake). And it was when they had finished a contest this morning, after she had pantingly pointed a green finger at the immature tomatoes evident in the lugs at the end of his row and he had returned the accusation (with justice), that he had startlingly brought up the matter of their possibly meeting outside the range of both their parents' dubious eyes.

"What for?" she had asked.

"I've got a secret I want to tell you," he said.

"Tell me now," she demanded.

"It won't be ready till tonight," he said.

She laughed. "Tell me tomorrow then."

"It'll be gone tomorrow," he threatened.

"Well, for seven hakes, what is it?" she had asked, more than twice, and when he had suggested that the packing shed would be an appropriate place to find out, she had cautiously answered maybe. She had not been certain she was going to keep the appointment until the arrival of mother's sister and her husband. Their coming seemed a sort of signal of permission, of grace, and she had definitely made up her mind to lie and leave as she was bowing them welcome.

So as soon as everyone appeared settled back for the evening, she announced loudly that she was going to the privy outside, "I'm going to the *benjo!*" and slipped out the door. And now that she was actually on her way, her heart pumped in such an undisciplined way that she could hear it with her ears. It's because I'm running, she told herself, slowing to a walk. The shed was up ahead, one more patch away, in the middle of the fields. Its bulk, looming in the dimness, took on a sinisterness that was funny when Rosie reminded herself that it was only a wooden frame with a canvas roof and three canvas walls that made a slapping noise on breezy days.

Jesus was sitting on the narrow plank that was the sorting platform and she went around to the other side and jumped backwards to seat herself on the rim of a packing stand. "Well, tell me," she said without greeting, thinking her voice sounded reassuringly familiar.

"I saw you coming out the door," Jesus said. "I heard you running part of the way, too."

"Uh-huh," Rosie said. "Now tell me the secret."

"I was afraid you wouldn't come," he said.

Rosie delved around on the chicken-wire bottom of the stall for number two tomatoes, ripe, which she was sitting beside, and came up with a left-over that felt edible. She bit into it and began sucking out the pulp and seeds. "I'm here," she pointed out.

"Rosie, are you sorry you came?"

"Sorry? What for?" she said. "You said you were going to tell me something."

"I will, I will," Jesus said, but his voice contained disappointment, and Rosie fleetingly felt the older of the two, realizing a brand-new power which vanished without category under her recognition.

"I have to go back in a minute," she said. "My aunt and uncle are here from Wintersburg. I told them I was going to the privy."

Jesus laughed. "You funny thing," he said. "You slay me!"

"Just because you have a bathroom *inside*," Rosie said. "Come on, tell me."

Chuckling, Jesus came around to lean on the stand facing her. They still could not see each other very clearly, but Rosie noticed that Jesus became very sober again as he took the hollow tomato from her hand and dropped it back into the stall. When he took hold of her empty hand, she could find no words to protest; her vocabulary had become distressingly constricted and she thought desperately that all that remained intact now was yes and no and oh, and even these few sounds would not easily out. Thus, kissed by Jesus, Rosie fell for the first time entirely victim to a helplessness delectable beyond speech. But the terrible, beautiful sensation lasted no more than a second, and the reality of Jesus' lips and tongue and teeth and hands made her pull away with such strength that she nearly tumbled.

Rosie stopped running as she approached the lights from the windows of home. How long since she had left? She could not guess, but gasping yet, she went to the privy in back and locked herself in. Her own breathing deafened her in the dark, close space, and she sat and waited until she could hear at last the nightly calling of the frogs and crickets. Even then, all she could think to say was oh, my, and the pressure of Jesus' face against her face would not leave.

No one had missed her in the parlor, however, and Rosie walked in and through quickly, announcing that she was next going to take a bath. "Your father's in the bathhouse," her mother said, and Rosie, in her room, recalled that she had not seen him when she entered. There had been only Aunt Taka and Uncle Gimpachi with her mother at the table, drinking tea. She got her robe and straw sandals and crossed the parlor again to go outside. Her mother was telling them about the *haiku* competition in the *Mainichi* and the poem she had entered.

Rosie met her father coming out of the bathhouse. "Are you through Father?" she asked. "I was going to ask you to scrub my back."

"Scrub your own back," he said shortly, going toward the main house.

"What have I done now?" she yelled after him. She suddenly felt like doing a lot of yelling. But he did not answer, and she went into the bathhouse. Turning on the dangling light, she removed her denims and T-shirt and threw them in the big carton for dirty clothes standing next to the washing machine. Her other things she took with her into the bath compartment to wash after her bath. After she had scooped a basin of hot water from the square wooden tub, she sat on the grey cement of the floor and soaped herself at exaggerated leisure, singing "Red Sails in the Sunset" at the top of her voice and using da-da-da where she suspected her words. Then, standing up, still singing, for she was possessed by the notion that any attempt now to analyze would result in spoilage and she believed that the larger her volume the less she would be able to hear herself think, she obtained more hot water and poured it on until she was free of lather. Only then did she allow herself to step into the steaming vat, one leg first, then the remainder of her body inch by inch until the water no longer stung and she could move around at will.

She took a long time soaking, afterwards remembering to go around outside to stoke the embers of the tin-lined fireplace beneath the tub and to throw on a few more sticks so that the water might keep its heat for her mother, and when she finally returned to the parlor, she found her mother still talking *haiku* with her aunt and uncle, the three of them on another round of tea. Her father was nowhere in sight.

At Japanese school the next day (Wednesday, it was), Rosie was grave and giddy by turns. Preoccupied at her desk in the row for students on Book Eight, she made up for it at recess by performing wild mimicry for the benefit of her friend Chizuko. She held her nose and whined a witticism or two in what she considered was the manner of Fred Allen; she assumed intoxication and a British accent to go over the climax of the Rudy Vallee recording of the pub conversation about William Ewart Gladstone; she was the child Shirley Temple piping, "On the Good Ship Lollipop"; she was the gentleman soprano of the Four Inkspots trilling, "If I Didn't Care." And she felt reasonably satisfied when Chizuko wept and gasped, "Oh, Rosie, you ought to be in the movies!"

Her father came after her at noon, bringing her sandwiches of minced ham and two nectarines to eat while she rode, so that she could pitch right into the sorting when they got home. The lugs were piling up, he said, and the ripe tomatoes in them would probably have to be taken to the cannery tomorrow if they were not ready for the produce haulers tonight. "This heat's not doing them any good. And we've got no time for a break today."

It *was* hot, probably the hottest day of the year, and Rosie's blouse stuck damply to her back even under the protection of the canvas. But she worked as efficiently as a flawless machine and kept the stalls heaped, with one part of her mind listening in to the parental murmuring about the heat and the tomatoes and with another part planning the exact words she would say to Jesus when he drove up with the first load of the afternoon. But when at last she saw that the pick-up was coming, her hands went berserk and the tomatoes started falling in the wrong stalls, and her father said, "Hey, hey! Rosie, watch what you're doing!"

"Well, I have to go to the *benjo*," she said, hiding panic.

"Go in the weeds over there," he said, only half-joking.

"Oh, Father!" she protested.

"Oh, go on home," her mother said. "We'll make out for awhile."

In the privy Rosie peered through a knothole toward the fields, watching as much as she could of Jesus. Happily she thought she saw him look in the direction of the house from time to time before he finished unloading and went back toward the patch where his mother and father worked. As she was heading for the shed, a very presentable black car purred up the dirt driveway to the house and its driver motioned to her. Was this the Hayashi home, he wanted to know. She nodded. Was she a Hayashi? Yes, she said, thinking that he was a good-looking man. He got out of the car with a huge, flat package and she saw that he warmly wore a business suit. "I have something here for your mother then," he said, in a more elegant Japanese than she was used to.

She told him where her mother was and he came along with her, patting his face with an immaculate white handkerchief and saying something about the coolness of San Francisco. To her surprised mother and father, he bowed and introduced himself as, among other things, the *haiku* editor of the *Mainichi Shimbun*, saying that since he had been coming as far as Los Angeles anyway, he had decided to bring her the first prize she had won in the recent contest.

"First prize?" her mother echoed, believing and not believing, pleased and overwhelmed. Handed the package with a bow, she bobbed her head up and down numerous times to express her utter gratitude.

"It is nothing much," he added, "but I hope it will serve as a token of our great appreciation for your contributions and our great admiration of your considerable talent."

"I am not worthy," she said, falling easily into his style. "It is I who should make some sign of my humble thanks for being permitted to contribute."

"No, no, to the contrary," he said, bowing again.

But Rosie's mother insisted, and then saying that she knew she was being unorthodox, she asked if she might open the package because her curiosity was so great. Certainly she might. In fact, he would like her reaction to it, for personally, it was one of his favorite *Hiroshiges*.

Rosie thought it was a pleasant picture, which looked to have been sketched with delicate quickness. There were pink clouds, containing some graceful calligraphy, and a sea that was a pale blue except at the edges, containing four sampans with indications of people in them. Pines edged the water and on the far-off beach there was a cluster of thatched huts towered over by pine-dotted mountains of grey and blue. The frame was scalloped and gilt.

After Rosie's mother pronounced it without peer and somewhat prodded her father into nodding agreement, she said Mr. Kuroda must at least have a cup of tea after coming all this way, and although Mr. Kuroda did not want to impose, he soon agreed that a cup of tea would be refreshing and went along with her to the house, carrying the picture for her.

"Ha, your mother's crazy!" Rosie's father said, and Rosie laughed uneasily as she resumed judgment on the tomatoes. She had emptied six lugs when he broke into an imaginary conversation with Jesus to tell her to go and remind her mother of the tomatoes, and she went slowly.

Mr. Kuroda was in his shirtsleeves expounding some *haiku* theory as he munched a rice cake, and her mother was rapt. Abashed in the great man's presence, Rosie stood next to her mother's chair until her mother looked up inquiringly, and then she started to whisper the message, but her mother pushed her gently away and reproached, "You are not being very polite to our guest."

"Father says the tomatoes . . ." Rosie said aloud, smiling foolishly.

"Tell him I shall only be a minute," her mother said, speaking the language of Mr. Kuroda.

When Rosie carried the reply to her father, he did not seem to hear and she said again, "Mother says she'll be back in a minute."

"All right, all right," he nodded, and they worked again in silence. But suddenly, her father uttered an incredible noise, exactly like the cork of a bottle popping, and the next Rosie knew, he was stalking angrily toward the house, almost running in fact, and she chased after him crying, "Father! Father! What are you going to do?"

He stopped long enough to order her back to the shed. "Never mind!" he shouted, "Get on with the sorting!"

And from the place in the fields where she stood, frightened and vacillating, Rosie saw her father enter the house. Soon Mr. Kuroda came out alone, putting on his coat. Mr. Kuroda got into his car and backed out down the driveway onto the highway. Next her father emerged, also alone, something in his arms (it was the picture, she realized), and, going over to the bathhouse woodpile, he threw the picture on the ground and picked up the axe. Smashing the picture, glass and all (she heard the explosion faintly), he reached over for the kerosene that was used to encourage the bath fire and poured it over the wreckage. I am dreaming, Rosie said to herself, I am dreaming, but her father, having made sure that his act of cremation was irrevocable, was even then returning to the fields.

Rosie ran past him and toward the house. What had become of her mother? She burst into the parlor and found her mother at the back window watching the dying fire. They watched together until there remained only a feeble smoke under the blazing sun. Her mother was very calm.

"Do you know why I married your father?" she said without turning.

"No," said Rosie. It was the most frightening question she had ever been called upon to answer. Don't tell me now, she wanted to say, tell me tomorrow, tell me next week, don't tell me today. But she knew she would be told now, that the telling would combine with the other violence of the hot afternoon to level her life, her world to the very ground.

It was like a story out of the magazines illustrated in sepia, which she had consumed so greedily for a period until the information had somehow reached her that those wretchedly unhappy autobiographies, offered to her as the testimonials of living men and women, were largely inventions: Her mother, at nineteen, had come to America and married her father as an alternative to suicide.

At eighteen she had been in love with the first son of one of the well-to-do families in her village. The two had met whenever and wherever they could, secretly, because it would not have done for his family to see him favor her—her father had no money; he was a drunkard and a gambler besides. She had learned she was with child; an excellent match had already been arranged for her lover. Despised by her family, she had given premature birth to a stillborn son, who would be seventeen now. Her family did not turn her out, but she could no longer project herself in any direction without refreshing in them the memory of her indiscretion. She wrote to Aunt Taka, her favorite sister in America, threatening to kill herself if Aunt Taka would not send for her. Aunt Taka hastily arranged a marriage with a young man of whom she knew, but lately arrived from Japan, a young man of simple mind, it was said, but of kindly heart. The young man was never told why his unseen betrothed was so eager to hasten the day of meeting.

The story was told perfectly, with neither groping for words nor untoward passion. It was as though her mother had memorized it by heart, reciting it to herself so many times over that its nagging vileness had long since gone.

"I had a brother then?" Rosie asked, for this was what seemed to matter now; she would think about the other later, she assured herself, pushing back the illumination which threatened all that darkness that had hitherto been merely mysterious or even glamorous. "A half-brother?"

"Yes."

"I would have liked a brother," she said.

Suddenly, her mother knelt on the floor and took her by the wrists. "Rosie," she said urgently, "Promise me you will never marry!" Shocked more by the request than the revelation, Rosie stared at her mother's face. Jesus, Jesus, she called silently, not certain whether she was invoking the help of the son of the Carrascos or of God, until there returned sweetly the memory of Jesus' hand, how it had touched her and where. Still her mother waited for an answer, holding her wrists so tightly that her hands were going numb. She tried to pull free. Promise, her mother whispered fiercely, promise. Yes, yes, I promise, Rosie said. But for an instant she turned away, and her mother, hearing the familiar glib agreement, released her. Oh, you, you, you, her eyes and twisted mouth said, you fool. Rosie, covering her face, began at last to cry, and the embrace and consoling hand came much later than she expected.

1949

ELIZABETH BISHOP
1911–1979

Elizabeth Bishop was the only child of William Thomas Bishop and Gertrude (Bulmer) Bishop. William, the oldest son of John W. Bishop of Prince Edward Island, was a contractor responsible for many public buildings in Boston (including the Museum of Fine Arts and the Boston Public Library). He married Gertrude Bulmer of Great Village, Nova Scotia, and died when Elizabeth was eight months old. When the poet was four years old, her mother, after years of nervous breakdowns, was permanently placed in a mental institution. Elizabeth spent summers with her maternal grandparents in Nova Scotia and was intermittently cared for by her paternal grandparents in Worcester and later by a married but childless aunt in and around Boston. Bishop's childhood was spent in the company of adults; in her early years, she had little opportunity for contact with members of her own generation.

Chronically ill with asthma, Bishop was unable to attend school until 1927, when she enrolled at Walnut Hill School in Natick, Massachusetts. Sailing (two months at the Nautical Camp for Girls on Cape Cod), reading, and music were her early and enduring enthusiasms. When she entered Vassar College in 1930, she was undecided as to whether she would major in music, literature, or medicine. Though that Vassar class would come to be known as a particularly literary group (Muriel Rukeyser and Mary McCarthy were coeditors with Bishop of the student literary magazine, *Con Spirito*), Bishop did not meet her literary mentor, Marianne Moore, at Vassar but in the entryway of the New York Public Library.

The Vassar College librarian had arranged a meeting after Bishop expressed an interest in Marianne Moore's poetry; the meeting led to a lifelong friendship.

Marianne Moore was Bishop's first life example, editor, confidante, and typist. In an age when women lacked women as role models, Moore emerged as one of the earliest as well as most significant reference points in the younger poet's world. As Bishop later recalled, Moore offered a rare confluence of manners and morals, a life as distinctly styled as her poetry. Correspondence between the poets reveals a protégée influenced by, yet resistant to, the poetic style of her mentor. While comparisons are inevitable, Bishop repeatedly distinguished her aesthetic as traditional in comparison with Moore's unique brand of modernism. Curiously, poets as diverse as George Herbert, Gerard Manley Hopkins, Emerson, Thoreau, and Pablo Neruda greatly influenced Bishop's early work.

Robert Lowell's intuitive and precise review of *North & South* (*Sewanee Review*, 1947) brought the poets together for a lifetime of correspondence. Though Lowell repeatedly confessed his debt to Bishop's poetry, her debt to his is less well known. For Bishop, Lowell represented the quintessential American: male and historically significant. Indeed, he became her "other." Even as *Questions of Travel* seems a reply to Lowell's earlier *Life Studies*, *Geography III* seems unimaginable without Lowell's struggle to place life at the center of the lyric.

Although Moore and Lowell served as her sponsors, Bishop returned that favor in correspondence, friendship, and support of May Swenson. The voluminous collection of letters between these poets (Washington University Library Special Collections) describes a mutual female bonding and support. Swenson is as tough-minded as the young Bishop was, but she refuses to see the role of mentor as exclusively Bishop's. Swenson enters into a lively critical discussion with Bishop, often assuming the role of teacher herself. The reserve that marks the Moore-Bishop letters fades into an eloquent democracy in the Bishop-Swenson letters.

Bishop's literary development is best known through letters because she spent most of her adult life in Brazil, away from the stresses and competitiveness of the New York literary world. Though Moore, Lowell, Randall Jarrell, and Swenson kept her informed about the American poetry world, she was able to live a life of tropical remove with her Brazilian friend, Lota Costellat de Macedo Soares. Witness to overwhelming poverty, political instability, and a mixture of foreign cultures, Bishop, armed with a small trust fund, could afford to keep these distractions at bay while she traveled, observed, and wrote.

Keenly observed description and a dependence on the things of this world characterize Bishop's work. In language, she is a direct descendant of what Perry Miller called the American plain stylists. Like Robert Frost, she effects a wide tonal range within a remarkably narrow range of words, often accomplished through formal means. In "Filling Station," Bishop uses the restrictions of form to impose limitations on the tone and atmosphere of the poem. Solitary figures in the landscape abound in her poems and suggest the familiar Romantic lyric of the isolated hero, the Wordsworthian self-discoverer; yet she systematically rejects epiphany, preferring the familiarity of the phenomenal world. Bishop's early interest in surrealism surfaces throughout her work in dreamscapes of different sorts. "The Man-Moth" explores the nightmarish uncertainties of the night world, while invoking the poet's interest in the perceptions of exiles. Like many American writers, she prizes the isolated moral force. As in Emerson's poetry, Bishop sees, names, and gives the landscape a moral form and purpose.

Much has been made of Bishop's reticence. Octavio Paz proclaimed it a power, a womanly strength; Sylvia Plath and Adrienne Rich, searching for appropriate women poets as models, rejected it as a kind of repression. Bishop's refusal to appear in women's anthologies did not stem from an avoidance of women's issues (she had lived her life as an independent artist), but rather from a lifelong commitment to the transcendent potential of art, a belief that literature should address that world beyond life's limitations.

C. K. Doreski
Boston University

PRIMARY WORKS

North & South, 1946; *Poems: North & South—A Cold Spring* (Pulitzer Prize, 1956); *Questions of Travel*, 1965; *The Complete Poems*, 1969; *Geography III*, 1976; *The Complete Poems, 1927–1979*, 1983; *The Collected Prose*, 1984.

The Fish

I caught a tremendous fish
and held him beside the boat
half out of water, with my hook
fast in a corner of his mouth.
He didn't fight.   5
He hadn't fought at all.
He hung a grunting weight,
battered and venerable
and homely. Here and there
his brown skin hung in strips   10
like ancient wallpaper,
and its pattern of darker brown
was like wallpaper:
shapes like full-blown roses
stained and lost through age.   15
He was speckled with barnacles,
fine rosettes of lime,
and infested
with tiny white sea-lice,
and underneath two or three   20
rags of green weed hung down.
While his gills were breathing in
the terrible oxygen
—the frightening gills,
fresh and crisp with blood,   25
that can cut so badly—
I thought of the coarse white flesh

packed in like feathers,
the big bones and the little bones,
the dramatic reds and blacks   30
of his shiny entrails,
and the pink swim-bladder
like a big peony.
I looked into his eyes
which were far larger than mine   35
but shallower, and yellowed,
the irises backed and packed
with tarnished tinfoil
seen through the lenses
of old scratched isinglass.   40
They shifted a little, but not
to return my stare.
—It was more like the tipping
of an object toward the light.
I admired his sullen face,   45
the mechanism of his jaw,
and then I saw
that from his lower lip
—if you could call it a lip—
grim, wet, and weaponlike,   50
hung five old pieces of fish-line,
or four and a wire leader
with the swivel still attached,
with all their five big hooks
grown firmly in his mouth.   55
A green line, frayed at the end
where he broke it, two heavier lines,
and a fine black thread
still crimped from the strain and snap
when it broke and he got away.   60
Like medals with their ribbons
frayed and wavering,
a five-haired beard of wisdom
trailing from his aching jaw.
I stared and stared   65
and victory filled up
the little rented boat,
from the pool of bilge
where oil had spread a rainbow
around the rusted engine   70
to the bailer rusted orange,
the sun-cracked thwarts,
the oarlocks on their strings,

the gunnels—until everything
was rainbow, rainbow, rainbow!   75
And I let the fish go.

                                                                 1946

The Man-Moth[1]

    Here, above,
cracks in the buildings are filled with battered moonlight.
The whole shadow of Man is only as big as his hat.
It lies at his feet like a circle for a doll to stand on,
and he makes an inverted pin, the point magnetized to the moon.   5
He does not see the moon; he observes only her vast properties,
feeling the queer light on his hands, neither warm nor cold,
of a temperature impossible to record in thermometers.

    But when the Man-Moth
pays his rare, although occasional, visits to the surface,   10
the moon looks rather different to him. He emerges
from an opening under the edge of one of the sidewalks
and nervously begins to scale the faces of the buildings.
He thinks the moon is a small hole at the top of the sky,
proving the sky quite useless for protection.   15
He trembles, but must investigate as high as he can climb.

    Up the façades,
his shadow dragging like a photographer's cloth behind him,
he climbs fearfully, thinking that this time he will manage
to push his small head through that round clean opening   20
and be forced through, as from a tube, in black scrolls on the
        light.
(Man, standing below him, has no such illusions.)
But what the Man-Moth fears most he must do, although
he fails, of course, and falls back scared but quite unhurt.   25

    Then he returns
to the pale subways of cement he calls his home. He flits,
he flutters, and cannot get aboard the silent trains
fast enough to suit him. The doors close swiftly.
The Man-Moth always seats himself facing the wrong way   30
and the train starts at once at its full, terrible speed,
without a shift in gears or a gradation of any sort.
He cannot tell the rate at which he travels backwards.

---

[1]Newspaper misprint for "mammoth."

Each night he must
be carried through artificial tunnels and dream recurrent dreams.   35
Just as the ties recur beneath his train, these underlie
his rushing brain. He does not dare look out the window,
for the third rail, the unbroken draught of poison,
runs there beside him. He regards it as a disease
he has inherited the susceptibility to. He has to keep   40
his hands in his pockets, as others must wear mufflers.

If you catch him,
hold up a flashlight to his eye. It's all dark pupil,
an entire night itself, whose haired horizon tightens
as he stares back, and closes up the eye. Then from the lids   45
one tear, his only possession, like the bee's sting, slips.
Slyly he palms it, and if you're not paying attention
he'll swallow it. However, if you watch, he'll hand it over,
cool as from underground springs and pure enough to drink.

1946

At the Fishhouses

Although it is a cold evening,
down by one of the fishhouses
an old man sits netting,
his net, in the gloaming almost invisible,
a dark purple-brown,   5
and his shuttle worn and polished.
The air smells so strong of codfish
it makes one's nose run and one's eyes water.
The five fishhouses have steeply peaked roofs
and narrow, cleated gangplanks slant up   10
to storerooms in the gables
for the wheelbarrows to be pushed up and down on.
All is silver: the heavy surface of the sea,
swelling slowly as if considering spilling over,
is opaque, but the silver of the benches,   15
the lobster pots, and masts, scattered
among the wild jagged rocks,
is of an apparent translucence
like the small old buildings with an emerald moss
growing on their shoreward walls.   20
The big fish tubs are completely lined
with layers of beautiful herring scales
and the wheelbarrows are similarly plastered
with creamy iridescent coats of mail,

with small iridescent flies crawling on them.   25
Up on the little slope behind the houses,
set in the sparse bright sprinkle of grass,
is an ancient wooden capstan,
cracked, with two long bleached handles
and some melancholy stains, like dried blood,   30
where the ironwork has rusted.
The old man accepts a Lucky Strike.
He was a friend of my grandfather.
We talk of the decline in the population
and of codfish and herring   35
while he waits for a herring boat to come in.
There are sequins on his vest and on his thumb.
He has scraped the scales, the principal beauty,
from unnumbered fish with that black old knife,
the blade of which is almost worn away.   40

Down at the water's edge, at the place
where they haul up the boats, up the long ramp
descending into the water, thin silver
tree trunks are laid horizontally
across the gray stones, down and down   45
at intervals of four or five feet.

Cold dark deep and absolutely clear,
element bearable to no mortal,
to fish and to seals . . . One seal particularly
I have seen here evening after evening.   50
He was curious about me. He was interested in music;
like me a believer in total immersion,
so I used to sing him Baptist hymns.
I also sang "A Mighty Fortress Is Our God."
He stood up in the water and regarded me   55
steadily, moving his head a little.
Then he would disappear, then suddenly emerge
almost in the same spot, with a sort of shrug
as if it were against his better judgment.
Cold dark deep and absolutely clear,   60
the clear gray icy water . . . Back, behind us,
the dignified tall firs begin.
Bluish, associating with their shadows,
a million Christmas trees stand
waiting for Christmas. The water seems suspended   65
above the rounded gray and blue-gray stones.
I have seen it over and over, the same sea, the same,
slightly, indifferently swinging above the stones,

icily free above the stones,
above the stones and then the world.   70
If you should dip your hand in,
your wrist would ache immediately,
your bones would begin to ache and your hand would burn
as if the water were a transmutation of fire
that feeds on stones and burns with a dark gray flame.   75
If you tasted it, it would first taste bitter,
then briny, then surely burn your tongue.
It is like what we imagine knowledge to be:
dark, salt, clear, moving, utterly free,
drawn from the cold hard mouth   80
of the world, derived from the rocky breasts
forever, flowing and drawn, and since
our knowledge is historical, flowing, and flown.

                                                                        1955

Filling Station

Oh, but it is dirty!
—this little filling station,
oil-soaked, oil-permeated
to a disturbing, over-all
black translucency.   5
Be careful with that match!

Father wears a dirty,
oil-soaked monkey suit
that cuts him under the arms,
and several quick and saucy   10
and greasy sons assist him
(it's a family filling station),
all quite thoroughly dirty.

Do they live in the station?
It has a cement porch   15
behind the pumps, and on it
a set of crushed and grease-
impregnated wickerwork;
on the wicker sofa
a dirty dog, quite comfy.   20

Some comic books provide
the only note of color—
of certain color. They lie

upon a big dim doily
draping a taboret[1]   25
(part of the set), beside
a big hirsute begonia.

Why the extraneous plant?
Why the taboret?
Why, oh why, the doily?   30
(Embroidered in daisy stitch
with marguerites, I think,
and heavy with gray crochet.)

Somebody embroidered the doily.
Somebody waters the plant,   35
or oils it, maybe. Somebody
arranges the rows of cans
so that they softly say:
ESSO—SO—SO—SO
to high-strung automobiles.   40
Somebody loves us all.

                                                                    1965

THEODORE ROETHKE
1908–1963

Theodore Roethke was born in Saginaw, Michigan, and spent his childhood in and around his father's large commercial greenhouses, with their luxuriance of protected natural growth. It was there, among the acres of roses and carnations and in cellars rank with rotten manure and rooting slips, that he developed his participatory awareness of the small things of nature. These two, the greenhouses and the almost godlike father directing a crew of skilled florists and helpers, became the most pervasive shaping presences in his poetry: the greenhouses a humanly created Eden surrounded by open fields of eternity, and the father a center of powerful conflicting emotions of love and hate.

Roethke apparently began to write poems during his undergraduate years at the University of Michigan, where he received a B.A. in 1929, but if so, he wrote in secret. His doing so is only one early instance of his habitual wearing of masks to hide an inner vulnerability and seriousness. It was not until his graduate school years, first at Michigan and then at Harvard, that he either discussed

---

[1]Small stand.

or wrote poetry openly. His first publications came in 1930 and 1931. His teaching career, which proved to be lifelong, began in the fall of 1931 at Lafayette College in Easton, Pennsylvania. Toward the end of his four-year term there, he served also as tennis coach, a game he played with intense aggressiveness. Later he taught at several other colleges and universities before settling, from 1947 until his death, at the University of Washington.

Another pattern that also proved to be lifelong emerged by 1931 or even before. By the time he went to Easton to teach, Roethke was already a heavy drinker, having frequent bouts of drunkenness during which he sometimes became rowdy and even destructive. Friends later recalled his drinking as a kind of search for oblivion. Certainly the drinking was both evidence and a contributing cause of the complex and severe emotional problems that led to his being hospitalized several times for what was usually diagnosed as manic-depression. Throughout his life he swung between extremes—of mood, of bravado or torturing self-doubt, of self-righteousness or guilt, of certainty that he was America's preeminent poet or despair over his supposed lack of achievement. He seems to have felt that nothing he did would have earned his father's approval.

In 1953, Roethke married Beatrice O'Connell, his former student and also a former fashion model. At the time of their marriage, Beatrice was unaware of his history of mental illness. Before a year was out, she had seen him through one of his typical crises, though a fairly mild one involving only two weeks of hospitalization. She rose to the need and supported him over the years, a real companion as well as caretaker. It must not have been easy. He was demanding, dependent, and a casual womanizer. His difficulties relating to women apparently sprang from complex feelings toward his mother, which, if less disturbing than those toward his father, were at any rate troubled. However, several of his late poems record Roethke's great care and concern for his wife, and one of his most significant works, "Meditations of an Old Woman," draws partly on his regard for his mother.

Besides its disciplined exploration of rhythmic variation and symbolist style, Roethke's poetry is characterized by a deep, even mystical, animism, a close attention to minute living things and natural processes, and a continuing use of childhood anxieties and his own ambivalent feelings toward his father in developing a motif of the soul journey. For Roethke, this journey went toward reconciliation and oneness. In his late poem "The Rose" (from "North American Sequence") his father is joined with an evocation of the greenhouse world as images of perfect beatitude: "What need for heaven, then, / With that man and those roses?" Among his many honors and awards were the Pulitzer Prize, the Bollingen Prize, a Fulbright Award, and two Guggenheim Fellowships.

Janis Stout
Texas A & M University

PRIMARY WORKS

Open House, 1941; *The Lost Son and Other Poems*, 1948; *Praise to the End!*, 1951; *The Waking: Poems 1933–53*, 1953; *Words for the Wind: The Collected Verse of Theodore Roethke*, 1957; *I Am! Says the Lamb*, 1961; *Party at the Zoo*, 1963; *The Far Field*, 1964; *Sequence, Sometimes Metaphysical*, 1964; *The Collected Poems of Theodore Roethke*, 1968.

Frau Bauman, Frau Schmidt, and Frau Schwartze[1]

Gone the three ancient ladies
Who creaked on the greenhouse ladders,
Reaching up white strings
To wind, to wind
The sweet-pea tendrils,[2] the smilax,[3]   5
Nasturtiums, the climbing
Roses, to straighten
Carnations, red
Chrysanthemums; the stiff
Stems, jointed like corn,   10
They tied and tucked,—
These nurses of nobody else.
Quicker than birds, they dipped
Up and sifted the dirt;
They sprinkled and shook;   15
They stood astride pipes,
Their skirts billowing out wide into tents,
Their hands twinkling with wet;
Like witches they flew along rows
Keeping creation at ease;   20
With a tendril for needle
They sewed up the air with a stem;
They teased out the seed that the cold kept asleep,—
All the coils, loops, and whorls.
They trellised[4] the sun; they plotted for more than themselves.   25

I remember how they picked me up, a spindly[5] kid,
Pinching and poking my thin ribs
Till I lay in their laps, laughing,
Weak as a whiffet;[6]
Now, when I'm alone and cold in my bed,   30
They still hover over me,
These ancient leathery crones,
With their bandannas stiffened with sweat,
And their thorn-bitten wrists,
And their snuff-laden breath blowing lightly over me in my first   35
    sleep.

1948

[1]Common German names; Roethke's family was German.
[2]Small twigs of vining plants.
[3]A climbing plant with prickly stems.
[4]Trained up on a frame, usually made of laths, as a plant is trained into a chosen shape.

Roethke's tribute to the three greenhouse workers/nature goddesses has reached mythic proportions.
[5]Skinny.
[6]A small, young, or unimportant person; probably a corruption of *whippet*, a small dog.

Root Cellar

Nothing would sleep in that cellar,[1] dank as a ditch,
Bulbs broke out of boxes hunting for chinks in the dark,
Shoots dangled and drooped,
Lolling obscenely from mildewed crates,
Hung down long yellow evil necks, like tropical snakes.   5
And what a congress[2] of stinks!—
Roots ripe as old bait,
Pulpy stems, rank, silo-rich,[3]
Leaf-mold, manure, lime, piled against slippery planks.
Nothing would give up life: 10
Even the dirt kept breathing a small breath.

1948

Big Wind

Where were the greenhouses going,
Lunging into the lashing
Wind driving water
So far down the river
All the faucets stopped?—   5
So we drained the manure-machine
For the steam plant,
Pumping the stale mixture
Into the rusty boilers,
Watching the pressure gauge   10
Waver over to red,
As the seams hissed
And the live steam
Drove to the far
End of the rose-house,   15
Where the worst wind was,
Creaking the cypress window-frames,
Cracking so much thin glass
We stayed all night,
Stuffing the holes with burlap;   20
But she rode it out,
That old rose-house,

[1]The cellar of the poet's father's commercial greenhouse in Saginaw, Michigan. "Root Cellar" is one of the famous "greenhouse poems."
[2]Literally, a coming together; thus a collection or assortment.

[3]Rank from long storage; a silo is a storage building for grain.

She hove[1] into the teeth of it,
The core and pith of that ugly storm,
Ploughing with her stiff prow,   25
Bucking into the wind-waves
That broke over the whole of her,
Flailing her sides with spray,
Flinging long strings of wet across the roof-top,
Finally veering, wearing themselves out, merely   30
Whistling thinly under the wind-vents;
She sailed until the calm morning,
Carrying her full cargo of roses.

                                                            1948

My Papa's Waltz

The whiskey on your breath
Could make a small boy dizzy;
But I hung on like death:
Such waltzing was not easy.

We romped until the pans   5
Slid from the kitchen shelf;
My mother's countenance
Could not unfrown itself.

The hand that held my wrist
Was battered on one knuckle;   10
At every step you missed
My right ear scraped a buckle.

You beat time on my head
With a palm caked hard by dirt,
Then waltzed me off to bed   15
Still clinging to your shirt.

                                                            1948

Elegy

Her face like a rain-beaten stone on the day she rolled off
With the dark hearse, and enough flowers for an alderman,[1]—
And so she was, in her way, Aunt Tilly.

---

[1]Past tense of *heave*; in nautical usage, to heave to is to keep the ship heading into the wind. Here, the term is part of an extended conceit of greenhouse as boat or ship.

[1]A public official, like a city councilman.

Sighs, sighs, who says they have sequence?
Between the spirit and the flesh,—what war?   5
She never knew;
For she asked no quarter[2] and gave none,
Who sat with the dead when the relatives left,
Who fed and tended the infirm, the mad, the epileptic,
And, with a harsh rasp of a laugh at herself,   10
Faced up to the worst.

I recall how she harried the children away all the late summer
From the one beautiful thing in her yard, the peachtree;
How she kept the wizened,[3] the fallen, the misshapen for herself,
And picked and pickled the best, to be left on rickety doorsteps.   15

And yet she died in agony,
Her tongue, at the last, thick, black as an ox's.

Terror of cops, bill collectors, betrayers of the poor,—
I see you[4] in some celestial[5] supermarket,
Moving serenely among the leeks and cabbages,   20
Probing the squash,
Bearing down, with two steady eyes,
On the quaking butcher.

1958

RALPH ELLISON
1914–1994

Ralph Waldo Ellison was born in Oklahoma City to parents who migrated from
South Carolina and Georgia. His father, Lewis, a construction foreman and later
the owner of a small ice and coal business, named his son after Emerson, hoping
he would be a poet. After losing his father when he was three, Ellison and his
younger brother, Herbert, were raised by their mother, Ida, who worked as a
nursemaid, janitress, and domestic and was active in politics. Ellison used to

---

[2] Mercy granted to a surrendering foe.
[3] Shriveled.
[4] The poet addresses his dead Aunt Tilly, whom he characterizes as a terror to three representative groups of oppressors—

policemen, bill collectors, and betrayers of the poor.
[5] Heavenly; he envisions Aunt Tilly in an afterlife very much like her accustomed life on earth.

enjoy telling how she had canvassed for Eugene V. Debs and other Socialist candidates and later been jailed for defying Oklahoma City's segregation ordinances.

Ellison was drawn to music, playing cornet and trumpet from an early age and, in 1933, going to study classical composition at Tuskegee Institute under William L. Dawson. Of his musical influences he later said, "The great emphasis in my school was upon classical music, but such great jazz musicians as Hot Lips Page, Jimmy Rushing, and Lester Young were living in Oklahoma City.... As it turned out, the perfection, the artistic dedication which helped me as a writer, was not so much in the classical emphasis as in the jazz itself."

In July 1936, after his junior year at Tuskegee, Ellison went to New York to earn money for his senior year and to study music and sculpture, and he stayed. In June 1937 his friendship with Richard Wright began and led him toward becoming a writer. Ellison also made the acquaintance of Langston Hughes and the painter Romare Bearden. In Dayton, Ohio, where he went to visit his ailing mother and remained for six months after her unexpected death in October 1937, he began to write seriously, mostly nights in the second-story law office of Attorney William O. Stokes, using Stokes's letterhead and typewriter.

Returning to New York, from 1938 until 1942 Ellison worked on the New York Federal Writers Project of the Works Progress Administration (WPA). Starting in the late 1930s, he contributed reviews, essays, and short fiction to *New Masses, Tomorrow, The Negro Quarterly* (of which he was for a time managing editor), *The New Republic, The Saturday Review, Antioch Review, The Reporter*, and other periodicals. During World War II he served in the merchant marine as a cook and baker and afterward worked at a variety of jobs, including freelance photography and the building and installation of audio systems.

Over a period of seven years, Ellison wrote *Invisible Man*, which was recognized upon its publication in 1952 as one of the most important works of fiction of its time. It was on the best-seller list for sixteen weeks and won the National Book Award. Its critical reputation and popularity have only continued to grow in the six decades since its publication. Ellison has described his novel's structure as that of a symphonic jazz composition with a central theme (or bass line) and harmonic variations (or riffs) often expressed in virtuoso solo performances. *Invisible Man* speaks for all readers, reflecting the contradictions and complexities of American life through the prism of African American experience.

Although an excerpt from a second novel was published in *Noble Savage* in 1960, and seven other selections in literary magazines between then and 1977, no other long work of fiction has yet appeared. *Shadow and Act* (1964) and *Going to the Territory* (1986) collect essays and interviews written over more than forty years. Since Ellison's death four posthumous works have appeared: *The Collected Essays of Ralph Ellison* (1995), *Conversations with Ralph Ellison* (1995), *Flying Home and Other Stories* (1996), and *Juneteenth* (1999).

"A Party Down at the Square" (undated), unpublished in Ellison's lifetime, is a tour de force. By narrating a lynching in the voice of a Cincinnati white boy visiting his uncle in Alabama, Ellison, while still a young writer, crosses the narrative color line and defies the "segregation of the word" he found lingering in American literature when he wrote "Twentieth-Century Fiction and the Black Mask of Humanity" (1946). Ellison's technique in "A Party Down at the Square" compels readers to experience the human condition in extremis, mediated by a stranger whose morality is a commitment to be noncommittal. The white boy's most telling response comes from his insides when, to his shame, he throws up. His sensations signify a resistance to values he has been taught not to question. There is nothing like this story in the rest of Ellison's work.

"Flying Home" (1944) anticipates the theme of invisibility and the technique of solos and breaks with which Ellison took flight in *Invisible Man*. Just when Todd, Ellison's northern protagonist, believes that he has learned to use his wiles to escape the limitations of race, language, and geography, circumstances force him to confront the strange "old country" of the South. A literary descendant of Icarus, as well as Joyce's Stephen Dedalus, Todd, one of the black eagles from the Negro flight school at Tuskegee, flies too close to the sun, collides with a buzzard (a "jimcrow"), and falls to earth in rural Alabama. There, he is saved by Jefferson, whose folktales and actions enable Todd to recognize where he is and who he is and to come back to life by following the old black peasant and his son out of a labyrinthine Alabama valley.

In "Brave Words for a Startling Occasion" (1953), his acceptance address for the National Book Award, Ellison celebrates the richness and diversity of American speech and the American language. He identifies the task of the American writer as "always to challenge the apparent forms of reality—that is, the fixed manners and values of the few—and to struggle with it until it reveals its mad, vari-implicated chaos, its false faces, and on until it surrenders its insight, its truth."

John F. Callahan
Lewis and Clark College

PRIMARY WORKS

Invisible Man, 1952; *Shadow and Act*, 1964; *Going to the Territory*, 1986; *The Collected Essays of Ralph Ellison*, 1995; *Flying Home and Other Stories*, 1996; *Juneteenth*, 1999.

A Party Down at the Square

I don't know what started it. A bunch of men came by my Uncle Ed's place and said there was going to be a party down at the Square, and my uncle hollered for me to come on and I ran with them through the dark and rain and there we were at the Square. When we got there everybody was mad and quiet and standing around looking at the nigger. Some of the men had guns, and one man kept goosing the nigger in his pants with the barrel of a shotgun, saying he ought to pull the trigger, but he never did. It was right in front of the courthouse, and the old clock in the tower was striking twelve. The rain was falling cold and freezing as it fell. Everybody was cold, and the nigger kept wrapping his arms around himself trying to stop the shivers.

Then one of the boys pushed through the circle and snatched off the nigger's shirt, and there he stood, with his black skin all shivering in the light from the fire, and looking at us with a scaired look on his face and putting his hands in his pants pockets. Folks started yelling to hurry up and kill the nigger. Somebody yelled: "Take your hands out of your pockets, nigger;

we gonna have plenty heat in a minnit." But the nigger didn't hear him and kept his hands where they were.

I tell you the rain was cold. I had to stick my hands in my pockets they got so cold. The fire was pretty small, and they put some logs around the platform they had the nigger on and then threw on some gasoline, and you could see the flames light up the whole Square. It was late and the street-lights had been off for a long time. It was so bright that the bronze statue of the general standing there in the Square was like something alive. The shadows playing on his moldy green face made him seem to be smiling down at the nigger.

They threw on more gas, and it made the Square bright like it gets when the lights are turned on or when the sun is setting red. All the wagons and cars were standing around the curbs. Not like Saturday though—the niggers weren't there. Not a single nigger was there except this Bacote nigger and they dragged him there tied to the back of Jed Wilson's truck. On Saturday there's as many niggers as white folks.

Everybody was yelling crazy 'cause they were about to set fire to the nig-ger, and I got to the rear of the circle and looked around the Square to try to count the cars. The shadows of the folks was flickering on the trees in the middle of the Square. I saw some birds that the noise had woke up fly-ing through the trees. I guess maybe they thought it was morning. The ice had started the cobblestones in the street to shine where the rain was fall-ing and freezing. I counted forty cars before I lost count. I knew folks must have been there from Phenix City by all the cars mixed in with the wagons.

God, it was a hell of a night. It was some night all right. When the noise died down I heard the nigger's voice from where I stood in the back, so I pushed my way up front. The nigger was bleeding from his nose and ears, and I could see him all red where the dark blood was running down his black skin. He kept lifting first one foot and then the other, like a chicken on a hot stove. I looked down at the platform they had him on, and they had pushed a ring of fire up close to his feet. It must have been hot to him with the flames almost touching his big black toes. Somebody yelled for the nig-ger to say his prayers, but the nigger wasn't saying anything now. He just kinda moaned with his eyes shut and kept moving up and down on his feet, first one foot and then the other.

I watched the flames burning the logs up closer and closer to the nig-ger's feet. They were burning good now, and the rain had stopped and the wind was rising, making the flames flare higher. I looked, and there must have been thirty-five women in the crowd, and I could hear their voices clear and shrill mixed in with those of the men. Then it happened. I heard the noise about the same time everyone else did. It was like the roar of a cyclone blowing up the gulf, and everyone was looking up into the air to see what it was. Some of the faces looked surprised and scaired, all but the nigger. He didn't even hear the noise. He didn't even look up. Then the roar came closer, right above our heads and the wind was blowing higher and higher and the sound seemed to be going in circles.

Then I saw her. Through the clouds and fog I could see a red and green light on her wings. I could see them just for a second; then she rose up into the low clouds. I looked out for the beacon over the tops of the buildings in the direction of the airfield that's forty miles away, and it wasn't circling around. You usually could see it sweeping around the sky at night, but it wasn't there. Then, there she was again, like a big bird lost in the fog. I looked for the red and green lights, and they weren't there anymore. She was flying even closer to the tops of the buildings than before. The wind was blowing harder, and leaves started flying about, making funny shadows on the ground, and tree limbs were cracking and falling.

It was a storm all right. The pilot must have thought he was over the landing field. Maybe he thought the fire in the Square was put there for him to land by. Gosh, but it scaired the folks. I was scaired too. They started yelling: "He's going to land. He's going to land." And: "He's going to fall." A few started for their cars and wagons. I could hear the wagons creaking and chains jangling and cars spitting and missing as they started the engines up. Off to my right, a horse started pitching and striking his hooves against a car.

I didn't know what to do. I wanted to run, and I wanted to stay and see what was going to happen. The plane was close as hell. The pilot must have been trying to see where he was at, and her motors were drowning out all the sounds. I could even feel the vibration, and my hair felt like it was standing up under my hat. I happened to look over at the statue of the general standing with one leg before the other and leaning back on a sword, and I was fixing to run over and climb between his legs and sit there and watch when the roar stopped some, and I looked up and she was gliding just over the top of the trees in the middle of the Square.

Her motors stopped altogether and I could hear the sound of branches cracking and snapping off below her landing gear. I could see her plain now, all silver and shining in the light of the fire with T.W.A. in black letters under her wings. She was sailing smoothly out of the Square when she hit the high power lines that follow the Birmingham highway through the town. It made a loud crash. It sounded like the wind blowing the door of a tin barn shut. She only hit with her landing gear, but I could see the sparks flying, and the wires knocked loose from the poles were spitting blue sparks and whipping around like a bunch of snakes and leaving circles of blue sparks in the darkness.

The plane had knocked five or six wires loose, and they were dangling and swinging, and every time they touched they threw off more sparks. The wind was making them swing, and when I got over there, there was a crackling and spitting screen of blue haze across the highway. I lost my hat running over, but I didn't stop to look for it. I was among the first and I could hear the others pounding behind me across the grass of the Square. They were yelling to beat all hell, and they came up fast, pushing and shoving, and someone got pushed against a swinging wire. It made a sound like when a blacksmith drops a red hot horseshoe into a barrel of water, and the steam comes up. I could smell the flesh burning. The first time I'd ever smelled it. I got up close and it was a woman. It must have killed her right off. She was lying in a puddle stiff as a board, with pieces of glass insulators that the plane had knocked off the poles lying all around her. Her white dress was torn, and I saw one of her tits hanging out in the water and her thighs. Some woman screamed and fainted and almost fell on a wire, but a man caught her. The sheriff and his men were yelling and driving folks back with guns shining in their hands, and everything was lit up blue by the sparks. The shock had turned the woman almost as black as the nigger. I was trying to see if she wasn't blue too, or if it was just the sparks, and the sheriff drove me away. As I backed off trying to see, I heard the motors of the plane start up again somewhere off to the right in the clouds.

The clouds were moving fast in the wind and the wind was blowing the smell of something burning over to me. I turned around, and the crowd was headed back to the nigger. I could see him standing there in the middle of the flames. The wind was making the flames brighter every minute. The crowd was running. I ran too. I ran back across the grass with the crowd. It wasn't so large now that so many had gone when the plane came. I tripped and fell over the limb of a tree lying in the grass and bit my lip. It ain't well yet I bit it so bad. I could taste the blood in my mouth as I ran over. I guess that's what made me sick. When I got there, the fire had caught the nigger's pants, and the folks were standing around watching, but not too close on account of the wind blowing the flames. Somebody hollered, "Well, nigger, it ain't so cold now, is it? You don't need to put your hands in your pockets now." And the nigger looked up with his great white eyes looking like they was 'bout to pop out of his head, and I had enough. I didn't want to see anymore. I wanted to run somewhere to puke, but I stayed. I stayed right there in the front of the crowd and looked.

The nigger tried to say something I couldn't hear for the roar of the wind in the fire, and I strained my ears. Jed Wilson hollered, "What you say there, nigger?" And it came back through the flames in his nigger voice: "Will one a you gentlemen please cut my throat?" he said. "Will somebody please cut my throat like a Christian?" And Jed hollered back, "Sorry, but ain't no Christians around tonight. Ain't no Jew-boys neither. We're just one hundred percent Americans."

Then the nigger was silent. Folks started laughing at Jed. Jed's right popular with the folks, and next year, my uncle says, they plan to run him for sheriff. The heat was too much for me, and the smoke was making my eyes to smart. I was trying to back away when Jed reached down and brought up a can of gasoline and threw it in the fire on the nigger. I could see the flames catching the gas in a puff as it went in in a silver sheet and some of it reached the nigger, making spurts of blue fire all over his chest.

Well, that nigger was tough. I have to give it to that nigger; he was really tough. He had started to burn like a house afire and was making the smoke smell like burning hides. The fire was up around his head, and the smoke was so thick and black we couldn't see him. And him not moving—we thought he was dead. Then he started out. The fire had burned the ropes they had tied him with, and he started jumping and kicking about like he was blind, and you could smell his skin burning. He kicked so hard that the platform, which was burning too, fell in, and he rolled out of the fire at my feet. I jumped back so he wouldn't get on me. I'll never forget it. Every time I eat barbeque I'll remember that nigger. His back was just like a barbecued hog. I could see the prints of his ribs where they start around from his back-bone and curve down and around. It was a sight to see, that nigger's back. He was right at my feet, and somebody behind pushed me and almost made me step on him, and he was still burning.

I didn't step on him though, and Jed and somebody else pushed him back into the burning planks and logs and poured on more gas. I wanted to leave, but the folks were yelling and I couldn't move except to look around and see the statue. A branch the wind had broken was resting on his hat. I tried to push out and get away because my guts were gone, and all I got was spit and hot breath in my face from the woman and two men standing directly behind me. So I had to turn back around. The nigger rolled out of the fire again. He wouldn't stay put. It was on the other side this time. I couldn't see him very well through the flames and smoke. They got some tree limbs and held him there this time and he stayed there till he was ashes. I guess he stayed there. I know he burned to ashes because I saw Jed a week later, and he laughed and showed me some white finger bones still held together with little pieces of the nigger's skin. Anyway, I left when somebody moved around to see the nigger. I pushed my way through the crowd, and a woman in the rear scratched my face as she yelled and fought to get up close.

I ran across the Square to the other side, where the sheriff and his depu-ties were guarding the wires that were still spitting and making a blue fog. My heart was pounding like I had been running a long ways, and I bent over and let my insides go. Everything came up and spilled in a big gush over the ground. I was sick, and tired, and weak, and cold. The wind was still high, and large drops of rain were beginning to fall. I headed down the street to my uncle's place past a store where the wind had broken a window, and glass lay over the sidewalk. I kicked it as I went by. I remember somebody's fool rooster crowing like it was morning in all that wind.

The next day I was too weak to go out, and my uncle kidded me and called me "the gutless wonder from Cincinnati." I didn't mind. He said you get used to it in time. He couldn't go out hisself. There was too much wind and rain. I got up and looked out of the window, and the rain was pouring down and dead sparrows and limbs of trees were scattered all over the yard. There had been a cyclone all right. It swept a path right through the county, and we were lucky we didn't get the full force of it.

It blew for three days steady, and put the town in a hell of a shape. The wind blew sparks and set fire to the white-and-green-trimmed house on Jackson Avenue that had the big concrete lions in the yard and burned it down to the ground. They had to kill another nigger who tried to run out of the county after they burned this Bacote nigger. My Uncle Ed said they always have to kill niggers in pairs to keep the other niggers in place. I don't know though, the folks seem a little skittish of the niggers. They all came back, but they act pretty sullen. They look mean as hell when you pass them down at the store. The other day I was down to Brinkley's store, and a white cropper said it didn't do no good to kill the niggers 'cause things don't get no better. He looked hungry as hell. Most of the croppers look hungry. You'd be surprised how hungry white folks can look. Somebody said that he'd better shut his damn mouth, and he shut up. But from the look on his face he won't stay shut long. He went out of the store muttering to himself and spit a big chew of tobacco right down on Brinkley's floor. Brinkley said he was sore 'cause he wouldn't let him have credit. Anyway, it didn't seem to help things. First it was the nigger and the storm, then the plane, then the woman and the wires, and now I hear the airplane line is investigating to find who set the fire that almost wrecked their plane. All that in one night, and all of it but the storm over one nigger. It was some night all right. It was some party too. I was right there, see. I was right there watching it all. It was my first party and my last. God, but that nigger was tough. That Bacote nigger was some nigger!

1997 (posthumously)

Flying Home

When Todd came to, he saw two faces suspended above him in a sun so hot and blinding that he could not tell if they were black or white. He stirred, feeling a pain that burned as though his whole body had been laid open to the sun, which glared into his eyes. For a moment an old fear of being touched by white hands seized him. Then the very sharpness of the pain began slowly to clear his head. Sounds came to him dimly. *He done come to*. Who are they? he thought. *Naw he ain't, I coulda sworn he was white*. Then he heard clearly:

"You hurt bad?"

Something within him uncoiled. It was a Negro sound.

"He's still out," he heard.

"Give 'im time.... Say, son, you hurt bad?"

Was he? There was that awful pain. He lay rigid, hearing their breathing and trying to weave a meaning between them and his being stretched painfully upon the ground. He watched them warily, his mind traveling back over a painful distance. Jagged scenes, swiftly unfolding as in a movie trailer, reeled through his mind, and he saw himself piloting a tailspinning plane and landing and falling from the cockpit and trying to stand. Then, as in a great silence, he remembered the sound of crunching bone and, now, looking up into the anxious faces of an old Negro man and a boy from where he lay in the same field, the memory sickened him and he wanted to remember no more.

"How you feel, son?"

Todd hesitated, as though to answer would be to admit an unacceptable weakness. Then, "It's my ankle," he said.

"Which one?"

"The left."

With a sense of remoteness he watched the old man bend and remove his boot, feeling the pressure ease.

"That any better?"

"A lot. Thank you."

He had the sensation of discussing someone else, that his concern was with some far more important thing, which for some reason escaped him.

"You done broke it bad," the old man said. "We have to get you to a doctor."

He felt that he had been thrown into a tailspin. He looked at his watch; how long had he been here? He knew there was but one important thing in the world, to get the plane back to the field before his officers were displeased.

"Help me up," he said. "Into the ship."

"But it's broke too bad . . ."

"Give me your arm!"

"But, son . . ."

Clutching the old man's arm, he pulled himself up, keeping his left leg clear, thinking, I'd never make him understand, as the leather-smooth face came parallel with his own.

"Now, let's see."

He pushed the old man back, hearing a bird's insistent shrill. He swayed, giddily. Blackness washed over him, like infinity.

"You best sit down."

"No, I'm okay."

"But, son. You jus gonna make it worse . . ."

It was a fact that everything in him cried out to deny, even against the flaming pain in his ankle. He would have to try again.

"You mess with that ankle they have to cut your foot off," he heard.

Holding his breath, he started up again. It pained so badly that he had to bite his lips to keep from crying out and he allowed them to help him down with a pang of despair.

"It's best you take it easy. We gon git you a doctor."

Of all the luck, he thought. Of all the rotten luck, now I have done it. The fumes of high-octane gasoline clung in the heat, taunting him.

"We kin ride him into town on old Ned," the boy said.

Ned? He turned, seeing the boy point toward an ox team, browsing where the buried blade of a plow marked the end of a furrow. Thoughts of himself riding an ox through the town, past streets full of white faces, down the concrete runways of the airfield, made swift images of humiliation in his mind. With a pang he remembered his girl's last letter. "Todd," she had written, "I don't need the papers to tell me you had the intelligence to fly. And I have always known you to be as brave as anyone else. The papers annoy me.

Don't you be contented to prove over and over again that you're brave or skillful just because you're black, Todd. I think they keep beating that dead horse because they don't want to say why you boys are not yet fighting. I'm really disappointed, Todd. Anyone with brains can learn to fly, but then what. What about using it, and who will you use it for? I wish, dear, you'd write about this. I sometimes think they're playing a trick on us. It's very humiliating...." He whipped cold sweat from his face, thinking, What does she know of humiliation? She's never been down South. *Now* the humiliation would come. When you must have them judge you, knowing that they never accept your mistakes as your own but hold it against your whole race—that was humiliation. Yes, and humiliation was when you could never be simply yourself; when you were always a part of this old black ignorant man. Sure, he's all right. Nice and kind and helpful. But he's not you. Well, there's one humiliation I can spare myself.

"No," he said. "I have orders not to leave the ship...."

"Aw," the old man said. Then turning to the boy, "Teddy, then you better hustle down to Mister Graves and get him to come...."

"No, wait!" he protested before he was fully aware. Graves might be white. "Just have him get word to the field, please. They'll take care of the rest."

He saw the boy leave, running.

"How far does he have to go?"

"Might' nigh a mile."

He rested back, looking at the dusty face of his watch. By now they know something has happened, he thought. In the ship there was a perfectly good radio, but it was useless. The old fellow would never operate it. That buzzard knocked me back a hundred years, he thought. Irony danced within him like the gnats circling the old man's head. With all I've learned, I'm dependent upon this "peasant's" sense of time and space. His leg throbbed. In the plane, instead of time being measured by the rhythms of pain and a kid's legs, the instruments would have told him at a glance. Twisting upon his elbows, he saw where dust had powdered the plane's fuselage, feeling the lump form in his throat that was always there when he thought of flight. It's crouched there, he thought, like the abandoned shell of a locust. I'm naked without it. Not a machine, a suit of clothes you wear. And with a sudden embarrassment and wonder he whispered, "It's the only dignity I have...."

He saw the old man watching, his torn overalls clinging limply to him in the heat. He felt a sharp need to tell the old man what he felt. But that would be meaningless. If I tried to explain why I need to fly back, he'd think I was simply afraid of white officers. But it's more than fear ... a sense of anguish clung to him like the veil of sweat that hugged his face. He watched the old man, hearing him humming snatches of a tune as he admired the plane. He felt a furtive sense of resentment. Such old men often came to the field to watch the pilots with childish eyes. At first it had made him proud; they had been a meaningful part of a new experience. But soon he realized they did not understand his accomplishments and they came to shame and embarrass him, like the distasteful praise of an idiot. A part of the meaning of flying had gone, then, and he had not been able to regain it. If I were a prize-fighter I would be more human, he thought. Not a monkey doing tricks, but a man. They were pleased simply that he was a Negro who could fly, and that was not enough. He felt cut off from them by age, by understanding, by sensibility, by technology, and by his need to measure himself against the mirror of other men's appreciation. Somehow he felt betrayed, as he had when as a child he grew to discover that his father was dead. Now, for him, any real appreciation lay with his white officers; and with them he could never be sure. Between ignorant black men and condescending whites, his course of flight seemed mapped by the nature of things away from all needed and natural landmarks. Under some sealed orders, couched in ever more technical and mysterious terms, his path curved swiftly away from both the shame the old man symbolized and the cloudy terrain of white man's regard. Flying blind, he knew but one point of landing and there he would receive his wings. After that the enemy would appreciate his skill and he would assume his deepest meaning, he thought sadly, neither from those who condescended nor from those who praised without understanding, but from the enemy who would recognize his manhood and skill in terms of hate....

He sighed, seeing the oxen making queer, prehistoric shadows against the dry brown earth.

"You just take it easy, son," the old man soothed. "That boy won't take long. Crazy as he is about airplanes."

"I can wait," he said.

"What kinda airplane you call this here'n?"

"An Advanced Trainer," he said, seeing the old man smile. His fingers were like gnarled dark wood against the metal as he touched the low-slung wing.

"'Bout how fast can she fly?"

"Over two hundred an hour."

"Lawd! That's so fast I bet it don't seem like you moving!"

Holding himself rigid, Todd opened his flying suit. The shade had gone and he lay in a ball of fire.

"You mind if I take a look inside? I was always curious to see ..."

"Help yourself. Just don't touch anything."

He heard him climb upon the metal wing, grunting. Now the questions would start. Well, so you don't have to think to answer....

He saw the old man looking over into the cockpit, his eyes bright as a child's.

"You must have to know a lot to work all these here things."

Todd was silent, seeing him step down and kneel beside him.

"Son, how come you want to fly way up there in the air?"

Because it's the most meaningful act in the world ... because it makes me less like you, he thought.

But he said: "Because I like it, I guess. It's as good a way to fight and die as I know."

"Yeah? I guess you right," the old man said. "But how long you think before they gonna let you all fight?"

He tensed. This was the question all Negroes asked, put with the same timid hopefulness and longing that always opened a greater void within him than that he had felt beneath the plane the first time he had flown. He felt lightheaded. It came to him suddenly that there was something sinister about the conversation, that he was flying unwillingly into unsafe and uncharted regions. If he could only be insulting and tell this old man who was trying to help him to shut up!

"I bet you one thing . . ."

"Yes?"

"That you was plenty scared coming down."

He did not answer. Like a dog on a trail the old man seemed to smell out his fears, and he felt anger bubble within him.

"You sho scared *me*. When I seen you coming down in that thing with it a-rollin' and a-jumpin' like a pitchin' hoss, I thought sho you was a goner. I almost had me a stroke!"

He saw the old man grinning. "Ever'thin's been happening round here this morning, come to think of it."

"Like what?" he asked.

"Well, first thing I know, here come two white fellers looking for Mister Rudolph, that's Mister Graves' cousin. That got me worked up right away. . . ."

"Why?"

"Why? 'Cause he done broke outa the crazy house, that's why. He liable to kill somebody," he said. "They oughta have him by now though. Then here *you* come. First I think it's one of them white boys. Then doggone if you don't fall outa there. Lawd, I'd done heard about you boys but I haven't never *seen* one o' you all. Caint tell you how it felt to see somebody what look like me in a airplane!"

The old man talked on, the sound streaming around Todd's thoughts like air flowing over the fuselage of a flying plane. You were a fool, he thought, remembering how before the spin the sun had blazed, bright against the billboard signs beyond the town, and how a boy's blue kite had bloomed beneath him, tugging gently in the wind like a strange, odd-shaped flower. He had once flown such kites himself and tried to find the boy at the end of the invisible cord. But he had been flying too high and too fast. He had climbed steeply away in exultation. Too steeply, he thought. And one of the first rules you learn is that if the angle of thrust is too steep the plane goes into a spin. And then, instead of pulling out of it and going into a dive you let a buzzard panic you. A lousy buzzard!

"Son, what made all that blood on the glass?"

"A buzzard," he said, remembering how the blood and feathers had sprayed back against the hatch. It had been as though he had flown into a storm of blood and blackness.

"Well, I declare! They's lots of 'em around here. They after dead things. Don't eat nothing what's alive."

"A little bit more and he would have made a meal out of me," Todd said grimly.

"They bad luck all right. Teddy's got a name for 'em, calls 'em jimcrows," the old man laughed.

"It's a damned good name."

"They the damnedest birds. Once I seen a hoss all stretched out like he was sick, you know. So I hollers, 'Gid up from there, suh!' Just to make sho! An,' doggone, son, if I don't see two old jimcrows come flying right up outa that hoss's insides! Yessuh! The sun was shinin' on 'em and they couldn'ta been no greasier if they'd been eating barbecue!"

Todd thought he would vomit; his stomach quivered.

"You made that up," he said.

"Nawsuh! Saw him just like you."

"Well, I'm glad it was you."

"You see lots a funny things down here, son."

"No, I'll let you see them," he said.

"By the way, the white folks round here don't like to see you boys up there in the sky. They ever bother you?"

"No."

"Well, they'd like to."

"Someone always wants to bother someone else," Todd said. "How do you know?"

"I just know."

"Well," he said defensively, "no one has bothered us."

Blood pounded in his ears as he looked away into space. He tensed, seeing a black spot in the sky, and strained to confirm what he could not clearly see.

"What does that look like to you?" he asked excitedly.

"Just another bad luck, son."

Then he saw the movement of wings with disappointment. It was gliding smoothly down, wings outspread, tail feathers gripping the air, down swiftly—gone behind the green screen of trees. It was like a bird he had imagined there, only the sloping branches of the pines remained, sharp against the pale stretch of sky. He lay barely breathing and stared at the point where it had disappeared, caught in a spell of loathing and admiration. Why did they make them so disgusting and yet teach them to fly so well? *It's like when I was up in heaven,* he heard, starting.

The old man was chuckling, rubbing his stubbled chin.

"What did you say?"

"Sho, I died and went to heaven ... maybe by time I tell you about it they be done come after you."

"I hope so," he said wearily.

"You boys ever sit around and swap lies?"

"Not often. Is this going to be one?"

"Well, I ain't so sho, on account of it took place when I was dead."

The old man paused. "That wasn't no lie 'bout the buzzards though."

"All right," he said.

"Sho you want to hear 'bout heaven?"

"Please," he answered, resting his head upon his arm.

"Well, I went to heaven and right away started to sproutin' me some wings. Six-foot ones, they was. Just like them the white angels had. I couldn't hardly believe it. I was so glad that I went off on some clouds by myself and tried 'em out. You know, 'cause I didn't want to make a fool outa myself the first thing ..."

It's an old tale, Todd thought. Told me years ago. Had forgotten. But at least it will keep him from talking about buzzards.

He closed his eyes, listening.

"... First thing I done was to git up on a low cloud and jump off. And doggone, boy, if them wings didn't work! First I tried the right; then I tried the left; then I tried 'em both together. Then, Lawd, I started to move on out among the folks. I let 'em see me ..."

He saw the old man gesturing flight with his arms, his face full of mock pride as he indicated an imaginary crowd, thinking, *It'll be in the newspapers*, as he heard, "... so I went and found me some colored angels—somehow I didn't believe I was an angel till I seen a real black one, ha, yes! Then I was sho—but they tole me I better come down 'cause us colored folks had to wear a special kin'a harness when we flew. That was how come *they* wasn't flyin'. Oh yes, an' you had to be extra strong for a black man even, to fly with one of them harnesses ..."

This is a new turn, Todd thought. What's he driving at?

"So I said to myself, I ain't gonna be bothered with no harness! Oh naw! 'Cause if God let you sprout wings you oughta have sense enough not to let nobody make you wear something what gits in the way of flyin'. So I starts to flyin'. Hecks, son," he chuckled, his eyes twinkling, "you know I had to let eve'body know that old Jefferson could fly good as anybody else. And I could too, fly smooth as a bird! I could even loop-the-loop—only I had to make sho to keep my long white robe down roun' my ankles ..."

Todd felt uneasy. He wanted to laugh at the joke, but his body refused, as of an independent will. He felt as he had as a child when after he had chewed a sugar-coated pill which his mother had given him, she had laughed at his efforts to remove the terrible taste.

"... Well," he heard. "I was doing all right till I got to speeding. Found out I could fan up a right strong breeze, I could fly so fast. I could do all kin'sa stunts too. I started flying up to the stars and divin' down and zoom-ing roun' the moon. Man, I like to scare the devil outa some ole white angels. I was raisin' hell. Not that I meant any harm, son. But I was just feel-ing good. It was so good to know I was free at last. I accidentally knocked the tips offa some stars and they tell me I caused a storm and a coupla lynchings down here in Macon County—though I swear I believe them boys what said that was making up lies on me ..."

He's mocking me, Todd thought angrily. He thinks it's a joke. Grinning down at me ... His throat was dry. He looked at his watch; why the hell didn't they come? Since they had to, why? *One day I was flying down one of them heavenly streets.* You got yourself into it, Todd thought. Like Jonah in the whale.

"Justa throwin' feathers in eve'body's face. An' ole Saint Peter called me in. Said, 'Jefferson, tell me two things, what you doin' flyin' without a harness; an' how come you flyin' so fast?' So I tole him I was flyin' without a harness 'cause it got in my way, but I couldn'ta been flyin' so fast, 'cause I wasn't usin' but one wing. Saint Peter said, 'You wasn't flyin' with but *one* wing?' 'Yessuh,' I says, scared-like. So he says, 'Well, since you got sucha extra fine pair of wings you can leave off yo harness awhile. But from now on none of that there one-wing flyin', 'cause you gittin' up too damn much speed!'"

And with one mouth full of bad teeth you're making too damned much talk, thought Todd. Why don't I send him after the boy? His body ached from the hard ground, and seeking to shift his position he twisted his ankle and hated himself for crying out.

"It gittin' worse?"

"I . . . I twisted it," he groaned.

"Try not to think about it, son. That's what I do."

He bit his lip, fighting pain with counter-pain as the voice resumed its rhythmical droning. Jefferson seemed caught in his own creation.

". . . After all that trouble I just floated roun' heaven in slow motion. But I forgot like colored folks will do and got to flyin' with one wing agin. This time I was restin' my ole broken arm and got to flyin' fast enough to shame the devil. I was comin' so fast, Lawd, I got myself called befo ole Saint Peter agin. He said, 'Jeff, didn't I warn you 'bout that speedin'?' 'Yessuh,' I says, 'but it was an accident.' He looked at me sad-like and shook his head and I knowed I was gone. He said, 'Jeff, you and that speedin' is a danger to the heavenly community. If I was to let you keep on flyin', heaven wouldn't be nothin' but uproar. Jeff, you got to go!' Son, I argued and pleaded with that old white man, but it didn't do a bit of good. They rushed me straight to them pearly gates and gimme a parachute and a map of the state of Alabama . . ."

Todd heard him laughing so that he could hardly speak, making a screen between them upon which his humiliation glowed like fire.

"Maybe you'd better stop a while," he said, his voice unreal.

"Ain't much more," Jefferson laughed. "When they gimme the parachute ole Saint Peter ask me if I wanted to say a few words before I went. I felt so bad I couldn't hardly look at him, specially with all them white angels standin' around. Then somebody laughed and made me mad. So I tole him, 'Well, you done took my wings. And you puttin' me out. You got charge of things so's I can't do nothin' about it. But you got to admit just this: While I was up here I was the flyin'est son-of-a-bitch what ever hit heaven!'"

At the burst of laughter Todd felt such an intense humiliation that only great violence would wash it away. The laughter which shook the old man like a boiling purge set up vibrations of guilt within him which not even the intricate machinery of the plane would have been adequate to transform and he heard himself screaming, "Why do you laugh at me this way?"

He hated himself at that moment, but he had lost control. He saw Jefferson's mouth fall open. "What—?"

"Answer me!"

His blood pounded as though it would surely burst his temples, and he tried to reach the old man and fell, screaming, "Can I help it because they won't let us actually fly? Maybe we are a bunch of buzzards feeding on a dead horse, but we can hope to be eagles, can't we? *Can't we?*"

He fell back, exhausted, his ankle pounding. The saliva was like straw in his mouth. If he had the strength he would strangle this old man. This grinning gray-headed clown who made him feel as he felt when watched by the white officers at the field. And yet this old man had neither power, prestige, rank, nor technique. Nothing that could rid him of this terrible feeling. He watched him, seeing his face struggle to express a turmoil of feeling.

"What you mean, son? What you talking 'bout . . . ?"

"Go away. Go tell your tales to the white folks."

"But I didn't mean nothing like that . . . I . . . I wasn't tryin' to hurt your feelings . . ."

"Please. Get the hell away from me!"

"But I didn't, son. I didn't mean all them things a-tall."

Todd shook as with a chill, searching Jefferson's face for a trace of the mockery he had seen there. But now the face was somber and tired and old. He was confused. He could not be sure that there had ever been laughter there, that Jefferson had ever really laughed in his whole life. He saw Jefferson reach out to touch him and shrank away, wondering if anything except the pain, now causing his vision to waver, was real. Perhaps he had imagined it all.

"Don't let it get you down, son," the voice said pensively.

He heard Jefferson sigh wearily, as though he felt more than he could say. His anger ebbed, leaving only the pain.

"I'm sorry," he mumbled.

"You just wore out with pain, was all . . ."

He saw him through a blur, smiling. And for a second he felt the embarrassed silence of understanding flutter between them.

"What was you doin' flyin' over this section, son? Wasn't you scared they might shoot you for a crow?"

Todd tensed. Was he being laughed at again? But before he could decide, the pain shook him and a part of him was lying calmly behind the screen of pain that had fallen between them, recalling the first time he had ever seen a plane. It was as though an endless series of hangars had been shaken ajar in the airbase of his memory and from each, like a young wasp emerging from its cell, arose the memory of the plane.

The first time I ever saw a plane I was very small and planes were new in the world. I was four and a half and the only plane that I had ever seen was a model suspended from the ceiling of the automobile exhibit at the state fair. But

I did not know that it was only a model. I did not know how large a real plane was, nor how expensive. To me it was a fascinating toy, complete in itself, which my mother said could only be owned by rich little white boys. I stood rigid with admiration, my head straining backward as I watched the gray little plane describing arcs above the gleaming tops of the automobiles. And I vowed that, rich or poor, some day I would own such a toy. My mother had to drag me out of the exhibit, and not even the merry-go-round, the Ferris wheel, or the racing horses could hold my attention for the rest of the fair. I was too busy imitating the tiny drone of the plane with my lips, and imitating with my hands the motion, swift and circling, that it made in flight.

After that I no longer used the pieces of lumber that lay about our backyard to construct wagons and autos . . . now it was used for airplanes. I built biplanes, using pieces of board for wings, a small box for the fuselage, another piece of wood for the rudder. The trip to the fair had brought something new into my small world. I asked my mother repeatedly when the fair would come back again. I'd lie in the grass and watch the sky and each flighting bird became a soaring plane. I would have been good a year just to have seen a plane again. I became a nuisance to everyone with my questions about airplanes. But planes were new to the old folks, too, and there was little that they could tell me. Only my uncle knew some of the answers. And better still, he could carve propellers from pieces of wood that would whirl rapidly in the wind, wobbling noisily upon oiled nails.

I wanted a plane more than I'd wanted anything; more than I wanted the red wagon with rubber tires, more than the train that ran on a track with its train of cars. I asked my mother over and over again:

"Mama?"

"What do you want, boy?" she'd say.

"Mama, will you get mad if I ask you?" I'd say.

"What do you want now, I ain't got time to be answering a lot of fool questions. What you want?"

"Mama, when you gonna get me one . . . ?" I'd ask.

"Get you one what?" she'd say.

"You know, Mama; what I been asking you . . ."

"Boy," she'd say, "if you don't want a spanking you better come on 'n tell me what you talking about so I can get on with my work."

"Aw, Mama, you know . . ."

"What I just tell you?" she'd say.

"I mean when you gonna buy me a airplane."

"AIRPLANE! Boy, is you crazy? How many times I have to tell you to stop that foolishness. I done told you them things cost too much. I bet I'm gon wham the living daylight out of you if you don't quit worrying me 'bout them things!"

But this did not stop me, and a few days later I'd try all over again.

Then one day a strange thing happened. It was spring and for some reason I had been hot and irritable all morning. It was a beautiful spring. I could feel it as I played barefoot in the backyard. Blossoms hung from the thorny black locust trees like clusters of fragrant white grapes. Butterflies flickered in the sunlight above the short new dew-wet grass. I had gone in the house for bread and butter and coming out I heard a steady unfamiliar drone. It was unlike anything I had ever heard before. I tried to place the sound. It was no use. It was a sensation like that I had when searching for my father's watch, heard ticking unseen in a room. It made me feel as though I had forgotten to perform some task that my mother had ordered ... then I located it, overhead. In the sky, flying quite low and about a hundred yards off, was a plane! It came so slowly that it seemed barely to move. My mouth hung wide; my bread and butter fell into the dirt. I wanted to jump up and down and cheer. And when the idea struck I trembled with excitement: Some little white boy's plane's done flew away and all I got to do is stretch out my hands and it'll be mine! It was a little plane like that at the fair, flying no higher than the eaves of our roof. Seeing it come steadily forward I felt the world grow warm with promise. I opened the screen and climbed over it and clung there, waiting. I would catch the plane as it came over and swing down fast and run into the house before anyone could see me. Then no one could come to claim the plane. It droned nearer. Then when it hung like a silver cross in the blue directly above me I stretched out my hand and grabbed. It was like sticking my finger through a soap bubble. The plane flew on, as though I had simply blown my breath after it. I grabbed again, frantically, trying to catch the tail. My fingers clutched the air and disappointment surged tight and hard in my throat. Giving one last desperate grasp, I strained forward. My fingers ripped from the screen. I was falling, the ground burst hard against me. I drummed the earth with my heels and when my breath returned, I lay there bawling.

My mother rushed through the door.

"What's the matter, chile! What on earth is wrong with you?"

"It's gone! It's gone!"

"What gone?"

"The airplane ..."

"Airplane?"

"Yessum, jus like the one at the fair ... I ... I tried to stop it an' it kep right on going ..."

"When, boy?"

"Just now," I cried through my tears.

"Where it go, boy, what way?"

"Yonder, there ..."

She scanned the sky, her arms akimbo and her checkered apron flapping in the wind, as I pointed to the fading plane. Finally she looked down at me, slowly shaking her head.

"It's gone! It's gone!" I cried.

"Boy, is you a fool?" she said. "Don't you see that there's a real airplane 'stead of one of them toy ones?"

"Real ... ?" I forgot to cry. "Real?"

"Yass, real. Don't you know that thing you reaching for is bigger'n a auto? You here trying to reach for it and I bet it's flying 'bout two hundred miles high-er'n this roof." She was disgusted with me. "You come on in this house before somebody else sees what a fool you done turned out to be. You must think these here li'l ole arms of your'n is mighty long ..."

I was carried into the house and undressed for bed and the doctor was called. I cried bitterly; as much from the disappointment of finding the plane so far beyond my reach as from the pain.

When the doctor came I heard my mother telling him about the plane and asking if anything was wrong with my mind. He explained that I had had a fever for several hours. But I was kept in bed for a week and I constantly saw the plane in my sleep, flying just beyond my fingertips, sailing so slowly that it seemed barely to move. And each time I'd reach out to grab it I'd miss and through each dream I'd hear my grandma warning:

"Young man, young man
Yo arm's too short
To box with God...."

"Hey, son!"

At first he did not know where he was and looked at the old man pointing, with blurred eyes.

"Ain't that one of you all's airplanes coming after you?"

As his vision cleared he saw a small black shape above a distant field, soaring through waves of heat. But he could not be sure and with the pain he feared that somehow a horrible recurring fantasy of being split in twain by the whirling blades of a propeller had come true.

"You think he sees us?" he heard.

"See? I hope so."

"He's coming like a bat outa hell!"

Straining, he heard the faint sound of a motor and hoped it would soon be over.

"How you feeling?"

"Like a nightmare," he said.

"Hey, he's done curved back the other way!"

"Maybe he saw us," he said. "Maybe he's gone to send out the ambulance and ground crew." And, he thought with despair, maybe he didn't even see us.

"Where did you send the boy?"

"Down to Mister Graves," Jefferson said. "Man what owns this land."

"Do you think he phoned?"

Jefferson looked at him quickly.

"Aw sho. Dabney Graves is got a bad name on accounta them killings, but he'll call though ..."

"What killings?"

"Them five fellers ... ain't you heard?" he asked with surprise.

"No."

"Eve'body knows 'bout Dabney Graves, especially the colored. He done killed enough of us."

Todd had the sensation of being caught in a white neighborhood after dark.

"What did they do?" he asked.

"Thought they was men," Jefferson said. "An' some he owed money, like he do me ..."

"But why do you stay here?"

"You black, son."

"I know, but ..."

"You have to come by the white folks, too."

He turned away from Jefferson's eyes, at once consoled and accused. And I'll have to come by them soon, he thought with despair. Closing his eyes, he heard Jefferson's voice as the sun burned blood-red upon his lids.

"I got nowhere to go," Jefferson said, "an' they'd come after me if I did. But Dabney Graves is a funny fellow. He's all the time making jokes. He can be mean as hell, then he's liable to turn right around and back the colored against the white folks. I seen him do it. But me, I hates him for that more'n anything else. 'Cause just as soon as he gits tired helping a man he don't care what happens to him. He just leaves him stone-cold. And then the other white folks is double hard on anybody he done helped. For him it's just a joke. He don't give a hilla beans for nobody—but hisself ..."

Todd listened to the thread of detachment in the old man's voice. It was as though he held his words at arm's length before him to avoid their destructive meaning.

"He'd just as soon do you a favor and then turn right around and have you strung up. Me, I stays outa his way 'cause down here that's what you gotta do."

If my ankle would only ease for a while, he thought. The closer I spin toward the earth the blacker I become, flashed through his mind. Sweat ran into his eyes and he was sure that he would never see the plane if his head continued whirling. He tried to see Jefferson, what it was that Jefferson held in his hand. It was a little black man, another Jefferson! A little black Jefferson that shook with fits of belly laughter while the other Jefferson looked on with detachment. Then Jefferson looked up from the thing in his hand and turned to speak but Todd was far away, searching the sky for a plane in a hot dry land on a day and age he had long forgotten. He was going mysteriously with his mother through empty streets where black faces peered from behind drawn shades and someone was rapping at a window and he was looking back to see a hand and a frightened face frantically beckoning from a cracked door and his mother was looking down the empty perspective of the street and shaking her head and hurrying him along and at first it was only a flash he saw and a motor was droning as through the sun's glare he saw it gleaming silver as it circled and he was seeing a burst like a puff of white smoke and hearing his mother yell, "Come along, boy, I got no time for them fool airplanes, I got no time," and he saw it a second time, the plane flying high, and the burst appeared suddenly and fell slowly, billowing out and sparkling like fireworks and he was watching and being hurried along as the air filled with a flurry of white pinwheeling cards that caught in the wind and scattered over the rooftops and into the gutters and a woman was running and snatching a card and reading it and screaming and he darted into the shower, grabbing as in winter he grabbed for snow-flakes and bounding away at his mother's, "Come on here, boy! Come on, I say!" And he was watching as she took the card away seeing her face grow puzzled and turning taut as her voice quavered, "Niggers Stay from the Polls," and died to a moan of terror as he saw the eyeless sockets of a white hood staring at him from the card and above he saw the plane spiraling gracefully, agleam in the sun like a fiery sword. And seeing it soar he was caught, transfixed between a terrible horror and a horrible fascination.

The sun was not so high now, and Jefferson was calling, and gradually he saw three figures moving across the curving roll of the field.

"Look like some doctors, all dressed in white," said Jefferson.

They're coming at last, Todd thought. And he felt such a release of tension within him that he thought he would faint. But no sooner did he close his eyes than he was seized and he was struggling with three white men who were forcing his arms into some kind of coat. It was too much for him, his arms were pinned to his sides and as the pain blazed in his eyes, he realized that it was a straitjacket. What filthy joke was this?

"That oughta hold him, Mister Graves," he heard.

His total energies seemed focused in his eyes as he searched for their faces. That was Graves, the other two wore hospital uniforms. He was poised between two poles of fear and hate as he heard the one called Graves saying,

"He looks kinda purty in that there suit, boys. I'm glad you dropped by."

"This boy ain't crazy, Mister Graves," one of the others said. "He needs a doctor, not us. Don't see how you led us way out here anyway. It might be a joke to you, but your cousin Rudolph liable to kill somebody. White folks or niggers don't make no difference . . ."

Todd saw the man turn red with anger. Graves looked down upon him, chuckling.

"This nigguh belongs in a straitjacket, too, boys. I knowed that the min-nit Jeff's kid said something 'bout a nigguh flyer. You all know you caint let the nigguh git up that high without his going crazy. The nigguh brain ain't built right for high altitudes . . ."

Todd watched the drawling red face, feeling that all the unnamed horror and obscenities that he had ever imagined stood materialized before him.

"Let's git outa here," one of the attendants said.

Todd saw the other reach toward him, realizing for the first time that he lay upon a stretcher as he yelled:

"Don't put your hands on me!"

They drew back, surprised.

"What's that you say, nigguh?" asked Graves.

He did not answer and thought that Graves' foot was aimed at his head. It landed in his chest and he could hardly breathe. He coughed helplessly, seeing Graves' lips stretch taut over his yellow teeth, and tried to shift his head. It was as though a half-dead fly was dragging slowly across his face, and a bomb seemed to burst within him. Blasts of hot, hysterical laughter tore from his chest, causing his eyes to pop, and he felt that the veins in his neck would surely burst. And then a part of him stood behind it all, watching the surprise in Graves' red face and his own hysteria. He thought he would never stop, he would laugh himself to death. It rang in his ears like Jefferson's laughter and he looked for him, centering his eyes desperately upon his face, as though somehow he had become his sole salvation in an insane world of outrage and humiliation. It brought a certain relief. He was suddenly aware that although his body was still contorted, it was an echo that no longer rang in his ears. He heard Jefferson's voice with gratitude.

"Mister Graves, the army done tole him not to leave his airplane."

"Nigguh, army or no, you gittin' off my land! That airplane can stay 'cause it was paid for by taxpayers' money. But you gittin' off. An' dead or alive, it don't make no difference to me."

Todd was beyond it now, lost in a world of anguish.

"Jeff," Graves said. "You and Teddy come and grab holt. I want you to take this here black eagle over to that nigguh airfield and leave him."

Jefferson and the boy approached him silently. He looked away, realizing and doubting at once that only they could release him from his overpowering sense of isolation.

They bent for the stretcher. One of the attendants moved toward Teddy.

"Think you can manage it, boy?"

"I think I can, suh," Teddy said.

"Well, you better go behind then, and let yo pa go ahead so's to keep that leg elevated."

He saw the white men walking ahead as Jefferson and the boy carried him along in silence. Then they were pausing, and he felt a hand wiping his face, then he was moving again. And it was as though he had been lifted out of his isolation, back into the world of men. A new current of communication flowed between the man and boy and himself. They moved him gently. Far away he heard a mocking-bird liquidly calling. He raised his eyes, seeing a buzzard poised unmoving in space. For a moment the whole afternoon seemed suspended, and he waited for the horror to seize him again. Then like a song within his head he heard the boy's soft humming and saw the dark bird glide into the sun and glow like a bird of flaming gold.

1944

Brave Words for a Startling Occasion[1]

First, as I express my gratitude for this honor which you have bestowed on me, let me say that I take it that you are rewarding my efforts rather than my not quite fully achieved attempt at a major novel. Indeed, if I were asked in all seriousness just what I considered to be the chief significance of

[1]Address for Presentation Ceremony, National Book Award, January 27, 1953.

Invisible Man as a fiction, I would reply: its experimental attitude, and its attempt to return to the mood of personal moral responsibility for democracy which typified the best of our nineteenth-century fiction. That my first novel should win this most coveted prize must certainly indicate that there is a crisis in the American novel. You as critics have told us so, and current fiction sales would indicate that the reading public agrees. Certainly the younger novelists concur. The explosive nature of events mocks our brightest efforts. And the very "facts" which the naturalists assumed would make us free have lost the power to protect us from despair. Controversy now rages over just what aspects of American experience are suitable for novelistic treatment. The prestige of the theorists of the so-called novel of manners has been challenged. Thus, after a long period of stability we find our assumptions concerning the novel being called into question. And though I was only vaguely aware of it, it was this growing crisis which shaped the writing of *Invisible Man.*

After the usual apprenticeship of imitation and seeking with delight to examine my experience through the discipline of the novel, I became gradually aware that the forms of so many of the works which impressed me were too restricted to contain the experience which I knew. The diversity of American life with its extreme fluidity and openness seemed too vital and alive to be caught for more than the briefest instant in the tight, well-made Jamesian novel, which was, for all its artistic perfection, too concerned with "good taste" and stable areas. Nor could I safely use the forms of the "hard-boiled" novel, with its dedication to physical violence, social cynicism and understatement. Understatement depends, after all, upon commonly held assumptions, and my minority status rendered all such assumptions questionable. There was also a problem of language, and even dialogue, which, with its hard-boiled stance and its monosyllabic utterance, is one of the shining achievements of twentieth-century American writing. For despite the notion that its rhythms were those of everyday speech, I found that when compared with the rich babel of idiomatic expression around me, a language full of imagery and gesture and rhetorical canniness, it was embarrassingly austere. Our speech I found resounding with an alive language swirling with over three hundred years of American living, a mixture of the folk, the Biblical, the scientific and the political. Slangy in one stance, academic in another, loaded poetically with imagery at one moment, mathematically bare of imagery in the next. As for the rather rigid concepts of reality which informed a number of the works which impressed me and to which I owe a great deal, I was forced to conclude that reality was far more mysterious and uncertain, and more exciting, and still, despite its raw violence and capriciousness, more promising. To attempt to express that American experience which has carried one back and forth and up and down the land and across, and across again the great river, from freight train to Pullman car, from contact with slavery to contact with a world of advanced scholarship, art and science, is simply to burst such neatly understated forms of the novel asunder.

A novel whose range was both broader and deeper was needed. And in my search I found myself turning to our classical nineteenth-century novelists. I felt that except for the work of William Faulkner something vital had gone out of American prose after Mark Twain. I came to believe that the writers of that period took a much greater responsibility for the condition of democracy and, indeed, their works were imaginative projections of the conflicts within the human heart which arose when the sacred principles of the Constitution and the Bill of Rights clashed with the practical exigencies of human greed and fear, hate and love. Naturally I was attracted to these writers as a Negro. Whatever they thought of my people per se, in their imaginative economy the Negro symbolized both the man lowest down and the mysterious, underground aspect of human personality. In a sense the Negro was the gauge of the human condition as it waxed and waned in our democracy. These writers were willing to confront the broad complexities of American life, and we are the richer for their having done so.

Thus to see America with an awareness of its rich diversity and its almost magical fluidity and freedom, I was forced to conceive of a novel unburdened by the narrow naturalism which has led, after so many triumphs, to the final and unrelieved despair which marks so much of our current fiction. I was to dream of a prose which was flexible, and swift as American change is swift, confronting the inequalities and brutalities of our society forthrightly, yet thrusting forth its images of hope, human fraternity and individual self-realization. It would use the richness of our speech, the idiomatic expression and the rhetorical flourishes from past periods which are still alive among us. And despite my personal failures, there must be possible a fiction which, leaving sociology to the scientists, can arrive at the truth about the human condition, here and now, with all the bright magic of a fairy tale.

What has been missing from so much experimental writing has been the passionate will to dominate reality as well as the laws of art. This will is the true source of the experimental attitude. We who struggle with form and with America should remember Eidothea's advice to Menelaus when in the *Odyssey* he and his friends are seeking their way home. She tells him to seize her father, Proteus, and to hold him fast "however he may struggle and fight. He will turn into all sorts of shapes to try you," she says, "into all the creatures that live and move upon the earth, into water, into blazing fire; but you must hold him fast and press him all the harder. When he is himself, and questions you in the same shape that he was when you saw him in his bed, let the old man go; and then, sir, ask which god it is who is angry, and how you shall make your way homewards over the fish-giving sea."

For the novelist, Proteus stands for both America and the inheritance of illusion through which all men must fight to achieve reality; the offended god stands for our sins against those principles we all hold sacred. The way home we seek is that condition of man's being at home in the world, which is called love, and which we term democracy. Our task then is always to challenge the apparent forms of reality—that is, the fixed manners and values of the few—and to struggle with it until it reveals its mad, vari-implicated chaos, its false faces, and on until it surrenders its insight, its truth. We are fortunate as American writers in that with our variety of racial and national traditions, idioms and manners, we are yet one. On its profoundest level American experience is of a whole. Its truth lies in its diversity and swiftness of change. Through forging forms of the novel worthy of it, we achieve not only the promise of our lives, but we anticipate the resolution of those world problems of humanity which for a moment seem to those who are in awe of statistics completely insoluble.

Whenever we as Americans have faced serious crises we have returned to fundamentals; this, in brief, is what I have tried to do.

1953

JOHN CHEEVER
1912–1982

Although his reputation has ebbed and flowed from the beginning of his career in the 1940s until now, no critic would deny John Cheever's impact on the mid-twentieth-century short story. In particular, Cheever was at the center of a tradition of writers, including Richard Yates, J. D. Salinger, John Updike, and Richard Ford, whose fiction concerned itself primarily with chronicling suburbia, usually peering beneath its veneer and discovering unhappiness, infidelity, alcoholism, narcissism, and a host of other discontents that belie the typical vision of the suburban American dream. Although he published a half dozen novels and novellas, Cheever was known primarily as a craftsman of the short story. His collection *The Stories of John Cheever*, published in 1978, was a best seller that won the Pulitzer Prize and the National Book Critics' Circle Award.

Like those of his characters, Cheever's life seemed happy from an outsider's perspective. He cultivated steady work habits in his early career and managed to earn a prosperous living on his stories alone. But his posthumously published journals and letters—as well as a critical memoir published by his daughter Susan, also a professional writer—reveal a wealth of unhappiness that nearly destroyed him and put great strain on his family. Alcoholism and latent bisexuality drove Cheever into a deep depression that he did not conquer until his waning years, when he achieved sobriety and wrote his novel *Falconer* (1977), which achieved much greater acclaim than any of his previous attempts at longer fiction.

The scion of a New England family that traced back to Puritan times, Cheever grew up in Wollaston, Massachusetts, south of Boston, but after a stint in the army transplanted himself to Westchester Country, New York, when he began to write for *The New Yorker*. Despite a state-sponsored trip to the Soviet Union in 1964 (where he met John Updike) and frequent trips to Italy, most of

Cheever's stories are local rather than global, many set in a fictional New York suburb called Shady Hill. Some of his stories achieve expansiveness through biblical and mythological allusion. Others gain texture through the fancifulness of the author's imagination; "The Country Husband," for instance, is a suburban tale that ends with the narrative observation, "Then it is dark; it is a night where kings in golden suits ride elephants over the mountains." The key to understanding Cheever's fiction might not be in the suburbs themselves, but rather in the perspective of the writer who observes them; in "The Worm in the Apple," after trying to imagine a number of horrible scenarios about his seemingly contented neighbors, the narrator admits, "one might wonder if the worm was not in the eye of the observer who, through timidity or moral cowardice, could not embrace the broad range of their natural enthusiasms and would not grant that, while Larry played neither Bach nor football very well, his pleasure in both was genuine."

This emphasis on an eccentric perspective accounts for the appeal of Cheever's most famous stories, "The Swimmer" and "The Enormous Radio" (included here). What might seem like typical suburban middle-class settings are distorted by something surreal in these stories. In "The Enormous Radio," one of his earliest stories, there is also a distinct emphasis on the anxieties of the post–World War II decades in which privacy was compromised by spying and many Americans felt scrutinized for their political beliefs, if not their domestic secrets. The American suburbs of the 1940s and 1950s were believed to be safe places, but the invasion of privacy in this story suggests an ironic reversal of that belief.

D. Quentin Miller
Suffolk University

PRIMARY WORKS

The Way Some People Live, 1943; *The Enormous Radio and Other Stories*, 1953; *The Wapshot Chronicle*, 1957; *The Housebreaker of Shady Hill and Other Stories*, 1958; *Some People, Places, and Things That Will Not Appear in My Next Novel*, 1961; *The Wapshot Scandal*, 1964; *The Brigadier and the Golf Widow*, 1964; *Bullet Park*, 1969; *The World of Apples*, 1973; *Falconer*, 1977; The *Stories of John Cheever*, 1978; *Oh, What a Paradise It Seems*, 1982; *The Letters of John Cheever*, 1988; *The Journals of John Cheever*, 1991.

The Enormous Radio

Jim and Irene Westcott were the kind of people who seem to strike that satisfactory average of income, endeavor, and respectability that is reached by the statistical reports in college alumni bulletins. They were the parents of two young children, they had been married nine years, they lived on the twelfth floor of an apartment house near Sutton Place, they went to the theatre on an average of 10.3 times a year, and they hoped someday to live in Westchester. Irene Westcott was a pleasant, rather plain girl with soft brown hair and a wide, fine forehead upon which nothing at all had been written, and in the cold weather she wore a coat of fitch skins dyed to resemble mink. You could not say that Jim Westcott looked younger than he was, but you could at least say of him that he seemed to feel younger. He wore his graying hair cut very short, he dressed in the kind of clothes his class had worn at Andover, and his manner was earnest, vehement, and intentionally naïve. The Westcotts differed from their friends, their classmates, and their neighbors only in an interest they shared in serious music. They went to a great many concerts—although they seldom mentioned this to anyone— and they spent a good deal of time listening to music on the radio.

Their radio was an old instrument, sensitive, unpredictable, and beyond repair. Neither of them understood the mechanics of radio—or of any of the other appliances that surrounded them—and when the instrument faltered, Jim would strike the side of the cabinet with his hand. This sometimes helped. One Sunday afternoon, in the middle of a Schubert quartet, the music faded away altogether. Jim struck the cabinet repeatedly, but there was no response; the Schubert was lost to them forever. He promised to buy Irene a new radio, and on Monday when he came home from work he told her that he had got one. He refused to describe it, and said it would be a surprise for her when it came.

The radio was delivered at the kitchen door the following afternoon, and with the assistance of her maid and the handyman Irene uncrated it and brought it into the living room. She was struck at once with the physical ugliness of the large gumwood cabinet. Irene was proud of her living room, she had chosen its furnishings and colors as carefully as she chose her clothes, and now it seemed to her that the new radio stood among her intimate possessions like an aggressive intruder. She was confounded by the number of dials and switches on the instrument panel, and she studied them thoroughly before she put the plug into a wall socket and turned the radio on. The dials flooded with a malevolent green light, and in the distance she heard the music of a piano quintet. The quintet was in the distance for only an instant; it bore down upon her with a speed greater than light and filled the apartment with the noise of music amplified so mightily that it knocked a china ornament from a table to the floor. She rushed to the instrument and reduced the volume. The violent forces that were snared in the ugly gumwood cabinet made her uneasy. Her children came home from school then, and she took them to the Park. It was not until later in the afternoon that she was able to return to the radio.

The maid had given the children their suppers and was supervising their baths when Irene turned on the radio, reduced the volume, and sat down to listen to a Mozart quintet that she knew and enjoyed. The music came through clearly. The new instrument had a much purer tone, she thought, than the old one. She decided that tone was most important and that she could conceal the cabinet behind a sofa. But as soon as she had made her peace with the radio, the interference began. A crackling sound like the noise of a burning powder fuse began to accompany the singing of the strings. Beyond the music, there was a rustling that reminded Irene unpleasantly of the sea, and as the quintet progressed, these noises were joined by many others. She tried all the dials and switches but nothing dimmed the interference, and she sat down, disappointed and bewildered, and tried to trace the flight of the melody. The elevator shaft in her building ran beside the living-room wall, and it was the noise of the elevator that gave her a clue to the character of the static. The rattling of the elevator cables and the opening and closing of the elevator doors were reproduced in her loudspeaker, and, realizing that the radio was sensitive to electrical currents of all sorts, she began to discern through the Mozart the ringing of telephone bells, the dialing of phones, and the lamentation of a vacuum cleaner. By listening more carefully, she was able to distinguish doorbells, elevator bells, electric razors, and Waring mixers, whose sounds had been picked up from the apartments that surrounded hers and transmitted through her loudspeaker. The powerful and ugly instrument, with its mistaken sensitivity to discord, was more than she could hope to master, so she turned the thing off and went into the nursery to see her children.

When Jim Westcott came home that night, he went to the radio confidently and worked the controls. He had the same sort of experience Irene had had. A man was speaking on the station Jim had chosen, and his voice swung instantly from the distance into a force so powerful that it shook the apartment. Jim turned the volume control and reduced the voice. Then, a minute or two later, the interference began. The ringing of telephones and doorbells set in, joined by the rasp of the elevator doors and the whir of cooking appliances. The character of the noise had changed since Irene had tried the radio earlier; the last of the electric razors was being unplugged, the vacuum cleaners had all been returned to their closets, and the static reflected that change in pace that overtakes the city after the sun goes down. He fiddled with the knobs but couldn't get rid of the noises, so he turned the radio off and told Irene that in the morning he'd call the people who had sold it to him and give them hell.

The following afternoon, when Irene returned to the apartment from a luncheon date, the maid told her that a man had come and fixed the radio. Irene went into the living room before she took off her hat or her furs and tried the instrument. From the loudspeaker came a recording of the "Missouri Waltz." It reminded her of the thin, scratchy music from an old-fashioned phonograph that she sometimes heard across the lake where she spent her summers. She waited until the waltz had finished, expecting an explanation of the recording, but there was none. The music was followed by silence, and then the plaintive and scratchy record was repeated. She turned the dial and got a satisfactory burst of Caucasian music—the thump of bare feet in the dust and the rattle of coin jewelry—but in the background she could hear the ringing of bells and a confusion of voices. Her children came home from school then, and she turned off the radio and went to the nursery.

When Jim came home that night, he was tired, and he took a bath and changed his clothes. Then he joined Irene in the living room. He had just turned on the radio when the maid announced dinner, so he left it on, and he and Irene went to the table.

Jim was too tired to make even a pretense of sociability, and there was nothing about the dinner to hold Irene's interest, so her attention wandered from the food to the deposits of silver polish on the candlesticks and from there to the music in the other room. She listened for a few minutes to a Chopin prelude and then was surprised to hear a man's voice break in. "For Christ's sake, Kathy," he said, "do you always have to play the piano when I get home?" The music stopped abruptly. "It's the only chance I have," a woman said. "I'm at the office all day." "So am I," the man said. He added something obscene about an upright piano, and slammed a door. The passionate and melancholy music began again.

"Did you hear that?" Irene asked.

"What?" Jim was eating his dessert.

"The radio. A man said something while the music was still going on—something dirty."

"It's probably a play."

"I don't think it is a play," Irene said.

They left the table and took their coffee into the living room. Irene asked Jim to try another station. He turned the knob. "Have you seen my garters?" a man asked. "Button me up," a woman said. "Have you seen my garters?" the man said again. "Just button me up and I'll find your garters," the woman said. Jim shifted to another station. "I wish you wouldn't leave apple cores in the ashtrays," a man said. "I hate the smell."

"This is strange," Jim said.

"Isn't it?" Irene said.

Jim turned the knob again. "'On the coast of Coromandel where the early pumpkins blow,'" a woman with a pronounced English accent said, "'in the middle of the woods lived the Yonghy-Bonghy-Bò. Two old chairs, and half a candle, one old jug without a handle ...'"

"My God!" Irene cried. "That's the Sweeneys' nurse."

"'These were all his worldly goods,'" the British voice continued.

"Turn that thing off," Irene said. "Maybe they can hear us." Jim switched the radio off. "That was Miss Armstrong, the Sweeneys' nurse," Irene said. "She must be reading to the little girl. They live in 17-B. I've talked with Miss Armstrong in the Park. I know her voice very well. We must be getting other people's apartments."

"That's impossible," Jim said.

"Well, that was the Sweeneys' nurse," Irene said hotly. "I know her voice. I know it very well. I'm wondering if they can hear us."

Jim turned the switch. First from a distance and then nearer, nearer, as if borne on the wind, came the pure accents of the Sweeneys' nurse again: "'Lady Jingly! Lady Jingly!'" she said, "'sitting where the pumpkins blow, will you come and be my wife? said the Yonghy-Bonghy-Bò ...'"

Jim went over to the radio and said "Hello" loudly into the speaker.

"'I am tired of living singly,'" the nurse went on, "'on this coast so wild and shingly, I'm a-weary of my life; if you'll come and be my wife, quite serene would be my life ...'"

"I guess she can't hear us," Irene said. "Try something else."

Jim turned to another station, and the living room was filled with the uproar of a cocktail party that had overshot its mark. Someone was playing the piano and singing the "Whiffenpoof Song," and the voices that surrounded the piano were vehement and happy. "Eat some more sandwiches," a woman shrieked. There were screams of laughter and a dish of some sort crashed to the floor.

"Those must be the Fullers, in 11-E," Irene said. "I knew they were giving a party this afternoon. I saw her in the liquor store. Isn't this too divine? Try something else. See if you can get those people in 18-C."

The Westcotts overheard that evening a monologue on salmon fishing in Canada, a bridge game, running comments on home movies of what had apparently been a fortnight at Sea Island, and a bitter family quarrel about an overdraft at the bank. They turned off their radio at midnight and went to bed, weak with laughter. Sometime in the night, their son began to call for a glass of water and Irene got one and took it to his room. It was very early. All the lights in the neighborhood were extinguished, and from the boy's window she could see the empty street. She went into the living room and tried the radio. There was some faint coughing, a moan, and then a man spoke. "Are you all right, darling?" he asked. "Yes," a woman said wearily. "Yes, I'm all right, I guess," and then she added with great feeling, "But, you know, Charlie, I don't feel like myself any more. Sometimes there are about fifteen or twenty minutes in the week when I feel like myself. I don't like to go to another doctor, because the doctor's bills are so awful already, but I just don't feel like myself, Charlie. I just never feel like myself." They were not young, Irene thought. She guessed from the timbre of their voices that they were middle-aged. The restrained melancholy of the dialogue and the draft from the bedroom window made her shiver, and she went back to bed.

The following morning, Irene cooked breakfast for the family—the maid didn't come up from her room in the basement until ten—braided her daughter's hair, and waited at the door until her children and her husband had been carried away in the elevator. Then she went into the living room and tried the radio. "I don't want to go to school," a child screamed. "I hate school. I won't go to school. I hate school." "You will go to school," an enraged woman said. "We paid eight hundred dollars to get you into that school and you'll go if it kills you." The next number on the dial produced the worn record of the "Missouri Waltz." Irene shifted the control and invaded the privacy of several breakfast tables. She overheard demonstrations of indigestion, carnal love, abysmal vanity, faith, and despair. Irene's life was nearly as simple and sheltered as it appeared to be, and the forthright and sometimes brutal language that came from the loudspeaker that morning astonished and troubled her. She continued to listen until her maid came in. Then she turned off the radio quickly, since this insight, she realized, was a furtive one.

Irene had a luncheon date with a friend that day, and she left her apartment at a little after twelve. There were a number of women in the elevator when it stopped at her floor. She stared at their handsome and impassive faces, their furs, and the cloth flowers in their hats. Which one of them had been to Sea Island? she wondered. Which one had overdrawn her bank account? The elevator stopped at the tenth floor and a woman with a pair of Skye terriers joined them. Her hair was rigged high on her head and she wore a mink cape. She was humming the "Missouri Waltz."

Irene had two Martinis at lunch, and she looked searchingly at her friend and wondered what her secrets were. They had intended to go shopping after lunch, but Irene excused herself and went home. She told the maid that she was not to be disturbed; then she went into the living room, closed the doors, and switched on the radio. She heard, in the course of the afternoon, the halting conversation of a woman entertaining her aunt, the hysterical conclusion of a luncheon party, and a hostess briefing her maid about some cocktail guests. "Don't give the best Scotch to anyone who hasn't white hair," the hostess said. "See if you can get rid of that liver paste before you pass those hot things, and could you lend me five dollars? I want to tip the elevator man."

As the afternoon waned, the conversations increased in intensity. From where Irene sat, she could see the open sky above the East River. There were hundreds of clouds in the sky, as though the south wind had broken the winter into pieces and were blowing it north, and on her radio she could hear the arrival of cocktail guests and the return of children and businessmen from their schools and offices. "I found a good-sized diamond on the bathroom floor this morning," a woman said. "It must have fallen out of that bracelet Mrs. Dunston was wearing last night." "We'll sell it," a man said. "Take it down to the jeweler on Madison Avenue and sell it. Mrs. Dunston won't know the difference, and we could use a couple of hundred bucks ..." "'Oranges and lemons, say the bells of St. Clement's,'" the Sweeneys' nurse sang. "'Halfpence and farthings, say the bells of St. Martin's. When will you pay me? say the bells at old Bailey ...'" "It's not a hat," a woman cried, and at her back roared a cocktail party. "It's not a hat, it's a love affair. That's what Walter Florell said. He said it's not a hat, it's a love affair," and then, in a lower voice, the same woman added, "Talk to somebody, for Christ's sake, honey, talk to somebody. If she catches you standing here not talking to anybody, she'll take us off her invitation list, and I love these parties."

The Westcotts were going out for dinner that night, and when Jim came home, Irene was dressing. She seemed sad and vague, and he brought her a drink. They were dining with friends in the neighborhood, and they walked to where they were going. The sky was broad and filled with light. It was one of those splendid spring evenings that excite memory and desire, and the air that touched their hands and faces felt very soft. A Salvation Army band was on the corner playing "Jesus Is Sweeter." Irene drew on her husband's arm and held him there for a minute, to hear the music. "They're really such nice people, aren't they?" she said. "They have such nice faces. Actually, they're so much nicer than a lot of the people we know." She took a bill from her purse and walked over and dropped it into the tambourine. There was in her face, when she returned to her husband, a look of radiant melancholy that he was not familiar with. And her conduct at the dinner party that night seemed strange to him, too. She interrupted her hostess rudely and stared at the people across the table from her with an intensity for which she would have punished her children.

It was still mild when they walked home from the party, and Irene looked up at the spring stars. "'How far that little candle throws its beams,'" she exclaimed. "'So shines a good deed in a naughty world.'" She waited that night until Jim had fallen asleep, and then went into the living room and turned on the radio.

Jim came home at about six the next night. Emma, the maid, let him in, and he had taken off his hat and was taking off his coat when Irene ran into the hall. Her face was shining with tears and her hair was disordered. "Go up to 16-C, Jim!" she screamed. "Don't take off your coat. Go up to 16-C. Mr. Osborn's beating his wife. They've been quarreling since four o'clock, and now he's hitting her. Go up there and stop him."

From the radio in the living room, Jim heard screams, obscenities, and thuds. "You know you don't have to listen to this sort of thing," he said. He strode into the living room and turned the switch. "It's indecent," he said. "It's like looking in windows. You know you don't have to listen to this sort of thing. You can turn it off."

"Oh, it's so horrible, it's so dreadful," Irene was sobbing. "I've been listening all day, and it's so depressing."

"Well, if it's so depressing, why do you listen to it? I bought this damned radio to give you some pleasure," he said. "I paid a great deal of money for it. I thought it might make you happy. I wanted to make you happy."

"Don't, don't, don't, don't quarrel with me," she moaned, and laid her head on his shoulder. "All the others have been quarreling all day. Everybody's been quarreling. They're all worried about money. Mrs. Hutchinson's mother is dying of cancer in Florida and they don't have enough money to send her to the Mayo Clinic. At least, Mr. Hutchinson says they don't have enough money. And some woman in this building is having an affair with the handyman—with that hideous handyman. It's too disgusting. And Mrs. Melville has heart trouble and Mr. Hendricks is going to lose his job in April and Mrs. Hendricks is horrid about the whole thing and that girl who plays the 'Missouri Waltz' is a whore, a common whore, and the elevator man has tuberculosis and Mr. Osborn has been beating Mrs. Osborn." She wailed, she trembled with grief and checked the stream of tears down her face with the heel of her palm.

"Well, why do you have to listen?" Jim asked again. "Why do you have to listen to this stuff if it makes you so miserable?"

"Oh, don't, don't, don't," she cried. "Life is too terrible, too sordid and awful. But we've never been like that, have we, darling? Have we? I mean, we've always been good and decent and loving to one another, haven't we? And we have two children, two beautiful children. Our lives aren't sordid, are they, darling? Are they?" She flung her arms around his neck and drew his face down to hers. "We're happy, aren't we, darling? We are happy, aren't we?"

"Of course we're happy," he said tiredly. He began to surrender his resentment. "Of course we're happy. I'll have that damned radio fixed or taken away tomorrow." He stroked her soft hair. "My poor girl," he said.

"You love me, don't you?" she asked. "And we're not hypercritical or worried about money or dishonest, are we?"

"No, darling," he said.

A man came in the morning and fixed the radio. Irene turned it on cautiously and was happy to hear a California-wine commercial and a recording of Beethoven's Ninth Symphony, including Schiller's "Ode to Joy." She kept the radio on all day and nothing untoward came from the speaker.

A Spanish suite was being played when Jim came home. "Is everything all right?" he asked. His face was pale, she thought. They had some cocktails and went in to dinner to the "Anvil Chorus" from Il Trovatore. This was followed by Debussy's "La Mer."

"I paid the bill for the radio today," Jim said. "It cost four hundred dollars. I hope you'll get some enjoyment out of it."

"Oh, I'm sure I will," Irene said.

"Four hundred dollars is a good deal more than I can afford," he went on. "I wanted to get something that you'd enjoy. It's the last extravagance we'll be able to indulge in this year. I see that you haven't paid your clothing bills yet. I saw them on your dressing table." He looked directly at her. "Why did you tell me you'd paid them? Why did you lie to me?"

"I just didn't want you to worry, Jim," she said. She drank some water. "I'll be able to pay my bills out of this month's allowance. There were the slipcovers last month, and that party."

"You've got to learn to handle the money I give you a little more intelligently, Irene," he said. "You've got to understand that we won't have as much money this year as we had last. I had a very sobering talk with Mitchell today. No one is buying anything. We're spending all our time promoting new issues, and you know how long that takes. I'm not getting any younger, you know. I'm thirty-seven. My hair will be gray next year. I haven't done as well as I'd hoped to do. And I don't suppose things will get any better."

"Yes, dear," she said.

"We've got to start cutting down," Jim said. "We've got to think of the children. To be perfectly frank with you, I worry about money a great deal. I'm not at all sure of the future. No one is. If anything should happen to me, there's the insurance, but that wouldn't go very far today. I've worked awfully hard to give you and the children a comfortable life," he said bitterly. "I don't like to see all of my energies, all of my youth, wasted in fur coats and radios and slipcovers and—"

"Please, Jim," she said. "Please. They'll hear us."

"Who'll hear us? Emma can't hear us."

"The radio."

"Oh, I'm sick!" he shouted. "I'm sick to death of your apprehensiveness. The radio can't hear us. Nobody can hear us. And what if they can hear us? Who cares?"

Irene got up from the table and went into the living room. Jim went to the door and shouted at her from there. "Why are you so Christly all of a sudden? What's turned you overnight into a convent girl? You stole your mother's jewelry before they probated her will. You never gave your sister a cent of that money that was intended for her—not even when she needed it. You made Grace Howland's life miserable, and where was all your piety and your virtue when you went to that abortionist? I'll never forget how cool you were. You packed your bag and went off to have that child murdered as if you were going to Nassau. If you'd had any reasons, if you'd had any good reasons—"

Irene stood for a minute before the hideous cabinet, disgraced and sickened, but she held her hand on the switch before she extinguished the music and the voices, hoping that the instrument might speak to her kindly, that she might hear the Sweeneys' nurse. Jim continued to shout at her from the door. The voice on the radio was suave and noncommittal. "An early-morning railroad disaster in Tokyo," the loudspeaker said, "killed twenty-nine people. A fire in a Catholic hospital near Buffalo for the care of blind children was extinguished early this morning by nuns. The temperature is forty-seven. The humidity is eighty-nine."

1947

SAUL BELLOW
1915–2005

The son of immigrant parents from Russia, Saul Bellow grew up in a Jewish ghetto of Montreal, Canada, where he learned Yiddish, Hebrew, English, and French. In 1924 his family moved to Chicago, a city that often appears in his fiction. After earning a bachelor's degree from Northwestern University, in 1937 he entered the University of Wisconsin at Madison to study anthropology but left there in December to become a writer. Employed for a brief period with the Works Progress Administration Writers Project, he led a bohemian life until World War II, when he served in the Merchant Marine. After the war he taught at the University of Minnesota in Minneapolis and other schools, traveled in Europe, and lived in Paris for a period of time. From 1963 until his death, he held academic positions at the University of Chicago and Boston University.

Bellow is usually considered to be one of America's most important contemporary writers; his work impresses one with its diversity of style, the profundity of its content, and its scope. Bellow published his first novel, *Dangling Man*, in 1944; it is a diary of a demoralized man who is left "dangling" with no real purpose as he waits to be drafted. Three years later, Bellow published *The Victim*, which borrows the technique of the Doppelgänger from Dostoevsky's *The Eternal Husband*. In this second novel, he depicts the intense psychological battle between the Jew Asa Leventhal and his "double," the Gentile Kirby Allbee.

In the late 1940s, Bellow became disenchanted with the "modernist victim literature" of his first two novels. Detached in tone, these restrained works followed "repressive" Flaubertian formal standards. With *The Adventures of Augie March* (1953), Bellow broke free from the "modernist" chains that bound him. In contrast to the two morose early novels, this open-ended, picaresque narrative with its flamboyant language, zany comedy, and exuberant hero affirms the potential of the individual, his imagination, and the worth of ordinary existence.

Bellow's subsequent novels develop the themes of *The Adventures of Augie March*. *Seize the Day* (1956) is a dark comedy that depicts the day of reckoning in the life of Tommy Wilhelm, a "loser" who is spiritually reborn at the very end of the work. *Henderson the Rain King* (1959) is the story of an eccentric, energetic millionaire who journeys to the heart of Africa and experiences fantastic adventures. *Herzog* (1964), an enormous critical and financial success, depicts the intense psychological struggles of a professor who is on the verge of a mental breakdown as a result of his divorce from his second wife and the betrayal of his best friend. *The Dean's December* (1982) confronts political and social problems more directly than any of his other novels; Bellow contrasts the near anarchy of the slums of Chicago with the authoritarianism of the Communist world and sees a "moral crisis" in both West and East. *Ravelstein* (2000) is a meditative and autobiographical novel that explores a variety of subjects but focuses on friendship, memory, and death.

Bellow also wrote short stories, some of which are collected in *Mosby's Memoirs and Other Stories* and *Him with His Foot in His Mouth and Other Stories*; a nonfiction book on Israel, *To Jerusalem and Back*; several plays; and a number of essays, some of which are collected in *It All Adds Up*. He received many awards for his writing, including the Nobel Prize for Literature in 1976.

Bellow was a master of narrative voice and perspective; he was a remarkable stylist who could move with ease from formal rhetoric to the language of the street. A great comic writer, perhaps America's greatest since Mark Twain, Bellow explored the tragicomic search of urban man for spiritual survival in a materialistic world hostile to the imagination and "higher meanings."

Allan Chavkin
Southwest Texas State University

PRIMARY WORKS

Dangling Man, 1944; *The Victim*, 1947; *The Adventures of Augie March*, 1953; *Seize the Day*, 1956; *Henderson the Rain King*, 1959; *Herzog*, 1964; *Mosby's Memoirs and Other Stories*, 1968; *Mr. Sammler's Planet*, 1970; *Humboldt's Gift*, 1975; *To Jerusalem and Back*, 1976; *The Dean's December*, 1982; *Him with His Foot in His Mouth and Other Stories*, 1984; *More Die of Heartbreak*, 1987; *A Theft*, 1989; *The Bellarosa Connection*, 1989; *Something to Remember Me By*, 1991; *It All Adds Up*, 1994; *The Actual*, 1997; *Ravelstein*, 2000.

Looking for Mr. Green

Whatsoever thy hand findeth to do, do it with thy might....[1]

Hard work? No, it wasn't really so hard. He wasn't used to walking and stair-climbing, but the physical difficulty of his new job was not what George Grebe felt most. He was delivering relief checks in the Negro district, and although he was a native Chicagoan this was not a part of the city he knew much about—it needed a depression to introduce him to it. No, it wasn't literally hard work, not as reckoned in foot-pounds, but yet he was beginning to feel the strain of it, to grow aware of its peculiar difficulty. He could find the streets and numbers, but the clients were not where they were supposed to be, and he felt like a hunter inexperienced in the camouflage of his game. It was an unfavorable day, too—fall, and cold, dark weather, windy. But, anyway, instead of shells in his deep trenchcoat pocket he had the cardboard of checks, punctured for the spindles of the file, the holes reminding him of the holes in player-piano paper. And he didn't look much like a hunter, either; his was a city figure entirely, belted up in this Irish conspirator's coat. He was slender without being tall, stiff in the back, his legs looking shabby in a pair of old tweed pants gone through and fringy at the cuffs. With this stiffness, he kept his head forward, so that his face was red from the sharpness of the weather; and it was an indoors sort of face with gray eyes that persisted in some kind of thought and yet seemed to avoid definiteness of conclusion. He wore sideburns that surprised you somewhat by the tough curl of the blond hair and the effect of assertion in their length. He was not so mild as he looked, nor so youthful; and nevertheless there was no effort on his part to seem what he was not. He was an educated man; he was a bachelor; he was in some ways simple; without lushing, he liked a drink; his luck had not been good. Nothing was deliberately hidden.

He felt that his luck was better than usual today. When he had reported for work that morning he had expected to be shut up in the relief office at a clerk's job, for he had been hired downtown as a clerk, and he was glad to have, instead, the freedom of the streets and welcomed, at least at first, the vigor of the cold and even the blowing of the hard wind. But on the other hand he was not getting on with the distribution of the checks. It was true that it was a city job; nobody expected you to push too hard at a city job. His supervisor, that young Mr. Raynor, had practically told him that. Still, he wanted to do well at it. For one thing, when he knew how quickly he could deliver a batch of checks, he would know also how much time he could expect to clip for himself. And then, too, the clients would be waiting for their money. That was not the most important consideration, though it certainly mattered to him. No, but he wanted to do well, simply for doing-well's sake, to acquit himself decently of a job because he so rarely had a job to do that required just this sort of energy. Of this peculiar energy he now had a

[1]Ecclesiastes 9:10 "Whatsoever thy hand findeth to do, do it with thy might; for there is no work, nor device, nor knowledge, nor wisdom, in the grave, whither thou goest."

superabundance; once it had started to flow, it flowed all too heavily. And, for the time being anyway, he was balked. He could not find Mr. Green.

So he stood in his big-skirted trenchcoat with a large envelope in his hand and papers showing from his pocket, wondering why people should be so hard to locate who were too feeble or sick to come to the station to collect their own checks. But Raynor had told him that tracking them down was not easy at first and had offered him some advice on how to proceed. "If you can see the postman, he's your first man to ask, and your best bet. If you can't connect with him, try the stores and tradespeople around. Then the janitor and the neighbors. But you'll find the closer you come to your man the less people will tell you. They don't want to tell you anything."

"Because I'm a stranger."

"Because you're white. We ought to have a Negro doing this, but we don't at the moment, and of course you've got to eat, too, and this is public employment. Jobs have to be made. Oh, that holds for me too. Mind you, I'm not letting myself out. I've got three years of seniority on you, that's all. And a law degree. Otherwise, you might be back of the desk and I might be going out into the field this cold day. The same dough pays us both and for the same, exact, identical reason. What's my law degree got to do with it? But you have to pass out these checks, Mr. Grebe, and it'll help if you're stubborn, so I hope you are."

"Yes, I'm fairly stubborn."

Raynor sketched hard with an eraser in the old dirt of his desk, left-handed, and said, "Sure, what else can you answer to such a question. Anyhow, the trouble you're going to have is that they don't like to give information about anybody. They think you're a plain-clothes dick or an installment collector, or summons-server or something like that. Till you've been seen around the neighborhood for a few months and people know you're only from the relief."

It was dark, ground-freezing, pre-Thanksgiving weather; the wind played hob with the smoke, rushing it down, and Grebe missed his gloves, which he had left in Raynor's office. And no one would admit knowing Green. It was past three o'clock and the postman had made his last delivery. The nearest grocer, himself a Negro, had never heard the name Tulliver Green, or said he hadn't. Grebe was inclined to think that it was true, that he had in the end convinced the man that he wanted only to deliver a check. But he wasn't sure. He needed experience in interpreting looks and signs and, even more, the will not to be put off or denied and even the force to bully if need be. If the grocer did know, he had got rid of him easily. But since most of his trade was with reliefers, why should he prevent the delivery of a check? Maybe Green, or Mrs. Green, if there was a Mrs. Green, patronized another grocer. And was there a Mrs. Green? It was one of Grebe's great handicaps that he hadn't looked at any of the case records. Raynor should have let him read files for a few hours. But he apparently saw no need for that, probably considering the job unimportant. Why prepare systematically to deliver a few checks?

But now it was time to look for the janitor. Grebe took in the building in the wind and gloom of the late November day—trampled, frost-hardened lots on one side; on the other, an automobile junk yard and then the infinite work of Elevated frames,[2] weak-looking, gaping with rubbish fires; two sets of leaning brick porches three stories high and a flight of cement stairs to the cellar. Descending, he entered the underground passage, where he tried the doors until one opened and he found himself in the furnace room. There someone rose toward him and approached, scraping on the coal grit and bending under the canvas-jacketed pipes.

"Are you the janitor?"

"What do you want?"

"I'm looking for a man who's supposed to be living here. Green."

"What Green?"

"Oh, you maybe have more than one Green?" said Grebe with new, pleasant hope. "This is Tulliver Green."

"I don't think I c'n help you, mister. I don't know any."

"A crippled man."

The janitor stood bent before him. Could it be that he was crippled? Oh, God! what if he was. Grebe's gray eyes sought with excited difficulty to see. But no, he was only very short and stooped. A head awakened from meditation, a strong-haired beard, low, wide shoulders. A staleness of sweat and coal rose from his black shirt and the burlap sack he wore as an apron.

"Crippled how?"

Grebe thought and then answered with the light voice of unmixed candor, "I don't know. I've never seen him." This was damaging, but his only other choice was to make a lying guess, and he was not up to it. "I'm delivering checks for the relief to shut-in cases. If he weren't crippled he'd come to collect himself. That's why I said crippled. Bedridden, chair-ridden—is there anybody like that?"

This sort of frankness was one of Grebe's oldest talents, going back to childhood. But it gained him nothing here.

"No suh. I've got four buildin's same as this that I take care of. I don' know all the tenants, leave alone the tenants' tenants. The rooms turn over so fast, people movin' in and out every day. I can't tell you."

The janitor opened his grimy lips but Grebe did not hear him in the piping of the valves and the consuming pull of air to flame in the body of the furnace. He knew, however, what he had said.

"Well, all the same, thanks. Sorry I bothered you. I'll prowl around upstairs again and see if I can turn up someone who knows him."

Once more in the cold air and early darkness he made the short circle from the cellarway to the entrance crowded between the brickwork pillars and began to climb to the third floor. Pieces of plaster ground under his feet; strips of brass tape from which the carpeting had been torn away

---

[2]The "El," or elevated railroad, which operates
on an elevated structure, as over streets.

marked old boundaries at the sides. In the passage, the cold reached him worse than in the street; it touched him to the bone. The hall toilets ran like springs. He thought grimly as he heard the wind burning around the building with a sound like that of the furnace, that this was a great piece of constructed shelter. Then he struck a match in the gloom and searched for names and numbers among the writings and scribbles on the walls. He saw WHOODY-DOODY GO TO JESUS, and zigzags, caricatures, sexual scrawls, and curses. So the sealed rooms of pyramids were also decorated, and the caves of human dawn.

The information on his card was, TULLIVER GREEN—APT 3D. There were no names, however, and no numbers. His shoulders drawn up, tears of cold in his eyes, breathing vapor, he went the length of the corridor and told himself that if he had been lucky enough to have the temperament for it he would bang on one of the doors and bawl out "Tulliver Green!" until he got results. But it wasn't in him to make an uproar and he continued to burn matches, passing the light over the walls. At the rear, in a corner off the hall, he discovered a door he had not seen before and he thought it best to investigate. It sounded empty when he knocked, but a young Negress answered, hardly more than a girl. She opened only a bit, to guard the warmth of the room.

"Yes suh?"

"I'm from the district relief station on Prairie Avenue. I'm looking for a man named Tulliver Green to give him his check. Do you know him?"

No, she didn't; but he thought she had not understood anything of what he had said. She had a dream-bound, dream-blind face, very soft and black, shut off. She wore a man's jacket and pulled the ends together at her throat. Her hair was parted in three directions, at the sides and transversely, standing up at the front in a dull puff.

"Is there somebody around here who might know?"

"I jus' taken this room las' week."

He observed that she shivered, but even her shiver was somnambulistic and there was no sharp consciousness of cold in the big smooth eyes of her handsome face.

"All right, miss, thank you. Thanks," he said, and went to try another place.

Here he was admitted. He was grateful, for the room was warm. It was full of people, and they were silent as he entered—ten people, or a dozen, perhaps more, sitting on benches like a parliament. There was no light, properly speaking, but a tempered darkness that the window gave, and everyone seemed to him enormous, the men padded out in heavy work clothes and winter coats, and the women huge, too, in their sweaters, hats, and old furs. And, besides, bed and bedding, a black cooking range, a piano piled towering to the ceiling with papers, a dining-room table of the old style of prosperous Chicago. Among these people Grebe, with his cold-heightened fresh color and his smaller stature, entered like a schoolboy. Even though he was met with smiles and good will, he knew, before a single word was spoken, that all the currents ran against him and that he would make no headway. Nevertheless he began. "Does anybody here know how I can deliver a check to Mr. Tulliver Green?"

"Green?" It was the man that had let him in who answered. He was in short sleeves, in a checkered shirt, and had a queer, high head, profusely overgrown and long as a shako;[3] the veins entered it strongly from his forehead. "I never heard mention of him. Is this where he live?"

"This is the address they gave me at the station. He's a sick man, and he'll need his check. Can't anybody tell me where to find him?"

He stood his ground and waited for a reply, his crimson wool scarf wound about his neck and drooping outside his trenchcoat, pockets weighted with the block of checks and official forms. They must have realized that he was not a college boy employed afternoons by a bill collector, trying foxily to pass for a relief clerk, recognized that he was an older man who knew himself what need was, who had had more than an average seasoning in hardship. It was evident enough if you looked at the marks under his eyes and at the sides of his mouth.

"Anybody know this sick man?"

"No suh." On all sides he saw heads shaken and smiles of denial. No one knew. And maybe it was true, he considered, standing silent in the earthen, musky human gloom of the place as the rumble continued. But he could never really be sure.

"What's the matter with this man?" said shako-head.

"I've never seen him. All I can tell you is that he can't come in person for his money. It's my first day in this district."

"Maybe they given you the wrong number?"

"I don't believe so. But where else can I ask about him?" He felt that this persistence amused them deeply, and in a way he shared their amusement that he should stand up so tenaciously to them. Though smaller, though slight, he was his own man, he retracted nothing about himself, and he looked back at them, gray-eyed, with amusement and also with a sort of courage. On the bench some man spoke in his throat, the words impossible to catch, and a woman answered with a wild, shrieking laugh, which was quickly cut off.

"Well, so nobody will tell me?"

"Ain't nobody who knows."

"At least, if he lives here, he pays rent to someone. Who manages the building?"

"Greatham Company. That's on Thirty-ninth Street."

Grebe wrote it in his pad. But, in the street again, a sheet of wind-driven paper clinging to his leg while he deliberated what direction to take next, it seemed a feeble lead to follow. Probably this Green didn't rent a flat, but a room. Sometimes there were as many as twenty people in an apartment; the

---

[3]A military cap in the shape of a cylinder with a visor and a pompon or plume.

real-estate agent would know only the lessee. And not even the agent could tell you who the renters were. In some places the beds were even used in shifts, watchmen or jitney drivers or short-order cooks in night joints turning out after a day's sleep and surrendering their beds to a sister, a nephew, or perhaps a stranger, just off the bus. There were large numbers of newcomers in this terrific, blight-bitten portion of the city between Cottage Grove and Ashland, wandering from house to house and room to room. When you saw them, how could you know them? They didn't carry bundles on their backs or look picturesque. You only saw a man, a Negro, walking in the street or riding in the car, like everyone else, with his thumb closed on a transfer. And therefore how were you supposed to tell? Grebe thought the Greatham agent would only laugh at his question.

But how much it would have simplified the job to be able to say that Green was old, or blind, or consumptive. An hour in the files, taking a few notes, and he needn't have been at such a disadvantage. When Raynor gave him the block of checks he asked, "How much should I know about these people?" Then Raynor had looked as though he were preparing to accuse him of trying to make the job more important than it was. He smiled, because by then they were on fine terms, but nevertheless he had been getting ready to say something like that when the confusion began in the station over Staika and her children.

Grebe had waited a long time for this job. It came to him through the pull of an old schoolmate in the Corporation Counsel's office, never a close friend, but suddenly sympathetic and interested—pleased to show, moreover, how well he had done, how strongly he was coming on even in these miserable times. Well, he was coming through strongly, along with the Democratic administration itself. Grebe had gone to see him in City Hall, and they had had a counter lunch or beers at least once a month for a year, and finally it had been possible to swing the job. He didn't mind being assigned the lowest clerical grade, nor even being a messenger, though Raynor thought he did.

This Raynor was an original sort of guy and Grebe had taken to him immediately. As was proper on the first day, Grebe had come early, but he waited long, for Raynor was late. At last he darted into his cubicle of an office as though he had just jumped from one of those hurtling huge red Indian Avenue cars. His thin, rough face was wind-stung and he was grinning and saying something breathlessly to himself. In his hat, a small fedora, and his coat, the velvet collar a neat fit about his neck, and his silk muffler that set off the nervous twist of his chin, he swayed and turned himself in his swivel chair, feet leaving the ground; so that he pranced a little as he sat. Meanwhile he took Grebe's measure out of his eyes, eyes of an unusual vertical length and slightly sardonic. So the two men sat for a while, saying nothing, while the supervisor raised his hat from his miscombed hair and put it in his lap. His cold-darkened hands were not clean. A steel beam passed through the little make-shift room, from which machine belts once had hung. The building was an old factory.

"I'm younger than you; I hope you won't find it hard taking orders from me," said Raynor. "But I don't make them up, either. You're how old, about?"

"Thirty-five."

"And you thought you'd be inside doing paper work. But it so happens I have to send you out."

"I don't mind."

"And it's mostly a Negro load we have in this district."

"So I thought it would be."

"Fine. You'll get along. *C'est un bon boulot.*[4] Do you know French?"

"Some."

"I thought you'd be a university man."

"Have you been in France?" said Grebe.

"No, that's the French of the Berlitz School. I've been at it for more than a year, just as I'm sure people have been, all over the world, office boys in China and braves in Tanganyika. In fact, I damn well know it. Such is the attractive power of civilization. It's overrated, but what do you want? *Que voulez-vous?*[5] I get *Le Rire*[6] and all the spicy papers, just like in Tanganyika. It must be mystifying, out there. But my reason is that I'm aiming at the diplomatic service. I have a cousin who's a courier, and the way he describes it is awfully attractive. He rides in the *wagon-lits*[7] and reads books. While we—What did you do before?"

"I sold."

"Where?"

"Canned meat at Stop and Shop. In the basement."

"And before that?"

"Window shades, at Goldblatt's."

"Steady work?"

"No, Thursdays and Saturdays. I also sold shoes."

"You've been a shoe-dog too. Well. And prior to that? Here it is in your folder." He opened the record. "Saint Olaf's College, instructor in classical languages. Fellow, University of Chicago, 1926–27. I've had Latin, too. Let's trade quotations—'*Dum spiro spero.*'"

"'*Da dextram misero.*'"

"'*Alea jacta est.*'"

"'*Excelsior.*'"[8]

Raynor shouted with laughter, and other workers came to look at him over the partition. Grebe also laughed, feeling pleased and easy. The luxury of fun on a nervous morning.

When they were done and no one was watching or listening, Raynor said rather seriously, "What made you study Latin in the first place? Was it for the priesthood?"

---

[4]"It's a good job."
[5]"What do you want?"
[6]French comic journal.
[7]Train sleeping-cars.

[8]"While I breathe, I hope"; "Give your right hand to the wretched"; "The die is cast"; "Higher!"

"No."

"Just for the hell of it? For the culture? Oh, the things people think they can pull!" He made his cry hilarious and tragic. "I ran my pants off so I could study for the bar, and I've passed the bar, so I get twelve dollars a week more than you as a bonus for having seen life straight and whole. I'll tell you, as a man of culture, that even though nothing looks to be real, and everything stands for something else, and that thing for another thing, and that thing for a still further one—there ain't any comparison between twenty-five and thirty-seven dollars a week, regardless of the last reality. Don't you think that was clear to your Greeks? They were a thoughtful people, but they didn't part with their slaves."

This was a great deal more than Grebe had looked for in his first interview with his supervisor. He was too shy to show all the astonishment he felt. He laughed a little, aroused, and brushed at the sunbeam that covered his head with its dust. "Do you think my mistake was so terrible?"

"Damn right it was terrible, and you know it now that you've had the whip of hard times laid on your back. You should have been preparing yourself for trouble. Your people must have been well off to send you to the university. Stop me, if I'm stepping on your toes. Did your mother pamper you? Did your father give in to you? Were you brought up tenderly, with permission to go and find out what were the last things that everything else stands for while everybody else labored in the fallen world of appearances?"

"Well, no, it wasn't exactly like that." Grebe smiled. *The fallen world of appearances!* no less. But now it was his turn to deliver a surprise. "We weren't rich. My father was the last genuine English butler in Chicago—"

"Are you kidding?"

"Why should I be?"

"In a livery?"

"In livery. Up on the Gold Coast."[9]

"And he wanted you to be educated like a gentleman?"

"He did not. He sent me to the Armour Institute to study chemical engineering. But when he died I changed schools."

He stopped himself, and considered how quickly Raynor had reached him. In no time he had your valise on the table and all your stuff unpacked. And afterward, in the streets, he was still reviewing how far he might have gone, and how much he might have been led to tell if they had not been interrupted by Mrs. Staika's great noise.

But just then a young woman, one of Raynor's workers, ran into the cubicle exclaiming, "Haven't you heard all the fuss?"

"We haven't heard anything."

"It's Staika, giving out with all her might. The reporters are coming. She said she phoned the papers, and you know she did."

---

[9] Lake Shore Drive, one of Chicago's richest areas.

"But what is she up to?" said Raynor.

"She brought her wash and she's ironing it here, with our current, because the relief won't pay her electric bill. She has her ironing board set up by the admitting desk, and her kids are with her, all six. They never are in school more than once a week. She's always dragging them around with her because of her reputation."

"I don't want to miss any of this," said Raynor, jumping up. Grebe, as he followed with the secretary, said, "Who is this Staika?"

"They call her the 'Blood Mother of Federal Street.' She's a professional donor at the hospitals. I think they pay ten dollars a pint. Of course it's no joke, but she makes a very big thing out of it and she and the kids are in the papers all the time."

A small crowd, staff and clients divided by a plywood barrier, stood in the narrow space of the entrance, and Staika was shouting in a gruff, mannish voice, plunging the iron on the board and slamming it on the metal rest.

"My father and mother came in a steerage, and I was born in our house, Robey by Huron. I'm no dirty immigrant. I'm a U.S. citizen. My husband is a gassed veteran from France with lungs weaker'n paper, that hardly can he go to the toilet by himself. These six children of mine, I have to buy the shoes for their feet with my own blood. Even a lousy little white Communion necktie, that a couple of drops of blood; a little piece of mosquito veil for my Vadja so she won't be ashamed in church for the other girls, they take my blood for it by Goldblatt. That's how I keep goin'. A fine thing if I had to depend on the relief. And there's plenty of people on the rolls— fakes! There's nothin' *they* can't get, that can go and wrap bacon at Swift and Armour any time. They're lookin' for them by the Yards. They never have to be out of work. Only they rather lay in their lousy beds and eat the public's money." She was not afraid, in a predominantly Negro station, to shout this way about Negroes.

Grebe and Raynor worked themselves forward to get a closer view of the woman. She was flaming with anger and with pleasure at herself, broad and huge, a golden-headed woman who wore a cotton cap laced with pink ribbon. She was barelegged and had on black gym shoes, her Hoover apron was open and her great breasts, not much restrained by a man's undershirt, hampered her arms as she worked at the kid's dress on the ironing board. And the children, silent and white, with a kind of locked obstinacy, in sheepskins and lumberjackets, stood behind her. She had captured the station, and the pleasure this gave her was enormous. Yet her grievances were true grievances. She was telling the truth. But she behaved like a liar. The look of her small eyes was hidden, and while she raged she also seemed to be spinning and planning.

"They send me out college case workers in silk pants to talk me out of what I got comin'. Are they better'n me? Who told them? Fire them. Let 'em go and get married, and then you won't have to cut electric from people's budget."

The chief supervisor, Mr. Ewing, couldn't silence her and he stood with folded arms at the head of his staff, bald, bald-headed, saying to his subordinates like the ex-school principal he was, "Pretty soon she'll be tired and go."

"No she won't," said Raynor to Grebe. "She'll get what she wants. She knows more about the relief even then Ewing. She's been on the rolls for years, and she always gets what she wants because she puts on a noisy show. Ewing knows it. He'll give in soon. He's only saving face. If he gets bad publicity, the Commissioner'll have him on the carpet, downtown. She's got him submerged; she'll submerge everybody in time, and that includes nations and governments."

Grebe replied with his characteristic smile, disagreeing completely. Who would take Staika's orders, and what changes could her yelling ever bring about?

No, what Grebe saw in her, the power that made people listen, was that her cry expressed the war of flesh and blood, perhaps turned a little crazy and certainly ugly, on this place and this condition. And at first, when he went out, the spirit of Staika somehow presided over the whole district for him, and it took color from her; he saw her color, in the spotty curb fires, and the fires under the El, the straight alley of flamy gloom. Later, too, when he went into a tavern for a shot of rye, the sweat of beer, association with West Side Polish streets, made him think of her again.

He wiped the corners of his mouth with his muffler, his handkerchief being inconvenient to reach for, and went out again to get on with the delivery of his checks. The air bit cold and hard and a few flakes of snow formed near him. A train struck by and left a quiver in the frames and a bristling icy hiss over the rails.

Crossing the street, he descended a flight of board steps into a basement grocery, setting off a little bell. It was a dark, long store and it caught you with its stinks of smoked meat, soap, dried peaches, and fish. There was a fire wrinkling and flapping in the little stove, and the proprietor was waiting, an Italian with a long, hollow face and stubborn bristles. He kept his hands warm under his apron.

No, he didn't know Green. You knew people but not names. The same man might not have the same name twice. The police didn't know, either, and mostly didn't care. When somebody was shot or knifed they took the body away and didn't look for the murderer. In the first place, nobody would tell them anything. So they made up a name for the coroner and called it quits. And in the second place, they didn't give a goddamn anyhow. But they couldn't get to the bottom of a thing even if they wanted to. Nobody would get to know even a tenth of what went on among these people. They stabbed and stole, they did every crime and abomination you ever heard of, men and men, women and women, parents and children, worse than the animals. They carried on their own way, and the horrors passed off like a smoke. There was never anything like it in the history of the whole world.

It was a long speech, deepening with every word in its fantasy and passion and becoming increasingly senseless and terrible: a swarm amassed by suggestion and invention, a huge, hugging, despairing knot, a human wheel of heads, legs, bellies, arms, rolling through his shop.

Grebe felt that he must interrupt him. He said sharply, "What are you talking about! All I asked was whether you knew this man."

"That isn't even the half of it. I been here six years. You probably don't want to believe this. But suppose it's true?"

"All the same," said Grebe, "there must be a way to find a person."

The Italian's close-spaced eyes had been queerly concentrated, as were his muscles, while he leaned across the counter trying to convince Grebe. Now he gave up the effort and sat down on his stool. "Oh—I suppose. Once in a while. But I been telling you, even the cops don't get anywhere."

"They're always after somebody. It's not the same thing."

"Well, keep trying if you want. I can't help you."

But he didn't keep trying. He had no more time to spend on Green. He slipped Green's check to the back of the block. The next name on the list was FIELD, WINSTON.

He found the back-yard bungalow without the least trouble; it shared a lot with another house, a few feet of yard between. Grebe knew these two-shack arrangements. They had been built in vast numbers in the days before the swamps were filled and the streets raised, and they were all the same—a boardwalk along the fence, well under street level, three or four ball-headed posts for clotheslines, greening wood, dead shingles, and a long, long flight of stairs to the rear door.

A twelve-year-old boy let him into the kitchen, and there the old man was, sitting by the table in a wheel chair.

"Oh, it's d' Government man," he said to the boy when Grebe drew out his checks. "Go bring me my box of papers." He cleared a space on the table.

"Oh, you don't have to go to all that trouble," said Grebe. But Field laid out his papers: Social Security card, relief certification, letters from the state hospital in Manteno, and a naval discharge dated San Diego, 1920.

"That's plenty," Grebe said. "Just sign."

"You got to know who I am," the old man said. "You're from the Government. It's not your check, it's a Government check and you got no business to hand it over till everything is proved."

He loved the ceremony of it, and Grebe made no more objections. Field emptied his box and finished out the circle of cards and letters.

"There's everything I done and been. Just the death certificate and they can close book on me." He said this with a certain happy pride and magnificence. Still he did not sign; he merely held the little pen upright on the golden-green corduroy of his thigh. Grebe did not hurry him. He felt the old man's hunger for conversation.

"I got to get better coal," he said. "I send my little gran'son to the yard with my order and they fill his wagon with screening. The stove ain't made for it. It fall through the grate. The order says Franklin County egg-size coal."

"I'll report it and see what can be done."

"Nothing can be done, I expect. You know and I know. There ain't no little ways to make things better, and the only big thing is money. That's the only sunbeams, money. Nothing is black where it shines, and the only place you see black is where it ain't shining. What we colored have to have is our own rich. There ain't no other way."

Grebe sat, his reddened forehead bridged levelly by his close-cut hair and his cheeks lowered in the wings of his collar—the caked fire shone hard within the isinglass-and-iron frames but the room was not comfortable—sat and listened while the old man unfolded his scheme. This was to create one Negro millionaire a month by subscription. One clever, good-hearted young fellow elected every month would sign a contract to use the money to start a business employing Negroes. This would be advertised by chain letters and word of mouth, and every Negro wage earner would contribute a dollar a month. Within five years there would be sixty millionaires.

"That'll fetch respect," he said with a throat-stopped sound that came out like a foreign syllable. "You got to take and organize all the money that gets thrown away on the policy wheel and horse race. As long as they can take it away from you, they got no respect for you. Money, that's d' sun of human kind!" Field was a Negro of mixed blood, perhaps Cherokee, or Natchez; his skin was reddish. And he sounded, speaking about a golden sun in this dark room, and looked, shaggy and slab-headed, with the mingled blood of his face and broad lips, the little pen still upright in his hand, like one of the underground kings of mythology, old judge Minos[10] himself.

And now he accepted the check and signed. Not to soil the slip, he held it down with his knuckles. The table budged and creaked, the center of the gloomy, heathen midden[11] of the kitchen covered with bread, meat, and cans, and the scramble of papers.

"Don't you think my scheme'd work?"

"It's worth thinking about. Something ought to be done, I agree."

"It'll work if people will do it. That's all. That's the only thing, any time. When they understand it in the same way, all of them."

"That's true," said Grebe, rising. His glance met the old man's.

"I know you got to go," he said. "Well, God bless you, boy, you ain't been sly with me. I can tell it in a minute."

He went back through the buried yard. Someone nursed a candle in a shed, where a man unloaded kindling wood from a sprawl-wheeled baby buggy and two voices carried on a high conversation. As he came up the sheltered passage he heard the hard boost of the wind in the branches and against the house fronts, and then, reaching the sidewalk, he saw the needle-eye red of cable towers in the open icy height hundreds of feet above

---

[10]According to classical mythology, a ruler of Crete, who directed Daedalus to construct the Labyrinth, a vast maze to house the monstrous Minotaur.

[11]Refuse pile.

the river and the factories—those keen points. From here, his view was obstructed all the way to the South Branch and its timber banks, and the cranes beside the water. Rebuilt after the Great Fire, this part of the city was, not fifty years later, in ruins again, factories boarded up, buildings deserted or fallen, gaps of prairie between. But it wasn't desolation that this made you feel, but rather a faltering of organization that set free a huge energy, an escaped, unattached, unregulated power from the giant raw place. Not only must people feel it but, it seemed to Grebe, they were compelled to match it. In their very bodies. He no less than others, he realized. Say that his parents had been servants in their time, whereas he was not supposed to be one. He thought that they had never done any service like this, which no one visible asked for, and probably flesh and blood could not even perform. Nor could anyone show why it should be performed; or see where the performance would lead. That did not mean that he wanted to be released from it, he realized with a grimly pensive face. On the contrary. He had something to do. To be compelled to feel this energy and yet have no task to do—that was horrible; that was suffering; he knew what that was. It was now quitting time. Six o'clock. He could go home if he liked, to his room, that is, to wash in hot water, to pour a drink, lie down on his quilt, read the paper, eat some liver paste on crackers before going out to dinner. But to think of this actually made him feel a little sick, as though he had swallowed hard air. He had six checks left, and he was determined to deliver at least one of these: Mr. Green's check.

So he started again. He had four or five dark blocks to go, past open lots, condemned houses, old foundations, closed schools, black churches, mounds, and he reflected that there must be many people alive who had once seen the neighborhood rebuilt and new. Now there was a second layer of ruins; centuries of history accomplished through human massing. Numbers had given the place forced growth; enormous numbers had also broken it down. Objects once so new, so concrete that it could have occurred to anyone they stood for other things, had crumbled. Therefore, reflected Grebe, the secret of them was out. It was that they stood for themselves by agreement, and were natural and not unnatural by agreement, and when the things themselves collapsed the agreement became visible. What was it, otherwise, that kept cities from looking peculiar? Rome, that was almost permanent, did not give rise to thoughts like these. And was it abidingly real? But in Chicago, where the cycles were so fast and the familiar died out, and again rose changed, and died again in thirty years, you saw the common agreement or covenant, and you were forced to think about appearances and realities. (He remembered Raynor and he smiled. Raynor was a clever boy.) Once you had grasped this, a great many things became intelligible. For instance, why Mr. Field should conceive such a scheme. Of course, if people were to agree to create a millionaire, a real millionaire would come into existence. And if you wanted to know how Mr. Field was inspired to think of this, why, he had within sight of his kitchen window the chart, the very bones of a successful scheme—the El with its blue and green confetti of signals. People consented to pay dimes and ride the crash-box cars, and so it was a success. Yet how absurd it looked; how little reality there was to start with. And yet Yerkes,[12] the great financier who built it, had known that he could get people to agree to do it. Viewed as itself, what a scheme of a scheme it seemed, how close to an appearance. Then why wonder at Mr. Field's idea? He had grasped a principle. And then Grebe remembered, too, that Mr. Yerkes had established the Yerkes Observatory and endowed it with millions. Now how did the notion come to him in his New York museum of a palace or his Aegean-bound yacht to give money to astronomers? Was he awed by the success of his bizarre enterprise and therefore ready to spend money to find out where in the universe being and seeming were identical? Yes, he wanted to know what abides; and whether flesh is Bible grass;[13] and he offered money to be burned in the fire of suns. Okay, then, Grebe thought further, these things exist because people consent to exist with them—we have got so far—and also there is a reality which doesn't depend on consent but within which consent is a game. But what about need, the need that keeps so many vast thousands in position? You tell me that, you *private* little gentleman and *decent* soul—he used these words against himself scornfully. Why is the consent given to misery? And why so painfully ugly? Because there is *something* that is dismal and permanently ugly? Here he sighed and gave it up, and thought it was enough for the present moment that he had a real check in his pocket for a Mr. Green who must be real beyond question. If only his neighbors didn't think they had to conceal him.

This time he stopped at the second floor. He struck a match and found a door. Presently a man answered his knock and Grebe had the check ready and showed it even before he began. "Does Tulliver Green live here? I'm from the relief."

The man narrowed the opening and spoke to someone at his back.

"Does he live here?"

"Uh-uh. No."

"Or anywhere in this building? He's a sick man and he can't come for his dough." He exhibited the check in the light, which was smoky—the air smelled of charred lard—and the man held off the brim of his cap to study it.

"Uh-uh. Never seen the name."

"There's nobody around here that uses crutches?"

[12]Charles Tyson Yerkes (1837–1905), American financier, who, by 1886, took control of the railway lines of the west and north sections of Chicago. By financial maneuvers and corrupt politics he acquired transportation franchises and constructed an empire. Yerkes's gift in 1892 to the University of Chicago resulted in the building of the Yerkes Observatory, which opened in 1897 in Williams Bay, Wisconsin. Dreiser's *The Financier*, *The Titan*, and *The Stoic* are based on Yerkes's life.

[13]See Isaiah 40:6–8. "All flesh is grass, And all the goodliness thereof is as the flower of the field; The grass withereth, the flower fadeth; Because the breath of the LORD bloweth upon it—Surely the people is grass. The grass withereth, the flower fadeth; But the word of our God shall stand for ever."

He seemed to think, but it was Grebe's impression that he was simply waiting for a decent interval to pass.

"No, suh. Nobody I ever see."

"I've been looking for this man all afternoon"—Grebe spoke out with sudden force—"and I'm going to have to carry this check back to the station. It seems strange not to be able to find a person to *give* him something when you're looking for him for a good reason. I suppose if I had bad news for him I'd find him quick enough."

There was a responsive motion in the other man's face. "That's right, I reckon."

"It almost doesn't do any good to have a name if you can't be found by it. It doesn't stand for anything. He might as well not have any," he went on, smiling. It was as much of a concession as he could make of his desire to laugh.

"Well, now, there's a little old knot-back man I see once in a while. He might be the one you lookin' for. Downstairs."

"Where? Right side or left? Which door?"

"I don't know which. Thin-face little knot-back with a stick."

But no one answered at any of the doors on the first floor. He went to the end of the corridor, searching by matchlight, and found only a stairless exit to the yard, a drop of about six feet. But there was a bungalow near the alley, an old house like Mr. Field's. To jump was unsafe. He ran from the front door, through the underground passage and into the yard. The place was occupied. There was a light through the curtains, upstairs. The name on the ticket under the broken, scoop-shaped mailbox was Green! He exultantly rang the bell and pressed against the locked door. Then the lock clicked faintly and a long staircase opened before him. Someone was slowly coming down—a woman. He had the impression in the weak light that she was shaping her hair as she came, making herself presentable, for he saw her arms raised. But it was for support that they were raised; she was feeling her way downward, down the wall, stumbling. Next he wondered about the pressure of her feet on the treads; she did not seem to be wearing shoes. And it was a freezing stairway. His ring had got her out of bed, perhaps, and she had forgotten to put them on. And then he saw that she was not only shoeless but naked; she was entirely naked, climbing down while she talked to herself, a heavy woman, naked and drunk. She blundered into him. The contact of her breasts, though they touched only his coat, made him go back against the door with a blind shock. See what he had tracked down, in his hunting game!

The woman was saying to herself, furious with insult, "So I cain't——k, huh? I'll show that son-of-a-bitch kin I, cain't I."

What should he do now? Grebe asked himself. Why, he should go. He should turn away and go. He couldn't talk to this woman. He couldn't keep her standing naked in the cold. But when he tried he found himself unable to turn away.

He said, "Is this where Mr. Green lives?"

But she was still talking to herself and did not hear him.

"Is this Mr. Green's house?"

At last she turned her furious drunken glance on him. "What do you want?"

Again her eyes wandered from him; there was a dot of blood in their enraged brilliance. He wondered why she didn't feel the cold.

"I'm from the relief."

"Awright, what?"

"I've got a check for Tulliver Green."

This time she heard and put out her hand.

"No, no, for *Mr*. Green. He's got to sign," he said. How was he going to get Green's signature tonight!

"I'll take it. He cain't."

He desperately shook his head, thinking of Mr. Field's precautions about identification. "I can't let you have it. It's for him. Are you Mrs. Green?"

"Maybe I is, and maybe I ain't. Who want to know?"

"Is he upstairs?"

"Awright. Take it up yourself, you goddamn fool."

Sure, he was a goddamn fool. Of course he could not go up because Green would probably be drunk and naked, too. And perhaps he would appear on the landing soon. He looked eagerly upward. Under the light was a high narrow brown wall. Empty! It remained empty!

"Hell with you, then!" he heard her cry. To deliver a check for coal and clothes, he was keeping her in the cold. She did not feel it, but his face was burning with frost and self-ridicule. He backed away from her.

"I'll come tomorrow, tell him."

"Ah, hell with you. Don' never come. What you doin' here in the night-time? Don' come back." She yelled so that he saw the breadth of her tongue. She stood astride in the long cold box of the hall and held on to the banister and the wall. The bungalow itself was shaped something like a box, a clumsy, high box pointing into the freezing air with its sharp, wintry lights.

"If you are Mrs. Green, I'll give you the check," he said, changing his mind.

"Give here, then." She took it, took the pen offered with it in her left hand, and tried to sign the receipt on the wall. He looked around, almost as though to see whether his madness was being observed, and came near believing someone was standing on a mountain of used tires in the auto-junking shop next door.

"But are you Mrs. Green?" he now thought to ask. But she was already climbing the stairs with the check, and it was too late, if he had made an error, if he was now in trouble, to undo the thing. But he wasn't going to worry about it. Though she might not be Mrs. Green, he was convinced that Mr. Green was upstairs. Whoever she was, the woman stood for Green, whom he was not to see this time. Well, you silly bastard, he said to himself, so you think you found him. So what? Maybe you really did find him—what of it? But it was important that there was a real Mr. Green whom they could not keep him from reaching because he seemed to come as an emissary from hostile appearances. And though the self-ridicule was slow to diminish, and his face still blazed with it, he had, nevertheless, a feeling of elation, too. "For after all," he said, "he *could* be found!"

1951

CHARLES OLSON
1910–1970

As poet, essayist, letter writer, and teacher, Charles Olson was a seminal figure in the generation after Ezra Pound and William Carlos Williams. His first book, *Call Me Ishmael*, is an interpretation of Melville's *Moby-Dick* that deserves a place beside D. H. Lawrence's *Studies in Classic American Literature*, Williams's *In the American Grain*, and Edward Dahlberg's *Can These Bones Live*. His long sequence, *The Maximus Poems*, is the major attempt at a "personal epic" after Pound's *Cantos* and Williams's *Paterson*. He increasingly thought of himself as a "mythographer" or "archaeologist of morning" who aimed to reconnect us with the natural process from which we have been alienated by the rationalist thought of the last 2,500 years.

Born in Worcester, Massachusetts, Olson grew up there while spending summers in Gloucester, the city he later celebrated in *The Maximus Poems*. He attended Wesleyan University, where he received a B.A. and an M.A. with a thesis on Melville. He then embarked on a search for Melville's library and tracked down many of his books, including his personally annotated Hawthorne and Shakespeare. Olson taught English for two years at Clark University, took a summer job on the schooner *Doris W. Hawkes*, and entered Harvard's American Civilization program, where he studied with the historian Frederick Merk and the literary scholar F. O. Matthiessen. After completing the coursework for the Ph.D., he returned to Gloucester to take up a Guggenheim Fellowship for studies on Melville. In 1940 he met Constance Wilcock, who became his common-law wife, and began working in New York for the American Civil Liberties Union and then for the Common Council for American Unity. From 1942 to 1944, he worked for the Office of War Information in Washington and then became director of the Foreign Nationalities Division of the Democratic National Committee. In 1945, disenchanted with politics, he decided to commit himself to writing. During that year he wrote *Call Me Ishmael* (based on his earlier Melville research), several poems, and an essay in qualified defense of Ezra Pound, the boldly mimetic "This Is Yeats Speaking."

Over the next three years, Olson met Pound and also the geographer Carl Sauer (an important influence on his thought), worked on a book about the American West, wrote a dance-play based on *Moby-Dick*, and began to lecture at Black Mountain College as a replacement for his friend and mentor, Edward

Dahlberg. In 1949 he wrote his important postmodernist poem "The King-fishers." In 1950 he began corresponding with Robert Creeley, wrote the first Maximus poem, and published "Projective Verse," in which he reasserted Cree-ley's principle, "Form is never more than an extension of content," and Dahl-berg's clue to poetic process, "One perception must immediately and directly lead to a further perception." In 1951 he began his association with Cid Corman and the magazine *Origin*, traveled to the Yucatán to study Mayan culture, and wrote "Human Universe," in which he argued that art "is the only twin life has" because it "does not seek to describe but to enact."

That year he also joined Black Mountain full-time, where he remained (except for a leave in 1952 for further research on Mayan glyphs) as faculty member and then rector until the college closed in 1956. While there he sepa-rated from Constance and took as common-law wife Elizabeth Kaiser. Olson effectively turned Black Mountain into an arts center. Among his associates were the painters Franz Kline and Robert Rauschenberg, the dancer Merce Cun-ningham, and the musician John Cage. In 1957 Olson returned to Gloucester, traveling from there to various colleges for lectures and readings. In 1963 he began to teach at the State University of New York at Buffalo. In 1964 his wife, Elizabeth, was killed in an automobile accident—a tragedy from which Olson never recovered. He returned to Gloucester in 1965 and in 1969 accepted a position at the University of Connecticut, where he taught for a few weeks before his death. During these years, he continued to work on *The Maximus Poems*, which he never completed. The third book of that sequence was posthu-mously arranged from his notes by his former students Charles Boer and George F. Butterick.

Olson's poetry is often elliptical and allusive, with a range that includes Sumerian myth, Heraclitus, Hesiod, the linguist B. L. Whorf, the cyberneticist Norbert Wiener, the philosopher Alfred North Whitehead, the psychologist C. G. Jung, and the details of both ancient and modern history. His style tends to be meditative and didactic, but with frequent lyricism. It is often made diffi-cult by incomplete syntax, heavy reliance on abstract terms, brief notations, and a disjunctive or paratactic forward motion that accumulates incremental mean-ings and produces an effect of continual self-revision. These traits are in accord with Olson's understanding of art as "enactment." His constantly twisting utter-ance seeks not to describe but to enact the movements of a speaker who is him-self in "process" as he grapples with the matter in hand. As Olson once said at Goddard College, "I myself would wish that all who spoke and wrote, spoke always from a place that is *new* at that moment that they do speak."

Thomas R. Whitaker
Yale University

PRIMARY WORKS

Poetry: *Y & X*, 1949; *In Cold Hell, In Thicket*, 1953; *The Maximus Poems / 1–10*, 1953; *The Maximus Poems / 11–22*, 1956; *The Maximus Poems*, 1960; *The Distances*, 1960; *The Maximus Poems IV, V, VI*, 1968; *Archaeologist of Morning*, 1973; *The Maximus Poems*, 1983; *The Collected Poems*, 1987; *A Nation of Nothing but Poetry: Supplemen-tary Poems*, 1989; *Selected Poems*, 1993. Prose: *Call Me Ishmael*, 1947; *A Bibliography* on *America for Ed Dorn*, 1964; *Human Universe and Other Essays*, 1965; *Proprioception*, 1965; *Stocking Cap*, 1966; *Causal Mythology*, 1969; *The Special View of History*, 1970; *Poetry and Truth: The Beloit Lectures and Poems*, 1971; *Additional Prose*, 1974; *The Post Office*, 1975.

For Sappho, Back[1]

I

With a dry eye, she
saw things out of the corner of,
with a bold
she looked on any man,
with a shy eye   5

With a cold eye, with her eye she looked on, she looked out, she
who was not so different as you might imagine from,
who had, as nature hath, an eye to look upon her makings, to,
in her womb, know
how red, and because it is red, how   10
handsome blood is, how, because it is unseen, how
because it goes about its business as she does,
as nature's things have that way of doing, as
in the delight of her eye she
creates constants   15

          And, in the thickness of her blood, some

variants

II

As blood is, as flesh can be
is she, self-housed, and moving
moving in impeccability to be   20
clear, clear! to be
as, what is rhythm but
her limpidity?

---

[1]Sappho was a Greek lyric poet, born c. 630 B.C., who lived and wrote on the island of Lesbos off the coast of Asia Minor, and who has been much admired by modern American poets. Except for three poems, her work is now known only in fragments, many of which were discovered in the twentieth century on papyrus that had been reused to make mummy shrouds. Her verse, both pas-sionate and detached, celebrates a love of women and of all delicate things. Olson read the translations by J. M. Edmonds in the Loeb Classical Library *Lyra Graeca* (Volume 1). Olson's tribute, which begins in the past tense but moves to a continuing present, makes of Sappho a trope for woman, poetry, dance, and creative nature beyond all rational analysis.

She
who is as certain as the morning is   25
when it arises, when it is spring, when, from wetness comes its
    brightness
as fresh as this beloved's fingers, lips
each new time she new turns herself to
tendernesses, she   30
turns her most objective, scrupulous attention, her own
self-causing
    each time it is,
    as is the morning, is
    the morning night and revelation of her   35
    nakedness, new
    forever new, as fresh as is the scruple of her eye, the accurate
    kiss

III

If you would know what woman is, what
strength the reed of man unknows, forever   40
cannot know, look, look! in these eyes, look
as she passes, on this moving thing, which moves
as grass blade by grass blade moves, as
syllable does throw light on fellow syllable, as,
in this rare creature, each hidden, each moving thing   45
is light to its known, unknown brother,
as objects stand one by one by another, so
is this universe, this flow, this woman, these eyes
are sign

IV

The intimate, the intricate, what shall perplex, forever   50
is a matter, is it not, not of confusions to be studied and made literal,
but of a dry dance by which, as shoots one day make leaves, as
the earth's crust, when ice draws back, wrings mountains
from itself, makes valleys in whose palms
root-eating fisher folk spring up—   55
by such a dance, in which the dancer contradicts
the waste and easy gesture, contains
the heave within,
within, because the human is so light a structure, within
a finger, say, or there   60
within the gentlest swaying of
                   (of your true hips)

In such containment
        And in search for that which is the shoot, the thrust
of what you are   65
        (of what you were so delicately born)
                                      of what fruits
of your own making you are
                    the hidden constance of which all the rest
is awkward variation   70
        this! this
        is what gives beauty to her eye, inhabitation
        to her tender-taken bones, is what illumines
        all her skin with satin glow
        when love blows over, turning   75
        as the leaf turns in the wind
        and, with that shock of recognition,[2] shows
        its other side, the joy, the sort of terror of

a dancer going off

                                              1951

I, Maximus of Gloucester, to You[1]

Off-shore, by islands hidden in the
      blood[2']
jewels & miracles, I, Maximus
a metal hot from boiling water, tell you
what is a lance, who obeys the figures of   5
the present dance

---

[2]A phrase made famous by Edmund Wilson's *The Shock of Recognition* (1943), which treats a self-consciousness among American writers that has manifested itself in "moments when genius becomes aware of its kin" (p. viii).

[1]The first "letter" of *The Maximus Poems*. Like "Paterson" in Williams's *Paterson*, Maximus is a complex figure. Most often, in this exploratory and self-corrective sequence, he is an aspect of the six-foot-eight-inch poet himself, probing the geography, history, and present needs of Gloucester, on Cape Ann in Massachusetts, which is for him "the last *polis* or city" in the northwestward migration of European culture from the eastern Mediterranean. But his name also suggests both Maximus of Tyre, a second-century A.D. Greek eclectic philosopher whom Olson encountered while reading about Sappho, and C. G.

Jung's "homo maximus" or Self, which includes the ego-consciousness and the unconscious collective archetypes and is the final goal of psychological "individuation." The title of this poem recalls the form of address used by St. Paul in his letters to the church-communities (e.g., *Colossians* 1:1–3); but Maximus's initial oracular stance will be undercut by the opening lines of "Letter 2": "... tell you? ha! who / can tell another how / to manage the swimming?"

[2']Suggesting an inner voice that projects itself to the east of Gloucester. *The Maximus Poems* later stress the fact that Maximus of Tyre lived on an island (offshore from Asia Minor) which was made into a peninsula by a mole built by Alexander the Great, even as Cape Ann is an island made into a peninsula by the highway bridge of Route 128.

1

the thing you're after
may lie around the bend
of the nest (second, time slain, the bird! the bird!

And there! (strong) thrust, the mast! flight   10

> (of the bird
> o kylix,[3] o
> Antony of Padua[4]
> sweep low, o bless

the roofs, the old ones, the gentle steep ones   15
on whose ridge-poles the gulls sit, from which they depart,

> And the flake-racks

of my city!

2

love is form, and cannot be without
important substance (the weight   20
say, 58 carats each one of us, perforce
our goldsmith's scale

> feather to feather added
> (and what is mineral, what
> is curling hair, the string   25
> you carry in your nervous beak, these

> make bulk, these, in the end, are
> the sum[5]
> (o my lady of good voyage[6]
> in whose arm, whose left arm rests   30
no boy but a carefully carved wood, a painted face, a schooner!
a delicate mast, as bow-sprit for

> forwarding

---

[3]An ancient Greek shallow cup with tall stem, evoked by the bird's flight and the shape of Gloucester harbor. These invocational lines recall and revise the seagull imagery that opens Hart Crane's modern "epic," The Bridge (see Volume D of this anthology).

[4]Franciscan friar and saint (1195–1231), patron of the Portuguese fishing community of Gloucester.

[5]An allusion to the preface of Williams's Paterson: "To make a start, / out of particulars / and make them general, rolling / up the sum, by defective means—."

[6]At the top of the Church of Our Lady of Good Voyage, in the Portuguese community of Gloucester, is a statue of Our Lady holding a schooner. She is the invoked muse of the poem, the guide on its voyage.

3

the underpart is, though stemmed, uncertain
is, as sex is, as moneys are, facts!   35
facts, to be dealt with, as the sea is, the demand
that they be played by, that they only can be, that they must
be played by, said he, coldly, the
ear!

By ear, he sd.   40
But that which matters, that which insists, that which will last,
that! o my people, where shall you find it, how, where, where shall
        you listen
when all is become billboards, when, all, even silence, is spray-gunned?

when even our bird, my roofs,   45
cannot be heard

when even you, when sound itself is neoned in?
when, on the hill, over the water
where she who used to sing,
when the water glowed,   50
black, gold, the tide
outward, at evening

when bells came like boats
over the oil-slicks, milkweed
hulls   55

And a man slumped,
attentionless,
against pink shingles

o sea city)

4

one loves only form,   60
and form only comes
into existence when
the thing is born

        born of yourself, born
        of hay and cotton struts,   65
        of street-pickings, wharves, weeds
        you carry in, my bird

of a bone of a fish
of a straw, or will
of a color, of a bell   70
of yourself, torn

5

love is not easy
but how shall you know,
New England, now
that pejorocracy is here, how   75
that street-cars, o Oregon, twitter[7]
in the afternoon, offend
a black-gold loin?

how shall you strike,[8]
o swordsman, the blue-red back   80
when, last night, your aim
was mu-sick, mu-sick, mu-sick[9]
And not the cribbage game?

(o Gloucester-man,
weave   85
your birds and fingers
new, your roof-tops,
clean shit upon racks
sunned on
American   90
braid
with others like you, such
extricable surface
as faun and oral,
satyr lesbos vase[10]   95

o kill kill kill kill kill[11]
those
who advertise you
out)

---

[7]At the time of the poem, streetcars in the East (though presumably not in Oregon) were piping in recorded music for the passengers.

[8]A "striker" is a swordfish harpooner.

[9]Recalling a popular song, "Music, Music, Music."

[10]The lines suggest the classical Greek ("oral culture" and the island of Lesbos) and also modes of sexuality.

[11]Echoing Shakespeare, *King Lear*, 4. 6. 191.

6

in! in! the bow-sprit, bird, the beak   100
in, the bend is, in, goes in, the form
that which you make, what holds, which is
the law of object, strut after strut, what you are, what you must be, what
the force can throw up, can, right now hereinafter erect,
the mast, the mast, the tender   105
mast!

       The nest, I say, to you, I Maximus, say
       under the hand, as I see it, over the waters
       from this place where I am, where I hear,
       can still hear   110

       from where I carry you a feather
       as though, sharp, I picked up,
       in the afternoon delivered you
       a jewel,
               it flashing more than a wing,   115

       than any old romantic thing,
       than memory, than place,
       than anything other than that which you carry

       than that which is,
       call it a nest, around the head of, call it   120
       the next second

       than that which you
       can do!

                      1953

Maximus, to Himself[1]

I have had to learn the simplest things
last. Which made for difficulties.
Even at sea I was slow, to get the hand out, or to cross
a wet deck.
       The sea was not, finally, my trade.   5

---

[1]The twelfth poem in *The Maximus Poems*.

But even my trade, at it, I stood estranged
from that which was most familiar.[2] Was delayed,
and not content with the man's argument
that such postponement
is now the nature of   10
obedience,

    that we are all late
    in a slow time,
    that we grow up many
    And the single   15
    is not easily
    known

It could be, though the sharpness (the *achiote*)[3]
I note in others,
makes more sense   20
than my own distances. The agilities

    they show daily
    who do the world's
    businesses
    And who do nature's   25
    as I have no sense
    I have done either

I have made dialogues,
have discussed ancient texts,
have thrown what light I could, offered   30
what pleasures
doceat[4] allows

    But the known?
This, I have had to be given,
a life, love, and from one man[5]   35
the world.

---

[2]Olson often quoted, and later chose as epigraph for *The Special View of History*, a dictum he attributed to Heraclitus: "Man is estranged from that [with] which he is most familiar." That seems to be Olson's own condensation of Heraclitus's Fragments 1 and 2, which he here ("the man's argument") paraphrases at greater length.

[3]Spanish: The seeds of the annatto tree, which are surrounded by a dark red pulp. When crushed to a paste, *achiote* can impart to food a deep, golden-yellow color. Delicate in flavor but often combined with further seasoning, *achiote* is widely used in Yucatán cooking, where Olson would have encountered it.

[4]Teaching, or to teach (from Latin *docere*). Pound, in *Make It New*, p. 8, quotes Rudolf Agricola's statement of the three proper functions of literature: "*Ut doceat, ut moveat, ut delectet*" ("to teach, to move, or to delight").

[5]Robert Creeley, Olson's friend and colleague, to whom (as "the Figure of Outward") he dedicated *The Maximus Poems*.

Tokens.
But sitting here
I look out as a wind
and water man, testing   40
And missing
some proof

    I know the quarters
of the weather, where it comes from,
where it goes. But the stem of me,   45
this I took from their welcome,
or their rejection, of me

    And my arrogance
was neither diminished
nor increased,   50
by the communication

2

    It is undone business
I speak of, this morning,
with the sea
stretching out   55
from my feet

1956

■ FLANNERY O'CONNOR ■
1925–1964

Grotesque, Catholic, Southern—each of these labels has been affixed to Flannery O'Connor's writing, yet none fully captures its scope. Her work is all of these and more.

    She did often make use of the grotesque, for instance, but its use was not, as one critic claimed, gratuitous. She wanted to push the reader to experience a sense of something beyond the ordinary, a sense of the mystery of life. She wanted to shock the reader into recognizing the distortions of modern life that we have come to consider natural: "for the almost-blind you draw large and startling figures," she has noted in an essay.

    O'Connor's writing was also fueled by her Roman Catholic beliefs. The something beyond the ordinary that she wanted the reader to experience, starkly, unsentimentally, was a sense of the sacred. But the reader of her fiction doesn't need to be Catholic to appreciate the extra-ordinary, to experience the mystery of life.

Her Catholicism probably contributed to O'Connor's sense of living in a fallen world. She also probably absorbed this sense of having fallen from past grandeur by growing up white in the post–Civil War South. Yet her characters are not so much fallen aristocrats as poor or middle-class whites, who often don't realize what their lives are lacking. Her portrayal of these characters, their thoughts, their speech, is true, funny, powerful—and devastating.

Like most of her characters, Mary Flannery O'Connor grew up in the South—in Georgia. The only child of Edward Francis O'Connor and Regina Cline O'Connor, she lived in Savannah her first thirteen years. Then her father was diagnosed with disseminated lupus erythematosis, a disease of the immune system so debilitating that he could not continue his real estate work. The family moved to Milledgeville, to the house where O'Connor's mother had grown up, a house that had been the governor's mansion when Milledgeville was the capital of Georgia a century before. O'Connor's father died three years later. The following year, when O'Connor was seventeen, she entered Georgia State College for Women, now Georgia College. There she majored in social science (she would later satirize social scientists mercilessly) and published cartoons in the school newspaper (since *The New Yorker* wouldn't publish them).

In 1945 O'Connor left Georgia to study creative writing at the Writers' Workshop of the State University of Iowa (now the University of Iowa), where she wrote a series of short stories and earned a master's degree in fine arts. She then embarked on her first novel, working on it at Yaddo, an artists' colony in upstate New York, in an apartment in New York City, and while boarding with friends in Ridgefield, Connecticut. Heading home for Christmas in 1950, O'Connor suffered an attack of lupus, the disease that had killed her father.

Severely weakened—she was too weak to climb stairs—O'Connor, with her mother and uncle, moved to the family farm near Milledgeville. Cortisone drugs kept the lupus largely under control but weakened her bones. During the next thirteen years she hobbled about with a cane or crutches, raised peafowl, and wrote for two or three hours a day. Sometimes she was well enough to travel within or beyond Georgia to give a speech or a reading or to accept an honorary degree; once she even traveled as far as Lourdes and Rome. But mostly she lived quietly on the farm—until surgery in February 1964 reactivated the lupus; she died in August, at the age of thirty-nine.

O'Connor completed two novels, *Wise Blood* and *The Violent Bear It Away*, but is better remembered for her two volumes of short stories, *A Good Man Is Hard to Find* and the posthumous *Everything That Rises Must Converge*. Several other volumes have been published since her death: a complete collection of stories and also collections of essays (*Mystery and Manners*), letters (including *The Habit of Being*), and book reviews (including *The Presence of Grace*).

"A Good Man Is Hard to Find" is typical of many of O'Connor's stories, with its jolting disruption of the mundane, its satire, its toughness. Yet even more than O'Connor's other work, this story provokes extreme reactions: it is funny but also horrifying.

Beverly Lyon Clark
Wheaton College

PRIMARY WORKS

Wise Blood, 1952; *A Good Man Is Hard to Find, and Other Stories*, 1955; *The Violent Bear It Away*, 1960; *Everything That Rises Must Converge*, 1965; *Mystery and Manners: Occasional Prose*, 1969; *The Complete Stories*, 1971; *The Habit of Being: The Letters of Flannery O'Connor*, 1979; *The Presence of Grace, and Other Book Reviews*, 1983; *Collected Works*, 1988.

A Good Man Is Hard to Find[1]

The grandmother didn't want to go to Florida. She wanted to visit some of her connections in east Tennessee and she was seizing at every chance to change Bailey's mind. Bailey was the son she lived with, her only boy. He was sitting on the edge of his chair at the table, bent over the orange sports section of the *Journal*. "Now look here, Bailey," she said, "see here, read this," and she stood with one hand on her thin hip and the other rattling the newspaper at his bald head. "Here this fellow that calls himself the Misfit is aloose from the Federal Pen and headed toward Florida and you read here what it says he did to these people. Just you read it. I wouldn't take my children in any direction with a criminal like that aloose in it. I couldn't answer to my conscience if I did."

Bailey didn't look up from his reading so she wheeled around then and faced the children's mother, a young woman in slacks, whose face was as broad and innocent as a cabbage and was tied around with a green head-kerchief that had two points on the top like rabbit's ears. She was sitting on the sofa, feeding the baby his apricots out of a jar. "The children have been to Florida before," the old lady said. "You all ought to take them somewhere else for a change so they would see different parts of the world and be broad. They never have been to east Tennessee."

The children's mother didn't seem to hear but the eight-year-old boy, John Wesley, a stocky child with glasses, said, "If you don't want to go to Florida, why dontcha stay at home?" He and the little girl, June Star, were reading the funny papers on the floor.

"She wouldn't stay at home to be queen for a day," June Star said without raising her yellow head.

"Yes and what would you do if this fellow, The Misfit, caught you?" the grandmother asked.

"I'd smack his face," John Wesley said.

"She wouldn't stay at home for a million bucks," June Star said. "Afraid she'd miss something. She has to go everywhere we go."

"All right, Miss," the grandmother said. "Just remember that the next time you want me to curl your hair."

June Star said her hair was naturally curly.

---

[1] Also the title of a blues song, composed by Eddie Green in 1918.

to marry Mr. Teagarden because he was a gentleman and had bought Coca-Cola stock when it first came out and that he had died only a few years ago, a very wealthy man.

They stopped at The Tower for barbecued sandwiches. The Tower was a part stucco and part wood filling station and dance hall set in a clearing outside of Timothy. A fat man named Red Sammy Butts ran it and there were signs stuck here and there on the building and for miles up and down the highway saying, TRY RED SAMMY'S FAMOUS BARBECUE. NONE LIKE FAMOUS RED SAMMY'S! RED SAM! THE FAT BOY WITH THE HAPPY LAUGH. A VETERAN! RED SAMMY'S YOUR MAN!

Red Sammy was lying on the bare ground outside The Tower with his head under a truck while a gray monkey about a foot high, chained to a small chinaberry tree, chattered nearby. The monkey sprang back into the tree and got on the highest limb as soon as he saw the children jump out of the car and run toward him.

Inside, The Tower was a long dark room with a counter at one end and tables at the other and dancing space in the middle. They all sat down at a board table next to the nickelodeon and Red Sam's wife, a tall burnt-brown woman with hair and eyes lighter than her skin, came and took their order. The children's mother put a dime in the machine and played "The Tennessee Waltz," and the grandmother said that tune always made her want to dance. She asked Bailey if he would like to dance but he only glared at her. He didn't have a naturally sunny disposition like she did and trips made him nervous. The grandmother's brown eyes were very bright. She swayed her head from side to side and pretended she was dancing in her chair. June Star said play something she could tap to so the children's mother put in another dime and played a fast number and June Star stepped out onto the dance floor and did her tap routine.

"Ain't she cute?" Red Sam's wife said, leaning over the counter. "Would you like to come be my little girl?"

"No I certainly wouldn't," June Star said. "I wouldn't live in a broken-down place like this for a million bucks!" and she ran back to the table.

"Ain't she cute?" the woman repeated, stretching her mouth politely.

"Aren't you ashamed?" hissed the grandmother.

Red Sam came in and told his wife to quit lounging on the counter and hurry up with these people's order. His khaki trousers reached just to his hip bones and his stomach hung over them like a sack of meal swaying under his shirt. He came over and sat down at a table nearby and let out a combination sigh and yodel. "You can't win," he said. "You can't win," and he wiped his sweating red face off with a gray handkerchief. "These days you don't know who to trust," he said. "Ain't that the truth?"

"People are certainly not nice like they used to be," said the grandmother.

"Two fellers come in here last week," Red Sammy said, "driving a Chrysler. It was a old beat-up car but it was a good one and these boys looked all right to me. Said they worked at the mill and you know I let them fellers charge the gas they bought? Now why did I do that?"

"Because you're a good man!" the grandmother said at once.

"Yes'm, I suppose so," Red Sam said as if he were struck with this answer.

His wife brought the orders, carrying the five plates all at once without a tray, two in each hand and one balanced on her arm. "It isn't a soul in this green world of God's that you can trust," she said. "And I don't count nobody out of that, not nobody," she repeated, looking at Red Sammy.

"Did you read about that criminal, The Misfit, that's escaped?" asked the grandmother.

"I wouldn't be a bit surprised if he didn't attact this place right here," said the woman. "If he hears about it being here, I wouldn't be none surprised to see him. If he hears it's two cent in the cash register, I wouldn't be a tall surprised if he . . ."

"That'll do," Red Sam said. "Go bring these people their Co'-Colas," and the woman went off to get the rest of the order.

"A good man is hard to find," Red Sammy said. "Everything is getting terrible. I remember the day you could go off and leave your screen door unlatched. Not no more."

He and the grandmother discussed better times. The old lady said that in her opinion Europe was entirely to blame for the way things were now. She said the way Europe acted you would think we were made of money and Red Sam said it was no use talking about it, she was exactly right. The children ran outside into the white sunlight and looked at the monkey in the lacy chinaberry tree. He was busy catching fleas on himself and biting each one carefully between his teeth as if it were a delicacy.

They drove off again into the hot afternoon. The grandmother took cat naps and woke up every few minutes with her own snoring. Outside of Toombsboro she woke up and recalled an old plantation that she had visited in this neighborhood once when she was a young lady. She said the house had six white columns across the front and that there was an avenue of oaks leading up to it and two little wooden trellis arbors on either side in front where you sat down with your suitor after a stroll in the garden. She recalled exactly which road to turn off to get to it. She knew that Bailey would not be willing to lose any time looking at an old house, but the more she talked about it, the more she wanted to see it once again and find out if the little twin arbors were still standing. "There was a secret panel in this house," she said craftily, not telling the truth but wishing that she were, "and the story went that all the family silver was hidden in it when Sherman[4] came through but it was never found . . ."

"Hey!" John Wesley said. "Let's go see it! We'll find it! We'll poke all the woodwork and find it! Who lives there? Where do you turn off at? Hey Pop, can't we turn off there?"

---

[4]Northern Civil War general, best known for his march through Georgia (starting in Tennessee), destroying houses and plantations on his way to the sea.

"We never have seen a house with a secret panel!" June Star shrieked. "Let's go to the house with the secret panel! Hey Pop, can't we go see the house with the secret panel!"

"It's not far from here, I know," the grandmother said. "It wouldn't take over twenty minutes."

Bailey was looking straight ahead. His jaw was as rigid as a horseshoe. "No," he said.

The children began to yell and scream that they wanted to see the house with the secret panel. John Wesley kicked the back of the front seat and June Star hung over her mother's shoulder and whined desperately into her ear that they never had any fun even on their vacation, that they could never do what THEY wanted to do. The baby began to scream and John Wesley kicked the back of the seat so hard that his father could feel the blows in his kidney.

"All right!" he shouted and drew the car to a stop at the side of the road. "Will you all shut up? Will you all just shut up for one second? If you don't shut up, we won't go anywhere."

"It would be very educational for them," the grandmother murmured.

"All right," Bailey said, "but get this: this is the only time we're going to stop for anything like this. This is the one and only time."

"The dirt road that you have to turn down is about a mile back," the grandmother directed. "I marked it when we passed."

"A dirt road," Bailey groaned.

After they had turned around and were headed toward the dirt road, the grandmother recalled other points about the house, the beautiful glass over the front doorway and the candle-lamp in the hall. John Wesley said that the secret panel was probably in the fireplace.

"You can't go inside this house," Bailey said. "You don't know who lives there."

"While you all talk to the people in front, I'll run around behind and get in a window," John Wesley suggested.

"We'll all stay in the car," his mother said.

They turned onto the dirt road and the car raced roughly along in a swirl of pink dust. The grandmother recalled the times when there were no paved roads and thirty miles was a day's journey. The dirt road was hilly and there were sudden washes in it and sharp curves on dangerous embankments. All at once they would be on a hill, looking down over the blue tops of trees for miles around, then the next minute, they would be in a red depression with the dust-coated trees looking down on them.

"This place had better turn up in a minute," Bailey said, "or I'm going to turn around."

The road looked as if no one had traveled on it in months.

"It's not much farther," the grandmother said and just as she said it, a horrible thought came to her. The thought was so embarrassing that she turned red in the face and her eyes dilated and her feet jumped up, upsetting her valise in the corner. The instant the valise moved, the newspaper top she had over the basket under it rose with a snarl and Pitty Sing, the cat, sprang onto Bailey's shoulder.

The children were thrown to the floor and their mother, clutching the baby, was thrown out the door onto the ground; the old lady was thrown into the front seat. The car turned over once and landed right-side-up in a gulch off the side of the road. Bailey remained in the driver's seat with the cat—gray-striped with a broad white face and an orange nose—clinging to his neck like a caterpillar.

As soon as the children saw they could move their arms and legs, they scrambled out of the car, shouting, "We've had an ACCIDENT!" The grandmother was curled up under the dashboard, hoping she was injured so that Bailey's wrath would not come down on her all at once. The horrible thought she had had before the accident was that the house she had remembered so vividly was not in Georgia but in Tennessee.

Bailey removed the cat from his neck with both hands and flung it out the window against the side of a pine tree. Then he got out of the car and started looking for the children's mother. She was sitting against the side of a red gutted ditch, holding the screaming baby, but she only had a cut down her face and a broken shoulder. "We've had an ACCIDENT!" the children screamed in a frenzy of delight.

"But nobody's killed," June Star said with disappointment as the grandmother limped out of the car, her hat still pinned to her head but the broken front brim standing up at a jaunty angle and the violet spray hanging off the side. They all sat down in the ditch, except the children, to recover from the shock. They were all shaking.

"Maybe a car will come along," said the children's mother hoarsely.

"I believe I have injured an organ," said the grandmother, pressing her side, but no one answered her. Bailey's teeth were clattering. He had on a yellow sport shirt with bright blue parrots designed in it and his face was as yellow as the shirt. The grandmother decided that she would not mention that the house was in Tennessee.

The road was about ten feet above and they could see only the tops of the trees on the other side of it. Behind the ditch they were sitting in there were more woods, tall and dark and deep. In a few minutes they saw a car some distance away on top of a hill, coming slowly as if the occupants were watching them. The grandmother stood up and waved both arms dramatically to attract their attention. The car continued to come on slowly, disappeared around a bend and appeared again, moving even slower, on top of the hill they had gone over. It was a big black battered hearse-like automobile. There were three men in it.

It came to a stop just over them and for some minutes, the driver looked down with a steady expressionless gaze to where they were sitting, and didn't speak. Then he turned his head and muttered something to the other two and they got out. One was a fat boy in black trousers and a red sweat shirt with a silver stallion embossed on the front of it. He moved around on the right side of them and stood staring, his mouth partly open in a kind of loose grin. The other had on khaki pants and a blue striped coat and a gray hat pulled down very low, hiding most of his face. He came around slowly on the left side. Neither spoke.

The driver got out of the car and stood by the side of it, looking down at them. He was an older man than the other two. His hair was just beginning to gray and he wore silver-rimmed spectacles that gave him a scholarly look. He had a long creased face and didn't have on any shirt or undershirt. He had on blue jeans that were too tight for him and he was holding a black hat and a gun. The two boys also had guns.

"We've had an ACCIDENT!" the children screamed.

The grandmother had the peculiar feeling that the bespectacled man was someone she knew. His face was as familiar to her as if she had known him all her life but she could not recall who he was. He moved away from the car and began to come down the embankment, placing his feet carefully so that he wouldn't slip. He had on tan and white shoes and no socks, and his ankles were red and thin. "Good afternoon," he said. "I see you all had you a little spill."

"We turned over twice!" said the grandmother.

"Oncet," he corrected. "We seen it happen. Try their car and see will it run, Hiram," he said quietly to the boy with the gray hat.

"What you got that gun for?" John Wesley asked. "Whatcha gonna do with that gun?"

"Lady," the man said to the children's mother, "would you mind calling them children to sit down by you? Children make me nervous. I want all you all to sit down right together there where you're at."

"What are you telling US what to do for?" June Star asked.

Behind them the line of woods gaped like a dark open mouth. "Come here," said the mother.

"Look here now," Bailey began suddenly, "we're in a predicament! We're in ..."

The grandmother shrieked. She scrambled to her feet and stood staring. "You're The Misfit!" she said. "I recognized you at once!"

"Yes'm," the man said, smiling slightly as if he were pleased in spite of himself to be known, "but it would have been better for all of you, lady, if you hadn't of reckernized me."

Bailey turned his head sharply and said something to his mother that shocked even the children. The old lady began to cry and The Misfit reddened.

"Lady," he said, "don't you get upset. Sometimes a man says things he don't mean. I don't reckon he meant to talk to you thataway."

"You wouldn't shoot a lady, would you?" the grandmother said and removed a clean handkerchief from her cuff and began to slap at her eyes with it.

The Misfit pointed the toe of his shoe into the ground and made a little hole and then covered it up again. "I would hate to have to," he said.

"Listen," the grandmother almost screamed, "I know you're a good man. You don't look a bit like you have common blood. I know you must come from nice people!"

"Yes mam," he said, "finest people in the world." When he smiled he showed a row of strong white teeth. "God never made a finer woman than my mother and my daddy's heart was pure gold," he said. The boy with the red sweat shirt had come around behind them and was standing with his gun at his hip. The Misfit squatted down on the ground. "Watch them children, Bobby Lee," he said. "You know they make me nervous." He looked at the six of them huddled together in front of him and he seemed to be embarrassed as if he couldn't think of anything to say. "Ain't a cloud in the sky," he remarked, looking up at it. "Don't see no sun but don't see no cloud neither."

"Yes, it's a beautiful day," said the grandmother. "Listen," she said, "you shouldn't call yourself The Misfit because I know you're a good man at heart. I can just look at you and tell."

"Hush!" Bailey yelled. "Hush! Everybody shut up and let me handle this!" He was squatting in the position of a runner about to sprint forward but he didn't move.

"I pre-chate that, lady," The Misfit said and drew a little circle in the ground with the butt of his gun.

"It'll take a half a hour to fix this here car," Hiram called, looking over the raised hood of it.

"Well, first you Bobby Lee get him and that little boy to step over yonder with you," The Misfit said, pointing to Bailey and John Wesley. "The boys want to ast you something," he said to Bailey. "Would you mind stepping back in them woods there with them?"

"Listen," Bailey began, "we're in a terrible predicament! Nobody realizes what this is," and his voice cracked. His eyes were as blue and intense as the parrots in his shirt and he remained perfectly still.

The grandmother reached up to adjust her hat brim as if she were going to the woods with him but it came off in her hand. She stood staring at it and after a second she let it fall on the ground. Hiram pulled Bailey up by the arm as if he were assisting an old man. John Wesley caught hold of his father's hand and Bobby Lee followed. They went off toward the woods and just as they reached the dark edge, Bailey turned and supporting himself against a gray naked pine trunk, he shouted, "I'll be back in a minute, Mamma, wait on me!"

"Come back this instant!" his mother shrilled but they all disappeared into the woods.

"Bailey Boy!" the grandmother called in a tragic voice but she found she was looking at The Misfit squatting on the ground in front of her. "I just know you're a good man," she said desperately. "You're not a bit common!"

"Nome, I ain't a good man," The Misfit said after a second as if he had considered her statement carefully, "but I ain't the worst in the world neither. My daddy said I was a different breed of dog from my brothers and sisters. 'You know,' Daddy said, 'it's some that can live their whole life without asking about it and it's others has to know why it is, and this boy is one of the latters. He's going to be into everything!'" He put on his black hat and looked up suddenly and then away deep into the woods as if he were embarrassed again. "I'm sorry I don't have on a shirt before you ladies," he said, hunching his shoulders slightly. "We buried our clothes that we had on when we escaped and we're just making do until we can get better. We borrowed these from some folks we met," he explained.

"That's perfectly all right," the grandmother said. "Maybe Bailey has an extra shirt in his suitcase."

"I'll look and see terrectly," The Misfit said.

"Where are they taking him?" the children's mother screamed.

"Daddy was a card himself," The Misfit said. "You couldn't put anything over on him. He never got in trouble with the Authorities though. Just had the knack of handling them."

"You could be honest too if you'd only try," said the grandmother. "Think how wonderful it would be to settle down and live a comfortable life and not have to think about somebody chasing you all the time."

The Misfit kept scratching in the ground with the butt of his gun as if he were thinking about it. "Yes'm, somebody is always after you," he murmured.

The grandmother noticed how thin his shoulder blades were just behind his hat because she was standing up looking down on him. "Do you ever pray?" she asked.

He shook his head. All she saw was the black hat wiggle between his shoulder blades. "Nome," he said.

There was a pistol shot from the woods, followed closely by another. Then silence. The old lady's head jerked around. She could hear the wind move through the tree tops like a long satisfied insuck of breath. "Bailey Boy!" she called.

"I was a gospel singer for a while," The Misfit said. "I been most everything. Been in the arm service, both land and sea, at home and abroad, been twict married, been an undertaker, been with the railroads, plowed Mother Earth, been in a tornado, seen a man burnt alive oncet," and he looked up at the children's mother and the little girl who were sitting close together, their faces white and their eyes glassy. "I even seen a woman flogged," he said.

"Pray, pray," the grandmother began, "pray, pray . . ."

"I never was a bad boy that I remember of," The Misfit said in an almost dreamy voice, "but somewheres along the line I done something wrong and got sent to the penitentiary. I was buried alive," and he looked up and held her attention to him by a steady stare.

"That's when you should have started to pray," she said, "What did you do to get sent to the penitentiary that first time?"

"Turn to the right, it was a wall," The Misfit said, looking up again at the cloudless sky. "Turn to the left, it was a wall. Look up it was a ceiling, look down it was a floor. I forget what I done, lady. I set there and set there, trying to remember what it was I done and I ain't recalled it to this day. Oncet in a while, I would think it was coming to me, but it never come."

"Maybe they put you in by mistake," the old lady said vaguely.

"Nome," he said. "It wasn't no mistake. They had the papers on me."

"You must have stolen something," she said.

The Misfit sneered slightly. "Nobody had nothing I wanted," he said. "It was a head-doctor at the penitentiary said what I had done was kill my daddy but I known that for a lie. My daddy died in nineteen ought nineteen of the epidemic flu and I never had a thing to do with it. He was buried in the Mount Hopewell Baptist churchyard and you can go there and see for yourself."

"If you would pray," the old lady said, "Jesus would help you."

"That's right," The Misfit said.

"Well then, why don't you pray?" she asked trembling with delight suddenly.

"I don't want no hep," he said. "I'm doing all right by myself."

Bobby Lee and Hiram came ambling back from the woods. Bobby Lee was dragging a yellow shirt with bright blue parrots in it.

"Thow me that shirt, Bobby Lee," The Misfit said. The shirt came flying at him and landed on his shoulder and he put it on. The grandmother couldn't name what the shirt reminded her of. "No, lady," The Misfit said while he was buttoning it up, "I found out the crime don't matter. You can do one thing or you can do another, kill a man or take a tire off his car, because sooner or later you're going to forget what it was you done and just be punished for it."

The children's mother had begun to make heaving noises as if she couldn't get her breath. "Lady," he asked, "would you and that little girl like to step off yonder with Bobby Lee and Hiram and join your husband?"

"Yes, thank you," the mother said faintly. Her left arm dangled helplessly and she was holding the baby, who had gone to sleep, in the other. "Hep that lady up, Hiram," The Misfit said as she struggled to climb out of the ditch, "and Bobby Lee, you hold onto that little girl's hand."

"I don't want to hold hands with him," June Star said. "He reminds me of a pig."

The fat boy blushed and laughed and caught her by the arm and pulled her off into the woods after Hiram and her mother.

Alone with The Misfit, the grandmother found that she had lost her voice. There was not a cloud in the sky nor any sun. There was nothing around her but woods. She wanted to tell him that he must pray. She opened and closed her mouth several times before anything came out. Finally she found herself saying, "Jesus. Jesus," meaning, Jesus will help you, but the way she was saying it, it sounded as if she might be cursing.

"Yes'm," The Misfit said as if he agreed. "Jesus thown everything off balance. It was the same case with Him as with me except He hadn't committed any crime and they could prove I had committed one because they had the papers on me. Of course," he said, "they never shown me my papers. That's why I sign myself now. I said long ago, you get you a signature and sign everything you do and keep a copy of it. Then you'll know what you done and you can hold up the crime to the punishment and see do they match and in the end you'll have something to prove you ain't been treated right. I call myself The Misfit," he said, "because I can't make what all I done wrong fit what all I gone through in punishment."

There was a piercing scream from the woods, followed closely by a pistol report. "Does it seem right to you, lady, that one is punished a heap and another ain't punished at all?"

"Jesus!" the old lady cried. "You've got good blood! I know you wouldn't shoot a lady! I know you come from nice people! Pray! Jesus, you ought not to shoot a lady. I'll give you all the money I've got!"

"Lady," The Misfit said, looking beyond her far into the woods, "there never was a body that give the undertaker a tip."

There were two more pistol reports and the grandmother raised her head like a parched old turkey hen crying for water and called, "Bailey Boy, Bailey Boy!" as if her heart would break.

"Jesus was the only One that ever raised the dead," The Misfit continued, "and He shouldn't have done it. He thown everything off balance. If He did what He said, then it's nothing for you to do but thow away everything and follow Him, and if He didn't, then it's nothing for you to do but enjoy the few minutes you got left the best way you can—by killing somebody or burning down his house or doing some other meanness to him. No pleasure but meanness," he said and his voice had become almost a snarl.

"Maybe He didn't raise the dead," the old lady mumbled, not knowing what she was saying and feeling so dizzy that she sank down in the ditch with her legs twisted under her.

"I wasn't there so I can't say He didn't," The Misfit said. "I wisht I had of been there," he said, hitting the ground with his fist. "It ain't right I wasn't there because if I had of been there I would of known. Listen lady," he said in a high voice, "if I had of been there I would of known and I wouldn't be like I am now." His voice seemed about to crack and the grandmother's head cleared for an instant. She saw the man's face twisted close to her own as if he were going to cry and she murmured, "Why you're one of my babies. You're one of my own children!" She reached out and touched him on the shoulder. The Misfit sprang back as if a snake had bitten him and shot her three times through the chest. Then he put his gun down on the ground and took off his glasses and began to clean them.

Hiram and Bobby Lee returned from the woods and stood over the ditch, looking down at the grandmother who half sat and half lay in a puddle of blood with her legs crossed under her like a child's and her face smiling up at the cloudless sky.

Without his glasses, The Misfit's eyes were red-rimmed and pale and defenseless-looking. "Take her off and thow her where you thown the others," he said, picking up the cat that was rubbing itself against his leg.

"She was a talker, wasn't she?" Bobby Lee said, sliding down the ditch with a yodel.

"She would of been a good woman," The Misfit said, "if it had been somebody there to shoot her every minute of her life."

"Some fun!" Bobby Lee said.
"Shut up, Bobby Lee," The Misfit said. "It's no real pleasure in life."

1953

■ BIENVENIDO N. SANTOS ■
1911–1996

Throughout his career, Bienvenido N. Santos meditated again and again on a condition that is perhaps best diagnosed by the narrator of his story "Scent of Apples": "certain ideals, certain beliefs, even illusions peculiar to the exile." For Santos, exile was much more than a literary trope. He often described himself and his work as indelibly marked by the alienation, loneliness, and longing that were produced by a lifetime of transnational experiences.

As a writer, Santos came to think of himself as "belong[ing] to the literature of two great countries: the Philippines, land of my birth; and the United States, sanctuary, a second home." Santos was one of the first Filipino writers to publish literature in English in both countries, and he had a prolific, noteworthy career. In 1941, after he completed his undergraduate education at the University of the Philippines, Santos was awarded a scholarship for study abroad and attended the University of Illinois at Urbana–Champaign, where he received a master of arts in English. But when the United States became involved World War II, many Filipinos were unable to return home. In 1942 the U.S. government summoned Santos to work for the war effort in Washington, D.C. He wrote speeches and articles as part of a public relations venture to educate Americans about the war in the Pacific, and he toured the country giving lectures about the Philippines. This experience became the autobiographical basis for stories like "Scent of Apples."

Although Santos eventually became a U.S. citizen, he lived, taught, and wrote in both countries until he died. He participated in creative writing workshops at Columbia, Harvard, and the University of Iowa, and he taught at a wide range of institutions, including Ohio State University, University of Iowa, Wichita State University, University of the Philippines, Ateneo de Manila University, and De La Salle University in Manila. He held honorary doctorates from institutions in both countries, and he received multiple awards, including the Manila Critics Circle National Book Award and fellowships from the Rockefeller Foundation, Guggenheim Foundation, and National Endowment for the Arts.

In the United States, "Scent of Apples" is Santos's best-known work. He originally published the story in the Philippines as part of the collection *You Lovely People* (1955), and he later included it in the warmly praised U.S.-published collection *Scent of Apples* (1979). "Scent of Apples" highlights recurring formal and thematic features in Santos's short stories. In the story, an unnamed "first class Filipino" narrator encounters Celestino Fabia, who describes himself as "just a Filipino farmer" in Michigan. Ultimately, the narrator sympathizes with Fabia's need to believe in an idealized memory of "our Filipino women" as a link to his lost home in the Philippines. Through the developing relationship between these men and the contrast in their narrative perspectives, the story reflects on Filipino immigration and exile; the tensions between an older group of Filipinos who migrated to the United States as laborers and a younger, mobile, and elite generation of Filipinos; and the place of women in the imaginations of Filipinos abroad.

Denise Cruz
Indiana University, Bloomington

PRIMARY WORKS

You Lovely People, 1955; *The Wounded Stag: Fifty-Four Poems*, 1956; *Brother My Brother*, 1960; *Villa Magdalena*, 1965; *The Volcano*, 1965; *The Day the Dancers Came*, 1967; *Scent of Apples*, 1979; *The Praying Man*, 1982; *The Man Who (Thought He) Looked Like Robert Taylor*, 1983; *Distances in Time*, 1983; *Dwell in the Wilderness*, 1985; *What the Hell for You Left Your Heart in San Francisco*, 1987; *Memory's Fictions: A Personal History*, 1993; *Postscript to a Saintly Life*, 1994; *Letters*, 1995.

Scent of Apples

When I arrived in Kalamazoo it was October and the war was still on. Gold and silver stars hung on pennants above silent windows of white and brick-red cottages. In a backyard an old man burned leaves and twigs while a grey-haired woman sat on the porch, her red hands quiet on her lap, watching the smoke rising above the elms, both of them thinking of the same thought perhaps, about a tall, grinning boy with blue eyes and flying hair, who went out to war: where could he be now this month when leaves were turning into gold and the fragrance of gathered apples was in the wind?

It was a cold night when I left my room at the hotel for a usual speaking arrangement. I walked but a little way. A heavy wind coming up from Lake Michigan was icy on the face. It felt like winter straying early in the northern woodlands. Under the lampposts the leaves shone like bronze. And they rolled on the pavements like the ghost feet of a thousand autumns long dead, long before the boys left for faraway lands without great icy winds and promise of winter early in the air, lands without apple trees, *the singing and the gold!*

It was the same night I met Celestino Fabia, "just a Filipino farmer" as he called himself, who had a farm about thirty miles east of Kalamazoo.

"You came all that way on a night like this just to hear me talk?" I asked.

"I've seen no Filipino for so many years now," he answered quickly. "So when I saw your name in the papers where it says you come from the Islands and that you're going to talk, I come right away."

Earlier that night I had addressed a college crowd, mostly women. It appeared that they wanted me to talk about my country; they wanted me to tell them things about it because my country had become a lost country. Everywhere in the land the enemy stalked. Over it a great silence hung; and their boys were there, unheard from, or they were on their way to some little known island on the Pacific, young boys all, hardly men, thinking of harvest moons and smell of forest fire.

It was not hard talking about our own people. I knew them well and I loved them. And they seemed so far away during those terrible years that I must have spoken of them with a little fervor, a little nostalgia.

In the open forum that followed, the audience wanted to know whether there was much difference between our women and the American women. I tried to answer the question as best as I could, saying, among other things, that I did not know much about American women, except that they looked friendly, but differences or similarities in inner qualities such as naturally belonged to the heart or to the mind, I could only speak about with vagueness.

While I was trying to explain away the fact that it was not easy to make comparisons, a man rose from the rear of the hall, wanting to say something. In the distance, he looked slight and old and very brown. Even before he spoke, I knew that he was, like me, a Filipino.

"I'm a Filipino," he began, loud and clear, in a voice that seemed used to wide open spaces, "I'm just a Filipino farmer out in the country." He waved his hand towards the door. "I left the Philippines more than twenty years ago and have never been back. Never will perhaps. I want to find out, sir, are our Filipino women the same like they were twenty years ago?"

As he sat down, the hall filled with voices, hushed and intrigued. I weighed my answer carefully. I did not want to tell a lie yet I did not want to say anything that would seem platitudinous, insincere. But more important than these considerations, it seemed to me that moment as I looked towards my countryman, I must give him an answer that would not make him so unhappy. Surely, all these years, he must have held on to certain ideals, certain beliefs, even illusions peculiar to the exile.

"First," I said as the voices gradually died down and every eye seemed upon me, "First, tell me what our women were like twenty years ago."

The man stood to answer. "Yes," he said, "you're too young ... Twenty years ago our women were nice, they were modest, they wore their hair long, they dressed proper and went for no monkey business. They were natural, they went to church regular, and they were faithful." He had spoken slowly, and now in what seemed like an afterthought, added, "It's the men who ain't."

Now I knew what I was going to say.

"Well," I began, "it will interest you to know that our women have changed—but definitely! The change, however, has been on the outside only. Inside, here," pointing to the heart, "they are the same as they were twenty years ago. God-fearing, faithful, modest, and *nice*."

The man was visibly moved. "I'm very happy, sir," he said, in the manner of one who, having stakes on the land, had found no cause to regret one's sentimental investment.

After this, everything that was said and done in that hall that night seemed like an anti-climax; and later, as we walked outside, he gave me his name and told me of his farm thirty miles east of the city.

We had stopped at the main entrance to the hotel lobby. We had not talked very much on the way. As a matter of fact, we were never alone. Kindly American friends talked to us, asked us questions, said goodnight. So now I asked him whether he cared to step into the lobby with me and talk.

"No, thank you," he said, "you are tired. And I don't want to stay out too late."

"Yes, you live very far."

"I got a car," he said, "besides ..."

Now he smiled, he truly smiled. All night I had been watching his face and I wondered when he was going to smile.

"Will you do me a favor, please," he continued smiling almost sweetly. "I want you to have dinner with my family out in the country. I'd call for you tomorrow afternoon, then drive you back. Will that be all right?"

"Of course," I said. "I'd love to meet your family." I was leaving Kalamazoo for Muncie, Indiana, in two days. There was plenty of time.

"You will make my wife very happy," he said.

"You flatter me."

"Honest. She'll be very happy. Ruth is a country girl and hasn't met many Filipinos. I mean Filipinos younger than I, cleaner looking. We're just poor farmer folk, you know, and we don't get to town very often. Roger, that's my boy, he goes to school in town. A bus takes him early in the morning and he's back in the afternoon. He's nice boy."

"I bet he is," I agreed. "I've seen the children of some of the boys by their American wives and the boys are tall, taller than the father, and very good looking."

"Roger, he'd be tall. You'll like him."

Then he said goodbye and I waved to him as he disappeared in the darkness.

The next day he came, at about three in the afternoon. There was a mild, ineffectual sun shining; and it was not too cold. He was wearing an old brown tweed jacket and worsted trousers to match. His shoes were polished, and although the green of his tie seemed faded, a colored shirt hardly accentuated it. He looked younger than he appeared the night before now that he was clean shaven and seemed ready to go to a party. He was grinning as we met.

"Oh, Ruth can't believe it. She can't believe it," he kept repeating as he led me to his car—a nondescript thing in faded black that had known better days and many hands. "I says to her, I'm bringing you a first class Filipino, and she says, aw, go away, quit kidding, there's no such thing as first class Filipino. But Roger, that's my boy, he believed me immediately. What's he like, daddy, he asks. Oh, you will see, I says, he's first class. Like you daddy? No, no, I laugh at him, your daddy ain't first class. Aw, but you are, daddy, he says. So you can see what a nice boy he is, so innocent. Then Ruth starts griping about the house, but the house is a mess, she says. True it's a mess, it's always a mess, but you don't mind, do you? We're poor folks, you know."

The trip seemed interminable. We passed through narrow lanes and disappeared into thickets, and came out on barren land overgrown with weeds in places. All around were dead leaves and dry earth. In the distance were apple trees.

"Aren't those apple trees?" I asked wanting to be sure.

"Yes, those are apple trees," he replied. "Do you like apples? I got lots of 'em. I got an apple orchard, I'll show you."

All the beauty of the afternoon seemed in the distance, on the hills, in the dull soft sky.

"Those trees are beautiful on the hills," I said.

"Autumn's a lovely season. The trees are getting ready to die, and they show their colors, proud-like."

"No such thing in our own country," I said.

That remark seemed unkind, I realized later. It touched him off on a long deserted tangent, but ever there perhaps. How many times did the lonely mind take unpleasant detours away from the familiar winding lanes towards home for fear of this, the remembered hurt, the long lost youth, the grim shadows of the years; how many times indeed, only the exile knows.

It was a rugged road we were travelling and the car made so much noise that I could not hear everything he said, but I understood him. He was telling his story for the first time in many years. He was remembering his own youth. He was thinking of home. In these odd moments there seemed no cause for fear, no cause at all, no pain. That would come later. In the night perhaps. Or lonely on the farm under the apple trees.

In this old Visyan town, the streets are narrow and dirty and strewn with corral shells. You have been there? You could not have missed our house, it was the biggest in town, one of the oldest, ours was a big family. The house stood right on the edge of the street. A door opened heavily and you enter a dark hall leading to the stairs. There is the smell of chickens roosting on the low-topped walls, there is the familiar sound they make and you grope your way up a massive staircase, the bannisters smooth upon the trembling hand. Such nights, they are no better than days, windows are closed against the sun; they close heavily.

Mother sits in her corner looking very white and sick. This was her world, her domain. In all these years I cannot remember the sound of her voice. Father was different. He moved about. He shouted. He ranted. He lived in the past and talked of honor as though it were the only thing.

I was born in that house. I grew up there into a pampered brat. I was mean. One day I broke their hearts. I saw mother cry wordlessly as father heaped his curses upon me and drove me out of the house, the gate closing heavily after me. And my brothers and sisters took up my father's hate for me and multiplied it numberless times in their own broken hearts. I was no good.

But sometimes, you know, I miss that house, the roosting chickens on the low-topped walls. I miss my brothers and sisters. Mother sitting in her chair, looking like a pale ghost in a corner of the room. I would remember the great live posts, massive tree trunks from the forests. Leafy plants grew on the sides, buds pointing downwards, wilted and died before they could become flowers. As they fell on the floor, father bent to pick them and throw them out into the corral streets. His hands were strong. I have kissed those hands ... many times, many times.

Finally we rounded a deep curve and suddenly came upon a shanty, all but ready to crumble in a heap on the ground, its plastered walls were rotting away, the floor was hardly a foot from the ground. I thought of the cottages of the poor colored folk in the south, the hovels of the poor everywhere in the land. This one stood all by itself as though by common consent all the folk that used to live here had decided to stay away, despising it, ashamed of it. Even the lovely season could not color it with beauty.

A dog barked loudly as we approached. A fat blonde woman stood at the door with a little boy by her side. Roger seemed newly scrubbed. He hardly took his eyes off me. Ruth had a clean apron around her shapeless waist. Now as she shook my hands in sincere delight I noticed shamefacedly (that I should notice) how rough her hands, how coarse and red with labor, how ugly! She was no longer young and her smile was pathetic.

As we stepped inside and the door closed behind us, immediately I was aware of the familiar scent of apples. The room was bare except for a few ancient pieces of second-hand furniture. In the middle of the room stood a stove to keep the family warm in winter. The walls were bare. Over the dining table hung a lamp yet unlighted.

Ruth got busy with the drinks. She kept coming in and out of a rear room that must have been the kitchen and soon the table was heavy with food, fried chicken legs and rice, and green peas and corn on the ear. Even as we ate, Ruth kept standing, and going to the kitchen for more food. Roger ate like a little gentleman.

"Isn't he nice looking?" his father asked.

"You are a handsome boy, Roger," I said.

The boy smiled at me. "You look like Daddy," he said.

Afterwards I noticed an old picture leaning on the top of a dresser and stood to pick it up. It was yellow and soiled with many fingerings. The faded figure of a woman in Philippine dress could yet be distinguished although the face had become a blur.

"Your ..." I began.

"I don't know who she is," Fabia hastened to say. "I picked that picture many years ago in a room on La Salle Street in Chicago. I have often wondered who she is."

"The face wasn't a blur in the beginning?"

"Oh, no. It was a young face and good."

Ruth came with a plate full of apples.

"Ah," I cried, picking out a ripe one, "I've been thinking where all the scent of apples come from. The room is full of it."

"I'll show you," said Fabia.

He showed me a backroom, not very big. It was half-full of apples.

"Every day," he explained, "I take some of them to town to sell to the groceries. Prices have been low. I've been losing on the trips."

"These apples will spoil," I said.

"We'll feed them to the pigs."

Then he showed me around the farm. It was twilight now and the apple trees stood bare against a glowing western sky. In apple blossom time it must be lovely here, I thought. But what about wintertime?

One day, according to Fabia, a few years ago, before Roger was born, he had an attack of acute appendicitis. It was deep winter. The snow lay heavy everywhere. Ruth was pregnant and none too well herself. At first she did not know what to do. She bundled him in warm clothing and put him on a cot near the stove. She shoveled the snow from their front door and practically carried the suffering man on her shoulders, dragging him through the newly made path towards the road where they waited for the U.S. Mail car to pass. Meanwhile snowflakes poured all over them and she kept rubbing the man's arms and legs as she herself nearly froze to death.

"Go back to the house, Ruth!" her husband cried, "you'll freeze to death."

But she clung to him wordlessly. Even as she massaged his arms and legs, her tears rolled down her cheeks. "I won't leave you, I won't leave you," she repeated.

Finally the U.S. Mail car arrived. The mailman, who knew them well, helped them board the car, and, without stopping on his usual route, took the sick man and his wife direct to the nearest hospital.

Ruth stayed in the hospital with Fabia. She slept in a corridor outside the patients' ward and in the day time helped in scrubbing the floor and washing the dishes and cleaning the men's things. They didn't have enough money and Ruth was willing to work like a slave.

"Ruth's a nice girl," said Fabia, "like our own Filipino women."

Before nightfall, he took me back to the hotel. Ruth and Roger stood at the door holding hands and smiling at me. From inside the room of the shanty, a low light flickered. I had a last glimpse of the apple trees in the orchard under the darkened sky as Fabia backed up the car. And soon we were on our way back to town. The dog had started barking. We could hear it for some time, until finally, we could not hear it anymore, and all was darkness around us, except where the head lamps revealed a stretch of road leading somewhere.

Fabia did not talk this time. I didn't seem to have anything to say myself. But when finally we came to the hotel and I got down, Fabia said, "Well, I guess I won't be seeing you again."

It was dimly lighted in front of the hotel and I could hardly see Fabia's face. Without getting off the car, he moved to where I had sat, and I saw him extend his hand. I gripped it.

"Tell Ruth and Roger," I said, "I love them."

He dropped my hand quickly. "They'll be waiting for me now," he said.

"Look," I said, not knowing why I said it, "one of these days, very soon, I hope, I'll be going home. I could go to your town."

"No," he said softly, sounding very much defeated but brave, "Thanks a lot. But, you see, nobody would remember me now."

Then he started the car, and as it moved away, he waved his hand.

"Goodbye," I said, waving back into the darkness. And suddenly the night was cold like winter straying early in these northern woodlands.

I hurried inside. There was a train the next morning that left for Muncie, Indiana, at a quarter after eight.

1979 (originally published in the Philippines in 1955)

■ # TILLIE LERNER OLSEN
1913–2007 ■

Tillie Olsen's parents, Samuel and Ida Lerner, took part in the 1905 revolution in Russia, fleeing to the United States when it failed. Her father worked at a variety of jobs, from farming to packinghouse work, and eventually became state secretary of the Nebraska Socialist Party. The young Tillie Lerner read avidly in her public library, becoming conversant with American and world literature. Forced to leave school after the eleventh grade to go to work, she pressed ties, trimmed meat in the packinghouses, and worked as a domestic and a waitress. She also became an activist in the Young Communist League, going to jail in Kansas City after attempting to organize packinghouse workers. At nineteen she began work on the novel that many years later would become *Yonnondio: From the Thirties*; in the same year, she bore her first child, a daughter. In the early thirties, she moved to northern California, where she continued to write and to do political work. She combined the two in reportage such as "The Strike," an essay about the great general strike that spread up and down the Coast from San Francisco in 1934.

In 1936 Tillie Lerner became involved with her YCL companion Jack Olsen, whom she eventually married. In the years that followed, she bore three more children, struggling to combine mothering with work out of the home to help support her growing family. During the 1950s, she and her family, like so many progressives of the thirties and forties, were harassed by the FBI. Nonetheless, Olsen began writing again: "I Stand Here Ironing," "Hey Sailor, What Ship?" and "O Yes," written in the mid-fifties, followed by "Tell Me a Riddle," which won the

O. Henry Award in 1961 for best short story of the year. These stories, originally conceived as part of a novel about three generations of a Russian Jewish family, celebrate the stubborn endurance of human love and of the passion for justice, in spite of the injuries inflicted by poverty, racism, and the patriarchal order.

The same theme informs *Yonnondio: From the Thirties*, a novel revised and published forty years after its inception by the "older writer in arduous partnership with that long ago younger one." The story of the Holbrook family's efforts to survive on the farms and in the packinghouses of the Midwest in the twenties, the novel creates in Mazie Holbrook and in her mother Anna a figure that reappears throughout Olsen's work, fiction and criticism alike: the potential female artist/activist silenced by poverty, by the willingly assumed burdens of caring for loved others, by the expectations associated with her sex. *Silences*, Olsen's collected critical essays, continues this theme. The book is a sustained prose poem about all the forms of silencing that befall writers—especially, though not exclusively, women; especially, though not exclusively, those who must struggle for sheer survival.

Concerned with the "circumstances" of class, race, and gender as the soil that nurtures or impedes human achievement, Olsen's work constitutes a vitally important link between the radical movements of the thirties and the culture, ideas, and literature of the women's liberation movement. Her fiction and essays, finely crafted and emotionally powerful, make an important contribution to American literature, an achievement acknowledged in the many prestigious awards and four honorary doctorates she received. She contributed to what she called "the larger tradition of social concern" not only as a writer but also as a scholar and teacher. Her efforts helped to reclaim many "lost" women writers and to initiate the democratization of the literary canon reflected in the contours of this anthology.

Deborah S. Rosenfelt
University of Maryland at College Park

PRIMARY WORKS

Tell Me a Riddle, 1961; *Yonnondio: From the Thirties*, 1974; *Silences*, 1978; *Mother to Daughter, Daughter to Mother: A Daybook and Reader*, 1984.

O Yes

1

They are the only white people there, sitting in the dimness of the Negro church that had once been a corner store, and all through the bubbling, swelling, seething of before the services, twelve-year-old Carol clenches tight her mother's hand, the other resting lightly on her friend, Parialee Phillips, for whose baptism she has come.

The white-gloved ushers hurry up and down the aisle, beckoning people to their seats. A jostle of people. To the chairs angled to the left for the youth choir, to the chairs angled to the right for the ladies' choir, even up to the platform, where behind the place for the dignitaries and the mixed choir,

The lady in front of her moaned, *"O yes"* and others were moaning *"O yes."*

"And when the earth mourned the Lord said, Weep not, for all will be returned to you, every dust, every atom. And the tired dust settles back, goes back. Until that Judgment Day. That great day."

"O yes."

The ushers were giving out fans. Carol reached for one and Parry said: "What *you* need one for?" but she took it anyway.

"You think Satchmo can blow; you think Muggsy can blow; you think Dizzy can blow?" He was straining to an imaginary trumpet now, his head far back and his voice coming out like a trumpet.

"Oh Parry, he's so good."

"Well. Jelly jelly."

"Nothing to Gabriel on that great getting-up morning. And the horn wakes up Adam and, Adam runs to wake up Eve, and Eve moans; Just one more minute, let me sleep, and Adam yells, Great Day, woman, don't you know it's the Great Day?"

"Great Day, Great Day," the mixed choir behind the preacher rejoices:

> *When our cares are past*
> *when we're home at last . . .*

"And Eve runs to wake up Cain." Running round the platform, stooping and shaking imaginary sleepers, "and Cain runs to wake up Abel." Looping, scalloping his voice—"Grea-aaa-aat Daaaay." All the choirs thundering:

> *Great Day*
> *When the battle's fought*
> *And the victory's won*

Exultant spirals of sound. And Carol caught into it (Eddie forgotten, the game forgotten) chanting with Lucy and Bubbie: *"Great Day."*

"Ohhhhhhhhhh," his voice like a trumpet again, "the re-unioning. Ohhhhhhhhh, the rejoicing. After the ages immemorial of longing."

Someone *was* screaming. And an awful thrumming sound with it, like feet and hands thrashing around, like a giant jumping of a rope.

"Great Day." And no one stirred or stared as the ushers brought a little woman out into the aisle, screaming and shaking, just a little shrunk-up woman, not much taller than Carol, the biggest thing about her her swollen hands and the cascades of tears wearing her face.

The shaking inside Carol too. Turning and trembling to ask: "What? . . . that lady?" But Parry still ponders the platform; little Lucy loops the chain of her bracelet round and round; and Bubbie sits placidly, dreamily. Alva Phillips is up fanning a lady in front of her; two lady ushers are fanning other people Carol cannot see. And her mother, her mother looks in a sleep.

Yes. He raised up the dead from the grave. He made old death behave.

Yes. Yes. From all over, hushed.

O Yes

He was your mother's rock. Your father's mighty tower. And he gave us a little baby. A little baby to love.

I am so glad

Yes, your friend, when you're friendless. Your father when you're fatherless.
Way maker. Door opener.

Yes

When it seems you can't go on any longer, he's there. You can, he says, you can.

Yes

And that burden you been carrying—ohhhhh that burden—not for always
will it be. No, not for always.

Stay with me, Lord

I will put my Word in you and it is power. I will put my Truth in you and it
is power.

O Yes

Out of your suffering I will make you to stand as a stone. A tried stone.
Hewn out of the mountains of ages eternal. Ohhhhhhhhhhh. Out of the
mire I will lift your feet. Your tired feet from so much wandering. From so
much work and wear and hard times.

Yes

From so much journeying—and never the promised land. And I'll wash
them in the well your tears made. And I'll shod them in the gospel of peace,
and of feeling good. Ohhhhhhhh.

O Yes.

Behind Carol, a trembling wavering scream. Then the thrashing. Up
above, the singing:

They taken my blessed Jesus and flogged him to the woods
And they made him hew out his cross and they dragged him to Calvary

Shout brother, Shout shout shout. He never cried a word.

Powerful throbbing voices. Calling and answering to each other.

They taken my blessed Jesus and whipped him up the hill
With a knotty whip and a raggedy thorn he never cried a word
Shout, sister. Shout shout shout. He never cried a word.

Go tell the people the Saviour has risen
Has risen from the dead and will live forevermore
And won't have to die no more.

Halleloo.

Shout, brother, shout
We won't have to die no more!

A single exultant lunge of shriek. Then the thrashing. All around a clapping. Shouts with it. The piano whipping, whipping air to a froth. Singing now.

I once was lost who now am found
Was blind who now can see

On Carol's fan, a little Jesus walked on wondrously blue waters to where bearded disciples spread nets out of a fishing boat. If she studied the fan—became it—it might make a wall around her. If she could make what was happening (*what* was happening?) into a record small and round to listen to far and far as if into a seashell—the stamp and rills and spirals all tiny (but never any screaming).

> *wade wade in the water*
>
> > *Jordan's water is chilly and wild*
> > *I've got to get home to the other side*
> > *God's going to trouble the waters*

The music leaps and prowls. Ladders of screamings. Drumming feet of ushers running. And still little Lucy fluffs her skirts, loops the chain on her bracelet; still Bubbie sits and rocks dreamily; and only eyes turn for an instant to the aisle as if nothing were happening. "Mother, let's go home," Carol begs, but her mother holds her so tight. Alva Phillips, strong Alva, rocking too and chanting, *O Yes*. No, do not look.

> *Wade,*
> *Sea of trouble all mingled with fire*
> *Come on my brethren it's time to go higher*
> *Wade wade*

The voices in great humming waves, slow, slow (when did it become the humming?), everyone swaying with it, too, moving like in slow waves and singing, and up where Eddie is, a new cry, wild and open, "O help me, Jesus," and when Carol opens her eyes she closes them again, quick, but still can see the new known face from school (not Eddie), the thrashing, writhing body, struggling against the ushers with the look of grave and loving support on their faces, and hear the torn, tearing cry: "Don't take me away, life everlasting, don't take me away."

And now the rhinestones in Parry's hair glitter wicked, the white hands of the ushers, fanning, foam in the air; the blue-painted waters of Jordan swell and thunder; Christ spirals on his cross in the window, and she is drowned under the sluice of the slow singing and the sway.

So high up and forgotten the waves and the world, so stirless the deep cool green and the wrecks of what had been. Here now Hostess Foods, where Alva Phillips works her nights—but different from that time Alva had taken them through before work, for it is all sunken under water, the creaking loading platform where they had left the night behind; the closet room where Alva's swaddles of sweaters, boots, and cap hung, the long hall lined with pickle barrels, the sharp freezer door swinging open.

Bubbles of breath that swell. A gulp of numbing air. She swims into the chill room where the huge wheels of cheese stand, and Alva swims too, deftly oiling each machine: slicers and wedgers and the convey, that at her touch start to roll and grind. The light of day blazes up and Alva is holding a cup, saying: Drink this, baby.

"DRINK IT." Her mother's voice and the numbing air demanding her to pay attention. Up through the waters and into the car.

"That's right, lambie, now lie back." Her mother's lap.

"Mother."

"Shhhhh. You almost fainted, lambie."

Alva's voice. "You gonna be all right, Carol … Lucy, I'm telling you for the last time, you and Buford get back into that church. Carol is *fine*."

"Lucyinda, if I had all your petticoats I could float." Crying. "Why didn't you let me wear my full skirt with the petticoats, Mother."

"Shhhhh, lamb." Smoothing her cheek. "Just breathe, take long deep breaths."

"… How you doing now, you little ol' consolation prize?" It is Parry, but she does not come in the car or reach to Carol through the open window: "No need to cuss and fuss. You going to be sharp as a tack, Jack."

Answering automatically: "And cool as a fool."

Quick, they look at each other.

"Parry, we have to go home now, don't we, Mother? I almost fainted, didn't I, Mother? … Parry, I'm sorry I got sick and have to miss your baptism."

"Don't feel sorry. I'll feel better you not there to watch. It was our mommas wanted you to be there, not me."

"Parry!" Three voices.

"Maybe I'll come over to play kickball after. If you feeling better. Maybe. Or bring the pogo." Old shared joys in her voice. "Or any little thing."

In just a whisper: "Or any little thing. Parry. Goodbye, Parry."

And why does Alva have to talk now?

"You all right? You breathin' deep like your momma said? Was it too close 'n hot in there? Did something scare you, Carrie?"

Shaking her head to lie, "No."

"I blame myself for not paying attention. You not used to people letting go that way. Lucy and Bubbie, Parialee, they used to it. They been coming since they lap babies."

"Alva, that's all right. Alva, Mrs. Phillips."

"You *was* scared. Carol, it's something to study about. You'll feel better if you understand."

Trying not to listen.

"You not used to hearing what people keeps inside, Carol. You know how music can make you feel things? Glad or sad or like you can't sit still? That was religion music, Carol."

"I have to breathe deep, Mother said."

"Not everybody feels religion the same way. Some it's in their mouth, but some it's like a hope in the blood, their bones. And they singing songs every word that's real to them, Carol, every word out of they own life. And the preaching finding lodgment in their hearts."

The screaming was tuning up in her ears again, high above Alva's patient voice and the waves lapping and fretting.

"Maybe somebody's had a hard week, Carol, and they locked up with it. Maybe a lot of hard weeks bearing down."

"Mother, my head hurts."

"And they're home, Carol, church is home. Maybe the only place they can feel how they feel and maybe let it come out. So they can go on. And it's all right."

"Please, Alva. Mother, tell Alva my head hurts."

"Get Happy, we call it, and most it's a good feeling, Carol. When you got all that locked up inside you."

"Tell her we have to go home. It's all right, Alva. Please, Mother. Say good-bye. Good-bye."

When I was carrying Parry and her father left me, and I fifteen years old, one thousand miles away from home, sin-sick and never really believing, as still I don't believe all, scorning, for what have it done to help, waiting there in the clinic and maybe sleeping, a voice called: Alva, Alva. So mournful and so sweet: Alva. Fear not, I have loved you from the foundation of the universe. And a little small child tugged on my dress. He was carrying a parade stick, on the end of it a star that outshined the sun. Follow me, he said. And the real sun went down and he hidden his stick. How dark it was, how dark. I could feel the darkness with my hands. And when I could see, I screamed. Dump trucks run, dumping bodies in hell, and a convey line run, never ceasing with souls, weary ones having to stamp and shove them along, and the air like fire. Oh I never want to hear such screaming. Then the little child jumped on a motorbike making a path no bigger than my little finger. But first he greased my feet with the hands of my momma when I was a knee baby. They shined like the sun was on them. Eyes he placed all around my head, and as I journeyed upward after him, it seemed I heard a mourning: "Mama Mama you must help carry the world." The rise and fall of nations I saw. And the voice called again Alva Alva, and I flew into a world of light, multitudes singing, Free, free, I am so glad.

2

Helen began to cry, telling her husband about it.

"You and Alva ought to have your heads examined, taking her there cold like that," Len said. "All right, wreck my best handkerchief. Anyway, now that she's had a bath, her Sunday dinner...."

"And been fussed over," seventeen-year-old Jeannie put in.

"She seems good as new. Now *you* forget it, Helen."

"I can't. Something ... deep happened. If only I or Alva had told her what it would be like.... But I didn't realize."

You don't realize a lot of things, Mother, Jeannie said, but not aloud.

"So Alva talked about it after instead of before. Maybe it meant more that way."

"Oh Len, she didn't listen."

"You don't know if she did or not. Or what there was in the experience for her...."

Enough to pull that kid apart two ways even more, Jeannie said, but still not aloud.

"I was so glad she and Parry were going someplace together again. Now that'll be between them too. Len, they really need, miss each other. What happened in a few months? When I think of how close they were, the hours of makebelieve and dressup and playing ball and collecting...."

"Grow up, Mother." Jeannie's voice was harsh. "Parialee's collecting something else now. Like her own crowd. Like jivetalk and rhythmandblues. Like teachers who treat her like a dummy and white kids who treat her like dirt; boys who think she's really something and chicks who...."

"Jeannie, I know. It hurts."

"Well, maybe it hurts Parry too. Maybe. At least she's got a crowd. Just don't let it hurt Carol though, 'cause there's nothing she can do about it. That's all through, her and Parialee Phillips, put away with their paper dolls."

"No, Jeannie, no."

"It's like Ginger and me. Remember Ginger, my best friend in Horace Mann. But you hardly noticed when it happened to us, did you ... because she was white? Yes, Ginger, who's got two kids now, who quit school year before last. Parry's never going to finish either. What's she got to do with Carrie any more? They're going different places. Different places, different crowds. And they're sorting...."

"Now wait, Jeannie. Parry's just as bright, just as capable."

"They're in junior high, Mother. Don't you know about junior high? How they sort? And it's all where you're going. Yes and Parry's colored and Carrie's white. And you have to watch everything, what you wear and how you wear it and who you eat lunch with and how much homework you do and how you act to the teacher and what you laugh at.... And run with your crowd."

"It's that final?" asked Len. "Don't you think kids like Carol and Parry can show it doesn't *have* to be that way."

"They can't. They can't. They don't let you."

"No need to shout," he said mildly. "And who do you mean by 'they' and what do you mean by 'sorting'?"

How they sort. A foreboding of comprehension whirled within Helen. What was it Carol had told her of the Welcome Assembly the first day in junior high? The models showing How to Dress and How Not to Dress and half the girls in their loved new clothes watching their counterparts up on the stage—*their* straight skirt, *their* sweater, *their* earrings, lipstick, hairdo—"How Not to Dress," "a bad reputation for your school." It was nowhere in Carol's description, yet picturing it now, it seemed to Helen that a mute cry of violated dignity hung in the air. Later there had been a story of going to another Low 7 homeroom on an errand and seeing a teacher trying to wipe the forbidden lipstick off a girl who was fighting back and cursing. Helen could hear Carol's frightened, self-righteous tones: ".... and I hope they expel her; she's the kind that gives Franklin Jr. a bad rep; she doesn't care about anything and always gets into fights." Yet there was nothing in these incidents to touch the heavy comprehension that waited.... Homework, the wonderings those times Jeannie and Carol needed help: "What if there's no one at home to give the help, and the teachers with their two hundred and forty kids a day can't or don't or the kids don't ask and they fall hopelessly behind, what then?"—but this too was unrelated. And what had it been that time about Parry? "Mother, Melanie and Sharon won't go if they know Parry's coming." Then of course you'll go with Parry, she's been your friend longer, she had answered, but where was it they were going and what had finally happened? Len, my head hurts, she felt like saying, in Carol's voice in the car, but Len's eyes were grave on Jeannie who was saying passionately:

"If you think it's so goddam important why do we have to live here where it's for real; why don't we move to Ivy like Betsy (yes, I know, money), where it's the deal to be buddies, in school anyway, three coloured kids and their father's a doctor or judge or something big wheel and one always gets elected President or head song girl or something to prove oh how we're democratic.... What do you want of that poor kid anyway? Make up your mind. Stay friends with Parry—but be one of the kids. Sure. Be a brain—but not a square. Rise on up, college prep, but don't get separated. Yes, stay one of the kids but...."

"Jeannie. You're not talking about Carol at all, are you, Jeannie? Say it again. I wasn't listening. I was trying to think."

"She will not say it again," Len said firmly, "you look about ready to pull a Carol. One a day's our quota. And you, Jeannie, we'd better cool it. Too much to talk about for one session.... Here, come to the window and watch the Carol and Parry you're both all worked up about."

In the wind and the shimmering sunset light, half the children of the block are playing down the street. Leaping, bouncing, hallooing, tugging the kites of spring. In the old synchronized understanding, Carol and Parry kick, catch, kick, catch. And now Parry jumps on her pogo stick (the last time), Carol shadowing her, and Bubbie, arching his body in a semicircle of joy, bounding after them, high, higher, higher.

And the months go by and supposedly it is forgotten, except for the now and then when, self-important, Carol will say: I really truly did nearly faint, didn't I, Mother, that time I went to church with Parry?

And now seldom Parry and Carol walk the hill together. Melanie's mother drives by to pick up Carol, and the several times Helen has suggested Parry, too, Carol is quick to explain: "She's already left" or "She isn't ready; she'll make us late."

And after school? Carol is off to club or skating or library or someone's house, and Parry can stay for kickball only on the rare afternoons when she does not have to hurry home where Lucy, Bubbie, and the cousins wait to be cared for, now Alva works the four to twelve-thirty shift.

No more the bending together over the homework. All semester the teachers have been different, and rarely Parry brings her books home, for where is there space or time and what is the sense? And the phone never rings with: what you going to wear tomorrow, are you bringing your lunch, or come on over, let's design some clothes for Katy Keane comic-book contest. And Parry never drops by with Alva for Saturday snack to or from grocery shopping.

And the months go by and the sorting goes on and seemingly it is over until that morning when Helen must stay home from work, so swollen and feverish is Carol with mumps.

> *The afternoon before, Parry had come by, skimming up the stairs, spilling books and binders on the bed: Hey frail, lookahere and wail, your momma askin for homework, what she got against YOU? . . . looking quickly once then not looking again and talking fast. . . . Hey, you bloomed. You gonna be your own pumpkin, hallowe'en? Your momma know yet it's mu-umps? And lumps. Momma says: no distress, she'll be by tomorrow morning see do you need anything while your momma's to work. . . . (Singing:* whole lotta shakin going on.*) All your 'signments is inside; Miss Rockface says the teachers to write 'em cause I mightn't get it right all right.*
>
> *But did not tell: Does your mother work for Carol's mother? Oh, you're neighbors! Very well, I'll send along a monitor to open Carol's locker but you're only to take these things I'm writing down, nothing else. Now say after me: Miss Campbell is trusting me to be a good responsible girl. And go right to Carol's house. After school. Not stop anywhere on the way. Not lose anything. And only take. What's written on the list.*
>
> *You really gonna mess with that book stuff? Sign on mine says do-not-open-until-eX-mas. . . . That Mrs. Fernandez doll she didn't send nothin, she was the only, says feel better and read a book to report if you feel like and I'm the most for takin care for you; she's my most, wish I could get her but she only teaches 'celerated. . . . Flicking the old read books on the shelf but not opening to mock-declaim as once she used to . . . Vicky, Eddie's g.f. in Rockface office, she's on suspended for sure, yellin to Rockface: you bitch-kitty don't you give me no more bad shit. That Vicky she can sure sling-ating-ring it. Staring out the window as if the tree not there in which they had hid out and rocked so often. . . . For sure. (Keep mo-o-vin.) Got me a new pink top and lilac skirt. Look sharp with this purple? Cinching in the wide belt as if delighted with what newly swelled above and swelled below. Wear it Saturday night to Sweet's, Modernaires Sounds of Joy, Leroy and Ginny and me goin if Momma'll stay home. IF. (Shake my baby shake.) How come old folks still likes to party? Huh? Asking of Rembrandt's weary old face looking from the wall. How come (softly) you long-gone you. Touching her face to his quickly, lightly. NEXT mumps is your buddybud Melanie's turn to tote your stuff. I'm gettin the hoovus goovus. Hey you so unneat, don't care what you bed with. Removing the books and binders, ranging them on the dresser one by one, marking lipstick faces—bemused or mocking or amazed—on each paper jacket. Better. Fluffing out smoothing the quilt with exaggerated energy. Any little thing I can get, cause I gotta blow.*

Tossing up and catching their year-ago, arm-in-arm graduation picture, replacing it deftly, upside down, into its mirror crevice. Joe. Bring your joy juice or fizz water or kickapoo? Adding a frown line to one bookface. Twanging the paper fishkite, the Japanese windbell overhead, setting the mobile they had once made of painted eggshells and decorated straws to twirling and rocking. And is gone.

She talked to the lipstick faces after, in her fever, tried to stand on her head to match the picture, twirled and twanged with the violent overhead.

Sleeping at last after the disordered night. Having surrounded herself with the furnishings of that world of childhood she no sooner learned to live in comfortably, then had to leave.

The dollhouse stands there to arrange and rearrange; the shell and picture card collections to re-sort and remember; the population of dolls given away to little sister, borrowed back, propped all around to dress and undress and caress.

She has thrown off her nightgown because of the fever, and her just budding breast is exposed where she reaches to hold the floppy plush dog that had been her childhood pillow.

Not anything would Helen have disturbed her. Except that in the unaccustomedness of a morning at home, in the bruised restlessness after the sleepless night, she clicks on the radio—and the storm of singing whirls into the room:

> *. . . of trouble all mingled with fire*
> *Come on my brethern we've got to go higher*
> *Wade, wade. . . .*

And Carol runs down the stairs, shrieking and shrieking. "Turn it off, Mother, turn it off." Hurling herself at the dial and wrenching it so it comes off in her hand.

"Ohhhhh," choked and convulsive, while Helen tries to hold her, to quiet.

"Mother, why did they sing and scream like that?"

"At Parry's church?"

"Yes." Rocking and strangling the cries. "I hear it all the time." Clinging and beseeching. ". . . What was it, Mother? Why?"

Emotion, Helen thought of explaining, *a characteristic of the religion of all oppressed peoples, yes your very own great-grandparents*—thought of saying. And discarded.

Aren't you now, haven't you had feelings in yourself so strong they had to come out some way? ("what howls restrained by decorum")—thought of saying. And discarded.

Repeat Alva: *hope . . . every word out of their own life. A place to let go. And church is home.* And discarded.

The special history of the Negro people—history?—just you try living what must be lived every day—thought of saying. And discarded.

And said nothing.

And said nothing.

And soothed and held.

"Mother, a lot of the teachers and kids don't like Parry when they don't even know what she's like. Just because...." Rocking again, convulsive and shamed. "And I'm not really her friend any more."

No news. Betrayal and shame. Who betrayed? Whose shame? Brought herself to say aloud: "But may be friends again. As Alva and I are."

The sobbing a whisper. "That girl Vicky who got that way when I fainted, she's in school. She's the one keeps wearing lipstick and they wipe it off and she's always in trouble and now maybe she's expelled. Mother."

"Yes, lambie."

"She acts so awful outside but I remember how she was in church and whenever I see her now I have to wonder. And hear ... like I'm her, Mother, like I'm her." Clinging and trembling. "Oh why do I have to feel it happens to me too?

"Mother, I want to forget about it all, and not care,—like Melanie. Why can't I forget? Oh why is it like it is and why do I have to care?"

Caressing, quieting.

Thinking: *caring asks doing. It is a long baptism into the seas of humankind, my daughter. Better immersion than to live untouched.... Yet how will you sustain?*

Why is it like it is?

Sheltering her daughter close, mourning the illusion of the embrace.

And why do I have to care?

While in her, her own need leapt and plunged for the place of strength that was not—where one could scream or sorrow while all knew and accepted, and gloved and loving hands waiting to support and understand.

1956

BERNARD MALAMUD
1914–1986

Author of eight novels and numerous short stories, Bernard Malamud preferred to view himself as a universal writer who "happened to be Jewish, also American." Malamud's diverse subjects, varied readers, and prestigious national awards underscore his status as a major twentieth-century writer and a prominent American Jewish author.

Malamud consistently transformed the raw materials of his life into imaginative fiction. Born in 1914 to Max and Bertha Malamud, hardworking Russian Jews who ran a Brooklyn grocery (the setting for *The Assistant*), the author attended Erasmus High School, then received a B.A. from City College and an

M.A. from Columbia University. After teaching evenings in New York City high schools for several years, Malamud moved to Oregon with his wife, Ann, and their young son, Paul. For a decade he taught at Oregon State University in Corvallis, the subject of his academic satire, *A New Life*. During that period, he published some of his finest fiction: *The Natural*, an allegorical baseball story later made into a film, *The Assistant*, and *The Magic Barrel*, a short story collection that won the National Book Award.

In 1961 Malamud accepted a teaching position at Bennington College that allowed him to spend the warm months in Vermont and the winters in New York City. The move was also conducive to his writing. *The Fixer*, somewhat based on Russian persecution of Mendel Beiliss, a Jew, won both a National Book Award and a Pulitzer Prize. Within the next decade, Malamud published *Pictures of Fidelman*, a series of stories connected by an Italian setting and Jewish American protagonist, *The Tenants*, a bleak encounter between an African American and Jewish American writer, and *Rembrandt's Hat*, a short story collection. *Dubin's Lives*, which appeared in 1979, includes a variety of familiar settings (Vermont, New York, and Italy) as well as characters and themes.

Although his last completed novel, *God's Grace* (1982), is his gloomiest, with its post–nuclear war setting and cast of island primates, it contains a reflective, tormented Jew who struggles to understand and to control his grim environment. In fact, though the settings and situations of Malamud's works vary, his bumbling, suffering, at times comic, heroes resemble one another. Whether a Jewish grocer, college professor, novelist, artist, or fixer, or even an Italian assistant or a black angel, all are students of life who learn the importance of being human. In Malamud's fiction, a good Jew is a good man. Malamud's world is peopled with Jews and non-Jews in frequently surprising ways. In *The Fixer*, a Jewish spy betrays an embattled prisoner, while a Russian guard attempts to save him. In *The Assistant*, a Jew transforms a Gentile into a good person and therefore into a good Jew.

Though Malamud's fiction reflects his immigrant Jewish background and American experience, above all it reveals a unique imagination that can mingle history and fantasy, comedy and tragedy. A combination of such elements seems to characterize *The People*, the novel Malamud was composing when he died. In contrast to his more pessimistic later works, *The People*, published posthumously in 1989, unites a lonely Jewish immigrant with a needy Indian tribe in what promises to be a mutually beneficial association.

Even without *The People*, Malamud's legacy is enormous. A leader of the post–World War II Jewish literary renaissance, Malamud changed the landscape of American literature, introducing mainstream America to marginal ethnic characters, to immigrant urban settings, to Jewish American dialect, and most important, to a world with which Americans could empathize. Something of a magician, Malamud transformed the particular into the universal so that poor Jews symbolized all individuals struggling to survive with dignity and humanity.

Evelyn Avery
Towson University

PRIMARY WORKS

The Natural, 1952; *The Assistant*, 1957; *The Magic Barrel*, 1958; *A New Life*, 1961; *Idiots First*, 1963; *The Fixer*, 1966; *Pictures of Fidelman: An Exhibition*, 1969; *The Tenants*, 1971; *Rembrandt's Hat*, 1973; *Dubin's Lives*, 1979; *God's Grace*, 1982; *The Stories of Bernard Malamud*, 1984; *The People and Uncollected Stories*, 1989; *The Complete Stories of Bernard Malamud*, 1997.

The Magic Barrel

Not long ago there lived in uptown New York, in a small, almost meager room, though crowded with books, *Leo Finkle*, a rabbinical student at the Yeshiva University. Finkle, after six years of study, was to be ordained in June and had been advised by an acquaintance that he might find it easier to win himself a congregation if he were married. Since he had no present prospects of marriage, after two tormented days of turning it over in his mind, he called in Pinye Salzman, a marriage broker whose two-line advertisement he had read in the *Forward*.

The matchmaker appeared one night out of the dark fourth-floor hallway of the graystone rooming house where Finkle lived, grasping a black, strapped portfolio that had been worn thin with use. Salzman, who had been long in the business, was of slight but dignified build, wearing an old hat, and an overcoat too short and tight for him. He smelled frankly of fish, which he loved to eat, and although he was missing a few teeth, his presence was not displeasing, because of an amiable manner curiously contrasted with mournful eyes. His voice, his lips, his wisp of beard, his bony fingers were animated, but give him a moment of repose and his mild blue eyes revealed a depth of sadness, a characteristic that put Leo a little at ease although the situation, for him, was inherently tense.

He at once informed Salzman why he had asked him to come, explaining that but for his parents, who had married comparatively late in life, he was alone in the world. He had for six years devoted himself almost entirely to his studies, as a result of which, understandably, he had found himself without time for social life and the company of young women. Therefore he thought it the better part of trial and error—of embarrassing fumbling—to call in an experienced person to advise him on these matters. He remarked in passing that the function of the marriage broker was ancient and honorable, highly approved in the Jewish community, because it made practical the necessary without hindering joy. Moreover, his own parents had been brought together by a matchmaker. They had made, if not a financially profitable marriage—since neither had possessed any worldly goods to speak of—at least a successful one in the sense of their everlasting devotion to each other. Salzman listened in embarrassed surprise, sensing a sort of apology. Later, however, he experienced a glow of pride in his work, an emotion that had left him years ago, and he heartily approved of Finkle.

The two went to their business. Leo had led Salzman to the only clear place in the room, a table near a window that overlooked the lamp-lit city. He seated himself at the matchmaker's side but facing him, attempting by an act of will to suppress the unpleasant tickle in his throat. Salzman eagerly unstrapped his portfolio and removed a loose rubber band from a thin packet of much-handled cards. As he flipped through them, a gesture and sound that physically hurt Leo, the student pretended not to see and gazed steadfastly out the window. Although it was still February, winter was on its last legs, signs of which he had for the first time in years begun to notice. He now observed the round white moon, moving high in the sky through a cloud menagerie, and watched with half-open mouth as it penetrated a huge hen, and dropped out of her like an egg laying itself. Salzman, though pretending through eyeglasses he had just slipped on to be engaged in scanning the writing on the cards, stole occasional glances at the young man's distinguished face, noting with pleasure the long, severe scholar's nose, brown eyes heavy with learning, sensitive yet ascetic lips, and a certain almost hollow quality of the dark cheeks. He gazed around at shelves upon shelves of books and let out a soft, contented sigh.

When Leo's eyes fell upon the cards, he counted six spread out in Salzman's hand.

"So few?" he asked in disappointment.

"You wouldn't believe me how much cards I got in my office," Salzman replied. "The drawers are already filled to the top, so I keep them now in a barrel, but is every girl good for a new rabbi?"

Leo blushed at this, regretting all he had revealed of himself in a curriculum vitae he had sent to Salzman. He had thought it best to acquaint him with his strict standards and specifications, but in having done so, felt he had told the marriage broker more than was absolutely necessary.

He hesitantly inquired, "Do you keep photographs of your clients on file?"

"First comes family, amount of dowry, also what kind promises," Salzman replied, unbuttoning his tight coat and settling himself in the chair. "After comes pictures, rabbi."

"Call me Mr. Finkle. I'm not yet a rabbi."

Salzman said he would, but instead called him doctor, which he changed to rabbi when Leo was not listening too attentively.

Salzman adjusted his horn-rimmed spectacles, gently cleared his throat, and read in an eager voice the contents of the top card:

"Sophie P. Twenty-four years. Widow one year. No children. Educated high school and two years college. Father promises eight thousand dollars. Has wonderful wholesale business. Also real estate. On the mother's side comes teachers, also one actor. Well known on Second Avenue."

Leo gazed up in surprise. "Did you say a widow?"

"A widow don't mean spoiled, rabbi. She lived with her husband maybe four months. He was a sick boy she made a mistake to marry him."

"Marrying a widow has never entered my mind."

"This is because you have no experience. A widow, especially if she is young and healthy like this girl, is a wonderful person to marry. She will be thankful to you the rest of her life. Believe me, if I was looking now for a bride, I would marry a widow."

Leo reflected, then shook his head.

Salzman hunched his shoulders in an almost imperceptible gesture of disappointment. He placed the card down on the wooden table and began to read another:

"Lily H. High school teacher. Regular. Not a substitute. Has savings and new Dodge car. Lived in Paris one year. Father is successful dentist thirty-five years. Interested in professional man. Well-Americanized family. Wonderful opportunity.

"I know her personally," said Salzman. "I wish you could see this girl. She is a doll. Also very intelligent. All day you could talk to her about books and theyater and what not. She also knows current events."

"I don't believe you mentioned her age?"

"Her age?" Salzman said, raising his brows. "Her age is thirty-two years."

Leo said after a while, "I'm afraid that seems a little too old."

Salzman let out a laugh. "So how old are you, rabbi?"

"Twenty-seven."

"So what is the difference, tell me, between twenty-seven and thirty-two? My own wife is seven years older than me. So what did I suffer?—Nothing. If Rothschild's daughter wants to marry you, would you say on account her age, no?"

"Yes," Leo said dryly.

Salzman shook off the no in the yes. "Five years don't mean a thing. I give you my word that when you will live with her for one week you will forget her age. What does it mean five years—that she lived more and knows more than somebody who is younger? On this girl, God bless her, years are not wasted. Each one that it comes makes better the bargain."

"What subject does she teach in high school?"

"Languages. If you heard the way she speaks French, you will think it is music. I am in the business twenty-five years, and I recommend her with my whole heart. Believe me, I know what I'm talking, rabbi."

"What's on the next card?" Leo said abruptly.

Salzman reluctantly turned up the third card:

"Ruth K. Nineteen years. Honor student. Father offers thirteen thousand cash to the right bridegroom. He is a medical doctor. Stomach specialist with marvelous practice. Brother-in-law owns own garment business. Particular people."

Salzman looked as if he had read his trump card.

"Did you say nineteen?" Leo asked with interest.

"On the dot."

"Is she attractive?" He blushed. "Pretty?"

Salzman kissed his fingertips. "A little doll. On this I give you my word. Let me call the father tonight and you will see what means pretty."

But Leo was troubled. "You're sure she's that young?"

"This I am positive. The father will show you the birth certificate."

"Are you positive there isn't something wrong with her?" Leo insisted.

"Who says there is wrong?"

"I don't understand why an American girl her age should go to a marriage broker."

A smile spread over Salzman's face.

"So for the same reason you went, she comes."

Leo flushed. "I am pressed for time."

Salzman, realizing he had been tactless, quickly explained. "The father came, not her. He wants she should have the best, so he looks around himself. When we will locate the right boy he will introduce him and encourage. This makes a better marriage than if a young girl without experience takes for herself. I don't have to tell you this."

"But don't you think this young girl believes in love?" Leo spoke uneasily.

Salzman was about to guffaw but caught himself and said soberly, "Love comes with the right person, not before."

Leo parted dry lips but did not speak. Noticing that Salzman had snatched a glance at the next card, he cleverly asked, "How is her health?"

"Perfect," Salzman said, breathing with difficulty. "Of course, she is a little lame on her right foot from an auto accident that it happened to her when she was twelve years, but nobody notices on account she is so brilliant and also beautiful."

Leo got up heavily and went to the window. He felt curiously bitter and upbraided himself for having called in the marriage broker. Finally, he shook his head.

"Why not?" Salzman persisted, the pitch of his voice rising.

"Because I detest stomach specialists."

"So what do you care what is his business? After you marry her do you need him? Who says he must come every Friday night in your house?"

Ashamed of the way the talk was going, Leo dismissed Salzman, who went home with heavy, melancholy eyes.

Though he had felt only relief at the marriage broker's departure, Leo was in low spirits the next day. He explained it as arising from Salzman's failure to produce a suitable bride for him. He did not care for his type of clientele. But when Leo found himself hesitating whether to seek out another matchmaker, one more polished than Pinye, he wondered if it could be—his protestations to the contrary, and although he honored his father and mother—that he did not, in essence, care for the matchmaking institution? This thought he quickly put out of mind yet found himself still upset. All day he ran around in the woods—missed an important appointment, forgot to give out his laundry, walked out of a Broadway cafeteria without paying and had to run back with the ticket in his hand; had even not recognized his landlady in the street when she passed with a friend and courteously called out, "A good evening to you, Doctor Finkle." By nightfall, however, he had regained sufficient calm to sink his nose into a book and there found peace from his thoughts.

Almost at once there came a knock on the door. Before Leo could say enter, Salzman, commercial cupid, was standing in the room. His face was gray and meager, his expression hungry, and he looked as if he would expire on his feet. Yet the marriage broker managed, by some trick of the muscles, to display a broad smile.

"So good evening. I am invited?"

Leo nodded, disturbed to see him again, yet unwilling to ask the man to leave.

Beaming still, Salzman laid his portfolio on the table. "Rabbi, I got for you tonight good news."

"I've asked you not to call me rabbi. I'm still a student."

"Your worries are finished. I have for you a first-class bride."

"Leave me in peace concerning this subject." Leo pretended lack of interest.

"The world will dance at your wedding."

"Please, Mr. Salzman, no more."

"But first must come back my strength," Salzman said weakly. He fumbled with the portfolio straps and took out of the leather case an oily paper bag, from which he extracted a hard, seeded roll and a small smoked whitefish. With a quick motion of his hand he stripped the fish out of its skin and began ravenously to chew. "All day in a rush," he muttered.

Leo watched him eat.

"A sliced tomato you have maybe?" Salzman hesitantly inquired.

"No."

The marriage broker shut his eyes and ate. When he had finished he carefully cleaned up the crumbs and rolled up the remains of the fish, in the paper bag. His spectacled eyes roamed the room until he discovered, amid some piles of books, a one-burner gas stove. Lifting his hat he humbly asked, "A glass tea you got, rabbi?"

Conscience-stricken, Leo rose and brewed the tea. He served it with a chunk of lemon and two cubes of lump sugar, delighting Salzman.

After he had drunk his tea, Salzman's strength and good spirits were restored.

"So tell me, rabbi," he said amiably, "you considered some more the three clients I mentioned yesterday?"

"There was no need to consider."

"Why not?"

"None of them suits me."

"What then suits you?"

Leo let it pass because he could give only a confused answer.

Without waiting for a reply, Salzman asked, "You remember this girl I talked to you—the high school teacher?"

"Age thirty-two?"

But, surprisingly, Salzman's face lit in a smile. "Age twenty-nine."

Leo shot him a look. "Reduced from thirty-two?"

"A mistake," Salzman avowed. "I talked today with the dentist. He took me to his safety deposit box and showed me the birth certificate. She was twenty-nine years last August. They made her a party in the mountains where she went for her vacation. When her father spoke to me the first time I forgot to write the age and I told you thirty-two, but now I remember this was a different client, a widow."

"The same one you told me about, I thought she was twenty-four?"

"A different. Am I responsible that the world is filled with widows?"

"No, but I'm not interested in them, nor, for that matter, in school-teachers."

Salzman pulled his clasped hands to his breast. Looking at the ceiling he devoutly exclaimed, "Yiddishe kinder, what can I say to somebody that he is not interested in high school teachers? So what then you are interested?"

Leo flushed but controlled himself.

"In what else will you be interested," Salzman went on, "if you not inter-ested in this fine girl that she speaks four languages and has personally in the bank ten thousand dollars? Also her father guarantees further twelve thousand. Also she has a new car, wonderful clothes, talks on all subjects, and she will give you a first-class home and children. How near do we come in our life to paradise?"

"If she's so wonderful, why wasn't she married ten years ago?"

"Why?" said Salzman with a heavy laugh. "—Why? Because she is *parti-kiler*. This is why. She wants the *best*."

Leo was silent, amused at how he had entangled himself. But Salzman had aroused his interest in Lily H., and he began seriously to consider calling on her. When the marriage broker observed how intently Leo's mind was at work on the facts he had supplied, he felt certain they would soon come to an agreement.

Late Saturday afternoon, conscious of Salzman, Leo Finkle walked with Lily Hirschorn along Riverside Drive. He walked briskly and erectly, wearing with distinction the black fedora he had that morning taken with trepidation out of the dusty hat box on his closet shelf, and the heavy black Saturday coat he had thoroughly whisked clean. Leo also owned a walking stick, a present from a distant relative, but quickly put temptation aside and did not use it. Lily, petite and not unpretty, had on something signifying the approach of spring. She was au courant, animatedly, with all sorts of subjects, and he weighed her words and found her surprisingly sound—score another for Salz-man, whom he uneasily sensed to be somewhere around, hiding perhaps high in a tree along the street, flashing the lady signals with a pocket mirror; or perhaps a cloven-hoofed Pan, piping nuptial ditties as he danced his invisible way before them, strewing wild buds on the walk and purple grapes in their path, symbolizing fruit of a union, though there was of course still none.

Lily startled Leo by remarking, "I was thinking of Mr. Salzman, a curious figure, wouldn't you say?"

Not certain what to answer, he nodded.

She bravely went on, blushing, "I for one am grateful for his introducing us. Aren't you?"

He courteously replied, "I am."

"I mean," she said with a little laugh—and it was all in good taste, or at least gave the effect of being not in bad—"do you mind that we came together so?"

He was not displeased with her honesty, recognizing that she meant to set the relationship aright, and understanding that it took a certain amount of experience in life, and courage, to want to do it quite that way. One had to have some sort of past to make that kind of beginning.

He said that he did not mind. Salzman's function was traditional and honorable—valuable for what it might achieve, which, he pointed out, was frequently nothing.

Lily agreed with a sigh. They walked on for a while and she said after a long silence, again with a nervous laugh, "Would you mind if I asked you something a little bit personal? Frankly, I find the subject fascinating." Although Leo shrugged, she went on half embarrassedly, "How was it that you came to your calling? I mean, was it a sudden passionate inspiration?"

Leo, after a time, slowly replied, "I was always interested in the Law."

"You saw revealed in it the presence of the Highest?"

He nodded and changed the subject. "I understand that you spent a little time in Paris, Miss Hirschorn?"

"Oh, did Mr. Salzman tell you, Rabbi Finkle?" Leo winced but she went on, "It was ages ago and almost forgotten. I remember I had to return for my sister's wedding."

And Lily would not be put off. "When," she asked in a slightly trembly voice, "did you become enamored of God?"

He stared at her. Then it came to him that she was talking not about Leo Finkle but a total stranger, some mystical figure, perhaps even passionate prophet that Salzman had dreamed up for her—no relation to the living or dead. Leo trembled with rage and weakness. The trickster had obviously sold her a bill of goods, just as he had him, who'd expected to become acquainted with a young lady of twenty-nine, only to behold, the moment he had laid eyes upon her strained and anxious face, a woman past thirty-five and aging rapidly. Only his self-control had kept him this long in her presence.

"I am not," he said gravely, "a talented religious person," and in seeking words to go on, found himself possessed by shame and fear. "I think," he said in a strained manner, "that I came to God not because I loved Him but because I did not."

This confession he spoke harshly because its unexpectedness shook him.

Lily wilted. Leo saw a profusion of loaves of bread go flying like ducks high over his head, not unlike the winged loaves by which he had counted himself to sleep last night. Mercifully, then, it snowed, which he would not put past Salzman's machinations.

He was infuriated with the marriage broker and swore he would throw him out of the room the moment he reappeared. But Salzman did not come that night, and when Leo's anger had subsided, an unaccountable despair grew in its place. At first he thought this was caused by his disappointment in Lily, but before long it became evident that he had involved himself with Salzman without a true knowledge of his own intent. He gradually realized—with an emptiness that seized him with six hands—that he had called in the broker to find him a bride because he was incapable of doing it himself. This terrifying insight he had derived as a result of his meeting and conversation with Lily Hirschorn. Her probing questions had somehow irritated him into revealing—to himself more than her—the true nature of his relationship to God, and from that it had come upon him, with shocking force, that apart from his parents, he had never loved anyone. Or perhaps it went the other way, that he did not love God so well as he might, because he had not loved man. It seemed to Leo that his whole life stood starkly revealed and he saw himself for the first time as he truly was—unloved and loveless. This bitter but somehow not fully unexpected revelation brought him to a point of panic, controlled only by extraordinary effort. He covered his face with his hands and cried.

The week that followed was the worst of his life. He did not eat and lost weight. His beard darkened and grew ragged. He stopped attending seminars and almost never opened a book. He seriously considered leaving the Yeshiva, although he was deeply troubled at the thought of the loss of all his years of study—saw them like pages torn from a book, strewn over the city—and at the devastating effect of this decision upon his parents. But he had lived without knowledge of himself, and never in the Five Books and all the Commentaries—mea culpa—had the truth been revealed to him. He did not know where to turn, and in all this desolating loneliness there was no *to whom*, although he often thought of Lily but not once could bring himself to go downstairs and make the call. He became touchy and irritable, especially with his landlady, who asked him all manner of personal questions; on the other hand, sensing his own disagreeableness, he waylaid her on the stairs and apologized abjectly, until, mortified, she ran from him. Out of this, however, he drew the consolation that he was a Jew and that a Jew suffered. But gradually, as the long and terrible week drew to a close, he regained his composure and some idea of purpose in life: to go on as planned. Although he was imperfect, the ideal was not. As for his quest of a bride, the thought of continuing afflicted him with anxiety and heartburn, yet perhaps with this new knowledge of himself he would be more successful than in the past. Perhaps love would now come to him and a bride to that love. And for this sanctified seeking who needed a Salzman?

The marriage broker, a skeleton with haunted eyes, returned that very night. He looked, withal, the picture of frustrated expectancy—as if he had steadfastly waited the week at Miss Lily Hirschorn's side for a telephone call that never came.

Casually coughing, Salzman came immediately to the point: "So how did you like her?"

Leo's anger rose and he could not refrain from chiding the matchmaker: "Why did you lie to me, Salzman?"

Salzman's pale face went dead white, the world had snowed on him.

"Did you not state that she was twenty-nine?" Leo insisted.

"I give you my word—"

"She was thirty-five, if a day. *At least* thirty-five."

"Of this don't be too sure. Her father told me—"

"Never mind. The worst of it is that you lied to her."

"How did I lie to her, tell me?"

"You told her things about me that weren't true. You made me out to be more, consequently less than I am. She had in mind a totally different person, a sort of semi-mystical Wonder Rabbi."

"All I said, you was a religious man."

"I can imagine."

Salzman sighed. "This is my weakness that I have," he confessed. "My wife says to me I shouldn't be a salesman, but when I have two fine people that they would be wonderful to be married, I am so happy that I talk too much." He smiled wanly. "This is why Salzman is a poor man."

Leo's anger left him. "Well, Salzman, I'm afraid that's all."

The marriage broker fastened hungry eyes on him.

"You don't want any more a bride?"

"I do," said Leo, "but I have decided to seek her in another way. I am no longer interested in an arranged marriage. To be frank, I now admit the necessity of premarital love. That is, I want to be in love with the one I marry."

"Love?" said Salzman, astounded. After a moment he remarked, "For us, our love is our life, not for the ladies. In the ghetto they—"

"I know, I know," said Leo. "I've thought of it often. Love, I have said to myself, should be a product of living and worship rather than its own end. Yet for myself I find it necessary to establish the level of my need and fulfill it."

Salzman shrugged but answered, "Listen, rabbi, if you want love, this I can find for you also. I have such beautiful clients that you will love them the minute your eyes will see them."

Leo smiled unhappily. "I'm afraid you don't understand."

But Salzman hastily unstrapped his portfolio and withdrew a manila packet from it.

"Pictures," he said, quickly laying the envelope on the table.

Leo called after him to take the pictures away, but as if on the wings of the wind, Salzman had disappeared.

March came. Leo had returned to his regular routine. Although he felt not quite himself yet—lacked energy—he was making plans for a more active social life. Of course it would cost something, but he was an expert in cutting corners; and when there were no corners left he would make circles rounder. All the while Salzman's pictures had lain on the table, gathering dust. Occasionally as Leo sat studying, or enjoying a cup of tea, his eyes fell on the manila envelope, but he never opened it.

The days went by and no social life to speak of developed with a member of the opposite sex—it was difficult, given the circumstances of his situation. One morning Leo toiled up the stairs to his room and stared out the window at the city. Although the day was bright his view of it was dark. For some time he watched the people in the street below hurrying along and then turned with a heavy heart to his little room. On the table was the packet. With a sudden relentless gesture he tore it open. For a half hour he stood by the table in a state of excitement, examining the photographs of the ladies Salzman had included. Finally, with a deep sigh he put them down. There were six, of varying degrees of attractiveness, but look at them long enough and they all became Lily Hirschorn: all past their prime, all starved behind bright smiles, not a true personality in the lot. Life, despite their frantic yoo-hooings, had passed them by; they were pictures in a briefcase that stank of fish. After a while, however, as Leo attempted to return the photographs into the envelope, he found in it another, a snapshot of the type taken by a machine for a quarter. He gazed at it a moment and let out a low cry.

Her face deeply moved him. Why, he could at first not say. It gave him the impression of youth—spring flowers, yet age—a sense of having been used to the bone, wasted; this came from the eyes, which were hauntingly familiar, yet absolutely strange. He had a vivid impression that he had met her before, but try as he might he could not place her although he could almost recall her name, as if he had read it in her own handwriting. No, this couldn't be; he would have remembered her. It was not, he affirmed, that she had an extraordinary beauty—no, though her face was attractive enough; it was that *something* about her moved him. Feature for feature, even some of the ladies of the photographs could do better; but she leaped forth to his heart—had *lived*, or wanted to—more than just wanted, perhaps regretted how she had lived—had somehow deeply suffered: it could be seen in the depths of those reluctant eyes, and from the way the light enclosed and shone from her, and within her, opening realms of possibility: this was her own. Her he desired. His head ached and eyes narrowed with the intensity of his gazing, then as if an obscure fog had blown up in the mind, he experienced fear of her and was aware that he had received an impression, somehow, of evil. He shuddered, saying softly, it is thus with us all. Leo brewed some tea in a small pot and sat sipping it without sugar, to calm himself. But before he had finished drinking, again with excitement he examined the face and found it good: good for Leo Finkle. Only such a one could understand him and help him seek whatever he was seeking. She might, perhaps, love him. How she had happened to be among the discards in Salzman's barrel he could never guess, but he knew he must urgently go find her.

Leo rushed downstairs, grabbed up the Bronx telephone book, and searched for Salzman's home address. He was not listed, nor was his office. Neither was he in the Manhattan book. But Leo remembered having written down the address on a slip of paper after he had read Salzman's advertisement in the "personals" column of the *Forward*. He ran up to his room and tore through his papers, without luck. It was exasperating. Just when he needed the matchmaker he was nowhere to be found. Fortunately Leo remembered to look in his wallet. There on a card he found his name written and a Bronx address. No phone number was listed, the reason—Leo now recalled—he had originally communicated with Salzman by letter. He got on his coat, put a hat on over his skullcap and hurried to the subway station. All the way to the far end of the Bronx he sat on the edge of his seat. He was more than once tempted to take out the picture and see if the girl's face was as he remembered, but he refrained, allowing the snapshot to remain in his inside coat pocket, content to have her so close. When the train pulled into the station he was waiting at the door and bolted out. He quickly located the street Salzman had advertised.

The building he sought was less than a block from the subway, but it was not an office building, nor even a loft, nor a store in which one could rent office space. It was a very old tenement house. Leo found Salzman's name in pencil on a soiled tag under the bell and climbed three dark flights to his apartment. When he knocked, the door was opened by a thin, asthmatic, gray-haired woman, in felt slippers.

"Yes?" she said, expecting nothing. She listened without listening. He could have sworn he had seen her, too, before but knew it was an illusion.

"Salzman—does he live here? Pinye Salzman," he said, "the matchmaker?"

She stared at him a long minute. "Of course."

He felt embarrassed. "Is he in?"

"No." Her mouth, though left open, offered nothing more.

"The matter is urgent. Can you tell me where his office is?"

"In the air." She pointed upward.

"You mean he has no office?" Leo asked.

"In his socks."

He peered into the apartment. It was sunless and dingy, one large room divided by a half-open curtain, beyond which he could see a sagging metal bed. The near side of the room was crowded with rickety chairs, old bureaus, a three-legged table, racks of cooking utensils, and all the apparatus of a kitchen. But there was no sign of Salzman or his magic barrel, probably also a figment of the imagination. An odor of frying fish made Leo weak to the knees.

"Where is he?" he insisted. "I've got to see your husband."

At length she answered, "So who knows where he is? Every time he thinks a new thought he runs to a different place. Go home, he will find you."

"Tell him Leo Finkle."

She gave no sign she had heard.

He walked downstairs, depressed.

But Salzman, breathless, stood waiting at his door.

Leo was astounded and overjoyed. "How did you get here before me?"

"I rushed."

"Come inside."

They entered. Leo fixed tea, and a sardine sandwich for Salzman. As they were drinking he reached behind him for the packet of pictures and handed them to the marriage broker.

Salzman put down his glass and said expectantly, "You found somebody you like?"

"Not among these."

The marriage broker turned away.

"Here is the one I want." Leo held forth the snapshot.

Salzman slipped on his glasses and took the picture into his trembling hand. He turned ghastly and let out a groan.

"What's the matter?" cried Leo.

"Excuse me. Was an accident this picture. She isn't for you."

Salzman frantically shoved the manila packet into his portfolio. He thrust the snapshot into his pocket and fled down the stairs.

Leo, after momentary paralysis, gave chase and cornered the marriage broker in the vestibule. The landlady made hysterical outcries but neither of them listened.

"Give me back the picture, Salzman."

"No." The pain in his eyes was terrible.

"Tell me who she is then."

"This I can't tell you. Excuse me."

He made to depart, but Leo, forgetting himself, seized the matchmaker by his tight coat and shook him frenziedly.

"Please," sighed Salzman. "*Please.*"

Leo ashamedly let him go. "Tell me who she is," he begged. "It's very important for me to know."

"She is not for you. She is a wild one—wild, without shame. This is not a bride for a rabbi."

"What do you mean wild?"

"Like an animal. Like a dog. For her to be poor was a sin. This is why to me she is dead now."

"In God's name, what do you mean?"

"Her I can't introduce to you," Salzman cried.

"Why are you so excited?"

"Why, he asks," Salzman said, bursting into tears. "This is my baby, my Stella, she should burn in hell."

Leo hurried up to bed and hid under the covers. Under the covers he thought his life through. Although he soon fell asleep he could not sleep her out of his mind. He woke, beating his breast. Though he prayed to be rid of her, his prayers went unanswered. Through days of torment he endlessly struggled not to love her; fearing success, he escaped it. He then concluded to convert her to goodness, himself to God. The idea alternately nauseated and exalted him.

He perhaps did not know that he had come to a final decision until he encountered Salzman in a Broadway cafeteria. He was sitting alone at a rear table, sucking the bony remains of a fish. The marriage broker appeared haggard, and transparent to the point of vanishing.

Salzman looked up at first without recognizing him. Leo had grown a pointed beard and his eyes were weighted with wisdom.

"Salzman," he said, "love has at last come to my heart."

"Who can love from a picture?" mocked the marriage broker.

"It is not impossible."

"If you can love her, then you can love anybody. Let me show you some new clients that they just sent me their photographs. One is a little doll."

"Just her I want," Leo murmured.

"Don't be a fool, doctor. Don't bother with her."

"Put me in touch with her, Salzman," Leo said humbly. "Perhaps I can be of service."

Salzman had stopped eating and Leo understood with emotion that it was now arranged.

Leaving the cafeteria, he was, however, afflicted by a tormenting suspicion that Salzman had planned it all to happen this way.

Leo was informed by letter that she would meet him on a certain corner, and she was there one spring night, waiting under a street lamp. He appeared, carrying a small bouquet of violets and rosebuds. Stella stood by the lamppost, smoking. She wore white with red shoes, which fitted his expectations, although in a troubled moment he had imagined the dress red, and only the shoes white. She waited uneasily and shyly. From afar he saw that her eyes—clearly her father's—were filled with desperate innocence. He pictured, in her, his own redemption. Violins and lit candles revolved in the sky. Leo ran forward with flowers outthrust.

Around the corner, Salzman, leaning against a wall, chanted prayers for the dead.

1958

ARTHUR MILLER
1915–2005

Until the age of fourteen, Arthur Miller lived on East 112th Street in Harlem, New York, the son of a prosperous manufacturer of women's coats. With the Depression, his father lost his business, and the family moved to a small but comfortable house in Brooklyn. Miller attended Abraham Lincoln High School, where he played football, sustaining a knee injury. Following graduation, he worked at various odd jobs ranging from singer on a local radio station to truck driver to clerk in an automobile parts warehouse. He saved his pay for two years to attend college but was unable to enroll because of poor grades in high school. On the long daily subway ride into Manhattan from Brooklyn, he began reading *The Brothers Karamazov* (which he thought was a detective story), the book that he later referred to as "the great book of wonder" and that presumably aroused his interest in serious literature.

After two attempts, in 1934 Miller finally was admitted to the University of Michigan in Ann Arbor, where he became a journalism major, working his way through college by waiting tables, feeding mice in the university laboratories, and gaining experience as a reporter and night editor of the student newspaper. During the spring of 1936, he wrote a play, *No Villain*, that won a Hopwood Award in Drama, an annual contest that carried an award of $250. Transferring his degree program to English, Miller began to study plays eagerly and revised *No Villain* for the Theatre Guild's Bureau of New Plays Contest with a new title, *They Too Arise*. In 1937 Miller enrolled in a playwriting class taught by Kenneth T. Rowe; that year *They Too Arise* received a major award of $1,250 from the Bureau of New Plays and was produced in Ann Arbor and Detroit. In June his second Hopwood entry earned him another $250 award, and Miller decided that playwriting was his future. After narrowly missing winning a third Hopwood Award for *The Great Disobedience*, Miller graduated in 1938 and returned to Brooklyn.

Over the next six years, Miller wrote radio plays and scripts while continuing to look for a play producer. In 1944 his first Broadway play, *The Man Who Had All the Luck*, opened—but closed after four performances. Two years later, Miller appeared on Broadway again with *All My Sons*, a play that, like most of his major dramas, explores relationships between family members, often between fathers, sons, and brothers. *All My Sons* won the New York Drama Critics' Circle Award. In 1945 Miller published a novel, *Focus*, that dealt with anti-Semitism. In 1949 *Death of a Salesman* was produced at the Morosco Theater in New York and firmly established its author as a major American playwright. The play won the Pulitzer Prize, the New York Drama Critics' Circle Award, the Antoinette Perry (Tony) Award, the Theater Club Award, and the Donaldson Award, among many others. As a study of the American character and culture, it remains one of the most definitive stage works of all time.

Because his dramatic themes and interests have always been closely related to what's "in the air," Miller has been described as a "social dramatist," but his plays range widely and experimentally in theme, form, and content. *The Crucible* (1953), *A View from the Bridge* (1956, two-act version), his film script for *The Misfits* (1960, now a classic film), *After the Fall* (1964, a dramatic representation of his family, political troubles, and marriage to Marilyn Monroe), *The Price* (1968), *The Archbishop's Ceiling* (1977), and *The American Clock* (1984), among others, deal directly or indirectly with the family, the 1930s Depression, politics, and the American dream.

Robert A. Martin
Michigan State University

PRIMARY WORKS

The Golden Years, 1939; *The Man Who Had All the Luck*, 1944; *Focus*, 1945; *All My Sons*, 1947; *Death of a Salesman*, 1949; *The Crucible*, 1953; *A View from the Bridge*, 1955; *Arthur Miller's Collected Plays*, 1957; *The Misfits*, 1961; *After the Fall*, 1964; *Incident at Vichy*, 1964; *I Don't Need You Any More*, 1967; *The Price*, 1968; *The Creation of the World and Other Business*, 1972; *The Theater Essays of Arthur Miller*, 1978; *Playing for Time*, 1980; *The American Clock*, 1983; *The Archbishop's Ceiling*, 1984; *The Two-Way Mirror* (*Elegy for a Lady* and *Some Kind of Love Story*), 1984; *Danger: Memory* (*I Can't Remember Anything* and *Clara*), 1986; *Timebends: A Life*, 1987; *The Ride down Mt. Morgan*, 1991; *The Last Yankee*, 1993; *Broken Glass*, 1994; *Mr. Peters' Connections*, 1998; *Resurrection Blues*, 2002; *Finishing the Picture*, 2004.

A View from the Bridge

A Play in Two Acts

THE CHARACTERS:

LOUIS	RODOLPHO
MIKE	FIRST IMMIGRATION OFFICER
ALFIERI	SECOND IMMIGRATION OFFICER
EDDIE	MR. LIPARI
CATHERINE	MRS. LIPARI
BEATRICE	TWO "SUBMARINES"
MARCO	NEIGHBORS
TONY	

ACT ONE

The street and house front of a tenement building. The front is skeletal entirely. The main acting area is the living room–dining room of Eddie's apartment. It is a worker's flat, clean, sparse, homely. There is a rocker down front; a round dining table at center, with chairs; and a portable phonograph.

At back are a bedroom door and an opening to the kitchen; none of these interiors are seen.

At the right, forestage, a desk. This is Mr. Alfieri's law office.

There is also a telephone booth. This is not used until the last scenes, so it may be covered or left in view.

A stairway leads up to the apartment, and then farther up to the next story, which is not seen.

Ramps, representing the street, run upstage and off to right and left.

As the curtain rises, Louis and Mike, longshoremen, are pitching coins against the building at left.

A distant foghorn blows.

Enter Alfieri, a lawyer in his fifties turning gray; he is portly, good-humored, and thoughtful. The two pitchers nod to him as he passes. He crosses the stage to his desk, removes his hat, runs his fingers through his hair, and grinning, speaks to the audience.

ALFIERI: You wouldn't have known it, but something amusing has just happened. You see how uneasily they nod to me? That's because I am a lawyer. In this neighborhood to meet a lawyer or a priest on the street is unlucky. We're only thought of in connection with disasters, and they'd rather not get too close.

I often think that behind that suspicious little nod of theirs lie three thousand years of distrust. A lawyer means the law, and in Sicily, from where their fathers came, the law has not been a friendly idea since the Greeks were beaten.

I am inclined to notice the ruins in things, perhaps because I was born in Italy.... I only came here when I was twenty-five. In those days, Al Capone, the greatest Carthaginian of all, was learning his trade on these pavements, and Frankie Yale himself was cut precisely in half by a machine gun on the corner of Union Street, two blocks away. Oh, there were many here who were justly shot by unjust men. Justice is very important here.

But this is Red Hook, not Sicily. This is the slum that faces the bay on the seaward side of Brooklyn Bridge. This is the gullet of New York swallowing the tonnage of the world. And now we are quite civilized, quite American. Now we settle for half, and I like it better. I no longer keep a pistol in my filing cabinet.

And my practice is entirely unromantic.

My wife has warned me, so have my friends; they tell me the people in this neighborhood lack elegance, glamour. After all, who have I dealt with in my life? Longshoremen and their wives, and fathers and grandfathers, compensation cases, evictions, family squabbles—the petty troubles of the poor—and yet ... every few years there is still a case, and as the parties tell me what the trouble is, the flat air in my office suddenly washes in with the green scent of the sea, the dust in this air is blown away and the thought comes that in some Caesar's year, in Calabria perhaps or on the cliff at Syracuse, another lawyer, quite differently dressed, heard the same complaint and sat there as powerless as I, and watched it run its bloody course.

Eddie has appeared and has been pitching coins with the men and is highlighted among them. He is forty—a husky, slightly overweight longshoreman.

This one's name was Eddie Carbone, a longshoreman working the docks from Brooklyn Bridge to the breakwater where the open sea begins.

Alfieri walks into darkness.

EDDIE, *moving up steps into doorway:* Well, I'll see ya, fellas.

Catherine enters from kitchen, crosses down to window, looks out.

LOUIS: You workin' tomorrow?

EDDIE: Yeah, there's another day yet on that ship. See ya, Louis.

Eddie goes into the house, as light rises in the apartment.
Catherine is waving to Louis from the window and turns to him.

CATHERINE: Hi, Eddie!

Eddie is pleased and therefore shy about it; he hangs up his cap and jacket.

EDDIE: Where you goin' all dressed up?

CATHERINE: *running her hands over her skirt:* I just got it. You like it?

EDDIE: Yeah, it's nice. And what happened to your hair?

CATHERINE: You like it? I fixed it different. *Calling to kitchen:* He's here, B.!

EDDIE: Beautiful. Turn around, lemme see in the back. *She turns for him.* Oh, if your mother was alive to see you now! She wouldn't believe it.

CATHERINE: You like it, huh?

EDDIE: You look like one of them girls that went to college. Where you goin'?

CATHERINE, *taking his arm:* Wait'll B. comes in, I'll tell you something. Here, sit down. *She is walking him to the armchair. Calling offstage:* Hurry up, will you, B.?

EDDIE, *sitting:* What's goin' on?

CATHERINE: I'll get you a beer, all right?

EDDIE: Well, tell me what happened. Come over here, talk to me.

CATHERINE: I want to wait till B. comes in. *She sits on her heels beside him.* Guess how much we paid for the skirt.

EDDIE: I think it's too short, ain't it?

CATHERINE, *standing:* No! not when I stand up.

EDDIE: Yeah, but you gotta sit down sometimes.

CATHERINE: Eddie, it's the style now. *She walks to show him.* I mean, if you see me walkin' down the street—

EDDIE: Listen, you been givin' me the willies the way you walk down the street, I mean it.

CATHERINE: Why?

EDDIE: Catherine, I don't want to be a pest, but I'm tellin' you you're walkin' wavy.

CATHERINE: I'm walkin' wavy?

EDDIE: Now don't aggravate me, Katie, you are walkin' wavy! I don't like the looks they're givin you in the candy store. And with them new high heels on the sidewalk—clack, clack, clack. The heads are turnin' like windmills.

CATHERINE: But those guys look at all the girls, you know that.

EDDIE: You ain't "all the girls."

CATHERINE, *almost in tears because he disapproves:* What do you want me to do? You want me to—

EDDIE: Now don't get mad, kid.

CATHERINE: Well, I don't know what you want from me.

EDDIE: Katie, I promised your mother on her deathbed. I'm responsible for you. You're a baby, you don't understand these things. I mean like when you stand here by the window, wavin' outside.

CATHERINE: I was wavin' to Louis!

EDDIE: Listen, I could tell you things about Louis which you wouldn't wave to him no more.

CATHERINE, *trying to joke him out of his warning:* Eddie, I wish there was one guy you couldn't tell me things about!

EDDIE: Catherine, do me a favor, will you? You're gettin' to be a big girl now, you gotta keep yourself more, you can't be so friendly, kid. *Calls:* Hey, B., what're you doin' in there? *To Catherine:* Get her in here, will you? I got news for her.

CATHERINE, *starting out:* What?

EDDIE: Her cousins landed.

CATHERINE, *clapping her hands together:* No! *She turns instantly and starts for the kitchen.* B.! Your cousins!

Beatrice enters, wiping her hands with a towel.

BEATRICE, *in the face of Catherine's shout:* What?

CATHERINE: Your cousins got in!

BEATRICE, *astounded, turns to Eddie:* What are you talkin' about? Where?

EDDIE: I was just knockin' off work before and Tony Bereli come over to me; he says the ship is in the North River.

BEATRICE—*her hands are clasped at her breast; she seems half in fear, half in unutterable joy:* They're all right?

EDDIE: He didn't see them yet, they're still on board. But as soon as they get off he'll meet them. He figures about ten o'clock they'll be here.

BEATRICE *sits, almost weak from tension:* And they'll let them off the ship all right? That's fixed, heh?

EDDIE: Sure, they give them regular seamen papers and they walk off with the crew. Don't worry about it, B., there's nothin' to it. Couple of hours they'll be here.

BEATRICE: What happened? They wasn't supposed to be till next Thursday.

EDDIE: I don't know; they put them on any ship they can get them out on. Maybe the other ship they was supposed to take there was some danger—What you cryin' about?

BEATRICE, *astounded and afraid:* I'm—I just—I can't believe it! I didn't even buy a new table cloth; I was gonna wash the walls—

EDDIE: Listen, they'll think it's a millionaire's house compared to the way they live. Don't worry about the walls. They'll be thankful. *To Catherine:* Whyn't you run down buy a table cloth. Go ahead, here. *He is reaching into his pocket.*

CATHERINE: There's no stores open now.

EDDIE, *to Beatrice:* You was gonna put a new cover on the chair.

BEATRICE: I know—well, I thought it was gonna be next week! I was gonna clean the walls, I was gonna wax the floors. *She stands disturbed.*

CATHERINE, *pointing upward:* Maybe Mrs. Dondero upstairs—

BEATRICE, *of the table cloth:* No, hers is worse than this one. *Suddenly:* My God, I don't even have nothin' to eat for them! *She starts for the kitchen.*

EDDIE, *reaching out and grabbing her arm:* Hey, hey! Take it easy.

BEATRICE: No, I'm just nervous, that's all. *To Catherine:* I'll make the fish.

EDDIE: You're savin' their lives, what're you worryin' about the table cloth? They probably didn't see a table cloth in their whole life where they come from.

BEATRICE, *looking into his eyes:* I'm just worried about you, that's all I'm worried.

EDDIE: Listen, as long as they know where they're gonna sleep.

BEATRICE: I told them in the letters. They're sleepin' on the floor.

EDDIE: Beatrice, all I'm worried about is you got such a heart that I'll end up on the floor with you, and they'll be in our bed.

BEATRICE: All right, stop it.

EDDIE: Because as soon as you see a tired relative, I end up on the floor.

BEATRICE: When did you end up on the floor?

EDDIE: When your father's house burned down I didn't end up on the floor?

BEATRICE: Well, their house burned down!

EDDIE: Yeah, but it didn't keep burnin' for two weeks!

BEATRICE: All right, look, I'll tell them to go someplace else. *She starts into the kitchen.*

EDDIE: Now wait a minute. Beatrice! *She halts. He goes to her.* I just don't want you bein' pushed around, that's all. You got too big a heart. *He touches her hand.* What're you so touchy?

BEATRICE: I'm just afraid if it don't turn out good you'll be mad at me.

EDDIE: Listen, if everybody keeps his mouth shut, nothin' can happen. They'll pay for their board.

BEATRICE: Oh, I told them.

EDDIE: Then what the hell. *Pause. He moves.* It's an honor, B. I mean it. I was just thinkin' before, comin' home, suppose my father didn't come to this country, and I was starvin' like them over there ... and I had people in America could keep me a couple of months? The man would be honored to lend me a place to sleep.

BEATRICE—*there are tears in her eyes. She turns to Catherine:* You see what he is? *She turns and grabs Eddie's face in her hands.* Mmm! You're an angel! God'll bless you. *He is gratefully smiling.* You'll see, you'll get a blessing for this!

EDDIE, *laughing:* I'll settle for my own bed.

BEATRICE: Go, Baby, set the table.

CATHERINE: We didn't tell him about me yet.

BEATRICE: Let him eat first, then we'll tell him. Bring everything in. *She hurries Catherine out.*

EDDIE, *sitting at the table:* What's all that about? Where's she goin'?

BEATRICE: Noplace. It's very good news, Eddie. I want you to be happy.

EDDIE: What's goin' on?

Catherine enters with plates, forks.

BEATRICE: She's got a job.

Pause. Eddie looks at Catherine, then back to Beatrice.

EDDIE: What job? She's gonna finish school.

CATHERINE: Eddie, you won't believe it—

EDDIE: No—no, you gonna finish school. What kinda job, what do you mean? All of a sudden you—

CATHERINE: Listen a minute, it's wonderful.

EDDIE: It's not wonderful. You'll never get nowheres unless you finish school. You can't take no job. Why didn't you ask me before you take a job?

BEATRICE: She's askin' you now, she didn't take nothin' yet.

CATHERINE: Listen a minute! I came to school this morning and the principal called me out of the class, see? To go to his office.

EDDIE: Yeah?

CATHERINE: So I went in and he says to me he's got my records, y'know? And there's a company wants a girl right away. It ain't exactly a secretary, it's a stenographer first, but pretty soon you get to be secretary. And he says to me that I'm the best student in the whole class—

BEATRICE: You hear that?

EDDIE: Well why not? Sure she's the best.

CATHERINE: I'm the best student, he says, and if I want, I should take the job and the end of the year he'll let me take the examination and he'll give me the certificate. So I'll save practically a year!

EDDIE, *strangely nervous:* Where's the job? What company?

CATHERINE: It's a big plumbing company over Nostrand Avenue.

EDDIE: Nostrand Avenue and where?

CATHERINE: It's someplace by the Navy Yard.

BEATRICE: Fifty dollars a week, Eddie.

EDDIE, *to Catherine, surprised:* Fifty?

CATHERINE: I swear.

Pause.

EDDIE: What about all the stuff you wouldn't learn this year, though?

CATHERINE: There's nothin' more to learn, Eddie, I just gotta practice from now on. I know all the symbols and I know the keyboard. I'll just get faster, that's all. And when I'm workin' I'll keep gettin' better and better, you see?

BEATRICE: Work is the best practice anyway.

EDDIE: That ain't what I wanted, though.

CATHERINE: Why! It's a great big company—

EDDIE: I don't like that neighborhood over there.

CATHERINE: It's a block and half from the subway, he says.

EDDIE: Near the Navy Yard plenty can happen in a block and a half. And a plumbin' company! That's one step over the water front. They're practically longshoremen.

BEATRICE: Yeah, but she'll be in the office, Eddie.

EDDIE: I know she'll be in the office, but that ain't what I had in mind.

BEATRICE: Listen, she's gotta go to work sometime.

EDDIE: Listen, B., she'll be with a lotta plumbers? And sailors up and down the street? So what did she go to school for?

CATHERINE: But it's fifty a week, Eddie.

EDDIE: Look, did I ask you for money? I supported you this long I support you a little more. Please, do me a favor, will ya? I want you to be with different kind of people. I want you to be in a nice office. Maybe a lawyer's office someplace in New York in one of them nice buildings. I mean if you're gonna get outa here then get out; don't go practically in the same kind of neighborhood.

Pause. Catherine lowers her eyes.

BEATRICE: Go, Baby, bring in the supper. *Catherine goes out.* Think about it a little bit, Eddie. Please. She's crazy to start work. It's not a little shop, it's a big company. Some day she could be a secretary. They picked her out of the whole class. *He is silent, staring down at the tablecloth, fingering the pattern.* What are you worried about? She could take care of herself. She'll get out of the subway and be in the office in two minutes.

EDDIE, *somehow sickened:* I know that neighborhood, B., I don't like it.

BEATRICE: Listen, if nothin' happened to her in this neighborhood it ain't gonna happen noplace else. *She turns his face to her.* Look, you gotta get used to it, she's no baby no more. Tell her to take it. *He turns his head away.* You hear me? *She is angering.* I don't understand you; she's seventeen years old, you gonna keep her in the house all her life?

EDDIE, *insulted:* What kinda remark is that?

BEATRICE, *with sympathy but insistent force:* Well, I don't understand when it ends. First it was gonna be when she graduated high school, so she graduated high school. Then it was gonna be when she learned stenographer, so she learned stenographer. So what're we gonna wait for now? I mean it, Eddie, sometimes I don't understand you; they picked her out of the whole class, it's an honor for her.

Catherine enters with food, which she silently sets on the table. After a moment of watching her face, Eddie breaks into a smile, but it almost seems that tears will form in his eyes.

EDDIE: With your hair that way you look like a madonna, you know that? You're the madonna type. *She doesn't look at him, but continues ladling out food onto the plates.* You wanna go to work, heh, Madonna?

CATHERINE, *softly:* Yeah.

EDDIE, *with a sense of her childhood, her babyhood, and the years:* All right, go to work. *She looks at him, then rushes and hugs him.* Hey, hey! Take it easy! *He holds her face away from him to look at her.* What're you cryin' about? *He is affected by her, but smiles his emotion away.*

CATHERINE, *sitting at her place:* I just—*Bursting out:* I'm gonna buy all new dishes with my first pay! *They laugh warmly.* I mean it. I'll fix up the whole house! I'll buy a rug!

EDDIE: And then you'll move away.

CATHERINE: No, Eddie!

EDDIE, *grinning:* Why not? That's life. And you'll come visit on Sundays, then once a month, then Christmas and New Year's, finally.

CATHERINE, *grasping his arm to reassure him and to erase the accusation:* No, please!

EDDIE, *smiling but hurt:* I only ask you one thing—don't trust nobody. You got a good aunt but she's got too big a heart, you learned bad from her. Believe me.

BEATRICE: Be the way you are, Katie, don't listen to him.

EDDIE, *to Beatrice—strangely and quickly resentful:* You lived in a house all your life, what do you know about it? You never worked in your life.

BEATRICE: She likes people. What's wrong with that?

EDDIE: Because most people ain't people. She's goin' to work; plumbers; they'll chew her to pieces if she don't watch out. *To Catherine:* Believe me, Katie, the less you trust, the less you be sorry.

Eddie crosses himself and the women do the same, and they eat.

CATHERINE: First thing I'll buy is a rug, heh, B.?

BEATRICE: I don't mind. *To Eddie:* I smelled coffee all day today. You unloadin' coffee today?

EDDIE: Yeah, a Brazil ship.

CATHERINE: I smelled it too. It smelled all over the neighborhood.

EDDIE: That's one time, boy, to be a longshoreman is a pleasure. I could work coffee ships twenty hours a day. You go down in the hold, y'know? It's like flowers, that smell. We'll bust a bag tomorrow, I'll bring you some.

BEATRICE: Just be sure there's no spiders in it, will ya? I mean it. *She directs this to Catherine, rolling her eyes upward.* I still remember that spider coming out of that bag he brung home. I nearly died.

EDDIE: You call that a spider? You oughta see what comes outa the bananas sometimes.

BEATRICE: Don't talk about it!

EDDIE: I seen spiders could stop a Buick.

BEATRICE, *clapping her hands over her ears:* All right, shut up!

EDDIE, *laughing and taking a watch out of his pocket:* Well, who started with spiders?

BEATRICE: All right, I'm sorry, I didn't mean it. Just don't bring none home again. What time is it?

EDDIE: Quarter nine. *Puts watch back in his pocket.*

They continue eating in silence.

CATHERINE: He's bringin' them ten o'clock, Tony?

EDDIE: Around, yeah. *He eats.*

CATHERINE: Eddie, suppose somebody asks if they're livin' here. *He looks at her as though already she had divulged something publicly. Defensively:* I mean if they ask.

EDDIE: Now look, Baby, I can see we're gettin' mixed up again here.

CATHERINE: No, I just mean . . . people'll see them goin' in and out.

EDDIE: I don't care who sees them goin' in and out as long as you don't see them goin' in and out. And this goes for you too, B. You don't see nothin' and you don't know nothin'.

BEATRICE: What do you mean? I understand.

EDDIE: You don't understand; you still think you can talk about this to somebody just a little bit. Now lemme say it once and for all, because you're makin' me nervous again, both of you. I don't care if somebody comes in the house and sees them sleepin' on the floor, it never comes out of your mouth who they are or what they're doin' here.

BEATRICE: Yeah, but my mother'll know—

EDDIE: Sure she'll know, but just don't you be the one who told her, that's all. This is the United States government you're playin' with now, this is the Immigration Bureau. If you said it you knew it, if you didn't say it you didn't know it.

CATHERINE: Yeah, but Eddie, suppose somebody—

EDDIE: I don't care what question it is. You—don't—know—nothin'. They got stool pigeons all over this neighborhood they're payin' them every week for information, and you don't know who they are. It could be your best friend. You hear? *To Beatrice:* Like Vinny Bolzano, remember Vinny?

BEATRICE: Oh, yeah. God forbid.

EDDIE: Tell her about Vinny. *To Catherine:* You think I'm blowin' steam here? *To Beatrice:* Go ahead, tell her. *To Catherine:* You was a baby then. There was a family lived next door to her mother, he was about sixteen—

BEATRICE: No, he was no more than fourteen, cause I was to his confirmation in Saint Agnes. But the family had an uncle that they were hidin' in the house, and he snitched to the Immigration.

CATHERINE: The kid snitched?

EDDIE: On his own uncle!

CATHERINE: What, was he crazy?

EDDIE: He was crazy after, I tell you that, boy.

BEATRICE: Oh, it was terrible. He had five brothers and the old father. And they grabbed him in the kitchen and pulled him down the stairs—three flights his head was bouncin' like a coconut. And they spit on him in the street, his own father and his brothers. The whole neighborhood was cryin'.

CATHERINE: Ts! So what happened to him?

BEATRICE: I think he went away. *To Eddie:* I never seen him again, did you?

EDDIE *rises during this, taking out his watch:* Him? You'll never see him no more, a guy do a thing like that? How's he gonna show his face? *To Catherine, as he gets up uneasily:* Just remember, kid, you can quicker get back a million dollars that was stole than a word that you gave away. *He is standing now, stretching his back.*

CATHERINE: Okay, I won't say a word to nobody, I swear.

EDDIE: Gonna rain tomorrow. We'll be slidin' all over the decks. Maybe you oughta put something on for them, they be here soon.

BEATRICE: I only got fish, I hate to spoil it if they ate already. I'll wait, it only takes a few minutes; I could broil it.

CATHERINE: What happens, Eddie, when that ship pulls out and they ain't on it, though? Don't the captain say nothin'?

EDDIE, *slicing an apple with his pocket knife:* Captain's pieced off, what do you mean?

CATHERINE: Even the captain?

EDDIE: What's the matter, the captain don't have to live? Captain gets a piece, maybe one of the mates, piece for the guy in Italy who fixed the papers for them, Tony here'll get a little bite. . . .

BEATRICE: I just hope they get work here, that's all I hope.

EDDIE: Oh, the syndicate'll fix jobs for them; till they pay 'em off they'll get them work every day. It's after the pay-off, then they'll have to scramble like the rest of us.

BEATRICE: Well, it be better than they got there.

EDDIE: Oh sure, well, listen. So you gonna start Monday, heh, Madonna?

CATHERINE, *embarrassed:* I'm supposed to, yeah.

Eddie is standing facing the two seated women. First Beatrice smiles, then Catherine, for a powerful emotion is on him, a childish one and a knowing fear, and the tears show in his eyes—and they are shy before the avowal.

EDDIE: *sadly smiling, yet somehow proud of her:* Well . . . I hope you have good luck. I wish you the best. You know that, kid.

CATHERINE, *rising, trying to laugh:* You sound like I'm goin' a million miles!

EDDIE: I know. I guess I just never figured on one thing.

CATHERINE, *smiling:* What?

EDDIE: That you would ever grow up. *He utters a soundless laugh at himself, feeling his breast pocket of his shirt.* I left a cigar in my other coat, I think. *He starts for the bedroom.*

CATHERINE: Stay there! I'll get it for you.

She hurries out. There is a slight pause, and Eddie turns to Beatrice, who has been avoiding his gaze.

EDDIE: What are you mad at me lately?

BEATRICE: Who's mad? *She gets up, clearing the dishes.* I'm not mad. *She picks up the dishes and turns to him.* You're the one is mad. *She turns and goes into the kitchen as Catherine enters from the bedroom with a cigar and a pack of matches.*

CATHERINE: Here! I'll light it for you! *She strikes a match and holds it to his cigar. He puffs. Quietly:* Don't worry about me, Eddie, heh?

EDDIE: Don't burn yourself. *Just in time she blows out the match.* You better go in help her with the dishes.

CATHERINE *turns quickly to the table, and, seeing the table cleared, she says, almost guiltily:* Oh! *She hurries into the kitchen, and as she exits there:* I'll do the dishes, B.!

Alone, Eddie stands looking toward the kitchen for a moment. Then he takes out his watch, glances at it, replaces it in his pocket, sits in the armchair, and stares at the smoke flowing out of his mouth.

The lights go down, then come up on Alfieri, who has moved onto the fore-stage.

ALFIERI: He was as good a man as he had to be in a life that was hard and even. He worked on the piers when there was work, he brought home his pay, and he lived. And toward ten o'clock of that night, after they had eaten, the cousins came.

The lights fade on Alfieri and rise on the street.

Enter Tony, escorting Marco and Rodolpho, each with a valise. Tony halts, indicates the house. They stand for a moment looking at it.

MARCO—*he is a square-built peasant of thirty-two, suspicious, tender, and quiet-voiced:* Thank you.
TONY: You're on your own now. Just be careful, that's all. Ground floor.
MARCO: Thank you.
TONY, *indicating the house:* I'll see you on the pier tomorrow. You'll go to work.

Marco nods. Tony continues on walking down the street.

RODOLPHO: This will be the first house I ever walked into in America! Imagine! She said they were poor!
MARCO: Ssh! Come. *They go to door.*

Marco knocks. The lights rise in the room. Eddie goes and opens the door. Enter Marco and Rodolpho, removing their caps. Beatrice and Catherine enter from the kitchen. The lights fade in the street.

EDDIE: You Marco?
MARCO: Marco.
EDDIE: Come on in! *He shakes Marco's hand.*
BEATRICE: Here, take the bags!
MARCO nods, looks to the women and fixes on Beatrice. Crosses to Beatrice. Are you my cousin?

She nods. He kisses her hand.

BEATRICE, *above the table, touching her chest with her hand:* Beatrice. This is my husband, Eddie. *All nod.* Catherine, my sister Nancy's daughter. *The Brothers nod.*
MARCO, *indicating Rodolpho:* My brother. Rodolpho. *Rodolpho nods. Marco comes with a certain formal stiffness to Eddie.* I want to tell you now Eddie—when you say go, we will go.
EDDIE: Oh, no . . . *Takes Marco's bag.*
MARCO: I see it's a small house, but soon, maybe, we can have our own house.
EDDIE: You're welcome, Marco, we got plenty of room here. Katie, give them supper, heh? *Exits into bedroom with their bags.*

CATHERINE: Come here, sit down. I'll get you some soup.

MARCO, *as they go to the table:* We ate on the ship. Thank you. *To Eddie, calling off to bedroom:* Thank you.

BEATRICE: Get some coffee. We'll all have coffee. Come sit down.

Rodolpho and Marco sit, at the table.

CATHERINE, *wondrously:* How come he's so dark and you're so light, Rodolpho?

RODOLPHO, *ready to laugh:* I don't know. A thousand years ago, they say, the Danes invaded Sicily.

Beatrice kisses Rodolpho. They laugh as Eddie enters.

CATHERINE, *to Beatrice:* He's practically blond!

EDDIE: How's the coffee doin'?

CATHERINE, *brought up:* I'm gettin' it. *She hurries out to kitchen.*

EDDIE *sits on his rocker:* Yiz have a nice trip?

MARCO: The ocean is always rough. But we are good sailors.

EDDIE: No trouble gettin' here?

MARCO: No. The man brought us. Very nice man.

RODOLPHO, *to Eddie:* He says we start to work tomorrow. Is he honest?

EDDIE, *laughing:* No. But as long as you owe them money, they'll get you plenty of work. *To Marco:* Yiz ever work on the piers in Italy?

MARCO: Piers? Ts!—no.

RODOLPHO, *smiling at the smallness of his town:* In our town there are no piers, only the beach, and little fishing boats.

BEATRICE: So what kinda work did yiz do?

MARCO, *shrugging shyly, even embarrassed:* Whatever there is, anything.

RODOLPHO: Sometimes they build a house, or if they fix the bridge—Marco is a mason and I bring him the cement. *He laughs.* In harvest time we work in the fields . . . if there is work. Anything.

EDDIE: Still bad there, heh?

MARCO: Bad, yes.

RODOLPHO, *laughing:* It's terrible! We stand around all day in the piazza listening to the fountain like birds. Everybody waits only for the train.

BEATRICE: What's on the train?

RODOLPHO: Nothing. But if there are many passengers and you're lucky you make a few lire to push the taxi up the hill.

Enter Catherine; she listens.

BEATRICE: You gotta push a taxi?

RODOLPHO, *laughing:* Oh, sure! It's a feature in our town. The horses in our town are skinnier than goats. So if there are too many passengers we help to push the carriages up to the hotel. *He laughs.* In our town the horses are only for show.

CATHERINE: Why don't they have automobile taxis?

RODOLPHO: There is one. We push that too. *They laugh.* Everything in our town, you gotta push!

BEATRICE, *to Eddie:* How do you like that!

EDDIE, *to Marco:* So what're you wanna do, you gonna stay here in this country or you wanna go back?

MARCO, *surprised:* Go back?

EDDIE: Well, you're married, ain't you?

MARCO: Yes. I have three children.

BEATRICE: Three! I thought only one.

MARCO: Oh, no. I have three now. Four years, five years, six years.

BEATRICE: Ah . . . I bet they're cryin' for you already, heh?

MARCO: What can I do? The older one is sick in his chest. My wife—she feeds them from her own mouth. I tell you the truth, if I stay there they will never grow up. They eat the sunshine.

BEATRICE: My God. So how long you want to stay?

MARCO: With your permission, we will stay maybe a—

EDDIE: She don't mean in this house, she means in the country.

MARCO: Oh. Maybe four, five, six years, I think.

RODOLPHO, *smiling:* He trusts his wife.

BEATRICE: Yeah, but maybe you'll get enough, you'll be able to go back quicker.

MARCO: I hope. I don't know. *To Eddie:* I understand it's not so good here either.

EDDIE: Oh, you guys'll be all right—till you pay them off, anyway. After that, you'll have to scramble, that's all. But you'll make better here than you could there.

RODOLPHO: How much? We hear all kinds of figures. How much can a man make? We work hard, we'll work all day, all night—

Marco raises a hand to hush him.

EDDIE—*he is coming more and more to address Marco only:* On the average a whole year? Maybe—well, it's hard to say, see. Sometimes we lay off, there's no ships three four weeks.

MARCO: Three, four weeks!—Ts!

EDDIE: But I think you could probably—thirty, forty a week, over the whole twelve months of the year.

MARCO, *rises, crosses to Eddie:* Dollars.

EDDIE: Sure dollars.

Marco puts an arm round Rodolpho and they laugh.

MARCO: If we can stay here a few months, Beatrice—

BEATRICE: Listen, you're welcome, Marco—

MARCO: Because I could send them a little more if I stay here.

BEATRICE: As long as you want, we got plenty a room.

MARCO, *his eyes are showing tears:* My wife—*To Eddie:* My wife—I want to send right away maybe twenty dollars—

EDDIE: You could send them something next week already.

MARCO—*he is near tears:* Eduardo . . . *He goes to Eddie, offering his hand.*

EDDIE: Don't thank me. Listen, what the hell, it's no skin off me. *To Catherine:* What happened to the coffee?

CATHERINE: I got it on. *To Rodolpho:* You married too? No.

RODOLPHO *rises:* Oh, no . . .

BEATRICE, *to Catherine:* I told you he—

CATHERINE: I know, I just thought maybe he got married recently.

RODOLPHO: I have no money to get married. I have a nice face, but no money. *He laughs.*

CATHERINE, *to Beatrice:* He's a real blond!

BEATRICE, *to Rodolpho:* You want to stay here too, heh? For good?

RODOLPHO: Me? Yes, forever! Me, I want to be an American. And then I want to go back to Italy when I am rich, and I will buy a motorcycle. *He smiles. Marco shakes him affectionately.*

CATHERINE: A motorcycle!

RODOLPHO: With a motorcycle in Italy you will never starve any more.

BEATRICE: I'll get you coffee. *She exits to the kitchen.*

EDDIE: What you do with a motorcycle?

MARCO: He dreams, he dreams.

RODOLPHO, *to Marco:* Why? *To Eddie:* Messages! The rich people in the hotel always need someone who will carry a message. But quickly, and with a great noise. With a blue motorcycle I would station myself in the courtyard of the hotel, and in a little while I would have messages.

MARCO: When you have no wife you have dreams.

EDDIE: Why can't you just walk, or take a trolley or sump'm?

Enter Beatrice with coffee.

RODOLPHO: Oh, no, the machine, the machine is necessary. A man comes into a great hotel and says, I am a messenger. Who is this man? He disappears walking, there is no noise, nothing. Maybe he will never come back, maybe he will never deliver the message. But a man who rides up on a great machine, this man is responsible, this man exists. He will be given messages. *He helps Beatrice set out the coffee things.* I am also a singer, though.

EDDIE: You mean a regular—?

RODOLPHO: Oh, yes. One night last year Andreola got sick. Baritone. And I took his place in the garden of the hotel. Three arias I sang without a mistake! Thousand-lire notes they threw from the tables, money was falling like a storm in the treasury. It was magnificent. We lived six months on that night, eh, Marco?

Marco nods doubtfully.

MARCO: Two months.

Eddie laughs.

BEATRICE: Can't you get a job in that place?

RODOLPHO: Andreola got better. He's a baritone, very strong.

Beatrice laughs.

MARCO, *regretfully, to Beatrice:* He sang too loud.

RODOLPHO: Why too loud?

MARCO: Too loud. The guests in that hotel are all Englishmen. They don't like too loud.

RODOLPHO, *to Catherine:* Nobody ever said it was too loud!

MARCO: I say. It was too loud. *To Beatrice:* I knew it as soon as he started to sing. Too loud.

RODOLPHO: Then why did they throw so much money?

MARCO: They paid for your courage. The English like courage. But once is enough.

RODOLPHO, *to all but Marco:* I never heard anybody say it was too loud.

CATHERINE: Did you ever hear of jazz?

RODOLPHO: Oh, sure! I *sing* jazz.

CATHERINE *rises:* You could sing jazz?

RODOLPHO: Oh, I sing Napolidan, jazz, bel canto—I sing "Paper Doll," you like "Paper Doll"?

CATHERINE: Oh, sure, I'm crazy for "Paper Doll." Go ahead, sing it.

RODOLPHO *takes his stance after getting a nod of permission from Marco, and with a high tenor voice begins singing:*

> "I'll tell you boys it's tough to be alone,
> And it's tough to love a doll that's not your own.
> I'm through with all of them,
> I'll never fall again,
> Hey, boy, what you gonna do?
> I'm gonna buy a paper doll that I can call my own,
> A doll that other fellows cannot steal.

Eddie rises and moves upstage.

> And then those flirty, flirty guys
> With their flirty, flirty eyes
> Will have to flirt with dollies that are real—

EDDIE: Hey, kid—hey, wait a minute—

CATHERINE, *enthralled:* Leave him finish, it's beautiful! *To Beatrice:* He's terrific! It's terrific, Rodolpho.

EDDIE: Look, kid; you don't want to be picked up, do ya?

MARCO: No—no! *He rises.*

EDDIE, *indicating the rest of the building:* Because we never had no singers here ... and all of a sudden there's a singer in the house, y'know what I mean?

MARCO: Yes, yes. You'll be quiet, Rodolpho.

EDDIE—*he is flushed:* They got guys all over the place, Marco. I mean.

MARCO: Yes. He'll be quiet. *To Rodolpho:* You'll be quiet.

Rodolpho nods.

Eddie has risen, with iron control, even a smile. He moves to Catherine.

EDDIE: What's the high heels for, Garbo?

CATHERINE: I figured for tonight—

EDDIE: DO me a favor, will you? Go ahead.

Embarrassed now, angered, Catherine goes out into the bedroom. Beatrice watches her go and gets up; in passing, she gives Eddie a cold look, restrained only by the strangers, and goes to the table to pour coffee.

EDDIE, *striving to laugh, and to Marco, but directed as much to Beatrice:* All actresses they want to be around here.

RODOLPHO, *happy about it:* In Italy too! All the girls.

Catherine emerges from the bedroom in low-heel shoes, comes to the table. Rodolpho is lifting a cup.

EDDIE—*he is sizing up Rodolpho, and there is a concealed suspicion:* Yeah, heh?

RODOLPHO: Yes! *Laughs, indicating Catherine:* Especially when they are so beautiful!

CATHERINE: You like sugar?

RODOLPHO: Sugar? Yes! I like sugar very much!

Eddie is downstage, watching as she pours a spoonful of sugar into his cup, his face puffed with trouble, and the room dies.
Lights rise on Alfieri.

ALFIERI: Who can ever know what will be discovered? Eddie Carbone had never expected to have a destiny. A man works, raises his family, goes bowling, eats, gets old, and then he dies. Now, as the weeks passed, there was a future, there was a trouble that would not go away.

The lights fade on Alfieri, then rise on Eddie standing at the doorway of the house. Beatrice enters on the street. She sees Eddie, smiles at him. He looks away. She starts to enter the house when Eddie speaks.

EDDIE: It's after eight.

BEATRICE: Well, it's a long show at the Paramount.

EDDIE: They must've seen every picture in Brooklyn by now. He's supposed to stay in the house when he ain't working. He ain't supposed to go advertising himself.

BEATRICE: Well that's his trouble, what do you care? If they pick him up they pick him up, that's all. Come in the house.

EDDIE: What happened to the stenography? I don't see her practice no more.

BEATRICE: She'll get back to it. She's excited, Eddie.

EDDIE: She tell you anything?

BEATRICE *comes to him, now the subject is opened:* What's the matter with you? He's a nice kid, what do you want from him?

EDDIE: That's a nice kid? He gives me the heeby-jeebies.

BEATRICE, *smiling:* Ah, go on, you're just jealous.

EDDIE: Of *him?* Boy, you don't think much of me.

BEATRICE: I don't understand you. What's so terrible about him?

EDDIE: You mean it's all right with you? That's gonna be her husband?

BEATRICE: Why? He's a nice fella, hard workin', he's a good-lookin' fella.

EDDIE: He sings on the ships, didja know that?

BEATRICE: What do you mean, he sings?

EDDIE: Just what I said, he sings. Right on the deck, all of a sudden, a whole song comes out of his mouth—with motions. You know what they're callin' him now? Paper Doll they're callin' him, Canary. He's like a weird. He comes out on the pier, one-two-three, it's a regular free show.

BEATRICE: Well, he's a kid; he don't know how to behave himself yet.

EDDIE: And with that wacky hair; he's like a chorus girl or sump'm.

BEATRICE: So he's blond, so—

EDDIE: I just hope that's his regular hair, that's all I hope.

BEATRICE: You crazy or sump'm? *She tries to turn him to her.*

EDDIE—*he keeps his head turned away:* What's so crazy? I don't like his whole way.

BEATRICE: Listen, you never seen a blond guy in your life? What about Whitey Balso?

EDDIE, *turning to her victoriously:* Sure, but Whitey don't sing; he don't do like that on the ships.

BEATRICE: Well, maybe that's the way they do in Italy.

EDDIE: Then why don't his brother sing? Marco goes around like a man; nobody kids Marco. *He moves from her, halts. She realizes there is a campaign solidified in him.* I tell you the truth I'm surprised I have to tell you all this. I mean I'm surprised, B.

BEATRICE—*she goes to him with purpose now:* Listen, you ain't gonna start nothin' here.

EDDIE: I ain't startin' nothin', but I ain't gonna stand around lookin' at that. For that character I didn't bring her up. I swear, B., I'm surprised at you; I sit there waitin' for you to wake up but everything is great with you.

BEATRICE: No, everything ain't great with me.

EDDIE: No?

BEATRICE: No. But I got other worries.

EDDIE: Yeah. *He is already weakening.*

BEATRICE: Yeah, you want me to tell you?

EDDIE, *in retreat:* Why? What worries you got?

BEATRICE: When am I gonna be a wife again, Eddie?

EDDIE: I ain't been feelin' good. They bother me since they came.

BEATRICE: It's almost three months you don't feel good; they're only here a couple of weeks. It's three months, Eddie.

EDDIE: I don't know, B. I don't want to talk about it.

BEATRICE: What's the matter, Eddie, you don't like me, heh?

EDDIE: What do you mean, I don't like you? I said I don't feel good, that's all.

BEATRICE: Well, tell me, am I doing something wrong? Talk to me.

EDDIE—*Pause. He can't speak, then:* I can't. I can't talk about it.

BEATRICE: Well tell me what—

EDDIE: I got nothin' to say about it!

She stands for a moment; he is looking off; she turns to go into the house.

EDDIE: I'll be all right, B.; just lay off me, will ya? I'm worried about her.

BEATRICE: The girl is gonna be eighteen years old, it's time already.

EDDIE: B., he's taking her for a ride!

BEATRICE: All right, that's her ride. What're you gonna stand over her till she's forty? Eddie, I want you to cut it out now, you hear me? I don't like it! Now come in the house.

EDDIE: I want to take a walk, I'll be in right away.

BEATRICE: They ain't goin' to come any quicker if you stand in the street. It ain't nice, Eddie.

EDDIE: I'll be in right away. Go ahead. *He walks off.*

She goes into the house. Eddie glances up the street, sees Louis and Mike coming, and sits on an iron railing. Louis and Mike enter.

LOUIS: Wanna go bowlin' tonight?

EDDIE: I'm too tired. Goin' to sleep.

LOUIS: How's your two submarines?

EDDIE: They're okay.

LOUIS: I see they're gettin' work allatime.

EDDIE: Oh yeah, they're doin' all right.

MIKE: That's what we oughta do. We oughta leave the country and come in under the water. Then we get work.

EDDIE: You ain't kiddin'.

LOUIS: Well, what the hell. Y'know?

EDDIE: Sure.

LOUIS—*sits on railing beside Eddie:* Believe me, Eddie, you got a lotta credit comin' to you.

EDDIE: Aah, they don't bother me, don't cost me nutt'n.

MIKE: That older one, boy, he's a regular bull. I seen him the other day liftin' coffee bags over the Matson Line. They leave him alone he woulda load the whole ship by himself.

EDDIE: Yeah, he's a strong guy, that guy. Their father was a regular giant, supposed to be.

LOUIS: Yeah, you could see. He's a regular slave.

MIKE, *grinning:* That blond one, though—*Eddie looks at him.* He's got a sense of humor. *Louis snickers.*

EDDIE, *searchingly:* Yeah. He's funny—

MIKE, *starting to laugh:* Well he ain't exackly funny, but he's always like makin' remarks like, y'know? He comes around, everybody's laughin'. *Louis laughs.*

EDDIE, *uncomfortably, grinning:* Yeah, well . . . he's got a sense of humor.

MIKE, *laughing:* Yeah, I mean, he's always makin' like remarks, like, y'know?

EDDIE: Yeah, I know. But he's a kid yet, y'know? He—he's just a kid, that's all.

MIKE, *getting hysterical with Louis:* I know. You take one look at him—everybody's happy. *Louis laughs.* I worked one day with him last week over the Moore-MacCormack Line, I'm tellin' you they was all hysterical. *Louis and he explode in laughter.*

EDDIE: Why? What'd he do?

MIKE: I don't know ... he was just humorous. You never can remember what he says, y'know? But it's the way he says it. I mean he gives you a look sometimes and you start laughin'!

EDDIE: Yeah. *Troubled:* He's got a sense of humor.

MIKE, *gasping:* Yeah.

LOUIS, *rising:* Well, we see ya, Eddie.

EDDIE: Take it easy.

LOUIS: Yeah. See ya.

MIKE: If you wanna come bowlin' later we're goin' Flatbush Avenue.

Laughing, they move to exit, meeting Rodolpho and Catherine entering on the street. Their laughter rises as they see Rodolpho, who does not understand but joins in. Eddie moves to enter the house as Louis and Mike exit. Catherine stops him at the door.

CATHERINE: Hey, Eddie—what a picture we saw! Did we laugh!

EDDIE—*he can't help smiling at sight of her:* Where'd you go?

CATHERINE: Paramount. It was with those two guys, y'know? That—

EDDIE: Brooklyn Paramount?

CATHERINE, *with an edge of anger, embarrassed before Rodolpho:* Sure, the Brooklyn Paramount. I told you we wasn't goin' to New York.

EDDIE, *retreating before the threat of her anger:* All right, I only asked you. *To Rodolpho:* I just don't want her hangin' around Times Square, see? It's full of tramps over there.

RODOLPHO: I would like to go to Broadway once, Eddie. I would like to walk with her once where the theaters are and the opera. Since I was a boy I see pictures of those lights.

EDDIE, *his little patience waning:* I want to talk to her a minute, Rodolpho. Go inside, will you?

RODOLPHO: Eddie, we only walk together in the streets. She teaches me.

CATHERINE: You know what he can't get over? That there's no fountains in Brooklyn!

EDDIE, *smiling unwillingly:* Fountains? *Rodolpho smiles at his own naïveté.*

CATHERINE: In Italy he says, every town's got fountains, and they meet there. And you know what? They got oranges on the trees where he comes from, and lemons. Imagine—on the trees? I mean it's interesting. But he's crazy for New York.

RODOLPHO, *attempting familiarity:* Eddie, why can't we go once to Broadway—?

EDDIE: Look, I gotta tell her something—

RODOLPHO: Maybe you can come too. I want to see all those lights. *He sees no response in Eddie's face. He glances at Catherine.* I'll walk by the river before I go to sleep. *He walks off down the street.*

CATHERINE: Why don't you talk to him, Eddie? He blesses you, and you don't talk to him hardly.

EDDIE, *enveloping her with his eyes:* I bless you and you don't talk to me. *He tries to smile.*

CATHERINE: *I don't talk to you? She hits his arm.* What do you mean?

EDDIE: I don't see you no more. I come home you're runnin' around someplace—

CATHERINE: Well, he wants to see everything, that's all, so we go.... You mad at me?

EDDIE: No. *He moves from her, smiling sadly.* It's just I used to come home, you was always there. Now, I turn around, you're a big girl. I don't know how to talk to you.

CATHERINE: Why?

EDDIE: I don't know, you're runnin', you're runnin', Katie. I don't think you listening any more to me.

CATHERINE, *going to him:* Ah, Eddie, sure I am. What's the matter? You don't like him?

Slight pause.

EDDIE, *turns to her:* You like him, Katie?

CATHERINE, *with a blush but holding her ground:* Yeah. I like him.

EDDIE—*his smile goes:* You like him.

CATHERINE, *looking down:* Yeah. *Now she looks at him for the consequences, smiling but tense. He looks at her like a lost boy.* What're you got against him? I don't understand. He only blesses you.

EDDIE *turns away:* He don't bless me, Katie.

CATHERINE: He does! You're like a father to him!

EDDIE *turns to her:* Katie.

CATHERINE: What, Eddie?

EDDIE: You gonna marry him?

CATHERINE: I don't know. We just been ... goin' around, that's all. *Turns to him:* What're you got against him, Eddie? Please, tell me. What?

EDDIE: He don't respect you.

CATHERINE: Why?

EDDIE: Katie ... if you wasn't an orphan, wouldn't he ask your father's permission before he run around with you like this?

CATHERINE: Oh, well, he didn't think you'd mind.

EDDIE: He knows I mind, but it don't bother him if I mind, don't you see that?

CATHERINE: No, Eddie, he's got all kinds of respect for me. And you too! We walk across the street he takes my arm—he almost bows to me! You got him all wrong, Eddie; I mean it, you—

EDDIE: Katie, he's only bowin' to his passport.

CATHERINE: His passport!

EDDIE: That's right. He marries you he's got the right to be an American citizen. That's what's goin' on here. *She is puzzled and surprised.* You understand what I'm tellin' you? The guy is lookin' for his break, that's all he's lookin' for.

CATHERINE, *pained:* Oh, no, Eddie, I don't think so.

EDDIE: You don't think so! Katie, you're gonna make me cry here. Is that a workin' man? What does he do with his first money? A snappy new jacket he buys, records, a pointy pair new shoes and his brother's kids are starvin' over there with tuberculosis? That's a hit-and-run guy, baby; he's got bright lights in his head, Broadway. Them guys don't think of nobody but theirself! You marry him and the next time you see him it'll be for divorce!

CATHERINE *steps toward him:* Eddie, he never said a word about his papers or—

EDDIE: You mean he's supposed to tell you that?

CATHERINE: I don't think he's even thinking about it.

EDDIE: What's better for him to think about! He could be picked up any day here and he's back pushin' taxis up the hill!

CATHERINE: No, I don't believe it.

EDDIE: Katie, don't break my heart, listen to me.

CATHERINE: I don't want to hear it.

EDDIE: Katie, listen . . .

CATHERINE: He loves me!

EDDIE, *with deep alarm:* Don't say that, for God's sake! This is the oldest racket in the country—

CATHERINE, *desperately, as though he had made his imprint:* I don't believe it! *She rushes to the house.*

EDDIE, *following her:* They been pullin' this since the Immigration Law was put in! They grab a green kid that don't know nothin' and they—

CATHERINE, *sobbing:* I don't believe it and I wish to hell you'd stop it!

EDDIE: Katie!

They enter the apartment. The lights in the living room have risen and Beatrice is there. She looks past the sobbing Catherine at Eddie, who in the presence of his wife, makes an awkward gesture of eroded command, indicating Catherine.

EDDIE: Why don't you straighten her out?

BEATRICE, *inwardly angered at his flowing emotion, which in itself alarms her:* When are you going to leave her alone?

EDDIE: B., the guy is no good!

BEATRICE, *suddenly, with open fright and fury:* You going to leave her alone? Or you gonna drive me crazy? *He turns, striving to retain his dignity, but nevertheless in guilt walks out of the house, into the street and away. Catherine starts into a bedroom.* Listen, Catherine. *Catherine halts, turns to her sheepishly.* What are you going to do with yourself?

CATHERINE: I don't know.

BEATRICE: Don't tell me you don't know; you're not a baby any more, what are you going to do with yourself?

CATHERINE: He won't listen to me.

BEATRICE: I don't understand this. He's not your father, Catherine. I don't understand what's going on here.

CATHERINE, *as one who herself is trying to rationalize a buried impulse:* What am I going to do, just kick him in the face with it?

BEATRICE: Look, honey, you wanna get married, or don't you wanna get married? What are you worried about, Katie?

CATHERINE, *quietly, trembling:* I don't know B. It just seems wrong if he's against it so much.

BEATRICE, *never losing her aroused alarm:* Sit down, honey, I want to tell you something. Here, sit down. Was there ever any fella he liked for you? There wasn't, was there?

CATHERINE: But he says Rodolpho's just after his papers.

BEATRICE: Look, he'll say anything. What does he care what he says? If it was a prince came here for you it would be no different. You know that, don't you?

CATHERINE: Yeah, I guess.

BEATRICE: So what does that mean?

CATHERINE *slowly turns her head to Beatrice:* What?

BEATRICE: It means you gotta be your own self more. You still think you're a little girl, honey. But nobody else can make up your mind for you any more, you understand? You gotta give him to understand that he can't give you orders no more.

CATHERINE: Yeah, but how am I going to do that? He thinks I'm a baby.

BEATRICE: Because *you* think you're a baby. I told you fifty times already, you can't act the way you act. You still walk around in front of him in your slip—

CATHERINE: Well I forgot.

BEATRICE: Well you can't do it. Or like you sit on the edge of the bathtub talkin' to him when he's shavin' in his underwear.

CATHERINE: When'd I do that?

BEATRICE: I seen you in there this morning.

CATHERINE: Oh . . . well, I wanted to tell him something and I—

BEATRICE: I know, honey. But if you act like a baby and he be treatin' you like a baby. Like when he comes home sometimes you throw yourself at him like when you was twelve years old.

CATHERINE: Well I like to see him and I'm happy so I—

BEATRICE: Look, I'm not tellin' you what to do honey, but—

CATHERINE: No, you could tell me, B.! Gee, I'm all mixed up. See, I—He looks so sad now and it hurts me.

BEATRICE: Well look Katie, if it's goin' to hurt you so much you're gonna end up an old maid here.

CATHERINE: No!

BEATRICE: I'm tellin' you, I'm not makin' a joke. I tried to tell you a couple of times in the last year or so. That's why I was so happy you were going to go out and get work, you wouldn't be here so much, you'd be a little more independent. I mean it. It's wonderful for a whole family to love each other, but you're a grown woman and you're in the same house with a grown man.

So you'll act different now, heh?

CATHERINE: Yeah, I will. I'll remember.

BEATRICE: Because it ain't only up to him, Katie, you understand? I told him the same thing already.

CATHERINE, *quickly:* What?

BEATRICE: That he should let you go. But, you see, if only I tell him, he thinks I'm just bawlin' him out, or maybe I'm jealous or somethin', you know?

CATHERINE, *astonished:* He said you was jealous?

BEATRICE: No, I'm just sayin' maybe that's what he thinks. *She reaches over to Catherine's hand; with a strained smile:* You think I'm jealous of you, honey?

CATHERINE: No! It's the first I thought of it.

BEATRICE, *with a quiet sad laugh:* Well you should have thought of it before ... but I'm not. We'll be all right. Just give him to understand; you don't have to fight, you're just—You're a woman, that's all, and you got a nice boy, and now the time came when you said good-bye. All right?

CATHERINE, *strangely moved at the prospect:* All right. . . . If I can.

BEATRICE: Honey ... you gotta.

Catherine, sensing now an imperious demand, turns with some fear, with a discovery, to Beatrice. She is at the edge of tears, as though a familiar world had shattered.

CATHERINE: Okay.

Lights out on them and up on Alfieri, seated behind his desk.

ALFIERI: It was at this time that he first came to me. I had represented his father in an accident case some years before, and I was acquainted with the family in a casual way. I remember him now as he walked through my doorway—

Enter Eddie down right ramp.

His eyes were like tunnels; my first thought was that he had committed a crime,

Eddie sits besides the desk, cap in hand, looking out.

but soon I saw it was only a passion that had moved into his body, like a stranger. *Alfieri pauses, looks down at his desk, then to Eddie as though he were continuing a conversation with him.* I don't quite understand what I can do for you. Is there a question of law somewhere?

EDDIE: That's what I want to ask you.

ALFIERI: Because there's nothing illegal about a girl falling in love with an immigrant.

EDDIE: Yeah, but what about it if the only reason for it is to get his papers?

ALFIERI: First of all you don't know that.

EDDIE: I see it in his eyes; he's laughin' at her and he's laughin' at me.

ALFIERI: Eddie, I'm a lawyer. I can only deal in what's provable. You understand that, don't you? Can you prove that?

EDDIE: I know what's in his mind, Mr. Alfieri!

ALFIERI: Eddie, even if you could prove that—

EDDIE: Listen . . . will you listen to me a minute? My father always said you was a smart man. I want you to listen to me.

ALFIERI: I'm only a lawyer, Eddie.

EDDIE: Will you listen a minute? I'm talkin' about the law. Lemme just bring out what I mean. A man, which he comes into the country illegal, don't it stand to reason he's gonna take every penny and put it in the sock? Because they don't know from one day to another, right?

ALFIERI: All right.

EDDIE: He's spendin'. Records he buys now. Shoes. Jackets. Y'understand me? This guy ain't worried. This guy is *here*. So it must be that he's got it all laid out in his mind already—he's stayin'. Right?

ALFIERI: Well? What about it?

EDDIE: All right. *He glances at Alfieri, then down to the floor.* I'm talking to you confidential, ain't I?

ALFIERI: Certainly.

EDDIE: I mean it don't go no place but here. Because I don't like to say this about anybody. Even my wife I didn't exactly say this.

ALFIERI: What is it?

EDDIE *takes a breath and glances briefly over each shoulder:* The guy ain't right, Mr. Alfieri.

ALFIERI: What do you mean?

EDDIE: I mean he ain't right.

ALFIERI: I don't get you.

EDDIE, *shifts to another position in the chair:* Dja ever get a look at him?

ALFIERI: Not that I know of, no.

EDDIE: He's a blond guy. Like . . . platinum. You know what I mean?

ALFIERI: No.

EDDIE: I mean if you close the paper fast—you could blow him over.

ALFIERI: Well that doesn't mean—

EDDIE: Wait a minute, I'm tellin' you sump'm. He sings, see. Which is—I mean it's all right, but sometimes he hits a note, see. I turn around. I mean—high. You know what I mean?

ALFIERI: Well, that's a tenor.

EDDIE: I know a tenor, Mr. Alfieri. This ain't no tenor. I mean if you came in the house and you didn't know who was singin', you wouldn't be lookin' for him you be lookin' for her.

ALFIERI: Yes, but that's not—

EDDIE: I'm tellin' you sump'm, wait a minute. Please, Mr. Alfieri. I'm tryin' to bring out my thoughts here. Couple of nights ago my niece brings out a dress which it's too small for her, because she shot up like a light this last year. He takes the dress, lays it on the table, he cuts it up; one-two-three, he makes a new dress. I mean he looked so sweet there, like an angel—you could kiss him he was so sweet.

ALFIERI: Now look, Eddie—

EDDIE: Mr. Alfieri, they're laughin' at him on the piers. I'm ashamed. Paper Doll they call him. Blondie now. His brother thinks it's because he's got a sense of humor, see—which he's got—but that ain't what they're laughin'. Which they're not goin' to come out with it because they know he's my relative, which they have to see me if they make a crack, y'know? But I know what they're laughin' at, and when I think of that guy layin' his hands on her I could—I mean it's eatin' me out, Mr. Alfieri, because I struggled for that girl. And now he comes in my house and—

ALFIERI: Eddie, look—I have my own children. I understand you. But the law is very specific. The law does not . . .

EDDIE, *with a fuller flow of indignation:* You mean to tell me that there's no law that a guy which he ain't right can go to work and marry a girl and—?

ALFIERI: You have no recourse in the law, Eddie.

EDDIE: Yeah, but if he ain't right, Mr. Alfieri, you mean to tell me—

ALFIERI: There is nothing you can do, Eddie, believe me.

EDDIE: Nothin'.

ALFIERI: Nothing at all. There's only one legal question here.

EDDIE: What?

ALFIERI: The manner in which they entered the country. But I don't think you want to do anything about that, do you?

EDDIE: You mean—?

ALFIERI: Well, they entered illegally.

EDDIE: Oh, Jesus, no, I wouldn't do nothin' about that, I mean—

ALFIERI: All right, then, let me talk now, eh?

EDDIE: Mr. Alfieri, I can't believe what you tell me. I mean there must be some kinda law which—

ALFIERI: Eddie, I want you to listen to me. *Pause.* You know, sometimes God mixes up the people. We all love somebody, the wife, the kids—every man's got somebody that he loves, heh? But sometimes . . . there's too much. You know? There's too much, and it goes where it mustn't. A man works hard, he brings up a child, sometimes it's a niece, sometimes even a daughter, and he never realizes it, but through the years—there is too much love for the daughter, there is too much love for the niece. Do you understand what I'm saying to you?

EDDIE, *sardonically:* What do you mean, I shouldn't look out for her good?

ALFIERI: Yes, but these things have to end, Eddie, that's all. The child has to grow up and go away, and the man has to learn to forget. Because after all, Eddie—what other way can it end? *Pause.* Let her go. That's my advice. You did your job, now it's her life; wish her luck, and let her go. *Pause.* Will you do that? Because there's no law, Eddie; make up your mind to it; the law is not interested in this.

EDDIE: You mean to tell me, even if he's a punk? If he's—

ALFIERI: There's nothing you can do.

Eddie stands.

BEATRICE: I just hope you ain't gonna do like some of them around here. They're here twenty-five years, some men, and they didn't get enough together to go back twice.

MARCO: Oh, I know. We have many families in our town, the children never saw the father. But I will go home. Three, four years, I think.

BEATRICE: Maybe you should keep more here. Because maybe she thinks it comes so easy you'll never get ahead of yourself.

MARCO: Oh, no, she saves. I send everything. My wife is very lonesome. *He smiles shyly.*

BEATRICE: She must be nice. She pretty? I bet, heh?

MARCO, *blushing:* No, but she understand everything.

RODOLPHO: Oh, he's got a clever wife!

EDDIE: I betcha there's plenty surprises sometimes when those guys get back there, heh?

MARCO: Surprises?

EDDIE, *laughing:* I mean, you know—they count the kids and there's a couple extra than when they left?

MARCO: No—no . . . The women wait, Eddie. Most. Most. Very few surprises.

RODOLPHO: It's more strict in our town. *Eddie looks at him now.* It's not so free.

EDDIE *rises, paces up and down:* It ain't so free here either, Rodolpho, like you think. I seen greenhorns sometimes get in trouble that way—they think just because a girl don't go around with a shawl over her head that she ain't strict, y'know? Girl don't have to wear black dress to be strict. Know what I mean?

RODOLPHO: Well, I always have respect—

EDDIE: I know, but in your town you wouldn't just drag off some girl without permission, I mean. *He turns.* You know what I mean, Marco? It ain't that much different here.

MARCO, *cautiously:* Yes.

BEATRICE: Well, he didn't exactly drag her off though, Eddie.

EDDIE: I know, but I seen some of them get the wrong idea sometimes. *To Rodolpho:* I mean it might be a little more free here but it's just as strict.

RODOLPHO: I have respect for her, Eddie. I do anything wrong?

EDDIE: Look, kid, I ain't her father, I'm only her uncle—

BEATRICE: Well then, be an uncle then. *Eddie looks at her, aware of her criticizing force.* I mean.

MARCO: No, Beatrice, if he does wrong you must tell him. *To Eddie:* What does he do wrong?

EDDIE: Well, Marco, till he came here she was never out on the street twelve o'clock at night.

MARCO, *to Rodolpho:* You come home early now.

BEATRICE, *to Catherine:* Well, you said the movie ended late, didn't you?

CATHERINE: Yeah.

BEATRICE: Well, tell him, honey. *To Eddie:* The movie ended late.

EDDIE: Look, B., I'm just sayin'—he thinks she always stayed out like that.

MARCO: You come home early now, Rodolpho.

RODOLPHO, *embarrassed:* All right, sure. But I can't stay in the house all the time, Eddie.

EDDIE: Look, kid, I'm not only talkin' about her. The more you run around like that the more chance you're takin'. *To Beatrice:* I mean suppose he gets hit by a car or something. *To Marco:* Where's his papers, who is he? Know what I mean?

BEATRICE: Yeah, but who is he in the daytime, though? It's the same chance in the daytime.

EDDIE, *holding back a voice full of anger:* Yeah, but he don't have to go lookin' for it, Beatrice. If he's here to work, then he should work; if he's here for a good time then he could fool around! *To Marco:* But I understood, Marco, that you was both comin' to make a livin' for your family. You understand me, don't you, Marco? *He goes to his rocker.*

MARCO: I beg your pardon, Eddie.

EDDIE: I mean, that's what I understood in the first place, see.

MARCO: Yes. That's why we came.

EDDIE *sits on his rocker:* Well, that's all I'm askin'.

Eddie reads his paper. There is a pause, an awkwardness. Now Catherine gets up and puts a record on the phonograph—"Paper Doll."

CATHERINE, *flushed with revolt:* You wanna dance, Rodolpho?

Eddie freezes.

RODOLPHO, *in deference to Eddie:* No, I—I'm tired.

BEATRICE: Go ahead, dance, Rodolpho.

CATHERINE: Ah, come on. They got a beautiful quartet, these guys. Come.

She has taken his hand and he stiffly rises, feeling Eddie's eyes on his back, and they dance.

EDDIE, *to Catherine:* What's that, a new record?

CATHERINE: It's the same one. We bought it the other day.

BEATRICE, *to Eddie:* They only bought three records. *She watches them dance; Eddie turns his head away. Marco just sits there, waiting. Now Beatrice turns to Eddie.* Must be nice to go all over in one of them fishin' boats. I would like that myself. See all them other countries?

EDDIE: Yeah.

BEATRICE, *to Marco:* But the women don't go along, I bet.

MARCO: No, not on the boats. Hard work.

BEATRICE: What're you got, a regular kitchen and everything?

MARCO: Yes, we eat very good on the boats—especially when Rodolpho comes along; everybody gets fat.

BEATRICE: Oh, he cooks?

MARCO: Sure, very good cook. Rice, pasta, fish, everything.

Eddie lowers his paper.

EDDIE: He's a cook, too! *Looking at Rodolpho:* He sings, he cooks . . .

Rodolpho smiles thankfully.

BEATRICE: Well it's good, he could always make a living.

EDDIE: It's wonderful. He sings, he cooks, he could make dresses . . .

CATHERINE: They get some high pay, them guys. The head chefs in all the big hotels are men. You read about them.

EDDIE: That's what I'm sayin'.

Catherine and Rodolpho continue dancing.

CATHERINE: Yeah, well, I mean.

EDDIE, *to Beatrice:* He's lucky, believe me. *Slight pause. He looks away, then back to Beatrice.* That's why the water front is no place for him. *They stop dancing. Rodolpho turns off phonograph.* I mean like me—I can't cook, I can't sing, I can't make dresses, so I'm on the water front. But if I could cook, if I could sing, if I could make dresses, I wouldn't be on the water front. *He has been unconsciously twisting the newspaper into a tight roll. They are all regarding him now; he senses he is exposing the issue and he is driven on.* I would be someplace else, I would be like in a dress store. *He has bent the rolled paper and it suddenly tears in two. He suddenly gets up and pulls his pants up over his belly and goes to Marco.* What do you say, Marco, we go to the bouts next Saturday night. You never seen a fight, did you?

MARCO, *uneasily:* Only in the moving pictures.

EDDIE, *going to Rodolpho:* I'll treat yiz. What do you say, Danish? You wanna come along? I'll buy the tickets.

RODOLPHO: Sure. I like to go.

CATHERINE *goes to Eddie; nervously happy now:* I'll make some coffee, all right?

EDDIE: Go ahead, make some! Make it nice and strong. *Mystified, she smiles and exits to kitchen. He is weirdly elated, rubbing his fists into his palms. He strides to Marco.* You wait, Marco, you see some real fights here. You ever do any boxing?

MARCO: NO, I never.

EDDIE, *to Rodolpho:* Betcha you have done some, heh?

RODOLPHO: No.

EDDIE: Well, come on, I'll teach you.

BEATRICE : What's he got to learn that for?

EDDIE: Ya can't tell, one a these days somebody's liable to step on his foot or sump'm. Come on, Rodolpho, I show you a couple a passes. *He stands below table.*

BEATRICE: Go ahead, Rodolpho. He's a good boxer, he could teach you.

RODOLPHO, *embarrassed:* Well, I don't know how to—*He moves down to Eddie.*

EDDIE: Just put your hands up. Like this, see? That's right. That's very good, keep your left up, because you lead with the left, see, like this. *He gently moves his left into Rodolpho's face.* See? Now what you gotta do is you gotta block me, so when I come in like that you—*Rodolpho parries his left.* Hey, that's very good! *Rodolpho laughs.* All right, now come into me. Come on.

RODOLPHO: I don't want to hit you, Eddie.

EDDIE: Don't pity me, come on. Throw it, I'll show you how to block it. *Rodolpho jabs at him, laughing. The others join.* 'At's it. Come on again. For the jaw right here. *Rodolpho jabs with more assurance.* Very good!

BEATRICE, *to Marco:* He's very good!

Eddie crosses directly upstage of Rodolpho.

EDDIE: Sure, he's great! Come on, kid, put sump'm behind it, you can't hurt me. *Rodolpho, more seriously, jabs at Eddie's jaw and grazes it.* Attaboy.

Catherine comes from the kitchen, watches.

Now I'm gonna hit you, so block me, see?

CATHERINE, *with beginning alarm:* What are they doin'?

They are lightly boxing now.

BEATRICE—*she senses only the comradeship in it now:* He's teachin' him; he's very good!

EDDIE: Sure, he's terrific! Look at him go! *Rodolpho lands a blow.* 'At's it! Now, watch out, here I come, Danish! *He feints with his left hand and lands with his right. It mildly staggers Rodolpho. Marco rises.*

CATHERINE, *rushing to Rodolpho:* Eddie!

EDDIE: Why? I didn't hurt him. Did I hurt you, kid? *He rubs the back of his hand across his mouth.*

RODOLPHO: No, no, he didn't hurt me. *To Eddie with a certain gleam and a smile:* I was only surprised.

BEATRICE, *pulling Eddie down into the rocker:* That's enough, Eddie; he did pretty good, though.

EDDIE: Yeah. *Rubbing his fists together:* He could be very good, Marco. I'll teach him again.

Marco nods at him dubiously.

RODOLPHO: Dance, Catherine. Come. *He takes her hand; they go to phonograph and start it. It plays "Paper Doll."*

Rodolpho takes her in his arms. They dance. Eddie in thought sits in his chair, and Marco takes a chair, places it in front of Eddie, and looks down at it. Beatrice and Eddie watch him.

MARCO: Can you lift this chair?

EDDIE: What do you mean?

MARCO: From here. *He gets on one knee with one hand behind his back, and grasps the bottom of one of the chair legs but does not raise it.*

EDDIE: Sure, why not? *He comes to the chair, kneels, grasps the leg, raises the chair one inch, but it leans over to the floor.* Gee, that's hard, I never knew that. *He tries again, and again fails.* It's on an angle, that's why, heh?

MARCO: Here. *He kneels, grasps, and with strain slowly raises the chair higher and higher, getting to his feet now. Rodolpho and Catherine have stopped dancing as Marco raises the chair over his head.*

Marco is face to face with Eddie, a strained tension gripping his eyes and jaw, his neck stiff, the chair raised like a weapon over Eddie's head—and he transforms what might appear like a glare of warning into a smile of triumph, and Eddie's grin vanishes as he absorbs his look.

CURTAIN

ACT TWO

Light rises on Alfieri at his desk.

ALFIERI: On the twenty-third of that December a case of Scotch whisky slipped from a net while being unloaded—as a case of Scotch whisky is inclined to do on the twenty-third of December on Pier Forty-one. There was no snow, but it was cold, his wife was out shopping. Marco was still at work. The boy had not been hired that day; Catherine told me later that this was the first time they had been alone together in the house.

Light is rising on Catherine in the apartment. Rodolpho is watching as she arranges a paper pattern on cloth spread on the table.

CATHERINE: You hungry?

RODOLPHO: Not for anything to eat. *Pause.* I have nearly three hundred dollars. Catherine?

CATHERINE: I heard you.

RODOLPHO: You don't like to talk about it any more?

CATHERINE: Sure, I don't mind talkin' about it.

RODOLPHO: What worries you, Catherine?

CATHERINE: I been wantin' to ask you about something. Could I?

RODOLPHO: All the answers are in my eyes, Catherine. But you don't look in my eyes lately. You're full of secrets. *She looks at him. She seems withdrawn.* What is the question?

CATHERINE: Suppose I wanted to live in Italy.

RODOLPHO, *smiling at the incongruity:* You going to marry somebody rich?

CATHERINE: No, I mean live there—you and me.

RODOLPHO, *his smile vanishing:* When?

CATHERINE: Well . . . when we get married.

RODOLPHO, *astonished:* You want to be an Italian?

CATHERINE: No, but I could live there without being Italian. Americans live there.

RODOLPHO: Forever?

CATHERINE: Yeah.

RODOLPHO *crosses to rocker:* You're fooling.

CATHERINE: No, I mean it.

RODOLPHO: Where do you get such an idea?

CATHERINE: Well, you're always saying it's so beautiful there, with the mountains and the ocean and all the—

RODOLPHO: You're fooling me.

CATHERINE: I mean it.

RODOLPHO *goes to her slowly:* Catherine, if I ever brought you home with no money, no business, nothing, they would call the priest and the doctor and they would say Rodolpho is crazy.

CATHERINE: I know, but I think we would be happier there.

RODOLPHO: Happier! What would you eat? You can't cook the view!

CATHERINE: Maybe you could be a singer, like in Rome or—

RODOLPHO: Rome! Rome is full of singers.

CATHERINE: Well, I could work then.

RODOLPHO: Where?

CATHERINE: God, there must be jobs somewhere!

RODOLPHO: There's nothing! Nothing, nothing, nothing. Now tell me what you're talking about. How can I bring you from a rich country to suffer in a poor country? What are you talking about? *She searches for words.* I would be a criminal stealing your face. In two years you would have an old, hungry face. When my brother's babies cry they give them water, water that boiled a bone. Don't you believe that?

CATHERINE, *quietly:* I'm afraid of Eddie here.

Slight pause.

RODOLPHO, *steps closer to her:* We wouldn't live here. Once I am a citizen I could work anywhere and I would find better jobs and we would have a house, Catherine. If I were not afraid to be arrested I would start to be something wonderful here!

CATHERINE, *steeling herself:* Tell me something. I mean just tell me, Rodolpho—would you still want to do it if it turned out we had to go live in Italy? I mean just if it turned out that way.

RODOLPHO: This is your question or his question?

CATHERINE: I would like to know, Rodolpho. I mean it.

RODOLPHO: To go there with nothing.

CATHERINE: Yeah.

RODOLPHO: No. *She looks at him wide-eyed.* No.

CATHERINE: You wouldn't?

RODOLPHO: No; I will not marry you to live in Italy. I want you to be my wife, and I want to be a citizen. Tell him that, or I will. Yes. *He moves about angrily.* And tell him also, and tell yourself, please, that I am not a beggar, and you are not a horse, a gift, a favor for a poor immigrant.

CATHERINE: Well, don't get mad!

RODOLPHO: I am furious! *Goes to her.* Do you think I am so desperate? My brother is desperate, not me. You think I would carry on my back the rest of my life a woman I didn't love just to be an American? It's so wonderful? You think we have no tall buildings in Italy? Electric lights? No wide streets? No flags? No automobiles? Only work we don't have. I want to be an American so I can work, that is the only wonder here—work! How can you insult me, Catherine?

CATHERINE: I didn't mean that—

RODOLPHO: My heart dies to look at you. Why are you so afraid of him?

CATHERINE, *near tears:* I don't know!

RODOLPHO: Do you trust me, Catherine? You?

CATHERINE: It's only that I—He was good to me, Rodolpho. You don't know him; he was always the sweetest guy to me. Good. He razzes me all the time but he don't mean it. I know. I would—just feel ashamed if I made him sad. 'Cause I always dreamt that when I got married he would be happy at the wedding, and laughin'—and now he's—mad all the time and nasty—*She is weeping.* Tell him you'd live in Italy—just tell him, and maybe he would start to trust you a little, see? Because I want him to be happy; I mean—I like him, Rodolpho—and I can't stand it!

RODOLPHO: Oh, Catherine—oh, little girl.

CATHERINE: I love you, Rodolpho, I love you.

RODOLPHO: Then why are you afraid? That he'll spank you?

CATHERINE: Don't, don't laugh at me! I've been here all my life.... Every day I saw him when he left in the morning and when he came home at night. You think it's so easy to turn around and say to a man he's nothin' to you no more?

RODOLPHO: I know, but—

CATHERINE: You don't know; nobody knows! I'm not a baby, I know a lot more than people think I know. Beatrice says to be a woman, but—

RODOLPHO: Yes.

CATHERINE: Then why don't she be a woman? If I was a wife I would make a man happy instead of goin' at him all the time. I can tell a block away when he's blue in his mind and just wants to talk to somebody quiet and nice.... I can tell when he's hungry or wants a beer before he even says anything. I know when his feet hurt him, I mean I *know* him and now I'm supposed to turn around and make a stranger out of him? I don't know why I have to do that, I mean.

RODOLPHO: Catherine. If I take in my hands a little bird. And she grows and wishes to fly. But I will not let her out of my hands because I love her so much, is that right for me to do? I don't say you must hate him; but anyway you must go, mustn't you? Catherine?

CATHERINE, *softly:* Hold me.

RODOLPHO, *clasping her to him:* Oh, my little girl.

CATHERINE: Teach me. *She is weeping.* I don't know anything, teach me, Rodolpho, hold me.

RODOLPHO: There's nobody here now. Come inside. Come. *He is leading her toward the bedrooms.* And don't cry any more.

Light rises on the street. In a moment Eddie appears. He is unsteady, drunk. He mounts the stairs. He enters the apartment, looks around, takes out a bottle from one pocket, puts it on the table. Then another bottle from another pocket, and a third from an inside pocket. He sees the pattern and cloth, goes over to it and touches it, and turns toward upstage.

EDDIE: Beatrice? *He goes to the open kitchen door and looks in.* Beatrice? Beatrice?

Catherine enters from bedroom; under his gaze she adjusts her dress.

CATHERINE: You got home early.

EDDIE: Knocked off for Christmas early. *Indicating the pattern:* Rodolpho makin' you a dress?

CATHERINE: No. I'm makin' a blouse.

Rodolpho appears in the bedroom doorway. Eddie sees him and his arm jerks slightly in shock. Rodolpho nods to him testingly.

RODOLPHO: Beatrice went to buy presents for her mother.

Pause.

EDDIE: Pack it up. Go ahead. Get your stuff and get outa here. *Catherine instantly turns and walks toward the bedroom, and Eddie grabs her arm.* Where you goin'?

CATHERINE, *trembling with fright:* I think I have to get out of here, Eddie.

EDDIE: No, you ain't goin' nowheres, he's the one.

CATHERINE: I think I can't stay here no more. *She frees her arm, steps back toward the bedroom.* I'm sorry, Eddie. *She sees the tears in his eyes.* Well, don't cry. I'll be around the neighborhood; I'll see you. I just can't stay here no more. You know I can't. *Her sobs of pity and love for him break her composure.* Don't you know I can't? You know that, don't you? *She goes to him.* Wish me luck. *She clasps her hands prayerfully.* Oh, Eddie, don't be like that!

EDDIE: You ain't goin' nowheres.

CATHERINE: Eddie, I'm not gonna be a baby any more! You—

He reaches out suddenly, draws her to him, and as she strives to free herself he kisses her on the mouth.

RODOLPHO: Don't! *He pulls on Eddie's arm.* Stop that! Have respect for her!

EDDIE, *spun round by Rodolpho:* You want something?

RODOLPHO: Yes! She'll be my wife. That is what I want. My wife!

EDDIE: But what're you gonna be?

RODOLPHO: I show you what I be!

CATHERINE: Wait outside; don't argue with him!

EDDIE: Come on, show me! What're you gonna be? Show me!

RODOLPHO, *with tears of rage:* Don't say that to me!

Rodolpho flies at him in attack. Eddie pins his arms, laughing, and suddenly kisses him.

CATHERINE: Eddie! Let go, ya hear me! I'll kill you! Leggo of him!

She tears at Eddie's face and Eddie releases Rodolpho. Eddie stands there with tears rolling down his face as he laughs mockingly at Rodolpho. She is staring at him in horror. Rodolpho is rigid. They are like animals that have torn at one another and broken up without a decision, each waiting for the other's mood.

EDDIE, *to Catherine:* You see? *To Rodolpho:* I give you till tomorrow, kid. Get outa here. Alone. You hear me? Alone.

CATHERINE: I'm going with him, Eddie. *She starts toward Rodolpho.*

EDDIE, *indicating Rodolpho with his head:* Not with that. *She halts, frightened. He sits, still panting for breath, and they watch him helplessly as he leans toward them over the table.* Don't make me do nuttin', Catherine. Watch your step, submarine. By rights they oughta throw you back in the water. But I got pity for you. *He moves unsteadily toward the door, always facing Rodolpho.* Just get outa here and don't lay another hand on her unless you wanna go out feet first. *He goes out of the apartment.*

The lights go down, as they rise on Alfieri.

ALFIERI: On December twenty-seventh I saw him next. I normally go home well before six, but that day I sat around looking out my window at the bay, and when I saw him walking through my doorway, I knew why I had waited. And if I seem to tell this like a dream, it was that way. Several moments arrived in the course of the two talks we had when it occurred to me how—almost transfixed I had come to feel. I had lost my strength somewhere. *Eddie enters, removing his cap, sits in the chair, looks thoughtfully out.* I looked in his eyes more than I listened—in fact, I can hardly remember the conversation. But I will never forget how dark the room became when he looked at me; his eyes were like tunnels. I kept wanting to call the police, but nothing had happened. Nothing at all had really happened. *He breaks off and looks down at the desk. Then he turns to Eddie.* So in other words, he won't leave?

EDDIE: My wife is talkin' about renting a room upstairs for them. An old lady on the top floor is got an empty room.

ALFIERI: What does Marco say?

EDDIE: He just sits there. Marco don't say much.

ALFIERI: I guess they didn't tell him, heh? What happened?

EDDIE: I don't know; Marco don't say much.

ALFIERI: What does your wife say?

EDDIE, *unwilling to pursue this:* Nobody's talkin' much in the house. So what about that?

ALFIERI: But you didn't prove anything about him. It sounds like he just wasn't strong enough to break your grip.

EDDIE: I'm tellin' you I know—he ain't right. Somebody that don't want it can break it. Even a mouse, if you catch a teeny mouse and you hold it in your hand, that mouse can give you the right kind of fight. He didn't give me the right kind of fight, I know it, Mr. Alfieri, the guy ain't right.

ALFIERI: What did you do that for, Eddie?

EDDIE: To show her what he is! So she would see, once and for all! Her mother'll turn over in the grave! *He gathers himself almost peremptorily.* So what do I gotta do now? Tell me what to do.

ALFIERI: She actually said she's marrying him?

EDDIE: She told me, yeah. So what do I do?

Slight pause.

ALFIERI: This is my last word, Eddie, take it or not, that's your business. Morally and legally you have no rights, you cannot stop it; she is a free agent.

EDDIE, *angering:* Didn't you hear what I told you?

ALFIERI, *with a tougher tone:* I heard what you told me, and I'm telling you what the answer is. I'm not only telling you now, I'm warning you—the law is nature. The law is only a word for what has a right to happen. When the law is wrong it's because it's unnatural, but in this case it is natural and a river will drown you if you buck it now. Let her go. And bless her. *A phone booth begins to glow on the opposite side of the stage; a faint, lonely blue. Eddie stands up, jaws clenched.* Somebody had to come for her, Eddie, sooner or later. *Eddie starts turning to go and Alfieri rises with new anxiety.* You won't have a friend in the world, Eddie! Even those who understand will turn against you, even the ones who feel the same will despise you! *Eddie moves off.* Put it out of your mind! Eddie! *He follows into the darkness, calling desperately.*

Eddie is gone. The phone is glowing in light now. Light is out on Alfieri. Eddie has at the same time appeared beside the phone.

EDDIE: Give me the number of the Immigration Bureau. Thanks. *He dials.* I want to report something. Illegal immigrants. Two of them. That's right. Four-forty-one Saxon Street, Brooklyn, yeah. Ground floor. Heh? *With greater difficulty:* I'm just around the neighborhood, that's all. Heh?

Evidently he is being questioned further, and he slowly hangs up. He leaves the phone just as Louis and Mike come down the street.

LOUIS: Go bowlin', Eddie?

EDDIE: No, I'm due home.

LOUIS: Well, take it easy.

EDDIE: I'll see yiz.

They leave him, exiting right, and he watches them go. He glances about, then goes up into the house. The lights go on in the apartment. Beatrice is taking down Christmas decorations and packing them in a box.

EDDIE: Where is everybody? *Beatrice does not answer.* I says where is everybody?

BEATRICE, *looking up at him, wearied with it, and concealing a fear of him:* I decided to move them upstairs with Mrs. Dondero.

EDDIE: Oh, they're all moved up there already?

BEATRICE: Yeah.

EDDIE: Where's Catherine? She up there?

BEATRICE: Only to bring pillow cases.

EDDIE: She ain't movin' in with them.

BEATRICE: Look, I'm sick and tired of it. I'm sick and tired of it!

EDDIE: All right, all right, take it easy.

BEATRICE: I don't wanna hear no more about it, you understand? Nothin'!

EDDIE: What're you blowin' off about? Who brought them in here?

BEATRICE: All right, I'm sorry; I wish I'd a drop dead before I told them to come. In the ground I wish I was.

EDDIE: Don't drop dead, just keep in mind who brought them in here, that's all. *He moves about restlessly.* I mean I got a couple of rights here. *He moves, wanting to beat down her evident disapproval of him.* This is my house here not their house.

BEATRICE: What do you want from me? They're moved out; what do you want now?

EDDIE: I want my respect!

BEATRICE: So I moved them out, what more do you want? You got your house now, you got your respect.

EDDIE—*he moves about biting his lip:* I don't like the way you talk to me, Beatrice.

BEATRICE: I'm just tellin' you I done what you want!

EDDIE: I don't like it! The way you talk to me and the way you look at me. This is my house. And she is my niece and I'm responsible for her.

BEATRICE: So that's why you done that to him?

EDDIE: I done what to him?

BEATRICE: What you done to him in front of her; you know what I'm talkin' about. She goes around shakin' all the time, she can't go to sleep! That's what you call responsible for her?

EDDIE, *quietly:* The guy ain't right, Beatrice. *She is silent.* Did you hear what I said?

BEATRICE: Look, I'm finished with it. That's all. *She resumes her work.*

EDDIE, *helping her to pack the tinsel:* I'm gonna have it out with you one of these days, Beatrice.

BEATRICE: Nothin' to have out with me, it's all settled. Now we gonna be like it never happened, that's all.

EDDIE: I want my respect, Beatrice, and you know what I'm talkin' about.

BEATRICE: What?

Pause.

EDDIE—*finally his resolution hardens:* What I feel like doin' in the bed and what I don't feel like doin'. I don't want no—

BEATRICE: When'd I say anything about that?

EDDIE: You said, you said, I ain't deaf. I don't want no more conversations about that, Beatrice. I do what I feel like doin' or what I don't feel like doin'.

BEATRICE: Okay.

Pause.

EDDIE: You used to be different, Beatrice. You had a whole different way.

BEATRICE: *I'm* no different.

EDDIE: You didn't used to jump me all the time about everything. The last year or two I come in the house I don't know what's gonna hit me. It's a shootin' gallery in here and I'm the pigeon.

BEATRICE: Okay, okay.

EDDIE: Don't tell me okay, okay, I'm tellin' you the truth. A wife is supposed to believe the husband. If I tell you that guy ain't right don't tell me he is right.

BEATRICE: But how do you know?

EDDIE: Because I know. I don't go around makin' accusations. He give me the heeby-jeebies the first minute I seen him. And I don't like you sayin' I don't want her marryin' anybody. I broke my back payin' her stenography lessons so she could go out and meet a better class of people. Would I do that if I didn't want her to get married? Sometimes you talk like I was a crazy man or sump'm.

BEATRICE: But she likes him.

EDDIE: Beatrice, she's a baby, how is she gonna know what she likes?

BEATRICE: Well, you kept her a baby, you wouldn't let her go out. I told you a hundred times.

Pause.

EDDIE: All right. Let her go out, then.

BEATRICE: She don't wanna go out now. It's too late, Eddie.

Pause.

EDDIE: Suppose I told her to go out. Suppose I—

BEATRICE: They're going to get married next week, Eddie.

EDDIE—*his head jerks around to her:* She said that?

BEATRICE: Eddie, if you want my advice, go to her and tell her good luck. I think maybe now that you had it out you learned better.

EDDIE: What's the hurry next week?

BEATRICE: Well, she's been worried about him bein' picked up; this way he could start to be a citizen. She loves him, Eddie. *He gets up, moves about uneasily, restlessly.* Why don't you give her a good word? Because I still think she would like you to be a friend, y'know? *He is standing, looking at the floor.* I mean like if you told her you'd go to the wedding.

EDDIE: She asked you that?

BEATRICE: I know she would like it. I'd like to make a party here for her. I mean there oughta be some kinda send-off. Heh? I mean she'll have trouble enough in her life, let's start it off happy. What do you say? Cause in her heart she still loves you, Eddie. I know it. *He presses his fingers against his eyes.* What're you, cryin'? *She goes to him, holds his face.* Go . . . whyn't you go tell her you're sorry? *Catherine is seen on the upper landing of the stairway, and they hear her descending.* There . . . she's comin' down. Come on, shake hands with her.

EDDIE, *moving with suppressed suddenness:* No, I can't, I can't talk to her.

BEATRICE: Eddie, give her a break; a wedding should be happy!

EDDIE: I'm goin', I'm goin' for a walk.

He goes upstage for his jacket. Catherine enters and starts for the bedroom door.

BEATRICE: Katie? . . . Eddie, don't go, wait a minute. *She embraces Eddie's arm with warmth.* Ask him, Katie. Come on, honey.

EDDIE: It's all right, I'm—*He starts to go and she holds him.*

BEATRICE: No, she wants to ask you. Come on, Katie, ask him. We'll have a party! What're we gonna do, hate each other? Come on!

CATHERINE: I'm gonna get married, Eddie. So if you wanna come, the wedding be on Saturday.

Pause.

EDDIE: Okay. I only wanted the best for you, Katie. I hope you know that.

CATHERINE: Okay. *She starts out again.*

EDDIE: Catherine? *She turns to him.* I was just tellin' Beatrice . . . if you wanna go out, like . . . I mean I realize maybe I kept you home too much. Because he's the first guy you ever knew, y'know? I mean now that you got a job, you might meet some fellas, and you get a different idea, y'know? I mean you could always come back to him, you're still only kids, the both of yiz. What's the hurry? Maybe you'll get around a little bit, you grow up a little more, maybe you'll see different in a couple of months. I mean you be surprised, it don't have to be him.

CATHERINE: No, we made it up already.

EDDIE, *with increasing anxiety:* Katie, wait a minute.

CATHERINE: No, I made up my mind.

EDDIE: But you never knew no other fella, Katie! How could you make up your mind?

CATHERINE: Cause I did. I don't want nobody else.

EDDIE: But, Katie, suppose he gets picked up.

CATHERINE: That's why we gonna do it right away. Soon as we finish the wedding he's goin' right over and start to be a citizen. I made up my mind, Eddie. I'm sorry. *To Beatrice:* Could I take two more pillow cases for the other guys?

BEATRICE: Sure, go ahead. Only don't let her forget where they came from.

Catherine goes into a bedroom.

EDDIE: She's got other boarders up there?

BEATRICE: Yeah, there's two guys that just came over.

EDDIE: What do you mean, came over?

BEATRICE: From Italy. Lipari the butcher—his nephew. They come from Bari, they just got here yesterday. I didn't even know till Marco and Rodolpho moved up there before. *Catherine enters, going toward exit with two pillow cases.* It'll be nice, they could all talk together.

EDDIE: Catherine! *She halts near the exit door. He takes in Beatrice too.* What're you, got no brains? You put them up there with two other submarines?

CATHERINE: Why?

EDDIE, *in a driving fright and anger:* Why! How do you know they're not trackin' these guys? They'll come up for them and find Marco and Rodolpho! Get them out of the house!

BEATRICE: But they been here so long already—

EDDIE: How do you know what enemies Lipari's got? Which they'd love to stab him in the back?

CATHERINE: Well what'll I do with them?

EDDIE: The neighborhood is full of rooms. Can't you stand to live a couple of blocks away from him? Get them out of the house!

CATHERINE: Well maybe tomorrow night I'll—

EDDIE: Not tomorrow, do it now. Catherine, you never mix yourself with somebody else's family! These guys get picked up, Lipari's liable to blame you or me and we got his whole family on our head. They got a temper, that family.

Two men in overcoats appear outside, start into the house.

CATHERINE: How'm I gonna find a place tonight?

EDDIE: Will you stop arguin' with me and get them out! You think I'm always tryin' to fool you or sump'm? What's the matter with you, don't you believe I could think of your good? Did I ever ask sump'm for myself? You think I got no feelin's? I never told you nothin' in my life that wasn't for your good. Nothin'! And look at the way you talk to me! Like I was an enemy! Like I—*A knock on the door. His head swerves. They all stand motionless. Another knock. Eddie, in a whisper, pointing upstage.* Go up the fire escape, get them out over the back fence.

Catherine stands motionless, uncomprehending.

FIRST OFFICER, *in the hall:* Immigration! Open up in there!

EDDIE: Go, go. Hurry up! *She stands a moment staring at him in a realized horror.* Well, what're you lookin' at!

FIRST OFFICER: Open up!

EDDIE, *calling toward door:* Who's that there?

FIRST OFFICER: Immigration, open up.

Eddie turns, looks at Beatrice. She sits. Then he looks at Catherine. With a sob of fury Catherine streaks into a bedroom.
   Knock is repeated.

EDDIE: All right, take it easy, take it easy. *He goes and opens the door. The Officer steps inside.* What's all this?

FIRST OFFICER: Where are they?

Second Officer sweeps past and, glancing about, goes into the kitchen.

EDDIE: Where's who?

FIRST OFFICER: Come on, come on, where are they? *He hurries into the bedrooms.*

EDDIE: Who? We got nobody here. *He looks at Beatrice, who turns her head away. Pugnaciously, furious, he steps toward Beatrice.* What's the matter with *you*?

First Officer enters from the bedroom, calls to the kitchen.

FIRST OFFICER: Dominick?

Enter Second Officer from kitchen.

SECOND OFFICER: Maybe it's a different apartment.

FIRST OFFICER: There's only two more floors up there. I'll take the front, you go up the fire escape. I'll let you in. Watch your step up there.

SECOND OFFICER: Okay, right, Charley. *First Officer goes out apartment door and runs up the stairs.* This is Four-forty-one, isn't it?

EDDIE: That's right.

Second Officer goes out into the kitchen.
    Eddie turns to Beatrice. She looks at him now and sees his terror.

BEATRICE, *weakened with fear:* Oh, Jesus, Eddie.

EDDIE: What's the matter with *you*?

BEATRICE, *pressing her palms against her face:* Oh, my God, my God.

EDDIE: What're you, accusin' me?

BEATRICE—*her final thrust is to turn toward him instead of running from him:* My God, what did you do?

Many steps on the outer stair draw his attention. We see the First Officer descending, with Marco, behind him Rodolpho, and Catherine and the two strange immigrants, followed by Second Officer. Beatrice hurries to door.

CATHERINE, *backing down stairs, fighting with First Officer; as they appear on the stairs:* What do yiz want from them? They work, that's all. They're boarders upstairs, they work on the piers.

BEATRICE, *to First Officer:* Ah, Mister, what do you want from them, who do they hurt?

CATHERINE, *pointing to Rodolpho:* They ain't no submarines, he was born in Philadelphia.

FIRST OFFICER: Step aside, lady.

CATHERINE: What do you mean? You can't just come in a house and—

FIRST OFFICER: All right, take it easy. *To Rodolpho:* What street were you born in Philadelphia?

CATHERINE: What do you mean, what street? Could you tell me what street you were born?

FIRST OFFICER: Sure. Four blocks away, One-eleven Union Street. Let's go fellas.

CATHERINE, *fending him off Rodolpho:* No, you can't! Now, get outa here!

FIRST OFFICER: Look, girlie, if they're all right they'll be out tomorrow. If they're illegal they go back where they came from. If you want, get yourself a lawyer, although I'm tellin' you now you're wasting your money. Let's get them in the car, Dom. *To the men:* Andiamo, Andiamo, let's go.

The men start, but Marco hangs back.

BEATRICE, *from doorway:* Who're they hurtin', for God's sake, what do you want from them? They're starvin' over there, what do you want! Marco!

Marco suddenly breaks from the group and dashes into the room and faces Eddie; Beatrice and First Officer rush in as Marco spits into Eddie's face.

    Catherine runs into hallway and throws herself into Rodolpho's arms. Eddie, with an enraged cry, lunges for Marco.

EDDIE: Oh, you mother's—!

First Officer quickly intercedes and pushes Eddie from Marco, who stands there accusingly.

FIRST OFFICER, *between them, pushing Eddie from Marco:* Cut it out!

EDDIE, *over the First Officer's shoulder, to Marco:* I'll kill you for that, you son of a bitch!

FIRST OFFICER: Hey! *Shakes him.* Stay in here now, don't come out, don't bother him. You hear me? Don't come out, fella.

For an instant there is silence. Then First Officer turns and takes Marco's arm and then gives a last, informative look at Eddie. As he and Marco are going out into the hall, Eddie erupts.

EDDIE: I don't forget that, Marco! You hear what I'm sayin'?

Out in the hall, First Officer and Marco go down the stairs. Now, in the street, Louis, Mike, and several neighbors including the butcher, Lipari—a stout, intense, middle-aged man—are gathering around the stoop.

    Lipari the butcher, walks over to the two strange men and kisses them. His wife, keening, goes and kisses their hands. Eddie is emerging from the house shouting after Marco. Beatrice is trying to restrain him.

EDDIE: That's the thanks I get? Which I took the blankets off my bed for yiz? You gonna apologize to me, Marco! *Marco!*

FIRST OFFICER, *in the doorway with Marco:* All right, lady, let them go. Get in the car, fellas, it's right over there.

Rodolpho is almost carrying the sobbing Catherine off up the street, left.

CATHERINE: He was born in Philadelphia! What do you want from him?

FIRST OFFICER: Step aside, lady, come on now ...

The Second Officer has moved off with the two strange men. Marco, taking advantage of the First Officer's being occupied with Catherine, suddenly frees himself and points back at Eddie.

MARCO: That one! I accuse that one!

Eddie brushes Beatrice aside and rushes out to the stoop.

FIRST OFFICER, *grabbing him and moving him quickly off up the left street:* Come on!

MARCO, *as he is taken off, pointing back at Eddie:* That one! He killed my children! That one stole the food from my children!

Marco is gone. The crowd has turned to Eddie.

EDDIE, *to Lipari and wife:* He's crazy! I give them the blankets off my bed. Six months I kept them like my own brothers!

Lipari, the butcher, turns and starts up left with his arm around his wife.

EDDIE: Lipari! *He follows Lipari up left.* For Christ's sake, I kept them, I give them the blankets off my bed!

Lipari and wife exit. Eddie turns and starts crossing down right to Louis and Mike.

EDDIE: Louis! *Louis!*

Louis barely turns, then walks off and exits down right with Mike. Only Beatrice is left on the stoop. Catherine now returns, blank-eyed, from offstage and the car. Eddie calls after Louis and Mike.

EDDIE: He's gonna take that back. He's gonna take that back or I'll kill him! You hear me? I'll kill him! I'll kill him! *He exits up street calling.*

There is a pause of darkness before the lights rise, on the reception room of a prison. Marco is seated; Alfieri, Catherine, and Rodolpho standing.

ALFIERI: I'm waiting, Marco, what do you say?

RODOLPHO: Marco never hurt anybody.

ALFIERI: I can bail you out until your hearing comes up. But I'm not going to do it, you understand me? Unless I have your promise. You're an honorable man, I will believe your promise. Now what do you say?

MARCO: In my country he would be dead now. He would not live this long.

ALFIERI: All right, Rodolpho—you come with me now.

RODOLPHO: No! Please, Mister. Marco—promise the man. Please, I want you to watch the wedding. How can I be married and you're in here? Please, you're not going to do anything; you know you're not.

Marco is silent.

CATHERINE, *kneeling left of Marco:* Marco, don't you understand?
He can't bail you out if you're gonna do something bad. To hell with Eddie. Nobody is gonna talk to him again if he lives to a hundred. Everybody knows you spit in his face, that's enough, isn't it? Give me the satisfaction—I want you at the wedding. You got a wife and kids, Marco. You could be workin' till the hearing comes up, instead of layin' around here.

MARCO, *to Alfieri:* I have no chance?

ALFIERI *crosses to behind Marco:* No, Marco. You're going back. The hearing is a formality, that's all.

MARCO: But him? There is a chance, eh?

ALFIERI: When she marries him he can start to become an American. They permit that, if the wife is born here.

MARCO, *looking at Rodolpho:* Well—we did something. *He lays a palm on Rodolpho's arm and Rodolpho covers it.*

RODOLPHO: Marco, tell the man.

MARCO, *pulling his hand away:* What will I tell him? He knows such a promise is dishonorable.

ALFIERI: To promise not to kill is not dishonorable.

MARCO, *looking at Alfieri:* No?

ALFIERI: No.

MARCO, *gesturing with his head—this is a new idea:* Then what is done with such a man?

ALFIERI: Nothing. If he obeys the law, he lives. That's all.

MARCO, *rises, turns to Alfieri:* The law? All the law is not in a book.

ALFIERI: Yes. In a book. There is no other law.

MARCO, *his anger rising:* He degraded my brother. My blood. He robbed my children, he mocks my work. I work to come here, mister!

ALFIERI: I know, Marco—

MARCO: There is no law for that? Where is the law for that?

ALFIERI: There is none.

MARCO, *shaking his head, sitting:* I don't understand this country.

ALFIERI: Well? What is your answer? You have five or six weeks you could work. Or else you sit here. What do you say to me?

MARCO *lowers his eyes. It almost seems he is ashamed.* All right.

ALFIERI: You won't touch him. This is your promise.

Slight pause.

MARCO: Maybe he wants to apologize to me.

Marco is staring away. Alfieri takes one of his hands.

ALFIERI: This is not God, Marco. You hear? Only God makes justice.

MARCO: All right.

ALFIERI, *nodding, not with assurance:* Good! Catherine, Rodolpho, Marco, let us go.

Catherine kisses Rodolpho and Marco, then kisses Alfieri's hand.

CATHERINE: I'll get Beatrice and meet you at the church. *She leaves quickly.*

Marco rises. Rodolpho suddenly embraces him. Marco pats him on the back and Rodolpho exits after Catherine. Marco faces Alfieri.

ALFIERI: Only God, Marco.

Marco turns and walks out. Alfieri with a certain processional tread leaves the stage. The lights dim out.

    The lights rise in the apartment. Eddie is alone in the rocker, rocking back and forth in little surges. Pause. Now Beatrice emerges from a bedroom. She is in her best clothes, wearing a hat.

BEATRICE, *with fear, going to Eddie:* I'll be back in about an hour, Eddie. All right?

EDDIE, *quietly, almost inaudibly, as though drained:* What, have I been talkin' to myself?

BEATRICE: Eddie, for God's sake, it's her wedding.

EDDIE: Didn't you hear what I told you? You walk out that door to that wedding you ain't comin' back here, Beatrice.

BEATRICE: Why! What do you want?

EDDIE: I want my respect. Didn't you ever hear of that? From my wife?

Catherine enters from bedroom.

CATHERINE: It's after three; we're supposed to be there already, Beatrice. The priest won't wait.

BEATRICE: Eddie. It's her wedding. There'll be nobody there from her family. For my sister let me go. I'm goin' for my sister.

EDDIE, *as though hurt:* Look, I been arguin' with you all day already, Beatrice, and I said what I'm gonna say. He's gonna come here and apologize to me or nobody from this house is goin' into that church today. Now if that's more to you than I am, then go. But don't come back. You be on my side or on their side, that's all.

CATHERINE, *suddenly:* Who the hell do you think you are?

BEATRICE: Sssh!

CATHERINE: You got no more right to tell nobody nothin'! Nobody! The rest of your life, nobody!

BEATRICE: Shut up, Katie! *She turns Catherine around.*

CATHERINE: You're gonna come with me!

BEATRICE: I can't Katie, I can't . . .

CATHERINE: How can you listen to him? This rat!

BEATRICE, *shaking Catherine:* Don't you call him that!

CATHERINE, *clearing from Beatrice:* What're you scared of? He's a rat! He belongs in the sewer!

BEATRICE: Stop it!

CATHERINE, *weeping:* He bites people when they sleep! He comes when nobody's lookin' and poisons decent people. In the garbage he belongs!

Eddie seems about to pick up the table and fling it at her.

BEATRICE: No, Eddie! Eddie! *To Catherine:* Then we all belong in the garbage. You, and me too. Don't say that. Whatever happened we all done it, and don't you ever forget it, Catherine. *She goes to Catherine.* Now go, go to your wedding, Katie, I'll stay home. Go. God bless you, God bless your children.

Enter Rodolpho.

RODOLPHO: Eddie?

EDDIE: Who said you could come in here? Get outa here!

RODOLPHO: Marco is coming, Eddie. *Pause. Beatrice raises her hands in terror.* He's praying in the church. You understand? *Pause. Rodolpho advances into the room.* Catherine, I think it is better we go. Come with me.

CATHERINE: Eddie, go away please.

BEATRICE, *quietly:* Eddie. Let's go someplace. Come. You and me. *He has not moved.* I don't want you to be here when he comes. I'll get your coat.

EDDIE: Where? Where am I goin'? This is my house.

BEATRICE, *crying out:* What's the use of it! He's crazy now, you know the way they get, what good is it! You got nothin' against Marco, you always liked Marco!

EDDIE: I got nothin' against Marco? Which he called me a rat in front of the whole neighborhood? Which he said I killed his children! Where you been?

RODOLPHO, *quite suddenly, stepping up to Eddie:* It is my fault, Eddie. Everything. I wish to apologize. It was wrong that I do not ask your permission. I kiss your hand. *He reaches for Eddie's hand, but Eddie snaps it away from him.*

BEATRICE: Eddie, he's apologizing!

RODOLPHO: I have made all our troubles. But you have insult me too. Maybe God understand why you did that to me. Maybe you did not mean to insult me at all—

BEATRICE: Listen to him! Eddie, listen what he's tellin' you!

RODOLPHO: I think, maybe when Marco comes, if we can tell him we are comrades now, and we have no more argument between us. Then maybe Marco will not—

EDDIE: Now, listen—

CATHERINE: Eddie, give him a chance!

BEATRICE: What do you want! Eddie, what do you want!

EDDIE: I want my name! He didn't take my name; he's only a punk. Marco's got my name—*to Rodolpho:* and you can run tell him, kid, that he's gonna give it back to me in front of this neighborhood, or we have it out. *Hoisting up his pants:* Come on, where is he? Take me to him.

BEATRICE: Eddie, listen—

EDDIE: I heard enough! Come on, let's go!

BEATRICE: Only blood is good? He kissed your hand!

EDDIE: What he does don't mean nothin' to nobody! *To Rodolpho:* Come on!

BEATRICE, *barring his way to the stairs:* What's gonna mean somethin'? Eddie, listen to me. Who could give you your name? Listen to me, I love you, I'm talkin' to you, I love you; if Marco'll kiss your hand outside, if he goes on his knees, what is he got to give you? That's not what you want.

EDDIE: Don't bother me!

BEATRICE: You want somethin' else, Eddie, and you can never have her!

CATHERINE, *in horror:* B.!

EDDIE, *shocked, horrified, his fists clenching:* Beatrice!

Marco appears outside, walking toward the door from a distant point.

BEATRICE, *crying out, weeping:* The truth is not as bad as blood, Eddie! I'm tellin' you the truth—tell her good-bye forever!

EDDIE, *crying out in agony:* That's what you think of me—that I would have such a thoughts? *His fists clench his head as though it will burst.*

MARCO, *calling near the door outside:* Eddie Carbone!

Eddie swerves about; all stand transfixed for an instant. People appear outside.

EDDIE, *as though flinging his challenge:* Yeah, Marco! Eddie Carbone. Eddie Carbone. Eddie Carbone. *He goes up the stairs and emerges from the apartment. Rodolpho streaks up and out past him and runs to Marco.*

RODOLPHO: No, Marco, please! Eddie, please, he has children! You will kill a family!

BEATRICE: Go in the house! Eddie, go in the house!

EDDIE—*he gradually comes to address the people:* Maybe he come to apologize to me. Heh, Marco? For what you said about me in front of the neighborhood? *He is incensing himself and little bits of laughter even escape him as his eyes are murderous and he cracks his knuckles in his hands with a strange sort of relaxation.* He knows that ain't right. To do like that? To a man? Which I put my roof over their head and my food in their mouth? Like in the Bible? Strangers I never seen in my whole life? To come out of the water and grab a girl for a passport? To go and take from your own family like from the stable—and never a word to me? And now accusations in the bargain! *Directly to Marco:* Wipin' the neighborhood with my name like a dirty rag! I want my name, Marco. *He is moving now, carefully, toward Marco.* Now gimme my name and we go together to the wedding.

BEATRICE AND CATHERINE, *keening:* Eddie! Eddie, don't! Eddie!

EDDIE: No, Marco knows what's right from wrong. Tell the people, Marco, tell them what a liar you are! *He has his arms spread and Marco is spreading his.* Come on, liar, you know what you done! *He lunges for Marco as a great hushed shout goes up from the people.*

Marco strikes Eddie beside the neck.

MARCO: Animal! You go on your knees to me!

Eddie goes down with the blow and Marco starts to raise a foot to stomp him when Eddie springs a knife into his hand and Marco steps back. Louis rushes in toward Eddie.

LOUIS: Eddie, for Christ's sake!

Eddie raises the knife and Louis halts and steps back.

EDDIE: You lied about me, Marco. Now say it. Come on now, say it!

MARCO: Anima-a-a-l!

Eddie lunges with the knife. Marco grabs his arm, turning the blade inward and pressing it home as the women and Louis and Mike rush in and separate them, and Eddie, the knife still in his hand, falls to his knees before Marco. The two women support him for a moment, calling his name again and again.

CATHERINE: Eddie I never meant to do nothing bad to you.

EDDIE: Then why—Oh, B.!

BEATRICE: Yes, yes!

EDDIE: My B.!

He dies in her arms, and Beatrice covers him with her body. Alfieri, who is in the crowd, turns out to the audience. The lights have gone down, leaving him in a glow, while behind him the dull prayers of the people and the keening of the women continue.

ALFIERI: Most of the time now we settle for half and I like it better. But the truth is holy, and even as I know how wrong he was, and his death useless, I tremble, for I confess that something perversely pure calls to me from his memory—not purely good, but himself purely, for he allowed himself to be wholly known and for that I think I will love him more than all my sensible clients. And yet, it is better to settle for half, it must be! And so I mourn him—I admit it—with a certain . . . alarm.

CURTAIN

1955

GWENDOLYN BROOKS
1917–2000

Gwendolyn Brooks, born in Topeka, Kansas, considered herself a lifelong Chicagoan. When she began writing at age seven, her mother predicted, "You are going to be the *lady* Paul Laurence Dunbar." First published at eleven, by sixteen Brooks was contributing poetry weekly to the *Chicago Defender*. In *Report from Part One*, she describes a happy childhood spent in black neighborhoods with her parents and younger brother Raymond. Her mother, "duty-loving" Keziah Wims Brooks, had been a fifth-grade teacher; she played the piano, wrote music, and published a book of stories at eighty-six. Her father, David Anderson Brooks, son of a runaway slave, was a janitor with "rich artistic abilities"; he sang, told stories, and worked hard to purchase a house and support his family. Both parents nurtured their daughter's precocious gifts. "I had always felt that to be black was good," Brooks wrote in her autobiography.

Her home environment supported her confidence and fostered her black musical heritage, whose creative center was the church. At church she met James Weldon Johnson and Langston Hughes; the latter became an inspiration and, later, a friend and mentor.

Following graduation from Wilson Junior College (now Kennedy-King) in 1936, Brooks worked for a month as a maid in a North Shore home and then spent four unhappy months as secretary to the spiritual adviser who became the prototype for Prophet Williams in "In the Mecca." In 1939 she married Henry Lowington Blakely II, a fellow member of Inez Cunningham Stark's poetry workshop at the South Side Community Art Center. In 1950 she won the Pulitzer Prize for Poetry with *Annie Allen*, the first black writer to be so honored.

That award was followed by two Guggenheim Fellowships, election to membership in the National Institute of Arts and Letters, and selection as Consultant in Poetry to the Library of Congress.

Finely crafted, influenced by Langston Hughes, T. S. Eliot, Emily Dickinson, and Robert Frost—and later by the 1960s Black Arts movement—Brooks's poetry was always a social act. *A Street in Bronzeville* addresses the realities of segregation for black Americans at home and in World War II military service; *Annie Allen* ironically explores postwar antiromanticism. *Maud Martha*, her prose masterpiece, sketches a bildungsroman of black womanhood; *The Bean Eaters* and later poems sound the urgencies of the civil rights movement. In 1967 she attended the Second Fisk University Writers' Conference and was deeply impressed with the activism of Amiri Baraka. Subsequently, although she had always experimented with various forms, her work opened more distinctly to free verse, a notable feature of *In the Mecca* (1968).

Returning to Chicago from the Fisk Conference, Brooks conducted a workshop with the Blackstone Rangers, a teen gang, and then with young writers like Carolyn M. Rodgers and Haki R. Madhubuti (then don l. lee). Her new Black Nationalist perspective impelled her commitment to black publishing. In 1969 she turned to Dudley Randall's Broadside Press for publication of *Riot*, followed by *Family Pictures* and *Aloneness*, and to Madhubuti's Third World Press for *The Tiger Who Wore White Gloves* and *To Disembark*. In 1971 she began publishing a literary annual, *The Black Position*, under her own aegis. Starting with *Primer for Blacks* in 1980, she took charge of her creative work. Although many of her earlier books now issue from Third World Press, *Children Coming Home* was published in 1991 by The David Company, her own imprint.

Brooks traveled widely and constantly, giving workshops and readings in schools, libraries, and prisons. Her visits to Africa in 1971 and 1974 deepened her sense of African heritage. Yet her poetry reflects the rich confluence and continuity of a dual stream: the black sermonic tradition and black music—the spiritual, the blues, and jazz—and white antecedents like the ballad, the sonnet, and conventional and free forms. It suggests connections with Anglo-Saxon alliteration and strong-stressed verse, with the Homeric bard and the African griot. Brooks's heroic and prophetic voice surfaces in what she called "preachments." Brooks intended that her work "'call' all black people."

D. H. Melhem
Independent Scholar

PRIMARY WORKS

A Street in Bronzeville, 1945; *Annie Allen*, 1949; *Maud Martha*, 1953; *Bronzeville Boys and Girls*, 1956; *The Bean Eaters*, 1960; *Selected Poems*, 1963; *In the Mecca*, 1968; *Riot*, 1969; *Family Pictures*, 1970; *Aloneness*, 1971; *Jump Bad*, 1971; *The World of Gwendolyn Brooks*, 1971; *Report from Part One*, 1972; *Beckonings*, 1975; *A Capsule Course in Black Poetry Writing*, 1975; *Primer for Blacks*, 1980; *Young Poet's Primer*, 1980; *To Disembark*, 1981; *Mayor Harold Washington and Chicago, the I Will City*, 1983; *Very Young Poets*, 1983; *The Near-Johannesburg Boy and Other Poems*, 1986; *Blacks* (omnibus), 1987; *Gottschalk and the Grande Tarantelle*, 1988; *Winnie*, 1991; *Children Coming Home*, 1991; *Report from Part Two*, 1996.

The Sundays of Satin-Legs Smith

Inamoratas, with an approbation,
Bestowed his title. Blessed his inclination.

He wakes, unwinds, elaborately: a cat
Tawny, reluctant, royal. He is fat
And fine this morning. Definite. Reimbursed.   5

He waits a moment, he designs his reign,
That no performance may be plain or vain.
Then rises in a clear delirium.

He sheds, with his pajamas, shabby days.
And his desertedness, his intricate fear, the   10
Postponed resentments and the prim precautions.

Now, at his bath, would you deny him lavender
Or take away the power of his pine?
What smelly substitute, heady as wine,
Would you provide? life must be aromatic.   15
There must be scent, somehow there must be some.
Would you have flowers in his life? suggest
Asters? a Really Good geranium?
A white carnation? would you prescribe a Show
With the cold lilies, formal chrysanthemum   20
Magnificence, poinsettias, and emphatic
Red of prize roses? might his happiest
Alternative (you muse) be, after all,
A bit of gentle garden in the best
Of taste and straight tradition? Maybe so.   25
But you forget, or did you ever know,
His heritage of cabbage and pigtails,
Old intimacy with alleys, garbage pails,
Down in the deep (but always beautiful) South
Where roses blush their blithest (it is said)   30
And sweet magnolias put Chanel to shame.

No! He has not a flower to his name.
Except a feather one, for his lapel.
Apart from that, if he should think of flowers
It is in terms of dandelions or death.   35
Ah, there is little hope. You might as well—
Unless you care to set the world a-boil
And do a lot of equalizing things,

Remove a little ermine, say, from kings,
Shake hands with paupers and appoint them men,   40
For instance—certainly you might as well
Leave him his lotion, lavender and oil.

Let us proceed. Let us inspect, together
With his meticulous and serious love,
The innards of this closet. Which is a vault   45
Whose glory is not diamonds, not pearls,
Not silver plate with just enough dull shine.
But wonder-suits in yellow and in wine,
Sarcastic green and zebra-striped cobalt.
All drapes. With shoulder padding that is wide   50
And cocky and determined as his pride;
Ballooning pants that taper off to ends
Scheduled to choke precisely.
                                        Here are hats
Like bright umbrellas; and hysterical ties   55
Like narrow banners for some gathering war.

People are so in need, in need of help.
People want so much that they do not know.
Below the tinkling trade of little coins
The gold impulse not possible to show   60
Or spend. Promise piled over and betrayed.

These kneaded limbs receive the kiss of silk.
Then they receive the brave and beautiful
Embrace of some of that equivocal wool.
He looks into his mirror, loves himself—   65
The neat curve here; the angularity
That is appropriate at just its place;
The technique of a variegated grace.

Here is all his sculpture and his art
And all his architectural design.   70
Perhaps you would prefer to this a fine
Value of marble, complicated stone.
Would have him think with horror of baroque,
Rococo. You forget and you forget.

He dances down the hotel steps that keep   75
Remnants of last night's high life and distress.
As spat-out purchased kisses and spilled beer.
He swallows sunshine with a secret yelp.

Passes to coffee and a roll or two.
Has breakfasted.   80
                    Out. Sounds about him smear,
Become a unit. He hears and does not hear
The alarm clock meddling in somebody's sleep;
Children's governed Sunday happiness;
The dry tone of a plane; a woman's oath;   85
Consumption's spiritless expectoration;
An indignant robin's resolute donation
Pinching a track through apathy and din;
Restaurant vendors weeping; and the L
That comes on like a slightly horrible thought.   90

Pictures, too, as usual, are blurred.
He sees and does not see the broken windows
Hiding their shame with newsprint; little girl
With ribbons decking wornness, little boy
Wearing the trousers with the decentest patch,   95
To honor Sunday; women on their way
From "service," temperate holiness arranged
Ably on asking faces; men estranged
From music and from wonder and from joy
But far familiar with the guiding awe   100
Of foodlessness.
                    He loiters.
                              Restaurant vendors
Weep, or out of them rolls a restless glee.
The Lonesome Blues, the Long-lost Blues, I Want A   105
Big Fat Mama. Down these sore avenues
Comes no Saint-Saëns, no piquant elusive Grieg,
And not Tschaikovsky's wayward eloquence
And not the shapely tender drift of Brahms.
But could he love them? Since a man must bring   110
To music what his mother spanked him for
When he was two: bits of forgotten hate,
Devotion: whether or not his mattress hurts:
The little dream his father humored: the thing
His sister did for money: what he ate   115
For breakfast—and for dinner twenty years
Ago last autumn: all his skipped desserts.

The pasts of his ancestors lean against
Him. Crowd him. Fog out his identity.
Hundreds of hungers mingle with his own,   120
Hundreds of voices advise so dexterously

He quite considers his reactions his,
Judges he walks most powerfully alone,
That everything is—simply what it is.

But movie-time approaches, time to boo   125
The hero's kiss, and boo the heroine
Whose ivory and yellow it is sin
For his eye to eat of. The Mickey Mouse,
However, is for everyone in the house.

Squires his lady to dinner at Joe's Eats.   130
His lady alters as to leg and eye,
Thickness and height, such minor points as these,
From Sunday to Sunday. But no matter what
Her name or body positively she's
In Queen Lace stockings with ambitious heels   135
That strain to kiss the calves, and vivid shoes
Frontless and backless, Chinese fingernails,
Earrings, three layers of lipstick, intense hat
Dripping with the most voluble of veils.
Her affable extremes are like sweet bombs   140
About him, whom no middle grace or good
Could gratify. He had no education
In quiet arts of compromise. He would
Not understand your counsels on control, nor
Thank you for your late trouble.   145
                                        At Joe's Eats
You get your fish or chicken on meat platters.
With coleslaw, macaroni, candied sweets,
Coffee and apple pie. You go out full.
(The end is—isn't it?—all that really matters.)   150

        And even and intrepid come
        The tender boots of night to home.

        Her body is like new brown bread
        Under the Woolworth mignonette.[1]
        Her body is a honey bowl   155
        Whose waiting honey is deep and hot.
        Her body is like summer earth,
        Receptive, soft, and absolute . . .

                                                        1945

---

[1]An herb, native to northern Africa; here it
refers to a narrow bobbin lace, having a scattered small design on a ground somewhat
like tulle and made especially by the French
and the Flemish in the sixteenth through the
nineteenth centuries.

The Mother

Abortions will not let you forget.
You remember the children you got that you did not get.
The damp small pulps with a little or with no hair,
The singers and workers that never handled the air.
You will never neglect or beat   5
Them, or silence or buy with a sweet.
You will never wind up the sucking-thumb
Or scuttle off ghosts that come.
You will never leave them, controlling your luscious sigh,
Return for a snack of them, with gobbling mother-eye.   10

I have heard in the voices of the wind the voices of my dim killed
    children.
I have contracted. I have eased
My dim dears at the breasts they could never suck.
I have said, Sweets, if I sinned, if I seized   15
Your luck
And your lives from your unfinished reach,
If I stole your births and your names,
Your straight baby tears and your games,
Your stilted or lovely loves, your tumults, your marriages, aches,   20
    and your deaths,
If I poisoned the beginnings of your breaths,
Believe that even in my deliberateness I was not deliberate.
Though why should I whine,
Whine that the crime was other than mine?—   25
Since anyhow you are dead.
Or rather, or instead,
You were never made.
But that too, I am afraid,
Is faulty: oh, what shall I say, how is the truth to be said?   30
You were born, you had body, you died.
It is just that you never giggled or planned or cried.

Believe me, I loved you all.
Believe me, I knew you, though faintly, and I loved, I loved you
All.   35

                                                                1945

We Real Cool

The Pool Players.
Seven at the Golden Shovel.

We real cool. We
Left school. We

Lurk late. We
Strike straight. We

Sing sin. We   5
Thin gin. We

Jazz June.[1] We
Die soon.

                                                                      1960

A Bronzeville Mother Loiters in Mississippi. Meanwhile, a Mississippi Mother Burns Bacon[1']

From the first it had been like a
Ballad. It had the beat inevitable. It had the blood.
A wildness cut up, and tied in little bunches,
Like the four-line stanzas of the ballads she had never quite
Understood—the ballads they had set her to, in school.   5

Herself: the milk-white maid, the "maid mild"
Of the ballad. Pursued
By the Dark Villain. Rescued by the Fine Prince.
The Happiness-Ever-After.
That was worth anything.   10
It was good to be a "maid mild."
That made the breath go fast.

Her bacon burned. She
Hastened to hide it in the step-on can, and
Drew more strips from the meat case. The eggs and sour-milk   15
    biscuits
Did well. She set out a jar
Of her new quince preserve.

. . . But there was a something about the matter of the Dark
    Villain.   20

[1] A reference to popular music and enjoying the summer of youth.
[1'] Both this poem and the next concern the murder of Emmett Louis Till, a fourteen-year-old Chicago youth who was murdered in Mississippi on August 28, 1955, because he had "wolf-whistled" at a white woman.

He should have been older, perhaps.
The hacking down of a villain was more fun to think about
When his menace possessed undisputed breadth, undisputed
    height,
And a harsh kind of vice.   25
And best of all, when his history was cluttered
With the bones of many eaten knights and princesses.

The fun was disturbed, then all but nullified
When the Dark Villain was a blackish child
Of fourteen, with eyes still too young to be dirty,   30
And a mouth too young to have lost every reminder
Of its infant softness.
That boy must have been surprised! For
These were grown-ups. Grown-ups were supposed to be wise.
And the Fine Prince—and that other—so tall, so broad, so   35
Grown! Perhaps the boy had never guessed
That the trouble with grown-ups was that under the magnificent
    shell of adulthood, just under,
Waited the baby full of tantrums.
It occurred to her that there may have been something   40
Ridiculous in the picture of the Fine Prince
Rushing (rich with the breadth and height and
Mature solidness whose lack, in the Dark Villain, was impressing
    her,
Confronting her more and more as this first day after the trial   45
And acquittal wore on) rushing
With his heavy companion to hack down (unhorsed)
That little foe.
So much had happened, she could not remember now what that
    foe had done   50
Against her, or if anything had been done.
The one thing in the world that she did know and knew
With terrifying clarity was that her composition
Had disintegrated. That, although the pattern prevailed,
The breaks were everywhere. That she could think   55
Of no thread capable of the necessary
Sew-work.

She made the babies sit in their places at the table.
Then, before calling Him, she hurried
To the mirror with her comb and lipstick. It was necessary   60
To be more beautiful than ever.
The beautiful wife.
For sometimes she fancied he looked at her as though
Measuring her. As if he considered, Had she been worth It?
Had *she* been worth the blood, the cramped cries, the little   65
    stuttering bravado,

The gradual dulling of those Negro eyes,
The sudden, overwhelming *little-boyness* in that barn?
Whatever she might feel or half-feel, the lipstick necessity was
    something apart. He must never conclude   70
That she had not been worth It.

He sat down, the Fine Prince, and
Began buttering a biscuit. He looked at his hands.
He twisted in his chair, he scratched his nose.
He glanced again, almost secretly, at his hands.   75
More papers were in from the North, he mumbled. More
    meddling headlines.
With their pepper-words, "bestiality," and "barbarism," and
"Shocking."
The half-sneers he had mastered for the trial worked across   80
His sweet and pretty face.

What he'd like to do, he explained, was kill them all.
The time lost. The unwanted fame.
Still, it had been fun to show those intruders   85
A thing or two. To show that snappy-eyed mother,
That sassy, Northern, brown-black——

Nothing could stop Mississippi.
He knew that. Big Fella
Knew that.   90
And, what was so good, Mississippi knew that.
Nothing and nothing could stop Mississippi.
They could send in their petitions, and scar
Their newspapers with bleeding headlines. Their governors
Could appeal to Washington. . . .   95

"What I want," the older baby said, "is 'lasses on my jam."
Whereupon the younger baby
Picked up the molasses pitcher and threw
The molasses in his brother's face. Instantly
The Fine Prince leaned across the table and slapped   100
The small and smiling criminal.

She did not speak. When the Hand
Came down and away, and she could look at her child,
At her baby-child,
She could think only of blood.   105
Surely her baby's cheek
Had disappeared, and in its place, surely,
Hung a heaviness, a lengthening red, a red that had no end.

She shook her head. It was not true, of course.
It was not true at all. The   110
Child's face was as always, the
Color of the paste in her paste-jar.

She left the table, to the tune of the children's lamentations, which
    were shriller
Than ever. She   115
Looked out of a window. She said not a word. *That*
Was one of the new Somethings—
The fear,
Tying her as with iron.

Suddenly she felt his hands upon her. He had followed her   120
To the window. The children were whimpering now.
Such bits of tots. And she, their mother,
Could not protect them. She looked at her shoulders, still
Gripped in the claim of his hands. She tried, but could not resist
    the idea   125
That a red ooze was seeping, spreading darkly, thickly, slowly,
Over her white shoulders, her own shoulders,
And over all of Earth and Mars.

He whispered something to her, did the Fine Prince, something
About love, something about love and night and intention.   130

She heard no hoof-beat of the horse and saw no flash of the
    shining steel.
He pulled her face around to meet
His, and there it was, close close,
For the first time in all those days and nights.   135
His mouth, wet and red,
So very, very, very red,
Closed over hers.

Then a sickness heaved within her. The courtroom Coca-Cola,
The courtroom beer and hate and sweat and drone,   140
Pushed like a wall against her. She wanted to bear it.
But his mouth would not go away and neither would the
Decapitated exclamation points in that Other Woman's eyes.

She did not scream.
She stood there.   145
But a hatred for him burst into glorious flower,
And its perfume enclasped them—big,
Bigger than all magnolias.

The last bleak news of the ballad.
The rest of the rugged music.   150
The last quatrain.

                                        1960

The Last Quatrain of the Ballad of Emmett Till

                              after the murder,
                              after the burial

Emmett's mother is a pretty-faced thing;
      the tint of pulled taffy.
She sits in a red room,   5
      drinking black coffee.
She kisses her killed boy.
      And she is sorry.
Chaos in windy grays
      through a red prairie.   10

                                        1960

Ulysses[1]

Religion

At home we pray every morning, we
get down on our knees in a circle,
holding hands, holding Love,
and we sing Hallelujah.

Then we go into the World.   5

Daddy *speeds*, to break bread with his Girl Friend.
Mommy's a Boss. And a lesbian.
(She too has a nice Girl Friend.)

My brothers and sisters and I come to school.
We bring knives pistols bottles, little boxes, and cans.   10

We talk to the man who's cool at the playground gate.
Nobody Sees us, nobody stops our sin.

[1]The name of one of the twenty children who are the personae represented by each poem in the book. Ulysses is the Roman name for Odysseus, a famous Greek warrior whose adventures and return home after twenty years are recounted in Homer's epic poem *The Odyssey*.

Our teachers feed us geography.
We spit it out in a hurry.

Now we are coming home.   15

At home, we pray every evening, we
get down on our knees in a circle,
holding hands, holding Love.

And we sing Hallelujah.

                                                         1991

MITSUYE YAMADA
B. 1923

Born on July 4, 1923, while her parents—both U.S. residents—were on a visit to Fukuoka, Japan, Mitsuye Yamada née Yasutake settled with her family in Seattle, Washington, in 1926. Her father was a poet and interpreter, and her mother was a seamstress. Along with other Japanese Americans, Yamada was incarcerated during World War II, as a result of Executive Order 9066, in the Puyallup Assembly Center (known as Camp Harmony) and the Minidoka Relocation Center in Idaho. From 1942 to 1944, Yamada recorded some of her impressions of the internment in poetic form. She did not publish these poems, however, until 1976. Since that time, Yamada has written more poems, short stories, and essays; taught literature and creative writing; and worked as a women's rights activist.

Like many other Japanese Americans, Yamada remained silent during the 1940s, 1950s, and 1960s regarding her years in internment (notable exceptions include writers Miné Okubo and John Okada). According to the speaker in her poem "Thirty Years Under," she had "sealed" her memories in a psychological "iron box." Having been granted clearance to leave internment in 1944, Yamada attended the University of Cincinnati. In 1947 she earned a B.A. in English and art from New York University, and in 1953 she earned an M.A. in English from the University of Chicago. She became a naturalized U.S. citizen in 1955 and taught at Fullerton and Cypress junior colleges and the University of California at Irvine. With her husband, Yoshikazu Yamada, she raised four children.

The civil rights and women's rights movements of the late 1960s and 1970s, as well as literature by E. L. Doctorow, Marge Piercy, and Tillie Olsen, inspired Yamada to tell her story. In a documentary titled *Mitsuye and Nellie: Asian American Poets* (1981), Yamada talks with her daughter about the code of silence that she chose to break with her first book of poems, *Camp Notes* (1976), which was released by the Shameless Hussy Press, an Oakland-based feminist publisher. This book traces various internees' points of view, from that of a young person being told to pack two bags for "a vacation / lasting forever" to that of an older man imprisoned as a POW to that of the dominant voice: a young woman who observes the irony of a watchtower guard who seems to be "in solitary / confined in the middle / of his land." The young female speaker eventually leaves for what she thinks will be "freedom" in Cincinnati but finds herself still virtually imprisoned by the racist treatment of others, who go so far as to call her a "dirty jap" and spit on her. Thirty years later, this speaker recognizes a kindred soul in a black man who struggles against similar humiliations, a figure perhaps of the civil rights movement, and who implicitly wakes her from her period of repression. In her subsequent volume, *Desert Run: Poems and Stories* (1988), and the expanded version of her first book, *Camp Notes and Other Poems* (1992), Yamada continues to share wry observations on the internment, represent some of the emotions of the experience, and consider the perspectives of others, including Japanese immigrants and Euro-Americans. Interested in uniting words with action, Yamada founded a group to encourage others called the Multicultural Women Writers of Orange County, served on the board of Amnesty International, and worked in the Japanese American redress movement. Besides poetry and short stories, Yamada also wrote essays, including "Invisibility Is an Unnatural Disaster: Reflections of an Asian American Woman" for *This Bridge Called My Back: Writings by Radical Women of Color* (1981). Yamada retired in 1989 from the University of California at Irvine, where her papers are held.

Floyd Cheung
Smith College

PRIMARY WORKS

Camp Notes, 1976; *Desert Run: Poems and Stories*, 1988; *Camp Notes and Other Poems*, 1992.

Evacuation

As we boarded the bus
bags on both sides
(I had never packed
two bags before
on a vacation   5
lasting forever)
the *Seattle Times*
photographer said
Smile!
so obediently I smiled   10
and the caption the next day
read:
Note smiling faces
a lesson to Tokyo.

1976 (composed in 1943)

Desert Storm

Near the mess hall
along the latrines
by the laundry
between the rows of
black tar papered barracks   5
the block captain galloped by.
Take cover everyone he said
here comes a twister.
Hundreds of windows
slammed shut.   10
Five pairs of hands
in our room
with mess hall
butter knives
stuffed   15
newspapers and rags
between the cracks.
But the Idaho dust
persistent and seeping
found us crouched   20
under the covers.
This was not
im
prison
ment.   25
This was
re
location.

                               1976 (composed in 1943)

Inside News

A small group
huddles around a contraband
radio
What?
We   5
are losing the war?
Who is we?
We are we the enemy
the enemy is the enemy.
Static sounds and we   10
cannot hear.
The enemy is confused

the enemy is determined
and winning.
Mess hall gossips   15
have it that
the parents
with samurai morals
are now the children.

                                                    1976 (composed in 1945)

The Question of Loyalty

I met the deadline
for alien registration
once before
was numbered fingerprinted
and ordered not to travel   5
without permit.
But alien still they said I must
foreswear allegiance to the emperor.
For me that was easy
I didn't even know him   10
but my mother who did cried out
    If I sign this
    What will I be?
    I am doubly loyal
    to my American children   15
    also to my own people.
    How can double mean nothing?
    I wish no one to lose this war.
    Everyone does.
I was poor   20
at math.
I signed
my only ticket out.

                                                    1976 (composed in 1947)

The Night before Good-Bye

Mama is mending
my underwear
while my brothers sleep.
Her husband taken away by the FBI
one son lured away by the Army   5
now another son and daughter
lusting for the free world outside.

She must let go.
The war goes on.
She will take one still small son   10
and join Papa in internment
to make a family.
Still sewing
squinting in the dim light
in room C barrack 4 block 4   15
she whispers
Remember
keep your underwear
in good repair
in case of accident   20
don't bring shame
on us.

                                    1976 (composed in 1945)

Thirty Years Under

I had packed up
my wounds in a cast
iron box
sealed it
labeled it   5
do not open . . .
ever . . .
and traveled blind
for thirty years
until one day I heard   10
a black man with huge bulbous eyes
say
there is nothing more
humiliating
more than beatings   15
more than curses
than being spat on
like a dog.

                                    1976 (composed in 1953)

Cincinnati

Freedom at last
in this town aimless
I walked against the rush
hour traffic

My first day
in a real city
where
no one knew me.
No one except one   5
hissing voice that said
dirty jap   10
warm spittle on my right cheek.
I turned and faced
the shop window
and my spittled face   15
spilled onto a hill
of books.
Words on display.
In Government Square
people criss-crossed   20
the street
like the spokes of
a giant wheel.
I lifted my right hand
but it would not obey me.   25
My other hand fumbled
for a hankie.
My tears would not
wash it. They stopped
and parted.   30
My hankie brushed
the forked
tears and spittle
together.
I edged toward the curb   35
loosened my fisthold
and the bleached laced
mother-ironed hankie blossomed in
the gutter atop teeth marked
gum wads and heeled candy wrappers.   40
Everyone knew me.

                                                                                    1976

To the Lady

The one in San Francisco who asked
Why did the Japanese Americans let
the government put them in
those camps without protest?
Come to think of it I   5

should've run off to Canada
should've hijacked a plane to Algeria
should've pulled myself up from my
bra straps
and kicked'm in the groin   10
should've bombed a bank
should've tried self-immolation
should've holed myself up in a
woodframe house
and let you watch me   15
burn up on the six o'clock news
should've run howling down the street
naked and assaulted you at breakfast
by AP wirephoto
should've screamed bloody murder   20
like Kitty Genovese
Then
YOU would've
come to my aid in shining armor
laid yourself across the railroad track   25
marched on Washington
tattooed a Star of David on your arm
written six million enraged
letters to Congress
But we didn't draw the line   30
anywhere
law and order Executive Order 9066
social order moral order internal order
YOU let'm
I let'm   35
All are punished.

1976

JAMES BALDWIN
1924–1987

Perhaps more than any other writer who came to prominence after 1950, James Baldwin represented the process by which a person at odds with the country of his birth seeks to reconcile him- or herself to it, as well as to a status as less than a first-class citizen. Through the essays that became his trademark, Baldwin pricked the conscience of an America that had distorted the original concepts of democracy. He encouraged Americans to retrieve those seeds and bring them to fruition. Through his life and his art, Baldwin repeatedly bore witness to the injustices heaped upon black Americans and consistently urged healing of the social fabric before it was torn beyond repair.

Born to Emma Berdis Jones (a single mother) in Harlem, New York, Baldwin would create art out of the pain of illegitimacy and the problems he had with his stepfather, David Baldwin, whom his mother married when he was three. As his mother bore eight more children, Baldwin helped care for them and tried to escape his stepfather's anger by excelling in school. Relationships between parents and children, particularly between fathers and sons, form the theme of many of Baldwin's works, including "Sonny's Blues" and other stories collected in *Going to Meet the Man*, 1965. The religious fanaticism of his stepfather also became a dominant subject for his early fiction.

Baldwin read voraciously, including Harriet Beecher Stowe's *Uncle Tom's Cabin*, Charles Dickens, and Horatio Alger. In fact, he read through the Harlem libraries and moved on to other parts of the city. He edited his junior high school newspaper and shared editorial duties on the *Magpie* at DeWitt Clinton High School, a predominantly white Bronx secondary school. When Baldwin was fourteen, he underwent a religious conversion, which led to ministerial duties until he was seventeen. This religious experience was partly a way of defying his stepfather, but its influence also recurs throughout his later writing.

Although Baldwin published some scattered pieces in the 1940s, he made his debut in 1953 with *Go Tell It on the Mountain*, a chronicle of three generations of a black family plagued by slavery and internal strife. Young John Grimes, in the present generation of the novel, serves as Baldwin's fictional representation of his crisis of the spirit. In subsequent fiction, he dealt with homosexuality (among white characters), racial and sexual identities, problems of the civil rights movement, life in Harlem, and religion. Although his fiction was well received, the essay may be Baldwin's strength, and his collections of essays were sometimes better sellers than his novels.

Of Baldwin's plays, two continue the religious and political themes of his other works. *The Amen Corner* focuses on the influence of the church in the lives of black Americans; *Blues for Mister Charlie* is loosely based on the case of Emmett Till, the fourteen-year-old black boy who was killed in Mississippi in 1955 for allegedly whistling at a white woman.

Although Baldwin was quite active in the civil rights movement, he participated only by returning to the United States in the 1950s and 1960s from France, a country to which he had bought a one-way ticket in 1948, and from Turkey, where he spent a considerable amount of time in the 1960s. After that time, he moved back and forth, never staying in the United States for an extended period and eventually settling in the south of France. Whatever his vantage point, Baldwin continued to prod Americans into better behavior, for he genuinely loved the country that was less willing to return that love.

Trudier Harris
University of North Carolina at Chapel Hill

PRIMARY WORKS

Go Tell It on the Mountain, 1953; *Notes of a Native Son*, 1955; *Giovanni's Room*, 1956; *Nobody Knows My Name*, 1961; *Another Country*, 1962; *The Fire Next Time*, 1963;

Blues for Mister Charlie, 1964; *Nothing Personal* (with Richard Avedon), 1964; *Going to Meet the Man*, 1965; *Tell Me How Long the Train's Been Gone*, 1968; *The Amen Corner*, 1968; *No Name in the Street*, 1972; *A Dialogue* (with Nikki Giovanni), 1973; *If Beale Street Could Talk*, 1974; *The Devil Finds Work*, 1976; *Just above My Head*, 1979; *Jimmy's Blues*, 1983; *The Evidence of Things Not Seen*, 1985.

Sonny's Blues

I read about it in the paper, in the subway, on my way to work. I read it, and I couldn't believe it, and I read it again. Then perhaps I just stared at it, at the newsprint spelling out his name, spelling out the story. I stared at it in the swinging lights of the subway car, and in the faces and bodies of the people, and in my own face, trapped in the darkness which roared outside.

It was not to be believed and I kept telling myself that, as I walked from the subway station to the high school. And at the same time I couldn't doubt it. I was scared, scared for Sonny. He became real to me again. A great block of ice got settled in my belly and kept melting there slowly all day long, while I taught my classes algebra. It was a special kind of ice. It kept melting, sending trickles of ice water all up and down my veins, but it never got less. Sometimes it hardened and seemed to expand until I felt my guts were going to come spilling out or that I was going to choke or scream. This would always be at a moment when I was remembering some specific thing Sonny had once said or done.

When he was about as old as the boys in my classes his face had been bright and open, there was a lot of copper in it; and he'd had wonderfully direct brown eyes, and great gentleness and privacy. I wondered what he looked like now. He had been picked up the evening before, in a raid on an apartment downtown, for peddling and using heroin.

I couldn't believe it: but what I mean by that is that I couldn't find any room for it anywhere inside me. I had kept it outside me for a long time. I hadn't wanted to know. I had had suspicions, but I didn't name them, I kept putting them away. I told myself that Sonny was wild, but he wasn't crazy. And he'd always been a good boy, he hadn't ever turned hard or evil or disrespectful, the way kids can, so quick, especially in Harlem. I didn't want to believe that I'd ever see my brother going down, coming to nothing, all that light in his face gone out, in the condition I'd already seen so many others. Yet it had happened and here I was, talking about algebra to a lot of boys who might, every one of them for all I knew, be popping off needles every time they went to the head. Maybe it did more for them than algebra could.

I was sure that the first time Sonny had ever had horse,[1] he couldn't have been much older than these boys were now. These boys, now, were living as we'd been living then, they were growing up with a rush and their heads bumped abruptly against the low ceiling of their actual possibilities. They were filled with rage. All they really knew were two darknesses, the

---

[1]Heroin.

darkness of their lives, which was now closing in on them, and the darkness of the movies, which had blinded them to that other darkness, and in which they now, vindictively, dreamed, at once more together than they were at any other time, and more alone.

When the last bell rang, the last class ended, I let out my breath. It seemed I'd been holding it for all that time. My clothes were wet—I may have looked as though I'd been sitting in a steam bath, all dressed up all afternoon. I sat alone in the classroom a long time. I listened to the boys outside, downstairs, shouting and cursing and laughing. Their laughter struck me for perhaps the first time. It was not the joyous laughter which— God knows why—one associates with children. It was mocking and insular, its intent was to denigrate. It was disenchanted, and in this, also, lay the authority of their curses. Perhaps I was listening to them because I was thinking about my brother and in them I heard my brother. And myself.

One boy was whistling a tune, at once very complicated and very simple, it seemed to be pouring out of him as though he were a bird, and it sounded very cool and moving through all that harsh, bright air, only just holding its own through all those other sounds.

I stood up and walked over to the window and looked down into the courtyard. It was the beginning of the spring and the sap was rising in the boys. A teacher passed through them every now and again, quickly, as though he or she couldn't wait to get out of that courtyard, to get those boys out of their sight and off their minds. I started collecting my stuff. I thought I'd better get home and talk to Isabel.

The courtyard was almost deserted by the time I got downstairs. I saw this boy standing in the shadow of a doorway, looking just like Sonny. I almost called his name. Then I saw that it wasn't Sonny, but somebody we used to know, a boy from around our block. He'd been Sonny's friend. He'd never been mine, having been too young for me, and, anyway, I'd never liked him. And now, even though he was a grown-up man, he still hung around that block, still spent hours on the street corners, was always high and raggy. I used to run into him from time to time and he'd often work around to asking me for a quarter or fifty cents. He always had some real good excuse too, and I always gave it to him, I don't know why.

But now, abruptly I hated him. I couldn't stand the way he looked at me, partly like a dog, partly like a cunning child. I wanted to ask him what the hell he was doing in the school courtyard.

He sort of shuffled over to me, and he said, "I see you got the papers. So you already know about it."

"You mean about Sonny? Yes, I already know about it. How come they didn't get you?"

He grinned. It made him repulsive and it also brought to mind what he'd looked like as a kid. "I wasn't there. I stay away from them people."

"Good for you." I offered him a cigarette and I watched him through the smoke. "You come all the way down here just to tell me about Sonny?"

"That's right." He was sort of shaking his head and his eyes looked strange, as though they were about to cross. The bright sun deadened his damp dark brown skin and it made his eyes look yellow and showed up the dirt in his kinked hair. He smelled funky. I moved a little way away from him and I said, "Well, thanks. But I already know about it and I got to get home."

"I'll walk you a little ways," he said. We started walking. There were a couple of kids still loitering in the courtyard and one of them said goodnight to me and looked strangely at the boy beside me.

"What're you going to do?" he asked me. "I mean, about Sonny?"

"Look. I haven't seen Sonny for over a year. I'm not sure I'm going to do anything. Anyway, what the hell *can* I do?"

"That's right," he said quickly, "ain't nothing you can do. Can't much help old Sonny no more, I guess."

It was what I was thinking and so it seemed to me he had no right to say it.

"I'm surprised at Sonny, though," he went on—he had a funny way of talking, he looked straight ahead as though he were talking to himself—"I thought Sonny was a smart boy, I thought he was too smart to get hung."

"I guess he thought so too," I said sharply, "and that's how he got hung. And how about you? You're pretty goddamn smart, I bet."

Then he looked directly at me, just for a minute. "I ain't smart," he said. "If I was smart, I'd have reached for a pistol a long time ago."

"Look. Don't tell *me* your sad story, if it was up to me, I'd give you one." Then I felt guilty—guilty, probably, for never having supposed that the poor bastard *had* a story of his own, much less a sad one, and I asked, quickly, "What's going to happen to him now?"

He didn't answer this. He was off by himself some place. "Funny thing," he said, and from his tone we might have been discussing the quickest way to get to Brooklyn, "when I saw the papers this morning, the first thing I asked myself was if I had anything to do with it. I felt sort of responsible."

I began to listen more carefully. The subway station was on the corner, just before us, and I stopped. He stopped, too. We were in front of a bar and he ducked slightly, peering in, but whoever he was looking for didn't seem to be there. The juke box was blasting away with something black and bouncy and I half watched the barmaid as she danced her way from the juke box to her place behind the bar. And I watched her face as she laughingly responded to something someone said to her, still keeping time to the music. When she smiled one saw the little girl, one sensed the doomed, still struggling woman beneath the battered face of the semi-whore.

"I never *give* Sonny nothing," the boy said finally, "but a long time ago I come to school high and Sonny asked me how it felt." He paused, I couldn't bear to watch him, I watched the barmaid, and I listened to the music which seemed to be causing the pavement to shake. "I told him it felt great." The music stopped, the barmaid paused and watched the juke box until the music began again. "It did."

All this was carrying me some place I didn't want to go. I certainly didn't want to know how it felt. It filled everything, the people, the houses, the music, the dark, quicksilver barmaid, with menace, and this menace was their reality.

"What's going to happen to him now?" I asked again.

"They'll send him away some place and they'll try to cure him." He shook his head. "Maybe he'll even think he's kicked the habit. Then they'll let him loose"—he gestured, throwing his cigarette into the gutter. "That's all."

"What do you mean that's *all*?"

But I knew what he meant.

"I *mean*, that's *all*." He turned his head and looked at me, pulling down the corners of his mouth. "Don't you know what I mean?" he asked, softly.

"How the hell *would* I know what you mean?" I almost whispered it, I don't know why.

"That's right," he said to the air, "how would *he* know what I mean?" He turned toward me again, patient and calm, and yet I somehow felt him shaking, shaking as though he were going to fall apart. I felt that ice in my guts again, the dread I'd felt all afternoon; and again I watched the barmaid, moving about the bar, washing glasses, and singing. "Listen. They'll let him out and then it'll just start all over again. That's what I mean."

"You mean—they'll let him out. And then he'll just start working his way back in again. You mean he'll never kick the habit. Is that what you mean?"

"That's right," he said cheerfully. "*You* see what I mean."

"Tell me," I said at last, "why does he want to die? He must want to die, he's killing himself, why does he want to die?"

He looked at me in surprise. He licked his lips. "He don't want to die. He wants to live. Don't nobody want to die, ever."

Then I wanted to ask him—too many things. He could not have answered, or if he had, I could not have borne the answers. I started walking. "Well, I guess it's none of my business."

"It's going to be rough on old Sonny," he said. We reached the subway station. "This is your station?" he asked. I nodded. I took one step down. "Damn!" he said suddenly. I looked up at him. He grinned again. "Damn it if I didn't leave all my money home. You ain't got a dollar on you, have you? Just for a couple of days, is all."

All at once something inside gave and threatened to come pouring out of me. I didn't hate him any more. I felt that in another moment I'd start crying like a child.

"Sure," I said. "Don't sweat." I looked in my wallet and didn't have a dollar, I only had five. "Here," I said. "That hold you?"

He didn't look at it—he didn't want to look at it. A terrible closed look came over his face, as though he were keeping the number on the bill a secret from him and me. "Thanks," he said, and now he was dying to see me go. "Don't worry about Sonny. Maybe I'll write him or something."

"Sure," I said. "You do that. So long."

"Be seeing you," he said. I went on down the steps.

And I didn't write Sonny or send him anything for a long time. When I finally did, it was just after my little girl died, he wrote me back a letter which made me feel like a bastard.

Here's what he said:

> Dear brother,
>
> You don't know how much I needed to hear from you. I wanted to write you many a time but I dug how much I must have hurt you and so I didn't write. But now I feel like a man who's been trying to climb up out of some deep, real deep and funky hole and just saw the sun up there, outside. I got to get outside.
>
> I can't tell you much about how I got here. I mean I don't know how to tell you. I guess I was afraid of something or I was trying to escape from something and you know I have never been very strong in the head (smile). I'm glad Mama and Daddy are dead and can't see what's happened to their son and I swear if I'd known what I was doing I would never have hurt you so, you and a lot of other fine people who were nice to me and who believed in me.
>
> I don't want you to think it had anything to do with me being a musician. It's more than that. Or maybe less than that. I can't get anything straight in my head down here and I try not to think about what's going to happen to me when I get outside again. Sometime I think I'm going to flip and never get outside and sometime I think I'll come straight back. I tell you one thing, though, I'd rather blow my brains out than go through this again. But that's what they all say, so they tell me. If I tell you when I'm coming to New York and if you could meet me, I sure would appreciate it. Give my love to Isabel and the kids and I was sure sorry to hear about little Gracie. I wish I could be like Mama and say the Lord's will be done, but I don't know it seems to me that trouble is the one thing that never does get stopped and I don't know what good it does to blame it on the Lord. But maybe it does some good if you believe it.
>
> Your brother,
> Sonny

Then I kept in constant touch with him and I sent him whatever I could and I went to meet him when he came back to New York. When I saw him many things I thought I had forgotten came flooding back to me. This was because I had begun, finally, to wonder about Sonny, about the life that Sonny lived inside. This life, whatever it was, had made him older and thinner and it had deepened the distant stillness in which he had always moved. He looked very unlike my baby brother. Yet, when he smiled, when we shook hands, the baby brother I'd never known looked out from the depths of his private life, like an animal waiting to be coaxed into the light.

"How you been keeping?" he asked me.

"All right. And you?"

"Just fine." He was smiling all over his face. "It's good to see you again."

"It's good to see you."

The seven years' difference in our ages lay between us like a chasm: I wondered if these years would ever operate between us as a bridge. I was remembering, and it made it hard to catch my breath, that I had been there when he was born; and I had heard the first words he had ever spoken. When he started to walk, he walked from our mother straight to me. I caught him just before he fell when he took the first steps he ever took in this world.

"How's Isabel?"

"Just fine. She's dying to see you."

"And the boys?"

"They're fine, too. They're anxious to see their uncle."

"Oh, come on. You know they don't remember me."

"Are you kidding? Of course they remember you."

He grinned again. We got into a taxi. We had a lot to say to each other, far too much to know how to begin.

As the taxi began to move, I asked, "You still want to go to India?"

He laughed. "You still remember that. Hell, no. This place is Indian enough for me."

"It used to belong to them," I said.

And he laughed again. "They damn sure knew what they were doing when they got rid of it."

Years ago, when he was around fourteen, he'd been all hipped on the idea of going to India. He read books about people sitting on rocks, naked, in all kinds of weather, but mostly bad, naturally, and walking barefoot through hot coals and arriving at wisdom. I used to say that it sounded to me as though they were getting away from wisdom as fast as they could. I think he sort of looked down on me for that.

"Do you mind," he asked, "if we have the driver drive alongside the park? On the west side—I haven't seen the city in so long."

"Of course not," I said. I was afraid that I might sound as though I were humoring him, but I hoped he wouldn't take it that way.

So we drove along, between the green of the park and the stony, lifeless elegance of hotels and apartment buildings, toward the vivid, killing streets of our childhood. These streets hadn't changed, though housing projects jutted up out of them now like rocks in the middle of a boiling sea. Most of the houses in which we had grown up had vanished, as had the stores from which we had stolen, the basements in which we had first tried sex, the rooftops from which we had hurled tin cans and bricks. But houses exactly like the houses of our past yet dominated the landscape, boys exactly like the boys we once had been found themselves smothering in these houses, came down into the streets for light and air and found themselves encircled by disaster. Some escaped the trap, most didn't. Those who got out always left something of themselves behind, as some animals amputate a leg and leave it in the trap. It might be said, perhaps, that I had escaped, after all, I was a school teacher; or that Sonny had, he hadn't lived in Harlem for years. Yet, as the cab moved uptown through streets which seemed, with a rush, to darken with dark people, and as I covertly studied Sonny's face, it came to me that what we both were seeking through our separate cab windows was that part of ourselves which had been left behind. It's always at the hour of trouble and confrontation that the missing member aches.

We hit 110th Street and started rolling up Lenox Avenue. And I'd known this avenue all my life, but it seemed to me again, as it had seemed on the day I'd first heard about Sonny's trouble, filled with a hidden menace which was its very breath of life.

"We almost there," said Sonny.

"Almost." We were both too nervous to say anything more.

We live in a housing project. It hasn't been up long. A few days after it was up it seemed uninhabitably new, now, of course, it's already rundown. It looks like a parody of the good, clean, faceless life—God knows the people who live in it do their best to make it a parody. The beat-looking grass lying around isn't enough to make their lives green, the hedges will never hold out the streets, and they know it. The big windows fool no one, they aren't big enough to make space out of no space. They don't bother with the windows, they watch the TV screen instead. The playground is most popular with the children who don't play at jacks, or skip rope, or roller skate, or swing, and they can be found in it after dark. We moved in partly because it's not too far from where I teach, and partly for the kids; but it's really just like the houses in which Sonny and I grew up. The same things happen, they'll have the same things to remember. The moment Sonny and I started into the house I had the feeling that I was simply bringing him back into the danger he had almost died trying to escape.

Sonny has never been talkative. So I don't know why I was sure he'd be dying to talk to me when supper was over the first night. Everything went fine, the oldest boy remembered him, and the youngest boy liked him, and Sonny had remembered to bring something for each of them; and Isabel, who is really much nicer than I am, more open and giving, had gone to a lot of trouble about dinner and was genuinely glad to see him. And she's always been able to tease Sonny in a way that I haven't. It was nice to see her face so vivid again and to hear her laugh and watch her make Sonny laugh. She wasn't, or, anyway, she didn't seem to be, at all uneasy or embarrassed. She chatted as though there were no subject which had to be avoided and she got Sonny past his first, faint stiffness. And thank God she was there, for I was filled with that icy dread again. Everything I did seemed awkward to me, and everything I said sounded freighted with hidden meaning. I was trying to remember everything I'd heard about dope addiction and I couldn't help watching Sonny for signs. I wasn't doing it out of malice. I was trying to find out something about my brother. I was dying to hear him tell me he was safe.

"Safe!" my father grunted, whenever Mama suggested trying to move to a neighborhood which might be safer for children. "Safe, hell! Ain't no place safe for kids, nor nobody."

He always went on like this, but he wasn't, ever, really as bad as he sounded, not even on weekends, when he got drunk. As a matter of fact, he was always on the lookout for "something a little better," but he died before he found it. He died suddenly, during a drunken weekend in the middle of the war, when Sonny was fifteen. He and Sonny hadn't ever got on too well. And this was partly because Sonny was the apple of his father's eye. It was because he loved Sonny so much and was frightened for him, that he was always fighting with him. It doesn't do any good to fight with Sonny. Sonny just moves back, inside himself, where he can't be reached. But the principal reason that they never hit it off is that they were so much alike. Daddy was big and rough and loud-talking, just the opposite of Sonny, but they both had—that same privacy.

Mama tried to tell me something about this, just after Daddy died. I was home on leave from the army.

This was the last time I ever saw my mother alive. Just the same, this picture gets all mixed up in my mind with pictures I had of her when she was younger. The way I always see her is the way she used to be on a Sunday afternoon, say, when the old folks were talking after the big Sunday dinner. I always see her wearing pale blue. She'd be sitting on the sofa. And my father would be sitting in the easy chair, not far from her. And the living room would be full of church folks and relatives. There they sit, in chairs all around the living room, and the night is creeping up outside, but nobody knows it yet. You can see the darkness growing against the window-panes and you hear the street noises every now and again, or maybe the jangling beat of a tambourine from one of the churches close by, but it's real quiet in the room. For a moment nobody's talking, but every face looks darkening, like the sky outside. And my mother rocks a little from the waist, and my father's eyes are closed. Everyone is looking at something a child can't see. For a minute they've forgotten the children. Maybe a kid is lying on the rug, half asleep. Maybe somebody's got a kid in his lap and is absent-mindedly stroking the kid's head. Maybe there's a kid, quiet and big-eyed, curled up in a big chair in the corner. The silence, the darkness coming, and the darkness in the faces frightens the child obscurely. He hopes that the hand which strokes his forehead will never stop—will never die. He hopes that there will never come a time when the old folks won't be sitting around the living room, talking about where they've come from, and what they've seen, and what's happened to them and their kinfolk.

But something deep and watchful in the child knows that this is bound to end, is already ending. In a moment someone will get up and turn on the light. Then the old folks will remember the children and they won't talk any more that day. And when light fills the room, the child is filled with darkness. He knows that every time this happens he's moved just a little closer to that darkness outside. The darkness outside is what the old folks have been talking about. It's what they've come from. It's what they endure. The child knows that they won't talk any more because if he knows too much about what's happening to *them*, he'll know too much too soon, about what's going to happen to *him*.

The last time I talked to my mother, I remember I was restless. I wanted to get out and see Isabel. We weren't married then and we had a lot to straighten out between us.

There Mama sat, in black, by the window. She was humming an old church song, *Lord you brought me from a long ways off*. Sonny was out somewhere. Mama kept watching the streets.

"I don't know," she said, "if I'll ever see you again, after you go off from here. But I hope you'll remember the things I tried to teach you."

"Don't talk like that," I said, and smiled. "You'll be here a long time yet."

She smiled, too, but she said nothing. She was quiet for a long time. And I said, "Mama, don't you worry about nothing. I'll be writing all the time, and you be getting the checks...."

"I want to talk to you about your brother," she said, suddenly. "If anything happens to me he ain't going to have nobody to look out for him."

"Mama," I said, "ain't nothing going to happen to you *or* Sonny. Sonny's all right. He's a good boy and he's got good sense."

"It ain't a question of his being a good boy," Mama said, "nor of his having good sense. It ain't only the bad ones, nor yet the dumb ones that gets sucked under." She stopped, looking at me. "Your Daddy once had a brother," she said, and she smiled in a way that made me feel she was in pain. "You didn't never know that, did you?"

"No," I said, "I never knew that," and I watched her face.

"Oh, yes," she said, "your Daddy had a brother." She looked out of the window again. "I know you never saw your Daddy cry. But *I* did—many a time, through all these years."

I asked her, "What happened to his brother? How come nobody's ever talked about him?"

This was the first time I ever saw my mother look old.

"His brother got killed," she said, "when he was just a little younger than you are now. I knew him. He was a fine boy. He was maybe a little full of the devil, but he didn't mean nobody no harm."

Then she stopped and the room was silent, exactly as it had sometimes been on those Sunday afternoons. Mama kept looking out into the streets.

"He used to have a job in the mill," she said, "and, like all young folks, he just liked to perform on Saturday nights. Saturday nights, him and your father would drift around to different places, go to dances and things like that, or just sit around with people they knew, and your father's brother would sing, he had a fine voice, and play along with himself on his guitar. Well, this particular Saturday night, him and your father was coming home from some place, and they were both a little drunk and there was a moon that night, it was bright like day. Your father's brother was feeling kind of good, and he was whistling to himself, and he had his guitar slung over his shoulder. They was coming down a hill and beneath them was a road that turned off from the highway. Well, your father's brother, being always kind of frisky, decided to run down this hill, and he did, with that guitar banging and clanging behind him, and he ran across the road, and he was making water behind a tree. And your father was sort of amused at him and he was still coming down the hill, kind of slow. Then he heard a car motor and that same minute his brother stepped from behind the tree, into the road, in the moonlight. And he started to cross the road. And your father started to run down the hill, he says he don't know why. This car was full of white men. They was all drunk, and when they seen your father's brother they let out a great whoop and holler and they aimed the car straight at him. They was having fun, they just wanted to scare him, the way they do sometimes, you know. But they was drunk. And I guess the boy, being drunk, too, and scared, kind of lost his head. By the time he jumped it was too late. Your father says he heard his brother scream when the car rolled over him, and he heard the wood of that guitar when it give, and he heard them strings go flying, and he heard them white men shouting, and the car kept on a-going and it ain't stopped till this day. And, time your father got down the hill, his brother weren't nothing but blood and pulp."

Tears were gleaming on my mother's face. There wasn't anything I could say.

"He never mentioned it," she said, "because I never let him mention it before you children. Your Daddy was like a crazy man that night and for many a night thereafter. He says he never in his life seen anything as dark as that road after the lights of that car had gone away. Weren't nothing, weren't nobody on that road, just your Daddy and his brother and that busted guitar. Oh, yes. Your Daddy never did really get right again. Till the day he died he weren't sure but that every white man he saw was the man that killed his brother."

She stopped and took out her handkerchief and dried her eyes and looked at me.

"I ain't telling you all this," she said, "to make you scared or bitter or to make you hate nobody. I'm telling you this because you got a brother. And the world ain't changed."

I guess I didn't want to believe this. I guess she saw this in my face. She turned away from me, toward the window again, searching those streets.

"But I praise my Redeemer," she said at last, "that He called your Daddy home before me. I ain't saying it to throw no flowers at myself, but, I declare, it keeps me from feeling too cast down to know I helped your father get safely through this world. Your father always acted like he was the roughest, strongest man on earth. And everybody took him to be like that. But if he hadn't had *me* there—to see his tears!"

She was crying again. Still I couldn't move. I said, "Lord, Lord, Mama, I didn't know it was like that."

"Oh, honey," she said, "there's a lot that you don't know. But you are going to find it out." She stood up from the window and came over to me. "You got to hold on to your brother," she said, "and don't let him fall, no matter what it looks like is happening to him and no matter how evil you gets with him. You going to be evil with him many a time. But don't you forget what I told you, you hear?"

"I won't forget," I said. "Don't you worry, I won't forget. I won't let nothing happen to Sonny."

My mother smiled as though she were amused at something she saw in my face. Then, "You may not be able to stop nothing from happening. But you got to let him know you's *there.*"

Two days later I was married, and then I was gone. And I had a lot of things on my mind and I pretty well forgot my promise to Mama until I got shipped home on a special furlough for her funeral.

And, after the funeral, with just Sonny and me alone in the empty kitchen, I tried to find out something about him.

"What do you want to do?" I asked him.

"I'm going to be a musician," he said.

For he had graduated, in the time I had been away, from dancing to the juke box to finding out who was playing what, and what they were doing with it, and he had bought himself a set of drums.

"You mean, you want to be a drummer?" I somehow had the feeling that being a drummer might be all right for other people but not for my brother Sonny.

"I don't think," he said, looking at me very gravely, "that I'll ever be a good drummer. But I think I can play a piano."

I frowned. I'd never played the role of the older brother quite so seriously before, had scarcely ever, in fact, *asked* Sonny a damn thing. I sensed myself in the presence of something I didn't really know how to handle, didn't understand. So I made my frown a little deeper as I asked: "What kind of musician do you want to be?"

He grinned. "How many kinds do you think there are?"

"Be *serious*," I said.

He laughed, throwing his head back, and then looked at me. "I *am* serious."

"Well, then, for Christ's sake, stop kidding around and answer a serious question. I mean, do you want to be a concert pianist, or want to play classical music and all that, or—or what?" Long before I finished he was laughing again. "For Christ's *sake*, Sonny!"

He sobered, but with difficulty. "I'm sorry. But you sound so—*scared!*" and he was off again.

"Well, you may think it's funny now, baby, but it's not going to be so funny when you have to make your living at it, let me tell you *that.*" I was furious because I knew he was laughing at me and I didn't know why.

"No," he said, very sober now, and afraid, perhaps, that he'd hurt me, "I don't want to be a classical pianist. That isn't what interests me. I mean"—he paused, looking hard at me, as though his eyes would help me to understand, and then gestured helplessly, as though perhaps his hand would help—"I mean, I'll have a lot of studying to do, and I'll have to study *everything*, but, I mean, I want to play *with*—jazz musicians." He stopped. "I want to play jazz," he said.

Well, the word had never before sounded as heavy, as real, as it sounded that afternoon in Sonny's mouth. I just looked at him and I was probably frowning a real frown by this time. I simply couldn't see why on earth he'd want to spend his time hanging around nightclubs, clowning around on bandstands, while people pushed each other around a dance floor. It seemed—beneath him, somehow. I had never thought about it before, had never been forced to, but I suppose I had always put jazz musicians in a class with what Daddy called "goodtime people."

"Are you *serious*?"

"Hell, *yes*, I'm serious."

He looked more helpless than ever, and annoyed, and deeply hurt.

I suggested helpfully: "You mean—like Louis Armstrong?"

His face closed as though I'd struck him. "No. I'm not talking about none of that old-time, down home crap."

"Well, look Sonny, I'm sorry, don't get mad. I just don't altogether get it, that's all. Name somebody—you know, a jazz musician you admire."

"Bird."

"Who?"

"Bird! Charlie Parker! Don't they teach you nothing in the god-damn army?"

I lit a cigarette. I was surprised and then a little amused to discover that I was trembling. "I've been out of touch," I said. "You'll have to be patient with me. Now. Who's this Parker character?"

"He's just one of the greatest jazz musicians alive," said Sonny, sullenly, his hands in his pockets, his back to me. "Maybe *the* greatest," he added, bitterly, "that's probably why *you* never heard of him."

"All right," I said, "I'm ignorant. I'm sorry. I'll go out and buy all the cat's records right away, all right?"

"It don't," said Sonny, with dignity, "make any difference to me. I don't care what you listen to. Don't do me no favors."

I was beginning to realize that I'd never seen him so upset before. With another part of my mind I was thinking that this would probably turn out to be one of those things kids go through and that I shouldn't make it seem important by pushing it too hard. Still, I didn't think it would do any harm to ask: "Doesn't all this take a lot of time? Can you make a living at it?"

He turned back to me and half leaned, half sat, on the kitchen table. "Everything takes time," he said, "and—well, yes, sure, I can make a living at it. But what I don't seem to be able to make you understand is that it's the only thing I want to do."

"Well, Sonny," I said gently, "you know people can't always do exactly what they *want* to do—"

"*No*, I don't know that," said Sonny, surprising me. "I think people *ought* to do what they want to do, what else are they alive for?"

"You are getting to be a big boy," I said desperately, "it's time you started thinking about your future."

"I'm thinking about my future," said Sonny, grimly. "I think about it all the time."

I gave up. I decided, if he didn't change his mind, that we could always talk about it later. "In the meantime," I said, "you got to finish school." We had already decided that he'd have to move in with Isabel and her folks. I knew this wasn't the ideal arrangement because Isabel's folks are inclined to be dicty[2] and they hadn't especially wanted Isabel to marry me. But I didn't know what else to do. "And we have to get you fixed up at Isabel's."

There was a long silence. He moved from the kitchen table to the window. "That's a terrible idea. You know it yourself."

"Do you have a *better* idea?"

He just walked up and down the kitchen for a minute. He was as tall as I was. He had started to shave. I suddenly had the feeling that I didn't know him at all.

He stopped at the kitchen table and picked up my cigarettes. Looking at me with a kind of mocking, amused defiance, he put one between his lips. "You mind?"

"You smoking already?"

He lit the cigarette and nodded, watching me through the smoke. "I just wanted to see if I'd have the courage to smoke in front of you." He grinned and blew a great cloud of smoke to the ceiling. "It was easy." He looked at my face. "Come on, now. I bet you was smoking at my age, tell the truth."

I didn't say anything but the truth was on my face, and he laughed. But now there was something very strained in his laugh. "Sure. And I bet that ain't all you was doing."

He was frightening me a little. "Cut the crap," I said. "We already decided that you was going to go and live at Isabel's. Now what's got into you all of a sudden?"

"*You* decided it," he pointed out. "*I* didn't decide nothing." He stopped in front of me, leaning against the stove, arms loosely folded. "Look, brother. I don't want to stay in Harlem no more, I really don't." He was very earnest. He looked at me, then over toward the kitchen window. There was something in his eyes I'd never seen before, some thoughtfulness, some worry all his own. He rubbed the muscle of one arm. "It's time I was getting out of here."

"Where do you want to *go*, Sonny?"

"I want to join the army. Or the navy, I don't care. If I say I'm old enough, they'll believe me."

Then I got mad. It was because I was so scared. "You must be crazy. You goddamn fool, what the hell do you want to go and join the *army* for?"

"I just told you. To get out of Harlem."

---

[2]Snobbish.

"Sonny, you haven't even finished *school*. And if you really want to be a musician, how do you expect to study if you're in the *army?*"

He looked at me, trapped, and in anguish. "There's ways. I might be able to work out some kind of deal. Anyway, I'll have the G.I. Bill when I come out."

"*If* you come out." We stared at each other. "Sonny, please. Be reasonable. I know the setup is far from perfect. But we got to do the best we can."

"I ain't learning nothing in school," he said. "Even when I go." He turned away from me and opened the window and threw his cigarette out into the narrow alley. I watched his back. "At least, I ain't learning nothing you'd want me to learn." He slammed the window so hard I thought the glass would fly out, and turned back to me. "And I'm sick of the stink of these garbage cans!"

"Sonny," I said, "I know how you feel. But if you don't finish school now, you're going to be sorry later that you didn't." I grabbed him by the shoulders. "And you only got another year. It ain't so bad. And I'll come back and I swear I'll help you do *whatever* you want to do. Just try to put up with it till I come back. Will you please do that? For me?"

He didn't answer and he wouldn't look at me.

"Sonny. You hear me?"

He pulled away. "I hear you. But you never hear anything *I* say."

I didn't know what to say to that. He looked out of the window and then back at me. "OK," he said, and sighed. "I'll try."

Then I said, trying to cheer him up a little, "They got a piano at Isabel's. You can practice on it."

And as a matter of fact, it did cheer him up for a minute. "That's right," he said to himself. "I forgot that." His face relaxed a little. But the worry, the thoughtfulness, played on it still, the way shadows play on a face which is staring into the fire.

But I thought I'd never hear the end of that piano. At first, Isabel would write me, saying how nice it was that Sonny was so serious about his music and how, as soon as he came in from school, or wherever he had been when he was supposed to be at school, he went straight to that piano and stayed there until suppertime. And, after supper, he went back to that piano and stayed there until everybody went to bed. He was at the piano all day Saturday and all day Sunday. Then he bought a record player and started playing records. He'd play one record over and over again, all day long sometimes, and he'd improvise along with it on the piano. Or he'd play one section of the record, one chord, one change, one progression, then he'd do it on the piano. Then back to the record. Then back to the piano.

Well, I really don't know how they stood it. Isabel finally confessed that it wasn't like living with a person at all, it was like living with sound. And the sound didn't make any sense to her, didn't make any sense to any of them—naturally. They began, in a way, to be afflicted by this presence that was living in their home. It was as though Sonny were some sort of god, or monster. He moved in an atmosphere which wasn't like theirs at all. They fed him and he ate, he washed himself, he walked in and out of their door; he certainly wasn't nasty or unpleasant or rude, Sonny isn't any of those things; but it was as though he were all wrapped up in some cloud, some fire, some vision all his own; and there wasn't any way to reach him.

At the same time, he wasn't really a man yet, he was still a child, and they had to watch out for him in all kinds of ways. They certainly couldn't throw him out. Neither did they dare to make a great scene about that piano because even they dimly sensed, as I sensed, from so many thousands of miles away, that Sonny was at that piano playing for his life.

But he hadn't been going to school. One day a letter came from the school board and Isabel's mother got it—there had, apparently, been other letters but Sonny had torn them up. This day, when Sonny came in, Isabel's mother showed him the letter and asked where he'd been spending his time. And she finally got it out of him that he'd been down in Greenwich Village, with musicians and other characters, in a white girl's apartment. And this scared her and she started to scream at him and what came up, once she began—though she denies it to this day—was what sacrifices they were making to give Sonny a decent home and how little he appreciated it.

Sonny didn't play the piano that day. By evening, Isabel's mother had calmed down but then there was the old man to deal with, and Isabel herself. Isabel says she did her best to be calm but she broke down and started crying. She says she just watched Sonny's face. She could tell, by watching him, what was happening with him. And what was happening was that they penetrated his cloud, they had reached him. Even if their fingers had been a thousand times more gentle than human fingers ever are, he could hardly help feeling that they had stripped him naked and were spitting on that nakedness. For he also had to see that his presence, that music, which was life or death to him, had been torture for them and that they had endured it, not at all for his sake, but only for mine. And Sonny couldn't take that. He can take it a little better today than he could then but he's still not very good at it and, frankly, I don't know anybody who is.

The silence of the next few days must have been louder than the sound of all the music ever played since time began. One morning, before she went to work, Isabel was in his room for something and she suddenly realized that all of his records were gone. And she knew for certain that he was gone. And he was. He went as far as the navy would carry him. He finally sent me a postcard from some place in Greece and that was the first I knew that Sonny was still alive. I didn't see him any more until we were both back in New York and the war had long been over.

He was a man by then, of course, but I wasn't willing to see it. He came by the house from time to time, but we fought almost every time we met. I didn't like the way he carried himself, loose and dreamlike all the time, and I didn't like his friends, and his music seemed to be merely an excuse for the life he led. It sounded just that weird and disordered.

Then we had a fight, a pretty awful fight, and I didn't see him for months. By and by I looked him up, where he was living, in a furnished room in the Village, and I tried to make it up. But there were lots of other people in the room and Sonny just lay on his bed, and he wouldn't come downstairs with me, and he treated these other people as though they were his family and I weren't. So I got mad and then he got mad, and then I told him that he might just as well be dead as live the way he was living. Then he stood up and he told me not to worry about him any more in life, that he *was* dead as far as I was concerned. Then he pushed me to the door and the other people looked on as though nothing were happening, and he slammed the door behind me. I stood in the hallway, staring at the door. I heard somebody laugh in the room and then the tears came to my eyes. I started down the steps, whistling to keep from crying, I kept whistling to myself, *You going to need me, baby, one of these cold, rainy days.*

I read about Sonny's trouble in the spring. Little Grace died in the fall. She was a beautiful little girl. But she only lived a little over two years. She died of polio and she suffered. She had a slight fever for a couple of days, but it didn't seem like anything and we just kept her in bed. And we would certainly have called the doctor, but the fever dropped, she seemed to be all right. So we thought it had just been a cold. Then, one day, she was up, play-ing, Isabel was in the kitchen fixing lunch for the two boys when they'd come in from school, and she heard Grace fall down in the living room. When you have a lot of children you don't always start running when one of them falls, unless they start screaming or something. And, this time, Grace was quiet. Yet, Isabel says that when she heard that *thump* and then that silence, something happened in her to make her afraid. And she ran to the living room and there was little Grace on the floor, all twisted up, and the reason she hadn't screamed was that she couldn't get her breath. And when she did scream, it was the worst sound, Isabel says, that she'd ever heard in all her life, and she still hears it sometimes in her dreams. Isabel will some-times wake me up with a low, moaning, strangled sound and I have to be quick to awaken her and hold her to me and where Isabel is weeping against me seems a mortal wound.

I think I may have written Sonny the very day that little Grace was bur-ied. I was sitting in the living room in the dark, by myself, and I suddenly thought of Sonny. My trouble made his real.

One Saturday afternoon, when Sonny had been living with us, or, any-way, been in our house, for nearly two weeks, I found myself wandering aimlessly about the living room, drinking from a can of beer, and trying to work up the courage to search Sonny's room. He was out, he was usually out whenever I was home, and Isabel had taken the children to see their grand-parents. Suddenly I was standing still in front of the living room window, watching Seventh Avenue. The idea of searching Sonny's room made me still. I scarcely dared to admit to myself what I'd be searching for. I didn't know what I'd do if I found it. Or if I didn't.

On the sidewalk across from me, near the entrance to a barbecue joint, some people were holding an old-fashioned revival meeting. The barbecue cook, wearing a dirty white apron, his conked hair reddish and metallic in the pale sun, and a cigarette between his lips, stood in the doorway, watching them. Kids and older people paused in their errands and stood there, along with some older men and a couple of very tough-looking women who watched everything that happened on the avenue, as though they owned it, or were maybe owned by it. Well, they were watching this, too. The revival was being carried on by three sisters in black, and a brother. All they had were their voices and their Bibles and a tambourine. The brother was testifying and while he testified two of the sisters stood together, seeming to say, amen, and the third sister walked around with the tambourine outstretched and a couple of people dropped coins into it. Then the brother's testimony ended and the sister who had been taking up the collection dumped the coins into her palm and transferred them to the pocket of her long black robe. Then she raised both hands, striking the tambourine against the air, and then against one hand, and she started to sing. And the two other sisters and the brother joined in.

It was strange, suddenly, to watch, though I had been seeing these street meetings all my life. So, of course, had everybody else down there. Yet, they paused and watched and listened and I stood still at the window. *"Tis the old ship of Zion,"* they sang, and the sister with the tambourine kept a steady, jangling beat, *"it has rescued many a thousand!"* Not a soul under the sound of their voices was hearing this song for the first time, not one of them had been rescued. Nor had they seen much in the way of rescue work being done around them. Neither did they especially believe in the holiness of the three sisters and the brother, they knew too much about them, knew where they lived, and how. The woman with the tambourine, whose voice dominated the air, whose face was bright with joy, was divided by very little from the woman who stood watching her, a cigarette between her heavy, chapped lips, her hair a cuckoo's nest, her face scarred and swollen from many beatings, and her black eyes glittering like coal. Perhaps they both knew this, which was why, when, as rarely, they addressed each other, they addressed each other as Sister. As the singing filled the air the watching, listening faces underwent a change, the eyes focusing on something within; the music seemed to soothe a poison out of them; and time seemed, nearly, to fall away from the sullen, belligerent, battered faces, as though they were fleeing back to their first condition, while dreaming of their last. The barbecue cook half shook his head and smiled, and dropped his cigarette and disappeared into his joint. A man fumbled in his pockets for change and stood holding it in his hand impatiently, as though he had just remembered a pressing appointment further up the avenue. He looked furious. Then I saw Sonny, standing on the edge of the crowd. He was carrying a wide, flat notebook with a green cover, and it made him look, from where I was standing, almost like a schoolboy. The coppery sun brought out the copper in his skin, he was very faintly smiling, standing very still. Then the singing stopped, the tambourine turned into a collection plate again. The furious man dropped in his coins and vanished, so did a couple of the women, and Sonny dropped some change in the plate, looking directly at the woman with a little smile. He started across the avenue, toward the house. He has a slow, loping walk, something like the way Harlem hipsters walk, only he's imposed on this his own half-beat. I had never really noticed it before.

I stayed at the window, both relieved and apprehensive. As Sonny disappeared from my sight, they began singing again. And they were still singing when his key turned in the lock.

"Hey," he said.

"Hey, yourself. You want some beer?"

"No. Well, maybe." But he came up to the window and stood beside me, looking out. "What a warm voice," he said.

They were singing *If I could only hear my mother pray again!*

"Yes," I said, "and she can sure beat that tambourine."

"But what a terrible song," he said, and laughed. He dropped his notebook on the sofa and disappeared into the kitchen. "Where's Isabel and the kids?"

"I think they went to see their grandparents. You hungry?"

"No." He came back into the living room with his can of beer. "You want to come some place with me tonight?"

I sensed, I don't know how, that I couldn't possibly say no. "Sure. Where?"

He sat down on the sofa and picked up his notebook and started leafing through it. "I'm going to sit in with some fellows in a joint in the Village."

"You mean, you're going to play, tonight?"

"That's right." He took a swallow of his beer and moved back, to the window. He gave me a sidelong look. "If you can stand it."

"I'll try," I said.

He smiled to himself and we both watched as the meeting across the way broke up. The three sisters and the brother, heads bowed, were singing *God be with you till we meet again*. The faces around them were very quiet. Then the song ended. The small crowd dispersed. We watched the three women and the lone man walk slowly up the avenue.

"When she was singing before," said Sonny, abruptly, "her voice reminded me for a minute of what heroin feels like sometimes—when it's in your veins. It makes you feel sort of warm and cool at the same time. And distant. And—and sure." He sipped his beer, very deliberately not looking at me. I watched his face. "It makes you feel—in control. Sometimes you've got to have that feeling."

"Do you?" I sat down slowly in the easy chair.

"Sometimes." He went to the sofa and picked up his notebook again. "Some people do."

"In order," I asked, "to play?" And my voice was very ugly, full of contempt and anger.

"Well"—he looked at me with great, troubled eyes, as though, in fact, he hoped his eyes would tell me things he could never otherwise say—"they *think* so. And *if* they think so—!"

"And what do *you* think?" I asked.

He sat on the sofa and put his can of beer on the floor. "I don't know," he said, and I couldn't be sure if he were answering my question or pursuing his thoughts. His face didn't tell me. "It's not so much to *play*. It's to *stand* it, to be able to make it at all. On any level." He frowned and smiled: "In order to keep from shaking to pieces."

"But these friends of yours," I said, "they seem to shake themselves to pieces pretty goddamn fast."

"Maybe." He played with the notebook. And something told me that I should curb my tongue, that Sonny was doing his best to talk, that I should listen. "But of course you only know the ones that've gone to pieces. Some don't—or at least they haven't *yet* and that's just about all *any* of us can say." He paused. "And then there are some who just live, really, in hell, and they know it and they see what's happening, and they go right on. I don't know." He sighed, dropped the notebook, folded his arms. "Some guys, you can tell from the way they play, they on something *all* the time. And you can see that, well, it makes something real for them. But of course," he picked up his beer from the floor and sipped it and put the can down again, "they *want* to, too, you've got to see that. Even some of them that say they don't—*some*, not all."

"And what about you?" I asked—I couldn't help it. "What about you? Do *you* want to?"

He stood up and walked to the window and remained silent for a long time. Then he sighed. "Me," he said. Then: "While I was downstairs before, on my way here, listening to that woman sing, it struck me all of a sudden how much suffering she must have had to go through—to sing like that. It's *repulsive* to think you have to suffer that much."

I said: "But there's no way not to suffer—is there, Sonny?"

"I believe not," he said and smiled, "but that's never stopped anyone from trying." He looked at me. "Has it?" I realized, with this mocking look, that there stood between us, forever, beyond the power of time or forgiveness, the fact that I had held silence—so long!—when he had needed human speech to help him. He turned back to the window. "No, there's no way not to suffer. But you try all kinds of ways to keep from drowning in it, to keep on top of it, and to make it seem—well, like *you*. Like you did something, all right, and now you're suffering for it. You know?" I said nothing. "Well you know," he said, impatiently, "why *do* people suffer? Maybe it's better to do something to give it a reason, *any* reason."

"But we just agreed," I said, "that there's no way not to suffer. Isn't it better, then, just to—take it?"

"But nobody just takes it," Sonny cried, "that's what I'm telling you! *Everybody* tries not to. You're just hung up on the *way* some people try—it's not *your* way!"

The hair on my face began to itch, my face felt wet. "That's not true," I said, "that's not true. I don't give a damn what other people do, I don't even care how they suffer. I just care how *you* suffer." And he looked at me. "Please believe me," I said. "I don't want to see you—die—trying not to suffer."

"I won't," he said, flatly, "die trying not to suffer. At least, not any faster than anybody else."

"But there's no need," I said, trying to laugh, "is there? in killing yourself."

I wanted to say more, but I couldn't. I wanted to talk about will power and how life could be—well, beautiful. I wanted to say that it was all within; but was it? or, rather, wasn't that exactly the trouble? And I wanted to promise that I would never fail him again. But it would all have sounded—empty words and lies.

So I made the promise to myself and prayed that I would keep it.

"It's terrible sometimes, inside," he said, "that's what's the trouble. You walk these streets, black and funky and cold, and there's not really a living ass to talk to, and there's nothing shaking, and there's no way of getting it out—that storm inside. You can't talk it and you can't make love with it, and when you finally try to get with it and play it, you realize *nobody's* listening. So *you've* got to listen. You got to find a way to listen."

And then he walked away from the window and sat on the sofa again, as though all the wind had suddenly been knocked out of him. "Sometimes you'll do *anything* to play, even cut your mother's throat." He laughed and looked at me. "Or your brother's." Then he sobered. "Or your own." Then: "Don't worry. I'm all right now and I think I'll *be* all right. But I can't forget—where I've been. I don't mean just the physical place I've been, I mean where I've *been*. And *what* I've been."

"What have you been, Sonny?" I asked.

He smiled—but sat sideways on the sofa, his elbow resting on the back, his fingers playing with his mouth and chin, not looking at me. "I've been something I didn't recognize, didn't know I could be. Didn't know anybody could be." He stopped, looking inward, looking helplessly young, looking old. "I'm not talking about it now because I feel *guilty* or anything like that—maybe it would be better if I did, I don't know. Anyway, I can't really talk about it. Not to you, not to anybody," and now he turned and faced me. "Sometimes, you know and it was actually when I was most *out* of the world. I felt that I was in it, that I was *with* it, really, and I could play or I didn't really have to *play*, it just came out of me, it was there. And I don't know how I played, thinking about it now, but I know I did awful things, those times, sometimes, to people. Or it wasn't that I *did* anything to them—it was that they weren't real." He picked up the beer can; it was empty; he rolled it between his palms: "And other times—well, I needed a fix, I needed to find a place to lean, I needed to clear a space to *listen*—and I couldn't find it, and I —went crazy, I did terrible things to *me*, I was terrible *for* me." He began pressing the beer can between his hands, I watched the metal begin to give. It glittered, as he played with it, like a knife, and I was afraid he would cut himself, but I said nothing. "Oh well. I can never tell you. I was all by myself at the bottom of something, stinking and sweating and crying and shaking, and I smelled it, you know? *my* stink, and I thought I'd die if I couldn't get away from it and yet, all the same, I knew that everything I was doing was just locking me in with it. And I didn't know," he paused, still flattening the beer can, "I didn't know, I still *don't* know, something kept telling me that maybe it was good to smell your own stink, but I didn't think that *that* was what I'd been trying to do—and—who can stand it?" and he abruptly dropped the ruined beer can, looking at me with a small, still smile, and then rose, walking to the window as though it were the lodestone rock. I watched his face, he watched the avenue. "I couldn't tell you when Mama died—but the reason I wanted to leave Harlem so bad was to get away from drugs. And then, when I ran away, that's what I was running from—really. When I came back, nothing had changed, I hadn't changed, I was just—older." And he stopped drumming with his fingers on the windowpane. The sun had vanished, soon darkness would fall. I watched his face. "It can come again," he said, almost as though speaking to himself. Then he turned to me. "It can come again," he repeated. "I just want you to know that."

"All right," I said, at last. "So it can come again, All right."

He smiled, but the smile was sorrowful. "I had to try to tell you," he said.

"Yes," I said. "I understand that."

"You're my brother," he said, looking straight at me, and not smiling at all.

"Yes," I repeated, "yes. I understand that."

He turned back to the window, looking out. "All that hatred down there," he said, "all that hatred and misery and love. It's a wonder it doesn't blow the avenue apart."

We went to the only nightclub on a short, dark street, downtown. We squeezed through the narrow, chattering, jam-packed bar to the entrance of the big room, where the bandstand was. And we stood there for a moment, for the lights were very dim in this room and we couldn't see. Then, "Hello, boy," said a voice and an enormous black man, much older than Sonny or myself, erupted out of all that atmospheric lighting and put an arm around Sonny's shoulder. "I been sitting right here," he said, "waiting for you."

He had a big voice, too, and heads in the darkness turned toward us.

Sonny grinned and pulled a little away, and said, "Creole, this is my brother. I told you about him."

Creole shook my hand. "I'm glad to meet you, son," he said, and it was clear that he was glad to meet me *there*, for Sonny's sake. And he smiled, "You got a real musician in *your* family," and he took his arm from Sonny's shoulder and slapped him, lightly, affectionately, with the back of his hand.

"Well. Now I've heard it all," said a voice behind us. This was another musician, and a friend of Sonny's, a coal-black, cheerful-looking man, built close to the ground. He immediately began confiding to me, at the top of his lungs, the most terrible things about Sonny, his teeth gleaming like a lighthouse and his laugh coming up out of him like the beginning of an earthquake. And it turned out that everyone at the bar knew Sonny, or almost everyone; some were musicians, working there, or nearby, or not working, some were simply hangers-on, and some were there to hear Sonny play. I was introduced to all of them and they were all very polite to me. Yet, it was clear that, for them, I was only Sonny's brother. Here, I was in Sonny's world. Or, rather: his kingdom. Here, it was not even a question that his veins bore royal blood.

They were going to play soon and Creole installed me, by myself, at a table in a dark corner. Then I watched them, Creole, and the little black man, and Sonny, and the others, while they horsed around, standing just below the bandstand. The light from the bandstand spilled just a little short of them and, watching them laughing and gesturing and moving about, I had the feeling that they, nevertheless, were being most careful not to step into that circle of light too suddenly: that if they moved into the light too suddenly, without thinking, they would perish in flame. Then, while I watched, one of them, the small, black man, moved into the light and crossed the bandstand and started fooling around with his drums. Then— being funny and being, also, extremely ceremonious—Creole took Sonny by the arm and led him to the piano. A woman's voice called Sonny's name and a few hands started clapping. And Sonny, also being funny and being cere- monious, and so touched, I think, that he could have cried, but neither hid- ing it nor showing it, riding it like a man, grinned, and put both hands to his heart and bowed from the waist.

Creole then went to the bass fiddle and a lean, very bright-skinned brown man jumped up on the bandstand and picked up his horn. So there they were, and the atmosphere on the bandstand and in the room began to change and tighten. Someone stepped up to the microphone and announced them. Then there were all kinds of murmurs. Some people at the bar shushed others. The waitress ran around, frantically getting in the last orders, guys and chicks got closer to each other, and the lights on the band- stand, on the quartet, turned to a kind of indigo. Then they all looked dif- ferent there. Creole looked about him for the last time, as though he were making certain that all his chickens were in the coop, and then he—jumped and struck the fiddle. And there they were.

All I know about music is that not many people ever really hear it. And even then, on the rare occasions when something opens within, and the music enters, what we mainly hear, or hear corroborated, are personal, pri- vate, vanishing evocations. But the man who creates the music is hearing something else, is dealing with the roar rising from the void and imposing order on it as it hits the air. What is evoked in him, then, is of another order, more terrible because it has no words, and triumphant, too, for that same reason. And his triumph, when he triumphs, is ours. I just watched Sonny's face. His face was troubled, he was working hard, but he wasn't with

it. And I had the feeling that, in a way, everyone on the bandstand was waiting for him, both waiting for him and pushing him along. But as I began to
watch Creole, I realized that it was Creole who held them all back. He had
them on a short rein. Up there, keeping the beat with his whole body, wailing on the fiddle, with his eyes half closed, he was listening to everything,
but he was listening to Sonny. He was having a dialogue with Sonny. He
wanted Sonny to leave the shoreline and strike out for the deep water.
He was Sonny's witness that deep water and drowning were not the
same thing—he had been there, and he knew. And he wanted Sonny to
know. He was waiting for Sonny to do the things on the keys which would
let Creole know that Sonny was in the water.

And, while Creole listened, Sonny moved, deep within, exactly like someone in torment. I had never before thought of how awful the relationship
must be between the musician and his instrument. He has to fill it, this
instrument, with the breath of life, his own. He has to make it do what he
wants it to do. And a piano is just a piano. It's made out of so much wood
and wires and little hammers and big ones, and ivory. While there's only so
much you can do with it, the only way to find this out is to try; to try and
make it do everything.

And Sonny hadn't been near a piano for over a year. And he wasn't on
much better terms with his life, not the life that stretched before him now.
He and the piano stammered, started one way, got scared, stopped; started
another way, panicked, marked time, started again; then seemed to have
found a direction, panicked again, got stuck. And the face I saw on Sonny
I'd never seen before. Everything had been burned out of it, and, at the
same time, things usually hidden were being burned in, by the fire and fury
of the battle which was occurring in him up there.

Yet, watching Creole's face as they neared the end of the first set, I had
the feeling that something had happened, something I hadn't heard. Then
they finished, there was scattered applause, and then, without an instant's
warning, Creole started into something else, it was almost sardonic, it was
Am I Blue. And, as though he commanded, Sonny began to play. Something
began to happen. And Creole let out the reins. The dry, low, black man said
something awful on the drums, Creole answered, and the drums talked
back. Then the horn insisted, sweet and high, slightly detached perhaps,
and Creole listened, commenting now and then, dry, and driving, beautiful
and calm and old. Then they all came together again, and Sonny was part
of the family again. I could tell this from his face. He seemed to have
found, right there beneath his fingers, a damn brand-new piano. It seemed
that he couldn't get over it. Then, for awhile, just being happy with Sonny,
they seemed to be agreeing with him that brand-new pianos certainly were
a gas.

Then Creole stepped forward to remind them that what they were playing was the blues. He hit something in all of them, he hit something in me,
myself, and the music tightened and deepened, apprehension began to beat
the air. Creole began to tell us what the blues were all about. They were

not about anything very new. He and his boys up there were keeping it new, at the risk of ruin, destruction, madness, and death, in order to find new ways to make us listen. For, while the tale of how we suffer, and how we are delighted, and how we may triumph is never new, it always must be heard. There isn't any other tale to tell, it's the only light we've got in all this darkness.

And this tale, according to that face, that body, those strong hands on those strings, has another aspect in every country, and a new depth in every generation. Listen, Creole seemed to be saying, listen. Now these are Sonny's blues. He made the little black man on the drums know it, and the bright, brown man on the horn. Creole wasn't trying any longer to get Sonny in the water. He was wishing him Godspeed. Then he stepped back, very slowly, filling the air with the immense suggestion that Sonny speak for himself.

Then they all gathered around Sonny and Sonny played. Every now and again one of them seemed to say, amen. Sonny's fingers filled the air with life, his life. But that life contained so many others. And Sonny went all the way back, he really began with the spare, flat statement of the opening phrase of the song. Then he began to make it his. It was very beautiful because it wasn't hurried and it was no longer a lament. I seemed to hear with what burning he had made it his, with what burning we had yet to make it ours, how we could cease lamenting. Freedom lurked around us and I understood, at last, that he could help us to be free if we would listen, that he would never be free until we did. Yet, there was no battle in his face now. I heard what he had gone through, and would continue to go through until he came to rest in earth. He had made it his: that long line, of which we knew only Mama and Daddy. And he was giving it back, as everything must be given back, so that, passing through death, it can live forever. I saw my mother's face again, and felt, for the first time, how the stones of the road she had walked on must have bruised her feet. I saw the moonlit road where my father's brother died. And it brought something else back to me, and carried me past it, I saw my little girl again and felt Isabel's tears again, and I felt my own tears begin to rise. And I was yet aware that this was only a moment, that the world waited outside, as hungry as a tiger, and that trouble stretched above us, longer than the sky.

Then it was over. Creole and Sonny let out their breath, both soaking wet, and grinning. There was a lot of applause and some of it was real. In the dark, the girl came by and I asked her to take drinks to the bandstand. There was a long pause, while they talked up there in the indigo light and after awhile I saw the girl put a Scotch and milk on top of the piano for Sonny. He didn't seem to notice it, but just before they started playing again he sipped from it and looked toward me, and nodded. Then he put it back on top of the piano. For me, then, as they began to play again, it glowed and shook above my brother's head like the very cup of trembling.

1957

PHILIP ROTH
B. 1933

Philip Roth is one of the most prolific and persistent American novelists of the past half century. His early fiction was highly controversial, both for its critique of post–World War II American Jewish identity and for its explicit sexual content. Although his work earned a number of critical prizes such as the National Book Award and the Pulitzer Prize, he remained a controversial figure through the 1980s. Since then he has published a startling amount of fiction that has earned him a place among elite American writers. In a 2006 *New York Times Book Review* retrospective of the best twenty-five novels of the previous twenty-five years, six were written by Roth. His willingness to dig beneath the surface of the American reality to explore its contradictions, difficulties, and invariable agony, mixed with humor, has earned him the status of one of the most important fiction writers of his time.

Roth was born in Newark, New Jersey, and his birthplace often serves as the setting for his fiction. He earned a B.A. from Bucknell University in Pennsylvania and an M.A. from the University of Chicago, where he taught fiction for a time. He has lived in near-seclusion in a restored farmhouse in Connecticut since the mid-1980s. His first book, *Goodbye, Columbus* (1959), contained a novella as well as five short stories, including "You Can't Tell a Man by the Song He Sings." This book earned Roth his first National Book Award, but it also initiated the controversy associated with the first half of his career. In particular, American Jews were upset by the depiction of a character in the story "Defender of the Faith" who apparently uses his religion as an excuse to shirk military duties. Roth's depiction of the well-to-do Patimkin family in the novella *Goodbye, Columbus* calls into question the notion of suburban, middle-class American success, couched again in terms of the Jewish experience.

Roth's 1969 novel, *Portnoy's Complaint*, eclipsed the controversy of his first book, however. Humorous from some perspectives, offensive from others, this novel uses psychoanalysis and masturbation as consistent touchstones in the life of a man consumed with the meaning of being an American Jew.

Although Roth's legacy rests to some degree on these two books, it could be argued that his breakthrough occurred with the publication of the novel *My Life as a Man* in 1974. Here Roth created a fictional protagonist named Nathan Zuckerman who is the author's close alter ego. Zuckerman has proved to be one of the longest-lived recurrent characters in contemporary fiction. Through him Roth has been able to find his own voice and his own subject matter. Zuckerman has been both a character and a chronicler of contemporary America, at times dispassionate and at times a sharp critic.

The early Zuckerman books were initially collected in *Zuckerman Bound* (1985), but Zuckerman has also resurfaced in the critically acclaimed American trilogy *American Pastoral* (1997), *I Married a Communist* (1998), and *The Human Stain* (2000). These mature works combine recent American history, social commentary, and human drama to paint a rich and complex portrait of what it means to be a late-twentieth-century American. In *The Human Stain*, a psychologically damaged Vietnam War veteran, who is likely responsible for the death of his former wife and her lover, asks Zuckerman what kind of books he writes, and he answers succinctly, "I write about people like you [and] their problems."

It makes sense that Roth's most enduring character is a writer because his work has always revealed a preoccupation with work. The story that follows, "You Can't Tell a Man by the Song He Sings," reveals that preoccupation, along with a number of Roth's other themes: the fragility of social respectability, the government's ability to monitor and control individuals, the individual's will to resist such control, and the human proclivity to misjudge others. Roth's characteristic humor is also apparent here, as is his predisposition to focus on the male experience, often with baseball as a backdrop.

D. Quentin Miller
Suffolk University

PRIMARY WORKS

Goodbye, Columbus, 1959; *Letting Go*, 1962; *When She Was Good*, 1967; *Portnoy's Complaint*, 1969; *Our Gang*, 1971; *The Breast*, 1972; *The Great American Novel*, 1973; *My Life as a Man*, 1974; *The Professor of Desire*, 1977; *The Ghost Writer*, 1979; *Zuckerman Unbound*, 1981; *The Anatomy Lesson*, 1983; *The Counterlife*, 1986; *The Facts: A Novelist's Autobiography*, 1988; *Deception: A Novel*, 1990; *Patrimony: A True Story*, 1991; *Operation Shylock: A Confession*, 1993; *Sabbath's Theater*, 1995; *The Prague Orgy*, 1996; *American Pastoral*, 1997; *I Married a Communist*, 1998; *The Human Stain*, 2000; *The Dying Animal*, 2001; *The Plot against America*, 2004; *Everyman*, 2006; *Exit, Ghost*, 2007; *Indignation*, 2008; *The Humbling*, 2009; *Nemesis*, 2010.

You Can't Tell a Man by the Song He Sings

It was in a freshman high school class called "Occupations" that, fifteen years ago, I first met the ex-con, Alberto Pelagutti. The first week my new classmates and I were given "a battery of tests" designed to reveal our skills, deficiencies, tendencies, and psyches. At the end of the week, Mr. Russo, the Occupations teacher, would add the skills, subtract the deficiencies, and tell us what jobs best suited our talents; it was all mysterious but scientific. I remember we first took a "Preference Test": "Which would you prefer to do, this, that, or the other thing ..." Albie Pelagutti sat one seat behind me and to my left, and while this first day of high school I strolled happily through the test, examining ancient fossils here, defending criminals there, Albie, like the inside of Vesuvius, rose, fell, pitched, tossed, and swelled in his chair. When he finally made a decision, he made it. You could hear his pencil drive the *x* into the column opposite the activity in which he thought it wisest to prefer to engage. His agony reinforced the legend that had preceded him: he was seventeen; had just left Jamesburg Reformatory; this was his third high school, his third freshman year; but now—I heard another *x* driven home—he had decided "to go straight."

Halfway through the hour Mr. Russo left the room. "I'm going for a drink," he said. Russo was forever at pains to let us know what a square-shooter he was and that, unlike other teachers we might have had, he would not go out the front door of the classroom to sneak around to the back door and observe how responsible we were. And sure enough, when he returned after going for a drink, his lips were wet; when he came back from the men's room, you could smell the soap on his hands. "Take your time, boys," he said, and the door swung shut behind him.

His black wingtipped shoes beat down the marble corridor and five thick fingers dug into my shoulder. I turned around; it was Pelagutti. "What?" I said. "Number twenty-six," Pelagutti said, "What's the answer?" I gave him the truth: "Anything." Pelagutti rose halfway over his desk and glared at me. He was a hippopotamus, big, black, and smelly; his short sleeves squeezed tight around his monstrous arms as though they were taking his own blood pressure—which at that moment was sky-bound: "What's the answer!" Menaced, I flipped back three pages in my question booklet and reread number twenty-six. "Which would you prefer to do: (1) Attend a World Trade Convention. (2) Pick cherries. (3) Stay with and read to a sick friend. (4) Tinker with automobile engines." I looked blank-faced back to Albie, and shrugged my shoulders. "It doesn't matter—there's no right answer. Anything." He almost rocketed out of his seat. "Don't give me that crap! What's the answer!" Strange heads popped up all over the room—thin-eyed glances, hissing lips, shaming grins—and I realized that any minute Russo, wet-lipped, might come back and my first day in high school I would be caught cheating. I looked again at number twenty-six; then back to Albie; and then propelled— as I always was towards him—by anger, pity, fear, love, vengeance, and an instinct for irony that was at the time delicate as a mallet, I whispered, "Stay and read to a sick friend." The volcano subsided, and Albie and I had met.

We became friends. He remained at my elbow throughout the testing, then throughout lunch, then after school. I learned that Albie, as a youth, had done all the things I, under direction, had not: he had eaten hamburgers in strange diners; he had gone out after cold showers, wet-haired, into winter weather; he had been cruel to animals; he had trafficked with whores; he had stolen, he had been caught, and he had paid. But now he told me, as I unwrapped my lunch in the candy store across the school, "No, I'm through crappin' around. I'm gettin' an education. I'm gonna—" and I think he picked up the figure from a movie musical he had seen the previous afternoon while the rest of us were in English class—"I'm gonna put my best foot forward." The following week when Russo read the results of the testing it appeared that Albie's feet were not only moving forward but finding strange, wonderful paths. Russo sat at his desk, piles of tests stacked before him like ammunition, charts and diagrams mounted huge on either side, and delivered our destinies. Albie and I were going to be lawyers.

Of all that Albie confessed to me that first week, one fact in particular fastened on my brain: I soon forgot the town in Sicily where he was born; the occupation of his father (he either made ice or delivered it); the year and model of the cars he had stolen. I did not forget though that Albie had apparently been the star of the Jamesburg Reformatory baseball team. When I was selected by the gym teacher, Mr. Hopper, to captain one of my gym class's softball teams (we played softball until the World Series was over, then switched to touch football), I knew that I had to get Pelagutti on my side. With those arms he could hit the ball a mile.

The day teams were to be selected Albie shuffled back and forth at my side, while in the lockerroom I changed into my gym uniform—jockstrap, khaki-colored shorts, T-shirt, sweat socks, and sneakers. Albie had already changed: beneath his khaki gym shorts he did not wear a support but retained his lavender undershorts; they hung down three inches below the outer shorts and looked like a long fancy hem. Instead of a T-shirt he wore a sleeveless undershirt; and beneath his high, tar-black sneakers he wore thin black silk socks with slender arrows embroidered up the sides. Naked he might, like some centuries-dead ancestor, have tossed lions to their death in the Colosseum; the outfit, though I didn't tell him, detracted from his dignity.

As we left the lockerroom and padded through the dark basement corridor and up onto the sunny September playing field, he talked continually, "I didn't play sports when I was a kid, but I played at Jamesburg and baseball came to me like nothing." I nodded my head. "What you think of Pete Reiser?" he asked. "He's a pretty good man," I said. "What you think of Tommy Henrich?" "I don't know," I answered, "he's dependable, I guess." As a Dodger fan I preferred Reiser to the Yankees' Henrich; and besides, my tastes have always been a bit baroque, and Reiser, who repeatedly bounced off outfield walls to save the day for Brooklyn, had won a special trophy in the Cooperstown of my heart. "Yeh," Albie said, "I like all them Yankees."

I didn't have a chance to ask Albie what he meant by that, for Mr. Hopper, bronzed, smiling, erect, was flipping a coin; I looked up, saw the glint in the sun, and I was calling "heads." It landed tails and the other captain had first choice. My heart flopped over when he looked at Albie's arms, but calmed when he passed on and chose first a tall, lean, first-baseman type. Immediately I said, "I'll take Pelagutti." You don't very often see smiles like the one that crossed Albie Pelagutti's face that moment: you would think I had paroled him from a life sentence.

The game began. I played shortstop—left-handed—and batted second; Albie was in center field and, at his wish, batted fourth. Their first man grounded out, me to the first baseman. The next batter hit a high, lofty fly ball to center field. The moment I saw Albie move after it I knew Tommy Henrich and Pete Reiser were only names to him; all he knew about baseball he'd boned up on the night before. While the ball hung in the air, Albie jumped up and down beneath it, his arms raised upward directly above his head; his wrists were glued together, and his two hands flapped open and closed like a butterfly's wings, begging the ball toward him.

"C'mon," he was screaming to the sky, "c'mon you bastard . . ." And his legs bicycle-pumped up and down, up and down. I hope the moment of my death does not take as long as it did for that damn ball to drop. It hung, it hung,

Albie cavorting beneath like a Holy Roller. And then it landed, smack into Albie's chest. The runner was rounding second and heading for third while Albie twirled all around, looking, his arms down now, stretched out, as though he were playing ring-around-a-rosy with two invisible children. "Behind you, Pelagutti!" I screamed. He stopped moving. "What?" he called back to me. I ran halfway out to center field. "Behind you—relay it!" And then, as the runner rounded third, I had to stand there defining "relay" to him.

At the end of the first half of the first inning we came to bat behind, 8–0—eight home runs, all relayed in too late by Pelagutti.

Out of a masochistic delight I must describe Albie at the plate: first, he *faced* the pitcher; then, when he swung at the ball—and he did, at every one—it was not to the side but down, as though he were driving a peg into the ground. Don't ask if he was right-handed or left-handed. I don't know.

While we changed out of our gym uniforms I was silent. I boiled as I watched Pelagutti from the corner of my eye. He kicked off those crazy black sneakers and pulled his pink gaucho shirt on over his undershirt— there was still a red spot above the U front of the undershirt where the first fly ball had hit him. Without removing his gym shorts he stuck his feet into his gray trousers—I watched as he hoisted the trousers over the red splotches where ground balls had banged off his shins, past the red splotches where pitched balls had smacked his knee caps and thighs.

Finally I spoke. "Damn you, Pelagutti, you wouldn't know Pete Reiser if you fell over him!" He was stuffing his sneakers into his locker; he didn't answer. I was talking to his mountainous pink shirt back. "Where do you come off telling me you played for that prison team?" He mumbled something. "What?" I said. "I did," he grumbled. "Bullshit!" I said. He turned and, black-eyed, glared at me: "I did!" "That must've been some team!" I said. We did not speak as we left the lockerroom. As we passed the gym office on our way up to Occupations, Mr. Hopper looked up from his desk and winked at me. Then he motioned his head at Pelagutti to indicate that he knew I'd picked a lemon, but how could I have expected a bum like Pelagutti to be an All-American boy in the first place? Then Mr. Hopper turned his sun-lamped head back to his desk.

"Now," I said to Pelagutti as we turned at the second floor landing, "now I'm stuck with you for the rest of the term." He shuffled ahead of me without answering; his oxlike behind should have had a tail on it to flick the flies away—it infuriated me. "You goddamn liar!" I said.

He spun around as fast as an ox can. "You ain't stuck with nobody." We were at the top of the landing headed into the locker-lined corridor; the kids who were piling up the stairs behind stopped, listened. "No you ain't, you snot-ass!" And I saw five hairy knuckles coming right at my mouth. I moved but not in time, and heard a crash inside the bridge of my nose. I felt my hips dip back, my legs and head come forward, and, curved like the letter *c*, I was swept fifteen feet backward before I felt cold marble beneath the palms of my hands. Albie stepped around me and into the Occupations room. Just then I looked up to see Mr. Russo's black wingtipped shoes enter the room. I'm almost sure he had seen Albie blast me but I'll never know. Nobody, including Albie and myself, ever mentioned it again. Perhaps it had been a mistake for me to call Albie a liar, but if he had starred at baseball, it was in some league I did not know.

By way of contrast I want to introduce Duke Scarpa, another ex-con who was with us that year. Neither Albie nor the Duke, incidentally, was a typical member of my high school community. Both lived at the other end of Newark, "down neck," and they had reached us only after the Board of Education had tried Albie at two other schools and the Duke at four. The Board hoped finally, like Marx, that the higher culture would absorb the lower.

Albie and Duke had no particular use for each other; where Albie had made up his mind to go straight, one always felt that the Duke, in his oily quietness, his boneless grace, was planning a job. Yet, though affection never lived between them, Duke wandered after Albie and me, aware, I suspect, that if Albie despised him it was because he was able to read his soul—and that such an associate was easier to abide than one who despises you because he does not know your soul at all. Where Albie was a hippopotamus, an ox, Duke was reptilian. Me? I don't know; it is easy to spot the animal in one's fellows.

During lunch hour, the Duke and I used to spar with each other in the hall outside the cafeteria. He did not know a hook from a jab and disliked having his dark skin roughened or his hair mussed; but he so delighted in moving, bobbing, coiling, and uncoiling, that I think he would have paid for the privilege of playing the serpent with me. He hypnotized me, the Duke; he pulled some slimy string inside me—where Albie Pelagutti sought and stretched a deeper and, I think, a nobler cord.

But I make Albie sound like peaches-and-cream. Let me tell you what he and I did to Mr. Russo.

Russo believed in his battery of tests as his immigrant parents (and Albie's, and maybe Albie himself) believed in papal infallibility. If the tests said Albie was going to be a lawyer then he was going to be a lawyer. As for Albie's past, it seemed only to increase Russo's devotion to the prophecy: he approached Albie with salvation in his eyes. In September, then, he gave Albie a biography to read, the life of Oliver Wendell Holmes; during October, once a week, he had the poor fellow speak impromptu before the class; in November he had him write a report on the Constitution, which I wrote; and then in December, the final indignity, he sent Albie and me (and two others who displayed a legal bent) to the Essex County Court House where he could see "real lawyers in action."

It was a cold, windy morning and as we flicked our cigarettes at the Lincoln statue on the courtyard plaza, and started up the long flight of white cement steps, Albie suddenly did an about-face and headed back across the plaza and out to Market Street. I called to him but he shouted back that he had seen it all before, and then he was not walking, but running towards the crowded downtown streets, pursued not by police, but by other days. It wasn't that he considered Russo an ass for having sent him to visit the

Court House—Albie respected teachers too much for that; rather I think he felt Russo had tried to rub his nose in it.

No surprise, then, when the next day after gym Albie announced his assault on the Occupations teacher; it was the first crime he had planned since his decision to go straight back in September. He outlined the action to me and indicated that I should pass the details on to the other members of the class. As liaison between Albie and the well-behaved, healthy nonconvicts like myself who made up the rest of the class, I was stationed at the classroom door and as each member passed in I unfolded the plot into his ear: "As soon after ten-fifteen as Russo turns to the blackboard, you bend over to tie your shoelace." If a classmate looked back at me puzzled, I would motion to Pelagutti hulking over his desk; the puzzled expression would vanish and another accomplice would enter the room. The only one who gave me any trouble was the Duke. He listened to the plan and then scowled back at me with the look of a man who's got his own syndicate, and, in fact, has never even heard of yours.

Finally the bell rang; I closed the door behind me and moved noiselessly to my desk. I waited for the clock to move to a quarter after; it did; and then Russo turned to the board to write upon it the salary range of aluminum workers. I bent to tie my shoelaces—beneath all the desks I saw other upside-down grinning faces. To my left behind me I heard Albie hissing; his hands fumbled about his black silk socks, and the hiss grew and grew until it was a rush of Sicilian, muttered, spewed, vicious. The exchange was strictly between Russo and himself. I looked to the front of the classroom, my fingers knotting and unknotting my shoelaces, the blood pumping now to my face. I saw Russo's legs turn. What a sight he must have seen—where there had been twenty-five faces, now there was nothing. Just desks. "Okay," I heard Russo say, "okay." And then he gave a little clap with his hands. "That's enough now, fellas. The joke is over. Sit up." And then Albie's hiss traveled to all the blood-pinked ears below the desks; it rushed about us like a subterranean stream—"Stay down!"

While Russo asked us to get up we stayed down. And we did not sit up until Albie told us to; and then under his direction we were singing—

> Don't sit under the apple tree
> With anyone else but me,
> Anyone else but me,
> Anyone else but me,
> Oh, no, no, don't sit under the apple tree . . .

And then in time to the music we clapped. What a noise!

Mr. Russo stood motionless at the front of the class, listening, astonished. He wore a neatly pressed dark blue pin-striped suit, a tan tie with a collie's head in the center, and a tieclasp with the initials R.R. engraved upon it; he had on the black wingtipped shoes; they glittered. Russo, who believed in neatness, honesty, punctuality, planned destinies—who believed in the future, in Occupations! And next to me, behind me, inside me, all over me—Albie! We looked at each other, Albie and I, and my lungs split with joy: *"Don't sit under the apple tree—"* Albie's monotone boomed out, and then a thick liquid crooner's voice behind Albie bathed me in sound: it was the Duke's; he clapped to a tango beat.

Russo leaned for a moment against a visual aids chart—"Skilled Laborers: Salaries and Requirements"—and then scraped back his chair and plunged down into it, so far down it looked to have no bottom. He lowered his big head to the desk and his shoulders curled forward like the ends of wet paper; and that was when Albie pulled his coup. He stopped singing "Don't Sit Under the Apple Tree"; we all stopped. Russo looked up at the silence; his eyes black and baggy, he stared at our leader, Alberto Pelagutti. Slowly Russo began to shake his head from side to side: this was no Capone, this was a Garibaldi! Russo waited, I waited, we all waited. Albie slowly rose, and began to sing *"Oh, say can you see, by the dawn's early light, what so proudly we hailed—"* And we all stood and joined him. Tears sparkling on his long black lashes, Mr. Robert Russo dragged himself wearily up from his desk, beaten, and as the Pelagutti basso boomed disastrously behind me, I saw Russo's lips begin to move, *"the bombs bursting in air, gave proof—"* God, did we sing!

Albie left school in June of that year—he had passed only Occupations—but our comradeship, that strange vessel, was smashed to bits at noon one day a few months earlier. It was a lunch hour in March, the Duke and I were sparring in the hall outside the cafeteria, and Albie, who had been more hospitable to the Duke since the day his warm, liquid voice had joined the others—Albie had decided to act as our referee, jumping between us, separating our clinches, warning us about low blows, grabbing out for the Duke's droopy crotch, in general having a good time. I remember that the Duke and I were in a clinch; as I showered soft little punches to his kidneys he squirmed in my embrace. The sun shone through the window behind him, lighting up his hair like a nest of snakes. I fluttered his sides, he twisted, I breathed hard through my nose, my eyes registered on his snaky hair, and suddenly Albie wedged between and knocked us apart—the Duke plunged sideways, I plunged forward, and my fist crashed through the window that Scarpa had been using as his corner. Feet pounded; in a second a wisecracking, guiltless, chewing crowd was gathered around me, just me. Albie and the Duke were gone. I cursed them both, the honorless bastards! The crowd did not drift back to lunch until the head dietitian, a huge, varicose-veined matron in a laundry-stiff white uniform had written down my name and led me to the nurse's office to have the glass picked out of my knuckles. Later in the afternoon I was called for the first and only time to the office of Mr. Wendell, the Principal.

Fifteen years have passed since then and I do not know what has happened to Albie Pelagutti. If he is a gangster he was not one with notoriety or money enough for the Kefauver Committee[1] to interest itself in several

---

[1] A U.S. Senate committee that investigated organized crime in 1950 and 1951.

years ago. When the Crime Committee reached New Jersey I followed their investigations carefully but never did I read in the papers the name Alberto Pelagutti or even Duke Scarpa—though who can tell what name the Duke is known by now. I do know, however, what happened to the Occupations teacher, for when another Senate Committee swooped through the state a while back it was discovered that Robert Russo—among others—had been a Marxist while attending Montclair State Teachers' College circa 1935. Russo refused to answer some of the Committee's questions, and the Newark Board of Education met, chastened, and dismissed him. I read now and then in the Newark *News* that Civil Liberties Union attorneys are still trying to appeal his case, and I have even written a letter to the Board of Education swearing that if anything subversive was ever done to my character, it wasn't done by my ex-high school teacher, Russo; if he was a Communist I never knew it. I could not decide whether or not to include in the letter a report of the "Star-Spangled Banner" incident: who knows what is and is not proof to the crotchety ladies and chainstore owners who sit and die on Boards of Education?

And if (to alter an Ancient's text) a man's history is his fate, who knows whether the Newark Board of Education will ever attend to a letter written to them by me. I mean, have fifteen years buried that afternoon I was called to see the Principal?

... He was a tall, distinguished gentleman and as I entered his office he rose and extended his hand. The same sun that an hour earlier had lit up snakes in the Duke's hair now slanted through Mr. Wendell's blinds and warmed his deep green carpet. "How do you do?" he said. "Yes," I answered, non sequiturly, and ducked my bandaged hand under my unbandaged hand. Graciously he said, "Sit down, won't you?" Frightened, unpracticed, I performed an aborted curtsy and sat. I watched Mr. Wendell go to his metal filing cabinet, slide one drawer open, and take from it a large white index card. He set the card on his desk and motioned me over so I might read what was typed on the card. At the top, in caps, was my whole name—last, first, and middle; below the name was a Roman numeral one, and beside it, "Fighting in corridor; broke window (3/19/42)." Already documented. And on a big card with plenty of space.

I returned to my chair and sat back as Mr. Wendell told me that the card would follow me through life. At first I listened, but as he talked on and on the drama went out of what he said, and my attention wandered to his filing cabinet. I began to imagine the cards inside, Albie's card and the Duke's, and then I understood—just short of forgiveness—why the two of them had zoomed off and left me to pay penance for the window by myself. Albie, you see, had always known about the filing cabinet and these index cards; I hadn't; and Russo, poor Russo, has only recently found out.

1958

■ TENNESSEE WILLIAMS ■
1911–1983

Although invariably ranked second (just behind Eugene O'Neill) among American dramatists, Tennessee Williams is indisputably the most important playwright yet to emerge from the American South. Born Thomas Lanier Williams in Columbus, Mississippi, where his much loved maternal grandfather was an Episcopalian minister, by 1919 he had been transplanted with his family to St. Louis, Missouri. The contrast between these two cultures—an agrarian South that looked back nostalgically to a partly mythical past of refinement and gentility and a forward-looking urban North that valued pragmatism and practicality over civility and beauty—would haunt Williams throughout his life, providing one of the enduring tensions in his plays.

After attending the University of Missouri and Washington University in St. Louis, Williams followed his graduation from the University of Iowa in 1938 with a period of wandering around the country and a succession of odd jobs, including an unsuccessful stint as a scriptwriter in Hollywood. One of those film scripts, however, became the genesis for his first great theatrical success during the 1944–1945 season, *The Glass Menagerie*. In that "memory play," the autobiographical narrator, Tom Wingfield, hopes that by reliving his desertion of his domineering mother and physically and psychically fragile sister, Laura, he will find release from the guilt of the past, thereby allowing his full maturation as a poet. Biographers Donald Spoto and Lyle Leverich remark (as have others before them) on Williams's lasting and decisive love for his schizophrenic sister Rose, clearly the model for Laura, and at least partially for Blanche in the classic *A Streetcar Named Desire* (1947), Catherine in *Suddenly Last Summer* (1958), the sister Clare in *Out Cry* (1973), and even for the largely factual Zelda Fitzgerald in his final Broadway play, *Clothes for a Summer Hotel* (1980). No other American dramatist has created female characters of such complexity, portrayed with such deep understanding and sensitivity.

In his opening narration in *Menagerie*, Tom speaks of "an emissary from a world of reality that we were somehow set apart from" who threatens to upset the fragile escape into illusion that serves repeatedly in Williams's dramas as a refuge for those who are physically, emotionally, or spiritually misbegotten and vulnerable and yet, because of this, somehow special. One of Williams's chief characteristics as a dramatist is his compassion for misfits and outsiders, perhaps fed early on by his own sexual orientation (he frankly discusses his homosexuality in the confessional *Memoirs*) and later, in the two decades before his death, by the increasingly negative critical reception of works that became excessively private. If there is a central ethical norm by which his characters must live, it is surely that espoused by the nonjudgmental artist Hannah in *Night of the Iguana* (1961): "Nothing human disgusts me unless it's unkind, violent."

Williams was a prolific author, a two-time winner of the Pulitzer Prize for Drama (for *Streetcar* and *Cat on a Hot Tin Roof* [1955]), and a four-time recipient of the New York Drama Critics' Circle Award (for those two plays as well as for *Menagerie* and *Iguana*). Along with two dozen full-length plays and two collections of one-acts, he wrote two novels, four collections of short fiction—among his finest stories, influenced by Hawthorne and Poe, are "Desire and the Black Masseur" and "One Arm"—two volumes of poetry, and several screenplays. Most are charged with a highly expressive symbolism and imbued with his recurrent attitudes and motifs: a somewhat sentimental valuation of the lost and lonely; a worship of sexuality as a means of transcending aloneness; a castigation of repression and excessive guilt; an abhorrence of the underdeveloped heart that refuses to reach out to others; a fear of time, the enemy that robs one of physical beauty and artistic vitality; and an insistence on the need for the courage to endure, to always continue onward—as Williams himself did as a writer.

Thomas P. Adler
Purdue University

PRIMARY WORKS

Battle of Angels, 1945; *The Glass Menagerie*, 1945; *Twenty-Seven Wagons Full of Cotton & Other One-Act Plays*, 1946; *You Touched Me!*, 1947; *A Streetcar Named Desire*, 1947; *One Arm and Other Short Stories*, 1948; *Summer and Smoke*, 1948; *American Blues: Five Short Stories*, 1948; *The Roman Spring of Mrs. Stone*, 1950; *The Rose Tattoo*, 1951; *I Rise in Flame, Cried the Phoenix*, 1951; *Camino Real*, 1953; *Hard Candy*, 1954; *Cat on a Hot Tin Roof*, 1955; *In the Winter of Cities*, 1956; *Baby Doll*, 1956; *Orpheus Descending*, 1958; *The Fugitive Kind*, 1958; *Suddenly Last Summer*, 1958; *Sweet Bird of Youth*, 1959; *Period of Adjustment*, 1960; *The Milk Train Doesn't Stop Here Any More*, 1964; *The Knightly Quest: A Novella & Four Short Stories*, 1966; *Kingdom of Earth*, 1967; *Two-Character Play*, 1969; *Dragon Country*, 1970; *Small Craft Warnings*, 1972; *Out Cry*, 1973; *Eight Mortal Ladies Possessed*, 1974; *Moise and the World of Reason*, 1975; *Memoirs*, 1975; *Eccentricities of a Nightingale*, 1976; *Where I Live: Selected Essays*, 1978; *Something Cloudy, Something Clear*, 1981; *Clothes for a Summer Hotel*, 1981; *A House Not Meant to Stand*, 1982; *In Masks Outrageous and Austere*, 1983; *Collected Stories*, 1986.

Suddenly Last Summer

Scene One

The set may be as unrealistic as the decor of a dramatic ballet. It represents part of a mansion of Victorian Gothic style in the Garden District of New Orleans on a late afternoon, between late summer and early fall. The interior is blended with a fantastic garden which is more like a tropical jungle, or forest, in the prehistoric age of giant fern-forests when living creatures had flippers turning to limbs and scales to skin. The colors of this jungle-garden are violent, especially since it is steaming with heat after rain. There are massive tree-flowers that suggest organs of a body, torn out, still glistening with undried blood; there are harsh cries and sibilant hissings and thrashing sounds in the garden as if it were inhabited by beasts, serpents and birds, all of savage nature. . . .

The jungle tumult continues a few moments after the curtain rises; then sub-sides into relative quiet, which is occasionally broken by a new outburst.

A lady enters with the assistance of a silver-knobbed cane. She has light or-ange or pink hair and wears a lavender lace dress, and over her withered bosom is pinned a starfish of diamonds.

She is followed by a young blond Doctor, all in white, glacially brilliant, very, very good-looking, and the old lady's manner and eloquence indicate her undelib-erate response to his icy charm.

MRS. VENABLE: Yes, this was Sebastian's garden. The Latin names of the plants were printed on tags attached to them but the print's fading out. Those ones there—[*She draws a deep breath*]—are the oldest plants on earth, survivors from the age of the giant fern-forests. Of course in this semi-tropical climate—[*She takes another deep breath*]—some of the rarest plants, such as the Venus flytrap—you know what this is, Doctor? The Venus flytrap?

DOCTOR: An insectivorous plant?

MRS. VENABLE: Yes, it feeds on insects. It has to be kept under glass from early fall to late spring and when it went under glass, my son, Sebastian, had to provide it with fruit flies flown in at great expense from a Florida labora-tory that used fruit flies for experiments in genetics. Well, I can't do that, Doctor. [*She takes a deep breath.*] I can't, I just can't do it! It's not the expense but the—

DOCTOR: Effort.

MRS. VENABLE: Yes. So goodbye, Venus flytrap!—like so much else ... Whew! ... [*She draws breath.*]—I don't know why, but—! I already feel I can lean on your shoulder, Doctor—Cu?—Cu?

DOCTOR: Cu-kro-wicz. It's a Polish word that mean sugar, so let's make it sim-ple and call me Doctor Sugar.

[*He returns her smile.*]

MRS. VENABLE: Well, now, Doctor Sugar, you've seen Sebastian's garden.

[*They are advancing slowly to the patio area.*]

DOCTOR: It's like a well-groomed jungle....

MRS. VENABLE: That's how he meant it to be, nothing was accidental, every-thing was planned and designed in Sebastian's life and his—[*She dabs her forehead with her handkerchief which she had taken from her reticule*]—work!

DOCTOR: What was your son's work, Mrs. Venable?—besides this garden?

MRS. VENABLE: As many times as I've had to answer that question! D'you know it still shocks me a little?—to realize that Sebastian Venable, the poet is still unknown outside of a small coterie of friends, including his mother.

DOCTOR: Oh.

MRS. VENABLE: You see, strictly speaking, his *life* was his occupation.

DOCTOR: I see.

MRS. VENABLE: No, you *don't* see, yet, but before I'm through, you will.—Sebastian was a poet! That's what I meant when I said his life was his work because the work of a poet is the life of a poet and—vice versa, the life of a poet is the work of a poet, I mean you can't separate them, I mean—well, for instance, a salesman's work is one thing and his life is another—or can be. The same thing's true of—doctor, lawyer, merchant, *thief*!—But a poet's life is his work and his work is his life in a special sense because—oh, I've already talked myself breathless and dizzy.

[*The Doctor offers his arm.*]

Thank you.

DOCTOR: Mrs. Venable, did your doctor okay this thing?

MRS. VENABLE [*breathless*]: What thing?

DOCTOR: Your meeting this girl that you think is responsible for your son's death?

MRS. VENABLE: I've waited months to face her because I couldn't get to St. Mary's to face her—I've had her brought here to my house. I won't collapse! She'll collapse! I mean her lies will collapse—not my truth—not the truth.... *Forward march, Doctor Sugar!*

[*He conducts her slowly to the patio.*]

Ah, we've *made* it, *ha ha*! I didn't know that I was so weak on my pins! Sit down, Doctor. I'm not afraid of using every last ounce and inch of my little, left-over strength in doing just what I'm doing. I'm devoting all that's left of my life, Doctor, to the defense of a dead poet's reputation. Sebastian had no public name as a poet, he didn't want one, he refused to have one. He *dreaded, abhorred*!—false values that come from being publicly known, from fame, from personal—exploitation.... Oh, he'd say to me: "Violet? Mother?—You're going to outlive me!!"

DOCTOR: What made him think that?

MRS. VENABLE: Poets are always clairvoyant!—And he had rheumatic fever when he was fifteen and it affected a heart-valve and he wouldn't stay off horses and out of water and so forth.... "Violet? Mother? You're going to live longer than me, and then, when I'm gone, it will be yours, in your hands, to do whatever you please with!"—Meaning, of course, his future recognition!—That he *did* want, he wanted it after his death when it couldn't disturb him; then he did want to offer his work to the world. All right. Have I made my point, Doctor? Well, here is my son's work, Doctor, here's his life going *on*!

[*She lifts a thin gilt-edged volume from the patio table as if elevating the Host before the altar. Its gold leaf and lettering catch the afternoon sun. It says* Poem of Summer. *Her face suddenly has a different look, the look of a visionary, an exalted* religieuse. *At the same instant a bird sings clearly and purely in the garden and the old lady seems to be almost young for a moment.*]

DOCTOR [*reading the title*]: Poem of Summer?

MRS. VENABLE: *Poem of Summer*, and the date of the summer, there are twenty-five of them, he wrote one poem a year which he printed himself on an eighteenth-century hand-press at his—atelier in the—French—Quarter—so no one but he could see it....

[*She seems dizzy for a moment.*]

DOCTOR: He wrote one poem a year?

MRS. VENABLE: One for each summer that we traveled together. The other nine months of the year were really only a preparation.

DOCTOR: Nine months?

MRS. VENABLE: The length of a pregnancy, yes....

DOCTOR: The poem was hard to deliver?

MRS. VENABLE: Yes, even with me. *Without* me, *impossible*, Doctor!—he wrote no poem last summer.

DOCTOR: He died last summer?

MRS. VENABLE: Without me he died last summer, that was his last summer's poem.

[*She staggers; he assists her toward a chair. She catches her breath with difficulty.*]

One long-ago summer—now, why am I thinking of this?—my son, Sebastian, said, "Mother?—Listen to this!"—He read me Herman Melville's description of the Encantadas, the Galapagos Islands: Quote—take five and twenty heaps of cinders dumped here and there in an outside city lot. Imagine some of them magnified into mountains, and the vacant lot, the sea. And you'll have a fit idea of the general aspect of the Encantadas, the Enchanted Isles—extinct volcanos, looking much as the world at large might look—after a last conflagration—end quote. He read me that description and said that we had to go there. And so we did go there that summer on a chartered boat, a four-masted schooner, as close as possible to the sort of a boat that Melville must have sailed on.... We saw the Encantadas, but on the Encantadas we saw something Melville *hadn't* written about. We saw the great sea-turtles crawl up out of the sea for their annual egg-laying.... Once a year the female of the sea-turtle crawls up out of the equatorial sea onto the blazing sand-beach of a volcanic island to dig a pit in the sand and deposit her eggs there. It's a long and dreadful thing, the depositing of the eggs in the sand-pits, and when it's finished the exhausted female turtle crawls back to the sea half-dead. She never sees her offspring, but we did. Sebastian knew exactly when the sea-turtle eggs would be hatched out and we returned in time for it....

DOCTOR: You went back to the—?

MRS. VENABLE: Terrible Encantadas, those heaps of extinct volcanos, in time to witness the hatching of the sea-turtles and their desperate flight to the sea!

[*There is a sound of harsh bird-cries in the air. She looks up.*]

—The narrow beach, the color of caviar, was all in motion! But the sky was in motion, too....

DOCTOR: The sky was in motion, too?

MRS. VENABLE:—Full of flesh-eating birds and the noise of the birds, the horrible savage cries of the—

DOCTOR: Carnivorous birds?

MRS. VENABLE: Over the narrow black beach of the Encantadas as the just hatched sea-turtles scrambled out of the sandpits and started their race to the sea. . . .

DOCTOR: Race to the sea?

MRS. VENABLE: To escape the flesh-eating birds that made the sky almost as black as the beach!

[*She gazes up again: we hear the wild, ravenous, harsh cries of the birds. The sound comes in rhythmic waves like a savage chant.*]

And the sand all alive, all alive, as the hatched sea-turtles made their dash for the sea, while the birds hovered and swooped to attack and hovered and—swooped to attack! They were diving down on the hatched sea-turtles, turning them over to expose their soft undersides, tearing the undersides open and rending and eating their flesh. Sebastian guessed that possibly only a hundredth of one per cent of their number would escape to the sea. . . .

DOCTOR: What was it about this that fascinated your son?

MRS. VENABLE: My son was looking for—[*She stops short with a slight gasp.*]— Let's just say he was interested in sea-turtles!

DOCTOR: That isn't what you started to say.

MRS. VENABLE: I stopped myself just in time.

DOCTOR: Say what you started to say.

MRS. VENABLE: I started to say that my son was looking for God and I stopped myself because I thought you'd think "Oh, a pretentious young crackpot!"—which Sebastian was *not*!

DOCTOR: Mrs. Venable, doctors look for God, too.

MRS. VENABLE: Oh?

DOCTOR: I think they have to look harder for him than priests since they don't have the help of such well-known guidebooks and well-organized expeditions as the priests have with their scriptures and—churches. . . .

MRS. VENABLE: You mean they go on a solitary safari like a poet?

DOCTOR: Yes. Some do. I do.

MRS. VENABLE: I believe, I *believe* you! [*She laughs, startled.*]

DOCTOR: Let me tell you something—the first operation I performed at Lion's View.—You can imagine how anxious and nervous I was about the outcome.

MRS. VENABLE: Yes.

DOCTOR: The patient was a young girl regarded as hopeless and put in the Drum—

MRS. VENABLE: Yes.

DOCTOR: The name for the violent ward at Lion's View because it looks like the inside of a drum with very bright lights burning all day and all night.—So the attendants can see any change of expression or movement among the inmates in time to grab them if they're about to attack. After the operation I stayed with the girl, as if I'd delivered a child that might stop breathing.—When they finally wheeled her out of surgery, I still stayed with her. I walked along by the rolling table holding onto her hand—with my heart in my throat....

[*We hear faint music.*]

—It was a nice afternoon, as fair as this one. And the moment we wheeled her outside, she whispered something, she whispered: "Oh, how blue the sky is!"—And I felt proud, I felt proud and relieved, because up till then her speech, everything that she'd babbled, was a torrent of obscenities!

MRS. VENABLE: Yes, well, now, I can tell you without any hesitation that my son *was* looking for God, I mean for a clear image of him. He spent that whole blazing equatorial day in the crow's-nest of the schooner watching this thing on the beach till it was too dark to see it, and when he came down the rigging he said "Well, now I've seen Him!," and he meant God.—And for several weeks after that he had a fever, he was delirious with it.—

[*The Encantadas music then fades in again, briefly, at a lower level, a whisper.*]

DOCTOR: I can see how he *might* be, I think he *would* be disturbed if he thought he'd seen God's image, an equation of God, in that spectacle you watched in the Encantadas: creatures of the air hovering over and swooping down to devour creatures of the sea that had had the bad luck to be hatched on land and weren't able to scramble back into the sea fast enough to escape that massacre you witnessed, yes, I can see how such a spectacle could be equated with a good deal of—*experience, existence!*— but not with *God!* Can *you*?

MRS. VENABLE: Dr. Sugar, I'm a reasonably loyal member of the Protestant Episcopal Church, but I understood what he meant.

DOCTOR: Did he mean we must rise above God?

MRS. VENABLE: He meant that God shows a savage face to people and shouts some fierce things at them, it's all we see or hear of Him. Isn't it all we ever really see and hear of Him, now?—Nobody seems to know why....

[*Music fades out again.*]

Shall I go on from there?

DOCTOR: Yes, do.

MRS. VENABLE: Well, next?—India—China—

[*Miss Foxhill appears with the medicine. Mrs. Venable sees her.*]

MISS FOXHILL: Mrs. Venable.

MRS. VENABLE: Oh, God—elixir—of—. [*She takes the glass.*] Isn't it kind of the drugstore to keep me alive. Where was I, Doctor?

DOCTOR: In the Himalayas.

MRS. VENABLE: Oh yes, that long-ago summer.... In the Himalayas he almost entered a Buddhist monastery, had gone so far as to shave his head and eat just rice out of a wood bowl on a grass mat. He'd promised those sly Buddhist monks that he would give up the world and himself and all his worldly possessions to their mendicant order.—Well, I cabled his father, "For God's sake notify bank to freeze Sebastian's accounts!"—I got back this cable from my late husband's lawyer: "Mr. Venable critically ill Stop Wants you Stop Needs you Stop Immediate return advised most strongly. Stop. Cable time of arrival. . . ."

DOCTOR: Did you go back to your husband?

MRS. VENABLE: I made the hardest decision of my life I stayed with my son. I got him through that crisis too. In less than a month he got up off the filthy grass mat and threw the rice bowl away—and booked us into Shepheard's Hotel in Cairo and the Ritz in Paris—. And from then on, oh, we—still lived in a—world of light and shadow. . . .

[*She turns vaguely with empty glass. He rises and takes it from her.*]

But the shadow was almost as luminous as the light.

DOCTOR: Don't you want to sit down now?

MRS. VENABLE: Yes, indeed I do, before I fall down.

[*He assists her into wheelchair.*]

—Are your hind-legs still on you?

DOCTOR [*still concerned over her agitation*]: —My what? Oh—hind legs!— Yes . . .

MRS. VENEABLE: Well, then you're not a donkey, you're certainly not a donkey because I've been talking the hind-legs off a donkey—several donkeys. . . . But I had to make it clear to you that the world lost a great deal too when I lost my son last summer. . . . You would have liked my son, he would have been charmed by you. My son, Sebastian, was not a family snob or a money snob but he was a snob, all right. He was a snob about personal charm in people, he insisted upon good looks in people around him, and, oh, he had a perfect little court of young and beautiful people around him always, wherever he was, here in New Orleans or New York or on the Riviera or in Paris and Venice, he always had a little entourage of the beautiful and the talented and the young!

DOCTOR: Your son was young, Mrs. Venable?

MRS. VENABLE: Both of us were young, and stayed young, Doctor.

DOCTOR: Could I see a photograph of your son, Mrs. Venable?

MRS. VENABLE: Yes, indeed you could, Doctor. I'm glad that you asked to see one. I'm going to show you not one photograph but two. Here. Here is my son, Sebastian, in a Renaissance pageboy's costume at a masked ball in Cannes. Here is my son, Sebastian, in the same costume at a masked ball in Venice. These two pictures were taken twenty years apart. Now which is the older one, Doctor?

DOCTOR: This photograph looks older.

MRS. VENABLE: The photograph looks older but not the subject. It takes character to refuse to grow old, Doctor—successfully to refuse to. It calls for discipline, abstention. One cocktail before dinner, not two, four, six—a single lean chop and lime juice on a salad in restaurants famed for rich dishes.

[*Foxhill comes from the house.*]

MISS FOXHILL: Mrs. Venable, Miss Holly's mother and brother are—

[*Simultaneously Mrs. Holly and George appear in the window.*]

GEORGE: Hi, Aunt Vi!

MRS. HOLLY: Violet dear, we're here.

MISS FOXHILL: They're here.

MRS. VENABLE: Wait upstairs in my upstairs living room for me.

[*To Miss Foxhill:*]

Get them upstairs. I don't want them at that window during this talk.

[*To the Doctor:*]

Let's get away from the window.

[*He wheels her to stage center.*]

DOCTOR: Mrs. Venable? Did your son have a—well—what kind of a *personal*, well, *private* life did—

MRS. VENABLE: That's a question I wanted you to ask me.

MISS FOXHILL: Why?

MRS. VENABLE: I haven't heard the girl's story except indirectly in a watered-down version, being too ill to go to hear it directly, but I've gathered enough to know that it's a hideous attack on my son's moral character which, being dead, he can't defend himself from. I have to be the defender. Now. Sit down. Listen to me . . .

[*The Doctor sits.*]

. . . before you hear whatever you're going to hear from the girl when she gets here. My son, Sebastian, was chaste. Not c-h-a-s-e-d! Oh, he was chased in that way of spelling it, too, we had to be very fleet-footed I can tell you, with his looks and his charm, to keep ahead of pursuers, every kind of pursuer!—I mean he was c-h-a-s-t-e!—Chaste.

DOCTOR: I understood what you meant, Mrs. Venable.

MRS. VENABLE: And you *believe* me, don't you?

DOCTOR: Yes, but—

MRS. VENABLE: But *what*?

DOCTOR: Chastity at—what age was your son last summer?

MRS. VENABLE: *Forty*, maybe. We really didn't count birthdays. . . .

DOCTOR: He lived a celibate life?

MRS. VENABLE: As strictly as if he'd *vowed* to! This sounds like vanity, Doctor, but really I was actually the only one in his life that satisfied the demands he made of people. Time after time my son would let people go, dismiss them!—because their, their, their!—*attitude* toward him was—

DOCTOR: Not pure as—

MRS. VENABLE: My son, Sebastian, demanded! We were a famous couple. People didn't speak of Sebastian and his mother or Mrs. Venable and her son, they said "Sebastian and Violet, Violet and Sebastian are staying at the Lido, they're at the Ritz in Madrid. Sebastian and Violet, Violet and Sebastian have taken a house at Biarritz for the season," and every appearance, every time we appeared, attention was centered on *us!*—*everyone else*! *Eclipsed*! Vanity? Ohhhh, no, Doctor, you can't call it that—

DOCTOR: I didn't call it that.

MRS. VENABLE:—It wasn't *folie de grandeur*, it was grandeur.

DOCTOR: I see.

MRS. VENABLE: An attitude toward life that's hardly been known in the world since the great Renaissance princes were crowded out of their palaces and gardens by successful shopkeepers!

DOCTOR: I see.

MRS. VENABLE: Most people's lives—what are they but trails of debris, each day more debris, more debris, long, long trails of debris with nothing to clean it all up but, finally, death . . .

[*We hear lyric music*]

My son, Sebastian, and I constructed our days, each day, we would—carve out each day of our lives like a piece of sculpture.—Yes, we left behind us a trail of days like a gallery of sculpture! But, last summer—

[*Pause: the music continues.*]

I can't forgive him for it, not even now that he's paid for it with his life!—he let in this—*vandal*! This—

DOCTOR: The girl that—?

MRS. VENABLE: That you're going to meet here this afternoon! Yes. He admitted this vandal and with her tongue for a hatchet she's gone about smashing our legend, the memory of—

DOCTOR: Mrs. Venable, what do you think is her reason?

MRS. VENABLE: Lunatics don't have reason!

DOCTOR: I mean what do you think is her—motive?

MRS. VENABLE: What a question!—We put the bread in her mouth and the clothes on her back. People that like you for that or even forgive you for it are, are—*hen's teeth*, Doctor. The role of the benefactor is worse than thankless, it's the role of a victim, Doctor, a sacrificial victim, yes, they want your blood, Doctor, they want your blood on the altar steps of their *outraged, outrageous* egos!

DOCTOR: Oh. You mean she resented the—

MRS. VENABLE: Loathed!—They can't shut her up at St. Mary's.

DOCTOR: I thought she'd been there for months.

MRS. VENABLE: I mean keep her *still* there. She *babbles*! They couldn't shut her up in Cabeza de Lobo or at the clinic in Paris—she babbled, babbled!—smashing my son's reputation.—On the Berengaria bringing her back to the States she broke out of the stateroom and babbled, babbled; even at the airport when she was flown down here, she babbled a bit of her story before they could whisk her into an ambulance to St. Mary's. This is a reticule, Doctor. [*She raises a cloth bag.*] A catch-all, carry-all bag for an elderly lady which I turned into last summer. . . . Will you open it for me, my hands are stiff, and fish out some cigarettes and a cigarette holder.

[*He does.*]

DOCTOR: I don't have matches.

MRS. VENABLE: I think there's a table-lighter on the table.

DOCTOR: Yes, there is.

[*He lights it, it flames up high.*]

My Lord, what a torch!

MRS. VENABLE [*with a sudden, sweet smile*]: "So shines a good deed in a naughty world," Doctor—Sugar. . . .

[*Pause. A bird sings sweetly in the garden.*]

DOCTOR: Mrs. Venable?

MRS. VENABLE: Yes?

DOCTOR: In your letter last week you made some reference to a, to a—fund of some kind, an endowment fund of—

MRS. VENABLE: I wrote you that my lawyers and bankers and certified public accountants were setting up the Sebastian Venable Memorial Foundation to subsidize the work of young people like you that are pushing out the frontiers of art and science but have a financial problem. You have a financial problem, don't you, Doctor?

DOCTOR: Yes, we do have that problem. My work is such a *new* and *radical* thing that people in charge of state funds are naturally a little scared of it and keep us on a small budget, so small that—. We need a separate ward for my patients, I need trained assistants, I'd like to marry a girl I can't afford to marry!—But there's also the problem of getting right patients, not just—criminal psychopaths that the State turns over to us for my operation!—because it's—well—risky. . . . I don't want to turn you against my work at Lion's View but I have to be honest with you. There is a good deal of risk in my operation. Whenever you enter the brain with a foreign object . . .

MRS. VENABLE: Yes.

DOCTOR:—Even a needle-thin knife . . .

MRS. VENABLE: Yes.

DOCTOR:—In a skilled surgeon's fingers . . .

MRS. VENABLE: Yes.

DOCTOR:—There is a good deal of risk involved in—the operation. . . .

MRS. VENABLE: You said that it pacifies them, it quiets them down, it suddenly makes them peaceful.

DOCTOR: Yes. It does that, that much we already know, but—

MRS. VENABLE: What?

DOCTOR: Well, it will be ten years before we can tell if the immediate benefits of the operation will be lasting or—passing or even if there'd still be— and this is what haunts me about it!—any possibility, afterwards, of reconstructing a—totally sound person, it may be that the person will always be limited afterwards, relieved of acute disturbances but—*limited,* Mrs Venable. . . .

MRS. VENABLE: Oh, but what a blessing to them, Doctor, to be just peaceful, to be just suddenly—peaceful. . . .

[*A bird sings sweetly in the garden.*]

After all that horror, after those nightmares: just to be able to lift up their eyes and see—[*She looks up and raises a hand to indicate the sky*]—a sky not as black with savage, devouring birds as the sky that we saw in the Encantadas, Doctor.

DOCTOR:—Mrs. Venable? I can't guarantee that a lobotomy would stop her— *babbling*!!

MRS. VENABLE: That may be, maybe not, but after the operation, who would *believe* her, Doctor?

[*Pause: faint jungle music*]

DOCTOR: [*quietly*]: My God. [*Pause.*]—Mrs. Venable, suppose after meeting the girl and observing the girl and hearing this story she babbles—I still shouldn't feel that her condition's—intractable enough! to justify the risks of—suppose I shouldn't feel that non-surgical treatment such as in- sulin shock and electric shock and—

MRS. VENABLE: SHE'S HAD ALL THAT AT SAINT MARY'S!! Nothing else is left for her.

DOCTOR: But if I disagreed with you? [*Pause.*]

MRS. VENABLE: That's just part of a question: finish the question, Doctor.

DOCTOR: Would you still be interested in my work at Lion's View? I mean would the Sebastian Venable Memorial Foundation still be interested in it?

MRS. VENABLE: Aren't we always more interested in a thing that concerns us personally, Doctor?

DOCTOR: Mrs. Venable!!

[*Catharine Holly appears between the lace window curtains.*]

You're such an innocent person that it doesn't occur to you, it obviously hasn't even occurred to you that anybody less innocent than you are could possibly interpret this offer of a subsidy as—well, as sort of a *bribe*?

MRS. VENABLE [*laughs throwing her head back*]: Name it that—I don't care—. There's just two things to remember. She's a destroyer. My son was a *cre- ator!* —Now if my honesty's shocked you—pick up your little black bag without the subsidy in it, and run away from this garden!—Nobody's heard our conversation but you and I, Doctor Sugar. . . .

[*Miss Foxhill comes out of the house and calls.*]

MISS FOXHILL: Mrs. Venable?

MRS. VENABLE: What is it, what do you want, Miss Foxhill?

MISS FOXHILL: Mrs. Venable? Miss Holly is here, with—

[*Mrs. Venable sees Catharine at the window.*]

MRS. VENABLE: Oh, my God. There she is, in the window!—I told you I didn't want her to enter my house again, I told you to meet them at the door and lead them around the side of the house to the garden and you didn't listen. I'm not ready to face her. I have to have my five o'clock cocktail first, to fortify me. Take my chair inside. Doctor? Are you still here? I thought you'd run out of the garden. I'm going back through the garden to the other entrance. Doctor? Sugar? You may stay in the garden if you wish to or run out of the garden if you wish to or go in this way if you wish to or do anything that you wish to but I'm going to have my five o'clock daiquiri, *frozen!*—before I face her....

[*All during this she has been sailing very slowly off through the garden like a stately vessel at sea with a fair wind in her sails, a pirate's frigate or a treasure-laden galleon. The young Doctor stares at Catharine framed by the lace window curtains. Sister Felicity appears beside her and draws her away from the window. Music: an ominous fanfare. Sister Felicity holds the door open for Catharine as the Doctor starts quickly forward. He starts to pick up his bag but doesn't. Catharine rushes out, they almost collide with each other.*]

CATHARINE: *Excuse me.*

DOCTOR: *I'm sorry....*

[*She looks after him as he goes into the house.*]

SISTER FELICITY: Sit down and be still till your family come outside.

DIM OUT

Scene Two

Catharine removes a cigarette from a lacquered box on the table and lights it. The following quick, cadenced lines are accompanied by quick, dancelike movement, almost formal, as the Sister in her sweeping white habit, which should be starched to make a crackling sound, pursues the girl about the white wicker patio table and among the wicker chairs: this can be accompanied by quick music.

SISTER: What did you take out of that box on the table?

CATHARINE: Just a cigarette, Sister.

SISTER: Put it back in the box.

CATHARINE: Too late, it's already lighted.

SISTER: Give it here.

CATHARINE: Oh, please, let me smoke, Sister!

SISTER: Give it here.

CATHARINE: *Please*, Sister Felicity.

SISTER: Catharine, give it here. You know that you're not allowed to smoke at Saint Mary's.

CATHARINE: We're not at Saint Mary's, this is an afternoon out.

SISTER: You're still in my charge. I can't permit you to smoke because the last time you smoked you dropped a lighted cigarette on your dress and started a fire.

CATHARINE: Oh, I did not start a fire. I just burned a hole in my skirt because I was half unconscious under medication. [*She is now back of a white wicker chair.*]

SISTER [*overlapping her*]: Catharine, give it here.

CATHARINE: Don't be such a bully!

SISTER: Disobedience has to be paid for later.

CATHARINE: All right, I'll pay for it later.

SISTER [*overlapping*]: Give me that cigarette or I'll make a report that'll put you right back on the violent ward, if you don't. [*She claps her hands twice and holds one hand out across the table.*]

CATHARINE [*overlapping*]: I'm not being violent, Sister.

SISTER [*overlapping*]: Give me that cigarette, I'm holding my hand out for it!

CATHARINE: All right, take it, here, take it!

[*She thrusts the lighted end of the cigarette into the palm of the Sister's hand. The Sister cries out and sucks her burned hand.*]

SISTER: *You burned me with it!*

CATHARINE: I'm sorry, I didn't mean to.

SISTER [*shocked, hurt*]: You deliberately burned me!

CATHARINE [*overlapping*]: You said give it to you and so I gave it to you.

SISTER [*overlapping*]: You stuck the lighted end of that cigarette in my hand!

CATHARINE [*overlapping*]: I'm *sick*, I'm *sick*—of being *bossed* and *bullied*!

SISTER [*commandingly*]: Sit down!

[*Catherine sits down stiffly in a white wicker chair on forestage, facing the audience. The sister resumes sucking the burned palm of her hand. Ten beats. Then from inside the house the whirr of a mechanical mixer.*]

CATHARINE: There goes the Waring Mixer, Aunt Violet's about to have her five o'clock frozen daiquiri, you could set a watch by it! [*She almost laughs. Then she draws a deep, shuddering breath and leans back in her chair, but her hands remain clenched on the white wicker arms.*]—We're in Sebastian's garden. *My God, I can still cry!*

SISTER: Did you have any medication before you went out?

CATHARINE: No. I didn't have any. Will you give me some, Sister?

SISTER [*almost gently*]: I can't. I wasn't told to. However, I think the doctor will give you something.

CATHARINE: The young blond man I bumped into?

SISTER: Yes. The young doctor's a specialist from another hospital.

CATHARINE: What hospital?

SISTER: A word to the wise is sufficient. . . .

[*The Doctor has appeared in the window.*]

CATHARINE [*rising abruptly*]: I knew I was being watched, he's in the window, staring out at me!

SISTER: Sit down and be still. Your family's coming outside.

CATHARINE [*overlapping*]: LION'S VIEW, IS IT! DOCTOR?

[*She has advanced toward the bay window. The Doctor draws back, letting the misty white gauze curtains down to obscure him.*]

SISTER [*rising with a restraining gesture which is almost pitying*]: Sit down, dear.

CATHARINE: IS IT LION'S VIEW? DOCTOR?!

SISTER: Be still. . . .

CATHARINE: WHEN CAN I STOP RUNNING DOWN THAT STEEP WHITE STREET IN CABEZA DE LOBO?

SISTER: Catharine, dear, sit down.

CATHARINE: I loved him, Sister! Why wouldn't he let me save him? I tried to hold onto his hand but he struck me away and ran, ran, ran in the wrong direction, Sister!

SISTER: Catharine, dear—be still.

[*The Sister sneezes.*]

CATHARINE: Bless you, Sister. [*She says this absently, still watching the window.*]

SISTER: Thank you.

CATHARINE: The Doctor's still at the window but he's too blond to hide behind window curtains, he catches the light, he shines through them. [*She turns from the window.*] —We were *going* to blonds, blonds were next on the menu.

SISTER: Be still now. Quiet, dear.

CATHARINE: Cousin Sebastian said he was famished for blonds, he was fed up with the dark ones and was famished for blonds. All the travel brochures he picked up were advertisements of the blond northern countries. I think he'd already booked us to—Copenhagen or—Stockholm.—Fed up with dark ones, famished for light ones: that's how he talked about people, as if they were—items on a menu.—"That one's delicious-looking, that one is appetizing," or "that one is *not* appetizing"—I think because he was really nearly half-starved from living on pills and salads. . . .

SISTER: *Stop it!*—Catharine, be still.

CATHARINE: He liked me and so I loved him. . . . [*She cries a little again.*] If he'd kept hold of my hand I could have saved him!—Sebastian suddenly said to me last summer: "Let's fly north, little bird—I want to walk under those radiant, cold northern lights—I've never *seen* the aurora borealis!"— Somebody said once or wrote, once: "We're all of us children in a vast kindergarten trying to spell God's name with the wrong alphabet blocks!"

MRS. HOLLY [*offstage*]: Sister?

[*The Sister rises.*]

CATHERINE [*rising*]: I think it's *me* they're calling, they call *me* "Sister," Sister!

Scene Three

The Sister resumes her seat impassively as the girl's mother and younger brother appear from the garden. The mother, Mrs. Holly, is a fatuous Southern lady who requires no other description. The brother, George, is typically good-looking, he has the best "looks" of the family, tall and elegant of figure. They enter.

MRS. HOLLY: Catharine, dear! Catharine—

[*They embrace tentatively.*]

Well, well! Doesn't she look fine, George?

GEORGE: Uh huh.

CATHARINE: They send you to the beauty parlor whenever you're going to have a family visit. Other times you look awful, you can't have a compact or lipstick or anything made out of metal because they're afraid you'll swallow it.

MRS. HOLLY [*giving a tinkly little laugh*]: I think she looks just splendid, don't you, George?

GEORGE: Can't we talk to her without the nun for a minute?

MRS. HOLLY: Yes, I'm sure it's all right to. Sister?

CATHARINE: Excuse me, Sister Felicity, this is my mother, Mrs. Holly, and my brother, George.

SISTER: How do you do.

GEORGE: How d'ya do.

CATHARINE: This is Sister Felicity. . . .

MRS. HOLLY: We're so happy that Catharine's at Saint Mary's! So very grateful for all you're doing for her.

SISTER [*sadly, mechanically*]: We do the best we can for her, Mrs. Holly.

MRS. HOLLY: I'm sure you do. Yes, well—I wonder if you would mind if we had a little private chat with our Cathie?

SISTER: I'm not supposed to let her out of my sight.

MRS. HOLLY: It's just for a minute. You can sit in the hall or the garden and we'll call you right back here the minute the private part of the little talk is over.

[*Sister Felicity withdraws with an uncertain nod and a swish of starched fabric.*]

GEORGE [*to Catherine*]: Jesus! What are you up to? Huh? Sister? Are you trying to RUIN us?!

MRS. HOLLY: GAWGE! WILL YOU BE QUIET. You're upsetting your sister!

[*He jumps up and stalks off a little, rapping his knee with his zipper-covered tennis racket.*]

CATHARINE: How elegant George looks.

MRS. HOLLY: George inherited Cousin Sebastian's wardrobe but everything else is in probate! Did you know that? That everything else is in probate and Violet can keep it in probate just as long as she wants to?

CATHARINE: Where is Aunt Violet?

MRS. HOLLY: *George, come back here!*

[*He does, sulkily.*]

Violet's on her way down.

GEORGE: Yeah. Aunt Violet has an elevator now.

MRS. HOLLY: Yais, she has, she's had an elevator installed where the back stairs were, and, Sister, it's the cutest little thing you ever did see! It's paneled in Chinese lacquer, black an' gold Chinese lacquer, with lovely bird-pictures on it. But there's only room for two people at a time in it. George and I came down on foot.—I think she's havin' her frozen daiquiri now, she still has a frozen daiquiri promptly at five o'clock ev'ry afternoon in the world ... in warm weather.... Sister, the horrible death of Sebastian just about *killed* her!—She's now slightly better ... but it's a question of time.—Dear, you know, I'm sure that you understand, why we haven't been out to see you at Saint Mary's. They said you were too disturbed, and a family visit might disturb you more. But I want you to know that nobody, absolutely nobody in the city, knows a thing about what you've been through. Have they, George? Not a thing. Not a soul even knows that you've come back from Europe. When people enquire, when they question us about you, we just say that you've stayed abroad to study something or other. [*She catches her breath.*] Now. Sister?—I want you to please be *very* careful what you say to your Aunt Violet about what happened to Sebastian in Cabeza de Lobo.

CATHARINE: What do you want me to say about what—?.

MRS. HOLLY: Just don't repeat that same fantastic story! For my sake and George's sake, the sake of your brother and mother, don't repeat that horrible story again! Not to Violet! Will you?

CATHARINE: Then I am going to have to tell Aunt Violet what happened to her son in Cabeza de Lobo?

MRS. HOLLY: Honey, that's why you're here. She has INSISTED on hearing it straight from YOU!

GEORGE: You were the only witness to it, Cathie.

CATHARINE: No, there were others. That *ran.*

MRS. HOLLY: Oh, Sister, you've just had a little sort of a—*nightmare* about it! Now, listen to me, will you, Sister? Sebastian has left, has BEQUEATHED!—to you an' Gawge in his *will*—

GEORGE [*religiously*]: *To each of us, fifty grand, each!*—AFTER! TAXES!—GET IT?

CATHARINE: Oh, yes, but if they give me an injection—I won't have any choice but to tell exactly what happened in Cabeza de Lobo last summer. Don't you see? I won't have any choice but to tell the truth. It makes you tell the truth because it shuts something off that might make you able not to and *everything* comes out, decent or *not* decent, you have no control, but always, always the truth!

MRS. HOLLY: Catharine, darling. I don't know the full story, but surely you're not too sick in your *head* to know in your *heart* that the story you've been telling is just—too—

GEORGE: [*cutting in*]: Cathie, Cathie, you got to forget that story! Can'tcha? For *your* fifty grand?

MRS. HOLLY: Because if Aunt Vi contests the will, and we know she'll contest it, she'll keep it in the courts forever!—We'll be—

GEORGE: It's in PROBATE NOW! And'll never get out of probate until you drop that story—we can't afford to hire lawyers good enough to contest it! So if you don't stop telling that crazy story, we won't have a pot to— cook *greens* in!

[*He turns away with a fierce grimace and a sharp, abrupt wave of his hand, as if slapping down something. Catharine stares at his tall back for a moment and laughs wildly.*]

MRS. HOLLY: Catharine, don't laugh like that, it scares me, Catharine.

[*Jungle birds scream in the garden.*]

GEORGE [*turning his back on his sister*]: Cathie, the money is all tied up.

[*He stoops over sofa, hands on flannel knees, speaking directly into Catharine's face as if she were hard of hearing. She raises a hand to touch his cheek affectionately; he seizes the hand and removes it but holds it tight.*]

If Aunt Vi decided to contest Sebastian's will that leaves us all of this cash?!—Am I coming through to you?

CATHARINE: Yes, little brother, you are.

GEORGE: You see, Mama, she's crazy like a coyote!

[*He gives her a quick cold kiss*]

We won't get a single damn penny, honest t' God we won't! So you've just GOT to stop tellin' that story about what you say happened to Cousin Sebastian in Cabeza de Lobo, even if it's what it *couldn't* be, TRUE!—You got to drop it, Sister, you can't tell such a story to civilized people in a civilized up-to-date country!

MRS. HOLLY: Cathie, why, why, why!—did you invent such a tale?

CATHARINE: But, Mother, I DIDN'T invent it. I know it's a hideous story but it's a true story of our time and the world we live in and what did truly happen to Cousin Sebastian in Cabeza de Lobo....

GEORGE: Oh, then you are going to tell it. Mama, she IS going to tell it! Right to Aunt Vi, and lose us a hundred thousand!—Cathie? You are a BITCH!

MRS. HOLLY: GAWGE!

GEORGE: I repeat it, a bitch! She isn't crazy, Mama, she's no more crazy than I am, she's just, just—PERVERSE! Was ALWAYS!—perverse....

[*Catharine turns away and breaks into quiet sobbing.*]

MRS. HOLLY: Gawge, Gawge, apologize to Sister, this is no way for you to talk to your sister. You come right back over here and tell your sweet little sister you're sorry you spoke like that to her!

GEORGE [*turning back to Catherine*]: I'm sorry, Cathie, but you know we NEED that money! Mama and me, we—Cathie? I got *ambitions!* And, Cathie, I'm

YOUNG!—I *want* things, I *need* them, Cathie! So will you please think about ME? Us?

MISS FOXHILL [*offstage*]: Mrs. Holly? Mrs. Holly?

MRS. HOLLY: Somebody's callin' fo' me. Catharine, Gawge put it very badly but you know that it's TRUE! WE DO HAVE TO GET WHAT SEBASTIAN HAS LEFT US IN HIS WILL, DEAREST! AND YOU WON'T LET US DOWN? PROMISE? YOU WON'T? LET US DOWN?

GEORGE [*fiercely shouting*]: HERE COMES AUNT VI! Mama, Cathie, Aunt Violet's—here is Aunt Vi!

Scene Four

Mrs. Venable enters downstage area. Entrance music.

MRS. HOLLY: *Cathie! Here's Aunt Vi!*

MRS. VENABLE: She sees me and I see her. That's all that's necessary. Miss Foxhill, put my chair in this corner. Crank the back up a little.

[*Miss Foxhill does this business.*]

More. More. Not that much!—Let it back down a little. All right. Now, then. I'll have my frozen daiquiri, now. . . . Do any of you want coffee?

GEORGE: I'd like a chocolate malt.

MRS. HOLLY: Gawge!

MRS. VENABLE: This isn't a drugstore.

MRS. HOLLY: Oh, Gawge is just being Gawge.

MRS. VENABLE: That's what I *thought* he was being!

[*An uncomfortable silence falls. Miss Foxhill creeps out like a burglar. She speaks in a breathless whisper, presenting a cardboard folder toward Mrs. Venable.*]

MISS FOXHILL: Here's the portfolio marked Cabeza de Lobo. It has all your correspondence with the police there and the American consul.

MRS. VENABLE: I asked for the *English transcript!* It's in a separate—

MISS FOXHILL: Separate, yes, here it is!

MRS. VENABLE: Oh . . .

MISS FOXHILL: And here's the report of the private investigators and here's the report of—

MRS. VENABLE: Yes, yes, yes! Where's the doctor?

MISS FOXHILL: On the phone in the library!

MRS. VENABLE: Why does he choose such a moment to make a phone-call?

MISS FOXHILL: He didn't make a phone-call, he received a phone-call from—

MRS. VENABLE: Miss Foxhill, why are you talking to me like a burglar!?

[*Miss Foxhill giggles a little desperately.*]

CATHARINE: Aunt Violet, she's frightened.—Can I move? Can I get up and move around till it starts?

MRS. HOLLY: Cathie, Cathie, dear, did Gawge tell you that he received bids from every good fraternity on the Tulane campus and went Phi Delt because Paul Junior did?

MRS. VENABLE: I see that he had the natural tact and good taste to come here this afternoon outfitted from head to foot in clothes that belonged to my son!

GEORGE: You gave 'em to me, Aunt Vi.

MRS. VENABLE: I didn't know you'd parade them in front of me, George.

MRS. HOLLY [*quickly*]: Gawge, tell Aunt Violet how grateful you are for—

GEORGE: I found a little Jew tailor on Britannia Street that makes alterations so good you'd never guess that they weren't cut *out* for me to *begin* with!

MRS. HOLLY: *AND* so reasonable!—Luckily, since it seems that Sebastian's wonderful, wonderful bequest to Gawge an' Cathie is going to be tied up a while!?

GEORGE: Aunt Vi? About the will?

[*Mrs. Holly coughs.*]

I was just wondering if we can't figure out some way to, to—

MRS. HOLLY: Gawge means to EXPEDITE it! To get through the red tape quicker?

MRS. VENABLE: I understand his meaning. Foxhill, get the Doctor.

[*She has risen with her cane and hobbled to the door.*]

MISS FOXHILL [*exits calling*]: Doctor!

MRS. HOLLY: Gawge, no more about money.

GEORGE: How do we know we'll ever see her again?

[*Catharine gasps and rises; she moves downstage, followed quickly by Sister Felicity.*]

SISTER [*mechanically*]: What's wrong, dear?

CATHARINE: I think I'm just dreaming this, it doesn't seem real!

[*Miss Foxhill comes back out, saying:*]

MISS FOXHILL: He had to answer an urgent call from Lion's View.

[*Slight, tense pause.*]

MRS. HOLLY: Violet! *Not* Lion's View!

[*Sister Felicity had started conducting Catharine back to the patio; she stops her, now.*]

SISTER: Wait, dear.

CATHARINE: What for? I know what's coming.

MRS. VENABLE [*at same time*]: Why? are you all prepared to put out a thousand a month plus extra charge for treatments to keep the girl at St. Mary's?

MRS. HOLLY: Cathie? Cathie, dear?

[*Catharine has returned with the Sister.*]

Tell Aunt Violet how grateful you are for her makin' it possible for you to rest an' recuperate at such a sweet, sweet place as St. Mary's!

CATHARINE: No place for lunatics is a sweet, sweet place.

MRS. HOLLY: But the food's good there. Isn't the food good there?

CATHARINE: Just give me written permission not to eat fried grits. I had yard privileges till I refused to eat fried grits.

SISTER: She lost yard privileges because she couldn't be trusted in the yard without constant supervision or even with it because she'd run to the fence and make signs to cars on the highway.

CATHARINE: Yes, I did, I did that because I've been trying for weeks to get a message out of that "sweet, sweet place."

MRS. HOLLY: What message, dear?

CATHARINE: I got panicky, Mother.

MRS. HOLLY: Sister, I don't understand.

GEORGE: What're you scared of, Sister?

CATHARINE: What they might do to me now, after they've done all the rest!— That man in the window's a specialist from Lion's View! We get newspapers. I know what they're . . .

[*The Doctor comes out.*]

MRS. VENABLE: Why, doctor, I thought you'd left us with just that little black bag to remember you by!

DOCTOR: Oh, no: Don't you remember our talk? I had to answer a call about a patient that—

MRS. VENABLE: This is Dr. Cukrowicz. He says it means "sugar" and we can call him "Sugar"—

[*George laughs.*]

He's a specialist from Lion's View.

CATHARINE [*cutting in*]: WHAT DOES HE SPECIALIZE IN?

MRS. VENABLE: Something new. When other treatments have failed.

[*Pause. The jungle clamor comes up and subsides again.*]

CATHARINE: *Do you want to bore a hole in my skull and turn a knife in my brain? Everything else was done to me!*

[*Mrs. Holly sobs. George raps his knee with the tennis racket.*]

You'd have to have my mother's permission for that.

MRS. VENABLE: I'm paying to keep you in a private asylum.

CATHARINE: You're not my legal guardian.

MRS. VENABLE: Your mother's dependent on me. All of you are!—Financially. . . .

CATHARINE: I think the situation is—clear to me, now. . . .

MRS. VENABLE: Good! In that case. . . .

DOCTOR: I think a quiet atmosphere will get us the best results.

MRS. VENABLE: I don't know what you mean by a quiet atmosphere. She shouted, I didn't.

DOCTOR: Mrs. Venable, let's try to keep things on a quiet level, now. Your niece seems to be disturbed.

MRS. VENABLE: She has every reason to be. She took my son from me, and then she—

CATHARINE: Aunt Violet, you're not being fair.

MRS. VENABLE: Oh, aren't I?

CATHARINE [*to the others*]: She's not being fair.

[*Then back to Mrs. Venable:*]

Aunt Violet, you know why Sebastian asked me to travel with him.

MRS. VENABLE: Yes, I *do* know why!

CATHARINE: You weren't able to travel. You'd had a—[*She stops short.*]

MRS. VENABLE: Go on! *What* had I had? Are you afraid to say it in front of the Doctor? She meant that I had a stroke. —I DID NOT HAVE A STROKE!—I had a slight aneurism. You know what that is, Doctor? A little vascular convulsion! Not a hemorrhage, just a little convulsion of a blood-vessel. I had it when I discovered that she was trying to take my son away from me. Then I had it. It gave a little temporary—muscular—contraction.—To one side of my face.... [*She crosses back into main acting area.*] These people are not blood-relatives of mine, they're my dead husband's relations. I always detested these people, my dead husband's sister and—her two worthless children. But I did more than my duty to keep their heads above water. To please my son, whose weakness was being excessively softhearted, I went to the expense and humiliation, yes, public humiliation, of giving this girl a debut which was a fiasco. Nobody liked her when I brought her out. Oh, she had some kind of—notoriety! She had a sharp tongue that some people mistook for wit. A habit of laughing in the faces of decent people which would infuriate them, and also reflected adversely on me and Sebastian, too. But, he, Sebastian, was amused by this girl. While I was disgusted, sickened. And halfway through the season, she was dropped off the party lists, yes, dropped off the lists in spite of my position. Why? Because she'd lost her head over a young married man, made a scandalous scene at a Mardi Gras ball, in the middle of the ballroom. Then everybody dropped her like a hot—rock, but—[*She loses her breath.*] My son, Sebastian, still felt sorry for her and took her with him last summer instead of me....

CATHARINE [*springing up with a cry*]: I can't change truth, I'm not God! I'm not even sure that He could, I don't think God can change truth! How can I change the story of what happened to her son in Cabeza de Lobo?

MRS. VENABLE [*at the same time*]: She was in love with my son!

CATHARINE [*overlapping*]: Let me go back to Saint Mary's. Sister Felicity, let's go back to Saint—

MRS. VENABLE [*overlapping*]: Oh, no! That's not where you'll go!

CATHARINE [*overlapping*]: All right, *Lion's View* but don't ask me to—

MRS. VENABLE [*overlapping*]: You *know* that you were!

CATHARINE [*overlapping*]: That I was *what*, Aunt Violet?

MRS. VENABLE [*overlapping*]: Don't call me "Aunt," you're the niece of my dead husband, not me!

MRS. HOLLY [*overlapping*]: Catharine, Catharine, don't upset your—Doctor? Oh, Doctor!

[*But the Doctor is calmly observing the scene, with detachment. The jungle garden is loud with the sounds of its feathered and scaled inhabitants.*]

CATHARINE: I don't want to, I didn't want to come here! I know what she thinks, she thinks I murdered her son, she thinks that I was responsible for his death.

MRS. VENABLE: That's right. I told him when he told me that he was going with you in my place last summer that I'd never see him again and I never did. And only you know why!

CATHARINE: Oh, my God, I—

[*She rushes out toward garden, followed immediately by the Sister.*]

SISTER: Miss Catharine, Miss Catharine—

DOCTOR [*overlapping*]: Mrs. Venable?

SISTER [*overlapping*]: Miss Catharine?

DOCTOR [*overlapping*]: Mrs. Venable?

MRS. VENABLE: What?

DOCTOR: I'd like to be left alone with Miss Catharine for a few minutes.

MRS. HOLLY: George, talk to her, George.

[*George crouches appealingly before the old lady's chair, peering close into her face, a hand on her knee.*]

GEORGE: Aunt Vi? Cathie can't go to Lion's View. Everyone in the Garden District would know you'd put your niece in a state asylum, Aunt Vi.

MRS. VENABLE: Foxhill!

GEORGE: What do you want, Aunt Vi?

MRS. VENABLE: Let go of my chair. Foxhill? Get me away from these people!

GEORGE: Aunt Vi, listen, think of the talk it—

MRS. VENABLE: I can't get up! Push me, push me away!

GEORGE [*rising but holding chair*]: I'll push her, Miss Foxhill.

MRS. VENABLE: Let go of my chair or—

MISS FOXHILL: Mr. Holly, I—

GEORGE: I got to talk to her.

[*He pushes her chair downstage.*]

MRS. VENABLE: Foxhill!

MISS FOXHILL: Mr. Holly, she doesn't want you to push her.

GEORGE: I know what I'm doing, leave me alone with Aunt Vi!

MRS. VENABLE: Let go me or I'll *strike* you!

GEORGE: Oh, Aunt Vi!

MRS. VENABLE: Foxhill!

MRS. HOLLY: George—

GEORGE: Aunt Vi?

[*She strikes at him with her cane. He releases the chair and Miss Foxhill pushes her off. He trots after her a few steps, then he returns to Mrs. Holly, who is sobbing into a handkerchief. He sighs, and sits down beside her, taking her hand. The scene fades as light is brought up on Catharine and the Sister in the garden. The Doctor comes up to them. Mrs. Holly stretches her arms out to George, sobbing, and he crouches before her chair and rests his head in her lap. She strokes his head. During this: the Sister has stood beside Catharine, holding onto her arm.*]

CATHARINE: You don't have to hold onto me. I can't run away.

DOCTOR: Miss Catharine?

CATHARINE: What?

DOCTOR: Your aunt is a very sick woman. She had a stroke last spring?

CATHARINE: Yes, she did, but she'll never admit it. . . .

DOCTOR: You have to understand why.

CATHARINE: I do, I understand why. I didn't want to come here.

DOCTOR: Miss Catharine, do you hate her?

CATHARINE: I don't understand what hate is. How can you hate anybody and still be sane? You see, I still think I'm sane!

DOCTOR: You think she did have a stroke?

CATHARINE: She had a slight stroke in April. It just affected one side, the left side, of her face ... but it was disfiguring, and after that, Sebastian couldn't use her.

DOCTOR: Use her? Did you say use her?

[*The sounds of the jungle garden are not loud but ominous.*]

CATHARINE: Yes, we all use each other and that's what we think of as love, and not being able to use each other is what's—*hate*. . . .

DOCTOR: Do you hate her, Miss Catharine?

CATHARINE: Didn't you ask me that, once? And didn't I say that I didn't understand hate. A ship struck an iceberg at sea—everyone sinking—

DOCTOR: Go on, Miss Catharine!

CATHARINE: But that's no reason for everyone drowning for hating everyone drowning! Is it, Doctor?

DOCTOR: Tell me: what was your feeling for your cousin Sebastian?

CATHARINE: He liked me and so I loved him.

DOCTOR: In what way did you love him?

CATHARINE: The only way he'd accept:—a sort of motherly way. I tried to save him, Doctor.

DOCTOR: From what? Save him from what?

CATHARINE: Completing—a sort of!—*image!*—he had of himself as a sort of!—*sacrifice* to a!—*terrible* sort of a—

DOCTOR:—God?

CATHARINE: Yes, a—*cruel* one, Doctor!

DOCTOR: How did you feel about that?

CATHARINE: Doctor, my feelings are the sort of feelings that you have in a dream. . . .

DOCTOR: Your life doesn't seem real to you?

CATHARINE: Suddenly last winter I began to write my journal in the third person.

[*He grasps her elbow and leads her out upon forestage. At the same time Miss Foxhill wheels Mrs. Venable off, Mrs. Holly weeps into a handkerchief and George rises and shrugs and turns his back to the audience.*]

DOCTOR: Something happened last winter?

CATHARINE: At a Mardi Gras ball some—some boy that took me to it got too drunk to stand up! [*A short, mirthless note of laughter.*] I wanted to go home. My coat was in the cloakroom, they couldn't find the check for it in his pockets. I said, "Oh, hell, let it go!"—I started out for a taxi. Somebody took my arm and said, "I'll drive you home." He took off his coat as we left the hotel and put it over my shoulders, and then I looked at him and—I don't think I'd ever seen him before then, really!—He took me home in his car but took me another place first. We stopped near the Duelling Oaks at the end of Esplanade Street. . . . Stopped!—I said, "What for?"—He didn't answer, just struck a match in the car to light a cigarette in the car and I looked at him in the car and I knew "what for"!—I think I got out of the car before he got out of the car, and we walked through the wet grass to the great misty oaks as if somebody was calling us for help there!

[*Pause. The subdued, toneless bird-cries in the garden turn to a single bird-song.*]

DOCTOR: After that?

CATHARINE: I lost him.—He took me home and said an awful thing to me. "We'd better forget it," he said, "my wife's expecting a child and—." —I just entered the house and sat there thinking a little and then I suddenly called a taxi and went right back to the Roosevelt Hotel ballroom. The ball was still going on. I thought I'd gone back to pick up my borrowed coat but that wasn't what I'd gone back for. I'd gone back to make a scene on the floor of the ballroom, yes, I didn't stop at the cloakroom to pick up Aunt Violet's old mink stole, no, I rushed right into the ballroom and spotted him on the floor and ran up to him and beat him as hard as I could in the face and chest with my fists till—Cousin Sebastian took me away.—After that, the next morning, I started writing my diary in the third person, singular, such as "She's still living this morning," meaning that *I* was. . . . —"WHAT'S NEXT FOR HER? GOD KNOWS!"—I couldn't go out any more.—However one morning my Cousin Sebastian came in my bedroom and said: "Get up!"—Well . . . if you're still alive after dying, well then, you're obedient, Doctor.—I got up. He took me downtown to a place for passport photos. Said: "Mother can't go abroad with me this summer. You're going to go with me this summer instead of Mother."—If

you don't believe me, read my journal of Paris!—"She woke up at daybreak this morning, had her coffee and dressed and took a brief walk—"
DOCTOR: *Who* did?
CATHARINE: *She* did. *I* did—from the Hotel Plaza Athénée to the Place de l'Etoile as if pursued by a pack of Siberian wolves! [*She laughs her tired, helpless laugh.*]—Went right through all stop signs—couldn't wait for green signals.—"Where did she think she was going? Back to the Duelling Oaks?"—Everything chilly and dim but his hot, ravenous mouth! on—
DOCTOR: Miss Catharine, let me give you something.

[*The others go out, leaving Catharine and the Doctor onstage.*]

CATHARINE: Do I have to have the injection again, this time? What am I going to be stuck with this time, Doctor? I don't care. I've been stuck so often that if you connected me with a garden hose I'd make a good sprinkler.
DOCTOR [*preparing needle*]: Please take off your jacket.

[*She does. The Doctor gives her an injection.*]

CATHARINE: I didn't feel it.
DOCTOR: That's good. Now sit down.

[*She sits down.*]

CATHARINE: Shall I start counting backwards from a hundred?
DOCTOR: Do you like counting backwards?
CATHARINE: Love it! Just love it! One hundred! Ninety-nine! Ninety-eight! Ninety-seven. Ninety-six. Ninety—five.—Oh!—I already feel it! How funny!
DOCTOR: That's right. Close your eyes for a minute.

[*He moves his chair closer to hers. Half a minute passes.*]

I want you to give me something.
CATHARINE: Name it and it's yours, Doctor Sugar.
DOCTOR: Give me all your resistance.
CATHARINE: Resistance to what?
DOCTOR: The truth. Which you're going to tell me.
CATHARINE: The truth's the one thing I have never resisted!
DOCTOR: Sometimes people just think they don't resist it, but still do.
CATHARINE: They say it's at the bottom of a bottomless well, you know.
DOCTOR: Relax.
CATHARINE: Truth.
DOCTOR: Don't talk.
CATHARINE: Where was I, now? At ninety?
DOCTOR: You don't have to count backwards.
CATHARINE: At ninety something?
DOCTOR: You can open your eyes.
CATHARINE: Oh, I do feel funny!

[*Silence, pause.*]

You know what I think you're doing? I think you're trying to hypnotize me. Aren't you? You're looking so straight at me and doing something to me with your eyes and your—eyes.... Is that what you're doing to me?

DOCTOR: Is that what you *feel* I'm doing?

CATHARINE: Yes! I feel so peculiar. And it's not just the drug.

DOCTOR: Give me all your resistance. See. I'm holding my hand out. I want you to put yours in mine and give me all your resistance. Pass all of your resistance out of your hand to mine.

CATHARINE: Here's my hand. But there's no resistance in it.

DOCTOR: You are totally passive.

CATHARINE: Yes, I am.

DOCTOR: You will do what I ask.

CATHARINE: Yes, I will try.

DOCTOR: You will tell the true story.

CATHARINE: Yes, I will.

DOCTOR: The absolutely true story. No lies, nothing not spoken. Everything told, exactly.

CATHARINE: Everything. Exactly. Because I'll have to. Can I—can I stand up?

DOCTOR: Yes, but be careful. You might feel a little bit dizzy.

[*She struggles to rise, then falls back.*]

CATHARINE: I can't get up! Tell me to. Then I think I could do it.

DOCTOR: Stand up.

[*She rises unsteadily.*]

CATHARINE: How funny! Now I can! Oh, I do feel dizzy! Help me, I'm—

[*He rushes to support her.*]

—about to fall over....

[*He holds her. She looks out vaguely toward the brilliant, steaming garden. Looks back at him. Suddenly sways toward him, against him.*]

DOCTOR: You see, you lost your balance.

CATHARINE: No, I didn't. I did what I wanted to do without you telling me to.

[*She holds him tight against her.*]

Let me! Let! Let! Let me! Let me, let me, oh, let me....

[*She crushes her mouth to his violently. He tries to disengage himself. She presses her lips to his fiercely, clutching his body against her. Her brother George enters.*]

Please hold me! I've been so lonely. It's lonelier than death, if I've gone mad, it's lonelier than death!

GEORGE [*shocked, disgusted*]: Cathie!—you've got a hell of a nerve.

[*She falls back, panting, covers her face, runs a few paces and grabs the back of a chair. Mrs. Holly enters.*]

MRS. HOLLY: What's the matter, George? Is Catharine ill?

GEORGE: No.

DOCTOR: Miss Catharine had an injection that made her a little unsteady.

MRS. HOLLY: What did he say about Catharine?

[*Catharine has gone out into the dazzling jungle of the garden.*]

SISTER [*returning*]: She's gone into the garden.

DOCTOR: That's all right, she'll come back when I call her.

SISTER: It may be all right for you. You're not responsible for her.

[*Mrs. Venable has re-entered.*]

MRS. VENABLE: Call her now!

DOCTOR: Miss Catharine! Come back.

[*To the Sister:*]

   Bring her back, please, Sister!

[*Catharine enters quietly, a little unsteady.*]

   Now, Miss Catharine, you're going to tell the true story.

CATHARINE: Where do I start the story?

DOCTOR: Wherever you think it started.

CATHARINE: I think it started the day he was born in this house.

MRS. VENABLE: Ha! You see!

GEORGE: Cathie.

DOCTOR: Let's start later than that. [*Pause.*] Shall we begin with last summer?

CATHARINE: Oh. Last summer.

DOCTOR: Yes. Last summer.

[*There is a long pause. The raucous sounds in the garden fade into a bird-song which is clear and sweet. Mrs. Holly coughs. Mrs. Venable stirs impatiently. George crosses downstage to catch Catharine's eye as he lights a cigarette.*]

CATHARINE: Could I—?

MRS. VENABLE: Keep that boy away from her!

GEORGE: She wants to smoke, Aunt Vi.

CATHARINE: Something helps in the—hands. . . .

SISTER: Unh unh!

DOCTOR: It's all right, Sister. [*He lights her cigarette.*] About last summer: how did it begin?

CATHARINE: It began with his kindness and the six days at sea that took me so far away from the—Duelling Oaks that I forgot them, nearly. He was affectionate with me, so sweet and attentive to me, that some people took us for a honeymoon couple until they noticed that we had—separate staterooms, and—then in Paris, he took me to Patou and Schiaparelli's— this is from Schiaparelli's! [*Like a child, she indicates her suit.*]—bought me so many new clothes that I gave away my old ones to make room for my new ones in my new luggage to—travel. . . . I turned into a peacock! Of course, so was *he* one, too. . . .

GEORGE: *Ha Ha!*

MRS. VENABLE: Shh!

CATHARINE: But then I made the mistake of responding too much to his kindness, of taking hold of his hand before he'd take hold of mine, of holding onto his arm and leaning on his shoulder, of appreciating his kindness more than he wanted me to, and, suddenly, last summer, he began to be restless, and—oh!

DOCTOR: Go on.

CATHARINE: The Blue Jay notebook!

DOCTOR: Did you say notebook?

MRS. VENABLE: I know what she means by that, she's talking about the school composition book with a Blue Jay trademark that Sebastian used for making notes and revisions on his *"Poem of Summer."* It went with him everywhere that he went, in his jacket pocket, even his dinner jacket. I have the one that he had with him last summer. *Foxhill! The Blue Jay notebook!*

[*Miss Foxhill rushes in with a gasp.*]

It came with his personal effects shipped back from Cabeza de Lobo.

DOCTOR: I don't quite get the connection between new clothes and so forth and the Blue Jay notebook.

MRS. VENABLE: I HAVE IT!—Doctor, tell her I've found it.

[*Miss Foxhill hears this as she comes back out of house: gasps with relief, retires.*]

DOCTOR: With all these interruptions it's going to be awfully hard to—

MRS. VENABLE: This is important. I don't know why she mentioned the Blue Jay notebook but I want you to see it. Here it is, here! [*She holds up a notebook and leafs swiftly through the pages.*] Title? *"Poem of Summer"* and the date of the summer—1935. After that: *what? Blank pages, blank pages,* nothing but *nothing*!—last summer. . . .

DOCTOR: What's that got to do with—?

MRS. VENABLE: His destruction? I'll tell you. A poet's vocation is something that rests on something as thin and fine as the web of a spider, Doctor. That's all that holds him *over*!—out of destruction. . . . Few, very few are able to do it alone! Great help is needed! I *did* give it! She *didn't*.

CATHARINE: She's right about that. I failed him. I wasn't able to keep the web from—breaking. . . . I saw it breaking but couldn't save or—repair it!

MRS. VENABLE: There now, the truth's coming out. We had an agreement between us, a sort of contract or covenant between us which he broke last summer when he broke away from me and took her with him, not me! When he was frightened and I knew when and what of, because his hands would shake and his eyes looked in, not out, I'd reach across a table and touch his hands and say not a word, just look, and touch his hands with my hand until his hands stopped shaking and his eyes looked out, not in, and in the morning, the poem would be continued. *Continued until it was finished!*

[*The following ten speeches are said very rapidly, overlapping.*]

CATHARINE: I—couldn't!

MRS. VENABLE: *Naturally* not! He was *mine!* I *knew* how to help him, I *could!* You didn't, you couldn't!

DOCTOR: These interruptions—

MRS. VENABLE: I would say "You *will*" and he *would*, I—!

CATHARINE: Yes, you see, I failed him! And so, last summer, we went to Cabeza de Lobo, we flew down there from where he gave up writing his poem last summer. . . .

MRS. VENABLE: Because he'd broken our—

CATHARINE: Yes! Yes, something had broken, that string of pearls that old mothers hold their sons by like a—sort of a—sort of—*umbilical* cord, long—after . . .

MRS. VENABLE: She means that I held him back from—

DOCTOR: *Please!*

MRS. VENABLE: *Destruction!*

CATHARINE: All I know is that suddenly, last summer, he wasn't young any more, and we went to Cabeza de Lobo, and he suddenly switched from the evenings to the beach. . . .

DOCTOR: From evenings? To beach?

CATHARINE: I mean from the evenings to the afternoons and from the fa— fash—

[*Silence: Mrs. Holly draws a long, long painful breath. George stirs impatiently.*]

DOCTOR: Fashionable! Is that the word you—?

CATHARINE: Yes. Suddenly, last summer Cousin Sebastian changed to the afternoons and the beach.

DOCTOR: What beach?

CATHARINE: In Cabeza de Lobo there is a beach that's named for Sebastian's name saint, it's known as La Playa San Sebastian, and that's where we started spending all afternoon, every day.

DOCTOR: What kind of beach was it?

CATHARINE: It was a big city beach near the harbor.

DOCTOR: It was a big public beach?

CATHARINE: Yes, public.

MRS. VENABLE: It's little statements like that that give her away.

[*The Doctor rises and crosses to Mrs. Venable without breaking his concentration on Catharine.*]

After all I've told you about his fastidiousness, can you accept such a statement?

DOCTOR: You mustn't interrupt her.

MRS. VENABLE [*overlapping him*]: That Sebastian would go every day to some dirty free public beach near a harbor? A man that had to go out a mile in a boat to find water to swim in?

DOCTOR: Mrs. Venable, no matter what she says you have to let her say it without any more interruptions or this interview will be useless.

MRS. VENABLE: I won't speak again. I'll keep still, if it kills me.

CATHARINE: I don't want to go on. . . .

DOCTOR: Go on with the story. Every afternoon last summer your Cousin Sebastian and you want out to this free public beach?

CATHARINE: No, it wasn't the free one, the free one was right next to it, there was a fence between the free beach and the one that we went to that charged a small charge of admission.

DOCTOR: Yes, and what did you do there?

[*He still stands beside Mrs. Venable and the light gradually changes as the girl gets deeper into her story: the light concentrates on Catharine, the other figures sink into shadow.*]

Did anything happen there that disturbed you about it?

CATHARINE: Yes!

DOCTOR: What?

CATHARINE: He bought me a swim-suit I didn't want to wear. I laughed. I said, "I can't wear that, it's a scandal to the jay-birds!"

DOCTOR: What did you mean by that? That the suit was immodest?

CATHARINE: My God, yes! It was a one-piece suit made of white lisle, the water made it transparent! [*She laughs sadly at the memory of it.*] —I didn't want to swim in it, but he'd grab my hand and drag me into the water, all the way in, and I'd come out looking naked!

DOCTOR: Why did he do that? Did you understand why?

CATHARINE:—Yes! To attract!—Attention.

DOCTOR: He wanted you to attract attention, did he, because he felt you were moody? Lonely? He wanted to shock you out of your depression last summer?

CATHARINE: Don't you understand? I was PROCURING for him!

[*Mrs. Venable's gasp is like the sound that a great hooked fish might make.*]

She used to do it, too.

[*Mrs. Venable cries out.*]

Not consciously! She didn't *know* that she was procuring for him in the smart, the fashionable places they used to go to before last summer! Sebastian was shy with people. She wasn't. Neither was I. We both did the same thing for him, made contacts for him, but she did it in nice places and in decent ways and I had to do it the way that I just told you!— Sebastian was lonely, Doctor, and the empty Blue Jay notebook got bigger and bigger, so big it was big and empty as that big empty blue sea and sky. . . . I knew what I was doing. I came out in the French Quarter years before I came out in the Garden District. . . .

MRS. HOLLY: Oh, Cathie! Sister . . .

DOCTOR: Hush!

CATHARINE: And before long, when the weather got warmer and the beach so crowded, he didn't need me any more for that purpose. The ones on the free beach began to climb over the fence or swim around it, bands of homeless young people that lived on the free beach like scavenger dogs, hungry children.... So now he let me wear a decent dark suit. I'd go to a faraway empty end of the beach, write postcards and letters and keep up my—third-person journal till it was—five o'clock and time to meet him outside the bathhouses, on the street.... He would come out, *followed*.

DOCTOR: Who would follow him out?

CATHARINE: The homeless, hungry young people that had climbed over the fence from the free beach that they lived on. He'd pass out tips among them as if they'd all—shined his shoes or called taxis for him.... Each day the crowd was bigger, noisier, greedier!—Sebastian began to be frightened.—At last we stopped going out there....

DOCTOR: And then? After that? After you quit going out to the public beach?

CATHARINE: Then one day, a few days after we stopped going out to the beach—it was one of those white blazing days in Cabeza de Lobo, not a blazing hot *blue* one but a blazing hot *white* one.

DOCTOR: Yes?

CATHARINE: We had a late lunch at one of those open-air restaurants on the sea there.—Sebastian was white as the weather. He had on a spotless white silk Shantung suit and a white silk tie and a white panama and white shoes, white—white lizard skin—pumps! He—[*She throws back her head in a startled laugh at the recollection*]—kept touching his face and his throat here and there with a white silk handkerchief and popping little white pills in his mouth, and I knew he was having a bad time with his heart and was frightened about it and that was the reason we hadn't gone out to the beach....

[*During the monologue the lights have changed, the surrounding area has dimmed out and a hot white spot is focused on Catharine.*]

"I think we ought to go north," he kept saying, "I think we've done Cabeza de Lobo, I think we've done it, don't you?" *I* thought we'd done it!—but I had learned it was better not to seem to have an opinion because if I did, well, Sebastian, well, you know Sebastian, he always preferred to do what no one else wanted to do, and I always tried to give the impression that I was agreeing reluctantly to his wishes ... it was a— game....

SISTER: She's dropped her cigarette.

DOCTOR: I've got it, Sister.

[*There are whispers, various movements in the penumbra. The Doctor fills a glass for her from the cocktail shaker.*]

CATHARINE: Where was I? Oh, yes, that five o'clock lunch at one of those fish-places along the harbor of Cabeza de Lobo, it was between the city and the sea, and there were naked children along the beach which was fenced off with barbed wire from the restaurant and we had our tables less than a yard from the barbed wire fence that held the beggars at bay.... There were naked children along the beach, a band of frightfully thin and dark naked children that looked like a flock of plucked birds, and they would come darting up to the barbed wire fence as if blown there by the wind, the hot white wind from the sea, all crying out, *"Pan, pan, pan!"*

DOCTOR [*quietly*]: What's *pan?*

CATHARINE: The word for bread, and they made gobbling noises with their little black mouths, stuffing their little black fists to their mouths and making those gobbling noises, with frightful grins!—Of course we were sorry that we had come to this place but it was too late to go....

DOCTOR [*quietly*]: Why was it "too late to go"?

CATHARINE: I told you Cousin Sebastian wasn't well. He was popping those little white pills in his mouth. I think he had popped in so many of them that they had made him feel weak.... His, his!—eyes looked—dazed, but he said: "Don't look at those little monsters. Beggars are a social disease in this country. If you look at them, you get sick of the country, it spoils the whole country for you...."

DOCTOR: Go on.

CATHARINE: I'm going on. I have to wait now and then till it gets clearer. Under the drug it has to be a vision, or nothing comes....

DOCTOR: All right?

CATHARINE: Always when I was with him I did what he told me. I didn't look at the band of naked children, not even when the waiters drove them away from the barbed wire fence with sticks!—Rushing out through a wicket gate like an assault party in war!—and beating them screaming away from the barbed wire fence with the sticks.... Then! [*Pause.*]

DOCTOR: Go on, Miss Catherine, what comes next in the vision?

CATHARINE: The, the the!—band of children began to—serenade us....

DOCTOR: Do what?

CATHARINE: Play for us! On instruments! Make music!—if you could call it music....

DOCTOR: Oh?

CATHARINE: Their, their—instruments were—instruments of percussion!—Do you know what I mean?

DOCTOR [*making a note*]: Yes. Instruments of percussion such as—*drums?*

CATHARINE: I stole glances at them when Cousin Sebastian wasn't looking, and as well as I could make out in the white blaze of the sand-beach, the instruments were tin cans strung together.

DOCTOR [*slowly, writing*]: Tin—cans—strung—together.

CATHARINE: *And, and, and, and—and!*—bits of metal, *other* bits of metal that had been flattened out, made into—

DOCTOR: What?

CATHARINE: *Cymbals!* You know? *Cymbals?*

DOCTOR: Yes. Brass plates hit together.

CATHARINE: That's right, Doctor.—Tin cans flattened out and clashed together!—Cymbals....

DOCTOR: Yes. I understand. What's after that, in the vision?

CATHARINE [*rapidly, panting a little*]: And others had paper bags, bags made out of—coarse paper!—with something on a string inside the bags which they pulled up and down, back and forth, to make a sort of a—

DOCTOR: Sort of a—?

CATHARINE: Noise like—

DOCTOR: Noise like?

CATHARINE [*rising stiffly from chair*]: Ooompa! Oompa! Ooooooompa!

DOCTOR: Ahhh ... a sound like a *tuba*?

CATHARINE: That's right!—they made a sound like a tuba....

DOCTOR: Oompa, oompa, oompa, like a tuba.

[*He is making a note of the description.*]

CATHARINE: Oompa, oompa, oompa, like a—

[*Short pause.*]

DOCTOR:—Tuba....

CATHARINE: All during lunch they stayed at a—a fairly *close—distance*....

DOCTOR: Go on with the vision, Miss Catharine.

CATHARINE [*striding about the table*]: Oh, I'm going on, nothing could stop it now!!

DOCTOR: Your Cousin Sebastian was *entertained* by this—*concert*?

CATHARINE: I think he was *terrified* of it!

DOCTOR: Why was he terrified of it?

CATHARINE: I think he recognized some of the musicians, some of the boys, between childhood and—older....

DOCTOR: What did he do? Did he do anything about it, Miss Catharine?—Did he complain to the manager about it?

CATHARINE: *What* manager? *God*? Oh, *no*!—The manager of the fishplace on the beach? Haha!—No!—You don't understand my cousin!

DOCTOR: What do you mean?

CATHARINE: *He!* —*accepted!* —*all!* —as —*how!* —*things!* —are! —And thought nobody had any right to complain or interfere in any way whatsoever, and even though he knew that what was awful was awful, that what was wrong was wrong, and my Cousin Sebastian was certainly never sure that anything was wrong!—He thought it unfitting to ever take any action about anything whatsoever!—except to go on doing as something in him directed....

DOCTOR: What did something in him direct him to do?—I mean on this occasion in Cabeza de Lobo.

CATHARINE: After the salad, before they brought the coffee, he suddenly pushed himself away from the table, and said, "They've got to stop that! Waiter, make them stop that. I'm not a well man, I have a heart condition, it's making me sick!"—This was the first time that Cousin Sebastian had ever attempted to correct a human situation!—I think perhaps that *that* was his fatal error.... It was then that the waiters, all eight or ten of them, charged out of the barbed wire wicket gate and beat the little musicians away with clubs and skillets and anything hard that they could snatch from the kitchen!—Cousin Sebastian left the table. He stalked out of the restaurant after throwing a handful of paper money on the table and he fled from the place. I followed. It was all white outside. White hot, a blazing white hot, hot blazing white, at five o'clock in the afternoon in the city of—Cabeza de Lobo. It looked as if—

DOCTOR: It looked as if?

CATHARINE: As if a huge white bone had caught on fire in the sky and blazed so bright it was white and turned the sky and everything under the sky white with it!

DOCTOR:—White ...

CATHARINE: Yes—white ...

DOCTOR: You followed your Cousin Sebastian out of the restaurant onto the hot white street?

CATHARINE: Running up and down hill....

DOCTOR: You ran up and down hill?

CATHARINE: No, no! *Didn't!*—move either *way!*—at first, we were—

[*During this recitation there are various sound effects. The percussive sounds described are very softly employed.*]

I rarely made any suggestion but *this* time I *did*....

DOCTOR: What did you suggest?

CATHARINE: Cousin Sebastian seemed to be paralyzed near the entrance of the café, so I said, "Let's go." I remember that it was a very wide and steep white street, and I said, "Cousin Sebastian, down that way is the waterfront and we are more likely to find a taxi near there.... Or why don't we go back in?—and have them *call* us a taxi! Oh, let's do! Let's do *that*, that's better!" And he said, "*Mad*, are you *mad*? Go back in that filthy, place? Never! That gang of kids shouted vile things about me to the waiters!" "Oh," I said, "then let's go down toward the docks, down there at the bottom of the hill, let's not try to climb the hill in this dreadful heat." And Cousin Sebastian shouted, "Please shut up, let me handle this situation, will you? I want to handle this thing." And he started up the steep street with a hand stuck in his jacket where I knew he was having a pain in his chest from his palpitations.... But he walked faster and faster, in panic, but the faster he walked the louder and closer it got!

DOCTOR: What got louder?

CATHARINE: The music.

DOCTOR: The music again.

CATHARINE: The oompa-oompa of the—following band.—They'd somehow gotten through the barbed wire and out on the street, and they were following, following!—up the blazing white street. The band of naked children pursued us up the steep white street in the sun that was like a great white bone of a giant beast that had caught on fire in the sky!—Sebastian started to run and they all screamed at once and seemed to fly in the air, they outran him so quickly. I screamed. I heard Sebastian scream, he screamed just once before this flock of black plucked little birds that pursued him and overtook him halfway up the white hill.

DOCTOR: And you, Miss Catharine, what did *you* do, then?

CATHARINE: Ran!

DOCTOR: Ran where?

CATHARINE: Down! Oh, I ran down, the easier direction to run was down, down, down, down!—The hot, white, blazing street, screaming out "Help" all the way, till—

DOCTOR: What?

CATHARINE:—Waiters, police, and others—ran out of buildings and rushed back up the hill with me. When we got back to where my Cousin Sebastian had disappeared in the flock of featherless little black sparrows, he—he was lying naked as they had been naked against a white wall, and this you won't believe, nobody *has* believed it, nobody *could* believe it, nobody, nobody on earth could possibly believe it, and I don't *blame* them!—They had *devoured* parts of him.

[*Mrs. Venable cries out softly.*]

Torn or cut parts of him away with their hands or knives or maybe those jagged tin cans they made music with, they had torn bits of him away and stuffed them into those gobbling fierce little empty black mouths of theirs. There wasn't a sound any more, there was nothing to see but Sebastian, what was left of him, that looked like a big white-paper-wrapped bunch of red roses had been *torn, thrown, crushed!*—against that blazing white wall. . . .

[*Mrs. Venable springs with amazing power from her wheelchair, stumbles erratically but swiftly toward the girl and tries to strike her with her cane. The Doctor snatches it from her and catches her as she is about to fall. She gasps hoarsely several times as he leads her toward the exit.*]

MRS. VENABLE [*offstage*]: Lion's View! State asylum, cut this hideous story out of her brain!

[*Mrs. Holly sobs and crosses to George, who turns away from her, saying:*]

GEORGE: Mom, I'll quit school, I'll get a job, I'll—

MRS. HOLLY: Hush son! Doctor, can't you say something?

[*Pause. The Doctor comes downstage. Catharine wanders out into the garden followed by the Sister.*]

DOCTOR [*after a while, reflectively, into space*]: I think we ought at least to consider the possibility that the girl's story could be true. . . .

1958

The Beat Movement

WHEN LAWRENCE FERLINGHETTI PUBLISHED ALLEN GINSBERG'S LONG POEM "Howl" at his San Francisco–based City Lights Books in 1956, the first widely circulated text of the anti-establishment Beat culture was born. *Howl and Other Poems* appeared in the highly visible white and black pocketbook format that was to showcase works by Jack Kerouac, Gregory Corso, Robert Creeley, Ginsberg, Ferlinghetti himself, and many others. The concept of a group identity may have begun at a 1955 poetry reading at the Six Gallery in San Francisco. Kenneth Rexroth was master of ceremonies, and readers were—besides Ginsberg—Philip Lamantia, Michael McClure, Gary Snyder, Lew Welsh, and Philip Whalen.

Responding to the restrictive and conservative post–World War II culture (the soporific 1950s), this group of poets—which often included Denise Levertov, Charles Olson, Robert Duncan, Neal Cassady, William Everson, and others—forced on the reading public an awareness of other cultures: drug experiences, lives in prison and mental institutions, homosexual and lesbian sexualities, liberal politics, spiritualism not necessarily housed in suburban Protestant environs. Admittedly intended to shock in some cases, the works—poetry, prose, and matrices of both—were descended from writers as disparate as Whitman, Rimbaud, William Carlos Williams, Antonin Artaud, William Burroughs, and other American writers not yet acknowledged as significant writers. One of the foremost characteristics of writing of the Beats was a sense of humor, long absent from United States writing, and a belief that spiritual life (*beat* meaning "beatific, holy") was essential to a person's existence.

ALLEN GINSBERG
1926–1997

Allen Ginsberg brought to American poetry not only a new self-consciousness but a rare sense of humor. While poets contemporary with him—W. D. Snodgrass, Robert Lowell, Theodore Roethke, and somewhat later Anne Sexton and Sylvia Plath—were mining the personal to unearth images that would speak for an "Everyperson" understanding, Ginsberg was exploring the psyche with a shrewd sense of humor. His dialogue with Walt Whitman, "A Supermarket in California," views the suburban scene of lush plenty with a wry vision that brings the elements of poetry and life together in a completely new perspective.

Ginsberg is best known for his first long-lined poem, "Howl," written after he left Columbia University and the New York avant-garde and moved to California. "Howl" lamented the wastes of the 1950s—good minds buried under layers of convention, stifling restrictions on art and sexual expression—reversing Whitman's catalogs of praise to chart uncountable griefs. Its irony and its all-too-real truths gave Ginsberg an immediate audience once City Lights published the poem, with a foreword by William Carlos Williams.

Though Ginsberg quickly became identified with the homosexual drug culture, his roots stretched back more directly to his New Jersey home, where his knowledge of social inequities and cultural frustrations mirrored that of his older Rutherford neighbor, Williams. His next major poem, "Kaddish," a lament for the health of his brilliant Jewish mother, Naomi Levy, reflected much of that social coercion, intensified by cultural alienation and the social response to mental instability.

Ginsberg was born to Naomi and Louis Ginsberg in Newark, where his father was a high school teacher and a poet. Before graduating from Columbia University in 1949, Ginsberg held jobs as a dishwasher, spot welder, copy boy on the *New York World-Telegram*, and reporter for a New Jersey paper. After he graduated with his A.B. degree, he traveled to California to find William Burroughs, who wrote from the tradition of prophetic, inspired voices (Ginsberg had had visions in which he saw William Blake, and he thought of himself as a seer in his art). After his comparative successes in California, determined to live on his income from writing, Ginsberg spent part of 1963 in India, traveling with his lover Peter Orlovsky. He returned to North America to participate in a poetry festival at the University of British Columbia, bringing with him a mantra-like chant that from then on enhanced the delivery of his poetry.

In 1963 Ginsberg was a Guggenheim Fellow. He received a National Institute of Arts and Letters award in 1969 and the National Book Award for *The Fall of America: Poems of These States* in 1973. In 1979 he received the National Arts Club Medal of Honor for Literature. Although he read frequently on university campuses and remained a spokesperson for the avant-garde, Ginsberg maintained a comparatively low-key profile during the last decade of his life. He returned to New Jersey, where he lived on a small farm, accessible to his friends and admirers, writing a remarkably constant poetry that hammered away at the problems faced not only by the United States but by most of the world's cultures. The "insane demands" he wrote of in his 1956 poem "America" are still rampant, and Ginsberg proved to be prophetic once more as he described himself staying with the country, trying to work through its aberrations to find some of its truth. In that endeavor, too, he echoed the efforts of William Carlos Williams. Though never accepted by the culture he was so critical of, Ginsberg never expatriated himself from it; rather, he preached, and sang, and chanted, lessons he thought might be helpful to its greatest dilemmas.

Linda Wagner-Martin
University of North Carolina at Chapel Hill

PRIMARY WORKS

Howl and Other Poems, 1956; *Kaddish and Other Poems 1958–60*, 1961; *Empty Mirror: Early Poems*, 1961; *Reality Sandwiches: 1953–1960*, 1963; *Wichita Vortex Sutra*, 1967; *Planet News*, 1968; *Iron Horse*, 1972; *The Fall of America: Poems of These States, 1965–1971*, 1973; *Mind Breaths: Poems, 1972–1977*, 1978; *Collected Poems, 1947–1980*, 1984; *Howl* (facsimile), 1986; *White Shroud: Poems 1980–1985*, 1986; *Cosmopolitan Greetings: Poems 1986–1992*, 1995; *Death and Fame: Poems, 1993–1997*, 1999.

A Supermarket in California

What thoughts I have of you tonight, Walt Whitman, for I
walked down the sidestreets under the trees with a headache
self-conscious looking at the full moon.

In my hungry fatigue, and shopping for images, I went into
the neon fruit supermarket, dreaming of your enumerations!   5

What peaches and what penumbras! Whole families
shopping at night! Aisles full of husbands! Wives in the
avocados, babies in the tomatoes!—and you, Garcia Lorca,[1]
what were you doing down by the watermelons?

I saw you, Walt Whitman, childless, lonely old grubber,   10
poking among the meats in the refrigerator and eyeing the
grocery boys.

I heard you asking questions of each: Who killed the pork
chops? What price bananas? Are you my Angel?

I wandered in and out of the brilliant stacks of cans   15
following you, and followed in my imagination by the store
detective.

We strode down the open corridors together in our solitary
fancy tasting artichokes, possessing every frozen delicacy, and
never passing the cashier.   20

Where are we going, Walt Whitman? The doors close in an
hour. Which way does your beard point tonight?

(I touch your book and dream of our odyssey in the
supermarket and feel absurd.)

Will we walk all night through solitary streets? The trees   25
add shade to shade, lights out in the houses, we'll both be
lonely.

Will we stroll dreaming of the lost America of love past
blue automobiles in driveways, home to our silent cottage?

---

[1]Spanish poet and playwright Federico García
Lorca (1899–1936), who was murdered at
the start of the Spanish Civil War.

Ah, dear father, graybeard, lonely old courage-teacher, what   30
America did you have when Charon[2] quit poling his ferry and
you got out on a smoking bank and stood watching the boat
disappear on the black waters of Lethe?

1956

Howl

for Carl Solomon[1]

I

I saw the best minds of my generation destroyed by madness,
    starving hysterical naked,
dragging themselves through the negro streets at dawn looking for
    an angry fix,
angelheaded hipsters burning for the ancient heavenly connection   5
    to the starry dynamo in the machinery of night,
who poverty and tatters and hollow-eyed and high sat up smoking
    in the supernatural darkness of cold-water flats floating across
    the tops of cities contemplating jazz,
who bared their brains to Heaven under the El[2] and saw   10
    Mohammedan angels staggering on tenement roofs
    illuminated,
who passed through universities with radiant cool eyes
    hallucinating Arkansas and Blake-light[3] tragedy among the
    scholars of war,   15
who were expelled from the academies for crazy & publishing
    obscene odes on the windows of the skull,[4]
who cowered in unshaven rooms in underwear, burning their
    money in wastebaskets and listening to the Terror through the
    wall,   20
who got busted in their pubic beards returning through Laredo
    with a belt of marijuana for New York,
who ate fire in paint hotels or drank turpentine in Paradise Alley,[5]
    death, or purgatoried their torsos night after night
with dreams, with drugs, with waking nightmares, alcohol and cock   25
    and endless balls,

---

[2]In Greek myth, Charon ferried the shades of the dead to Hades over Lethe, river of forgetfulness.

[1]Friend of Ginsberg and fellow psychiatric patient in 1949.

[2]The elevated railway.

[3]Refers to English poet William Blake (1757–1827).

[4]Ginsberg was expelled from Columbia for writing an obscenity on his windowpane.

[5]A slum courtyard on the East Side.

incomparable blind streets of shuddering cloud and lightning in
the mind leaping toward poles of Canada & Paterson,
illuminating all the motionless world of Time between,

Peyote solidities of halls, backyard green tree cemetery dawns,   30
wine drunkenness over the rooftops, storefront boroughs of
teahead joyride neon blinking traffic light, sun and moon and
tree vibrations in the roaring winter dusks of Brooklyn, ashcan
rantings and kind king light of mind,

who chained themselves to subways for the endless ride from   35
Battery to holy Bronx on benzedrine until the noise of wheels
and children brought them down shuddering mouth-wracked
and battered bleak of brain all drained of brilliance in the
drear light of Zoo,

who sank all night in submarine light of Bickford's[6] floated out   40
and sat through the stale beer afternoon in desolate
Fugazzi's,[7] listening to the crack of doom on the hydrogen
jukebox,

who talked continuously seventy hours from park to pad to bar to
Bellevue[8] to museum to the Brooklyn Bridge,   45

a lost battalion of platonic conversationalists jumping down the
stoops off fire escapes off windowsills off Empire State out of
the moon,

yacketayakking screaming vomiting whispering facts and memories
and anecdotes and eyeball kicks and shocks of hospitals and   50
jails and wars,

whole intellects disgorged in total recall for seven days and nights
with brilliant eyes, meat for the Synagogue cast on the
pavement,

who vanished into nowhere Zen New Jersey leaving a trail of   55
ambiguous picture postcards of Atlantic City Hall,

suffering Eastern sweats and Tangerian bone-grindings and
migraines of China under junk-withdrawal in Newark's bleak
furnished room,

who wandered around and around at midnight in the railroad yard   60
wondering where to go, and went, leaving no broken hearts,

who lit cigarettes in boxcars boxcars boxcars racketing through
snow toward lonesome farms in grandfather night,

who studied Plotinus Poe St. John of the Cross[9] telepathy and bop
kaballa[10] because the cosmos instinctively vibrated at their feet 65
in Kansas,

---

[6]Cafeteria.
[7]Bar in Greenwich Village.
[8]New York City public hospital.
[9]Plotinus (205–270), Roman philosopher;
Edgar Allan Poe (1809–1849); St. John of
the Cross (1542–1591), Spanish poet.

[10]Cf. Cabala: esoteric interpretation of Hebrew scriptures.

who loned it through the streets of Idaho seeking visionary indian
    angels who were visionary indian angels,

who thought they were only mad when Baltimore gleamed in
    supernatural ecstasy,   70

who jumped in limousines with the Chinaman of Oklahoma on the
    impulse of winter midnight streetlight smalltown rain,

who lounged hungry and lonesome through Houston seeking jazz
    or sex or soup, and followed the brilliant Spaniard to
    converse about America and Eternity, a hopeless task, and so   75
    took ship to Africa,

who disappeared into the volcanoes of Mexico leaving behind
    nothing but the shadow of dungarees and the lava and ash of
    poetry scattered in fireplace Chicago,

who reappeared on the West Coast investigating the F.B.I. in   80
    beards and shorts with big pacifist eyes sexy in their dark skin
    passing out incomprehensible leaflets,

who burned cigarette holes in their arms protesting the narcotic
    tobacco haze of Capitalism,

who distributed Supercommunist pamphlets in Union Square   85
    weeping and undressing while the sirens of Los Alamos wailed
    them down, and wailed down Wall, and the Staten Island
    ferry also wailed,

who broke down crying in white gymnasiums naked and trembling
    before the machinery of other skeletons,   90

who bit detectives in the neck and shrieked with delight in
    policecars for committing no crime but their own wild
    cooking pederasty and intoxication,

who howled on their knees in the subway and were dragged off
    the roof waving genitals and manuscripts,   95

who let themselves be fucked in the ass by saintly motorcyclists,
    and screamed with joy,

who blew and were blown by those human seraphim, the sailors,
    caresses of Atlantic and Caribbean love,

who balled in the morning in the evenings in rosegardens and the   100
    grass of public parks and cemeteries scattering their semen
    freely to whomever come who may,

who hiccupped endlessly trying to giggle but wound up with a sob
    behind a partition in a Turkish Bath when the blonde &
    naked angel came to pierce them with a sword,   105

who lost their loveboys to the three old shrews of fate the one
    eyed shrew of the heterosexual dollar the one eyed shrew that
    winks out of the womb and the one eyed shrew that does
    nothing but sit on her ass and snip the intellectual golden
    threads of the craftsman's loom,   110

who copulated ecstatic and insatiate with a bottle of beer a
    sweetheart a package of cigarettes a candle and fell off the
    bed, and continued along the floor and down the hall and
    ended fainting on the wall with a vision of ultimate cunt and
    come eluding the last gyzym of consciousness,   115
who sweetened the snatches of a million girls trembling in the
    sunset, and were red eyed in the morning but prepared to
    sweeten the snatch of the sunrise, flashing buttocks under
    barns and naked in the lake,
who went out whoring through Colorado in myriad stolen night-   120
    cars, N.C.,[11] secret hero of these poems, cocksman and
    Adonis of Denver—joy to the memory of his innumerable lays
    of girls in empty lots & diner backyards, moviehouses' rickety
    rows, on mountaintops in caves or with gaunt waitresses in
    familiar roadside lonely petticoat upliftings & especially secret 125
    gas-station solipsisms of johns, & hometown alleys too,
who faded out in vast sordid movies, were shifted in dreams, woke
    on a sudden Manhattan, and picked themselves up out of
    basements hungover with heartless Tokay and horrors of
    Third Avenue iron dreams & stumbled to unemployment   130
    offices,
who walked all night with their shoes full of blood on the
    snowbank docks waiting for a door in the East River to open
    to a room full of steamheat and opium,
who created great suicidal dramas on the apartment cliff-banks of 135
    the Hudson under the wartime blue floodlight of the moon &
    their heads shall be crowned with laurel in oblivion,
who ate the lamb stew of the imagination or digested the crab at
    the muddy bottom of the rivers of Bowery,
who wept at the romance of the streets with their pushcarts full of 140
    onions and bad music,
who sat in boxes breathing in the darkness under the bridge, and
    rose up to build harpsichords in their lofts,
who coughed on the sixth floor of Harlem crowned with flame
    under the tubercular sky surrounded by orange crates of   145
    theology,
who scribbled all night rocking and rolling over lofty incantations
    which in the yellow morning were stanzas of gibberish,
who cooked rotten animals lung heart feet tail borscht & tortillas
    dreaming of the pure vegetable kingdom,   150
who plunged themselves under meat trucks looking for an egg,

[11]Neal Cassady, friend of Ginsberg and Jack
  Kerouac.

who threw their watches off the roof to cast their ballot for
Eternity outside of Time, & alarm clocks fell on their heads
every day for the next decade,

who cut their wrists three times successively unsuccessfully, gave   155
up and were forced to open antique stores where they thought
they were growing old and cried,

who were burned alive in their innocent flannel suits on Madison
Avenue amid blasts of leaden verse & the tanked-up clatter of
the iron regiments of fashion & the nitroglycerine shrieks of   160
the fairies of advertising & the mustard gas of sinister
intelligent editors, or were run down by the drunken taxicabs
of Absolute Reality,

who jumped off the Brooklyn Bridge this actually happened and
walked away unknown and forgotten into the ghostly daze of   165
Chinatown soup alleyways & firetrucks, not even one free
beer,

who sang out of their windows in despair, fell out of the subway
window, jumped in the filthy Passaic, leaped on negroes, cried
all over the street, danced on broken wineglasses barefoot   170
smashed phonograph records of nostalgic European 1930's
German jazz finished the whiskey and threw up groaning into
the bloody toilet, moans in their ears and the blast of colossal
steamwhistles,

who barreled down the highways of the past journeying to each   175
other's hotrod-Golgotha[12] jail-solitude watch or Birmingham
jazz incarnation,

who drove crosscountry seventytwo hours to find out if I had a
vision or you had a vision or he had a vision to find out
Eternity,   180

who journeyed to Denver, who died in Denver, who came back to
Denver & waited in vain, who watched over Denver &
brooded & loned in Denver and finally went away to find out
the Time, & now Denver is lonesome for her heroes,

who fell on their knees in hopeless cathedrals praying for each   185
other's salvation and light and breasts, until the soul
illuminated its hair for a second,

who crashed through their minds in jail waiting for impossible
criminals with golden heads and the charm of reality in their
hearts who sang sweet blues to Alcatraz,   190

who retired to Mexico to cultivate a habit, or Rocky Mount to
tender Buddha or Tangiers to boys or Southern Pacific to the
black locomotive or Harvard to Narcissus to Woodlawn[13] to
the daisychain or grave,

---

[12]Scene of Jesus' crucifixion.   [13]Bronx cemetery.

who demanded sanity trials accusing the radio of hypnotism &   195
    were left with their insanity & their hands & a hung jury,
who threw potato salad at CCNY lecturers on Dadaism and
    subsequently presented themselves on the granite steps of the
    madhouse with shaven heads and harlequin speech of suicide,
    demanding instantaneous lobotomy,   200
and who were given instead the concrete void of insulin metrasol
    electricity hydrotherapy psychotherapy occupational therapy
    pingpong & amnesia,
who in humorless protest overturned only one symbolic pingpong
    table, resting briefly in catatonia,   205
returning years later truly bald except for a wig of blood, and tears
    and fingers, to the visible madman doom of the wards of the
    madtowns of the East,
Pilgrim State's Rockland's and Greystone's[14] foetid halls, bickering
    with the echoes of the soul, rocking and rolling in the   210
    midnight solitude-bench dolmen-realms of love, dream of life
    a nightmare, bodies turned to stone as heavy as the moon,
with mother finally ******, and the last fantastic book flung out of
    the tenement window, and the last door closed at 4 AM and
    the last telephone slammed at the wall in reply and the last   215
    furnished room emptied down to the last piece of mental
    furniture, a yellow paper rose twisted on a wire hanger in the
    closet, and even that imaginary, nothing but a hopeful little
    bit of hallucination—
ah, Carl, while you are not safe I am not safe, and now you're   220
    really in the total animal soup of time—
and who therefore ran through the icy streets obsessed with a
    sudden flash of the alchemy of the use of the ellipse the
    catalog the meter & the vibrating plane,
who dreamt and made incarnate gaps in Time & Space through   225
    images juxtaposed, and trapped the archangel of the soul
    between 2 visual images and joined the elemental verbs and
    set the noun and dash of consciousness together jumping with
    sensation of Pater Omnipotens Aeterna Deus[15]
to recreate the syntax and measure of poor human prose and stand 230
    before you speechless and intelligent and shaking with shame,
    rejected yet confessing out the soul to conform to the rhythm
    of thought in his naked and endless head,
the madman bum and angel beat in Time, unknown, yet putting
    down here what might be left to say in time come after death, 235

---

[14]Mental hospitals in New York and New Jersey.
[15]Latin: "Omnipotent Father Eternal God,"
from a letter of French painter Paul
Cézanne (1839–1906).

and rose incarnate in the ghostly clothes of jazz in the goldhorn
    shadow of the band and blew the suffering of America's
    naked mind for love into an eli eli lamma lamma sabacthani[16]
    saxophone cry that shivered the cities down to the last radio
with the absolute heart of the poem of life butchered out of their   240
    own bodies good to eat a thousand years.

II

What sphinx of cement and aluminum bashed open their skulls
    and ate up their brains and imagination?
Moloch![17] Solitude! Filth! Ugliness! Ashcans and unobtainable
    dollars! Children screaming under the stairways! Boys   245
    sobbing in armies! Old men weeping in the parks!
Moloch! Moloch! Nightmare of Moloch! Moloch the loveless!
    Mental Moloch! Moloch the heavy judger of men!
Moloch the incomprehensible prison! Moloch the crossbone
    soulless jailhouse and Congress of sorrows! Moloch whose   250
    buildings are judgement! Moloch the vast stone of war!
    Moloch the stunned governments!
Moloch whose mind is pure machinery! Moloch whose blood is
    running money! Moloch whose fingers are ten armies!
    Moloch whose breast is a cannibal dynamo! Moloch whose   255
    ear is a smoking tomb!
Moloch whose eyes are a thousand blind windows! Moloch whose
    skyscrapers stand in the long streets like endless Jehovahs!
    Moloch whose factories dream and croak in the fog!
    Moloch whose smokestacks and antennae crown the cities!   260
Moloch whose love is endless oil and stone! Moloch whose soul is
    electricity and banks! Moloch whose poverty is the
    specter of genius! Moloch whose fate is a cloud of sexless
    hydrogen! Moloch whose name is the Mind!
Moloch in whom I sit lonely! Moloch in whom I dream Angels!   265
    Crazy in Moloch! Cocksucker in Moloch! Lacklove and manless in
      Moloch!
Moloch who entered my soul early! Moloch in whom I am a
    consciousness without a body! Moloch who frightened me
    out of my natural ecstasy! Moloch whom I abandon!   270
    Wake up in Moloch! Light streaming out of the sky!
Moloch! Moloch! Robot apartments! invisible suburbs!
    skeleton treasuries! blind capitals! demonic industries!
    spectral nations! invincible madhouses! granite cocks!
    monstrous bombs!   275

---

[16]Hebrew: "My God, my God, why hast thou forsaken me?" Christ's words on the cross (Matthew 27:46).

[17]Semitic god to whom children were sacrificed.

They broke their backs lifting Moloch to Heaven! Pavements,
    trees, radios, tons! lifting the city to Heaven which exists
    and is everywhere about us!
Visions! omens! hallucinations! miracles! ecstasies! gone down
    the American river!   280
Dreams! adorations! illuminations! religions! the whole
    boatload of sensitive bullshit!
Breakthroughs! over the river! flips and crucifixions! gone down
    the flood! Highs! Epiphanies! Despairs! Ten years'
    animal screams and suicides! Minds! New loves! Mad   285
    generation! down on the rocks of Time!
Real holy laughter in the river! They saw it all! the wild eyes!
    the holy yells! They bade farewell! They jumped off the
    roof! to solitude! waving! carrying flowers! Down to
    the river! into the street!   290

III

Carl Solomon! I'm with you in Rockland
    where you're madder than I am
I'm with you in Rockland
    where you must feel very strange
I'm with you in Rockland   295
    where you imitate the shade of my mother
I'm with you in Rockland
    where you've murdered your twelve secretaries
I'm with you in Rockland
    where you laugh at this invisible humor   300
I'm with you in Rockland
    where we are great writers on the same dreadful
    typewriter
I'm with you in Rockland
    where your condition has become serious and   305
    is reported on the radio
I'm with you in Rockland
    where the faculties of the skull no longer admit
    the worms of the senses
I'm with you in Rockland   310
    where you drink the tea of the breasts of the
    spinsters of Utica
I'm with you in Rockland
    where you pun on the bodies of your nurses the
    harpies of the Bronx   315

I'm with you in Rockland
    where you scream in a straightjacket that you're
    losing the game of the actual pingpong of the
    abyss
I'm with you in Rockland   320
    where you bang on the catatonic piano the soul
    is innocent and immortal it should never die
    ungodly in an armed madhouse
I'm with you in Rockland
    where fifty more shocks will never return your   325
    soul to its body again from its pilgrimage to a
    cross in the void
I'm with you in Rockland
    where you accuse your doctors of insanity and
    plot the Hebrew socialist revolution against the   330
    fascist national Golgotha[18]
I'm with you in Rockland
    where you split the heavens of Long Island
    and resurrect your living human Jesus from
    the superhuman tomb   335
I'm with you in Rockland
    where there are twenty-five-thousand mad com-
    rades all together singing the final stanzas of
    the Internationale
I'm with you in Rockland   340
    where we hug and kiss the United States under
    our bedsheets the United States that coughs all
    night and won't let us sleep
I'm with you in Rockland
    where we wake up electrified out of the coma   345
    by our own souls' airplanes roaring over the
    roof they've come to drop angelic bombs the
    hospital illuminates itself imaginary walls col-
    lapse O skinny legions run outside O starry-
    spangled shock of mercy the eternal war is   350
    here O victory forget your underwear
    we're free
I'm with you in Rockland
    in my dreams you walk dripping from a sea-
    journey on the highway across America in tears   355
    to the door of my cottage in the Western night

                                         1955–56

---

[18]Same as Calvary, the hill where Jesus was
crucified.

America

America I've given you all and now I'm nothing.
America two dollars and twentyseven cents January 17, 1956.
I can't stand my own mind.
America when will we end the human war?
Go fuck yourself with your atom bomb.   5
I don't feel good don't bother me.
I won't write my poem till I'm in my right mind.
America when will you be angelic?
When will you take off your clothes?
When will you look at yourself through the grave?   10
When will you be worthy of your million Trotskyites?[1]
America why are your libraries full of tears?
America when will you send your eggs to India?
I'm sick of your insane demands.
When can I go into the supermarket and buy what I need with my   15
    good looks?
America after all it is you and I who are perfect not the next
    world.
Your machinery is too much for me.
You made me want to be a saint.   20
There must be some other way to settle this argument.
Burroughs[2] is in Tangiers I don't think he'll come back it's sinister.
Are you being sinister or is this some form of practical joke?
I'm trying to come to the point.
I refuse to give up my obsession.   25
America stop pushing I know what I'm doing.
America the plum blossoms are falling.
I haven't read the newspapers for months, everyday somebody goes
    on trial for murder.
America I feel sentimental about the Wobblies.[3]   30
America I used to be a communist when I was a kid I'm not sorry.
I smoke marijuana every chance I get.
I sit in my house for days on end and stare at the roses in the
    closet.
When I go to Chinatown I get drunk and never get laid.   35
My mind is made up there's going to be trouble.
You should have seen me reading Marx.
My psychoanalyst thinks I'm perfectly right.
I won't say the Lord's Prayer.
I have mystical visions and cosmic vibrations.   40

---

[1] Communist idealists, followers of Leon Trotsky (1879–1940).
[2] William Burroughs (1914–1997), author of *Naked Lunch.*

[3] Nickname for Industrial Workers of the World, a militant labor organization strong in the 1910s.

America I still haven't told you what you did to Uncle Max after
    he came over from Russia.

I'm addressing you.
Are you going to let your emotional life be run by Time
    Magazine?   45
I'm obsessed by Time Magazine.
I read it every week.
Its cover stares at me every time I slink past the corner candystore.
I read it in the basement of the Berkeley Public Library.
It's always telling me about responsibility. Businessmen are serious. 50
    Movie producers are serious. Everybody's serious but me.
It occurs to me that I am America.
I am talking to myself again.

Asia is rising against me.
I haven't got a chinaman's chance.   55
I'd better consider my national resources.
My national resources consist of two joints of marijuana millions of
    genitals an unpublished private literature that goes 1400 miles
    an hour and twentyfive-thousand mental institutions.
I say nothing about my prisons nor the millions of underprivileged 60
    who live in my flowerpots under the light of five hundred
    suns.
I have abolished the whorehouses of France, Tangiers is the next
    to go.
My ambition is to be President despite the fact that I'm a   65
    Catholic.

America how can I write a holy litany in your silly mood?
I will continue like Henry Ford my strophes are as individual as
    his automobiles more so they're all different sexes.
America I will sell you strophes $2500 apiece $500 down on your 70
    old strophe
America free Tom Mooney[4]
America save the Spanish Loyalists[5]
America Sacco & Vanzetti[6] must not die.
America I am the Scottsboro boys.[7]   75

---

[4]Labor leader sentenced to death for killings in 1916; the sentence was commuted and he was eventually pardoned.

[5]Opponents of Franco's Fascists in the Spanish Civil War.

[6]Anarchists executed in Massachusetts for murder (1927) in a case that aroused much controversy.

[7]Nine blacks falsely convicted in Alabama for the rape of two white women (1931). The defense was undertaken by the Communist Party, and the case became a cause for liberals and radicals, who believed it to be a miscarriage of justice.

America when I was seven momma took me to Communist Cell
    meetings they sold us garbanzos a handful per ticket a ticket
    cost a nickel and the speeches were free everybody was
    angelic and sentimental about the workers it was all so sincere
    you have no idea what a good thing the party was in 1935   80
    Scott Nearing was a grand old man a real mensch Mother
    Bloor made my cry I once saw Israel Amter[8] plain. Everybody
    must have been a spy.
America you don't really want to go to war.
America it's them bad Russians   85
Them Russians them Russians and them Chinamen. And them
    Russians.
The Russia wants to eat us alive. The Russia's power mad. She
    wants to take our cars from out our garages.
Her wants to grab Chicago. Her needs a Red Reader's Digest. Her   90
    wants our auto plants in Siberia. Him big bureaucracy
    running our fillingstations.
That no good. Ugh. Him make Indians learn read. Him need big
    black niggers. Hah. Her make us all work sixteen hours a day.
    Help.   95
America this is quite serious.
America this is the impression I get from looking in the television
    set.
America is this correct?
I'd better get right down to the job.   100
It's true I don't want to join the Army or turn lathes in precision
parts factories, I'm nearsighted and psychopathic anyway.
America I'm putting my queer shoulder to the wheel.

            1956

JACK KEROUAC
1922–1969

Jack Kerouac transformed his life into a modern myth, one that appeals anew
to each generation discovering his classic *On the Road* (1957). While romanticiz-
ing his cross-country travels and writing frankly about the sex, drugs, and drinking that took up so much of his time, Kerouac also infused his books with a
literary consciousness and brooding spirituality, proof that he was smarter and

[8]Nearing, Bloor, and Amter were active in
  Socialist and radical causes.

deeper than detractors such as Truman Capote (who claimed Kerouac's writing was mere "typing") wanted him to be.

Though known as a novelist of the open road, he also wrote at length about his childhood in Lowell, Massachusetts, the provincial New England mill town where he was born Jean Louis Lebris de Kerouac to French Canadian immigrant parents. Lowell is the basis for the town in *The Town and the City* (1950), his first and most traditional novel, modeled after the work of Thomas Wolfe, and it provides the mystical atmosphere for several of his other novels, including *Visions of Gerard* (1963), the account of his nine-year-old brother Gerard's illness and death. This book effectively blends the Catholicism of his youth with the Buddhist principles informing his later years; its free-flowing style epitomizes the "spontaneous prose" that grew out of the author's faith in "the unspeakable visions of the individual."

After graduating from Lowell High School, Kerouac earned a football scholarship to Columbia College by way of a year at the Horace Mann Preparatory School in New York. At Horace Mann he enjoyed a charmed life as an athlete and scholar. His subsequent years at Columbia did not go so smoothly. An injury derailed his football career, and he eventually dropped out of school and enlisted in the U.S. Navy and later the Merchant Marine. In the midst of this indecisive time, he made the friends with whom he would instigate the literary trend and liberal lifestyle known as the Beat movement.

Allen Ginsberg and William S. Burroughs (a Harvard graduate) were, like Kerouac himself, brilliant, driven, and often self-tormented. In New York City's jazz clubs and gay bars and among the criminal elements of Times Square, they found a bracing alternative to workaday jobs and conventional family life. The hustler Herbert Huncke introduced them to "beat," a slang term for a drug deal gone bad. Kerouac applied the musically resonant word to his down-and-out but spiritually questing ("beatific") peers. In 1948 he told his friend John Clellon Holmes that their postwar generation of outsiders evinced "a weariness with all the forms, all the conventions of the world. . . . So I guess you might say we're a beat generation."

The following year, Kerouac took to the road with Neal Cassady, a charismatic con man who personified all things beat. The model for Dean Moriarty in *On the Road* and Cody in *Visions of Cody* (1972), Cassady lived as spontaneously as Kerouac wanted to write. In *On the Road*, he applauds the fictional counterparts of Cassady and Ginsberg, "the ones who are mad to live, mad to talk, mad to be saved, desirous of everything at the same time, the ones who never yawn or say a commonplace thing."

After the publication of *On the Road* and *The Dharma Bums* (1958), the successful follow-up novel based on his friendship with the poet Gary Snyder, Kerouac drifted on a sea of distracting fame. Though he continued to publish both prose and poetry, his drinking and often outlandish behavior cost him the critical recognition that he craved. He died of stomach hemorrhaging at age forty-seven in St. Petersburg, Florida, in the company of his mother and his third wife, Stella Sampas Kerouac of Lowell.

Kerouac embodied many of the contradictions and paradoxes that have long animated American society. He was a homebody and vagabond, bottle-swigging hedonist and Thoreau-quoting hermit, all-American hero and hard-luck hobo.

All of these personae make their appearance in his compelling, recklessly honest writing.

Hilary Holladay
James Madison University

PRIMARY WORKS

The Town and the City, 1950; *On the Road*, 1957; *The Dharma Bums*, 1958; *The Subterraneans*, 1958; *Doctor Sax: Faust Part Three*, 1959; *Maggie Cassidy*, 1959; *Mexico City Blues*, 1959; *The Scripture of the Golden Eternity*, 1960; *Tristessa*, 1960; *Lonesome Traveler*, 1960; *Book of Dreams*, 1961; *Pull My Daisy*, 1961; *Big Sur*, 1962; *Visions of Gerard*, 1963; *Desolation Angels*, 1965; *Satori in Paris*, 1966; *Vanity of Duluoz: An Adventurous Education*, 1968; *Scattered Poems*, 1971; *Pic*, 1971; *Visions of Cody*, 1972; *Heaven and Other Poems*, 1977; *Pomes All Sizes*, 1992; *Old Angel Midnight*, 1993; *Good Blonde & Others*, 1993; *Some of the Dharma*, 1997; *Selected Letters: 1940–1956*, 1995; *Selected Letters: 1957–1969*, 1999; *Atop an Underwood: Early Stories and Other Writings*, 1999; *Book of Sketches*, 2006; *Windblown World (Journals)*, 2006.

The Vanishing American Hobo

The American hobo has a hard time hoboing nowadays due to the increase in police surveillance of highways, railroad yards, sea shores, river bottoms, embankments and the thousand-and-one hiding holes of industrial night.— In California, the pack rat, the original old type who goes walking from town to town with supplies and bedding on his back, the "Homeless Brother," has practically vanished, along with the ancient gold-panning desert rat who used to walk with hope in his heart through struggling Western towns that are now so prosperous they dont want old bums any more.—"Man dont want no pack rats here even though they founded California" said an old man hiding with a can of beans and an Indian fire in a river bottom outside Riverside California in 1955.—Great sinister tax-paid police cars (1960 models with humorless searchlights) are likely to bear down at any moment on the hobo in his idealistic lope to freedom and the hills of holy silence and holy privacy.—There's nothing nobler than to put up with a few inconveniences like snakes and dust for the sake of absolute freedom.

I myself was a hobo but only of sorts, as you see, because I knew someday my literary efforts would be rewarded by social protection—I was not a real hobo with no hope ever except that secret eternal hope you get sleeping in empty boxcars flying up the Salinas Valley in hot January sunshine full of Golden Eternity toward San Jose where mean-looking old bo's 'll look at you from surly lips and offer you something to eat and a drink too—down by the tracks or in the Guadaloupe Creekbottom.

The original hobo dream was best expressed in a lovely little poem mentioned by Dwight Goddard in his *Buddhist Bible:*

> *Oh for this one rare occurrence*
> *Gladly would I give ten thousand pieces of gold!*
> *A hat is on my head, a bundle on my back,*
> *And my staff, the refreshing breeze and the full moon.*

In America there has always been (you will notice the peculiarly Whitmanesque tone of this poem, probably written by old Goddard) a definite special idea of footwalking freedom going back to the days of Jim Bridger and Johnny Appleseed and carried on today by a vanishing group of hardy old timers still seen sometimes waiting in a desert highway for a short bus ride into town for panhandling (or work) and grub, or wandering the Eastern part of the country hitting Salvation Armies and moving on from town to town and state to state toward the eventual doom of big-city skid rows when their feet give out.—Nevertheless not long ago in California I did see (deep in the gorge by a railroad track outside San Jose buried in eucalyptus leaves and the blessed oblivion of vines) a bunch of cardboard and jerrybuilt huts at evening in front of one of which sat an aged man puffing his 15¢ Granger tobacco in his corncob pipe (Japan's mountains are full of free huts and old men who cackle over root brews waiting for Supreme Enlightenment which is only obtainable through occasional complete solitude.)

In America camping is considered a healthy sport for Boy Scouts but a crime for mature men who have made it their vocation.—Poverty is considered a virtue among the monks of civilized nations—in America you spend a night in the calaboose if you're caught short without your vagrancy change (it was fifty cents last I heard of, Pard—what now?)

In Brueghel's time children danced around the hobo, he wore huge and raggy clothes and always looked straight ahead indifferent to the children, and the families didnt mind the children playing with the hobo, it was a natural thing.—But today mothers hold tight their children when the hobo passes through town, because of what newspapers made the hobo to be— the rapist, the strangler, child-eater.—Stay away from strangers, they'll give you poison candy. Though the Brueghel hobo and the hobo today are the same, the children are different.—Where is even the Chaplinesque hobo? The old Divine Comedy hobo? The hobo is Virgil, he leadeth.—The hobo enters the child's world (like in the famous painting by Brueghel of a huge hobo solemnly passing through the washtub village being barked at and laughed at by children, St. Pied Piper) but today it's an adult world, it's not a child's world.—Today the hobo's made to slink—everybody's watching the cop heroes on TV.

Benjamin Franklin was like a hobo in Pennsylvania; he walked through Philly with three big rolls under his arms and a Massachusetts halfpenny on his hat.—John Muir was a hobo who went off into the mountains with a pocketful of dried bread, which he soaked in creeks.

Did Whitman terrify the children of Louisiana when he walked the open road?

What about the Black Hobo? Moonshiner? Chicken snatcher? Remus? The black hobo in the South is the last of the Brueghel bums, children pay tribute and stand in awe making no comment. You see him coming out of the piney barren with an old unspeakable sack. Is he carrying coons? Is he carrying Br'er Rabbit? Nobody knows what he's carrying.

The Forty Niner, the ghost of the plains, Old Zacatecan Jack the Walking Saint, the prospector, the spirits and ghosts of hoboism are gone—but

they (the prospectors) wanted to fill their unspeakable sacks with gold.—
Teddy Roosevelt, political hobo—Vachel Lindsay, troubadour hobo, seedy
hobo—how many pies for one of *his* poems? The hobo lives in a Disneyland,
Pete-the-Tramp land, where everything is human lions, tin men, moondogs
with rubber teeth, orange-and-purple paths, emerald castles in the distance
looming, kind philosophers of witches.—No witch ever cooked a hobo.—
The hobo has two watches you can't buy in Tiffany's, on one wrist the sun,
on the other wrist the moon, both bands are made of sky.

> *Hark! Hark! The dogs do bark,*
> *The beggars are coming to town;*
> *Some in rags, some in tags,*
> *And some in velvet gowns.*

The Jet Age is crucifying the hobo because how can he hop a freight jet?
Does Louella Parsons look kindly upon hobos, I wonder? Henry Miller would
allow the hobos to swim in his swimming pool.—What about Shirley Temple,
to whom the hobo gave the Bluebird? Are the young Temples bluebirdless?

Today the hobo has to hide, he has fewer places to hide, the cops are looking for him, *calling all cars, calling all cars, hobos seen in the vicinity of Bird-in-
Hand*—Jean Valjean weighed with his sack of candelabra, screaming to youth,
"There's your *sou*, your *sou!*" Beethoven was a hobo who knelt and listened to
the light, a deaf hobo who could not hear other hobo complaints.—Einstein
the hobo with his ratty turtleneck sweater made of lamb, Bernard Baruch the
disillusioned hobo sitting on a park bench with voice-catcher plastic in his ear
waiting for John Henry, waiting for somebody very mad, waiting for the Persian epic.—

Sergei Esenin was a great hobo who took advantage of the Russian Revolution to rush around drinking potato juice in the backward villages of Russia (his most famous poem is called *Confessions of a Bum*) who said at the
moment they were storming the Czar "Right now I feel like pissing through
the window at the moon." It is the egoless hobo that will give birth to a
child someday—Li Po was a mighty hobo.—ego is the greatest hobo—Hail
Hobo Ego! Whose monument someday will be a golden tin coffee can.

Jesus was a strange hobo who walked on water.—

Buddha was also a hobo who paid no attention to the other hobo.—

Chief Rain-In-The-Face, weirder even.—

W. C. Fields—his red nose explained the meaning of the triple world,
Great Vehicle, Lesser Vehicle, Diamond Vehicle.

The hobo is born of pride, having nothing to do with a community but
with himself and other hobos and maybe a dog.—Hobos by the railroad
embankments cook at night huge tin cans of coffee.—Proud was the way
the hobo walked through a town by the back doors where pies were cooling
on window sills, the hobo was a mental leper, he didnt need to beg to eat,
strong Western bony mothers knew his tinkling beard and tattered toga,
come and get it! But proud be proud, still there was some annoyance because

sometimes when she called *come and get it*, hordes of hobos came, ten or twenty at a time, and it was kind of hard to feed that many, sometimes hobos were inconsiderate, but not always, but when they were, they no longer held their pride, they became bums—they migrated to the Bowery in New York, to Scollay Square in Boston, to Pratt Street in Baltimore, to Madison Street in Chicago, to 12th Street in Kansas City, to Larimer Street in Denver, to South Main Street in Los Angeles, to downtown Third Street in San Francisco, to Skid Road in Seattle ("blighted areas" all)—

The Bowery is the haven for hobos who came to the big city to make the big time by getting pushcarts and collecting cardboard.—Lots of Bowery bums are Scandinavian, lots of them bleed easily because they drink too much.—When winter comes bums drink a drink called smoke, it consists of wood alcohol and a drop of iodine and a scab of lemon, this they gulp down and wham! they hibernate all winter so as not to catch cold, because they dont live anywhere, and it gets very cold outside in the city in winter.— Sometimes hobos sleep arm-in-arm to keep warm, right on the sidewalk. Bowery Mission veterans say that the beer-drinking bums are the most belligerent of the lot.

Fred Bunz is the great Howard Johnson's of the bums—it is located on 277 Bowery in New York. They write the menu in soap on the windows.— You see the bums reluctantly paying fifteen cents for pig brains, twenty-five cents for goulash, and shuffling out in thin cotton shirts in the cold November night to go and make the lunar Bowery with a smash of broken bottle in an alley where they stand against a wall like naughty boys.—Some of them wear adventurous rainy hats picked up by the track in Hugo Colorado or blasted shoes kicked off by Indians in the dumps of Juarez, or coats from the lugubrious salon of the seal and fish.—Bum hotels are white and tiled and seem as though they were upright johns.—Used to be bums told tourists that they once were successful doctors, now they tell tourists they were once guides for movie stars or directors in Africa and that when TV came into being they lost their safari rights.

In Holland they dont allow bums, the same maybe in Copenhagen. But in Paris you can be a bum—in Paris bums are treated with great respect and are rarely refused a few francs.—There are various kinds of classes of bums in Paris, the high-class bum has a dog and a baby carriage in which he keeps all his belongings, and that usually consists of old *France Soirs*, rags, tin cans, empty bottles, broken dolls.—This bum sometimes has a mistress who follows him and his dog and carriage around.—The lower bums dont own a thing, they just sit on the banks of the Seine picking their nose at the Eiffel Tower.—

The bums in England have English accents, and it makes them seem strange—they don't understand bums in Germany.—America is the motherland of bumdom.—

American hobo Lou Jenkins from Allentown Pennsylvania was interviewed at Fred Bunz's on The Bowery.—"What you wanta know all this info for, what you want?"

"I understand that you've been a hobo travelin' around the country."

"How about givin' a fella few bits for some wine before we talk."

"Al, go get the wine."

"Where's this gonna be in, the *Daily News?*"

"No, in a book."

"What are you young kids doing here, I mean where's the drink?"

"Al's gone to the liquor store—You wanted Thunderbird, wasnt it?"

"Yair."

Lou Jenkins then grew worse—"How about a few bits for a flop tonight?"

"Okay, we just wanta ask you a few questions like why did you leave Allentown?"

"My wife.—My wife,—Never get married. You'll never live it down. You mean to say it's gonna be in a book hey what I'm sayin'?"

"Come on say something about bums or something.—"

"Well whattaya wanta know about bums? Lot of 'em around, kinda tough these days, no money—lissen, how about a good meal?"

"See you in the Sagamore." (Respectable bums' cafeteria at Third and Cooper Union.)

"Okay kid, thanks a lot."—He opens the Thunderbird bottle with one expert flip of the plastic seal.—Glub, as the moon rises resplendent as a rose he swallows with big ugly lips thirsty to gulp the throat down, Sclup! and down goes the drink and his eyes be-pop themselves and he licks tongue on top lip and says "H-a-h!" And he shouts "Dont forget my name is spelled Jenkins, J-e-n-k-y-n-s.—"

Another character—"You say that your name is Ephram Freece of Pawling New York?"

"Well, no, my name is James Russell Hubbard."

"You look pretty respectable for a bum."

"My grandfather was a Kentucky colonel."

"Oh?"

"Yes."

"Whatever made you come here to Third Avenue?"

"I really cant do it, I dont care, I cant be bothered, I feel nothing, I dont care any more. I'm sorry but—somebody stole my razor blade last night, if you can lay some money on me I'll buy myself a Schick razor."

"Where will you plug it in? Do you have such facilities?"

"A Schick injector."

"Oh."

"And I always carry this book with me—*The Rules of St. Benedict*. A dreary book, but well I got another book in my pack. A dreary book too I guess."

"Why do you read it then?"

"Because I found it—I found it in Bristol last year."

"What are you interested in? You like interested in something?"

"Well, this other book I got there is er, yee, er, a big strange book—you shouldnt be interviewing me. Talk to that old nigra fella over there with the harmonica—I'm no good for nothing, all I want is to be left alone—"

"I see you smoke a pipe."

"Yeah—Granger tobacco. Want some?"

"Will you show me the book?"

"No I aint got it with me, I only got this with me."—He points to his pipe and tobacco.

"Can you say something?"

"Lightin flash."

The American Hobo is on the way out as long as sheriffs operate with as Louis-Ferdinand Céline said, "One line of crime and nine of boredom," because having nothing to do in the middle of the night with everybody gone to sleep they pick on the first human being they see walking.—They pick on lovers on the beach even. They just dont know what to do with themselves in those five-thousand-dollar police cars with the twoway Dick Tracy radios except pick on anything that moves in the night and in the daytime on anything that seems to be moving independently of gasoline, power, Army or police.—I myself was a hobo but I had to give it up around 1956 because of increasing television stories about the abominableness of strangers with packs passing through by themselves independently—I was surrounded by three squad cars in Tucson Arizona at 2 A.M. as I was walking pack-on-back for a night's sweet sleep in the red moon desert:

"Where you goin'?"

"Sleep."

"Sleep where?"

"On the sand."

"Why?"

"Got my sleeping bag."

"Why?"

"Studyin' the great outdoors."

"Who are you? Let's see your identification."

"I just spent a summer with the Forest Service."

"Did you get paid?"

"Yeah."

"Then why dont you go to a hotel?"

"I like it better outdoors and it's free."

"Why?"

"Because I'm studying hobo."

"What's so good about that?"

They wanted an *explanation* for my hoboing and came close to hauling me in but I was sincere with them and they ended up scratching their heads and saying "Go ahead if that's what you want."—They didnt offer me a ride four miles out to the desert.

And the sheriff of Cochise allowed me to sleep on the cold clay outside Bowie Arizona only because he didnt know about it.—

There's something strange going on, you cant even be alone any more in the primitive wilderness ("primitive areas" so-called), there's always a helicopter comes and snoops around, you need camouflage.—Then they begin to demand that you observe strange aircraft for Civil Defense as though you knew the difference between regular strange aircraft and any kind of strange aircraft.—As far as I'm concerned the only thing to do is sit in a room and get drunk and give up your hoboing and your camping ambitions because there aint a sheriff or fire warden in any of the new fifty states who will let you cook a little meal over some burning sticks in the tule brake or the hidden valley or anyplace any more because he has nothing to do but pick on what he sees out there on the landscape moving independently of the gasoline power army police station.—I have no ax to grind: I'm simply going to another world.

Ray Rademacher, a fellow staying at the Mission in the Bowery, said recently, "I wish things was like they was when my father was known as Johnny the Walker of the White Mountains.—He once straightened out a young boy's bones after an accident, for a meal, and left. The French around there called him '*Le Passant.*'" (He who passes through.)

The hobos of America who can still travel in a healthy way are still in good shape, they can go hide in cemeteries and drink wine under cemetery groves of trees and micturate and sleep on cardboards and smash bottles on the tombstones and not care and not be scared of the dead but serious and humorous in the cop-avoiding night and even amused and leave litters of their picnic between the grizzled slabs of Imagined Death, cussing what they think are real days, but Oh the poor bum of the skid row! There he sleeps in the doorway, back to wall, head down, with his right hand palm-up as if to receive from the night, the other hand hanging, strong, firm, like Joe Louis hands, pathetic, made tragic by unavoidable circumstance—the hand like a beggar's upheld with the fingers forming a suggestion of what he deserves and desires to receive, shaping the alms, thumb almost touching finger tips, as though on the tip of the tongue he's about to say in sleep and with that gesture what he couldnt say awake: "Why have you taken this away from me, that I cant draw my breath in the peace and sweetness of my own bed but here in these dull and nameless rags on this humbling stoop I have to sit waiting for the wheels of the city to roll," and further, "I dont want to show my hand but in sleep I'm helpless to straighten it, yet take this opportunity to see my plea, I'm alone, I'm sick, I'm dying—see my hand up-tipped, learn the secret of my human heart, give me the thing, give me your hand, take me to the emerald mountains beyond the city, take me to the safe place, be kind, be nice, smile—I'm too tired now of everything else, I've had enough, I give up, I quit, I want to go home, take me home O brother in the night—take me home, lock me in safe, take me to where all is peace and amity, to the family of life, my mother, my father, my sister, my wife and you my brother and you my friend—but no hope, no hope, no hope, I wake up and I'd give a million dollars to be in my own bed—O Lord save me—" In evil roads behind gas tanks where murderous dogs snarl from behind wire fences cruisers suddenly leap out like getaway cars but from a crime more secret, more baneful than words can tell.

The woods are full of wardens.

1960

from **Mexico City Blues**

43rd Chorus

Mexico City Bop
I got the huck bop
I got the floogle mock
I got the thiri chiribim
    bitchy bitchy bitchy   5
    batch batch
  Chippely bop
      Noise like that
      Like fallin off porches   10
      Of Tenement Petersburg
      Russia Chicago O Yay.
Like, when you see,
    the trumpet kind, horn
    shiny in his hand, raise   15
    it in smoke among heads
    he bespeaks, elucidates,
    explains and drops out,
    end of chorus, staring
    at the final wall   20
    where in Africa
    the old men petered
    out on their own account
    using their own Immemorial
      Salvation Mind   25
      SLIPPITY BOP

                    1959

211th Chorus

The wheel of the quivering meat
      conception
Turns in the void expelling human beings,
Pigs, turtles, frogs, insects, nits,
Mice, lice, lizards, rats, roan   5
Racinghorses, poxy bucolic pigtics,
Horrible unnameable lice of vultures,
Murderous attacking dog-armies
Of Africa, Rhinos roaming in the
         jungle,   10
Vast boars and huge gigantic bull
Elephants, rams, eagles, condors,

Pones and Porcupines and Pills —
All the endless conception of living
                    beings   15
Gnashing everywhere in Consciousness
Throughout the ten directions of space
Occupying all the quarters in & out,
From supermicroscopic no-bug
To huge Galaxy Lightyear Bowell   20
Illuminating the sky of one Mind —
    Poor! I wish I was free
    of that slaving meat wheel
    and safe in heaven dead

                                       1959

■   # LAWRENCE FERLINGHETTI   ■

B. 1919

A prominent voice of the Beat poetry movement of the 1950s, whose primary aim was to bring poetry back to the people, Lawrence Ferlinghetti has greatly extended that objective in his prolific career as editor and publisher of the renowned City Lights Books press in San Francisco. His literary production has embraced many areas: translation, fiction writing, travelogues, playwriting, film narration, and essays. Yet his impact and importance remain as a poet and as a voice of dissent, reflected in his political self-description as "an enemy of the State."

Following graduation from the University of North Carolina and service in World War II, Ferlinghetti received a master's degree from Columbia University in 1948 and a doctorate from the Sorbonne in 1951. From 1951 to 1953, when he settled in San Francisco, he taught French in an adult education program. In 1953 he became co-owner of the City Lights Bookshop, the first all-paperback bookstore in the country, and by 1955 had founded and become editor of the City Lights Books publishing house. City Lights served as a meeting place for Beat writers. His press published and promoted Beat writings, and he personally encouraged them—in the case of Diane di Prima, writing the introduction for her first collection, *This Kind of Bird Flies Backward*.

Ferlinghetti's publication of Allen Ginsberg's *Howl* in 1956 led to his arrest on obscenity charges. The trial that followed (he was acquitted) drew national attention to the Beat movement and established Ferlinghetti as its prominent voice. In fact, Ferlinghetti own *A Coney Island of the Mind* was, along with *Howl*, the most popular poetry book of the 1950s. Often concerned with political and social issues, Ferlinghetti's poetry set out to dispute the literary elite's definition of art and the artist's role in the world. Though imbued with the commonplace, his poetry cannot be dismissed as polemic or personal protest, for it stands on his craftsmanship, thematics, and grounding in tradition.

Ferlinghetti described his one novel, *Her*, as "a surreal semi-autobiographical blackbook." It deals with a young man's search for his identity, but its free-association experimentation proved baffling to critics.

Known for his political poetry, he explains his commitment in art as well as life by saying "Only the dead are disengaged." Well aware of the incongruity between his social dissent and his success as a publisher, Ferlinghetti, in an interview for the Los Angeles *Times*, remarked on "the enormous capacity of society to ingest its own most dissident elements.... It happens to everyone successful within the system. I'm ingested myself."

Helen Barolini
Independent scholar

PRIMARY WORKS

Pictures of the Gone World, 1955, 1973, 1995; *A Coney Island of the Mind*, 1958; *Her* (novel), 1960; *Starting from San Francisco*, 1961, 1967; *Unfair Arguments with Existence*, 1963; *Routines*, 1964; *Tyrannus Nix?*, 1969; *The Secret Meaning of Things*, 1969; *The Mexican Night: Travel Journal*, 1970; *Back Roads to Far Places*, 1971; *Love Is No Stone on the Moon: Automatic Poem*, 1971; *Open Eye, Open Heart*, 1973; *Who Are We Now?*, 1976; *Landscapes of Living and Dying*, 1979; *Literary San Francisco*, 1980; *Endless Life: Selected Poems*, 1981; *Over All the Obscene Boundaries*, 1984; *The Canticle of Jack Kerouac*, 1987; *Love in the Days of Rage*, 1988; *European Poems and Transitions*, 1988; *Ascending over Ohio*, 1989; *A Buddha in the Woodpile*, 1993; *These Are My Rivers: New and Selected Poems*, 1993; *A Far Rockaway of the Heart*, 1997; *How to Paint Sunlight: Lyric Poems and Others 1997–2000*, 2001; *San Francisco Poems*, 2001; *Americus: Part 1*, 2004; *Poetry as Insurgent Art*, 2007.

from **I Am Waiting**

I am waiting for my case to come up
and I am waiting
for a rebirth of wonder
and I am waiting for someone
to really discover America   5
and wail
and I am waiting
for the discovery
of a new symbolic western frontier
and I am waiting   10
for the American Eagle
to really spread its wings
and straighten up and fly right
and I am waiting
for the Age of Anxiety   15
to drop dead
and I am waiting

for the war to be fought
which will make the world safe
for anarchy   20
and I am waiting
for the final withering away
of all governments
and I am perpetually awaiting
a rebirth of wonder   25

I am waiting for the Second Coming
and I am waiting
for a religious revival
to sweep thru the state of Arizona
and I am waiting   30
for the Grapes of Wrath to be stored
and I am waiting
for them to prove
that God is really American
and I am seriously waiting   35
for Billy Graham and Elvis Presley
to exchange roles seriously
and I am waiting
to see God on television
piped onto church altars   40
if only they can find
the right channel
to tune in on
and I am waiting
for the Last Supper to be served again   45
with a strange new appetizer
and I am perpetually awaiting
a rebirth of wonder

I am waiting for my number to be called
and I am waiting   50
for the living end
and I am waiting
for dad to come home
his pockets full
of irradiated silver dollars   55
and I am waiting
for the atomic tests to end
and I am waiting happily
for things to get much worse
before they improve   60
and I am waiting
for the Salvation Army to take over

and I am waiting
for the human crowd
to wander off a cliff somewhere   65
clutching its atomic umbrella
and I am waiting
for Ike to act
and I am waiting
for the meek to be blessed   70
and inherit the earth
without taxes
and I am waiting
for forests and animals
to reclaim the earth as theirs   75
and I am waiting
for a way to be devised
to destroy all nationalisms
without killing anybody
and I am waiting   80
for linnets and planets to fall like rain
and I am waiting for lovers and weepers
to lie down together again
in a new rebirth of wonder

I am waiting for the Great Divide to be crossed   85
and I am anxiously waiting
for the secret of eternal life to be discovered
by an obscure general practitioner
and save me forever from certain death
and I am waiting   90
for life to begin
and I am waiting
for the storms of life
to be over
and I am waiting   95
to set sail for happiness
and I am waiting
for a reconstructed Mayflower
to reach America
with its picture story and tv rights   100
sold in advance to the natives
and I am waiting
for the lost music to sound again
in the Lost Continent
in a new rebirth of wonder   105

I am waiting for the day
that maketh all things clear

and I am waiting
for Ole Man River
to just stop rolling along   110
past the country club
and I am waiting
for the deepest South
to just stop Reconstructing itself
in its own image   115
and I am waiting
for a sweet desegregated chariot
to swing low
and carry me back to Ole Virginie
and I am waiting   120
for Ole Virginie to discover
just why Darkies are born
and I am waiting
for God to lookout
from Lookout Mountain   125
and see the Ode to the Confederate Dead
as a real farce
and I am awaiting retribution
for what America did
to Tom Sawyer   130
and I am perpetually awaiting
a rebirth of wonder

I am waiting for Tom Swift to grow up
and I am waiting
for the American Boy   135
to take off Beauty's clothes
and get on top of her
and I am waiting
for Alice in Wonderland
to retransmit to me   140
her total dream of innocence
and I am waiting
for Childe Roland to come
to the final darkest tower
and I am waiting   145
for Aphrodite
to grow live arms
at a final disarmament conference
in a new rebirth of wonder

I am waiting   150
to get some intimations
of immortality

by recollecting my early childhood
and I am waiting
for the green mornings to come again   155
youth's dumb green fields come back again
and I am waiting
for some strains of unpremeditated art
to shake my typewriter
and I am waiting to write   160
the great indelible poem
and I am waiting
for the last long careless rapture
and I am perpetually waiting
for the fleeing lovers on the Grecian Urn   165
to catch each other up at last
and embrace
and I am waiting
perpetually and forever
a renaissance of wonder   170

                                                        1958

Dove Sta Amore . . .

Dove sta amore
Where lies love
Dove sta amore
  Here lies love
The ring dove love   5
In lyrical delight
Hear love's hillsong
Love's true willsong
Love's low plainsong
Too sweet painsong   10
In passages of night
  Dove sta amore
    Here lies love
The ring dove love
  Dove sta amore   15
    Here lies love

                                                        1958

The Old Italians Dying

For years the old Italians have been dying
all over America
For years the old Italians in faded felt hats

have been sunning themselves and dying
You have seen them on the benches   5
in the park in Washington Square
the old Italians in their black high button shoes
the old men in their old felt fedoras
                              with stained hatbands
have been dying and dying   10
                    day by day
You have seen them
every day in Washington Square San Francisco
the slow bell
tolls in the morning   15
in the Church of Peter & Paul
in the marzipan church on the plaza
toward ten in the morning the slow bell tolls
in the towers of Peter & Paul
and the old men who are still alive   20
sit sunning themselves in a row
on the wood benches in the park
and watch the processions in and out
funerals in the morning
weddings in the afternoon   25
slow bell in the morning Fast bell at noon
In one door out the other
the old men sit there in their hats
and watch the coming & going
You have seen them   30
the ones who feed the pigeons
                    cutting the stale bread
                         with their thumbs & penknives
the ones with old pocketwatches
the old ones with gnarled hands   35
                    and wild eyebrows
the ones with the baggy pants
                         with both belt & suspenders
the grappa drinkers with teeth like corn
the Piemontesi the Genovesi the Sicilianos   40
                    smelling of garlic & pepperonis
the ones who loved Mussolini
the old fascists
the ones who loved Garibaldi
the old anarchists reading *L'Umanita Nova*   45
the ones who loved Sacco & Vanzetti
They are almost all gone now
They are sitting and waiting their turn
and sunning themselves in front of the church

over the doors of which is inscribed   50
a phrase which would seem to be unfinished
from Dante's *Paradiso*
about the glory of the One
            who moves everything . . .
The old men are waiting   55
for it to be finished
for their glorious sentence on earth
              to be finished
the slow bell tolls & tolls
the pigeons strut about   60
not even thinking of flying
the air too heavy with heavy tolling
The black hired hearses draw up
the black limousines with black windowshades
shielding the widows   65
the widows with the long black veils
who will outlive them all
You have seen them
madre di terra, madre di mare
The widows climb out of the limousines   70
The family mourners step out in stiff suits
The widows walk so slowly
up the steps of the cathedral
fishnet veils drawn down
leaning hard on darkcloth arms   75
Their faces do not fall apart
They are merely drawn apart
They are still the matriarchs
outliving everyone
the old dagos dying out   80
in Little Italys all over America
the old dead dagos
hauled out in the morning sun
that does not mourn for anyone
One by one Year by year   85
they are carried out
The bell
never stops tolling
The old Italians with lapstrake faces
are hauled out of the hearses   90
by the paid pallbearers
in mafioso mourning coats & dark glasses
The old dead men are hauled out
in their black coffins like small skiffs
They enter the true church   95

for the first time in many years
in these carved black boats
          ready to be ferried over
The priests scurry about
          as if to cast off the lines   100
The other old men
          still alive on the benches
watch it all with their hats on

You have seen them sitting there
waiting for the bocci ball to stop rolling   105
waiting for the bell
          to stop tolling & tolling
for the slow bell
          to be finished tolling
telling the unfinished *Paradiso* story   110
as seen in an unfinished phrase
          on the face of a church
as seen in a fisherman's face
in a black boat without sails
making his final haul   115

          1979

BRENDA (BONNIE) FRAZER
B. 1939

Bonnie Frazer has lived along a border of American mainstream culture, dropping out for writing and hipster adventure and dropping in for work and family life several times over. Similarly, her writing probes a fault line of literary invention, the point at which confession borders fiction. Writing of the people and panoramas of the road, amalgamating art and life in her tales, combining personal confession with artistic composition, Frazer expresses quintessential Beat literary impulses.

Frazer was born in Washington, D.C. After studying briefly at Sweet Briar College, in 1959 she met the Beat poet Ray Bremser and married him three weeks later. In 1961, she, Bremser, and their baby daughter, Rachel, fled to Mexico to evade New Jersey prison authorities, who were pursuing Bremser for parole violation. A year later Frazer, who had given up her child for adoption in Mexico and resorted to prostitution to survive, produced *Troia: Mexican Memoirs* (under the name Bonnie Bremser) from letters to Ray while he was again in prison in New Jersey. Bremser, along with the book's editor, Michael Perkins, arranged the letters into a narrative, and *Troia* was published at his insistence in 1969. It was published in Great Britain under the title *For Love of Ray* in 1971. Frazer eventually left both Bremser and the Beat counterculture, obtained a master's degree in soil science, and worked for the U.S. Department of Agriculture as a soil surveyor to support herself and her children. Now retired, she lives in Michigan, where she has returned to writing, expanding her narrative of life in the Beat movement.

Troia, Frazer's major published work, advances the movement's signature aesthetics while integrating female sexuality, consciousness, and desire, as well as motherhood and a woman's artistic ambition, into the Beat literary and cultural domain. Its composition and character follow the Beat movement's aesthetics of immersion in memory and imagination and its reliance on spontaneous expression and free association. Frazer wrote *Troia* in two-page daily installments, letters to Ray that were memories of the previous year in emulation of Kerouac's method for composing poetry and prose. However, Frazer's poetics modify Beat avant-garde ideals by demanding that sexual freedom and freedom of expression be permitted equally to women as to men. *Troia* means sexual adventurer, and this story of a woman's experience on the road violates long-held patriarchal constraints on women's lives and conduct, echoing contemporaneous claims of second-wave feminism for female equality and sexual self-determination. *Troia* alters the male-centered road tale by introducing domestic elements, bringing to Beat generation legends a mobile female protagonist whose picaresque adventures defy the male model by the presence of her baby. Through its focus on motherhood and gender, *Troia* critiques hipster marriage and sexual politics, just as the narrator jettisons the guilt and shame associated with her sexual promiscuity, open prostitution, and relinquishment of her child. Modifying *On the Road*, *Troia* explicitly asks what existential and sexual adventuring can mean for women under laws of male dominance and ideas of women as caretakers and sexual objects. A revolutionary text of women's liberation, *Troia* is an original, radical example of antiestablishment Beat generation writing.

Ronna C. Johnson
Tufts University

PRIMARY WORK

Troia: Mexican Memoirs, 1969.

from **Troia: Mexican Memoirs**

Once across, we were quickly tired of Matamoros and purchased tickets to Mexico City. Transportes Del Norte, maroon buses, nothing to complain of in these first class accommodations, we had enough money to get safely to Mexico City from where we were somehow to get safely to Veracruz, where we were to find our refuge ... had I already exchanged one fear for another? Had the cold damp night of Matamoros put another chill into my heart? Was my fear at this time all composed of not being able to handle external circumstances, afraid I would not be able to keep Rachel healthy, or at least

not crying, (and that was a feat I didn't often succeed in,) and not to be able
to satisfy Ray—what was happening in his head, something similar? And it
all was so extremely personal, this service of responsibility, that the failure
of it and maybe the success I have not had much chance to experience up to
this point was a very lonely thing; we were not really helping each other too
much now. Each of us was just clinging as well as possible to what shreds of
strength were left in the confidential self. The bus ride to Mexico City, full
of this, I am constantly with the baby on my lap, broken hearted at every
spell of crying, the frustration of not being a very good mother really—
trying to groove, trying to groove under the circumstances—and in spite of
it I have impressions of dark shrouded nights of passage through the hills,
of an oasis of light in a restaurant stop. 2 A.M. with everyone sitting around
the narrow lighted room—with a sense of it being the only lighted room for
fifty miles around—eating eggs Mexican style for the first time. Ray got his
huevos rancheros and me eggs scrambled with fried beans and this was sort
of a prelude to our Mexican trip. . . .

The trip—maroon bus awaits us beside the low immigration building,
near the broken-down bridge—beer cans clatter in the dusty road afternoon
no sunlight but the approaching lowering clouds of a thunderstorm spreading out over the sky into gray vastness of a depressing stand-still underneath any tree; lonely your reality here in Matamoros, the streets which
carry through the center of town growing in importance to the four central
parallels which cut out the square of the plaza, where afternoon bistek eaters and shoe-shine boys eye each other from across the unpaved streets;
these same streets spread outward into the still mathematically correct city
layout but sidewalks disappear and houses rise in midst of a block shacked
upwards from a broken down fence entryway by eroded paths; a house may
take any shape or position within a block and weeds of menacing aspect care
little for the store on the corner so drawn into its cache of paper candies
and orange soda signs it has shrunk to the stature of a poverty-struck doll
house—the incredible ironies of Mexico—the wild-flung filth of Matamoros.
Leaving town on the bus, mud hole crossroads fifty yards wide of rutting
and industry—some International Harvester or reaping machine showroom
with its economic splendor surveying the city; it will grow on, and the sky
disapproves. Pass Sta. Teresa, a cafe faces east on the flat land. Look across
to the Gulf, and nothing looks back, save the mesquite bushes, a mangy dog
chases a couple of not promising cows across a landscape you would not
expect to carry even that much vision of life. Seen from the air, Transportes
Del Norte carries on, a vision of good service, sixty people burning up the
dust on the first stretch of the roads which do indeed all lead to Mexico
City—San Fernando, Tres Palos, Encinal. The sun shines briefly as I change
the baby's diaper and we have a cup of coffee and head back to the bus. San-
tandar Jimeniz, we do not know yet that from here dots one of those
"almost" roads perpendicular to the route of travelling civilization. A road
which grows out of the solid surety of modern highway dotting in weak secrecy into the plain to Abasolo where another almost not to be seen road,

goes nowhere, but goes—we want to see where all the roads go, since then, but this first trip just get us there and quick, get us there where we are going, and we don't know yet that nothing waits but the bottom waiting to be scraped in our own whimsical and full-of-love fashion—got to get there and quick—damn the crying and wet diapers and laps full of Gerbers on the bus, of leg cramps and not much to view—Padilla, Guemez, Ciudad Victoria, chicken salad sandwiches and the unknown feeling of a waterfall. In all of these places we stop, passing through, rushing downward, seeking our level, slowly dying, get it over, let's get there. Ciudad Monte, non-stop Valles, passing in the night the bus driver picks up on lack of sleep, answers on the wheeling whispering pavement. We take our first curves into the hills, the roads start to swing—Tamazunchale, lights seen across a valley, Jacala, pencil marks on maps of future excitement. We turn East in the night approaching Ixmiquilpan, herald Indian feathers, the driver mutters incoherent names over the sleeping passageway, the bus careens as we shoot through Actopan, come another and final turning point at Pachuca. The driver announces the last lap and everyone stirs and gets excited at the news, not realizing it is more than 3 hours of approach to Mexico City. I look out and God drops from his hand the myriad stars and constellations I have never seen before, plumb to the horizon flat landed out beneath the giant horoscopic screen of Mexican heaven....

Two o'clock *en la mañana*, we arrive in Mexico City and the bus leaves us off at ADO and not at the Transportes Del Norte bus terminal. In a swelter of homeless appearing people whom we don't recognize there are many who are waiting for the morning bus perhaps, and though they look disreputable something will eventually be brought out of their packs to make them proud—like us, our records, our chevrons at that point I guess, on our way to make the scene at P's and it couldn't be too soon for me. I was cold, tired and ready for the new day to dawn with everything O.K., as usual. Taxi drivers, *caldo* eaters of the night, our soon-to-be-compadres of doubtful reckonings on Mexico City taxi meters. When the meter registers two pesos, the passenger somehow must pay four and even more surprisingly we find out this is not just tourist graft and that the taxi in Mexico is one of the cheapest rides anywhere with privacy like a king; cheapest except for the bus ride, if you are game, but that is more rollercoaster thrills....

Ray was perhaps responding to the illusion of everything being beautiful. He always was ahead of me in that respect, and I do respect, although it in fact leaves me behind. He decided to stay in Mexico City for twenty-four hours more while it is decided for me that I will travel to Veracruz by bus with N and the baby. Ah bitter, I was not about to accept with grace my maidenly burdened-by-baby responsibility at this particular time. I should have put my foot down instead of being shuffled because see what it did in rebellion (sure! almost sure! suspecting something really wrong since Matamoros—that Ray had already set his eye on something that didn't include me—what could it be—my perceptions were not sharp) and my survival reflexes were working overtime, I guess. But I go—midway between holding the baby on the eight hour bus trip, the night quickly sets in and I decide to try my seductive powers on N, and the mistaken blue jeans, not to survive this episode, did indeed entice his hand where it should have by any standards stayed away from, the baby on my lap, we arrive in Mexico, me zipping up alone, my lonely pleasure, had I known I could have got in any restroom by my own mechanics—damn N.

If I could only do more than grab at a passing branch over my head, but the trouble with that is everything up until now has taken place fast on the go, the screeching terror of speed of everything falling out from underneath you—the recurring dream of bridges falling and falling away from beneath your very feet into rushing water, the resulting social shock, but more than that, knowing what it is to fall for the last time forever.

1969

JOYCE JOHNSON
B. 1934

With the 1983 publication of *Minor Characters*, Joyce Johnson's memoir of her experiences as a young writer in the New York Beat scene of the 1950s, women associated with the movement became visible. Johnson's writing of women's lives in the era just before second-wave feminism epitomizes the "cool" Beat style of cerebral detachment. All her works—two memoirs, three novels, a collection of letters, and a nonfiction book—bear her signature tone and style: restrained, ironic, witty inflections; an understated scrutiny that refuses easy compromise; a Beat weariness of inflated claims that is still open to possibilities of redemption and relief. Her observant, lucid prose shows that Johnson, recalling the maxim of her model, Henry James, is a writer on whom nothing has been lost; aloof acuity is her Beat style.

Born Joyce Glassman in New York City, she left Barnard College in 1954 one course short of graduation, found a job in publishing, and began to focus on becoming a novelist. She earned a book contract in her early twenties—before becoming involved with Jack Kerouac in 1957—and, as Joyce Glassman, published her first novel, *Come and Join the Dance*, in 1962. Johnson's second novel was published in 1978 after a hiatus from writing during which she was widowed, remarried, had a child, and began her publishing career as an editor at such houses as William Morrow, Dial, Atlantic Monthly, and McGraw-Hill. Johnson writes regularly for magazines and newspapers and continues to produce her own books; the most recent, *Missing Men* (2004), is a memoir of her life before and after the Beat generation heyday.

Her novels, and especially her hipster protagonists, reconfigure dominant Beat themes and, through depictions of women's sexual self-determination, challenge sexist constructions of female inferiority and marginality. Johnson's

Come and Join the Dance, the first Beat novel by and about a woman, insists that women of the fifties had deeper ambitions that the M-R-S degree. It fills in Beat generation narratives with hipster women's existential and personal ethics, aesthetics, beliefs, and conduct. *Bad Connections* (1978) portrays the turmoil of its white middle-class protagonist as she struggles to maintain a home for her child and participate in the liberation movements of the 1960s. *In the Night Café* (1989) returns to Beat themes and venues through a young female protagonist who is married to a destructive and talented abstract painter in the fifties. These three novels form a trilogy about hipster New York that offsets the Beat men's well-known tales by representing women in the movement.

In a similar vein, *Minor Characters* recounts Beat history through women who were Johnson's close friends, colleagues, and fellow writers, including the self-destructive poet Elise Cowen; Edie Parker, Kerouac's first wife; Joan Vollmer Adams Burroughs, murdered by William S. Burroughs in 1951; the sculptor Mary Frank; and late-blooming poet Hettie Jones. Johnson tells of these bohemian women's struggles to write and to be recognized, raise children, produce art, and survive in the subsistence economies and downward mobility of Beat culture. Johnson's remarkable 1957–1958 correspondence with Kerouac, published in *Door Wide Open* (2000), testifies to the real-life trials of women's exclusion from full social and political life and, through the art of the letter, evinces the wellsprings of the trademark Beat confessionalism that informs all her work.

Ronna C. Johnson
Tufts University

PRIMARY WORKS

Come and Join the Dance, 1962; *Bad Connections*, 1978; *Minor Characters*, 1983; *In the Night Café*, 1989; *What Lisa Knew: The Truth and Lies of the Steinberg Case*, 1991; *Door Wide Open*, 2000; *Missing Men*, 2004.

from **Door Wide Open**

July 26, 1957

Dear Jack,

Yes, yes I will come to Mexico!

I wish you hadn't been afraid to write me. I know you have to do what you have to do, and that isn't being a bum—don't put yourself down like that. Elise wrote me that you'd left, but her letter was so vague that it sounded as though you were in some terrible trouble and had decided to disappear, and I've spent a sad week, wanting so much to write you not to disappear and not know where to write—so that it was just too much to get your letter. I walked out of the hotel with it in my hand, ordered on enormous breakfast that I couldn't eat, and *flew* downtown in the IRT, which I think I imagined as somehow bound for Mexico that minute. Yes, and I bought a learning-Spanish-phonetically-thru-pictures type book and can already say Yo soy muchacha, a sentence which I am sure will come in very handy eventually. I wish it were September.

It worries me, Jack, to think of you with $33 to your name while Viking's machinery works out a way of feeding you. And I've really got all this money—so would you like some in the meanwhile? Let me know, and I'll send you a money order or whatever.

I got a review copy of ON THE ROAD, read it, and think it's a great, beautiful book. I think you write with the same power and freedom that Dean Moriarty drives a car. Well, it's terrific, and very moving and affirmative. Don't know why, but it made me remember Mark Twain. Ed Stringham has read it too and thinks it "one of the best books since World War II" and is going to write you a long letter and tell you all this, much more coherently than I can.

Saw [Sheila] off to Europe Wednesday on a little white ship not much bigger than a ferry boat, full of waving singing young kids. Everybody smiling and throwing streamers, [Sheila] too, but I didn't know how she felt. It's funny the way you and Allen and Peter came to town this winter and shook us all up. Just think—we had been here all our lives, and now suddenly Elise is in Frisco, [Sheila] in Paris, and I'm going to Mexico—most peculiar. I feel rather friendless in New York at present, miss talking to Elise a lot, especially. She called me collect from San Francisco this week because she needed money and we tried to talk but couldn't hear each other and kept screaming "Wh-a-a-t? Wh-a-a-t." But then I remember walking with you at night through the Brooklyn docks and seeing the white steam rising from the ships against the black sky and how beautiful it was and I'd never seen it before—imagine!—but if I'd walked through it with anyone else, I wouldn't have seen it either, because I wouldn't have felt safe in what my mother would categorically call "a bad neighborhood," I would have been thinking "Where's the subway?" and missed everything. But with you—I felt as though nothing could touch me, and if anything happened, the Hell with it. You don't know what narrow lives girls have, how few real adventures there are for them; misadventures, yes, like abortions and little men following them in subways, but seldom anything like seeing ships at night. So that's why we've all taken off like this, and that's also part of why I love you.

Take care.

Love,
Joyce

P.S. When you write next maybe you could say something about the Mexican climate, whether it ever gets cold, so I'll know what to bring with me. As you've probably gathered by now, I'm incredibly vague about geography.

from **Minor Characters**

In a "dream letter" from John Clellon Holmes recorded by Allen Ginsberg in 1954 are the words: "The social organization which is most true of itself to the artist is the boy gang." To which Allen, awakening, writing into his journal, added sternly, "Not society's perfum'd marriage."

The messages of the real Holmes seem to have remained consistent with those of the dream one. Even in 1977, after years of a stable and sustaining second marriage, after all the messages of Women's Liberation that so battered the consciousness of the seventies, Holmes wrote in his preface to a new edition of *Go*: "Did we really resemble these feverish young men, these centerless young women, awkwardly reaching out for love, for hope, for comprehension of their lives and times?" And whereas he scrupulously matches each of the male characters in his roman à clef to their originals, the "girls" are variously "amalgams of several people"; "accurate to the young women of the time"; "a type rather than an individual." He can't quite remember them—they were mere anonymous passengers on the big Greyhound bus of experience. Lacking centers, how could they burn with the fever that infected his young men? What they did, I guess, was fill up the seats.

It's a crisp September morning, the beginning of yet another academic year. The grey-haired, craggy-faced, perhaps self-consciously Lincolnesque professor enters the small classroom where his girl students await him. There's a proper hush as he takes his place behind the oak table, circa 1910, lays out his sharpened pencils, his roll book containing their names, his two slim volumes of something or other—must be the latest in criticism. Intimidated in advance, the girl students study this man's glamorously American Gothic features, looking for signs of humor or mercy. Can he be gotten around? They will be judged by this Professor X, the big fish in the rather smallish pond that is the Barnard English Department.

Picture this middle-aged man, who no doubt wishes he were standing before a class at Harvard—*that* would count for something. There will be few compensations for the spirit here, much less the eye, in teaching this new frumpy lot of young females—rumpled, pasty girls who've dived into the laundry bag for something to wear to class. Only one slouching beauty with a tangle of auburn hair and a glory of freckles, as well as—perhaps he notices immediately—extraordinary knees, can possibly redeem this semester for him.

He wrenches his gaze away from her and begins. Ha! Let's try this question on 'em, he thinks. He rises to his full six feet, the more to heighten the little drama of this opening moment.

"Well"—his tone is as dry as the crackers in the American cultural barrel—"how many of you girls want to be writers?"

He watches with sardonic amusement as one hand flies up confusedly, then another, till all fifteen are flapping. Here and there an engagement ring sparkles.

The air is thick with the uneasiness of the girl students. Why is Professor X asking this? He knows his course is required of all creative-writing majors.

"Well, I'm sorry to see this," says Professor X, the Melville and Hawthorne expert. "Very sorry. Because"—there's a steel glint in his cold eye—"first of all, if you were going to be writers, you wouldn't be enrolled in this class. You couldn't even be enrolled in school. You'd be hopping freight trains, riding through America."

The received wisdom of 1953.

The young would-be writers in this room have understood instantly that of course there is no hope. One by one their hands have all come down.

I was one of those who'd raised hers.

The social organization which is most true of itself to the artist is the girl gang.

Why, everyone would agree, that's absolutely absurd! ...

...

I moved out of 116th Street on Independence Day, 1955—a date I'd chosen not for its symbolism but because it was the first day of a long weekend. I'd taken a tiny maid's room in an apartment on Amsterdam Avenue five blocks away, to which I planned to move all my things, going back and forth with my mother's shopping cart.

I got up early that morning and started putting books into shopping bags. When I thought my parents would be awake, I walked into their room. They were dozing in their twin beds, an oscillating fan whirring between them. I said, "I have something to tell you. I'm moving out today." I felt sick to my stomach, as if I had murdered these two mild people. I could see their blood on the beige summer covers.

Two weeks earlier I'd found the room. With the first paychecks from my new job, I'd bought an unpainted rocking chair, a small desk, two sheets, and a poster of Picasso's *Blue Boy*—the furnishings of my first freedom. I knew children did not own furniture.

All this had been accomplished in secret, like the arrangements for a coup d'état. I wouldn't speak until it was time to leave. There was nothing to discuss. I was terribly afraid of being talked out of it.

"I need to borrow the cart," I said to my mother, "for my clothes and books."

"Don't think—" she said. "Don't think you can just come around here for dinner any time you want."

All day long I dragged the cart back and forth over the hot red brick sidewalks of the Columbia campus. No one shouted. No one stood at the door on 116th Street and tried to bar my way. In the stillness of their house, my parents moved slowly around the rooms as if injured.

I was done by evening. On my way out for the last time, I wrote my address on a piece of paper and left it on the kitchen table. From my new apartment, I called Elise and Sheila, who were sharing a place in Yorkville. "I really did it, I guess," I said.

Everyone knew in the 1950s why a girl from a nice family left home. The meaning of her theft of herself from her parents was clear to all—as well as what she'd be up to in that room of her own.

On 116th Street the superintendent knew it. He'd seen my comings and goings with the cart. He spread the word among the neighbors that the

Glassmans' daughter was "bad." His imagination rendered me pregnant. He wrote my parents a note to that effect. My mother called and, weeping over the phone, asked if this was true.

The crime of sex was like guilt by association—not visible to the eye of the outsider, but an act that could be rather easily conjectured. Consequences would make it manifest.

I, too, knew why I'd left—better than anyone. It was to be with Alex. He was the concrete embodiment of my more abstract desire to be "free." By which I meant—if I'd been pressed to admit it—sexually free. The desire for this kind of freedom subsumed every other. For this I was prepared to make my way in the world at the age of nineteen, incurring all the risks of waifdom on fifty dollars a week. In fact, fifty dollars seemed a lot to me, since I'd never had more than ten dollars in my pocket all at once. I opened a charge account at Lord and Taylor....

My boss, Naomi Burton, who'd hired me despite my lack of a B.A., took an interest in me. I was talented, she told me. I could become a literary agent myself if I worked for her for a few more years. She persuaded me to show her a story I'd written at Barnard and published in the college literary magazine. "You're a writer," she said. "You should try your hand at a novel." She rang up a friend of hers, an editor named Hiram Haydn who ran a famous novel workshop at the New School for Social Research, and asked him to let me into the course.

It was thrilling but terrifying—as if I were really in danger of fulfilling the destiny my mother had wanted for me, which I had gone to such lengths to avoid. It seemed to be happening to a person outside the person I really was. I'd hidden from my mother's eyes the story Naomi Burton was sending Hiram Haydn—a story I'd written over and over again in various forms ever since my high-school days—about a thirteen-year-old girl whose mother confides in her one day her bitter disappointment with her marriage.

1983

GARY SNYDER
B. 1930

Gary Snyder has said that his work "has been driven by the insight that all is connected and interdependent—nature, societies; rocks, stars." Growing up on a small farm north of Seattle, Washington, he was devoted to hiking and camping. At Reed College he wrote poetry, majored in literature and anthropology, read Chinese and Indian Buddhist philosophy, and prepared a thesis on a Native American myth of the Northwest Coast. After studying linguistics and anthropology for a term at Indiana University, he broke off his academic career—

ending also the marriage with Alison Gass that had begun at Reed—and went to San Francisco. He spent two summers as a forest fire lookout—at Crater Mountain and Sourdough Mountain—and then entered the University of California in 1953 as a student of Oriental languages, preparing himself to go to Asia.

The American West and ancient China came together in his translations from "Cold Mountain," by the Zen hermit Han Shan. In 1955, having met Kenneth Rexroth, Jack Kerouac, and Allen Ginsberg, he took part in the poetry reading at the Six Gallery that launched the "San Francisco Renaissance." A lively if rather superficial portrait of him, as Japhy Ryder, is central to Kerouac's novel *The Dharma Bums*.

In 1956 Snyder went to Japan, where he learned Japanese and studied Zen Buddhism with Miura Isshu. Over the next twelve years he spent much time there, continuing his studies with Oda Sesso. He also spent brief interludes working in a ship's engine room, traveling through India with Ginsberg and Peter Orlovsky, teaching at Berkeley, and reading his poetry on American college campuses. From 1960 to 1965, he was married to Joanne Kyger. In 1967, while living at Banyan Ashram on Suwa-No-Se Island off the coast of Kyushu, Japan, he married Masa Uehara. After their son Kai was born the following year, the family came to the United States, where a second son, Gen, was born in 1969. In 1971 Snyder built a home (Kitkitdizze) in the foothills of the Sierra Nevada in California, where the family lived together for many years. In 1988 Snyder and Masa Uehara separated, and he was joined at Kitkitdizze by Carole Korda, whom he married in 1991.

During the last two decades—in poetry, prose, political action, and personal example—Snyder has been an advocate for ecological awareness. With *Earth House Hold* and *Turtle Island* (awarded the Pulitzer Prize for Poetry in 1975) his vision of cosmic interdependence or community assumed forceful and comprehensive literary form. Since 1985 he has been teaching at the University of California at Davis.

Snyder's poetry recovers values important to Thoreau and Whitman but does so in ways that have been influenced by the darker perspective of Robinson Jeffers; the pansexuality of D. H. Lawrence; the imagist discipline of Ezra Pound and William Carlos Williams; related disciplines in Japanese and Chinese poetry; the structural use of myth in the long poem, from Eliot's *The Waste Land* to Williams's *Paterson* and Olson's *The Maximus Poems*; the sound shaping and shamanism in oral poetry; and the analytical insights of psychology, anthropology, and biology. All this is grounded in the serious practice of Zen. The poetics of *Riprap* is a craft of placing verbal details to make a path for the attention. That of the early *Myths & Texts* and of *Mountains and Rivers without End*—a text composed over a forty-year period—involves the counterpointing of personal experience, meditation, exploration of myth, and song. In *Regarding Wave*, his attention turned more sharply to words—their sounds, etymologies, proliferating meanings—as offering a field of generative energies like those that shape the cosmos itself. With urgency and detachment, seriousness and humor, Snyder continues as poet and essayist to explore the primal activities through which we participate in the "Great Family" whose habitation is Mind.

Thomas R. Whitaker
Yale University

PRIMARY WORKS

Riprap, 1959; *Myths & Texts*, 1960; *Riprap, and Cold Mountain Poems*, 1965; *A Range of Poems*, 1966; *The Back Country*, 1968; *Earth House Hold: Technical Notes & Queries to Fellow Dharma Revolutionaries*, 1969; *Regarding Wave*, 1969, 1970; *Turtle Island*, 1974; *The Old Ways: Six Essays*, 1977; *Axe Handles*, 1983; *Passage through India*, 1984; *Left Out in the Rain: New Poems 1947–1985*, 1986; *The Practice of the Wild: Essays*, 1990; *No Nature: New and Selected Poems*, 1992; *A Place in Space: Ethics, Aesthetics, and Watersheds: New and Selected Prose*, 1995; *Mountains and Rivers without End*, 1996; *The Gary Snyder Reader: Prose, Poetry, and Translations, 1952–1998*, 1999; *Look Out: A Selection of New Writings*, 2002; *Danger on Peaks*, 2005; *Back on the Fire: Essays*, 2007; *Tamalpais Walking* (with Tom Killion), 2009.

from **Riprap**[1]

Lay down these words
Before your mind like rocks.
          placed solid, by hands
In choice of place, set
Before the body of the mind   5
          in space and time:
Solidity of bark, leaf, or wall
          riprap of things:
Cobble of milky way,
          straying planets,   10
These poems, people,
          lost ponies with
Dragging saddles—
          and rocky sure-foot trails.
The worlds like an endless   15
          four-dimensional
Game of *Go*.[2]
          ants and pebbles
In the thin loam, each rock a word
          a creek-washed stone   20
Granite: ingrained
          with torment of fire and weight
Crystal and sediment linked hot
          all change, in thoughts,
As well as things.   25

          1959

---

[1] Snyder's own annotation: "a cobble of stone laid on steep slick rock to make a trail for horses in the mountains."

[2] A Japanese game played with black and white stones on a board marked with nineteen vertical and nineteen horizontal lines to make 361 intersections.

Vapor Trails

Twin streaks twice higher than cumulus,
Precise plane icetracks in the vertical blue
Cloud-flaked light-shot shadow-arcing
Field of all future war, edging off to space.

Young expert U.S. pilots waiting   5
The day of criss-cross rockets
And white blossoming smoke of bomb,
The air world torn and staggered for these
Specks of brushy land and ant-hill towns—

I stumble on the cobble rockpath,   10
Passing through temples,
Watching for two-leaf pine
—spotting that design.
    in Daitoku-ji[1]

                                             1951

Wave

Grooving clam shell,
        streakt through marble,
    sweeping down ponderosa pine bark-scale
      rip-cut tree grain
          sand-dunes, lava   5
            flow
Wave   wife.
      woman—wyfman[1']—
"veiled; vibrating; vague"
sawtooth ranges pulsing;   10
    veins on the back of the hand.

Forkt out; birdsfoot-alluvium
    wash

      great dunes rolling
Each inch rippld, every grain a wave.   15

Leaning against sand cornices til they blow away

[1] The Japanese site of the poem's experience.
[1'] Anglo-Saxon: "female human being," an
early form of "woman."

<pre>
        —wind, shake
        still thorns of cholla, ocotillo
        sometimes I get stuck in thickets—
Ah, trembling spreading radiating wyf   20
            racing zebra
        catch me and fling me wide
To the dancing grain of things
                    of my mind!
</pre>

1969

It Was When

<pre>
We harked up the path in the dark
        to the bamboo house
            green strokes down my back
            arms over your doubled hips
    under cow-breath thatch   5
        bent   cool
                    breasts brush my chest
—and Naga walked in with a candle,
        "I'm sleepy"
Or jungle ridge by a snag—   10
        banyan canyon—a Temminck's Robin
            whirled down the waterfall gorge
in zazen,[1] a poncho spread out on the stones.
            below us the overturning
                silvery   15
            brush-bamboo slopes—
rainsqualls came up on us naked
            brown nipples in needles of ocean-
                cloud
                    rain.   20

    Or the night in the farmhouse
        with Franco on one side, or Pon
    Miko's head against me, I swung you
            around and came into you
    careless and joyous,   25
            late
        when Antares[2] had set

    Or out on the boulders
        south beach at noon
</pre>

[1]The practice in Zen Buddhism of sitting cross-legged in sustained contemplation.   [2]A bright red star in the constellation Scorpio.

        rockt by surf   30
burnd under by stone
burnd over by sun
            saltwater caked
   skin   swing
        hips on my eyes   35
            burn   between;

That we caught: sprout
      took grip in your womb and it held.
      new power in your breath called its place.
      blood of the moon   stoppt;   40
      you pickt your steps well.
   Waves
      and the
            prevalent easterly
                breeze.   45
            whispering into you,
                through us,
                    the grace.

                                                1969

■   ALBERT SAIJO   ■
                     1926–2011

Albert Saijo is best known to readers by a different name. In *Big Sur* (1962), Jack Kerouac refers to his friend George Baso as a "Zen master," one whose "answers come like an old man's." As the inspiration for the fictional Baso, Saijo often served as the racially visible alternative that the Beats sought throughout the 1950s and 1960s in, among many things, Zen Buddhism. He is sprinkled in many of the Beats' longer meditations on their physical and psychic journeys, and Saijo's name emerges from shadow occasionally in letters from major figures of the Beat movement. But even as he seemed to embody for his fellow Beats the ambivalent status of what Jane Iwamura calls the "Oriental Monk," Saijo maintained a relative literary silence during the movement's heyday. Nevertheless, he played a pivotal role in the Beat movement, and his reflective and sometimes critical poetic vision was informed, but not subsumed, by the machinations of Beat culture.

   Born in the United States to a minister father and schoolteacher mother, the young Saijo grew up near Los Angeles. Like other Japanese Americans living on the West Coast, Saijo was interned early in World War II. His family was removed to the Heart Mountain Relocation Center in northern Wyoming, where he completed high school and was immediately drafted into the U.S. Army. As a member of the famed and later celebrated all-Nisei 442nd Regimental Combat Unit, Saijo participated in missions in Italy and France until the end of the war in Europe. He returned to the United States and eventually to Los Angeles, where he began to study Zen Buddhism and earned a degree from the University of Southern California.

In the 1950s, Saijo moved to the San Francisco Bay area, where he met Beat poets and Zen practitioners. As Kerouac, Gary Snyder, and Lew Welch deepened their interest in Zen Buddhism, they often turned to Saijo's expertise. Saijo helped Snyder establish Marin-An, a meditation hall or floating *zendo*, in 1958 and lived with fellow Beats Welch and Phillip Walen at Hyphen House in San Francisco. Saijo traveled with Kerouac and Welch on a cross-country road trip that later was chronicled in the collectively assembled *Trip Trap* (1973), an extended haiku about the three men's experiences between San Francisco and New York. Saijo also spent time in the High Sierras, an experience that formed the basis of his first book, *The Backpacker* (1972). A primer on the West Coast wilderness, *The Backpacker* is by turns a practical guide to surviving in the wild and a meditation on the visionary possibilities of escaping the stultifying environment of industrialized society.

In his seventies, Saijo published his first book of poetry, *Outspeaks: A Rhapsody* (1997), which he describes as a kind of "slanguage." Printed entirely in capital letters, Saijo's style is jarring, perhaps revealing the exuberant, even explosive, possibilities of language and culture that simmer below the surface of someone considered a Zen master by his former associates. His poetics of shock (which should not be misconstrued as expressions of utter autonomy) leads him at one point to sit "ON THE FLOOR CUZ CHAIRS SEEMED A FORM OF REPRESSION." In other moments, Saijo turns himself into the Bodhisattva, a figure on the brink of achieving the state of nirvana, or ascending to the level of Buddha, but who remains in human form. A fitting, perhaps wistful (and grumpy), recasting of his role as Zen master to the more famous Beats might well be that of helping others, over and over, off a sinking ship. And that may be his legacy.

James Kyung-Jin Lee
University of California, Santa Barbara

PRIMARY WORKS

The Backpacker, 1972; *Trip, Trap* (with Jack Kerouac and Lew Welch), 1973; *Outspeaks: A Rhapsody*, 1997.

Bodhisattva Vows

BODHISATTVA VOWS TO BE THE LAST ONE OFF THE SINKING SHIP—
YOU SIGN UP & FIND OUT IT'S FOREVER—PASSENGER LIST END-
LESS—SHIP NEVER EMPTIES—SHIP KEEPS SINKING BUT DOESN'T GO
QUITE UNDER—ON BOARD ANGST PANIC & DESPERATION HOLD
SWAY—TURNS OUT BODHISATTVAHOOD IS A FUCKING JOB LIKE ANY

OTHER BUT DIFFERENT IN THAT THERE'S NO WEEKENDS HOLIDAYS
VACATIONS NO GOLDEN YEARS OF RETIREMENT—YOU'RE SPENDING
ALL YOUR TIME & ENERGY GETTING OTHER PEOPLE OFF THE SINK-
ING SHIP INTO LIFEBOATS BOUND GAILY FOR NIRVANA WHILE THERE
YOU ARE SINKING—& OF COURSE YOU HAD TO GO & GIVE YOUR LIFE-
JACKET AWAY—SO NOW LET US BE CHEERFUL AS WE SINK—OUR SPI-
RIT EVER BUOYANT AS WE SINK

1972

from Trip Trap (with Lew Welch and Jack Kerouac)

Lew's Haiku

I turned into
    a gas station
—The engine stopped

In the desert
    sun, a yellow   5
Caboose

1973

Albert

Seems like stealing
    candy
from a baby,
    this road

The new moon   5
    is
the toenail of God

1973

Albert

It's us humans
    give things
Back and front

1973

Jack & Lew

Mormons who had
narrow little wagons
      have left us
    very wide streets

and
      temples
          with
            no
              nails   5

                                                  1973

Lew

I always take
      more keen,
I cook it in a rifle
      and shoot myself

                                                  1973

Albert
Fucking with the Muse in Texas

The country is blond
      and flat.
For fifty miles
couldn't think
of anything but that whore   5
in Chicago and the tub
            of oysters

                                                  1973

from **The Backpacker**

Backpacking into wilderness is a change, and a vivid change at that. It is a nearly total separation from the normal context of your life. The supportive context. The context within which you know who you are. This is my home. This is my family. This is my job. This is the newspaper I read. These are the things I like and dislike. Suddenly you are not home but in the middle of wilderness. The first reaction is generally one of exhilaration, even euphoria. If this is your first trip, you may also feel some uncertainty, since you don't know what to expect. Then there's that heavy pack and that rough walking. It's no joke. It's strenuous. It can be toilsome and irritating.

Should you have taken this trail? Does your friend and guide—say this is your first trip—know what he's doing? You're beginning to feel the altitude. Your head feels like your skull is too small. Isn't the pace a little fast? There must be an easier trail. The heel of one foot is starting to get sore and you realize that you haven't broken in your boots enough. Stop. A blister already. The trail begins to ascend. Are you really expected to climb that wall? Your pack seems to be getting heavier. You feel like a beast of burden. And it's hot besides. The mosquitoes gather to you like cows to a feeding trough.

You begin to yearn for the familiar context of who you know yourself to be. What are you doing out here anyhow?

This negative chain of thought might be avoided if you were to start out with a different attitude. Perhaps the trip could be thought of as a pilgrimage. Like the pilgrimage to the Virgin of Guadalupe where the pilgrims make their way on their knees, or by one full-length prostration after another. Like the pilgrimage of Harding and Caldwell up the Wall of the Early Morning Light in Yosemite. Or like the pilgrimage of Lama Govinda to Kailasa. Well, is wilderness a shrine? And is backpacking a form of devotion?

As you descend a trail and look at the faces of the people coming up, you get the feeling that you are all involved in some mystery or vaster allegory, in which you are all devotees of a space. A space not even outside, perhaps. What you might be doing is a pilgrimage to a more authentic outback inside yourself. But is there an inside and an outside? And you thought you were just backpacking?

Don't let yourself get bogged down in a negative space. When you're doing a tough stretch, you need to boost your body with a certain psychic drive. Do your mantra, if you have a mantra. Take a rosary and say it as you walk. If you have a koan, work on it. Isn't walking a form of meditation?

Say you're climbing a pass and find it rough going. You're thinking of how far you've come and of the thousand feet you still have to go. Take it a step at a time. As a psychic booster, you might think of each step as bringing you one step closer to the time and place of your death. Not in a morbid sense, but in the sense that your life is a journey from one place to another place, and that this wilderness trip is a short segment of that journey, a thing you have to do, a place you have to come to in order to reach the next place. You can't hold back. You've got to go on. If you weren't supposed to be in wilderness, you wouldn't be there. It is a step-by-step revelation of your fate. Let each step be whole, conscious and clear. Keep your head wide open. You get to the top of the pass, or top of the mountain—so where are you?

Here is that cirque with lake. You made it. Now to find your spot and set out your camp.

1972

THE 1960s: POSTMODERNISM AND OTHER VIOLENT CHANGES

No one can agree on the number of hippies who attended a massive concert in a field at Bethel, New York, in August 1969, but Joni Mitchell's song "Woodstock" estimates "half a million strong," and most estimates are not far from that number. Seen by many as the most harmonious gathering of a crowd that size in history, Woodstock (as the festival has come to be known) remains a fascinating event, preserved in a lengthy documentary film, of an era when hair was long, nudity was encouraged, marijuana was abundant, music was full of youthful exuberance, and a generation seemed united behind one goal: peace. The concert became free when organizers realized there was no way to stem the tide of the surging crowd. Rock music and its variants constituted a nearly unprecedented cultural force.

Another free concert staged just over two months later by the Rolling Stones at Altamont Speedway in San Francisco has come to represent a darker, more sinister vision of the late 1960s. There, under the dubious crowd control tactics of the motorcycle gang known as Hell's Angels, violence erupted, and a man brandishing a gun was stabbed just in front of the stage by one of the motorcyclists. Despite the ripples of exuberance emanating from Woodstock, Altamont reminded Americans that there had been much violence throughout this decade: the assassinations of Martin Luther King, Malcolm X, and John and Robert Kennedy; the murder spree led by California cult leader Charles Manson; race riots in cities such as Los Angeles, Newark, and Chicago; and, of course, the ongoing American military involvement in Vietnam. The insistence on peace at Woodstock was either an anomaly or an emphatic reaction to the predominant tone of the rest of the decade. Altamont was probably closer to the prevailing mood of chaos and violence.

The word *revolution* was in the air throughout the 1960s. In terms of literature, the revolution took several forms: aesthetic, political, and topical. The second half of the decade saw the experimental literature of the late 1950s—the Beats, Black Mountain College, the European-inspired Theater of the Absurd—develop into a series of even more iconoclastic experiments. But the first half was a little tamer, marked by a turn inward before cultural and political events catalyzed a turn outward.

A significant and lasting school of poetry that developed in the early 1960s was known as confessional poetry. Its leading figure was Robert Lowell, an influential poet who had written in a more traditional modernist style through the early 1950s. In 1960, with the publication of his *Life Studies*, Lowell paved the way for a generation of poets to follow. Confessional poetry focuses on subjective experience, often connected to a perceived broader social ill. The "I" of the poem is central—not as a mask or persona, as it had been in modern poetry, but as a subject for deep scrutiny. In this sense, confessional poetry parallels

Beat poetry, which flourished at the same time and which also renders personal experience in writing, but the confessional style is more influenced by classical poetic forms than by the jazz rhythms and spontaneity that dictate the form of Beat poetry. Confessional poetry tends to privilege extreme emotional states or psychological ruin. Its speakers tend toward neurosis. Sylvia Plath and Anne Sexton, both students of Lowell at Boston University, wrote in the confessional mode, and both committed suicide. All three poets are represented early in this section, and their influence on later poets is profound.

The confessional mode of writing tends to showcase middle-class domestic voices, but as the events of the decade became increasingly violent, beginning with the assassination of President Kennedy in 1963, American writers became acutely sensitive to their rapidly changing nation. Many of the writers we call "postmodern" reflect this chaos in their work. There is little agreement on the definition of "postmodernism," though its chief practitioners have a few clear traits in common. The works of Kurt Vonnegut, John Barth, Donald Barthelme, Thomas Pynchon, Ishmael Reed, John Ashbery, and Don DeLillo, all represented in this volume, are classic examples of postmodern fiction and poetry. These writers accepted randomness and chaos as principles of our contemporary life, and therefore of the literature that reflects it. Critics have used chaos theory and systems theory to analyze the fiction of Barthelme, Pynchon, and DeLillo, all of whom are preoccupied with the tendency, in the postmodern world, for systems to overwhelm the agency of individuals. Reed and Barth are perhaps less concerned with the world of physics and more concerned with the history of literature and, in Reed's case, with racial discrimination. All five writers, along with many other postmodernists, consistently point to their own fictions as fiction, revealing (often humorously) the inner workings of their stories or novels. Barth's story "Lost in the Funhouse," included in this section, is one of the best-known examples of this postmodern self-reflexiveness and self-consciousness. There is also a dark strain of human insignificance in these works.

The changes in style and taste of 1960s literature are evident in the works we have selected by African American writers. The transition from the confessional/modernist poems of Robert Hayden to the politically charged verse of Amiri Baraka is dramatic. Baraka was a particularly influential figure in the Black Arts Movement of the late-1960s that sought to express the political aims of radical Black activism in art. The inclusion of works by the decade's most prominent Black leaders, Martin Luther King and Malcolm X, reveals the increasing confluence of the literary and the social during the 1960s, and the fiction of Ernest J. Gaines and a number of works by African American writers in the 1970s demonstrate the changes in sensibility that occurred during this period.

The "In Focus" section on the Vietnam War and its aftermath not only demonstrates the increased politicization of poetry and prose but also indicates a genre development. The so-called new journalism of the late 1960s was a hybrid of nonfiction and fiction advanced by such figures as Joan Didion, Tom Wolfe, Norman Mailer, and Michael Herr; the latter two are represented here. These authors and their cohorts sought to blur the lines between the subjective and the objective by describing real events in fanciful language.

Early in the 1960s, Bob Dylan famously sang, "The Times They Are A-Changin'." Halfway through the decade, having ushered in these changes through his conversion from traditional folk to edgier rock music, Dylan sang to a bewildered everyman persona, "something is happening here/But you don't know what it is/Do you, Mr. Jones?" The changes of the decade were so dramatic and so unpredictable that Mr. Jones's lack of comprehension was widespread. After the assassinations, riots, war, and various cultural revolutions, the American mood by the end of the decade was a mixture of excitement and fear. After the grand display of peace at Woodstock and deterioration into violence at Altamont, Americans barely had time to ask, "What was that?" before turning to the question of what would happen next.

ROBERT LOWELL, JR.
1917–1977

Born to Charlotte Winslow and Robert Traill Spence Lowell in Boston, Robert Lowell was the great-grandnephew of James Russell Lowell and a distant cousin of Amy Lowell. He attended St. Marks School and then Harvard (1935–1937) but completed his undergraduate education at Kenyon College in Ohio, receiving his degree *summa cum laude* in 1940. An avid student of poetry, he chose his friends from an artistic coterie and in 1940 married fiction writer Jean Stafford. During World War II, Lowell declared himself a conscientious objector and was imprisoned in 1943–1944. In 1947 he received a Guggenheim Fellowship and the Pulitzer Prize for Poetry (for *Lord Weary's Castle*). He also was chosen Consultant in Poetry for the Library of Congress for 1947–1948. In 1948 he and Stafford were divorced, and in 1949 he married critic Elizabeth Hardwick.

Lowell's life was devoted to poetry—writing and teaching—but it was marred by emotional breakdowns that required hospitalization. His periodic instability made relationships troublesome; he tended to find his greatest solace in friendships with other writers, including Delmore Schwartz, John Berryman, Randall Jarrell, Elizabeth Bishop, William Carlos Williams, Anne Sexton, and the countless younger writers who studied with him at Boston University, Harvard, and the University of Iowa. His writing charted his cycles of change: from the rebellion of the elite Brahmin to the immersion in art experienced at Kenyon, where Lowell studied with John Crowe Ransom and developed his penchant for allusive, densely referential poetry. In 1940 he became a Catholic; in 1950 he left the church.

After giving a series of readings on the West Coast in 1957, Lowell became dissatisfied with his tightly structured poems and began the process of self-exploration that led to his masterful autobiographical work, *Life Studies* and *For the Union Dead*. The latter drew together the autobiographical and Lowell's fascination with history, and the two works marked the apex of Lowell's influence on the poetry scene. He also moved to New York, where he became politically active, marching against the Pentagon in 1967 and continuing to scrutinize his life against the canvas of world and national events.

In the early 1970s, Lowell and Hardwick divorced and Lowell married Lady Caroline Blackwood. He then divided his life between her home in England and periods of teaching at Harvard, a pattern that allowed him to explore the consequences of his New England roots and his need to cut himself off from that locale. When he died of a heart attack at age sixty, he was considered the most important and most influential poet of his generation.

Some critics reacted harshly to his last poetry, in which his divorce from Hardwick and separation from their child became the subject of his art. There is a limit to a reader's interest in seeing self-destruction portrayed in poetry. Like many of his peers, Lowell led a life of difficult and often broken human relationships, and the poems that chart those relationships are often less than great.

Linda Wagner-Martin
University of North Carolina at Chapel Hill

PRIMARY WORKS

Land of Unlikeness, 1944; *Lord Weary's Castle*, 1946; *The Mills of the Kavanaughs*, 1951; *Life Studies*, 1959; *Imitations*, 1961; *For the Union Dead*, 1964; *The Old Glory* (plays), 1965; *Selected Poems*, 1965; *Near the Ocean*, 1967; *Notebook 1967–68*, 1969; *The Dolphin*, 1973; *History*, 1973; *For Lizzie and Harriet*, 1973; *Selected Poems*, 1976; *Day by Day*, 1977; *The Collected Prose*, 1987.

Skunk Hour
(For Elizabeth Bishop)

Nautilus Island's[1] hermit
heiress still lives through winter in her Spartan cottage;
her sheep still graze above the sea.
Her son's a bishop. Her farmer
is first selectman in our village;   5
she's in her dotage.

Thirsting for
the hierarchic privacy
of Queen Victoria's century,
she buys up all   10
the eyesores facing her shore,
and lets them fall.

[1]In Maine.

The season's ill—
we've lost our summer millionaire,
who seemed to leap from an L.L. Bean[2]   15
catalogue. His nine-knot yawl
was auctioned off to lobstermen.
A red fox stain covers Blue Hill.

And now our fairy
decorator brightens his shop for fall;   20
his fishnet's filled with orange cork,
orange, his cobbler's bench and awl;
there is no money in his work,
he'd rather marry.

One dark night,   25
my Tudor Ford climbed the hill's skull;
I watched for love-cars. Lights turned down,
they lay together, hull to hull,
where the graveyard shelves on the town. . . .
My mind's not right.   30

A car radio bleats,
"Love, O careless Love. . . ." I hear
my ill-spirit sob in each blood cell,
as if my hand were at its throat. . . .
I myself am hell;   35
nobody's here—

only skunks, that search
in the moonlight for a bite to eat.
They march on their soles up Main Street:
white stripes, moonstruck eyes' red fire   40
under the chalk-dry and spar spire
of the Trinitarian Church.

I stand on top
of our back steps and breathe the rich air—
a mother skunk with her column of kittens swills the garbage pail.   45
She jabs her wedge-head in a cup
of sour cream, drops her ostrich tail,
and will not scare.

                                                        1960

---

[2]Freeport, Maine, mail order house.

For Theodore Roethke

1908–1963

All night you wallowed through my sleep,
then in the morning you were lost
in the Maine sky—close, cold and gray,
smoke and smoke-colored cloud.

Sheeplike, unsociable reptilian, two   5
hell-divers splattered squawking on the water,
loons devolving to a monochrome.
You honored nature,

helpless, elemental creature.
The black stump of your hand   10
just touched the waters under the earth,
and left them quickened with your name. . . .

Now, you honor the mother,
Omnipresent,
she made you nonexistent,   15
the ocean's anchor, our high tide.

                                                                    1963

For the Union Dead

"Relinquunt Omnia Servare Rem Publicam."[1]

The old South Boston Aquarium stands
in a Sahara of snow now. Its broken windows are boarded.
The bronze weathervane cod has lost half its scales.
The airy tanks are dry.

Once my nose crawled like a snail on the glass;   5
my hand tingled
to burst the bubbles
drifting from the noses of the cowed, compliant fish.

My hand draws back. I often sigh still
for the dark downward and vegetating kingdom   10
of the fish and reptile. One morning last March,
I pressed against the new barbed and galvanized

---

[1]"They give up all else to serve the republic."

fence on the Boston Common. Behind their cage,
yellow dinosaur steamshovels were grunting
as they cropped up tons of mush and grass   15
to gouge their underworld garage.

Parking spaces luxuriate like civic
sandpiles in the heart of Boston.
A girdle of orange, Puritan-pumpkin colored girders
braces the tingling Statehouse,   20

shaking over the excavations, as it faces Colonel Shaw
and his bell-cheeked Negro infantry
on St. Gaudens' shaking Civil War relief,[2]
propped by a plank splint against the garage's earthquake.

Two months after marching through Boston,   25
half the regiment was dead;
at the dedication,
William James could almost hear the bronze Negroes breathe.

Their monument sticks like a fishbone
in the city's throat.   30
Its Colonel is as lean
as a compass-needle.

He has an angry wrenlike vigilance,
a greyhound's gentle tautness;
he seems to wince at pleasure,   35
and suffocate for privacy.

He is out of bounds now. He rejoices in man's lovely,
peculiar power to choose life and die—
when he leads his black soldiers to death,
he cannot bend his back.   40

On a thousand small town New England greens,
the old white churches hold their air
of sparse, sincere rebellion; frayed flags
quilt the graveyards of the Grand Army of the Republic.

The stone statues of the abstract Union Soldier   45
grow slimmer and younger each year—

[2]On the edge of Boston Common stands a monument honoring Colonel Robert Shaw (1837–1863) and the African American troops of the 54th Massachusetts by the sculptor Augustus Saint-Gaudens (1848–1907). Shaw was killed, with many of his men, in South Carolina on July 18, 1863.

wasp-waisted they doze over muskets
and muse through their sideburns . . .

Shaw's father wanted no monument
except the ditch,   50
where his son's body was thrown
and lost with his "niggers."

The ditch is nearer.
There are no statues for the last war here;
on Boylston Street, a commercial photograph   55
shows Hiroshima boiling

over a Mosler Safe, the "Rock of Ages"
that survived the blast. Space is nearer.
When I crouch to my television set,
the drained faces of Negro school-children rise like balloons.   60

Colonel Shaw
is riding on his bubble,
he waits
for the blessèd break.

The Aquarium is gone. Everywhere,   65
giant finned cars nose forward like fish;
a savage servility
slides by on grease.

                                                                          1960

Near the Ocean

(For E.H.L.)[1]

The house is filled. The last heartthrob
thrills through her flesh. The hero stands,
stunned by the applauding hands,
and lifts her head to please the mob . . .
No, young and starry-eyed, the brother   5
and sister wait before their mother,
old iron-bruises, powder, "Child,
these breasts . . ." He knows. And if she's killed

---

[1]Elizabeth Hardwick Lowell, the poet's former
wife.

his treadmill heart will never rest—
his wet mouth pressed to some slack breast,   10
or shifting over on his back . . .
the severed radiance filters back,
athirst for nightlife—gorgon head,
fished up from the Aegean dead,
with all its stranded snakes uncoiled,   15
here beheaded and despoiled.

We hear the ocean. Older seas
and deserts give asylum, peace
to each abortion and mistake.
Lost in the Near Eastern dreck,   20
the tyrant and tyrannicide
lie like the bridegroom and the bride;
the battering ram, abandoned, prone,
beside the apeman's phallic stone.

Betrayals! Was it the first night?   25
They stood against a black and white
inland New England backdrop. No dogs
there, horse or hunter, only frogs
chirring from the dark trees and swamps.
Elms watching like extinguished lamps.   30
Knee-high hedges of black sheep
encircling them at every step.

Some subway-green coldwater flat,
its walls tattooed with neon light,
then high delirious squalor, food   35
burned down with vodka . . . menstrual blood
caking the covers, when they woke
to the dry, childless Sunday walk,
saw cars on Brooklyn Bridge descend
through steel and coal dust to land's end.   40

Was it years later when they met,
and summer's coarse last-quarter drought
had dried the hardveined elms to bark—
lying like people out of work,
dead sober, cured, recovered, on   45
the downslope of some gritty green,
all access barred with broken glass;
and dehydration browned the grass?

Is it this shore? Their eyes worn white
as moons from hitting bottom? Night,   50
the sandfleas scissoring their feet,
the sandbed cooling to concrete,
one borrowed blanket, lights of cars
shining down at them like stars? . . .
Sand built the lost Atlantis . . . sand,   55
Atlantic ocean, condoms, sand.

Sleep, sleep. The ocean, grinding stones,
can only speak the present tense;
nothing will age, nothing will last,
or take corruption from the past.   60
A hand, your hand then! I'm afraid
to touch the crisp hair on your head—
Monster loved for what you are,
till time, that buries us, lay bare.

1967

Thomas Pynchon
B. 1937

Very few American writers have been accorded, while still alive, the somewhat dubious honor of having their last name turned into an adjective. Even fewer have seen the resulting adjective become a buzzword in highbrow popular culture, associated with everything from film and literature to advertising campaigns, pop music, and underground publications. Thomas Ruggles Pynchon, Jr., entered the collective consciousness of late-twentieth- and early-twenty-first-century American culture largely through the use (and abuse) of the labels "Pynchonian" and "Pynchonesque." These two adjectives, which sprang up after the publication of his mammoth novel *Gravity's Rainbow*, connote extreme intellectualism, an encyclopedic frame of reference, paranoia, spiraling conspiracy theories, reclusiveness, dark humor, or a combination of all these. Perhaps unfairly, these have also been the dominant themes in criticism of Pynchon's work.

Few of Pynchon's biographical details are known. He was born on Long Island in Oyster Bay, New York, on May 8, 1937. His family is descended from the Puritan Pyncheons who provided Nathaniel Hawthorne with material for *The House of the Seven Gables*. After a brief stint in the U.S. Navy, Pynchon attended Cornell University, where he majored in engineering before switching to English; he took classes from Vladimir Nabokov and befriended Richard Fariña, whose 1966 novel *Been Down So Long It Looks like Up to Me* anticipated many of the themes that Pynchon would later treat. Having passed up an opportunity to go to graduate school, he worked as a technical writer for Boeing Aircraft in Seattle from 1960 to 1962. His subsequent public biography consists almost entirely of his publication history.

Pynchon's first novel, *V.*, published in 1963, won the Faulkner First Novel Award. In 1966 *The Crying of Lot 49*, a shorter but no less complex novel, garnered the Rosenthal Memorial Award. *Gravity's Rainbow*, published in 1973, nearly won the Pulitzer Prize until several jurors rejected it on the grounds of "obscenity and obscurity." In 1975 Pynchon was awarded the Howells Medal of the American Academy but turned it down without giving a reason. His literary output for the remainder of the 1970s and '80s was limited to *Slow Learner*, a collection of five short stories ("Entropy" among them) originally published between 1959 and 1964, and a small number of essays and reviews.

It is generally believed that Pynchon lived in Aptos, a small town in northern California, for much of the 1980s, during which he produced his novel *Vineland* (1990) and possibly wrote a series of letters to a small local newspaper using the pseudonym Wanda Tinasky. Since then he has apparently lived in New York City. He is married to his literary agent, Melanie Jackson; they have one son. His most recent novel is *Inherent Vice*, published in 2009.

Whatever the facts of his life may be, Pynchon's small but important body of work—seven novels and a collection of short stories over the course of more than forty years—has had a profound effect on the development of American literature. Many readers have been tempted to categorize Pynchon's individual works as products of a certain place and time, especially *The Crying of Lot 49* and *Vineland*, which are often criticized for being generational pieces "about" California in the 1960s and 1980s, respectively. Examination of his entire body of work, though, leads to an understanding of both the depth of Pynchon's encyclopedic erudition and his wide-ranging cultural satire.

"Entropy" initially appeared in the *Kenyon Review* in the spring of 1960. Pynchon himself evinced considerable disdain for the story in the introduction to *Slow Learner*: "The story is a fine example of a procedural error beginning writers are always cautioned against. It is simply wrong to begin with a theme, symbol or other abstract unifying agent, and then to try to force characters and events to conform to it." Despite this harsh self-criticism, the story represents his first extensive treatment of the concept of entropy in its thermodynamic, informational, and cosmic forms. This theme recurs notably in the "Whole Sick Crew" episodes of *V.* and throughout *The Crying of Lot 49*, most tellingly in the "Maxwell's Demon" portions.

"Entropy" does not have the intricately organized and at times maddeningly allusive structure of *Gravity's Rainbow*, but it is possible to see Pynchon's authorial voice taking shape in this story. The blending of near-farcical comic elements with a dark, even brooding satirical impulse leaves the reader with an ambiguous message, another hallmark of his later works. Critics disagree about whether Pynchon is more sympathetic to Meatball Mulligan, who attempts to make order out of chaos despite the unavoidable force of entropy, or to Callisto, who walls himself off from the outside world and seems to have resigned himself to its "heat-death." One's interpretation largely determines whether the dual endings of the story represent an affirmation of life like that of the Beats (whose works and language Pynchon cites as an early influence) or an acquiescence to the inevitability of death, a theme that existentialist philosophers/novelists such as Albert Camus and Jean-Paul Sartre had popularized during Pynchon's adolescence.

Derek C. Maus
University of North Carolina at Chapel Hill

PRIMARY WORKS

V., 1963; *The Crying of Lot 49,* 1966; *Gravity's Rainbow,* 1973; *Slow Learner,* 1984; *Vineland,* 1990; *Mason & Dixon,* 1997; *Against the Day,* 2006; *Inherent Vice,* 2009.

Entropy

Boris has just given me a summary of his views. He is a weather prophet.
The weather will continue bad, he says. There will be more calamities, more
death, more despair. Not the slightest indication of a change anywhere. . . .
We must get into step, a lockstep toward the prison of death. There is no
escape. The weather will not change.

—Tropic of Cancer

Downstairs, Meatball Mulligan's lease-breaking party was moving into its 40th hour. On the kitchen floor, amid a litter of empty champagne fifths, were Sandor Rojas and three friends, playing spit in the ocean and staying awake on Heidseck and benzedrine pills. In the living room Duke, Vincent, Krinkles and Paco sat crouched over a 15-inch speaker which had been bolted into the top of a wastepaper basket, listening to 27 watts' worth of *The Heroes' Gate at Kiev.* They all wore hornrimmed sunglasses and rapt expressions, and smoked funny-looking cigarettes which contained not, as you might expect, tobacco, but an adulterated form of *cannabis sativa.* This group was the Duke di Angelis quartet. They recorded for a local label called Tambú and had to their credit one 10" LP entitled *Songs of Outer Space.* From time to time one of them would flick the ashes from his cigarette into the speaker cone to watch them dance around. Meatball himself was sleeping over by the window, holding an empty magnum to his chest as if it were a teddy bear. Several government girls, who worked for people like the State Department and NSA, had passed out on couches, chairs and in one case the bathroom sink.

This was in early February of '57 and back then there were a lot of American expatriates around Washington, D.C., who would talk, every time they met you, about how someday they were going to go over to Europe for real but right now it seemed they were working for the government. Everyone saw a fine irony in this. They would stage, for instance, polyglot parties where the newcomer was sort of ignored if he couldn't carry on simultaneous conversations in three or four languages. They would haunt Armenian delicatessens for weeks at a stretch and invite you over for bulghour and lamb in tiny kitchens whose walls were covered with bullfight posters. They would have affairs with sultry girls from Andalucía or the Midi who studied economics at Georgetown. Their Dôme was a collegiate Rathskeller out on Wisconsin Avenue called the Old Heidelberg and they had to settle for cherry blossoms instead of lime trees when spring came, but in its lethargic way their life provided, as they said, kicks.

At the moment, Meatball's party seemed to be gathering its second wind. Outside there was rain. Rain splatted against the tar paper on the roof and was fractured into a fine spray off the noses, eyebrows and lips of wooden gargoyles under the eaves, and ran like drool down the window-panes. The day before, it had snowed and the day before that there had been winds of gale force and before that the sun had made the city glitter bright as April, though the calendar read early February. It is a curious season in Washington, this false spring. Somewhere in it are Lincoln's Birthday and the Chinese New Year, and a forlornness in the streets because cherry blossoms are weeks away still and, as Sarah Vaughan has put it, spring will be a little late this year. Generally crowds like the one which would gather in the Old Heidelberg on weekday afternoons to drink Würtzburger and to sing Lili Marlene (not to mention The Sweetheart of Sigma Chi) are inevitably and incorrigibly Romantic. And as every good Romantic knows, the soul (*spiritus, ruach, pneuma*) is nothing, substantially, but air; it is only natural that warpings in the atmosphere should be recapitulated in those who breathe it. So that over and above the public components—holidays, tourist attractions—there are private meanderings, linked to the climate as if this spell were a *stretto* passage in the year's fugue: haphazard weather, aimless loves, unpredicted commitments: months one can easily spend *in* fugue, because oddly enough, later on, winds, rains, passions of February and March are never remembered in that city, it is as if they had never been.

The last bass notes of *The Heroes' Gate* boomed up through the floor and woke Callisto from an uneasy sleep. The first thing he became aware of was a small bird he had been holding gently between his hands, against his body. He turned his head sidewise on the pillow to smile down at it, at its blue hunched-down head and sick, lidded eyes, wondering how many more nights he would have to give it warmth before it was well again. He had been holding the bird like that for three days: it was the only way he knew to restore its health. Next to him the girl stirred and whimpered, her arm thrown across her face. Mingled with the sounds of the rain came the first tentative, querulous morning voices of the other birds, hidden in philodendrons and small fan palms: patches of scarlet, yellow and blue laced through this Rousseau-like fantasy, this hothouse jungle it had taken him seven years to weave together. Hermetically sealed, it was a tiny enclave of regularity in the city's chaos, alien to the vagaries of the weather, of national politics, of any civil disorder. Through trial-and-error Callisto had perfected its ecological balance, with the help of the girl its artistic harmony, so that the swayings of its plant life, the stirrings of its birds and human inhabitants were all as integral as the rhythms of a perfectly-executed mobile. He and the girl could no longer, of course, be omitted from that sanctuary; they had become necessary to its unity. What they needed from outside was delivered. They did not go out.

"Is he all right," she whispered. She lay like a tawny question mark facing him, her eyes suddenly huge and dark and blinking slowly. Callisto ran a finger beneath the feathers at the base of the bird's neck; caressed it gently. "He's going to be well, I think. See: he hears his friends beginning to wake up." The girl had heard the rain and the birds even before she was fully awake. Her name was Aubade: she was part French and part Annamese, and she lived on her own curious and lonely planet, where the clouds and the odor of poincianas, the bitterness of wine and the accidental fingers at the small of her back or feathery against her breasts came to her reduced inevitably to the terms of sound: of music which emerged at intervals from a howling darkness of discordancy. "Aubade," he said, "go see." Obedient, she arose; padded to the window, pulled aside the drapes and after a moment said: "It is 37. Still 37." Callisto frowned. "Since Tuesday, then," he said. "No change." Henry Adams, three generations before his own, had stared aghast at Power; Callisto found himself now in much the same state over Thermodynamics, the inner life of that power, realizing like his predecessor that the Virgin and the dynamo stand as much for love as for power; that the two are indeed identical; and that love therefore not only makes the world go round but also makes the boccie ball spin, the nebula precess. It was this latter or sidereal element which disturbed him. The cosmologists had predicted an eventual heat-death for the universe (something like Limbo: form and motion abolished, heat-energy identical at every point in it); the meteorologists, day-to-day, staved it off by contradicting with a reassuring array of varied temperatures.

But for three days now, despite the changeful weather, the mercury had stayed at 37 degrees Fahrenheit. Leery at omens of apocalypse, Callisto shifted beneath the covers. His fingers pressed the bird more firmly, as if needing some pulsing or suffering assurance of an early break in the temperature.

It was that last cymbal crash that did it. Meatball was hurled wincing into consciousness as the synchronized wagging of heads over the wastebasket stopped. The final hiss remained for an instant in the room, then melted into the whisper of rain outside. "Aarrgghh," announced Meatball in the silence, looking at the empty magnum. Krinkles, in slow motion, turned, smiled and held out a cigarette. "Tea time, man," he said. "No, no," said Meatball. "How many times I got to tell you guys. Not at my place. You ought to know, Washington is lousy with Feds." Krinkles looked wistful. "Jeez, Meatball," he said, "you don't want to do nothing no more." "Hair of dog," said Meatball. "Only hope. Any juice left?" He began to crawl toward the kitchen. "No champagne, I don't think," Duke said. "Case of tequila behind the icebox." They put on an Earl Bostic side. Meatball paused at the kitchen door, glowering at Sandor Rojas. "Lemons," he said after some thought. He crawled to the refrigerator and got out three lemons and some cubes, found the tequila and set about restoring order to his nervous system. He drew blood once cutting the lemons and had to use two hands squeezing them and his foot to crack the ice tray but after about ten minutes he found himself, through some miracle, beaming down into a monster tequila sour. "That looks yummy," Sandor Rojas said. "How about you make me one." Meatball blinked at him. "*Kitchi lofass a shegitbe,*" he replied automatically, and wandered away into the bathroom. "I say," he called out a moment later to no one in particular. "I say, there seems to be a girl or something sleeping in the sink." He took her by the shoulders and shook. "Wha," she said. "You don't look too comfortable," Meatball said. "Well," she agreed. She stumbled to the shower, turned on the cold water and sat down crosslegged in the spray. "That's better," she smiled.

"Meatball," Sandor Rojas yelled from the kitchen. "Somebody is trying to come in the window. A burglar, I think. A second-story man." "What are you worrying about," Meatball said. "We're on the third floor." He loped back into the kitchen. A shaggy woebegone figure stood out on the fire escape, raking his fingernails down the windowpane. Meatball opened the window. "Saul," he said.

"Sort of wet out," Saul said. He climbed in, dripping. "You heard, I guess."

"Miriam left you," Meatball said, "or something, is all I heard."

There was a sudden flurry of knocking at the front door. "Do come in," Sandor Rojas called. The door opened and there were three coeds from George Washington, all of whom were majoring in philosophy. They were each holding a gallon of Chianti. Sandor leaped up and dashed into the living room. "We heard there was a party," one blonde said. "Young blood," Sandor shouted. He was an ex-Hungarian freedom fighter who had easily the worst chronic case of what certain critics of the middle class have called Don Giovannism in the District of Columbia. *Purche porti la gonnella, voi sapete quel che fa.* Like Pavlov's dog: a contralto voice or a whiff of Arpège and Sandor would begin to salivate. Meatball regarded the trio blearily as they filed into the kitchen; he shrugged. "Put the wine in the icebox," he said "and good morning."

Aubade's neck made a golden bow as she bent over the sheets of fools-cap, scribbling away in the green murk of the room. "As a young man at Princeton," Callisto was dictating, nestling the bird against the gray hairs of his chest, "Callisto had learned a mnemonic device for remembering the Laws of Thermodynamics: you can't win, things are going to get worse before they get better, who says they're going to get better. At the age of 54, confronted with Gibbs' notion of the universe, he suddenly realized that undergraduate cant had been oracle, after all. That spindly maze of equations became, for him, a vision of ultimate, cosmic heat-death. He had known all along, of course, that nothing but a theoretical engine or system ever runs at 100% efficiency; and about the theorem of Clausius, which states that the entropy of an isolated system always continually increases. It was not, however, until Gibbs and Boltzmann brought to this principle the methods of statistical mechanics that the horrible significance of it all dawned on him: only then did he realize that the isolated system—galaxy, engine, human being, culture, whatever—must evolve spontaneously toward the Condition of the More Probable. He was forced, therefore, in the sad dying fall of middle age, to a radical reevaluation of everything he had learned up to then; all the cities and seasons and casual passions of his days had now to be looked at in a new and elusive light. He did not know if he was equal to the task. He was aware of the dangers of the reductive fallacy and, he hoped, strong enough not to drift into the graceful decadence of an enervated fatalism. His had always been a vigorous, Italian sort of pessimism: like Machiavelli, he allowed the forces of *virtù* and *fortuna* to be about 50/50; but the equations now introduced a random factor which pushed the odds to some unutterable and indeterminate ratio which he found himself afraid to calculate." Around him loomed vague hothouse shapes; the pitifully small heart fluttered against his own. Counterpointed against his words the girl heard the chatter of birds and fitful car honkings scattered along the wet morning and Earl Bostic's alto rising in occasional wild peaks through the floor. The architectonic purity of her world was constantly threatened by such hints of anarchy: gaps and excrescences and skew lines, and a shifting or tilting of planes to which she had continually to readjust lest the whole structure shiver into a disarray of discrete and meaningless signals. Callisto had described the process once as a kind of "feedback": she crawled into dreams each night with a sense of exhaustion, and a desperate resolve never to relax that vigilance. Even in the brief periods when Callisto made love to her, soaring above the bowing of taut nerves in haphazard doublestops would be the one singing string of her determination.

"Nevertheless," continued Callisto, "he found in entropy or the measure of disorganization for a closed system an adequate metaphor to apply to certain phenomena in his own world. He saw, for example, the younger generation responding to Madison Avenue with the same spleen his own had once reserved for Wall Street: and in American 'consumerism' discovered a similar tendency from the least to the most probable, from differentiation to sameness, from ordered individuality to a kind of chaos. He found himself, in short, restating Gibbs' prediction in social terms, and envisioned a heat-death for his culture in which ideas, like heat-energy, would no longer be transferred, since each point in it would ultimately have the same quantity of energy; and intellectual motion would, accordingly, cease." He glanced up suddenly. "Check it now," he said. Again she rose and peered out at the thermometer. "37," she said. "The rain has stopped." He bent his head quickly and held his lips against a quivering wing. "Then it will change soon," he said, trying to keep his voice firm.

Sitting on the stove Saul was like any big rag doll that a kid has been taking out some incomprehensible rage on. "What happened," Meatball said. "If you feel like talking, I mean."

"Of course I feel like talking," Saul said. "One thing I did, I slugged her."

"Discipline must be maintained."

"Ha, ha. I wish you'd been there. Oh Meatball, it was a lovely fight. She ended up throwing a *Handbook of Chemistry and Physics* at me, only it missed and went through the window, and when the glass broke I reckon something in her broke too. She stormed out of the house crying, out in the rain. No raincoat or anything."

"She'll be back."

"No."

"Well." Soon Meatball said: "It was something earth-shattering, no doubt. Like who is better, Sal Mineo or Ricky Nelson."

"What it was about," Saul said, "was communication theory. Which of course makes it very hilarious."

"I don't know anything about communication theory."

"Neither does my wife. Come right down to it, who does? That's the joke."

When Meatball saw the kind of smile Saul had on his face he said: "Maybe you would like tequila or something."

"No. I mean, I'm sorry. It's a field you can go off the deep end in, is all. You get where you're watching all the time for security cops: behind bushes, around corners, MUFFET is top secret."

"Wha."

"Multi-unit factorial field electronic tabulator."

"You were fighting about that."

"Miriam has been reading science fiction again. That and *Scientific American*. It seems she is, as we say, bugged at this idea of computers acting like people. I made the mistake of saying you can just as well turn that around, and talk about human behavior like a program fed into an IBM machine."

"Why not," Meatball said.

"Indeed, why not. In fact it is sort of crucial to communication, not to mention information theory. Only when I said that she hit the roof. Up went the balloon. And I can't figure out *why*. If anybody should know why, I should. I refuse to believe the government is wasting taxpayers' money on me, when it has so many bigger and better things to waste it on."

Meatball made a moue. "Maybe she thought you were acting like a cold, dehumanized amoral scientist type."

"My god," Saul flung up an arm. "Dehumanized. How much more human can I get? I worry, Meatball, I do. There are Europeans wandering around North Africa these days with their tongues torn out of their heads because those tongues have spoken the wrong words. Only the Europeans thought they were the right words."

"Language barrier," Meatball suggested.

Saul jumped down off the stove. "That," he said, angry, "is a good candidate for sick joke of the year. No, ace, it is *not* a barrier. If it is anything it's a kind of leakage. Tell a girl: 'I love you.' No trouble with two-thirds of that, it's a closed circuit. Just you and she. But that nasty four-letter word in the middle, *that's* the one you have to look out for. Ambiguity. Redundance. Irrelevance, even. Leakage. All this is noise. Noise screws up your signal, makes for disorganization in the circuit."

Meatball shuffled around. "Well, now, Saul," he muttered, "you're sort of, I don't know, expecting a lot from people. I mean, you know. What it is is, most of the things we say, I guess, are mostly noise."

"Ha! Half of what you just said, for example."

"Well, you do it too."

"I know." Saul smiled grimly. "It's a bitch, ain't it."

"I bet that's what keeps divorce lawyers in business. Whoops."

"Oh I'm not sensitive. Besides," frowning, "you're right. You find I think that most 'successful' marriages—Miriam and me, up to last night—are sort of founded on compromises. You never run at top efficiency, usually all you have is a minimum basis for a workable thing. I believe the phrase is Togetherness."

"Aarrgghh."

"Exactly. You find that one a bit noisy, don't you. But the noise content is different for each of us because you're a bachelor and I'm not. Or wasn't. The hell with it."

"Well sure," Meatball said, trying to be helpful, "you were using different words. By 'human being' you meant something that you can look at like it was a computer. It helps you think better on the job or something. But Miriam meant something entirely—"

"The hell with it."

Meatball fell silent. "I'll take that drink," Saul said after a while.

The card game had been abandoned and Sandor's friends were slowly getting wasted on tequila. On the living room couch, one of the coeds and Krinkles were engaged in amorous conversation. "No," Krinkles was saying, "no, I can't put Dave *down*. In fact I give Dave a lot of credit, man. Especially considering his accident and all." The girl's smile faded. "How terrible," she said. "What accident?" "Hadn't you heard?" Krinkles said. "When Dave was in the army, just a private E-2, they sent him down to Oak Ridge on special duty. Something to do with the Manhattan Project. He was handling hot stuff one day and got an overdose of radiation. So now he's got to wear lead gloves all the time." She shook her head sympathetically. "What an awful break for a piano-player."

Meatball had abandoned Saul to a bottle of tequila and was about to go to sleep in a closet when the front door flew open and the place was invaded by five enlisted personnel of the U.S. Navy, all in varying stages of abomination. "This is the place," shouted a fat, pimply seaman apprentice who had lost his white hat. "This here is the hoorhouse that chief was telling us about." A stringy-looking 3rd class boatswain's mate pushed him aside and cased the living room. "You're right, Slab," he said. "But it don't look like much, even for Stateside. I seen better tail in Naples, Italy." "How much, hey," boomed a large seaman with adenoids, who was holding a Mason jar full of white lightning. "Oh, my god," said Meatball.

Outside the temperature remained constant at 37 degrees Fahrenheit. In the hothouse Aubade stood absently caressing the branches of a young mimosa, hearing a motif of sap-rising, the rough and unresolved anticipatory theme of those fragile pink blossoms which, it is said, insure fertility. That music rose in a tangled tracery: arabesques of order competing fugally with the improvised discords of the party downstairs, which peaked sometimes in cusps and ogees of noise. That precious signal-to-noise ratio, whose delicate balance required every calorie of her strength, seesawed inside the small tenuous skull as she watched Callisto, sheltering the bird. Callisto was trying to confront any idea of the heat-death now, as he nuzzled the feathery lump in his hands. He sought correspondences. Sade, of course. And Temple Drake, gaunt and hopeless in her little park in Paris, at the end of *Sanctuary*. Final equilibrium. *Nightwood*. And the tango. Any tango, but more than any perhaps the sad sick dance in Stravinsky's *L'Histoire du Soldat*. He thought back: what had tango music been for them after the war, what meanings had he missed in all the stately coupled automatons in the *cafés-dansants*, or in the metronomes which had ticked behind the eyes of his own partners? Not even the clean constant winds of Switzerland could cure the *grippe espagnole:* Stravinsky had had it, they all had had it. And how many musicians were left after Passchendaele, after the Marne? It came down in this case to seven: violin, double-bass. Clarinet, bassoon. Cornet, trombone. Tympani. Almost as if any tiny troupe of saltimbanques had set about conveying the same information as a full pit-orchestra. There was hardly a full complement left in Europe. Yet with violin and tympani Stravinsky had managed to communicate in that tango the same exhaustion, the same airlessness one saw in the slicked-down youths who were trying to imitate Vernon Castle, and in their mistresses, who simply did not care. *Ma maîtresse.* Celeste. Returning to Nice after the second war he had found that café replaced by a perfume shop which catered to American tourists. And no secret vestige of her in the cobblestones or in the old pension next door; no perfume to match her breath heavy with the sweet Spanish wine she always drank. And so instead he had purchased a Henry Miller novel and left for Paris, and read the book on the train so that when he arrived he had been given at least a little forewarning. And saw that Celeste and the others and even Temple Drake were not all that had changed. "Aubade," he said, "my head aches." The sound of his voice generated in the girl an answering scrap of melody. Her movement toward the kitchen, the towel, the cold water, and his eyes following her formed a weird and intricate canon; as she placed the compress on his forehead his sigh of gratitude seemed to signal a new subject, another series of modulations.

"No," Meatball was still saying, "no, I'm afraid not. This is not a house of ill repute. I'm sorry, really I am." Slab was adamant. "But the chief said," he kept repeating. The seaman offered to swap the moonshine for a good piece. Meatball looked around frantically, as if seeking assistance. In the middle of the room, the Duke di Angelis quartet were engaged in a historic moment. Vincent was seated and the others standing: they were going through the motions of a group having a session, only without instruments. "I say," Meatball said. Duke moved his head a few times, smiled faintly, lit a cigarette, and eventually caught sight of Meatball. "Quiet, man," he whispered. Vincent began to fling his arms around, his fists clenched; then, abruptly, was still, then repeated the performance. This went on for a few minutes while Meatball sipped his drink moodily. The navy had withdrawn to the kitchen. Finally at some invisible signal the group stopped tapping their feet and Duke grinned and said, "At least we ended together."

Meatball glared at him. "I say," he said. "I have this new conception, man," Duke said. "You remember your namesake. You remember Gerry."

"No," said Meatball. "I'll remember April, if that's any help."

"As a matter of fact," Duke said, "it was Love for Sale. Which shows how much you know. The point is, it was Mulligan, Chet Baker and that crew, way back then, out yonder. You dig?"

"Baritone sax," Meatball said. "Something about a baritone sax."

"But no piano, man. No guitar. Or accordion. You know what that means."

"Not exactly," Meatball said.

"Well first let me just say, that I am no Mingus, no John Lewis. Theory was never my strong point. I mean things like reading were always difficult for me and all—"

"I know," Meatball said drily. "You got your card taken away because you changed key on Happy Birthday at a Kiwanis Club picnic."

"Rotarian. But it occurred to me, in one of these flashes of insight, that if that first quartet of Mulligan's had no piano, it could only mean one thing."

"No chords," said Paco, the baby-faced bass.

"What he is trying to say," Duke said, "is no root chords. Nothing to listen to while you blow a horizontal line. What one does in such a case is, one *thinks* the roots."

A horrified awareness was dawning on Meatball. "And the next logical extension," he said.

"Is to think everything," Duke announced with simple dignity. "Roots, line, everything."

Meatball looked at Duke, awed. "But," he said.

"Well," Duke said modestly, "there are a few bugs to work out."

"But," Meatball said.

"Just listen," Duke said. "You'll catch on." And off they went again into orbit, presumably somewhere around the asteroid belt. After a while Krinkles made an embouchure and started moving his fingers and Duke clapped his hand to his forehead. "Oaf!" he roared. "The new head we're using, you remember, I wrote last night?" "Sure," Krinkles said, "the new head. I come in on the bridge. All your heads I come in then." "Right," Duke said. "So why—" "Wha," said Krinkles, "16 bars, I wait, I come in—" "16?" Duke said. "No. No, Krinkles. Eight you waited. You want me to sing it? A cigarette that bears a lipstick's traces, an airline ticket to romantic places." Krinkles scratched his head. "These Foolish Things, you mean." "Yes," Duke said, "yes, Krinkles. Bravo." "Not I'll Remember April," Krinkles said. "*Minghe morte,*" said Duke. "I *figured* we were playing it a little slow," Krinkles said. Meatball chuckled. "Back to the old drawing board," he said. "No, man," Duke said, "back to the airless void." And they took off again, only it seemed

Paco was playing in G sharp while the rest were in E flat, so they had to start all over.

In the kitchen two of the girls from George Washington and the sailors were singing Let's All Go Down and Piss on the Forrestal. There was a two-handed, bilingual *morra* game on over by the icebox. Saul had filled several paper bags with water and was sitting on the fire escape, dropping them on passersby in the street. A fat government girl in a Bennington sweatshirt, recently engaged to an ensign attached to the Forrestal, came charging into the kitchen, head lowered, and butted Slab in the stomach. Figuring this was as good an excuse for a fight as any, Slab's buddies piled in. The *morra* players were nose-to-nose, screaming *trois, sette* at the tops of their lungs. From the shower the girl Meatball had taken out of the sink announced that she was drowning. She had apparently sat on the drain and the water was now up to her neck. The noise in Meatball's apartment had reached a sustained, ungodly crescendo.

Meatball stood and watched, scratching his stomach lazily. The way he figured, there were only about two ways he could cope: (a) lock himself in the closet and maybe eventually they would all go away, or (b) try to calm everybody down, one by one. (a) was certainly the more attractive alternative. But then he started thinking about that closet. It was dark and stuffy and he would be alone. He did not feature being alone. And then this crew off the good ship Lollipop or whatever it was might take it upon themselves to kick down the closet door, for a lark. And if that happened he would be, at the very least, embarrassed. The other way was more a pain in the neck, but probably better in the long run.

So he decided to try and keep his lease-breaking party from deteriorating into total chaos: he gave wine to the sailors and separated the *morra* players; he introduced the fat government girl to Sandor Rojas, who would keep her out of trouble; he helped the girl in the shower to dry off and get into bed; he had another talk with Saul; he called a repairman for the refrigerator, which someone had discovered was on the blink. This is what he did until nightfall, when most of the revellers had passed out and the party trembled on the threshold of its third day.

Upstairs Callisto, helpless in the past, did not feel the faint rhythm inside the bird begin to slacken and fail. Aubade was by the window, wandering the ashes of her own lovely world; the temperature held steady, the sky had become a uniform darkening gray. Then something from downstairs—a girl's scream, an overturned chair, a glass dropped on the floor, he would never know what exactly—pierced that private time-warp and he became aware of the faltering, the constriction of muscles, the tiny tossing of the bird's head; and his own pulse began to pound more fiercely, as if trying to compensate. "Aubade," he called weakly, "he's dying." The girl, flowing and rapt, crossed the hothouse to gaze down at Callisto's hands. The two remained like that, poised, for one minute, and two, while the heartbeat ticked a graceful diminuendo down at last into stillness. Callisto raised his head slowly. "I held him," he protested, impotent with the wonder of it, "to give him the warmth of my body. Almost as if I were communicating life to him, or a sense of life. What has happened? Has the transfer of heat ceased to work? Is there no more ..." He did not finish.

"I was just at the window," she said. He sank back, terrified. She stood a moment more, irresolute; she had sensed his obsession long ago, realized somehow that that constant 37 was now decisive. Suddenly then, as if seeing the single and unavoidable conclusion to all this she moved swiftly to the window before Callisto could speak; tore away the drapes and smashed out the glass with two exquisite hands which came away bleeding and glistening with splinters; and turned to face the man on the bed and wait with him until the moment of equilibrium was reached, when 37 degrees Fahrenheit should prevail both outside and inside, and forever, and the hovering, curious dominant of their separate lives should resolve into a tonic of darkness and the final absence of all motion.

1960

ROBERT CREELEY
1926–2005

Robert Creeley grew up on a small farm in West Acton, Massachusetts, where his mother worked as a public health nurse. After graduating from Holderness School in New Hampshire, he attended Harvard, drove an ambulance in India for the American Field Service, returned to Harvard, and then left without a degree in 1947. By that time he had married Ann MacKinnon, with whom he tried subsistence farming for a while near Littleton, New Hampshire. He began to correspond with Cid Corman, later editor of *Origin*, in 1949 and in 1950 with Charles Olson, who continued to be a mentor. The Creeleys moved to southern France and then to Mallorca—the scene of his later novel, *The Island*. In 1954 Creeley joined Olson at Black Mountain College, North Carolina, where he received a B.A., taught, and edited *Black Mountain Review*. After a divorce, he left Black Mountain for the West, settling in Albuquerque, where he taught at a boys' school. In 1957 he married Bobbie Hall, who over the next two decades would provide many occasions for poems. After spending two years as a tutor in Guatemala and earning an M.A. from the University of New Mexico, Creeley became an instructor of English at that institution in 1961. During the 1950s he published widely in low-circulation magazines and with small presses, but in the 1960s he gained a national reputation. A divorce from Bobbie was followed in 1977 by marriage to Penelope Highton. In 1978 he was named Gray Professor of Poetry and Letters at the State University of New York at Buffalo and, later, Capen Professor of Poetry and Humanities. He was New York State Poet for 1989–1991.

Creeley has been widely recognized as a central figure in contemporary American writing. His poetry is shaped by his New England childhood; his early admiration for Wallace Stevens, Paul Valéry, and classical poetry; his wide reading in European love poetry; his years of discussion with Charles Olson; his assimilation of the Whitman tradition as modified by William Carlos Williams, Ezra Pound, and Hart Crane; and by his own experimental openness, his remarkable ear, his obsessive self-examination, and his firm sense of the poem as an act of responsibility. He has a classicist's respect for poetic forms and also a Projectivist's insistence that form must be an extension of freshly perceived content. Though his poems may at first seem thin or abstract, they express with honesty and precision a quite specific interior drama: the struggle of consciousness to articulate its movements in response to an ungraspable and "broken" world. Whether arising from occasions of loss, perplexity, ironic reflection, gratitude, or brief ecstasy, the poems render that drama in their groping diction, tortured syntax, wry echoes and rhymes, strategic line breaks, and stammering pace. Following the writing of *Pieces*, Creeley often constructed from brief poems or prose notations a larger form that might trace the difficult passage of such a consciousness through its continuing present. *Memory Gardens* modulates his lifelong concerns into a more quietly elegiac and meditative mode, and *Windows* engages more fully both the "inside" and the "outside" worlds.

Thomas R. Whitaker
Yale University

PRIMARY WORKS

The Gold Diggers, 1954; *Four Poems from A Form of Women*, 1959; *For Love: Poems 1950–1960*, 1962; *The Island*, 1963; *Words*, 1967; *The Charm: Early and Uncollected Poems*, 1967; *Pieces*, 1969; *A Quick Graph: Collected Notes & Essays*, 1970; *A Day Book*, 1972; *Listen*, 1972; *A Sense of Measure*, 1973; *Contexts of Poetry: Interviews 1961–1972*, 1973; *Thirty Things*, 1974; *Away*, 1976; *Presences*, 1976; *Mabel: A Story*, 1976; *Hello: A Journal*, 1978; *Later*, 1979; *Was That a Real Poem and Other Essays*, 1979; *The Collected Poems 1945–1975*, 1982; *Echoes*, 1982; *Mirrors*, 1983; *Going On: Selected Poems 1958–1980*, 1983; *The Collected Prose*, 1984; *Memory Gardens*, 1986; *The Company*, 1988; *The Collected Essays*, 1989; *Windows*, 1990; *Selected Poems*, 1991; *Life & Death*, 1998; *Personal*, 1998; *Day Book of a Virtual Poet*, 1998; *So There: Poems 1976–1983*, 1998; *Just in Time: Poems 1984–1994*, 2001; *Collected Prose*, 2001; *On Earth: Last Poems and an Essay*, 2006.

Hart Crane

for Slater Brown[1]

1

He had been stuttering, by the edge
of the street, one foot still
on the sidewalk, and the other
in the gutter . . .

---

[1]A friend of Hart Crane who also became a
friend of Creeley.

like a bird, say, wired to flight, the 5
wings, pinned to their motion, stuffed.

The words, several, and for each, several
senses.
            "It is very difficult to sum up
briefly ..." 10
            It always was.

(Slater, let me come home.
The letters have proved insufficient.
The mind cannot hang to them as it could
to the words. 15

There are ways beyond
what I have here to work with,
what my head cannot push to any kind
of conclusion.

But my own ineptness 20
cannot bring them to hand,
the particulars of those times
we had talked.)

"Men kill themselves because they are
afraid of death, he says ..." 25

The push
            beyond and
into

Respect, they said he respected the
ones with the learning, lacking it 30
himself
            (Waldo Frank[2] & his
6 languages)
            What had seemed
important 35
While Crane sailed to Mexico I was writing
(so that one betrayed
            himself)

---

[2]Critic, novelist, and friend of Hart Crane.

He slowed
      (without those friends to keep going, to   40
keep up), stopped
        dead and the head could not
go further
       without those friends
. . . And so it was I entered the broken world[3]   45

Hart Crane.

    Hart

                          1962

I Know a Man

As I sd to my
friend, because I am
always talking,—John, I

sd, which was not his
name, the darkness sur-   5
rounds us, what

can we do against
it, or else, shall we &
why not, buy a goddam big car,

drive, he sd, for   10
christ's sake, look
out where yr going.

                          1962

For Love

                    for Bobbie[1]

Yesterday I wanted to
speak of it, that sense above
the others to me
important because all

---

[3]Quoted from Crane's late poem "The Broken Tower."

[1]Creeley's second wife.

that I know derives
from what it teaches me.
Today, what is it that
is finally so helpless,   5

different, despairs of its own
statement, wants to   10
turn away, endlessly
to turn away.

If the moon did not ...
no, if you did not
I wouldn't either, but   15
what would I not

do, what prevention, what
thing so quickly stopped.
That is love yesterday
or tomorrow, not   20

now. Can I eat
what you give me. I
have not earned it. Must
I think of everything
as earned. Now love also   25
becomes a reward so
remote from me I have
only made it with my mind.

Here is tedium,
despair, a painful
sense of isolation and   30
whimsical if pompous

self-regard. But that image
is only of the mind's
vague structure, vague to me   35
because it is my own.

Love, what do I think
to say. I cannot say it.
What have you become to ask,
what have I made you into,   40

companion, good company,
crossed legs with skirt, or

soft body under
the bones of the bed.

Nothing says anything   45
but that which it wishes
would come true, fears
what else might happen in

some other place, some
other time not this one.   50
A voice in my place, an
echo of that only in yours,

Let me stumble into
not the confession but
the obsession I begin with   55
now. For you

also (also)
some time beyond place, or
place beyond time, no
mind left to   60

say anything at all,
that face gone, now.
Into the company of love[2]
it all returns.

                                                         1962

Words

You are always
with me,
there is never
a separate

place. But if   5
in the twisted
place I
cannot speak,

not indulgence
or fear only,   10

---

[2]A phrase from Hart Crane's "The Broken
Tower."

but a tongue
rotten with what

it tastes—There is
a memory
of water, of   15
food, when hungry.

Some day
will not be
this one, then
to say   20

words like a
clear, fine
ash sifts,
like dust,

from nowhere.   25
                                                              1967

America

America, you ode for reality![1]
Give back the people you took.

Let the sun shine again
on the four corners of the world

you thought of first but do not   5
own, or keep like a convenience.

People are your own word, you
invented that locus and term.

Here, you said and say, is
where we are. Give back   10

what we are, these people you made,
us, and nowhere but you to be.

                                                              1969

---

[1]Cf. Walt Whitman, in Preface to *Leaves of
Grass*: "The United States themselves are
essentially the greatest poem."

FRANK O'HARA
1926–1966

Joe LeSueur, a playwright and Frank O'Hara's roommate for nearly a decade, wrote in a memoir, "as far as I could tell, writing poetry was something Frank did in his spare time.... For that reason, I didn't realize right away that if you took poetry as much for granted as you did breathing it might mean you felt that it was essential to your life."[1] For many readers, the enormous appeal of Frank O'Hara's work—and he is among the most appealing of all American poets—is that he combines a seeming effortlessness of expression with a life-sustaining intensity of purpose. The poems were often dashed off, almost always on the typewriter—*The Lunch Poems*, for example, got their title because they were written on O'Hara's lunch hour—but they came out of the wholeness of O'Hara's experience and emotions. As funny as they often are, they always indicate a shrewd awareness of people, places, and history. And although O'Hara is one of the most joyous poets America has produced, a darkness always hovers below the surface, accentuating the brightness above.

Frank O'Hara was born in Baltimore, Maryland, and grew up in Worcester, Massachusetts. He attended Harvard University, where he studied music, and the graduate school of the University of Michigan. But he is most associated with New York City and the Long Island coast, especially Fire Island, where he died in a freak accident—run over by a jeep on an island where cars are banned. With John Ashbery (a friend from his undergraduate days), James Schuyler, and Kenneth Koch, O'Hara formed the central core of what has been dubbed the New York School. Although what primarily bound these poets was personal friendship, they also share certain poetic similarities: (1) They all emphasize the immediacy of the individual poetic voice rather than the impersonal presentation of images. (2) They playfully combine elements from high and low culture, incorporating into their works the most mundane aspects of urban life and such features of popular culture as comic strip characters, Hollywood movies, and popular songs. (3) They fearlessly court the comic, the slapstick, the vulgar, and the sentimental. (4) They experiment with surrealism, although the dreamlike often dissolves into the quite ordinary.

O'Hara, Ashbery, and Schuyler are also united by their involvement in the visual arts. All three worked at various times for *Art News*, writing articles and reviews. O'Hara worked for the Museum of Modern Art, first as a ticket taker and then as a curator, organizing major exhibitions by the end of his life. He was a personal friend of many important artists, including Larry Rivers, Willem de Kooning, Grace Hartigan, and Fairfield Porter. The directness and energy that many of these artists wished to bring to painting, O'Hara sought to register in his own work.

---

[1]Joe LeSueur, "Four Apartments," in *Homage to Frank O'Hara*, eds. Bill Berkson and Joe LeSueur (New York: Big Sky, 1978), p. 47.

One of the typical modes in which O'Hara worked was what he called the "I do this I do that" poem. Many lesser poets have attempted to imitate O'Hara's seemingly documentary style, but few have caught his eye for detail, his ear for the music of American English, or his sensitivity to the wide fluctuation of mood. O'Hara was also among the earliest poets to write unself-consciously of his homosexual relationships. His love poems—and he wrote many of them—have a frankness, a joy, and a pathos that would seem more revolutionary if they did not appear so natural and easy.

David Bergman
Towson University

PRIMARY WORKS

A City Winter and Other Poems, 1952; *Meditations in an Emergency,* 1957; *Jackson Pollack,* 1959; *Lunch Poems,* 1964; *Collected Poems,* 1971; *Art Chronicles 1954–1966,* 1975; *Early Writing,* 1977; *Poems Retrieved, 1951–1966,* 1977; *Selected Plays,* 1978; *Standing Still and Walking in New York,* 1983; *Collected Poems of Frank O'Hara,* 1995; *Poems Retrieved,* 1996; *Amorous Nightmares of Delay: Selected Plays,* 1997.

My Heart

I'm not going to cry all the time
nor shall I laugh all the time,
I don't prefer one "strain" to another.
I'd have the immediacy of a bad movie,
not just a sleeper,[1] but also the big,   5
overproduced first-run kind. I want to be
at least as alive as the vulgar. And if
some aficionado[2] of my mess says "That's
not like Frank!", all to the good! I
don't wear brown and grey suits all the time,   10
do I? No. I wear workshirts to the opera,
often. I want my feet to be bare,
I want my face to be shaven, and my heart—
you can't plan on the heart, but
the better part of it, my poetry, is open.   15

    1970

---

[1]A "sleeper" is film jargon for an unexpectedly successful movie, usually a low-budget film that proves to be of artistic and commercial value.

[2]An aficionado is a person devoted to someone, or his or her works; a fan with more than an average level of expertise in a subject.

The Day Lady Died[1]

It is 12:20 in New York a Friday
three days after Bastille day,[2] yes
it is 1959 and I go get a shoeshine
because I will get off the 4:19 in Easthampton,[3]
at 7:15 and then go straight to dinner   5
and I don't know the people who will feed me

I walk up the muggy street beginning to sun
and have a hamburger and a malted and buy
an ugly NEW WORLD WRITING to see what the poets
in Ghana are doing these days   10
                    I go on to the bank
and Miss Stillwagon (first name Linda I once heard)
doesn't even look up my balance for once in her life
and in the GOLDEN GRIFFIN I get a little Verlaine,[4]
for Patsy with drawings by Bonnard,[5] although I do   15
think of Hesiod, trans. Richmond Lattimore,[6] or
Brendan Behan's new play,[7] or *Le Balcon* or *Les Nègres*
of Genet,[8] but I don't, I stick with Verlaine
after practically going to sleep with quandariness

and for Mike I just stroll into the PARK LANE   20
Liquor Store and ask for a bottle of Strega and
then I go back where I came from to 6th Avenue
and the tobacconist in the Ziegfeld Theatre and
casually ask for a carton of Gauloises and a carton
of Picayunes[9] and a NEW YORK POST with her face on it   25

[1]The poem is an homage to the great blues singer Billie Holiday (1915–1959), whose nickname, "Lady Day," is alluded to in the title.

[2]Bastille Day, July 14, is French Independence Day.

[3]Easthampton is a town on the south shore of Long Island, and a stop on the Long Island Railroad. O'Hara is going to visit Patsy Southgate and her husband at the time, Mike Goldberg (they are referred to in lines 15 and 20; Mike Goldberg is also the painter referred to in "Why I Am Not a Painter"). They lived in Southampton, a nearby community, where "Getting Up Ahead of Someone (Sun)" is set. The Hamptons have now become a rather exclusive area, but in the 1950s, they were a group of farming communities and an inexpensive place for artists to live and work.

[4]Paul Verlaine (1844–1896) was one of the great French poets of the nineteenth century.

[5]Pierre Bonnard (1867–1947) was one of the major French post-Impressionist painters. He illustrated Verlaine's *Parallelement* in 1902.

[6]Hesiod was an ancient Greek poet. Richmond Lattimore, a prolific Greek translator, published his *Hesiod* in 1959.

[7]Brendan Behan (1923–1964) was a controversial Irish playwright, author of *The Quare Fellow* (1956) and *The Hostage* (1958).

[8]Jean Genêt (1910–1986) was one of France's greatest twentieth-century writers. His plays *Le Balcon* (The Balcony) and *Les Nègres* (The Blacks), produced in the 1950s, created enormous controversy because of their sexual, racial, and political subject matter.

[9]Gauloises and Picayunes are brands of French cigarettes. The emphasis on French culture stands in contrast to Billie Holiday, the subject of the poem. The effect is to suggest how far away O'Hara's thoughts are from Holiday until he sees her face in the newspaper.

and I am sweating a lot by now and thinking of
leaning on the john door in the 5 SPOT
while she whispered a song along the keyboard
to Mal Waldron[10] and everyone and I stopped breathing

1964

Why I Am Not a Painter

I am not a painter, I am a poet.
Why? I think I would rather be
a painter, but I am not. Well,

for instance, Mike Goldberg[1]
is starting a painting. I drop in.   5
"Sit down and have a drink" he
says. I drink; we drink. I look
up. "You have SARDINES in it."
"Yes, it needed something there."
"Oh." I go and the days go by   10
and I drop in again. The painting
is going on, and I go, and the days
go by. I drop in. The painting is
finished. "Where's SARDINES?"
All that's left is just   15
letters, "It was too much," Mike says.

But me? One day I am thinking of
a color: orange. I write a line
about orange. Pretty soon it is a
whole page of words, not lines.   20
Then another page. There should be
so much more, not of orange, of
words, of how terrible orange is
and life. Days go by. It is even in
prose, I am a real poet. My poem   25
is finished and I haven't mentioned
orange yet. It's twelve poems, I call
it ORANGES. And one day in a gallery
I see Mike's painting, called SARDINES.

1971

---

[10]Mal Waldron (1925–2002) was Billie Holiday's
pianist.

[1]Mike Goldberg (1924–2007) was a painter
who worked with O'Hara on several projects.

Poem

"À la recherche de Gertrude Stein"[1]

When I am feeling depressed and anxious sullen[2]
all you have to do is take your clothes off
and all is wiped away revealing life's tenderness
that we are flesh and breathe and are near us
as you are really as you are I become as I   5
really am alive and knowing vaguely what is
and what is important to me above the intrusions
of incident and accidental relationships
which have nothing to do with my life
when I am in your presence I feel life is strong   10
and will defeat all its enemies and all of mine
and all of yours and yours in you and mine in me
sick logic and feeble reasoning are cured
by the perfect symmetry of your arms and legs
spread out making an eternal circle together   15
creating a golden pillar beside the Atlantic
the faint line of hair dividing your torso
gives my mind rest and emotions their release
into the infinite air where since once we are
together we always will be in this life come what may   20

1965

■ # ROBERT HAYDEN ■
1913–1980

Born Asa Bundy Sheffey in Detroit, Michigan, Hayden grew up in a poor, racially mixed neighborhood. Because his parents were divorced when he was quite young, his mother left him with neighbors, William and Sue Ellen Hayden, who gave him their name and raised him. His mother's periodic reappearances

---

[1]"*A la recherche de Gertrude Stein*" is French for "in remembrance of Gertrude Stein" (1874–1946), the American expatriate writer, whose experimental works and involvement with painters mirrors O'Hara's own career. The phrase alludes to Marcel Proust's multivolume novel *A la recherche du temps perdu*, often translated as *Remembrance of Things Past*.

[2]The opening line recalls the opening of Shakespeare's sonnet "When in disgrace with fortune and men's eyes," which, according to Patsy Southgate, was O'Hara's favorite Shakespeare sonnet.

coupled with the jealousy of his foster mother made him "a divided person," and his art includes images of warring forces within the self.

Nearsighted and introverted, Hayden spent many hours reading and writing; he published his first poem at eighteen. Between 1932 and 1936, he attended Detroit City College (now Wayne State University); between 1936 and 1938, he worked for the Federal Writers Project of the Works Progress Administration (WPA); and in 1944 he completed an M.A. in English at the University of Michigan. He married Erma Morris, a musician and teacher, in 1940. In 1946 he began teaching at Fisk University, and in 1969 he joined the English Department of the University of Michigan, where he taught until his death.

For much of his life, Hayden wrote good poetry with little recognition. He was sustained by some awards and by friendships with other poets: a Rosenwald Fellowship in 1947, a Ford Foundation grant to write and travel in Mexico in 1954–1955, and the Grand Prize for Poetry at the First World Festival of Negro Arts in 1966. During the 1970s, he was published by Liveright (*Angle of Ascent*, 1975) and elected a fellow of the American Academy of Poets. In 1976 he was chosen as Consultant in Poetry to the Library of Congress, the first African American ever to hold that post.

Hayden's philosophy of art remained constant throughout his life. Opposed to ethnocentrism, he refused to allow race to define subject matter. He also refused to believe that black social and political frustrations demanded poetry aimed exclusively at a black readership. Two criteria pertained for all artists: expert craft and universal subject matter. Universality did not mean denial of racial material; it meant building out of personal and ethnic experience to human insights that could reach across group lines. Hayden's Baha'i faith, which he adopted in the 1940s, helped him believe in the unity of people and in the spiritual importance of art.

Some of the major themes of Hayden's poetry are the tension between the imagination and the tragic nature of life, the past in the present, art as a form of spiritual redemption, and the nurturing power of early life and history. Most of his work falls into the categories of "spirit of place" poems, folk character poems, Detroit neighborhood poems, and historical poems. This last group, best known by the long poem "Middle Passage," is aimed at "correcting the misconceptions and destroying some of the stereotypes and clichés which surround Negro history." In the context of the racial militance of the 1960s and 1970s, Hayden's work has sometimes been found wanting by younger poets. His output over more than forty years, however, suggests the deepest of commitments both to his own race and to humanity as a whole.

Robert M. Greenberg
Temple University

PRIMARY WORKS

Heart-Shape in the Dust, 1940; *The Lion and the Archer* (with Myron O'Higgins), 1948; *Figure of Time*, 1955; *A Ballad of Remembrance*, 1962; *Selected Poems*, 1966; *Words in the Mourning Time*, 1970; *The Night-Blooming Cereus*, 1972; *Angle of Ascent: New and Selected Poems*, 1975; *American Journal*, 1982; *Collected Prose*, 1984; *Collected Poems*, 1985.

Those Winter Sundays

Sundays too my father got up early
and put his clothes on in the blueblack cold,
then with cracked hands that ached
from labor in the weekday weather made
banked fires blaze. No one ever thanked him.   5

I'd wake and hear the cold splintering, breaking.
When the rooms were warm, he'd call,
and slowly I would rise and dress,
fearing the chronic angers of that house,

Speaking indifferently to him,   10
who had driven out the cold
and polished my good shoes as well.
What did I know, what did I know
of love's austere and lonely offices?

                                                        1962

Summertime and the Living . . .[1]

Nobody planted roses, he recalls,
but sunflowers gangled there sometimes,
tough-stalked and bold
and like the vivid children there unplanned.
There circus-poster horses curveted   5
in trees of heaven
above the quarrels and shattered glass,
and he was bareback rider of them all.

No roses there in summer—
oh, never roses except when people died—   10
and no vacations for his elders,
so harshened after each unrelenting day
that they were shouting-angry.
But summer was, they said, the poor folks' time
of year. And he remembers   15
how they would sit on broken steps amid

---

[1]Lyric ("Summertime and the living is easy")
from George and Ira Gershwin's *Porgie and
Bess*.

The fevered tossings of the dusk, the dark,
wafting hearsay with funeral-parlor fans
or making evening solemn by
their quietness. Feels their Mosaic eyes   20
upon him, though the florist roses
that only sorrow could afford
long since have bidden them Godspeed.
Oh, summer summer summertime—

Then grim street preachers shook   25
their tambourines and Bibles in the face
of tolerant wickedness;
then Elks parades and big splendiferous
Jack Johnson[2] in his diamond limousine
set the ghetto burgeoning   30
with fantasies
of Ethiopia spreading her gorgeous wings.[3]

                                                                 1962

Mourning Poem for the Queen of Sunday

Lord's lost Him His mockingbird,
His fancy warbler;
Satan sweet-talked her,
four bullets hushed her.
Who would have thought   5
she'd end that way?

Four bullets hushed her. And the world a-clang with evil.
Who's going to make old hardened sinner men tremble now
and the righteous rock?
Oh who and oh who will sing Jesus down   10
to help with struggling and doing without and being colored
all through blue Monday?
Till way next Sunday?

All those angels
in their cretonne clouds and finery   15
the true believer saw
when she rared back her head and sang,

---

[2] A black folk hero, Jack Johnson (1878–1946) won the world heavyweight boxing championship in 1908. He was the subject of the Broadway play and Hollywood movie *The Great White Hope*.

[3] Adapts an often quoted biblical reference to Ethiopia.

all those angels are surely weeping.
Who would have thought
she'd end that way?   20

Four holes in her heart. The gold works wrecked.
But she looks so natural in her big bronze coffin
among the Broken Hearts and Gates-Ajar,
it's as if any moment she'd lift her head
from its pillow of chill gardenias   25
and turn this quiet into shouting Sunday
and make folks forget what she did on Monday.

Oh, Satan sweet-talked her,
and four bullets hushed her.
Lord's lost Him His diva,   30
His fancy warbler's gone.
Who would have thought,
who would have thought she'd end that way?

                                                       1962

ANNE SEXTON
1928–1974

Anne Gray Harvey Sexton was born in Newton, Massachusetts, the third daughter of Mary Gray and Ralph Harvey. Sexton's great-uncle had been governor of Maine, and her grandfather, editor of Maine's *Lewiston Evening Journal*, was a respected journalist. The family's primary emphasis by the time of Sexton's birth was mercantile; Sexton's father and later her husband were both wool merchants. The Harveys lived in the Boston suburbs but spent the summers on Squirrel Island, Maine. Her childhood was both privileged and difficult. Sexton felt she could not fulfill her family's expectations, which were both high and vague. She was implicitly expected to marry at the right time and to behave decorously—neither of which she did—but not necessarily to distinguish herself professionally or intellectually.

Anne Harvey was a spirited and demanding child, a romantic and popular adolescent, and an undistinguished student (she attended a finishing school for women in Boston). In 1948 she eloped with Alfred Sexton, to whom she remained married until 1973. Shortly after the birth of each of her two daughters, in 1953 and 1955, Sexton was hospitalized for the recurring emotional disturbances that continued to plague her for the rest of her life. After a suicide attempt in 1956, on the advice of her doctor, she began writing poetry. In 1957 Sexton enrolled in

John Holmes's poetry workshop in Boston, where she met Maxine Kumin, her closest personal friend. In 1958–1959 she was a student in Robert Lowell's writing seminar at Boston University, where she met Sylvia Plath.

Her first collection, *To Bedlam and Part Way Back* (1960), was controversial and established Sexton's reputation as a confessional poet. Popularity and something approaching notoriety accompanied Sexton's poetic career. She received numerous awards, including a nomination for the National Book Award; fellowships from the American Academy of Arts and Letters, the Ford Foundation, and the Guggenheim Foundation; several honorary doctorates; and, in 1967, the Pulitzer Prize for *Live or Die*. She taught at Harvard and Radcliffe, lectured at the Breadloaf Writers' Conference, held the Crashaw Chair at Colgate University, and was a full professor at Boston University by 1972. Her celebrated readings on the poetry circuit were criticized as the flamboyant, dramatic performances they were. When Sexton killed herself in 1974, she was still professionally successful and productive. Diane Wood Middlebrook's *Anne Sexton: A Biography* tells readers much more about a life that seems, but clearly is not, fully disclosed in the poetry.

Sexton used the personal to speak to cultural concerns, many of which apply to women's conflicts and transitions in modern American society. If Lowell and Snodgrass are the fathers of confessional poetry, Sexton is perhaps its first mother. The gender distinction is worth making. Snodgrass gave her "permission," as she phrased it, to write about loss, neurosis, even madness, but no one had extended the permission to write about such experiences from a female point of view. For that bold stroke there was no precedent. Many feminist poets and critics find in her work a set of resonant and enabling myths, as well as a critique of those that disabled Sexton herself.

Sexton's early work was preoccupied with formal structure and lyric discipline, while the later work became what critics have variously called surreal, mythic, or visionary. Anne Sexton's poems articulate some of the deepest dilemmas of her contemporaries about their—our—most fundamental wishes and fears.

Diana Hume George
Pennsylvania State University—Erie, Behrend College

PRIMARY WORKS

To Bedlam and Part Way Back, 1960; *All My Pretty Ones*, 1962; *Selected Poems*, 1964; *Live or Die*, 1966; *Love Poems*, 1969; *Transformations*, 1971; *The Book of Folly*, 1972; *The Death Notebooks*, 1974; *The Awful Rowing Toward God*, 1975; *45 Mercy Street*, 1976; *Anne Sexton: A Self-Portrait in Letters*, 1977; *Words for Dr. Y: Uncollected Poems with Three Stories*, 1978; *The Complete Poems*, 1981; *No Evil Star: Selected Essays, Interviews, and Prose*, 1985; *Selected Poems of Anne Sexton*, 1988.

Her Kind

I have gone out, a possessed witch,
haunting the black air, braver at night;
dreaming evil, I have done my hitch
over the plain houses, light by light:

lonely thing, twelve-fingered, out of mind.   5
A woman like that is not a woman, quite.
I have been her kind.

I have found the warm caves in the woods,
filled them with skillets, carvings, shelves,
closets, silks, innumerable goods;   10
fixed the suppers for the worms and the elves:
whining, rearranging the disaligned.
A woman like that is misunderstood.
I have been her kind.

I have ridden in your cart, driver,   15
waved my nude arms at villages going by,
learning the last bright routes, survivor
where your flames still bite my thigh
and my ribs crack where your wheels wind.
A woman like that is not ashamed to die.   20
I have been her kind.

                                                              1960

Housewife

Some women marry houses.
It's another kind of skin; it has a heart,
a mouth, a liver and bowel movements.
The walls are permanent and pink.
See how she sits on her knees all day,   5
faithfully washing herself down.
Men enter by force, drawn back like Jonah
into their fleshy mothers.
A woman *is* her mother.
That's the main thing.   10

                                                              1962

Young

A thousand doors ago
when I was a lonely kid
in a big house with four
garages and it was summer
as long as I could remember,   5
I lay on the lawn at night,
clover wrinkling under me,

the wise stars bedding over me,
my mother's window a funnel
of yellow heat running out,   10
my father's window, half shut,
an eye where sleepers pass,
and the boards of the house
were smooth and white as wax
and probably a million leaves   15
sailed on their strange stalks
as the crickets ticked together
and I, in my brand new body,
which was not a woman's yet,
told the stars my questions   20
and thought God could really see
the heat and the painted light,
elbows, knees, dreams, goodnight.

                                                                    1961

Somewhere in Africa

Must you leave, John Holmes,[1] with the prayers and psalms
you never said, said over you? Death with no rage
to weigh you down? Praised by the mild God, his arm
over the pulpit, leaving you timid, with no real age,
whitewashed by belief, as dull as the windy preacher!   5
Dead of a dark thing, John Holmes, you've been lost
in the college chapel, mourned as father and teacher,
mourned with piety and grace under the University Cross.

Your last book unsung, your last hard words unknown,
abandoned by science, cancer blossomed in your throat,   10
rooted like bougainvillea into your gray backbone,
ruptured your pores until you wore it like a coat.

The thick petals, the exotic reds, the purples and whites
covered up your nakedness and bore you up with all
their blind power. I think of your last June nights   15
in Boston, your body swollen but light, your eyes small

---

[1]John Holmes was a mid-twentieth-century American poet who died in 1962. In 1957 Sexton enrolled in his poetry workshop at the Boston Center for Adult Education, where she also met Maxine Kumin and George Starbuck. The group continued meeting for several years after the initial workshop. Sexton's troubled, ambivalent relationship with her first teacher produced two of her poems, "Somewhere in Africa" and "For John, Who Begs Me Not to Enquire Further."

as you let the nurses carry you into a strange land.
. . . If this is death and God is necessary let him be hidden
from the missionary, the well-wisher and the glad hand.
Let God be some tribal female who is known but forbidden.   20

Let there be this God who is a woman who will place you
upon her shallow boat, who is a woman naked to the waist,
moist with palm oil and sweat, a woman of some virtue
and wild breasts, her limbs excellent, unbruised and chaste.

Let her take you. She will put twelve strong men at the oars   25
for you are stronger than mahogany and your bones fill
the boat high as with fruit and bark from the interior.
She will have you now, you whom the funeral cannot kill.

John Holmes, cut from a single tree, lie heavy in her hold
and go down that river with the ivory, the copra and the gold.   30

1966

SYLVIA PLATH
1932–1963

Sylvia Plath was the precocious child of well-educated Boston parents, Otto and
Aurelia Schoeber Plath. Otto, who taught German and zoology at Boston University, died when Sylvia was eight of complications following the amputation of
his leg. An authority on bees, he had been ill the previous four years from
untreated diabetes mellitus. Finances were slim, so Sylvia's mother returned to
teaching; to help care for the children, her maternal grandparents moved into
the Plath home, where they remained until their deaths. In order to take a position at Boston University herself, Aurelia moved the family to Wellesley.

Plath's childhood and adolescence were a series of high academic achievements. She published poetry, fiction, and journalism in a number of places even
before attending Smith College on a partial scholarship. An English major at
Smith, she continued her consistent prize winning, but she was also very much
a woman of the 1950s, plagued with thoughts that she had to marry and have
children or else she would never be a "complete" female. Some of her conflicts
over direction (career versus marriage, sexual experience versus chastity) combined with a strain of depression in her paternal line to cause a breakdown in
the summer of 1953, shortly after she had served as a *Mademoiselle* College
Board editor. The outpatient electroconvulsive shock treatments she received
then probably led to her subsequent suicide attempt in August 1953, and she

spent the next four months under psychiatric care before returning to Smith. She graduated *summa cum laude* in June 1955 and then earned an M.A. on a Fulbright Fellowship at Cambridge University in England.

On June 16, 1956, she married Ted Hughes, who later became Poet Laureate of England. In 1957 they returned to the United States, where Plath taught freshman English at Smith. She and Hughes lived for another year in Boston, establishing themselves as professional writers; late in 1959, they returned to England. In the next three years, Plath bore two children, published *The Colossus and Other Poems*, established a home in Devon, and separated from Hughes. She was living with her children in a flat in Yeats's house in London when she committed suicide, just a few weeks after publication of *The Bell Jar* in 1963. *Ariel*, a collection of some of her last poems, was published in 1965.

Plath's poems show a steadily developing sense of her own voice, speaking of subjects that before the 1960s were seldom considered appropriate for poetry: anger, macabre humor, and defiance, contrasted with a rarer joy and a poignant understanding of women's various roles. "Three Women," which is set in a maternity ward, *The Bell Jar*, and many of her late 1962 poems were unlike any of the expert literature that, until the last years of her life, she had so carefully imitated. Her breaking out of the conventional patterns—her reliance on metaphor, the rapid shifts from image to image, a frantic yet always controlled pace that mirrored the tensions of her single-parent life during 1962—set an example that shaped a great deal of poetry for the next forty years. In contrast to late poems like "Daddy" and "Lady Lazarus," Plath's final poems were icily mystic, solemn, and resigned. The full range of her work is evident in the 1981 *Collected Poems*, which won the Pulitzer Prize for Poetry in 1982.

Linda Wagner-Martin
University of North Carolina at Chapel Hill

PRIMARY WORKS

The Colossus, 1960; *The Bell Jar*, 1963 (published under "Victoria Lucas"); *Ariel*, 1965; *Crossing the Water*, 1971; *Winter Trees*, 1972; *Johnny Panic and the Bible of Dreams and Other Prose Writings*, 1977; *The Collected Poems*, 1981; *The Journals of Sylvia Plath*, 1982.

For a Fatherless Son

You will be aware of an absence, presently,
Growing beside you, like a tree,
A death tree, color gone, an Australian gum tree—
Balding, gelded by lightning—an illusion,
And a sky like a pig's backside, an utter lack of attention.   5

But right now you are dumb.
And I love your stupidity,
The blind mirror of it. I look in
And find no face but my own, and you think that's funny.
It is good for me   10

To have you grab my nose, a ladder rung.
One day you may touch what's wrong—
The small skulls, the smashed blue hills, the godawful hush.
Till then your smiles are found money.

1962

Daddy

You do not do, you do not do
Any more, black shoe
In which I have lived like a foot
For thirty years, poor and white,
Barely daring to breathe or Achoo.   5

Daddy, I have had to kill you.
You died before I had time——
Marble-heavy, a bag full of God,
Ghastly statue with one gray toe
Big as a Frisco seal[1]   10

And a head in the freakish Atlantic
Where it pours bean green over blue
In the waters off beautiful Nauset.[2]
I used to pray to recover you.
Ach, du.[3]   15

In the German tongue, in the Polish town
Scraped flat by the roller
Of wars, wars, wars.
But the name of the town is common.
My Polack friend   20

Says there are a dozen or two.
So I never could tell where you
Put your foot, your root,
I never could talk to you.
The tongue stuck in my jaw.   25

It stuck in a barb wire snare.
Ich, ich, ich, ich,[4]
I could hardly speak.
I thought every German was you.
And the language obscene   30

[1]San Francisco Seal Rocks.   [3]German: Ah, you.
[2]Cape Cod harbor.   [4]German: I.

An engine, an engine
Chuffing me off like a Jew.
A Jew to Dachau, Auschwitz, Belsen.[5]
I began to talk like a Jew.
I think I may well be a Jew.   35

The snows of the Tyrol,[6] the clear beer of Vienna
Are not very pure or true.
With my gipsy ancestress and my weird luck
And my Taroc[7] pack and my Taroc pack
I may be a bit of a Jew.   40

I have always been scared of *you*,
With your Luftwaffe,[8] your gobbledygoo.
And your neat mustache
And your Aryan[9] eye, bright blue.
Panzer-man, panzer-man,[10] O You——   45

Not God but a swastika
So black no sky could squeak through.
Every woman adores a Fascist,
The boot in the face, the brute
Brute heart of a brute like you.   50

You stand at the blackboard, daddy,
In the picture I have of you,
A cleft in your chin instead of your foot
But no less a devil for that, no not
Any less the black man who   55

Bit my pretty red heart in two.
I was ten when they buried you.
At twenty I tried to die
And get back, back, back to you.
I thought even the bones would do.   60

But they pulled me out of the sack,
And they stuck me together with glue.
And then I knew what to do.
I made a model of you,
A man in black with a Meinkampf[11] look   65

---

[5]Nazi concentration camps of Holocaust.
[6]Austrian Alps.
[7]Tarot fortune-telling cards.
[8]Nazi air force.

[9]Caucasian Gentile, the Nazi ideal race.
[10]*Panzer* is German for armor: Nazi World
War II armored divisions.
[11]Hitler's manifesto, "My Battle."

And a love of the rack and the screw.
And I said I do, I do.
So daddy, I'm finally through.
The black telephone's off at the root,
The voices just can't worm through.   70

If I've killed one man, I've killed two——
The vampire who said he was you
And drank my blood for a year,
Seven years, if you want to know.
Daddy, you can lie back now.   75

There's a stake in your fat black heart
And the villagers never liked you.
They are dancing and stamping on you.
They always *knew* it was you.
Daddy, daddy, you bastard, I'm through.   80

                                                            1965

Lady Lazarus

I have done it again.
One year in every ten
I manage it——

A sort of walking miracle, my skin
Bright as a Nazi lampshade,   5
My right foot

A paperweight,
My face a featureless, fine
Jew linen.

Peel off the napkin   10
O my enemy.
Do I terrify?——

The nose, the eye pits, the full set of teeth?
The sour breath
Will vanish in a day.   15

Soon, soon the flesh
The grave cave ate will be
At home on me

And I a smiling woman.
I am only thirty.
And like the cat I have nine times to die.   20

This is Number Three.
What a trash
To annihilate each decade.

What a million filaments.
The peanut-crunching crowd   25
Shoves in to see

Them unwrap me hand and foot——
The big strip tease.
Gentlemen, ladies   30

These are my hands,
My knees.
I may be skin and bone,

Nevertheless, I am the same, identical woman.
The first time it happened I was ten.   35
It was an accident.

The second time I meant
To last it out and not come back at all.
I rocked shut

As a seashell.   40
They had to call and call
And pick the worms off me like sticky pearls.

Dying
Is an art, like everything else.
I do it exceptionally well.   45

I do it so it feels like hell.
I do it so it feels real.
I guess you could say I've a call.

It's easy enough to do it in a cell.
It's easy enough to do it and stay put.   50
It's the theatrical

Comeback in broad day
To the same place, the same face, the same brute
Amused shout:

"A miracle!"   55
That knocks me out.
There is a charge

For the eyeing of my scars, there is a charge
For the hearing of my heart——
It really goes.   60

And there is a charge, a very large charge
For a word or a touch
Or a bit of blood

Or a piece of my hair or my clothes.
So, so, Herr Doktor.   65
So, Herr Enemy.

I am your opus,
I am your valuable,
The pure gold baby

That melts to a shriek.   70
I turn and burn.
Do not think I underestimate your great concern.

Ash, ash—
You poke and stir.
Flesh, bone, there is nothing there——   75

A cake of soap,
A wedding ring,
A gold filling.

Herr God, Herr Lucifer,
Beware   80
Beware.

Out of the ash
I rise with my red hair
And I eat men like air.

                                                         1965

KURT VONNEGUT
1922–2007

The work of Kurt Vonnegut—a prodigious body of short stories, plays, novels, and essays—testifies to the burden of bearing witness to history. In an era when American fiction became enamored either with the small dramas of small lives or with the self-reflexive endgame of experimenting with narrative form itself, Vonnegut returned narrative to its ancient privilege, testifying to its moment in history. Vonnegut, across six tumultuous decades, perceived writing as a public service, using the enthralling pull of storytelling both to indict postwar America—for its unexamined enslavement to the depersonalizing effects of technology, its blind allegiance to authority embodied in bumbling government bureaucracies and crooked politicians, its curious worship of a capricious and hapless Christian God, its embrace of the soulless materialism of consumer capitalism, and above all its tragic fascination with violence and the rabbit-hole logic of war—and to offer it the slenderest of hope, kindness tempered with respect and compassion.

Vonnegut was raised in Middle America (Indianapolis, Indiana) in middle-class comfort (his father was a respected architect). He matriculated at Cornell University in 1940. His father insisted that he study something practical and Vonnegut chose biochemistry, but he found working on the student newspaper, writing biting editorial columns, more appealing. He left Cornell during his junior year and enlisted in the Army, where he studied engineering. An infantry private, Vonnegut was captured by the Germans in December 1944 and held as a POW near Dresden, where he witnessed the horrific Allied firebombing of February 1945 that reduced that beautiful (and undefended) city to rubble. After his discharge, Vonnegut struggled. He attended the graduate program in cultural anthropology at the University of Chicago but left without completing the degree. Over the next six years, he worked as a crime reporter, opened a car dealership, taught English to emotionally handicapped high school students, worked in advertising, and finally, in 1947, accepted a position as a technical writer for General Electric near Schenectady, New York (his brother, a respected scientist, worked there). Through it all, Vonnegut crafted short stories, highly imaginative science fiction tales of time travel and aliens. The stories sold, and by the late 1950s he had published a series of sci-fi paperback novels that enjoyed underground success but little critical attention.

In the mid-1960s, Vonnegut decided it was time to bear witness to his Dresden experience. The result—the landmark 1969 novel *Slaughterhouse-Five*, named for the underground meat locker where he was incarcerated as a POW—catapulted him into prominence. The book tapped into the widening counterculture resistance to the Vietnam War and secured his position as a provocative voice of liberal dissent. Vonnegut struggled with the burden of celebrity (he attempted suicide in 1984) and with the vitriolic attacks from the literary establishment that dismissed him as a lightweight. But he maintained a fiercely loyal following among readers who relished his caustic satires, his unadorned writing style, his extravagant imagination that conjured alternate universes and marvelous gadgets, his penchant for hand-drawn illustrations, his compassion-ate humanism that refused to surrender to the obvious conclusion that human-ity was simply too stupid to help itself, his quirky cartoonish characters; his curmudgeonly authorial intrusions into his own stories, and above all his scath-ing black humor. Those fans found in Vonnegut an uncompromising voice of tonic honesty in tumultuous times, a public position he maintained until his death in 2007 at age 84. "Harrison Bergeron," a dystopian satire from Vonne-gut's most productive period during the height of the Cold War, addresses para-noid apprehensions over totalitarian governments and enforced conformity.

Joseph Dewey
University of Pittsburgh at Johnstown

PRIMARY WORKS

Player Piano, 1952; *The Sirens of Titan*, 1959; *Canary in a Cathouse*, 1961; *Mother Night*, 1962; *Cat's Cradle*, 1963; *God Bless You, Mr. Rosewater: or Pearls before Swine*, 1965; *Welcome to the Monkey House*, 1968; *Slaughterhouse-Five, or The Children's Cru-sade: A Duty-Dance with Death*, 1969; *Breakfast of Champions: or Goodbye, Blue Mon-day*, 1973; *Wampeters, Foma, and Granfalloons (Opinions)*, 1974; *Slapstick: or Lonesome No More!*, 1976; *Jailbird*, 1979; *Palm Sunday: An Autobiographical Collage*, 1981; *Dead-eye Dick*, 1982; *Nothing Is Lost Save Honor: Two Essays*, 1984; *Galapagos: A Novel*, 1985; *Bluebeard: The Autobiography of Rabo Karabekian (1916–1988)*, 1987; *Hocus Pocus*, 1990; *Fates Worse than Death: An Autobiographical Collage*, 1991; *Timequake*, 1997; *Bagomobo Snuff Box: Uncollected Short Fiction*, 1999; *God Bless You, Dr. Kevor-kian*, 1999; *A Man without a Country*, 2005; *Armageddon in Retrospect and Other New and Unpublished Writings on War and Peace*, 2008; *Look at the Birdie: Unpublished Fic-tion*, 2009; *While Mortals Sleep: Unpublished Fiction*, 2011.

Harrison Bergeron

The year was 2081, and everybody was finally equal. They weren't only equal before God and the law. They were equal every which way. Nobody was smarter than anybody else. Nobody was better looking than anybody else. Nobody was stronger or quicker than anybody else. All this equality was due to the 211th, 212th, and 213th Amendments to the Constitution, and to the unceasing vigilance of agents of the United States Handicapper General.

Some things about living still weren't quite right, though. April, for instance, still drove people crazy by not being springtime. And it was in that clammy month that the H-G men took George and Hazel Bergeron's fourteen-year-old son, Harrison, away.

It was tragic, all right, but George and Hazel couldn't think about it very hard. Hazel had a perfectly average intelligence, which meant she couldn't think about anything except in short bursts. And George, while his intelli-gence was way above normal, had a little mental handicap radio in his ear. He was required by law to wear it at all times. It was tuned to a government transmitter. Every twenty seconds or so, the transmitter would send out some sharp noise to keep people like George from taking unfair advantage of their brains.

George and Hazel were watching television. There were tears on Hazel's cheeks, but she'd forgotten for the moment what they were about.

On the television screen were ballerinas.

A buzzer sounded in George's head. His thoughts fled in panic, like bandits from a burglar alarm.

"That was a real pretty dance, that dance they just did," said Hazel.

"Huh?" said George.

"That dance—it was nice," said Hazel.

"Yup," said George. He tried to think a little about the ballerinas. They weren't really very good—no better than anybody else would have been, anyway. They were burdened with sashweights and bags of birdshot, and their faces were masked, so that no one, seeing a free and graceful gesture or a pretty face, would feel like something the cat drug in. George was toying with the vague notion that maybe dancers shouldn't be handicapped. But he didn't get very far with it before another noise in his ear radio scattered his thoughts.

George winced. So did two out of the eight ballerinas.

Hazel saw him wince. Having no mental handicap herself, she had to ask George what the latest sound had been.

"Sounded like somebody hitting a milk bottle with a ball peen hammer," said George.

"I'd think it would be real interesting, hearing all the different sounds," said Hazel, a little envious. "All the things they think up."

"Um," said George.

"Only, if I was Handicapper General, you know what I would do?" said Hazel. Hazel, as a matter of fact, bore a strong resemblance to the Handicapper General, a woman named Diana Moon Glampers. "If I was Diana Moon Glampers," said Hazel, "I'd have chimes on Sunday—just chimes. Kind of in honor of religion."

"I could think, if it was just chimes," said George.

"Well—maybe make 'em real loud," said Hazel. "I think I'd make a good Handicapper General."

"Good as anybody else," said George.

"Who knows better'n I do what normal is?" said Hazel.

"Right," said George. He began to think glimmeringly about his abnormal son who was now in jail, about Harrison, but a twenty-one-gun salute in his head stopped that.

"Boy!" said Hazel, "that was a doozy, wasn't it?"

It was such a doozy that George was white and trembling, and tears stood on the rims of his red eyes. Two of the eight ballerinas had collapsed to the studio floor, were holding their temples.

"All of a sudden you look so tired," said Hazel. "Why don't you stretch out on the sofa, so's you can rest your handicap bag on the pillows, honeybunch." She was referring to the forty-seven pounds of birdshot in a canvas bag, which was padlocked around George's neck. "Go on and rest the bag for a little while," she said. "I don't care if you're not equal to me for a while."

George weighed the bag with his hands. "I don't mind it," he said. "I don't notice it any more. It's just a part of me."

"You been so tired lately—kind of wore out," said Hazel. "If there was just some way we could make a little hole in the bottom of the bag, and just take out a few of them lead balls. Just a few."

"Two years in prison and two thousand dollars fine for every ball I took out," said George. "I don't call that a bargain."

"If you could just take a few out when you came home from work," said Hazel. "I mean—you don't compete with anybody around here. You just set around."

"If I tried to get away with it," said George, "then other people'd get away with it—and pretty soon we'd be right back to the dark ages again, with everybody competing against everybody else. You wouldn't like that, would you?"

"I'd hate it," said Hazel.

"There you are," said George. "The minute people start cheating on laws, what do you think happens to society?"

If Hazel hadn't been able to come up with an answer to this question, George couldn't have supplied one. A siren was going off in his head.

"Reckon it'd fall all apart," said Hazel.

Screams and barking cries of consternation came from the television set. The photograph of Harrison Bergeron on the screen jumped again and again, as though dancing to the tune of an earthquake.

George Bergeron correctly identified the earthquake, and well he might have—for many was the time his own home had danced to the same crashing tune. "My God—" said George, "that must be Harrison!"

The realization was blasted from his mind instantly by the sound of an automobile collision in his head.

When George could open his eyes again, the photograph of Harrison was gone. A living, breathing Harrison filled the screen.

Clanking, clownish, and huge, Harrison stood in the center of the studio. The knob of the uprooted studio door was still in his hand. Ballerinas, technicians, musicians, and announcers cowered on their knees before him, expecting to die.

"I am the Emperor!" cried Harrison. "Do you hear? I am the Emperor! Everybody must do what I say at once!" He stamped his foot and the studio shook.

"Even as I stand here—" he bellowed, "crippled, hobbled, sickened—I am a greater ruler than any man who ever lived! Now watch me become what I *can* become!"

Harrison tore the straps of his handicap harness like wet tissue paper, tore straps guaranteed to support five thousand pounds.

Harrison's scrap-iron handicaps crashed to the floor.

Harrison thrust his thumbs under the bar of the padlock that secured his head harness. The bar snapped like celery. Harrison smashed his headphones and spectacles against the wall.

He flung away his rubber-ball nose, revealed a man that would have awed Thor, the god of thunder.

"I shall now select my Empress!" he said, looking down on the cowering people. "Let the first woman who dares rise to her feet claim her mate and her throne!"

A moment passed, and then a ballerina arose, swaying like a willow.

Harrison plucked the mental handicap from her ear, snapped off her physical handicaps with marvelous delicacy. Last of all, he removed her mask.

She was blindingly beautiful.

"Now—" said Harrison, taking her hand, "shall we show the people the meaning of the word dance? Music!" he commanded.

The musicians scrambled back into their chairs, and Harrison stripped them of their handicaps, too. "Play your best," he told them, "and I'll make you barons and dukes and earls."

The music began. It was normal at first—cheap, silly, false. But Harrison snatched two musicians from their chairs, waved them like batons as he sang the music as he wanted it played. He slammed them back into their chairs.

The music began again and was much improved.

Harrison and his Empress merely listened to the music for a while— listened gravely, as though synchronizing their heartbeats with it.

"What would?" said George blankly.

"Society," said Hazel uncertainly. "Wasn't that what you just said?"

"Who knows?" said George.

The television program was suddenly interrupted for a news bulletin. It wasn't clear at first as to what the bulletin was about, since the announcer, like all announcers, had a serious speech impediment. For about half a minute, and in a state of high excitement, the announcer tried to say, "Ladies and gentlemen—"

He finally gave up, handed the bulletin to a ballerina to read.

"That's all right—" Hazel said of the announcer, "he tried. That's the big thing. He tried to do the best he could with what God gave him. He should get a nice raise for trying so hard."

"Ladies and gentlemen—" said the ballerina, reading the bulletin. She must have been extraordinarily beautiful, because the mask she wore was hideous. And it was easy to see that she was the strongest and most graceful of all the dancers, for her handicap bags were as big as those worn by two-hundred-pound men.

And she had to apologize at once for her voice, which was a very unfair voice for a woman to use. Her voice was a warm, luminous, timeless melody. "Excuse me—" she said, and she began again, making her voice absolutely uncompetitive.

"Harrison Bergeron, age fourteen," she said in a grackle squawk, "has just escaped from jail, where he was held on suspicion of plotting to overthrow the government. He is a genius and an athlete, is under-handicapped, and should be regarded as extremely dangerous."

A police photograph of Harrison Bergeron was flashed on the screen upside down, then sideways, upside down again, then right side up. The picture showed the full length of Harrison against a background calibrated in feet and inches. He was exactly seven feet tall.

The rest of Harrison's appearance was Halloween and hardware. Nobody had ever borne heavier handicaps. He had outgrown hindrances faster than the H-G men could think them up. Instead of a little ear radio for a mental handicap, he wore a tremendous pair of earphones, and spectacles with thick wavy lenses. The spectacles were intended to make him not only half blind, but to give him whanging headaches besides.

Scrap metal was hung all over him. Ordinarily, there was a certain symmetry, a military neatness to the handicaps issued to strong people, but Harrison looked like a walking junkyard. In the race of life, Harrison carried three hundred pounds.

And to offset his good looks, the H-G men required that he wear at all times a red rubber ball for a nose, keep his eyebrows shaved off, and cover his even white teeth with black caps at snaggle-tooth random.

"If you see this boy," said the ballerina, "do not—I repeat, do not—try to reason with him."

There was the shriek of a door being torn from its hinges.

They shifted their weights to their toes.

Harrison placed his big hands on the girl's tiny waist, letting her sense the weightlessness that would soon be hers.

And then, in an explosion of joy and grace, into the air they sprang!

Not only were the laws of the land abandoned, but the law of gravity and the laws of motion as well.

They reeled, whirled, swiveled, flounced, capered, gamboled, and spun.

They leaped like deer on the moon.

The studio ceiling was thirty feet high, but each leap brought the dancers nearer to it.

It became their obvious intention to kiss the ceiling.

They kissed it.

And then, neutralizing gravity with love and pure will, they remained suspended in air inches below the ceiling, and they kissed each other for a long, long time.

It was then that Diana Moon Glampers, the Handicapper General, came into the studio with a double-barreled ten-gauge shotgun. She fired twice, and the Emperor and the Empress were dead before they hit the floor.

Diana Moon Glampers loaded the gun again. She aimed it at the musicians and told them they had ten seconds to get their handicaps back on.

It was then that the Bergerons' television tube burned out.

Hazel turned to comment about the blackout to George. But George had gone out into the kitchen for a can of beer.

George came back in with the beer, paused while a handicap signal shook him up. And then he sat down again. "You been crying?" he said to Hazel.

"Yup," she said.

"What about?" he said.

"I forget," she said. "Something real sad on television."

"What was it?" he said.

"It's all kind of mixed up in my mind," said Hazel.

"Forget sad things," said George.

"I always do," said Hazel.

"That's my girl," said George. He winced. There was the sound of a riveting gun in his head.

"Gee—I could tell that one was a doozy," said Hazel.

"You can say that again," said George.

"Gee—" said Hazel, "I could tell that one was a doozy."

1968

JOHN ASHBERY
B. 1927

John Ashbery was born in Rochester, New York, and attended Harvard University, where he met the poets Frank O'Hara and Kenneth Koch. Later these college friends moved to New York City, where they formed the core of the so-called New York School, noted for its use of popular imagery, surrealistic turns of thought, and high-spirited humor. After college Ashbery worked for Oxford University Press and McGraw-Hill. "The Instruction Manual" dates from those days.

Awarded a Fulbright Fellowship, in 1956 Ashbery moved to France and worked as an art journalist, a profession he followed for the next thirty years, writing for magazines such as *Art International*, *New York*, and *Newsweek*. In 1965 he returned to New York to become executive editor of *Art News*. In 1974 he joined the faculty of Brooklyn College, where he served as Distinguished Professor. From 1990 until his retirement in 2008, he was the Charles P. Stevenson Professor of Languages and Literature at Bard College.

Ashbery is one of the few poets who has been able to gain the admiration of both experimental artists and conservative academicians, winning virtually all the major literary prizes this country has to offer. In "Farm Implements and Rutabagas in a Landscape," for example, he sets his outrageous installment of Popeye in the form of a sestina, one of the most difficult poetic forms. Thus the poem combines untraditional subject matter with highly traditional form.

Many of Ashbery's chief preoccupations are also traditional ones, which he treats in an unusually charged and avant-garde manner. One important theme running through virtually all of his work is "mutability," a central theme of the English Renaissance and American Transcendentalists. For older writers and thinkers, the mutable or changeable world of human and natural affairs is contrasted to the eternal, fixed world of the spirit and ideas. Some poets, including Wallace Stevens—one of the strongest influences on Ashbery—prefer the mutable to the eternal.

Yet another topic informed by the theme of mutability is the self: is our consciousness fixed and unitary or fluid and multiple? Many poems try to catch the mind even as it changes shape, for what is empathy but the power to take on another person's consciousness, or the imagination but the ability to transform the experiences around us into something very different? Reality for Ashbery is not a hard, fixed, or certain entity but an awareness brimming with impressions, memories, and desires that are constantly transformed, repeated, blurred, and blotted out.

David Bergman
Towson University

PRIMARY WORKS

Some Trees, 1956; *The Tennis Court Oath,* 1962; *Rivers and Mountains,* 1966; *A Nest of Ninnies* (novel with James Schuyler), 1969; *The Double Dream of Spring,* 1970; *Three Poems,* 1972; *The Vermont Notebook,* 1975; *Self-Portrait in a Convex Mirror,* 1975; *Houseboat Days,* 1978; *Three Plays,* 1978; *As We Know,* 1979; *Shadow Train,* 1981; *A Wave,* 1984; *Selected Poems,* 1985; *April Galleons,* 1987; *Reported Sightings: Art Chronicles 1957–1987,* 1989; *Flow Chart,* 1991; *Hotel L'Autréamont,* 1993; *Three Books,* 1993; *And the Stars Were Shining,* 1994; *Can You Hear, Bird,* 1995; *The Mooring of Starting Out: The First Five Books of Poetry,* 1997; *Wakefulness,* 1998; *Girls on the Run,* 1999; *Other Traditions,* 2000; *Your Name Here,* 2000; *The Vermont Notebook,* 2001; *Chinese Whispers,* 2002; *Where Shall I Wander,* 2005; *A Worldly Country,* 2007; *Planisphere,* 2009.

The Instruction Manual

As I sit looking out of a window of the building
I wish I did not have to write the instruction manual on the uses
    of a new metal.
I look down into the street and see people, each walking with an
    inner peace,   5
And envy them—they are so far away from me!
Not one of them has to worry about getting out this manual on
    schedule.
And, as my way is, I begin to dream, resting my elbows on the
    desk and leaning out of the window a little,   10
Of dim Guadalajara![1] City of rose-colored flowers!
City I wanted most to see, and most did not see, in Mexico!
But I fancy I see, under the press of having to write the
    instruction manual,
Your public square, city, with its elaborate little bandstand!   15
The band is playing *Scheherazade* by Rimsky-Korsakov.[2]

---

[1]Guadalajara is the second largest city in Mexico, 275 miles west-northwest of Mexico City. Mariachi bands originated in Guadalajara.
[2]Rimsky-Korsakov (1844–1908) was one of the finest Russian composers of his time. *Schehera-* zade (1888) was composed for the Russian Ballet and celebrates the dancing-girl who preserved her life by weaving the thousand-and-one stories of the *Arabian Nights.*

Around stand the flower girls, handing out rose- and lemon-
    colored flowers,
Each attractive in her rose-and-blue striped dress (Oh! such shades
    of rose and blue),   20
And nearby is the little white booth where women in green serve
    you green and yellow fruit.
The couples are parading; everyone is in a holiday mood.
First, leading the parade, is a dapper fellow
Clothed in deep blue. On his head sits a white hat   25
And he wears a mustache, which has been trimmed for the
    occasion.
His dear one, his wife, is young and pretty; her shawl is rose,
    pink, and white.
Her slippers are patent leather, in the American fashion,   30
And she carries a fan, for she is modest, and does not want the
    crowd to see her face too often.
But everybody is so busy with his wife or loved one
I doubt they would notice the mustachioed man's wife.
Here come the boys! They are skipping and throwing little things   35
    on the sidewalk
Which is made of gray tile. One of them, a little older, has a
    toothpick in his teeth.
He is silenter than the rest, and affects not to notice the pretty
    young girls in white.   40
But his friends notice them, and shout their jeers at the laughing girls.
Yet soon all this will cease, with the deepening of their years,
And love bring each to the parade grounds for another reason.
But I have lost sight of the young fellow with the toothpick.
Wait—there he is—on the other side of the bandstand,   45
Secluded from his friends, in earnest talk with a young girl
Of fourteen or fifteen. I try to hear what they are saying
But it seems they are just mumbling something—shy words of
    love, probably.
She is slightly taller than he, and looks quietly down into his   50
    sincere eyes.
She is wearing white. The breeze ruffles her long fine black hair
    against her olive cheek.
Obviously she is in love. The boy, the young boy with the
    toothpick, he is in love too;   55
His eyes show it. Turning from this couple,
I see there is an intermission in the concert.
The paraders are resting and sipping drinks through straws
(The drinks are dispensed from a large glass crock by a lady in
    dark blue),   60
And the musicians mingle among them, in their creamy white
    uniforms, and talk
About the weather, perhaps, or how their kids are doing at school.

Let us take this opportunity to tiptoe into one of the side streets.
Here you may see one of those white houses with green trim 65
That are so popular here. Look—I told you!
It is cool and dim inside, but the patio is sunny.
An old woman in gray sits there, fanning herself with a palm leaf
    fan.
She welcomes us to her patio, and offers us a cooling drink. 70
"My son is in Mexico City," she says? "He would welcome you
    too
If he were here. But his job is with a bank there.
Look, here is a photograph of him."
And a dark-skinned lad with pearly teeth grins out at us from the 75
    worn leather frame.
We thank her for her hospitality, for it is getting late
And we must catch a view of the city, before we leave, from a
    good high place.
That church tower will do—the faded pink one, there against the 80
    fierce blue of the sky. Slowly we enter.
The caretaker, an old man dressed in brown and gray, asks us how
    long we have been in the city, and how we like it here.
His daughter is scrubbing the steps—she nods to us as we pass
    into the tower. 85
Soon we have reached the top, and the whole network of the city
    extends before us.
There is the rich quarter, with its houses of pink and white, and
    its crumbling, leafy terraces.
There is the poorer quarter, its homes a deep blue. 90
There is the market, where men are selling hats and swatting flies
And there is the public library, painted several shades of pale
    green and beige.
Look! There is the square we just came from, with the
    promenaders. 95
There are fewer of them, now that the heat of the day has
    increased,
But the young boy and girl still lurk in the shadows of the
    bandstand.
And there is the home of the little old lady— 100
She is still sitting in the patio, fanning herself.
How limited, but how complete withal, has been our experience of
    Guadalajara!
We have seen young love, married love, and the love of an aged
    mother for her son. 105
We have heard the music, tasted the drinks, and looked at colored
    houses.
What more is there to do, except stay? And that we cannot do.

And as a last breeze freshens the top of the weathered old tower, I
   turn my gaze   110
Back to the instruction manual which has made me dream of
   Guadalajara.

                                                    1956

Farm Implements and Rutabagas in a Landscape[1]

The first of the undecoded messages read: "Popeye sits in
   thunder,[2]
Unthought of. From that shoebox of an apartment,
From livid curtain's hue, a tangram emerges: a country."
Meanwhile the Sea Hag was relaxing on a green couch: "How   5
   pleasant
To spend one's vacation *en la casa de Popeye*,"[3] she scratched
Her cleft chin's solitary hair. She remembered spinach

And was going to ask Wimpy if he had bought any spinach.
"M'love," he intercepted, "the plains are decked out in thunder   10
Today, and it shall be as you wish." He scratched
The part of his head under his hat. The apartment
Seemed to grow smaller. "But what if no pleasant
Inspiration plunge us now to the stars? *For this is my country.*"

Suddenly they remembered how it was cheaper in the country.   15
Wimpy was thoughtfully cutting open a number 2 can of spinach
When the door opened and Swee'pea crept in. "How pleasant!"
But Swee'pea looked morose. A note was pinned to his bib.
   "Thunder
And tears are unavailing," it read. "Henceforth shall Popeye's   20
   apartment
Be but remembered space, toxic or salubrious, whole or
   scratched."

---

[1] When he was an editor for *Art News*, Ashbery and the poet James Schuyler amused themselves by inventing funny titles for imaginary paintings and prints.

[2] Popeye was the main character in a comic strip created by Segar and was transformed into animated films by Max Fleisher. In the 1930s, Popeye rivaled Mickey Mouse in popularity. In an interview, Ashbery explained: "I go back to my earliest impressions a great deal when writing poetry. All poets do, I think. To me, it was always a great event. On Saturday night we got colored comics."

[3] Spanish for "in Popeye's house." Ashbery explains: "The reason that the Spanish phrase is in the poem is because [Popeye is] now published in New York only in *El Diario*, the Spanish-language paper.... I just liked the way it looks, and the fact of the characters speaking Spanish, seems so funny. I used to follow it also in French newspapers, where Popeye's dislocations of the English language are reproduced charmingly in French.... I tend to dislocate the language myself."

Olive came hurtling through the window; its geraniums scratched
Her long thigh. "I have news!" she gasped. "Popeye, forced as   25
    you know to flee the country
One musty gusty evening, by the schemes of his wizened, duplicate
    father, jealous of the apartment
And all that it contains, myself and spinach
In particular, heave bolts of loving thunder   30
At his own astonished becoming, rupturing the pleasant

Arpeggio of our years. No more shall pleasant
Rays of the sun refresh your sense of growing old, nor the
    scratched
Tree-trunks and mossy foliage, only immaculate darkness and   35
    thunder."
She grabbed Swee'pea. "I'm taking the brat to the country."
"But you can't do that—he hasn't even finished his spinach."
Urged the Sea Hag, looking fearfully around at the apartment.

But Olive was already out of earshot. Now the apartment   40
Succumbed to a strange new hush. "Actually it's quite pleasant
Here," thought the Sea Hag. "If this is all we need fear from
    spinach
Then I don't mind so much. Perhaps we could invite Alice the
    Goon over"—she scratched   45
One dug pensively—"but Wimpy is such a country
Bumpkin, always burping like that." Minute at first, the thunder

Soon filled the apartment. It was domestic thunder,
The color of spinach. Popeye chuckled and scratched
his balls: it sure was pleasant to spend a day in the country.   50

                                                                    1970

As You Came from the Holy Land

of western New York state[1]
were the graves all right in their bushings
was there a note of panic in the late August air
because the old man had peed in his pants again
was there turning away from the late afternoon glare   5
as though it too could be wished away
was any of this present

---

[1]Western New York State may be a "holy land" for Ashbery because it is his birthplace, the area where Joseph Smith in 1827 discovered the mystical tablets that form the basis of the Mormon religion, and the location of the Oneida Community, a Utopian society founded in 1847 by John Humphrey Noyes.

and how could this be
the magic solution to what you are in now
whatever has held you motionless   10
like this so long through the dark season
until now the women come out in navy blue
and the worms come out of the compost to die
it is the end of any season

you reading there so accurately   15
sitting not wanting to be disturbed
as you came from that holy land
what other signs of earth's dependency were upon you
what fixed sign at the crossroads
what lethargy in the avenues   20
where all is said in a whisper
what tone of voice among the hedges
what tone under the apple trees
the numbered land stretches away
and your house is built in tomorrow   25
but surely not before the examination
of what is right and will befall
not before the census
and the writing down of names

remember you are free to wander away   30
as from other times other scenes that were taking place
the history of someone who came too late
the time is ripe now and the adage
is hatching as the seasons change and tremble
it is finally as though that thing of monstrous interest   35
were happening in the sky
but the sun is setting and prevents you from seeing it

out of night the token emerges
its leaves like birds alighting all at once under a tree
taken up and shaken again   40
put down in weak rage
knowing as the brain does it can never come about
not here not yesterday in the past
only in the gap of today filling itself
as emptiness is distributed   45
in the idea of what time it is
when that time is already past

1975

MARTIN LUTHER KING, JR.
1929–1968

The son and grandson of Baptist preachers, Martin Luther King, Jr., grew up in a middle-class home in Atlanta. He graduated with a B.A. from Morehouse College, completed ministerial studies at Crozer Theological Seminary, and earned a Ph.D. at Boston University.

After King became a pastor in Montgomery, Alabama, Rosa Parks was arrested for refusing to yield her bus seat to a white man. Her jailing spurred Jo Ann Robinson and the Women's Political Council to initiate the Montgomery Bus Boycott, a yearlong nonviolent protest in that city. King's eloquent leadership of that struggle earned him the national spotlight. By outlawing bus segregation in Montgomery, the Supreme Court gave King an important victory.

After others launched the lunch counter sit-ins of 1960 and the Freedom Rides of 1961, King directed a well-publicized racial protest in Birmingham, Alabama. National television cameras recorded scenes of nonviolent black marchers, including children, being attacked by the fire hoses and police dogs of Birmingham's city government. Arrested, King penned his "Letter from Birmingham Jail." Winning the battle for American public opinion, he successfully pushed business leaders to outlaw segregation in downtown Birmingham.

In August 1963, some 250,000 protesters heard King deliver "I Have a Dream" at the Lincoln Memorial in Washington, D.C. This electrifying address helped build momentum for the Civil Rights Act of 1964, a sweeping measure that banned racial discrimination in hotels, restaurants, and other public accommodations. King won the Nobel Peace Prize in that same year. In 1965 his march from Selma, Alabama, to Montgomery prompted passage of the Voting Rights Act, which guaranteed African Americans the right to vote.

In 1967 King condemned American participation in the Vietnam War. A previously sympathetic press vilified him for this stance, which also earned the contempt of a once friendly President Lyndon Johnson.

King also railed against poverty. Planning his most ambitious protest, he envisioned thousands of blacks, Hispanics, Indians, and poor whites converging on the nation's capital. A strike by garbage workers in Memphis diverted him from this effort. After galvanizing supporters with "I've Been to the Mountaintop," he was assassinated the next day.

King's fame has obscured the contributions of James Farmer, Ella Baker, John Lewis, Fannie Lou Hamer, and others, who, like King, mastered Gandhian strategy in the quest for racial justice. But King's fiery yet magisterial language convinced whites to tear down the walls of legalized segregation. He triumphed by reviving the slaves' vivid identification with the biblical Hebrews trapped in Egyptian bondage, a strategy especially evident in "I've Been to the Mountaintop." Trained by African American folk preachers, he adopted their assumption that language is a shared treasure, not private property. King often borrowed sermons without acknowledgment from Harry Emerson Fosdick and other liberal preachers. This borrowed material appears in scores of King's published and unpublished addresses and essays, including "Letter from Birmingham Jail," "I

Have a Dream," the Nobel Prize Address, and "I've Been to the Mountaintop."
By synthesizing black and white pulpit traditions, King persuaded whites to hear
the slaves' cry, "Let my people go!"

Keith D. Miller
Arizona State University

PRIMARY WORKS

Stride Toward Freedom: The Montgomery Story, 1958; *Strength to Love*, 1963; *Why We
Can't Wait*, 1965; *Where Do We Go from Here? Chaos or Community*, 1967; *A Testament
of Hope: The Essential Writings of Martin Luther King, Jr.*, 1986; *The Papers of Martin
Luther King, Jr.*, vols. 1–4, 1992, 1994, 1997, 2000.

I Have a Dream

I am happy to join with you today in what will go down in history as the
greatest demonstration for freedom in the history of our nation.

Five score years ago a great American in whose symbolic shadow we stand
today signed the Emancipation Proclamation.[1] This momentous decree came
as a great beacon light of hope to millions of Negro slaves who had been
seared in the flames of withering injustice. It came as a joyous daybreak to
end the long night of their captivity. But one hundred years later the Negro
still is not free. One hundred years later the life of the Negro is still sadly
crippled by the manacles of segregation and the chains of discrimination. One
hundred years later the Negro lives on a lonely island of poverty in the midst
of a vast ocean of material prosperity. One hundred years later the Negro is
still languished in the corners of American society and finds himself in exile
in his own land. So we've come here today to dramatize a shameful condition.

In a sense we've come to our nation's capital to cash a check. When the
architects of our Republic wrote the magnificent words of the Constitution
and the Declaration of Independence, they were signing a promissory note
to which every American was to fall heir. This note was a promise that all
men—yes, black men as well as white men—would be guaranteed the
unalienable rights of life, liberty and the pursuit of happiness.[2] It is obvious
today that America has defaulted on this promissory note insofar as her citizens of color are concerned. Instead of honoring this sacred obligation,
America has given the Negro people a bad check, a check which has come
back marked "insufficient funds."

But we refuse to believe that the bank of justice is bankrupt. We refuse
to believe that there are insufficient funds in the great vaults of opportunity
of this nation. So we've come to cash this check, a check that will give us
upon demand the riches of freedom and the security of justice.

---

[1]King delivered this speech on the steps of the
Lincoln Memorial, which houses a giant marble statue of Abraham Lincoln, whose Emancipation Proclamation freed American slaves.
"Five score years ago ..." echoes the beginning of Lincoln's famous Gettysburg Address.

[2]The phrase "unalienable rights of life, liberty,
and the pursuit of happiness" appears in the
Declaration of Independence, written by
Thomas Jefferson.

We have also come to this hallowed spot to remind America of the fierce urgency of now. This is no time to engage in the luxury of cooling off or to take the tranquilizing drug of gradualism. Now is the time to make real the promises of democracy. Now is the time to rise from the dark and desolate valley of segregation to the sunlit path of racial justice. Now is the time to lift our nation from the quicksands of racial injustice to the solid rock of brotherhood.

Now is the time to make justice a reality for all of God's children. It would be fatal for the nation to overlook the urgency of the moment. This sweltering summer of the Negro's legitimate discontent[3] will not pass until there is an invigorating autumn of freedom and equality—nineteen sixty-three is not an end but a beginning. Those who hope that the Negro needed to blow off steam and will now be content will have a rude awakening if the nation returns to business as usual.

There will be neither rest nor tranquility in America until the Negro is granted his citizenship rights. The whirlwinds of revolt will continue to shake the foundations of our nation until the bright day of justice emerges.

But there is something that I must say to my people who stand on the worn threshold which leads into the palace of justice. In the process of gaining our rightful place we must not be guilty of wrongful deeds. Let us not seek to satisfy our thirst for freedom by drinking from the cup of bitterness and hatred.

We must forever conduct our struggle on the high plane of dignity and discipline. We must not allow our creative protests to degenerate into physical violence. Again and again we must rise to the majestic heights of meeting physical force with soul force.[4] The marvelous new militancy which has engulfed the Negro community must not lead us to a distrust of all white people, for many of our white brothers, as evidenced by their presence here today, have come to realize that their destiny is tied up with our destiny. They have come to realize that their freedom is inextricably bound to our freedom. We cannot walk alone. And as we walk we must make the pledge that we shall always march ahead. We cannot turn back.

There are those who are asking the devotees of civil rights, "When will you be satisfied?"

We can never be satisfied as long as the Negro is the victim of the unspeakable horrors of police brutality.

We can never be satisfied as long as our bodies, heavy with the fatigue of travel, cannot gain lodging in the motels of the highways and the hotels of the cities.[5]

We cannot be satisfied as long as the Negro's basic mobility is from a smaller ghetto to a larger one.[6] We can never be satisfied as long as our

---

[3]King turns inside out Shakespeare's "Now is the winter of our discontent/Made glorious summer by this sun of York. . . ." See *Richard III*, Act I, Scene 1.

[4]Following the example of Gandhi, King consistently practiced and preached nonviolence, even though his opponents often resorted to violence against him.

[5]Throughout the South, most motels and hotels were reserved for whites only.

[6]Throughout much of the nation blacks experienced racial discrimination in housing.

children are stripped of their selfhood and robbed of their dignity by signs stating "For Whites Only."

We cannot be satisfied as long as the Negro in Mississippi cannot vote and the Negro in New York believes he has nothing for which to vote.

No, no, we are not satisfied, and we will not be satisfied until justice rolls down like waters and righteousness like a mighty stream.[7]

I am not unmindful that some of you have come here out of great trials and tribulations. Some of you have come fresh from narrow jail cells.[8] Some of you have come from areas where your quest for freedom left you battered by the storms of persecution and staggered by the winds of police brutality. You have been the veterans of creative suffering.

Continue to work with the faith that unearned suffering is redemptive. Go back to Mississippi, go back to Alabama, go back to South Carolina, go back to Georgia, go back to Louisiana, go back to the slums and ghettos of our Northern cities, knowing that somehow this situation can and will be changed. Let us not wallow in the valley of despair.

I say to you today, my friends, so even though we face the difficulties of today and tomorrow, I still have a dream. It is a dream deeply rooted in the American dream. I have a dream that one day this nation will rise up, live out the true meaning of its creed: "We hold these truths to be self-evident, that all men are created equal."[9]

I have a dream that one day on the red hills of Georgia sons of former slaves and the sons of former slave-owners will be able to sit down together at the table of brotherhood. I have a dream that one day even the state of Mississippi, a state sweltering with the heat of injustice, sweltering with the heat of oppression, will be transformed into an oasis of freedom and justice.

I have a dream that my four little children will one day live in a nation where they will not be judged by the color of their skin but by the content of their character. I have a dream today. I have a dream that one day down in Alabama, with its vicious racists, with its governor having his lips dripping with the words of interposition and nullification,[10] one day right there in Alabama little black boys and black girls will be able to join hands with little white boys and white girls as sisters and brothers.

I have a dream today. I have a dream that one day every valley shall be exalted, every hill and mountain shall be made low. The rough places will be made plain, and the crooked places will be made straight. And the glory of the Lord shall be revealed, and all flesh shall see it together.[11] This is our

[7]This statement includes a renowned biblical declaration from the Hebrew prophet Amos ("Let justice roll down . . ."). See Amos 5:24.

[8]Violating local laws, King and other civil rights protesters voluntarily went to jail to dramatize their cause.

[9]"We hold these truths . . ." is the most famous sentence of the Declaration of Independence.

[10]Governor George Wallace of Alabama attempted to interpose state authority to nullify federal orders to integrate his state.

[11]This passage incorporates visionary language from the Hebrew prophet Isaiah ("Every valley shall be exalted . . .") that reappears in the Christian New Testament. Handel includes it in the *Messiah*, a popular, long piece of Christian music. See Isaiah 40:4 and Luke 3:5. Biblical quotations remind listeners of King's status as a minister.

hope. This is the faith that I go back to the South with. With this faith we will be able to hew out of the mountain of despair a stone of hope. With this faith we will be able to transform the jangling discords of our nation into a beautiful symphony of brotherhood. With this faith we will be able to work together, to pray together, to struggle together, to go to jail together, to stand up for freedom together, knowing that we will be free one day.

This will be the day, this will be the day when all of God's children will be able to sing with new meaning, "My country, 'tis of thee, sweet land of liberty, of thee I sing. Land where my fathers died, land of the pilgrim's pride, from every mountainside, let freedom ring."[12] And if America is to be a great nation, this must become true. So let freedom ring from the prodigious hilltops of New Hampshire. Let freedom ring from the mighty mountains of New York. Let freedom ring from the heightening Alleghenies of Pennsylvania. Let freedom ring from the snowcapped Rockies of Colorado. Let freedom ring from the curvaceous slopes of California.

But not only that. Let freedom ring from Stone Mountain of Georgia. Let freedom ring from Lookout Mountain of Tennessee. Let freedom ring from every hill and molehill of Mississippi, from every mountainside.[13] Let freedom ring.

And when this happens, when we allow freedom [to] ring—when we let it ring from every village and every hamlet, from every state and every city, we will be able to speed up that day when all of God's children, black men and white men, Jews and Gentiles, Protestants and Catholics, will be able to join hands and sing in the words of the old Negro spiritual, "Free at last, Free at last, Thank God a-mighty, We are free at last."

1963

Letter from Birmingham Jail

April 16, 1963

My Dear Fellow Clergymen:

While confined here in the Birmingham city jail, I came across your recent statement calling my present activities "unwise and untimely." Seldom do I pause to answer criticism of my work and ideas. If I sought to answer all the criticisms that cross my desk, my secretaries would have little time for anything other than such correspondence in the course of the day, and I would have no time for constructive work. But since I feel that you are men of genuine good will and that your criticisms are sincerely set forth, I

[12]These are the opening lines of "America," our unofficial national anthem. King's use of the phrase "Let freedom ring" seems to extend the lyrics of the song.

[13]King borrowed and adapted the "Let freedom ring" litany from a speech at the 1952 Republican Convention by Archibald Carey, an African American minister from Chicago and friend of King.

want to try to answer your statement in what I hope will be patient and reasonable terms.

I think I should indicate why I am here in Birmingham, since you have been influenced by the view which argues against "outsiders coming in." I have the honor of serving as president of the Southern Christian Leadership Conference, an organization operating in every southern state, with headquarters in Atlanta, Georgia. We have some eighty-five affiliated organizations across the South, and one of them is the Alabama Christian Movement for Human Rights. Frequently we share staff, educational, and financial resources with our affiliates. Several months ago the affiliate here in Birmingham asked us to be on call to engage in a nonviolent direct-action program if such were deemed necessary. We readily consented, and when the hour came we lived up to our promise. So I, along with several members of my staff, am here because I was invited here. I am here because I have organizational ties here.

But more basically, I am in Birmingham because injustice is here. Just as the prophets of the eighth century B.C. left their villages and carried their "thus saith the Lord" far beyond the boundaries of their home towns, and just as the Apostle Paul[1] left his village of Tarsus and carried the gospel of Jesus Christ to the far corners of the Greco-Roman world, so am I compelled to carry the gospel of freedom beyond my own home town. Like Paul, I must constantly respond to the Macedonian call for aid.

Moreover, I am cognizant of the interrelatedness of all communities and states. I cannot sit idly by in Atlanta and not be concerned about what happens in Birmingham. Injustice anywhere is a threat to justice everywhere. We are caught in an inescapable network of mutuality, tied in a single garment of destiny. Whatever affects one directly, affects all indirectly. Never again can we afford to live with the narrow, provincial, "outside agitator" idea. Anyone who lives inside the United States can never be considered an outsider anywhere within its bounds.

You deplore the demonstrations taking place in Birmingham. But your statement, I am sorry to say, fails to express a similar concern for the conditions that brought about the demonstrations. I am sure that none of you would want to rest content with the superficial kind of social analysis that deals merely with the effects and does not grapple with underlying causes. It is unfortunate that demonstrations are taking place in Birmingham, but it is even more unfortunate that the city's white power structure left the Negro community with no alternative.

In any nonviolent campaign there are four basic steps: collection of the facts to determine whether injustices exist; negotiation; self-purification; and direct action. We have gone through all these steps in Birmingham. There can be no gainsaying the fact that racial injustice engulfs this community.

[1]Saint Paul, originally Saul of Tarsus, was a follower of Jesus who went on a mission after seeing a vision that the Macedonian people needed his help. Martin Luther King is also following in Paul's tradition as a writer of inspirational letters.

Birmingham is probably the most thoroughly segregated city in the United States. Its ugly record of brutality is widely known. Negroes have experienced grossly unjust treatment in the courts. There have been more unsolved bombings of Negro homes and churches in Birmingham than in any other city in the nation. These are the hard brutal facts of the case. On the basis of these conditions, Negro leaders sought to negotiate with the city fathers. But the latter consistently refused to engage in good-faith negotiation.

Then, last September, came the opportunity to talk with leaders of Birmingham's economic community. In the course of the negotiations, certain promises were made by the merchants—for example, to remove the stores' humiliating racial signs. On the basis of these promises, the Reverend Fred Shuttlesworth[2] and the leaders of the Alabama Christian Movement for Human Rights agreed to a moratorium on all demonstrations. As the weeks and months went by, we realized that we were the victims of a broken promise. A few signs, briefly removed, returned; the others remained.

As in so many past experiences, our hopes had been blasted, and the shadows of deep disappointment settled upon us. We had no alternative except to prepare for direct action, whereby we would present our very bodies as a means of laying our case before the conscience of the local and the national community. Mindful of the difficulties involved, we decided to undertake a process of self-purification. We began a series of workshops on nonviolence, and we repeatedly asked ourselves: "Are you able to accept blows without retaliating?" "Are you able to endure the ordeal of jail?" We decided to schedule our direct-action program for the Easter season, realizing that except for Christmas, this is the main shopping period of the year. Knowing that a strong economic-withdrawal program would be the by-product of direct action, we felt that this would be the best time to bring pressure to bear on the merchants for the needed change.

Then it occurred to us that Birmingham's mayoral election was coming up in March, and we speedily decided to postpone action until after election day. When we discovered that the Commissioner of Public Safety, Eugene "Bull" Connor, had piled up enough votes to be in the run-off, we decided again to postpone action until the day after the run-off so that the demonstration could not be used to cloud the issues. Like many others, we waited to see Mr. Connor defeated, and to this end we endured postponement after postponement. Having aided in this community need, we felt that our direct-action program could be delayed no longer.

You may well ask, "Why direct action? Why sit-ins, marches, and so forth? Isn't negotiation a better path?" You are quite right in calling for negotiation. Indeed, this is the very purpose of direct action. Nonviolent direct action seeks to create such a crisis and foster such a tension that a community which has constantly refused to negotiate is forced to confront the issue. It seeks so to dramatize the issue that it can no longer be ignored.

[2]Fred Shuttlesworth (1922–2011) was a civil
rights activist who fought against segregation.

My citing the creation of tension as part of the work of the nonviolent resister may sound rather shocking. But I must confess that I am not afraid of the word "tension." I have earnestly opposed violent tension, but there is a type of constructive, non-violent tension which is necessary for growth. Just as Socrates felt that it was necessary to create a tension in the mind so that individuals could rise from the bondage of myths and half truths to the unfettered realm of creative analysis and objective appraisal, so must we see the need for nonviolent gadflies to create the kind of tension in society that will help men rise from the dark depths of prejudice and racism to the majestic heights of understanding and brotherhood.

The purpose of our direct-action program is to create a situation so crisis-packed that it will inevitably open the door to negotiation. I therefore concur with you in your call for negotiation. Too long has our beloved Southland been bogged down in a tragic effort to live in monologue rather than dialogue.

One of the basic points in your statement is that the action that I and my associates have taken in Birmingham is untimely. Some have asked: "Why didn't you give the new city administration time to act?" The only answer that I can give to this query is that the new Birmingham administration must be prodded about as much as the outgoing one, before it will act. We are sadly mistaken if we feel that the election of Albert Boutwell as mayor will bring the millennium to Birmingham. While Mr. Boutwell is a much more gentle person than Mr. Connor, they are both segregationists, dedicated to maintenance of the status quo. I have hoped that Mr. Boutwell will be reasonable enough to see the futility of massive resistance to desegregation. But he will not see this without pressure from devotees of civil rights. My friends, I must say to you that we have not made a single gain in civil rights without determined legal and nonviolent pressure. Lamentably, it is an historical fact that privileged groups seldom give up their privileges voluntarily. Individuals may see the moral light and voluntarily give up their unjust posture; but, as Reinhold Niebuhr[3] has reminded us, groups tend to be more immoral than individuals.

We know through painful experience that freedom is never voluntarily given by the oppressor; it must be demanded by the oppressed. Frankly, I have yet to engage in a direct-action campaign that was "well timed" in the view of those who have not suffered unduly from the disease of segregation. For years now I have heard the word "Wait!" It rings in the ear of every Negro with piercing familiarity. This "Wait" has almost always meant "Never." We must come to see, with one of our distinguished jurists, that "justice too long delayed is justice denied."

We have waited for more than 340 years for our constitutional and God-given rights. The nations of Asia and Africa are moving with jet-like speed toward gaining political independence, but we still creep at horse-and-buggy

---

[3]Reinhold Niebuhr (1892–1971) was a Protestant theologian and philosopher who attempted to reconcile Christianity and pacifism with the need to fight against injustice.

pace toward gaining a cup of coffee at a lunch counter. Perhaps it is easy for those who have never felt the stinging darts of segregation to say, "Wait." But when you have seen vicious mobs lynch your mothers and fathers at will and drown your sisters and brothers at whim; when you have seen hate-filled policemen curse, kick, and even kill your black brothers and sisters; when you see the vast majority of your twenty million Negro brothers smothering in an airtight cage of poverty in the midst of an affluent society; when you suddenly find your tongue twisted and your speech stammering as you seek to explain to your six-year-old daughter why she can't go to the public amusement park that has just been advertised on television, and see tears welling up in her eyes when she is told that Funtown is closed to colored children, and see ominous clouds of inferiority beginning to form in her little mental sky, and see her beginning to distort her personality by developing an unconscious bitterness toward white people; when you have to concoct an answer for a five-year-old son who is asking, "Daddy, why do white people treat colored people so mean?"; when you take a cross-country drive and find it necessary to sleep night after night in the uncomfortable corners of your automobile because no motel will accept you; when you are humiliated day in and day out by nagging signs reading "white" and "colored"; when your first name becomes "nigger," and your middle name becomes "boy" (however old you are) and your last name becomes "John," and your wife and mother are never given the respected title "Mrs."; when you are harried by day and haunted by night by the fact that you are a Negro, living constantly at tiptoe stance, never quite knowing what to expect next, and are plagued with inner fears and outer resentments; when you are forever fighting a degenerating sense of "nobodiness"—then you will understand why we find it difficult to wait. There comes a time when the cup of endurance runs over, and men are no longer willing to be plunged into the abyss of despair. I hope, sirs, you can understand our legitimate and unavoidable impatience.

You express a great deal of anxiety over our willingness to break laws. This is certainly a legitimate concern. Since we so diligently urge people to obey the Supreme Court's decision of 1954 outlawing segregation in the public schools, at first glance it may seem rather paradoxical for us consciously to break laws. One may well ask: "How can you advocate breaking some laws and obeying others?" The answer lies in the fact that there are two types of laws: just and unjust. I would be the first to advocate obeying just laws. One has not only a legal but a moral responsibility to obey just laws. Conversely, one has a moral responsibility to disobey unjust laws. I would agree with St. Augustine that "an unjust law is no law at all."

Now, what is the difference between the two? How does one determine whether a law is just or unjust? A just law is a man-made code that squares with the moral law or the law of God. An unjust law is a code that is out of harmony with the moral law. To put it in the terms of St. Thomas Aquinas: An unjust law is a human law that is not rooted in eternal law and natural law. Any law that uplifts human personality is just. Any law that degrades human personality is unjust. All segregation statutes are unjust because segregation distorts the soul and damages the personality. It gives the segregator a false sense of superiority and the segregated a false sense of inferiority. Segregation, to use the terminology of the Jewish philosopher Martin Buber, substitutes an "I-it" relationship for an "I-thou" relationship and ends up relegating persons to the status of things. Hence segregation is not only politically, economically, and sociologically unsound, it is morally wrong and sinful. Paul Tillich has said that sin is separation. Is not segregation an existential expression of man's tragic separation, his awful estrangement, his terrible sinfulness? Thus it is that I can urge men to obey the 1954 decision of the Supreme Court, for it is morally right; and I can urge them to disobey segregation ordinances, for they are morally wrong.

Let us consider a more concrete example of just and unjust laws. An unjust law is a code that a numerical or power majority group compels a minority group to obey but does not make binding on itself. This is *difference* made legal. By the same token, a just law is a code that a majority compels a minority to follow and that it is willing to follow itself. This is *sameness* made legal.

Let me give another explanation. A law is unjust if it is inflicted on a minority that, as a result of being denied the right to vote, had no part in enacting or devising the law. Who can say that the legislature of Alabama which set up that state's segregation laws was democratically elected? Throughout Alabama all sorts of devious methods are used to prevent Negroes from becoming registered voters, and there are some counties in which, even though Negroes constitute a majority of the population, not a single Negro is registered. Can any law enacted under such circumstances be considered democratically structured?

Sometimes a law is just on its face and unjust in its application. For instance, I have been arrested on a charge of parading without a permit. Now, there is nothing wrong in having an ordinance which requires a permit for a parade. But such an ordinance becomes unjust when it is used to maintain segregation and to deny citizens the First Amendment privilege of peaceful assembly and protest.

I hope you are able to see the distinction I am trying to point out. In no sense do I advocate evading or defying the law, as would the rabid segregationist. That would lead to anarchy. One who breaks an unjust law must do so openly, lovingly, and with a willingness to accept the penalty. I submit that an individual who breaks a law that conscience tells him is unjust, and who willingly accepts the penalty of imprisonment in order to arouse the conscience of the community over its injustice, is in reality expressing the highest respect for law.

Of course, there is nothing new about this kind of civil disobedience. It was evidenced sublimely in the refusal of Shadrach, Meshach, and Abednego to obey the laws of Nebuchadnezzar,[4] on the ground that a higher moral

---

[4]Nebuchadnezzar was a leader of Babylon who helped build his empire through conquests of Jerusalem and Judah. In the Book of Daniel, he ordered Shadrach, Meshach, and Abednego to worship a golden idol, and when they refused, he threw them into a furnace, but they were miraculously unharmed.

law was at stake. It was practiced superbly by the early Christians, who were willing to face hungry lions and the excruciating pain of chopping blocks rather than submit to certain unjust laws of the Roman Empire. To a degree, academic freedom is a reality today because Socrates practiced civil disobedience. In our own nation, the Boston Tea Party represented a massive act of civil disobedience.

We should never forget that everything Adolf Hitler did in Germany was "legal" and everything the Hungarian freedom fighters did in Hungary was "illegal." It was "illegal" to aid and comfort a Jew in Hitler's Germany. Even so, I am sure that, had I lived in Germany at the time, I would have aided and comforted my Jewish brothers. If today I lived in a Communist country where certain principles dear to the Christian faith are suppressed, I would openly advocate disobeying that country's antireligious laws.

I must make two honest confessions to you, my Christian and Jewish brothers. First, I must confess that over the past few years I have been gravely disappointed with the white moderate. I have almost reached the regrettable conclusion that the Negro's great stumbling block in his stride toward freedom is not the White Citizen's Counciler or the Ku Klux Klanner, but the white moderate, who is more devoted to "order" than to justice, who prefers a negative peace which is the absence of tension to a positive peace which is the presence of justice; who constantly says, "I agree with you in the goal you seek, but I cannot agree with your methods of direct action"; who paternalistically believes he can set the timetable for another man's freedom; who lives by a mythical concept of time and who constantly advises the Negro to wait for a "more convenient season." Shallow understanding from people of good will is more frustrating than absolute misunderstanding from people of ill will. Lukewarm acceptance is much more bewildering than outright rejection.

I had hoped that the white moderate would understand that law and order exist for the purpose of establishing justice and that when they fail in this purpose they become the dangerously structured dams that block the flow of social progress. I had hoped that the white moderate would understand that the present tension in the South is a necessary phase of the transition from an obnoxious negative peace, in which the Negro passively accepted his unjust plight, to a substantive and positive peace, in which all men will respect the dignity and worth of human personality. Actually, we who engage in nonviolent direct action are not the creators of tension. We bring it out in the open, where it can be seen and dealt with. Like a boil that can never be cured so long as it is covered up but must be opened with all its ugliness to the natural medicines of air and light, injustices must be exposed, with all the tension its exposure creates, to the light of human conscience and the air of national opinion, before it can be cured.

In your statement you assert that our actions, even though peaceful, must be condemned because they precipitate violence. But is this a logical assertion? Isn't this like condemning a robbed man because his possession of money precipitated the evil act of robbery? Isn't this like condemning

Socrates because his unswerving commitment to truth and his philosophical inquiries precipitated the act by the misguided populace in which they made him drink hemlock? Isn't this like condemning Jesus because his unique God-consciousness and never-ceasing devotion to God's will precipitated the evil act of crucifixion? We must come to see that, as the federal courts have consistently affirmed, it is wrong to urge an individual to cease his efforts to gain his basic constitutional rights because the quest may precipitate violence. Society must protect the robbed and punish the robber.

I had also hoped that the white moderate would reject the myth concerning time in relation to the struggle for freedom. I have just received a letter from a white brother in Texas. He writes: "All Christians know that the colored people will receive equal rights eventually, but it is possible that you are in too great a religious hurry. It has taken Christianity almost two thousand years to accomplish what it has. The teachings of Christ take time to come to earth." Such an attitude stems from a tragic misconception of time, from the strangely irrational notion that there is something in the very flow of time that will inevitably cure all ills. Actually, time itself is neutral; it can be used either destructively or constructively. More and more I feel that the people of ill will have used time much more effectively than have the people of good will. We will have to repent in this generation not merely for the hateful words and actions of the bad people, but for the appalling silence of the good people. Human progress never rolls in on wheels inevitability; it comes through the tireless efforts of men willing to be co-workers with God, and without this hard work, time itself becomes an ally of the forces of social stagnation. We must use time creatively, in the knowledge that the time is always ripe to do right. Now is the time to make real the promise of democracy and transform our pending national elegy into a creative psalm of brotherhood. Now is the time to lift our national policy from the quicksand of racial injustice to the solid rock of human dignity.

You speak of our activity in Birmingham as extreme. At first I was rather disappointed that fellow clergymen would see my nonviolent efforts as those of an extremist. I began thinking about the fact that I stand in the middle of two opposing forces in the Negro community. One is a force of complacency made up in part of Negroes who, as a result of long years of oppression, are so drained of self-respect and a sense of "somebodiness" that they have adjusted to segregation; and in part of a few middle-class Negroes who, because of a degree of academic and economic security and because in some ways they profit by segregation, have become insensitive to the problems of the masses. The other force is one of bitterness and hatred, and it comes perilously close to advocating violence. It is expressed in the various black nationalist groups that are springing up across the nation, the largest and best known being Elijah Muhammad's Muslim movement. Nourished by the Negro's frustration over the continued existence of racial discrimination, this movement is made up of people who have lost faith in America, who have absolutely repudiated Christianity, and who have concluded that the white man is an incorrigible "devil."

I have tried to stand between these two forces, saying that we need emulate neither the "do-nothingism" of the complacent nor the hatred and despair of the black nationalist. For there is the more excellent way of love and nonviolent protest. I am grateful to God that, through the influence of the Negro church, the way of nonviolence became an integral part of our struggle.

If this philosophy had not emerged, by now many streets of the South would, I am convinced, be flowing with blood. And I am further convinced that if our white brothers dismiss as "rabble rousers" and "outside agitators" those of us who employ nonviolent direct action, and if they refuse to support our nonviolent efforts, millions of Negroes will, out of frustration and despair, seek solace and security in black nationalist ideologies—a development that would inevitably lead to a frightening racial nightmare.

Oppressed people cannot remain oppressed forever. The yearning for freedom eventually manifests itself, and that is what has happened to the American Negro. Something within has reminded him of his birthright of freedom, and something without has reminded him that it can be gained. Consciously or unconsciously, he has been caught up by the Zeitgeist,[5] and with his black brothers of Africa and his brown and yellow brothers of Asia, South America, and the Caribbean, the United States Negro is moving with a sense of great urgency toward the promised land of racial justice. If one recognizes this vital urge that has engulfed the Negro community, one should readily understand why public demonstrations are taking place. The Negro has many pent-up resentments and latent frustrations, and he must release them. So let him march; let him make prayer pilgrimages to the city hall, let him go on freedom rides—and try to understand why he must do so. If his repressed emotions are not released in nonviolent ways, they will seek expression through violence; this is not a threat but a fact of history. So I have not said to my people, "Get rid of your discontent." Rather, I have tried to say that this normal and healthy discontent can be channeled into the creative outlet of nonviolent direct action. And now this approach is being termed extremist.

But though I was initially disappointed at being categorized as an extremist, as I continued to think about the matter I gradually gained a measure of satisfaction from the label. Was not Jesus an extremist for love: "Love your enemies, bless them that curse you, do good to them that hate you, and pray for them which despitefully use you, and persecute you." Was not Amos an extremist for justice: "Let justice roll down like waters and righteousness like an ever-flowing stream." Was not Paul an extremist for the Christian gospel: "I bear in my body the marks of the Lord Jesus." Was not Martin Luther[6] an extremist: "Here I stand; I cannot do otherwise, so help me God." And John Bunyan:[7] "I will stay in jail to the end of my days

---

[5]Spirit of the times (German).
[6]Martin Luther (1483–1546) was a German monk and religious dissident whose "95 Theses" nailed to a church door in 1517 marked the beginning of the Protestant Reformation in Europe.

[7]John Bunyan (1628–1688) was an English writer and preacher who wrote *Pilgrim's Progress* (published in 1678 and 1684), a highly influential Christian allegory.

before I make a butchery of my conscience." And Abraham Lincoln: "This nation cannot survive half slave and half free." And Thomas Jefferson: "We hold these truths to be self-evident, that all men are created equal...." So the question is not whether we will be extremists, but what kind of extremists we will be. Will we be extremists for hate or for love? Will we be extremists for the preservation of injustice or for the extension of justice? In that dramatic scene on Calvary's hill three men were crucified. We must never forget that all three were crucified for the same crime—the crime of extremism. Two were extremists for immorality, and thus fell below their environment. The other, Jesus Christ, was an extremist for love, truth, and goodness, and thereby rose above his environment. Perhaps the South, the nation, and the world are in dire need of creative extremists.

I had hoped that the white moderate would see this need. Perhaps I was too optimistic; perhaps I expected too much. I suppose I should have realized that few members of the oppressor race can understand the deep groans and passionate yearnings of the oppressed race, and still fewer have the vision to see that injustice must be rooted out by strong, persistent, and determined action. I am thankful, however, that some of our white brothers in the South have grasped the meaning of this social revolution and committed themselves to it. They are still all too few in quantity, but they are big in quality. Some—such as Ralph McGill, Lillian Smith, Harry Golden, James McBride Dabbs, Ann Braden, and Sarah Patton Boyle—have written about our struggle in eloquent and prophetic terms. Others have marched with us down nameless streets of the South. They have languished in filthy, roach-infested jails, suffering the abuse and brutality of policemen who view them as "dirty nigger-lovers." Unlike so many of their moderate brothers and sisters, they have recognized the urgency of the moment and sensed the need for powerful "action" antidotes to combat the disease of segregation.

Let me take note of my other major disappointment. I have been so greatly disappointed with the white church and its leadership. Of course, there are some notable exceptions. I am not unmindful of the fact that each of you has taken some significant stands on this issue. I commend you, Reverend Stallings, for your Christian stand on this past Sunday, in welcoming Negroes to your worship service on a non-segregated basis. I commend the Catholic leaders of this state for integrating Spring Hill College[8] several years ago.

But despite these notable exceptions, I must honestly reiterate that I have been disappointed with the church. I do not say this as one of those negative critics who can always find something wrong with the church. I say this as a minister of the gospel, who loves the church; who was nurtured in its bosom; who has been sustained by its spiritual blessings and who will remain true to it as long as the cord of life shall lengthen.

[8]The first Catholic Jesuit college in the South, Spring Hill College (located in Mobile, Alabama) was desegregated in 1954, just before the United States Supreme Court's landmark decision banning segregation.

When I was suddenly catapulted into the leadership of the bus protest in Montgomery, Alabama, a few years ago, I felt we would be supported by the white church. I felt that the white ministers, priests, and rabbis of the South would be among our strongest allies. Instead, some have been outright opponents, refusing to understand the freedom movement and misrepresenting its leaders; all too many others have been more cautious than courageous and have remained silent behind the anesthetizing security of stained-glass windows.

In spite of my shattered dreams, I came to Birmingham with the hope that the white religious leadership of this community would see the justice of our cause and, with deep moral concerns, would serve as the channel through which our just grievances could reach the power structure. I had hoped that each of you would understand. But again I have been disappointed. . . .

There was a time when the church was very powerful—in the time when the early Christians rejoiced at being deemed worthy to suffer for what they believed. In those days the church was not merely a thermometer that recorded the ideas and principles of popular opinion; it was a thermostat that transformed the mores of society. Whenever the early Christians entered a town, the people in power became disturbed and immediately sought to convict the Christians for being "disturbers of the peace" and "outside agitators." But the Christians pressed on, in the conviction that they were a "colony of heaven," called to obey God rather than man. Small in number, they were big in commitment. They were too God intoxicated to be "astronomically intimidated." By their effort and example they brought an end to such ancient evils as infanticide and gladiatorial contests.

Things are different now. So often the contemporary church is a weak, ineffectual voice with an uncertain sound. So often it is an archdefender of the status quo. Far from being disturbed by the presence of the church, the power structure of the average community is consoled by the church's silent—and often even vocal—sanction of things as they are.

But the judgment of God is upon the church as never before. If today's church does not recapture the sacrificial spirit of the early church, it will lose its authenticity, forfeit the loyalty of millions, and be dismissed as an irrelevant social club with no meaning for the twentieth century. Every day I meet young people whose disappointment with the church has turned into outright disgust.

Perhaps I have once again been too optimistic. Is organized religion too inextricably bound to the status quo to save our nation and the world? Perhaps I must turn my faith to the inner spiritual church, the church within the church, as the true ekklesia and the hope of the world. But again I am thankful to God that some noble souls from the ranks of organized religion have broken loose from the paralyzing chains of conformity and joined us as active partners in the struggle for freedom. They have left their secure congregations and walked the streets of Albany, Georgia, with us. They have gone down the highways of the South on torturous rides for freedom. Yes, they have gone to jail with us. Some have been dismissed from their churches, have lost the support of their bishops and fellow ministers. But they have acted in the faith that right defeated is strong than evil triumphant. Their witness has been the spiritual salt that has preserved the true meaning of the gospel in these troubled times. They have carved a tunnel of hope through the dark mountain of disappointment.

I hope the church as a whole will meet the challenge of this decisive hour. But even if the church does not come to the aid of justice, I have no despair about the future. I have no fear about the outcome of our struggle in Birmingham, even if our motives are at present misunderstood. We will reach the goal of freedom in Birmingham and all over the nation, because the goal of America is freedom. Abused and scorned though we may be, our destiny is tied up with America's destiny. Before the pilgrims landed at Plymouth, we were here. Before the pen of Jefferson etched the majestic words of the Declaration of Independence across the pages of history, we were here. For more than two centuries our forebears labored in this country without wages; they made cotton king; they built the homes of their masters while suffering gross injustice and shameful humiliation— and yet out of a bottomless vitality they continued to thrive and develop. If the inexpressible cruelties of slavery could not stop us, the opposition we now face will surely fail. We will win our freedom because the sacred heritage of our nation and the eternal will of God are embodied in our echoing demands.

Before closing I feel impelled to mention one other point in your statement that has troubled me profoundly. You warmly commended the Birmingham police force for keeping "order" and "preventing violence." I doubt that you would have so warmly commended the police force if you had seen its dogs sinking their teeth into unarmed, non-violent Negroes. I doubt that you would so quickly commend the policemen if you were to observe their ugly and inhumane treatment of Negroes here in the city jail; if you were to watch them push and curse old Negro women and young Negro girls; if you were to see them slap and kick old Negro men and young boys; if you were to observe them, as they did on two occasions, refuse to give us food because we wanted to sing our grace together. I cannot join you in your praise of the Birmingham police department.

It is true that the police have exercised a degree of discipline in handling the demonstrations. In this sense they have conducted themselves rather "nonviolently" in public. But for what purpose? To preserve the evil system of segregation. Over the past few years I have consistently preached that nonviolence demands that the means we use must be as pure as the ends we seek. I have tried to make clear that it is wrong to use immoral means to attain moral ends. But now I must affirm that it is just as wrong, or perhaps even more so, to use moral means to preserve immoral ends. Perhaps Mr. Connor and his policemen have been rather nonviolent in public, as was Chief Pritchett in Albany, Georgia, but they have used the moral means of nonviolence to maintain the immoral end of racial injustice. As T. S. Eliot has said, "The last temptation is the greatest treason: To do the right deed for the wrong reason."

I wish you had commended the Negro sit-inners and demonstrators of Birmingham for their sublime courage, their willingness to suffer, and their amazing discipline in the midst of great provocation. One day the South will recognize its real heroes. They will be the James Merediths,[9] with the noble sense of purpose that enables them to face jeering and hostile mobs, and with the agonizing loneliness that characterizes the life of the pioneer. They will be old, oppressed, battered Negro women, symbolized in a seventy-two-year-old woman in Montgomery, Alabama, who rose up with a sense of dignity and with her people decided not to ride segregated buses, and who responded with ungrammatical profundity to one who inquired about her weariness: "My feets is tired, but my soul is at rest." They will be the young high school and college students, the young ministers of the gospel and a host of their elders, courageously and nonviolently sitting in at lunch counters and willingly going to jail for conscience' sake. One day the South will know that when these disinherited children of God sat down at lunch counters, they were in reality standing up for what is best in the American dream and for the most sacred values in our Judaeo-Christian heritage, thereby bringing our nation back to those great wells of democracy which were dug deep by the founding fathers in their formulation of the Constitution and the Declaration of Independence.

Never before have I written so long a letter. I'm afraid it is much too long to take your precious time. I can assure you that it would have been much shorter if I had been writing from a comfortable desk, but what else can one do when he is alone in a narrow jail cell, other than write long letters, think long thoughts, and pray long prayers?

If I have said anything in this letter that overstates the truth and indicates an unreasonable impatience, I beg you to forgive me. If I have said anything that understates the truth and indicates my having a patience that allows me to settle for anything less than brotherhood, I beg God to forgive me.

I hope this letter finds you strong in the faith. I also hope that circumstances will soon make it possible for me to meet each of you, not as an integrationist or a civil rights leader but as a fellow clergyman and a Christian brother. Let us all hope that the dark clouds of racial prejudice will soon pass away and the deep fog of misunderstanding will be lifted from our fear-drenched communities, and in some not too distant tomorrow the radiant stars of love and brotherhood will shine over our great nation with all their scintillating beauty.

Yours in the cause of Peace and Brotherhood,
Martin Luther King, Jr.

1963

---

[9]James Meredith (b. 1933) was an African American student whose enrollment in the University of Mississippi in 1962 set off riots at the campus in Oxford, Mississippi.

MALCOLM X
1925–1965

Malcolm X was born Malcolm Little, the son of Earl and Louise Little, in Omaha, Nebraska. His father was a follower of Marcus Garvey, who instilled racial pride among masses of African Americans. Earl Little died at a relatively young age, leaving his wife and eight children in extreme poverty. "We would be so hungry," Malcolm X later reported, "we were dizzy." Malcolm Little quit school at age fifteen and moved to Harlem, where, he recalled, he became a thief and a drug dealer.

When Little entered prison at age twenty, he began to educate himself. He learned about the Nation of Islam (or Black Muslims), led by Elijah Muhammad, and became an eager convert. Accepting Elijah Muhammad's doctrine that white people were devils, he rejoiced in a newfound racial identity. After leaving prison, he met Elijah Muhammad and replaced his own last name with "X," which stands for the African name his ancestors lost when they were brought to the United States in slave ships.

Malcolm X became an extremely popular evangelist for the Nation of Islam, recruiting new members and emphasizing African American pride. With brilliant fables, analogies, and turns of speech, he elevated the spirits of urban blacks trapped by segregation. He condemned hypocritical whites for preaching love and democracy while treating blacks as subhuman. In "Message to the Grass Roots," he criticized African Americans for their submission to whites:

> As long as the white man sent you to Korea, you bled. He sent you to Germany, you bled. He sent you to the South Pacific to fight the Japanese, you bled. You bleed for white people, but when it comes to seeing your own churches being bombed and little black girls murdered, you haven't got any blood. You bleed when the white man says bleed; you bite when the white man says bite; and you bark when the white man says bark. I hate to say this about us, but it's true.

Malcolm X also castigated Martin Luther King, Jr., but his fiery, uncompromising militance helped prepare whites to accept King's message, which, by contrast, seemed moderate and palatable.

"The Ballot or the Bullet" is an address delivered in 1964, shortly after Malcolm X announced his break with the Nation of Islam. He had learned of Elijah Muhammad's flaws and became bitterly disenchanted with the man who "had virtually raised me from the dead." Recovering from disillusionment, he made a pilgrimage to Mecca, met white followers of Islam, and became more accepting of some whites. After returning to the United States, he formed the Organization of Afro-American Unity. In 1965, however, black assailants murdered him in a hail of gunfire.

Mourned by Harlemites and praised by portions of the Third World press, Malcolm X was damned by the established American media. The *New York Times*, for example, branded him an "irresponsible demagogue." The eloquent

Malcolm X, however, had the last word. He had dictated his life story to Alex Haley. The posthumous *Autobiography of Malcolm X* portrays a person capable of the most startling self-transformation: from a starving child to a parasitic criminal to an angry but uplifting orator to a notably more tolerant leader worthy of a world stage. Though challenged over some of its details, the best-selling *Autobiography of Malcolm X* brilliantly portrays American race relations.

Keith D. Miller
Arizona State University

PRIMARY WORKS

Autobiography of Malcolm X (with Alex Haley), 1965; *Malcolm X Speaks*, 1965; *By Any Means Necessary*, 1970; *The End of White World Supremacy: Four Speeches*, 1971; *The Last Speeches*, 1989.

from The Autobiography of Malcolm X

from Chapter 19: 1965

I kept having all kinds of troubles trying to develop the kind of Black Nationalist organization I wanted to build for the American Negro. Why Black Nationalism? Well, in the competitive American society, how can there ever be any white-black solidarity before there is first some black solidarity? If you will remember, in my childhood I had been exposed to the Black Nationalist teachings of Marcus Garvey—which, in fact, I had been told had led to my father's murder. Even when I was a follower of Elijah Muhammad, I had been strongly aware of how the Black Nationalist political, economic and social philosophies had the ability to instill within black men the racial dignity, the incentive, and the confidence that the black race needs today to get up off its knees, and to get on its feet, and get rid of its scars, and to take a stand for itself.

One of the major troubles that I was having in building the organization that I wanted—an all-black organization whose ultimate objective was to help create a society in which there could exist honest white-black brotherhood—was that my earlier public image, my old so-called "Black Muslim" image, kept blocking me. I was trying to gradually reshape that image. I was trying to turn a corner, into a new regard by the public, especially Negroes: I was no less angry than I had been, but at the same time the true brotherhood I had seen in the Holy World had influenced me to recognize the anger can blind human vision.

Every free moment I could find, I did a lot of talking to key people whom I knew around Harlem, and I made a lot of speeches, saying: "True Islam taught me that it takes *all* of the religious, political, economic, psychological, and racial ingredients, or characteristics, to make the Human Family and the Human Society complete.

"Since I learned the *truth* in Mecca, my dearest friends have come to include *all* kinds—some Christians, Jews, Buddhists, Hindus, agnostics, and even atheists! I have friends who are called Capitalists, Socialists, and Communists! Some of my friends are moderates, conservatives, extremists—some are even Uncle Toms! My friends today are black, brown, red, yellow, and *white!*"

I said to Harlem street audiences that only when mankind would submit to the One God who created all—only then would mankind even approach the "peace" of which so much *talk* could be heard ... but toward which so little *action* was seen.

I said that on the American racial level, we had to approach the black man's struggle against the white man's racism as a human problem, that we had to forget hypocritical politics and propaganda. I said that both races, as human beings, had the obligation, the responsibility, of helping to correct America's human problem. The well-meaning white people, I said, had to combat, actively and directly, the racism in other white people. And the black people had to build within themselves much greater awareness that along with equal rights there had to be the bearing of equal responsibilities.

I knew, better than most Negroes, how many white people truly wanted to see American racial problems solved. I knew that many whites were as frustrated as Negroes. I'll bet I got fifty letters some days from white people. The white people in meeting audiences would throng around me, asking me, after I had addressed them somewhere, "What *can* a sincere white person do?"

When I say that here now, it makes me think about the little co-ed I told you about, the one who flew from her New England college down to New York and came up to me in the Nation of Islam's restaurant in Harlem, and I told her that there was "nothing" she could do. I regret that I told her that. I wish that now I knew her name, or where I could telephone her, or write to her, and tell her what I tell white people now when they present themselves as being sincere, and ask me, one way or another, the same thing that she asked.

The first thing I tell them is that at least where my own particular Black Nationalist organization, the Organization of Afro-American Unity, is concerned, they can't join us. I have these very deep feelings that white people who want to join black organizations are really just taking the escapist way to salve their consciences. By visibly hovering near us, they are "proving" that they are "with us." But the hard truth is this isn't helping to solve America's racist problem. The Negroes aren't the racists. Where the really sincere white people have got to do their "proving" of themselves is not among the black victims, but on the battle lines of where America's racism really is—and that's in their own home communities; America's racism is among their own fellow whites. That's where the sincere whites who really mean to accomplish something have got to work.

Aside from that, I mean nothing against any sincere whites, when I say that as members of black organizations, generally whites' very presence subtly renders the black organization automatically less effective. Even the best white members will slow down the Negroes' discovery of what they need to do, and particularly of what they can do—for themselves, working by themselves, among their own kind, in their own communities.

I sure don't want to hurt anybody's feelings, but in fact I'll even go so far as to say that I never really trust the kind of white people who are always so anxious to hang around Negroes, or to hang around in Negro communities. I don't trust the kind of whites who love having Negroes always hanging around them. I don't know—this feeling may be a throwback to the years when I was hustling in Harlem and all of those red-faced, drunk whites in the after-hours clubs were always grabbing hold of some Negroes and talking about "I just want you to know you're just as good as I am—" And then they got back in their taxicabs and black limousines and went back downtown to the places where they lived and worked, where no blacks except servants had better get caught. But, anyway, I know that every time that whites join a black organization, you watch, pretty soon the blacks will be leaning on the whites to support it, and before you know it a black may be up front with a title, but the whites, because of their money, are the real controllers.

I tell sincere white people, "Work in conjunction with us—each of us working among our own kind." Let sincere white individuals find all other white people they can who feel as they do—and let them form their own all-white groups, to work trying to convert other white people who are thinking and acting so racist. Let sincere whites go and teach non-violence to white people!

We will completely respect our white co-workers. They will deserve every credit. We will give them every credit. We will meanwhile be working among our own kind, in our own black communities—showing and teaching black men in ways that other black men can—that the black man has got to help himself. Working separately, the sincere white people and sincere black people actually will be together.

In our mutual sincerity we might be able to show a road to the salvation of America's very soul. It can only be salvaged if human rights and dignity, in full, are extended to black men. Only such real, meaningful actions as those which are sincerely motivated from a deep sense of humanism and moral responsibility can get at the basic causes that produce the racial explosions in America today. Otherwise, the racial explosions are only going to grow worse. Certainly nothing is ever going to be solved by throwing upon me and other so-called black "extremists" and "demagogues" the blame for the racism that is in America.

Sometimes, I have dared to dream to myself that one day, history may even say that my voice—which disturbed the white man's smugness, and his arrogance, and his complacency—that my voice helped to save America from a grave, possibly even a fatal catastrophe.

The goal has always been the same, with the approaches to it as different as mine and Dr. Martin Luther King's non-violent marching, that dramatizes the brutality and the evil of the white man against defenseless blacks. And in the racial climate of this country today, it is anybody's guess which of the "extremes" in approach to the black man's problems might *personally* meet a fatal catastrophe first—"non-violent" Dr. King, or so-called "violent" me.

Anything I do today, I regard as urgent. No man is given but so much time to accomplish whatever is his life's work. My life in particular never has stayed fixed in one position for very long. You have seen how throughout my life, I have often known unexpected drastic changes.

I am only facing the facts when I know that any moment of any day, or any night, could bring me death. This is particularly true since the last trip that I made abroad. I have seen the nature of things that are happening, and I have heard things from sources which are reliable.

To speculate about dying doesn't disturb me as it might some people. I never have felt that I would live to become an old man. Even before I was a Muslim—when I was a hustler in the ghetto jungle, and then a criminal in prison, it always stayed on my mind that I could die a violent death. In fact, it runs in my family. My father and most of his brothers died by violence— my father because of what he believed in. To come right down to it, if I take the kind of things in which I believe, then add to that the kind of temperament that I have, plus the one hundred percent dedication I have to whatever I believe in—these are ingredients which make it just about impossible for me to die of old age.

I have given to this book so much of whatever time I have because I feel, and I hope, that if I honestly and fully tell my life's account, read objectively it might prove to be a testimony of some social value.

I think that an objective reader may see how in the society to which I was exposed as a black youth here in America, for me to wind up in a prison was really just about inevitable. It happens to so many thousands of black youth.

I think than an objective reader may see how when I heard "The white man is the devil," when I played back what had been my own experiences, it was inevitable that I would respond positively: then the next twelve years of my life were devoted and dedicated to propagating that phrase among the black people.

I think, I hope, that the objective reader, in following my life—the life of only one ghetto-created Negro—may gain a better picture and understanding than he has previously had of the black ghettoes which are shaping the lives and the thinking of almost all of the 22 million Negroes who live in America.

Thicker each year in these ghettoes is the kind of teenager that I was— with the wrong kinds of heroes, and the wrong kinds of influences. I am not saying that all of them become the kind of parasite that I was. Fortunately, by far most do not. But still, the small fraction who do add up to an annual total of more and more costly, dangerous youthful criminals. The F.B.I. not long ago released a report of a shocking rise in crime each successive year since the end of World War II—ten to twelve percent each year. The report did not say so in so many words, but I am saying that the majority of that crime increase in annually spawned in the black ghettoes which the American racist society permits to exist. In the 1964 "long, hot summer" riots in major cities across the United States, the socially disinherited black ghetto youth were always at the forefront.

In this year, 1965, I am certain that more—and worse—riots are going to erupt, in yet more cities, in spite of the conscience-salving Civil Rights Bill. The reason is that the *cause* of these riots, the racist malignancy in America, has been too long unattended.

I believe that it would be almost impossible to find anywhere in America a black man who has lived further down in the mud of human society than I have; or a black man who has been any more ignorant than I have been; or a black man who has suffered more anguish during his life than I have. But it is only after the deepest darkness that the greatest joy can come; it is only after slavery and prison that the sweetest appreciation of freedom can come.

For the freedom of my twenty-two million black brothers and sisters here in America, I do believe that I have fought the best that I knew how, and the best that I could, with the shortcomings that I have had. I know that my shortcomings are many.

My greatest lack has been, I believe, that I don't have the kind of academic education I wish I had been able to get—to have been a lawyer, perhaps. I do believe that I might have made a good lawyer. I have always loved verbal battle, and challenge. You can believe me that if I had the time right now, I would not be one bit ashamed to go back into any New York City public school and start where I left off at the ninth grade, and go on through a degree. Because I don't begin to be academically equipped for so many of the interests that I have. For instance, I love languages. I wish I were an accomplished linguist. I don't know anything more frustrating than to be around people talking something you can't understand. Especially when they are people who look just like you. In Africa, I heard original mother tongues, such as Hausa, and Swahili, being spoken, and there I was standing like some little boy, waiting for someone to tell me what had been said; I never will forget how ignorant I felt.

Aside from the basic African dialects, I would try to learn Chinese, because it looks as if Chinese will be the most powerful political language of the future. And already I have begun studying Arabic, which I think is going to be the most powerful spiritual language of the future.

I would just like to study. I mean ranging study, because I have a wide-open mind. I'm interested in almost any subject you can mention. I know this is the reason I have come to really like, as individuals, some of the hosts of radio or television panel programs I have been on, and to respect their minds—because even if they have been almost steadily in disagreement with me on the race issue, they still kept their minds open and objective about the truths of things happening in this world. Irv Kupcinet in Chicago, and Barry Farber, Barry Gray and Mike Wallace in New York—people like them. They also let me see that they respected my mind—in a way I know they never realized. The way I knew was that often they would invite my opinion on subjects off the race issue. Sometimes, after the programs, we would sit around and talk about all kinds of things, current events and other things, for an hour or more. You see, most whites, even when they credit a Negro with some intelligence, will still feel that all he can talk about is the race issue; most whites never feel that Negroes can contribute anything to other areas of thought, and ideas. You just notice how rarely you will ever hear whites asking any Negroes what they thing about the problem of world health, or the space race to land men on the moon.

Every morning when I wake up, now, I regard it as having another borrowed day. In any city, wherever I go, making speeches, holding meetings of my organization, or attending to other business, black men are watching every move I make, awaiting their chance to kill me. I have said publicly many times that I know that they have their orders. Anyone who chooses not to believe what I am saying doesn't know the Muslims in the Nation of Islam.

But I am also blessed with faithful followers who are, I believe, as dedicated to me as I once was to Mr. Elijah Muhammad. Those who would hunt a man need to remember that a jungle also contains those who hunt the hunters.

I know, too, that I could suddenly die at the hands of some white racists. Or I could die at the hands of some Negro hired by the white man. Or it could be some brainwashed Negro acting on his own idea that by eliminating me he would be helping out the white man, because I talk about the white man the way I do.

Anyway, now, each day I live as if I am already dead, and I tell you what I would like for you to do. when I *am* dead—I say it that way because from the things I *know*, I do not expect to live long enough to read this book in its finished form—I want you to just watch and see if I'm not right in what I say: that the white man, in his press, is going to identify me with "hate."

He will make use of me dead, as he has made use of me alive, as a convenient symbol of "hatred"—and that will help him to escape facing the truth that all I have been doing is holding up a mirror to reflect, to show, the history of unspeakable crimes that his race has committed against my race.

You watch. I will be labeled as, at best, an "irresponsible" black man. I have always felt about this accusation that the black "leader" whom white men consider to be "responsible" is invariably the black "leader" who never gets any results. You only get action as a black man if you are regarded by the white man as "irresponsible." In fact, this much I had learned when I was just a little boy. And since I have been some kind of a "leader" of black people here in the racist society of America, I have been more reassured each time the white man resisted me, or attacked me harder—because each time made me more certain that I was on the right track in the American black man's best interests. The racist white man's opposition automatically made me know that I did offer the black man something worthwhile.

Yes, I have cherished my "demagogue" role. I know that societies often have killed the people who have helped to change those societies. And if I can die having brought any light, having exposed any meaningful truth that will help to destroy the racist cancer that is malignant in the body of America—then, all of the credit is due to Allah. Only the mistakes have been mine.

1965

AMIRI BARAKA (LEROI JONES)
B. 1934

Amiri Baraka, born Everett LeRoy Jones to Coyt LeRoy and Anna Lois Jones in Newark, New Jersey, grew up in a middle-class environment. He attended a predominantly black elementary school, but his college-prep high school, from which he graduated with honors in 1951, was mainly white. About 1951 he changed the spelling of his middle name from "LeRoy" to "LeRoi." From 1952 to 1954 he attended Howard University, where he studied with Sterling Brown and Nathan Scott. After flunking out of school, he enlisted in the U.S. Air Force. In 1957, however, he was dishonorably discharged because of suspicions of communism along with such other "suspicious activities" as voracious reading, journal keeping, poetry writing, and subscribing to avant-garde journals.

Free to live the avant-garde life that had become his preference, he moved to New York's Greenwich Village. Among his associates there were Charles Olson, Frank O'Hara, and Allen Ginsberg. In 1958 he married Hettie Cohn, a Jewish woman who was also part of the Beat scene, and together they edited *Yugen*, a literary journal that published the work of Kerouac, Ginsberg, and many others.

The next decade was marked by a significant change from things aesthetic to things political. His 1960 visit to Cuba marks the genesis of political awareness of blackness and a new frame of reference: the Third World. The year after his trip saw the inauguration of another avant-garde journal, this time coedited with poet Diane di Prima, and the publication of his first volume of poetry, but by 1964 the tensions between his early poetic asceticism and more recent racial didacticism become apparent in the poems of *The Dead Lecturer* as well as in his play *Dutchman*, whose off-Broadway production won an Obie Award.

Radically affected by the assassination of Malcolm X in 1965, LeRoi Jones left Hettie and the bohemian life of the Village and moved to Harlem, where he established the Black Arts Repertory Theater/School. In 1966 he returned to Newark, where he founded a similar venture, Spirit House, and married Sylvia Robinson, a black woman. Again a change of name signaled a reshaping of identity: LeRoi Jones became Imamu Amiri Baraka, as he was known through the racial upheavals of the 1960s. By the early 1970s, he had dropped the title "Imamu," indicating yet another shift, this time from black nationalism to international socialism. His published poetry of the late 1970s reflects this shift in thought.

In 1979 he joined the African Studies Department at SUNY Stony Brook, where he was promoted to associate professor with tenure in 1982 and to full professor in 1984 following the publication of *Autobiography* and *Daggers and Javelins*. He continues to work on *Wise/Whys*, an African American poetic-historical odyssey.

The sense of flux and process, of intensity and explosion, of rebellion and reconstruction, and always the *sound* of it, are everywhere present in his poetry and in his prose. *Dutchman*, included here, has come to be seen as his signature work.

Marcellette Williams
University of Massachusetts Amherst

PRIMARY WORKS

Preface to a Twenty Volume Suicide Note . . ., 1961; *Blues People: Negro Music in White America*, 1963; *Dutchman* and *The Slave*, 1964; *The Dead Lecturer*, 1964; *Home: Social Essays*, 1966; *The Baptism* and *The Toilet*, 1967; *Black Music*, 1967; *Tales*, 1967; *Black Magic*, 1969; *In Our Terribleness*, 1970; *It's Nation Time*, 1970; *Jello*, 1970; *Raise, Race, Rays, Raze: Essays Since 1965*, 1971; *Spirit Reach*, 1972; *The Floating Bear*, 1973; *Hard Facts*, 1975; *The Motion of History and Other Plays*, 1978; *Selected Poetry of Amiri Baraka/LeRoi Jones*, 1979; *Selected Plays and Prose of Amiri Baraka/LeRoi Jones*, 1979; *The Autobiography of LeRoi Jones/Amiri Baraka*, 1984; *Daggers and Javelins: Essays, 1974–1979*, 1984; *The Music: Reflections on Jazz and Blues*, 1987; *The LeRoi Jones/Amiri Baraka Reader*, 1991; *Transbluesency: Selected Poems*, 1995; *Funk Lore: New Poems*, 1996; *The Fiction of LeRoi Jones/Amiri Baraka*, 2000; *Somebody Blew Up America*, 2001; *Tales of the Out and the Gone*, 2006.

An Agony. As Now.

I am inside someone
who hates me. I look
out from his eyes. Smell
what fouled tunes come in
to his breath. Love his   5
wretched women.

Slits in the metal, for sun. Where
my eyes sit turning, at the cool air
the glance of light, or hard flesh
rubbed against me, a woman, a man,   10
without shadow, or voice, or meaning.

This is the enclosure (flesh,
where innocence is a weapon. An
abstraction. Touch. (Not mine.
Or yours, if you are the soul I had   15
and abandoned when I was blind and had
my enemies carry me as a dead man
(if he is beautiful, or pitied.

It can be pain. (As now, as all his
flesh hurts me.) It can be that. Or   20

pain. As when she ran from me into
that forest.
                Or pain, the mind
silver spiraled whirled against the
sun, higher than even old men thought   25
God would be. Or pain. And the other. The
yes. (Inside his books, his fingers. They
are withered yellow flowers and were never
beautiful.) The yes. You will, lost soul, say
"beauty." Beauty, practiced, as the tree. The   30
slow river. A white sun in its wet sentences.

Or, the cold men in their gale. Ecstasy. Flesh
or souls. The yes. (Their robes blown. Their bowls
empty. They chant at my heels, not at yours.) Flesh
or soul, as corrupt. Where the answer moves too quickly.   35
Where the God is a self, after all.)

Cold air blown through narrow blind eyes. Flesh,
white hot metal. Glows as the day with its sun.
It is a human love, I live inside. A bony skeleton
you recognize as words or simple feeling.   40

But it has no feeling. As the metal, is hot, it is not,
given to love.

It burns the thing
inside it. And that thing
screams.   45

                                              1964

Ka 'Ba[1]

A closed window looks down
on a dirty courtyard, and black people
call across or scream across or walk across
defying physics in the stream of their will

Our world is full of sound   5
Our world is more lovely than anyone's
tho we suffer, and kill each other
and sometimes fail to walk the air

[1]Relating to the sacred Islamic shrine in Mecca.

We are beautiful people
with african imaginations   10
full of masks and dances and swelling chants
with african eyes, and noses, and arms,
though we sprawl in grey chains in a place
full of winters, when what we want is sun.
We have been captured,   15
brothers. And we labor
to make our getaway, into
the ancient image, into a new

correspondence with ourselves
and our black family. We need magic   20
now we need the spells, to raise up
return, destroy, and create. What will be

the sacred words?

                                                                  1969

Black People: This Is Our Destiny

The road runs straight with no turning, the circle
runs complete as it is in the storm of peace, the all
embraced embracing in the circle complete turning road
straight like a burning straight with the circle complete
as in a peaceful storm, the elements, the niggers' voices   5
harmonized with creation on a peak in the holy black man's
eyes that we rise, whose race is only direction up, where
we go to meet the realization of makers knowing who we are
and the war in our hearts but the purity of the holy world
that we long for, knowing how to live, and what life is, and   10
who God is, and the many revolutions we must spin through in our
seven adventures in the endlessness of all existing feeling, all
existing forms of life, the gases, the plants, the ghost minerals
the spirits the souls the light in the stillness where the storm
the glow the nothing in God is complete except there is nothing   15
to be incomplete the pulse and change of rhythm, blown flight
to be anything at all ... vibration holy nuance beating against
itself, a rhythm a playing re-understood now by one of the 1st race
the primitives the first men who evolve again to civilize the
world   20

                                                                  1969

A Poem Some People Will Have to Understand

Dull unwashed windows of eyes
and buildings of industry. What
industry do I practice? A slick
colored boy, 12 miles from his
home. I practice no industry.   5
I am no longer a credit
to my race. I read a little,
scratch against silence slow spring
afternoons.
        I had thought, before, some years ago   10
that I'd come to the end of my life.
        Watercolor ego. Without the preciseness
a violent man could propose.
        But the wheel, and the wheels,
won't let us alone. All the fantasy   15
        and justice, and dry charcoal winters
All the pitifully intelligent citizens
        I've forced myself to love.

We have awaited the coming of a natural
phenomenon. Mystics and romantics, knowledgeable   20
workers
of the land.

But none has come.
(Repeat)
           but none has come.   25

Will the machinegunners please step forward?

                1969

Numbers, Letters

If you're not home, where
are you? Where'd you go? What
were you doing when gone? When
you come back, better make it good.
What was you doing down there, freakin' off[1]   5
with white women, hangin' out
with Queens, say it straight, to be
understood straight, put it flat and real

[1]Going crazy.

in the street where the sun comes and the
moon comes and the cold wind in winter   10
waters your eyes. Say what you mean, dig
it out put it down, and be strong
about it.

I cant say who I am
unless you agree I'm real   15

I cant be anything I'm not
Except these words pretend
to life not yet explained,
so here's some feeling for you
see how you like it, what it   20
reveals, and that's me.

Unless you agree I'm real
that I can feel
whatever beats hardest
at our black souls   25

I am real, and I can't say who
I am. Ask me if I know, I'll say
yes, I might say no. Still, ask.

I'm Everett LeRoi Jones, 30 yrs old.
A black nigger in the universe. A long breath singer,   30
wouldbe dancer, strong from years of fantasy
and study. All this time then, for what's happening
now. All that spilling of white ether, clocks in ghostheads
lips drying and rewet, eyes opening and shut, mouths churning.

I am a meditative man. And when I say something it's all of me   35
saying, and all the things that make me, have formed me, colored me
this brilliant reddish night. I will say nothing that I feel is
lie, or unproven by the same ghostclocks, by the same riders
always move so fast with the word slung over their backs or
in saddlebags, charging down Chinese roads. I carry some words,   40
some feeling, some life in me. My heart is large as my mind
this is a messenger calling, over here, over here, open your eyes
and your ears and your souls; today is the history we must learn
to desire. There is no guilt in love

1969

Dutchman

CHARACTERS

CLAY, *twenty-year-old Negro*
LULA, *thirty-year-old white woman*
RIDERS OF COACH, *white and black*
YOUNG NEGRO
CONDUCTOR

In the flying underbelly of the city. Steaming hot, and summer on top, outside. Underground. The subway heaped in modern myth.

Opening scene is a man sitting in a subway seat, holding a magazine but looking vacantly just above its wilting pages. Occasionally he looks blankly toward the window on his right. Dim lights and darkness whistling by against the glass. (Or paste the lights, as admitted props, right on the subway windows. Have them move, even dim and flicker. But give the sense of speed. Also stations, whether the train is stopped or the glitter and activity of these stations merely flashes by the windows.)

The man is sitting alone. That is, only his seat is visible, though the rest of the car is outfitted as a complete subway car. But only his seat is shown. There might be, for a time, as the play begins, a loud scream of the actual train. And it can recur throughout the play, or continue on a lower key once the dialogue starts.

The train slows after a time, pulling to a brief stop at one of the stations. The man looks idly up, until he sees a woman's face staring at him through the window; when it realizes that the man has noticed the face, it begins very premeditatedly to smile. The man smiles too, for a moment, without a trace of self-consciousness. Almost an instinctive though undesirable response. Then a kind of awkwardness or embarrassment sets in, and the man makes to look away, is further embarrassed, so he brings back his eyes to where the face was, but by now the train is moving again, and the face would seem to be left behind by the way the man turns his head to look back through the other windows at the slowly fading platform. He smiles then; more comfortably confident, hoping perhaps that his memory of this brief encounter will be pleasant. And then he is idle again.

SCENE I

Train roars. Lights flash outside the windows.

LULA enters from the rear of the car in bright, skimpy summer clothes and sandals. She carries a net bag full of paper books, fruit, and other anonymous articles. She is wearing sunglasses, which she pushes up on her forehead from time to time. LULA is a tall, slender, beautiful woman with long red hair hanging straight down her back, wearing only loud lipstick in somebody's good taste. She is eating an apple, very daintily. Coming down the car toward CLAY.

She stops beside CLAY'*s seat and hangs languidly from the strap, still managing to eat the apple. It is apparent that she is going to sit in the seat next to* CLAY, *and that she is only waiting for him to notice her before she sits.*

CLAY *sits as before, looking just beyond his magazine, now and again pulling the magazine slowly back and forth in front of his face in a hopeless effort to fan himself. Then he sees the woman hanging there beside him and he looks up into her face, smiling quizzically.*

LULA: Hello.

CLAY: Uh, hi're you?

LULA: I'm going to sit down. . . . O.K.?

CLAY: Sure.

LULA:

[Swings down onto the seat, pushing her legs straight out as if she is very weary]

Oooof! Too much weight.

CLAY: Ha, doesn't look like much to me.

[Leaning back against the window, a little surprised and maybe stiff]

LULA: It's so anyway.

[And she moves her toes in the sandals, then pulls her right leg up on the left knee, better to inspect the bottoms of the sandals and the back of her heel. She appears for a second not to notice that CLAY *is sitting next to her or that she has spoken to him just a second before.* CLAY *looks at the magazine, then out the black window. As he does this, she turns very quickly toward him]*

Weren't you staring at me through the window?

CLAY:

[Wheeling around and very much stiffened]

What?

LULA: Weren't you staring at me through the window? At the last stop?

CLAY: Staring at you? What do you mean?

LULA: Don't you know what staring means?

CLAY: I saw you through the window . . . if that's what it means. I don't know if I was staring. Seems to me you were staring through the window at me.

LULA: I was. But only after I'd turned around and saw you staring through that window down in the vicinity of my ass and legs.

CLAY: Really?

LULA: Really. I guess you were just taking those idle potshots. Nothing else to do. Run your mind over people's flesh.

CLAY: Oh boy. Wow, now I admit I was looking in your direction. But the rest of that weight is yours.

LULA: I suppose.

CLAY: Staring through train windows is weird business. Much weirder than staring very sedately at abstract asses.

LULA: That's why I came looking through the window ... so you'd have more than that to go on. I even smiled at you.

CLAY: That's right.

LULA: I even got into this train, going some other way than mine. Walked down the aisle ... searching you out.

CLAY: Really? That's pretty funny.

LULA: That's pretty funny.... God, you're dull.

CLAY: Well, I'm sorry, lady, but I really wasn't prepared for party talk.

LULA: No, you're not. What are you prepared for?

[Wrapping the apple core in a Kleenex and dropping it on the floor]

CLAY:

[Takes her conversation as pure sex talk. He turns to confront her squarely with this idea]

I'm prepared for anything. How about you?

LULA:

[Laughing loudly and cutting it off abruptly]

What do you think you're doing?

CLAY: What?

LULA: You think I want to pick you up, get you to take me somewhere and screw me, huh?

CLAY: Is that the way I look?

LULA: You look like you been trying to grow a beard. That's exactly what you look like. You look like you live in New Jersey with your parents and are trying to grow a beard. That's what. You look like you've been reading Chinese poetry and drinking lukewarm sugarless tea.

[Laughs, uncrossing and recrossing her legs]

You look like death eating a soda cracker.

CLAY:

[Cocking his head from one side to the other, embarrassed and trying to make some comeback, but also intrigued by what the woman is saying ... even the sharp city coarseness of her voice, which is still a kind of gentle sidewalk throb]

Really? I look like all that?

LULA: Not all of it.

[She feints a seriousness to cover an actual somber tone]

I lie a lot.

[Smiling]

It helps me control the world.

CLAY:

[Relieved and laughing louder than the humor]

Yeah, I bet.

LULA: But it's true, most of it, right? Jersey? Your bumpy neck?

CLAY: How'd you know all that? Huh? Really, I mean about Jersey ... and even the beard. I met you before? You know Warren Enright?

LULA: You tried to make it with your sister when you were ten.

[CLAY *leans back hard against the back of the seat, his eyes opening now, still trying to look amused*]

But I succeeded a few weeks ago.

[She starts to laugh again]

CLAY: What're you talking about? Warren tell you that? You're a friend of Georgia's?

LULA: I told you I lie. I don't know your sister. I don't know Warren Enright.

CLAY: You mean you're just picking these things out of the air?

LULA: Is Warren Enright a tall skinny black black boy with a phony English accent?

CLAY: I figured you knew him.

LULA: But I don't. I just figured you would know somebody like that.

[Laughs]

CLAY: Yeah, yeah.

LULA: You're probably on your way to his house now.

CLAY: That's right.

LULA:

[Putting her hand on CLAY's *closest knee, drawing it from the knee up to the thigh's hinge, then removing it, watching his face very closely and continuing to laugh, perhaps more gently than before*]

Dull, dull, dull. I bet you think I'm exciting.

CLAY: You're O.K.

LULA: Am I exciting you now?

CLAY: Right. That's not what's supposed to happen?

LULA: How do I know?

[She returns her hand, without moving it, then takes it away and plunges it in her bag to draw out an apple]

You want this?

CLAY: Sure.

LULA:

[She gets one out of the bag for herself]

Eating apples together is always the first step. Or walking up uninhabited Seventh Avenue in the twenties on weekends.

[Bites and giggles, glancing at CLAY *and speaking in loose sing-song*]

Can get you involved ... boy! Get us involved. Um-huh.

[*Mock seriousness*]

Would you like to get involved with me, Mister Man?

CLAY:

[*Trying to be as flippant as* LULA, *whacking happily at the apple*]

Sure. Why not? A beautiful woman like you. Huh, I'd be a fool not to.

LULA: And I bet you're sure you know what you're talking about.

[*Taking him a little roughly by the wrist, so he cannot eat the apple, then shaking the wrist*]

I bet you're sure of almost everything anybody ever asked you about ... right?

[*Shakes his wrist harder*]

Right?

CLAY: Yeah, right.... Wow, you're pretty strong, you know? Whatta you, a lady wrestler or something?

LULA: What's wrong with lady wrestlers? And don't answer because you never knew any. Huh.

[*Cynically*]

That's for sure. They don't have any lady wrestlers in that part of Jersey. That's for sure.

CLAY: Hey, you still haven't told me how you know so much about me.

LULA: I told you I didn't know anything about *you* ... you're a well-known type.

CLAY: Really?

LULA: Or at least I know the type very well. And your skinny English friend too.

CLAY: Anonymously?

LULA:

[*Settles back in seat, single-mindedly finishing her apple and humming snatches of rhythm and blues song*]

What?

CLAY: Without knowing us specifically?

LULA: Oh boy.

[*Looking quickly at Clay*]

What a face. You know, you could be a handsome man.

CLAY: I can't argue with you.

LULA:

[*Vague, off-center response*]

What?

CLAY:

[Raising his voice, thinking the train noise has drowned part of his sentence]

I can't argue with you.

LULA: My hair is turning gray. A gray hair for each year and type I've come through.

CLAY: Why do you want to sound so old?

LULA: But it's always gentle when it starts.

[Attention drifting]

Hugged against tenements, day or night.

CLAY: What?

LULA:

[Refocusing]

Hey, why don't you take me to that party you're going to?

CLAY: You must be a friend of Warren's to know about the party.

LULA: Wouldn't you like to take me to the party?

[Imitates clinging vine]

Oh, come on, ask me to your party.

CLAY: Of course I'll ask you to come with me to the party. And I'll bet you're a friend of Warren's.

LULA: Why not be a friend of Warren's? Why not?

[Taking his arm]

Have you asked me yet?

CLAY: How can I ask you when I don't know your name?

LULA: Are you talking to my name?

CLAY: What is it, a secret?

LULA: I'm Lena the Hyena.[1]

CLAY: The famous woman poet?

LULA: Poetess! The same!

CLAY: Well, you know so much about me ... what's my name?

LULA: Morris the Hyena.

CLAY: The famous woman poet?

LULA: The same.

[Laughing and going into her bag]

You want another apple?

CLAY: Can't make it, lady. I only have to keep one doctor away a day.

---

[1]Character in Al Capp's comic strip, *Li'l Abner* (1934–1977). The ugliest woman who ever lived, Lena drove anyone who looked at her instantly mad, so no sane person could reliably describe her. She was the subject of a famous national drawing contest sponsored by Capp in 1945.

LULA: I bet your name is . . . something like . . . uh, Gerald or Walter. Huh?

CLAY: God, no.

LULA: Lloyd, Norman? One of those hopeless colored names creeping out of New Jersey. Leonard? Gag. . . .

CLAY: Like Warren?

LULA: Definitely. Just exactly like Warren. Or Everett.

CLAY: Gag. . . .

LULA: Well, for sure, it's not Willie.

CLAY: It's Clay.

LULA: Clay? Really? Clay what?

CLAY: Take your pick. Jackson, Johnson, or Williams.

LULA: Oh, really? Good for you. But it's got to be Williams. You're too pretentious to be a Jackson or Johnson.

CLAY: Thass right.

LULA: But Clay's O.K.

CLAY: So's Lena.

LULA: It's Lula.

CLAY: Oh?

LULA: Lula the Hyena.

CLAY: Very good.

LULA:

[Starts laughing again]

Now you say to me, "Lula, Lula, why don't you go to this party with me tonight?" It's your turn, and let those be your lines.

CLAY: Lula, why don't you go to this party with me tonight, Huh?

LULA: Say my name twice before you ask, and no huh's.

CLAY: Lula, Lula, why don't you go to this party with me tonight?

LULA: I'd like to go, Clay, but how can you ask me to go when you barely know me?

CLAY: That is strange, isn't it?

LULA: What kind of reaction is that? You're supposed to say, "Aw, come on, we'll get to know each other better at the party."

CLAY: That's pretty corny.

LULA: What are you into anyway?

[Looking at him half sullenly but still amused]

What thing are you playing at, Mister? Mister Clay Williams?

[Grabs his thigh, up near the crotch]

What are *you* thinking about?

CLAY: Watch it now, you're gonna excite me for real.

LULA:

[Taking her hand away and throwing her apple core through the window]

I bet.

[She slumps in the seat and is heavily silent]

CLAY: I thought you knew everything about me? What happened?

[LULA looks at him, then looks slowly away, then over where the other aisle would be. Noise of the train. She reaches in her bag and pulls out one of the paper books. She puts it on her leg and thumbs the pages listlessly. CLAY cocks his head to see the title of the book. Noise of the train. LULA flips pages and her eyes drift. Both remain silent]

Are you going to the party with me, Lula?

LULA:

[Bored and not even looking]

I don't even know you.

CLAY: You said you know my type.

LULA:

[Strangely irritated]

Don't get smart with me, Buster. I know you like the palm of my hand.

CLAY: The one you eat the apples with?

LULA: Yeh. And the one I open doors late Saturday evening with. That's my door. Up at the top of the stairs. Five flights. Above a lot of Italians and lying Americans. And scrape carrots with. Also . . .

[Looks at him]

the same hand I unbutton my dress with, or let my skirt fall down. Same hand. Lover.

CLAY: Are you angry about anything? Did I say something wrong?

LULA: Everything you say is wrong.

[Mock smile]

That's what makes you so attractive. Ha. In that funnybook jacket with all the buttons.

[More animate, taking hold of his jacket]

What've you got that jacket and tie on in all this heat for? And why're you wearing a jacket and tie like that? Did your people ever burn witches or start revolutions over the price of tea? Boy, those narrow-shoulder clothes come from a tradition you ought to feel oppressed by. A three-button suit. What right do you have to be wearing a three-button suit and striped tie? Your grandfather was a slave, he didn't go to Harvard.

CLAY: My grandfather was a night watchman.

LULA: And you went to a colored college where everybody thought they were Averell Harriman.[2]

[2]Wealthy U.S. businessman and public official (1891–1986). Harriman was undersecretary of state in 1964, when *Dutchman* was first performed.

CLAY: All except me.

LULA: And who did you think you were? Who do you think you are now?

CLAY:

[Laughs as if to make light of the whole trend of the conversation]

Well, in college I thought I was Baudelaire.[3] But I've slowed down since.

LULA: I bet you never once thought you were a black nigger.

[Mock serious, then she howls with laughter. CLAY is stunned but after initial reaction, he quickly tries to appreciate the humor. LULA almost shrieks]

A black Baudelaire.

CLAY: That's right.

LULA: Boy, are you corny. I take back what I said before. Everything you say is not wrong. It's perfect. You should be on television.

CLAY: You act like you're on television already.

LULA: That's because I'm an actress.

CLAY: I thought so.

LULA: Well, you're wrong. I'm no actress. I told you I always lie. I'm nothing, honey, and don't you ever forget it.

[Lighter]

Although my mother was a Communist. The only person in my family ever to amount to anything.

CLAY: My mother was a Republican.

LULA: And your father voted for the man[4] rather than the party.[5]

CLAY: Right!

LULA: Yea for him. Yea, yea for him.

CLAY: Yea!

LULA: And yea for America where he is free to vote for the mediocrity of his choice! Yea!

CLAY: Yea!

LULA: And yea for both your parents who even though they differ about so crucial a matter as the body politic still forged a union of love and sacrifice that was destined to flower at the birth of the noble Clay ... what's your middle name?

CLAY: Clay.

LULA: A union of love and sacrifice that was destined to flower at the birth of the noble Clay Clay Williams. Yea! And most of all yea yea for you, Clay Clay. The Black Baudelaire! Yes!

[3]Charles Baudelaire (1821–1867), French poet and critic unappreciated during his lifetime (he was fined for "offenses against public morals" after the publication of one book), now considered a landmark French literary figure.

[4]Slang for "the white man," or the system of institutionalized racism that oppresses black Americans.

[5]The International Communist Party, which recruited heavily among the American black population in the mid-twentieth century by promising complete racial equality.

[And with knifelike cynicism]

> My Christ. My Christ.

CLAY: Thank you, ma'am.

LULA: May the people accept you as a ghost of the future. And love you, that you might not kill them when you can.

CLAY: What?

LULA: You're a murderer, Clay, and you know it.

[Her voice darkening with significance]

> You know goddamn well what I mean.

CLAY: I do?

LULA: So we'll pretend the air is light and full of perfume.

CLAY:

[Sniffing at her blouse]

> It is.

LULA: And we'll pretend the people cannot see you. That is, the citizens. And that you are free of your own history. And I am free of my history. We'll pretend that we are both anonymous beauties smashing along through the city's entrails.

[She yells as loud as she can]

> GROOVE!
> *Black*

SCENE II

Scene is the same as before, though now there are other seats visible in the car. And throughout the scene other people get on the subway. There are maybe one or two seated in the car as the scene opens, though neither CLAY nor LULA notices them. CLAY's tie is open. LULA is hugging his arm.

CLAY: The party!

LULA: I know it'll be something good. You can come in with me, looking casual and significant. I'll be strange, haughty, and silent, and walk with long slow strides.

CLAY: Right.

LULA: When you get drunk, pat me once, very lovingly on the flanks, and I'll look at you cryptically, licking my lips.

CLAY: It sounds like something we can do.

LULA: You'll go around talking to young men about your mind, and to old men about your plans. If you meet a very close friend who is also with someone like me, we can stand together, sipping our drinks and exchanging codes of lust. The atmosphere will be slithering in love and half-love and very open moral decision.

CLAY: Great. Great.

LULA: And everyone will pretend they don't know your name, and then ...

[*She pauses heavily*]

later, when they have to, they'll claim a friendship that denies your sterling character.

CLAY:

[*Kissing her neck and fingers*]

And then what?

LULA: Then? Well, then we'll go down the street, late night, eating apples and winding very deliberately toward my house.

CLAY: Deliberately?

LULA: I mean, we'll look in all the shopwindows, and make fun of the queers. Maybe we'll meet a Jewish Buddhist and flatten his conceits over some very pretentious coffee.

CLAY: In honor of whose God?

LULA: Mine.

CLAY: Who is ... ?

LULA: Me ... and you?

CLAY: A corporate Godhead.

LULA: Exactly. Exactly.

[*Notices one of the other people entering*]

CLAY: Go on with the chronicle. Then what happens to us?

LULA:

[*A mild depression, but she still makes her description triumphant and increasingly direct*]

To my house, of course.

CLAY: Of course.

LULA: And up the narrow steps of the tenement.[6]

CLAY: You live in a tenement?

LULA: Wouldn't live anywhere else. Reminds me specifically of my novel form of insanity.

CLAY: Up the tenement stairs.

LULA: And with my apple-eating hand I push open the door and lead you, my tender big-eyed prey, into my ... God, what can I call it ... into my hovel.

CLAY: Then what happens?

LULA: After the dancing and games, after the long drinks and long walks, the real fun begins.

CLAY: Ah, the real fun.

[*Embarrassed, in spite of himself*]

[6]Apartment house, but with connotations of overcrowding, poor sanitation, safety hazards, and discomfort. Generally used to refer to the housing of impoverished urban immigrants during the early twentieth century.

Which is . . .?

LULA:

[Laughs at him]

Real fun in the dark house. Hah! Real fun in the dark house, high up above the street and the ignorant cowboys. I lead you in, holding your wet hand gently in my hand . . .

CLAY: Which is not wet?

LULA: Which is dry as ashes.

CLAY: And cold?

LULA: Don't think you'll get out of your responsibility that way. It's not cold at all. You Fascist![7] Into my dark living room. Where we'll sit and talk endlessly, endlessly.

CLAY: About what?

LULA: About what? About your manhood, what do you think? What do you think we've been talking about all this time?

CLAY: Well, I didn't know it was that. That's for sure. Every other thing in the world but that.

[Notices another person entering, looks quickly, almost involuntarily up and down the car, seeing the other people in the car]

Hey, I didn't even notice when those people got on.

LULA: Yeah, I know.

CLAY: Man, this subway is slow.

LULA: Yeah, I know.

CLAY: Well, go on. We were talking about my manhood.

LULA: We still are. All the time.

CLAY: We were in your living room.

LULA: My dark living room. Talking endlessly.

CLAY: About my manhood.

LULA: I'll make you a map of it. Just as soon as we get to my house.

CLAY: Well, that's great.

LULA: One of the things we do while we talk. And screw.

CLAY:

[Trying to make his smile broader and less shaky]

We finally got there.

LULA: And you'll call my rooms black as a grave. You'll say, "This place is like Juliet's tomb."[8]

---

[7]An adherent of fascism, a totalitarian political system organized around fidelity to a dictatorial leader, social and economic centralization, and the violent suppression of resistance.
[8]From William Shakespeare's *Romeo and Juliet*. Because her parents opposed her marriage to

Romeo, Juliet feigned death with a sleeping potion in order to be reunited with him, thus spending several days alive in her family's tomb.

CLAY:

[*Laughs*]

I might.

LULA: I know. You've probably said it before.

CLAY: And is that all? The whole grand tour?

LULA: Not all. You'll say to me very close to my face, many, many times, you'll say, even whisper, that you love me.

CLAY: Maybe I will.

LULA: And you'll be lying.

CLAY: I wouldn't lie about something like that.

LULA: Hah. It's the only kind of thing you will lie about. Especially if you think it'll keep me alive.

CLAY: Keep you alive? I don't understand.

LULA:

[*Bursting out laughing, but too shrilly*]

Don't understand? Well, don't look at me. It's the path I take, that's all. Where both feet take me when I set them down. One in front of the other.

CLAY: Morbid. Morbid. You sure you're not an actress? All that self-aggrandizement.

LULA: Well, I told you I wasn't an actress . . . but I also told you I lie all the time. Draw your own conclusions.

CLAY: Morbid. Morbid. You sure you're not an actress? All scribed? There's no more?

LULA: I've told you all I know. Or almost all.

CLAY: There's no funny parts?

LULA: I thought it was all funny.

CLAY: But you mean peculiar, not ha-ha.

LULA: You don't know what I mean.

CLAY: Well, tell me the almost part then. You said almost all. What else? I want the whole story.

LULA:

[*Searching aimlessly through her bag. She begins to talk breathlessly, with a light and silly tone*]

All stories are whole stories. All of 'em. Our whole story . . . nothing but change. How could things go on like that forever? Huh?

[*Slaps him on the shoulder, begins finding things in her bag, taking them out and throwing them over her shoulder into the aisle*]

Except I do go on as I do. Apples and long walks with deathless intelligent lovers. But you mix it up. Look out the window, all the time. Turning pages. Change change change. Till, shit, I don't know you. Wouldn't, for that matter. You're too serious. I bet you're even too serious to be psychoanalyzed. Like all those Jewish poets from Yonkers,[9] who leave their mothers looking for other mothers, or others' mothers, on whose baggy tits they lay their fumbling heads. Their poems are always funny, and all about sex.

CLAY: They sound great. Like movies.

LULA: But you change.

[Blankly]

And things work on you till you hate them.

[More people come into the train. They come closer to the couple, some of them not sitting, but swinging drearily on the straps, staring at the two with uncertain interest]

CLAY: Wow. All these people, so suddenly. They must all come from the same place.

LULA: Right. That they do.

CLAY: Oh? You know about them too?

LULA: Oh yeah. About them more than I know about you. Do they frighten you?

CLAY: Frighten me? Why should they frighten me?

LULA: 'Cause you're an escaped nigger.

CLAY: Yeah?

LULA: 'Cause you crawled through the wire and made tracks to my side.

CLAY: Wire?

LULA: Don't they have wire around plantations?

CLAY: You must be Jewish. All you can think about is wire.[10] Plantations didn't have any wire. Plantations were big open whitewashed places like heaven, and everybody on 'em was grooved to be there. Just strummin' and hummin' all day.

LULA: Yes, yes.

CLAY: And that's how the blues was born.

LULA: Yes, yes. And that's how the blues was born.

[Begins to make up a song that becomes quickly hysterical. As she sings she rises from her seat, still throwing things out of her bag into the aisle, beginning a rhythmical shudder and twistlike wiggle, which she continues up and down the aisle, bumping into many of the standing people and tripping over the feet of those sitting. Each time she runs into a person she lets out a very vicious piece of profanity, wiggling and stepping all the time]

---

[9]Suburb of Manhattan in southern Westchester County, New York.

[10]Reference to the barbed wire fences surrounding Nazi concentration camps during the Holocaust.

And that's how the blues was born. Yes. Yes. Son of a bitch, get out of the way. Yes. Quack. Yes. Yes. And that's how the blues was born. Ten little niggers sitting on a limb, but none of them ever looked like him.[11]

[Points to CLAY, *returns toward the seat, with her hands extended for him to rise and dance with her]*

And that's how blues was born. Yes. Come on, Clay. Let's do the nasty. Rub bellies. Rub bellies.

CLAY:

[Waves his hands to refuse. He is embarrassed, but determined to get a kick out of the proceedings]

Hey, what was in those apples? Mirror, mirror on the wall, who's the fairest one of all? Snow White,[12] baby, and don't you forget it.

LULA:

[Grabbing for his hands, which he draws away]

Come on, Clay. Let's rub bellies on the train. The nasty. The nasty. Do the gritty grind, like your ol' rag-head mammy. Grind till you lose your mind. Shake it, shake it, shake it, shake it! OOOOweeee! Come on, Clay. Let's do the choo-choo train shuffle, the navel scratcher.

CLAY: Hey, you coming on like the lady who smoked up her grass skirt.

LULA:

[Becoming annoyed that he will not dance, and becoming more animated as if to embarrass him still further]

Come on, Clay . . . let's do the thing. Uhh! Uhh! Clay! Clay! You middle-class black bastard. Forget your social-working mother for a few seconds and let's knock stomachs. Clay, you liver-lipped white man. You would-be Christian. You ain't no nigger, you're just a dirty white man. Get up, Clay. Dance with me, Clay.

CLAY: Lula! Sit down, now. Be cool.

LULA:

[Mocking him, in wild dance]

Be cool. Be cool. That's all you know . . . shaking that wildroot cream-oil on your knotty head, jackets buttoning up to your chin, so full of white man's words. Christ. God. Get up and scream at these people. Like scream meaningless shit in these hopeless faces.

[She screams at people in train, still dancing]

---

[11]Parody of a British nursery rhyme, "Ten Little Niggers" (also known as "Ten Little Indians"), in which each of the ten is sequentially killed—for example, "Ten little niggers going out to dine/One choked his little self and then there were nine." In Lula's version, all ten are lynching victims who were hanged from a tree limb.
[12]Slang reference to cocaine.

Red trains cough Jewish underwear for keeps! Expanding smells of silence. Gravy snot whistling like sea birds. Clay. Clay, you got to break out. Don't sit there dying the way they want you to die. Get up.

CLAY: Oh, sit the fuck down.

[He moves to restrain her]

Sit down, goddamn it.

LULA:

[Twisting out of his reach]

Screw yourself, Uncle Tom.[13] Thomas Woolly-head.

[Begins to dance a kind of jig, mocking CLAY with loud forced humor]

There is Uncle Tom ... I mean, Uncle Thomas Woolly-Head. With old white matted mane. He hobbles on his wooden cane. Old Tom. Old Tom. Let the white man hump his ol' mama, and he jes' shuffle off in the woods and hide his gentle gray head. Ol' Thomas Woolly-Head.

[Some of the other riders are laughing now. A drunk gets up and joins LULA in her dance, singing, as best he can, her "song." CLAY gets up out of his seat and visibly scans the faces of the other riders]

CLAY: Lula! Lula!

[She is dancing and turning, still shouting as loud as she can. The drunk too is shouting, and waving his hands wildly]

Lula ... you dumb bitch. Why don't you stop it?

[He rushes half stumbling from his seat, and grabs one of her flailing arms]

LULA: Let me go! You black son of a bitch.

[She struggles against him]

Let me go! Help!

[CLAY is dragging her towards her seat, and the drunk seeks to interfere. He grabs CLAY around the shoulders and begins wrestling with him. CLAY clubs the drunk to the floor without releasing LULA, who is still screaming. CLAY finally gets her to the seat and throws her into it]

CLAY: Now you shut the hell up.

[Grabbing her shoulders]

Just shut up. You don't know what you're talking about. You don't know anything. So just keep your stupid mouth closed.

LULA: You're afraid of white people. And your father was. Uncle Tom Big Lip!

---

[13]Slang term for a servile black man, taken from the docile, pious black slave and title character of Harriet Beecher Stowe's 1852 novel *Uncle Tom's Cabin*.

CLAY:

[Slaps her as hard as he can, across the mouth. LULA's *head bangs against the back of the seat. When she raises it again,* CLAY *slaps her again]*

Now shut up and let me talk.

[He turns toward the other riders, some of whom are sitting on the edge of their seats. The drunk is on one knee, rubbing his head, and singing softly the same song. He shuts up too when he sees CLAY *watching him. The others go back to newspapers or stare out the windows]*

Shit, you don't have any sense, Lula, nor feelings either. I could murder you now. Such a tiny ugly throat. I could squeeze it flat, and watch you turn blue, on a humble. For dull kicks. And all these weak-faced ofays[14] squatting around here, staring over their papers at me. Murder them too. Even if they expected it. That man there . . .

[Points to well-dressed man]

I could rip that *Times* right out of his hand, as skinny and middle-classed as I am, I could rip that paper out of his hand and just as easily rip out his throat. It takes no great effort. For what? To kill you soft idiots? You don't understand anything but luxury.

LULA: You fool!

CLAY:

[Pushing her against the seat]

I'm not telling you again, Tallulah Bankhead![15] Luxury. In your face and your fingers. You telling me what I ought to do.

[Sudden scream frightening the whole coach]

Well, don't! Don't you tell me anything! If I'm a middle-class fake white man . . . let me be. And let me be in the way I want.

[Through his teeth]

I'll rip your lousy breasts off! Let me be who I feel like being. Uncle Tom. Thomas. Whoever. It's none of your business. You don't know anything except what's there for you to see. An act. Lies. Device. Not the pure heart, the pumping black heart. You don't ever know that. And I sit here, in this buttoned-up suit, to keep myself from cutting all your throats. I mean wantonly. You great liberated whore! You fuck some black man, and right away you're an expert on black people. What a lotta shit that is. The only thing you know is that you come if he bangs you hard enough. And that's all. The belly rub? You wanted to do the belly rub? Shit, you don't even know how. You don't know how. That ol' dipty-dip shit you do,

---

[14]Derogatory black slang for white people.
[15]Flamboyant American stage and film actress (1903–1968), notorious for glamorous parties, heavy drinking, chain smoking, and public nudity.

rolling your ass like an elephant. That's not my kind of belly rub. Belly rub is not Queens. Belly rub is dark places, with big hats and overcoats held up with one arm. Belly rub hates you. Old bald-headed four-eyed ofays popping their fingers . . . and don't know yet what they're doing. They say, "I love Bessie Smith."[16] And don't even understand that Bessie Smith is saying, "Kiss my ass, kiss my black unruly ass." Before love, suffering, desire, anything you can explain, she's saying, and very plainly, "Kiss my black ass." And if you don't know that, it's you that's doing the kissing.

Charlie Parker?[17] Charlie Parker. All the hip white boys scream for Bird. And Bird saying, "Up your ass, feeble-minded ofay! Up your ass." And they sit there talking about the tortured genius of Charlie Parker. Bird would've played not a note of music if he just walked up to East Sixty-seventh Street and killed the first ten white people he saw. Not a note! And I'm the great would-be poet. Yes. That's right! Poet. Some kind of bastard literature . . . all it needs is a simple knife thrust. Just let me bleed you, you loud whore, and one poem vanished. A whole people of neurotics, struggling to keep from being sane. And the only thing that would cure the neurosis would be your murder. Simple as that. I mean if I murdered you, then other white people would begin to understand me. You understand? No. I guess not. If Bessie Smith had killed some white people she wouldn't have needed that music. She could have talked very straight and plain about the world. No metaphors. No grunts. No wiggles in the dark of her soul. Just straight two and two are four. Money. Power. Luxury. Like that. All of them. Crazy niggers turning their backs on sanity. When all it needs is that simple act. Murder. Just murder! Would make us all sane.

[Suddenly weary]

Ahhh. Shit. But who needs it? I'd rather be a fool. Insane. Safe with my words, and no deaths, and clean, hard thoughts, urging me to new conquests. My people's madness. Hah! That's a laugh. My people. They don't need me to claim them. They got legs and arms of their own. Personal insanities. Mirrors. They don't need all those words. They don't need any defense. But listen, though, one more thing. And you tell this to your father, who's probably the kind of man who needs to know at once. So he can plan ahead. Tell him not to preach so much rationalism and cold logic to these niggers. Let them alone. Let them sing curses at you in code and see your filth as simple lack of style. Don't make the mistake, through some irresponsible surge of Christian charity, of talking too much about the advantages of Western rationalism, or the great intellectual legacy of the white man, or maybe they'll begin to listen. And then, maybe one day, you'll find

---

[16]Legendary American blues singer and enormously influential musician (1895–1937) who achieved stardom in the 1920s with both black and white audiences.
[17]Known as "Bird," brilliant jazz saxophonist (1920–1955) who pioneered bebop and

improvisational forms, changing popular music forever. Almost as well known for his lifelong drug use as for his music, Parker collaborated with nearly every major jazz musician of the mid-twentieth century before his untimely death at 34.

they actually do understand exactly what you are talking about, all these fantasy people. All these blues people. And on that day, as sure as shit, when you really believe you can "accept" them into your fold, as half-white trusties late of the subject peoples. With no more blues, except the very old ones, and not a watermelon in sight, the great missionary heart will have triumphed, and all of those ex-coons will be stand-up Western men, with eyes for clean hard useful lives, sober, pious and sane, and they'll murder you. They'll murder you, and have very rational explanations. Very much like your own. They'll cut your throats, and drag you out to the edge of your cities so the flesh can fall away from your bones, in sanitary isolation.

LULA:

[Her voice takes on a different, more businesslike quality]

I've heard enough.

CLAY:

[Reaching for his books]

I bet you have. I guess I better collect my stuff and get off this train. Looks like we won't be acting out that little pageant you outlined before.

LULA: No. We won't. You're right about that, at least.

[She turns to look quickly around the rest of the car]

All right!

[The others respond]

CLAY:

[Bending across the girl to retrieve his belongings]

Sorry, baby, I don't think we could make it.

[As he is bending over her, the girl brings up a small knife and plunges it into CLAY's *chest. Twice. He slumps across her knees, his mouth working stupidly]*

LULA: Sorry is right.

[Turning to the others in the car who have already gotten up from their seats]

Sorry is the rightest thing you've said. Get this man off me! Hurry, now!

[The others come and drag CLAY's *body down the aisle]*

Open the door and throw his body out.

[They throw him off]

And all of you get off at the next stop.

[LULA busies herself straightening her things. Getting everything in order. She takes out a notebook and makes a quick scribbling note. Drops it in her bag. The train apparently stops and all the others get off, leaving her alone in the coach.

Very soon a young Negro of about twenty comes into the coach, with a couple of books under his arm. He sits a few seats in back of LULA. When he is seated she turns and gives him a long slow look. He looks up from his book and drops the book on his lap. Then an old Negro conductor comes into the car, doing a sort of restrained soft shoe, and half mumbling the words of some song. He looks at the young man, briefly, with a quick greeting]

CONDUCTOR: Hey, brother!
YOUNG MAN: Hey.

[The conductor continues down the aisle with his little dance and the mumbled song. LULA turns to stare at him and follows his movements down the aisle. The conductor tips his hat when he reaches her seat, and continues out the car]

Curtain

1964

JOYCE CAROL OATES
B. 1938

Critic, teacher, short story writer, poet, playwright, novelist, editor, and publisher, Joyce Carol Oates is an artist of amazing versatility, productivity, and range. She has written more than forty novels and hundreds of shorter works; several of her plays have been produced off-Broadway; and at least two of her stories have been made into films. Writing about men and women struggling for existence in "Eden Valley," a region strikingly like her own birthplace in upstate New York, Oates has been variously classified as a realist, a naturalist, a "gothic" artist, and "the dark lady of American Letters." She has won many prizes, including the National Book Award, a Guggenheim Fellowship, an O. Henry Award for Special Achievement, and an award from the Lotos Club, and has been elected to the National Institute of Arts and Letters. While she calls herself a feminist, she prefers to be considered "a woman who writes." She has a wide readership: her work is as likely to be found on an academic syllabus as on the best-seller list.

Oates has often been considered a realist in the tradition of Dreiser; she is indeed a social critic, focusing on contemporary events and issues in fiction and essays. But she also tests classical myths and established literary conventions beyond the limits of any one genre. Curiously, as if to expand her own boundaries, Oates has published fiction—a series of harrowing psychological mysteries—under a pseudonym, Rosamond Smith.

Perhaps Oates is best understood as an artist in residence—in the largest sense of that term. She studied at Syracuse and then in graduate school at the University of Wisconsin; she has taught literature and writing at Detroit and Windsor. As a scholar, she has written several collections of literary criticism, including *New Heaven, New Earth, (Woman) Writer*, and *The Profane Art*. She is on the Advisory Board of *The Kenyon Review* and is a frequent reviewer of contemporary literature. Currently she is Roger S. Berlind Distinguished Professor of English at Princeton, where she lives and writes and works at the press she founded with her late husband, Professor Raymond Smith.

Oates draws upon this complex and varied background in her fiction. In one way or another, all of her characters struggle to find a place in a changing and often threatening world. In her early novels *With Shuddering Fall* and *A Garden of Earthly Delights*, she writes about rural America with its migrants, ragged prophets, and automobile junkyards; in contrast, *Expensive People* mocks the suburbanite, and her novel *them* dramatizes the violent lives of the urban poor. *Wonderland* is a novel of lost generations: the hero barely escapes from the gunfire of his crazed father; as a father himself, he is in danger of losing his daughter in the turbulence of the sixties. *Childwold* is a lyrical and experimental portrait of an artist as a young woman. Oates satirizes doctors, lawyers, and preachers; she casts an especially critical eye on professors and resident artists in *Unholy Loves, Solstice, American Appetites*, and *Marya: A Life*.

Fascinated by the literary past and the work of other writers, Oates has tried her hand at "imitations"—reimagining stories of Joyce, Thoreau, James, Chekhov, and Kafka. She produced a group of novels that represent her own imaginative view of nineteenth-century conventions, with particular emphasis on the constraints placed upon women both as writers and as hapless heroines. But she also inscribes the history of the present, memorializing the paranoia of the fifties in *You Must Remember This*, dramatizing explosive American race relations in *Because It Is Bitter, and Because It Is My Heart*, and publishing essays on boxing that have won her infrequent spots as a ringside commentator.

Joyce Carol Oates may be best known for her short stories, frequently included in the annual O. Henry Prize Selection and widely anthologized. Like her novels, many of her stories are experiments in form and character. Most focus on the personality at risk—on seemingly ordinary people whose lives are vulnerable to powerful threats from external society and the inner self.

"Where Are You Going, Where Have You Been?" is one of these. A frightening view of "coming of age" written in 1967, the story has appeared in several collections, including *The Wheel of Love*; it has also been adapted for the screen (*Smooth Talk*, 1986). Its central character, Connie, is a young woman fatally at ease in the world of adolescent ritual: high school flirtations, hamburger hangouts and drive-ins, movies and fan magazines, her dreams shaped by popular song lyrics. She seems destined for a conventional future very much like her mother's, evident in their half-affectionate bickering. Yet as Oates deftly and gradually reveals, this sense of security is at best illusory; even the familiar language of popular song becomes the agency of seduction, making Connie the helpless victim of a grotesque and demonic caller she mistakes for a "friend." Asking the question posed by the sixties balladeer and youth culture cult figure Bob Dylan (to whom this story is dedicated), "Where Are You Going, Where Have You Been?" powerfully represents the complex, open-ended literary project of author Joyce Carol Oates.

Eileen T. Bender
Indiana University

PRIMARY WORKS

By the North Gate, 1963; *With Shuddering Fall*, 1964; *A Garden of Earthly Delights*, 1967; *Expensive People*, 1968; *them*, 1969; *The Wheel of Love*, 1970; *Love and Its Derangements*, 1970; *Wonderland*, 1971; *Marriages and Infidelities*, 1972; *Angel Fire*, 1973; *Do with Me What You Will*, 1973; *New Heaven, New Earth*, 1974; *The Goddess and Other Women*, 1974; *The Hungry Ghosts*, 1974; *The Fabulous Beasts*, 1975; *The Seduction and Other Stories*, 1975; *The Assassins*, 1975; *Childwold*, 1976; *Crossing the Border*, 1976; *Triumph of the Spider Monkey*, 1976; *Night Side*, 1977; *Son of the Morning*, 1978; *All the Good People I've Left Behind*, 1978; *Cybele*, 1979; *Unholy Loves*, 1979; *Bellefleur*, 1980; *A Sentimental Education*, 1980; *Celestial Timepiece*, 1980; *Three Plays*, 1980; *Contraries*, 1981; *Angel of Light*, 1981; *A Bloodsmoor Romance*, 1982; *Invisible Woman*, 1982; *The Profane Art*, 1983; *Last Days*, 1984; *Mysteries of Winterhurn*, 1984; *Solstice*, 1985; *Raven's Wing*, 1986; *Marya: A Life*, 1986; *(Woman) Writer*, 1986; *You Must Remember This*, 1987; *On Boxing*, 1988; *The Assignation*, 1988; *American Appetites*, 1989; *The Time Traveler*, 1989; *I Lock My Door upon Myself*, 1990; *Expensive People*, 1990; *Because It Is Bitter, and Because It Is My Heart*, 1991; *In Darkest America*, 1991; *Twelve Plays*, 1991; *The Rise of Life on Earth*, 1991; *Where Is Here?*, 1992; *Heat and Other Stories*, 1992; *Black Water*, 1992; *Where Are You Going, Where Have You Been?: Selected Early Stories*, 1993; *Foxfire*, 1993; *Haunted*, 1994; *What I Lived For*, 1994; *Zombie*, 1995; *The Perfectionist and Other Plays*, 1995; *First Love: A Gothic Tale*, 1996; *Will You Always Love Me?*, 1996; *Tenderness*, 1996; *We Were the Mulvaneys*, 1996; *Mancrazy*, 1997; *My Heart Laid Bare*, 1998; *The Collector of Hearts*, 1998; *New Plays*, 1998; *Broke Heart Blues*, 1999; *Where I've Been, and Where I'm Going*, 1999; *Blonde*, 2000; *Faithless*, 2001; *Middle Age*, 2001; *Beasts*, 2002; *I'll Take You There*, 2002; *The Tattooed Girl*, 2003; *Rope: A Love Story*, 2003; *The Falls*, 2004; *The Corn Maiden*, 2005; *Missing Mom*, 2005; *Black Girl/White Girl*, 2006; *The Gravedigger's Daughter*, 2007; *My Sister, My Love*, 2008; *Dear Husband*, 2009; *Little Bird of Heaven*, 2009; *A Fair Maiden*, 2010; *Sourland: Stories*, 2010; *Give Me Your Heart: Tales of Mystery and Suspense*, 2011.

Where Are You Going, Where Have You Been?

For Bob Dylan

Her name was Connie. She was fifteen and she had a quick, nervous giggling habit of craning her neck to glance into mirrors or checking other people's faces to make sure her own was all right. Her mother, who noticed everything and knew everything and who hadn't much reason any longer to look at her own face, always scolded Connie about it. "Stop gawking at yourself. Who are you? You think you're so pretty?" she would say. Connie would raise her eyebrows at these familiar old complaints and look right through her mother, into a shadowy vision of herself as she was right at that moment: she knew she was pretty and that was everything. Her mother had been pretty once too, if you could believe those old snapshots in the album, but now her looks were gone and that was why she was always after Connie.

"Why don't you keep your room clean like your sister? How've you got your hair fixed—what the hell stinks? Hair spray? You don't see your sister using that junk."

Her sister June was twenty-four and still lived at home. She was a secretary in the high school Connie attended, and if that wasn't bad enough—with her in the same building—she was so plain and chunky and steady that Connie had to hear her praised all the time by her mother and her mother's sisters. June did this, June did that, she saved money and helped clean the house and cooked and Connie couldn't do a thing, her mind was all filled with trashy daydreams. Their father was away at work most of the time and when he came home he wanted supper and he read the newspaper at supper and after supper he went to bed. He didn't bother talking much to them, but around his bent head Connie's mother kept picking at her until Connie wished her mother was dead and she herself was dead and it was all over. "She makes me want to throw up sometimes," she complained to her friends. She had a high, breathless, amused voice that made everything she said sound a little forced, whether it was sincere or not.

There was one good thing: June went places with girl friends of hers, girls who were just as plain and steady as she, and so when Connie wanted to do that her mother had no objections. The father of Connie's best girl friend drove the girls the three miles to town and left them at a shopping plaza so they could walk through the stores or go to a movie, and when he came to pick them up again at eleven he never bothered to ask what they had done.

They must have been familiar sights, walking around the shopping plaza in their shorts and flat ballerina slippers that always scuffed the sidewalk, with charm bracelets jingling on their thin wrists; they would lean together to whisper and laugh secretly if someone passed who amused or interested them. Connie had long dark blond hair that drew anyone's eye to it, and she wore part of it pulled up on her head and puffed out and the rest of it she let fall down her back. She wore a pull-over jersey blouse that looked one way when she was at home and another way when she was away from home. Everything about her had two sides to it, one for home and one for anywhere that was not home: her walk, which could be childlike and bobbing, or languid enough to make anyone think she was hearing music in her head; her mouth, which was pale and smirking most of the time, but bright and pink on these evenings out; her laugh, which was cynical and drawling at home—"Ha, ha, very funny,"—but high-pitched and nervous anywhere else, like the jingling of the charms on her bracelet.

Sometimes they did go shopping or to a movie, but sometimes they went across the highway, ducking fast across the busy road, to a drive-in restaurant where older kids hung out. The restaurant was shaped like a big bottle, though squatter than a real bottle, and on its cap was a revolving figure of a grinning boy holding a hamburger aloft. One night in midsummer they ran across, breathless with daring, and right away someone leaned out a car window and invited them over, but it was just a boy from high school they didn't like. It made them feel good to be able to ignore him. They went up through the maze of parked and cruising cars to the bright-lit, fly-infested restaurant, their faces pleased and expectant as if they were entering a sacred building that loomed up out of the night to give them what haven and blessing they yearned for. They sat at the counter and crossed their legs at the ankles, their thin shoulders rigid with excitement, and listened to the music that made everything so good: the music was always in the background, like music at a church service; it was something to depend upon.

A boy named Eddie came in to talk with them. He sat backwards on his stool, turning himself jerkily around in semicircles and then stopping and turning back again, and after a while he asked Connie if she would like something to eat. She said she would and so she tapped her friend's arm on her way out—her friend pulled her face up into a brave, droll look—and Connie said she would meet her at eleven, across the way. "I just hate to leave her like that," Connie said earnestly, but the boy said that she wouldn't be alone for long. So they went out to his car, and on the way Connie couldn't help but let her eyes wander over the windshields and faces all around her, her face gleaming with a joy that had nothing to do with Eddie or even this place; it might have been the music. She drew her shoulders up and sucked in her breath with the pure pleasure of being alive, and just at that moment she happened to glance at a face just a few feet from hers. It was a boy with shaggy black hair, in a convertible jalopy painted gold. He stared at her and then his lips widened into a grin. Connie slit her eyes at him and turned away, but she couldn't help glancing back and there he was, still watching her. He wagged a finger and laughed and said, "Gonna get you, baby," and Connie turned away again without Eddie noticing anything.

She spent three hours with him, at the restaurant where they ate hamburgers and drank Cokes in wax cups that were always sweating, and then down an alley a mile or so away, and when he left her off at five to eleven only the movie house was still open at the plaza. Her girl friend was there, talking with a boy. When Connie came up, the two girls smiled at each other and Connie said, "How was the movie?" and the girl said, "*You* should know." They rode off with the girl's father, sleepy and pleased, and Connie couldn't help but look back at the darkened shopping plaza with its big empty parking lot and its signs that were faded and ghostly now, and over at the drive-in restaurant where cars were still circling tirelessly. She couldn't hear the music at this distance.

Next morning June asked her how the movie was and Connie said, "So-so."

She and that girl and occasionally another girl went out several times a week, and the rest of the time Connie spent around the house—it was summer vacation—getting in her mother's way and thinking, dreaming about the boys she met. But all the boys fell back and dissolved into a single face that was not even a face but an idea, a feeling, mixed up with the urgent insistent pounding of the music and the humid night air of July. Connie's mother kept dragging her back to the daylight by finding things for her to do or saying suddenly, "What's this about the Pettinger girl?"

And Connie would say nervously, "Oh, her. That dope." She always drew thick clear lines between herself and such girls, and her mother was simple and kind enough to believe it. Her mother was so simple, Connie thought, that it was maybe cruel to fool her so much. Her mother went scuffling around the house in old bedroom slippers and complained over the telephone to one sister about the other, then the other called up and the two of them complained about the third one. If June's name was mentioned her mother's tone was approving, and if Connie's name was mentioned it was disapproving. This did not really mean she disliked Connie, and actually Connie thought that her mother preferred her to June just because she was prettier, but the two of them kept up a pretense of exasperation, a sense that they were tugging and struggling over something of little value to either of them. Sometimes, over coffee, they were almost friends, but something would come up—some vexation that was like a fly buzzing suddenly around their heads—and their faces went hard with contempt.

One Sunday Connie got up at eleven—none of them bothered with church—and washed her hair so that it could dry all day long in the sun. Her parents and sister were going to a barbecue at an aunt's house and Connie said no, she wasn't interested, rolling her eyes to let her mother know just what she thought of it. "Stay home alone then," her mother said sharply. Connie sat out back in a lawn chair and watched them drive away, her father quiet and bald, hunched around so that he could back the car out, her mother with a look that was still angry and not at all softened through the windshield, and in the back seat poor old June, all dressed up as if she didn't know what a barbecue was, with all the running yelling kids and the flies. Connie sat with her eyes closed in the sun, dreaming and dazed with the warmth about her as if this were a kind of love, the caresses of love, and her mind slipped over onto thoughts of the boy she had been with the night before and how nice he had been, how sweet it always was, not the way someone like June would suppose but sweet, gentle, the way it was in movies and promised in songs; and when she opened her eyes she hardly knew where she was, the back yard ran off into weeds and a fence-like line of trees and behind it the sky was perfectly blue and still. The asbestos "ranch house" that was now three years old startled her—it looked small. She shook her head as if to get awake.

It was too hot. She went inside the house and turned on the radio to drown out the quiet. She sat on the edge of her bed, barefoot, and listened for an hour and a half to a program called XYZ Sunday Jamboree, record after record of hard, fast, shrieking songs she sang along with, interspersed by exclamations from "Bobby King": "An' look here, you girls at Napoleon's—Son and Charley want you to pay real close attention to this song coming up!"

And Connie paid close attention herself, bathed in a glow of slow-pulsed joy that seemed to rise mysteriously out of the music itself and lay languidly about the airless little room, breathed in and breathed out with each gentle rise and fall of her chest.

After a while she heard a car coming up the drive. She sat up at once, startled, because it couldn't be her father so soon. The gravel kept crunching all the way in from the road—the driveway was long—and Connie ran to the window. It was a car she didn't know. It was an open jalopy, painted a bright gold that caught the sunlight opaquely. Her heart began to pound and her fingers snatched at her hair, checking it, and she whispered, "Christ. Christ," wondering how bad she looked. The car came to a stop at the side door and the horn sounded four short taps, as if this were a signal Connie knew.

She went into the kitchen and approached the door slowly, then hung out the screen door, her bare toes curling down off the step. There were two boys in the car and now she recognized the driver: he had shaggy, shabby black hair that looked crazy as a wig and he was grinning at her.

"I ain't late, am I?" he said.

"Who the hell do you think you are?" Connie said.

"Toldja I'd be out, didn't I?"

"I don't even know who you are."

She spoke sullenly, careful to show no interest or pleasure, and he spoke in a fast, bright monotone. Connie looked past him to the other boy, taking her time. He had fair brown hair, with a lock that fell onto his forehead. His sideburns gave him a fierce, embarrassed look, but so far he hadn't even bothered to glance at her. Both boys wore sunglasses. The driver's glasses were metallic and mirrored everything in miniature.

"You wanta come for a ride?" he said.

Connie smirked and let her hair fall loose over one shoulder.

"Don'tcha like my car? New paint job," he said. "Hey."

"What?"

"You're cute."

She pretended to fidget, chasing flies away from the door.

"Don'tcha believe me, or what?" he said.

"Look, I don't even know who you are," Connie said in disgust.

"Hey, Ellie's got a radio, see. Mine broke down." He lifted his friend's arm and showed her the little transistor radio the boy was holding, and now Connie began to hear the music. It was the same program that was playing inside the house.

"Bobby King?" she said.

"I listen to him all the time. I think he's great."

"He's kind of great," Connie said reluctantly.

"Listen, that guy's *great*. He knows where the action is."

Connie blushed a little, because the glasses made it impossible for her to see just what this boy was looking at. She couldn't decide if she liked him or if he was just a jerk, and so she dawdled in the doorway and wouldn't come down or go back inside. She said, "What's all that stuff painted on your car?"

"Can'tcha read it?" He opened the door very carefully, as if he were afraid it might fall off. He slid out just as carefully, planting his feet firmly on the ground, the tiny metallic world in his glasses slowing down like gelatine hardening, and in the midst of it Connie's bright green blouse. "This here is my name, to begin with," he said. ARNOLD FRIEND was written in tarlike black letters on the side, with a drawing of a round, grinning face that reminded Connie of a pumpkin, except it wore sunglasses. "I wanta introduce myself, I'm Arnold Friend and that's my real name and I'm gonna be your friend, honey, and inside the car's Ellie Oscar, he's kinda shy." Ellie brought his transistor radio up to his shoulder and balanced it there. "Now, these numbers are a secret code, honey," Arnold Friend explained. He read off the numbers 33, 19, 17 and raised his eyebrows at her to see what she thought of that, but she didn't think much of it. The left rear fender had been smashed and around it was written, on the gleaming gold background: DONE BY CRAZY WOMAN DRIVER. Connie had to laugh at that. Arnold Friend was pleased at her laughter and looked up at her. "Around the other side's a lot more—you wanta come and see them?"

"No."

"Why not?"

"Why should I?"

"Don'tcha wanta see what's on the car? Don'tcha wanta go for a ride?"

"I don't know."

"Why not?"

"I got things to do."

"Like what?"

"Things."

He laughed as if she had said something funny. He slapped his thighs. He was standing in a strange way, leaning back against the car as if he were balancing himself. He wasn't tall, only an inch or so taller than she would be if she came down to him. Connie liked the way he was dressed, which was the way all of them dressed: tight faded jeans stuffed into black, scuffed boots, a belt that pulled his waist in and showed how lean he was, and a white pull-over shirt that was a little soiled and showed the hard small muscles of his arms and shoulders. He looked as if he probably did hard work, lifting and carrying things. Even his neck looked muscular. And his face was a familiar face, somehow: the jaw and chin and cheeks slightly darkened because he hadn't shaved for a day or two, and the nose long and hawk-like, sniffing as if she were a treat he was going to gobble up and it was all a joke.

"Connie, you ain't telling the truth. This is your day set aside for a ride with me and you know it," he said, still laughing. The way he straightened and recovered from his fit of laughing showed that it had been all fake.

"How do you know what my name is?" she said suspiciously.

"It's Connie."

"Maybe and maybe not."

"I know my Connie," he said, wagging his finger. Now she remembered him even better, back at the restaurant, and her cheeks warmed at the thought of how she had sucked in her breath just at the moment she passed him—how she must have looked to him. And he had remembered her. "Ellie and I come out here especially for you," he said. "Ellie can sit in back. How about it?"

"Where?"

"Where what?"

"Where're we going?"

He looked at her. He took off the sunglasses and she saw how pale the skin around his eyes was, like holes that were not in shadow but instead in light. His eyes were like chips of broken glass that catch the light in an amiable way. He smiled. It was as if the idea of going for a ride somewhere, to someplace, was a new idea to him.

"Just for a ride, Connie sweetheart."

"I never said my name was Connie," she said.

"But I know what it is. I know your name and all about you, lots of things," Arnold Friend said. He had not moved yet but stood still leaning back against the side of his jalopy. "I took a special interest in you, such a pretty girl, and found out all about you—like I know your parents and sister are gone somewheres and I know where and how long they're going to be gone, and I know who you were with last night, and your best girl friend's name is Betty. Right?"

He spoke in a simple lilting voice, exactly as if he were reciting the words to a song. His smile assured her that everything was fine. In the car Ellie turned up the volume on his radio and did not bother to look around at them.

"Ellie can sit in the back seat," Arnold Friend said. He indicated his friend with a casual jerk of his chin, as if Ellie did not count and she should not bother with him.

"How'd you find out all that stuff?" Connie said.

"Listen: Betty Schultz and Tony Fitch and Jimmy Pettinger and Nancy Pettinger," he said in a chant. "Raymond Stanley and Bob Hutter—"

"Do you know all those kids?"

"I know everybody."

"Look, you're kidding. You're not from around here."

"Sure."

"But—how come we never saw you before?"

"Sure you saw me before," he said. He looked down at his boots, as if he were a little offended. "You just don't remember."

"I guess I'd remember you," Connie said.

"Yeah?" He looked up at this, beaming. He was pleased. He began to mark time with the music from Ellie's radio, tapping his fists lightly together. Connie looked away from his smile to the car, which was painted so bright it almost hurt her eyes to look at it. She looked at that name, ARNOLD FRIEND. And up at the front fender was an expression that was familiar—MAN THE FLYING SAUCERS. It was an expression kids had used the year before but didn't use this year. She looked at it for a while as if the words meant something to her that she did not yet know.

"What're you thinking about? Huh?" Arnold Friend demanded. "Not worried about your hair blowing around in the car, are you?"

"No."

"Think I maybe can't drive good?"

"How do I know?"

"You're a hard girl to handle. How come?" he said. "Don't you know I'm your friend? Didn't you see me put my sign in the air when you walked by?"

"What sign?"

"My sign." And he drew an X in the air, leaning out toward her. They were maybe ten feet apart. After his hand fell back to his side the X was still in the air, almost visible. Connie let the screen door close and stood perfectly still inside it, listening to the music from her radio and the boy's blend together. She stared at Arnold Friend. He stood there so stiffly relaxed, pretending to be relaxed, with one hand idly on the door handle as if he were keeping himself up that way and had no intention of ever moving again. She recognized most things about him, the tight jeans that showed his thighs and buttocks and the greasy leather boots and the tight shirt, and even that slippery friendly smile of his, that sleepy dreamy smile that all the boys used to get across ideas they didn't want to put into words. She recognized all this and also the singsong way he talked, slightly mocking, kidding, but serious and a little melancholy, and she recognized the way he tapped one fist against the other in homage to the perpetual music behind him. But all these things did not come together.

She said suddenly, "Hey, how old are you?"

His smile faded. She could see then that he wasn't a kid, he was much older—thirty, maybe more. At this knowledge her heart began to pound faster.

"That's a crazy thing to ask. Can'tcha see I'm your own age?"

"Like hell you are."

"Or maybe a coupla years older. I'm eighteen."

"Eighteen?" she said doubtfully.

He grinned to reassure her and lines appeared at the corners of his mouth. His teeth were big and white. He grinned so broadly his eyes became slits and she saw how thick the lashes were, thick and black as if painted with a black tarlike material. Then, abruptly, he seemed to become embarrassed and looked over his shoulder at Ellie. "*Him*, he's crazy," he said. "Ain't he a riot? He's a nut, a real character." Ellie was still listening to the music. His sunglasses told nothing about what he was thinking. He wore a bright orange shirt unbuttoned halfway to show his chest, which was a pale, bluish chest and not muscular like Arnold Friend's. His shirt collar was turned up all around and the very tips of the collar pointed out past his chin as if they were protecting him. He was pressing the transistor radio up against his ear and sat there in a kind of a daze, right in the sun.

"He's kinda strange," Connie said.

"Hey, she says you're kinda strange! Kinda strange!" Arnold Friend cried. He pounded on the car to get Ellie's attention. Ellie turned for the first time and Connie saw with shock that he wasn't a kid either—he had a fair, hairless face, cheeks reddened slightly as if the veins grew too close to the surface of his skin, the face of a forty-year-old baby. Connie felt a wave of dizziness rise in her at this sight and she stared at him as if waiting for something to change the shock of the moment, make it all right again. Ellie's lips kept shaping words, mumbling along with the words blasting in his ear.

"Maybe you two better go away," Connie said faintly.

"What? How come?" Arnold Friend cried. "We come out here to take you for a ride. It's Sunday." He had the voice of the man on the radio now. It was the same voice, Connie thought. "Don'tcha know it's Sunday all day? And honey, no matter who you were with last night, today you're with Arnold Friend and don't you forget it! Maybe you better step out here," he said, and this last was in a different voice. It was a little flatter, as if the heat was finally getting to him.

"Hey."

"You two better leave."

"We ain't leaving until you come with us."

"Like hell I am—"

"Connie, don't fool around with me. I mean—I mean, don't fool *around*," he said shaking his head. He laughed incredulously. He placed his sunglasses on top of his head, carefully, as if he were indeed wearing a wig, and brought the stems down behind his ears. Connie stared at him, another wave of dizziness and fear rising in her so that for a moment he wasn't even in focus but was just a blur standing there against his gold car, and she had the idea that he had driven up the driveway all right but had come from nowhere before that and belonged nowhere and that everything about him and even about the music that was so familiar to her was only half real.

"If my father comes and sees you—"

"He ain't coming. He's at a barbecue."

"How do you know that?"

"Aunt Tillie's. Right now they're—uh—they're drinking. Sitting around," he said vaguely, squinting as if he were staring all the way to town and over to Aunt Tillie's back yard. Then the vision seemed to get clear and he nodded energetically. "Yeah. Sitting around. There's your sister in a blue dress, huh? And high heels, the poor sad bitch—nothing like you, sweetheart! And your mother's helping some fat woman with the corn, they're cleaning the corn—husking the corn—"

"What fat woman?" Connie cried.

"How do I know what fat woman, I don't know every goddamn fat woman in the world!" Arnold Friend laughed.

"Oh, that's Mrs. Hornsby.... Who invited her?" Connie said. She felt a little lightheaded. Her breath was coming quickly.

"She's too fat. I don't like them fat. I like them the way you are, honey," he said, smiling sleepily at her. They stared at each other for a while through the screen door. He said softly, "Now, what you're going to do is this: you're going to come out that door. You're going to sit up front with me and Ellie's going to sit in the back, the hell with Ellie, right? This isn't Ellie's date. You're my date. I'm your lover, honey."

"What? You're crazy—"

"Yes, I'm your lover. You don't know what that is but you will," he said. "I know that too. I know all about you. But look: it's real nice and you couldn't ask for nobody better than me, or more polite. I always keep my word. I'll tell you how it is, I'm always nice at first, the first time. I'll hold you so tight you won't think you have to try to get away or pretend anything because you'll know you can't. And I'll come inside you where it's all secret and you'll give in to me and you'll love me—"

"Shut up! You're crazy!" Connie said. She backed away from the door. She put her hands up against her ears as if she'd heard something terrible, something not meant for her. "People don't talk like that, you're crazy," she muttered. Her heart was almost too big now for her chest and its pumping made sweat break out all over her. She looked out to see Arnold Friend pause and then take a step toward the porch, lurching. He almost fell. But, like a clever drunken man, he managed to catch his balance. He wobbled in his high boots and grabbed hold of one of the porch posts.

"Honey?" he said. "You still listening?"

"Get the hell out of here!"

"Be nice, honey. Listen."

"I'm going to call the police—"

He wobbled again and out of the side of his mouth came a fast spat curse, an aside not meant for her to hear. But even this "Christ!" sounded forced. Then he began to smile again. She watched this smile come, awkward as if he were smiling from inside a mask. His whole face was a mask, she thought wildly, tanned down to his throat but then running out as if he had plastered make-up on his face but had forgotten about his throat.

"Honey—? Listen, here's how it is. I always tell the truth and I promise you this: I ain't coming in that house after you."

"You better not! I'm going to call the police if you—if you don't—"

"Honey," he said, talking right through her voice, "honey, I'm not coming in there but you are coming out here. You know why?"

She was panting. The kitchen looked like a place she had never seen before, some room she had run inside but that wasn't good enough, wasn't going to help her. The kitchen window had never had a curtain, after three years, and there were dishes in the sink for her to do—probably—and if you ran your hand across the table you'd probably feel something sticky there.

"You listening, honey? Hey?"

"—going to call the police—"

"Soon as you touch the phone I don't need to keep my promise and can come inside. You won't want that."

She rushed forward and tried to lock the door. Her fingers were shaking. "But why lock it," Arnold Friend said gently, talking right into her face. "It's just a screen door. It's just nothing." One of his boots was at a strange angle, as if his foot wasn't in it. It pointed out to the left, bent at the ankle. "I mean, anybody can break through a screen door and glass and wood and iron or anything else if he needs to, anybody at all, and specially Arnold

Friend. If the place got lit up with a fire, honey, you'd come runnin' out into my arms, right into my arms an' safe at home—like you knew I was your lover and'd stopped fooling around. I don't mind a nice shy girl but I don't like no fooling around." Part of those words were spoken with a slight rhythmic lilt, and Connie somehow recognized them—the echo of a song from last year, about a girl rushing into her boy friend's arms and coming home again—

Connie stood barefoot on the linoleum floor, staring at him. "What do you want?" she whispered.

"I want you," he said.

"What?"

"Seen you that night and thought, that's the one, yes sir. I never needed to look anymore."

"But my father's coming back. He's coming to get me. I had to wash my hair first—" She spoke in a dry, rapid voice, hardly raising it for him to hear.

"No, your daddy is not coming and yes, you had to wash your hair and you washed it for me. It's nice and shining and all for me. I thank you, sweetheart," he said with a mock bow, but again he almost lost his balance. He had to bend and adjust his boots. Evidently his feet did not go all the way down; the boots must have been stuffed with something so that he would seem taller. Connie stared out at him and behind him at Ellie in the car, who seemed to be looking off toward Connie's right, into nothing. This Ellie said, pulling the words out of the air one after another as if he were just discovering them, "You want me to pull out the phone?"

"Shut your mouth and keep it shut," Arnold Friend said, his face red from bending over or maybe from embarrassment because Connie had seen his boots. "This ain't none of your business."

"What—what are you doing? What do you want?" Connie said. "If I call the police they'll get you, they'll arrest you—"

"Promise was not to come in unless you touch that phone, and I'll keep that promise," he said. He resumed his erect position and tried to force his shoulders back. He sounded like a hero in a movie, declaring something important. But he spoke too loudly and it was as if he were speaking to someone behind Connie. "I ain't made plans for coming in that house where I don't belong but just for you to come out to me, the way you should. Don't you know who I am?"

"You're crazy," she whispered. She backed away from the door but did not want to go into another part of the house, as if this would give him permission to come through the door. "What do you . . . you're crazy, you. . . ."

"Huh? What're you saying, honey?"

Her eyes darted everywhere in the kitchen. She could not remember what it was, this room.

"This is how it is, honey: you come out and we'll drive away, have a nice ride. But if you don't come out we're gonna wait till your people come home and then they're all going to get it."

"You want that telephone pulled out?" Ellie said. He held the radio away from his ear and grimaced, as if without the radio the air was too much for him.

"I toldja shut up, Ellie," Arnold Friend said, "you're deaf, get a hearing aid, right? Fix yourself up. This little girl's no trouble and's gonna be nice to me, so Ellie keep to yourself, this ain't your date—right? Don't hem in on me, don't hog, don't crush, don't bird dog, don't trail me," he said in a rapid, meaningless voice, as if he were running through all the expressions he'd learned but was no longer sure which of them was in style, then rushing on to new ones, making them up with his eyes closed. "Don't crawl under my fence, don't squeeze in my chipmunk hole, don't sniff my glue, suck my popsicle, keep your own greasy fingers on yourself!" He shaded his eyes and peered in at Connie, who was backed against the kitchen table. "Don't mind him, honey, he's just a creep. He's a dope. Right? I'm the boy for you and like I said, you come out here nice like a lady and give me your hand, and nobody else gets hurt, I mean, your nice old bald-headed daddy and your mummy and your sister in her high heels. Because listen: why bring them in this?"

"Leave me alone," Connie whispered.

"Hey, you know that old woman down the road, the one with the chickens and stuff—you know her?"

"She's dead!"

"Dead? What? You know her?" Arnold Friend said.

"She's dead—"

"Don't you like her?"

"She's dead—she's—she isn't here any more—"

"But don't you like her, I mean, you got something against her? Some grudge or something?" Then his voice dipped as if he were conscious of a rudeness. He touched the sunglasses perched up on top of his head as if to make sure they were still there. "Now, you be a good girl."

"What are you going to do?"

"Just two things, or maybe three," Arnold Friend said. "But I promise it won't last long and you'll like me the way you get to like people you're close to. You will. It's all over for you here, so come on out. You don't want your people in any trouble, do you?"

She turned and bumped against a chair or something, hurting her leg, but she ran into the back room and picked up the telephone. Something roared in her ear, a tiny roaring, and she was so sick with fear that she could do nothing but listen to it—the telephone was clammy and very heavy and her fingers groped down to the dial but were too weak to touch it. She began to scream into the phone, into the roaring. She cried out, she cried for her mother, she felt her breath start jerking back and forth in her lungs as if it were something Arnold Friend was stabbing her with again and again with no tenderness. A noisy sorrowful wailing rose all about her and she was locked inside it the way she was locked inside this house.

After a while she could hear again. She was sitting on the floor with her wet back against the wall.

Arnold Friend was saying from the door, "That's a good girl. Put the phone back."

She kicked the phone away from her.

"No, honey. Pick it up. Put it back right."

She picked it up and put it back. The dial tone stopped.

"That's a good girl. Now, you come outside."

She was hollow with what had been fear but what was now just an emptiness. All that screaming had blasted it out of her. She sat, one leg cramped under her, and deep inside her brain was something like a pinpoint of light that kept going and would not let her relax. She thought, I'm not going to see my mother again. She thought, I'm not going to sleep in my bed again. Her bright green blouse was all wet.

Arnold Friend said, in a gentle-loud voice that was like a stage voice, "The place where you came from ain't there any more, and where you had in mind to go is cancelled out. This place you are now—inside your daddy's house—is nothing but a cardboard box I can knock down any time. You know that and always did know it. You hear me?"

She thought, I have got to think. I have got to know what to do.

"We'll go out to a nice field, out in the country here where it smells so nice and it's sunny," Arnold Friend said. "I'll have my arms tight around you so you won't need to try to get away and I'll show you what love is like, what it does. The hell with this house! It looks solid all right," he said. He ran a fingernail down the screen and the noise did not make Connie shiver, as it would have the day before. "Now, put your hand on your heart, honey. Feel that? That feels solid too but we know better. Be nice to me, be sweet like you can because what else is there for a girl like you but to be sweet and pretty and give in?—and get away before her people come back?"

She felt her pounding heart. Her hand seemed to enclose it. She thought for the first time in her life that it was nothing that was hers, that belonged to her, but just a pounding, living thing inside this body that wasn't really hers either.

"You don't want them to get hurt," Arnold Friend went on. "Now, get up, honey. Get up all by yourself."

She stood.

"Now, turn this way. That's right. Come over here to me.—Ellie, put that away, didn't I tell you? You dope. You miserable creepy dope," Arnold Friend said. His words were not angry but only part of an incantation. The incantation was kindly. "Now, come out through the kitchen to me, honey, and let's see a smile, try it, you're a brave, sweet little girl and now they're eating corn and hot dogs cooked to bursting over an outdoor fire, and they don't know one thing about you and never did and honey, you're better than them because not a one of them would have done this for you."

Connie felt the linoleum under her feet; it was cool. She brushed her hair back out of her eyes. Arnold Friend let go of the post tentatively and opened his arms for her, his elbows pointing in toward each other and his wrists limp, to show that this was an embarrassed embrace and a little mocking, he didn't want to make her self-conscious.

She put out her hand against the screen. She watched herself push the door slowly open as if she were back safe somewhere in the other doorway, watching this body and this head of long hair moving out into the sunlight where Arnold Friend waited.

"My sweet little blue-eyed girl," he said in a half-sung sigh that had nothing to do with her brown eyes but was taken up just the same by the vast sunlit reaches of the land behind him and on all sides of him—so much land that Connie had never seen before and did not recognize except to know that she was going to it.

1966

LUÍS VALDEZ
B. 1940

A Chicano born to a farmworker family in Delano, California, Luís Valdez excelled in mathematics and physics as a high school and university student but eventually pursued his passion for political theater at San Jose State University, where he received an English B.A. in 1964. The San Jose State University Drama Department performed Valdez's first full-length play, *The Shrunken Head of Pancho Villa* (1963), an experimental production that foreshadowed his theatrical innovations as cofounder of Teatro Campesino (Farmworker Theater). After a brief membership with the San Francisco Mime Troup, a politically charged, agitprop guerrilla theater group, Valdez developed his signature theatrical form: the Acto, a short minimalist agitprop skit that used nonprofessional actors to demonstrate issues directly related to the community from which the performers were recruited. Renowned for Valdez's proclamation, "if we can't bring the people to the theater, we'll bring the theater to the people," Actos initially were performed on the back of a flatbed truck that traveled throughout farmworker communities as part of United Farmworker Workers efforts to unionize agricultural laborers during the political mobilizations of the 1960s and 1970s that later came to be known as the Chicano Movement. Valdez's populist poetics coincided with radical fusions of theater and political action throughout the postcolonial world, such as Agusto Boal's Marxist-inspired community-based Theater of the Oppressed in Brazil and Ngugi wa Thiong'o's indigenous anticolonialist theater in Kenya.

Valdez's magnum opus is *Zoot Suit*, an historical musical that premiered in 1978 at the Mark Taper Forum in Los Angeles and traveled to Broadway the following year. Though not a financial success, the play was lauded by critics and scholars as a groundbreaking event in contemporary American theater. The play launched many acting careers, most notably that of Edward James Olmos, who played the existentialist Pachuco alter ego of Hank Reyna (played by Valdez's brother Daniel), the angst-ridden countercultural Chicano zoot-suiter protagonist who is framed for murder but remains defiant throughout his ordeal. *Zoot Suit* and Luís Valdez's tutelage of Teatro Campesino found themselves at the center of critical interrogations of the masculinist dimensions of Chicano Movement poetics, particularly the celebratory treatment of the Chicano male warrior hero archetype, which some artists embedded with Mayan and Aztec cosmology as a counterpoint to racist imperialist stereotypes in mainstream media.

Teatro Campesino eventually morphed into a multifaceted theater and film enterprise that remained grounded in populist arts while also producing crossover cinema with blockbuster films such as *La Bamba* (1987) and *Stand and Deliver* (1988). Despite this Hollywood success, Luís Valdez and Teatro Campesino continue to be based in a building that once served as an agricultural produce packing shed. Teatro Campesino continues to have a profound impact as an incubator of Chicana/o community theater and experimental film. Beneficiaries of Teatro Campesino patronage include playwrights and filmmakers Judith and Severo Pérez as well as Luís Valdez's sons Kinan and Anahuac Valdez, who directed and produced *Ballad of a Soldier* (1999), a feature film based on their father's play *Soldado Razo* (1970), part of Teatro Campesino's Vietnam War Trilogy that also includes *Vietnam Campesino* and *Dark Root of a Scream*.

Luís Valdez's plays for Teatro Campesino have been staged throughout the world, and several have been adapted as films. *Los Vendidos (The Sellouts)*, written in 1967 and filmed in 1972, is one of the most politically complex Chicano Movement plays. It takes its title from a common epithet used among immigrant and minority groups in the United States, including Latina/os, that arises from skepticism about the potential group benefits from individual assimilation and upward class mobility into mainstream society. Contrary to the binary socialist realist overtones of some Actos, in which the oppressed farmworkers ultimately overcome the power of evil growers, labor contractors, and police enforcers of the status quo, *Los Vendidos* involves metacritical inquiry at multiple levels. Through a Brechtian aesthetic that presents viscerally displeasing protagonists, *Los Vendidos* deploys multiple stereotypes to critique the very idea of a stereotype. The play further adds to our understanding about the complexity of power exchanges by disrupting conventional theatrical notions of a singular protagonist. The play, grounded in a specific time and place, ultimately offers unique opportunities to meditate on timeless universal themes of identity and ideology, culture and power, gender and class, as well as the individual vis-à-vis the collective.

B. V. Olguín
University of Texas at San Antonio

PRIMARY WORKS

Theft, 1961; *The Shrunken Head of Pancho Villa*, 1963; *Las Dos Caras del Patroncito* (The Two Faces of the Owner), 1965; *La Quinta Temporada* (The Fifth Season), 1966; *Los Vendidos* (The Sellouts), 1967; *La Conquista de Mexico* (The Conquest of Mexico),

1968; *No Saco Nada de la Escuela* (I Don't Get Anything Out of School), 1969; *The Militants*, 1969; *Bernabe*, 1970; *Huelguistas* (Strikers), 1970; *Vietnam Campesino* (Vietnam Peasant), 1970; *Soldado Razo* (Chicano Buck Private), 1971; *Dark Root of a Scream*, 1971; *La Gran Carpa de la Familia Rascuachi* (The Great Tent of the Rascuachi Family), 1971; *Actos* (with El Teatro Compesino), 1971; *Luis Valdez—Early Works: Actos, Bernabe and Pensamiento Serpentino*, 1971 [reprinted 1990]; *Aztlan: An Anthology of Mexican American Literature* (ed. with Stan Steiner), 1972; *El Fin del Mundo* (The End of the World), 1972; *Pensamiento Serpentino: A Chicano Approach to the Theater of Reality*, 1973; *El Baile de los Gigantes* (The Dance of the Giants), 1974; *Zoot Suit*, 1978; *Zoot Suit* [film], 1981; *Bandido* (Bandit), 1981; *Corridos* (Ballads), 1982; *I Don't Have to Show You No Stinking Badges*, 1986; *Zoot Suit and Other Plays*, 1992.

Los Vendidos

CHARACTERS

HONEST SANCHO
SECRETARY
FARMWORKER
PACHUCO
REVOLUCIONARIO
MEXICAN-AMERICAN

SCENE: HONEST SANCHO'S *Used Mexican Lot and Mexican Curio Shop. Three models are on display in* HONEST SANCHO'S *shop. To the right, there is a* REVOLUCIONARIO, *complete with sombrero, carrilleras and carabina 30-30. At center, on the floor, there is the* FARMWORKER, *under a broad straw sombrero. At stage left is the* PACHUCO, *filero in hand.* HONEST SANCHO *is moving among his models, dusting them off and preparing for another day of business.*

SANCHO: Bueno, bueno, mis monos, vamos a ver a quién vendemos ahora, ¿no? (*To audience.*) ¡Quihubo! I'm Honest Sancho and this is my shop. Antes fui contratista, pero ahora logré tener mi negocito. All I need now is a customer. (*A bell rings offstage.*) Ay, a customer!

SECRETARY: (*Entering.*) Good morning, I'm Miss Jimenez from ...

SANCHO: Ah, una chicana! Welcome, welcome Señorita Jiménez.

SECRETARY: (*Anglo pronunciation.*) JIM-enez.

SANCHO: ¿Qué?

SECRETARY: My name is Miss JIM-enez. Don't you speak English? What's wrong with you?

SANCHO: Oh, nothing, Señorita JIM-enez. I'm here to help you.

SECRETARY: That's better. As I was starting to say, I'm a secretary from Governor Reagan's office, and we're looking for a Mexican type for the administration.

SANCHO: Well, you come to the right place, lady. This is Honest Sancho's Used Mexican Lot, and we got all types here. Any particular type you want?

SECRETARY: Yes, we were looking for somebody suave ...

SANCHO: Suave.

SECRETARY: Debonaire.

SANCHO: De buen aire.

SECRETARY: Dark.

SANCHO: Prieto.

SECRETARY: But of course, not too dark.

SANCHO: No muy prieto.

SECRETARY: Perhaps, beige.

SANCHO: Beige, just the tone. Así como cafecito con leche, ¿no?

SECRETARY: One more thing. He must be hard-working.

SANCHO: That could only be one model. Step right over here to the center of the shop, lady. (*They cross to the* FARMWORKER.) This is our standard farmworker model. As you can see, in the words of our beloved Senator George Murphy, he is "built close to the ground." Also, take special notice of his 4-ply Goodyear huaraches, made from the rain tire. This wide-brimmed sombrero is an extra added feature; keeps off the sun, rain and dust.

SECRETARY: Yes, it does look durable.

SANCHO: And our farmworker model is friendly. Muy amable. Watch. (*Snaps his fingers.*)

FARMWORKER: (*Lifts his head.*) Buenos días, señorita. (*His head drops.*)

SECRETARY: My, he is friendly.

SANCHO: Didn't I tell you? Loves his patrones! But his most attractive feature is that he's hard-working. Let me show you. (*Snaps fingers.* FARMWORKER *stands.*)

FARMWORKER: ¡El jale! (*He begins to work.*)

SANCHO: As you can see he is cutting grapes.

SECRETARY: Oh, I wouldn't know.

SANCHO: He also picks cotton. (*Snaps.* FARMWORKER *begins to pick cotton.*)

SECRETARY: Versatile, isn't he?

SANCHO: He also picks melons. (*Snaps.* FARMWORKER *picks melons.*) That's his slow speed for late in the season. Here's his fast speed. (*Snap.* FARMWORKER *picks faster.*)

SECRETARY: Chihuahua . . . I mean, goodness, he sure is a hard worker.

SANCHO: (*Pulls the* FARMWORKER *to his feet.*) And that isn't half of it. Do you see these little holes in his arms that appear to be pores? During those hot sluggish days in the field when the vines or the branches get so entangled, it's almost impossible to move, these holes emit a certain grease that allows our model to slip and slide right through the crop with no trouble at all.

SECRETARY: Wonderful. But is he economical?

SANCHO: Economical? Señorita, you are looking at the Volkswagen of Mexicans. Pennies a day is all it takes. One plate of beans and tortillas will keep him going all day. That, and chile. Plenty of chile. Chile jalapeños, chile verde, chile colorado. But, of course, if you do give him chile, (*Snap.* FARMWORKER *turns left face. Snap.* FARMWORKER *bends over.*) then you have to change his oil filter once a week.

SECRETARY: What about storage?

SANCHO: No problem. You know these new farm labor camps our Honorable Governor Reagan has built out by Palier or Raisin City? They were designed with our model in mind. Five, six, seven, even ten in one of those shacks will give you no trouble at all. You can also put him in old barns, old cars, riverbanks. You can even leave him out in the field over night with no worry!

SECRETARY: Remarkable.

SANCHO: And here's an added feature: every year at the end of the season, this model goes back to Mexico and doesn't return, automatically, until next Spring.

SECRETARY: How about that. But tell me, does he speak English?

SANCHO: Another outstanding feature is that last year this model was programmed to go out on STRIKE! (*Snap.*)

FARMWORKER: ¡Huelga! ¡Huelga! Hermanos, sálganse de esos files. (*Snaps. He stops.*)

SECRETARY: NO! Oh no, we can't strike in the State Capitol.

SANCHO: Well, he also scabs. (*Snap.*)

FARMWORKER: Me vendo barato, ¿y qué? (*Snap.*)

SECRETARY: That's much better, but you didn't answer my question. Does he speak English?

SANCHO: Bueno . . . no, pero he has other . . .

SECRETARY: No.

SANCHO: Other features.

SECRETARY: No! He just won't do!

SANCHO: Okay, okay, pues. We have other models.

SECRETARY: I hope so. What we need is something a little more sophisticated.

SANCHO: Sophiti-qué?

SECRETARY: An urban model.

SANCHO: Ah, from the city! Step right back. Over here in this corner of the shop is exactly what you're looking for. Introducing our new 1969 JOHNNY PACHUCO model! This is our fast-back model. Streamlined. Built for speed, low-riding, city life. Take a look at some of these features. Mag shoes, dual exhausts, green chartreuse paint-job, dark-tint windshield, a little poof on top. Let me just turn him on. (*Snap.* JOHNNY *walks to stage center with a* PACHUCO *bounce.*)

SECRETARY: What was that?

SANCHO: That, señorita, was the Chicano shuffle.

SECRETARY: Okay, what does he do?

SANCHO: Anything and everything necessary for city life. For instance, survival: he knife fights. (*Snaps.* JOHNNY *pulls out a switchblade and swings at* SECRETARY. SECRETARY *screams.*) He dances. (*Snap.*)

JOHNNY: (*Singing.*) "Angel Baby, my Angel Baby . . ." (*Snap.*)

SANCHO: And here's a feature no city model can be without. He gets arrested, but not without resisting, of course. (*Snap.*)

JOHNNY: En la madre, la placa. I didn't do it! I didn't do it! (JOHNNY *turns and stands up against an imaginary wall, legs spread out, arms behind his back.*)

SECRETARY: Oh no, we can't have arrests! We must maintain law and order.

SANCHO: But he's bilingual.

SECRETARY: Bilingual?

SANCHO: Simón que yes. He speaks English! Johnny, give us some English. (*Snap.*)

JOHNNY: (*Comes downstage.*) Fuck-you!

SECRETARY: (*Gasps.*) Oh! I've never been so insulted in my whole life!

SANCHO: Well, he learned it in your school.

SECRETARY: I don't care where he learned it.

SANCHO: But he's economical.

SECRETARY: Economical?

SANCHO: Nickels and dimes. You can keep Johnny running on hamburgers, Taco Bell tacos, Lucky Lager beer, Thunderbird wine, yesca . . .

SECRETARY: Yesca?

SANCHO: Mota.

SECRETARY: Mota?

SANCHO: Leños . . . marijuana. (*Snap.* JOHNNY *inhales on an imaginary joint.*)

SECRETARY: That's against the law!

JOHNNY: (*Big smile, holding his breath*) Yeah.

SANCHO: He also sniffs glue. (*Snap.* JOHNNY *inhales glue, big smile.*)

JOHNNY: Tha's too much man, ese.

SECRETARY: No, Mr. Sancho, I don't think this . . .

SANCHO: Wait a minute, he has other qualities I know you'll love. For example, an inferiority complex. (*Snap.*)

JOHNNY: (To SANCHO.) You think you're better than me, huh, ese? (*Swings switchblade.*)

SANCHO: He can also be beaten and he bruises. Cut him and he bleeds, kick him *and* he . . . (*He beats, bruises and kicks* PACHUCO.) Would you like to try it?

SECRETARY: Oh, I couldn't.

SANCHO: Be my guest. He's a great escape goat.

SECRETARY: No really.

SANCHO: Please.

SECRETARY: Well, all right. Just once. (*She kicks* PACHUCO.) Oh, he's so soft.

SANCHO: Wasn't that good? Try again.

SECRETARY: (*Kicks* PACHUCO.) Oh, he's so wonderful! (*She kicks him again.*)

SANCHO: Okay, that's enough, lady. You'll ruin the merchandise. Yes, our Johnny Pachuco model can give you many hours of pleasure. Why, the LAPD just bought 20 of these to train their rookie cops on. And talk about maintenance. Señorita, you are looking at an entirely self-supporting machine. You're never going to find our Johnny Pachuco model on the relief rolls. No, sir, this model knows how to liberate.

SECRETARY: Liberate?

SANCHO: He steals. (*Snap.* JOHNNY *rushes to* SECRETARY *and steals her purse.*)

JOHNNY: ¡Dame esa bolsa, vieja! (*He grabs the purse and runs. Snap by* SANCHO, *he stops.* SECRETARY *runs after* JOHNNY *and grabs purse away from him, kicking him as she goes.*)

SECRETARY: No, no, no! We can't have any more thieves in the State Administration. Put him back.

SANCHO: Okay, we still got other models. Come on, Johnny, we'll sell you to some old lady. (SANCHO *takes* JOHNNY *back to his place.*)

SECRETARY: Mr. Sancho, I don' think you quite understand what we need. What we need is something that will attract the women voters. Something more traditional, more romantic.

SANCHO: Ah, a lover. (*He smiles meaningfully.*) Step right over here, señorita. Introducing our standard Revolucionario and/or Early California Bandit type. As you can see, he is well-built, sturdy, durable. This is the International Harvester of Mexicans.

SECRETARY: What does he do?

SANCHO: You name it, he does it. He rides horses, stays in the mountains, crosses deserts, plains, rivers, leads revolutions, follows revolutions, kills, can be killed, serves as a martyr, hero, movie star. Did I say movie star? Did you ever see *Viva Zapata? Viva Villa, Villa Rides, Pancho Villa Returns, Pancho Villa Goes Back, Pancho Villa Meets Abbott and Costello?*

SECRETARY: I've never seen any of those.

SANCHO: Well, he was in all of them. Listen to this. (*Snap.*)

REVOLUCIONARIO: (*Scream.*) ¡Viva Villaaaa!

SECRETARY: That's awfully loud.

SANCHO: He has volume control. (*He adjusts volume. Snap.*)

REVOLUCIONARIO: (*Mousey voice.*) Viva Villa.

SECRETARY: That's better.

SANCHO: And even if you didn't see him in the movies, perhaps you saw him on TV. He makes commercials. (*Snap.*)

REVOLUCIONARIO: Is there a Frito Bandito in your house?

SECRETARY: Oh yes, I've seen that one!

SANCHO: Another feature about this one is that he is economical. He runs on raw horse-meat and tequila!

SECRETARY: Isn't that rather savage?

SANCHO: Al contrario, it makes him a lover. (*Snap.*)

REVOLUCIONARIO: (*To* SECRETARY.) Ay, mamasota, cochota, ven pa 'ca! (*He grabs* SECRETARY *and folds her back, Latin-lover style.*)

SANCHO: (*Snap.* REVOLUCIONARIO *goes back upright.*) Now wasn't that nice?

SECRETARY: Well, that was rather nice.

SANCHO: And finally, there is one outstanding feature about this model I know the ladies are going to love: he's a genuine antique! He was made in Mexico in 1910!

SECRETARY: Made in Mexico?

SANCHO: That's right. Once in Tijuana, twice in Guadalajara, three times in Cuernavaca.

SECRETARY: Mr. Sancho, I thought he was an American product.

SANCHO: No, but . . .

SECRETARY: No, I'm sorry. We can't buy anything but American made products. He just won't do.

SANCHO: But he's an antique!

SECRETARY: I don't care. You still don't understand what we need. It's true we need Mexican models, such as these, but it's more important that he be American.

SANCHO: American?

SECRETARY: That's right, and judging from what you've shown me, I don't think you have what we want. Well, my lunch hour's almost over, I better . . .

SANCHO: Wait a minute! Mexican but American?

SECRETARY: That's correct.

SANCHO: Mexican but . . . (*A sudden flash.*) American! Yeah, I think we've got exactly what you want. He just came in today! Give me a minute. (*He exits. Talks from backstage.*) Here he is in the shop. Let me just get some papers off. There. Introducing our new 1970 Mexican-American! Ta-ra-ra-raaaa! (SANCHO *brings out the* MEXICAN-AMERICAN *model, a clean-shaven middle class type in a business suit, with glasses.*)

SECRETARY: (*Impressed.*) Where have you been hiding this one?

SANCHO: He just came in this morning. Ain't he a beauty? Feast your eyes on him! Sturdy U.S. Steel Frame, streamlined, modern. As a matter of fact, he is built exactly like our Anglo models, except that he comes in a variety of darker shades: naugahide, leather or leatherette.

SECRETARY: Naugahide.

SANCHO: Well, we'll just write that down. Yes, señorita, this model represents the apex of American engineering! He is bilingual, college educated, ambitious! Say the word "acculturate" and he accelerates. He is intelligent, well-mannered, clean. Did I say clean? (*Snap.* MEXICAN-AMERICAN *raises his arm.*) Smell.

SECRETARY: (*Smells.*) Old Sobaco, my favorite.

SANCHO: (*Snap.* MEXICAN-AMERICAN *turns toward* SANCHO.) Eric? (*To* SECRETARY.) We call him Eric Garcia. (*To* ERIC.) I want you to meet Miss JIM-enez, Eric.

MEXICAN-AMERICAN: Miss Jim-enez, I am delighted to make your acquaintance. (*He kisses her hand.*)

SECRETARY: Oh, my, how charming!

SANCHO: Did you feel the suction? He has seven especially engineered suction cups right behind his lips. He's a charmer all right!

SECRETARY: How about boards, does he function on boards?

SANCHO: You name them, he is on them. Parole boards, draft boards, school boards, taco quality control boards, surf boards, two by fours.

SECRETARY: Does he function in politics?

SANCHO: Señorita, you are looking at a political machine. Have you ever heard of the OEO, EOC, COD, WAR ON POVERTY? That's our model! Not only that, he makes political speeches.

SECRETARY: May I hear one?

SANCHO: With pleasure. (*Snap.*) Eric, give us a speech.

MEXICAN-AMERICAN: Mr. Congressman, Mr. Chairman, members of the board, honored guests, ladies and gentlemen. (SANCHO *and* SECRETARY *applaud.*) Please, please I come before you as a Mexican-American to tell you about the problems of the Mexican. The problems of the Mexican stem from one thing and one thing only; he's stupid. He's uneducated. He needs to stay in school. He needs to be ambitious, forward-looking harder-working. He needs to think American, American, American, American, American! God bless America! God bless America! God bless America! (*He goes out of control* SANCHO *snaps frantically and the* MEXICAN-AMERICAN *finally slumps forward bending at the waist.*)

SECRETARY: Oh my, he's patriotic too!

SANCHO: Sí, señorita, he loves his country. Let me just make a little adjustment here (*Stands* MEXICAN-AMERICAN *up.*)

SECRETARY: What about upkeep? Is he economical?

SANCHO: Well, no, I won't lie to you. The Mexican-American costs a little bit more, but you get what you pay for. He's worth every extra cent. You can keep him running on dry Martinis, Langerdorf bread ...

SECRETARY: Apple pie?

SANCHO: Only Mom's. Of course, he's also programmed to eat Mexican food at ceremonial functions, but I must warn you, an overdose of beans will plug his exhaust.

SECRETARY: Fine! There's just one more question. How much do you want for him?

SANCHO: Well, I tell you what I'm gonna do. Today and today only, because you've been so sweet, I'm gonna let you steal this model from me! I'm gonna let you drive him off the lot for the simple price of, let's see, taxes and license included, $15,000.

SECRETARY: Fifteen thousand dollars? For a Mexican!!!!

SANCHO: Mexican? What are you talking about? This is a Mexican-American! We had to melt down two pachucos, a farmworker and three gabachos to make this model! You want quality, but you gotta pay for it! This is no cheap run-about. He's got class!

SECRETARY: Okay, I'll take him.

SANCHO: You will?

SECRETARY: Here's your money.

SANCHO: You mind if I count it?

SECRETARY: Go right ahead.

SANCHO: Well, you'll get your pink slip in the mail. Oh, do you want me to wrap him up for you? We have a box in the back.

SECRETARY: No, thank you. The Governor is having a luncheon this afternoon, and we need a brown face in the crowd. How do I drive him?

SANCHO: Just snap your fingers. He'll do anything you want. (SECRETARY *snaps.* MEXICAN-AMERICAN *steps forward.*)

MEXICAN-AMERICAN: ¡Raza querida, vamos levantando armas para liberarnos de estos desgraciados gabachos que nos explotan! Vamos ...

SECRETARY: What did he say?

SANCHO: Something about taking up arms, killing white people, etc.

SECRETARY: But he's not supposed to say that!

SANCHO: Look, lady, don't blame me for bugs from the factory. He's your Mexican-American, you bought him, now drive him off the lot!

SECRETARY: But he's broken!

SANCHO: Try snapping another finger. (SECRETARY *snaps*. MEXICAN-AMERICAN *comes to life again*.)

MEXICAN-AMERICAN: ¡Esta gran humanidad ha dicho basta! ¡Y se ha puesto en marcha! Basta! ¡Basta! ¡Viva la raza! ¡Viva la causa! ¡Viva la huelga! ¡Vivan los brown berets! Vivan los estudiantes! ¡Chicano power! (*The* MEXICAN-AMERICAN *turns toward the* SECRETARY, *who gasps and backs up. He keeps turning toward the* PACHUCO, FARMWORKER, *and* REVOLUCIONARIO, *snapping his fingers and turning each of them on, one by one*.)

PACHUCO: (*Snap. To* SECRETARY.) I'm going to get you, baby! ¡Viva la raza!

FARMWORKER: (*Snap. To* SECRETARY.) ¡Viva la huelga! ¡Viva la huelga! ¡Viva la huelga!

REVOLUCIONARIO: (*Snap. To* SECRETARY.) ¡Viva la revolución! (*The three models join together and advance toward the* SECRETARY, *who backs up and runs out of the shop screaming.* SANCHO *is at the other end of the shop holding his money in his hand. All freeze. After a few seconds of silence, the* PACHUCO *moves and stretches, shaking his arms and loosening up. The* FARMWORKER *and* REVOLUCIONARIO *do the same.* SANCHO *stays where he is, frozen to his spot*.)

JOHNNY: Man, that was a long one, ese. (*Others agree with him*.)

FARMWORKER: How did we do?

JOHNNY: Pretty good, look at all that lana, man! (*He goes over to* SANCHO *and removes the money from his hand.* SANCHO *stays where he is*.)

REVOLUCIONARIO: En la madre, look at all the money.

JOHNNY: We keep this up, we're going to be rich.

FARMWORKER: They think we're machines.

REVOLUCIONARIO: Burros.

JOHNNY: Puppets.

MEXICAN-AMERICAN: The only thing I don't like is how come I always get to play the goddamn Mexican-American?

JOHNNY: Here it comes right now. $3,000 for you, $3,000 for you, $3,000 for you and $3,000 for me. The rest we put back into the business.

MEXICAN-AMERICAN: Too much, man. Heh, where you vatos going tonight?

FARMWORKER: I'm going over to Concha's. There's a party.

JOHNNY: Wait a minute, vatos. What about our salesman? I think he needs an oil job.

REVOLUCIONARIO: Leave him to me. (*The* PACHUCO, FARMWORKER, *and* MEXICAN-AMERICAN *exit, talking loudly about their plans for the night. The* REVOLUCIONARIO *goes over to* SANCHO, *removes his derby hat and cigar, lifts him up and throws him over his shoulder.* SANCHO *hangs loose, lifeless. To audience*.) He's the best model we got ¡Ajúa! (*Exit*.)

1967

JOHN BARTH
B. 1930

John Barth's birth in Cambridge, a small town on the Eastern Shore of Maryland, established his claim to one of the strongest literary heritages in twentieth-century America, the modernist tradition that took root in the American South through the novels of William Faulkner and Thomas Wolfe in the 1920s and 1930s. Despite an early focus on music, Barth, who in 1953 became a college writing instructor, absorbed this tradition well enough to give his first two novels, *The Floating Opera* (1956) and *The End of the Road* (1958), the strong sense of place and fate commonly found in modern Southern fiction.

Barth's first two books, however, also exhibit a playfulness closer to the improvisations of modern jazz, his earlier passion, and to the black humor emerging in the fifties, than to modern Southern fiction. The novels parody the existential movement, the dominant tendency of European writing during the late modernist period; *The Floating Opera* expresses Barth's comic response to Camus's earnest and familiar defense of suicide while *The End of the Road* pushes Sartre's views of commitment and protean freedom to sardonic extremes. In short, Barth was already experimenting with one of his favorite devices: framing seemingly exhausted literary modes by reworking them from radically different perspectives to renew them and thereby replenish the literary tradition. Eventually, his use of parody and frames would be his major contribution to the (then) undetected emergence of postmodernism, the dominant cultural development of the second half of the twentieth century and a movement in which Barth is regarded as the major American literary practitioner and advocate.

In *The Sot-Weed Factor* (1960)—taking a cue from a short work of fiction, "Pierre Menard, Author of Don Quixote," by Jorge Luis Borges, the modern writer from whom he appears to have learned the most—Barth again parodies established modes of writing, creating a gigantic eighteenth-century Anglo-Southern novel out of comic characters and themes appropriate to the mid-twentieth century. In *Giles Goat-Boy, or The Revised New Syllabus* (1966), he takes a decisive step toward postmodernism, freeing himself from both memory and history by creating an imaginary university parodying the universe in which earthlings found themselves during the Cold War.

The experiments collected in 1968 in *Lost in the Funhouse* mark Barth's emergence as leader of the American wing of the movement called postmodernism. As a contribution to the postmodern, the title story, reprinted here, generates special excitement, for it is difficult to imagine a more self-referential metafiction. Here the author frames a seemingly heartfelt parody of a coming-of-age story about a small-town boy, a subject typical of the Southern modernists, with the fatalistic thoughts of a beginning or blocked writer who struggles to obey the best-intended formulas of creative writing classes. Writer's block became a major theme, and likely a metaphor for contemporary culture, in such later works as *Chimera* (a masterpiece of the postmodern in America, published in 1972) and *LETTERS: A Novel* (1979).

After the seemingly (perhaps deliberately) botched experiment with narration and point of view in *Sabbatical: A Romance* (1982), Barth's jazzlike powers of improvisation return full force in his joy-filled metafiction *The Tidewater Tales* (1987). The temporal pastiche of *The Last Voyage of Somebody the Sailor* (1991) throws the assumptions of modern realist fiction into confusion by making the adventures of Sinbad seem to the audience that hears them examples of traditional realism while competing journalistic accounts of modern events appear to be sheer fiction. *On with the Story: Stories* (1996) complements the *Lost in the Funhouse* collection in its attempt to jump-start experimental postmodern fiction, which in the 1990s was losing ground to several retro tendencies. *The Friday Book* and *Further Fridays*, Barth's essays and nonfiction gathered together in 1984 and 1995, may be the best year-by-year record in existence of the emergence—from modernism, existentialism, black humor, and "irrealism"—of American literary postmodernism.

Julius Rowan Raper
University of North Carolina at Chapel Hill

PRIMARY WORKS

The Floating Opera, 1956 [rev. 1967]; *The End of the Road*, 1958 [rev. 1967]; *The Sot-Weed Factor*, 1960 [rev. 1967]; *Giles Goat-Boy, or The Revised New Syllabus*, 1966; *Lost in the Funhouse: Fiction for Print, Tape, Live Voice*, 1968; *Chimera*, 1972; *LETTERS: A Novel*, 1979; *Sabbatical: A Romance*, 1982; *The Friday Book: Essays and Other Nonfiction*, 1984; *The Tidewater Tales: A Novel*, 1987; *The Last Voyage of Somebody the Sailor*, 1991; *Once upon a Time: A Floating Opera*, 1994; *Further Fridays: Essays, Lectures, and Other Nonfiction, 1984–1994*, 1995; *On with the Story: Stories*, 1996; *The Book of Ten Nights and a Night*, 2004; *Where Three Roads Meet*, 2005; *The Development*, 2008; *Every Third Thought: A Novel in Five Seasons*, 2011.

Lost in the Funhouse

For whom is the funhouse fun? Perhaps for lovers. For Ambrose it is *a place of fear and confusion*. He has come to the seashore with his family for the holiday, *the occasion of their visit is Independence Day, the most important secular holiday of the United States of America*. A single straight underline is the manuscript mark for italic type, *which in turn* is the printed equivalent to oral emphasis of words and phrases as well as the customary type for titles of complete works, not to mention. Italics are also employed, in fiction stories especially, for "outside," intrusive, or artificial voices, such as radio announcements, the texts of telegrams and newspaper articles, et cetera. They should be used *sparingly*. If passages originally in roman type are italicized by someone repeating them, it's customary to acknowledge the fact. *Italics mine.*

Ambrose was "at that awkward age." His voice came out high-pitched as a child's if he let himself get carried away; to be on the safe side, therefore, he moved and spoke with *deliberate calm* and *adult gravity*. Talking soberly of unimportant or irrelevant matters and listening consciously to the sound of your own voice are useful habits for maintaining control in this difficult interval. *En route* to Ocean City he sat in the back seat of the family car with his brother Peter, age fifteen, and Magda G‾‾‾‾, age fourteen, a pretty girl an exquisite young lady, who lived not far from them on B‾‾‾Street in the town of D‾‾‾, Maryland. Initials, blanks, or both were often substituted for proper names in nineteenth-century fiction to enhance the illusion of reality. It is as if the author felt it necessary to delete the names for reasons of tact or legal liability. Interestingly, as with other aspects of realism, it is an *illusion* that is being enhanced, by purely artificial means. Is it likely, does it violate the principle of verisimilitude, that a thirteen-year-old boy could make such a sophisticated observation? A girl of fourteen is *the psychological coeval* of a boy of fifteen or sixteen; a thirteen-year-old boy, therefore, even one precocious in some other respects, might be three years *her emotional junior.*

Thrice a year—on Memorial, Independence, and Labor Days—the family visits Ocean City for the afternoon and evening. When Ambrose and Peter's father was their age, the excursion was made by train, as mentioned in the novel *The 42nd Parallel* by John Dos Passos. Many families from the same neighborhood used to travel together, with dependent relatives and often with Negro servants; schoolfuls of children swarmed through the railway cars; everyone shared everyone else's Maryland fried chicken, Virginia ham, deviled eggs, potato salad, beaten biscuits, iced tea. Nowadays (that is, in 19——, the year of our story) the journey is made by automobile—more comfortably and quickly though without the extra fun though without the *camaraderie* of a general excursion. It's all part of the deterioration of American life, their father declares; Uncle Karl supposes that when the boys take *their* families to Ocean City for the holidays they'll fly in Autogiros. Their mother, sitting in the middle of the front seat like Magda in the second, only with her arms on the seat-back behind the men's shoulders, wouldn't want the good old days back again, the steaming trains and stuffy long dresses; on the other hand she can do without Autogiros, too, if she has to become a grandmother to fly in them.

Description of physical appearance and mannerisms is one of several standard methods of characterization used by writers of fiction. It is also important to "keep the senses operating"; when a detail from one of the five senses, say visual, is "crossed" with a detail from another, say auditory, the reader's imagination is oriented to the scene, perhaps unconsciously. This procedure may be compared to the way surveyors and navigators determine their positions by two or more compass bearings, a process known as triangulation. The brown hair on Ambrose's mother's forearms gleamed in the sun like. Though right-handed, she took her left arm from the seat-back to press the dashboard cigar lighter for Uncle Karl. When the glass bead in its handle glowed red, the lighter was ready for use. The smell of Uncle Karl's cigar smoke reminded one of. The fragrance of the ocean came strong to the picnic ground where they always stopped for lunch, two miles inland from Ocean City. Having to pause for a full hour almost within the sound of the breakers was difficult for Peter and Ambrose when they were younger; even at their present age it was not easy to keep their anticipation, *stimulated by the briny spume*, from turning into short temper. The Irish author James Joyce, in his unusual novel entitled *Ulysses*, now available in this country, uses the adjectives *snot-green* and *scrotum-tightening* to describe the sea. Visual, auditory, tactile, olfactory, gustatory. Peter and Ambrose's father, while steering their black 1936 LaSalle sedan with one hand, could with the other remove the first cigarette from a white pack of Lucky Strikes and, more remarkably, light it with a match forefingered from its book and thumbed against the flint paper without being detached. The matchbook cover merely advertised U.S. War Bonds and Stamps. A fine metaphor, simile, or other figure of speech, in addition to its obvious "first-order" relevance to the thing it describes, will be seen upon reflection to have a second order of significance: it may be drawn from the *milieu* of the action, for example, or be particularly appropriate to the sensibility of the narrator, even hinting to the reader things of which the narrator is unaware; or it may cast further and subtler lights upon the thing it describes, sometimes ironically qualifying the more evident sense of the comparison.

To say that Ambrose's and Peter's mother was *pretty* is to accomplish nothing; the reader may acknowledge the proposition, but his imagination is not engaged. Besides, Magda was also pretty, yet in an altogether different way. Although she lived on B——Street she had very good manners and did better than average in school. Her figure was very well developed for her age. Her right hand lay casually on the plush upholstery of the seat, very near Ambrose's left leg, on which his own hand rested. The space between their legs, between her right and his left leg, was out of the line of sight of anyone sitting on the other side of Magda, as well as anyone glancing into the rearview mirror. Uncle Karl's face resembled Peter's—rather, vice versa. Both had dark hair and eyes, short husky statures, deep voices. Magda's left hand was probably in a similar position on her left side. The boy's father is difficult to describe; no particular feature of his appearance or manner stood out. He wore glasses and was principal of a T——County grade school. Uncle Karl was a masonry contractor.

Although Peter must have known as well as Ambrose that the latter, because of his position in the car, would be the first to see the electrical towers of the power plant at V——, the halfway point of their trip, he leaned forward and slightly toward the center of the car and pretended to be looking for them through the flat pinewoods and tuckahoe creeks along the highway. For as long as the boys could remember, "looking for the Towers" had been a feature of the first half of their excursions to Ocean City, "looking for the standpipe" of the second. Though the game was childish, their mother preserved the tradition of rewarding the first to see the Towers with a candybar or piece of fruit. She insisted now that Magda play the game; the prize, she said, was "something hard to get nowadays." Ambrose decided not to join in; he sat far back in his seat. Magda, like Peter, leaned forward. Two sets of straps were discernible through the shoulders of her sun dress; the inside right one, a brassiere-strap, was fastened or shortened with a small safety pin. The right armpit of her dress, presumably the left as well, was damp with perspiration. The simple strategy for being first to espy the Towers, which Ambrose had understood by the age of four, was to sit on the right-hand side of the car. Whoever sat there, however, had also to put up with the worst of the sun, and so Ambrose, without mentioning the matter, chose sometimes the one and sometimes the other. Not impossibly Peter had never caught on to the trick, or thought that his brother hadn't simply because Ambrose on occasion preferred shade to a Baby Ruth or tangerine.

The shade-sun situation didn't apply to the front seat, owing to the windshield; if anything the driver got more sun, since the person on the passenger side not only was shaded below by the door and dashboard but might swing down his sunvisor all the way too.

"Is that them?" Magda asked. Ambrose's mother teased the boys for letting Magda win, insinuating that "somebody [had] a girlfriend." Peter and Ambrose's father reached a long thin arm across their mother to butt his cigarette in the dashboard ashtray, under the lighter. The prize this time for seeing the Towers first was a banana. Their mother bestowed it after chiding their father for wasting a half-smoked cigarette when everything was so scarce. Magda, to take the prize, moved her hand from so near Ambrose's that he could have touched it as though accidentally. She offered to share the prize, things like that were so hard to find; but everyone insisted it was hers alone. Ambrose's mother sang an iambic trimeter couplet from a popular song, femininely rhymed:

> *"What's good is in the Army;*
> *What's left will never harm me."*

Uncle Karl tapped his cigar ash out the ventilator window; some particles were sucked by the slipstream back into the car through the rear window on the passenger side. Magda demonstrated her ability to hold a banana in one hand and peel it with her teeth. She still sat forward; Ambrose pushed his glasses back onto the bridge of his nose with his left hand, which he then negligently let fall to the seat cushion immediately behind her. He even permitted the single hair, gold, on the second joint of his thumb to brush the fabric of her skirt. Should she have sat back at that instant, his hand would have been caught under her.

Plush upholstery prickles uncomfortably through gabardine slacks in the July sun. The function of the *beginning* of a story is to introduce the principal characters, establish their initial relationships, set the scene for the main action, expose the background of the situation if necessary, plant motifs and foreshadowings where appropriate, and initiate the first complication or whatever of the "rising action." Actually, if one imagines a story called "The Funhouse," or "Lost in the Funhouse," the details of the drive to Ocean City don't seem especially relevant. The *beginning* should recount the events between Ambrose's first sight of the funhouse early in the afternoon and his entering it with Magda and Peter in the evening. The *middle* would narrate all relevant events from the time he goes in to the time he loses his way; middles have the double and contradictory function of delaying the climax while at the same time preparing the reader for it and fetching him to it. Then the *ending* would tell what Ambrose does while he's lost, how he finally finds his way out, and what everybody makes of the experience. So far there's been no real dialogue, very little sensory detail, and nothing in the way of a *theme*. And a long time has gone by already without anything happening; it makes a person wonder. We haven't even reached Ocean City yet: we will never get out of the funhouse.

The more closely an author identifies with the narrator, literally or metaphorically, the less advisable it is, as a rule, to use the first-person narrative viewpoint. Once three years previously the young people *aforementioned* played Niggers and Masters in the backyard; when it was Ambrose's turn to be Master and theirs to be Niggers Peter had to go serve his evening papers; Ambrose was afraid to punish Magda alone but she led him to the whitewashed Torture Chamber between the woodshed and the privy in the Slaves Quarters; there she knelt sweating among bamboo rakes and dusty Mason jars, pleadingly embraced his knees, and while bees droned in the lattice as if on an ordinary summer afternoon, purchased clemency at a surprising price set by herself. Doubtless she remembered nothing of this event; Ambrose on the other hand seemed unable to forget the least detail of his life. He even recalled how, standing beside himself with awed impersonality in the reeky heat, he'd stared the while at an empty cigar box in which Uncle Karl kept stone-cutting chisels: beneath the words *El Producto*, a laureled, loose-toga'd lady regarded the sea from a marble bench; beside her, forgotten or not yet turned to, was a five-stringed lyre. Her chin reposed on the back of her right hand; her left depended negligently from the bench-arm. The lower half of scene and lady was peeled away; the words EXAMINED BY——were inked there into the wood. Nowadays cigar boxes are made of pasteboard. Ambrose wondered what Magda would have done, Ambrose wondered what Magda would do when she sat back on his hand as he resolved she should. Be angry. Make a teasing joke of it. Give no sign at all. For a long time she leaned forward, playing cow-poker with Peter against Uncle Karl and Mother and watching for the first sign of Ocean City. At nearly the same instant, picnic ground and Ocean City standpipe hove into view; an Amoco filling station on their side of the road cost Mother and Uncle Karl fifty cows and the game; Magda bounced back, clapping her right hand on Mother's right arm; Ambrose moved clear "in the nick of time."

At this rate our hero, at this rate our protagonist will remain in the funhouse forever. Narrative ordinarily consists of alternating dramatization and summarization. One symptom of nervous tension, paradoxically, is repeated and violent yawning; neither Peter nor Magda nor Uncle Karl nor Mother reacted in this manner. Although they were no longer small children, Peter and Ambrose were each given a dollar to spend on boardwalk amusements in addition to what money of their own they'd brought along. Magda too, though she protested she had ample spending money. The boys' mother made a little scene out of distributing the bills; she pretended that her sons and Magda were small children and cautioned them not to spend the sum too quickly or in one place. Magda promised with a merry laugh and, having both hands free, took the bill with her left. Peter laughed also and pledged in a falsetto to be a good boy. His imitation of a child was not clever. The boys' father was tall and thin, balding, fair-complexioned. Assertions of that sort are not effective; the reader may acknowledge the proposition, but. We should be much farther along than we are; something has gone wrong; not much of this preliminary rambling seems relevant. Yet everyone begins in the same place; how is it that most go along without difficulty but a few lose their way?

"Stay out from under the boardwalk," Uncle Karl growled from the side of his mouth. The boys' mother pushed his shoulder *in mock annoyance*. They were all standing before Fat May the Laughing Lady who advertised the funhouse. Larger than life, Fat May mechanically shook, rocked on her heels, slapped her thighs while recorded laughter—uproarious, female—came amplified from a hidden loudspeaker. It chuckled, wheezed, wept; tried in vain to catch its breath; tittered, groaned, exploded raucous and anew. You couldn't hear it without laughing yourself, no matter how you felt. Father came back from talking to a Coast-Guardsman on duty and reported that the surf was spoiled with crude oil from tankers recently torpedoed offshore. Lumps of it, difficult to remove, made tarry tidelines on the beach and stuck on swimmers. Many bathed in the surf nevertheless and came out speckled; others paid to use a municipal pool and only sunbathed on the beach. We would do the latter. We would do the latter. We would do the latter.

Under the boardwalk, matchbook covers, grainy other things. What is the story's theme? Ambrose is ill. He perspires in the dark passages; candied apples-on-a-stick, delicious-looking, disappointing to eat. Funhouses need men's and ladies' room at intervals. Others perhaps have also vomited in corners and corridors; may even have had bowel movements liable to be stepped in in the dark. The word *fuck* suggests suction and/or and/or flatulence. Mother and Father; grandmothers and grandfathers on both sides; great-grandmothers and great-grandfathers on four sides, et cetera. Count a generation as thirty years: in approximately the year when Lord Baltimore was granted charter to the province of Maryland by Charles I, five hundred twelve women—English, Welsh, Bavarian, Swiss—of every class and character, received into themselves the penises the intromittent organs of five hundred twelve men, ditto, in every circumstance and posture, to conceive the five hundred twelve ancestors of the two hundred fifty-six ancestors of the et cetera et cetera et cetera et cetera et cetera et cetera et cetera et cetera of the author, of the narrator, of this story, *Lost in the Funhouse*. In alleyways, ditches, canopy beds, pinewoods, bridal suites, ship's cabins, coach-and-fours, coaches-and-four, sultry toolsheds; on the cold sand under boardwalks, littered with *El Producto* cigar butts, treasured with Lucky Strike cigarette stubs, Coca-Cola caps, gritty turds, cardboard lollipop sticks, matchbook covers warning that A Slip of the Lip Can Sink a Ship. The shluppish whisper, continuous as seawash round the globe, tidelike falls and rises with the circuit of dawn and dusk.

Magda's teeth. She *was* left-handed. Perspiration. They've gone all the way, through, Magda and Peter, they've been waiting for hours with Mother and Uncle Karl while Father searches for his lost son; they draw french-fried potatoes from a paper cup and shake their heads. They've named the children they'll one day have and bring to Ocean City on holidays. Can spermatozoa properly be thought of as male animalcules when there are no female spermatozoa? They grope through hot, dark windings, past Love's Tunnel's fearsome obstacles. Some perhaps lose their way.

Peter suggested then and there that they do the funhouse; he had been through it before, so had Magda, Ambrose hadn't and suggested, his voice cracking on account of Fat May's laughter, that they swim first. All were chuckling, couldn't help it; Ambrose's father, Ambrose's and Peter's father came up grinning like a lunatic with two boxes of syrup-coated popcorn, one for Mother, one for Magda; the men were to help themselves. Ambrose walked on Magda's right: being by nature left-handed, she carried the box in her left hand. Up front the situation was reversed.

"What are you limping for?" Magda inquired of Ambrose. He supposed in a husky tone that his foot had gone to sleep in the car. Her teeth flashed. "Pins and needles?" It was the honeysuckle on the lattice of the former privy that drew the bees. Imagine being stung there. How long is this going to take?

The adults decided to forgo the pool; but Uncle Karl insisted they change into swimsuits and do the beach. "He wants to watch the pretty girls," Peter teased, and ducked behind Magda from Uncle Karl's pretended wrath. "You've got all the pretty girls you need right here," Magda declared, and Mother said: "Now that's the gospel truth." Magda scolded Peter, who reached over her shoulder to sneak some popcorn. "Your brother and father aren't getting any." Uncle Karl wondered if they were going to have fireworks that night, what with the shortages. It wasn't the shortages, Mr. M_____replied; Ocean City had fireworks from pre-war. But it was too risky on account of the enemy submarines, some people thought.

"Don't seem like Fourth of July without fireworks," said Uncle Karl. The inverted tag in dialogue writing is still considered permissible with proper names or epithets, but sounds old-fashioned with personal pronouns. "We'll have 'em again soon enough," predicted the boys' father. Their mother declared she could do without fireworks: they reminded her too much of the real thing. Their father said all the more reason to shoot off a few now and again. Uncle Karl asked *rhetorically* who needed reminding, just look at people's hair and skin.

"The oil, yes," said Mrs. M_____.

Ambrose had a pain in his stomach and so didn't swim but enjoyed watching the others. He and his father burned red easily. Magda's figure was exceedingly well developed for her age. She too declined to swim, and got mad, and became angry when Peter attempted to drag her into the pool.

She always swam, he insisted; what did she mean not swim? Why did a person come to Ocean City?

"Maybe I want to lay here with Ambrose," Magda teased.

Nobody likes a pedant.

"Aha," said Mother. Peter grabbed Magda by one ankle and ordered Ambrose to grab the other. She squealed and rolled over on the beach blanket. Ambrose pretended to help hold her back. Her tan was darker than even Mother's and Peter's. "Help out, Uncle Karl!" Peter cried. Uncle Karl went to seize the other ankle. Inside the top of her swimsuit, however, you could see the line where the sunburn ended and, when she hunched her shoulders and squealed again, one nipple's auburn edge. Mother made them behave themselves. "*You* should certainly know," she said to Uncle Karl. Archly. "That when a lady says she doesn't feel like swimming, a gentleman doesn't ask questions." Uncle Karl said excuse *him*; Mother winked at Magda; Ambrose blushed; stupid Peter kept saying "Phooey on *feel like!*" and tugging at Magda's ankle; then even he got the point, and cannonballed with a holler into the pool.

"I swear," Magda said, in mock *in feigned* exasperation.

The diving would make a suitable literary symbol. To go off the high board you had to wait in a line along the poolside and up the ladder. Fellows tickled girls and goosed one another and shouted to the ones at the top to hurry up, or razzed them for bellyfloppers. Once on the springboard some took a great while posing or clowning or deciding on a dive or getting up their nerve; others ran right off. Especially among the younger fellows the idea was to strike the funniest pose or do the craziest stunt as you fell, a thing that got harder to do as you kept on and kept on. But whether you hollered *Geronimo!* or *Sieg heil!*, held your nose or "rode a bicycle," pretended to be shot or did a perfect jackknife or changed your mind halfway down and ended up with nothing, it was over in two seconds, after all that wait. Spring, pose, splash. Spring, neat-o, splash. Spring, aw fooey, splash.

The grown-ups had gone on; Ambrose wanted to converse with Magda; she was remarkably well developed for her age; it was said that that came from rubbing with a turkish towel, and there were other theories. Ambrose could think of nothing to say except how good a diver Peter was, who was showing off for her benefit. You could pretty well tell by looking at their bathing suits and arm muscles how far along the different fellows were. Ambrose was glad he hadn't gone in swimming, the cold water shrank you up so. Magda pretended to be uninterested in the diving; she probably weighed as much as he did. If you knew your way around in the funhouse like your own bedroom, you could wait until a girl came along and then slip away without ever getting caught, even if her boyfriend was right with her. She'd think *he* did it! It would be better to be the boyfriend, and act outraged, and tear the funhouse apart.

Not act; *be*.

"He's a master diver," Ambrose said. In feigned admiration. "You really have to slave away at it to get that good." What would it matter anyhow if he asked her right out whether she remembered, even teased her with it as Peter would have?

There's no point in going farther; this isn't getting anybody anywhere; they haven't even come to the funhouse yet. Ambrose is off the track, in some new or old part of the place that's not supposed to be used; he strayed into it by some one-in-a-million chance, like the time the roller-coaster car left the tracks in the nineteen-teens against all the laws of physics and sailed over the boardwalk in the dark. And they can't locate him because they don't know where to look. Even the designer and operator have forgotten this other part, that winds around on itself like a whelk shell. That winds around the right part like the snakes on Mercury's caduceus. Some people, perhaps, don't "hit their stride" until their twenties, when the growing-up business is over and women appreciate other things besides wisecracks and teasing and strutting. Peter didn't have one-tenth the imagination *he* had, not one-tenth. Peter did this naming-their-children thing as a joke, making up names like Aloysius and Murgatroyd, but Ambrose knew *exactly* how it would feel to be married and have children of your own, and be a loving husband and father, and go comfortably to work in the mornings and to bed with your wife at night, and wake up with her there. With a breeze coming through the sash and birds and mockingbirds singing in the Chinese-cigar trees. His eyes watered, there aren't enough ways to say that. He would be quite famous in his line of work. Whether Magda was his wife or not, one evening when he was wise-lined and gray at the temples he'd smile gravely, at a fashionable dinner party, and remind her of his youthful passion. The time they went with his family to Ocean City; the *erotic fantasies* he used to have about her. How long ago it seemed, and childish! Yet tender, too, *n'est-ce pas?* Would she have imagined that the world-famous whatever remembered how many strings were on the lyre on the bench beside the girl on the label of the cigar box he'd stared at in the toolshed at age ten while she, age eleven. Even then he had felt *wise beyond his years*; he'd stroked her hair and said in his deepest voice and correctest English, as to a dear child: "I shall never forget this moment."

But though he had breathed heavily, groaned as if ecstatic, what he'd really felt throughout was an odd detachment, as though someone else were Master. Strive as he might to be transported, he heard his mind take notes upon the scene: *This is what they call* passion. *I am experiencing it.* Many of the digger machines were out of order in the penny arcades and could not be repaired or replaced for the duration. Moreover the prizes, made now in USA, were less interesting than formerly, pasteboard items for the most part, and some of the machines wouldn't work on white pennies. The gypsy fortune-teller machine might have provided a foreshadowing of the climax of this story if Ambrose had operated it. It was even dilapidateder than most: the silver coating was worn off the brown metal handles, the glass windows around the dummy were cracked and taped, her kerchiefs and silks long-faded. If a man lived by himself, he could take a department-store mannequin with flexible joints and modify her in certain ways. *However:* by the time he was that old he'd have a real woman. There was a machine that stamped your name around a white-metal coin with a star in the middle: A_____. His son would be the second, and when the lad reached thirteen or so he would put a strong arm around his shoulder and tell him calmly: "It is perfectly normal. We have all been through it. It will not last forever." Nobody knew how to be what they were right. He'd smoke a pipe, teach his son how to fish and softcrab, assure him he needn't worry about himself. Magda would certainly give, Magda would certainly yield a great deal of milk, although guilty of occasional solecisms. It don't taste so bad. Suppose the lights came on now!

The day wore on. You think you're yourself, but there are other persons in you. Ambrose gets hard when Ambrose doesn't want to, *and obversely.* Ambrose watches them disagree; Ambrose watches him watch. In the funhouse mirror-room you can't see yourself go on forever, because no matter how you stand, your head gets in the way. Even if you had a glass periscope, the image of your eye would cover up the thing you really wanted to see. The police will come; there'll be a story in the papers. That must be where it happened. Unless he can find a surprise exit, an unofficial backdoor or escape hatch opening on an alley, say, and then stroll up to the family in front of the funhouse and ask where everybody's been; *he's* been out of the place for ages. That's just where it happened, in that last lighted room: Peter and Magda found the right exit; he found one that you weren't supposed to find and strayed off into the works somewhere. In a perfect funhouse you'd be able to go only one way, like the divers off the highboard; getting lost would be impossible; the doors and halls would work like minnow traps or the valves in veins.

On account of German U-boats, Ocean City was "browned out": streetlights were shaded on the seaward side; shop-windows and boardwalk amusement places were kept dim, not to silhouette tankers and Liberty-ships for torpedoing. In a short story about Ocean City, Maryland, during World War II, the author could make use of the image of sailors on leave in the penny arcades and shooting galleries, sighting through the crosshairs of toy machine guns at swastika'd subs, while out in the black Atlantic a U-boat skipper squints through his periscope at real ships outlined by the glow of penny arcades. After dinner the family strolled back to the amusement end of the boardwalk. The boys' father had burnt red as always and was masked with Noxzema, a minstrel in reverse. The grownups stood at the end of the boardwalk where the Hurricane of '33 had cut an inlet from the ocean to Assawoman Bay.

"Pronounced with a long *o*," Uncle Karl reminded Magda with a wink. His short sleeves were rolled up; Mother punched his brown biceps with the arrowed heart on it and said his mind was naughty. Fat May's laugh came suddenly from the funhouse, as if she'd just got the joke; the family laughed too at the coincidence. Ambrose went under the boardwalk to search for out-of-town matchbook covers with the aid of his pocket flashlight; he looked out from the edge of the North American continent and wondered how far their laughter carried over the water. Spies in rubber rafts; survivors in lifeboats. If the joke had been beyond his understanding, he could have said: *"The laughter was over his head."* And let the reader see the serious wordplay on second reading.

He turned the flashlight on and then off at once even before the woman whooped. He sprang away, heart athud, dropping the light. What had the man grunted? Perspiration drenched and chilled him by the time he scrambled up to the family. "See anything?" his father asked. His voice wouldn't come; he shrugged and violently brushed sand from his pants legs.

"Let's ride the old flying horses!" Magda cried. I'll never be an author. It's been forever already, everybody's gone home, Ocean City's deserted, the ghost-crabs are tickling across the beach and down the littered cold streets. And the empty halls of clapboard hotels and abandoned funhouses. A tidal wave; an enemy air raid; a monster-crab swelling like an island from the sea. *The inhabitants fled in terror.* Magda clung to his trouser leg; he alone knew the maze's secret. "He gave his life that we might live," said Uncle Karl with a scowl of pain, as he. The fellow's hands had been tattooed; the woman's legs, the woman's fat white legs had. *An astonishing coincidence.* He yearned to tell Peter. He wanted to throw up for excitement. They hadn't even chased him. He wished he were dead.

One possible ending would be to have Ambrose come across another lost person in the dark. They'd match their wits together against the funhouse, struggle like Ulysses past obstacle after obstacle, help and encourage each other. Or a girl. By the time they found the exit they'd be closest friends, sweethearts if it were a girl; they'd know each other's inmost souls, be bound together *by the cement of shared adventure*; then they'd emerge into the light and it would turn out that his friend was a Negro. A blind girl. President Roosevelt's son. Ambrose's former archenemy.

Shortly after the mirror room he'd groped along a musty corridor, his heart already misgiving him at the absence of phosphorescent arrows and other signs. He'd found a crack of light—not a door, it turned out, but a seam between the plyboard wall panels—and squinting up to it, espied a small old man, *in appearance not unlike* the photographs at home of Ambrose's late grandfather, nodding upon a stool beneath a bare, speckled bulb. A crude panel of toggle- and knife-switches hung beside the open fuse box near his head; elsewhere in the little room were wooden levers and ropes belayed to boat cleats. At the time, Ambrose wasn't lost enough to rap or call; later he couldn't find that crack. Now it seemed to him that he'd possibly dozed off for a few minutes somewhere along the way; certainly he was exhausted from the afternoon's sunshine and the evening's problems; he couldn't be sure he hadn't dreamed part or all of the sight. Had an old black wall fan droned like bees and shimmied two flypaper streamers? Had the funhouse operator—gentle, somewhat sad and tired-appearing, in expression not unlike the photographs at home of Ambrose's late Uncle Konrad—murmured in his sleep? Is there really such a person as Ambrose, or is he a figment of the author's imagination? Was it Assawoman Bay or Sinepuxent?

Are there other errors of fact in this fiction? Was there another sound besides the little slap slap of thigh on ham, like water sucking at the chineboards of a skiff?

When you're lost, the smartest thing to do is stay put till you're found, hollering if necessary. But to holler guarantees humiliation as well as rescue; keeping silent permits some saving of face—you can act surprised at the fuss when your rescuers find you and swear you weren't lost, if they do. What's more you might find your own way yet, *however belatedly*.

"Don't tell me your foot's still asleep!" Magda exclaimed as the three young people walked from the inlet to the area set aside for ferris wheels, carrousels, and other carnival rides, they having decided in favor of the vast and ancient merry-go-round instead of the funhouse. What a sentence, everything was wrong from the outset. People don't know what to make of him, he doesn't know what to make of himself, he's only thirteen, *athletically and socially inept*, not astonishingly bright, but there are antennae; he has … some sort of receivers in his head; things speak to him, he understands more than he should, the world winks at him through its objects, grabs grinning at his coat. Everybody else is in on some secret he doesn't know; they've forgotten to tell him. Through simple *procrastination* his mother put off his baptism until this year. Everyone else had it done as a baby; he'd assumed the same of himself, as had his mother, so she claimed, until it was time for him to join Grace Methodist-Protestant and the oversight came out. He was mortified, but pitched sleepless through his private catechizing, intimidated by the ancient mysteries, a thirteen year old would never say that, resolved to experience conversion like St. Augustine. When the water touched his brow and Adam's sin left him, he contrived by a strain like defecation to bring tears into his eyes—but felt nothing. There was some simple, radical difference about him; he hoped it was genius, feared it was madness, devoted himself to amiability and inconspicuousness. Alone on the seawall near his house he was seized by the terrifying transports he'd thought to find in toolshed, in Communion-cup. The grass was alive! The town, the river, himself, were not imaginary; time roared in his ears like wind; the world was *going on!* This part ought to be dramatized. The Irish author James Joyce once wrote. Ambrose M——is going to scream.

There is no *texture of rendered sensory detail*, for one thing. The faded distorting mirrors beside Fat May; the impossibility of choosing a mount when one had but a single ride on the great carrousel; the *vertigo attendant on his recognition* that Ocean City was worn out, the place of fathers and grandfathers, straw-boatered men and parasoled ladies survived by their amusements. Money spent, the three paused at Peter's insistence beside Fat May to watch the girls get their skirts blown up. The object was to tease Magda, who said: "I swear, Peter M——, you've got a one-track mind! Amby and me aren't *interested* in such things." In the tumbling-barrel, too, just inside the Devil's-mouth entrance to the funhouse, the girls were upended and their boyfriends and others could see up their dresses if they cared to. Which was the whole point. Ambrose realized. Of the entire funhouse! If you looked around, you noticed that almost all the people on the boardwalk were paired off into couples except the small children; in a way, that was the whole point of Ocean City! If you had X-ray eyes and could see everything going on at that instant under the boardwalk and in all the hotel rooms and cars and alleyways, you'd realize that all that normally *showed*, like restaurants and dance halls and clothing and test-your-strength machines, was merely preparation and intermission. Fat May screamed.

Because he watched the goings-on from the corner of his eye, it was Ambrose who spied the half-dollar on the boardwalk near the tumbling-barrel. Losers weepers. The first time he'd heard some people moving through a corridor not far away, just after he'd lost sight of the crack of light, he'd decided not to call to them, for fear they'd guess he was scared and poke fun; it sounded like roughnecks; he'd hoped they'd come by and he could follow in the dark without their knowing. Another time he'd heard just one person, unless he imagined it, bumping along as if on the other side of the plywood; perhaps Peter coming back for him, or Father, or Magda lost too. Or the owner and operator of the funhouse. He'd called out once, as though merrily: "Anybody know where the heck we are?" But the query was too stiff, his voice cracked, when the sounds stopped he was terrified: maybe it was a queer who waited for fellows to get lost, or a longhaired filthy monster that lived in some cranny of the funhouse. He stood rigid for hours it seemed like, scarcely respiring. His future was shockingly clear, in outline. He tried holding his breath to the point of unconsciousness. There ought to be a button you could push to end your life absolutely without pain; disappear in a flick, like turning out a light. He would push it instantly! He despised Uncle Karl. But he despised his father too, for not being what he was supposed to be. Perhaps his father hated *his* father, and so on, and his son would hate him, and so on. Instantly!

Naturally he didn't have nerve enough to ask Magda to go through the funhouse with him. With incredible nerve and to everyone's surprise he invited Magda, quietly and politely, to go through the funhouse with him. "I warn you, I've never been through it before," he added, *laughing easily*; "but I reckon we can manage somehow. The important thing to remember, after all, is that it's meant to be a *fun*house; that is, a place of amusement. If people really got lost or injured or too badly frightened in it, the owner'd go out of business. There'd even be lawsuits. No character in a work of fiction can make a speech this long without interruption or acknowledgment from the other characters."

Mother teased Uncle Karl: "Three's a crowd, I always heard." But actually Ambrose was relieved that Peter now had a quarter too. Nothing was what it looked like. Every instant, under the surface of the Atlantic Ocean, millions of living animals devoured one another. Pilots were falling in flames over Europe; women were being forcibly raped in the South Pacific. His father should have taken him aside and said: "There is a simple secret to getting through the funhouse, as simple as being first to see the Towers. Here it is. Peter does not know it; neither does your Uncle Karl.

You and I are different. Not surprisingly, you've often wished you weren't. Don't think I haven't noticed how unhappy your childhood has been! But you'll understand, when I tell you, why it had to be kept secret until now. And you won't regret not being like your brother and your uncle. *On the contrary!*" If you knew all the stories behind all the people on the boardwalk, you'd see that *nothing* was what it looked like. Husbands and wives often hated each other; parents didn't necessarily love their children; et cetera. A child took things for granted because he had nothing to compare his life to and everybody acted as if things were as they should be. Therefore each saw himself as the hero of the story, when the truth might turn out to be that he's the villain, or the coward. And there wasn't one thing you could do about it!

Hunchbacks, fat ladies, fools—that no one chose what he was was unbearable. In the movies he'd meet a beautiful young girl in the funhouse; they'd have hairsbreadth escapes from real dangers; he'd do and say the right things; she also; in the end they'd be lovers; their dialogue lines would match up; he'd be perfectly at ease; she'd not only like him well enough, she'd think he was *marvelous*; she'd lie awake thinking about *him*, instead of vice versa—the way *his* face looked in different lights and how he stood and exactly what he'd said—and yet that would be only one small episode in his wonderful life, among many many others. Not a *turning point* at all. What had happened in the toolshed was nothing. He hated, he loathed his parents! One reason for not writing a lost-in-the-funhouse story is that either everybody's felt what Ambrose feels, in which case it goes without saying, or else no normal person feels such things, in which case Ambrose is a freak. "Is anything more tiresome, in fiction, than the problems of sensitive adolescents?" And it's all too long and rambling, as if the author. For all a person knows the first time through, the end could be just around any corner; perhaps, *not impossibly* it's been within reach any number of times. On the other hand he may be scarcely past the start, with everything yet to get through, an intolerable idea.

Fill in: His father's raised eyebrows when he announced his decision to do the funhouse with Magda. Ambrose understands now, but didn't then, that his father was wondering whether he knew what the funhouse was *for*—especially since he didn't object, as he should have, when Peter decided to come along too. The ticket-woman, witchlike, mortifying him when inadvertently he gave her his name-coin instead of the half-dollar, then unkindly calling Magda's attention to the birthmark on his temple: "Watch out for him, girlie, he's a marked man!" She wasn't even cruel, he understood, only vulgar and insensitive. Somewhere in the world there was a young woman with such splendid understanding that she'd see him entire, like a poem or story, and find his words so valuable after all that when he confessed his apprehensions she would explain why they were in fact the very things that made him precious to her . . . and to Western Civilization! There was no such girl, the simple truth being. Violent yawns as they approached the mouth. Whispered advice from an old-timer on a bench near the barrel: "Go crabwise and ye'll get an eyeful without upsetting!" Composure vanished at the first pitch: Peter hollered joyously, Magda tumbled, shrieked, clutched her skirt; Ambrose scrambled crabwise, tight-lipped with terror, was soon out, watched his dropped name-coin slide among the couples. Shame-faced he saw that to get through expeditiously was not the point; Peter feigned assistance in order to trip Magda up, shouted "I see Christmas!" when her legs went flying. The old man, his latest betrayer, cacked approval. A dim hall then of black-thread cobwebs and recorded gibber: he took Magda's elbow to steady her against revolving discs set in the slanted floor to throw your feet out from under, and explained to her in a calm, deep voice his theory that each phase of the funhouse was triggered either automatically, by a series of photoelectric devices, or else manually by operators stationed at peepholes. But he lost his voice thrice as the discs unbalanced him; Magda was anyhow squealing; but at one point she clutched him about the waist to keep from falling, and her right cheek pressed for a moment against his belt-buckle. Heroically he drew her up, it was his chance to clutch her close as if for support and say: "I love you." He even put an arm lightly about the small of her back before a sailor-and-girl pitched into them from behind, sorely treading his left big toe and knocking Magda asprawl with them. The sailor's girl was a string-haired hussy with a loud laugh and light blue drawers; Ambrose realized that he wouldn't have said "I love you" anyhow, and was smitten with self-contempt. How much better it would be to be that common sailor! A wiry little Seaman 3rd, the fellow squeezed a girl to each side and stumbled hilarious into the mirror room, closer to Magda in thirty seconds than Ambrose had got in thirteen years. She giggled at something the fellow said to Peter; she drew her hair from her eyes with a movement so womanly it struck Ambrose's heart; Peter's smacking her backside then seemed particularly coarse. But Magda made a pleased indignant face and cried, "All right for *you*, mister!" and pursued Peter into the maze without a backward glance. The sailor followed after, leisurely, drawing his girl against his hip; Ambrose understood not only that they were all so relieved to be rid of his burdensome company that they didn't even notice his absence, but that he himself shared their relief. Stepping from the treacherous passage at last into the mirror-maze, he saw once again, more clearly than ever, how readily he deceived himself into supposing he was a person. He even foresaw, wincing at his dreadful self-knowledge, that he would repeat the deception, at ever-rarer intervals, all his wretched life, so fearful were the alternatives. Fame, madness, suicide; perhaps all three. It's not believable that so young a boy could articulate that reflection, and in fiction the merely true must always yield to the plausible. Moreover, the symbolism is in places heavy-footed. Yet Ambrose M——understood, as few adults do, that the famous loneliness of the great was no popular myth but a general truth—furthermore, that it was as much cause as effect.

All the preceding except the last few sentences is exposition that should've been done earlier or interspersed with the present action instead of lumped together. No reader would put up with so much with such *prolixity*. It's interesting that Ambrose's father, though presumably an intelligent man (as indicated by his role as grade-school principal), neither encouraged nor discouraged his sons at all in any way—as if he either didn't care about them or cared all right but didn't know how to act. If this fact should contribute to one of them's becoming a celebrated but wretchedly unhappy scientist, was it a good thing or not? He too might someday face the question; it would be useful to know whether it had tortured his father for years, for example, or never once crossed his mind.

In the maze two important things happened. First, our hero found a name-coin someone else had lost or discarded: AMBROSE, suggestive of the famous lightship and of his late grandfather's favorite dessert, which his mother used to prepare on special occasions out of coconut, oranges, grapes, and what else. Second, as he wondered at the endless replication of his image in the mirrors, second, as he *lost himself in the reflection* that the necessity for an observer makes perfect observation impossible, better make him eighteen at least, yet that would render other things unlikely, he heard Peter and Magda chuckling somewhere together in the maze. "Here!" "No, here!" they shouted to each other; Peter said, "Where's Amby?" Magda murmured. "Amb?" Peter called. In a pleased, friendly voice. He didn't reply. The truth was, his brother was a *happy-go-lucky youngster* who'd've been better off with a regular brother of his own, but who seldom complained of his lot and was generally cordial. Ambrose's throat ached; there aren't enough different ways to say that. He stood quietly while the two young people giggled and thumped through the glittering maze, hurrah'd their discovery of its exit, cried out in joyful alarm at what next beset them. Then he set his mouth and followed after, as he supposed, took a wrong turn, strayed into the pass *wherein he lingers yet*.

The action of conventional dramatic narrative may be represented by a diagram called Freitag's Triangle:

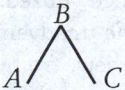

or more accurately by a variant of that diagram:

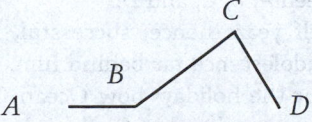

in which *AB* represents the exposition, *B* the introduction of conflict, *BC* the "rising action," complication, or development of the conflict, *C* the climax, or turn of the action, *CD* the dénouement, or resolution of the conflict. While there is no reason to regard this pattern as an absolute necessity, like many other conventions it became conventional because great numbers of people over many years learned by trial and error that it was effective; one ought not to forsake it, therefore, unless one wishes to forsake as well the effect of drama or has clear cause to feel that deliberate violation of the "normal" pattern can better can better effect that effect. This can't go on much longer; it can go on forever. He died telling stories to himself in the dark; years later, when that vast unsuspected area of the funhouse came to light, the first expedition found his skeleton in one of its labyrinthine corridors and mistook it for part of the entertainment. He died of starvation telling himself stories in the dark; but unbeknownst unbeknownst to him, an assistant operator of the funhouse, happening to overhear him, crouched just behind the plyboard partition and wrote down his every word. The operator's daughter, an exquisite young woman with a figure unusually well developed for her age, crouched just behind the partition and transcribed his every word. Though she had never laid eyes on him, she recognized that here was one of Western Culture's truly great imaginations, the eloquence of whose suffering would be an inspiration to unnumbered. And her heart was torn between her love for the misfortunate young man (yes, she loved him, though she had never laid though she knew him only—but how well!—through his words, and the deep, calm voice in which he spoke them) between her love et cetera and her womanly intuition that only in suffering and isolation could he give voice et cetera. Lone dark dying. Quietly she kissed the rough plyboard, and a tear fell upon the page. Where she had written in shorthand *Where she had written in shorthand* Where she had written in shorthand *Where she* et cetera. A long time ago we should have passed the apex of Freitag's Triangle and made brief work of the *dénouement*; the plot doesn't rise by meaningful steps but winds upon itself, digresses, retreats, hesitates, sighs, collapses, expires. The climax of the story must be its protagonist's discovery of a way to get through the funhouse. But he has found none, may have ceased to search.

What relevance does the war have to the story? Should there be fireworks outside or not?

Ambrose wandered, languished, dozed. Now and then he fell into his habit of rehearsing to himself the unadventurous story of his life, narrated from the third-person point of view, from his earliest memory parenthesis of maple leaves stirring in the summer breath of tidewater Maryland end of parenthesis to the present moment. Its principal events, on this telling, would appear to have been A, B, C, and D.

He imagined himself years hence, successful, married, at ease in the world, the trials of his adolescence far behind him. He has come to the seashore with his family for the holiday: how Ocean City has changed! But at one seldom at one ill-frequented end of the boardwalk a few derelict amusements survive from times gone by: the great carrousel from the turn of the century, with its monstrous griffins and mechanical concert band; the roller coaster rumored since 1916 to have been condemned; the mechanical shooting gallery in which only the image of our enemies changed. His own son laughs with Fat May and wants to know what a funhouse is; Ambrose hugs the sturdy lad close and smiles around his pipestem at his wife.

The family's going home. Mother sits between Father and Uncle Karl, who teases him good-naturedly who chuckles over the fact that the comrade with whom he'd fought his way shoulder to shoulder through the funhouse had turned out to be a blind Negro girl—to their mutual discomfort, as they'd opened their souls. But such are the walls of custom, which even. Whose arm is where? How must it feel. He dreams of a funhouse vaster by far than any yet constructed; but by then they may be out of fashion, like steamboats and excursion trains. Already quaint and seedy: the draperied ladies on the frieze of the carrousel are his father's father's moon-cheeked dreams; if he thinks of it more he will vomit his apple-on-a-stick.

He wonders: will he become a regular person? Something has gone wrong; his vaccination didn't take; at the Boy-Scout initiation campfire he only pretended to be deeply moved, as he pretends to this hour that it is not so bad after all in the funhouse, and that he has a little limp. How long will it last? He envisions a truly astonishing funhouse, incredibly complex yet utterly controlled from a great central switchboard like the console of a pipe organ. Nobody had enough imagination. He could design such a place himself, wiring and all, and he's only thirteen years old. He would be its operator: panel lights would show what was up in every cranny of its cunning of its multifarious vastness; a switch-flick would ease this fellow's way, complicate that's, to balance things out; if anyone seemed lost or frightened, all the operator had to do was.

He wishes he had never entered the funhouse. But he has. Then he wishes he were dead. But he's not. Therefore he will construct funhouses for others and be their secret operator—though he would rather be among the lovers for whom funhouses are designed.

1968

The U.S. War in Vietnam and Its Aftermath

IN A MODEST ATTEMPT TO FOCUS ATTENTION ON LITERATURE RESPONDING TO THE United States–Vietnam military conflict, this section includes prose by Michael Herr, Tim O'Brien, Norman Mailer, and Le Ly Hayslip and poetry by Yusef Komunyakaa, Denise Levertov, and Robert Bly. Komunyakaa came to prominence during the 1990s; Bly was one of the leaders of the very active Poets and Writers against Vietnam, along with Muriel Rukeyser, Denise Levertov, W. S. Merwin, James Wright, Hayden Carruth, Adrienne Rich, Galway Kinnell, Robert Lowell, Allen Ginsberg, and others. Mailer's *Armies of the Night*, his meditative account of an important antiwar demonstration has become a classic. The works by Tim O'Brien and Yusef Komunyakaa express veterans' view of the horrors of combat.

As Michael Bibby has reminded us, this literature is central to our view of mid-century American life, "considering that the Vietnam war was the longest overseas military conflict in U.S. history and that practically every working writer from 1965 to 1975 had something to say about it ..." (see Bibby's 1996 *Hearts and Minds: Bodies, Poetry, and Resistance in the Vietnam Era*).

MICHAEL HERR

B. 1940

Among the most private of contemporary writers, Michael Herr has revealed little of his personal life. He was born and raised in Syracuse, New York, and attended Syracuse University. He then moved to New York City, where he worked in the editorial offices of *Holiday* magazine and produced articles and film criticism for such periodicals as *Mademoiselle* and the *New Leader*. In 1967 he persuaded Harold Hayes, the editor of *Esquire* magazine, to send him to Vietnam. He stayed there for more than a year and witnessed some of the most intense fighting of the war. For a writer, Herr's situation in Vietnam was ideal: he had no specific assignment, he was relatively free to travel where he liked, and he was unencumbered by deadlines. Herr initially intended to write a monthly column from Vietnam but soon realized the idea was "horrible." In fact,

Herr published only a few Vietnam pieces in *Esquire* and did not get his war experiences into a book until 1977.

After the war, Herr lived in New York for a time. After finishing *Dispatches*, he collaborated on the screenplay for *Apocalypse Now* and, later, for *Full Metal Jacket*. At last report, Herr was living in London.

Dispatches is perhaps the most brilliant American literary treatment of the Vietnam War. Ostensibly journalistic, *Dispatches* is more properly regarded as a painstakingly executed product of the author's imagination—if not quite a novel, then certainly a literary work whose most dominant and satisfying qualities are novelistic. *Dispatches* is organized tautly, provides rich characterization, and evinces an extraordinary style thoroughly compatible with its subject. As Herr tells it, the Vietnam War was very much a 1960s spectacle: part John Wayne movie, part rock-and-roll concert, part redneck riot, part media event, and part bad drug trip. Herr's style, so perfectly grounded in the popular culture of the time, pulls at the reader with great power and unmistakable authenticity. After a particularly terrible battle, a young Marine glared at Herr, knowing he was a writer, and snarled: "Okay, man, you go on, you go on out of here, you cocksucker, but I mean it, you tell it! You tell it, man." And so Herr did.

The excerpt from *Dispatches* printed here comes from the beginning of the first section, called "Breathing In." Herr immediately establishes the hallucinatory quality of the war, against which he depicts the violence and remarkable array of characters. Herr's field of vision is broad but always at its center are the "grunts," the infantrymen who invariably carried themselves through the war with dignity and a carefully cultivated and life-sustaining combination of humor and cynicism.

Raymund Paredes
University of California, Los Angeles

PRIMARY WORKS

Dispatches, 1977; *The Big Room* (with Guy Peellaert), 1986; *Walter Winchell*, 1990; *Kubrick*, 2000.

from **Dispatches**

I

Going out at night the medics gave you pills, Dexedrine breath like dead snakes kept too long in a jar. I never saw the need for them myself, a little contact or anything that even sounded like contact would give me more speed than I could bear. Whenever I heard something outside of our clenched little circle I'd practically flip, hoping to God that I wasn't the only one who'd noticed it. A couple of rounds fired off in the dark a kilometer away and the Elephant would be there kneeling on my chest, sending me down into my boots for a breath. Once I thought I saw a light moving in the jungle and I caught myself just under a whisper saying, "I'm not ready for this, I'm not ready for this." That's when I decided to drop it and do something else with my nights. And I wasn't going out like the night ambushers did, or the Lurps, long-range recon patrollers who did it night after night for weeks and months, creeping up on VC base camps or around moving columns of North Vietnamese. I was living too close to my bones as it was, all I had to do was accept it. Anyway, I'd save the pills for later, for Saigon and the awful depressions I always had there.

I knew one 4th Division Lurp[1] who took his pills by the fistful, downs from the left pocket of his tiger suit and ups from the right, one to cut the trail for him and the other to send him down it. He told me that they cooled things out just right for him, that he could see that old jungle at night like he was looking at it through a starlight scope. "They sure give you the range," he said.

This was his third tour. In 1965 he'd been the only survivor in a platoon of the Cav wiped out going into the Ia Drang Valley. In '66 he'd come back with the Special Forces and one morning after an ambush he'd hidden under the bodies of his team while the VC walked all around them with knives, making sure. They stripped the bodies of their gear, the berets too, and finally went away, laughing. After that, there was nothing left for him in the war except the Lurps.

"I just can't hack it back in the World," he said. He told me that after he'd come back home the last time he would sit in his room all day, and sometimes he'd stick a hunting rifle out the window, leading people and cars as they passed his house until the only feeling he was aware of was all up in the tip of that one finger. "It used to put my folks real uptight," he said. But he put people uptight here too, even here.

"No man, I'm sorry, he's just too crazy for me," one of the men in his team said. "All's you got to do is look in his eyes, that's the whole fucking story right there."

"Yeah, but you better do it quick," someone else said. "I mean, you don't want to let him catch you at it."

But he always seemed to be watching for it, I think he slept with his eyes open, and I was afraid of him anyway. All I ever managed was one quick look in, and that was like looking at the floor of an ocean. He wore a gold earring and a headband torn from a piece of camouflage parachute material, and since nobody was about to tell him to get his hair cut it fell below his shoulders, covering a thick purple scar. Even at division he never went anywhere without at least a .45 and a knife, and he thought I was a freak because I wouldn't carry a weapon.

"Didn't you ever meet a reporter before?" I asked him.

"Tits on a bull," he said. "Nothing personal."

But what a story he told me, as one-pointed and resonant as any war story I ever heard, it took me a year to understand it:

"Patrol went up the mountain. One man came back. He died before he could tell us what happened."

[1]Lurp = Long Range Reconnaissance Patrol (LRRP)

I waited for the rest, but it seemed not to be that kind of story; when I asked him what had happened he just looked like he felt sorry for me, fucked if he'd waste time telling stories to anyone dumb as I was.

His face was all painted up for night walking now like a bad hallucination, not like the painted faces I'd seen in San Francisco only a few weeks before, the other extreme of the same theater. In the coming hours he'd stand as faceless and quiet in the jungle as a fallen tree, and God help his opposite numbers unless they had at least half a squad along, he was a good killer, one of our best. The rest of his team were gathered outside the tent, set a little apart from the other division units, with its own Lurp-designated latrine and its own exclusive freeze-dry rations, three-star war food, the same chop they sold at Abercrombie & Fitch. The regular division troops would almost shy off the path when they passed the area on their way to and from the mess tent. No matter how toughened up they became in the war, they still looked innocent compared to the Lurps. When the team had grouped they walked in a file down the hill to the lz[2] across the strip to the perimeter and into the treeline.

I never spoke to him again, but I saw him. When they came back in the next morning he had a prisoner with him, blindfolded and with his elbows bound sharply behind him. The Lurp area would definitely be off limits during the interrogation, and anyway, I was already down at the strip waiting for a helicopter to come and take me out of there.

"Hey, what're you guys, with the USO? Aw, we thought you was with the USO 'cause your hair's so long." Page took the kid's picture, I got the words down and Flynn laughed and told him we were the Rolling Stones. The three of us traveled around together for about a month that summer. At one lz the brigade chopper came in with a real foxtail hanging off the aerial, when the commander walked by us he almost took an infarction.

"Don't you men salute officers?"

"We're not men," Page said. "We're correspondents."

When the commander heard that, he wanted to throw a spontaneous operation for us, crank up his whole brigade and get some people killed. We had to get out on the next chopper to keep him from going ahead with it, amazing what some of them would do for a little ink. Page liked to augment his field gear with freak paraphernalia, scarves and beads, plus he was English, guys would stare at him like he'd just come down off a wall on Mars. Sean Flynn could look more incredibly beautiful than even his father, Errol, had thirty years before as Captain Blood, but sometimes he looked more like Artaud coming out of some heavy heart-of-darkness trip, overloaded on the information, the input! The input! He'd give off a bad sweat and sit for hours, combing his mustache through with the saw blade of his Swiss Army knife. We packed grass and tape: Have You Seen Your Mother Baby Standing in the Shadows, Best of the Animals, Strange Days, Purple Haze, Archie Bell and the Drells, "C'mon now everybody, do the Tighten Up...." Once in a

[2]lz = landing zone

while we'd catch a chopper straight into one of the lower hells, but it was a quiet time in the war, mostly it was lz's and camps, grunts hanging around, faces, stories.

"Best way's to just keep moving, one of them told us. "Just keep moving, stay in motion, you know what I'm saying?"

We knew. He was a moving-target-survivor subscriber, a true child of the war, because except for the rare times when you were pinned or stranded the system was geared to keep you mobile, if that was what you thought you wanted. As a technique for staying alive it seemed to make as much sense as anything, given naturally that you went there to begin with and wanted to see it close; it started out sound and straight but it formed a cone as it progressed, because the more you moved the more you saw, the more you saw the more besides death and mutilation you risked, and the more you risked of that the more you would have to let go of one day as a "survivor." Some of us moved around the war like crazy people until we couldn't see which way the run was even taking us anymore, only the war all over its surface with occasional, unexpected penetration. As long as we could have choppers like taxis it took real exhaustion or depression near shock or a dozen pipes of opium to keep us even apparently quiet, we'd still be running around inside our skins like something was after us, ha ha, La Vida Loca.

In the months after I got back the hundreds of helicopters I'd flown in began to draw together until they'd formed a collective meta-chopper, and in my mind it was the sexiest thing going; saver-destroyer, provider-waster, right hand–left hand, nimble, fluent, canny and human; hot steel, grease, jungle-saturated canvas webbing, sweat cooling and warming up again, cassette rock and roll in one ear and door-gun fire in the other, fuel, heat, vitality and death, death itself, hardly an intruder. Men on the crews would say that once you'd carried a dead person he would always be there, riding with you. Like all combat people they were incredibly superstitious and invariably self-dramatic, but it was (I knew) unbearably true that close exposure to the dead sensitized you to the force of their presence and made for long reverberations; long. Some people were so delicate that one look was enough to wipe them away; but even bone-dumb grunts seemed to feel that something weird and extra was happening to them.

Helicopters and people jumping out of helicopters, people so in love they'd run to get on even when there wasn't any pressure. Choppers rising straight out of small cleared jungle spaces, wobbling down onto city rooftops, cartons of rations and ammunition thrown off, dead and wounded loaded on. Sometimes they were so plentiful and loose that you could touch down at five or six places in a day, look around, hear the talk, catch the next one out. There were installations as big as cities with 30,000 citizens, once we dropped in to feed supply to one man. God knows what kind of Lord Jim phoenix numbers he was doing in there, all he said to me was, "You didn't see a thing, right Chief? You weren't even here." There were posh fat air-conditioned camps like comfortable middle-class scenes with the violence tacit, "far away"; camps named for commanders' wives, LZ Thelma, LZ Betty

Lou; number-named hilltops in trouble where I didn't want to stay; trail, paddy, swamp, deep hairy bush, scrub, swale, village, even city, where the ground couldn't drink up what the action spilled, it made you careful where you walked.

Sometimes the chopper you were riding in would top a hill and all the ground in front of you as far as the next hill would be charred and pitted and still smoking, and something between your chest and your stomach would turn over. Frail gray smoke where they'd burned off the rice fields around a free-strike zone, brilliant white smoke from phosphorus ("Willy Peter/Make you a buh liever"), deep black smoke from 'palm, they said that if you stood at the base of a column of napalm smoke it would such the air right out of your lungs. Once we fanned over a little ville that had just been airstruck and the words of a song by Wingy Manone that I'd heard when I was a few years old snapped into my head, "Stop the War, These Cats Is Killing Themselves." Then we dropped, hovered, settled down into purple lz smoke, dozens of children broke from their hootches to run in toward the focus of our landing, the pilot laughing and saying, "Vietnam, man, Bomb 'em and feed 'em, bomb 'em and feed 'em."

Flying over jungle was almost pure pleasure, doing it on foot was nearly all pain. I never belonged in there. Maybe it really was what its people had always called it, Beyond; at the very least it was serious, I gave up things to it I probably never got back. ("Aw, jungle's okay. If you know her you can live in her real good, if you don't she'll take you down in an hour. Under.") Once in some thick jungle corner with some grunts standing around, a correspondent said, "Gee, you must really see some beautiful sunsets in here," and they almost pissed themselves laughing. But you could fly up and into hot tropic sunsets that would change the way you thought about light forever. You could also fly out of places that were so grim they turned to black and white in your head five minutes after you'd gone.

That could be the coldest one in the world, standing at the edge of a clearing watching the chopper you'd just come in on taking off again, leaving you there to think about what it was going to be for you now: if this was a bad place, the wrong place, maybe even the last place, and whether you'd made a terrible mistake this time.

There was a camp at Soc Trang where a man at the lz said, "If you come looking for a story this is your lucky day, we got Condition Red here," and before the sound of the chopper had faded out, I knew I had it too.

"That's affirmative," the camp commander said, "we are *definitely* expecting rain. Glad to see you." He was a young captain, he was laughing and taping a bunch of sixteen clips together bottom to bottom for faster reloading, "grease." Everyone there was busy at it, cracking crates, squirreling away grenades, checking mortar pieces, piling rounds, clicking banana clips into automatic weapons that I'd never even seen before. They were wired into their listening posts out around the camp, into each other, into themselves, and when it got dark it got worse. The moon came up nasty and full, a fat moist piece of decadent fruit. It was soft and saffron-misted when you looked up at it, but its light over the sandbags and into the jungle was harsh and bright. We were all rubbing Army-issue nightfighter cosmetic under our eyes to cut the glare and the terrible things it made you see. (Around midnight, just for something to do, I crossed to the other perimeter and looked at the road running engineer-straight toward Route 4 like a yellow frozen ribbon out of sight and I saw it move, the whole road.) There were a few sharp arguments about who the light really favored, attackers or defenders, men were sitting around with Cinemascope eyes and jaws stuck out like they could shoot bullets, moving and antsing and shifting around inside their fatigues. "No sense us getting too relaxed, Charlie don't relax, just when you get good and comfortable is when he comes over and takes a giant shit on you." That was the level until morning, I smoked a pack an hour all night long, and nothing happened. Ten minutes after daybreak I was down at the lz asking about choppers.

A few days later Sean Flynn and I went up to a big firebase in the Americal TAOR that took it all the way over to another extreme, National Guard weekend. The colonel in command was so drunk that day that he could barely get his words out, and when he did, it was to say things like, "We aim to make good and goddammit sure that if *those guys* try *anything cute* they won't catch us with our pants down." The main mission there was to fire H&I, but one man told us that their record was the worst in the whole Corps, probably the whole country, they'd harassed and interdicted a lot of sleeping civilians and Korean Marines, even a couple of Americal patrols, but hardly any Viet Cong. (The colonel kept calling it "artillerary." The first time he said it Flynn and I looked away from each other, the second time we blew beer through our noses, but the colonel fell in laughing right away and more than covered us.) No sandbags, exposed shells, dirty pieces, guys going around giving us that look, "We're cool, how come you're not?" At the strip Sean was talking to the operator about it and the man got angry. "Oh *yeah*? Well fuck *you*, how tight do you think you want it? There ain't been any veecees around here in three months."

"So far so good," Sean said. "Hear anything on that chopper yet?"

But sometimes everything stopped, nothing flew, you couldn't even find out why. I got stuck for a chopper once in some lost patrol outpost in the Delta where the sergeant chain-ate candy bars and played country-and-western tapes twenty hours a day until I heard it in my sleep, some sleep, *Up on Wolverton Mountain* and *Lonesome as the bats and the bears in Miller's Cave* and *I fell into a burning ring of fire*, surrounded by strungout rednecks who weren't getting much sleep either because they couldn't trust one of their 400 mercenary troopers or their own handpicked perimeter guards or anybody else except maybe Baby Ruth and Johnny Cash, they'd been waiting for it so long now they were afraid they wouldn't know it when they finally got it, *and it burns burns burns*.... Finally on the fourth day a helicopter came in to deliver meat and movies to the camp and I went out on it, so happy to get back to Saigon that I didn't crash for two days.

Airmobility, dig it, you weren't going anywhere. It made you feel safe, it made you feel Omni, but it was only a stunt, technology. Mobility was just mobility, it saved lives or took them all the time (saved mine I don't know how many times, maybe dozens, maybe none), what you really needed was a flexibility far greater than anything the technology could provide, some generous, spontaneous gift for accepting surprises, and I didn't have it. I got to hate surprises, control freak at the crossroads, if you were one of those people who always thought they had to know what was coming next, the war could cream you. It was the same with your ongoing attempts at getting used to the jungle or the blow-you-out climate or the saturating strangeness of the place which didn't lessen with exposure so often as it fattened and darkened in accumulating alienation. It was great if you could adapt, you had to try, but it wasn't the same as making a discipline, going into your own reserves and developing a real war metabolism, slow yourself down when your heart tried to punch its way through your chest, get swift when everything went to stop and all you could feel of your whole life was the entropy whipping through it. Unlovable terms.

The ground was always in play, always being swept. Under the ground was his, above it was ours. We have the air, we could get up in it but not disappear in *to* it, we could run but we couldn't hide, and he could do each so well that sometimes it looked like he was doing them both at once, while our finder just went limp. All the same, one place or another it was always going on, rock around the clock, we had the days and he had the nights. You could be in the most protected space in Vietnam and still know that your safety was provisional, that early death, blindness, loss of legs, arms or balls, major and lasting disfigurement—the whole rotten deal— could come in on the freaky-fluky as easily as in the so-called expected ways, you heard so many of those stories it was a wonder anyone was left alive to die in firefights and mortar-rocket attacks. After a few weeks, when the nickel had jarred loose and dropped and I saw that everyone around me was carrying a gun, I also saw that any one of them could go off at any time, putting you where it wouldn't matter whether it had been an accident or not. The roads were mined, the trails booby-trapped, satchel charges and grenades blew up jeeps and movie theaters, the VC got work inside all the camps as shoeshine boys and laundresses and honey-dippers, they'd starch your fatigues and burn your shit and then go home and mortar your area. Saigon and Cholon and Danang held such hostile vibes that you felt you were being dry-sniped every time someone looked at you, and choppers fell out of the sky like fat poisoned birds a hundred times a day. After a while I couldn't get on one without thinking that I must be out of my fucking mind.

Fear and motion, fear and standstill, no preferred cut there, no way even to be clear about which was really worse, the wait or the delivery. Combat spared far more men than it wasted, but everyone suffered the time between contact, especially when they were going out every day looking for it; bad going on foot, terrible in trucks and APC's,[3] awful in helicopters, the worst, traveling so fast toward something so frightening. I can remember times when I went half dead with my fear of the motion, the speed and direction already fixed and pointed one way. It was painful enough just fly-ing "safe" hops between firebases and lz's; if you were ever on a helicopter that had been hit by ground fire your deep, perpetual chopper anxiety was guaranteed. At least actual contact when it was happening would draw long ragged strands of energy out of you, it was juicy, fast and refining, and trav-eling toward it was hollow, dry, cold and steady, it never let you alone. All you could do was look around at the other people on board and see if they were as scared and numbed out as you were. If it looked like they weren't you thought they were insane, if it looked like they were it made you feel a lot worse.

I went through that thing a number of times and only got a fast return on my fear once, a too classic hot landing with the heat coming from the trees about 300 yards away, sweeping machine-gun fire that sent men head down into swampy water, running on their hands and knees toward the grass where it wasn't blown flat by the rotor blades, not much to be running for but better than nothing. The helicopter pulled up before we'd all gotten out, leaving the last few men to jump twenty feet down between the guns across the paddy and the gun on the chopper door. When we'd all reached the cover of the wall and the captain had made a check, we were amazed to see that no one had even been hurt, except for one man who'd sprained both his ankles jumping. Afterwards, I remembered that I'd been down in the muck worrying about leeches. I guess you could say that I was refusing to accept the situation.

"Boy, you sure get offered some shitty choices," a Marine once said to me, and I couldn't help but feel that what he really meant was that you didn't get offered any at all. Specifically, he was just talking about a couple of C-ration cans, "dinner," but considering his young life you couldn't blame him for thinking that if he knew one thing for sure, it was that there was no one anywhere who cared less about what *he* wanted. There wasn't any-body he wanted to thank for his food, but he was grateful that he was still alive to eat it, that the mother-fucker hadn't scarfed him up first. He hadn't been anything but tired and scared for six months and he'd lost a lot, mostly people, and seen far too much, but he was breathing in and breathing out, some kind of choice all by itself.

He had one of those faces, I saw that face at least a thousand times at a hundred bases and camps, all the youth sucked out of the eyes, the color drawn from the skin, cold white lips, you knew he wouldn't wait for any of it to come back. Life had made him old, he'd live it out old. All those faces, sometimes it was like looking into faces at a rock concert, locked in, the event had them; or like students who were very heavily advanced, serious beyond what you'd call their years if you didn't know for yourself what the

---

[3]APC = armored personnel carrier

minutes and hours of those years were made up of. Not just like all the ones you saw who looked like they couldn't drag their asses through another day of it. (How do you feel when a nineteen-year-old kid tells you from the bottom of his heart that he's gotten too old for this kind of shit?) Not like the faces of the dead or wounded either, they could look more released than overtaken. These were the faces of boys whose whole lives seemed to have backed up on them, they'd be a few feet away but they'd be looking back at you over a distance you knew you'd never really cross. We'd talk, sometimes fly together, guys going out on R&R, guys escorting bodies, guys who'd flipped over into extremes of peace or violence. Once I flew with a kid who was going home, he looked back down once at the ground where he'd spent the year and spilled his whole load of tears. Sometimes you even flew with the dead.

Once I jumped on a chopper that was full of them. The kid in the op shack had said that there would be a body on board, but he'd been given some wrong information. "How bad do you want to get to Danang?" he'd asked me, and I'd said, "Bad."

When I saw what was happening I didn't want to get on, but they'd made a divert and a special landing for me, I had to go with the chopper I'd drawn, I was afraid of looking squeamish. (I remember, too, thinking that a chopper full of dead men was far less likely to get shot down than one full of living.) They weren't even in bags. They'd been on a truck near one of the firebases in the DMZ that was firing support for Khe Sanh, and the truck had hit a Command-detonated mine, then they'd been rocketed. The Marines were always running out of things, even food, ammo and medicine, it wasn't so strange that they'd run out of bags too. The men had been wrapped around in ponchos, some of them carelessly fastened with plastic straps, and loaded on board. There was a small space cleared for me between one of them and the door gunner, who looked pale and so tremendously furious that I thought he was angry with me and I couldn't look at him for a while. When we went up the wind blew through the ship and made the ponchos shake and tremble until the one next to me blew back in a fast brutal flap, uncovering the face. They hadn't even closed his eyes for him.

The gunner started hollering as loud as he could, "Fix it! Fix it!," maybe he thought the eyes were looking at him, but there wasn't anything I could do. My hand went there a couple of times and I couldn't, and then I did. I pulled the poncho tight, lifted his head carefully and tucked the poncho under it, and then I couldn't believe that I'd done it. All during the ride the gunner kept trying to smile, and when we landed at Dong Ha he thanked me and ran off to get a detail. The pilots jumped down and walked away without looking back once, like they'd never seen that chopper before in their lives. I flew the rest of the way to Danang in a general's plane.

1977

TIM O'BRIEN
B. 1946

After a small-town Minnesota childhood and a college education at Macalaster (class president, summa cum laude, Phi Beta Kappa), Tim O'Brien was drafted into the U.S. Army in 1968 and served one year as an infantryman in the American conflict in Vietnam. The war, which appears in all seven of his published books, constitutes a central focus of his uncollected writings; yet in interviews O'Brien repeatedly objects to being labeled a Vietnam War writer: "It's like calling Toni Morrison a black writer or Shakespeare a king writer." His concerns as a writer resonate beyond the battlefield: the subjective nature of experience, the life of the imagination, the grip of the past, control and its loss, love, betrayal, obsession, language, guilt, rage, death, moral ambiguity, mental and emotional instability, and storytelling as a means of coping with it all. Nevertheless, his personal experience of that war, along with his Midwestern background, provided him a site for his literary explorations of the human condition in late-twentieth-century American life.

Three of his books—one work of nonfiction and two works of fiction—deal directly with the war experience: *If I Die in a Combat Zone, Box Me Up and Ship Me Home* (1973), *Going after Cacciato* (1978), and *The Things They Carried* (1990). *Going after Cacciato*, his third book and second novel, won the National Book Award. The book takes place largely in the mind of Paul Berlin as he keeps himself awake on guard duty by remembering actual events and fancifully imagining what might have been. Berlin imagines his squad chasing the deserting Cacciato all the way to Paris, and his imagination transforms this initial act of *what if* into a tale that includes an echo of *Alice in Wonderland* and a Socratic exchange on the morality of the war, a tale that dramatizes Berlin's own desire to escape the war and to deny his own culpability. O'Brien's intellectual approach to the war is significantly informed by his political science graduate study at Harvard in the early 1970s; his unfinished doctoral dissertation is titled "Case Studies in American Military Interventions."

O'Brien's fourth work of fiction, *The Things They Carried*, is a collection of previously published and new stories, brought together, revised, and arranged to make a thematically unified work much like Hemingway's *In Our Time* and Joyce's *Dubliners*. The story printed here, "In the Field," comes from this book. Several of its stories are narrated by a character named "Tim O'Brien," who remains distinct from the author. The presence of "Tim O'Brien" underscores one of the novel's major conceits: the difference between "happening-truth" and "story-truth," or what actually happened versus what we say happened as factual events are received through our limited perspective and then transformed by memory, by the nature of storytelling, and by quasi-willful acts of reinvention for psychic survival.

O'Brien's other novels, including *Tomcat in Love* (1997), turn from war to romantic love between men and women as another source of conflict, ambiguity, shame, and haunting history. *Northern Lights* (1975), his first and by his own judgment his worst novel, pits two brothers—one a recently returned veteran—against each other, against the women in their lives, and against mother nature. Set in the future of 1995, *The Nuclear Age* (1985) presents a man struggling with his wife's adultery and his own obsession with nuclear war while simultaneously reliving a turbulent past of being in love with a militant antiwar activist. Paul Wade, the protagonist of *In the Lake of the Woods* (1994), is a politician who, having lost an election after the newspapers exposed his presence during the atrocities against Vietnamese civilians at My Lai, wakes one morning to find that his wife has vanished.

What happened to Paul Wade's wife? What happened to bring about Kiowa's death in the story that follows? Tim O'Brien's fiction frequently resists answering the *what happened* questions to emphasize that who we are is far more manifold, layered, and mysterious than such questions pretend.

Alex Vernon
Hendrix College

PRIMARY WORKS

If I Die in a Combat Zone, Box Me Up and Ship Me Home, 1973, rev. 1983; *Northern Lights,* 1975; *Going after Cacciato,* 1978, rev. 1989; *The Nuclear Age,* 1985, 1993; *The Things They Carried,* 1990; *In the Lake of the Woods,* 1994; *Tomcat in Love,* 1997; *July, July,* 2002.

In the Field

At daybreak the platoon of eighteen soldiers formed into a loose rank and began wading side by side through the deep muck of the shit field. They moved slowly in the rain. Leaning forward, heads down, they used the butts of their weapons as probes, wading across the field to the river and then turning and wading back again. They were tired and miserable; all they wanted now was to get it finished. Kiowa was gone. He was under the mud and water, folded in with the war, and their only thought was to find him and dig him out and then move on to someplace dry and warm. It had been a hard night. Maybe the worst ever. The rains had fallen without stop, and the Song Tra Bong had overflowed its banks, and the muck had now risen thigh-deep in the field along the river. A low, gray mist hovered over the land. Off to the west there was thunder, soft little moaning sounds, and the monsoons seemed to be a lasting element of the war. The eighteen soldiers moved in silence. First Lieutenant Jimmy Cross went first, now and then straightening out the rank, closing up the gaps. His uniform was dark with mud; his arms and face were filthy. Early in the morning he had radioed in the MIA report, giving the name and circumstances, but he was now determined to find his man, no matter what, even if it meant flying in slabs of concrete and damming up the river and draining the entire field. He would not lose a member of his command like this. It wasn't right. Kiowa had been a fine soldier and a fine human being, a devout Baptist, and there was no way Lieutenant Cross would allow such a good man to be lost under the slime of a shit field.

Briefly, he stopped and watched the clouds. Except for some occasional thunder it was a deeply quiet morning, just the rain and the steady sloshing sounds of eighteen men wading through the thick waters. Lieutenant Cross wished the rain would let up. Even for an hour, it would make things easier.

But then he shrugged. The rain was the war and you had to fight it.

Turning, he looked out across the field and yelled at one of his men to close up the rank. Not a man, really—a boy. The young soldier stood off by himself at the center of the field in knee-deep water, reaching down with both hands as if chasing some object just beneath the surface. The boy's shoulders were shaking. Jimmy Cross yelled again but the young soldier did not turn or look up. In his hooded poncho, everything caked with mud, the boy's face was impossible to make out. The filth seemed to erase identities, transforming the men into identical copies of a single soldier, which was exactly how Jimmy Cross had been trained to treat them, as interchangeable units of command. It was difficult sometimes, but he tried to avoid that sort of thinking. He had no military ambitions. He preferred to view his men not as units but as human beings. And Kiowa had been a splendid human being, the very best, intelligent and gentle and quiet-spoken. Very brave, too. And decent. The kid's father taught Sunday school in Oklahoma City, where Kiowa had been raised to believe in the promise of salvation under Jesus Christ, and this conviction had always been present in the boy's smile, in his posture toward the world, in the way he never went anywhere without an illustrated New Testament that his father had mailed to him as a birthday present back in January.

A crime, Jimmy Cross thought.

Looking out toward the river, he knew for a fact that he had made a mistake setting up here. The order had come from higher, true, but still he should've exercised some field discretion. He should've moved to higher ground for the night, should've radioed in false coordinates. There was nothing he could do now, but still it was a mistake and a hideous waste. He felt sick about it. Standing in the deep waters of the field, First Lieutenant Jimmy Cross began composing a letter in his head to the kid's father, not mentioning the shit field, just saying what a fine soldier Kiowa had been, what a fine human being, and how he was the kind of son that any father could be proud of forever.

The search went slowly. For a time the morning seemed to brighten, the sky going to a lighter shade of silver, but then the rains came back hard and steady. There was the feel of permanent twilight.

At the far left of the line, Azar and Norman Bowker and Mitchell Sanders waded along the edge of the field closest to the river. They were tall men, but at times the muck came to midthigh, other times to the crotch.

Azar kept shaking his head. He coughed and shook his head and said, "Man, talk about irony. I bet if Kiowa was here, I bet he'd just laugh. Eating shit—it's your classic irony."

"Fine," said Norman Bowker. "Now pipe down."

Azar sighed. "Wasted in the waste," he said. "A shit field. You got to admit, it's pure world-class irony."

The three men moved with slow, heavy steps. It was hard to keep balance. Their boots sank into the ooze, which produced a powerful downward suction, and with each step they would have to pull up hard to break the hold. The rain made quick dents in the water, like tiny mouths, and the stink was everywhere.

When they reached the river, they shifted a few meters to the north and began wading back up the field. Occasionally they used their weapons to test the bottom, but mostly they just searched with their feet.

"A classic case," Azar was saying. "Biting the dirt, so to speak, that tells the story."

"Enough," Bowker said.

"Like those old cowboy movies. One more redskin bites the dust."

"I'm serious, man. Zip it shut."

Azar smiled and said, "Classic."

The morning was cold and wet. They had not slept during the night, not even for a few moments, and all three of them were feeling the tension as they moved across the field toward the river. There was nothing they could do for Kiowa. Just find him and slide him aboard a chopper. Whenever a man died it was always the same, a desire to get it over with quickly, no fuss or ceremony, and what they wanted now was to head for a ville and get under a roof and forget what had happened during the night.

Halfway across the field Mitchell Sanders stopped. He stood for a moment with his eyes shut, feeling along the bottom with a foot, then he passed his weapon over to Norman Bowker and reached down into the muck. After a second he hauled up a filthy green rucksack.

The three men did not speak for a time. The pack was heavy with mud and water, dead-looking. Inside were a pair of moccasins and an illustrated New Testament.

"Well," Mitchell Sanders finally said, "the guy's around here somewhere."

"Better tell the LT."

"Screw him."

"Yeah, but—"

"Some lieutenant," Sanders said. "Camps us in a toilet. Man don't *know* shit."

"Nobody knew," Bowker said.

"Maybe so, maybe not. Ten billion places we could've set up last night, the man picks a latrine."

Norman Bowker stared down at the rucksack. It was made of dark green nylon with an aluminum frame, but now it had the curious look of flesh.

"It wasn't the LT's fault," Bowker said quietly.

"Whose then?"

"Nobody's. Nobody knew till afterward."

Mitchell Sanders made a sound in his throat. He hoisted up the rucksack, slipped into the harness, and pulled the straps tight. "All right, but this much for sure. The man knew it was raining. He knew about the river. One plus one. Add it up, you get exactly what happened."

Sanders glared at the river.

"Move it," he said. "Kiowa's waiting on us."

Slowly then, bending against the rain, Azar and Norman Bowker and Mitchell Sanders began wading again through the deep waters, their eyes down, circling out from where they had found the rucksack.

First Lieutenant Jimmy Cross stood fifty meters away. He had finished writing the letter in his head, explaining things to Kiowa's father, and now he folded his arms and watched his platoon crisscrossing the wide field. In a funny way, it reminded him of the municipal golf course in his hometown in New Jersey. A lost ball, he thought. Tired players searching through the rough, sweeping back and forth in long systematic patterns. He wished he were there right now. On the sixth hole. Looking out across the water hazard that fronted the small flat green, a seven iron in his hand, calculating wind and distance, wondering if he should reach instead for an eight. A tough decision, but all you could ever lose was a ball. You did not lose a player. And you never had to wade out into the hazard and spend the day searching through the slime.

Jimmy Cross did not want the responsibility of leading these men. He had never wanted it. In his sophomore year at Mount Sebastian College he had signed up for the Reserve Officer Training Corps without much thought. An automatic thing: because his friends had joined, and because it was worth a few credits, and because it seemed preferable to letting the draft take him. He was unprepared. Twenty-four years old and his heart wasn't in it. Military matters meant nothing to him. He did not care one way or the other about the war, and he had no desire to command, and even after all these months in the bush, all the days and nights, even then he did not know enough to keep his men out of a shit field.

What he should've done, he told himself, was follow his first impulse. In the late afternoon yesterday, when they reached the night coordinates, he should've taken one look and headed for higher ground. He should've known. No excuses. At one edge of the field was a small ville, and right away a couple of old mama-sans had trotted out to warn him. Number ten, they'd said. Evil ground. Not a good spot for good GIs. But it was a war, and he had his orders, so they'd set up a perimeter and crawled under their ponchos and tried to settle in for the night. The rain never stopped. By midnight the Song Tra Bong had overflowed its banks. The field turned to slop, everything soft and mushy. He remembered how the water kept rising, how a terrible stink began to bubble up out of the earth. It was a dead-fish smell, partly, but something else, too, and then later in the night Mitchell Sanders had crawled through the rain and grabbed him hard by the arm and asked what he was doing setting up in a shit field. The village toilet, Sanders said. He remembered the look on Sanders's face. The guy stared for a moment and then wiped his mouth and whispered, "Shit," and then crawled away into the dark.

A stupid mistake. That's all it was, a mistake, but it had killed Kiowa.

Lieutenant Jimmy Cross felt something tighten inside him. In the letter to Kiowa's father he would apologize point-blank. Just admit to the blunders.

He would place the blame where it belonged. Tactically, he'd say, it was indefensible ground from the start. Low and flat. No natural cover. And so late in the night, when they took mortar fire from across the river, all they could do was snake down under the slop and lie there and wait. The field just exploded. Rain and slop and shrapnel, it all mixed together, and the field seemed to boil. He would explain this to Kiowa's father. Carefully, not covering up his own guilt, he would tell how the mortar rounds made craters in the slush, spraying up great showers of filth, and how the craters then collapsed on themselves and filled up with mud and water, sucking things down, swallowing things, weapons and entrenching tools and belts of ammunition, and how in this way his son Kiowa had been combined with the waste and the war.

My own fault, he would say.

Straightening up, First Lieutenant Jimmy Cross rubbed his eyes and tried to get his thoughts together. The rain fell in a cold, sad drizzle.

Off toward the river he again noticed the young soldier standing alone at the center of the field. The boy's shoulders were shaking. Maybe it was something in the posture of the soldier, or the way he seemed to be reaching for some invisible object beneath the surface, but for several moments Jimmy Cross stood very still, afraid to move, yet knowing he had to, and then he murmured to himself, "My fault," and he nodded and waded out across the field toward the boy.

The young soldier was trying hard not to cry.

He, too, blamed himself. Bent forward at the waist, groping with both hands, he seemed to be chasing some creature just beyond reach, something elusive, a fish or a frog. His lips were moving. Like Jimmy Cross, the boy was explaining things to an absent judge. It wasn't to defend himself. The boy recognized his own guilt and wanted only to lay out the full causes.

Wading sideways a few steps, he leaned down and felt along the soft bottom of the field.

He pictured Kiowa's face. They'd been close buddies, the tightest, and he remembered how last night they had huddled together under their ponchos, the rain cold and steady, the water rising to their knees, but how Kiowa had just laughed it off and said they should concentrate on better things. And so for a long while they'd talked about their families and hometowns. At one point, the boy remembered, he'd been showing Kiowa a picture of his girlfriend. He remembered switching on his flashlight. A stupid thing to do, but he did it anyway, and he remembered Kiowa leaning in for a look at the picture—"Hey, she's *cute*," he'd said—and then the field exploded all around them.

Like murder, the boy thought. The flashlight made it happen. Dumb and dangerous. And as a result his friend Kiowa was dead.

That simple, he thought.

He wished there were some other way to look at it, but there wasn't. Very simple and very final. He remembered two mortar rounds hitting close by. Then a third, even closer, and off to his left he'd heard somebody scream. The voice was ragged and clotted up, but he knew instantly that it was Kiowa.

He remembered trying to crawl toward the screaming. No sense of direction, though, and the field seemed to suck him under, and everything was black and wet and swirling, and he couldn't get his bearings, and then another round hit nearby, and for a few moments all he could do was hold his breath and duck down beneath the water.

Later, when he came up again, there were no more screams. There was an arm and a wristwatch and part of a boot. There were bubbles where Kiowa's head should've been.

He remembered grabbing the boot. He remembered pulling hard, but how the field seemed to pull back, like a tug-of-war he couldn't win, and how finally he had to whisper his friend's name and let go and watch the boot slide away. Then for a long time there were things he could not remember. Various sounds, various smells. Later he'd found himself lying on a little rise, face-up, tasting the field in his mouth, listening to the rain and explosions and bubbling sounds. He was alone. He'd lost everything. He'd lost Kiowa and his weapon and his flashlight and his girlfriend's picture. He remembered this. He remembered wondering if he could lose himself.

Now, in the dull morning rain, the boy seemed frantic. He waded quickly from spot to spot, leaning down and plunging his hands into the water. He did not look up when Lieutenant Jimmy Cross approached.

"Right here," the boy was saying. "Got to be right here."

Jimmy Cross remembered the kid's face but not the name. That happened sometimes. He tried to treat his men as individuals but sometimes the names just escaped him.

He watched the young soldier shove his hands into the water. "Right *here*," he kept saying. His movements seemed random and jerky.

Jimmy Cross waited a moment, then stepped closer. "Listen," he said quietly, "the guy could be anywhere."

The boy glanced up. "Who could?"

"Kiowa. You can't expect—"

"Kiowa's *dead*."

"Well, yes."

The young soldier nodded. "So what about Billie?"

"Who?"

"My girl. What about her? This picture, it was the only one I had. Right here, I lost it."

Jimmy Cross shook his head. It bothered him that he could not come up with a name.

"Slow down," he said. "I don't—"

"Billie's *picture*. I had it all wrapped up, I had it in plastic, so it'll be okay if I can ... Last night we were looking at it, me and Kiowa. Right here. I know for sure it's right here somewhere."

Jimmy Cross smiled at the boy. "You can ask her for another one. A better one."

"She won't *send* another one. She's not even my *girl* anymore, she won't ... Man, I got to find it."

The boy yanked his arm free.

He shuffled sideways and stooped down again and dipped into the muck with both hands. His shoulders were shaking. Briefly, Lieutenant Cross wondered where the kid's weapon was, and his helmet, but it seemed better not to ask.

He felt some pity come on him. For a moment the day seemed to soften. So much hurt, he thought. He watched the young soldier wading through the water, bending down and then standing and then bending down again, as if something might finally be salvaged from all the waste.

Jimmy Cross silently wished the boy luck.

Then he closed his eyes and went back to working on the letter to Kiowa's father.

Across the field Azar and Norman Bowker and Mitchell Sanders were wading alongside a narrow dike at the edge of the field. It was near noon now.

Norman Bowker found Kiowa. He was under two feet of water. Nothing showed except the heel of a boot.

"That's him?" Azar said.

"Who else?"

"I don't know." Azar shook his head. "I don't know."

Norman Bowker touched the boot, covered his eyes for a moment, then stood up and looked at Azar.

"So where's the joke?" he said.

"No joke."

"Eating shit. Let's hear that one."

"Forget it."

Mitchell Sanders told them to knock it off. The three soldiers moved to the dike, put down their packs and weapons, then waded back to where the boot was showing. The body lay partly wedged under a layer of mud beneath the water. It was hard to get traction; with each movement the muck would grip their feet and hold tight. The rain had come back harder now. Mitchell Sanders reached down and found Kiowa's other boot, and they waited a moment, then Sanders sighed and said, "Okay," and they took hold of the two boots and pulled up hard. There was only a slight give. They tried again, but this time the body did not move at all. After the third try they stopped and looked down for a while. "One more time," Norman Bowker said. He counted to three and they leaned back and pulled.

"Stuck," said Mitchell Sanders.

"I see that. Christ."

They tried again, then called over Henry Dobbins and Rat Kiley, and all five of them put their arms and backs into it, but the body was jammed in tight.

Azar moved to the dike and sat holding his stomach. His face was pale.

The others stood in a circle, watching the water, then after a time somebody said, "We can't just *leave* him there," and the men nodded and got out their entrenching tools and began digging. It was hard, sloppy work. The mud seemed to flow back faster than they could dig, but Kiowa was their friend and they kept at it anyway.

Slowly, in little groups, the rest of the platoon drifted over to watch. Only Lieutenant Jimmy Cross and the young soldier were still searching the field.

"What we should do, I guess," Norman Bowker said, "is tell the LT."

Mitchell Sanders shook his head. "Just mess things up. Besides, the man looks happy out there, real content. Let him be."

After ten minutes they uncovered most of Kiowa's lower body. The corpse was angled steeply into the muck, upside down, like a diver who plunged headfirst off a high tower. The men stood quietly for a few seconds. There was a feeling of awe. Mitchell Sanders finally nodded and said, "Let's get it done," and they took hold of the legs and pulled up hard, then pulled again, and after a moment Kiowa came sliding to the surface. A piece of his shoulder was missing; the arms and chest and face were cut up with shrapnel. He was covered with bluish green mud. "Well," Henry Dobbins said, "it could be worse," and Dave Jensen said, "How, man? Tell me *how*." Carefully, trying not to look at the body, they carried Kiowa over to the dike and laid him down. They used towels to clean off the scum. Rat Kiley went through the kid's pockets, placed his personal effects in a plastic bag, taped the bag to Kiowa's wrist, then used the radio to call in a dustoff.

Moving away, the men found things to do with themselves, some smoking, some opening up cans of C rations, a few just standing in the rain.

For all of them it was a relief to have it finished. There was the promise now of finding a hootch somewhere, or an abandoned pagoda, where they could strip down and wring out their fatigues and maybe start a hot fire. They felt bad for Kiowa. But they also felt a kind of giddiness, a secret joy, because they were alive, and because even the rain was preferable to being sucked under a shit field, and because it was all a matter of luck and happenstance.

Azar sat down on the dike next to Norman Bowker.

"Listen," he said. "Those dumb jokes—I didn't mean anything."

"We all say things."

"Yeah, but when I saw the guy, it made me feel—I don't know—like he was listening."

"He wasn't."

"I guess not. But I felt sort of guilty almost, like if I'd kept my mouth shut none of it would've ever happened. Like it was my fault."

Norman Bowker looked out across the wet field. "Nobody's fault," he said. "Everybody's."

Near the center of the field First Lieutenant Jimmy Cross squatted in the muck, almost entirely submerged. In his head he was revising the letter to Kiowa's father. Impersonal this time. An officer expressing an officer's condolences. No apologies were necessary, because in fact it was one of those freak things, and the war was full of freaks, and nothing could ever change it anyway. Which was the truth, he thought. The exact truth.

Lieutenant Cross went deeper into the muck, the dark water at his throat, and tried to tell himself it was the truth.

Beside him, a few steps off to the left, the young soldier was still searching for his girlfriend's picture. Still remembering how he had killed Kiowa.

The boy wanted to confess. He wanted to tell the lieutenant how in the middle of the night he had pulled out Billie's picture and passed it over to Kiowa and then switched on the flashlight, and how Kiowa had whispered, "Hey, she's *cute*," and how for a second the flashlight had made Billie's face sparkle, and how right then the field had exploded all around them. The flashlight had done it. Like a target shining in the dark.

The boy looked up at the sky, then at Jimmy Cross.

"Sir?" he said.

The rain and mist moved across the field in broad, sweeping sheets of gray. Close by, there was thunder.

"Sir," the boy said, "I got to explain something."

But Lieutenant Jimmy Cross wasn't listening. Eyes closed, he let himself go deeper into the waste, just letting the field take him. He lay back and floated.

When a man died, there had to be blame. Jimmy Cross understood this. You could blame the war. You could blame the idiots who made the war. You could blame Kiowa for going to it. You could blame the rain. You could blame the river. You could blame the field, the mud, the climate. You could blame the enemy. You could blame the mortar rounds. You could blame people who were too lazy to read a newspaper, who were bored by the daily body counts, who switched channels at the mention of politics. You could blame whole nations. You could blame God. You could blame the munitions makers or Karl Marx or a trick of fate or an old man in Omaha who forgot to vote.

In the field, though, the causes were immediate. A moment of carelessness or bad judgment or plain stupidity carried consequences that lasted forever.

For a long while Jimmy Cross lay floating. In the clouds to the east there was the sound of a helicopter, but he did not take notice. With his eyes still closed, bobbing in the field, he let himself slip away. He was back home in New Jersey. A golden afternoon on the golf course, the fairways lush and green, and he was teeing it up on the first hole. It was a world without responsibility. When the war was over, he thought, maybe then he would write a letter to Kiowa's father. Or maybe not. Maybe he would just take a couple of practice swings and knock the ball down the middle and pick up his clubs and walk off into the afternoon.

1990

■   # NORMAN MAILER   ■
1923–2007

Norman Kingsley Mailer was born in Long Branch, New Jersey, and raised in Brooklyn, New York. He entered Harvard at the age of sixteen. There he majored in aeronautical engineering but soon became fascinated by literature, especially the work of Steinbeck, Farrell, and Dos Passos. Active in Harvard literary groups, he won *Story* magazine's College Award in 1941.

Drafted into the U.S. Army in 1944, he served as a rifleman with the 112th Cavalry out of San Antonio, Texas, an alien milieu for an unprepossessing Jewish boy from Brooklyn. He served for eighteen months in the Philippines and Japan, from which experience grew his first novel, *The Naked and the Dead* (1948). An enormous popular and critical success, this book made Mailer a celebrity at the age of twenty-five and set in motion a complex series of public responses.

Controversy dogged Mailer through his personal and professional life. The father of nine children, he was married six times and at the center of numerous political storms. His sometimes bizarre behavior during his youth and early middle age (fistfights, arrests, above all the nonfatal stabbing of his second wife, Adele Morales, in 1960), coupled with his involvement in political life (cofounding the *Village Voice* in 1956, running for mayor of New York City in 1969, being arrested for civil disobedience during the 1967 March on the Pentagon), made him a convenient target for the media. Simultaneously his work and its critical reception proceeded through various stages.

The Armies of the Night (1968), which won both the Pulitzer Prize for general nonfiction and the National Book Award for Arts and Letters, recounts Mailer's vision of the March on the Pentagon. This book is paradigmatic of various lines of development in his life and work. In this "nonfiction novel," subtitled *History as a Novel, The Novel as History*, Mailer's fictional voice, his political activism, and his flamboyant public image converge.

After *The Naked and the Dead*, a powerful but derivative naturalistic novel, Mailer developed an existential fictional voice that peaked in *An American Dream* (1965). This controversial novel treats allegorically the protagonist's murder of his wife, presenting a sophisticated and profoundly disturbing vision of the violence endemic in America.

Although Mailer remained paradoxical and flamboyant, *The Armies of the Night* forced the literary establishment to take him seriously once again. In the forty years following that book, he matured as an artist, producing a large body of important work and becoming a truly major figure in American letters. In 1979 he won his second Pulitzer Prize, for *The Executioner's Song*, the "true-life novel" of the murderer Gary Gilmore, which led to further criticism of Mailer's obsession with (some say glamorizing of) American violence. The year 1991 saw the publication of the massive *Harlot's Ghost*, steeped in Mailer's obsessive themes of sexuality, violence, and existential choice.

If his work did not cease to engender intense reactions, the former *enfant terrible* unquestionably mellowed personally and grew into the role of senior statesman of American letters. Happily married to his sixth wife, Norris Church, Mailer seemed to have found tranquillity. As president of PEN, an international organization of writers, he led the fight for freedom of expression. And in every arena of American life, he left his distinctive and indelible mark.

Barry H. Leeds
Central Connecticut State University

PRIMARY WORKS

The Naked and the Dead, 1948; *Barbary Shore*, 1951; *The Deer Park*, 1955; *The White Negro*, 1958; *Advertisements for Myself*, 1959; *Deaths for the Ladies and Other Disasters*, 1962; *The Presidential Papers*, 1963; *An American Dream*, 1965; *Cannibals and Christians*, 1966; *Why Are We in Vietnam?*, 1967; *Short Fiction of Norman Mailer*, 1967; *Miami and the Siege of Chicago*, 1968; *The Armies of the Night*, 1968; *Of a Fire on the Moon*, 1970; *The Prisoner of Sex*, 1971; *St. George and the Godfather*, 1972; *Essential Errands*, 1972; *Marilyn*, 1973; *The Faith of Graffiti*, 1974; *The Fight*, 1975; *Some Honorable Men*, 1976; *Genius and Lust*, 1976; *The Executioner's Song*, 1979; *Of Women and Their Elegance*, 1980; *Pieces and Pontifications*, 1982; *Ancient Evenings*, 1983; *Tough Guys Don't Dance*, 1984; *The Last Night*, 1984; *Harlot's Ghost*, 1991; *Oswald: An American Mystery*, 1995; *Portrait of Picasso as a Young Man*, 1996; *The Gospel according to the Son*, 1997; *The Time of Our Time*, 1998; *The Spooky Art: Some Thoughts on Writing*, 2003; *The Castle in the Forest*, 2007.

from **The Armies of the Night**

... "We are gathered here"—shades of Lincoln in hippieland—"to make a move on Saturday to invest the Pentagon and halt and slow down its workings, and this will be at once a symbolic act and a real act"—he was roaring—"for real heads may possibly get hurt, and soldiers will be there to hold us back, and some of us may be arrested"—how, wondered the wise voice at the rear of this roaring voice, could one ever leave Washington now without going to jail?—"some blood conceivably will be shed. If I were the man in the government responsible for controlling this March, I would not know what to do." Sonorously—"I would not wish to arrest too many or hurt anyone for fear the repercussions in the world would be too large for my bureaucrat's heart to bear—it's so full of shit." Roars and chills from the audience again. He was off into obscenity. It gave a heartiness like the blood of beef tea to his associations. There was no villainy in obscenity for him, just paradoxically, characteristically—his love for America: he had first come to love America when he served in the U.S. Army, not the America of course of the flag, the patriotic unendurable fix of the television programs and the newspapers, no, long before he was ever aware of the institutional oleo of the most suffocating American ideas he had come to love what editorial writers were fond of calling the democratic principle with its faith in the common man. He found that principle and that man in the Army, but what none of the editorial writers ever mentioned was that that noble common man was obscene as an old goat, and his obscenity was what saved him. The sanity of said common democratic man was in his humor, his humor was in his obscenity. And his philosophy as well—a reductive philosophy which looked to restore the hard edge of proportion to the overblown values overhanging each small military existence—viz, being forced to salute an overconscientious officer with your back stiffened into an exaggerated posture. "That Lieutenant is chicken-shit," would be the platoon verdict, and a blow had somehow been struck for democracy and the sanity of good temper. Mailer once heard a private end an argument about the merits of a general by saying, "his spit don't smell like ice cream either," only the private was not speaking of spit. Mailer thought enough of the line to put it into *The Naked and the Dead*, along with a good many other such lines the characters in his mind and his memory of the Army had begun to offer him. The common discovery of America was probably that Americans were the first people on earth to live for their humor; nothing was so important to Americans as humor. In Brooklyn, he had taken this for granted, at Harvard he had thought it was a by-product of being at Harvard, but in the Army he discovered that the humor was probably in the veins and the roots of the local history of every state and county in America—the truth of the way it really felt over the years passed on a river of obscenity from small-town storyteller to storyteller there down below the bankers and the books and the educators and the legislators—so Mailer never felt more like an American than when he was naturally obscene—all the gifts of the American language came out in the happy play of obscenity upon concept, which enabled one to go back to concept again. What was magnificent about the word shit is that it enabled you to use the word noble: a skinny Southern cracker with a beatific smile on his face saying in the dawn in a Filipino rice paddy, "Man, I just managed to take me a noble shit." Yeah, that was Mailer's America. If he was going to love something in the country, he would love that. So after years of keeping obscene language off to one corner of his work, as if to prove after *The Naked and the Dead* that he had many an arrow in his literary quiver, he had come back to obscenity again in the last year—he had kicked goodbye in his novel *Why Are We In Vietnam?* to the old literary corset of good taste, letting his sense of language play on obscenity as freely as it wished, so discovering that everything he knew about the American language (with its incommensurable resources) went flying in and out of the line of his prose with the happiest beating of wings—it was the first time his style seemed at once very American to him and very literary in the best way, at least as he saw the best way. But the reception of the book had been disappointing. Not because many of the reviews were bad (he had learned, despite all sudden discoveries of sorrow, to live with that as one lived with smog) no, what was disappointing was the crankiness across the country. Where fusty conservative old critics had once defended the obscenity in *The Naked and the Dead*, they, or their sons, now condemned it in the new book, and that *was* disappointing. The country was not growing up so much as getting a premature case of arthritis.

At any rate, he had come to the point where he liked to use a little obscenity in his public speaking. Once people got over the shock, they were sometimes able to discover that the humor it provided was not less powerful than the damage of the pain. Of course he did not do it often and tried not to do it unless he was in good voice—Mailer was under no illusion that public speaking was equal to candid conversation; an obscenity uttered in a voice too weak for its freight was obscene, since obscenity probably resides in the quick conversion of excitement to nausea—which is why Lyndon Johnson's speeches are called obscene by some. The excitement of listening to the American President alters abruptly into the nausea of wandering down the blind alleys of his voice.

This has been a considerable defense of the point, but then the point was at the center of his argument and it could be put thus: the American corporation executive, who was after all the foremost representative of Man in the world today, was perfectly capable of burning unseen women and children in the Vietnamese jungles, yet felt a large displeasure and fairly final disapproval at the generous use of obscenity in literature and in public. . . .

In a little more than a half hour, the students were done. Now began the faculty. They too came up one by one, but now there was no particular sense offered of an internal organization. Unlike the students, they had not debated these matters in open forum for months, organized, proselyted, or been overcome by argument, no, most of them had served as advisers to the students, had counseled them, and been picked up, many of them, and brought along by the rush of this moral stream much as a small piece of river bank might separate from the shore and go down the line of the flood. It must have been painful for these academics. They were older, certainly less suited for jail, aware more precisely of how and where their careers would be diverted or impeded, they had families many of them, they were liberal academics, technologues, they were being forced to abdicate from the machines they had chosen for their life. Their decision to turn in draft cards must have come for many in the middle of the night; for others it must have come even last night, or as they stood here debating with themselves. Many of them seemed to stand irresolutely near the steps for long periods, then move up at last. Rogoff, standing next to Mailer, hugging his thin chest in the October air, now cold, finally took out his card and, with a grin at Mailer, said, "I guess I'm going to turn this in. But you know the ridiculous part of it is that I'm 4-F."[2] So they came up one by one, not in solidarity, but as individuals, each breaking the shield or the fence or the mold or the home or even the construct of his own security. And as they did this, a deep gloom began to work on Mailer, because a deep modesty was on its way to him, he could feel himself becoming more and more of a modest man as he stood there in the cold with his hangover, and he hated this because modesty was an old family relative, he had been born to a modest family, had been a modest boy, a modest young man, and he hated that, he loved the pride and the arrogance and the confidence and the egocentricity he had acquired over the years, that was his force and his luxury and the iron in his greed, the richest sugar of his pleasure, the strength of his competitive force, he had lived long enough to know that the intimation one was being steeped in a new psychical condition (like this oncoming modest grace) was never to be disregarded, permanent new states could come into one on just so light a breeze. He stood in the cold watching the faculty men come up, yes always one by one, and felt his hangover which had come in part out of his imperfectly swallowed contempt for them the night before, and in part out of his fear, yes now he saw it, fear of the consequences of this weekend in Washington, for he had known from the beginning it could disrupt his life for a season or more and in some way the danger was there it could change him forever. He was forty-four years old, and it had taken him most of those forty-four years to begin to be able to enjoy his pleasures where he found them, rather than worry about his pleasures which eluded him—it was obviously no time to embark on ventures which would eventually give one more than a few years in jail. Yet, there was no escape. As if some final cherished rare innocence of childhood still preserved intact in him was brought finally to the surface and there expired, so he lost at that instant the last secret delight he retained in life as a game where finally you never got hurt if you played the game well enough. For years he had envisioned himself in some final cataclysm,[3] as an underground leader in the city, or a guerrilla with a gun in the hills, and had scorned the organizational aspects of revolution, the speeches, mimeograph machines, the hard dull forging of new parties and programs, the dull maneuvering to keep power, the intolerable obedience required before the over-all intellectual necessities of each objective period, and had scorned it, yes, had spit at it, and perhaps had been right, certainly had been right, such revolutions were the womb and cradle of technology land, no the only revolutionary truth was a gun in the hills, and that would not be his, he would be too old by then, and too incompetent, yes, too incompetent said the new modesty, and too showboat, too lacking in essential judgment—besides, he was too well-known! He would pay for the pleasures of his notoriety in the impossibility of disguise. No gun in the hills, no taste for organization, no, he was a figurehead, and therefore he was expendable, said the new modesty—not a future leader,

---

[2]Military term for individuals who are medically unfit for service.

[3]A violent upheaval.

but a future victim: *there* would be his real value. He could go to jail for protest, and spend some years if it came to it, possibly his life, for if the war
went on, and America put its hot martial tongue across the Chinese border,
well, jail was the probable perspective, detention camps, dissociation centers, liquidation alleys, that would be his portion, and it would come about
the time he had learned how to live.

The depth of this gloom and this modesty came down on Mailer, and he
watched the delegation take the bag into the Department of Justice with
994 cards contained inside, and listened to the speeches while they waited,
and was eventually called up himself to make a speech, and made a modest
one in a voice so used by the stentorian demonstrations of the night before
that he was happy for the mike since otherwise he might have communicated in a whisper. He said a little of what he had thought while watching
the others: that he had recognized on this afternoon that the time had come
when Americans, many Americans, would have to face the possibility of
going to jail for their ideas, and this was a prospect with no cheer because
prisons were unattractive places where much of the best in oneself was
slowly extinguished, but it could be there was no choice. The war in Vietnam
was an obscene war, the worst war the nation had ever been in, and so its
logic might compel sacrifice from those who were not so accustomed. And,
out of hardly more than a sense of old habit and old anger, he scolded the
press for their lies, and their misrepresentation, for their guilt in creating a
psychology over the last twenty years in the average American which made
wars like Vietnam possible; then he surrendered the mike and stepped down
and the applause was pleasant.

... out from that direction came the clear bitter-sweet excitation of a
military trumpet resounding in the near distance, one peal which seemed to
go all the way back through a galaxy of bugles to the cries of the Civil War
and the first trumpet note to blow the attack. The ghosts of old battles were
wheeling like clouds over Washington today.

The trumpet sounded again. It was calling the troops. "Come here," it
called from the steps of Lincoln Memorial over the two furlongs of the long
reflecting pool, out to the swell of the hill at the base of Washington Monument, "come here, come here, come here. The rally is on!" And from the
north and the east, from the direction of the White House and the Smithso-
nian and the Capitol, from Union Station and the Department of Justice
the troops were coming in, the volunteers were answering the call. They
came walking up in all sizes, a citizens' army not ranked yet by height, an
army of both sexes in numbers almost equal, and of all ages, although most
were young. Some were well-dressed, some were poor, many were conventional in appearance, as often were not. The hippies were there in great
number, perambulating down the hill, many dressed like the legions of Sgt.
Pepper's Band,[4] some were gotten up like Arab sheiks, or in Park Avenue's

---

[4]Fictional band made famous by the British
rock group, The Beatles.

doormen's greatcoats, others like Rogers and Clark of the West, Wyatt Earp, Kit Carson, Daniel Boone in buckskin, some had grown mustaches to look like *Have Gun, Will Travel*—Paladin's[5] surrogate was here!—and wild Indians with feathers, a hippie gotten up like Batman, another like Claude Rains in *The Invisible Man*—his face wrapped in a turban of bandages and he wore a black satin top hat. A host of these troops wore capes, beat-up khaki capes, slept on, used as blankets, towels, improvised duffel bags; or fine capes, orange linings, or luminous rose linings, the edges ragged, near a tatter, the threads ready to feather, but a musketeer's hat on their head. One hippie may have been dressed like Charles Chaplin; Buster Keaton and W.C. Fields[6] could have come to the ball; there were Martians and Moon-men and a knight unhorsed who stalked about in the weight of real armor. There were to be seen a hundred soldiers in Confederate gray, and maybe there were two or three hundred hippies in officer's coats of Union dark-blue. They had picked up their costumes where they could, in surplus stores, and Blow-your-mind shops, Digger free emporiums, and psychedelic caches of Hindu junk. There were soldiers in Foreign Legion uniforms, and tropical bush jackets, San Quentin and Chino, California striped shirt and pants, British copies of Eisenhower jackets, hippies dressed like Turkish shepherds and Roman senators, gurus, and samurai in dirty smocks. They were close to being assembled from all the intersections between history and the comic books, between legend and television, the Biblical archetypes and the movies. The sight of these troops, this army with a thousand costumes, fulfilled to the hilt our General's oldest idea of war which is that every man should dress as he pleases if he is going into battle, for that is his right, and variety never hurts the zest of the hardiest workers in every battalion (here today by thousands in plain hunting jackets, corduroys or dungarees, ready for assault!) if the sight of such masquerade lost its usual happy connotation of masked ladies and starving children outside the ball, it was not only because of the shabbiness of the costumes (up close half of them must have been used by hippies for everyday wear) but also because the aesthetic at last was in the politics—the dress ball was going into battle. Still, there were nightmares beneath the gaiety of these middle-class runaways, these Crusaders, going out to attack the hard core of technology land with less training than armies were once offered by a medieval assembly ground. The nightmare was in the echo of those trips which had fractured their sense of past and present. If nature was a veil whose tissue had been ripped by static, screams of jet motors, the highway grid of the suburbs, smog, defoliation, pollution of streams, overfertilization of earth, anti-fertilization of women, and the radiation of two decades of near blind atom busting, then perhaps the history of the past was another tissue, spiritual, no doubt, without physical embodiment, unless its embodiment was in the cuneiform hieroglyphics of the chromosome (so much like primitive writing!) but that tissue of past

---

[5]Various fictional and nonfictional American folk heroes.   [6]American comedians and early stars of film.

history, whether traceable in the flesh, or merely palpable in the collective underworld of the dream, was nonetheless being bombed by the use of LSD as outrageously as the atoll of Eniwetok, Hiroshima, Nagasaki, and the scorched foliage of Vietnam. The history of the past was being exploded right into the present: perhaps there were now lacunae in the firmament of the past, holes where once had been the psychic reality of an era which was gone. Mailer was haunted by the nightmare that the evils of the present not only exploited the present, but consumed the past, and gave every promise of demolishing whole territories of the future. The same villains who, promiscuously, wantonly, heedlessly, had gorged on LSD and consumed God knows what essential marrows of history, wearing indeed the history of all eras on their back as trophies of this gluttony, were now going forth (conscience-struck?) to make war on those other villains, corporation-land villains, who were destroying the promise of the present in their self-righteousness and greed and secret lust (often unknown to themselves) for some sexo-technological variety of neo-fascism.[7]

Mailer's final allegiance, however, was with the villains who were hippies. They would never have looked to blow their minds and destroy some part of the past if the authority had not brainwashed the mood of the present until it smelled like deodorant. (To cover the odor of burning flesh in Vietnam?) So he continued to enjoy the play of costumes, but his pleasure was now edged with a hint of the sinister. Not inappropriate for battle. He and Lowell,[8] were still in the best of moods. The morning was so splendid— it spoke of a vitality in nature which no number of bombings in space nor innerspace might ever subdue; the rustle of costumes warming up for the war spoke of future redemptions as quickly as they reminded of hog-swillings from the past, and the thin air! wine of Civil War apples in the October air! edge of excitement and awe—how would this day end? No one could know. Incredible spectacle now gathering—tens of thousands traveling hundreds of miles to attend a symbolic battle. In the capital of technology land beat a primitive drum. New drum of the Left! And the Left had been until this year the secret unwitting accomplice of every increase in the power of the technicians, bureaucrats, and labor leaders who ran the governmental military-industrial complex of super-technology land....

6: A Confrontation by the River

It was not much of a situation to study. The MPs stood in two widely spaced ranks. The first rank was ten yards behind the rope, and each MP in that row was close to twenty feet from the next man. The second rank, similarly spaced, was ten yards behind the first rank and perhaps thirty yards behind them a cluster appeared, every fifty yards or so, of two or three U.S. Marshals in white helmets and dark blue suits. They were out there waiting. Two moods confronted one another, two separate senses of a private silence.

[7]A new or recent form of fascism, a type of right-wing dictatorship.

[8]Robert Lowell, major American poet (1917–1977).

It was not unlike being a boy about to jump from one garage roof to an adjoining garage roof. The one thing not to do was wait. Mailer looked at Macdonald[9] and Lowell. "Let's go," he said. Not looking again at them, not pausing to gather or dissipate resolve, he made a point of stepping neatly and decisively over the low rope. Then he headed across the grass to the nearest MP he saw.

It was as if the air had changed, or light had altered; he felt immediately much more alive—yes, bathed in air—and yet disembodied from himself, as if indeed he were watching himself in a film where this action was taking place. He could feel the eyes of the people behind the rope watching him, could feel the intensity of their existence as spectators. And as he walked forward, he and the MP looked at one another with the naked stricken lucidity which comes when absolute strangers are for the moment absolutely locked together.

The MP lifted his club to his chest as if to bar all passage. To Mailer's great surprise—he had secretly expected the enemy to be calm and strong, why should they not? they had every power, all the guns—to his great surprise, the MP was trembling. He was a young Negro, part white, who looked to have come from some small town where perhaps there were not many other Negroes; he had at any rate no Harlem smoke, no devil swish, no black, no black power for him, just a simple boy in an Army suit with a look of horror in his eye, "Why, why did it have to happen to me?" was the message of the petrified marbles in his face.

"Go back," he said hoarsely to Mailer.

"If you don't arrest me, I'm going to the Pentagon."

"No. Go back."

The thought of a return—"since they won't arrest me, what can I do?"—over these same ten yards was not at all suitable.

As the MP spoke, the raised club quivered. He did not know if it quivered from the desire of the MP to strike him, or secret military wonder was he now possessed of a moral force which implanted terror in the arms of young soldiers? Some unfamiliar current, now gyroscopic, now a sluggish whirlpool, was evolving from that quiver of the club, and the MP seemed to turn slowly away from his position confronting the rope, and the novelist turned with him, each still facing the other until the axis of their shoulders was now perpendicular to the rope, and still they kept turning in this psychic field, not touching, the club quivering, and then Mailer was behind the MP, he was free of him, and he wheeled around and kept going in a half run to the next line of MPs and then on the push of a sudden instinct, sprinted suddenly around the nearest MP in the second line, much as if he were a back cutting around the nearest man in the secondary to break free—that was actually his precise thought—and had a passing perception of how simple it was to get past the MPs. They looked petrified. Stricken faces as he went by. They

[9]Dwight Macdonald, major American critic (1906–1982).

did not know what to do. It was his dark pinstripe suit, his vest, the maroon and blue regimental tie, the part in his hair, the barrel chest, the early paunch—he must have looked like a banker himself, a banker, gone ape! And then he saw the Pentagon to his right across the field, not a hundred yards away, and a little to his left, the marshals, and he ran on a jog toward them, and came up, and they glared at him and shouted, "Go back."

He had a quick impression of hard-faced men with gray eyes burning some transparent fuel for flame, and said, "I won't go back. If you don't arrest me, I'm going on to the Pentagon," and knew he meant it, some absolute certainty had come to him, and then two of them leaped on him at once in the cold clammy murderous fury of all cops at the existential moment of making their bust—all cops who secretly expect to be struck at that instant for their sins—and a supervising force came to his voice, and he roared, to his own distant pleasure in new achievement and new authority—"Take your hands off me, can't you see? I'm not resisting arrest," and one then let go of him, and the other stopped trying to pry his arm into a lock, and contented himself with a hard hand under his armpit, and they set off walking across the field at a rabid intent quick rate, walking parallel to the wall of the Pentagon, fully visible on his right at last, and he was arrested, he had succeeded in that, and without a club on his head, the mountain air in his lungs as thin and fierce as smoke, yes, the livid air of tension on this livid side promised a few events of more interest than the routine wait to be free, yes he was more than a visitor, he was in the land of the enemy now, he would get to see their face. . . .

But now a tall U.S. Marshal who had the body and insane look of a very good rangy defensive end in professional football—that same hard high-muscled build, same coiled spring of wrath, same livid conviction that everything opposing the team must be wrecked, sod, turf, grass, uniforms, helmets, bodies, yes even bite the football if it will help—now leaped into the truck and jumped between them. "Shut up," he said, "or I'll wreck both of you." He had a long craggy face somewhere in the physiognomical land between Steve McQueen and Robert Mitchum, but he would never have made Hollywood, for his skin was pocked with the big boiling craters of a red lunar acne, and his eyes in Cinemascope would have blazed an audience off their seat for such gray-green flame could only have issued from a blowtorch. Under his white Marshal's helmet, he was one impressive piece of gathered wrath.

Speaking to the Marshal at this point would have been dangerous. The Marshal's emotions had obviously been marinating for a week in the very special bile waters American Patriotism reserves for its need. His feelings were now caustic as a whip—too gentle the simile!—he was in agonies of frustration because the honor of his profession kept him from battering every prisoner's head to a Communist pulp. Mailer looked him over covertly to see what he could try if the Marshal went to work on him. All reports: negative. He would not stand a chance with this Marshal—there seemed no place to hit him where he'd be vulnerable; stone larynx, leather testicles, ice cubes for eyes. And he had his Marshal's club in his hand as well. Brother! Bring back the Nazi!

Whether the Marshal had been once in the Marine Corps, or in Vietnam, or if half his family were now in Vietnam, or if he just hated the sheer New York presumption of that slovenly, drug-ridden weak contaminating America-hating army of termites outside this fortress' walls, he was certainly any upstanding demonstrator's nightmare. Because he was full of American rectitude and was fearless, and savage, savage as the exhaust left in the wake of a motorcycle club, gasoline and cheap perfume were one end of his spectrum, yeah, this Marshal loved action, but he was also in that no man's land between the old frontier and the new ranch home—as they, yes *they*—the enemies of the Marshal—tried to pass bills to limit the purchase of hunting rifles, so did *they* try to kill America, inch by inch, all the forces of evil, disorder, mess and chaos in the world, and *cowardice!* and city ways, and slick shit, and despoliation of national resources, all the subtle invisible creeping paralyses of Communism which were changing America from a land where blood was red to a land where water was foul—yes in this Marshal's mind—no lesser explanation could suffice for the Knight of God light in the flame of his eye—the evil was without, America was threatened by a foreign disease and the Marshal was threatened to the core of his sanity by any one of the first fifty of Mailer's ideas which would insist that the evil was within, that the best in America was being destroyed by what in itself seemed next best, yes American heroism corrupted by American know-how—no wonder murder stood out in his face as he looked at the novelist—for the Marshal to lose his sanity was no passing psychiatric affair: think rather of a rifleman on a tower in Texas and a score of his dead on the street.[10] . . .

It may be obvious by now that a history of the March on the Pentagon which is not unfair will never be written, any more than a history which could prove dependable in details!

As it grew dark there was the air of carnival as well. The last few thousand Marchers to arrive from Lincoln Memorial did not even bother to go to the North Parking Area, but turned directly to the Mall and were cheered by the isolated detachments who saw them from a ledge of the wall at the plaza. Somewhere, somebody lit his draft card, and as it began to burn he held it high. The light of the burning card traveled through the crowd until it found another draft card someone else was ready to burn and this was lit, and then another in the distance. In the gathering dark it looked like a dusting of fireflies over the great shrub of the Mall.

By now, however, the way was open again to the North Parking. The chartered buses were getting ready to leave. That portion of this revolution which was Revolution on Excursion Ticket was now obliged to leave. Where once there had been thirty thousand people in the Mall, there were now

---

[10]A reference to Charles Whitman, who shot numerous pedestrians from atop a Texas clock tower on August 1, 1966.

suddenly twenty thousand people, ten thousand people, less. As the busses ground through the interlockings of their gears and pulled out into a mournful wheezing acceleration along the road, so did other thousands on the Mall look at one another and decide it was probably time to catch a cab or take the long walk back to Washington—they were in fact hungry for a meal. So the Mall began to empty, and the demonstrators on the steps must have drawn a little closer. The mass assault was over.

A few thousand, however, were left, and they were the best. The civil disobedience might be far from done. On the Mall, since the oncoming night was cold, bonfires were lit. On the stairs, a peace pipe was passed. It was filled with hashish. Soon the demonstrators were breaking out marijuana, handing it back and forth, offering it even to the soldiers here and there. The Army after all had been smoking marijuana since Korea, and in Vietnam—by all reports—were gorging on it. The smell of the drug, sweet as the sweetest leaves of burning tea, floated down to the Mall where its sharp bite of sugar and smoldering grass pinched the nose, relaxed the neck. Soon most of the young on the Mall were smoking as well. Can this be one of the moments when the Secretary of Defense looks out from his window in the Pentagon at the crowd on the Mall and studies their fires below? They cannot be unreminiscent of other campfires in Washington and Virginia little more than a century ago.[11]

... this passage through the night was a rite of passage, and these disenchanted heirs of the Old Left, this rabble of American Vietcong, and hippies, and pacifists, and whoever else was left were afloat on a voyage whose first note had been struck with the first sound of the trumpet Mailer had heard crossing Washington Monument in the morning. "Come here, come here, come here," the trumpet had said, and now eighteen hours later, in the false dawn, the echo of far greater rites of passage in American history, the light reflected from the radiance of greater more heroic hours may have come nonetheless to shine along the inner space and the caverns of the freaks, some hint of a glorious future may have hung in the air, some refrain from all the great American rites of passage when men and women manacled themselves to a lost and painful principle and survived a day, a night, a week, a month, a year, a celebration of Thanksgiving—the country had been founded on a rite of passage. Very few had not emigrated here without the echo of that rite, even if it were no more (and no less!) than eight days in the stink, bustle, fear, and propinquity of steerage on an ocean crossing (or the eighty days of dying on a slave ship) each generation of Americans had forged their own rite, in the forest of the Alleghenies and the Adirondacks, at Valley Forge, at New Orleans in 1812, with Rogers and Clark or at Sutter's Mill, at Gettysburg, the Alamo, the Klondike, the Argonne, Normandy, Pusan,[12]—the engagement at the Pentagon was a pale rite of passage next

---

[11]An allusion to the Civil War.
[12]References to various major American battles and explorations.

to these, and yet it was probably a true one, for it came to the spoiled children of a dead de-animalized middle class who had chosen most freely, out of the incomprehensible mysteries of moral choice, to make an attack and then hold a testament before the most authoritative embodiment of the principle that America was right, America was might, America was the true religious war of Christ against the Communist. So it became a rite of passage for these tender drug-vitiated jargon-mired children, they endured through a night, a black dark night which began in joy, near foundered in terror, and dragged on through empty apathetic hours while glints of light came to each alone. Yet the rite of passage was invoked, the moral ladder was climbed, they were forever different in the morning than they had been before the night, which is the meaning of a rite of passage, one has voyaged through a channel of shipwreck and temptation, and so some of the vices carried from another nether world into life itself (on the day of one's birth) may have departed, or fled, or quit; some part of the man has been born again, and is better, just as some hardly so remarkable area of the soul may have been in some miniscule sweet fashion reborn on the crossing of the marchers over Arlington Memorial Bridge, for the worst of them and the most timid were moving nonetheless to a confrontation they could only fear, they were going to the land of the warmakers. Not so easy for the timid when all is said.

11: The Metaphor Delivered

Whole crisis of Christianity in America that the military heroes were on one side, and the unnamed saints on the other! Let the bugle blow. The death of America rides in on the smog. America—the land where a new kind of man was born from the idea that God was present in every man not only as compassion but as power, and so the country belonged to the people; for the will of the people—if the locks of their life could be given the art to turn—was then the will of God. Great and dangerous idea! If the locks did not turn, then the will of the people was the will of the Devil. Who by now could know where was what? Liars controlled the locks.

Brood on that country who expresses our will. She is America, once a beauty of magnificence unparalleled, now a beauty with a leprous skin. She is heavy with child—no one knows if legitimate—and languishes in a dungeon whose walls are never seen. Now the first contractions of her fearsome labor begin—it will go on: no doctor exists to tell the hour. It is only known that false labor is not likely on her now, no, she will probably give birth, and to what?—the most fearsome totalitarianism the world has ever known? or can she, poor giant, tormented lovely girl, deliver a babe of a new world brave and tender, artful and wild? Rush to the locks. God writhes in his bonds. Rush to the locks. Deliver us from our curse. For we must end on the road to that mystery where courage, death, and the dream of love give promise of sleep.

1968

ROBERT BLY

B. 1926

Few American poets have explored so many facets of the creative—and the human—experience as Robert Bly. After graduating from Harvard, he returned to the Minnesota of his childhood and became one of the leading midcentury poets. Along with James Wright and William Stafford, Bly was one of the preeminent poets of nature, simplicity, and the reality of human experience. In a line of descent from William Carlos Williams, with overtones of the exact language drawn from Wallace Stevens, these poets forced readers back to an encounter with the truly human that had sometimes been obscured in the highly formalist poetry of Richard Eberhart, Richard Wilbur, and even Robert Lowell. Despite his geographically remote location, Bly influenced what was happening in United States poetry through his editing of a series of respected (if idiosyncratic) little magazines—first *The Fifties*, then *The Sixties*. His reviews, signed "Crunk," were read avidly.

Like Williams before him, Bly assumed a posture of stability: his address didn't change, his keen appreciation for the poetry of others was a given, and he was open to friendships with people who might have been seen as his competitors—such as his relationship with James Wright. Also, like the best of the world's poets, Bly was immensely influential in bringing readers, as well as other poets, to appreciate the work of non-English writers. From early in his career through the present, Bly has translated, published, and proselytized about the writings of Vallejo, Neruda, Machado, Jimánez, Rilke, Ponge, Tranströmer, Lagerlöf, Kabir, and (since his translations in 1981) Maulana Jalal al-Din Rumi, a thirteenth-century Persian poet.

Bly's poetry became one of search. Not only was he poised to become a leading poet for ecological preservation—given his immersion in the beauties and violence of the natural world—but he was intent on finding the richest poetic traditions from which to draw. His skill with translating was enhanced by his willingness to work with native speakers or scholars of the languages of the poems: Bly's contributions to what the art of translation could become have yet to be appreciated. But what gave Bly's career its most public visibility was U.S. involvement in the Vietnam conflict. Two of his best-known poems— "Counting Small-Boned Bodies," which stresses the macho superiority of U.S. physical size dominating the stature of the Vietnamese soldiers, and "The Teeth Mother Naked at Last," which presents his Jungian understanding of the divided female principle, welcoming mother set against destructive female—were published as antiwar works. With Denise Levertov, Muriel Rukeyser, and many other writers, Bly was an active proponent of Writers and Artists against the Vietnam War.

Bly's later publishing history continues to promote the psychological exploration of the human consciousness. His poetry, as well as his series of popular books that began with *Iron John* in 1990, insists on the ways men (in this stridently gendered world) must come to terms with their conflicted—or, perhaps, richly ambivalent—psyches. As a spokesperson for the archetypal, the Jungian, and the mystical, Bly travels and speaks widely: he may well be America's most visible poet. Such visibility draws mixed responses, but at heart Robert Bly continues to be the poet we welcomed so heartily at the time of the publication of his first collection, *Silence in the Snowy Fields*.

Linda Wagner-Martin
University of North Carolina at Chapel Hill

PRIMARY WORKS

Silence in the Snowy Fields, 1962; *The Light around the Body*, 1967; *Forty Poems Touching on Recent American History*, 1970; *The Sea and the Honeycomb*, 1971; *Jumping out of Bed*, 1973; *Sleepers Joining Hands*, 1973; *For the Stomach: Selected Poems*, 1974; *Old Man Rubbing His Eyes*, 1975; *The Morning Glory*, 1975; *This Body Is Made of Camphor and Gopherwood*, 1977; *The Kabir Book*, 1977; *This Tree Will Be Here for a Thousand Years*, 1979; *News of the Universe*, 1980; *Talking All Morning*, 1980; *The Man in the Black Coat Turns*, 1981; *Loving a Woman in Two Worlds*, 1985; *Selected Poems*, 1986; *American Poetry: Wilderness and Domesticity*, 1990; *Iron John: A Book about Men*, 1990; *What Have I Ever Lost by Dying: Collected Prose Poems*, 1992; *Gratitude to Old Teachers*, 1993; *Meditations on the Insatiable Soul*, 1994; *The Sibling Society*, 1996; *Morning Poems*, 1997; *Holes the Crickets Have Eaten in Blankets: A Sequence of Poems*, 1997; *The Maiden King: The Reunion of Masculine and Feminine*, 1998; *Eating the Honey of Words*, 1999; *The Night Abraham Called to the Stars*, 2001; *My Sentence Was a Thousand Years of Joy*, 2005; *The Urge to Travel Long Distances*, 2005; *Turkish Pears in August*, 2007; *Talking into the Ear of a Donkey: Poems*, 2011.

Counting Small-Boned Bodies

Let's count the bodies over again.

If we could only make the bodies smaller,
The size of skulls,
We could make a whole plain white with skulls in the moonlight!

If we could only make the bodies smaller,
Maybe we could get   5
A whole year's kill in front of us on a desk!

If we could only make the bodies smaller,
We could fit
A body into a finger-ring, for a keepsake forever.   10

1967

The Teeth Mother Naked at Last

I

Massive engines lift beautifully from the deck.
Wings appear over the trees, wings with eight hundred rivets.

Engines burning a thousand gallons of gasoline a minute sweep over
    the huts with dirt floors.

The chickens feel the new fear deep in the pits of their beaks.
Buddha with Padma Sambhava.   5

Meanwhile, out on the China Sea,
immense gray bodies are floating,
born in Roanoke,
the ocean on both sides expanding, "buoyed on the dense marine."

Helicopters flutter overhead. The death-   10
bee is coming. Super Sabres
like knots of neurotic energy sweep
around and return.
This is Hamilton's triumph.
This is the advantage of a centralized bank.   15
B-52s come from Guam. All the teachers
die in flames. The hopes of Tolstoy fall asleep in the ant heap.
Do not ask for mercy.

Now the time comes to look into the past-tunnels,
the hours given and taken in school,   20
the scuffles in coatrooms,
foam leaps from his nostrils,
now we come to the scum you take from the mouths of the dead,
now we sit beside the dying, and hold their hands, there is hardly time
    for good-bye,
the staff sergeant from North Carolina is dying—you hold his hand, 25
he knows the mansions of the dead are empty, he has an empty place
inside him, created one night when his parents came home drunk,
he uses half his skin to cover it,
as you try to protect a balloon from sharp objects . . .

Artillery shells explode. Napalm canisters roll end over end.   30
800 steel pellets fly through the vegetable walls.
The six-hour infant puts his fists instinctively to his eyes to keep out
    the light.
But the room explodes,

the children explode.
Blood leaps on the vegetable walls.   35

Yes, I know, blood leaps on the walls—
Don't cry at that—
Do you cry at the wind pouring out of Canada?
Do you cry at the reeds shaken at the edge of the sloughs?
The Marine battalion enters.   40
This happens when the seasons change,
This happens when the leaves begin to drop from the trees too early
"Kill them: I don't want to see anything moving."
This happens when the ice begins to show its teeth in the ponds
This happens when the heavy layers of lake water press down on the   45
    fish's head, and send him deeper, where his tail swirls slowly, and
    his brain passes him pictures of heavy reeds, of vegetation fallen
    on vegetation....
Hamilton saw all this in detail:

"Every banana tree slashed, every cooking utensil smashed, every
    mattress cut."

Now the Marine knives sweep around like sharp-edged jets; how
    beautifully they slash open the rice bags,
the mattresses ...
ducks are killed with $150 shotguns.   50

Old women watch the soldiers as they move.

II

Excellent Roman knives slip along the ribs.

A stronger man starts to jerk up the strips of flesh.

"Let's hear it again, you believe in the Father, the Son, and the Holy Ghost?"

A long scream unrolls.   55

More.

"From the political point of view, democratic institutions are being built
    in Vietnam, wouldn't you agree?"

A green parrot shudders under the fingernails.
Blood jumps in the pocket.
The scream lashes like a tail.   60

"Let us not be deterred from our task by the voices of dissent...."

The whines of the jets
pierce like a long needle.

As soon as the President finishes his press conference, black wings
    carry off the words,
bits of flesh still clinging to them.   65

The ministers lie, the professors lie, the television lies, the priests
    lie....
These lies mean that the country wants to die.
Lie after lie starts out into the prairie grass,
like enormous caravans of Conestoga wagons....

And a long desire for death flows out, guiding the enormous caravans 70
    from beneath,
stringing together the vague and foolish words.
It is a desire to eat death,
to gobble it down,
to rush on it like a cobra with mouth open

It's a desire to take death inside,   75
to feel it burning inside, pushing out velvety hairs,
like a clothes brush in the intestines—

This is the thrill that leads the President on to lie

Now the Chief Executive enters; the press conference begins:
First the President lies about the date the Appalachian Mountains rose. 80
Then he lies about the population of Chicago, then he lies about the
    weight of the adult eagle, then about the acreage of the Everglades

He lies about the number of fish taken every year in the Arctic, he has
    private information about which city *is* the capital of Wyoming, he
    lies about the birthplace of Attila the Hun.

He lies about the composition of the amniotic fluid, and he insists
    that Luther was never a German, and that only the Protestants sold
    indulgences,

That Pope Leo X *wanted* to reform the church, but the "liberal
    elements" prevented him,
that the Peasants' War was fomented by Italians from the North. 85

And the Attorney General lies about the time the sun sets.

These lies are only the longing we all feel to die.
It is the longing for someone to come and take you by the hand to
    where they all are sleeping:
where the Egyptian pharaohs are asleep, and your own mother,
and all those disappeared children, who used to go around with you   90
    in the rings at grade school.....

Do not be angry at the President—he is longing to take in his hand
the locks of death hair—
to meet his own children dead, or unborn....
He is drifting sideways toward the dusty places

III

This is what it's like for a rich country to make war   95
this is what it's like to bomb huts (afterwards described as "structures")
this is what it's like to kill marginal farmers (afterwards described as
    "Communists")

this is what it's like to watch the altimeter needle going mad

*Baron 25, this is 81. Are there any friendlies in the area? 81 from 25,
negative on the friendlies. I'd like you to take out as many structures
as possible located in those trees within 200 meters east and west of
my smoke mark.*

diving, the green earth swinging, cheeks hanging back, red pins   100
    blossoming ahead of us, 20-millimeter cannon fire, leveling off, rice
    fields shooting by like telephone poles, smoke rising, hut roofs
    loom up huge as landing fields, slugs going in, half the huts on fire,
    small figures running, palm trees burning, shooting past, up again; ...
    blue sky ... cloud mountains

This is what it's like to have a gross national product.

It's because the aluminum window shade business is doing so well in
    the United States that we roll fire over entire villages
It's because a hospital room in the average American city now costs
    $90 a day that we bomb hospitals in the North

It's because the milk trains coming into New Jersey hit the right
    switches every day that the best Vietnamese men are cut in two by
    American bullets that follow each other like freight cars

This is what it's like to send firebombs down from air-conditioned   105
    cockpits.

This is what it's like to be told to fire into a reed hut with an
    automatic weapon.

It's because we have new packaging for smoked oysters that bomb
    holes appear in the rice paddies

It is because we have so few women sobbing in back rooms,
because we have so few children's heads torn apart by high-velocity
    bullets,
Because we have so few tears falling on our own hands   110
    that the Super Sabre turns and screams down toward the earth.

It's because taxpayers move to the suburbs that we transfer
    populations.
The Marines use cigarette lighters to light the thatched roofs of huts
because so many Americans own their own homes.

IV

I see a car rolling toward a rock wall.   115
The treads in the face begin to crack.
We all feel like tires being run down roads under heavy cars.

The teen-ager imagines herself floating through the Seven Spheres.
Oven doors are found
open.   120
Soot collects over the doorframe, has children, takes courses,
goes mad, and dies.

There is a black silo inside our bodies, revolving fast.
Bits of black paint are flaking off,
where the motorcycles roar, around and around,   125
rising higher on the silo walls,
the bodies bent toward the horizon,
driven by angry women dressed in black.

* * *

I know that books are tired of us.
I *know* they are chaining the Bible to chairs.   130
Books don't want to remain in the same room with us anymore.

New Testaments are escaping ... dressed as women ... they go off
    after dark.
And Plato! Plato ... Plato wants to go backwards....
He wants to hurry back up the river of time, so he can end as some
    blob of sea flesh rotting on an Australian beach.

V

Why are they dying? I have written this so many times.   135
They are dying because the President has opened a Bible again.
They are dying because gold deposits have been found among the
    Shoshoni Indians.

They are dying because money follows intellect!
And intellect is like a fan opening in the wind—

The Marines think that unless they die the rivers will not move.   140
They are dying so that the mountain shadows will continue to fall east
    in the afternoon,
so that the beetle can move along the ground near the fallen twigs.

VI

But if one of those children came near that we have set on fire,
came toward you like a gray barn, walking,
you would howl like a wind tunnel in a hurricane,   145
you would tear at your shirt with blue hands,
you would drive over your own child's wagon trying to back up,
the pupils of your eyes would go wild—

If a child came by burning, you would dance on a lawn,
trying to leap into the air, digging into your cheeks,   150
you would ram your head against the wall of your bedroom
like a bull penned too long in his moody pen—

If one of those children came toward me with both hands
in the air, fire rising along both elbows,
I would suddenly go back to my animal brain,   155
I would drop on all fours, screaming,
my vocal chords would turn blue, so would yours,
it would be two days before I could play with my own children again.

VII

I want to sleep awhile in the rays of the sun slanting over the snow.
Don't wake me.   160
Don't tell me how much grief there is in the leaf with its natural oils.
Don't tell me how many children have been born with stumpy hands
    all those years we lived in St. Augustine's shadow.

Tell me about the dust that falls from the yellow daffodil shaken in
    the restless winds.
Tell me about the particles of Babylonian thought that still pass
    through the earthworm every day.
Don't tell me about "the frightening laborers who do not read books." 165

Now the whole nation starts to whirl,
the end of the Republic breaks off,
Europe comes to take revenge,
the mad beast covered with European hair rushes through the mesa
    bushes in Mendocino County,
pigs rush toward the cliff,   170
the waters underneath part: in one ocean luminous globes float up
    (in them hairy and ecstatic men—)
in the other, the teeth mother, naked at last.

Let us drive cars
up
the light beams   175
to the stars . . .

And return to earth crouched inside the drop of sweat
that falls
from the chin of the Protestant tied in the fire.

1970

YUSEF KOMUNYAKAA
B. 1947

Born in Bogalusa, Louisiana, the oldest of five children, Komunyakaa is the son of a carpenter and of a mother who bought a set of encyclopedias for her children. When he was sixteen, he discovered James Baldwin's essays and decided to become a writer.

From 1965 to 1968, Komunyakaa served a tour of duty in Vietnam as an information specialist, editing a military newspaper called the *Southern Cross*. In Vietnam he won the Bronze Star. After military service, he enrolled at the University of Colorado (double major in English and sociology) and began writing poetry. Upon graduation in 1980, he studied further at both Colorado State University (where he received an M.A. in creative writing) and the University of California, Irvine (where he received an M.F.A.) and taught at various universities before moving to New Orleans. In 1985, while teaching at the University of New Orleans, he married Australian novelist Mandy Sayer. Only then, nearly twenty years after his Vietnam experiences, did Komunyakaa write his important war poems, published in 1988 as *Dien Cai Dau*.

The violence of war, the pain of identifying with the Vietnamese, and the anguish of returning to the United States had seldom been so eloquently and hauntingly expressed. By 1994, when these poems were included in *Neon Vernacular: New and Selected Poems, 1977–1989*, Komunyakaa had won two creative writing fellowships from the National Endowment for the Arts and the San Francisco Poetry Center Award and had held the Lilly Professorship of Poetry at Indiana University. *Neon Vernacular* received the Pulitzer Prize for Poetry, as well as the Kingsley-Tufts Poetry Award from the Claremont Graduate School, leading to a reevaluation of his earlier eight collections of work.

In 1998 his poetry collection *Thieves of Paradise* was a finalist for the 1999 National Book Critics Circle Award, and that same year saw the publication of his recording, *Love Notes from the Madhouse*. In 2000 Radicloni Clytus edited a book of Komunyakaa's prose, *Blue Notes: Essays, Interviews, and Commentaries*, as part of a series published by the University of Michigan Press. In an essay from that collection, "Control Is the Mainspring," the poet writes, "I learned that the body and the mind are indeed connected: good writing is physical and mental. I welcomed the knowledge of this because I am from a working-class people who believe that physical labor is sacred and spiritual." This combination of the realistic and the spiritual runs throughout Komunyakaa's poems, whether they are about his childhood, the father-son relationship, the spiritual journey each of us takes—alone, and in whatever circumstances life hands us—or the various conflicts of war. He has become an important poet for our times.

Linda Wagner-Martin
University of North Carolina at Chapel Hill

PRIMARY WORKS

Dedications and Other Darkhorses, 1977; *Lost in the Bonewheel Factory*, 1979; *Copacetic*, 1984; *I Apologize for the Eyes in My Head*, 1986; *Toys in the Field*, 1987; *Dien Cai Dau*, 1988; *February in Sydney*, 1989; *Magic City*, 1992; *Neon Vernacular*, 1994; *Thieves of Paradise*, 1998; *Blue Notes: Essays, Interviews, and Commentaries*, ed. Radicloni Clytus, 2000; *Talking Dirty to the Gods*, 2000; *Pleasure Dome*, 2000; *Taboo*, 2004; *Gilgamesh*, 2006; *Warhorses*, 2008; *The Chameleon Couch*, 2011.

Tu Do Street[1]

Music divides the evening.
I close my eyes & can see
men drawing lines in the dust.
America pushes through the membrane
of mist & smoke, & I'm a small boy   5
again in Bogalusa.[2] *White Only*
signs & Hank Snow.[3] But tonight
I walk into a place where bar girls
fade like tropical birds. When
I order a beer, the mama-san   10
behind the counter acts as if she
can't understand, while her eyes
skirt each white face, as Hank Williams[4]
calls from the psychedelic jukebox.
We have played Judas where   15
only machine-gun fire brings us
together. Down the street
black GIs hold to their turf also.
An off-limits sign pulls me
deeper into alleys, as I look   20
for a softness behind these voices
wounded by their beauty & war.
Back in the bush at Dak To[5]
& Khe Sanh,[6] we fought
the brothers of these women   25
we now run to hold in our arms.
There's more than a nation
inside us, as black & white
soldiers touch the same lovers
minutes apart, tasting   30
each other's breath,
without knowing these rooms
run into each other like tunnels
leading to the underworld.

1988

[1]Street packed with bars and brothels at the center of Saigon, capital of South Vietnam; American Army headquarters during the Vietnam War, 1956–1975.

[2]The Louisiana town where the poet grew up.

[3]Country singer on Nashville's *Grand Ole Opry* program.

[4]American composer, singer, guitarist; one of the most influential figures in country music.

[5]Site of one of the most violent battles of the war in November 1967; located in northwest South Vietnam.

[6]Location of U.S. Marine base near the Laotian border; attacked by North Vietnamese Army on January 21, 1968, and kept under siege until April 7.

Prisoners

Usually at the helipad
I see them stumble-dance
across the hot asphalt
with crokersacks over their heads,
moving toward the interrogation huts,   5
thin-framed as box kites
of sticks & black silk
anticipating a hard wind
that'll tug & snatch them
out into space. I think   10
some must be laughing
under their dust-colored hoods,
knowing rockets are aimed
at Chu Lai[1]—that the water's
evaporating & soon the nail   15
will make contact with metal.
How can anyone anywhere love
these half-broken figures
bent under the sky's brightness?
The weight they carry   20
is the soil we tread night & day.
Who can cry for them?
I've heard the old ones
are the hardest to break.
An arm twist, a combat boot   25
against the skull, a .45
jabbed into the mouth, nothing
works. When they start talking
with ancestors faint as camphor
smoke in pagodas, you know   30
you'll have to kill them
to get an answer.
Sunlight throws
scythes against the afternoon.
Everything's a heat mirage; a river   35
tugs at their slow feet.
I stand alone & amazed,
with a pill-happy door gunner
signaling for me to board the Cobra.[2]

[1]Northern coastal town fifty miles south of   [2]Type of U.S. helicopter.
Danang; in 1965, the site of a major U.S. am-
phibious operation.

I remember how one day 40
I almost bowed to such figures
walking toward me, under
a corporal's ironclad stare.
I can't say why.
From a half-mile away 45
trees huddle together,
& the prisoners look like
marionettes hooked to strings of light.

1988

Thanks

Thanks for the tree
between me & a sniper's bullet.
I don't know what made the grass
sway seconds before the Viet Cong
raised his soundless rifle. 5
Some voice always followed,
telling me which foot
to put down first.
Thanks for deflecting the ricochet
against that anarchy of dusk. 10
I was back in San Francisco
wrapped up in a woman's wild colors,
causing some dark bird's love call
to be shattered by daylight
when my hands reached up 15
& pulled a branch away
from my face. Thanks
for the vague white flower
that pointed to the gleaming metal
reflecting how it is to be broken 20
like mist over the grass,
as we played some deadly
game for blind gods.
What made me spot the monarch
writhing on a single thread 25
tied to a farmer's gate,
holding the day together
like an unfingered guitar string,
is beyond me. Maybe the hills
grew weary & leaned a little in the heat. 30
Again, thanks for the dud
hand grenade tossed at my feet

outside Chu Lai. I'm still
falling through its silence.
I don't know why the intrepid   35
sun touched the bayonet,
but I know that something
stood among those lost trees
& moved only when I moved.

                                                                  1988

Facing It

My black face fades,
hiding inside the black granite.
I said I wouldn't,
dammit: No tears.
I'm stone. I'm flesh.   5
My clouded reflection eyes me
like a bird of prey, the profile of night
slanted against morning. I turn
this way—the stone lets me go.
I turn that way—I'm inside   10
the Vietnam Veterans Memorial
again, depending on the light
to make a difference.
I go down the 58,022 names,
half-expecting to find   15
my own in letters like smoke.
I touch the name Andrew Johnson;
I see the booby trap's white flash.
Names shimmer on a woman's blouse
but when she walks away   20
the names stay on the wall.
Brushstrokes flash, a red bird's
wings cutting across my stare.
The sky. A plane in the sky.
A white vet's image floats   25
closer to me, then his pale eyes
look through mine. I'm a window.
He's lost his right arm
inside the stone. In the black mirror
a woman's trying to erase names: 30
No, she's brushing a boy's hair.

                                                                  1988

Fog Galleon

Horse-headed clouds, flags
& pennants tied to black
Smokestacks in swamp mist.
From the quick green calm
Some nocturnal bird calls   5
Ship ahoy, ship ahoy!
I press against the taxicab
Window. I'm back here, interfaced
With a dead phosphorescence;
The whole town smells   10
Like the world's oldest anger.
Scabrous residue hunkers down under
Sulfur & dioxide, waiting
For sunrise, like cargo
On a phantom ship outside Gaul.   15
Cool glass against my cheek
Pulls me from the black schooner
On a timeless sea—everything
Dwarfed beneath the papermill
Lights blinking behind the cloudy   20
Commerce of wheels, of chemicals
That turn workers into pulp
When they fall into vats
Of steamy serenity.

                                                        1993

■ DENISE LEVERTOV ■
1923–1997

Denise Levertov, one of America's foremost contemporary poets, was born in Essex, England; was privately educated except for ballet school and a wartime nursing program; served as a nurse during World War II; and emigrated to the United States in 1948. She taught at Vassar, Drew, City College of New York, M.I.T., Tufts, and Brandeis and retired as a full professor at Stanford University in 1994. Levertov was a scholar at the Radcliffe Institute for Independent Study; received the Lenore Marshall Poetry Prize, a Guggenheim Fellowship, and the Elmer Holmes Bobst Award; and was a member of the American Institute of Arts and Letters.

Levertov was influenced by the poetry and poetic theory of William Carlos Williams. Though she was earlier considered an aesthetic compatriot of some of the poets of the Black Mountain School, she did not consider herself part of any particular school of poetry. She brought her own unmistakably distinctive voice to poems concerned with several dimensions of the human experience: love, motherhood, nature, war, the nuclear arms race, mysticism, poetry, and the role of the poet. In her essay "Poetry, Prophecy, Survival," Levertov cites a William Carlos Williams verse: "It is difficult/to get news from poems/yet men die miserably every day/for lack/of what is found there." She tells us in this essay that people turn to poems for "some kind of illumination, for revelations that help them to survive, to survive in spirit not only in body." She believed that these revelations are usually not of strange or distant things but of what lies around us, unseen and forgotten—like "Flowers of Sophia" in her 1996 volume of poetry. And she believed that poems and/or dreams, as she poignantly muses in "Dream Instruction," can "illuminate what we feel but don't *know* we feel until it is articulated."

"Poetry, Prophecy, Survival" reiterates a theme that Levertov articulated on several occasions throughout her career: the poet or artist's call "to summon the divine." She speaks clearly of this "vocation" in "The Origins of a Poem" and "The Sense of Pilgrimage" essays in *The Poet in the World* (1973); in "On the Edge of Darkness: What Is Political Poetry?" in *Light up the Cave* (1981); and in "A Poet's View" (1984). Levertov's awareness of the truly awesome nature of the poet's task is evident in "A Poet's View":

> To believe, as an artist, in inspiration or the intuitive, to know that without Imagination ... no amount of acquired craft or scholarship or of brilliant reasoning will suffice, is to live with a door of one's life open to the transcendent, the numinous. Not every artist, clearly, acknowledges that fact—yet all, in the creative act, experience mystery. The concept of "inspiration" presupposes a power that enters the individual and is not a personal attribute; and it is linked to a view of the artist's life as one of obedience to a vocation.[1]

Levertov's poems, most notably those after *The Jacob's Ladder* in 1958, reflect her serious commitment to this concept. In "Dream Instruction," one observes the poet's sensitive awareness of the rich depth of her inheritance and the important influence of the "cultural ambiance" of her family—those other "travellers/gone into dark." The Hasidic ancestry of her father, Paul Levertoff, his being steeped in Jewish and, after his conversion, Christian scholarship and mysticism, and the Welsh intensity and lyric feeling for nature of her mother, Beatrice Levertoff, are significant parts of the poet's finest works.

An interest in humanitarian politics came early into Levertov's life. Her father was active in protesting Mussolini's invasion of Abyssinia, and both he and her sister Olga protested Britain's lack of support for Spain. Long before these events, her mother canvassed on behalf of the League of Nations Union, and all three worked on behalf of German and Austrian refugees from 1933 onward. (One is not surprised, then, to find among her later poems wrenching reflections on the Gulf War.) This strong familial blend of the mystical with a firm commitment to social issues undoubtedly contributed to Levertov's being placed in the American visionary tradition. Rather than deliberately attempting to

---

[1]See *New and Selected Essays*, 1992, p. 241.

integrate social and political themes with lyricism, her approach was to fuse them, believing as she did that they are not antithetical. As is evident in the poetry of her last years, though Levertov's range of subject matter remained by no means exclusively "engaged," she believed, as she tells us in "Making Peace," that "each act of living/[is] one of its words, each word/a vibration of light—facets/of the forming crystal." Thus, along with other poets such as Pablo Neruda and Muriel Rukeyser, she confronted the social and political issues of our time. Levertov was named the sixty-first winner of the Academy of American Poets Fellowship in 1995.

Joan F. Hallisey
Regis College

PRIMARY WORKS

The Double Image, 1946; *Here and Now*, 1957; *The Jacob's Ladder*, 1958; *Overland to the Islands*, 1958; *With Eyes at the Back of Our Heads*, 1959; *O Taste and See*, 1964; *The Sorrow Dance*, 1966; *Relearning the Alphabet*, 1970; *To Stay Alive*, 1971; *The Poet in the World*, 1973; *Footprints*, 1975; *The Freeing of the Dust*, 1975; *Life in the Forest*, 1978; *Collected Earlier Poems 1940–1960*, 1979; *Light Up the Cave*, 1981; *Candles in Babylon*, 1982; *Poems 1960–1967*, 1983; *Oblique Prayers*, 1984; *Breathing the Water*, 1987; *Poems 1968–1972*, 1987; *The Menaced World*, 1985; *A Door in the Hive*, 1989; *Batterers*, 1990; *Evening Train*, 1992; *New and Selected Essays*, 1992; *Tasserae: Memories and Suppositions*, 1995; *Sands in the Well*, 1996; *Stream & the Sapphire*, 1997; *The Great Unknowing*, 1999; *Poems 1972–1982*, 2001; *Selected Poems*, 2002.

Overheard over S. E. Asia

"White phosphorus, white phosphorus,
mechanical snow,
where are you falling?"

"I am falling impartially on roads and roofs,
on bamboo thickets, on people.   5
My name recalls rich seas on rainy nights,
each drop that hits the surface eliciting
luminous response from a million algae.
My name is a whisper of sequins. Ha!
Each of them is a disk of fire,   10
I am the snow that burns.
                    I fall
wherever men send me to fall—
but I prefer flesh, so smooth, so dense:
I decorate it in black, and seek   15
the bone."

The theater of war. Offstage
a cast of thousands weeping.

Left center, well-lit, a mound
of unburied bodies,   20

or parts of bodies. Right,
near some dead bamboo that serves as wings,

a whole body, on which
a splash of napalm is working.

Enter the Bride.   25

She has one breast, one eye,
half of her scalp is bald.

She hobbles towards center front.
Enter the Bridegroom,

a young soldier, thin, but without   30
visible wounds. He sees her.

Slowly at first, then faster and faster,
he begins to shudder, to shudder,

to ripple with shudders.   Curtain.

                                                                       1970

In Thai Binh (Peace) Province

for Muriel and Jane

I've used up all my film on bombed hospitals,
bombed village schools, the scattered
lemon-yellow cocoons at the bombed silk-factory,

and for the moment all my tears too
are used up, having seen today   5
yet another child with its feet blown off,
          a girl, this one, eleven years old,
patient and bewildered in her home, a fragile
small house of mud bricks among rice fields.

So I'll use my dry burning eyes   10
to photograph within me
dark sails of the river boats,
warm slant of afternoon light
apricot on the brown, swift, wide river,

village towers—church and pagoda—on the far shore,   15
and a boy and small bird both
perched, relaxed, on a quietly grazing
buffalo.   Peace within the
          long war.

It is that life, unhurried, sure, persistent,   20
I must bring home when I try to bring
the war home.
            Child, river, light.

Here the future, fabled bird
that has migrated away from America,   25
nests, and breeds, and sings,

common as any sparrow.

                               1974

Fragrance of Life, Odor of Death

All the while among
the rubble even, and in
the hospitals, among the wounded,
        not only beneath
        lofty clouds   5

                in temples
           by the shores of lotus-dreaming
           lakes

a fragrance:
flowers, incense, the earth-mist rising   10
of mild daybreak in the delta—good smell
of life.

It's in America
where no bombs ever
have screamed down smashing   15
the buildings, shredding the people's bodies,
tossing the fields of Kansas or Vermont or Maryland into
                          the air

to land wrong way up, a gash of earth-guts …
it's in America, everywhere, a faint seepage,   20
I smell death.

                     Hanoi–Boston–Maine, November 1972

A Poem at Christmas, 1972,
during the Terror-Bombing of North Vietnam

Now I have lain awake imagining murder.
At first my pockets were loaded with rocks, with knives,
wherever I ran windows smashed, but I was swift
                                        and unseen,
    I was saving the knives until I reached   5
certain men ...
        Yes, Kissinger's smile faded,
he clutched his belly, he reeled ...
But as the night
wore on, what I held   10
hidden—under a napkin perhaps,
    I as a waitress at the inaugural dinner—
was a container of napalm:
and as I threw it in Nixon's face
and his crowd leapt back from the flames with crude   15
                                        yells of horror,
and some came rushing to seize me:
    quick as thought I had ready
a round of those small bombs designed
to explode at the pressure of a small child's weight,   20
and these instantly
dealt with the feet of Nixon's friends and henchmen,
who fell in their own blood
while the foul smoke of his body-oils
blackened the hellish room ...   25
It was of no interest
to imagine further. Instead,
the scene recommenced.
Each time around, fresh details,
variations of place and weapon.   30
All night to imagining murder.
O, to kill
the killers!

It is
to this extremity   35

the infection of their evil

thrusts us ...

1974

LE LY HAYSLIP
B. 1949

Le Ly Hayslip, born in 1949 as Phung Thi Le Ly in the village of Ky La, South Vietnam, is a memoirist. Hayslip married an American engineer in 1972, during the waning days of U.S. involvement in Vietnam, and emigrated to the United States. She wrote two autobiographical books, *When Heaven and Earth Changed Places* (1989) and *Child of War, Woman of Peace* (1993), which were published when memories of the divisive Vietnam War were still vivid for many Americans. Though American authors had produced a voluminous literature about Vietnam, it was centered on the experiences of Americans and of men. Hayslip addressed the silences in this literature by speaking from the perspective of a Vietnamese woman. In doing so, she became the first Vietnamese American writer to gain national prominence.

When Heaven and Earth Changed Places, cowritten with Jay Wurts, established her reputation. The book is a highly readable account that intercuts stories of Hayslip's youth in South Vietnam with a narrative about her eventual return to a reunified Vietnam in 1986. Hayslip's life was influenced both by French colonization, which ended in 1954, and by the conflict that the Vietnamese call the American War (1964–1973). As a young peasant girl in the south, Hayslip finds herself caught between the guerrilla forces of the National Liberation Front, commonly known as the Vietcong, and the U.S. Army with its South Vietnamese allies. After fleeing the war-torn countryside to the relative safety of Da Nang, the teenage Hayslip is impregnated by the man who has hired her to be his maid. This begins a long string of relationships that continues throughout her young life and into the second volume of her autobiography, *Child of War, Woman of Peace*. Written with her oldest son, James Hayslip, this book is divided between her life in suburban San Diego as a struggling immigrant mother of three boys and her second return to her native land. In postwar Vietnam, she reunites with her mother, sisters, and older brother, who had fought on the Communist side, and concludes her narrative with a call to her readers to forgive their enemies.

This narrative of forgiveness, in conjunction with Hayslip's representation of herself as a successful American immigrant, has helped the popularity of her book with American readers. The appeal of her writing can be measured by the adaption of her books by director Oliver Stone (well known for his Vietnam War film *Platoon*) into the movie *Heaven and Earth* (1993). Since then, a younger generation of Vietnamese American writers, including Monique Truong and le thi diem thuy, has joined Hayslip, but her works remain valuable for their unique perspective. Hayslip's books are based on the experiences of peasants, who comprise the overwhelming majority of Vietnamese, presenting stories that are rarely heard by U.S. audiences and rarely told by Vietnamese American writers.

Viet Thanh Nguyen
University of Southern California

PRIMARY WORKS

When Heaven and Earth Changed Places, 1989; *Child of War, Woman of Peace*, 1993.

from **When Heaven and Earth Changed Places**

from 7. A Different View

My wartime "souvenir" business lasted almost two years. During this time, my mother tried to look after Hung while she fretted over her two other Danang daughters, our various aunts and uncles who lived in the area, and, whenever possible, my father in Ky La. Because I was preoccupied with my business—making money to pay for our needs, saving for emergencies and for better times—I spent very little time at home. Because of our joint neglect, little Hung came to look like a typical Danang street urchin. His skin always suffered from one rash or another and his belly ballooned like a pregnant woman's from eating sand to comfort his feelings. I felt bad for my baby but I didn't know what to do. If I stayed home, we would lose our house and be forced to live again on the street or on the charity of others. Besides, my mother had raised six strong children already. If she couldn't keep Hung healthy, how could I do any better?

There seemed no solution until one day I learned from a girlfriend that a new American firebase had been set up outside Ky La. Because I now felt safer around Americans than ever before, this seemed an ideal time to go back to the village, visit my father—as I had longed to do for years—and see if it might be possible for Hung to live and grow up in the house where I myself had been raised. Failing that, of course, I could always make some sales.

I left my mother at sunrise praying for my safety. Both she and Ba had tried to discourage me from making the trip—saying there were rumors that my father had been beaten and that danger was everywhere—but they understood neither the risks I had already taken in my business nor the fact that I now knew Americans to be a bit less brutal and more trustworthy than either the Vietnamese or Viet Cong forces. To avoid combatants on either side, I traced the route I had taken in the storm almost three years before, through the swamps, jungle, hills, and brush country from Danang to Marble Mountain to Ky La but this time the weather was fine and I had plenty of time to think about my father and what to do when I got home. When I arrived, however, the village I remembered no longer existed.

Half of Ky La had been leveled to give the Americans a better "killing zone" when defending the village. Their camp, which was a complex of bunkers and trenches with tin roofs, sandbags, radio antennas, and tents, lorded over the village from a hilltop outside of town. Around its slopes, homeless peasants and little kids poked through the American garbage in hopes of finding food or something to sell. In the distance, through a screen of withered trees (which had been defoliated now by chemicals as well as bombs), I could see that Bai Gian had not been rebuilt, and that the few remaining temples, pagodas, and wayside shrines—even my old schoolhouse and the guardsmen's awful prison—had been wiped away by the hand of war. Beautiful tropical forests had been turned into a bomb-cratered desert. It was as if the American giant, who had for so long been taunted and annoyed by the Viet Cong ants, had finally come to stamp its feet—to drive the painted, smiling Buddha from his house and substitute instead the khaki, glowering God of Abraham.

With the sickening feeling that I was now a stranger in my own homeland, I crossed the last few yards to my house with a lump in my throat and a growing sense of dread. Houses could be rebuilt and damaged dikes repaired—but the loss of our temples and shrines meant the death of our culture itself. It meant that a generation of children would grow up without fathers to teach them about their ancestors or the rituals of worship. Families would lose records of their lineage and with them the umbilicals to the very root of our society—not just old buildings and books, but *people* who once lived and loved like them. Our ties to our past were being severed, setting us adrift on a sea of borrowed Western materialism, disrespect for the elderly, and selfishness. The war no longer seemed like a fight to see which view would prevail. Instead, it had become a fight to see just how much and how far the Vietnam of my ancestors would be transformed. It was as if I was standing by the cradle of a dying child and speculating with its aunts and uncles on what the doomed baby would have looked like had it grown up. By tugging on their baby so brutally, both parents had wound up killing it. Even worse, the war now attacked Mother Earth—the seedbed of us all. This, to me, was the highest crime—the frenzied suicide of cannibals. How shall one mourn a lifeless planet?

Inside, the neat, clean home of my childhood was a hovel. What few furnishings and tools were left after the battles had been looted or burned for fuel. Our household shrine, which always greeted new arrivals as the centerpiece of our family's pride, was in shambles. Immediately I saw the bag of bones and torn sinew that was my father lying in his bed. Our eyes met briefly but there was no sign of recognition in his dull face. Instead, he rolled away from me and asked:

"Where is your son?"

I crossed the room and knelt by his bed. I was afraid to touch him for fear of disturbing his wounds or tormenting his aching soul even more. He clutched his side as if his ribs hurt badly and I could see that his face was bruised and swollen.

"I am alone," I answered, swallowing back my tears. "Who did this to you?"

"Dich." (The enemy.) It was a peasant's standard answer.

I went to the kitchen and made some tea from a few dried leaves. It was as if my father knew he was dying and did not wish the house or its stores to survive him. If one must die alone, it should be in an empty place without wasting a thing.

When I returned, he was on his back. I held his poor, scabbed head and helped him drink some tea. I could see he was dehydrated, being unable to draw water from the well or get up to drink it even when neighbors brought some to the house.

"Where were you taken? What was the charge?" I asked.

"It doesn't matter." My father drank gratefully and lay back on the bed. "The Americans came to examine our family bunker. Because it was so big, they thought Viet Cong might be hiding inside and ordered me to go in first. When I came out and told them no one was there, they didn't believe me and threw in some grenades. One of them didn't go off right away and the two Americans who went in afterward were killed. They were just boys—" My father coughed up blood. "I don't blame them for being angry. That's what war is all about, isn't it? Bad luck. Bad karma."

"So they beat you up?"

"They pinned a paper on my back that said 'VC' and took me to Hoa Cam District for interrogation. I don't have to tell you what happened after that. I'm just lucky to be alive."

As sad as I felt about my father's misfortune, growing fury now burned inside me. There was no reason to beat this poor man almost to death because of a soldier's tragic mistake.

I made my father as comfortable as possible and climbed the hill to the American fortress with my bucket of merchandise, intent on making a different kind of sale.

"Honcho?" I asked the first soldier I saw on the trail. I didn't understand his answer, but eventually I made myself understood well enough to impress him with my harmlessness: "You buy? Very nice? No *bum-bum!* See captain. Where honcho?"

Eventually I made my way to an officer who poked around my bucket, which by now had been searched four or five times by Americans for explosives. When he finally understood I wanted to talk to him about more than the price of bracelets, he called for the camp's Vietnamese translator.

"Thank god!" I said, bowing politely to the frowning Republican soldier who was not from the Central Coast. I explained the situation quickly to him in Vietnamese. I told him there had been a terrible mistake and that my father lay badly wounded in our house down the hill. I told him I wanted the Americans to take him to a hospital where he would be cared for and to help repair his house when he came back. I told him I knew the Americans were required to do all these things by their own regulations.

The Republican translator only laughed at me. "Look, missy," he said, "the Americans do what they damn well please around here. They don't take orders from anybody, especially little Vietnamese girls. Now, if you're smart, you'll take your father and get the hell out of here!"

"But you didn't even translate what I said to the captain!" I protested. "Come on—give the American a chance to speak for himself!"

"Look—" the translator exploded. "You'd better get out of here now or I'll denounce you as VC! If you have a complaint, go to the district headquarters like everyone else! Put your request through channels—and be prepared to spend some money. Now run along before I get mad!"

I gathered my things and went back down the hill. Although some GIs tried to wave me over, I was too upset to make a sale. I just wanted to help my father and keep things from getting worse.

Because the Americans so dominated the area, I felt comparatively safe staying near my house and tending to my father. Unlike the Republicans, who commandeered civilian houses for their quarters, the Americans kept their distance and so managed to avoid a lot of friction with the peasants. I no longer tried to sell anything (the villagers still hated anyone who dealt with the invaders) and pretended I didn't speak English when their troops stopped me from time to time. Although people going to the toilet or gathering firewood were still shot occasionally by jumpy soldiers, things remained blessedly quiet. It had been months since a major Viet Cong attack and a new, if smaller, generation of children now played in Ky La's streets. More dangerous were the Koreans who now patrolled the American sector. Because a child from our village once walked into their camp and exploded a Viet Cong bomb wired to his body, the Koreans took terrible retribution against the children themselves (whom they saw simply as little Viet Cong). After the incident, some Korean soldiers went to a school, snatched up some boys, threw them into a well, and tossed a grenade in afterward as an example to the others. To the villagers, these Koreans were like the Moroccans— tougher and meaner than the white soldiers they supported. Like the Japanese of World War II, they seemed to have no conscience and went about their duties as ruthless killing machines. No wonder they found my country a perfect place to ply their terrible trade.

I discovered that most of the kids I grew up with (those who had not been killed in the fighting) had married or moved away. Girls my age, if they had not yet married, were considered burdens on their family—old maids who consumed food without producing children. They also attracted the unsavory attention of soldiers, which always led to trouble. One reason so many of our young women wound up in the cities was because the shortage of available men made them liabilities to their families. At least a dutiful grown-up daughter could work as a housekeeper, nanny, hostess, or prostitute and send back money to the family who no longer wanted her. Many families, too, had been uprooted—like the refugees from Bai Gian or those who had been moved so that their houses could be bulldozed to provide a better fire zone for the Americans. For every soldier who went into battle, a hundred civilians moved ahead of him—to get out of the way; or behind him—following in his wake the way leaves are pulled along in a cyclone, hoping to live off his garbage, his money, and when all else failed, his mercy.

This is not to say that rubble and refugees were the only by-products of our war. Hundreds of thousands of tons of rice and countless motorbikes, luxury cars, TVs, stereos, refrigerators, air conditioners, and crates of cigarettes, liquor, and cosmetics were imported for the Vietnamese elite and the Americans who supported them. This created a new class of privileged people—wealthy young officers, officials, and war profiteers—who supplanted the elderly as objects of veneration. Consequently, displaced farmers—old people, now, as well as young—became their servants, working as maids to the madams or bootblacks for fuzz-cheeked GIs. It was a common sight to see old people prostrate themselves before these young demigods, crying *lay ong*—I beg you, sir!—where before such elderly people paid homage to no one but their ancestors. It was a world turned on its head.

Of those villagers who remained in Ky La, many were disfigured from the war, suffering amputated limbs, jagged scars, or the diseases that followed malnutrition or took over a body no longer inhabited by a happy human spirit.

Saddest of all these, perhaps, was Ong Xa Quang, a once-wealthy man who had been like a second father to me in the village. Quang was a handsome, good-natured man who sent two sons north in 1954. Of his two remaining sons, one was drafted by the Republican army and the other, much later, joined the Viet Cong. His two daughters married men who also went north, and so were left widows for at least the duration of the war. When I went to visit Quang I found his home and his life in ruins. He had lost both legs to an American mine, and every last son had been killed in battle. His wife now neglected him (she wasn't home when I called) because he was so much trouble to care for and he looked malnourished and on the verge of starvation. Still, he counted himself lucky. Fate had spared his life while it took the lives of so many others around him. All his suffering was part of his life's education—but for what purpose, he admitted he was still not wise enough to know. Nonetheless, Quang said I should remember everything he told me, and to forget none of the details of the tragedies I myself had seen and was yet to see. I gave him a daughter's tearful hug and left, knowing I would probably never see him alive again.

I walked to the hill behind my house where my father had taken me when I was a little girl—the hill where he told me about my destiny and duty as a Phung Thi woman. I surveyed the broken dikes and battered crops and empty animal pens of my once flourishing village. I saw the ghosts of my friends and relatives going about their work and a generation of children who would never be born playing in the muddy fields and dusty streets. I wondered about the martyrs and heroes of our ancient legends—shouldn't they be here to throw back the invaders and punish the Vietnamese on both sides who were making our country not just a graveyard, but a sewer of corruption and prison of fear? Could a god who made such saints as well as ordinary people truly be a god if he couldn't feel our suffering with us? For that matter, what use was god at all when people, not deities, seemed to cause our problems on earth?

I shut my eyes and called on my spirit sense to answer but I heard no reply. It was as if life's cycle was no longer birth, growth, and death but only endless dying brought about by endless war. I realized that I, along with so many of my countrymen, had been born into war and that my soul knew nothing else. I tried to imagine people somewhere who knew only peace—what a paradise! How many souls in that world were blessed with the simple privilege of saying good-bye to their loved ones before they died? And how many of those loved ones died with the smile of a life well lived on their lips—knowing that their existence added up to something more than a number in a "body count" or another human brick on a towering wall of corpses? Perhaps such a place was America, although American wives and mothers, too, were losing husbands and sons every day in the evil vortex between heaven and hell that my country had become.

I sat on the hill for a very long time, like a vessel waiting to be filled up with rain—soft wisdom from heaven—but the sun simply drifted lower in the west and the insects buzzed and the tin roofs of the American camps shimmered in the heat and my village and the war sat heavily—unmoved and unmovable like an oppressive gravestone—on my land and in my heart. I got up and dusted off my pants. It was time to feed my father.

Back home, I told him about my visit to "our hilltop." I said I now regretted fleeing Ky La. Perhaps it would have been better to stay and fight—to fight the Americans with the Viet Cong or the Viet Cong with the Republicans or to fight both together by myself and with anyone else who would join me.

My father stopped eating and looked at me intently. "Bay Ly, you were born to be a wife and mother, not a killer. That is your duty. For as long as you live, you must remember what I say. You and me—we weren't born to make enemies. Don't make vengeance your god, because such gods are satisfied only by human sacrifice."

"But there has been so much suffering—so much destruction!" I replied, again on the verge of tears, "Shouldn't someone be punished?"

"Are you so smart that you truly know who's to blame? If you ask the Viet Cong, they'll blame the Americans. If you ask the Americans, they'll blame the North. If you ask the North, they'll blame the South. If you ask the South, they'll blame the Viet Cong. If you ask the monks, they'll blame the Catholics, or tell you our ancestors did something terrible and so brought this endless suffering on our heads. So tell me, who would you punish? The common soldier on both sides who's only doing his duty? Would you ask the French or Americans to repay our Vietnamese debt?"

"But generals and politicians give orders—orders to kill and destroy. And our own people cheat each other as if there's nothing to it. I know— I've seen it! And nobody has the right to destroy Mother Earth!"

"Well then, Bay Ly, go out and do the same, eh? Kill the killers and cheat the cheaters. That will certainly stop the war, won't it? Perhaps that's been our problem all along—not enough profiteers and soldiers!"

Despite my father's reasoning, my anger and confusion were so full-up that they burst forth, not with new arguments, but tears. He took me in his arms. "Shhh—listen, little peach blossom, when you see all those young Americans out there being killed and wounded in our war—in a war that fate or luck or god has commanded us to wage for our redemption and education—you must thank them, at least in your heart, for helping to put us back on our life's course. Don't wonder about right and wrong. Those are weapons as deadly as bombs and bullets. Right is the goodness you carry in your heart—love for your ancestors and your baby and your family and for everything that lives. Wrong is anything that comes between you and that love. Go back to your little son. Raise him the best way you can. That is the battle you were born to fight. That is the victory you must win."

1989

RALPH MOLINA
B. 1947

"Ralph Molina" is the pseudonym of a Vietnam veteran who was drafted into the U.S. Army in 1968 and served near Bien Hoa, South Vietnam, in 1969. He is the grandson of Mexican immigrants who migrated in the first decade of the twentieth century to California, where they established roots in East Los Angeles. His father served as a U.S. Marine in the Pacific theater during World War II.

The historical record clearly shows that throughout the twentieth and into the twenty-first century, Mexican Americans have served in the U.S. armed forces in high numbers. It is estimated that half a million men of Mexican descent fought in World War II. Their sons and daughters have served in every war since then and continue to enlist and die in U.S. wars today.

One factor that complicates the military service of this particular community is the thorny issue of assimilation, its connection to patriotism and to the promise of full citizenship in the nation. For a working-class and racialized community subject to Jim Crow-like restrictions from 1848 until long after World War II, military service often was riddled with irony: why should one fight for a country that too often marked you and your family as foreigners? Nevertheless, Chicanos in massive numbers, faced with the prospect of going to Vietnam, reacted with the same sense of duty and/or fatalism that had inspired their fathers, cousins, and uncles in previous wars.

The small town of Silvis, Illinois, exemplifies the sacrifices made by ethnic Mexicans in the U.S. armed forces. The town, which sits along the Mississippi River near the Iowa border, became home to Mexican railroad workers who had journeyed north to labor on the Rock Island line. During World War II and the U.S. wars in Korea and Vietnam, a single block in that community (renamed "Hero Street" in the 1960s) sent eighty-seven young men to war. Among those who died were men like Tony Pompa, a Mexican citizen who enlisted under an assumed name. As of 1994, more than one hundred residents of Hero Street had served in the U.S. military.

The paradox for Mexican Americans serving in the U.S. military has been powerful throughout this long history of service and sacrifice. Reflecting on the World War II period, Mexican American scholar and publisher Octavio I. Romano wrote about the contradictions for young Mexican American men fighting for democracy in 1943 as U.S. sailors and police harassed and beat young Mexican zoot-suiters in the streets of several major California cities. It is from Romano's text that Molina draws his inspiration.

In the two sections of his poem titled "Dos Recuerdos" (Two Memories), Molina represents those same contradictions as they were lived by his generation—the Chicano generation of the late 1960s. In the first section, the poetic voice evokes the growing sense among many Vietnam veterans that they had been used in an unnecessary and even illegal war. The sarcasm of one soldier becomes the rage of the Chicano soldier whose community still waits for first-class citizenship. In the second section, a Chicano soldier home on leave experiences racism in his hometown just a few months before he is sent to Vietnam. While he is in the combat zone, he learns of the police riot that destroyed a peaceful anti-war demonstration led by Chicanas and Chicanos in East Los Angeles—the Chicano Moratorium of August 29, 1970.

Molina's poem resonates today as young Latinas and Latinos—many of them noncitizens—fight and die in foreign wars even as their families in the United States live in fear of immigration raids and deportation.

Jorge Mariscal
University of California, San Diego

Dos Recuerdos (after Octavio I. Romano)

1

It is January, 1968, and the Viet Nam War is still raging.
After one year overseas, I return. We land in Oakland.
I get a pass and walk a street, any street. I stop at the first hamburger
    stand I encounter. I enter and order a big double cheeseburger.
For months and months and months and months I have dreamed of
    this moment.
Enjoy.
The place is full of soldiers. Apparently they had the same dream.
The soldier sitting next to me turns, and, with ketchup on his upper lip,
    he says, "Worth fighting for, huh?" There is a look of pure sarcasm
    on his face.
"Yeah," I reply. I don't know about my face, but I have a deep feeling of
    rage inside.
Tomorrow I leave for L.A., and home.

2

It is Spring of 1970.
Pam and I are on a date. She is Irish, red-haired. I am a Chicano GI on
    leave. We met at work at a bookstore before I was drafted. We talk
    a lot about the war, and should we get married. We are in a coffee
    shop on Atlantic Blvd., eating lunch. Two cops enter the restaurant.
All of a sudden Pam says, "Let's get out of here." I am surprised. We
    each still have a full plate of food in front of us. She insists.
When we are out on the street I ask, "Why leave now?"
"Didn't you hear those two cops behind us?"
"No. Why?"
"They were talking about hassling that spic with the redhead. They
    meant you."
Four months later, I am sent to fight communism overseas. In Viet Nam
    I read about the members of the Sheriff's Department and the LAPD
    who repeatedly attacked Chicanos and Chicanas in East Los Angeles.

PAULE MARSHALL

B. 1929

Paule Marshall, née Valenza Pauline Burke, was born in Brooklyn, New York. Her parents, Ada and Samuel Burke, were emigrants from Barbados, West Indies. At the age of nine, Marshall made an extended visit to the native land of her parents and discovered for herself the quality of life peculiar to that tropical isle. Although she then wrote a series of poems reflecting her impressions, creative writing did not become a serious pursuit until much later in her young adult life. The selection included here is a mature reminiscence and symbolic expansion of that childhood visit.

A quiet and retiring child ("living her old days first," her mother used to say), Marshall was an avid reader who spent countless hours in her neighborhood library. This, it seems, was at least a partial escape from the pressures of growing up, for the author admits going through a painful childhood period in which she rejected her West Indian heritage. Easily identified by the heavy silver bangles that girls from "the islands" wore on their wrists, she felt even more estranged from her classmates when she returned from Barbados with a noticeable accent. During early adolescence, reading also helped ease the longing for her father, who, having become a devoted follower of Father Divine, left home to live in the Harlem "kingdom."

Marshall had been attending Hunter College, majoring in social work, when illness necessitated a one-year stay in a sanatorium in upstate New York. There, in a tranquil lake setting, she wrote letters describing her surroundings so vividly that a friend encouraged her to think of a career in writing. Upon her release from the sanatorium, she transferred to Brooklyn College, changed her major to English literature, and graduated Phi Beta Kappa in 1953. Her first marriage, in 1957, was to Kenneth Marshall, with whom she had a son, Evan Keith. She divorced in 1963 and in 1970 wed a second time, to Haitian businessman Nourry Ménard.

Formerly a researcher and staff writer for *Our World* magazine in New York City, Marshall traveled on assignment to Brazil and to the West Indies. Once her literary career was launched, she contributed short stories and articles to numerous magazines and anthologies and began lecturing at several colleges and universities within the United States and abroad. The recipient of several prestigious awards, including the John D. and Catherine T. MacArthur Fellowship, Marshall continues to write and to teach. She is professor emerita of English and creative writing at Virginia Commonwealth University and resides in Richmond, Virginia.

Marshall's artistic vision evolves in a clear progression as she moves, through her creations, from an American to an African American/African Caribbean and, finally, a Pan-African sensibility. Indeed, the chronological order of her publications suggests an underlying design to follow the "middle passage" in reverse; that is, she examines the experience of blacks not in transit from Africa to the New World, but from the New World toward Africa. Thus, her first major work, *Brown Girl, Brownstones*, considers the coming of age of a young West Indian girl and simultaneously explores the black emigrant experience in America. *Soul Clap Hands and Sing*, a collection of novellas, is a lyrical depiction of the lives of four aging men coming to grips with the decline of Western values. The geographical setting changes from Brooklyn to Barbados to British Guiana and then to Brazil. Marshall next moves, in *The Chosen Place, the Timeless People*, to an imaginary Caribbean island that, on one side, faces the continent of Africa. In this epic novel, she traces the development and perpetuation of colonialism. In *Praisesong for the Widow*, Marshall shows increasing reliance on African images as she presents the portrait of an elderly black American widow who, on a cruise to Grenada, confronts her African heritage. In her novel *Daughters*, Marshall moves her geographical setting back and forth between the Caribbean and the United States to suggest the bicultural ties of her protagonist as well as the political strategies affecting both nations. She further establishes the centrality of women in transforming self, community, and nation.

Throughout her fiction, Marshall is preoccupied with black cultural history. Additionally, her emphasis on black female characters addresses contemporary feminist issues from an Afrocentric perspective. She insists that African peoples take a "journey back" through time to understand the political, social, and economic structures on which contemporary societies are based. As her vision expands to include oppressed peoples (men and women) all over the world, she develops a sensibility that values cultural differences while it celebrates the triumph of the human spirit.

Dorothy L. Denniston
Brown University

PRIMARY WORKS

Brown Girl, Brownstones, 1959; *Soul Clap Hands and Sing*, 1961; *The Chosen Place, the Timeless People*, 1969; *Praisesong for the Widow*, 1983; *Reena and Other Short Stories*, 1983; *Daughters*, 1991; *The Fisher King: A Novel*, 2001; *The Triangular Road*, 2009.

To Da-duh, in Memoriam

This is the most autobiographical of the stories, a reminiscence largely of a visit I paid to my grandmother (whose nickname was Da-duh) on the island of Barbados when I was nine. Ours was a complex relationship—close, affectionate yet rivalrous. During the year I spent with her a subtle kind of power struggle went on between us. It was as if we both knew, at a level beyond words, that I had come into the world not only to love her and to continue her line but to take her very life in order that I might live.

Years later, when I got around to writing the story, I tried giving the contest I had sensed between us a wider meaning. I wanted the basic theme of youth and old age to suggest rivalries, dichotomies of a cultural and political nature, having to do with the relationship of western civilization and the Third World.

Apart from this story, Da-duh also appears in one form or another in my other work as well. She's the old hairdresser, Mrs. Thompson, in BROWN GIRL, BROWNSTONES, *who offers Selina total, unquestioning love. She's Leesy Walkes and the silent cook, Carrington, "whose great breast ... had been used it seemed to suckle the world" in* THE CHOSEN PLACE, THE TIMELESS PEOPLE. *She's Aunt Vi in "Reena" and Medford, the old family retainer in "British Guiana" from* SOUL CLAP HANDS AND SING. *And she's Avey Johnson's Great-aunt Cuney in* PRAISE-SONG FOR THE WIDOW. *Da-duh turns up everywhere.*

She's an ancestor figure, symbolic for me of the long line of black women and men—African and New World—who made my being possible, and whose spirit I believe continues to animate my life and work. I wish to acknowledge and cele-brate them. I am, in a word, an unabashed ancestor worshipper.

> "... *Oh Nana! all of you is not involved in this evil business Death,*
> *Nor all of us in life.*"

—FROM "AT MY GRANDMOTHER'S GRAVE," BY LEBERT BETHUNE

I did not see her at first I remember. For not only was it dark inside the crowded disembarkation shed in spite of the daylight flooding in from out-side, but standing there waiting for her with my mother and sister I was still somewhat blinded from the sheen of tropical sunlight on the water of the bay which we had just crossed in the landing boat, leaving behind us the ship that had brought us from New York lying in the offing. Besides, being only nine years of age at the time and knowing nothing of islands I was busy attending to the alien sights and sounds of Barbados, the unfamiliar smells.

I did not see her, but I was alerted to her approach by my mother's hand which suddenly tightened around mine, and looking up I traced her gaze through the gloom in the shed until I finally made out the small, purposeful, painfully erect figure of the old woman headed our way.

Her face was drowned in the shadow of an ugly rolled-brim brown felt hat, but the details of her slight body and of the struggle taking place within it were clear enough—an intense, unrelenting struggle between her back which was beginning to bend ever so slightly under the weight of her eighty-odd years and the rest of her which sought to deny those years and hold that back straight, keep it in line. Moving swiftly toward us (so swiftly it seemed she did not intend stopping when she reached us but would sweep past us out the doorway which opened onto the sea and like Christ walk upon the water!)[1] she was caught between the sunlight at her end of the building and the darkness inside—and for a moment she appeared to con-tain them both: the light in the long severe old-fashioned white dress she wore which brought the sense of a past that was still alive into our bustling present and in the snatch of white at her eye; the darkness in her black high-top shoes and in her face which was visible now that she was closer.

It was as stark and fleshless as a death mask, that face. The maggots might have already done their work, leaving only the framework of bone beneath the ruined skin and deep wells at the temple and jaw. But her eyes were alive, unnervingly so for one so old, with a sharp light that flicked out of the dim clouded depths like a lizard's tongue to snap up all in her view.

[1]Biblical allusion, Matthew 14:22–33.

Those eyes betrayed a child's curiosity about the world, and I wondered vaguely seeing them, and seeing the way the bodice of her ancient dress had collapsed in on her flat chest (what had happened to her breasts?), whether she might not be some kind of child at the same time that she was a woman, with fourteen children, my mother included, to prove it. Perhaps she was both, both child and woman, darkness and light, past and present, life and death—all the opposites contained and reconciled in her.

"My Da-duh," my mother said formally and stepped forward. The name sounded like thunder fading softly in the distance.

"Child," Da-duh said, and her tone, her quick scrutiny of my mother, the brief embrace in which they appeared to shy from each other rather than touch, wiped out the fifteen years my mother had been away and restored the old relationship. My mother, who was such a formidable figure in my eyes, had suddenly with a word been reduced to my status.

"Yes, God is good," Da-duh said with a nod that was like a tic. "He has spared me to see my child again."

We were led forward then, apologetically because not only did Da-duh prefer boys but she also liked her grandchildren to be "white," that is, fair-skinned; and we had, I was to discover, a number of cousins, the outside children[2] of white estate managers and the like, who qualified. We, though, were as black as she.

My sister being the oldest was presented first. "This one takes after the father," my mother said and waited to be reproved.

Frowning, Da-duh tilted my sister's face toward the light. But her frown soon gave way to a grudging smile, for my sister with her large mild eyes and little broad winged nose, with our father's high-cheeked Barbadian cast to her face, was pretty.

"She's goin' be lucky," Da-duh said and patted her once on the cheek. "Any girl child that takes after the father does be lucky."

She turned then to me. But oddly enough she did not touch me. Instead leaning close, she peered hard at me, and then quickly drew back. I thought I saw her hand start up as though to shield her eyes. It was almost as if she saw not only me, a thin truculent child who it was said took after no one but myself, but something in me which for some reason she found disturbing, even threatening. We looked silently at each other for a long time there in the noisy shed, our gaze locked. She was the first to look away.

"But Adry," she said to my mother and her laugh was cracked, thin, apprehensive. "Where did you get this one here with this fierce look?"

"We don't know where she came out of, my Da-duh," my mother said, laughing also. Even I smiled to myself. After all I had won the encounter. Da-duh had recognized my small strength—and this was all I ever asked of the adults in my life then.

"Come, soul," Da-duh said and took my hand. "You must be one of those New York terrors you hear so much about."

---

[2]Children born outside marriage.

She led us, me at her side and my sister and mother behind, out of the shed into the sunlight that was like a bright driving summer rain and over to a group of people clustered beside a decrepit lorry. They were our relatives, most of them from St. Andrews although Da-duh herself lived in St. Thomas, the women wearing bright print dresses, the colors vivid against their darkness, the men rusty black suits that encased them like straitjackets. Da-duh, holding fast to my hand, became my anchor as they circled round us like a nervous sea, exclaiming, touching us with their calloused hands, embracing us shyly. They laughed in awed bursts: "But look Adry got big-big children!"/ "And see the nice things they wearing, wrist watch and all!"/ "I tell you, Adry has done all right for sheself in New York. . . ."

Da-duh, ashamed at their wonder, embarrassed for them, admonished them the while. "But oh Christ," she said, "why you all got to get on like you never saw people from 'Away' before? You would think New York is the only place in the world to hear wunna. That's why I don't like to go anyplace with you St. Andrews people, you know. You all ain't been colonized."[3]

We were in the back of the lorry finally, packed in among the barrels of ham, flour, cornmeal and rice and the trunks of clothes that my mother had brought as gifts. We made our way slowly through Bridgetown's clogged streets, part of a funereal procession of cars and open-sided buses, bicycles and donkey carts. The dim little limestone shops and offices along the way marched with us, at the same mournful pace, toward the same grave ceremony—as did the people, the women balancing huge baskets on top their heads as if they were no more than hats they wore to shade them from the sun. Looking over the edge of the lorry I watched as their feet slurred the dust. I listened, and their voices, raw and loud and dissonant in the heat, seemed to be grappling with each other high overhead.

Da-duh sat on a trunk in our midst, a monarch amid her court. She still held my hand, but it was different now. I had suddenly become her anchor, for I felt her fear of the lorry with its asthmatic motor (a fear and distrust, I later learned, she held of all machines)[4] beating like a pulse in her rough palm.

As soon as we left Bridgetown behind though, she relaxed, and while the others around us talked she gazed at the canes standing tall on either side of the winding marl road. "C'dear,"[5] she said softly to herself after a time. "The canes this side are pretty enough."

They were too much for me. I thought of them as giant weeds that had overrun the island, leaving scarcely any room for the small tottering houses of sunbleached pine we passed or the people, dark streaks as our lorry hurtled by. I suddenly feared that we were journeying, unaware that we were, toward some dangerous place where the canes, grown as high and thick as a

---

[3]Malapropism.

[4]The same dread of the mechanical appears in Leesy Walkes, a character in Marshall's *The Chosen Place, the Timeless People* (1969). Here the author symbolically establishes the con-

flict engendered when Western technology encroaches upon Da-duh's Edenic garden.

[5]A form of address spoken with a hard "C." Loosely translated as "Come dear" or "Good dear."

forest, would close in on us and run us through with their stiletto blades. I longed then for the familiar: for the street in Brooklyn where I lived, for my father who had refused to accompany us ("Blowing out good money on foolishness," he had said of the trip), for a game of tag with my friends under the chestnut tree outside our aging brownstone house.

"Yes, but wait till you see St. Thomas canes," Da-duh was saying to me. "They's canes father, bo," she gave a proud arrogant nod. "Tomorrow, God willing, I goin' take you out in the ground and show them to you."

True to her word Da-duh took me with her the following day out into the ground. It was a fairly large plot adjoining her weathered board and shingle house and consisting of a small orchard, a good-sized canepiece and behind the canes, where the land sloped abruptly down, a gully. She had purchased it with Panama money[6] sent her by her eldest son, my uncle Joseph, who had died working on the canal. We entered the ground along a trail no wider than her body and as devious and complex as her reasons for showing me her land. Da-duh strode briskly ahead, her slight form filled out this morning by the layers of sacking petticoats she wore under her working dress to protect her against the damp. A fresh white cloth, elaborately arranged around her head, added to her height, and lent her a vain, almost roguish air.

Her pace slowed once we reached the orchard, and glancing back at me occasionally over her shoulder, she pointed out the various trees.

"This here is a breadfruit," she said. "That one yonder is a papaw. Here's a guava. This is a mango. I know you don't have anything like these in New York. Here's a sugar apple." (The fruit looked more like artichokes than apples to me.) "This one bears limes...." She went on for some time, intoning the names of the trees as though they were those of her gods. Finally, turning to me, she said, "I know you don't have anything this nice where you come from." Then, as I hesitated: "I said I know you don't have anything this nice where you come from...."

"No," I said and my world did seem suddenly lacking.

Da-duh nodded and passed on. The orchard ended and we were on the narrow cart road that led through the canepiece, the canes clashing like swords above my cowering head. Again she turned and her thin muscular arms spread wide, her dim gaze embracing the small field of canes, she said—and her voice almost broke under the weight of her pride, "Tell me, have you got anything like these in that place where you were born?"

"No."

"I din' think so. I bet you don't even know that these canes here and the sugar you eat is one and the same thing. That they does throw the canes into some damn machine at the factory and squeeze out all the little life in them to make sugar for you all so in New York to eat. I bet you don't know that."

[6]Because of poor economic conditions in Barbados, many islanders worked abroad and sent money home to support their families.

"I've got two cavities and I'm not allowed to eat a lot of sugar."

But Da-duh didn't hear me. She had turned with an inexplicably angry motion and was making her way rapidly out of the canes and down the slope at the edge of the field which led to the gully below. Following her apprehensively down the incline amid a stand of banana plants whose leaves flapped like elephants ears in the wind, I found myself in the middle of a small tropical wood—a place dense and damp and gloomy and tremulous with the fitful play of light and shadow as the leaves high above moved against the sun that was almost hidden from view. It was a violent place, the tangled foliage fighting each other for a chance at the sunlight, the branches of the trees locked in what seemed an immemorial struggle, one both necessary and inevitable. But despite the violence, it was pleasant, almost peaceful in the gully, and beneath the thick undergrowth the earth smelled like spring.

This time Da-duh didn't even bother to ask her usual question, but simply turned and waited for me to speak.

"No," I said, my head bowed. "We don't have anything like this in New York."

"Ah," she cried, her triumph complete. "I din' think so. Why, I've heard that's a place where you can walk till you near drop and never see a tree."

"We've got a chestnut tree in front of our house," I said.

"Does it bear?" She waited. "I ask you, does it bear?"

"Not anymore," I muttered. "It used to, but not anymore."

She gave the nod that was like a nervous twitch. "You see," she said, "Nothing can bear there." Then, secure behind her scorn, she added, "But tell me, what's this snow like that you hear so much about?"

Looking up, I studied her closely, sensing my chance, and then I told her, describing at length and with as much drama as I could summon not only what snow in the city was like, but what it would be like here, in her perennial summer kingdom.

"... And you see all these trees you got here," I said. "Well, they'd be bare. No leaves, no fruit, nothing. They'd be covered in snow. You see your canes. They'd be buried under tons of snow. The snow would be higher than your head, higher than your house, and you wouldn't be able to come down into this here gully because it would be snowed under...."

She searched my face for the lie, still scornful but intrigued. "What a thing, huh?" she said finally, whispering it softly to herself.

"And when it snows you couldn't dress like you are now," I said. "Oh no, you'd freeze to death. You'd have to wear a hat and gloves and galoshes and ear muffs so your ears wouldn't freeze and drop off, and a heavy coat. I've got a Shirley Temple coat with fur on the collar. I can dance. You wanna see?"

Before she could answer I began, with a dance called the Truck which was popular back then in the 1930's. My right forefinger waving, I trucked around the nearby trees and around Da-duh's awed and rigid form. After the Truck I did the Suzy-Q, my lean hips swishing, my sneakers sidling zigzag over the ground. "I can sing," I said and did so, starting with "I'm Gonna Sit Right Down and Write Myself a Letter," then without pausing, "Tea For Two," and ending with "I Found a Million Dollar Baby in a Five and Ten Cent Store."

For long moments afterwards Da-duh stared at me as if I were a creature from Mars, an emissary from some world she did not know but which intrigued her and whose power she both felt and feared. Yet something about my performance must have pleased her, because bending down she slowly lifted her long skirt and then, one by one, the layers of petticoats until she came to a drawstring purse dangling at the end of a long strip of cloth tied round her waist. Opening the purse she handed me a penny. "Here," she said half-smiling against her will. "Take this to buy yourself a sweet at the shop up the road. There's nothing to be done with you, soul."

From then on, whenever I wasn't taken to visit relatives, I accompanied Da-duh out into the ground, and alone with her amid the canes or down in the gully I told her about New York. It always began with some slighting remark on her part: "I know they don't have anything this nice where you come from," or "Tell me, I hear those foolish people in New York does do such and such...." But as I answered, recreating my towering world of steel and concrete and machines for her, building the city out of words, I would feel her give way. I came to know the signs of her surrender: the total stillness that would come over her little hard dry form, the probing gaze that like a surgeon's knife sought to cut through my skull to get at the images there, to see if I were lying; above all, her fear, a fear nameless and profound, the same one I had felt beating in the palm of her hand that day in the lorry.

Over the weeks I told her about refrigerators, radios, gas stoves, elevators, trolley cars, wringer washing machines, movies, airplanes, the cyclone at Coney Island, subways, toasters, electric lights: "At night, see, all you have to do is flip this little switch on the wall and all the lights in the house go on. Just like that. Like magic. It's like turning on the sun at night."

"But tell me," she said to me once with a faint mocking smile, "do the white people have all these things too or it's only the people looking like us?"

I laughed. "What d'ya mean," I said. "The white people have even better." Then: "I beat up a white girl in my class last term."

"Beating up white people!" Her tone was incredulous.

"How you mean!" I said, using an expression of hers. "She called me a name."

For some reason Da-duh could not quite get over this and repeated in the same hushed, shocked voice, "Beating up white people now! Oh, the lord, the world's changing up so I can scarce recognize it anymore."

One morning toward the end of our stay, Da-duh led me into a part of the gully that we had never visited before, an area darker and more thickly overgrown than the rest, almost impenetrable. There in a small clearing amid the dense bush, she stopped before an incredibly tall royal palm which rose cleanly out of the ground, and drawing the eye up with it, soared high above the trees around it into the sky. It appeared to be touching the blue dome of sky, to be flaunting its dark crown of fronds right in the blinding white face of the late morning sun.

Da-duh watched me a long time before she spoke, and then she said, very quietly, "All right, now, tell me if you've got anything this tall in that place you're from."

I almost wished, seeing her face, that I could have said no. "Yes," I said. "We've got buildings hundreds of times this tall in New York. There's one called the Empire State Building that's the tallest in the world. My class visited it last year and I went all the way to the top. It's got over a hundred floors. I can't describe how tall it is. Wait a minute. What's the name of that hill I went to visit the other day, where they have the police station?"

"You mean Bissex?"

"Yes, Bissex. Well, the Empire State Building is way taller than that."

"You're lying now!" she shouted, trembling with rage. Her hand lifted to strike me.

"No, I'm not," I said. "It really is, if you don't believe me I'll send you a picture postcard of it soon as I get back home so you can see for yourself. But it's way taller than Bissex."

All the fight went out of her at that. The hand poised to strike me fell limp to her side, and as she stared at me, seeing not me but the building that was taller than the highest hill she knew, the small stubborn light in her eyes (it was the same amber as the flame in the kerosene lamp she lit at dusk) began to fail. Finally, with a vague gesture that even in the midst of her defeat still tried to dismiss me and my world, she turned and started back through the gully, walking slowly, her steps groping and uncertain, as if she were suddenly no longer sure of the way, while I followed triumphant yet strangely saddened behind.

The next morning I found her dressed for our morning walk but stretched out on the Berbice chair in the tiny drawing room where she sometimes napped during the afternoon heat, her face turned to the window beside her. She appeared thinner and suddenly indescribably old.

"My Da-duh," I said.

"Yes, nuh," she said. Her voice was listless and the face she slowly turned my way was, now that I think back on it, like a Benin mask the features drawn and almost distorted by an ancient abstract sorrow.

"Don't you feel well?" I asked.

"Girl, I don't know."

"My Da-duh, I goin' boil you some bush tea," my aunt, Da-duh's youngest child, who lived with her, called from the shed roof kitchen.

"Who tell you I need bush tea?" she cried, her voice assuming for a moment its old authority. "You can't even rest nowadays without some malicious person looking for you to be dead. Come girl," she motioned me to a place beside her on the old-fashioned lounge chair, "give us a tune."

I sang for her until breakfast at eleven, all my brash irreverent Tin Pan Alley songs, and then just before noon we went out into the ground. But it was a short, dispirited walk. Da-duh didn't even notice that the mangoes were beginning to ripen and would have to be picked before the village boys got to them. And when she paused occasionally and looked out across the canes or up at her trees it wasn't as if she were seeing them but something else. Some huge, monolithic shape had imposed itself, it seemed, between her and the land, obstructing her vision. Returning to the house she slept the entire afternoon on the Berbice chair.

She remained like this until we left, languishing away the mornings on the chair at the window gazing out at the land as if it were already doomed; then, at noon, taking the brief stroll with me through the ground during which she seldom spoke, and afterwards returning home to sleep till almost dusk sometimes.

On the day of our departure she put on the austere, ankle length white dress, the black shoes and brown felt hat (her town clothes she called them), but she did not go with us to town. She saw us off on the road outside her house and in the midst of my mother's tearful protracted farewell, she leaned down and whispered in my ear, "Girl, you're not to forget now to send me the picture of that building, you hear."

By the time I mailed her the large colored picture postcard of the Empire State building she was dead. She died during the famous '37 strike which began shortly after we left. On the day of her death England sent planes flying low over the island in a show of force—so low, according to my aunt's letter, that the downdraft from them shook the ripened mangoes from the trees in Da-duh's orchard. Frightened, everyone in the village fled into the canes. Except Da-duh. She remained in the house at the window so my aunt said, watching as the planes came swooping and screaming like monstrous birds down over the village, over her house, rattling her trees and flattening the young canes in her field. It must have seemed to her lying there that they did not intend pulling out of their dive, but like the hardback beetles which hurled themselves with suicidal force against the walls of the house at night, those menacing silver shapes would hurl themselves in an ecstasy of self-immolation onto the land, destroying it utterly.

When the planes finally left and the villagers returned they found her dead on the Berbice chair at the window.

She died and I lived, but always, to this day even, within the shadow of her death. For a brief period after I was grown I went to live alone, like one doing penance, in a loft above a noisy factory in downtown New York and there painted seas of sugar-cane and huge swirling Van Gogh suns and palm trees striding like brightly-plumed Tutsi warriors across a tropical landscape, while the thunderous tread of the machines downstairs jarred the floor beneath my easel, mocking my efforts.

1967

ERNEST J. GAINES
B. 1933

Ernest J. Gaines was born in Pointe Coupee Parish on "The Quarters" of River Lake Plantation, a few miles from New Roads, Louisiana. "Until I was fifteen years old," Gaines recounts, "I had been raised by an aunt, Miss Augusteen Jefferson, a lady who had never walked a day in her life," but who, as he says in the dedication to *The Autobiography of Miss Jane Pittman*, "taught me the importance of standing." As a boy Gaines worked in the cane fields "where all my people before me worked."

In 1948 Gaines left Louisiana to join his mother and stepfather in Vallejo, California. There, as a teenager, he began to "read all the Southern writers I could find in the Vallejo library; then I began to read any writer who wrote about nature or about people who worked the land—anyone who would say something about dirt and trees, clear streams, and open sky." After a two-year stint in the army, Gaines earned his B.A. degree at San Francisco State College in 1957. He then won a Wallace Stegner Creative Writing Fellowship at Stanford and also received the Joseph Henry Jackson Literary Award there in 1959.

Gaines's novels and short fiction are set in an imaginary Louisiana that evokes and re-creates the world of his childhood and the changes he has observed on his many returns to Louisiana. Although he has a drawer full of San Francisco–inspired fiction, Gaines's published work is exclusively about Louisiana. "I wanted," he says of his intention as a writer, "to smell that Louisiana earth, feel that Louisiana sun, sit under the shade of one of those Louisiana oaks, search for pecans in that Louisiana grass in one of those Louisiana yards next to one of those Louisiana bayous, not far from a Louisiana river. I wanted to see on paper those Louisiana black children walking to school on cold days while yellow Louisiana buses passed them by. I wanted to see on paper those black parents going to work before the sun came up and coming back home to look after their children after the sun went down. I wanted to see on paper the true reason why those black fathers left home—not because they were trifling or shiftless—but because they were tired of putting up with certain conditions. I wanted to see on paper the small country churches (schools during the week), and I wanted to hear those simple religious songs, those simple prayers—that true devotion. (It was Faulkner, I think, who said that if God were to stay alive in the country, the blacks would have to keep Him so.) And I wanted to hear that Louisiana dialect—that combination of English, Creole, Cajun, Black. For me there's no more beautiful sound anywhere."

Through the act of writing, Gaines reexperiences Louisiana. Once there in imagination, he puts on paper the historical but alterable society that exists in the midst of nature's abiding reality. The instrument behind the passage of the spoken word onto the page is the writer's healing human voice. Like his storytellers, Gaines breaks down the barriers between his voice and the voices of his characters. As a writer for his people, Gaines keeps faith with the oral tradition—a tradition of responsibility and change and, despite violent opposition, a tradition of citizenship.

"The Sky Is Gray" and the other stories in Gaines's *Bloodline* mediate two complementary facts of life: first, that very little changed in his remote parish between the Civil War and his departure after World War II; and second, that even rural Louisiana could not resist the racial upheaval of the 1950s and 1960s. According to Gaines's speech-driven donnée of fiction, for the writer to be free, his characters must be free, and an independent, individual voice is the first test of freedom.

John F. Callahan
Lewis and Clark College

PRIMARY WORKS

Catherine Carmier, 1964; *Of Love and Dust*, 1967; *Bloodline*, 1968; *The Autobiography of Miss Jane Pittman*, 1971; *In My Father's House*, 1978; *A Gathering of Old Men*, 1983; *A Lesson before Dying*, 1993; *Mozart and Leadbelly*, 2005.

The Sky Is Gray

1

Go'n be coming in a few minutes. Coming round that bend down there full speed. And I'm go'n get out my handkerchief and wave it down, and we go'n get on it and go.

I keep on looking for it, but Mama don't look that way no more. She's looking down the road where we just come from. It's a long old road, and far 's you can see you don't see nothing but gravel. You got dry weeds on both sides, and you got trees on both sides, and fences on both sides, too. And you got cows in the pastures and they standing close together. And when we was coming out here to catch the bus I seen the smoke coming out of the cows' noses.

I look at my mama and I know what she's thinking. I been with Mama so much, just me and her, I know what she's thinking all the time. Right now it's home—Auntie and them. She's thinking if they got enough wood—if she left enough there to keep them warm till we get back. She's thinking if it go'n rain and if any of them go'n have to go out in the rain. She's thinking 'bout the hog—if he go'n get out, and if Ty and Val be able to get him back in. She always worry like that when she leaves the house. She don't worry too much if she leave me there with the smaller ones, 'cause she know I'm go'n look after them and look after Auntie and everything else. I'm the oldest and she say I'm the man.

I look at my mama and I love my mama. She's wearing that black coat and that black hat and she's looking sad. I love my mama and I want put my arm round her and tell her. But I'm not supposed to do that. She say that's weakness and that's crybaby stuff, and she don't want no crybaby round her. She don't want you to be scared, either. 'Cause Ty's scared of ghosts and she's always whipping him. I'm scared of the dark, too, but I make 'tend I ain't. I make 'tend I ain't 'cause I'm the oldest, and I got to set a good sample for the rest. I can't ever be scared and I can't ever cry. And that's why I never said nothing 'bout my teeth. It's been hurting me and hurting me close to a month now, but I never said it. I didn't say it 'cause I didn't want act like a crybaby, and 'cause I know we didn't have enough money to go have it pulled. But, Lord, it been hurting me. And look like it wouldn't start till at night when you was trying to get yourself little sleep. Then soon 's you shut your eyes—ummm-ummm, Lord, look like it go right down to your heartstring.

"Hurting, hanh?" Ty'd say.

I'd shake my head, but I wouldn't open my mouth for nothing. You open your mouth and let that wind in, and it almost kill you.

I'd just lay there and listen to them snore. Ty there, right 'side me, and Auntie and Val over by the fireplace. Val younger than me and Ty, and he sleeps with Auntie. Mama sleeps round the other side with Louis and Walker.

I'd just lay there and listen to them, and listen to that wind out there, and listen to that fire in the fireplace. Sometimes it'd stop long enough to let me get little rest. Sometimes it just hurt, hurt, hurt. Lord, have mercy.

2

Auntie knowed it was hurting me. I didn't tell nobody but Ty, 'cause we buddies and he ain't go'n tell nobody. But some kind of way Auntie found out. When she asked me, I told her no, nothing was wrong. But she knowed it all the time. She told me to mash up a piece of aspirin and wrap it in some cotton and jugg it down in that hole. I did it, but it didn't do no good. It stopped for a little while, and started right back again. Auntie wanted to tell Mama, but I told her, "Uh-uh." 'Cause I knowed we didn't have any money, and it just was go'n make her mad again. So Auntie told Monsieur Bayonne, and Monsieur Bayonne came over to the house and told me to kneel down 'side him on the fireplace. He put his finger in his mouth and made the Sign of the Cross on my jaw. The tip of Monsieur Bayonne's finger is some hard, 'cause he's always playing on that guitar. If we sit outside at night we can always hear Monsieur Bayonne playing on his guitar. Sometimes we leave him out there playing on the guitar.

Monsieur Bayonne made the Sign of the Cross over and over on my jaw, but that didn't do no good. Even when he prayed and told me to pray some, too, that tooth still hurt me.

"How you feeling?" he say.

"Same," I say.

He kept on praying and making the Sign of the Cross and I kept on praying, too.

"Still hurting?" he say.

"Yes, sir."

Monsieur Bayonne mashed harder and harder on my jaw. He mashed so hard he almost pushed me over on Ty. But then he stopped.

"What kind of prayers you praying, boy?" he say.

"Baptist," I say.

"Well, I'll be—no wonder that tooth still killing him. I'm going one way and he pulling the other. Boy, don't you know any Catholic prayers?"

"I know 'Hail Mary,'" I say.

"Then you better start saying it."

"Yes, sir."

He started mashing on my jaw again, and I could hear him praying at the same time. And, sure enough, after while it stopped hurting me.

Me and Ty went outside where Monsieur Bayonne's two hounds was and we started playing with them. "Let's go hunting," Ty say. "All right," I say; and we went on back in the pasture. Soon the hounds got on a trail, and me and Ty followed them all 'cross the pasture and then back in the woods, too. And then they cornered this little old rabbit and killed him, and me and Ty made them get back, and we picked up the rabbit and started on back home. But my tooth had started hurting me again. It was hurting me plenty now, but I wouldn't tell Monsieur Bayonne. That night I didn't sleep a bit, and first thing in the morning Auntie told me to go back and let Monsieur Bayonne pray over me some more. Monsieur Bayonne was in his kitchen making coffee when I got there. Soon 's he seen me he knowed what was wrong.

"All right, kneel down there 'side that stove," he say. "And this time make sure you pray Catholic. I don't know nothing 'bout that Baptist, and I don't want know nothing 'bout him."

3

Last night Mama say, "Tomorrow we going to town."

"It ain't hurting me no more," I say. "I can eat anything on it."

"Tomorrow we going to town," she say.

And after she finished eating, she got up and went to bed. She always go to bed early now. 'Fore Daddy went in the Army, she used to stay up late. All of us sitting out on the gallery or round the fire. But now, look like soon 's she finish eating she go to bed.

This morning when I woke up, her and Auntie was standing 'fore the fireplace. She say: "Enough to get there and get back. Dollar and a half to have it pulled. Twenty-five for me to go, twenty-five for him. Twenty-five for me to come back, twenty-five for him. Fifty cents left. Guess I get little piece of salt meat with that."

"Sure can use it," Auntie say. "White beans and no salt meat ain't white beans."

"I do the best I can," Mama say.

They was quiet after that, and I made 'tend I was still asleep.

"James, hit the floor," Auntie say.

I still made 'tend I was asleep. I didn't want them to know I was listening.

"All right," Auntie say, shaking me by the shoulder. "Come on. Today's the day."

I pushed the cover down to get out, and Ty grabbed it and pulled it back.

"You, too, Ty," Auntie say.

"I ain't getting no teef pulled," Ty say.

"Don't mean it ain't time to get up," Auntie say. "Hit it, Ty."

Ty got up grumbling.

"James, you hurry up and get in your clothes and eat your food," Auntie say. "What time y'all coming back?" she say to Mama.

"That 'leven o'clock bus," Mama say. "Got to get back in that field this evening."

"Get a move on you, James," Auntie say.

I went in the kitchen and washed my face, then I ate my breakfast. I was having bread and syrup. The bread was warm and hard and tasted good. And I tried to make it last a long time.

Ty came back there grumbling and mad at me.

"Got to get up," he say. "I ain't having no teefes pulled. What I got to be getting up for?"

Ty poured some syrup in his pan and got a piece of bread. He didn't wash his hands, neither his face, and I could see that white stuff in his eyes.

"You the one getting your teef pulled," he say. "What I got to get up for. I bet if I was getting a teef pulled, you wouldn't be getting up. Shucks; syrup again. I'm getting tired of this old syrup. Syrup, syrup, syrup. I'm go'n take with the sugar diabetes. I want me some bacon sometime."

"Go out in the field and work and you can have your bacon," Auntie say. She stood in the middle door looking at Ty. "You better be glad you got syrup. Some people ain't got that—hard 's time is."

"Shucks," Ty say. "How can I be strong."

"I don't know too much 'bout your strength," Auntie say; "but I know where you go'n be hot at, you keep that grumbling up. James, get a move on you; your mama waiting."

I ate my last piece of bread and went in the front room. Mama was standing 'fore the fireplace warming her hands. I put on my coat and my cap, and we left the house.

4

I look down there again, but it still ain't coming. I almost say, "It ain't coming yet," but I keep my mouth shut. 'Cause that's something else she don't like. She don't like for you to say something just for nothing. She can see it ain't coming, I can see it ain't coming, so why say it ain't coming. I don't say it, I turn and look at the river that's back of us. It's so cold the smoke's just raising up from the water. I see a bunch of pool-doos not too far out—just on the other side the lilies. I'm wondering if you can eat pool-doos. I ain't too sure, 'cause I ain't never ate none. But I done ate owls and blackbirds, and I done ate redbirds, too. I didn't want kill the redbirds, but she made me kill them. They had two of them back there. One in my trap, one in Ty's trap. Me and Ty was go'n play with them and let them go, but she made me kill them 'cause we needed the food.

"I can't," I say. "I can't."

"Here," she say. "Take it."

"I can't," I say. "I can't. I can't kill him, Mama, please."

"Here," she say. "Take this fork, James."

"Please, Mama, I can't kill him," I say.

I could tell she was go'n hit me. I jerked back, but I didn't jerk back soon enough.

"Take it," she say.

I took it and reached in for him, but he kept on hopping to the back.

"I can't, Mama," I say. The water just kept on running down my face. "I can't," I say.

"Get him out of there," she say.

I reached in for him and he kept on hopping to the back. Then I reached in farther, and he pecked me on the hand.

"I can't, Mama," I say.

She slapped me again.

I reached in again, but he kept on hopping out my way. Then he hopped to one side and I reached there. The fork got him on the leg and I heard his leg pop. I pulled my hand out 'cause I had hurt him.

"Give it here," she say, and jerked the fork out my hand.

She reached in and got the little bird right in the neck. I heard the fork go in his neck, and I heard it go in the ground. She brought him out and helt him right in front of me.

"That's one," she say. She shook him off and gived me the fork. "Get the other one."

"I can't, Mama," I say. "I'll do anything, but don't make me do that."

She went to the corner of the fence and broke the biggest switch over there she could find. I knelt 'side the trap, crying.

"Get him out of there," she say.

"I can't, Mama."

She started hitting me 'cross the back. I went down on the ground, crying.

"Get him," she say.

"Octavia?" Auntie say.

'Cause she had come out of the house and she was standing by the tree looking at us.

"Get him out of there," Mama say.

"Octavia," Auntie say, "explain to him. Explain to him. Just don't beat him. Explain to him."

But she hit me and hit me and hit me.

I'm still young—I ain't no more than eight; but I know now; I know why I had to do it. (They was so little though. They was so little. I 'member how

I picked the feathers off them and cleaned them and helt them over the fire.
Then we all ate them. Ain't had but a little bitty piece each, but we all had a
little bitty piece, and everybody just looked at me 'cause they was so proud.)
Suppose she had to go away? That's why I had to do it. Suppose she had to
go away like Daddy went away? Then who was go'n look after us? They had
to be somebody left to carry on. I didn't know it then, but I know it now.
Auntie and Monsieur Bayonne talked to me and made me see.

5

Time I see it I get out my handkerchief and start waving. It's still 'way down
there, but I keep waving anyhow. Then it come up and stop and me and
Mama get on. Mama tell me go sit in the back while she pay. I do like she
say, and the people look at me. When I pass the little sign that say "White"
and "Colored," I start looking for a seat. I just see one of them back there,
but I don't take it, 'cause I want my mama to sit down herself. She comes in
the back and sit down, and I lean on the seat. They got seats in the front,
but I know I can't sit there, 'cause I have to sit back of the sign. Anyhow, I
don't want sit there if my mama go'n sit back here.

They got a lady sitting 'side my mama and she looks at me and smiles
little bit. I smile back, but I don't open my mouth, 'cause the wind'll get in
and make that tooth ache. The lady take out a pack of gum and reach me a
slice, but I shake my head. The lady just can't understand why a little boy'll
turn down gum, and she reach me a slice again. This time I point to my jaw.
The lady understands and smiles little bit, and I smile little bit, but I don't
open my mouth, though.

They got a girl sitting 'cross from me. She got on a red overcoat and her
hair's plaited in one big plait. First, I make 'tend I don't see her over there,
but then I start looking at her little bit. She make 'tend she don't see me, either, but I catch her looking that way. She got a cold, and every now and
then she h'ist that little handkerchief to her nose. She ought to blow it, but
she don't. Must think she's too much a lady or something.

Every time she h'ist that little handkerchief, the lady 'side her say something in her ear. She shakes her head and lays her hands in her lap again.
Then I catch her kind of looking where I'm at. I smile at her little bit. But
think she'll smile back? Uh-uh. She just turn up her little old nose and turn
her head. Well, I show her both of us can turn us head. I turn mine too and
look out at the river.

The river is gray. The sky is gray. They have pool-doos on the water. The
water is wavy, and the pool-doos go up and down. The bus go round a turn,
and you got plenty trees hiding the river. Then the bus go round another
turn, and I can see the river again.

I look toward the front where all the white people sitting. Then I look at
that little old gal again. I don't look right at her, 'cause I don't want all them
people to know I love her. I just look at her little bit, like I'm looking out
that window over there. But she knows I'm looking that way, and she kind

of look at me, too. The lady sitting 'side her catch her this time, and she leans over and says something in her ear.

"I don't love him nothing," that little old gal says out loud.

Everybody back there hear her mouth, and all of them look at us and laugh.

"I don't love you, either," I say. "So you don't have to turn up your nose, Miss."

"You the one looking," she say.

"I wasn't looking at you," I say. "I was looking out that window, there."

"Out that window, my foot," she say. "I seen you. Everytime I turned round you was looking at me."

"You must of been looking yourself if you seen me all them times," I say.

"Shucks," she say, "I got me all kind of boyfriends."

"I got girlfriends, too," I say.

"Well, I just don't want you getting your hopes up," she say.

I don't say no more to that little old gal 'cause I don't want have to bust her in the mouth. I lean on the seat where Mama sitting, and I don't even look that way no more. When we get to Bayonne, she jugg her little old tongue out at me. I make 'tend I'm go'n hit her, and she duck down 'side her mama. And all the people laugh at us again.

6

Me and Mama get off and start walking in town. Bayonne is a little bitty town. Baton Rouge is a hundred times bigger than Bayonne. I went to Baton Rouge once—me, Ty, Mama, and Daddy. But that was 'way back yonder, 'fore Daddy went in the Army. I wonder when we go'n see him again. I wonder when. Look like he ain't ever coming back home.... Even the pavement all cracked in Bayonne. Got grass shooting right out the sidewalk. Got weeds in the ditch, too; just like they got at home.

It's some cold in Bayonne. Look like it's colder than it is home. The wind blows in my face, and I feel that stuff running down my nose. I sniff. Mama says use that handkerchief. I blow my nose and put it back.

We pass a school and I see them white children playing in the yard. Big old red school, and them children just running and playing. Then we pass a café, and I see a bunch of people in there eating. I wish I was in there 'cause I'm cold. Mama tells me keep my eyes in front where they belong.

We pass stores that's got dummies, and we pass another café, and then we pass a shoe shop, and that bald-head man in there fixing on a shoe. I look at him and I butt into that white lady, and Mama jerks me in front and tells me stay there.

We come up to the courthouse, and I see the flag waving there. This flag ain't like the one we got at school. This one here ain't got but a handful of stars.[1] One at school got a big pile of stars—one for every state. We pass it

---

[1] Up through the 1940s and beyond, the Confederate flag with its stars and bars was displayed outside public schools, courthouses, and other official buildings in many southern states.

and we turn and there it is—the dentist office. Me and Mama go in, and they got people sitting everywhere you look. They even got a little boy in there younger than me.

Me and Mama sit on that bench, and a white lady come in there and ask me what my name is. Mama tells her and the white lady goes on back. Then I hear somebody hollering in there. Soon 's that little boy hear him hollering, he starts hollering, too. His mama pats him and pats him, trying to make him hush up, but he ain't thinking 'bout his mama.

The man that was hollering in there comes out holding his jaw. He is a big old man and he's wearing overalls and a jumper.

"Got it, hanh?" another man asks him.

The man shakes his head—don't want open his mouth.

"Man, I thought they was killing you in there," the other man says. "Hollering like a pig under a gate."

The man don't say nothing. He just heads for the door, and the other man follows him.

"John Lee," the white lady says. "John Lee Williams."

The little boy juggs his head down in his mama's lap and holler more now. His mama tells him go with the nurse, but he ain't thinking 'bout his mama. His mama tells him again, but he don't even hear her. His mama picks him up and takes him in there, and even when the white lady shuts the door I can still hear little old John Lee.

"I often wonder why the Lord let a child like that suffer," a lady says to my mama. The lady's sitting right in front of us on another bench. She's got on a white dress and a black sweater. She must be a nurse or something herself, I reckon.

"Not us to question," a man says.

"Sometimes I don't know if we shouldn't," the lady says.

"I know definitely we shouldn't," the man says. The man looks like a preacher. He's big and fat and he's got on a black suit. He's got a gold chain, too.

"Why?" the lady says.

"Why anything?" the preacher says.

"Yes," the lady says. "Why anything?"

"Not us to question," the preacher says.

The lady looks at the preacher a little while and looks at Mama again.

"And look like it's the poor who suffers the most," she says. "I don't understand it."

"Best not to even try," the preacher says. "He works in mysterious ways—wonders to perform."

Right then little John Lee bust out hollering, and everybody turn they head to listen.

"He's not a good dentist," the lady says. "Dr. Robillard is much better. But more expensive. That's why most of the colored people come here. The white people go to Dr. Robillard. Y'all from Bayonne?"

"Down the river," my mama says. And that's all she go'n say, 'cause she don't talk much. But the lady keeps on looking at her, and so she says, "Near Morgan."

"I see," the lady says.

7

"That's the trouble with the black people in this country today," somebody else says. This one here's sitting on the same side me and Mama's sitting, and he is kind of sitting in front of that preacher. He looks like a teacher or somebody that goes to college. He's got on a suit, and he's got a book that he's been reading. "We don't question is exactly our problem," he says. "We should question and question and question—question everything."

The preacher just looks at him a long time. He done put a toothpick or something in his mouth, and he just keeps on turning it and turning it. You can see he don't like that boy with that book.

"Maybe you can explain what you mean," he says.

"I said what I meant," the boy says. "Question everything. Every stripe, every star, every word spoken. Everything."

"It 'pears to me that this young lady and I was talking 'bout God, young man," the preacher says.

"Question Him, too," the boy says.

"Wait," the preacher says. "Wait now."

"You heard me right," the boy says. "His existence as well as everything else. Everything."

The preacher just looks across the room at the boy. You can see he's getting madder and madder. But mad or no mad, the boy ain't thinking 'bout him. He looks at that preacher just 's hard 's the preacher looks at him.

"Is this what they coming to?" the preacher says. "Is this what we educating them for?"

"You're not educating me," the boy says. "I wash dishes at night so that I can go to school in the day. So even the words you spoke need questioning."

The preacher just looks at him and shakes his head.

"When I come in this room and seen you there with your book, I said to myself, 'There's an intelligent man.' How wrong a person can be."

"Show me one reason to believe in the existence of a God," the boy says.

"My heart tells me," the preacher says.

"'My heart tells me,'" the boy says. "'My heart tells me.' Sure, 'My heart tells me.' And as long as you listen to what your heart tells you, you will have only what the white man gives you and nothing more. Me, I don't listen to my heart. The purpose of the heart is to pump blood throughout the body, and nothing else."

"Who's your paw, boy?" the preacher says.

"Why?"

"Who is he?"

"He's dead."

"And your mom?"

"She's in Charity Hospital with pneumonia. Half killed herself, working for nothing."

"And 'cause he's dead and she's sick, you mad at the world?"

"I'm not mad at the world. I'm questioning the world. I'm questioning it with cold logic, sir. What do words like Freedom, Liberty, God, White, Colored mean? I want to know. That's why *you* are sending us to school, to read and to ask questions. And because we ask these questions, you call us mad. No sir, it is not us who are mad."

"You keep saying 'us'?"

"'Us.' Yes—us. I'm not alone."

The preacher just shakes his head. Then he looks at everybody in the room—everybody. Some of the people look down at the floor, keep from looking at him. I kind of look 'way myself, but soon 's I know he done turn his head, I look that way again.

"I'm sorry for you," he says to the boy.

"Why?" the boy says. "Why not be sorry for yourself? Why are you so much better off than I am? Why aren't you sorry for these other people in here? Why not be sorry for the lady who had to drag her child into the dentist office? Why not be sorry for the lady sitting on that bench over there? Be sorry for them. Not for me. Some way or other I'm going to make it."

"No, I'm sorry for you," the preacher says.

"Of course, of course," the boy says, nodding his head. "You're sorry for me because I rock that pillar you're leaning on."

"You can't ever rock the pillar I'm leaning on, young man. It's stronger than anything man can ever do."

"You believe in God because a man told you to believe in God," the boy says. "A white man told you to believe in God. And why? To keep you ignorant so he can keep his feet on your neck."

"So now we the ignorant?" the preacher says.

"Yes," the boy says. "Yes." And he opens his book again.

The preacher just looks at him sitting there. The boy done forgot all about him. Everybody else make 'tend they done forgot the squabble, too.

Then I see that preacher getting up real slow. Preacher's a great big old man and he got to brace himself to get up. He comes over where the boy is sitting. He just stands there a little while looking down at him, but the boy don't raise his head.

"Get up, boy," preacher says.

The boy looks up at him, then he shuts his book real slow and stands up. Preacher just hauls back and hit him in the face. The boy falls back 'gainst the wall, but he straightens himself up and looks right back at that preacher.

"You forgot the other cheek," he says.

The preacher hauls back and hit him again on the other side. But this time the boy braces himself and don't fall.

"That hasn't changed a thing," he says.

The preacher just looks at the boy. The preacher's breathing real hard like he just run up a big hill. The boy sits down and opens his book again.

"I feel sorry for you," the preacher says. "I never felt so sorry for a man before."

The boy makes 'tend he don't even hear that preacher. He keeps on reading his book. The preacher goes back and gets his hat off the chair.

"Excuse me," he says to us. "I'll come back some other time. Y'all, please excuse me."

And he looks at the boy and goes out the room. The boy h'ist his hand up to his mouth one time to wipe 'way some blood. All the rest of the time he keeps on reading. And nobody else in there say a word.

8

Little John Lee and his mama come out the dentist office, and the nurse calls somebody else in. Then little bit later they come out, and the nurse calls another name. But fast 's she calls somebody in there, somebody else comes in the place where we sitting, and the room stays full.

The people coming in now, all of them wearing big coats. One of them says something 'bout sleeting, another one says he hope not. Another one says he think it ain't nothing but rain. 'Cause, he says, rain can get awful cold this time of year.

All round the room they talking. Some of them talking to people right by them, some of them talking to people clear 'cross the room, some of them talking to anybody'll listen. It's a little bitty room, no bigger than us kitchen, and I can see everybody in there. The little old room's full of smoke, 'cause you got two old men smoking pipes over by that side door. I think I feel my tooth thumping me some, and I hold my breath and wait. I wait and wait, but it don't thump me no more. Thank God for that.

I feel like going to sleep, and I lean back 'gainst the wall. But I'm scared to go to sleep. Scared 'cause the nurse might call my name and I won't hear her. And Mama might go to sleep, too, and she'll be mad if neither one of us heard the nurse.

I look up at Mama. I love my mama. I love my mama. And when cotton come I'm go'n get her a new coat. And I ain't go'n get a black one, either. I think I'm go'n get her a red one.

"They got some books over there," I say. "Want read one of them?"

Mama looks at the books, but she don't answer me.

"You got yourself a little man there," the lady says.

Mama don't say nothing to the lady, but she must've smiled, 'cause I seen the lady smiling back. The lady looks at me a little while, like she's feeling sorry for me.

"You sure got that preacher out here in a hurry," she says to that boy.

The boy looks up at her and looks in his book again. When I grow up I want be just like him. I want clothes like that and I want keep a book with me, too.

"You really don't believe in God?" the lady says.

"No," he says.

"But why?" the lady says.

"Because the wind is pink," he says.

"What?" the lady says.

The boy don't answer her no more. He just reads in his book.

"Talking 'bout the wind is pink," that old lady says. She's sitting on the same bench with the boy and she's trying to look in his face. The boy makes 'tend the old lady ain't even there. He just keeps on reading. "Wind is pink," she says again. "Eh, Lord, what children go'n be saying next?"

The lady 'cross from us bust out laughing.

"That's a good one," she says. "The wind is pink. Yes sir, that's a good one."

"Don't you believe the wind is pink?" the boy says. He keeps his head down in the book.

"Course I believe it, honey," the lady says. "Course I do." She looks at us and winks her eye. "And what color is grass, honey?"

"Grass? Grass is black."

She bust out laughing again. The boy looks at her.

"Don't you believe grass is black?" he says.

The lady quits her laughing and looks at him. Everybody else looking at him, too. The place quiet, quiet.

"Grass is green, honey," the lady says. "It was green yesterday, it's green today, and it's go'n be green tomorrow."

"How do you know it's green?"

"I know because I know."

"You don't know it's green," the boy says. "You believe it's green because someone told you it was green. If someone had told you it was black you'd believe it was black."

"It's green," the lady says. "I know green when I see green."

"Prove it's green," the boy says.

"Sure, now," the lady says. "Don't tell me it's coming to that."

"It's coming to just that," the boy says. "Words mean nothing. One means no more than the other."

"That's what it all coming to?" that old lady says. That old lady got on a turban and she got on two sweaters. She got a green sweater under a black sweater. I can see the green sweater 'cause some of the buttons on the other sweater's missing.

"Yes ma'am," the boy says. "Words mean nothing. Action is the only thing. Doing. That's the only thing."

"Other words, you want the Lord to come down here and show Hisself to you?" she says.

"Exactly, ma'am," he says.

"You don't mean that, I'm sure?" she says.

"I do, ma'am," he says.

"Done, Jesus," the old lady says, shaking her head.

"I didn't go 'long with that preacher at first," the other lady says; "but now—I don't know. When a person say the grass is black, he's either a lunatic or something's wrong."

"Prove to me that it's green," the boy says.

"It's green because the people say it's green."

"Those same people say we're citizens of these United States," the boy says.

"I think I'm a citizen," the lady says.

"Citizens have certain rights," the boy says. "Name me one right that you have. One right, granted by the Constitution, that you can exercise in Bayonne."

The lady don't answer him. She just looks at him like she don't know what he's talking 'bout. I know I don't.

"Things changing," she says.

"Things are changing because some black men have begun to think with their brains and not their hearts," the boy says.

"You trying to say these people don't believe in God?"

"I'm sure some of them do. Maybe most of them do. But they don't believe that God is going to touch these white people's hearts and change things tomorrow. Things change through action. By no other way."

Everybody sit quiet and look at the boy. Nobody says a thing. Then the lady 'cross the room from me and Mama just shakes her head.

"Let's hope that not all your generation feel the same way you do," she says.

"Think what you please, it doesn't matter," the boy says. "But it will be men who listen to their heads and not their hearts who will see that your children have a better chance than you had."

"Let's hope they ain't all like you, though," the old lady says. "Done forgot the heart absolutely."

"Yes ma'am, I hope they aren't all like me," the boy says. "Unfortunately, I was born too late to believe in your God. Let's hope that the ones who come after will have your faith—if not in your God, then in something else, something definitely that they can lean on. I haven't anything. For me, the wind is pink, the grass is black."

9

The nurse comes in the room where we all sitting and waiting and says the doctor won't take no more patients till one o'clock this evening. My mama jumps up off the bench and goes up to the white lady.

"Nurse, I have to go back in the field this evening," she says.

"The doctor is treating his last patient now," the nurse says. "One o'clock this evening."

"Can I at least speak to the doctor?" my mama asks.

"I'm his nurse," the lady says.

"My little boy's sick," my mama says. "Right now his tooth almost killing him."

The nurse looks at me. She's trying to make up her mind if to let me come in. I look at her real pitiful. The tooth ain't hurting me at all, but Mama say it is, so I make 'tend for her sake.

"This evening," the nurse says, and goes on back in the office.

"Don't feel 'jected, honey," the lady says to Mama. "I been round them a long time—they take you when they want to. If you was white, that's something else; but we the wrong color."

Mama don't say nothing to the lady, and me and her go outside and stand 'gainst the wall. It's cold out there. I can feel that wind going through my coat. Some of the other people come out of the room and go up the street. Me and Mama stand there a little while and we start walking. I don't know where we going. When we come to the other street we just stand there.

"You don't have to make water, do you?" Mama says.

"No, ma'am," I say.

We go on up the street. Walking real slow. I can tell Mama don't know where she's going. When we come to a store we stand there and look at the dummies. I look at a little boy wearing a brown overcoat. He's got on brown shoes, too. I look at my old shoes and look at his'n again. You wait till summer, I say.

Me and Mama walk away. We come up to another store and we stop and look at them dummies, too. Then we go on again. We pass a café where the white people in there eating. Mama tells me keep my eyes in front where they belong, but I can't help from seeing them people eat. My stomach starts to growling 'cause I'm hungry. When I see people eating, I get hungry; when I see a coat, I get cold.

A man whistles at my mama when we go by a filling station. She makes 'tend she don't even see him. I look back and I feel like hitting him in the mouth. If I was bigger, I say; if I was bigger, you'd see.

We keep on going. I'm getting colder and colder, but I don't say nothing. I feel that stuff running down my nose and I sniff.

"That rag," Mama says.

I get it out and wipe my nose. I'm getting cold all over now—my face, my hands, my feet, everything. We pass another little café, but this'n for white people, too, and we can't go in there, either. So we just walk. I'm so cold now I'm 'bout ready to say it. If I knowed where we was going I wouldn't be so cold, but I don't know where we going. We go, we go, we go. We walk clean out of Bayonne. Then we cross the street and we come back. Same thing I seen when I got off the bus this morning. Same old trees, same old walk, same old weeds, same old cracked pave—same old everything.

I sniff again.

"That rag," Mama says.

I wipe my nose real fast and jugg that handkerchief back in my pocket 'fore my hand gets too cold. I raise my head and I can see David's hardware store. When we come up to it, we go in. I don't know why, but I'm glad.

It's warm in there. It's so warm in there you don't ever want to leave. I look for the heater, and I see it over by them barrels. Three white men standing round the heater talking in Creole. One of them comes over to see what my mama want.

"Got any axe handles?" she says.

Me, Mama and the white man start to the back, but Mama stops me when we come up to the heater. She and the white man go on. I hold my hands over the heater and look at them. They go all the way to the back, and I see the white man pointing to the axe handles 'gainst the wall. Mama takes one of them and shakes it like she's trying to figure how much it weighs. Then she rubs her hand over it from one end to the other end. She turns it over and looks at the other side, then she shakes it again, and shakes her head and puts it back. She gets another one and she does it just like she did the first one, then she shakes her head. Then she gets a brown one and do it that, too. But she don't like this one, either. Then she gets another one, but 'fore she shakes it or anything, she looks at me. Look like she's trying to say something to me, but I don't know what it is. All I know is I done got warm now and I'm feeling right smart better. Mama shakes this axe handle just like she did the others, and shakes her head and says something to the white man. The white man just looks at his pile of axe handles, and when Mama pass him to come to the front, the white man just scratch his head and follows her. She tells me come on and we go on out and start walking again.

We walk and walk, and no time at all I'm cold again. Look like I'm colder now 'cause I can still remember how good it was back there. My stomach growls and I suck it in to keep Mama from hearing it. She's walking right 'side me, and it growls so loud you can hear it a mile. But Mama don't say a word.

10

When we come up to the courthouse, I look at the clock. It's got quarter to twelve. Mean we got another hour and a quarter to be out here in the cold. We go and stand 'side a building. Something hits my cap and I look up at the sky. Sleet's falling.

I look at Mama standing there. I want stand close 'side her, but she don't like that. She say that's crybaby stuff. She say you got to stand for yourself, by yourself.

"Let's go back to that office," she says.

We cross the street. When we get to the dentist office I try to open the door, but I can't. I twist and twist, but I can't. Mama pushes me to the side and she twist the knob, but she can't open the door, either. She turns 'way from the door. I look at her, but I don't move and I don't say nothing. I done seen her like this before and I'm scared of her.

"You hungry?" she says. She says it like she's mad at me, like I'm the cause of everything.

"No, ma'am," I say.

"You want eat and walk back, or you rather don't eat and ride?"

"I ain't hungry," I say.

I ain't just hungry, but I'm cold, too. I'm so hungry and cold I want to cry. And look like I'm getting colder and colder. My feet done got numb. I try to work my toes, but I don't even feel them. Look like I'm go'n die. Look like I'm go'n stand right here and freeze to death. I think 'bout home. I think 'bout Val and Auntie and Ty and Louis and Walker. It's 'bout twelve o'clock and I know they eating dinner now. I can hear Ty making jokes. He done forgot 'bout getting up early this morning and right now he's probably making jokes. Always trying to make somebody laugh. I wish I was right there listening to him. Give anything in the world if I was home round the fire.

"Come on," Mama says.

We start walking again. My feet so numb I can't hardly feel them. We turn the corner and go on back up the street. The clock on the courthouse starts hitting for twelve.

The sleet's coming down plenty now. They hit the pave and bounce like rice. Oh, Lord; oh, Lord, I pray. Don't let me die, don't let me die, don't let me die, Lord.

11

Now I know where we going. We going back of town where the colored people eat. I don't care if I don't eat. I been hungry before. I can stand it. But I can't stand the cold.

I can see we go'n have a long walk. It's 'bout a mile down there. But I don't mind. I know when I get there I'm go'n warm myself. I think I can hold out. My hands numb in my pockets and my feet numb, too, but if I keep moving I can hold out. Just don't stop no more, that's all.

The sky's gray. The sleet keeps on falling. Falling like rain now—plenty, plenty. You can hear it hitting the pave. You can see it bouncing. Sometimes it bounces two times 'fore it settles.

We keep on going. We don't say nothing. We just keep on going, keep on going.

I wonder what Mama's thinking. I hope she ain't mad at me. When summer come I'm go'n pick plenty cotton and get her a coat. I'm go'n get her a red one.

I hope they'd make it summer all the time. I'd be glad if it was summer all the time—but it ain't. We got to have winter, too. Lord, I hate the winter. I guess everybody hate the winter.

I don't sniff this time. I get out my handkerchief and wipe my nose. My hands's so cold I can hardly hold the handkerchief.

I think we getting close, but we ain't there yet. I wonder where everybody is. Can't see a soul but us. Look like we the only two people moving round today. Must be too cold for the rest of the people to move round in.

I can hear my teeth. I hope they don't knock together too hard and make that bad one hurt. Lord, that's all I need, for that bad one to start off.

I hear a church bell somewhere. But today ain't Sunday. They must be ringing for a funeral or something.

I wonder what they doing at home. They must be eating. Monsieur Bayonne might be there with his guitar. One day Ty played with Monsieur Bayonne's guitar and broke one of the strings. Monsieur Bayonne was some mad with Ty. He say Ty wasn't go'n ever 'mount to nothing. Ty can go just like Monsieur Bayonne when he ain't there. Ty can make everybody laugh when he starts to mocking Monsieur Bayonne.

I used to like to be with Mama and Daddy. We used to be happy. But they took him in the Army. Now, nobody happy no more.... I be glad when Daddy comes home.

Monsieur Bayonne say it wasn't fair for them to take Daddy and give Mama nothing and give us nothing. Auntie say, "Shhh, Etienne. Don't let them hear you talk like that." Monsieur Bayonne say, "It's God truth. What they giving his children? They have to walk three and a half miles to school hot or cold. That's anything to give for a paw? She's got to work in the field rain or shine just to make ends meet. That's anything to give for a husband?" Auntie say, "Shhh, Etienne, shhh." "Yes, you right," Monsieur Bayonne say. "Best don't say it in front of them now. But one day they go'n find out. One day." "Yes, I suppose so," Auntie say. "Then what, Rose Mary?" Monsieur Bayonne say. "I don't know, Etienne," Auntie say. "All we can do is us job, and leave everything else in His hand ..."

We getting closer, now. We getting closer. I can even see the railroad tracks.

We cross the tracks, and now I see the café. Just to get in there, I say. Just to get in there. Already I'm starting to feel little better.

12

We go in. Ahh, it's good. I look for the heater; there 'gainst the wall. One of them little brown ones. I just stand there and hold my hands over it. I can't open my hands too wide 'cause they almost froze.

Mama's standing right 'side me. She done unbuttoned her coat. Smoke rises out of the coat, and the coat smells like a wet dog.

I move to the side so Mama can have more room. She opens out her hands and rubs them together. I rub mine together, too, 'cause this keep them from hurting. If you let them warm too fast, they hurt you sure. But if you let them warm just little bit at a time, and you keep rubbing them, they be all right every time.

They got just two more people in the café. A lady back of the counter, and a man on this side the counter. They been watching us ever since we come in.

Mama gets out the handkerchief and count up the money. Both of us know how much money she's got there. Three dollars. No, she ain't got three dollars, 'cause she had to pay us way up here. She ain't got but two dollars and a half left. Dollar and a half to get my tooth pulled, and fifty cents for us to go back on, and fifty cents worth of salt meat.

She stirs the money round with her finger. Most of the money is change 'cause I can hear it rubbing together. She stirs it and stirs it. Then she looks at the door. It's still sleeting. I can hear it hitting 'gainst the wall like rice.

"I ain't hungry, Mama," I say.

"Got to pay them something for they heat," she says.

She takes a quarter out the handkerchief and ties the handkerchief up again. She looks over her shoulder at the people, but she still don't move. I hope she don't spend the money. I don't want her spending it on me. I'm hungry, I'm almost starving I'm so hungry, but I don't want her spending the money on me.

She flips the quarter over like she's thinking. She's must be thinking 'bout us walking back home. Lord, I sure don't want walk home. If I thought it'd do any good to say something, I'd say it. But Mama makes up her own mind 'bout things.

She turns 'way from the heater right fast, like she better hurry up and spend the quarter 'fore she change her mind. I watch her go toward the counter. The man and the lady look at her, too. She tells the lady something and the lady walks away. The man keeps on looking at her. Her back's turned to the man, and she don't even know he's standing there.

The lady puts some cakes and a glass of milk on the counter. Then she pours up a cup of coffee and sets it 'side the other stuff. Mama pays her for the things and come on back where I'm standing. She tells me sit down at the table 'gainst the wall.

The milk and the cakes's for me; the coffee's for Mama. I eat slow and I look at her. She's looking outside at the sleet. She's looking real sad. I say to myself, I'm go'n make all this up one day. You see, one day, I'm go'n make all this up. I want say it now; I want tell her how I feel right now; but Mama don't like for us to talk like that.

"I can't eat all this," I say.

They ain't got but just three little old cakes there. I'm so hungry right now, the Lord knows I can eat a hundred times three, but I want my mama to have one.

Mama don't even look my way. She knows I'm hungry, she knows I want it. I let it stay there a little while, then I get it and eat it. I eat just on my front teeth, though, 'cause if cake touch that back tooth I know what'll happen. Thank God it ain't hurt me at all today.

After I finish eating I see the man go to the juke box. He drops a nickel in it, then he just stand there a little while looking at the record. Mama tells me keep my eyes in front where they belong. I turn my head like she say, but then I hear the man coming toward us.

"Dance, pretty?" he says.

Mama gets up to dance with him. But 'fore you know it, she done grabbed the little man in the collar and done heaved him 'side the wall. He hit the wall so hard he stop the juke box from playing.

"Some pimp," the lady back of the counter says. "Some pimp."

The little man jumps up off the floor and starts toward my mama. 'Fore you know it, Mama done sprung open her knife and she's waiting for him.

"Come on," she says. "Come on. I'll gut you from your neighbo to your throat. Come on."

I go up to the little man to hit him, but Mama makes me come and stand 'side her. The little man looks at me and Mama and goes on back to the counter.

"Some pimp," the lady back of the counter says. "Some pimp." She starts laughing and pointing at the little man. "Yes sir, you a pimp, all right. Yes sir-ree."

13

"Fasten that coat, let's go," Mama says.

"You don't have to leave," the lady says.

Mama don't answer the lady, and we right out in the cold again. I'm warm right now—my hands, my ears, my feet—but I know this ain't go'n last too long. It done sleet so much now you got ice everywhere you look.

We cross the railroad tracks, and soon's we do, I get cold. That wind goes through this little old coat like it ain't even there. I got on a shirt and a sweater under the coat, but that wind don't pay them no mind. I look up and I can see we got a long way to go. I wonder if we go'n make it 'fore I get too cold.

We cross over to walk on the sidewalk. They got just one sidewalk back here, and it's over there.

After we go just a little piece, I smell bread cooking. I look, then I see a baker shop. When we get closer, I can smell it more better. I shut my eyes and make 'tend I'm eating. But I keep them shut too long and I butt up 'gainst a telephone post. Mama grabs me and see if I'm hurt. I ain't bleeding or nothing and she turns me loose.

I can feel I'm getting colder and colder, and I look up to see how far we still got to go. Uptown is 'way up yonder. A half mile more, I reckon. I try to think of something. They say think and you won't get cold. I think of that poem, "Annabel Lee."[2] I ain't been to school in so long—this bad weather—I reckon they done passed "Annabel Lee" by now. But passed it or not, I'm sure Miss Walker go'n make me recite it when I get there. That woman don't never forget nothing. I ain't never seen nobody like that in my life.

I'm still getting cold. "Annabel Lee" or no "Annabel Lee," I'm still getting cold. But I can see we getting closer. We getting there gradually.

Soon 's we turn the corner, I see a little old white lady up in front of us. She's the only lady on the street. She's all in black and she's got a long black rag over her head.

[2]An 1849 poem by Edgar Allan Poe from the point of view of a speaker whose love for a girl does not abate after her death. It was once a common poem for schoolchildren to recite.

"Stop," she says.

Me and mama stop and look at her. She must be crazy to be out in all this bad weather. Ain't got but a few other people out there, and all of them's men.

"Y'll done ate?" she says.

"Just finish," Mama says.

"Y'all must be cold then?" she says.

"We headed for the dentist," Mama says. "We'll warm up when we get there."

"What dentist?" the old lady says. "Mr. Bassett?"

"Yes, ma'am," Mama says.

"Come on in," the old lady says. "I'll telephone him and tell him y'all coming."

Me and Mama follow the old lady in the store. It's a little bitty store, and it don't have much in there. The old lady takes off her head rag and folds it up.

"Helena?" somebody calls from the back.

"Yes, Alnest?" the old lady says.

"Did you see them?"

"They're here. Standing beside me."

"Good. Now you can stay inside."

The old lady looks at Mama. Mama's waiting to hear what she brought us in here for. I'm waiting for that, too.

"I saw y'all each time you went by," she says. "I came out to catch you, but you were gone."

"We went back of town," Mama says.

"Did you eat?"

"Yes, ma'am."

The old lady looks at Mama a long time, like she's thinking Mama might be just saying that. Mama looks right back at her. The old lady looks at me to see what I have to say. I don't say nothing. I sure ain't going 'gainst my mama.

"There's food in the kitchen," she says to Mama. "I've been keeping it warm."

Mama turns right around and starts for the door.

"Just a minute," the old lady says. Mama stops. "The boy'll have to work for it. It isn't free."

"We don't take no handout," Mama says.

"I'm not handing out anything," the old lady says. "I need my garbage moved to the front. Ernest has a bad cold and can't go out there."

"James'll move it for you," Mama says.

"Not unless you eat," the old lady says. "I'm old, but I have my pride, too, you know."

Mama can see she ain't go'n beat this old lady down, so she just shakes her head.

"All right," the old lady says. "Come into the kitchen."

She leads the way with that rag in her hand. The kitchen is a little bitty little old thing, too. The table and the stove just 'bout fill it up. They got a little room to the side. Somebody in there laying 'cross the bed—'cause I can see one of his feet. Must be the person she was talking to: Ernest or Alnest—something like that.

"Sit down," the old lady says to Mama. "Not you," she says to me. "You have to move the cans."

"Helena?" the man says in the other room.

"Yes, Alnest?" the old lady says.

"Are you going out there again?"

"I must show the boy where the garbage is, Alnest," the old lady says.

"Keep that shawl over your head," the old man says.

"You don't have to remind me, Alnest. Come, boy," the old lady says.

We go out in the yard. Little old back yard ain't no bigger than the store or the kitchen. But it can sleet here just like it can sleet in any big back yard. And 'fore you know it, I'm trembling.

"There," the old lady says, pointing to the cans. I pick up one of the cans and set it right back down. The can's so light, I'm go'n see what's inside of it.

"Here," the old lady says. "Leave that can alone."

I look back at her standing there in the door. She's got that black rag wrapped round her shoulders, and she's pointing one of her little old fingers at me.

"Pick it up and carry it to the front," she says. I go by her with the can, and she's looking at me all the time. I'm sure the can's empty. I'm sure she could've carried it herself—maybe both of them at the same time. "Set it on the sidewalk by the door and come back for the other one," she says.

I go and come back, and Mama looks at me when I pass her. I get the other can and take it to the front. It don't feel a bit heavier than that first one. I tell myself I ain't go'n be nobody's fool, and I'm go'n look inside this can to see just what I been hauling. First, I look up the street, then down the street. Nobody coming. Then I look over my shoulder toward the door. That little old lady done slipped up there quiet 's mouse, watching me again. Look like she knowed what I was go'n do.

"Ehh, Lord," she says. "Children, children. Come in here, boy, and go wash your hands."

I follow her in the kitchen. She points toward the bathroom, and I go in there and wash up. Little bitty old bathroom, but it's clean, clean. I don't use any of her towels; I wipe my hands on my pants legs.

When I come back in the kitchen, the old lady done dished up the food. Rice, gravy, meat—and she even got some lettuce and tomato in a saucer. She even got a glass of milk and a piece of cake there, too. It looks so good, I almost start eating 'fore I say my blessing.

"Helena?" the old man says.

"Yes, Alnest?"

"Are they eating?"

"Yes," she says.

"Good," he says. "Now you'll stay inside."

The old lady goes in there where he is and I can hear them talking. I look at Mama. She's eating slow like she's thinking. I wonder what's the matter now. I reckon she's thinking 'bout home.

The old lady comes back in the kitchen.

"I talked to Dr. Bassett's nurse," she says. "Dr. Bassett will take you as soon as you get there."

"Thank you, ma'am," Mama says.

"Perfectly all right," the old lady says. "Which one is it?"

Mama nods toward me. The old lady looks at me real sad. I look sad, too.

"You're not afraid, are you?" she says.

"No, ma'am," I say.

"That's a good boy," the old lady says. "Nothing to be afraid of. Dr. Bassett will not hurt you."

When me and Mama get through eating, we thank the old lady again.

"Helena, are they leaving?" the old man says.

"Yes, Alnest."

"Tell them I say good-bye."

"They can hear you, Alnest."

"Good-bye both mother and son," the old man says. "And may God be with you."

Me and Mama tell the old man good-bye, and we follow the old lady in the front room. Mama opens the door to go out, but she stops and comes back in the store.

"You sell salt meat?" she says.

"Yes."

"Give me two bits worth."

"That isn't very much salt meat," the old lady says.

"That's all I have," Mama says.

The old lady goes back of the counter and cuts a big piece off the chunk. Then she wraps it up and puts it in a paper bag.

"Two bits," she says.

"That looks like awful lot of meat for a quarter," Mama says.

"Two bits," the old lady says. "I've been selling salt meat behind this counter twenty-five years. I think I know what I'm doing."

"You got a scale there," Mama says.

"What?" the old lady says.

"Weigh it," Mama says.

"What?" the old lady says. "Are you telling me how to run my business?"

"Thanks very much for the food," Mama says.

"Just a minute," the old lady says.

"James," Mama says to me. I move toward the door.

"Just one minute, I said," the old lady says.

Me and Mama stop again and look at her. The old lady takes the meat out of the bag and unwraps it and cuts 'bout half of it off. Then she wraps it up again and juggs it back in the bag and gives the bag to Mama. Mama lays the quarter on the counter.

"Your kindness will never be forgotten," she says. "James," she says to me.

We go out, and the old lady comes to the door to look at us. After we go a little piece I look back, and she's still there watching us.

The sleet's coming down heavy, heavy now, and I turn up my coat collar to keep my neck warm. My mama tells me turn it right back down.

"You not a bum," she says. "You a man."

1968

N. SCOTT MOMADAY (KIOWA)
B. 1934

N. Scott Momaday often attributes the diversity of his forms of expression to his rich cultural inheritance and varied life experiences. From his father's family he received Kiowa storytelling traditions and a love of the Rainy Mountain area of Oklahoma. His mother, whose paternal great-grandmother was Cherokee, gave him admiration for literature written in English and the example of how a willful act of imagination could create an "Indian" identity. As Momaday recounts in *The Names*, during his childhood he lived in non-Indian communities as well as with several Southwestern tribes, especially the Jemez Pueblo. He attended reservation, public, and parochial schools, a Virginia military academy, the University of New Mexico (political science), the University of Virginia (to study law briefly), and Stanford, where he received his M.A. and Ph.D. and was strongly influenced by his mentor, Yvor Winters. Momaday's teaching career includes professorships at Berkeley, Stanford, and the University of Arizona. He has been recognized by both non-Indian and Indian worlds with a Guggenheim Fellowship, a Pulitzer Prize (for *House Made of Dawn*), and membership in the Kiowa Gourd Clan.

The tendency toward diverse forms of expression is obvious in most of Momaday's works. In *The Names*, he used fictional as well as traditional autobiographical techniques. The poems in *The Gourd Dancer*, *In the Presence of the Sun*, and *In the Bear's House* range from forms close to American Indian oral traditions ("The Delight Song of Tsoai-talee") to poems using highly structured written conventions ("Before an Old Painting of the Crucifixion") to free or open verse ("Comparatives") and dialogues ("The Bear-God Dialogues"). *House Made of Dawn*, a powerful novel about an alienated Jemez Pueblo World War II veteran, is told from different viewpoints and exhibits styles as direct as Hemingway's, as dense as Faulkner's, and as resonant as the songs of the Navajo Nightway ceremony, the source of the novel's title. Several of his works—most notably *In the Presence of the Sun* and *Circle of Wonder*—combine written and visual expressions. His second novel, *The Ancient Child*, juxtaposes ancient Kiowa bear narratives, a contemporary artist's male midlife crisis story, and Billy the Kid fantasies.

It is *The Way to Rainy Mountain*, however, that more than any of his other works demonstrates Momaday's ability to break through generic boundaries. In his essay "The Man Made of Words" (available in *The Remembered Earth*, ed. Geary Hobson, 1979/1981), Momaday describes the composition process that began with a desire to comprehend his Kiowa identity and with the collecting of stories from Kiowa elders. To all but a few of these brief tribal and family stories he added short historical and personal commentaries. Momaday then arranged twenty-four of these three-voice sections into three divisions ("The Setting Out," "The Going On," "The Closing In") to suggest several physical and spiritual journeys, the two most obvious being the migration and history of the Kiowa and the gradual development of his Kiowa identity. The three divisions are framed by two poems and three lyric essays (Prologue, Introduction, Epilogue) that combine mythic, historic, and personal perspectives.

The following selections, taken from each of the three divisions of *Rainy Mountain*, suggest the nature of the form and themes—themes that reappear in most of Momaday's works: celebrating the importance of the imagination, memory, and oral traditions; seeing the land as a crucial aspect of identity; acknowledging the power of American Indian concepts of sacredness, beauty, and harmony; and revering a sense of language that encompasses economy, power, delight, and wonder.

Kenneth M. Roemer
University of Texas at Arlington

PRIMARY WORKS

House Made of Dawn, 1968; *The Way to Rainy Mountain*, 1969; *The Gourd Dancer*, 1976; *The Names: A Memoir*, 1976; *The Ancient Child*, 1989; *In the Presence of the Sun*, 1992; *Circle of Wonder: A Native American Christmas Story*, 1994; *The Man Made of Words*, 1997; *In the Bear's House*, 1999.

from **The Way to Rainy Mountain**

Headwaters

Noon in the intermountain plain:
There is scant telling of the marsh—
A log, hollow and weather-stained,
An insect at the mouth, and moss—
Yet waters rise against the roots,
Stand brimming to the stalks. What moves?
What moves on this archaic force
Was wild and welling at the source.

Prologue

The journey began one day long ago on the edge of the northern Plains. It was carried on over a course of many generations and many hundreds of miles. In the end there were many things to remember, to dwell upon and talk about.

"You know, everything had to begin. . . ." For the Kiowas the beginning was a struggle for existence in the bleak northern mountains. It was there, they say, that they entered the world through a hollow log. The end, too, was a struggle, and it was lost. The young Plains culture of the Kiowas withered and died like grass that is burned in the prairie wind. There came a day like destiny; in every direction, as far as the eye could see, carrion lay out in the land. The buffalo was the animal representation of the sun, the essential and sacrificial victim of the Sun Dance. When the wild herds were destroyed, so too was the will of the Kiowa people; there was nothing to sustain them in spirit. But these are idle recollections, the mean and ordinary agonies of human history. The interim was a time of great adventure and nobility and fulfillment.

Tai-me came to the Kiowas in a vision born of suffering and despair.[1] "Take me with you," Tai-me said, "and I will give you whatever you want." And it was so. The great adventure of the Kiowas was a going forth into the heart of the continent. They began a long migration from the headwaters of the Yellowstone River eastward to the Black Hills and south to the Wichita Mountains. Along the way they acquired horses, the religion of the Plains, a love and possession of the open land. Their nomadic soul was set free. In alliance with the Comanches they held dominion in the southern Plains for a hundred years. In the course of that long migration they had come of age as a people. They had conceived a good idea of themselves; they had dared to imagine and determine who they were.

In one sense, then, the way to Rainy Mountain is preeminently the history of an idea, man's idea of himself, and it has old and essential being in language. The verbal tradition by which it has been preserved has suffered a deterioration in time. What remains is fragmentary: mythology, legend, lore, and hearsay—and of course the idea itself, as crucial and complete as it ever was. That is the miracle.

The journey herein recalled continues to be made anew each time the miracle comes to mind, for that is peculiarly the right and responsibility of the imagination. It is a whole journey, intricate with motion and meaning; and it is made with the whole memory, that experience of the mind which is legendary as well as historical, personal as well as cultural. And the journey is an evocation of three things in particular: a landscape that is incomparable, a time that is gone forever, and the human spirit, which endures. The

---

[1]Tai-me (or Tai-may) appears primarily in two manifestations in this book: as the legendary being who appeared to the Kiowas during "bad times," offering to help them, and as the revered Sun Dance doll, "less than 2 feet in length, representing a human figure dressed in a robe of white feathers" (*The Way to Rainy Mountain*, Sec. 10).

imaginative experience and the historical express equally the traditions of man's reality. Finally, then, the journey recalled is among other things the revelation of one way in which these traditions are conceived, developed, and interfused in the human mind. There are on the way to Rainy Mountain many landmarks, many journeys in the one. From the beginning the migration of the Kiowas was an expression of the human spirit, and that expression is most truly made in terms of wonder and delight: "There were many people, and oh, it was beautiful. That was the beginning of the Sun Dance. It was all for Tai-me, you know, and it was a long time ago."[2]

from Introduction[3]

Houses are like sentinels in the plain, old keepers of the weather watch. There, in a very little while, wood takes on the appearance of great age. All colors wear soon away in the wind and rain, and then the wood is burned gray and the grain appears and the nails turn red with rust. The window-panes are black and opaque; you imagine there is nothing within, and indeed there are many ghosts, bones given up to the land. They stand here and there against the sky, and you approach them for a longer time than you expect. They belong in the distance; it is their domain.

Once there was a lot of sound in my grandmother's house, a lot of coming and going, feasting and talk. The summers there were full of excitement and reunion. The Kiowas are a summer people; they abide the cold and keep to themselves, but when the season turns and the land becomes warm and vital they cannot hold still; an old love of going returns upon them. The aged visitors who came to my grandmother's house when I was a child were made of lean and leather, and they bore themselves upright. They wore great black hats and bright ample shirts that shook in the wind. They rubbed fat upon their hair and wound their braids with strips of colored cloth. Some of them painted their faces and carried the scars of old and cherished enmities. They were an old council of warlords, come to remind and be reminded of who they were. Their wives and daughters served them well. The women might indulge themselves; gossip was at once the mark and compensation of their servitude. They made loud and elaborate talk among themselves, full of jest and gesture, fright and false alarm. They went abroad in fringed and flowered shawls, bright beadwork and German silver. They were at home in the kitchen, and they prepared meals that were banquets.

There were frequent prayer meetings, and great nocturnal feasts. When I was a child I played with my cousins outside, where the lamplight fell upon the ground and the singing of the old people rose up around us and carried

---

[2]These words, spoken by an old Kiowa woman, Ko-sahn, are repeated near the conclusion of the Epilogue, which is included in this excerpt.
[3]The following paragraphs conclude the Introduction. They are preceded by Momaday's moving descriptions of the Rainy Mountain area of southwestern Oklahoma, his tribe's migration from mountainous western Montana, and his own retracing of that journey, which concluded with his pilgrimage to his grandmother's (Aho's) house and her grave.

away into the darkness. There were a lot of good things to eat, a lot of laughter and surprise. And afterwards, when the quiet returned, I lay down with my grandmother and could hear the frogs away by the river and feel the motion of the air.

Now there is a funeral silence in the rooms, the endless wake of some final word. The walls have closed in upon my grandmother's house. When I returned to it in mourning, I saw for the first time in my life how small it was. It was late at night, and there was a white moon, nearly full. I sat for a long time on the stone steps by the kitchen door. From there I could see out across the land; I could see the long row of trees by the creek, the low light upon the rolling plains, and the stars of the Big Dipper. Once I looked at the moon and caught sight of a strange thing. A cricket had perched upon the handrail, only a few inches away from me. My line of vision was such that the creature filled the moon like a fossil. It had gone there, I thought, to live and die, for there, of all places, was its small definition made whole and eternal. A warm wind rose up and purled like the longing within me.

The next morning I awoke at dawn and went out on the dirt road to Rainy Mountain. It was already hot, and the grasshoppers began to fill the air. Still, it was early in the morning, and the birds sang out of the shadows. The long yellow grass on the mountain shone in the bright light, and a scissortail hied above the land. There, where it ought to be, at the end of a long and legendary way, was my grandmother's grave. Here and there on the dark stones were ancestral names. Looking back once, I saw the mountain and came away.

IV

They lived at first in the mountains. They did not yet know of Tai-me, but this is what they knew: There was a man and his wife. They had a beautiful child, a little girl whom they would not allow to go out of their sight. But one day a friend of the family came and asked if she might take the child outside to play. The mother guessed that would be all right, but she told the friend to leave the child in its cradle and to place the cradle in a tree. While the child was in the tree, a redbird came among the branches. It was not like any bird that you have seen; it was very beautiful, and it did not fly away. It kept still upon a limb, close to the child. After a while the child got out of its cradle and began to climb after the redbird. And at the same time the tree began to grow taller, and the child was borne up into the sky. She was then a woman, and she found herself in a strange place. Instead of a redbird, there was a young man standing before her. The man spoke to her and said: "I have been watching you for a long time, and I knew that I would find a way to bring you here. I have brought you here to be my wife." The woman looked all around; she saw that he was the only living man there. She saw that he was the sun.

There the land itself ascends into the sky. These mountains lie at the top of the continent, and they cast a long rain shadow on the sea of grasses to the east. They arise out of the last North American wilderness, and they have wilderness names: Wasatch, Bitterroot, Bighorn, Wind River.[4]

> *I have walked in a mountain meadow bright with Indian paintbrush, lupine, and wild buckwheat, and I have seen high in the branches of a lodgepole pine the male pine grosbeak, round and rose-colored, its dark, striped wings nearly invisible in the soft, mottled light. And the uppermost branches of the tree seemed very slowly to ride across the blue sky.*

XVI

There was a strange thing, a buffalo with horns of steel. One day a man came upon it in the plain, just there where once upon a time four trees stood close together. The man and the buffalo began to fight. The man's hunting horse was killed right away, and the man climbed one of the trees. The great bull lowered its head and began to strike the tree with its black metal horns, and soon the tree fell. But the man was quick, and he leaped to the safety of the second tree. Again the bull struck with its unnatural horns, and the tree soon splintered and fell. The man leaped to the third tree and all the while he shot arrows at the beast; but the arrows glanced away like sparks from its dark hide. At last there remained only one tree and the man had only one arrow. He believed then that he would surely die. But something spoke to him and said: "Each time the buffalo prepares to charge, it spreads its cloven hooves and strikes the ground. Only there in the cleft of the hoof is it vulnerable; it is there you must aim." The buffalo went away and turned, spreading its hooves, and the man drew the arrow to his bow. His aim was true and the arrow struck deep into the soft flesh of the hoof. The great bull shuddered and fell, and its steel horns flashed once in the sun.

Forty years ago the townspeople of Carnegie, Oklahoma, gathered about two old Kiowa men who were mounted on work horses and armed with bows and arrows. Someone had got a buffalo, a poor broken beast in which there was no trace left of the wild strain. The old men waited silently amid the laughter and talk; then, at a signal, the buffalo was let go. It balked at first, more confused, perhaps, than afraid, and the horses had to be urged and then brought up short. The people shouted, and at last the buffalo wheeled and ran. The old men gave chase, and in the distance they were lost to view in a great, red cloud of dust. But they ran that animal down and killed it with arrows.

> *One morning my father and I walked in Medicine Park, on the edge of a small herd of buffalo. It was late in the spring, and many of the cows had newborn calves. Nearby a calf lay in the tall grass; it was red-orange in color, delicately beautiful with new life. We approached, but suddenly the cow was there in our way, her great dark head low and fearful-looking. Then she came at us, and we turned and ran as hard as we could. She gave up after a short run, and I think we had not been in any real danger. But the spring morning*

---

[4]These mountain ranges are located in Wyoming, Utah, Idaho, and Montana.

was deep and beautiful and our hearts were beating fast and we knew just then what it was to be alive.

XVII

Bad women are thrown away. Once there was a handsome young man. He was wild and reckless, and the chief talked to the wind about him. After that, the man went hunting. A great whirlwind passed by, and he was blind. The Kiowas have no need of a blind man; they left him alone with his wife and child. The winter was coming on and food was scarce. In four days the man's wife grew tired of caring for him. A herd of buffalo came near, and the man knew the sound. He asked his wife to hand him a bow and an arrow. "You must tell me," he said, "when the buffalo are directly in front of me." And in that way he killed a bull, but his wife said that he had missed. He asked for another arrow and killed another bull, but again his wife said that he had missed. Now the man was a hunter, and he knew the sound an arrow makes when it strikes home, but he said nothing. Then his wife helped herself to the meat and ran away with her child. The man was blind; he ate grass and kept himself alive. In seven days a band of Kiowas found him and took him to their camp. There in the firelight a woman was telling a story. She told of how her husband had been killed by enemy warriors. The blind man listened, and he knew her voice. That was a bad woman. At sunrise they threw her away.

In the Kiowa calendars[5] there is graphic proof that the lives of women were hard, whether they were "bad women" or not. Only the captives, who were slaves, held lower status. During the Sun Dance of 1843, a man stabbed his wife in the breast because she accepted Chief Dohasan's invitation to ride with him in the ceremonial procession. And in the winter of 1851–52, Big Bow stole the wife of a man who was away on a raiding expedition. He brought her to his father's camp and made her wait outside in the bitter cold while he went in to collect his things. But his father knew what was going on, and he held Big Bow and would not let him go. The woman was made to wait in the snow until her feet were frozen.

Mammedaty's[6] grandmother, Kau-au-ointy, was a Mexican captive, taken from her homeland when she was a child of eight or ten years. I never knew her, but I have been to her grave at Rainy Mountain.

KAU-AU-OINTY
BORN 1834
DIED 1929
AT REST

She raised a lot of eyebrows, they say, for she would not play the part of a Kiowa woman. From slavery she rose up to become a figure in the tribe.

[5]Kiowa history was kept on pictorial calendars. [6]Momaday's paternal grandfather.
For example, see James Mooney's *Calendar History of the Kiowa Indians* (rpt. 1979).

She owned a great herd of cattle, and she could ride as well as any man. She had blue eyes.

XXIV

East of my grandmother's house, south of the pecan grove, there is buried a woman in a beautiful dress. Mammedaty used to know where she is buried, but now no one knows. If you stand on the front porch of the house and look eastward towards Carnegie, you know that the woman is buried somewhere within the range of your vision. But her grave is unmarked. She was buried in a cabinet, and she wore a beautiful dress. How beautiful it was! It was one of those fine buckskin dresses, and it was decorated with elk's teeth and beadwork. That dress is still there, under the ground.

Aho's high moccasins are made of softest, cream-colored skins. On each in-step there is a bright disc of beadwork—an eight-pointed star, red and pale blue on a white field—and there are bands of beadwork at the soles and ankles. The flaps of the leggings are wide and richly ornamented with blue and red and green and white and lavender beads.

East of my grandmother's house the sun rises out of the plain. Once in his life a man ought to concentrate his mind upon the remembered earth, I believe. He ought to give himself up to a particular landscape in his experience, to look at it from as many angles as he can, to wonder about it, to dwell upon it. He ought to imagine that he touches it with his hands at every season and listens to the sounds that are made upon it. He ought to imagine the creatures there and all the faintest motions of the wind. He ought to recollect the glare of noon and all the colors of the dawn and dusk.

Epilogue

During the first hours after midnight on the morning of November 13, 1833, it seemed that the world was coming to an end. Suddenly the stillness of the night was broken; there were brilliant flashes of light in the sky, light of such intensity that people were awakened by it. With the speed and density of a driving rain, stars were falling in the universe. Some were brighter than Venus; one was said to be as large as the moon.

That most brilliant shower of Leonid meteors has a special place in the memory of the Kiowa people. It is among the earliest entries in the Kiowa calendars, and it marks the beginning as it were of the historical period in the tribal mind. In the preceding year Tai-me had been stolen by a band of Osages, and although it was later returned, the loss was an almost unimaginable tragedy; and in 1837 the Kiowas made the first of their treaties with the United States. The falling stars seemed to image the sudden and violent disintegration of an old order.

But indeed the golden age of the Kiowas had been short-lived, ninety or a hundred years, say, from about 1740. The culture would persist for a while in decline, until about 1875, but then it would be gone, and there would be very little material evidence that it had ever been. Yet it is within the reach of memory still, though tenuously now, and moreover it is even defined in a remarkably rich and living verbal tradition which demands to be preserved for its own sake. The living memory and the verbal tradition which transcends it were brought together for me once and for all in the person of Ko-sahn.

A hundred-year-old woman came to my grandmother's house one afternoon in July. Aho was dead; Mammedaty had died before I was born. There were very few Kiowas left who could remember the Sun Dances; Ko-sahn was one of them; she was a grown woman when my grandparents came into the world. Her body was twisted and her face deeply lined with age. Her thin white hair was held in place by a cap of black netting, though she wore braids as well, and she had but one eye. She was dressed in the manner of a Kiowa matron, a dark, full-cut dress that reached nearly to the ankles, full, flowing sleeves, and a wide, apron-like sash. She sat on a bench in the arbor so concentrated in her great age that she seemed extraordinarily small. She was quiet for a time—she might almost have been asleep—and then she began to speak and to sing. She spoke of many things, and once she spoke of the Sun Dance:

> My sisters and I were very young; that was a long time ago. Early one morning they came to wake us up. They had brought a great buffalo in from the plain. Everyone went out to see and to pray. We heard a great many voices. One man said that the lodge was almost ready. We were told to go there, and someone gave me a piece of cloth. It was very beautiful. Then I asked what I ought to do with it, and they said that I must tie it to the Tai-me tree. There were other pieces of cloth on the tree, and so I put mine there as well.
>
> When the lodge frame was finished, a woman—sometimes a man—began to sing. It was like this:
>
> Everything is ready.
> Now the four societies must go out.
> They must go out and get the leaves,
>   the branches for the lodge.
>
> And when the branches were tied in place, again there was singing:
>
> Let the boys go out.
> Come on, boys, now we must get the earth.
>
> The boys began to shout. Now they were not just ordinary boys, not all of them; they were those for whom prayers had been made, and they were dressed in different ways. There was an old, old woman. She had something on her back. The boys went out to see. The old woman had a bag full of earth on her back. It was a certain kind of sandy earth. That is what they must have in the lodge. The dancers must dance upon the sandy earth. The old woman held a digging tool in her hand. She turned towards the south and pointed with her lips. It was like a kiss, and she began to sing:
>
> We have brought the earth,
> Now it is time to play;

As old as I am, I still have the feeling of play.
That was the beginning of the Sun Dance. The dancers treated themselves
with buffalo medicine, and slowly they began to take their steps ... And all
the people were around, and they wore splendid things—beautiful buckskin
and beads. The chiefs wore necklaces, and their pendants shone like the sun.
There were many people, and oh, it was beautiful! That was the beginning of
the Sun Dance. It was all for Tai-me, you know, and it was a long time ago.

It was—all of this and more—a quest, a going forth upon the way to
Rainy Mountain. Probably Ko-sahn too is dead now. At times, in the quiet
of evening, I think she must have wondered, dreaming, who she was. Was
she become in her sleep that old purveyor of the sacred earth, perhaps, that
ancient one who, old as she was, still had the feeling of play? And in her
mind, at times, did she see the falling stars?

Rainy Mountain Cemetery

Most is your name the name of this dark stone.
Deranged in death, the mind to be inheres
Forever in the nominal unknown,
The wake of nothing audible he hears
Who listens here and now to hear your name.

The early sun, red as a hunter's moon,
Runs in the plain. The mountain burns and shines;
And silence is the long approach of noon
Upon the shadow that your name defines—
And death this cold, black density of stone.

1969

Aesthetics and Politics of the 1960s and 1970s—Black, Brown, Yellow, Red

FOR ALL THE REVOLUTIONARY ZEAL THAT INFORMED THE CONTENT AND MANNER in which U.S. writers of color composed works of deliberate difference, Russell Leong reminds us that authors during this period turned most often to the poetic form for its sheer practicality. "Poems are portable," Leong reflected about two decades after the emergence of "movement aesthetics." "They are easily held, do not require a light projector, a picture frame, a wind or percussion instrument to carry their images or produce their sounds." All that the poet required to produce this kind of writing was to put pen to paper and an audience ready and willing to listen and see anew what it already implicitly knew—that people have stories and are ready to tell them anywhere and everywhere despite the fetters of industry, institution, and technology.

This call to a poetic expression (and, by extension, a general creative expression) that is readily accessible to everyone nonetheless was perhaps an impossible goal. It demanded simultaneously that the poet craft different slants of light *and* maintain a watchful relationship with the people whose stories the poet distilled into new, dynamic arrangements.

Leong calls the artists of this generation simply storytellers who "live in communities where they write for family and friends. The relationship between the teller and listener is neighborly, because the teller of the stories must also listen. Storytellers, in their work, utilize the beliefs, feelings, and common dialects of those around them." A sense of responsibility informed the practical nature of movement aesthetics and led to writings that moved bodies as much as they moved hearts.

These writers witnessed the tectonic upheavals that permeated the decades of the 1960s and 1970s. The lines that society had drawn to regulate how people walked through the world were being redrawn or broken. No sooner had the United States begun to recover from the assassination of President John F. Kennedy in 1963 than the country witnessed the fall of others—Malcolm X, Martin Luther King, Jr., Robert Kennedy. Meanwhile, the water hoses that had been turned on peaceful protesters in Selma in the early part of the decade were soon directed at burning cars and storefronts. In the summers of 1965 and 1967, the urban fires of revolt reminded some Americans—and informed others—of the despair and misery that plagued communities of color in cities throughout the United States.

Unlike politicians and police officers, who struggled to keep pace with the ferment, artists scrambled to find the language to walk with the national ferment and perhaps even become its prophets. But how would they find the poetic word or line that improved on the one already heard on the streets? "Burn, baby, burn!" Established writers like former-Beat-turned-black-nationalist LeRoi Jones/Amiri Baraka convened conferences, and Gwendolyn Brooks recalibrated her stanzas to the vibrant syncopation of the times to move closer to the spirit of the movement. Larry Neal's reflections on the black aesthetic might best articulate the movement writers' desire to bring together politics and aesthetics, responsibility and creativity: the black aesthetic, as he puts it, is "[m]ore concerned with the vibration of the Word than the Word itself."

It wasn't just black artists who wanted to feel the vibration of the word. Others sensed the reverberations, too. Vine Deloria wrote of the difficulties that Native Americans face because their history has been controlled by European Americans who see only the stereotyped and misunderstood versions of real Native Americans.

While black aesthetic practitioners looked to the collective history of African Americans and the mythos of Africa as sources of creative and political unity, Asian Americans decided to stop listening to the siren song touting their status as "model minorities" whose exemplary behavior implicitly scorned the calls for immediate social change by other groups. What this meant most immediately was that Asian Americans looked in the mirror and did not see a white reflection, as the anonymous, presumably female, writer of "White Male Qualities" satirically suggests.

This rejection of whiteness would not be completed overnight, nor was such renunciation done without humor. Like the author of "White Male Qualities," Ron Tanaka inveighs against the extent to which an Asian American culture must first shed its allegiance to white standards. Because Tanaka's untitled polemic is written primarily in blank verse, a centuries-old Anglo-American poetic form, it allows us to read the struggle against "Western standards" or "White qualities" as one that is much more deep-seated, complex, and fraught than simple reversals or rejections. This kind of ambiguity between content and form makes the movement aesthetic and the struggle to find "voice" perhaps more fun, as Wing Tek Lum's slicing of the proverbial American apple pie suggests.

Many in the artistic communities of color during this period appealed for unity. Others asserted alternative visions, maintaining that the movement demanded stories and poetics to fight not only racism and classism but also sexism, homophobia, and their intersections.

The "Black Feminist Statement" of the Combahee River Collective signals a moment in the history of feminist theory when a politics and poetics of "intersectional analysis" dispelled the notion that social change required a hierarchy of oppression. Maybe, as Rita Sánchez discovers in her "Chicana Writer Breaking Out of Silence," the practicality of organizing around and writing about those made most marginal by U.S. society is the true calling of poetry. Maybe the most revolutionary legacy of the movement and its aesthetics is the confidence that her capacity and willingness to write herself into history and community can indeed speak for an entire people and change the world.

James Kyung-Jin Lee
University of California, Santa Barbara

LARRY NEAL
1937–1981

Some Reflections on the Black Aesthetic

This outline below is a rough overview of some categories and elements that constituted a "Black Aesthetic" outlook. All of these categories need further elaboration, so I am working on a larger essay that will tie them all together.

Mythology	*formal manifestation*	
Spirit worship, Orishas, ancestors, African Gods. Syncretism/catholic voodoo, macumba, Holy Ghost, Jesus as somebody you might know, like a personal deity. River spirits.	Samba, Calypso, Batucada, Cha-Cha, juba, gospel songs, jubilees, work song, spirituals.	1. RACE MEMORY (Africa, Middle Passage) Rhythm as an expression of race memory; rhythm as a basic creative principle; rhythm as an existence; creative force as vector of existence. Swinging.
		2. MIDDLE PASSAGE (Diaspora) Race memory: terror, landlessness, claustrophobia: "America is a prison . . ." Malcolm X.
Neo-Mythology	*formal manifestation*	
Shamans: Preachers, poets, blues singers, musicians, mack-daddies, and politicians.	All aspects of Black dance styles in the New World. Pelvic. Dress and walk.	3. TRANSMUTATION AND SYNTHESIS Funky Butt, Stomps, Jump Jim Crow, Buck n' Wing, Jigs, Snake, Grind, slow drag, jitterbug, twist, Watusi, fish, swim, boogaloo, etc. Dance to the *after* beat. Dance as race memory; transmitted through the collective folk consciousness.

Neo-Mythology

Legba, Oshun, Yemaya, Urzulie, Soul Momma, Evil women, Good loving women, woman as primarily need/man as doer. Blues singer as poet and moral judge; bad man Earth centered, but directed cosmologically. Folk poet, philosopher, priest, priestess, conjurer, preacher, teacher, hustler, seer, soothsayer . . .

4. BLUES GOD/TONE AS MEANING AND MEMORY

Sound as racial memory, primeval. Life breath. Word is perceived as energy or force. Call and response Blues perceived as an emanation outside of man, but yet a manifestation of his being/reality. Same energy source as Gospel, field holler, but delineated in narrative song. The African voice transplanted. This God must be the meanest and the strongest. He survives and persists Once perceived as an evil force: ". . . and I (Dude Botley) got to thinking about how many thousand of people (Buddy) Bolden had made happy and all of them women who used to idolize him. 'Where are they now?' I say to myself. Then I hear Bolden's cornet. I look through the crack and there he is, relaxed back in the chair, blowing that silver cornet softly, just above a whisper, and I see he's got his hat over the bell of the horn. I put my ear close to the keyhole. I thought I heard Bolden play the blues before, and play hymns at funerals, but what he is playing now is real strange and I listen carefully, because he's playing something that, for a while sounds like the blues, then like a hymn. I cannot make out the tune, but after awhile I catch on. He is mixing up the blues with the hymns. He plays the blues real sad and the hymn sadder than the blues and then the blues sadder than the hymn. That is the first time that I had ever heard hymns and blues cooked up together. A strange cold feeling comes over me; I get sort of scared because I know the Lord don't like that mixing the Devil's music with his music. . . . It sounded like a battle between the Good Lord and the Devil. Something tells me to listen and see who wins. If Bolden stops on the hymn, the Good Lord wins; if he stops on the blues, the Devil wins."

HISTORY AS
UNITARY MYTH

Shango, Nat Turner, Denmark, Vesey, Brer' Rabbit, High John the Conqueror, Jack Johnson, Ray Robinson, Signifying Monkey, Malcolm X, Adam Clayton Powell, Garvey, DuBois, Hon. Elijah Muhammed, Martin L. King, Rap Brown, Rev. Franklin, Charlie Parker, Duke Ellington, James Brown, Bessie Smith, Moms Mabley, King Pleasure, Maefilt Johnson, Son House. Louis Armstrong.... Voodoo again/Ishmael Reed's Hoodoo. Islamic suffis. Third World's destiny. The East as the Womb and the Tomb. Fanon's Third World, Bandung Humanism. Revolution is the operational mythology. Symbol change. Expanded metaphors as in the poetry of Curtis Lyle and Stanley Crouch; or L. Barrett's *Song for MuMu* ... Nigger styles and masks such as Rinehart in the *Invisible Man*. Style as in James P. Johnson description of stride pianists in the twenties. Bobby Blue Bland wearing a dashiki and a process. All of this links up with the transmutation of African styles and the revitalization of these styles on the West.

5. **BLACK ARTS MOVEMENT/BLACK ART AESTHETIC**

Feeling/contemporary and historical. Energy intensifies. Non-matrixed art forms: Coltrane, Ornette, Sun Ra. More concerned with the vibrations of the Word, than with the Word itself. Like signifying.

The Black Nation as Poem. Ethical stance as aesthetic. The synthesis of the above presented outline. The integral unity of culture, politics, and art. Spiritual. Despises alienation in the European sense. Art consciously committed; art addressed primarily to Black and Third World people. Black attempts to realize the world as art by making Man more compatible to it and it more compatible to Man. Styles itself from nigger rhythms to cosmic sensibility. Black love, conscious and affirmed. Change.

1972

WING TEK LUM
B. 1946

Minority Poem

For George Lee

Why
we're just as American
as apple pie—
that is, if you count
the leftover peelings   5
lying on the kitchen counter
which the cook has forgotten about
or doesn't know
quite what to do with
except hope that the maid   10
when she cleans off the chopping block
will chuck them away
into a garbage can she'll take out
on leaving for the night.

1973

RON TANAKA
1944–2007

I Hate My Wife for Her Flat Yellow Face

I hate my wife for her flat yellow face
and her fat cucumber legs, but mostly
for her lack of elegance and lack of
intelligence compared to judith gluck.

I married my wife, daughter of a rich   5
east los angeles banker, for money,
of course, I thought I deserved better, but
suffering is something else altogether.

She married me for love but she can't love
me, since no one who went to Fresno State   10
knows anything about Warhol or Ginsberg or
Viet Nam. She has no jewish friends.

She's like a stupid water buffalo from
the old country, slowly plodding between
muddy furrows, and that's all she knows of   15
love beneath my curses and sometimes blows.

I thought I could love her at first, that she
could teach me to be myself again, free
from years of bopping round LA ghettos,
western civilization and the playmate of the month   20

since she was raised a buddhist with all
the arts of dancing, arranging and the
serving of tea, and I thought I saw in my
arrogance some long forgotten warrior prince.

But I wanted to be an anglican   25
too much and listened too long to dylan
or maybe it was the playmate of the
month or poetry and judith gluck.

So I hate my gentle wife for her flat
yellow face and her soft cucumber legs   30
bearing the burden of the love she has
borne for centuries, centuries before
        anglicans and dylans
        playmates and rock
        before   35
        me or judith gluck

            1969

■ COMBAHEE RIVER COLLECTIVE* ■

A Black Feminist Statement

We are a collective of Black feminists who have been meeting together since 1974.[1] During that time we have been involved in the process of defining and clarifying our politics, while at the same time doing political work within our own group and in coalition with other progressive organizations and movements. The most general statement of our politics at the present time would be that we are actively committed to struggling against racial, sexual, heterosexual, and class oppression and see as our particular task the development of integrated analysis and practice based upon the fact that the major systems of oppression are interlocking. The synthesis of these oppressions creates the conditions of our lives. As Black women we see Black feminism as the logical political movement to combat the manifold and simultaneous oppressions that all women of color face.

We will discuss four major topics in the paper that follows: (1) the genesis of contemporary black feminism; (2) what we believe, i.e., the specific province of our politics; (3) the problems in organizing Black feminists, including a brief history of our collective; and (4) Black feminist issues and practice.

1. The Genesis of Contemporary Black Feminism

Before looking at the recent development of Black feminism we would like to affirm that we find our origins in the historical reality of Afro-American women's continuous life-and-death struggle for survival and liberation. Black women's extremely negative relationship to the American political system (a system of white male rule) has always been determined by our membership in two oppressed racial and sexual castes. As Angela Davis points out in "Reflections on the Black Woman's Role in the Community of Slaves," Black women have always embodied, if only in their physical manifestation, an adversary stance to white male rule and have actively resisted its inroads upon them and their communities in both dramatic and subtle ways. There have always been Black women activists—some known, like Sojourner Truth, Harriet Tubman, Frances E. W. Harper, Ida B. Wells Barnett, and Mary Church Terrell, and thousands upon thousands unknown—who had a shared awareness of how their sexual identity combined with their racial identity to make their whole life situation and the focus of their political struggles unique.

---

*The Combahee River Collective is a Black feminist group in Boston whose name comes from the guerrilla action conceptualized and led by Harriet Tubman on June 2, 1863, in the Port Royal region of South Carolina. This action freed more than 750 slaves and is the only military campaign in American history planned and led by a woman.

[1] This statement is dated April 1977.

Contemporary Black feminism is the outgrowth of countless generations of personal sacrifice, militancy, and work by our mothers and sisters.

A Black feminist presence has evolved most obviously in connection with the second wave of the American women's movement beginning in the late 1960s. Black, other Third World, and working women have been involved in the feminist movement from its start, but both outside reactionary forces and racism and elitism within the movement itself have served to obscure our participation. In 1973 Black feminists, primarily located in New York, felt the necessity of forming a separate Black feminist group. This became the National Black Feminist Organization (NBFO).

Black feminist politics also have an obvious connection to movements for Black liberation, particularly those of the 1960s and 1970s. Many of us were active in those movements (civil rights, Black nationalism, the Black Panthers), and all of our lives were greatly affected and changed by their ideology, their goals, and the tactics used to achieve their goals. It was our experience and disillusionment within these liberation movements, as well as the experience on the periphery of the white male left, that led to the need to develop a politics that was antiracist, unlike those of white women, and antisexist, unlike those of Black and white men.

There is also undeniably a personal genesis for Black feminism, that is, the political realization that comes from the seemingly personal experiences of individual Black women's lives. Black feminists and many more Black women who do not define themselves as feminists have all experienced sexual oppression as a constant factor in our day-to-day existence. As children we realized that we were different from boys and that we were treated differently. For example, we were told in the same breath to be quiet both for the sake of being "ladylike" and to make us less objectionable in the eyes of white people. As we grew older we became aware of the threat of physical and sexual abuse by men. However, we had no way of conceptualizing what was so apparent to us, what we *knew* was really happening.

Black feminists often talk about their feelings of craziness before becoming conscious of the concepts of sexual politics, patriarchal rule, and most importantly, feminism, the political analysis and practice that we women use to struggle against our oppression. The fact that racial politics and indeed racism are pervasive factors in our lives did not allow us, and still does not allow most Black women, to look more deeply into our own experiences and, from that sharing and growing consciousness, to build a politics that will change our lives and inevitably end our oppression. Our development must also be tied to the contemporary economic and political position of Black people. The post–World War II generation of Black youth was the first to be able to minimally partake of certain educational and employment options, previously closed completely to Black people. Although our economic position is still at the very bottom of the American capitalistic economy, a handful of us have been able to gain certain tools as a result of tokenism in education and employment which potentially enable us to more effectively fight our oppression.

A combined antiracist and antisexist position drew us together initially, and as we developed politically we addressed ourselves to heterosexism and economic oppression under capitalism.

2. What We Believe

Above all else, our politics initially sprang from the shared belief that Black women are inherently valuable, that our liberation is a necessity not as an adjunct to somebody else's but because of our need as human persons for autonomy. This may seem so obvious as to sound simplistic, but it is apparent that no other ostensibly progressive movement has ever considered our specific oppression as a priority or worked seriously for the ending of that oppression. Merely naming the pejorative stereotypes attributed to Black women (e.g., mammy, matriarch, Sapphire, whore, bulldagger), let alone cataloguing the cruel, often murderous, treatment we receive, indicates how little value has been placed upon our lives during four centuries of bondage in the Western hemisphere. We realize that the only people who care enough about us to work consistently for our liberation is us. Our politics evolve from a healthy love for ourselves, our sisters and our community which allows us to continue our struggle and work.

This focusing upon our own oppression is embodied in the concept of identity politics. We believe that the most profound and potentially the most radical politics come directly out of our own identity, as opposed to working to end somebody else's oppression. In the case of Black women this is a particularly repugnant, dangerous, threatening, and therefore revolutionary concept because it is obvious from looking at all the political movements that have preceded us that anyone is more worthy of liberation than ourselves. We reject pedestals, queenhood, and walking ten paces behind. To be recognized as human, levelly human, is enough.

We believe that sexual politics under patriarchy is as pervasive in Black women's lives as are the politics of class and race. We also often find it difficult to separate race from class from sex oppression because in our lives they are most often experienced simultaneously. We know that there is such a thing as racial-sexual oppression which is neither solely racial nor solely sexual, e.g., the history of rape of Black women by white men as a weapon of political repression.

Although we are feminists and lesbians, we feel solidarity with progressive Black men and do not advocate the fractionalization that white women who are separatists demand. Our situation as Black people necessitates that we have solidarity around the fact of race, which white women of course do not need to have with white men, unless it is their negative solidarity as racial oppressors. We struggle together with Black men against racism, while we also struggle with Black men about sexism.

We realize that the liberation of all oppressed peoples necessitates the destruction of the political-economic systems of capitalism and imperialism as well as patriarchy. We are socialists because we believe the work must be organized for the collective benefit of those who do the work and create the products, and not for the profit of the bosses. Material resources must be equally distributed among those who create these resources. We are not convinced, however, that a socialist revolution that is not also a feminist and antiracist revolution will guarantee our liberation. We have arrived at the necessity for developing an understanding of class relationships that takes into account the specific class position of Black women who are generally marginal in the labor force, while at this particular time some of us are temporarily viewed as doubly desirable tokens at white-collar and professional levels. We need to articulate the real class situation of persons who are not merely raceless, sexless workers, but for whom racial and sexual oppression are significant determinants in their working/ economic lives. Although we are in essential agreement with Marx's theory as it applied to the very specific economic relationships he analyzed, we know that his analysis must be extended further in order for us to understand our specific economic situation as Black women.

A political contribution which we feel we have already made is the expansion of the feminist principle that the personal is political. In our consciousness-raising sessions, for example, we have in many ways gone beyond white women's revelations because we are dealing with the implications of race and class as well as sex. Even our Black women's style of talking/testifying in Black language about what we have experienced has a resonance that is both cultural and political. We have spent a great deal of energy delving into the cultural and experiential nature of our oppression out of necessity because none of these matters has ever been looked at before. No one before has ever examined the multilayered texture of Black women's lives. An example of this kind of revelation/conceptualization occurred at a meeting as we discussed the ways in which our early intellectual interests had been attacked by our peers, particularly Black males. We discovered that all of us, because we were "smart" had also been considered "ugly," i.e., "smart-ugly." "Smart-ugly" crystallized the way in which most of us had been forced to develop our intellects at great cost to our "social" lives. The sanctions in the Black and white communities against Black women thinkers is comparatively much higher than for white women, particularly ones from the educated middle and upper classes.

As we have already stated, we reject the stance of lesbian separatism because it is not a viable political analysis or strategy for us. It leaves out far too much and far too many people, particularly Black men, women, and children. We have a great deal of criticism and loathing for what men have been socialized to be in this society: what they support, how they act, and how they oppress. But we do not have the misguided notion that it is their maleness, per se—i.e., their biological maleness—that makes them what they are. As Black women we find any type of biological determinism a particularly dangerous and reactionary basis upon which to build a politic. We must also question whether lesbian separatism is an adequate and progressive political analysis and strategy, even for those who practice it, since it is so completely denies any but the sexual sources of women's oppression, negating the facts of class and race.

3. Problems in Organizing Black Feminists

During our years together as a Black feminist collective we have experienced success and defeat, joy and pain, victory and failure. We have found that it is very difficult to organize around Black feminist issues, difficult even to announce in certain contexts that we *are* Black feminists. We have tried to think about the reasons for our difficulties, particularly since the white women's movement continues to be strong and to grow in many directions. In this section we will discuss some of the general reasons for the organizing problems we face and also talk specifically about the stages in organizing in our own collective.

The major source of difficulty in our political work is that we are not just trying to fight oppression on one front or even two, but instead to address a whole range of oppressions. We do not have racial, sexual, hetero-sexual, or class privilege to rely upon, nor do we have even the minimal access to resources and power that groups who possess any one of these types of privilege have.

The psychological toll of being a Black woman and the difficulties this presents in reaching political consciousness and doing political work can never be underestimated. There is a very low value placed upon Black wom-en's psyches in this society, which is both racist and sexist. As an early group member once said, "We are all damaged people merely by virtue of being Black women." We are dispossessed psychologically and on every other level, and yet we feel the necessity to struggle to change the condition of all Black women. In "A Black Feminist's Search for Sisterhood," Michele Wallace arrives at this conclusion:

> We exist as women who are Black who are feminists, each stranded for the moment, working independently because there is not yet an environment in this society remotely congenial to our struggle—because, being on the bottom, we would have to do what no one else has done: we would have to fight the world.[2]

Wallace is pessimistic but realistic in her assessment of Black feminists' position, particularly in her allusion to the nearly classic isolation most of us face. We might use our position at the bottom, however, to make a clear leap into revolutionary action. If Black women were free, it would mean that everyone else would have to be free since our freedom would necessitate the destruction of all the systems of oppression.

Feminism is, nevertheless, very threatening to the majority of Black peo-ple because it calls into question some of the most basic assumptions about our existence, i.e., that sex should be a determinant of power relationships. Here is the way male and female voices were defined in a Black nationalist pamphlet from the early 1970's.

[2]Michele Wallace, "A Black Feminist's Search
for Sisterhood," *Village Voice*, July 28, 1975,
pp. 6–7.

We understand that it is and has been traditional that the man is the head of the house. He is the leader of the house/nation because his knowledge of the world is broader, his awareness is greater, his understanding is fuller and his application of this information is wiser ... After all, it is only reasonable that the man be the head of the house because he is able to defend and protect the development of his home ... Women cannot do the same things as men—they are made by nature to function differently. Equality of men and women is something that cannot happen even in the abstract world. Men are not equal to other men, i.e. ability, experience or even understanding. The value of men and women can be seen as in the value of gold and silver—they are not equal but both have great value. We must realize that men and women are a complement to each other because there is no house/family without a man and his wife. Both are essential to the development of any life.[3]

The material conditions of most Black women would hardly lead them to upset both economic and sexual arrangements that seem to represent some stability in their lives. Many Black women had a good understanding of both sexism and racism, but because of the everyday constrictions of their lives cannot risk struggling against them both.

The reaction of Black men to feminism has been notoriously negative. They are, of course, even more threatened than Black women by the possibility that Black feminists might organize around our own needs. They realize that they might not only lose valuable and hard-working allies in their struggles but that they might also be forced to change their habitually sexist ways of interacting with and oppressing Black women. Accusations that Black feminism divides the Black struggles are powerful deterrents to the growth of an autonomous Black women's movement.

Still, hundreds of women have been active at different times during the three-year existence of our group. And every Black woman who came, came out of a strongly-felt need for some level of possibility that did not previously exist in her life.

When we first started meeting early in 1974 after the NBFO first eastern regional conference, we did not have a strategy for organizing, or even a focus. We just wanted to see what we had. After a period of months of not meeting, we began to meet again late in the year and started doing an intense variety of consciousness-raising. The overwhelming feeling that we had is that after years and years we had finally found each other. Although we were not doing political work as a group, individuals continued their involvement in Lesbian politics, sterilization abuse and abortion rights work, Third World Women's International Women's Day activities, and support activity for the trials of Dr. Kenneth Edelin, Joan Little, and Inéz García. During our first summer, when membership had dropped off considerably, those of us remaining devoted serious discussions to the

[3]The Mumininas of the Committee for Unified Newark, "Mwanamke Mwanachi" (The Nationalist Woman), Newark, N.J., c. 1971, pp. 4–5.

possibility of opening a refuge for battered women in a Black community. (There was no refuge in Boston at that time.) We also decided around that time to become an independent collective since we had serious disagreements with NBFO's bourgeois-feminist stance and their lack of a clear political focus.

We also were contacted at that time by socialist feminists, with whom we had worked on abortion rights activities, who wanted to encourage us to attend the National Socialist Feminist Conference in Yellow Springs. One of our members did attend and despite the narrowness of the ideology that was promoted at that particular conference, we became more aware of the need for us to understand our own economic situation and to make our own economic analysis.

In the fall, when some members returned, we experienced several months of comparative inactivity and internal disagreements which were first conceptualized as a Lesbian-straight split but which were also the result of class and political differences. During the summer those of us who were still meeting had determined the need to do political work and to move beyond consciousness-raising and serving exclusively as an emotional support group. At the beginning of 1976, when some of the women who had not wanted to do political work and who also had voiced disagreements stopped attending of their own accord, we again looked for a focus. We decided at that time, with the addition of new members, to become a study group. We had always shared our reading with each other, and some of us had written papers on Black feminism for group discussion a few months before this decision was made. We began functioning as a study group and also began discussing the possibility of starting a Black feminist publication. We had a retreat in the late spring which provided a time for both political discussion and working our interpersonal issues. Currently we are planning to gather together a collection of Black feminist writing. We feel that it is absolutely essential to demonstrate the reality of our politics to other Black women and believe that we can do this through writing and distributing our work. The fact that individual Black feminists are living in isolation all over the country, that our own numbers are small, and that we have some skills in writing, printing, and publishing makes us want to carry out these kinds of projects as a means of organizing Black feminists as we continue to do political work in coalition with other groups.

4. Black Feminist Issues and Projects

During our time together we have identified and worked on many issues of particular relevance to Black women. The inclusiveness of our politics makes us concerned with any situation that impinges upon the lives of women, Third World and working people. We are of course particularly committed to working on those struggles in which race, sex and class are simultaneous factors in oppression. We might, for example, become involved in workplace organizing at a factory that employs Third World women or picket a hospital that is cutting back on already inadequate health care to a Third World community, or set up a rape crisis center in a Black neighborhood. Organizing around welfare and daycare concerns might also be a focus. The work to be done and the countless issues that this work represents merely reflect the pervasiveness of our oppression.

Issues and projects that collective members have actually worked on are sterilization abuse, abortion rights, battered women, rape and health care. We have also done many workshops and educationals on black feminism on college campuses, at women's conferences, and most recently for high school women. One issue that is of major concern to us and that we have begun to publicly address is racism in the white women's movement. As black feminists we are made constantly and painfully aware of how little effort white women have made to understand and combat their racism, which requires among other things that they have a more than superficial comprehension of race, color, and black history and culture. Eliminating racism in the white women's movement is by definition work for white women to do, but we will continue to speak to and demand accountability on this issue.

In the practice of our politics we do not believe that the end always justifies the means. Many reactionary and destructive acts have been done in the name of achieving "correct" political goals. As feminists we do not want to mess over people in the name of politics. We believe in collective process and a nonhierarchical distribution of power with our own group and in our vision of a revolutionary society. We are committed to a continual examination of our politics as they develop through criticism and self-criticism as an essential aspect of our practice. As black feminists and lesbians we know that we have a very definite revolutionary task to perform and we are ready for the lifetime of work and struggle before us.

1977

RITA SÁNCHEZ

B. 1952

Chicana Writer Breaking Out of the Silence

The Chicana writer, by the fact that she is even writing in today's society, is making a revolutionary act. Embodied in the act of writing is her voice against others' definitions of who she is and what she should be. There is, in her open expression and in the very nature of this act of opening up, a refusal to submit to a quality of silence that has been imposed upon her for centuries. In the act of writing, the Chicana is saying "No," and by doing so she becomes the revolutionary, a source of change, and a real force for humanization.

By becoming a writer, the Chicana has to have already rebelled against a socialization process that would have her remain merely the silent helpmate. Everything in her society, the schools, the church, the home, has sought this goal for her: she must be sheltered from the evils, noise, confusion, from the realities of the outside world, from sex to politics, even at times from intellectual dialogue, to be considered acceptable. In short, she should make no intrusion into adult or male conversation. Now, the Chicana, by voicing her own brand of expression has rejected the latter in favor of telling anyone who wishes to read her work, hear her voice, exactly what she is not, and who she, in fact, is.

Courageously, La Chicana writer, by understanding the condition of colonization under which she was born, the images of betrayal that surround her, and the forces of racism that still exist for her, has exhibited her strength by the very denial of these impositions. By her refusal to accept the myths, misinterpretations and the stereotypes of herself as presented by another, she has transcended the bounds of tradition, made a choice to determine her own life, and finally, has become the revolutionary voice. The reality of her history reveals La Mujer Chicana as the central core and basis of Chicana struggle. The Cuban film, *Lucia*, depicts the epic struggle of an entire people, and at the center: La Mujer. The rape of a woman in this story symbolized the colonization of the country. La Mujer has suffered the violation, but has emerged as the visionary who awakens her people. The Chicana is the same woman.

In her act of self expression shared in writing with others like herself she is saying what she feels and who she is; every time she puts down on paper her words; and every time those words are read by another Chicana, she has defined further who we Chicanas truly are. Her voice, in expressing a Chicana view, comes closer to expressing a collective Chicana voice. We, her readers, through reading what she has to say, through reading about her, are reading about ourselves and our own experiences. This phenomenon takes place simply because by writing she has put a name to what we have felt—a name to the feelings of anger, pain, love, joy, sympathy, strength, celebration. Every poem, essay, story becomes more than a work of art in this vital combination of writer and reader. Each work becomes an expression of life. The Chicana writer, like the revolutionary, is a creator and the result is twofold. She becomes the creator of a work of art and the creator of a destiny.

Although the Chicana voice is only recently emerging in writing, her presence, like the presence of the river in [Rodolfo] Anaya's *Bless Me, Ultima*, has always surrounded us; and when this presence reveals itself, finally, as it does to the protagonist, Antonio, it is an awesome revelation, one, like life itself, to be both revered and heeded. At first, what appears to be only a silence, in reality carries with it an underlying depth, strength, and volume, constantly moving, constantly alive; it is unable to be stopped and is not to be taken lightly.

In this sense the new Chicana poet, writer, the new voice you are hearing is not new at all. It has encompassed us since time immemorial only to have revealed itself in a more profound and real way. In Dorinda Moreno's *La Mujer en Pie de Lucha*, poet Viola Correa reveals the drama and fervor of this startling reality of the Chicana presence coming to life, in her poem, "la Nueva Chicana." This voice does not come from the elite, the women with the college degrees or titles, nor is it clad like one may have expected Jesus to have been clad, with royal robes. Her grandeur is of a different kind. Her presence is clothed in the voice of *tu hermana, tu madre, tu tia* [your sister, your mother, your aunt]. And by coming to us in this way, the voice is even more real to us; it comes from midst ourselves and not from above, as poets often do. More significantly, it comes from out of our own very real struggles: the picket lines, the factories, the fields, the *barrios*, the streets, *la casa* [the home].

The Chicana voice of today is reflective of the Aztec poets long ago. It binds us to a beauty of the past. Antonia Castañeda, co-editor of *Literature Chicana*, one of the first Chicanas to teach "*La Mujer de la Raza*" at the University of Washington, speaks of the depth of a Chicano collective voice as it comes to us from a long-ago voice of the Aztec poet, Temilotzín. Temilotzín, in his poetry, speaks not only for himself, but to all the people. *Literatura Chicana* says that his mission is to create flower and song while seeking *humanidad* [humanity] with the community. Antonia Casteñeda translates, "*en prestamos los unos a los otros,*" to mean, literally, that we are on loan to one another. The Chicana presence, the Chicana voice reaffirms this concept when she speaks. In so doing, she is reaching out to all Chicanas, "with song to encircle the community."

Writing, breaking the silence, subjective as it may appear, becomes a monumental and collective act because it signifies overcoming, freeing oneself from the confines and conditions of history. The collective act may not even be expressed in the words themselves, but is manifest in the act of writing down these words. Writing is the tool which allows the Chicana to implement action, critical thought, change. It signifies a voice, a dimension beyond just a presence. It allows us a voice that reaches out to yet another, spurring critical questions while creating empathy. By this process involving writer and reader, both participants are breaking out of silence, no longer are they mere presences, but instruments for change, visionaries awakening the people.

All of Chicana literature crys out to make the world, to make relationships human again. Although living in our own communities has sheltered us in a sense from the atrocities of the outside world, we are still confronted with the technocratic society that surrounds us. And in many ways, this society is worse than the physical poverty we might have known in our communities. It is more destructive because it leaves us spiritually poor. It attempts to strip us of those elements with which we grew up within our communities that allowed us to hold on to our humanidad [humanity]; our language, our culture, our family unity. Our responses of anger are against such dehumanization; they are a reaction against a kind of violence that already exists.

More and more the Chicana woman is emerging out of a traditionally imposed silence. Her already awesome presence becomes more awesome when it speaks. It becomes the conscience of the people; from one who is a participant in history. It is the writing process that will facilitate the goal we seek: that in writing, our effects may be far-reaching and that it will bring each one of us to our fullest human potential.

As long as we remain silent, no voice exists. Our right to speak, to voice ourselves is stripped from us; if you do not hear us, no voice exists and no one will notice our absence.

Verónica Cunningham through poetry admonishes our silence. If we do not speak out, the indictment is of ourselves and we must harbor the guilt of our own rape. If, in our silence, we make no rebellion our sentence, she says, will be our own silence; in itself, the worst possible punishment. Importantly, she begins this indictment with "I" and in so doing, her poem becomes all-encompassing. But she speaks to all women who would remain silent: "Chicana, Black, Asian, White, any woman, any age, child, sister, wife, aunt, or friend." As long as you are silent you are yourself guilty:

> You women are guilty of
> being victim, guilty of being raped
> And you are guilty of laying
>   yourself down
> to your courts of justice
> and your sentence has been silence . . .

Chicanas are being called upon today to put their thoughts down in writing, to share their emotions with others, thus beginning the process, the chain reaction that might spur others to self-expression and creativity. Our depth as Chicana women must be shared, in fact, is urgently needed so that others might hear the prophetic voice. This sharing is essential; it is the spirit of our people. This process creates a new awakening, a breaking out of silence, a revolutionary act. The burden is finally on us, on all Chicanas to break out of silence, to be present to all others who may themselves benefit from a voice, one that is both fearless and the penetrating conscience of the people.

1977

VINE DELORIA
1933–2005

from Custer Died for Your Sins

1. Indians Today, the Real and the Unreal

Indians are like the weather. Everyone knows all about the weather, but none can change it. When storms are predicted, the sun shines. When picnic weather is announced, the rain begins. Likewise, if you count on the unpredictability of Indian people, you will never be sorry.

One of the finest things about being an Indian is that people are always interested in you and your "plight." Other groups have difficulties, predicaments, quandaries, problems, or troubles. Traditionally we Indians have a "plight."

Our foremost plight is our transparency. People can tell just by looking at us what we want, what should be done to help us, how we feel, and what a "real" Indian is really like. Indian life, as it relates to the real world, is a continuous attempt not to disappoint people who know us. Unfulfilled expectations cause grief and we have already had our share.

Because people can see right through us, it becomes impossible to tell the truth from fiction or fact from mythology. Experts paint us as they would like us to be. Often we paint ourselves as we wish we were or as we might have been.

The more we try to be ourselves the more we are forced to defend what we have never been. The American public feels most comfortable with the mythical Indians of stereotype-land who were always THERE. These Indians are fierce, they wear feathers and grunt. Most of us don't fit this idealized figure since we grunt only when overeating, which is seldom.

To be an Indian in modern American society is in a very real sense to be unreal and ahistorical. In this book we will discuss the other side—the unrealities that face *us* as Indian people. It is this unreal feeling that has been welling up inside us and threatens to make this decade the most decisive in history for Indian people. In so many ways, Indian people are re-examining themselves in an effort to redefine a new social structure for their people. Tribes are reordering their priorities to account for the obvious discrepancies between their goals and the goals whites have defined for them.

Indian reactions are sudden and surprising. One day at a conference we were singing "My Country 'Tis of Thee" and we came across the part that goes:

> Land where our fathers died
> Land of the Pilgrims' pride ...

Some of us broke out laughing when we realized that our fathers undoubtedly died trying to keep those Pilgrims from stealing our land. In fact, many of our fathers died because the Pilgrims killed them as witches. We didn't feel much kinship with those Pilgrims, regardless of who they did in.

We often hear "give it back to the Indians" when a gadget fails to work. It's a terrible thing for a people to realize that society has set aside all non-working gadgets for their exclusive use.

During my three years as Executive Director of the National Congress of American Indians it was a rare day when some white didn't visit my office and proudly proclaim that he or she was of Indian descent.

Cherokee was the most popular tribe of their choice and many people placed the Cherokees anywhere from Maine to Washington State. Mohawk, Sioux, and Chippewa were next in popularity. Occasionally I would be told about some mythical tribe from lower Pennsylvania, Virginia, or Massachusetts which had spawned the white standing before me.

At times I became quite defensive about being a Sioux when these white people had a pedigree that was so much more respectable than mine. But eventually I came to understand their need to identify as partially Indian and did not resent them. I would confirm their wildest stories about their Indian ancestry and would add a few tales of my own hoping that they would be able to accept themselves someday and leave us alone.

Whites claiming Indian blood generally tend to reinforce mythical beliefs about Indians. All but one person I met who claimed Indian blood claimed it on their grandmother's side. I once did a projection backward and discovered that evidently most tribes were entirely female for the first three hundred years of white occupation. No one, it seemed, wanted to claim a male Indian as a forebear.

It doesn't take much insight into racial attitudes to understand the real meaning of the Indian-grandmother complex that plagues certain whites. A male ancestor has too much of the aura of the savage warrior, the unknown primitive, the instinctive animal, to make him a respectable member of the family tree. But a young Indian princess? Ah, there was royalty for the taking. Somehow the white was linked with a noble house of gentility and culture if his grandmother was an Indian princess who ran away with an intrepid pioneer. And royalty has always been an unconscious but all-consuming goal of the European immigrant.

The early colonists, accustomed to life under benevolent despots, projected their understanding of the European political structure onto the Indian tribe in trying to explain its political and social structure. European royal houses were closed to ex-convicts and indentured servants, so the colonists made all Indian maidens princesses, then proceeded to climb a social ladder of their own creation. Within the next generation, if the trend continues, a large portion of the American population will eventually be related to Powhattan.

While a real Indian grandmother is probably the nicest thing that could happen to a child, why is a remote Indian princess grandmother so necessary for many whites? Is it because they are afraid of being classed as foreigners? Do they need some blood tie with the frontier and its dangers in order to experience what it means to be an American? Or is it an attempt to avoid facing the guilt they bear for the treatment of the Indian?

The phenomenon seems to be universal. Only among the Jewish community, which has a long tribal-religious tradition of its own, does the mysterious Indian grandmother, the primeval princess, fail to dominate the family tree. Otherwise, there's not much to be gained by claiming Indian blood or publicly identifying as an Indian. The white believes that there is a great danger the lazy Indian will eventually corrupt God's hardworking people. He is still suspicious that the Indian way of life is dreadfully wrong. There is, in fact, something *un-American* about Indians for most whites.

I ran across a classic statement of this attitude one day in a history book which was published shortly after the turn of the century. Often have I wondered how many Senators, Congressmen, and clergymen of the day accepted the attitudes of that book as a basic fact of life in America. In no uncertain terms did the book praise God that the Indian had not yet been able to corrupt North America as he had South America:

> It was perhaps fortunate for the future of America that the Indians of the North rejected civilization. Had they accepted it the whites and Indians might have intermarried to some extent as they did in Mexico. That would have given us a population made up in a measure of shiftless half-breeds.

I never dared to show this passage to my white friends who had claimed Indian blood, but I often wondered why they were so energetic if they did have some of the bad seed in them.

Those whites who dare not claim Indian blood have an asset of their own. They *understand* Indians.

Understanding Indians is not an esoteric art. All it takes is a trip through Arizona or New Mexico, watching a documentary on TV, having known *one* in the service, or having read a popular book on *them*.

There appears to be some secret osmosis about Indian people by which they can magically and instantaneously communicate complete knowledge about themselves to these interested whites. Rarely is physical contact required. Anyone and everyone who knows an Indian or who is *interested*, immediately and thoroughly understands them.

You can verify this great truth at your next party. Mention Indians and you will find a person who saw some in a gas station in Utah, or who attended the Gallup ceremonial celebration, or whose Uncle Jim hired one to cut logs in Oregon, or whose church had a missionary come to speak last Sunday on the plight of Indians and the mission of the church.

There is no subject on earth so easily understood as that of the American Indian. Each summer, work camps disgorge teenagers on various reservations. Within one month's time the youngsters acquire a knowledge of Indians that would astound a college professor.

Easy knowledge about Indians is a historical tradition. After Columbus "discovered" America he brought back news of a great new world which he assumed to be India and, therefore, filled with Indians. Almost at once

European folklore devised a complete explanation of the new land and its inhabitants which feature the Fountain of Youth, the Seven Cities of Gold, and other exotic attractions. The absence of elephants apparently did not tip off the explorers that they weren't in India. By the time they realized their mistake, instant knowledge of Indians was a cherished tradition.

Missionaries, after learning some of the religious myths of tribes they encountered, solemnly declared that the inhabitants of the new continent were the Ten Lost Tribes of Israel. Indians thus received a religious-historical identity far greater than they wanted or deserved. But it was an impossible identity. Their failure to measure up to Old Testament standards doomed them to a fall from grace and they were soon relegated to the status of a picturesque species of wildlife.

Like the deer and the antelope, Indians seemed to play rather than get down to the serious business of piling up treasures upon the earth where thieves break through and steal. Scalping, introduced prior to the French and Indian War by the English,* confirmed the suspicion that Indians were wild animals to be hunted and skinned. Bounties were set and an Indian scalp became more valuable than beaver, otter, marten, and other animal pelts.

American blacks had become recognized as a species of human being by amendments to the Constitution shortly after the Civil War. Prior to emancipation they had been counted as three-fifths of a person in determining population for representation in the House of Representatives. Early Civil Rights bills nebulously state that other people shall have the same rights as "white people," indicating there *were* "other people." But Civil Rights bills passed during and after the Civil War systematically excluded Indian people. For a long time an Indian was not presumed capable of initiating an action in a court of law, of owning property, or of giving testimony against whites in court. Nor could an Indian vote or leave his reservation. Indians were America's captive people without any defined rights whatsoever.

---

*Notice, for example the following proclamation:

"Given at the Council Chamber in Boston this third day of November 1755 in the twenty-ninth year of the Reign of our Sovereign Lord George the Second by the Grace of God of Great Britain, France, and Ireland, King Defender of the Faith.

By His Honour's command
J. Willard, Secry.
God Save the King

"Whereas the tribe of Penobscot Indians have repeatedly in a perfidious manner acted contrary to their solemn submission unto his Majesty long since made and frequently renewed.

"I have, therefore, at the desire of the House of Representatives ... thought fit to issue this Proclamation and to declare the Penobscot Tribe of Indians to be enemies, rebels and traitors to his Majesty.... And I do hereby require his Majesty's subjects of the Province to embrace all opportunities of pursuing, captivating, killing and destroy-all and every of the aforesaid Indians.

"And whereas the General Court of this Province have voted that a bounty ... be granted and allowed to be paid out of the Province Treasury ... the premiums of bounty following viz:

"For every scalp of a male Indian brought in as evidence of their being killed as aforesaid, forty pounds.

"For every scalp of such female Indian or male Indian under the age of twelve years that shall be killed and brought in as evidence of their being killed as aforesaid, twenty pounds."

Then one day the white man discovered that the Indian tribes still owned some 135 million acres of land. To his horror he learned that much of it was very valuable. Some was good grazing land, some was farm land, some mining land, and some covered with timber.

Animals could be herded together on a piece of land, but they could not sell it. Therefore it took no time at all to discover that Indians were really people and should have the right to sell their lands. Land was the means of recognizing the Indian as a human being. It was the method whereby land could be stolen legally and not blatantly.

Once the Indian was thus acknowledged, it was fairly simple to determine what his goals were. If, thinking went, the Indian was just like the white, he must have the same outlook as the white. So the future was planned for the Indian people in public and private life. First in order was allotting them reservations so that they could sell their lands. God's foreordained plan to repopulate the continent fit exactly with the goals of the tribes as they were defined by their white friends.

It is fortunate that we were never slaves. We gave up land instead of life and labor. Because the Negro labored, he was considered a draft animal. Because the Indian occupied large areas of land, he was considered a wild animal. Had we given up anything else, or had anything else to give up, it is certain that we would have been considered some other thing.

Whites have had different attitudes toward the Indians and the blacks since the Republic was founded. Whites have always refused to give non-whites the respect which they have been found to legally possess. Instead there has always been a contemptuous attitude that although the law says one thing, "we all know better."

Thus whites steadfastly refused to allow blacks to enjoy the fruits of full citizenship. They systematically closed schools, churches, stores, restaurants, and public places to blacks or made insulting provisions for them. For one hundred years every program of public and private white America was devoted to the exclusion of the black. It was, perhaps, embarrassing to be rubbing shoulders with one who had not so long before been defined as a field animal.

The Indian suffered the reverse treatment. Law after law was passed requiring him to conform to white institutions. Indian children were kidnapped and forced into boarding schools thousands of miles from their homes to learn the white man's ways. Reservations were turned over to different Christian denominations for governing. Reservations were for a long time church operated. Everything possible was done to ensure that Indians were forced into American life. The wild animal was made into a household pet whether or not he wanted to be one.

Policies for both black and Indian failed completely. Blacks eventually began the Civil Rights movement. In doing so they assured themselves some rights in white society. Indians continued to withdraw from the overtures of white society and tried to maintain their own communities and activities.

Actually both groups had little choice. Blacks, trapped in a world of white symbols, retreated into themselves. And people thought comparable Indian withdrawal unnatural because they expected Indians to behave like whites.

The white world of abstract symbols became a nightmare for Indian people. The words of the treaties, clearly stating that Indians should have "free and undisturbed" use of their lands under the protection of the federal government, were cast aside by the whites as if they didn't exist. The Sioux once had a treaty plainly stating that it would take the signature or marks of three-fourths of the adult males to amend it. Yet through force the government obtained only 10 percent of the required signatures and declared the new agreement valid.

Indian solutions to problems which had been defined by the white society were rejected out of hand and obvious solutions discarded when they called for courses of action that were not proper in white society. When Crow Dog assassinated Spotted Tail the matter was solved under traditional Sioux customs. Yet an outraged public, furious because Crow Dog had not been executed, pressured for the Seven Major Crimes Act for the federal government to assume nearly total criminal jurisdiction over the reservations. Thus foreign laws and customs using the basic concepts of justice came to dominate Indian life. If, Indians reasoned, justice is for society's benefit, why isn't our justice accepted? Indians became convinced they were the world's stupidest people.

Words and situations never seemed to fit together. Always, it seemed, the white man chose a course of action that did not work. The white man preached that it was good to help the poor, yet he did nothing to assist the poor in his society. Instead he put constant pressure on the Indian people to hoard their worldly goods, and when they failed to accumulate capital but freely gave to the poor, the white man reacted violently. . . .

1969

THE 1970S: DECADE OF DISILLUSIONMENT

Even through the turbulent 1960s, the United States had always regarded itself as a young, even innocent nation. This was, of course, a myth. The nation that grew rich on the labor of slaves and on the land of displaced indigenous peoples had always been selective in its understanding of itself rather than truly innocent. But even the myth could not be sustained in the 1970s, a decade that saw the resignation of President Nixon over the Watergate scandal, the defeated return of U.S. troops from Vietnam (minus the more than 60,000 American fatalities), and the deterioration of cities nationwide. It could be said that the United States grew up in the 1970s, but that the dominant feeling was of loss rather than maturity.

Popular culture reflected a shift away from the earnest, progressive, community spirit of the 1960s. The most popular television comedy, *All in the Family*, centered around an intolerant bigot named Archie Bunker who routinely berated his feminist daughter, his intimidated wife, his underachieving son-in-law, and everyone who surrounded them, particularly those not of his race or socioeconomic class. Disco dancing and music—certainly less ambitious and less creative than some of the great accomplishments of popular music of the 1960s—as well as imitative "stadium rock" bands, dominated the music scene by the end of the decade, reflecting a shift away from the spiritual and intellectual possibilities achieved in the greatest works of the previous decade. It was considered a great decade for American film, but only because filmmakers seemed willing to dig into the depraved underbelly of the American experience in such acclaimed yet unsettling films as *The Godfather*, *Taxi Driver*, and *Apocalypse Now*. Films of the decade indulged in excess, whether it was psychological terror (*The Exorcist*), natural disasters (*Jaws*, *The Poseidon Adventure*, or any of the *Airport* movies), or intergalactic warfare (beginning with the budget-shattering *Star Wars* in 1978).

Indulgence and excess can be seen as watchwords of the 1970s, often dubbed the "Me decade." It should not have come as a surprise, then, that the nation faced a two-pronged economic crisis at the end of the decade: inflation and an oil shortage. As American drivers waited in long lines to buy gas, restricted to certain days based on the number or letter at the beginning of their license plates, President Jimmy Carter appeared on television in a cardigan sweater urging the nation to find ways to cut back on their oil consumption, including turning down the thermostat. He was not elected to a second term. Carter's presidency, which followed the scandal of Nixon's and the bland, sometimes bumbling management of Gerald Ford who served out Nixon's second term, was marked in the end not only by economic woes but also by international turmoil. An Islamist revolution in Iran deposed the Shah, who was in the United States for medical treatment and was granted asylum, and 52 American hostages were seized in Iran and detained for more than a year. They were released on the day of Ronald Reagan's inauguration in 1981.

One of the most significant literary works of the decade reflected the trend toward excess that marked the early years of the decade. Thomas Pynchon's 1973 postmodernist masterpiece *Gravity's Rainbow* pushed the boundaries of the literary novel in terms of length, taste, and experimentation. Even as it drew the reader deeper and deeper into its familiar but sometimes nightmarish universe, the novel maintained a darkly humorous distance from its subject, the absurdity of post–World War II existence and the inability of the individual to maintain control over his or her identity in a culture gone mad with corporate and governmental control. The main character, Slothrop, if he in fact is the main character, literally falls apart as the novel progresses, and Pynchon reveals late in the tome that we may have been watching a crude experimental film the whole time we thought we were reading a novel. Many of Pynchon's contemporaries, who might be called high postmodernists, had long been anxious that mass media such as film and television were obscuring literature. Their 1970s response seemed to be to surrender: literature could not be debased by pop culture if it admitted that literature was not really much different from pop culture. Like Andy Warhol's paintings of soup cans or statues of laundry detergent boxes, some writers were coming to terms with the fact that literature was another product to be consumed (if not discarded). Perhaps distraught by this idea, after publishing *Gravity's Rainbow* Pynchon went into a nearly twenty-year period of silence during which he published nothing. Other leading postmodernists such as John Barth kept producing lengthy novels through the 1970s, but their audiences didn't seem as impressed as they had been with earlier experiments in the form.

Yet against the tide of excess and (in Barth's words) exhaustion, a number of new, younger writers were discovering and displaying their voices. As postmodernism was beginning to solidify as something that could be recognized and defined in the 1960s, American writers from racial and ethnic minority groups were modifying, reacting to, rejecting, or embracing postmodern techniques for their own ends (notably Ishmael Reed, whose 1972 novel *Mumbo Jumbo* approaches African American cultural history through postmodern techniques). Yet it is limiting to connect all of the writers in the late twentieth and early twenty-first centuries to postmodernism, regardless of race or ethnicity. As has always been true, some prominent writers produce work that is traditional, or that does not fit neatly into any definition of postmodernism. The significance of many of the multiethnic voices in the final part of this volume is that they document experiences that had been invisible, or difficult to see, in earlier historical periods. On the other hand, difference is a postmodern characteristic. Following the cultural turbulence of the 1960s, America was better prepared than it had ever been to comprehend its own diversity, especially where literature was concerned.

One significant development was the rise of Latino/a poetry in the early 1970s. The epicenter of this movement was the Nuyorican Poets' Café in the East Village section of New York City. Following a high period of Puerto Rican immigration in the 1950s and 1960s, New York's ethnic makeup had been radically transformed from its previous influxes of European immigrants in the late nineteenth and early twentieth centuries and African Americans during the Great Migration of the early twentieth century. In the early 1970s, this growing population discovered its literary voice in such poets as Pedro Pietri and Tato Laviera, represented in this volume. The Nuyorican Poets' Café was the foundation for a number of similar public urban sites in cities throughout the country where Hispanic and Latino populations have grown. The establishment in 1967 in Berkeley, California, of Quinto Sol Publications, whose sole mission was to publish Mexican American writing, provided a forum for publication that complemented performative spaces such as the Nuyorican Poets' Café.

The decade also witnessed a louder than usual cry of defiance from Native Americans, who had formed solidarity groups based on 1960s activism. The American Indian Movement (A.I.M.), founded in 1968, became involved in a number of standoffs with the federal government, including the occupation of Alcatraz Island in San Francisco Harbor from 1969 to 1971 and the Wounded Knee incident at the Pine Ridge Reservation in South Dakota in 1973. The latter was an armed, bloody standoff that initially left two dead and led to dozens of additional deaths over the next few years. Native Americans were asserting their political voices, and their literary voices followed in what could be seen as a renaissance. Our "In Focus" section on the Ojibway Nation reveals this confluence of literary and political voices.

The beginning of Toni Morrison's illustrious career in the 1970s is significant for the trends it signals in contemporary American literature. As the most recent American recipient of the Nobel Prize in Literature (in 1993) and the first African American recipient of that prestigious award, Morrison demonstrates that black writers in America were finally beginning to gain proper recognition for their achievements as the twentieth century came to a close. Her celebrated novels *The Bluest Eye* (1970), *Sula* (1973), and *Song of Solomon* (1977) and her edited volume *The Black Book* (1974) are complex looks at African American identity and history that led to the publication of *Beloved* (1987), arguably the most important work of American literature in the twentieth century. Race is only one of Morrison's concerns, though; gender is another. The most prominent black writers of the mid-twentieth century—Richard Wright, Ralph Ellison, James Baldwin, and Amiri Baraka—were men. The female African American experience is given deep consideration in the 1970s in the works of Alice Walker, Toni Cade Bambara, and Audre Lorde, all represented here. (Morrison's short story "Recitatif" was published in 1983 and is thus included later in this volume.)

Lorde and Walker are deeply associated with the feminist movement of the late 1960s and early 1970s, as are other writers who came to prominence in the 1970s represented here, Adrienne Rich and Maxine Hong Kingston. This movement represents an ongoing struggle to advocate for the recognition of women's rights and the need to fight against injustice and inequality. Following the mantra "the personal is political," a phrase advanced by the activist and scholar Carol Hanisch, feminist artists and writers in the early 1970s sought to call attention to this struggle in poetic, dramatic, and narrative forms. Rich's creation of an androgynous myth in "Diving into the Wreck" and Kingston's deep consideration of her aunt, persecuted to the point of suicide because she was impregnated by a man who was not her husband, are subtle and resonant explorations of feminist thought.

An undisputedly turbulent decade, the 1970s revealed a number of cultural anxieties about the direction of the nation after the revolutions, assassinations, triumphs, and failures of the 1960s. Literature remained a powerful means of addressing those anxieties, providing a forum for previously unheard or muted voices and preparing the way for a more tolerant future. The nation learned to transcend disillusionment and to laugh at the ridiculous Archie Bunker who claimed that anyone who "can't speak poifect English oughta be de-exported the hell out of here!" So much for poifect English. American writers continued to be more interested in language's hidden possibilities, which are best unlocked when we listen to the "varied carols" (as Whitman put it) of the American song.

■ ALICE WALKER ■
B. 1944

Alice Walker was born in Eatonton, Georgia, the youngest of eight children of Minnie and Willie Lee Walker, black sharecroppers. Her early life in the South was marked by the pressures of segregation and economic hardship, on the one hand, and the nurturing refuge of family, church, and black community, on the other. Summer visits with her older brothers who had settled in the North gave Walker her first glimpses of the world beyond the rural South. Her poetry, often quite personal and at times starkly intimate in its themes of family connections, romantic passion, and political integrity, draws frequently on remembrances of childhood.

In 1961 Walker entered Spelman College, a black women's school in Atlanta, Georgia. Finding Spelman too traditional, Walker transferred in 1963 to Sarah Lawrence College in Bronxville, New York, a school noted for its avant-garde curriculum in the arts. There, under the tutelage of poet Muriel Rukeyser and others, she began her writing career.

After college, Walker worked briefly for the New York City Welfare Department and in 1967 married Mel Leventhal, a civil rights attorney. The couple moved to Mississippi, where he prosecuted school desegregation cases and she taught at Jackson State College and also conducted adult education courses in black history. Their life in Mississippi as an interracial, activist couple was harrowing; they lived with constant threats of lethal violence against themselves and their infant daughter. During that time Walker published *The Third Life of Grange Copeland*, a novel of personal and political confrontation and transformation in the lives of three generations of a Southern black family. A later novel, *Meridian*, explores the complex psychological burden borne throughout the rest of their lives by those young men and women, black and white, who came of age living and working at the center of the civil rights movement of the 1960s.

In 1971 Walker accepted a fellowship from the Radcliffe Institute in Cambridge, Massachusetts, where she worked on poetry and short fiction, as well as on her landmark essay *In Search of Our Mothers' Gardens*. In 1982 she published *The Color Purple*, an epistolary novel about the lives of two sisters, Celie and Nettie, raised in a rural Southern black community and separated through years of tragedy, pain, struggle, and ultimate triumph. The novel was awarded both the American Book Award and the Pulitzer Prize in 1983.

From the start of her career, Alice Walker has been a prolific and diversified writer, adept at poetry, novels, short stories, and essays. A central theme throughout her work is the courage, resourcefulness, and creativity of black women of various ages, circumstances, and conditions. Whether rescuing from oblivion the writing and reputation of novelist, folklorist, and anthropologist Zora Neale Hurston or producing her own portraits, unique in American letters, of black women whose rich and complex lives have been little known and frequently devalued, Alice Walker continues to be a central figure in reshaping and expanding the canon of American literature.

Marilyn Richardson
Independent Scholar

PRIMARY WORKS

Once, 1968; *The Third Life of Grange Copeland*, 1970; *Revolutionary Petunias*, 1973; *In Love & Trouble*, 1973; *Meridian*, 1976; *Goodnight, Willie Lee, I'll See You in the Morning*, 1979; *You Can't Keep a Good Woman Down*, 1981; *The Color Purple*, 1982; *In Search of Our Mothers' Gardens*, 1983; *Horses Make a Landscape Look More Beautiful*, 1984; *The Temple of My Familiar*, 1989; *Possessing the Secret of Joy*, 1992; *Warrior Marks: Her Blue Body Everything We Knew: Earthling Poems, 1965–1990*, 1991; *Female Genital Mutilation and the Sexual Blinding of Women*, 1993; *The Same River Twice: Honoring the Difficult*, 1996; *Anything We Love Can Be Saved: A Writer's Activism*, 1997; *By the Light of My Father's Smile: A Novel*, 1998; *The Way Forward Is with a Broken Heart*, 2000; *Sent by Earth: A Message from the Grandmother Spirit after the Bombing of the World Trade Center and Pentagon*, 2002; *Absolute Trust in the Goodness of the Earth: New Poems*, 2003; *Collected Poems*, 2005; *Now Is the Time to Open Your Heart*, 2005; *Devil's My Enemy*, 2008.

Laurel

It was during that summer in the mid-sixties that I met Laurel.

There was a new radical Southern newspaper starting up ... it was only six months old at the time, and was called *First Rebel*. The title referred, of course, to the black slave who was rebelling all over the South long before the white rebels fought the Civil War. Laurel was in Atlanta to confer with the young people on its staff, and, since he wished to work on a radical, racially mixed newspaper himself, to see if perhaps *First Rebel* might be it.

I was never interested in working on a newspaper, however radical. I agree with Leonard Woolf that to write against a weekly deadline deforms the brain. Still, I attended several of the editorial meetings of *First Rebel* because while wandering out of the first one, fleeing it, in fact, I bumped into Laurel, who, squinting at me through cheap, fingerprint-smudged blue-and-gray-framed bifocals, asked if I knew where the meeting was.

He seemed a parody of the country hick; he was tall, slightly stooped, with blackish hair cut exactly as if someone had put a bowl over his head. Even his ears stuck out, and were large and pink.

Really, I thought.

Though he was no more than twenty-two, two years older than me, he seemed older. No doubt his bifocals added to this impression, as did his nonchalant gait and slouchy posture. His eyes were clear and brown and filled with an appropriate country slyness. It was his voice that held me. It had a charming lilt to it.

"Would you say that again?" I asked.

"Sure," he said, making it two syllables, the last syllable a higher pitch than the first. "I'm looking for where *First Rebel*, the newspaper, is meeting. What are *you* doing?"

The country slyness was clumsily replaced by a look of country seduction.

Have mercy! I thought. And burst into laughter.

Laurel grinned, his ears reddening.

And so we became involved in planning a newspaper that was committed to combating racism and other violence in the South ... (until it ran out of funds and folded three years and many pieces of invaluable investigative journalism later).

Laurel's was not a variation of a Southern accent, as I'd first thought. His ancestors had immigrated to the United States in the early 1800s. They had settled in California because there they found the two things they liked best: wine grapes and apples.

I'd never heard anything like Laurel's speech. He could ask a question like "How d'you happen t' be here?" and it sounded as if two happy but languid children were slowly jumping rope under apple trees in the sun. And on Laurel himself, while he spoke, I seemed to smell apples and the faint woodruffy bouquet of May wine.

He was also effortlessly complimentary. He would say, as we went through the cafeteria line, "You're beaut-ti-ful, reel-i," and it was like hearing it and caring about hearing it for the first time. Laurel, who loved working among the grapes, and had done so up to the moment of leaving the orchards for Atlanta, had dirt, lots of it, under his nails.

That's it, I thought. I can safely play here. No one brings such dirty nails home to dinner. That was Monday. By Tuesday I thought that dirty nails were just the right nonbourgeois attribute and indicated a lack of personal concern for appearances that included the smudged bifocals and the frazzled but beautifully fitting jeans; in a back pocket of which was invariably a half-rolled, impressively battered paperback book. It occurred to me that I could not look at Laurel without wanting to make love with him.

He was the same.

For a while, I blamed it on Atlanta in the spring ... the cherry trees that blossomed around the campus buildings, the wonderful honeysuckle smells of our South, the excitement of being far away from New York City and its never-to-be-gotten-used-to dirt. But it was more: if we both walked into a room from separate doors, even if we didn't see each other, a current dragged us together. At breakfast neither of us could eat, except chokingly, so intense was our longing to be together. Minus people, table, food.

A veritable movie.

Throughout the rest of the week we racked our brains trying to think of a place to make love. But the hotels were still segregated, and once, after a Movement party at somebody's house, we were severely reprimanded for walking out into the Southern night, blissfully hand in hand.

"Don't you know this is outrageous?" a young black man asked us, pulling us into his car, where I sat on Laurel's lap in a kind of sensual stupor—hearing his words, agreeing with them, knowing the bloody History behind them … but not caring in the least.

In short, there was no place for us to make love, as that term is popularly understood. We were housed in dormitories. Men in one. Women in another. Interracial couples were under surveillance wherever the poor things raised their heads anywhere in the city. We were reduced to a kind of sexual acrobatics on a bench close beside one of the dormitories. And, as lovers know, acrobatics of a sexual sort puts a strain on one's power of physical ingenuity while making one's lust all the more a resident of the brain, where it quickly becomes all-pervading, insatiable, and profound.

The state of lust itself is not a happy one if there is no relief in sight. Though I am happy enough to enter that state whenever it occurs, I have learned to acknowledge its many and often devastating limitations. For example, the most monumental issues fade from one's consciousness as if erased by a swift wind. Movements of great social and political significance seem but backdrops to one's daily exchanges—be they ever so muted and circumscribed—with the Object of One's Desire. (I at least was not yet able to articulate how the personal is the political, as was certainly true in Laurel's and my case. Viz., nobody wanted us to go to bed with each other, except us, and they had made laws to that effect. And of course whether we slept together or not was nobody's business, except ours.)

The more it became impossible to be with Laurel, to make love fully and naturally, the more I wanted nothing but that. If the South had risen again during one of our stolen kisses—his hands on my breasts, my hands on his (his breasts were sensitive, we discovered quite by acrobatic invention and accident)—we would have been hard pressed to notice. This is "criminal" to write, of course, given the myths that supposedly make multiracial living so much easier to bear, but it is quite true. And yet, after our week together— passionate, beautiful, haunting, and never, never to be approximated between us again, our desire to make love never to be fulfilled (though we did not know this then), we went our separate ways. Because in fact, while we kissed and said Everything Else Be Damned! the South *was* rising again. *Was* murdering people. Was imprisoning our colleagues and friends. Was keeping us from strolling off to a clean, cheap hotel.

It was during our last night together that he told me about his wife. We were dancing in a local Movement-oriented nightclub. What would today be called a disco. He had an endearing way of dancing, even to slow tunes (during which we clung together shamelessly); he did a sort of hop, fast or slow depending on the music, from one foot to the other, almost in time with the music—and that was dance to him. It didn't bother me at all. Our bodies easily found their own rhythms anyway, and touching alone was our reason for being on the floor. *There* we could make a sort of love, in a dark enough corner, that was not exactly grace but was not, was definitely not, acrobatics.

He peered at me through the gray-and-blue-framed glasses.

"I've got a wife back home."

What I've most resented as "the other woman" is being made responsible for the continued contentment and happiness of the wife. On our last night together, our lust undiminished and apparently not to be extinguished, given our surroundings, what was I supposed to do with this information?

All I could think was: She's not *my* wife.

She was, from what he said, someone admirable. She was away from home for the summer, studying for an advanced degree. He seemed perplexed by this need of hers to continue her education instead of settling down to have his children, but lonely rather than bitter.

So it was *just sex* between us, after all, I thought.

(To be fair, I was engaged to a young man in the Peace Corps. I didn't mind if it *was* just sex, since by that time our mutual lust had reached a state, almost, of mysticism.)

Laurel, however, was tormented.

(I never told him about my engagement. As far as I was concerned, it remained to be seen whether my engagement was relevant to my relationship with others. I thought not, but realized I was still quite young.)

That night, Laurel wrung his hands, pulled his strangely cut hair and cried, as we brazenly walked out along Atlanta's dangerous, cracker-infested streets.

I cried because he did, and because in some odd way it relieved my lust. Besides, I enjoyed watching myself pretend to suffer ... Such moments of emotional dishonesty are always paid for, however, and that I did not know this at the time attests to my willingness to believe our relationship would not live past the moment itself.

And yet.

There was one letter from him to me after I'd settled in a small Georgia town (a) to picket the jailhouse where a local schoolteacher was under arrest for picketing the jailhouse where a local parent was under arrest for picketing the jailhouse where a local child was under arrest for picketing ... and (b) to register voters.

He wrote that he missed me.

I missed him. He was the principal other actor in all my fantasies. I wrote him that I was off to Africa, but would continue to write. I gave him the address of my school, to which he could send letters.

Once in Africa, my fiancé (who was conveniently in the next country from mine and free to visit) and I completed a breakup that had been coming for our entire two- year period of engagement. He told me, among other things, that it was not uncommon for Peace Corps men to sleep with ten-year-old African girls. *At that age, you see, they were still attractive.* I wrote about that aspect of the Peace Corps' activities to Laurel, as if I'd heard about it from a stranger.

Laurel, I felt, would never take advantage of a ten-year-old child. And I loved him for it.

Loving him, I was not prepared for the absence of letters from him, back at my school. Three months after my return I still had heard nothing. Out of depression over this and the distraction schoolwork provided, I was a practicing celibate. Only rarely did I feel lustful, and then of course I always thought of Laurel, as of a great opportunity, much missed. I thought of his musical speech and his scent of apples and May wine with varying degrees of regret and tenderness. However, our week of passion—magical, memorable, but far too brief—gradually assumed a less than central place even in my most sanguine recollections.

In late November, six months after Laurel and I met, I received a letter from his wife.

My first thought, when I saw the envelope, was: She has the same last name as his. It was the first time their marriage was real for me. I was also frightened that she wrote to accuse me of disturbing her peace. Why else would a wife write?

She wrote that on July fourth of the previous summer (six weeks after Laurel and I met) Laurel had had an automobile accident. He was driving his van, delivering copies of *First Rebel.* He had either fallen asleep at the wheel or been run off the road by local rebels of the other kind. He had sustained a broken leg, a fractured back, and a severely damaged brain. He had been in a coma for the past four months. Nothing could rouse him. She had found my letter in his pocket. Perhaps I would come to see him.

(I was never to meet Laurel's wife, but I admired this gesture then, and I admire it now.)

It was a small Catholic hospital in Laurel's hometown. In the entryway a bloody, gruesome, ugly Christ the color of a rutabaga, stood larger than life. Nuns dressed in black and white habits reminded one of giant flies. Floating moonlike above their "wings," their pink, cherubic faces were kind and comical.

Laurel's father looked very much like Laurel. The same bifocals, the same plain clothing, the same open-seeming face—but on closer look, wide rather than open. The same lilt to his voice. Laurel's sister was also there. She, unaccountably, embraced me.

"We're so glad you came," she said.

She was like Laurel too. Smaller, pretty, with short blond hair and apple cheeks.

She reached down and took Laurel's hand.

Laurel alone did not look like Laurel. He who had been healthy, firm-fleshed, virile, lay now on his hospital bed a skeleton with eyes. Tubes entered his body everywhere. His head was shaved, a bandage covering the hole that had been drilled in the top. His breathing was hardly a whistle through a hole punched in his throat.

I took the hands that had given such pleasure to my breasts, and they were bones, unmoving, cold, in mine. I touched the face I'd dreamed about for months as I would the face of someone already in a coffin.

His sister said, "Annie is here," her voice carrying the lilt.

Laurel's eyes were open, jerking, twitching, in his head. His mouth was open. But he was not there. Only his husk, his shell. His father looked at me—as he would look at any other treatment. Speculatively. Will it work? Will it revive my son?

I did not work. I did not revive his son. Laurel lay, wheezing through the hole in his throat, helpless, insensate. I was eager to leave.

Two years later, the letters began to arrive. Exactly as if he thought I still waited for them at school.

"My darling," he wrote, "I am loving you. Missing you and out of coma after a year and everybody given up on me. My brain damaged. Can you come to me? I am still bedridden."

But I was not in school. I was married, living in the South.

"Tell him you're married now," my husband advised. "He should know not to hurt himself with dreaming."

I wrote that I was not only married but "happily."

My marital status meant nothing to Laurel.

"Please come," he wrote. "There are few black people here. You would be lonesome but I will be here loving you."

I wrote again. This time I reported I was married, pregnant, and had a dog for protection.

"I dream of your body so luscious and fertile. I want so much to make love to you as we never could do. I hope you know how I lost part of my brain working for your people in the South. I miss you. Come soon."

I wrote: "Dear Laurel, I am so glad you are better. I'm sorry you were hurt. So sorry. I cannot come to you because I am married. I love my husband. I cannot bear to come. I am pregnant—nauseous all the time and anxious because of the life I/We lead." Etc., etc.

To which he replied: "You married a jew. [I had published a novel and apparently reviewers had focused on my marriage instead of my work as they often did.] There are no jews here either. I guess you have a taste for the exotic though I was not exotic. I am a cripple now with part of my brain in somebody's wastepaper basket. We could have children if you will take responsibility for bringing them up. I cannot be counted on. Ha Ha."

I asked my husband to intercept the letters that came to our house. I asked the president of my college to collect and destroy those sent to me there. I dreaded seeing them.

"I dream of your body, so warm and brown, whereas mine is white and cold to me now. I could take you as my wife here the people are prejudiced against blacks they were happy martin luther king was killed. I want you here. We can be happy and black and beautiful and crippled and missing part of my brain together. I want you but I guess you are tied up with that jew husband of yours. I mean no disrespect to him but we belong together and you know that."

"Dear Laurel, I am a mother. [I hoped this would save me. It didn't.] I have a baby daughter. I hope you are well. My husband sends his regards."

Most of Laurel's letters I was not shown. Assuming that my husband confiscated his letters without my consent, Laurel telegraphed: ANNIE, I AM COMING BY GREY-HOUND BUS DON'T LET YOUR DOG BITE ME, LAUREL.

My husband said: "Fine, let him come. Let him see that you are not the woman he remembers. His memory is frozen on your passion for each other. Let him see how happy you and I are."

I waited, trembling.

It was a cold, clear evening. Laurel hobbled out of the taxi on crutches, one leg shorter than the other. He had regained his weight and, though pale, was almost handsome. He glanced at my completely handsome husband once and dismissed him. He kept his eyes on me. He smiled on me happily, pleased with me.

I knew only one dish then, chicken tarragon; I served it.

I was frightened. Not of Laurel, exactly, but of feeling all the things I felt.

(My husband's conviction notwithstanding, I suspected marriage could not keep me from being, in some ways, exactly the woman Laurel remembered.)

I woke up my infant daughter and held her, disgruntled, flushed and ludicrously alert, in front of me.

While we ate, Laurel urged me to recall our acrobatic nights on the dormitory bench, our intimate dancing. Before my courteous husband, my cheeks flamed. Those nights that seemed so far away to me seemed all he clearly remembered; he recalled less well how his accident occurred. Everything before and after that week had been swept away. The moment was real to him. I was real to him. Our week together long ago was very real to him. But that was all. His speech was as beautifully lilting as ever, with a zaniness that came from a lack of connective knowledge. But he was hard to listen to: he was both overconfident of his success with me—based on what he recalled of our mutual passion—and so intense that his gaze had me on the verge of tears.

Now that he was here and almost well, I must drop everything, including the baby on my lap—whom he barely seemed to see—and come away with him. Had I not flown off to Africa, though it meant leaving the very country in which he lived?

Finally, after the riddles within riddles that his words became (and not so much riddles as poems, and disturbing ones), my husband drove Laurel back to the bus station. He had come over a thousand miles for a two-hour visit.

My husband's face was drawn when he returned. He loved me, I was sure of that. He was glad to help me out. Still, he wondered.

"It lasted a week!" I said. "Long before I met you."

"I know," he said. "Sha, sha, baby," he comforted me. I had crept into his arms, trembling from head to foot. "It's all right. We're safe."

But *were we?*

And Laurel? Zooming through the night back to his home? The letters continued. Sometimes I asked to read one that came to the house.

"I am on welfare now. I hate being alive. Why didn't my father let me die? The people are prejudiced here. If you came they would be cruel to us but maybe it would help them see something. You are more beautiful than ever. You are so sexy you make me ache—it is not only because you are black that would be racism but because when you are in the same room with me the room is full of color and scents and I am all alive."

He offered to adopt my daughter, shortly after he received a divorce from his wife.

After my husband and I were divorced (some seven years after Laurel's visit and thirteen years after Laurel and I met), we sat one evening discussing Laurel. He recalled him perfectly, with characteristic empathy and concern.

"If I hadn't been married to you, I would have gone off with him," I said, "Maybe."

"Really?" He seemed surprised.

Out of habit I touched his arm. "I loved him, in a way."

"I know," he said, and smiled.

"A lot of love was lust. That threw me off for years until I realized lust can be a kind of love."

He nodded.

"I felt guilty about Laurel. When he wrote me, I became anxious. When he came to visit us, I was afraid."

"He was not the man you knew."

"I don't think I knew him well enough to tell. Even so, I was afraid the love and lust would come flying back, along with the pity. And that even if they didn't come back, I would run off with him anyway, because of the pity—*and for the adventure.*"

It was the word "adventure" and the different meaning it had for each of us that finally separated us. We had come to understand that, and to accept it without bitterness.

"I wanted to ask you to let me go away with him, for just a couple of months," I said. *"To let me go ..."*

"He grew steadily worse, you know. His last letters were brutal. He blamed you for everything, even the accident, accusing you of awful, nasty things. He became a bitter, vindictive man."

He knew me well enough to know I heard this and I did not hear it.

He sighed. "It would have been tough for me," he said. "Tough for our daughter. Tough for you. Toughest of all for Laurel."

(*"Tell me it's all right that I didn't go!"* I wanted to plead, but didn't.)

"Right," I said instead, shrugging, and turning our talk to something else.

1971

■ TONI CADE BAMBARA ■
1939–1995

In a revealing essay called "Black English" (1972), Toni Cade Bambara summarized those attitudes that by 1970 had become the dramatic center of the fifteen stories included in her first short story collection, *Gorilla, My Love*. One of those attitudes, that "language is [as often] used to mis-inform, to mis-direct, to smoke out, to screen out, to block out, to intimidate as it is to inform," is one theme of the title story of that collection; another, that "language certainly determines how we perceive the world" (limiting or expanding it), is the thematic core of "Playing with Punjab," "Maggie of the Green Bottles," and especially "My Man Bovanne." As superb a linguist as she was satirist, as splendid a storyteller as she was cultural ecologist, and as crucial a thinker as she was intrepid force for social transformation, Toni Cade—who adopted the name Bambara, which she discovered as a signature on a sketchbook in her great-grandmother's trunk—grew up, like most of the narrators of her fiction, in an urban neighborhood whose rituals shaped her critical imagination.

In the New York City neighborhoods of Harlem, Bedford-Stuyvesant, and Queens, she and her brother Walter (now a painter) cut through the pernicious urban miasma that her fiction rigorously, often humorously, assails. Here in the "games, chants, jingles" of her peers, in the eloquence of the Seventh Avenue street speakers, in the elegance of the church-inspired club-inspired music of her neighborhood, in the talk and humor at home, and in the "space" allowed her by her parents, Walter and Helen (Henderson) Cade—who understood the necessity of encouraging a child's interior life—Toni Cade Bambara began to forge the language characteristic of the folk-based music, poetry, and prose of African American blues-jazz expressive modes. She earned a bachelor's degree in theater and literature from Queens College in 1959 and a master's in modern American literature from the City College of New York in 1963. She subsequently studied at the Commedia del' Arte in Milan and also studied filmmaking in England.

It is not surprising that during the period of tremendous political activism in which she matured—the struggle for civil rights in America, along with the struggle for the economic, political, and cultural empowerment of black Americans; international resistance to colonialism, with its demands for political and cultural self-determination in the Caribbean and on the continents of Africa and

Asia; and vigorous protests against war and nuclear weaponry—many young African American intellectuals like Toni Cade Bambara found common cause. Still, her personal voice continues to find its deepest resonance in the cadences of the womanly themes of re-creation and renewal found in "My Man Bovanne," the story that opens *Gorilla, My Love.* The pervasive melody harmonizing her work and embracing the specific emphasis of recent African American women writers is the theme of "a certain way of being in the world," nowhere more fully orchestrated than in her first novel, *The Salt Eaters* (1980), and in her second book of short stories, *The Sea Birds Are Still Alive* (1977).

Eleanor W. Traylor
Howard University

PRIMARY WORKS

The Black Woman: An Anthology, 1970; *Tales and Stories for Black Folks,* 1971; *Gorilla, My Love,* 1972; *The Sea Birds Are Still Alive: Collected Stories,* 1977; *The Salt Eaters,* 1980; *Raymond's Run,* 1990; *These Bones Are Not My Child,* 1999; *Deep Sightings and Rescue Missions: Fiction, Essays, and Conversations,* 1999.

My Man Bovanne

Blind people got a hummin jones if you notice. Which is understandable completely once you been around one and notice what no eyes will force you into to see people, and you get past the first time, which seems to come out of nowhere, and it's like you in church again with fat-chest ladies and old gents gruntin a hum low in the throat to whatever the preacher be saying. Shakey Bee bottom lip all swole up with Sweet Peach and me explainin how come the sweet-potato bread was a dollar-quarter this time stead of dollar regular and he say uh hunh he understand, then he break into this *thizzin* kind of hum which is quiet, but fiercesome just the same, if you ain't ready for it. Which I wasn't. But I got used to it and the onliest time I had to say somethin bout it was when he was playin checkers on the stoop one time and he commenst to hummin quite churchy seem to me. So I says, "Look here Shakey Bee, I can't beat you and Jesus too." He stop.

So that's how come I asked My Man Bovanne to dance. He ain't my man mind you, just a nice ole gent from the block that we all know cause he fixes things and the kids like him. Or used to fore Black Power got hold their minds and mess em around till they can't be civil to ole folks. So we at this benefit for my niece's cousin who's runnin for somethin with this Black party somethin or other behind her. And I press up close to dance with Bovanne who blind and I'm hummin and he hummin, chest to chest like talkin. Not jammin my breasts into the man. Wasn't bout tits. Was bout vibrations. And he dug it and asked me what color dress I had on and how my hair was fixed and how I was doin without a man, not nosy but nice-like, and who was at this affair and was the canapés dainty-stingy or healthy enough to get hold of proper. Comfy and cheery is what I'm tryin to get across. Touch talkin like the heel of the hand on the tambourine or on a drum.

But right away Joe Lee come up on us and frown for dancin so close to the man. My own son who knows what kind of warm I am about; and don't grown men call me long distance and in the middle of the night for a little Mama comfort? But he frown. Which ain't right since Bovanne can't see and defend himself. Just a nice old man who fixes toasters and busted irons and bicycles and things and changes the lock on my door when my men friends get messy. Nice man. Which is not why they invited him. Grass roots you see. Me and Sister Taylor and the woman who does heads at Mamies and the man from the barber shop, we all there on account of we grass roots. And I ain't never been souther than Brooklyn Battery and no more country than the window box on my fire escape. And just yesterday my kids tellin me to take them countrified rags off my head and be cool. And now can't get Black enough to suit em. So everybody passin sayin My Man Bovanne. Big deal, keep steppin and don't even stop a minute to get the man a drink or one of them cute sandwiches or tell him what's goin on. And him standin there with a smile ready case someone do speak he want to be ready. So that's how come I pull him on the dance floor and we dance squeezin past the tables and chairs and all them coats and people standin round up in each other face talkin bout this and that but got no use for this blind man who mostly fixed skates and scooters for all these folks when they was just kids. So I'm pressed up close and we touch talkin with the hum. And here come my daughter cuttin her eye at me like she do when she tell me about my "apolitical" self like I got hoof and mouf disease and there ain't no hope at all. And I don't pay her no I mind and just look up in Bovanne shadow face and tell him his stomach like a drum and he laugh. Laugh real loud. And here come my youngest, Task, with a tap on my elbow like he the third grade monitor and I'm cuttin up on the line to assembly.

"I was just talkin on the drums," I explained when they hauled me into the kitchen. I figured drums was my best defense. They can get ready for drums what with all this heritage business. And Bovanne stomach just like that drum Task give me when he come back from Africa. You just touch it and it hum thizzm, thizzm. So I stuck to the drum story. "Just drummin that's all."

"Mama, what are you talkin about?"

"She had too much to drink," say Elo to Task cause she don't hardly say nuthin to me direct no more since that ugly argument about my wigs.

"Look here Mama," say Task, the gentle one. "We just tryin to pull your coat. You were makin a spectacle of yourself out there dancing like that."

"Dancin like what?"

Task run a hand over his left ear like his father for the world and his father before that.

"Like a bitch in heat," say Elo.

"Well uhh, I was goin to say like one of them sex-starved ladies gettin on in years and not too discriminating. Know what I mean?"

I don't answer cause I'll cry. Terrible thing when your own children talk to you like that. Pullin me out the party and hustlin me into some stranger's kitchen in the back of a bar just like the damn police. And ain't like I'm old old. I can still wear me some sleeveless dresses without the meat hangin off my arm. And I keep up with some thangs through my kids. Who ain't kids no more. To hear them tell it. So I don't say nuthin.

"Dancin with that tom," say Elo to Joe Lee, who leanin on the folks' freezer. "His feet can smell a cracker a mile away and go into their shuffle number post haste. And them eyes. He could be a little considerate and put on some shades. Who wants to look into them blown-out fuses that—"

"Is this what they call the generation gap?" I say.

"Generation gap," spits Elo, like I suggested castor oil and fricassee possum in the milk-shakes or somethin. "That's a white concept for a white phenomenon. There's no generation gap among Black people. We are a col—"

"Yeh, well never mind," says Joe Lee. "The point is Mama ... well, it's pride. You embarrass yourself and us too dancin like that."

"I wasn't shame." Then nobody say nuthin. Them standin there in they pretty clothes with drinks in they hands and gangin up on me, and me in the third-degree chair and nary a olive to my name. Felt just like the police got hold to me.

"First of all," Task say, holdin up his hand and tickin off the offenses, "the dress. Now that dress is too short, Mama, and too low-cut for a woman your age. And Tamu's going to make a speech tonight to kick off the campaign and will be introducin you and expecting you to organize the council of elders—"

"Me? Didn nobody ask me nuthin. You mean Nisi? She change her name?"

"Well, Norton was supposed to tell you about it. Nisi wants to introduce you and then encourage the older folks to form a Council of the Elders to act as an advisory—"

"And you going to be standing there with your boobs out and that wig on your head and that hem up to your ass. And people'll say, 'Ain't that the horny bitch that was grindin with the blind dude?' "

"Elo, be cool a minute," say Task, gettin to the next finger. "And then there's the drinkin. Mama, you know you can't drink cause next thing you know you be laughin loud and carryin on," and he grab another finger for the loudness. "And then there's the dancin. You been tattooed on the man for four records straight and slow draggin even on the fast numbers. How you think that look for a woman your age?"

"What's my age?"

"What?"

"I'm axin you all a simple question. You keep talkin bout what's proper for a woman my age. How old am I anyhow?" And Joe Lee slams his eyes shut and squinches up his face to figure. And Task run a hand over his ear and stare into his glass like the ice cubes goin calculate for him. And Elo just starin at the top of my head like she goin rip the wig off any minute now.

"Is your hair braided up under that thing? If so, why don't you take it off? You always did do a neat cornroll."

"Uh huh," cause I'm thinkin how she couldn't undo her hair fast enough talking bout cornroll so countrified. None of which was the subject. "How old, I say?"

"Sixtee-one or—"

"You a damn lie Joe Lee Peoples."

"And that's another thing," say Task on the fingers.

"You know what you all can kiss," I say, gettin up and brushin the wrinkles out my lap.

"Oh, Mama," Elo say, puttin a hand on my shoulder like she hasn't done since she left home and the hand landin light and not sure it supposed to be there. Which hurt me to my heart. Cause this was the child in our happiness fore Mr. Peoples die. And I carried that child strapped to my chest till she was nearly two. We was close is what I'm tryin to tell you. Cause it was more me in the child than the others. And even after Task it was the girlchild I covered in the night and wept over for no reason at all less it was she was a chub-chub like me and not very pretty, but a warm child. And how did things get to this, that she can't put a sure hand on me and say Mama we love you and care about you and you entitled to enjoy yourself cause you a good woman?

"And then there's Reverend Trent," say Task, glancin from left to right like they hatchin a plot and just now lettin me in on it. "You were suppose to be talking with him to night, Mama, about giving us his basement for campaign headquarters and—"

"Didn nobody tell me nuthin. If grass roots mean you kept in the dark I can't use it. I really can't. And Reven Trent a fool anyway the way he tore into the widow man up there on Edgecomb cause he wouldn't take in three of them foster children and the woman not even comfy in the ground yet and the man's mind messed up and—"

"Look here," say Task. "What we need is a family conference so we can get all this stuff cleared up and laid out on the table. In the meantime I think we better get back into the other room and tend to business. And in the meantime, Mama, see if you can't get to Reverend Trent and—"

"You want me to belly rub with the Reven, that it?"

"Oh damn," Elo say and go through the swingin door.

"We'll talk about all this at dinner. How's tomorrow night, Joe Lee?" While Joe Lee being self-important I'm wonderin who's doin the cookin and how come no body ax me if I'm free and do I get a corsage and things like that. Then Joe nod that it's O.K. and he go through the swingin door and just a little hubbub come through from the other room. Then Task smile his smile, lookin just like his daddy and he leave. And it just me in this stranger's kitchen, which was a mess I wouldn't never let my kitchen look like. Poison you just to look at the pots. Then the door swing the other way and it's My Man Bovanne standin there sayin Miss Hazel but lookin at the deep fry and then at the steam table, and most surprised when I come up on him from the other direction and take him on out of there. Pass the folks pushin up towards the stage where Nisi and some other people settin and ready to talk, and folks gettin to the last of the sandwiches and the booze fore they settle down in one spot and listen serious. And I'm thinkin bout tellin Bovanne what a lovely long dress Nisi got on and the earrings and her hair piled up in a cone and the people bout to hear how we all gettin screwed and gotta form our own party and everybody there listenin and lookin. But instead I just haul the man on out of there, and Joe Lee and his wife look at me like I'm terrible, but they ain't said boo to the man yet. Cause he blind and old and don't nobody there need him since they grown up and don't need they skates fixed no more.

"Where we goin, Miss Hazel?" Him knowin all the time.

"First we gonna buy you some dark sunglasses. Then you comin with me to the supermarket so I can pick up tomorrow's dinner, which is goin to be a grand thing proper and you invited. Then we goin to my house."

"That be fine. I surely would like to rest my feet." Bein cute, but you got to let men play out they little show, blind or not. So he chat on bout how tired he is and how he appreciate me takin him in hand this way. And I'm thinkin I'll have him change the lock on my door first thing. Then I'll give the man a nice warm bath with jasmine leaves in the water and a little Epsom salt on the sponge to do his back. And then a good rubdown with rose water and olive oil. Then a cup of lemon tea with a taste in it. And a little talcum, some of that fancy stuff Nisi mother sent over last Christmas. And then a massage, a good face massage round the forehead which is the worryin part. Cause you gots to take care of the older folks. And let them know they still needed to run the mimeo machine and keep the spark plugs clean and fix the mailboxes for folks who might help us get the breakfast program goin, and the school for the little kids and the campaign and all. Cause old folks is the nation. That what Nisi was sayin and I mean to do my part.

"I imagine you are a very pretty woman, Miss Hazel."

"I surely am," I say just like the hussy my daughter always say I was.

1972

RUDOLFO A. ANAYA

B. 1937

Bless Me, Ultima (1972), Rudolfo Anaya's first novel, is the single literary work most responsible not only for introducing American readers to Mexican American experience but for suggesting something of its vast imaginative potential. *Bless Me, Ultima* compelled its readers to discard the traditional American stereotype of Mexican American culture as a minor regional phenomenon, a curious, even degraded blend of customs and values drawn haphazardly from either side of the United States–Mexico border. Anaya delineates instead a distinctive culture rooted in the rich traditions of pre-Columbian aboriginal America and golden-age Spain. To be sure, Anaya's fictional terrain is a highly individualized and relatively remote region of east-central New Mexico; nevertheless, *Bless Me, Ultima* has had the effect of validating Mexican American culture from California to Texas and beyond.

Like many first novels, *Bless Me, Ultima* contains autobiographical elements. Anaya is himself from east-central New Mexico, having been born in Pastura. He attended school in nearby Santa Rosa and later in Albuquerque, where he has lived most of his adult life. He earned several degrees in English and in guidance and counseling and taught for seven years in the Albuquerque public schools. Anaya had become director of counseling at the University of Albuquerque when *Bless Me, Ultima* appeared. Two years later, in 1974, Anaya joined the faculty of the University of New Mexico, where he is now professor emeritus of English.

Since *Bless Me, Ultima*, Anaya has published a steady sequence of novels, short stories, plays, and even a travel book titled *A Chicano in China*. Despite the subject of this last book, Anaya retains his fascination with New Mexico, its clash and blending of cultures and its unique qualities as a setting for the engagement of fundamental religious and moral questions. The drama *Matachines* explores the cultural meaning of a ritual dance combining Moorish, Spanish, and Indian elements; the novel *Alburquerque* (spelled as in the original Spanish) concerns a young man's search for his father against the backdrop of a city losing its cultural moorings and beset by urban problems. None of Anaya's subsequent writing, however, has matched either the appeal or the power of his first novel.

Bless Me, Ultima focuses on the experiences of Antonio Marez as he begins school at the conclusion of World War II. As the last of four sons in the family, Antonio carries the burden of his parents' increasingly desperate hopes. His mother, from a sedentary, tradition-bound clan of farmers, wishes Antonio to become a priest to absolve the indiscretions of one of her forebears. The father, equally alert to tradition, wants his son to maintain the *vaquero* customs of his family, most notably their fierce independence and self-reliance. As the battle lines for control of Antonio's destiny are drawn, the revered Ultima appears to nurture the boy in her own extraordinary way. Ultima is a *curandera*, a folk healer who joins the Marez household ostensibly to merely live out the rest of her days. Under Ultima's tutelage, Antonio flourishes and begins preparations to fulfill his true destiny: to write, record, and thus preserve the traditions of his father's and mother's families alike.

Bless Me, Ultima is a novel rich in folklore. Anaya appropriates legends such as *La Llorona* (the crying woman), folk medicine, and superstition to convey a feeling of Mexican American culture in rural New Mexico. For Antonio, the folklore transmitted to him by Ultima serves as the very core of his cultural identity.

In the passage from *Bless Me, Ultima* presented here, Antonio recalls events surrounding his first communion. Even as a very young boy, Antonio has doubts about the Catholic Church—its morbid emphasis on sinfulness, the unintelligibility of some of its practices, and its inability to justify God's treatment of his friend Florence who, just a boy himself, has already lost his parents and watched helplessly as his older sisters drifted into prostitution. Antonio finds himself attracted to the stories of the Golden Carp, a local pagan symbol of benevolence. But for all his growing doubts, Antonio is still very much the product of his mother's religious training, so for now he acquiesces and participates in the church's rituals.

Raymund A. Paredes
University of California, Los Angeles

PRIMARY WORKS

Bless Me, Ultima, 1972; *Heart of Aztlan*, 1976; *Tortuga*, 1979; *The Silence of the Llano: Short Stories*, 1982; *The Legend of La Llorona*, 1984; *The Adventures of Juan Chicaspatas*, 1985; *A Chicano in China*, 1986; *Lord of the Dawn: The Legend of Quetzalcóatl*, 1987; *The Season of La Llorona* (play), 1987; *Matachines* (play), 1992; *Alburquerque*, 1992; *The Anaya Reader*, 1995; *Zia Summer*, 1995; *Rio Grande Fall*, 1996; *Jalamanta: A Message from the Desert*, 1996; *Shaman Winter*, 1998; *The Curse of the Chupacabra*, 2003; *The Man Who Could Fly and Other Stories*, 2006.

from **Bless Me, Ultima**

Dieciocho

Ash Wednesday. There is no other day like Ash Wednesday. The proud and the meek, the arrogant and the humble are all made equal on Ash Wednesday. The healthy and the sick, the assured and the sick in spirit, all make their way to church in the gray morning or in the dusty afternoon. They line up silently, eyes downcast, bony fingers counting the beads of the rosary, lips mumbling prayers. All are repentant, all are preparing themselves for the shock of the laying of the ashes on the forehead and the priest's agonizing words, "Thou art dust, and to dust thou shalt return."

The anointment is done, and the priest moves on, only the dull feeling of helplessness remains. The body is not important. It is made of dust; it is made of ashes. It is food for the worms. The winds and the waters dissolve it and scatter it to the four corners of the earth. In the end, what we care most for lasts only a brief lifetime, then there is eternity. Time forever. Millions of worlds are born, evolve, and pass away into nebulous, unmeasured skies; and there is still eternity. Time always. The body becomes dust and trees and exploding fire, it becomes gaseous and disappears, and still there is eternity. Silent, unopposed, brooding, forever . . .

But the soul survives. The soul lives on forever. It is the soul that must be saved, because the soul endures. And so when the burden of being nothing lifts from one's thoughts the idea of the immortality of the soul is like a light in a blinding storm. Dear God! the spirit cries out, my soul will live forever!

And so we hurried to catechism! The trying forty days of Lent lay ahead of us, then the shining goal, Easter Sunday and first holy communion! Very little else mattered in my life. School work was dull and uninspiring compared to the mysteries of religion. Each new question, each new catechism chapter, each new story seemed to open up a thousand facets concerning the salvation of my soul. I saw very little of Ultima, or even of my mother and father. I was concerned with myself. I knew that eternity lasted forever, and a soul because of one mistake could spend that eternity in hell.

The knowledge of this was frightful. I had many dreams in which I saw myself or different people burning in the fires of hell. One person especially continually haunted my nightmares. It was Florence. Inevitably it was he whom I saw burning in the roaring inferno of eternal damnation.

But why? I questioned the hissing fires, Florence knows all the answers!

But he does not accept, the flames lisped back.

"Florence," I begged him that afternoon, "try to answer."

He smiled. "And lie to myself," he answered.

"Don't lie! Just answer!" I shouted with impatience.

"You mean, when the priest asks where is God, I am to say God is everywhere: He is the worms that await the summer heat to eat Narciso, He shares the bed with Tenorio and his evil daughters—"

"Oh, God!" I cried in despair.

Samuel came up and touched me on the shoulder. "Perhaps things would not be so difficult if he believed in the golden carp," he said softly.

"Does Florence know?" I asked.

"This summer he shall know," Samuel answered wisely.

"What's that all about?" Ernie asked.

"Nothing," I said.

"Come on!" Abel shouted, "bell's ringing—"

It was Friday and we ran to attend the ritual of the Stations of the Cross. The weather was beginning to warm up but the winds still blew, and the whistling of the wind and the mournful cou-rouing of the pigeons and the burning incense made the agony of Christ's journey very sad. Father Byrnes stood at the first station and prayed to the bulto on the wall that showed Christ being sentenced by Pilate. Two high-school altar boys accompanied the priest, one to hold the lighted candle and the other to hold the incense burner. The hushed journeyers with Christ answered the priest's prayer. Then there was an interlude of silence while the priest and his attendants moved to the second station, Christ receiving the cross.

Horse sat by me. He was carving his initials into the back of the seat in front of us. Horse never prayed all of the stations, he waited until the priest came near, then he prayed the one he happened to be sitting by. I looked at the wall and saw that today he had picked to sit by the third fall of Christ.

The priest genuflected and prayed at the first fall of Christ. The incense was thick and sweet. Sometimes it made me sick inside and I felt faint. Next Friday would be Good Friday. Lent had gone by fast. There would be no stations on Good Friday, and maybe no catechism. By then we would be ready for confession Saturday and then the receiving of the sacrament on the most holy of days, Easter Sunday.

"What's Immmm-ack-que-let Con-sep-shion?" Abel asked. And Father Byrnes moved to the station where Christ meets his mother. I tried to concentrate. I felt sympathy for the Virgin.

"Immaculate Conception," Lloyd whispered.

"Yeah?"

"The Virgin Mary—"

"But what does it mean?"

"Having babies without—"

"What?"

I tried to shut my ears, I tried to hear the priest, but he was moving away, moving to where Simon helped Christ carry the cross. Dear Lord, I will help.

"I don't know—" Everybody giggled.

"Shhh!" Agnes scowled at us. The girls always prayed with bowed heads throughout the stations.

"A man and a woman, it takes a man and a woman," Florence nodded.

But the Virgin! I panicked, the Virgin Mary was the mother of God! The priest had said she was a mother through a miracle.

The priest finished the station where Veronica wiped the bloodied face of Christ, and he moved to Christ's second fall. The face of Christ was imprinted on the cloth. Besides the Virgin's blue robe, it was the holiest cloth on earth. The cross was heavy, and when He fell the soldiers whipped Him and struck Him with clubs. The people laughed. His agony began to fill the church and the women moaned their prayers, but the kids would not listen.

"The test is Saturday morning—"

Horse left his carving and looked up. The word "test" made him nervous.

"I, I, I'll pass," he nodded. Bones growled.

"Everybody will pass," I said, trying to be reassuring.

"Florence doesn't believe!" Rita hissed behind us.

"Shhhh! The priest is turning." Father Byrnes was at the back of the church, the seventh station. Now he would come down this side of the aisle for the remaining seven. Christ was speaking to the women.

Maybe that's why they prayed so hard, Christ spoke to them.

In the bell tower the pigeons cou-rouing made a mournful sound.

The priest was by us now. I could smell the incense trapped in his frock, like the fragrance of Ultima's herbs was part of her clothes. I bowed my head. The burning incense was sweet and suffocating; the glowing candle was hypnotizing. Horse had looked at it too long. When the priest moved on Horse leaned on me. His face was white.

"A la chingada," he whispered, "voy a tirar tripas—"

The priest was at the station of the Crucifixion. The hammer blows were falling on the nails that ripped through the flesh. I could almost hear the murmuring of the crowd as they craned their necks to see. But today I could not feel the agony.

"Tony—" Horse was leaning on me and gagging.

I struggled under his weight. People turned to watch me carrying the limp Horse up the aisle. Florence left his seat to help me and together we dragged Horse outside. He threw up on the steps of the church.

"He watched the candle too long," Florence said.

"Yes," I answered.

Horse smiled weakly. He wiped the hot puke from his lips and said, "ah la veca, I'm going to try that again next Friday—"

We managed to get through the final week of catechism lessons. The depression that comes with fasting and strict penance deepened as Lent drew to its completion. On Good Friday there was no school. I went to church with my mother and Ultima. All of the saints' statues in the church were covered with purple sheaths. The church was packed with women in black, each one stoically suffering the three hours of the Crucifixion with the tortured Christ. Outside the wind blew and cut off the light of the sun with its dust, and the pigeons cried mournfully in the tower. Inside the prayers were like muffled cries against a storm which seemed to engulf the world. There seemed to be no one to turn to for solace. And when the dying Christ cried, "My God, my God, why hast Thou forsaken me?" the piercing words seemed to drive through to my heart and make me feel alone and lost in a dying universe.

Good Friday was forlorn, heavy and dreary with the death of God's son and the accompanying sense of utter hopelessness.

But on Saturday morning our spirits lifted. We had been through the agony and now the ecstasy of Easter was just ahead. Then too we had our first confession to look forward to in the afternoon. In the morning my mother took me to town and bought me a white shirt and dark pants and jacket. It was the first suit I ever owned, and I smiled when I saw myself in the store mirror. I even got new shoes. Everything was new, as it should be for the first communion.

My mother was excited. When we returned from town she would not allow me to go anywhere or do anything. Every five minutes she glanced at the clock. She did not want me to be late for confession.

"It's time!" she finally called, and with a kiss she sent me scampering down the goat path, to the bridge where I raced the Vitamin Kid and lost, then waited to walk to church with Samuel.

"You ready?" I asked. He only smiled. At the church all the kids were gathered around the steps, waiting for the priest to call us.

"Did you pass?" everyone asked. "What did the priest ask you?" He had given each one of us a quiz, asking us to answer questions on the catechism lessons or to recite prayers.

"He asked me how many persons in one God?" Bones howled.

"Wha'daya say?"

"Four! Four! Four!" Bones cried. Then he shook his head vigorously. "Or five! I don't know."

"And you passed?" Lloyd said contemptuously.

"I got my suit, don't I?" Bones growled. He would fight anyone who said he didn't pass.

"Okay, okay, you passed," Lloyd said to avoid a fight.

"Whad' did he ask you, Tony?"

"I had to recite the Apostles' Creed and tell what each part meant, and I had to explain where we get original sin—"

"¡Oh sí!" "¡Ah la veca!" "¡Chingada!"

"Bullshit!" Horse spit out the grass he had been chewing.

"Tony could do it," Florence defended me, "if he wanted to."

"Yeah, Tony knows more about religion and stuff like that than any-one—"

"Tony's gonna be a priest!"

"Hey, let's practice going to confession and make Tony the priest!" Ernie shouted.

"Yeahhhhh!" Horse reared up. Bones snarled and grabbed my pant leg in his teeth.

"Tony be the priest! Tony be the priest!" they began to chant.

"No, no," I begged, but they surrounded me. Ernie took off his sweater and draped it around me. "His priest's dress!" he shouted, and the others followed. They took off their jackets and sweaters and tied them around my waist and neck. I looked in vain for help but there was none.

"Tony is the priest, Tony is the priest, yah-yah-yah-ya-ya!" they sang and danced around me. I grew dizzy. The weight of the jackets on me was heavy and suffocating.

"All right!" I cried to appease them, "I shall be your priest!" I looked at Samuel. He had turned away.

"Yea-aaaaaaaye!" A great shout went up. Even the girls drew closer to watch.

"Hail to our priest!" Lloyd said judiciously.

"Do it right!" Agnes shouted.

"Yeah! Me first! Do it like for reals!" Horse shouted and threw himself at my feet.

"Everybody quiet!" Ernie held up his hands. They all drew around the kneeling Horse and myself, and the wall provided the enclosure but not the privacy of the confessional.

"Bless me, father—" Horse said, but as he concentrated to make the sign of the cross he forgot his lines. "Bless me, father—" he repeated desperately.

"You have sinned," I said. It was very quiet in the enclosure.

"Yes," he said. I remembered hearing the confession of the dying Narciso.

"It's not right to hear another person's confession," I said, glancing at the expectant faces around me.

"Go on!" Ernie hissed and hit me on the back. Blows fell on my head and shoulders. "Go on!" they cried. They really wanted to hear Horse's confession.

"It's only a game!" Rita whispered.

"How long has it been since your last confession?" I asked Horse.

"Always," he blurted out, "since I was born!"

"What are your sins?" I asked. I felt hot and uncomfortable under the weight of the jackets.

"Tell him only your worst one," Rita coaxed the Horse. "Yeah!" all the rest agreed.

The Horse was very quiet, thinking. He had grabbed one of my hands and he clutched it tightly, as if some holy power was going to pass through it and absolve him of his sins. His eyes rolled wildly, then he smiled and opened his mouth. His breath fouled the air.

"I know! I know!" he said excitedly, "one day when Miss Violet let me go to the bathroom I made a hole in the wall! With a nail! Then I could see into the girls' bathroom! I waited a long time! Then one of the girls came and sat down, and I could see everything! Her ass! Everything! I could even hear the pee!" he cried out.

"Horse, you're dirty!" June exclaimed. Then the girls looked shyly at each other and giggled.

"You have sinned," I said to Horse. Horse freed my hand and began rubbing at the front of his pants.

"There's more!" he cried, "I saw a teacher!"

"No!"

"Yes! Yes!" He rubbed harder.

"Who?" one of the girls asked.

"Mrs. Harrington!" Everyone laughed. Mrs. Harrington weighed about two hundred pounds. "It was bigggggggg—!" he exploded and fell trembling on the ground.

"Give him a penance!" the girls chanted and pointed accusing fingers at the pale Horse. "You are dirty, Horse," they cried, and he whimpered and accepted their accusations.

"For your penance say a rosary to the Virgin," I said weakly. I didn't feel good. The weight of the jackets was making me sweat, and the revelation of Horse's confession and the way the kids were acting was making me sick. I wondered how the priest could shoulder the burden of all the sins he heard.

. . . the weight of the sins will sink the town into the lake of the golden carp . . .

I looked for Samuel. He was not joining in the game. Florence was calmly accepting the sacrilegious game we were playing, but then it didn't matter to him, he didn't believe.

"Me next! Me next!" Bones shouted. He let go of my leg and knelt in front of me. "I got a better sin than Horse! Bless me, father! Bless me, father! Bless me, father!" he repeated. He kept making the sign of the cross over and over. "I got a sin! I got to confess! I saw a high school boy and a girl fucking in the grass by the Blue Lake!" He smiled proudly and looked around.

"Ah, I see them every night under the railroad bridge," the Vitamin Kid scoffed.

"What do you mean?" I asked Bones.

"Naked! Jumping up and down!" he exclaimed.

"You lie, Bones!" Horse shouted. He didn't want his own sin bettered.

"No I don't!" Bones argued. "I don't lie, father, I don't lie!" he pleaded.

"Who was it?" Rita asked.

"It was Larry Saiz, and that dumb gabacha whose father owns the Tex-aco station—please father, it's my sin! I saw it! I confess!" He squeezed my hand very hard.

"Okay, Bones, okay," I nodded my head, "it's your sin."

"Give me a penance!" he growled.

"A rosary to the Virgin," I said to be rid of him.

"Like Horse?" he shouted.

"Yes."

"But my sin was bigger!" he snarled and leaped for my throat. "Whagggggghhh—" he threw me down and would have strangled me if the others hadn't pulled him away.

"Another rosary for daring to touch the priest!" I shouted in self-defense and pointed an accusing finger at him. That made him happy and he settled down.

"Florence next!" Abel cried.

"Nah, Florence ain't goin' make it anyway," Lloyd argued.

"That's enough practice," I said and started to take off the cumbersome costume, but they wouldn't let me.

"Abel's right," Ernie said emphatically, "Florence needs the practice! He didn't make it because he didn't practice!"

"He didn't make it because he doesn't believe!" Agnes taunted.

"Why doesn't he believe?" June asked.

"Let's find out!" "Make him tell!" "¡Chingada!"

They grabbed tall Florence before he could bolt away and made him kneel in front of me.

"No!" I protested.

"Confess him!" they chanted. They held him with his arms pinned behind his back. I looked down at him and tried to let him know we might as well go along with the game. It would be easier that way.

"What are your sins?" I asked.

"I don't have any," Florence said softly.

"You do, you bastard!" Ernie shouted and pulled Florence's head back.

"You have sins," Abel agreed.

"Everybody has sins!" Agnes shouted. She helped Ernie twist Florence's head back. Florence tried to struggle but he was pinned by Horse and Bones and Abel. I tried to pull their hands away from him to relieve the pain I saw in his face, but the trappings of the priest's costume entangled me and so I could do very little.

"Tell me one sin," I pleaded with Florence. His face was very close to mine now, and when he shook his head to tell me again that he didn't have sins I saw a frightening truth in his eyes. He was telling the truth! He did not believe that he had ever sinned against God! "Oh my God!" I heard myself gasp.

"Confess your sins or you'll go to hell!" Rita cried out. She grabbed his blonde hair and helped Ernie and Agnes twist his head.

"Confess! Confess!" they cried. Then with one powerful heave and a groan Florence shook off his tormentors. He was long and sinewy, but because of his mild manner we had always underestimated his strength. Now the girls and Ernie and even Horse fell off him like flies.

"I have not sinned!" he shouted, looking me square in the eyes, challenging me, the priest. His voice was like Ultima's when she had challenged Tenorio, or Narciso's when he had tried to save Lupito.

"It is God who has sinned against me!" his voice thundered, and we fell back in horror at the blasphemy he uttered.

"Florence," I heard June whimper, "don't say that—"

Florence grinned. "Why? Because it is the truth?" he questioned. "Because you refuse to see the truth, or to accept me because I do not believe in your lies! I say God has sinned against me because he took my father and mother from me when I most needed them, and he made my sisters whores—He has punished all of us without just cause, Tony," his look pierced me, "He took Narciso! And why? What harm did Narciso ever do—"

"We shouldn't listen to him," Agnes had the courage to interrupt Florence, "we'll have to confess what we heard and the priest will be mad."

"The priest was right in not passing Florence, because he doesn't believe!" Rita added.

"He shouldn't even be here if he is not going to believe in the laws we learn," Lloyd said.

"Give him a penance! Make him ask for forgiveness for those terrible things he said about God!" Agnes insisted. They were gathering behind me now, I could feel their presence and their hot, bitter breath. They wanted me to be their leader; they wanted me to punish Florence.

"Make his penance hard," Rita leered.

"Make him kneel and we'll all beat him," Ernie suggested.

"Yeah, beat him!" Bones said wildly.

"Stone him!"

"Beat him!"

"Kill him!"

They circled around me and advanced on Florence, their eyes flashing with the thought of the punishment they would impose on the non-believer. It was then that the fear left me, and I knew what I had to do. I spun around and held out my hands to stop them.

"No!" I shouted, "there will be no punishment, there will be no penance! His sins are forgiven!" I turned and made the sign of the cross. "Go in peace, my son," I said to Florence.

"No!" they shouted, "don't let him go free!"

"Make him do penance! That's the law!"

"Punish him for not believing in God!"

"I am the priest!" I shouted back, "and I have absolved him of his sins!" I was facing the angry kids and I could see that their hunger for vengeance was directed at me, but I didn't care, I felt relieved. I had stood my ground for what I felt to be right and I was not afraid. I thought that perhaps it was this kind of strength that allowed Florence to say he did not believe in God.

"You are a bad priest, Tony!" Agnes lashed out at me.

"We do not want you for our priest!" Rita followed.

"Punish the priest!" they shouted and they engulfed me like a wave. They were upon me, clawing, kicking, tearing off the jackets, defrocking me. I fought back but it was useless. They were too many. They spread me out and held me pinned down to the hard ground. They had torn my shirt off so the sharp pebbles and stickers cut into my back.

"Give him the Indian torture!" someone shouted.

"Yeah, the Indian torture!" they chanted.

They held my arms while Horse jumped on my stomach and methodically began to pound with his fist on my chest. He used his sharp knuckles and aimed each blow directly at my breastbone. I kicked and wiggled and struggled to get free from the incessant beating, but they held me tight and I could not throw them off.

"No! No!" I shouted, but the raining blows continued. The blows of the knuckles coming down again and again on my breastbone were unbearable, but Horse knew no pity, and there was no pity on the faces of the others.

"God!" I cried, "God!" But the jarring blows continued to fall. I jerked my head from side to side and tried to kick or bite, but I could not get loose. Finally I bit my lips so I wouldn't cry, but my eyes filled with tears anyway. They were laughing and pointing down at the red welt that raised on my chest where the Horse was pounding.

"Serves him right," I heard, "he let the sinner go—"

Then, after what seemed an eternity of torture, they let me go. The priest was calling from the church steps, so they ran off to confession. I slowly picked myself up and rubbed the bruises on my chest. Florence handed me my shirt and jacket.

"You should have given me a penance," he said.

"You don't have to do any penance," I answered. I wiped my eyes and shook my head. Everything in me seemed loose and disconnected.

"Are you going to confession?" he asked.

"Yes," I answered and finished buttoning my shirt.

"You could never be their priest," he said.

I looked at the open door of the church. There was a calm in the wind and the bright sunlight made everything stark and harsh. The last of the kids went into the church and the doors closed.

"No," I nodded. "Are you going to confession?" I asked him.

"No," he muttered. "Like I said, I only wanted to be with you guys—I cannot eat God," he added.

"I have to," I whispered. I ran up the steps and entered the dark, musky church. I genuflected at the font of holy water, wet my fingertips, and made the sign of the cross. The lines were already formed on either side of the confessional, and the kids were behaving and quiet. Each one stood with bowed head, preparing himself to confess all of his sins to Father Byrnes. I walked quietly around the back pew and went to the end of one line. I made the sign of the cross again and began to say my prayers. As each kid finished his confession the line shuffled forward. I closed my eyes and tried not to be distracted by anything around me. I thought hard of all the sins I had ever committed, and I said as many prayers as I could remember. I begged God forgiveness for my sins over and over. After a long wait, Agnes, who had been in front of me came out of the confessional. She held the curtain as I stepped in, then she let it drop and all was dark. I knelt on the rough board and leaned against the small window. I prayed. I could hear whisperings from the confessional on the other side. My eyes grew accustomed to the gloom and I saw a small crucifix nailed to the side of the window. I kissed the feet of the hanging Jesus. The confessional smelled of old wood. I thought of the million sins that had been revealed in this small, dark space.

Then abruptly my thoughts were scattered. The small wooden door of the window slid open in front of me, and in the dark I could make out the head of Father Byrnes. His eyes were closed, his head bowed forward. He mumbled something in Latin then put his hand on his forehead and waited.

I made the sign of the cross and said, "Forgive me, Father, for I have sinned," and I made my first confession to him.

1972

PEDRO PIETRI
1944–2004

Born in Ponce, Puerto Rico, Pedro Pietri lived most of his life in New York City. He wrote poetry and plays, some of which have been presented in off-Broadway theaters. *Illusions of a Revolving Door*, a collection of his plays in English, was published in Puerto Rico in 1992, the first time a Nuyorican writer published his work in English on the island.

His texts illustrate the literature of protest and denunciation that characterizes the work of Nuyorican writers, who address their literature to Puerto Rican readers in order to raise consciousness of social and political oppression within American society. Nuyorican poets began to read at the Nuyorican Poets Cafe, at 505 East Sixth Street in New York City, where they met with other writers, artists, and community people. Their "poetic" language is antilyrical and harsh; it is the street language of blacks and Puerto Ricans in El Barrio. Such a stylistic choice implies a resistance to Americanization and an expression of dignity and pride in the *puertorriqueño's* heritage.

In *Puerto Rican Obituary*, a key text for Nuyorican poets, Pietri creates a mock epic of the Puerto Rican community in the United States. Through humor, sarcasm, and an irreverent irony, the poet presents the American Dream—which motivated many Puerto Ricans to emigrate to this country—not as a dream but as a nightmare and, ultimately, as death. The *puertorriqueños* find themselves shut out of America's economic opportunities and lifestyle and realize that they are unemployed, living on welfare, bitter, degraded. Pietri's image of a collective death is symbolic, denouncing the death of the Puerto Ricans' dignity as a people and individually. Yet Pietri is not altogether pessimistic, for the poem proposes a utopian symbolic space of Puerto Rican identity.

In *Traffic Violations*, Pietri moves away from the specificity of the social conditions of Puerto Ricans in New York and expresses a broader poetic vision of life as absurd. As his title indicates, his poetry reaffirms the need to break away from norms, the healthy rupturing of expectations, logic, and civilization. By inverting many American idiomatic expressions and clichés, he surprises and moves the reader. This book presents the poet as a self-willed outcast who drinks and uses drugs in order to avoid falling into any mechanization of the self. It is a surrealist work.

Representative of the literature of protest in Nuyorican culture, Pedro Pietri's work is a strong denunciation of the American system and of Western capitalism. To struggle against these forces, Pietri's poetry invites *puertorriqueños* to acquire a sense of dignity and pride in their heritage and to avoid complete cultural assimilation.

Frances R. Aparicio
University of Illinois at Chicago

PRIMARY WORKS

Puerto Rican Obituary, 1973; *Lost in the Museum of Natural History/Perdido en el Museo de Historia Natural*, 1981; *Traffic Violations*, 1983; *The Masses Are Asses*, 1984; *Illusions of a Revolving Door: Plays, Teatro*, 1992.

Puerto Rican Obituary

They worked
They were always on time
They were never late
They never spoke back
when they were insulted   5
They worked
They never took days off
that were not on the calendar
They never went on strike
without permission   10

They worked
ten days a week
and were only paid for five
They worked
They worked   15
They worked
and they died
They died broke
They died owing
They died never knowing   20
what the front entrance
of the first national city bank looks like
Juan
Miguel
Milagros   25
Olga
Manuel
All died yesterday today
and will die again tomorrow
passing their bill collectors   30
on to the next of kin
All died
waiting for the garden of eden
to open up again
under a new management   35
All died
dreaming about america
waking them up in the middle of the night
screaming: *Mira Mira*[1]
your name is on the winning lottery ticket   40
for one hundred thousand dollars
All died
hating the grocery stores
that sold them makebelieve steak
and bulletproof rice and beans   45
All died waiting dreaming and hating

Dead Puerto Ricans
Who never knew they were Puerto Ricans
Who never took a coffee break
from the ten commandments   50
to KILL KILL KILL
the landlords of their cracked skulls
and communicate with their latino souls

[1]Spanish: Look, Look.

Juan
Miguel
Milagros
Olga
Manuel   55
From the nervous breakdown streets
where the mice live like millionaires
and the people do not live at all   60
are dead and were never alive

Juan
died waiting for his number to hit
Miguel   65
died waiting for the welfare check
to come and go and come again
Milagros
died waiting for her ten children
to grow up and work   70
so she could quit working
Olga
died waiting for a five dollar raise
Manuel
died waiting for his supervisor to drop dead   75
so he could get a promotion

It's a long ride
from Spanish Harlem
to long island cemetery
where they were buried   80
First the train
and then the bus
and the cold cuts for lunch
and the flowers
that will be stolen   85
when visiting hours are over
It's very expensive
It's very expensive
But they understand
Their parents understood   90
It's a long nonprofit ride
from Spanish Harlem
to long island cemetery

Juan
Miguel   95
Milagros

Olga
Manuel
All died yesterday today
and will die again tomorrow   100
Dreaming
Dreaming about queens
Cleancut lilywhite neighborhood
Puerto Ricanless scene
Thirty thousand dollar home   105
The first spics on the block
Proud to belong to a community
of gringos who want them lynched
Proud to be a long distance away
from the sacred phrase: *Qué Pasa*[2]   110
These dreams
These empty dreams
from the makebelieve bedrooms
their parents left them
are the aftereffects   115
of television programs
about the ideal
white american family
with black maids
and latino janitors   120
who are well trained
to make everyone
and their bill collectors
laugh at them
and the people they represent   125

Juan
died dreaming about a new car
Miguel
died dreaming about new antipoverty programs

Milagros   130
died dreaming about a trip to Puerto Rico
Olga
died dreaming about real jewelry
Manuel
died dreaming about the irish sweepstakes   135

They all died
like a hero sandwich dies

[2]Spanish: What's happening?

in the garment district
at twelve o'clock in the afternoon
social security number to ashes   140
union dues to dust

They knew
they were born to weep
and keep the morticians employed
as long as they pledge allegiance   145
to the flag that wants them destroyed
They saw their names listed
in the telephone directory of destruction
They were trained to turn
the other cheek by newspapers   150
that mispelled mispronounced
and misunderstood their names
and celebrated when death came
and stole their final laundry ticket
They were born dead   155
and they died dead

It's time
to visit sister lópez again
the number one healer
and fortune card dealer   160
in Spanish Harlem
She can communicate
with your late relatives
for a reasonable fee

Good news is guaranteed   165

Rise Table Rise Table
death is not dumb and disabled
Those who love you want to know
the correct number to play
Let them know this right away   170
Rise Table Rise Table
death is not dumb and disabled
Now that your problems are over
and the world is off your shoulders
help those who you left behind   175
find financial peace of mind
Rise Table Rise Table
death is not dumb and disabled
If the right number we hit

all our problems will split 180
and we will visit your grave
on every legal holiday
Those who love you want to know
the correct number to play
Let them know this right away 185
We know your spirit is able
Death is not dumb and disabled
RISE TABLE RISE TABLE

Juan
Miguel 190
Milagros
Olga
Manuel
All died yesterday today
and will die again tomorrow 195
Hating fighting and stealing
broken windows from each other
Practicing a religion without a roof
The old testament
The new testament 200
according to the gospel
of the internal revenue
the judge and jury and executioner
protector and eternal bill collector

Secondhand shit for sale 205
Learn how to say *Cómo Está Usted*[3]
and you will make a fortune
They are dead
They are dead
and will not return from the dead 210
until they stop neglecting
the art of their dialogue
for broken english lessons
to impress the mister goldsteins
who keep them employed 215
as *lavaplatos*[4] porters messenger boys
factory workers maids stock clerks
shipping clerks assistant mailroom
assistant, assistant assistant
to the assistant's assistant 220
assistant lavaplatos and automatic

[3]Spanish: How are you?   [4]Spanish: Dishwashers.

artificial smiling doormen
for the lowest wages of the ages
and rages when you demand a raise
because it's against the company policy   225
to promote SPICS SPICS SPICS

Juan
died hating Miguel because Miguel's
used car was in better running condition
than his used car   230
Miguel
died hating Milagros because Milagros
had a color television set
and he could not afford one yet
Milagros   235
died hating Olga because Olga
made five dollars more on the same job
Olga
died hating Manuel because Manuel
had hit the numbers more times   240
than she had hit the numbers
Manuel
died hating all of them
Juan
Manuel   245
Milagros
and Olga
because they all spoke broken english
more fluently than he did

And now they are together   250
in the main lobby of the void
Addicted to silence
Off limits to the wind
Confined to worm supremacy
in long island cemetery   255
This is the groovy hereafter
the protestant collection box
was talking so loud and proud about

Here lies Juan
Here lies Miguel
Here lies Milagros   260
Here lies Olga
Here lies Manuel
who died yesterday today

and will die again tomorrow 265
Always broke
Always owing
Never knowing
that they are beautiful people
Never knowing 270
the geography of their complexion

PUERTO RICO IS A BEAUTIFUL PLACE
PUERTORRIQUEÑOS ARE A BEAUTIFUL RACE

If only they
had turned off the television 275
and tuned into their own imaginations
If only they
had used the white supremacy bibles
for toilet paper purpose
and made their latino souls 280
the only religion of their race
If only they
had returned to the definition of the sun
after the first mental snowstorm
on the summer of their senses 285
If only they
had kept their eyes open
at the funeral of their fellow employees
who came to this country to make a fortune
and were buried without underwear 290

Juan
Miguel
Milagros
Olga
Manuel 295
will right now be doing their own thing
where beautiful people sing
and dance and work together
where the wind is a stranger
to miserable weather conditions 300
where you do not need a dictionary
to communicate with your people
Aquí[5] *Se habla Español*[6] all the time
Aquí you salute your flag first
Aquí there are no dial soap commercials 305

[5]Spanish: Here.   [6]Spanish: We speak Spanish.

Aquí everybody smells good
Aquí tv dinners do not have a future
Aquí the men and women admire desire
and never get tired of each other
Aquí Qué Pasa Power is what's happening   310
Aquí to be called *negrito*[7]
means to be called LOVE

1973

Traffic Violations

you go into chicken delight
and order dinosaurs
because you are hungry
and want something different
now that you no longer   5
eat meat or fish or vegetables
you are told politely
is against company policies
to be that different
so you remove a button off   10
your absentminded overcoat
the scenery changes
you are waiting in line
to take a mean leak
at one of those public toilets   15
in the times square area
the line is 3 weeks long
many waited with their lunch
inside brown paper bags
singing the battle hymn   20
of the republic to keep warm

you remove another button off
your absentminded overcoat
all you can see now are
high heels and low quarter shoes   25
coming at your eyeballs
disappearing when they come
close enough to make contact

you try to get up off the floor
but you forgot how to move   30

[7]Spanish: Black (diminutive form).

umbrellas open up inside your head
you start screaming backwards
your legs behave like flat tires
your mind melts in slow motion

you remove another button off   35
your absentminded overcoat
is late in the evening
according to everybody
who keeps track of time
you are about to jump off the roof   40
emergency sirens are heard

A crowd of skilled & unskilled
Laborers on their mental lunch break
congregate on the street below
the roof you are about to jump from   45
they are laughing hysterically
nobody tries to talk you out of it
everybody wants you to jump
so they can get some sleep tonight—
should you change your mind about jumping   50
All the spectators will get uptight

red white and blue representatives
from the suicide prevention bureau
order you to jump immediately
you refuse to obey their orders   55
they sendout a helicopter to push you
off the roof into the morning headlines
the laughter from the crowd
on the street breaks the sound barrier

you try removing another button off   60
your absentminded overcoat
but that button is reported missing
the helicopter pushes you off the roof
everybody is feeling much better
you are losing your memory real fast   65
the clouds put on black arm bands
it starts raining needles and thread

a few seconds before having breakfast
at a cafeteria in the hereafter
you remove your absentminded overcoat   70

you are on the front and back seat
of a bi-lingo spaceship
smoking grass with your friends
from the past present and future
nothing unusual is happening   75
you are all speeding
without moving an inch
making sure nobody does the driving

1983

ADRIENNE RICH
1929–2012

The daughter of Helen Jones and Arnold Rich, a professor of pathology at Johns Hopkins University, Adrienne Rich grew up in Baltimore. Her father, an exacting tutor, required that his daughter master complex poetic meters and rhyme schemes. Her mother, who had been a concert pianist before marriage, conveyed to her child a love of the lyrical as well as the rhythmic.

Educated at Radcliffe College, Rich graduated Phi Beta Kappa and shortly after won distinction when her first book of poems, *A Change of World*, won the Yale Younger Poets award and was published with a laudatory preface by W. H. Auden. After traveling and writing in Europe on a Guggenheim fellowship, Rich married Alfred Conrad, an economics professor at Harvard. As a wife and the mother of three sons during the 1950s, Rich was expected to conform to a life of domestic femininity, which meant that she had little time for serious writing. Her *Snapshots of a Daughter-in-Law* conveys the anger and confusion she felt during those years of confinement. In her 1963 book of verse, Rich smashes the icons of domesticity: the coffee pot and raked gardens.

The conflict and distress experienced by creative, intellectual women in a culture that too often devalues female experience is a recurring theme in Rich's poetry. In the fifty years of her career, her poems and her essays chronicle the evolution of feminist consciousness and illuminate the phases of her personal growth from self-analysis and individual accomplishment to lesbian/feminist activism and the collective shaping of a feminist vision of community that is perhaps strangely rooted in the Puritan ideal of the city on a hill. The personal and political converge in her belief that politics is "not something 'out there' but something 'in here' and of the essence of [her] condition."

Adrienne Rich is a poet whose work has influenced the lives of many of her readers. She acknowledged that it is a profound responsibility and privilege to be a poet whose work is read by so many. As a radical feminist, Rich wrote poetry that is politically charged, refusing to accept the criticism that art and activism are antithetical. Her poems combine lyricism and tightly constructed lines characterized by the use of elegant assonance, consonance, slant rhyme, and onomatopoeia with quotations and slogans from antiwar and feminist statements.

Influenced by the open styles of Pound, Williams, and Levertov and the confessional mode of Lowell, Plath, Sexton, and Berryman, Rich created a poetic voice that is distinctive and powerful. Her unusual combination of artistic excellence and committed activism has been internationally praised; she has won numerous awards, including the 1974 National Book Award, the 1986 Ruth Lilly Poetry Prize, the 1997 Tanning Prize, and the 1999 Lannan Foundation's Lifetime Achievement Award, as well as two Guggenheim Fellowships and a MacArthur Fellowship. As a poet who committed herself to writing poetry that will change lives, Rich observed in her collected essays, *Lies, Secrets, and Silences*, "Poetry is, among other things, a criticism of language. Poetry is above all a concentration of the power of language, which is the power of our ultimate relationship to everything in the universe."

Wendy Martin
Claremont Graduate University

PRIMARY WORKS

A Change of World, 1951; *Snapshots of a Daughter-in-Law*, 1963; *Necessities of Life*, 1966; *Leaflets*, 1969; *The Will to Change*, 1971; *Diving into the Wreck: Poems 1971–1972*, 1973; *Poems Selected and New*, 1975; *Of Woman Born: Motherhood as Experience and Institution*, 1976, 1986; *The Dream of a Common Language: Poems 1974–1977*, 1978; *On Lies, Secrets, and Silence: Selected Prose 1966–1978*, 1979; *A Wild Patience Has Taken Me This Far: Poems 1978–1981*, 1981; *Sources*, 1983; *The Fact of a Doorframe: Poems Selected and New 1950–1984*, 1984; *Your Native Land, Your Life*, 1986; *Blood, Bread, and Poetry: Selected Prose 1979–1985*, 1986; *Time's Power: Poems 1985–1988*, 1989; *Women and Honor: Some Notes on Lying*, 1990; *An Atlas of the Difficult World: Poems 1988–1991*, 1991; *What Is Found There?: Notebooks on Poetry and Politics*, 1993; *Collected Early Poems, 1950–1970*, 1995; *Dark Fields of the Republic: Poems, 1991–1995*, 1995; *Selected Poems*, 1996; *Midnight Salvage: Poems, 1995–1998*, 1999; *Arts of the Possible: Essays and Conversation*, 2001; *Fox: Poems 1998–2000*, 2001; *Selected Poems*, 2004; *Telephone Ringing in the Labyrinth*, 2007; *A Human Eye: Essays on Art in Society, 1997–2008*, 2009; *Tonight No Poetry Will Serve: Poems 2007–2010*, 2010.

Diving into the Wreck

First having read the book of myths,
and loaded the camera,
and checked the edge of the knife-blade,
I put on
the body-armor of black rubber   5
the absurd flippers
the grave and awkward mask.
I am having to do this

not like Cousteau[1] with his
assiduous team   10
aboard the sun-flooded schooner
but here alone.

There is a ladder.
The ladder is always there
hanging innocently   15
close to the side of the schooner.
We know what it is for,
we who have used it.
Otherwise
it's a piece of maritime floss   20
some sundry equipment.

I go down.
Rung after rung and still
the oxygen immerses me
the blue light   25
the clear atoms
of our human air.
I go down.
My flippers cripple me,
I crawl like an insect down the ladder   30
and there is no one
to tell me when the ocean
will begin.

First the air is blue and then
it is bluer and then green and then   35
black I am blacking out and yet
my mask is powerful
it pumps my blood with power
the sea is another story
the sea is not a question of power   40
I have to learn alone
to turn my body without force
in the deep element.

And now: it is easy to forget
what I came for   45
among so many who have always
lived here
swaying their crenellated fans

---

[1]Jacques Cousteau (1910–1997), French under-
water explorer and environmentalist.

between the reefs
and besides   50
you breathe differently down here.

I came to explore the wreck.
The words are purposes.
The words are maps.
I came to see the damage that was done   55
and the treasures that prevail.
I stroke the beam of my lamp
slowly along the flank
of something more permanent
than fish or weed   60

the thing I came for:
the wreck and not the story of the wreck
the thing itself and not the myth
the drowned face always staring
toward the sun   65
the evidence of damage
worn by salt and sway into this threadbare beauty
the ribs of the disaster
curving their assertion
among the tentative haunters.   70

This is the place.
And I am here, the mermaid whose dark hair
streams black, the merman in his armored body
We circle silently
about the wreck   75
we dive into the hold.
I am she: I am he

whose drowned face sleeps with open eyes
whose breasts still bear the stress
whose silver, copper, vermeil cargo lies   80
obscurely inside barrels
half-wedged and left to rot
we are the half-destroyed instruments
that once held to a course
the water-eaten log   85
the fouled compass

We are, I am, you are
by cowardice or courage
the one who find our way
back to this scene   90

carrying a knife, a camera
a book of myths
in which
our names do not appear.

1972

From a Survivor

The pact that we made was the ordinary pact
of men & women in those days

I don't know who we thought we were
that our personalities
could resist the failures of the race   5

Lucky or unlucky, we didn't know
the race had failures of that order
and that we were going to share them

Like everybody else, we thought of ourselves as special

Your body is as vivid to me   10
as it ever was: even more

since my feeling for it is clearer:
I know what it could and could not do

it is no longer
the body of a god   15
or anything with power over my life

Next year it would have been 20 years
and you are wastefully dead[1]
who might have made the leap
we talked, too late, of making   20

which I live now
not as a leap
but a succession of brief, amazing movements

each one making possible the next

1972

[1]Adrienne Rich's husband, Alfred Conrad, committed suicide in 1970.

Power

Living   in the earth-deposits   of our history

Today a backhoe divulged   out of a crumbling flank of earth
one bottle   amber   perfect   a hundred-year-old
cure for fever   or melancholy   a tonic
for living on this earth   in the winters of this climate   5

Today I was reading about Marie Curie:[1]
she must have known she suffered   from radiation sickness
her body bombarded for years   by the element
she had purified
It seems she denied to the end   10
the source of the cataracts on her eyes
the cracked and suppurating skin   of her finger-ends
till she could no longer hold   a test-tube or a pencil

She died   a famous woman   denying
her wounds   15
denying
her wounds   came   from the same source as her power

                                                                                    1974

Not Somewhere Else, but Here

Courage   Her face in the leaves   the polygons
of the paving   Her   out of touch
Courage to breathe   The death of October
Spilt wine   The unbuilt house   The unmade life
Graffiti   without memory   grown conventional   5
scrawling the least wall   *god loves you   voice of the ghetto*
Death of the city   Her face
sleeping   Her quick stride   Her
running   Search for a private space   The city
caving in from within   The lessons badly   10
learned   Or not at all   The unbuilt world
This one love flowing   Touching other
lives   Spilt love   The least wall caving

To have enough courage   The life that must be lived
in terrible October   15

[1]Marie Curie (1867–1934) won a Nobel Prize
for her research on radioactive elements. She
died of leukemia.

Sudden immersion in yellows   streaked blood   The fast rain
Faces   Inscriptions   Trying to teach
unlearnable lessons   October   This one love
Repetitions   from other lives   The deaths
that must be lived   Denials   Blank walls   20
Our quick stride side by side   Her fugue
Bad air in the tunnels   *voice of the ghetto   god loves you*
My face   pale in the window   anger is pale
the blood shrinks to the heart
the head severed   it does not pay to feel   25

Her face   The fast rain tearing   Courage
to feel this   To tell of this   to be alive
Trying to learn   unteachable lessons

The fugue   Blood in my eyes   The careful sutures
ripped open   The hands that touch me   Shall it be said   30
I am not alone
Spilt love   seeking its level   flooding other
lives   that must be lived   not somewhere else
but here   seeing through blood   nothing is lost

                                                                       1974

Coast to Coast

There are days when housework seems the only
outlet   old funnel I've poured caldrons through
old servitude   In grief and fury bending
to the accustomed tasks   the vacuum cleaner plowing
realms of dust   the mirror scoured   grey webs   5
behind framed photographs   brushed away
the grey-seamed sky enormous in the west
snow gathering in corners   of the north

Seeing through the prism
you who gave it me   10
                You, bearing ceaselessly
yourself   the witness
Rainbow dissolves the Hudson   This chary, stinting
skin of late winter   ice   forming and breaking up
The unprotected seeing it through   15
with their ordinary valor

Rainbow composed of ordinary light
February-flat
grey-white of a cheap enamelled pan

breaking into veridian, azure, violet   20
You write: *Three and a half weeks lost from writing . . . .*
I think of the word *protection*
who it is we try to protect   and why

Seeing through the prism   Your face, fog-hollowed   burning
cold of eucalyptus hung with butterflies   25
lavender of rockbloom
O and your anger uttered in silence word and stammer
shattering the fog   lances of sun
piercing the grey Pacific   unanswerable tide
carving itself in clefts and fissures of the rock   30
Beauty of your breasts   your hands
turning a stone a shell a week a prism   in coastal light
traveller and witness
the passion of the speechless
driving your speech   35
protectless

If you can read and understand this poem
send something back: a burning strand of hair
a still-warm, still-liquid drop of blood
a shell   40
thickened from being battered year on year
send something back.

                                                                       1978

Frame

Winter twilight. She comes out of the lab-
oratory, last class of the day
a pile of notebooks slung in her knapsack, coat
zipped high against the already swirling
evening sleet. The wind is wicked and the   5
busses slower than usual. On her mind
is organic chemistry and the issue
of next month's rent and will it be possible to
bypass the professor with the coldest eyes
to get a reference for graduate school,   10
and whether any of them, even those who smile
can see, looking at her, a biochemist
or a marine biologist, which of the faces
can she trust to see her at all, either today
or in any future. The busses are worm-slow in the   15
quickly gathering dark. *I don't know her. I am*
standing though somewhere just outside the frame

of all this, trying to see. At her back
the newly finished building suddenly looks
like shelter, it has glass doors, lighted halls   20
presumably heat. The wind is wicked. She throws a
glance down the street, sees no bus coming and runs
up the newly constructed steps into the newly
constructed hallway. *I am standing all this time*
just beyond the frame, trying to see. She runs   25
her hand through the crystals of sleet about to melt
on her hair. She shifts the weight of the books
on her back. It isn't warm here exactly but it's
out of that wind. Through the glass
door panels she can watch for the bus through the thickening   30
weather. Watching so, she is not
watching for the white man who watches the building
who has been watching her. This is Boston 1979.
I am standing somewhere at the edge of the frame
watching the man, we are both white, who watches the building   35
telling her to move on, get out of the hallway.
I can hear nothing because I am not supposed to be
present but I can see her gesturing
out toward the street at the wind-raked curb
I see her drawing her small body up   40
against the implied charges. The man
goes away. Her body is different now.
It is holding together with more than a hint of fury
and more than a hint of fear. She is smaller, thinner
more fragile-looking than I am. *But I am not supposed to be*   45
there. I am just outside the frame
of this action when the anonymous white man
returns with a white police officer. Then she starts
to leave into the windraked night but already
the policeman is going to work, the handcuffs are on her   50
wrists he is throwing her down his knee has gone into
her breast he is dragging her down the stairs *I am unable*
to hear a sound of all this all that I know is what
I can see from this position there is no soundtrack
to go with this and I understand at once   55
it is meant to be in silence that this happens
in silence that he pushes her into the car
banging her head in silence that she cries out
in silence that she tries to explain she was only
waiting for a bus   60
in silence that he twists the flesh of her thigh
with his nails in silence that her tears begin to flow
that she pleads with the other policeman as if

he could be trusted to see her at all
in silence that in the precinct she refuses to give her name   65
in silence that they throw her into the cell
in silence that she stares him
straight in the face in silence that he sprays her
in her eyes with Mace in silence that she sinks her teeth
into his hand in silence that she is charged   70
with trespass assault and battery in
silence that at the sleet-swept corner her bus
passes without stopping and goes on
in silence. *What I am telling you*
is told by a white woman who they will say   75
was never there. I say I am there.

1980

ISHMAEL REED

B. 1938

Ishmael Reed is a poet, novelist, actor, journalist, dramatist, and editor; his works reflect his artistic, ethnic, political, religious, and social interests. He spotlights black issues, but his themes are universal. His satiric barbs intentionally provoke his audiences with irony and humor. Experimental forms, innovative style, and radical ideas place him in the forefront of contemporary writers. From black history to black humor, from Black Power to black magic, Reed integrates diverse themes and nontraditional styles.

Born on February 22, 1938, in Chattanooga, Tennessee, to Ben and Thelma (Coleman) Reed, he was raised in a blue-collar environment in Buffalo, New York, where the family moved when he was a child. From 1956 to 1960, he attended the University of New York at Buffalo. After moving to New York City, he founded the *East Village Other*, an independent newspaper, and published his first novel in 1967. This was followed by numerous books of poetry and fiction in addition to articles, plays, and songs, as well as very active editing after moving to Oakland, California, in 1968. Reed has won a National Endowment Fellowship and a Guggenheim Award, and he has been nominated twice for the National Book Award, once in poetry for *Conjure* and once in fiction for *Mumbo Jumbo*.

Although Reed is indebted to all the humorous, satiric, and bawdy writers from Ovid to Chaucer to Swift to Blake to Joyce, he emphasizes his debt to minority artists, especially black writers. He relies on African mythology, black sports heroes, and even rhythm and blues for his symbols and metaphors. Reed also weaves motifs of literary and contemporary allusions throughout his work: Amos and Andy, Egyptian gods, and famous figures past and present all appear in his mirror of society.

Controversial about race, sex, politics, freedom, religion, and everything else, Reed satirizes most institutions: "My main job I felt was to humble Judeo-Christian culture." In Reed's Neo-Hoo Doo Church, all poets are priests and historians. One of his favorite issues is that minority contributions to Western civilization seldom receive due credit. He stokes the fires of discord by distorting popular history. One function of the artist is to re-rewrite history to reveal the "truth," so Reed gleefully points out that cowboys were predominantly minorities; that Alexandre Dumas, the nineteenth-century French novelist who wrote *The Three Musketeers*, had African ancestry; and even that *Uncle Tom's Cabin* was stolen by Harriet Beecher Stowe from *The Life of Josiah Henson, Formerly a Slave*. But Reed is not a single-issue writer; he is a universal writer. His books are not solely about race issues, although these issues frequently serve as focal points. He attacks the black establishment as harshly as he does the white.

The comic tone and joyous outlook of Reed's parodies make us laugh at our foibles. Many of his works are comedies in the classical sense: Evil is punished and Good rewarded. Viewing life as a struggle between Dionysian and Apollonian forces, Reed chooses laughter, dance, music, and joy: "I see life as mysterious, holy, profound, exciting, serious, and fun." So is his writing.

Michael Boccia
University of Southern Maine

PRIMARY WORKS

The Free Lance Pallbearers, 1967; *The Rise and Fall of …? Adam Clayton Powell* (as Emmett Coleman), 1967; *Yellow Back Radio Broke-Down*, 1969; *19 Necromancers from Now*, 1970; *Catechism of D Neoamerican Hoo Doo Church*, 1970; *Mumbo Jumbo*, 1972; *Conjure*, 1972; *Chattanooga*, 1973; *The Last Days of Louisiana Red*, 1974; *A Secretary to the Spirits*, 1975; *Flight to Canada*, 1976; *Shrovetide in Old New Orleans*, 1978; *The Ace Booms*, 1980; *Mother Hubbard* (previously *Hell Hath No Fury*), 1982; *The Terrible Twos*, 1982; *God Made Alaska for the Indians*, 1982; *Savage Walls*, 1985. *Reckless Eyeballing*, 1986; *Points of View*, 1988; *Writin' Is Fightin'*, 1988; *New and Collected Poems*, 1989; *The Terrible Threes*, 1989; *The Freelance Pallbearers*, 1990; *Japanese by Spring*, 1993; *Airing Dirty Laundry*, 1993; *The Reed Reader*, 2000; *Another Day at the Front*, 2003; *New and Collected Poems 1964–2007*, 2007; *Mixing It Up*, 2008; *Juice!*, 2011.

Badman of the Guest Professor

For Joe Overstreet, David Henderson,
Albert Ayler & D Mysterious
'H' Who Cut Up D Rembrandts

i

    u worry me whoever u are
    i know u didnt want me to
    come here but here i am just
    d same; hi-jacking yr stagecoach,

hauling in yr pocket watches & mak   5
ing u hoof it all d way to
town. black bard, a robber w/ an
art: i left some curses in d cash
box so ull know its me

listen man, i cant help it if   10
yr thing is over, kaput,
   finis
no matter how u slice it dick
u are done. a dead duck all out
of quacks. d nagging hiccup dat   15
goes on & on w/out a simple glass
   of water for relief

ii

uve been teaching shakespeare for
20 years only to find d joke
   on u   20
d eavesdropping rascal who got it
in d shins because he didnt know
enough to keep his feet behind d cur
tains: a sad-sacked head served on a
platter in titus andronicus or falstaff   25
   too fat to make a go of it
   anymore

iii

its not my fault dat yr tradition
was knocked off wop style & left in
d alley w/ pricks in its mouth. i   30
read abt it in d papers but it was no
   skin off my nose
wasnt me who opened d gates & allowed
d rustlers to slip thru unnoticed. u
ought to do something abt yr security or   35
   mend yr fences partner
dont look at me if all dese niggers
are ripping it up like deadwood dick;
doing art d way its never been done. mak
ing wurlitzer sorry he made d piano dat   40
will drive mozart to d tennis
   courts
making smith-corona feel like d red

faced university dat has just delivered china
　　some 50 e-leben h bomb experts　　　　　　　　　　45

i didnt deliver d blow dat drove d
abstract expressionists to my ladies
linoleum where dey sleep beneath tons of
wax & dogshit & d muddy feet of children or
because some badassed blackpainter done sent　　　　50
french impressionism to d walls of highrise
　　lobbies where dey belong is not my fault
martha graham will never do d jerk
shes a sweet ol soul but her hips
cant roll; as stiff as d greek　　　　　　　　　　　　55
statues she loves so much

iv

dese are d reasons u did me nasty
j alfred prufrock, d trick u pull
d in d bookstore today; stand in d
corner no peaches for a week, u lemon　　　　　　　　60
u must blame me because yr wife is
ugly. 86-d by a thousand discriminating
saunas. dats why u did dat sneaky thing
i wont tell d townsfolk because u hv
to live here and im just passing thru　　　　　　　　65

v

u got one thing right tho. i did say
dat everytime i read william faulkner i
go to sleep.

fitzgerald wdnt hv known a gangster if one
had snatched zelda & made her a moll tho　　　　　　70
　　she wd hv been grateful i bet

bonnie of clyde wrote d saga of suicide
sal just as d feds were closing in. it is
worth more than d collected works of ts
elliot a trembling anglican whose address　　　　　　75
is now d hell dat thrilld him so
last word from down there he was open
ing a publishing co dat will bore d
devil back to paradise

vi

& by d way did u hear abt grammar?   80
cut to ribbons in a photo finish by
stevie wonder, a blindboy who dances
on a heel. he just came out of d slang
& broke it down before millions.
    it was bloody murder   85

vii

to make a long poem shorter—3 things
    moleheaded lame w/4 or 5 eyes

1) yr world is riding off into d sunset
2) d chips are down & nobody will chance yr i.o.u.s.
3) d last wish was a fluke so now u hv to re   90
turn to being a fish
p.s. d enchantment has worn off
dats why u didnt like my reading list—right?
it didnt include anyone on it dat u cd in
vite to a cocktail party & shoot a lot of   95
    bull—right?
so u want to take it out on my hide—right?
well i got news for u professor nothing—i
am my own brand while u must be d fantasy of
    a japanese cartoonist   100

a strangekind of dinosaurmouse
i can see it all now. d leaves
are running low. its d eve of
extinction & dere are no holes to
accept yr behind. u wander abt yr   105
long neck probing a tree. u think
its a tree but its really a trap. a
cry of victory goes up in d kitchen of
d world. a pest is dead. a prehis
toric pest at dat. a really funnytime   110
prehistoric pest whom we will lug into
a museum to show everyone how really funny
u are
    yr fate wd make a good
scenario but d plot is between u &   115
charles darwin.

as i said, im passing thru, just sing
ing my song. get along little doggie &
jazz like dat. word has it dat a big gold
shipment is coming to californy. i hv to   120
ride all night if im to meet my pardners
dey want me to help score d ambush

                                                  1969

Bitter Chocolate

I

Only the red-skins know what
I know, and they ain't talkin
So I keep good friends with
turkey whiskey
Or try to do some walkin   5
Don't want no lovin
Ain't anxious to play
And you want to know how
I got that way
Bitter Chocolate   10
Bitter Chocolate
Blood like ice water
Kisses taste like snuff
Why are all of my women
so jive and full of stuff   15

They call me a runaway father
But they won't give me no job
They say I'm a thief
when I'm the one gettin
robbed   20
Most of me was missing when
They brought me back from
Nam
My mama and my sister
cried for me   25
But my government didn't give
a damn
Bitter Chocolate
Bitter Chocolate
Sullied and sullen black   30
man

II

When they come to lynch somebody
Always breaking down my door
When they lay somebody off
I'm the first one off the floor   35
Bitter Chocolate
Bitter Chocolate
Veins full of brine
Skin sweatin turpentine
Cold and unfriendly   40
Got ways like a lizard

III

Well, it's winter in Chicago on
a February day
O'Hare airport is empty and
I call you on the line   45
It's 9:00 A.M. where you are
and the phone rings seven times
Hello, who is this? you say
in a sleeping heaving sigh
Your woman in the background yells   50
Who in the hell is that guy
Bitter Chocolate
Bitter Chocolate
I'm standing in the rain
All my love is all squeezed   55
out
All that I can give is pain
All that I can give is pain

1984

■   MAXINE HONG KINGSTON   ■

B. 1940

Born in Stockton, California, in 1940, Maxine Ting Ting Hong is the eldest of
six surviving children of Tom Hong (scholar, laundry man, and manager of
a gambling house) and Ying Lan Chew (midwife, laundress, field hand). She

earned a B.A. from the University of California at Berkeley in 1962 and a teaching certificate in 1965. She has lived and worked both in California and in Honolulu, Hawaii.

Author of three award-winning books, *The Woman Warrior* (1976), *China Men* (1980), and *Tripmaster Monkey* (1989), Maxine Hong Kingston is undoubtedly the most recognized Asian American writer today. Her work attracts attention in many arenas: Chinese Americans, feminist scholars, literary critics, and the media. Kingston won the *Mademoiselle Magazine* Award in 1977 and the Anisfield-Wolf Book Award in 1978. In 1980 she was proclaimed a Living Treasure of Hawaii. *The Woman Warrior* received the National Book Critics' Circle Award for the best nonfiction book of 1976, and *Time* magazine proclaimed it one of the top ten nonfiction works of the decade. It is, however, a collage of fiction and fact, memory and imagination—a hybrid genre of Kingston's own devising. Through the Chinese legends and family stories that marked her childhood and the mysterious old-world customs that her mother enforced but did not explain, through Kingston's own experiences and her imaginative and poetic flights, *The Woman Warrior* details the complexities and difficulties in Kingston's development as a woman and as a Chinese American. It focuses on a difficult and finally reconciled mother/daughter relationship.

Kingston's second book, *China Men*, focuses on men and is shaped by a rather uncommunicative father/daughter relationship. It depends heavily on family history, American laws, and imaginative projections based loosely on historical fact. Its purpose, Kingston has stated, is to "claim America" for Chinese Americans by showing how indebted America is to the labor of Chinese men, her great-grandfathers and grandfathers, who cleared jungle for the sugar plantations in Hawaii, who split rock and hammered steel to build railroads in the United States, who created fertile farmland out of swamp and desert, yet faced fierce discrimination and persecution. In this text, too, Kingston blends myth and fact, autobiography and fiction, blurring the usual dividing lines.

In *Tripmaster Monkey*, her first novel, Kingston again blends Chinese myth with American reality. She combines allusions to a Chinese classic, *Monkey* or *Journey to the West*—the story of a magical, mischievous monkey who accompanies a monk to India for the sacred books of Buddhism—with the life of a 1960s Berkeley beatnik playwright.

Amy Ling
University of Wisconsin at Madison
King-Kok Cheung
University of California, Los Angeles

PRIMARY WORKS

The Woman Warrior: Memoirs of a Girlhood among Ghosts, 1976; *China Men,* 1980; *Hawai'i One Summer,* 1987; *Tripmaster Monkey: His Fake Book,* 1989; *To Be the Poet,* 2002; *The Fifth Book of Peace,* 2003; *I Love a Broad Margin to My Life,* 2011.

No Name Woman

"You must not tell anyone," my mother said, "what I am about to tell you. In China your father had a sister who killed herself. She jumped into the family well. We say that your father has all brothers because it is as if she had never been born.

"In 1924 just a few days after our village celebrated seventeen hurry-up weddings—to make sure that every young man who went 'out on the road' would responsibly come home—your father and his brothers and your grandfather and his brothers and your aunt's new husband sailed for America, the Gold Mountain. It was your grandfather's last trip. Those lucky enough to get contracts waved good-bye from the decks. They fed and guarded the stowaways and helped them off in Cuba, New York, Bali, Hawaii. 'We'll meet in California next year,' they said. All of them sent money home.

"I remember looking at your aunt one day when she and I were dressing; I had not noticed before that she had such a protruding melon of a stomach. But I did not think, 'She's pregnant,' until she began to look like other pregnant women, her shirt pulling and the white tops of her black pants showing. She could not have been pregnant, you see, because her husband had been gone for years. No one said anything. We did not discuss it. In early summer she was ready to have the child, long after the time when it could have been possible.

"The village had also been counting. On the night the baby was to be born the villagers raided our house. Some were crying. Like a great saw, teeth strung with lights, files of people walked zigzag across our land, tearing the rice. Their lanterns doubled in the disturbed black water, which drained away through the broken bunds. As the villagers closed in, we could see that some of them, probably men and women we knew well, wore white masks. The people with long hair hung it over their faces. Women with short hair made it stand up on end. Some had tied white bands around their foreheads, arms, and legs.

"At first they threw mud and rocks at the house. Then they threw eggs and began slaughtering our stock. We could hear the animals scream their deaths—the roosters, the pigs, a last great roar from the ox. Familiar wild heads flared in our night windows; the villagers encircled us. Some of the faces stopped to peer at us, their eyes rushing like searchlights. The hands flattened against the panes, framed heads, and left red prints.

"The villagers broke in the front and the back doors at the same time, even though we had not locked the doors against them. Their knives dripped with the blood of our animals. They smeared the blood on the doors and walls. One woman swung a chicken, whose throat she had slit, splattering blood in red arcs about her. We stood together in the middle of our house, in the family hall with the pictures and tables of the ancestors around us, and looked straight ahead.

"At that time the house had only two wings. When the men came back, we would build two more to enclose our courtyard and a third one to begin a second courtyard. The villagers pushed through both wings, even your grandparents' rooms, to find your aunt's, which was also mine until the men returned. From this room a new wing for one of the younger families would grow. They ripped up her clothes and shoes and broke her combs, grinding them underfoot. They tore her work from the loom. They scattered the cooking fire and rolled the new weaving in it. We could hear them in the kitchen breaking our bowls and banging the pots. They overturned the great waist-high earthenware jugs; duck eggs, pickled fruits, vegetables burst out and mixed in acrid torrents. The old woman from the next field swept a broom through the air and loosed the spirits-of-the-broom over our heads. 'Pig.' 'Ghost.' 'Pig,' they sobbed and scolded while they ruined our house.

"When they left, they took sugar and oranges to bless themselves. They cut pieces from the dead animals. Some of them took bowls that were not broken and clothes that were not torn. Afterward we swept up the rice and sewed it back up into sacks. But the smells from the spilled preserves lasted. Your aunt gave birth in the pigsty that night. The next morning when I went for the water, I found her and the baby plugging up the family well.

"Don't let your father know that I told you. He denies her. Now that you have started to menstruate, what happened to her could happen to you. Don't humiliate us. You wouldn't like to be forgotten as if you had never been born. The villagers are watchful."

Whenever she had to warn us about life, my mother told stories that ran like this one, a story to grow up on. She tested our strength to establish realities. Those in the emigrant generations who could not reassert brute survival died young and far from home. Those of us in the first American generations have had to figure out how the invisible world the emigrants built around our childhoods fits in solid America.

The emigrants confused the gods by diverting their curses, misleading them with crooked streets and false names. They must try to confuse their offspring as well, who, I suppose, threaten them in similar ways—always trying to get things straight, always trying to name the unspeakable. The Chinese I know hide their names; sojourners take new names when their lives change and guard their real names with silence.

Chinese-Americans, when you try to understand what things in you are Chinese, how do you separate what is peculiar to childhood, to poverty, insanities, one family, your mother who marked your growing up with stories, from what is Chinese? What is Chinese tradition and what is the movies?

If I want to learn what clothes my aunt wore, whether flashy or ordinary, I would have to begin, "Remember Father's drowned-in-the-well sister?" I cannot ask that. My mother has told me once and for all the useful parts. She will add nothing unless powered by Necessity, a riverbank that guides her life. She plants vegetable gardens rather than lawns; she carries the odd-shaped tomatoes home from the fields and eats food left for the gods.

Whenever we did frivolous things, we used up energy; we flew high kites. We children came up off the ground over the melting cones our parents brought home from work and the American movie on New Year's Day—*Oh, You Beautiful Doll* with Betty Grable one year, and *She Wore a Yellow Ribbon* with John Wayne another year. After the one carnival ride each, we paid in guilt; our tired father counted his change on the dark walk home.

Adultery is extravagance. Could people who hatch their own chicks and eat the embryos and the heads for delicacies and boil the feet in vinegar for party food, leaving only the gravel, eating even the gizzard lining—could such people engender a prodigal aunt? To be a woman, to have a daughter in starvation time was a waste enough. My aunt could not have been the lone romantic who gave up everything for sex. Women in the old China did not choose. Some man had commanded her to lie with him and be his secret evil. I wonder whether he masked himself when he joined the raid on her family.

Perhaps she had encountered him in the fields or on the mountain where the daughters-in-law collected fuel. Or perhaps he first noticed her in the marketplace. He was not a stranger because the village housed no strangers. She had to have dealings with him other than sex. Perhaps he worked an adjoining field, or he sold her the cloth for the dress she sewed and wore. His demand must have surprised, then terrified her. She obeyed him; she always did as she was told.

When the family found a young man in the next village to be her husband, she had stood tractably beside the best rooster, his proxy, and promised before they met that she would be his forever. She was lucky that he was her age and she would be the first wife, an advantage secure now. The night she first saw him, he had sex with her. Then he left for America. She had almost forgotten what he looked like. When she tried to envision him, she only saw the black and white face in the group photograph the men had had taken before leaving.

The other man was not, after all, much different from her husband. They both gave orders: she followed. "If you tell your family, I'll beat you. I'll kill you. Be here again next week." No one talked sex, ever. And she might have separated the rapes from the rest of living if only she did not have to buy her oil from him or gather wood in the same forest. I want her fear to have lasted just as long as rape lasted so that the fear could have been contained. No drawn-out fear. But women at sex hazarded birth and hence lifetimes. The fear did not stop but permeated everywhere. She told the man, "I think I'm pregnant." He organized the raid against her.

On nights when my mother and father talked about their life back home, sometimes they mentioned an "outcast table" whose business they still seemed to be settling, their voices tight. In a commensal tradition, where food is precious, the powerful older people made wrongdoers eat alone. Instead of letting them start separate new lives like the Japanese, who could become samurais and geishas, the Chinese family, faces averted but eyes glowering sideways, hung on to the offenders and fed them leftovers. My aunt must have lived in the same house as my parents and eaten at an outcast table. My mother spoke about the raid as if she had seen it, when she and my aunt, a daughter-in-law to a different household, should not have been living together at all. Daughters-in-law lived with their husbands' parents, not their own; a synonym for marriage in Chinese is "taking a daughter-in-law." Her husband's parents could have sold her, mortgaged her, stoned her. But they had sent her back to her own mother and father, a mysterious act hinting at disgraces not told me. Perhaps they had thrown her out to deflect the avengers.

She was the only daughter; her four brothers went with her father, husband, and uncles "out on the road" and for some years became western men. When the goods were divided among the family, three of the brothers took land, and the youngest, my father, chose an education. After my grandparents gave their daughter away to her husband's family, they had dispensed all the adventure and all the property. They expected her alone to keep the traditional ways, which her brothers, now among the barbarians, could fumble without detection. The heavy, deep-rooted women were to maintain the past against the flood, safe for returning. But the rare urge west had fixed upon our family, and so my aunt crossed boundaries not delineated in space.

The work of preservation demands that the feelings playing about in one's guts not be turned into action. Just watch their passing like cherry blossoms. But perhaps my aunt, my forerunner, caught in a slow life, let dreams grow and fade and after some months or years went toward what persisted. Fear at the enormities of the forbidden kept her desires delicate, wire and bone. She looked at a man because she liked the way the hair was tucked behind his ears, or she liked the question-mark line of a long torso curving at the shoulder and a straight at the hip. For warm eyes or a soft voice or a slow walk—that's all—a few hairs, a line, a brightness, a sound, a pace, she gave up family. She offered us up for a charm that vanished with tiredness, a pigtail that didn't toss when the wind died. Why, the wrong lighting could erase the dearest thing about him.

It could very well have been, however, that my aunt did not take subtle enjoyment of her friend, but, a wild woman, kept rollicking company. Imagining her free with sex doesn't fit, though. I don't know any women like that, or men either. Unless I see her life branching into mine, she gives me no ancestral help.

To sustain her being in love, she often worked at herself in the mirror, guessing at the colors and shapes that would interest him, changing them frequently in order to hit on the right combination. She wanted him to look back.

On a farm near the sea, a woman who tended her appearance reaped a reputation for eccentricity. All the married women blunt-cut their hair in flaps about their ears or pulled it back in tight buns. No nonsense. Neither style blew easily into heart-catching tangles. And at their weddings they displayed themselves in their long hair for the last time. "It brushed the backs of my knees," my mother tells me. "It was braided, and even so, it brushed the backs of my knees."

At the mirror my aunt combed individuality into her bob. A bun could have been contrived to escape into black streamers blowing in the wind or in quiet wisps about her face, but only the older women in our picture album wear buns. She brushed her hair back from her forehead, tucking the flaps behind her ears. She looped a piece of thread, knotted into a circle between her index fingers and thumbs, and ran the double strand across her forehead. When she closed her fingers as if she were making a pair of shadow geese bite, the string twisted together catching the little hairs. Then she pulled the thread away from her skin, ripping the hairs out neatly, her eyes watering from the needles of pain. Opening her fingers, she cleaned the thread, then rolled it along her hairline and the tops of her eyebrows. My mother did the same to me and my sisters and herself. I used to believe that the expression "caught by the short hairs" meant a captive held with a depilatory string. It especially hurt at the temples, but my mother said we were lucky we didn't have to have our feet bound when we were seven. Sisters used to sit on their beds and cry together, she said, as their mothers or their slaves removed the bandages for a few minutes each night and let the blood gush back into their veins. I hope that the man my aunt loved appreciated a smooth brow, that he wasn't just a tits-and-ass man.

Once my aunt found a freckle on her chin, at a spot that the almanac said predestined her for unhappiness. She dug it out with a hot needle and washed the wound with peroxide.

More attention to her looks than these pullings of hairs and pickings at spots would have caused gossip among the villagers. They owned work clothes and good clothes, and they wore good clothes for feasting the new seasons. But since a woman combing her hair hexes beginnings, my aunt rarely found an occasion to look her best. Women looked like great sea snails—the corded wood, babies, and laundry they carried were the whorls on their backs. The Chinese did not admire a bent back; goddesses and warriors stood straight. Still there must have been a marvelous freeing of beauty when a worker laid down her burden and stretched and arched.

Such commonplace loveliness, however, was not enough for my aunt. She dreamed of a lover for the fifteen days of New Year's, the time for families to exchange visits, money, and food. She plied her secret comb. And sure enough she cursed the year, the family, the village, and herself.

Even as her hair lured her imminent lover, many other men looked at her. Uncles, cousins, nephews, brothers would have looked, too, had they been home between journeys. Perhaps they had already been restraining their curiosity, and they left, fearful that their glances, like a field of nesting birds, might be startled and caught. Poverty hurt, and that was their first reason for leaving. But another, final reason for leaving the crowded house was the never-said.

She may have been unusually beloved, the precious daughter, spoiled and mirror gazing because of the affection the family lavished on her. When her husband left, they welcomed the chance to take her back from the in-laws; she could live like the little daughter for just a while longer. There are stories that my grandfather was different from other people, "crazy ever since the little Jap bayoneted him in the head." He used to put his naked penis on the dinner table, laughing. And one day he brought home a baby girl, wrapped up inside his brown western-style greatcoat. He had traded one of his sons, probably my father, the youngest, for her. My grandmother made him trade back. When he finally got a daughter of his own, he doted on her. They must have all loved her, except perhaps my father, the only brother who never went back to China, having once been traded for a girl.

Brothers and sisters, newly men and women, had to efface their sexual color and present plain miens. Disturbing hair and eyes, a smile like no other, threatened the ideal of five generations living under one roof. To focus blurs, people shouted face to face and yelled from room to room. The immigrants I know have loud voices, unmodulated to American tones even after years away from the village where they called their friendships out across the fields. I have not been able to stop my mother's screams in public libraries or over telephones. Walking erect (knees straight, toes pointed forward, no pigeon-toed, which is Chinese-feminine) and speaking in an inaudible voice, I have tried to turn myself American-feminine. Chinese communication was loud, public. Only sick people had to whisper. But at the dinner table, where the family members came nearest one another, no one could talk, not the outcasts nor any eaters. Every word that falls from the mouth is a coin lost. Silently they gave and accepted food with both hands. A preoccupied child who took his bowl with one hand got a sideways glare. A complete moment of total attention is due everyone alike. Children and lovers have no singularity here, but my aunt used a secret voice, a separate attentiveness.

She kept the man's name to herself throughout her labor and dying; she did not accuse him that he be punished with her. To save her inseminator's name she gave silent birth.

He may have been somebody in her own household, but intercourse with a man outside the family would have been no less abhorrent. All the village were kinsmen, and the titles shouted in loud country voices never let kinship be forgotten. Any man within visiting distance would have been neutralized as a lover—"brother," "younger brother," "older brother"—one hundred and fifteen relationship titles. Parents researched birth charts probably not so much to assure good fortune as to circumvent incest in a population that has but one hundred surnames. Everybody has eight million relatives. How useless then sexual mannerisms, how dangerous.

As if it came from an atavism deeper than fear, I used to add "brother" silently to boys' names. It hexed the boys, who would or would not ask me to dance, and made them less scary and as familiar and deserving of benevolence as girls.

But, of course, I hexed myself also—no dates. I should have stood up, both arms waving, and shouted out across the libraries, "Hey you! Love me back." I had no idea, though, how to make attraction selective, how to control its direction and magnitude. If I made myself American-pretty so that the five or six Chinese boys in the class fell in love with me, everyone else—the Caucasian, Negro, and Japanese boys—would too. Sisterliness, dignified and honorable, made much more sense.

Attraction eludes control so stubbornly that whole societies designed to organize relationships among people cannot keep order, not even when they bind people to one another from childhood and raise them together. Among the very poor and the wealthy, brothers married their adopted sisters, like doves. Our family allowed some romance, paying adult brides' prices and providing dowries so that their sons and daughters could marry strangers. Marriages promises to turn strangers into friendly relatives—a nation of siblings.

In the village structure, spirits shimmered among the live creatures, balanced and held in equilibrium by time and land. But one human being flaring up into violence could open up a black hole, a maelstrom that pulled in the sky. They frightened villagers, who depended on one another to maintain the real, went to my aunt to show her a personal, physical representation of the break she had made in the "roundness." Misallying couples snapped off the future, which was to be embodied in true offspring. The villagers punished her for acting as if she could have a private life, secret and apart from them.

If my aunt had betrayed the family at a time of large grain yields and peace, when many boys were born, and wings were being built on many houses, perhaps she might have escaped such severe punishment. But the men—hungry, greedy, tired of planting in dry soil—had been forced to leave the village in order to send food-money home. There were ghost plagues, bandit plagues, wars with the Japanese, floods. My Chinese brother and sister had died of an unknown sickness. Adultery, perhaps only a mistake during good times, became a crime when the village needed food.

The round moon cakes and round doorways, the round tables of graduated sizes that fit one roundness inside another, round windows and rice bowls—these talismans had lost their power to warn this family of the law: a family must be whole, faithfully keeping the descent line by having sons to feed the old and the dead, who in turn look after the family. The villagers came to show my aunt and her lover-in-hiding a broken house. The villagers were speeding up the circling of events because she was too shortsighted to see that her infidelity had already harmed the village, that waves of consequences would return unpredictably, sometimes in disguise, as now, to hurt her. This roundness had to be made coin-sized so that she would see its circumference: punish her at the birth of her baby. Awaken her to the inexorable. People who refused fatalism because they could invent small resources insisted on culpability. Deny accidents and wrest fault from the stars.

After the villagers left, their lanterns now scattering in various directions toward home, the family broke their silence and cursed her. "Aiaa, we're going to die. Death is coming. Death is coming. Look what you've done. You've killed us. Ghost! Dead ghost! Ghost! You've never been born." She ran out into the fields, far enough from the house so that she could no longer hear their voices, and pressed herself against the earth, her own land no more. When she felt the birth coming, she thought that she had been hurt. Her body seized together. "They've hurt me too much," she thought. "This is gall, and it will kill me." With forehead and knees against the earth, her body convulsed and then relaxed. She turned on her back, lay on the ground. The black well of sky and stars went out and out and out forever; her body and her complexity seemed to disappear. She was one of the stars, a bright dot in blackness, without home, without a companion, in eternal cold and silence. An agoraphobia rose in her, speeding higher and higher, bigger and bigger; she would not be able to contain it; there would no end to fear.

Flayed, unprotected against space, she felt pain return, focusing her body. This pain chilled her—a cold, steady kind of surface pain. Inside, spasmodically, the other pain, the pain of the child, heated her. For hours she lay on the ground, alternately body and space. Sometimes a vision of normal comfort obliterated reality: she saw the family in the evening gambling at the dinner table, the young people massaging their elders' backs. She saw them congratulating one another, high joy on the morning the rice shoots came up. When these pictures burst, the stars drew yet further apart. Black space opened.

She got to her feet to fight better and remembered that old-fashioned women gave birth in their pigsties to fool the jealous, pain-dealing gods, who do not snatch piglets. Before the next spasm could stop her, she ran to the pigsty, each step a rushing out into emptiness. She climbed over the fence and knelt in the dirt. It was good to have a fence enclosing her, a tribal person alone.

Laboring, this woman who had carried her child as a foreign growth that sickened her every day, expelled it at last. She reached down to touch the hot, wet, moving mass, surely smaller than anything human, and could feel that it was human after all—fingers, toes, nails, nose. She pulled it up on to her belly, and it lay curled there, butt in the air, feet precisely tucked on under the other. She opened her loose shirt and buttoned the child inside. After resting, it squirmed and thrashed and she pushed it up to her breast. It turned its head this way and that until it found her nipple. There, it made little snuffling noises. She clenched her teeth at its preciousness, lovely as a young calf, a piglet, a little dog.

She may have gone to the pigsty as a last act of responsibility: she would protect this child as she had protected its father. It would look after her soul, leaving supplies on her grave. But how would this tiny child without family find her grave when there would be no marker for her anywhere, neither in the earth nor the family hall? No one would give her a family hall name. She had taken the child with her into the wastes. At its birth the two of them had felt the same raw pain of separation, a wound that only the family pressing tight could close. A child with no descent line would not soften her life but only trail after her ghostlike, begging her to give it purpose. At dawn the villagers on their way to the fields would stand around the fence and look.

Full of milk, the little ghost slept. When it awoke, she hardened her breasts against the milk that crying loosens. Toward morning she picked up the baby and walked toward the well.

Carrying the baby to the well shows loving. Otherwise abandon it. Turn its face into the mud. Mothers who love their children take them along. It was probably a girl; there is some hope of forgiveness for boys.

"Don't tell anyone you had an aunt. Your father does not want to hear her name. She has never been born." I have believed that sex was unspeakable and words so strong and fathers so frail that "aunt" would do my father mysterious harm. I have thought my family, having settled among immigrants who had also been their neighbors in the ancestral land, needed to clean their name, and a wrong word would incite the kinspeople even here. But there is more to this silence: they want me to participate in her punishment. And I have.

In the twenty years since I heard this story I have not asked for details nor said my aunt's name. I do not know it. People who can comfort the dead can also chase after them to hurt them further—a reverse ancestor worship. The real punishment was not the raid swiftly inflicted by the villagers, but the family's deliberate forgetting her. Her betrayal so maddened them, they saw to it that she would suffer forever, even after death. Always hungry, always needing, she would have to beg food from other ghosts, snatch and steal it from those whose living descendants give them gifts. She would have to fight the ghosts massed at the crossroads for the buns a few thoughtful citizens leave to decoy her away from the village and home so that the ancestral spirits could feast unharassed. At peace, they could act like gods, not ghosts, their descent lines providing them with paper suits and dresses, spirit money, paper houses, paper automobiles, chicken, meat, and rice into eternity—essences delivered up in smoke and flames, steam and incense rising from each rice bowl. In an attempt to make the Chinese care for people outside the family, Chairman Mao encourages us now to give our paper replicas to the spirits of outstanding soldiers and workers, no matter whose ancestors they may be. My aunt remains forever hungry. Goods are not distributed evenly among the dead.

My aunt haunts me—her ghost drawn to me because now, after fifty years of neglect, I alone devote pages of paper to her, though not origamied into houses and clothes. I do not think she always means me well. I am telling on her, and she was a spite suicide, drowning herself in the drinking water. The Chinese are always very frightened of the drowned one, whose weeping ghost, wet hair hanging and skin bloated, waits silently by the water to pull down a substitute.

1975–1976

JESSICA HAGEDORN
B. 1949

Born in the Santa Mesa section of Manila in 1949, Jessica Hagedorn traces her early inspiration to a mother devoted to painting and a maternal grandfather who was an accomplished writer and political cartoonist. Situated within a Philippines colonial heritage of Catholic schooling and U.S. cultural hegemony, Hagedorn found herself drawn to Hollywood movies and Western literary classics—but equally to melodramas and radio serials in Tagalog. This predilection for crossing boundaries defines Hagedorn's cultural productions, which include poetry and fiction, theater pieces and performance art, music and screenplays.

Moving to San Francisco at the age of fourteen proved pivotal in shaping Hagedorn's consciousness. Although she eventually attended the American Conservatory Theater, Hagedorn attributes a substantial part of her artistic development to her early exposure to San Francisco's social and literary scene. The family's frequent moves through diverse neighborhoods contributed, along with her unimpeded appetite for browsing bookstores, to her sense of multiculturalism. She cites Bienvenido Santos, Amiri Baraka, Ishmael Reed, Jayne Cortez, and Víctor Hernández Cruz, as well as Gabriel García Márquez, Manuel Puig, and Stéphane Mallarmé, among her literary influences. No less vital was her participation in San Francisco's Kearny Street Writers' Workshop, which introduced her to Asian American history and literature and helped infuse her with the spirit, passion, and social commitment of the late 1960s.

Hagedorn's urban American experience also stimulated an abiding interest in music, particularly rock, jazz, and rhythm and blues. Her poetry propels itself along rhythms inflected by music and urban vernacular. In 1973 her poetry appeared in *Four Young Women: Poems*, an anthology edited by Kenneth Rexroth. She continued experimenting in *Dangerous Music*, a 1975 collection whose poetry occasionally resembles a literal "dance" of words and whose offbeat prose fiction opens a space for the rewriting of immigration narratives.

In 1975, along with Thulani Davis and Ntozake Shange, Hagedorn formed a band called the West Coast Gangster Choir, rechristened the Gangster Choir in 1978 when she moved to New York, where she also participated in the Basement Workshop. Earlier experiments using dramatic sketches during the pauses between songs contributed to the development of her performance art. Following the production of several theatrical works and teleplays, in 1981 she published *Pet Food & Tropical Apparitions*, which featured sexually charged poems and, in the title story, took a hard but sympathetic look at the capacity of inner-city culture to evince simultaneously an incomparable vitality and a lurid self-destructiveness. Between 1988 and 1992, she participated in the performance/theater trio Thought Music.

In 1990 Hagedorn produced her first novel, *Dogeaters*, a mordant exploration of class and ethnic divisions, rampant commercialism, plutocratic machinations, revolutionary insurgency, and the varieties of corruption in a country caught in the grasp of a Marcos-like regime and laboring in the shadow of Western colonialism.

Nominated for the National Book Award and recipient of the American Book Award, *Dogeaters* is also noteworthy for its stylistic daring. Playfully splicing together book and letter excerpts, poetry, a gossip column, dramatic dialogue, and news items in a conventional storytelling frame, the novel explores the possibilities of combining postmodern narrative practices with a postcolonial political agenda.

In 1993 Hagedorn edited *Charlie Chan Is Dead: An Anthology of Contemporary Asian American Fiction*. Significantly, although the book included many well-known Asian American writers, such as Carlos Bulosan, Hisaye Yamamoto, Maxine Hong Kingston, Amy Tan, and Bharati Mukherjee, nearly half of the forty-eight writers enjoyed publication in a major collection for the first time.

Hagedorn's second novel, *The Gangster of Love*, appeared in 1996. It experiments with shifting points of view and engages dream as a supplementary narrative strategy but otherwise tells a conventional story of a young woman from the Philippines struggling to establish her musical and artistic career in America and later grappling with the encroachments of age.

Hagedorn remains ideologically aligned with the radical 1960s politics that helped shape her sensibility, but ultimately she is interested not in social realism but in reinvention and the varieties of liberation. Just as her work resists easy categorization into "high" or "pop" culture, it seeks to cross conventional boundaries of self and country and of writing and art.

George Uba
California State University, Northridge

PRIMARY WORKS

Dangerous Music, 1975; *Pet Food & Tropical Apparitions,* 1981; *Teenytown* (performance piece), 1988; *Dogeaters,* 1990; *Danger and Beauty,* 1993; *Airport Music* (performance piece), 1994; *The Gangster of Love,* 1996; *Burning Heart: A Portrait of the Philippines,* 1999; *Dream Jungle,* 2003.

The Death of Anna May Wong

My mother is very beautiful
And not yet old.
A Twin,
Color of two continents:

I stroll through Irish tenderloin   5
Nightmare doors—drunks spill out
Saloon alleys falling asleep
At my feet ...
My mother wears a beaded
Mandarin coat: 10
In the dryness
Of San Diego's mediterrannean parody
I see your ghost, Belen
As you clean up
After your sweet señora's   15

mierda

Jazz,
Don't do me like that.
Mambo,
Don't do me like that.   20
Samba, calypso, funk and
Boogie
Don't cut me up like that

Move my gut so high up
Inside my throat   25
I can only strangle you
To keep from crying . . .

My mother serves crêpes suzettes
With a smile
And a puma   30
Slithers down
              19th street and Valencia
Gabriel o.d.'s on reds
As we dance together

Dorothy Lamour undrapes   35
Her sarong
And Bing Crosby ignores
The mierda.

My mother's lavender lips
Stretch in a slow smile.   40
And beneath
The night's cartoon sky
Cold with rain
              Alice Coltrane
Kills the pain   45
And I know
I can't go home again.

                                                     1971

Filipino Boogie

Under a ceiling-high Christmas tree
I pose
     in my Japanese kimono
My mother hands me

                    a Dale Evans cowgirl skirt   5
and
    baby cowgirl boots

Mommy and daddy split
No one else is home

I take some rusty scissors   10
                    and cut the skirt up

        in
            little pieces

(don't give me no bullshit fringe,
Mama)   15

Mommy and daddy split
No one else is home

    I take my baby cowgirl boots
                    and flush them
                                    down   20
                            the
                                toilet

(don't hand me no bullshit fringe,
Papa)

I seen the Indian Fighter   25
Too many times

            dug on Sitting Bull
                    before Donald Duck

In my infant dream
These warriors weaved a magic spell   30
        more blessed than Tinker Bell

(Kirk Douglas rubs his chin
and slays Minnehaha by the campfire)

Mommy and daddy split
There ain't no one else home   35

        I climb a mango tree
            and wait for Mohawk drums

(Mama—World War II
is over . . . why you cryin'?)

Is this San Francisco?   40
Is this San Francisco?
Is this Amerika?

buy me Nestle's Crunch
       buy me Pepsi in a can

Ladies' Home Journal   45
      and *Bonanza*

I seen Little Joe in Tokyo
I seen Little Joe in Manila
I seen Laramie in Hong Kong
I seen Yul Brynner in San Diego   50
and the bloated ghost
          of Desi Arnaz

dancing
     in Tijuana

Rip-off synthetic ivory   55
         to send
              the natives
   back home

and

    North Beach boredom   60
   escapes
   the barber shops
  on Kearny street

        where
          they spit out   65
            red tobacco

      patiently
    waiting
      in 1930s suits
and in another dream   70
       I climb a mango tree
and Saturday
    afternoon

Jack Palance

bazooka 75

the krauts

and

the YELLOW PERIL

bombs

Pearl Harbor 80

1971

Homesick

Blame it on the mambo and the cha-cha, voodoo amulets worn on the same chain with tiny crucifixes and scapulars blessed by the Pope. Chains of love, medals engraved with the all-seeing Eye, ascending Blessed Virgins floating toward heaven surrounded by erotic cherubs and archangels, the magnificent torso of a tormented, half-naked Saint Sebastian pierced by arrows dripping blood. A crown of barbed-wire thorns adorns the holy subversive's head, while we drown in the legacy of brutal tropical generals stuffed in khaki uniforms, their eyes shielded by impenetrable black sunglasses, Douglas MacArthur style.

And Douglas MacArthur and Tom Cruise are painted on billboards lining Manila's highways, modeling *Ray-Ban* shades and Jockey underwear. You choose between the cinema version starring Gregory Peck smoking a corncob pipe, or the real thing. "I shall return," promised the North American general, still revered by many as the savior of the Filipino people, who eagerly awaited his return. As the old saying goes, this is how we got screwed, screwed real good. According to Nick Joaquin, "The Philippines spent three hundred years trapped in a convent, and fifty years in Hollywood . . ." Or was it four hundred years? No matter—there we were, seduced and abandoned in a confusion of identities, then granted our independence. Hollywood pretended to leave us alone. An African American saying also goes: "Nobody's *given* freedom." Being granted our independence meant we were owned all along by someone other than ourselves.

I step off the crowded plane onto the tarmac of the newly named Ninoy Aquino Airport. It is an interesting appropriation of the assassinated senator's name, don't you think? So I think, homesick for this birthplace, my country of supreme ironies and fatalistic humor, mountains of foul garbage and breathtaking women, men with the fierce faces of wolves and steamy streets teeming with abandoned children.

The widow of the assassinated senator is Corazon Aquino, now president of the Republic of the Philippines in a deft stroke of irony that left the world stunned by a sudden turn of events in February 1986. She is a beloved figure, a twentieth-century icon who has inherited a bundle of cultural contradictions and an economic nightmare in a lush paradise of corrupt, warring factions. In a Manila department store, one of the first souvenirs I buy my daughter is a rather homely Cory Aquino doll made out of brown cloth; the doll wears crooked wire eyeglasses, a straw shoulder bag, plastic high-heeled shoes, and Cory's signature yellow dress, with "I Love Cory" embroidered on the front. My daughter seems delighted with her doll, and the notion of a woman president.

Soldiers in disguise, patrol the countryside ... Jungle not far away. So goes a song I once wrote, pungent as the remembered taste of mangoes overripe as my imagination, the memory of Manila the central character of the novel I am writing, the novel that brings me back to this torrid zone, my landscape haunted by ghosts and movie-lovers.

Nietzsche once said, "A joke is an epitaph for an emotion." Our laughter is pained, self-mocking. Blame it on *Rambo, Platoon*, and *Gidget Goes Hawaiian*. Cory Aquino has inherited a holy war, a class war, an amazing nation of people who've endured incredible poverty and spiritual loss with inherent humor and grace. Member of the ruling class, our pious president has also inherited an army of divided, greedy men. Yet probably no one will bother assassinating her, as icons are always useful.

My novel sits in its black folder, an obsession with me for over ten years. Home is now New York, but home in my heart will also always be Manila, and the rage of a marvelous culture stilled, confused, and diverted. Manila is my river of dreams choked with refuse, the refuse of refusal and denial, a denial more profound than the forbidding Catholic Church in all its ominous presence.

Blame it on the mambo and the cha-cha, a cardinal named Sin, and an adviser named Joker. Blame it on a former beauty queen with a puffy face bailed out of a jam by Doris Duke. Blame it on *Imeldification*. Blame it on children named Lourdes, Maria, Jesus, Carlos, Peachy, Baby, and Elvis. Blame it on the rich, who hang on in spite of everything. Blame it on the same people who are still in power, before Marcos, after Marcos. You name it, we'll blame it. The NPA, the vigilantes, rebel colonels nicknamed "Gringo," and a restless army plotting coups. Blame it on signs in nightclubs that warn: NO GUNS OR DRUGS.

Cards have been reshuffled, roles exchanged. The major players are the same, even those who suffered long years in prison under one regime, even those who died by the bullet. Aquino, Lopez, Cojuangco, Zobel, Laurel, Enrile, etc. etc. Blood against blood, controlling the destinies of so many disparate tribes in these seven thousand islands.

I remember my grandmother, Lola Tecla, going for drives with me as a child down the boulevard along Manila Bay. The boulevard led to Luneta Park, where Rizal was executed by the Spanish colonizers; it was then known as Dewey Boulevard, after an American admiral. From history books forced on me as a child at a convent school run by strict nuns, I learned a lopsided history of myself, one full of lies and blank spaces, a history of omission—a colonial version of history which scorned the "savage" ways of precolonial Filipinos. In those days even our language was kept at a distance; Tagalog was studied in a course called "National Language" (*sic*), but it was English that was spoken, English that was preferred. Tagalog was a language used to address servants. I scorned myself, and it was only later, after I had left the Philippines to settle in the country of my oppressor, that I learned to confront my demons and reinvent my own history.

I am writing a novel set in contemporary Philippines. It is a journey back I am always taking. I leave one place for the other, welcomed and embraced by the family I have left—fathers and brothers and cousins and uncles and aunts. Childhood sweethearts, now with their own children. I am unable to stay. I make excuses, adhere to tight schedules. I return, only to depart, weeks or months later, depending on finances and the weather, obligations to my daughter, my art, my addiction to life in the belly of one particular beast. I am the other, the exile within, afflicted with permanent nostalgia for the mud. I return, only to depart: Manila, New York, San Francisco, Manila, Honolulu, Detroit, Manila, Guam, Hong Kong, Zamboanga, Manila, New York, San Francisco, Tokyo, Manila again, Manila again, Manila again.

1992

DONALD BARTHELME
1931–1989

Born in Philadelphia but raised in Houston, Texas, Donald Barthelme began writing stories and poems in high school and continued writing (journalism as well as fiction and poetry) at the University of Houston. After army service in Japan and Korea, he returned to the university and worked locally as a reporter. He then became director of Houston's Contemporary Arts Museum.

In 1962 Barthelme moved to New York and soon found his own voice and style. He became a regular contributor to the *New Yorker* and began to find in his fiction the innovation that was occurring in film and graphic art. He was influenced by the French Symbolists and worked frequently with myth and spatial techniques (perhaps because of the visionary influence of his father, an architect). His vision was comic, surreal, macabre, and his play with language—giving the reader the unexpected, the grotesque, and above all the fragmented—marked him as a postmodernist even before that classification existed.

With a montage style reminiscent of John Dos Passos, Barthelme drew phrases and lines from advertising, songs, and stereotyped phrases of the times and created from those borrowings new structures and new perspectives. His first novel, *Snow White*, retold the classic fairytale, but with a wit and acerbity that surprised readers of the 1960s. Structural experimentation in *The Dead*

Fathers made that novel another treasure house of narrative technique and brought a patina of fashion to a more serious theme. Even more than a montage of materials, "At the End of the Mechanical Age" represents a parody of fictional traditions and the various structures of storytelling they employ. By juxtaposing such structures, Barthelme exposes—to both scrutiny and laughter—the historical consciousness of the modern age. When biblical or creation myths jostle with "true romance" materials, then the modernist belief that we stand at the end of a long historical process, and thereby derive a certain cultural and social advantage, is given the lie. At the same time, the themes of divorce, repression, and secular self-doubt enter the mix, as they do in the tradition of nineteenth-century realist novels, but in a telegraphed way that some critics see as one of the hallmarks of Barthelme's style. He not only parodies his characters and their concerns, he also mocks the very possibilities and burdens of storytelling itself. Because he calls into question the mechanics of this central cultural activity, and by extension the ability of language to represent reality, he is often credited with influencing many aspects of postmodernism.

Charles Molesworth
Queens College, CUNY

PRIMARY WORKS

Come Back, Dr. Caligari (stories), 1964; *Snow White*, 1967; *Unspeakable Practices, Unnatural Acts* (stories), 1968; *City Life* (stories), 1970; *Sadness*, 1972; *Guilty Pleasures*, 1974; *The Dead Father*, 1975; *Amateurs* (stories), 1976; *Great Days* (stories), 1979; *Sixty Stories*, 1981; *Overnight to Many Distant Cities*, 1983; *Paradise*, 1986; *Forty Stories*, 1989; *The King*, 1990; *The Teachings of Don B.: The Satires, Parodies, Fables, Illustrated Stories, and Plays of Donald Barthelme*, 1992.

At the End of the Mechanical Age

I went to the grocery store to buy some soap. I stood for a long time before the soaps in their attractive boxes, RUB and FAB and TUB and suchlike, I couldn't decide so I closed my eyes and reached out blindly and when I opened my eyes I found her hand in mine.

Her name was Mrs. Davis, she said, and TUB was best for important cleaning experiences, in her opinion. So we went to lunch at a Mexican restaurant which as it happened she owned, she took me into the kitchen and showed me her stacks of handsome beige tortillas and the steam tables which were shiny-brite. I told her I wasn't very good with women and she said it didn't matter, few men were, and that nothing mattered, now that Jake was gone, but I would do as an interim project and sit down and have a Carta Blanca. So I sat down and had a cool Carta Blanca, God was standing in the basement reading the meters to see how much grace had been used up in the month of June. Grace is electricity, science has found, it is not *like* electricity, it *is* electricity and God was down in the basement reading the meters in His blue jump suit with the flashlight stuck in the back pocket.

"The mechanical age is drawing to a close," I said to her.

"Or has already done so," she replied.

"It was a good age," I said. "I was comfortable in it, relatively. Probably I will not enjoy the age to come quite so much. I don't like its look."

"One must be fair. We don't know yet what kind of an age the next one will be. Although I feel in my bones that it will be an age inimical to personal well-being and comfort, and that is what I like, personal well-being and comfort."

"Do you suppose there is something to be done?" I asked her.

"Huddle and cling," said Mrs. Davis. "We can huddle and cling. It will pall, of course, everything palls, in time ..."

Then we went back to my house to huddle and cling, most women are two different colors when they remove their clothes especially in summer but Mrs. Davis was all one color, an ocher. She seemed to like huddling and clinging, she stayed for many days. From time to time she checked the restaurant keeping everything shiny-brite and distributing sums of money to the staff, returning with tortillas in sacks, cases of Carta Blanca, buckets of guacamole, but I paid her for it because I didn't want to feel obligated.

There was a song I sang her, a song of great expectations.

"Ralph is coming," I sang, *"Ralph is striding in his suit of lights over moons and mountains, over parking lots and fountains, toward your silky side. Ralph is coming, he has a coat of many colors and all major credit cards and he is striding to meet you and culminate your foggy dreams in an explosion of blood and soil, at the end of the mechanical age. Ralph is coming preceded by fifty running men with spears and fifty dancing ladies who are throwing leaf spinach out of little baskets, in his path. Ralph is perfect,"* I sang, *"but he is also full of interesting tragic flaws, and he can drink fifty running men under the table without breaking his stride and he can have congress with fifty dancing ladies without breaking his stride, even his socks are ironed, so natty is Ralph, but he is also right down in the mud with the rest of us, he markets the mud at high prices for specialized industrial uses and he is striding, striding, striding, toward your waiting heart. Of course you may not like him, some people are awfully picky ... Ralph is coming,"* I sang to her, *"he is striding over dappled plains and crazy rivers and he will change your life for the better, probably, you will be fainting with glee at the simple touch of his grave gentle immense hand although I am aware that some people can't stand prosperity, Ralph is coming, I hear his hoofsteps on the drumhead of history, he is striding as he has been all his life toward you, you, you."*

"Yes," Mrs. Davis said, when I had finished singing, "that is what I deserve, all right. But probably I will not get it. And in the meantime, there is you."

God then rained for forty days and forty nights, when the water tore away the front of the house we got into the boat, Mrs. Davis liked the way I maneuvered the boat off the trailer and out of the garage, she was provoked into a memoir of Jake.

"Jake was a straight-ahead kind of man," she said, "he was simple-minded and that helped him to be the kind of man that he was." She was staring into her Scotch-and-floodwater rather moodily I thought, debris bouncing on the waves all around us but she paid no attention. "That is the type of man I like," she said, "a strong and simple-minded man. The case-study method was not Jake's method, he went right through the middle of the line and never failed to gain yardage, no matter what the game was. He had a lust for life, and life had a lust for him. I was inconsolable when Jake passed away." Mrs. Davis was drinking the Scotch for her nerves, she had no nerves of course, she was nerveless and possibly heartless also but that is another question, gutless she was not, she had a gut and a very pretty one ocher in color but that was another matter. God was standing up to His neck in the raging waters with a smile of incredible beauty on His visage, He seemed to be enjoying His creation, the disaster, the waters all around us were raging louder now, raging like a mighty tractor-trailer tailgating you on the highway.

Then Mrs. Davis sang to me, a song of great expectations.

"Maude is waiting for you," Mrs. Davis sang to me, *"Maude is waiting for you in all her seriousness and splendor, under her gilded onion dome, in that city which I cannot name at this time, Maude waits. Maude is what you lack, the pro-foundest of your lacks. Your every yearn since the first yearn has been a yearn for Maude, only you did not know it until I, your dear friend, pointed it out. She is going to heal your scrappy and generally unsatisfactory life with the balm of her Maudeness, luckiest of dogs, she waits only for you. Let me give you just one instance of Maude's inhuman sagacity. Maude named the tools. It was Maude who thought of calling the rattail file a rattail file. It was Maude who christened the needle-nose pliers. Maude named the rasp. Think of it. What else could a rasp be but a rasp? Maude in her wisdom went right to the point, and called it* rasp. *It was Maude who named the maul. Similarly the sledge, the wedge, the ball-peen hammer, the adz, the shim, the hone, the strop. The handsaw, the hacksaw, the bucksaw, and the fretsaw were named by Maude, peering into each saw and intuiting at once its specialness. The scratch awl, the scuffle hoe, the prick punch and the countersink—I could go on and on. The tools came to Maude, tool by tool in a long respectful line, she gave them their names. The vise. The gimlet. The cold chisel. The reamer, the router, the gouge. The plumb bob. How could she have thought up the rough justice of these wonderful cognomens? Looking lan-guidly at a pair of tin snips, and then deciding to call them* tin snips—*what a burst of glory! And I haven't even cited the bush hook, the grass snath, or the plumber's snake, or the C-clamp, or the nippers, or the scythe. What a tall achievement, naming the tools! And this is just one of Maude's contributions to our worldly estate, there are others. What delights will come crowding,"* Mrs. Davis sang to me, *"delight upon delight, when the epithalamium is ground out by the hundred organ grinders who are Maude's constant attendants, on that good-quality day of her own choosing, which you have desperately desired all your lean life, only you weren't aware of it until I, your dear friend, pointed it out. And Maude is young but not too young,"* Mrs. Davis sang to me, *"she is not too old either, she is just right and she is waiting for you with her tawny limbs and horse sense, when you receive Maude's nod your future and your past will begin."*

There was a pause, or pall.

"Is that true," I asked, "that song?"

"It is a metaphor," said Mrs. Davis, "it has metaphorical truth."

"And the end of the mechanical age," I said, "is that a metaphor?"

"The end of the mechanical age," said Mrs. Davis, "is in my judgment an actuality straining to become a metaphor. One must wish it luck, I suppose. One must cheer it on. Intellectual rigor demands that we give these damned metaphors every chance, even if they are inimical to personal well-being and comfort. We have a duty to understand everything, whether we like it or not—a duty I would scant if I could." At that moment the water jumped into the boat and sank us.

At the wedding Mrs. Davis spoke to me kindly.

"Tom," she said, "you are not Ralph, but you are all that is around at the moment. I have taken in the whole horizon with a single sweep of my practiced eye, no giant figure looms there and that is why I have decided to marry you, temporarily, with Jake gone and an age ending. It will be a marriage of convenience all right, and when Ralph comes, or Maude nods, then our arrangement will automatically self-destruct, like the tinted bubble that it is. You were very kind and considerate, when we were drying out, in the tree, and I appreciated that. That counted for something. Of course kindness and consideration are not what the great songs, the Ralph-song and the Maude-song, promise. They are merely flaky substitutes for the terminal experience. I realize that and want you to realize it. I want to be straight with you. That is one of the most admirable things about me, that I am always straight with people, from the sweet beginning to the bitter end. Now I will return to the big house where my handmaidens will proceed with the robing of the bride."

It was cool in the meadow by the river, the meadow Mrs. Davis had selected for the travesty, I walked over to the tree under which my friend Blackie was standing, he was the best man, in a sense.

"This disgusts me," Blackie said, "this hollow pretense and empty sham and I had to come all the way from Chicago."

God came to the wedding and stood behind a tree with just part of His effulgence showing, I wondered whether He was planning to bless this makeshift construct with His grace, or not. It's hard to imagine what He was thinking of in the beginning when He planned everything that was ever going to happen, planned everything exquisitely right down to the tiniest detail such as what I was thinking at this very moment, my thought about His thought, planned the end of the mechanical age and detailed the new age to follow, and then the bride emerged from the house with her train, all ocher in color and very lovely.

"And do you, Anne," the minister said, "promise to make whatever mutually satisfactory accommodations necessary to reduce tensions and arrive at whatever previously agreed-upon goals both parties have harmoniously set in the appropriate planning sessions?"

"I do," said Mrs. Davis.

"And do you, Thomas, promise to explore all differences thoroughly with patience and inner honesty ignoring no fruitful avenues of discussion and seeking at all times to achieve rapprochement while eschewing advantage in conflict situations?"

"Yes," I said.

"Well, now we are married," said Mrs. Davis, "I think I will retain my present name if you don't mind, I have always been Mrs. Davis and your name is a shade graceless, no offense, dear."

"O.K.," I said.

Then we received the congratulations and good wishes of the guests, who were mostly employees of the Mexican restaurant, Raul was there and Consuelo, Pedro, and Pepe came crowding around with outstretched hands and Blackie came crowding around with outstretched hands, God was standing behind the caterer's tables looking at the enchiladas and chalupas and chile con queso and chicken mole as if He had never seen such things before but that was hard to believe.

I started to speak to Him as all of the world's great religions with a few exceptions urge, from the heart, I started to say "Lord, Little Father of the Poor, and all that, I was just wondering now that an age, the mechanical age, is ending and a new age beginning or so they say, I was just wondering if You could give me a hint, sort of, not a Sign, I'm not asking for a Sign, but just the barest hint as to whether what we have been told about Your nature and our nature is, forgive me and I know how You feel about doubt or rather what we have been told you feel about it, but if You could just let drop the slightest indication as to whether what we have been told is authentic or just a bunch of apocryphal heterodoxy—"

But He had gone away with an insanely beautiful smile on His lighted countenance, gone away to read the meters and get a line on the efficacy of grace in that area, I surmised, I couldn't blame Him, my question had not been so very elegantly put, had I been able to express it mathematically He would have been more interested, maybe, but I have never been able to express anything mathematically.

After the marriage Mrs. Davis explained marriage to me.

Marriage, she said, an institution deeply enmeshed with the mechanical age.

Pairings smiled upon by law were but reifications of the laws of mechanics, inspired by unions of a technical nature, such as nut with bolt, wood with wood screw, aircraft with Plane-Mate.

Permanence or impermanence of the bond a function of (1) materials and (2) technique.

Growth of literacy a factor, she said.

Growth of illiteracy also.

The center will not hold if it has been spot-welded by an operator whose deepest concern is not with the weld but with his lottery ticket.

God interested only in grace—keeping things humming.

Blackouts, brownouts, temporary dimmings of household illumination all portents not of Divine displeasure but of Divine indifference to executive-development programs at middle-management levels.

He likes to get out into the field Himself, she said. With His flashlight. He is doing the best He can.

We two, she and I, no exception to general ebb/flow of world juice and its concomitant psychological effects, she said.

Bitter with the sweet, she said.

After the explanation came the divorce.

"Will you be wanting to contest the divorce?" I asked Mrs. Davis.

"I think not," she said calmly, "although I suppose one of us should, for the fun of the thing. An uncontested divorce always seems to me contrary to the spirit of divorce."

"That is true," I said, "I have had the same feeling myself, not infrequently."

After the divorce the child was born. We named him A.F. of L. Davis and sent him to that part of Russia where people live to be one hundred and ten years old. He is living there still, probably, growing in wisdom and beauty. Then we shook hands, Mrs. Davis and I, and she set out Ralphward, and I, Maudeward, the glow of hope not yet extinguished, the fear of pall not yet triumphant, standby generators ensuring the flow of grace to all of God's creatures at the end of the mechanical age.

1977

AUDRE LORDE
1934–1992

Audre Lorde, a black lesbian feminist warrior poet, was the youngest of three daughters born to Linda and Frederic Byron Lorde, who immigrated to New York City from Granada, the West Indies. Lorde's parents came to the United States with two plans. First they hoped to reap the financial rewards of hard work, and then they planned to return to their island home in grand style. But with the stock market crash of 1929, they were forced to abandon both dreams.

As a child, Lorde was inarticulate; in fact, she didn't speak until she was five years old. Even when she began talking, she spoke in poetry; that is, she would recite a poem in order to express herself. Hence, poetry literally became her language of communication. She believed that "the sensual content of life was masked and cryptic, but attended in well-coded phrases." She also learned to see herself as "a reflection of [her] mother's secret poetry as well as of her hidden anger." Giving expression to this reflection was the impetus for much of her work.

Lorde attended Hunter High School, received a B.A. in 1959 from Hunter College, and earned her M.L.S. in 1961 from Columbia University. In 1962 she married Edwin Ashley Rollins, with whom she had two children, Elizabeth and Jonathan. The marriage ended in divorce. In 1968 Lorde decided to become a full-time poet, leaving her job as head librarian of the City University of New York to become a poet-in-residence at Tougaloo College in Mississippi. Before her death, Lorde was Poet and Professor of English at Hunter College of the City University of New York.

Lorde insisted that she wrote to fulfill her responsibility "to speak the truth as [she felt] it, and to attempt to speak it with as much precision and beauty as possible." She described her life's work in terms of survival and teaching, two themes that dominate her prose and verse. Her power and high productivity arose from her living out these ambitions by confronting her own mortality, her own fear, and the opposition of those who tried to silence her.

All of her work resonates with courage, as she advises us "Not to be afraid of difference. To be real, tough, loving." "Even if you are afraid," she adds, "do it anyway because we learn to work when we are tired, so we can learn to work when we are afraid." In Lorde's later works, her vision arises from celebrating the legends of strong black women, especially her mother. In *Zami: A New Spelling of My Name*, she combines autobiography, history, and myth to create a new literary form that she calls "biomythography." *Zami* and *Our Dead behind Us*, in particular, signify the "strong triad of grandmother mother daughter" and "re-create in words the women who helped give [her] substance." They are her "mattering core," invigorating Lorde's visions of life and art with power.

Claudia Tate
George Washington University

PRIMARY WORKS

The First Cities, 1970; *Cables to Rage*, 1973; *From a Land Where Other People Live*, 1973 (nominated for the National Book Award in 1974); *New York Head Shop and Museum*, 1974; *Coal*, 1976; *Between Ourselves*, 1976; *The Black Unicorn*, 1978; *The Erotic as Power*, 1978; *The Cancer Journals*, 1980 (received a 1981 Book Award from the American Library Association Gay Caucus); *Zami: A New Spelling of My Name*, 1982; *Chosen Poems: Old and New*, 1982; *Sister Outsider*, 1984; *Our Dead behind Us*, 1986; *Apartheid USA*, 1986; *I Am Your Sister*, 1986; *Need: A Chorale for Black Woman Voices*, 1990; *A Burst of Light: Essays*, 1992; *Undersong: Chosen Poems, Old and New*, 1992; *The Marvelous Arithmetics of Distance*, 1993; *The Collected Poems*, 1997.

Power

The difference between poetry and rhetoric
is being
ready to kill
yourself
instead of your children.   5

I am trapped on a desert of raw gunshot wounds
and a dead child dragging his shattered black
face off the edge of my sleep

blood from his punctured cheeks and shoulders
is the only liquid for miles and my stomach   10
churns at the imagined taste while
my mouth splits into dry lips
without loyalty or reason
thirsting for the wetness of his blood
as it sinks into the whiteness   15
of the desert where I am lost
without imagery or magic
trying to make power out of hatred and destruction
trying to heal my dying son with kisses
only the sun will bleach his bones quicker.   20

The policeman who shot down a 10-year-old in Queens
stood over the boy with his cop shoes in childish blood
and a voice said "Die you little motherfucker" and
there are tapes to prove that. At his trial
this policeman said in his own defense   25
"I didn't notice the size or nothing else
only the color," and
there are tapes to prove that, too.

Today that 37-year-old white man with 13 years of police forcing
has been set free   30
by 11 white men who said they were satisfied
justice had been done
and one black woman who said
"They convinced me" meaning
they had dragged her 4′10″ black woman's frame   35
over the hot coals of four centuries of white male approval
until she let go the first real power she ever had
and lined her own womb with cement
to make a graveyard for our children.

I have not been able to touch the destruction within me.   40
But unless I learn to use
the difference between poetry and rhetoric
my power too will run corrupt as poisonous mold
or lie limp and useless as an unconnected wire
and one day I will take my teenaged plug   45
and connect it to the nearest socket
raping an 85-year-old white woman
who is somebody's mother
and as I beat her senseless and set a torch to her bed
a greek chorus will be singing in 3/4 time   50
"Poor thing. She never hurt a soul. What beasts they are."

1978

Never Take Fire from a Woman

My sister and I
have been raised to hate
genteelly
each other's silences
sear up our tongues   5
like flame
we greet each other
with respect
meaning
from a watchful distance   10
while we dream of lying
in the tender of passion
to drink from a woman
who smells like love.

1978

The Art of Response

The first answer was incorrect
the second was
sorry   the third trimmed its toenails
on the Vatican steps
the fourth went mad   5
the fifth
nursed a grudge until it bore twins
that drank poisoned grape juice in Jonestown
the sixth   wrote a book about it
the seventh   10
argued a case before the Supreme Court
against taxation on Girl Scout Cookies
the eighth held a news conference
while four Black babies
and one other   picketed New York City   15
for a hospital bed to die in
the ninth and tenth swore
Revenge on the Opposition
and the eleventh dug their graves
next to Eternal Truth   20
the twelfth
processed funds from a Third World country
that provides doctors for Central Harlem
the thirteenth
refused   25

the fourteenth sold cocaine and shamrocks
near a toilet in the Big Apple circus
the fifteenth
changed the question.

1986

Stations

Some women love
to wait
for life   for a ring
in the June light   for a touch
of the sun to heal them   for another   5
woman's voice   to make them whole
to untie their hands
put words in their mouths
form to their passages   sound
to their screams for   some other sleeper   10
to remember   their future   their past.

Some women wait for their right
train   in the wrong station
in the alleys of morning
for the noon to holler   15
the night come down.

Some women wait for love
to rise up
the child of their promise
to gather from earth   20
what they do not plant
to claim pain for labor
to become
the tip of an arrow   to aim
at the heart of now   25
but it never stays.

Some women wait for visions
that do not return
where they were not welcome
naked   30
for invitations to places
they always wanted
to visit
to be repeated.

Some women wait for themselves   35
around the next corner
and call the empty spot peace
but the opposite of living
is only not living
and the stars do not care.   40

Some women wait for something
to change   and nothing
does change
so they change
themselves.   45

                                                                1986

The Master's Tools Will Never Dismantle the Master's House[1]

I agreed to take part in a New York University Institute for the Humanities
conference a year ago, with the understanding that I would be commenting
upon papers dealing with the role of difference within the lives of american
women: difference of race, sexuality, class, and age. The absence of these
considerations weakens any feminist discussion of the personal and the
political.

It is a particular academic arrogance to assume any discussion of feminist theory without examining our many differences, and without a significant input from poor women, Black and Third World women, and lesbians.
And yet, I stand here as a Black lesbian feminist, having been invited to
comment within the only panel at this conference where the input of Black
feminists and lesbians is represented. What this says about the vision of this
conference is sad, in a country where racism, sexism, and homophobia are
inseparable. To read this program is to assume that lesbian and Black
women have nothing to say about existentialism, the erotic, women's culture and silence, developing feminist theory, or heterosexuality and power.
And what does it mean in personal and political terms when even the two
Black women who did present here were literally found at the last hour?
What does it mean when the tools of a racist patriarchy are used to examine
the fruits of that same patriarchy? It means that only the most narrow
perimeters of change are possible and allowable.

The absence of any consideration of lesbian consciousness or the consciousness of Third World women leaves a serious gap within this conference and within the papers presented here. For example, in a paper on

[1]Comments at "The Personal and the Political
Panel," Second Sex Conference, New York,
September 29, 1979.

material relationships between women, I was conscious of an either/or model of nurturing which totally dismissed my knowledge as a Black lesbian. In this paper there was no examination of mutuality between women, no systems of shared support, no interdependence as exists between lesbians and women-identified women. Yet it is only in the patriarchal model of nurturance that women "who attempt to emancipate themselves pay perhaps too high a price for the results," as this paper states.

For women, the need and desire to nurture each other is not pathological but redemptive, and it is within that knowledge that our real power is rediscovered. It is this real connection which is so feared by a patriarchal world. Only within a patriarchal structure is maternity the only social power open to women.

Interdependency between women is the way to a freedom which allows the *I* to *be*, not in order to be used, but in order to be creative. This is a difference between the passive *be* and the active *being*.

Advocating the mere tolerance of difference between women is the grossest reformism. It is a total denial of the creative function of difference in our lives. Difference must be not merely tolerated, but seen as a fund of necessary polarities between which our creativity can spark like a dialectic. Only then does the necessity for interdependency become unthreatening. Only within that interdependency of different strengths, acknowledged and equal, can the power to seek new ways of being in the world generate, as well as the courage and sustenance to act where there are no charters.

Within the interdependence of mutual (nondominant) differences lies that security which enables us to descend into the chaos of knowledge and return with true visions of our future, along with the concomitant power to effect those changes which can bring that future into being. Difference is that raw and powerful connection from which our personal power is forged.

As women, we have been taught either to ignore our differences, or to view them as causes for separation and suspicion rather than as forces for change. Without community there is no liberation, only the most vulnerable and temporary armistice between an individual and her oppression. But community must not mean a shedding of our differences, nor the pathetic pretense that these differences do not exist.

Those of us who stand outside the circle of this society's definition of acceptable women; those of us who have been forged in the crucibles of difference—those of us who are poor, who are lesbians, who are Black, who are older—know that *survival is not an academic skill*. It is learning how to stand alone, unpopular and sometimes reviled, and how to make common cause with those others identified as outside the structures in order to define and seek a world in which we can all flourish. It is learning how to take our differences and make them strengths. *For the master's tools will never dismantle the master's house*. They may allow us temporarily to beat him at his own game, but they will never enable us to bring about genuine change. And this fact is only threatening to those women who still define the master's house as their only source of support.

Poor women and women of Color know there is a difference between the daily manifestations of marital slavery and prostitution because it is our daughters who line 42nd Street. If white american feminist theory need not deal with the differences between us, and the resulting difference in our oppressions, then how do you deal with the fact that the women who clean your houses and tend your children while you attend conferences on feminist theory are, for the most part, poor women and women of Color? What is the theory behind racist feminism?

In a world of possibility for us all, our personal visions help lay the groundwork for political action. The failure of academic feminists to recognize difference as a crucial strength is a failure to reach beyond the first patriarchal lesson. In our world, divide and conquer must become define and empower.

Why weren't other women of Color found to participate in this conference? Why were two phone calls to me considered a consultation? Am I the only possible source of names of Black feminists? And although the Black panelist's paper ends on an important and powerful connection of love between women, what about interracial cooperation between feminists who don't love each other?

In academic feminist circles, the answer to these questions is often, "We did not know who to ask." But that is the same evasion of responsibility, the same cop-out, that keeps Black women's art out of women's exhibitions, Black women's work out of most feminist publications except for the occasional "Special Third World Women's Issue," and Black women's texts off your reading lists. But as Adrienne Rich pointed out in a recent talk, white feminists have educated themselves about such an enormous amount over the past ten years, how come you haven't also educated yourselves about Black women and the differences between us—white and Black—when it is key to our survival as a movement?

Women of today are still being called upon to stretch across the gap of male ignorance and to educate men as to our existence and our needs. This is an old and primary tool of all oppressors to keep the oppressed occupied with the master's concerns. Now we hear that it is the task of women of Color to educate white women—in the face of tremendous resistance—as to our existence, our differences, our relative roles in our joint survival. This is a diversion of energies and a tragic repetition of racist patriarchal thought.

Simone de Beauvoir once said: "It is in the knowledge of the genuine conditions of our lives that we must draw our strength to live and our reasons for acting."

Racism and homophobia are real conditions of all our lives in this place and time. *I urge each one of us here to reach down into that deep place of knowledge inside herself and touch that terror and loathing of any difference that lives there. See whose face it wears.* Then the personal as the political can begin to illuminate all our choices.

1979

MICHAEL S. HARPER
B. 1938

The poetry of Michael S. Harper resists easy categorization. Alternately metaphysical and reflective, historical and biographical, musical and autobiographical, Harper's poetry demonstrates a "both/and" sensibility. He views poetry as a place where "the microcosm and the cosmos are united." Harper's poetic project occurs, then, in a conceptual space where he maintains the sacred nature of speech as a form of human connection, evidenced by his assertion that "the tongue is the customer of the ear." Harper's work is oriented toward performance. His poems are heavily indebted to African American musical traditions such as jazz and the blues, for he is interested above all in the ways we improvise on the themes that compose human experience.

Born in Brooklyn, Harper spent the first thirteen years of his life in New York before his family relocated to Los Angeles. His father worked as a post office supervisor, his mother as a medical stenographer. Growing up in the 1940s and 1950s, Harper experienced the great cultural and artistic vitality manifested at that time in the African American community: Jackie Robinson's entry into major-league baseball, the music of Billie Holiday (she played piano in the Harper home), the birth and growth of bebop, and the boxing prowess of Sugar Ray Robinson. Harper's poetry often celebrates African American examples of artistic and athletic excellence.

After graduating from high school, Harper continued his education at Los Angeles State College and later the University of Iowa, where he received an M.A. in English and did work at the Iowa Writer's Workshop. But he claims that his education also took place at the facing table in the post office, where he worked full-time to put himself through college. It was there that he encountered black men and women trained as doctors, lawyers, and teachers whose race made the post office the only place they could find employment.

Harper is the author of many collections of poems, two of which, *Dear John, Dear Coltrane* (1970) and *Images of Kin* (1977), have been nominated for the National Book Award. He is coeditor of a critically acclaimed anthology, *Chant of Saints* (1979), and is responsible for bringing poet Sterling A. Brown's *Collected Poems* into print. Harper's books offer the reader a pantheon of heroes and heroines and a variety of geographical settings (often portraying aspects of Harper's travels through Mexico and West and South Africa, as well as New England and the American South) that demonstrate his affinity for different personas and idioms, each of which allows him to create modes of address that call for a more cohesive sensibility.

Harper's poems also explore his connections to other artists—jazz saxophonists John Coltrane and Charlie Parker and writers Ralph Ellison, Sterling Brown, Robert Hayden, and James Wright—and what they have taught him about the inherent responsibility of survival (a subject he has confronted in poems that concern the deaths of two of his children at birth and, more recently, of his brother). They provide models for his own poetic expressions.

Jazz provides the "architectonic impulse" that informs the structures of his poems. The writers offer models of enduring craft and seriousness. All of these heroes exemplify the concept of modality that runs through the Harper oeuvre. It represents, in part, the act of resisting the Western impulse to compartmentalize knowledge and experience and thus culture as well.

Herman Beavers
University of Pennsylvania

PRIMARY WORKS

Dear John, Dear Coltrane, 1970; *History Is Your Own Heartbeat,* 1971; *Photographs: Negatives; History as Apple Tree,* 1972; *Song: I Want a Witness,* 1972; *Debridement,* 1973; *Nightmare Begins Responsibility,* 1975; *Images of Kin,* 1977; *Healing Song for the Inner Ear,* 1985; *Honorable Amendments,* 1995; *Songlines in Michaeltree,* 2000.

Song: I Want a Witness

Blacks in frame houses
call to the helicopters,
their antlered arms
spinning; jeeps pad
these glass-studded streets;   5
on this hill are tanks painted gold.
Our children sing
spirituals of *Motown,*
idioms these streets suckled
on a southern road.   10
This scene is about power,
terror, producing
love and pain and pathology;
in an army of white dust,
blacks here to *testify*   15
and *testify,* and *testify,*
and *redeem,* and *redeem,*
in black smoke coming,
as they wave their arms,
as they wave their tongues.   20

1972

Nightmare Begins Responsibility

I place these numbed wrists to the pane
watching white uniforms whisk over
him in the tube-kept
prison

fear what they will do in experiment   5
watch my gloved stickshifting gasolined hands
breathe *boxcar-information-please* infirmary tubes
distrusting white-pink mending paperthin
silkened end hairs, distrusting tubes
shrunk in his *trunk-skincapped*   10
shaven head, in thighs
distrusting-white-hands-picking-baboon-light
on this son who will not make his second night
of this wardstrewn intensive airpocket
where his father's asthmatic   15
hymns of *night-train*, train done gone
his mother can only know that he has flown
up into essential calm unseen corridor
going boxscarred home, *mamaborn, sweetsonchild*
gonedowntown into *researchtestingwarehousebatteryacid*   20
mama-son-done-gone/me telling her 'nother
train tonight, no music, no breathstroked
heartbeat in my infinite distrust of them:

and of my distrusting self
white-doctor-who-breathed-for-him-all-night   25
say it for two sons gone,
say nightmare, say it loud
panebreaking heartmadness:
nightmare begins responsibility.

                                                                               1975

Here Where Coltrane Is

Soul and race
are private dominions,
memories and modal
songs, a tenor blossoming,
which would paint suffering   5
a clear color but is not in
this Victorian house
without oil in zero degree
weather and a forty-mile-an-hour wind;
it is all a well-knit family: 10
a love supreme.
Oak leaves pile up on walkway
and steps, catholic as apples
in a special mist of clear white
children who love my children.   15

I play "Alabama"
on a warped record player
skipping the scratches
on your faces over the fibrous
conical hairs of plastic   20
under the wooden floors.

Dreaming on a train from New York
to Philly, you hand out six
notes which become an anthem
to our memories of you: 25
oak, birch, maple,
apple, cocoa, rubber.
For this reason Martin is dead;
for this reason Malcolm is dead;
for this reason Coltrane is dead;   30
in the eyes of my first son are the browns
of these men and their music.

                                                              1977

Camp Story

I look over the old photos
for the US Hotel fire,
1900 Saratoga Springs,
where your grandfather
was chef on loan   5
from Catskill
where you were born.

The grapes from his arbor
sing in my mouth:
the smoke from the trestle   10
of his backyard,
the engine so close
to the bedroom
I can almost touch it,
make bricks from the yards   15
of perfection,
the clear puddles from the Hudson River,
where you would make change
at the dayline,
keep the change from the five   20
Jackleg Diamonds would leave
on the counter top or the stool.

Where is the CCC camp
you labored in
to send the money home to the family,   25
giving up your scholarship
so you could save the family
homestead from the banks of the river.

All across America the refugees
find homes in these camps   30
and are made to eat
at a table of liberty
you could have had
if you could not spell
or count, or keep time.   35

I see you, silent, wordfully
talking to my brother, Jonathan,
as he labors on the chromatic
respirator; you kiss his brown
temple where his helmet left   40
a slight depression
near a neat line of stitches
at the back of his skull.

As he twitches to chemicals
the Asian nurses catheter   45
into the cavities and caves
of his throat and lungs:
the doctor repeats the story
of his chances.

                                                    1985

Ojibway Writing and Activism in the Red Power Years

IN THE YEARS SURROUNDING AND FOLLOWING WORLD WAR II, U.S. INDIAN POLICY was focused on two intersecting assimilation policies: termination and relocation. Termination was a policy whereby the U.S. government unilaterally cut political ties with a number of smaller tribes, stripped them of treaty rights and protections, and undermined the social and familial structures that had kept many of these communities stable during otherwise difficult struggles against ever-encroaching demands on their lands and resources. Relocation involved encouraging rural and reservation Indian individuals and families to move to urban areas for employment and educational opportunities. The promised opportunities rarely materialized; many of the families struggled to find adequate jobs and housing in an unfamiliar and often racist environment that was disconnected from the kinship networks and lands they knew.

Cities were not unfamiliar to Native peoples in the Americas—as demonstrated by the grandeur of great city-states such as Cahokia, Tenochtitlán, and Qosqo (Cuzco), as well as smaller but similarly significant urban centers both pre- and post-European invasion—and there were small but continuous populations in all major cities in the hemisphere. What distinguished the relocation era was the focused and deliberate public policy that brought together American Indians from many different tribal nations in American cities such as San Francisco, Los Angeles, Denver, Minneapolis–St. Paul, and Chicago. Facing white hostility and limited access to economic and political resources, American Indian families developed supportive, pantribal service organizations, social and employment networks, religious groups, and activist communities that reached across linguistic, cultural, ceremonial, and political differences to build stronger communities and offer resources and encouragement. By the 1960s, urban Indian communities were well established in cities across the United States. Some families remained connected to their rural and reservation homes and families; others became increasingly separated and identified not with tribally specific communities but with a developing pan-Native culture that drew from shared traditions as well as generalized American expectations of Indian identity.

As the burgeoning civil rights movement of the 1960s and '70s brought growing attention to African American disenfranchisement, activism in response to the Vietnam War made many Americans increasingly critical of the uses and abuses of U.S. military power while feminist concerns about sexism and gender inequality found a ready and growing audience in both activist circles and, to varying degrees, in mainstream media and politics. Young American Indians were fully part of this heady mix of cultural critique, experimentation, and rebellion and brought their own concerns to the broader social movement. Urban Indians and Native veterans were particularly prominent in the growing anger against entrenched attitudes and policies that discriminated against Native peoples, here and elsewhere in the world. Indian activists not only critiqued the discriminatory policies that had led to the termination and relocation periods, but also challenged the longer brutal history of U.S. colonialism against American Indian nations.

A number of political groups emerged from these activist currents, but prominent among them was the American Indian Movement (AIM), founded in the late 1960s by members of the Minneapolis Indian community, many of whom were Ojibways. AIM members engaged in both behind-the-scenes and high-profile interventions to protect Indians and their rights, while also bringing public attention to historical and continuing wrongs against Native peoples. Among their more dramatic actions were the occupation of the federal offices of the Bureau of Indian Affairs (1971); a gathering in Washington, D.C., to protest the "Trail of Broken Treaties" (1972); and, in 1973, an armed confrontation with U.S. federal agents on the Pine Ridge Reservation, which began when AIM members were asked by Oglala Lakota tribal members to intervene against the contested leadership of chief Dick Wilson. In the 1980s and '90s, AIM and other organizations focused much of their more public work on treaty rights activism, especially regarding fishing and harvesting rights around the Great Lakes.

The Red Power movement—AIM and beyond—was deeply influenced by, but also distinct from, other social justice movements of the time, drawing on the revolutionary and liberationist rhetoric of the time to advance American Indian land, treaty, and political concerns. Many prominent Native scholars, writers, activists, and leaders would be deeply influenced by the ideas that emerged from this period, including legal scholar Vine Deloria, Jr., Congressman Ben Nighthorse Campbell, Cherokee Nation principal chief Wilma Mankiller, and poet Simon J. Ortiz. Although AIM and other primarily urban-founded activist organizations did not speak for all Indian people or communities, especially in rural areas, they nevertheless brought important attention to the concerns of American Indian peoples and a greater sense of shared solidarity among Indians of diverse tribal backgrounds.

That diversity, however, can obscure the substantial impact that one specific culture has had on American Indian politics, then and now. While not the only tribal nation to be influential in Red Power activism, the Ojibways and their linguistic and cultural kin of the Great Lakes region and environs have been particularly prominent in this movement. Significant both historically and today among the Algonquian-speaking communities of the border regions between Canada and the United States, the Ojibways are also known by the plural Anishinaabeg, which includes other related peoples, such as the Odawas and Potawatomies, who with the Ojibways make up the Three Fires Confederacy. This influence is in part due to their historical prominence in the upper Midwest, where some of the most significant urban Indian populations later developed (notably in Minneapolis and Chicago) and where there continue to be numerous reservation communities. Various dialects of Anishinaabemowin are spoken throughout the region, both on reservations and in cities. Coming from scores of distinct communities, with tens of thousands of members in both the United States and Canada, there are perhaps more Ojibway educators, scholars, writers, and political leaders of local, national, and international reputation than from any other tribal nation in North America. Most of the founders of AIM were urban or mixed urban-reservation Ojibways, and their often very context-specific understanding of Indian identity had a profound influence on pan-Native identities and cultural expression, then and now. Many of today's most celebrated Native writers are Ojibway, albeit from very different and distinct communities, and they have brought their specific and highly influential aesthetic and ideological perspectives to the larger archive of North American indigenous literary expression.

This "In Focus" feature brings together a group of diverse Ojibway writers to comment on a more broadly pan-Native era in U.S. history—namely, the Red Power movement and its legacies. Some of these writings emerged from that period; others are more current and reflect back to that time, directly or more obliquely, from a more removed perspective. Poetry and short fiction combine with autobiography, reportage, creative nonfiction, and an excerpt from a novel. Whether in debate, conversation, or reflection, all these selections by contemporary Ojibway writers engage the rich and complicated period of Native political activism. They offer rich and often powerful commentary on the lives, concerns, and commitments of American Indian people during a time of immense personal and social change.

■ DIANE BURNS ■
1957–2006

Sure You Can Ask Me a Personal Question

How do you do?
No, I'm not Chinese.
No, not Spanish.
No, I'm American Indi—uh, Native American.
No, not from India.   5
No, we're not extinct.
No, not Navajo.
No, not Sioux.
Yes, Indian.
Oh, so you've had an Indian friend?   10
   That close.
Oh, so you've had an Indian lover?
   That tight.
Oh, so you've had an Indian servant?
   That much.   15

Oh, so that's where you got those high cheekbones.
Your great-grandmother, eh?
Hair down to there?
Let me guess—Cherokee?
Oh, an Indian Princess.   20
No, I didn't make it rain tonight.
No, I don't know where you can get Navajo rugs real cheap.
No, I don't know where you can get peyote.
No, I didn't make this—I bought it at Bloomingdale's.
Yes, some of us drink too much.   25
Some of us can't drink enuf.
This ain't no stoic look.
This is my face.

                                                                 1989

LOUISE ERDRICH
B. 1954

The Red Convertible: Lyman Lamartine

from Love Medicine

I was the first one to drive a convertible on my reservation. And of course it was red, a red Olds. I owned that car along with my brother Henry Junior. We owned it together until his boots filled with water on a windy night and he bought out my share. Now Henry owns the whole car, and his youngest brother Lyman (that's myself), Lyman walks everywhere he goes.

How did I earn enough money to buy my share in the first place? My own talent was I could always make money. I had a touch for it, unusual in a Chippewa. From the first I was different that way, and everyone recognized it. I was the only kid they let in the American Legion Hall to shine shoes, for example, and one Christmas I sold spiritual bouquets for the mission door to door. The nuns let me keep a percentage. Once I started, it seemed the more money I made the easier the money came. Everyone encouraged it. When I was fifteen I got a job washing dishes at the Joliet Café, and that was where my first big break happened.

It wasn't long before I was promoted to bussing tables, and then the short-order cook quit and I was hired to take her place. No sooner than you know it I was managing the Joliet. The rest is history. I went on managing. I soon became part owner, and of course there was no stopping me then. It wasn't long before the whole thing was mine.

After I'd owned the Joliet for one year, it blew over in the worst tornado ever seen around here. The whole operation was smashed to bits. A total loss. The fryalator was up in a tree, the grill torn in half like it was paper. I was only sixteen. I had it all in my mother's name, and I lost it quick, but before I lost it I had every one of my relatives, and their relatives, to dinner, and I also bought that red Olds I mentioned, along with Henry.

The first time we saw it! I'll tell you when we first saw it. We had gotten a ride up to Winnipeg, and both of us had money. Don't ask me why, because we never mentioned a car or anything, we just had all our money. Mine was cash, a big bankroll from the Joliet's insurance. Henry had two checks—a week's extra pay for being laid off, and his regular check from the Jewel Bearing Plant.

We were walking down Portage anyway, seeing the sights, when we saw it. There it was, parked, large as life. Really as *if* it was alive. I thought of the word *repose*, because the car wasn't simply stopped, parked, or whatever. That car reposed, calm and gleaming, a FOR SALE sign in its left front window. Then, before we had thought it over at all, the car belonged to us and our pockets were empty. We had just enough money for gas back home.

We went places in that car, me and Henry. We took off driving all one whole summer. We started off toward the Little Knife River and Mandaree in Fort Berthold and then we found ourselves down in Wakpala somehow, and then suddenly we were over in Montana on the Rocky Boys, and yet the summer was not even half over. Some people hang on to details when they travel, but we didn't let them bother us and just lived our everyday lives here to there.

I do remember this one place with willows. I remember I laid under those trees and it was comfortable. So comfortable. The branches bent down all around me like a tent or a stable. And quiet, it was quiet, even though there was a powwow close enough so I could see it going on. The air was not too still, not too windy either. When the dust rises up and hangs in the air around the dancers like that, I feel good. Henry was asleep with his arms thrown wide. Later on, he woke up and we started driving again. We were somewhere in Montana, or maybe on the Blood Reserve—it could have been anywhere. Anyway it was where we met the girl.

All her hair was in buns around her ears, that's the first thing I noticed about her. She was posed alongside the road with her arm out, so we stopped. That girl was short, so short her lumber shirt looked comical on her, like a nightgown. She had jeans on and fancy moccasins and she carried a little suitcase.

"Hop on in," says Henry. So she climbs in between us.

"We'll take you home," I says. "Where do you live?"

"Chicken," she says.

"Where the hell's that?" I ask her.

"Alaska."

"Okay," says Henry, and we drive.

We got up there and never wanted to leave. The sun doesn't truly set there in summer, and the night is more a soft dusk. You might doze off, sometimes, but before you know it you're up again, like an animal in nature. You never feel like you have to sleep hard or put away the world. And things would grow up there. One day just dirt or moss, the next day flowers and long grass. The girl's name was Susy. Her family really took to us. They fed us and put us up. We had our own tent to live in by their house, and the kids would be in and out of there all day and night. They couldn't get over me and Henry being brothers, we looked so different. We told them we knew we had the same mother, anyway.

One night Susy came in to visit us. We sat around in the tent talking of this thing and that. The season was changing. It was getting darker by that time, and the cold was even getting just a little mean. I told her it was time for us to go. She stood up on a chair.

"You never seen my hair," Susy said.

That was true. She was standing on a chair, but still, when she unclipped her buns the hair reached all the way to the ground. Our eyes opened. You couldn't tell how much hair she had when it was rolled up so neatly. Then my brother Henry did something funny. He went up to the chair and said, "Jump on my shoulders." So she did that, and her hair reached down past his waist, and he started twirling, this way and that, so her hair was flung out from side to side.

"I always wondered what it was like to have long pretty hair," Henry says. Well we laughed. It was a funny sight, the way he did it. The next morning we got up and took leave of those people.

On to greener pastures, as they say. It was down through Spokane and across Idaho then Montana and very soon we were racing the weather right along under the Canadian border through Columbus, Des Lacs, and then we were in Bottineau County and soon home. We'd made most of the trip, that summer, without putting up the car hood at all. We got home just in time, it turned out, for the army to remember Henry had signed up to join it.

I don't wonder that the army was so glad to get my brother that they turned him into a Marine. He was built like a brick outhouse anyway. We liked to tease him that they really wanted him for his Indian nose. He had a nose big and sharp as a hatchet, like the nose on Red Tomahawk, the Indian who killed Sitting Bull, whose profile is on signs all along the North Dakota highways. Henry went off to training camp, came home once during Christmas, then the next thing you know we got an overseas letter from him. It was 1970, and he said he was stationed up in the northern hill country. Whereabouts I did not know. He wasn't such a hot letter writer, and only got off two before the enemy caught him. I could never keep it straight, which direction those good Vietnam soldiers were from.

I wrote him back several times, even though I didn't know if those letters would get through. I kept him informed all about the car. Most of the time I had it up on blocks in the yard or half taken apart, because that long trip did a hard job on it under the hood.

I always had good luck with numbers, and never worried about the draft myself. I never even had to think about what my number was. But Henry was never lucky in the same way as me. It was at least three years before Henry came home. By then I guess the whole war was solved in the government's mind, but for him it would keep on going. In those years I'd put his car into almost perfect shape. I always thought of it as his car while he was gone, even though when he left he said, "Now it's yours," and threw me his key.

"Thanks for the extra key," I'd say. "I'll put it up in your drawer just in case I need it." He laughed.

When he came home, though, Henry was very different, and I'll say this: the change was no good. You could hardly expect him to change for the better, I know. But he was quiet, so quiet, and never comfortable sitting still anywhere but always up and moving around. I thought back to times we'd sat still for whole afternoons, never moving a muscle, just shifting our weight along the ground, talking to whoever sat with us, watching things. He'd always had a joke, then, too, and now you couldn't get him to laugh, or when he did it was more the sound of a man choking, a sound that stopped up the throats of other people around him. They got to leaving him alone most of the time, and I didn't blame them. It was a fact: Henry was jumpy and mean.

I'd bought a color TV set for my mom and the rest of us while Henry was away. Money still came very easy. I was sorry I'd ever bought it though, because of Henry. I was also sorry I'd bought color, because with black-and-white the pictures seem older and farther away. But what are you going to do? He sat in front of it, watching it, and that was the only time he was completely still. But it was the kind of stillness that you see in a rabbit when it freezes and before it will bolt. He was not easy. He sat in his chair gripping the armrests with all his might, as if the chair itself was moving at a high speed and if he let go at all he would rocket forward and maybe crash right through the set.

Once I was in the room watching TV with Henry and I heard his teeth click at something. I looked over, and he'd bitten through his lip. Blood was going down his chin. I tell you right then I wanted to smash that tube to pieces. I went over to it but Henry must have known what I was up to. He rushed from his chair and shoved me out of the way, against the wall. I told myself he didn't know what he was doing.

My mom came in, turned the set off real quiet, and told us she had made something for supper. So we went and sat down. There was still blood going down Henry's chin, but he didn't notice it and no one said anything, even though every time he took a bit of his bread his blood fell onto it until he was eating his own blood mixed in with the food.

While Henry was not around we talked about what was going to happen to him. There were no Indian doctors on the reservation, and my mom was afraid of trusting Old Man Pillager because he courted her long ago and was jealous of her husbands. He might take revenge through her son. We were afraid that if we brought Henry to a regular hospital they would keep him.

"They don't fix them in those places," Mom said; "they just give them drugs."

"We wouldn't get him there in the first place," I agreed, "so let's just forget about it."

Then I thought about the car.

Henry had not even looked at the car since he'd gotten home, though like I said, it was in tip-top condition and ready to drive. I thought the car might bring the old Henry back somehow. So I bided my time and waited for my chance to interest him in the vehicle.

One night Henry was off somewhere. I took myself a hammer. I went out to that car and I did a number on its underside. Whacked it up. Bent the tail pipe double. Ripped the muffler loose. By the time I was done with the car it looked worse than any typical Indian car that has been driven all its life on reservation roads, which they always say are like government promises—full of holes. It just about hurt me, I'll tell you that! I threw dirt in the carburetor and I ripped all the electric tape off the seats. I made it look just as beat up as I could. Then I sat back and waited for Henry to find it.

Still, it took him over a month. That was all right, because it was just getting warm enough, not melting, but warm enough to work outside.

"Lyman," he says, walking in one day, "that red car looks like shit."

"Well it's old," I says. "You got to expect that."

"No way!" says Henry, "That car's a classic! But you went and ran the piss right out of it, Lyman, and you know it don't deserve that. I kept that car in A-one shape. You don't remember. You're too young. But when I left, that car was running like a watch. Now I don't even know if I can get it to start again, let alone get it anywhere near its old condition."

"Well you try," I said, like I was getting mad, "but I say it's a piece of junk."

Then I walked out before he could realize I knew he'd strung together more than six words at once.

After that I thought he'd freeze himself to death working on that car. He was out there all day, and at night he rigged up a little lamp, ran a cord out the window, and had himself some light to see by while he worked. He was better than he had been before, but that's still not saying much. It was easier for him to do the things the rest of us did. He ate more slowly and didn't jump up and down during the meal to get this or that or look out the window. I put my hand in the back of the TV set, I admit, and fiddled around with it good, so that it was almost impossible now to get a clear picture. He didn't look at it very often anyway. He was always out with that car or going off to get parts for it. By the time it was really melting outside, he had it fixed.

I had been feeling down in the dumps about Henry around this time. We had always been together before. Henry and Lyman. But he was such a loner now that I didn't know how to take it. So I jumped at the chance one day when Henry seemed friendly. It's not that he smiled or anything. He just said, "Let's take that old shitbox for a spin." Just the way he said it made me think he could be coming around.

We went out to the car. It was spring. The sun was shining very bright. My only sister, Bonita, who was just eleven years old, came out and made us stand together for a picture. Henry leaned his elbow on the red car's windshield, and he took his other arm and put it over my shoulder, very carefully, as though it was heavy for him to lift and he didn't want to bring the weight down all at once.

"Smile," Bonita said, and he did.

That picture, I never look at it anymore. A few months ago, I don't know why, I got his picture out and tacked it on the wall. I felt good about Henry at the time, close to him. I felt good having his picture on the wall, until one night when I was looking at television. I was a little drunk and stoned. I looked up at the wall and Henry was staring at me. I don't know what it was, but his smile had changed, or maybe it was gone. All I know is I couldn't stay in the same room with that picture. I was shaking. I got up, closed the door, and went into the kitchen. A little later my friend Ray came over and we both went back into that room. We put the picture in a brown bag, folded the bag over and over tightly, then put it way back in a closet.

I still see that picture now, as if it tugs at me, whenever I pass that closet door. The picture is very clear in my mind. It was so sunny that day Henry had to squint against the glare. Or maybe the camera Bonita held flashed like a mirror, blinding him, before she snapped the picture. My face is right out in the sun, big and round. But he might have drawn back, because the shadows on his face are deep as holes. There are two shadows curved like little hooks around the ends of his smile, as if to frame it and try to keep it there—that one, first smile that looked like it might have hurt his face. He has his field jacket on and the worn-in clothes he'd come back in and kept wearing ever since. After Bonita took the picture, she went into the house and we got into the car. There was a full cooler in the trunk. We started off, east, toward Pembina and the Red River because Henry said he wanted to see the high water.

The trip over there was beautiful. When everything starts changing, drying up, clearing off, you feel like your whole life is starting. Henry felt it, too. The top was down and the car hummed like a top. He'd really put it back in shape, even the tape on the seats was very carefully put down and glued back in layers. It's not that he smiled again or even joked, but his face looked to me as if it was clear, more peaceful. It looked as though he wasn't thinking of anything in particular except the bare fields and windbreaks and houses we were passing.

The river was high and full of winter trash when we got there. The sun was still out, but it was colder by the river. There were still little clumps of dirty snow here and there on the banks. The water hadn't gone over the banks yet, but it would, you could tell. It was just at its limit, hard swollen glossy like an old gray scar. We made ourselves a fire, and we sat down and watched the current go. As I watched it I felt something squeezing inside me and tightening and trying to let go all at the same time. I knew I was not just feeling it myself; I knew I was feeling what Henry was going through at that moment. Except that I couldn't stand it, the closing and opening. I jumped to my feet. I took Henry by the shoulders and I started shaking him. "Wake up," I says, "wake up, wake up, wake up!" I didn't know what had come over me. I sat down beside him again.

His face was totally white and hard. Then it broke, like stones break all of a sudden when water boils up inside them.

"I know it," he says. "I know it. I can't help it. It's no use."

We start talking. He said he knew what I'd done with the car. It was obvious it had been whacked out of shape and not just neglected. He said he wanted to give the car to me for good now, it was no use. He said he'd fixed it just to give it back and I should take it.

"No way," I says, "I don't want it."

"That's okay," he says, "you take it."

"I don't want it, though," I says back to him, and then to emphasize, just to emphasize, you understand, I touch his shoulder. He slaps my hand off.

"Take that car," he says.

"No," I say, "make me," I say, and then he grabs my jacket and rips the arm loose. That jacket is a class act, suede with tags and zippers. I push Henry backwards, off the log. He jumps up and bowls me over. We go down in a clinch and come up swinging hard, for all we're worth, with our fists. He socks my jaw so hard I feel like it swings loose. Then I'm at his ribcage and land a good one under his chin so his head snaps back. He's dazzled. He looks at me and I look at him and then his eyes are full of tears and blood and at first I think he's crying. But no, he's laughing. "Ha! Ha!" he says. "Ha! Ha! Take good care of it."

"Okay," I says, "okay, no problem. Ha! Ha!"

I can't help it, and I start laughing, too. My face feels fat and strange, and after a while I get a beer from the cooler in the trunk, and when I hand it to Henry he takes his shirt and wipes my germs off. "Hoof-and-mouth disease," he says. For some reason this cracks me up, and so we're really laughing for a while, and then we drink all the rest of the beers one by one and throw them in the river and see how far, how fast, the current takes them before they fill up and sink.

"You want to go on back?" I ask after a while. "Maybe we could snag a couple nice Kashpaw girls."

He says nothing. But I can tell his mood is turning again.

"They're all crazy, the girls up here, every damn one of them."

"You're crazy too," I say, to jolly him up. "Crazy Lamartine boys!"

He looks as though he will take this wrong at first. His face twists, then clears, and he jumps up on his feet. "That's right!" he says. "Crazier'n hell. Crazy Indians!"

I think it's the old Henry again. He throws off his jacket and starts swinging his legs out from the knees like a fancy dancer. He's down doing something between a grouse dance and a bunny hop, no kind of dance I ever saw before, but neither has anyone else on all this green growing earth. He's wild. He wants to pitch whoopee! He's up and at me and all over. All this time I'm laughing so hard, so hard my belly is getting tied up in a knot.

"Got to cool me off!" he shouts all of a sudden. Then he runs over to the river and jumps in.

There's boards and other things in the current. It's so high. No sound comes from the river after the splash he makes, so I run right over. I look around. It's getting dark. I see he's halfway across the water already, and I know he didn't swim there but the current took him. It's far. I hear his voice, though, very clearly across it.

"My boots are filling," he says.

He says this in a normal voice, like he just noticed and he doesn't know what to think of it. Then he's gone. A branch comes by. Another branch. And I go in.

By the time I get out of the river, off the snag I pulled myself onto, the sun is down. I walk back to the car, turn on the high beams, and drive it up the bank. I put it in first gear and then I take my foot off the clutch. I get out, close the door, and watch it plow softly into the water. The headlights reach in as they go down, searching, still lighted even after the water swirls over the back end. I wait. The wires short out. It is all finally dark. And then there is only the water, the sound of it going and running and going and running and running.

1984

DENNIS BANKS
B. 1937
WITH RICHARD ERDOES
1912–2008

from **Ojibwa Warrior**

CHAPTER 4
Interlude

A reservation is a parcel of land inhabited by Indians and surrounded by thieves.

—GEN. WILLIAM TECUMSEH SHERMAN

The two years after I ran away from boarding school and came back to the rez was the one time I was really involved in the traditional life of my people. When I got back I was taken around and introduced to all my relatives, many of whom I had not seen for years. I met my cousins, Aunt Sarah's boys, and I joined her family. I stayed at Aunt Sarah's house and she and I became very close.

My first winter back was spent getting reacquainted with the reservation and the people, and with pitching in to help with the chores around the house. Before winter set in, we needed to chop a lot of wood, maybe five or six cords. Chopping wood was an endless chore. Wood was our only source of heat and fuel for cooking. We dragged in dry wood, sawed it up, chopped it into chunks, and stacked it by the house. In winter we'd get up around five every morning to get the fires going and start our chores. The house was a small, simple two-bedroom structure with a good-sized living room. With all of Aunt Sarah's family and me, we were pretty crowded. There were seven of us living together in that house, and I liked that. To me it meant a lot because I had a home and a family. Sometimes I even shared my bed with a cousin and experienced what sharing in a family meant.

That winter I also began to learn things from the older men on the rez. They taught me about the different trees, plants, and herbs. When spring came, I remembered the old natural rhythm of life—from sugaring in the early spring to the rice harvest in the fall. It all came back to me.

Along with those memories came the shock that I had forgotten most of my native Anishinabe language. At school, English overpowered everything—I had to think in English to avoid being punished for accidentally speaking in my own language. The suppression of our native languages was a tragedy that affected several generations of Indian children forced into the BIA boarding schools. It brought several tribal languages close to extinction. After all those years, when I listened to my relatives speaking our language, it touched a resonance in me. But most of it I couldn't understand. Grandpa Josh and Grandma Jenny would be talking in Indian and they'd ask me to say something, almost making fun of me. I'd say a word in English and then say it in Indian, and they laughed as they corrected me. Years later I tried to study my language but I never became fluent in it.

For a while I enrolled in the high school at Walker to get my diploma. It was not a BIA boarding institution, but a public school. Up to that time, I had only gone to school with Indian kids, never with white students. And on my first day there, I had an uneasy feeling that I had never experienced before. I was surrounded by white kids, and it made me uncomfortable. For the first time in my life I could sense that there was a difference between these students and me. They kept to themselves and excluded me from their discussions in the hallway or lunchroom. We had a lot of reservation kids at that school but only three were in my class. I didn't have any white friends at Walker. There was a wall between us and them.

I was still interested in sports and wanted to participate regardless of whether the other kids were white or Indian, but the racial segregation at Walker was not easy to avoid. The bus picked us Indian kids up every morning. A couple of times I missed the bus from the rez and had to walk the thirteen miles to school. One time in the winter I had to cross the lake. It was three miles across and I ran all the way. There were thin spots in the ice so it was a little scary but also exciting. Though I could not participate in school sports, I got plenty of exercise.

The first winter I stayed at Aunt Sarah's, I put in a trap line for rabbits. Every morning before I went to school I would go out and check the traps, which were about a mile from the house, and bring in whatever rabbits I found in the snares. Then I would go to school. When I came back I would check the traps again. I was getting five or six rabbits a day, which I would skin and dress myself. Or I would leave them outside in the cold where they wouldn't spoil.

There were usually three or four dogs or cats around, and by the time I got back with the rabbits, the dogs would be following me. One time I had seven or eight dogs after me, and one of them managed to grab a rabbit and run. I chased him then thought, "Well, he deserved it," and let him get away. All the dogs fought over that rabbit—it was a free-for-all with tremendous snarling, growling, and howling. When I cleaned the rabbits, I would throw scraps to the dogs and cats. The cats got all the guts. Sometimes we would cook the heads; sometimes the dogs got them. We had rabbit stew almost every night. That was my little contribution to the family, and it made me feel good.

I didn't get into trapping for muskrats because I did not have the big traps that needed to be set up in the water. I never trapped beavers because I felt they were more purposeful creatures; whereas the only purpose rabbits had was to be caught in my snares for the soup pot. I wanted to protect the beavers. I enjoyed watching them building their dams.

I remember tracking a porcupine once for about two miles, watching him crawl up a big tree. I told him not to worry. I didn't have the heart to shoot him. I once shot and killed a porcupine and still felt very badly about it. I left it there and kind of apologized for what I had done, but took a bag of quills from it because the women used them for decorative embroidery. Aunt Sarah had said, "You should have brought it home. We could have cooked it. Porcupine makes good eating." Until that time it had never occurred to me to be eating porcupine.

I hunted. Grandpa Josh taught me, "If you meet an owl or a fox when you start out on a hunt, it means bad luck. You might just as well go home. Never kill an animal wantonly. Don't say anything that could hurt the feelings of a deer. Don't boast, 'Today I'll bag two deer!' The Great Spirit who created the deer does not like it. Rather, sprinkle sacred tobacco around your kill and thank the deer for having given itself so that people may live."

Hunting is best when the leaves are falling and the deer are fat. When they held a deer fry, a family would invite everybody over for big cookouts. Always the dogs would be there. They lucked out every hunting season. We would have to hang deer and other game from high tree branches so that the dogs and cats could not get at it. They got enough scraps to gorge themselves without getting at the best parts.

Much later, when I came back from the military, the old happy hunting days were at an end. The BIA and the state began to regulate everything. Under Public Law 280, we had to take out fishing and hunting licenses and compete with the wealthy tourists who dominated what had been—for all our known history—our livelihood. Constantly we felt this oppressive federal presence and we resented it. Grandpa Drumbeater hated the BIA and insisted he would go on in his old accustomed way, never taking out a hunting or fishing license "like some goddam white tourist!" He flatly ignored the new law, and he looked down upon those who obeyed the white man's crazy regulations.

The sugaring season started around the end of March, when there was still lots of snow on the ground, and ended during the last days of April. Our family has its own maple grove we return to year after year, but the groves are not "owned." The concept of ownership, either of land or of whatever grows or lives upon it, is not part of what Native people believe. If one particular family has done its sugaring in one place for a generation, then others will not intrude into that place. But when a family does not do its sugaring there for a year or two, others can make their maple sugar there. The Drumbeater clan had a big sugar camp near Federal Dam. We had about one hundred and fifty trees to tap. Sugaring was part of our subsistence and livelihood.

During the first spring back on the rez, I spent two weeks at the sugar camp doing much the same thing I had done as a little kid before I was sent to boarding school. Remembering back to when I was a kid who was so proud to help, I thought about those early impressions of life. I collected the sap from one-gallon cans on the trees, emptied them into five-gallon buckets, and then I put the empty cans back on the trees. The older boys took the five-gallon buckets to where we had a big fire. Grandpa Josh was in charge of the big pot on that fire where sap boiled down into maple sugar. As children, we watched the boiling and bubbling as the syrup thickened, and we begged for a little curl of syrup on a piece of birch bark. We dropped it into the clean snow to turn it into snow candy. I recall Grandpa Josh telling me to put a pinch of tobacco on the fire before eating the year's first maple sugar, and to do the same before eating the first fish or wild rice of the season. So that was our sugar camp.

The year I returned to the sugar camp, I was the big boy and did the heavy work. I chopped the wood for the kettle fires, built lean-tos, hauled water, dragged around the full five-gallon buckets, and snared rabbits for our simple camp meals. I breathed in the unforgettable scent of the wood fires and the rich, mouthwatering aromas of good things bubbling in the big, soot-covered pots. I watched the women cooking every day—I liked to hang around them while they made pan bread and biscuits.

But the main reason for being there was syrup and sugar. The sap was collected, boiled, evaporated, and refined. It had to be closely watched while boiling. Just as soon as it began to "make eyes," it had to be taken off the fire and worked with a kind of wooden board that looks like a small canoe paddle. If you boil the sap, you get maple syrup; if you keep boiling it, you get sugar cakes that can be ground into sugar. In our homes we used this natural sugar.

We had to bundle up in the evenings because it was always very cold at that time of year. One thing I liked about our sugar camp was when we wrapped ourselves in blankets to go sit around the fire in the darkness, listening to the elders tell the old tales. There was always a lot of storytelling. Some of the old-timers told stories of how bears would come into the camp to lick sap from the trees. Then the men would put some sugar cakes well outside the camp so that if bears were attracted by the sweet smell of boiling sap, they would find these stashes of sugar cakes and not bother us. That was our offering to Brother Bear. It is strange how we coexisted out there, but that is how it was done. And I know if I ever again organize a sugar camp in the spring, I'll put out sugar cakes for the spirits and the bears. I have many good memories of those sugar camps—of the sugar, the snow, and the stories—to last me for the rest of my life. We usually stayed out there for about ten days after the sap began to run. Then everybody would put the cans back in the shack until the next year.

Last summer, some forty-five years after my first spring back on the rez, I went back there. I found our old one-gallon cans lying around, most of them rusted out. I took two home as a reminder of those long gone days. Families no longer camp out there. A few people still tap the trees, but they're no longer bothered by the men with their badges and green uniforms who came to the sugar camps. They swaggered around with their clipboards and told our families which trees we could tap, that only the trees they had marked were for us. They would ask how many gallons of sap we had and mumble something about taxes. They had not imposed taxes on us, not on the Drumbeaters, but it was the assumption of control over our affairs that we resented so much. Every time I see a badge, it represents to me the police, a bureaucrat, or some government agent trying to control us.

Much of our activities, fishing in particular, centered around the lake. In late summer we would set up our fish camps. Again, nobody "owned" any part of the lakeshore, but families fished at the same spot over the years. Others did not intrude on that part of the shore. During my childhood I went along with my family to our fishing camp. The whole family would be there—my grandparents, my mother, Aunt Sarah, and all the kids belonging to my mother and my aunt. I would watch the bigger kids spearing fish and observe my mother setting out nets. I remember the nets filled with fish, and, small as I was, I tried to help by taking the fish out of the nets and putting them away. In the evenings we would have a big fire to roast or fry our fish. The old people would tell stories until we fell asleep.

When my grandparents were young the nets were still made by women who spun the cords from various plant fibers. But by the time I was a toddler, almost all the nets were factory-made. A dozen or so stones were tied to the nets to serve as sinkers, and big stones were used to hold the nets down across the lake bottom. Some nets were up to three hundred feet long. They had to be dried after each use. Almost everything that had to do with the care of nets was done by women. It was they who repaired, cleaned, and dried the nets.

We ate many kinds of fish, but the only fish we smoked were the whitefish. We split the fish down the back and removed the bones and guts before we placed the fillets upon racks to smoke over slow fires. Fishing was not only done with nets—we fished with hooks, spears, and traps. Just as with our hunting and sugaring rights, our fishing rights were restricted when agents from the Bureau of Fisheries made us pay for fishing licenses. There was nothing left that didn't have the government's handprint on it.

One of the most important events on the reservation was the wild rice harvest, which takes place in the early fall. The rice grows near the lakeshore or in slow-moving streams. We always went to the same place near Headquarters Bay where our families had traditionally harvested rice. Ours was only one of many ricing camps around the lake. The camp of the Drumbeater Clan consisted of between twenty and thirty people. Everybody went to the ricing camps, even the smaller children.

During the rice harvests before Mark, Audrey, and I were sent to boarding school, we had to stay back in camp. Even though we were so young, we tried to help take care of the campsite. There was always an older man who would stay behind with us to protect us from bears that might be attracted by the food in the camp. That food usually consisted of roast duck because ducks were always around the rice. Grandma Drumbeater was the boss lady who kept the whole camp busy—cooking, cleaning up, and washing clothes.

The rice had to be harvested just before it was totally ripe. If we waited too long, the rice kernels would drop from the stem into the water. We could lose a lot of the harvest by waiting too long.

I remember the first time I stood on the dock watching the boats go out for rice. The rice sticks out of the water, which is about ten feet deep. Stalks of wild rice can be fifteen or even twenty feet tall. There are always two men in each boat—one sits in front with a long pole to move the boat along while the other bends the rice stalks to knock the kernels into the boat with two sticks called "knockers." He pulls the stalks in with one stick and hits them twice with the other, knocking most of the rice kernels into the boat. A lot of rice drops back into the lake, and that is as it should be—it replenishes the rice field.

The rice stalks have sharp slivers on them that fly around during the knocking, so we had to wear bandannas around our faces to protect our eyes. If you got a sliver in your eye, you would have to tell someone about it quick and they would get it out for you. If you rubbed it, the sliver would just push itself further into the eye and get stuck. That was the first lesson ricers had to learn.

When the boat was filled it was time to go back to shore. The men would row back to the dock and we would all help lift the rice out and load it into big bags. After the rice gathering was done, all the bags were laid out to dry. When the rice was dry, we poured it into big buckets and the men and women would stand around them together loosening the hulls. Then the rice would be put into big frying pans to be parched. Afterward, a woman holding a big screen basket full of rice would stand against the wind and toss the rice up into the air. The hulls would fly off in the wind. The woman had to wear a bandanna to protect her eyes, and she sang a special song about the rice. Sometimes two or three women would sing along. The men would sit around the drum, which was beaten in rhythm with the singing.

Wild rice is not just a delicacy. It is our sacred food. It is saved up for winter ceremonies when we bring out food for the spirits. It is a wild plant, an uncultivated plant, the Creator's gift to our people.

The ricing would last for about ten days. At the end of the season we had huge gatherings. We would put on our finest quilled and beaded outfits—beautiful buckskins, bustles, ankle bells, and vests and jackets with beaded designs. Some men would wear a sacred eagle feather tied to their hair. Dances would go on for days. We always held a great ceremony to give thanks to the Great Spirit.

There were also social events. Fifteen or twenty rice camps were located in the Federal Dam area alone, and there were many more camps all around the shores of both Leech Lake and Cass Lake. There was a lot of visiting back and forth between camps and chances for boys and girls to meet, a beginning of relationships. Men and women of all ages sang and danced, and the young people and little children were all included. I remember my mother getting me dressed to dance when I was only four years old. I had on a wonderful head roach made of porcupine hair decorated with the quills and a round-dance bustle made of feathers. I can still hear the tinkling of my dance bells. Our rice harvest festivals are unforgettable.

Wild rice was a blessing in still another way. It bought for us our clothing, shoes, and other things we needed. It played a very important part in the Ojibwa economy. We took half the rice home, and the other half my mother and grandfather took to town to sell. Sometimes rice buyers came to the landings and bought directly from the camps. The price fluctuated between twenty-five and thirty cents a pound. Nowadays the price would be about one dollar and twenty-five cents or more per pound. People loved our wild rice. It is more nutritious then regular rice and tastes better.

Of course, the government agents would be there too, weighing the rice, tagging it, fixing the price, and trying to get a piece of the action by buying our rice to sell through government channels. But there were white buyers who ignored the BIA and its regulations. Now, in addition to regulations, we have some competition. White growers have begun cultivating a genetically engineered variation of wild rice and selling it as "wild rice," but it does not taste the same. Something is missing from it. Our wild rice has *always* been there; the wildness is there. The rice beds are still right where the Creator planted them.

I had been lucky. In my youth I had had the chance to glimpse our old traditional life, but it was only a glimpse. Already, during my two years back at home, that way of life—of interdependence and harmony with the natural world—was coming to an end. After eleven years at boarding school, I had come home to a bad situation. The white sportsmen had killed off the game. Our rice had to compete with commercially cultivated "wild" rice. There were no jobs for Indians. Many of our people were sick. The food available to us was bad and insufficient. Suddenly we were living on junk food, drowning in Coke and Pepsi.

It seems the makers of soft drinks discovered that Indians were good customers for the stuff. My younger sister, Terry, from my mother's second marriage, always used to have a Coke or Pepsi in her hand. It is addictive. You've got to have it. Overindulgence in soft drinks brought about an outbreak of diabetes. People started dying of it. Terry passed away at forty-two years of age from the disease. It was heartbreaking to see our people dying in this way. In the end, the doctors chop off their toes. Then they chop off a foot; then they cut off a leg from the knee down. After that it's from the hip down until you die from gangrene. I believe this comes from the food and drink that has replaced our old traditional fare.

Because the reservation seemed to be going to hell, I became restless. I wanted to cut loose and travel. Someday, I thought, I will be getting on a Greyhound bus. To me that was the ultimate high in traveling—getting into that huge bus and going with the roar of the engine, the shifting of gears, and looking back to wave at somebody waving at me. I think back to all those times when I was young and watched buses go by, waving and hollering and hoping somebody on that bus would wave back at me. I figured, some day it will be me on that bus, and if somebody waves up at me, I am going to slide the window open and wave back. And I'll yell, "Come on, let's go! Pick yourself up, go where you want to go!"

When I bought my first bus ticket, though it was only from Cass Lake to Bemidji, it got my adrenaline surging, and I thought, "Wow, man, I want to save this forever!" I meant the ticket stub. Dreams come true. Throughout my life I have traveled many miles around this earth and have been in the strangest places. But at age seventeen, I thought only of getting away and going to a place different from the place I was in.

I stayed on at Federal Dam on the rez even though I didn't know what to do with myself. I felt a yearning for something spiritual but had no clue what this could be. I started going to wakes, not even knowing who the deceased was, because I just wanted to hear the songs. And when they started chanting in Indian, I knew that is who I was. That was me. Songs mean much to me. I am a good singer now. For many years I did not sing at all—I just sat around the drum with Grandpa Josh feeling my heart beat in rhythm with the drums and listening to the ancient chants. There were songs learned from birds, in visions, and in dreams. We had no concept of people being "songwriters." The melodies come from the spirits and are only captured by those most closely connected to them. Such songs belong to the people rather than being someone's private copyrighted property.

The drum is the heart of Indian music. In Mohawk country a man talks to his drum, asking for its help during a ceremony. People will dance, adding the sound of their feet to the rhythm of the drum. It is the instrument around which people gather. I always felt that drums were living beings. As people gather in a circle around a drum, the power of the circle moves outward from the drum to the people and draws them into the circle. Then the people are as one. Both spiritually and politically the drum represents a power. So that was something I could have to comfort me as I set out into the unknown, the memory of our songs and the drum. The roots of my spirituality come from there.

I hitchhiked twice to Minneapolis to visit my sister Audrey, who had settled there. I ran into my old friend Floyd Westerman, who had just enlisted in the Marine Corps. We talked about the guys we knew who were already in Korea or in Germany. So I enlisted in the Air Force. For me, as with many other Indian kids, it was the only way out, the only chance for three meals and a warm place to sleep. I went home and talked to my mother about it. She said, "Fine, if that's what you want to do." I was only seventeen and had to have my parents' permission to join up.

Before I left, my Uncle Jim came to me and gave me a little pouch to wear around my neck. He said, "Keep this with you at all times," and I did. My Air Force buddies thought it was a good luck charm and kidded me about being a superstitious heathen. A medicine bundle has great spiritual meaning for its wearer. Prayers go into it, and it is worn for spiritual protection. Mine was a small medicine bundle on a cord around my neck. I took good care of it.

On the night I went into the military, a ceremony was held by all the people living near us. Men and women sang, and some smoked the pipe for me. As I savored the smoke and the fragrance of the sacred red willow bark tobacco, I closed my eyes and recalled Grandma and my childhood. Three men sitting on the ground were smoking the sacred pipe. I never spoke to them but I knew they were smoking and praying for me. I got down beside them, knowing that they were smoking for my coming back safe and in one piece.

2004

GERALD VIZENOR
B. 1934

Dennis of Wounded Knee

Prophets are seldom honored among a people who feel that they are masters of their own destiny. A social atmosphere which stimulates a spirit of self-confidence is not one to encourage reliance upon superhuman forces. It is only when the shocks and perils of existence are overwhelming that the individual feels the need for something to support his mortal weakness.

—HOMER BARNETT, INDIAN SHAKERS
February 12, 1974

Dennis Banks was dressed in secular vestments. He wore beads, bones, leathers, ribbons, and a cultural frown for his appearance in court where he was on trial for alleged violations of federal laws in connection with the occupation of Wounded Knee on the Pine Ridge Reservation in South Dakota.

Banks seldom smiles in public. He looked down that afternoon as he stood alone before twelve federal jurors. His focus seemed to shift from table to chair, past the rims and rails in the courtroom, and then he raised his head and told the jurors in his opening statement that he was at Wounded Knee, as charged, and that he was "guilty of asking that the Senate investigate all the conditions that the federal government has imposed upon our people. . . ."

Banks, who is Anishinaabe, a mixed blood from the Leech Lake Reservation in Minnesota, and one of the founders of the American Indian Movement, was on trial with Russell Means from the Pine Ridge Reservation.

Means, who seems to move in mythic time, overbearing at the brink of ritualism, thrust his chest forward that morning in court and explained to the jurors that he would produce evidence to show how the "United States of America has set up a public tribal government under the foam and the heel of the Interior Department and the Bureau of Indian Affairs, but before we get into some of the more specific evidence that we will introduce, one has to understand what the Indian psyche is all about, that we have a completely different value system than that of the larger society. . . . We will introduce evidence of how we've had to go underground in order to maintain our traditional religion, our traditional philosophy. . . .

"The Oglala people themselves will be the ones testifying. The Oglala, some of them will need interpreters, some of them won't be able to speak very good English, and they will all be scared. . . . We will prove that at the direction of our traditional chiefs and headmen, just as the treaty provides, at their direction and with their support, we were directed into Wounded Knee. . . .

"First of all, we believe that all living things come from our sacred mother earth, all living things, the green things, the winged things of the air, the four leggeds, the things that crawl and swim and, of course the two leggeds. . . . But the important thing in our philosophy is that we believe we're the weakest things on earth, that the two legged is the weakest thing on earth because we have no direction. . . .

"Now, because we are the weakest things on earth, we do not have a license to exploit or manipulate our brothers and sisters and we also know, because of our role in life, that the buffalo and all other relatives of ours teach us, and so we built our civilization. . . .

"Of course, there is another way. That is to grab the bottle, drink it, go down to the other bar and fight your brothers and sisters just to say, 'Look, I'm a man,' or take the bottle again and go home and mistreat your wife and tell her, 'Look, I'm a man.'

"And there is another way, the way that we will prove that the United States of America, in its genocidal policies against Indian people, forced us to be red-white people. That is the other way, is to cut our hair, put on the ties and become facsimiles of the white man. . . .

"There has been . . . a new way to express our manhood, and that's been the American Indian Movement to express our Indianness. . . . I was an accountant by trade in Cleveland, Ohio, and in the Lakota way, if you cut your hair, that means you're in mourning. And it is our contention that a lot of Dakotas now who are misguided cut their hair because they're mourning because they lost their Indianness.

"Also, when I had my hair cut," Russell Means told the jurors, "I was mistaken for a Chicano, for an Arab, a Hawaiian, a Pakistanian, everything but an American Indian. I'm very proud to be Lakota, and when I walk down the street, I want people to know I'm Indian."

Dennis Banks told the federal jurors that he was a member of the traditional Oglala Sioux Sun Dance religion, which, he explained in a gentle voice, is a "very sacred religious event where men warriors offer themselves to the great spirit to seek a vision, that we have to go through it for four years and somewhere through those four years we will find that vision; that there must be fasting, that we must give up water, and that we must prove to Mother Earth and all the female objects of this planet, to all the female things, that we would like to share some of the pain. The men warriors would like to share some of the pain that our mothers, that our mothers had, when we were born."

The Sun Dance is a ceremony in which vows are made in sacred preparation for a personal vision. Some participants in the ritual puncture the skin on their chest with wooden skewers which are tied to a sacred tree. Those who seek a vision, dance in the circle of the sun until the skewers are torn from their flesh.

"The piercing of the skin," Banks told the jurors that afternoon in federal court, "is a reminder to me that I truly owe myself to Mother Earth and to all the female things of this planet. The most sacred of all Oglala events is the Oglala Sun Dance; and when the flesh was torn from me I suddenly realized what a great sin, what a great injustice it would be to lose the Oglala Sioux religion."

Banks seems to represent the dominant male view in his references to women as "objects" and "things" while at the same time he presents himself as a tribal traditionalist and a man of peace and spiritual visions.

Banks told the federal jurors that he was called to a meeting on Monday, February 27, 1972, at Calico Hall on the Pine Ridge Reservation. "I attended this meeting, and the evidence will show that those who were in attendance at that meeting were Oglala Sioux chiefs, traditional headmen, medicine men and councilmen. . . .

"I heard an Oglala Sioux woman, two women, address their chiefs and headmen in their own language. . . . The plea that they made to the American Indian Movement, two women who were truly the real warriors of Indian society, who saw their own sons dying on the reservations, who saw their own children dying on the way to the hospital. . . . They asked the medicine men and the headmen, they asked them, where were the spirits of so long ago that made this nation great, where was that Indian spirit that the Oglala Sioux nation so many years ago stood up against the United States Army, and these two women demanded an answer from the chiefs and those of us who were present, demanded to know if there were any Indians left in this country, if there were any Indians left in the United States, Indians who were descendants of those great Indian heroes of long ago...."

Banks was not seen at Calico Hall on the Pine Ridge Reservation where five traditional leaders and more than a hundred other tribal people had gathered to consider a scheme to seize Wounded Knee village. Russell Means was at the meeting, but Banks was at Cherry Creek on the Cheyenne River Reservation with a television news reporter. Banks was chauffeured to Wounded Knee by the reporter, but she departed when federal marshals surrounded the area.

Monday evening, February 27, 1973, Means was perched on a platform behind a large table at the end of Calico Hall. Lower, in front of him, the five traditional, or hereditary, leaders were seated in a row on benches. Means, who did not speak a tribal language then, spoke to the leaders through Leonard Crow Dog, an interpreter. The traditional leaders listened to radical entreaties in translation and then retired to the basement of the small bulding to consider their approval of a plan to seize Wounded Knee. The leaders conferred for two hours, but postponed their decision until a second meeting could be held with elected reservation officials. Means was not pleased with their indecision, he had expected the support of the hereditary leaders; he told them not to overlook his response to their needs on the reservation. We have been invited here, but remember, he admonished the leaders through a translator, we can leave to help people in other places.

Banks has denied the mortal limits of his time on the earth; his radical visage will endure; he will be remembered in cold footnotes and in humorous stories. Seven years before Wounded Knee, Banks had short hair and wore a dark suit and narrow necktie. He had been paroled from prison and posed in conservative clothes then; he did not braid his hair or express his aspirations to become an urban tribal radical until he and others realized that the church and state would subsidize protest organizations. It seems ironic now that Banks once opposed the first protest of the area office of the Bureau of Indian Affairs in Minneapolis. "Demonstrations are not the Indian way," he said then as he wagged his finger at the director of the American Indian Employment Center who had organized the protest to demand equal federal services for urban tribal people.

The American Indian Movement is a radical urban organization whose members have tried from time to time to return to the reservations as the warrior heroes of tribal people. To some, the radicals are the heroes of dominant histories, but to others the leaders of the movement are the freebooters of racism. The leaders have been paid well for their activities.

The American Indian Movement was founded in a storefront in Minneapolis about five years before the occupation of Wounded Knee. Banks,

Clyde Bellecourt, Harold Goodsky, George Mitchell, and others, organized a patrol to monitor the activities of police officers in urban tribal communities. As the police watched the program grew from foot soldiers to expensive mobile radio units. The serious issue was police harassment, but the method of trailing police cars in expensive convertibles became an extravagant satire. The rhetoric was colonial oppression, the press coverage was excellent then, and thousands of dollars of guilt money rolled in from church groups, but the organizers of the movement argued about philosophies and ideologies. Mitchell, an intense individualist, was dedicated to service in urban communities, while Goodsky worked in corrections before returning to the reservation.

Banks and several others remained in the organization to continue the confrontation politics with the intellectual and legal assistance of dozens of romantic white radicals and liberals from the peace movement. Those tribal people who followed the ideologies of confrontation were in conflict at times with those who believed that negotiations lead to institutional changes. These differences in ideologies and radical practices were emphasized in media coverage. News reports created the heroes of confrontation for an imaginative white audience, while those dedicated to negotiations were ignored. Reporters have their own professional needs to discover and present adventurous characters and events. Banks, and other radical leaders, have become the warriors of headlines, but not the heart of the best stories that turn the remembered tribal world.

The political ideologies of the radical tribal leaders are reactions to racism and cultural adversities, that much all tribal people have in common, but the radical rhetoric of the leaders was not learned from traditional tribal people on reservations or in tribal communities. Some of the militant leaders were radicalized in prison where they found white inmates eager to listen. The poses of tribal radicals seem to mimic the romantic pictorial images in old photographs taken by Edward Curtis for a white audience. The radicals never seem to smile, an incautious throwback to a stoical tribal visage when camera shutters and film speeds were slower. The new radicals frown, even grimace at cameras, and claim the atrocities endured by all tribal cultures in first person pronouns.

Some militants decorate themselves in pastiche pantribal vestments, and pose, at times, as traditionalists, and speak a language of confrontation and urban politics. The radical figures were not elected to speak for tribal reservation people, nor were they appointed to represent the interests and political views of elected tribal officials. In response to this criticism several tribal radicals returned to reservations. Vernon Bellecourt, for example, a member of the American Indian Movement, returned to the White Earth Reservation where he was elected a representative. Bellecourt was an ambitious reservation politician, no less outspoken than he had been in urban tribal politics, and he served his constituents with distinction.

Banks, however, has never faced tribal constituencies in a legitimate election. His influence is media borne; he has carried numerous administrative titles in the past, but his power seems to be ideological, material, and institutional. His most recent academic position, for example, was as chancellor of Daganawidah-Quetzalcoatl University located near Davis, California, where he lived for several years. Banks had become a civil hero in exile, a new banished word warrior, when Governor Jerry Brown denied his extradition to South Dakota where he had been convicted of riot and assault charges and was wanted on a fugitive warrant.

Leech Lake Reservation:
Nine months before the occupation of Wounded Knee several hundred members of the American Indian Movement carried weapons for the first time in preparation for an armed confrontation with white people on the opening day of fishing on the Leech Lake Reservation in Minnesota. The militants were prepared and determined to battle for tribal control of hunting and fishing rights on the reservation, rights which had been won in federal court. Their threats were not needed.

Dennis Banks and a dozen armed leaders were invited to a meeting in a tribal center on the first day they arrived on the reservation. The militants marched into a classroom where the meeting was scheduled and sat on little chairs, their knees tucked under their chins. Banks remained in motion, with one hand at his neck, in serious thought. He was dressed in hunks of fur, his mountain man outfit that spring.

Simon Howard, then president of the Minnesota Chippewa Tribe, entered the classroom last. He sat on a little chair at the head of the circle and twirled his thumbs over his stomach and considered the arguments between the militants about their places in the radical chain of command. Howard wore a bowling jacket and a floral print porkpie fishing hat, cocked back on his head, in contrast to the new pantribal vestments worn by the militants. Howard was born on the reservation, he had lived there all his life. He called the meeting as an elected reservation official to maintain peace between white people and the urban tribal militants; a proper start with the militants in little chairs.

"All right boys, quiet down now and take your seats again," said Howard. "Now, I don't know everyone here, so let's go around the room and introduce ourselves. . . . Let's start with you over there, stand up and introduce yourself."

The man pushed his feet forward, swung his rifle around, and stood in front of his little chair. "My name is Delano Western, and I'm from Kansas," he said in a trembling voice as he leaned forward and looked down toward the floor. He was dressed in a wide black hat with an imitation silver headband, dark green sunglasses with round lenses, a sweatshirt with "Indian Power" printed on the front, two bandoliers of heavy ammunition, none of which matched the bore of his rifle, a black leather jacket, and a large military bayonet strapped to his waist next to his revolver.

"We came here to die," he said and sat down.

"The white man has stolen our sacred land and violated our treaties time and time again. . . ." Banks said as he paced outside the circle of little chairs.

"Banks, this is a reservation not a church basement," said a visitor, "save your speech for the white people out back with the cash."

The militants had been invited to live at a church camp which was located on the reservation. The land had been given to the church by the federal government to encourage the establishment of missions and schools to "civilize" the tribes. Several hundred militants lived there for about a week.

The militants had demanded money from white public officials in the area, and when they refused to be bribed, radical leaders held a press conference on a rifle range to scare the public.

Banks, dressed in a black velvet shirt, posed for television cameras with La Donna Harris, wife of Senator Fred Harris from Okilahoma, before he attempted to fire his short-barrel shotgun which was looped to his waist with rope. While the cameras recorded the event, Banks faced the food cans placed at a distance on the target range, dropped to one knee and drew his shotgun, but the trigger housing caught in the rope holster. Banks stood and tried to draw again, but it stuck a second time. While he untied the rope, the television focused on Russell Means who was firing what he called his "white people shooter," a small-caliber pistol.

The confrontations at the Leech Lake Reservation, unlike those confrontations which followed on other reservations, were, for the most part, little more than verbal battles. Several shots were exchanged one night near the church camp, but no one was injured. An investigation of the incident revealed that several militants had decided to shine for deer that night and seeing what they thought were the eyes of a deer they opened fire. The animal in the dark was a cow owned by a local farmer who fired back at the militants. The cow, the militants, and the farmer were unharmed.

Simon Howard, David Munnell, and other elected reservation officials, attorney Kent Tupper, and officials from the United States Department of Justice, were responsible for a peaceful resolution to potential armed violence in the area. Tensions were high in the militant church camp, even higher, perhaps, in white communities around the reservation.

"We must go on living on this reservation after you leave," Howard told the militants at their last meeting.

"We are making changes in the courts, not by violence," said Munnell. "We are building for ourselves an economic system and we will continue to fight in the courts for our rights."

Tupper, who represented the Leech Lake Reservation in federal court, told the militants several times during the week that the rights of tribal people must be won according to the law and not by violence.

Some local satirists, however, attributed the mellow verbal confrontation to the weather. The cold rain, some resolved, was all that could distract the urban tribal militants who were armed for the first time with new rifles and pitols. Myles Olson, a Minnesota Highway Patrolman for the area, explained that "two days of rain was worth two slop buckets of mace."

* * *

Washington to Wounded Knee:

Six months later, Dennis Banks and the American Indian Movement mustered the Trial of Broken Treaties which earned broad support from urban tribal communities and from church bodies and white liberal organizations. The favors of vicarious constituencies held when the new tribal militants seized the national offices of the Bureau of Indian Affairs, but enthusiasm eroded when it was revealed that the radicals had caused two million dollars in senseless damage to the building and that the leaders had accepted more than sixty-thousand dollars in cash to leave town.

Three months later the militants gathered in Custer, and Rapid City, South Dakota, for a few weeks before their assault on Wounded Knee.

The leaders of the American Indian Movement, with the exception of Dennis Banks on this occasion, were registered at a comfortable downtown motel in Rapid City while their followers, many of whom were on probation and parole and truant from public schools, were stuck at the Mother Butler Center with no food or funds. Local merchants reached an informal agreement that it was better to tolerate shoplifting than to detain the militants and risk possible personal harm and property damage. The leaders, meanwhile, were evicted from the motel when they refused to pay more than two thousand dollars in room and restaurant charges.

"I think you have a good message for this country," said Mayor Donald Barnett when he first met the radical tribal leaders. Later, however, when he had read their criminal records and discovered that they were armed, and unwilling to cover their debts, he changed is verbs and metaphors. "People working for civil rights do not carry guns. I have seen the records of these men and you can't sit and negotiate with a man who has a gun.... Are these men serious civil rights workers, or are they a bunch of bandits?"

Dennis Banks has never earned high salaries as a laborer or professional, but as a radical entrepreneur he has been bankrolled by the federal government and various church organizations. Banks never had so much cash as he did when he took to the road as a word warrior with a profound cultural frown.

John Peterson, an investigative reporter for the *Detroit News*, writes that the occupation of Wounded Knee "has been financed almost exclusively by federal money." In an article dated March 25, 1973, he quotes a federal official who said that the "Justice Department was all set to move in and made arrests" at Wounded Knee, but when American Indian Movement leaders "threatened to call a press conference and disclose exactly how much financing" they had received from the federal government, the "Justice Department backed off and tried to play for a standoff," hoping the militants would "tire and leave voluntarily." American Indian Movement leaders "have just dusted off and updated the old militant tactic of intimidating government officials until they come through with grants...." Peterson points out that during the year before the occupation of Wounded Knee the American Indian Movement had received about three hundred thousand dollars from the federal government for various programs.

The *Omaha World-Herald*, in an article published March 14, 1973, revealed that three national church organizations had contributed close to three hundred thousand dollars to the American Indian Movement, in addition to the federal funds.

The informer was a pilot:

Douglass Durham, an informer for the Federal Bureau of Investigation, and at the same time an advisor to Dennis Banks, reported that in the two years following the occupation of Wounded Knee, the American Indian Movement received more than one million dollars in contributions from various public and private sources. Columbia Studios, for example, paid Banks twenty-five thousand dollars for his consultation on a script about Wounded Knee. The actor Marlon Brando contributed cash, real estate, and properties, to the militant leaders.

The Wounded Knee Legal Defense-Offense Committee circulated hundreds of letters to raise funds. "In the interest of justice, and in the belief that everyone is entitled to a fair trial," one letter explained, "we are asking you to contribute. . . ."

United States District Judge Fred Nichol considered the financial condition of Russell Means and Dennis Banks and ruled that the court would appoint two attorneys for each defendant and pay incidental expenses including travel, parking fees, and living expenses during the Wounded Knee trail in Saint Paul.

Leonard Cavise, an attorney responsible for the financial accounting of contributions and expenditures of the legal committee, stated in an affidavit to the court that as of January 8, 1974, the committee had a balance of $316.99 in a checking account at the National Bank of South Dakota in Sioux Falls. Cavise explained that "No religious organizations, church or social-welfare group has contributed any funds to the committee for anything other than bail-bond purposes."

Dennis Banks is a pauper of sorts: he lives, it seems, on contributions from public and private charities, but he is not poor. He is not poor like thousands of tribal people who are malnourished and must live on less than a few thousand dollars a year. Banks has gained fame and relative wealth on the collective name of the tribal poor and on the ideologies of oppression; despite these ironies, he has been provided with court appointed attorneys for all his troubles, and he was issued a food stamp identification card by the Ramsey County Welfare Department, according to documents published in a report by the United States Senate Committee on the Judiciary.

Those who believe that the American Indian Movement is a new tribal spiritual movement could be disillusioned by some information critical of the radical leaders and their activities. In a report published and distributed by the militants, the American Indian Movement is defined as "first a spiritual movement, a religious rebirth, and then a rebirth of Indian dignity ... attempting to connect the realities of the past with the promises of tomorrow." However, in other documents identified as confidential by the militants, the future policies of the American Indian Movement did not include references to religion or spiritual movements. The American Indian Movement "should prepare a manifesto on the goals and political thought which constitutes the movement," the document reveals. The movement will also "formulate an international coordination with world powers ... create a Latin American liberation organization ... establish working contacts with all liberation fronts in South America ... establish a political action committee to fully exploit the democratic American system as long as it exists to utilize the system for Indian gains ... create an action arm to unify all resistance groups operating in the United States so as to form a functioning coalition with all ... create a labor relations committee ... prepare a detailed plan for the abolition" of Bureau of Indian Affairs control over one "major reservation and fight for this freedom through the courts...." Other documents explain that the "natural evolution" of the American Indian Movement "will result in the establishment of Indian member states based on tribal boundaries. These member states could form a coalition or a congress of Indian peoples. Reservations are the natural beginning of state formations." These ideas were imposed, not elected by tribal people.

During the summer, following the occupation of Wounded Knee on the Pine Ridge Reservation, Dennis Banks drove to Yellowknife on Great Slave Lake in Northwest Territories. There, to avoid possible arrest, Banks lived with the director of the Native Indian Brotherhood of Canada, according to information provided by Douglass Durham at a senate hearing before the Subcommittee to Investigate the Administration of the Internal Security Act, of the Committee of the Judiciary. Senator James Eastland, chairman of the subcommittee, called but one witness on April 6, 1976. The purpose of the hearing, the chairman explained, was "to try to establish whether there is, in fact, reason for believing that the American Indian Movement is a radical subversive organization rather than an organization committed to improving the lot of the American Indians." Based on the testimony of Durham, and various documents and reports, the subcommittee, in a report published in September 1976, concluded that "The American Indian Movement does not speak for the American Indians.... It is a frankly revolutionary organization which is committed to violence, calls for the arming of American Indians, has cached explosives and illegally purchased arms, plans kidnappings.... It has many foreign ties, direct and indirect – with Castro's Cuba, with China ... with the Palestine Liberation Organization," and with the Irish Republican Army. The subcommittee also found that the American Indian Movement has "maintained contact with and has received propaganda and other support from a large number of left extremist organizations, including the Weather Underground, the Communist Party, the Trotskyists, the Symbionese Liberation Army, the Black Panther Party," and other radical organizations in the United States.

Douglass Frank Durham was the national security director of the American Indian Movement when he was exposed as an informer for the Federal

Bureau of Investigation. He was a former patrolman with the Des Moines, Iowa, police department; in March 1973, he traveled to Wounded Knee as a photographer for the newspaper *Pax Today*. Six months later he had assisted Dennis Banks in his one month escape to the wilderness. Durham pretended that he was a tribal mixedblood from the Lac Courte Oreille Reservation in Wisconsin.

Banks was free on bond for his involvement in the occupation of Wounded Knee when he was indicted by a grand jury for his participation in a riot at Custer, South Dakota, six months earlier. Durham told the subcommittee that Banks instructed him, while he was at Yellowknife, to establish and maintain a "railroad" for tribal militants, "a means whereby you can move people, warriors, weapons," in overnight accommodations between states. Banks promoted Durham to his personal security director and pilot for the American Indian Movement. The informer testified that he was the only person who knew that Banks had moved from Yellowknife to Rae Lakes, a remote island in Northwest Territories near the Arctic Circle. He hid there with several friends for about one month while Durham raised money for his second bond.

Durham told the subcommittee that Banks assumed the name Sherman Eagle and was given false identification to return to the United States. Durham, a licensed pilot, rented a small airplane for the return trip. Banks, who was wanted on a fugitive warrant, was concerned, even with false identification, that he would be arrested at the international border. Durham testified that "he was concerned about radar and other devices picking us up because he felt they were on our trail. So, we flew below the systems through inclement weather, and did make it back into a small abandoned field out at the edge of town, where we landed. We sneaked Dennis Banks into Rapid City and into the courtroom," where he posted his bond before he was arrested.

Durham further testified that "George Roberts advocated spiriting Dennis Banks to Cuba, and in my presence called Dr. Faustino Perez, in New Mexico, to establish contact with Fidel Castro. Perez was an old friend of Ahmed Ben Bella from Algeria, and was quite involved in the landing in Cuba."

"The Bay of Pigs?" asked the subcommittee counsel.

"No; when Castro first obtained power in Cuba," Durham responded.

"All right, when he came out of the mountains."

"Right, out of the mountains," Durham contined. "Dr. Fausto – as he is referred to – advised Roberts that he would have the information sent in a diplomatic pouch to Cuba and at that point Roberts," who was from Venice, California, and the owner of the Inca Manufacturing Company, "advised his wife to travel to Mexico City to meet Faustino Perez, who was supposedly, or allegedly, a friend of hers. Anyway, she returned with the information that Castro had rejected the plan because he felt that there would be increasing relations with the United States...."

"He was expecting this to disturb the increasingly better relations with the United States?" the subcommittee counsel asked the witness.

"That's correct, sir," Durham responded to the counsel who asked most of the questions at the hearing. "A suggestion was issued, allegedly from Dr. Faustino Perez, that Banks should approach the People's Republic of China for a move in the direction they would indicate, which would later allow him to go to Latin America and become the new Che Guevara because he was a Native American person."

"Was all this arrangement in contemplation that he would be found guilty at the trial?" asked the subcommittee counsel.

"In contemplation not of his being found guilty at the trial," the witness explained, "but rather being seized at the end of the trial by the Custer County authorities and jailed until they held a trial for him. It was later decided that we would return and if Dennis Banks were to be found either guilty or not guilty, if there was a motion by Custer County authorities in South Dakota to arrest him, he would make a stand at Rosebud. Groups of Indians around the country started gathering arms and moving toward Rosebud, South Dakota...."

Sanctuaries from vengeance:

"Judge Nichol dismissed the charges, and the attorneys, William Kunstler, and Mark Lane, specifically Mark Lane, started a 'jurors and others for reconciliation movement' where he got the jurors and others to write letters...." Dennis Banks did not make his last stand at Rosebud, however, He moved to California where, Durham testified, "we were brought out at the expense of Columbia Studios, put up at the Hilton Hotel ... limousine service and chateaubriand dinners, and were just the victims of 'horrifying oppression' for quite some time there. I might add that during all this time, though, Banks was still drawing three-hundred dollars a month in food stamps...."

The Federal Bureau of Investigation, acting on a warrant from South Dakota, arrested Banks near San Francisco where he had been in hiding for several months. Marlon Brando, Jane Fonda, and others, publicized his cause; a petition signed by more than a million citizens supported Dennis Banks. The Attorney General of South Dakota, William Janklow, who was later elected governor of the state, assumed that the extradition law would be upheld and the militant leader would be returned to face a prison sentence on assault and riot convictions. California Governor Edmund G. Brown, Jr., however, denied extradition, which meant that Banks could live free in California so long as Brown was governor. Banks was a political prisoner, in a comfortable sense, because he could not leave California without fear of arrest and extradition from a state where the governor would not be so sympathetic.

Constance Matthiessen and Ron Sokol reported in the *Los Angeles Times* that Alice Lytle, the extradition secretary at the time extradition was denied, explained that the decision was based on the poor race relations in South Dakota at the time, and when you "balance that against the relatively light conviction – he wasn't convicted of murder or armed robbery, he was convicted of riot and assault without intent to kill, and these are typical charges that arise out of demonstrations – when you balance the circumstances against the need that South Dakota had to imprison him behind these charges, the danger to his life seems significant enought to refuse the extradition request."

Dennis Banks lost his pacific santuary when George Deukmejian was elected governor of California; he would allow extradition to South Dakota. Matthiessen and Sokol point out that, "besides the danger that Banks faces in South Dakota, Deukmejian should consider the fact that Banks has been a productive and law-abiding citizen during his time in California. . . . He has lectured at high schools and colleges throughout the state. A number of California cities have commended him for his work, and various groups have urged Deukmejian to allow Banks to stay." Banks did not take the chance; he moved from California to the Onondaga Nation, a reservation near Syracuse, New York which claims to be a sovereign nation where neither state nor federal agents have jurisdiction.

There are tribal people who will continue to believe in the sudden slogans of protest, a form of symbolic association; and there are people who are convinced that the expressions of internal rage by tribal militants was a real revolution. There are also tribal people who will forever revise the vain advertisements of peripatetic mouth warriors as statements of traditional visions. When the word wars of the putative warriors mumble down to the last exclamation points in newspaper columns, however, the radical dramas will best be remembered in personal metaphors: the lovers at the rim of time, children late at breakfast, people touched in mythic dreams, humor in the dark parks, undone poems. The miles traveled underground, photographic icons, violence at familiar intersections, and the paper-cuts from radical broadsides, are grim memories and spiritual burdens, denials of humor and trickeries, distractions from the spontaneous pleasures of imagination.

1984

■ # KIMBERLY BLAESER ■

B. 1955

Apprenticed to Justice

The weight of ashes
from burned out camps.
Lodges smoulder in fire,
animal hides wither
their mythic images shrinking
pulling in on themselves,   5

all incinerated
fragments
of breath bone and basket
rest heavy   10
sink deep
like wintering frogs.
And no dustbowl wind
can lift
this history   15
of loss.

Now fertilized by generations—
ashes upon ashes,
this old earth erupts.
Medicine voices rise like mists   20
white buffalo memories
teeth marks on birch bark
forgotten forms
tremble into wholeness.

And the grey weathered stumps,   25
trees and treaties
cut down
trampled for wealth.
Flat potlatch plateaus
of ghost forests   30
raked by bears
soften rot inward
until tiny arrows of green
sprout
rise erect   35
rootfed
from each crumbling center.

Some will never laugh
as easily.
Will hide knives   40
silver as fish in their boots,
hoard names
as if they could be stolen
as easily as land,
will paper their walls   45
with maps and broken promises,
scar their flesh
with this badge
heavy as ashes.

And this is a poem   50
for those
apprenticed
from birth.
In the womb
of your mother nation   55
heartbeats
sound like drums
drums like thunder
thunder like twelve thousand
walking   60
then ten thousand
then eight
walking away
from stolen homes
from burned out camps   65
from relatives fallen
as they walked
then crawled
then fell.
This is the woodpecker sound   70
of an old retreat.
It becomes an echo,
an accounting
to be reconciled.
This is the sound   75
of trees falling in the woods
when they are heard,
of red nations falling
when they are remembered.
This is the sound   80
we hear
when fist meets flesh
when memories rattle hollow in stomachs.

And we turn this sound
over and over again   85
until it becomes
fertile ground
from which we will build
new nations
upon the ashes of our ancestors.   90
Until it becomes
the rattle of a new revolution
these fingers
drumming on keys.

"Native Americans" vs. "The Poets"

Some thoughts I had while reading *Poetry East*

You know that solitary Indian
sitting in his fringed leathers
on his horse at the rise of the hill
face painted, holding a lance
there just at the horizon?   5
That guy's got a Ph.D.
He's *the* Indian for Mankato State or Carroll College

Indian professors at universities throughout the country
Exhibit A,
No B, no C, just solitary romanticized A   10
Not much of a threat that way

Real trouble is
America
still doesn't know what to do with Indians

Looked for your books lately in Powell's   15
or 57th St. Books?
Check first in folklore or anthropology
Found Louis' *Wolfsong* in black literature
Hell, no wonder we all got an identity crisis

You a poet?   20
No, I just write Indian stuff.

                                                                       1994

Jim Northrup

b. 1953

Veteran's Dance

Don't sweat the small shit, Lug thought, it's all small shit unless they're
shooting at you.

The tall, skinny Shinnob finished changing the tire on his car. It took
longer than usual because he had to improvise with the jack, Summer in
Minnesota and Lug, Luke Warmwater's cousin, was on his way to a powwow.

The powwow was on its second day. The dancers were getting ready for their third grand entry. Singers around the various drutns had found their rhythm. Old bones were loosening up. The M.C. was entertaining the crowd with jokes. Some of the jokes brought laughs and others brought groans. Kids wove through the people that circled the dance arena. The drum sound knitted the people together.

Lug brushed his long hair away from his face as he looked into the sky for eagles. He had been away from home a long time and was looking forward to seeing his friends and relatives again.

He really enjoyed powwows although he didn't dance. Lug was content to be with his people again. Ever since the war he felt disconnected from the things that made people happy.

The first time he walked around the arena he just concentrated on faces. He was looking for family. While walking along, he grazed at the food stands. He smelled, then sampled the fry bread, moose meat, and wild rice soup.

The Shinnobs walking around the dance arena looked like a river flowing two directions. Groups of people would stop and talk. Lug smiled at the laughing circles of Shinnobs. He looked at faces and eyes.

That little one there, she looked like his sister Judy when she was that age. Lug wondered if he would see her here. Judy was a jingledress dancer and should be at this powwow. After all, she lived only a mile away from the powwow grounds.

The guy walking in front of him looked like his cousin who had gone to Vietnam. Nope, couldn't be him. Lug had heard that he died in a single-car accident last fall.

Sitting in a red-and-white-striped powwow chair was an old lady who looked like his grandma. She wore heavy brown stockings held up with a big round knot at the knees. She chewed Copenhagen and spit the juice in a coffee can just like his gram. Of course, Lug's grandma had been dead for ten years, but it was still a good feeling to see someone who looked like her.

Lug recognized the woman walking towards him. She was his old used-to-be girlfriend. He hoped she didn't want to talk about what went wrong with them. She didn't, just snapped her eyes and looked away. Lug knew it was his fault he couldn't feel close to anyone. His face was a wooden mask as they passed each other. He could feel her looking at him out of the corner of her eyes. Maybe, he thought, just maybe.

He stopped at a food stand called Stand Here. Lug had black coffee and a bag of mini-donuts. The sugar and cinnamon coating stuck to his fingers. He brushed off his hands and lit a smoke. Lug watched the snaggers eight to sixty-eight cruising through the river of Shinnobs.

That jingledress dancer walking towards him looked like his sister Judy. Yup it was her. The maroon dress made a tinkling, jingling sound as she came closer. She looks healthy, Lug thought. A few more gray hairs but she moves like she was twenty years younger. They both smiled hard as their eyes met. Warm brown eyes reached for wary ones.

She noticed the lines on his face were deeper. The lines fanned out from the edges of his eyes. He looked like he had lost some weight since the last time she had seen him. His blue jean jacket is just hanging on him, she thought.

Lug and Judy shook hands and hugged each other. Her black beaded bag hit him on the back as they embraced. They were together again after a long time apart. Both leaned back to get a better look at each other.

"C'mon over to the house when they break for supper," she said.

"Got any cornbread?" he asked.

"I can whip some up for you," she promised.

"Sounds good," he said.

Eating cornbread was a reminder of when they were young together. Sometimes it was the only thing to eat in the house. Cornbread was the first thing she made him when he came back from Vietnam.

"I have to get in line for the grand entry. So, I'll see you later, I want to talk to you about something," she said.

"Okay, dance a round for me," Lug said.

"I will, just like I always do."

Lug watched the grand entry. He saw several relatives in their dance outfits. He nodded to friends standing around the dance arena. Lug sipped hot coffee as the grand entry song was sung. Judy came dancing by. Lug turned and looked at his car.

He walked to it as the flag song started. He moved in time to the beat as he walked. Lug decided to get his tire fixed at the truck stop. He got in and closed the car door as the veteran's song came over the public address system.

Lug left the powwow grounds and slipped a tape in his cassette player. The Animals singing "Sky Pilot" filled the car. Lug sang along with the vintage music.

He drove to the truck stop and read the newspaper while the mechanic fixed his tire. Lug put the tire in his trunk, paid the guy, and drove to his sister's house. He listened to the Righteous Brothers do "Soul and Inspiration" on the way.

Judy's car was in the driveway so he knew she was home. He parked and walked up to the front door. Lug rang the doorbell and walked in. He smelled cornbread.

She was in the kitchen making coffee. He sat at the kitchen table as she took the cornbread out of the oven. The steaming yellow bread made his mouth moist. Judy poured him a cup of coffee and sat down at the table.

"How have you been!" she asked.

"Okay, my health is okay."

"Where have, you been? I haven't heard from you in quite a while."

"Oh you know, just traveling here and there. I'd work a little bit and then move on. For a while there I was looking for guys I knew in the war."

"Where was that you called from last March?" she asked.

"D.C., I was in Washington, D.C. I went to the Wall and after being there I felt like I had to talk to someone I knew."

"You did sound troubled about something."

"I found a friend's name on the Wall. He died after I left Vietnam. I felt like killing myself."

"I'm glad you didn't."

"Me too, we wouldn't be having this conversation if I had gone through with it."

She got up, cut the cornbread, and brought it to the table. He buttered a piece and began taking bites from the hot bread. She refilled his cup.

"Remember when we used to haul water when we were kids? I was thinking about it the other day, that one time it was thirty below and the cream cans fell off the sled? You somehow convinced me it was my fault. I had to pump the water to fill the cans again. You told me it was so I could stay warm. I guess in your own way you were looking out for me," she said.

"Nahh, I just wanted to see if I could get you to do all the work." Lug smiled at his sister.

"I though it was good of you to send the folks money from your first military paycheck so we could get our own pump. We didn't have to bum water from the neighbors after that."

"I had to. I didn't want you to break your back, lugging those cream cans around."

"Yah, I really hated wash days. Ma had me hauling water all day when she washed clothes."

She got up and got a glass of water from the kitchen faucet. As she came back to the table she said,

"I've been talking to a spiritual leader about you. He wants you to come and see him. Don't forget to take him tobacco."

"That sounds like a good idea. I've been wanting to talk to someone," he said.

"What was it like in the war? You never talk much about it."

Lug started deep into his black medicine water as if expecting an answer to scroll across. He trusted his sister, but it was still difficult talking about the terrible memories.

His eyes retreated into his head as he told her what happened to him, what he did in the war. She later learned that this was called the thousand-yard stare. His eyes looked like he was trying to see something far away. The laugh lines were erased from his face.

"Sometimes I'd get so scared I couldn't get scared anymore," he said, hunched over his coffee cup.

Judy touched his arm. Her face said she was ready to listen to her brother.

"One night they were shooting at us. No one was getting hurt. It got to be a drag ducking every time they fired. The gunfire wasn't very heavy, just a rifle round every couple of minutes. We didn't know if it was the prelude to a big attack or just one guy out there with a case of ammo and a hard-on. We laid in our holes, counted the rounds going by, and tried to shrink inside our helmets. The bullets went by for a least a half hour. I counted seventeen of them. The ones that went high made a buzzing noise. The close ones made a *crack* sound. First you'd hear the bullet go by, then the sound of where it came from.

"I got tired of that shit. I crawled out of my hole and just stood there. I wanted to see where the bad guy was shooting from. The guys in the next hole told me to get down, but I was in a 'fuck it' mood. I didn't care what happened, didn't care if I lived or died."

Lug stood up to show his sister what it was like standing in the dark. He leaned forward trying to see through the night. His hands clutched an imaginary rifle. Lug's head swiveled back and forth as he looked for the hidden rifleman. He jerked as a rifle bullet came close to him. He turned his head towards the sound.

Judy watched Lug. She could feel her eyes burning and the tears building up. Using only willpower, she held the tears back. Judy somehow knew the tears would stop the flood of memories coming out of her brother. She waited.

"I finally saw the muzzle flash. I knew where the bastard was firing from. After he fired the next time we all returned fire. We must have shot five hundred rounds at him. The bad guy didn't shoot anymore. We either killed him or scared the shit out of him. After the noise died down I started getting scared. I realized I could have been killed standing up like that."

He paused before speaking again.

"That shows you how dangerous a 'fuck it' attitude is. I guess I have been living my life with a 'fuck it' attitude."

Lug sat back down and reached for another piece of cornbread. He ate it silently. When he finished the cornbread he lit a cigarette.

She touched his shoulder as she poured more coffee. Lug accepted this as permission to continue fighting the war. Judy sat down and lit her own cigarette.

"It was really crazy at times. One time we were caught out in this big rice paddy. They started shooting at us. I was close to the front of the formation so I got inside the treeline quick. The bad guys couldn't see me. When I leaned over to catch my breath I heard the *snick, snick, bang* sound of someone firing a bolt-action rifle. The enemy soldier was firing at the guys still out in the rice paddy. I figured out where the bad guy was from the sound—*snick, snick, bang*. I fired a three-round burst at the noise. That asshole turned and fired at me. I remember the muzzle flash and the bullet going by together. I fired again as I moved closer. Through a little opening in the brush I could see what looked like a pile of rags, bloody rags. I fired another round into his head. We used to do that all the time—one in the head to make sure. The 7.62 bullet knocked his hat off. When the hat came off hair came spilling out. It was a woman."

Lug slumped at the kitchen table unable to continue his story. He held his coffee cup as if warming his hands. Judy sat there looking at him. Tears ran down her cheeks and puddled up on the table.

Lug coughed and lit a cigarette. Judy reached for one of her own and Lug lit it for her. Their eyes met. She got up to blow her nose and wipe her eyes. Judy was trembling as she came back and sat at the table. She wanted to cradle her brother but couldn't.

"Her hair looked like grandma's hair used to look. Remember her long, black, shiny hair? This woman had hair like that. I knew killing people was wrong somehow but this made it worse when it turned out to be a woman."

Lug slowly rocked his head back and forth.

When it looked like Lug was not going to talk anymore, Judy got up and opened the back door. She poured more coffee and sat there looking at him. He couldn't meet her eyes.

"Tell me how you got wounded; you never did talk about it. All we knew was that you won a Purple Heart," she probed.

After a long silence, Lug answered,

"Ha, won a Purple Heart? We used to call them Idiot Awards. It meant that you fucked up somehow. Standing in the wrong place at the wrong time, something like that."

Lug's shoulders tightened as he began telling her about his wounds. He reached down for his leg.

"I don't know what happened to my leg. It was a long firefight, lots of explosions. After it was over, after the medivac choppers left, we were sitting around talking about what happened.

"I looked down and noticed blood on my leg. I thought it was from the guys we carried in from the listening post. The pain started about then. I rolled up my pants and saw a piece of shrapnel sticking out. Doc came over and pulled it out. He bandaged it up and must have written me up for a Heart. I remember it took a long time to heal because we were always in the water of the rice paddies."

Lug was absently rubbing his leg as he told his sister about his wound.

He suddenly stood up and changed the subject. He didn't talk about his other wounds. He drained his cup.

"I gotta go, I think I talked too much already. I don't want you to think I am crazy because of what I did in the war. I'll see you at the powwow," said Lug, walking to the door.

As she looked at his back she wished there was something she could do to ease his memories of the war.

"Wait a minute," Judy told her brother.

She lit some sage and smudged him with an eagle feather. He stood there with his eyes closed, palms facing out.

He thanked her and walked out the door.

While cleaning up after her brother left, Judy remembered the ads on TV for the Vet's Center. She looked the number up in the book and called. Judy spoke to a counselor who listened. The counselor suggested an inpatient Post Traumatic Stress Disorder program.

The closest one was located in St. Cloud, Minnesota. Judy got the address for her brother.

She went back to the powwow and found Lug standing on the edge of the crowd.

"They have a program for treating PTSD," she told Lug.

"Yah, I saw something on TV about PTSD."

"What did you think of it? What do you think of entering a treatment program?"

"It might do some good. I was talking to a guy who went through it. He said it helped him. It might be worth a shot," Lug said.

"I talked to a counselor after you left. She said you can come in anytime."

"How about right now? Do you think they are open right now?"

"Sure, they must keep regular hours."

When she saw him walking to his car she thought, it didn't take much to get him started.

Lug left the powwow and drove to the Vet's Center. On the way he listened to Dylan singing "Blowing in the Wind."

At the Vet's Center Lug found out he could enter the program in a couple of days. His stay would be about a month.

Lug talked to the spiritual man before he went in for the program. He remembered to bring him a package of Prince Albert tobacco and a pair of warm socks.

In talking with the man, Lug learned that veterans were respected because of the sacrifices they had made in the war. The man told Lug he would pray for him. He told Lug to come back and see him when he got out of the Veteran's Hospital.

Lug went to see the counselor and she helped him complete the paperwork. He thanked her and drove to his sister's house. He parked his car and went inside. Judy showed him where he could leave his car parked while he was gone.

Judy drove Lug to the brick hospital. Lug took his bag of clothes and walked up the steps. Judy waved from her car. Lug noticed she was parked under an American flag.

He walked into the building. The smell of disinfectant reminded him of other official buildings he had been through.

Lug was ready for whatever was to come. Don't sweat the small shit, he thought.

Lug quickly learned that he was not the only one having trouble coping with memories of the war. He felt comfortable talking with other vets who had similar experiences.

Living in the Vet's Hospital felt like being in the military again. He slept in a warm bed and ate warm food. Lug spent most of his time with guys his age who had been to Vietnam. His time was structured for him.

In the group therapy sessions they told war stories at first. After a while together they began to talk, about feelings. Lug became aware that he had been acting normal in what was an abnormal situation. He felt like he was leaving some of his memories at the hospital.

In spite of the camaraderie he felt, Lug was anxious to rejoin his community. He wanted to go home. Lug knew he would complete the program but didn't expect to spend one extra minute at the hospital.

While he was gone, Judy was busy. She made Lug a pair of moccasins. The toes had the traditional beaded floral design. Around the cuffs she stitched the colors of the Vietnam campaign ribbon. She called the counselor at the Vet's Center to make sure the colors were right. It was green, then yellow with three red stripes, yellow, then green again. The smoke-tanned hide smell came to her as she sewed.

The hardest part was going down in the basement for the trunk her husband left when he went to Vietnam. The trunk contained his traditional dance outfit. It had been packed away since he hadn't come back from the war.

Judy drove to the hospital and picked Lug up when he completed the PTSD program. Looks like he put on some weight, she thought when she first saw him.

She drove to the spiritual man's house. Judy was listening to a powwow tape while driving. Lug tapped his hand on his knee in time to the drum. On the way, Lug told hospital stories. She could see his laugh lines as he talked about the month with other vets.

At the house Judy waited outside while the two men talked and smoked. She listened to both sides of the tape twice before Lug came out. He had a smile and walked light on his feet. Lug got in the car.

Judy drove to her house. They listened to the powwow on the way. She could see that he was enjoying the music.

"I've got that extra bedroom downstairs. You can stay there until you get your own place," she told him.

"Sounds like a winner. Combread every day?"

"Nope, special occasions only."

"I might be eligible for a disability pension but I'd rather get a job," Lug said.

"Do what you want to do," she said.

"Where are we going now?" Lug asked.

"We're going to a powwow. I got my tent set up already and I want to dance in the first grand entry."

"Okay, it'll feel good to see familiar faces again."

"Did the hospital do anything for you?" she asked.

"I think so, but it felt better talking to the spiritual man," he answered.

When they got to the powwow grounds Judy drove to her tent. Lug perched on the fender when she went inside to change into her jingledress.

Sure, the hospital was nice, but it feels better being here with relatives, Lug thought. He breathed the cool air in deeply. He could hear his sister's jingledress as she got dressed. He was trying to decide which food stand to start with when his sister came out.

"Tie this up for me, will you?" she asked.

Judy handed him the eagle fluff and medicine wheel. He used rawhide to tie it to her small braid. After she checked to make sure it was the way she wanted it, Judy said,

"Go in the tent and get your present."

"Okay," he said, jumping off the fender and unzipping the tent.

Inside the tent he saw a pair of moccasins on top of a traditional dance outfit. The colors of the campaign ribbon on the moccasins caught his eye. He took off his sneakers and put on the moccasins.

"Hey, thanks a lot, I needed some moccasins," said Lug.

"The rest of the outfit belongs to you too," she said.

"Really?" He recognized the dance outfit. He knew who used to own it. He thought of his brother-in-law and the Vietnam War.

"Hurry up and put it on, it's almost time for grand entry," Judy told him.

Lug put on the dance outfit and walked out for the inspection he knew she would give. He did a couple of steps to show her how it fit. She smiled her approval.

They walked to where the people were lining up. He was laughing as he joined the traditional dancers. He saw his cousin Fuzzy, who was a Vietnam vet.

"Didja hear? They got a new flavor for Vietnam vets," Lug said.

"Yah, what is it?" asked Fuzzy, who had been in Khe Sahn in '68.

"Agent Grape," said Lug.

They both laughed at themselves for laughing.

Lug danced the grand entry song with slow dignity. He felt proud. Lug moved with the drum during the flag song.

When the veteran's song began Lug moved back to join his sister. Both of them had tears as they danced the Veteran's honor song together.

1997

GORDON HENRY

B. 1955

Arthur Boozhoo on the Nature of Magic

I'm different, you may have noticed. I was raised far away in a city my father went there under relocation to work for a utility company, electrical people. After a few years he died; he was falling, they say, and to save himself he reached up and grabbed at some wires and was electrocuted on the spot. I was ten. We moved around quite a bit after that. We lived with my aunties and uncles, but there were so many of us we caused hardship, so we didn't stay in one place long. About four years later, my mother met a man some-where when she was out drinking with her sisters. They married, but the man didn't want anything to do with us, so they sent all the kids away to live with our grandparents. By then I was seventeen, and I made up my mind to stay in the city.

While my brothers and sisters returned to the rez, I got work part-time in a candy factory, and I was doing pretty good for a while. In a few months I bought a car and I could drive all over. I drove to see my mother once at a place in San Francisco, but the visit didn't seem to mean much to her so I left. After a year or so I got letters from my grandparents here asking me to come back, but I had already decided to go to college part-time. After I wrote back to tell them about my plans, they wrote and told me I could go to school full-time with tribal funding, at a school closer to the reservation. Instead I applied and got financial aid to attend college at San Jose State the next fall. At first I wanted to study everything, but after two or three terms, a counselor told me I should consider one field. I chose drama. I felt I could act, and that if I chose many different roles maybe I'd find the one I was closest to and live it. While I was taking the drama course work, I got involved with a group of people who believed that everyone has a personal magic that they can ignore or use. We'd all meet once a week to discuss those mystical concepts and study magic. By the end of the year all but two people had dropped out of the group. So there was just me and one woman. At our last meeting she told me the only reason she stayed in the group was because she loved me. I didn't know what she meant, and I told her I thought she was a very magical person, but I didn't think I loved her. That was the last I saw of her.

But I was in love with magic. So I quit school and I went around the city seeking out magicians and gathering an assortment of tricks and teachings from each one. I also studied magic books, every one I could find. In time I knew enough to make a living from magic, with illusion and memory tricks. But I wasn't sure about things. I kept getting letters from my grandparents and my brothers and sisters. They all wanted me to return to this place, the place of my grandparents, my ancestors. One letter brought me back. My youngest sister was sick. Doctors found no cure, and she was next to death. I got in my car and drove for two days straight.

When I got to my grandparents' house they took me into the room where the girl was dying. The light was such that her head was a shadow growing up from the bed with the floral print of the sheets.

I spoke to her: "Do you know who I am? Can you see me?"

The shadow turned from the window and became a face. I knew then her eyes didn't register. I was unrecognizable, so I moved closer. Grand-mother tried to pull me back.

"It's catching, trachoma," she said. "Young people all over the reserva-tion are dying."

But the child's voice moved me forward to the edge of the bed.

"Do you know magic?" she said. "Show me some magic, brother."

"Can you see me?" I said.

"No," she said, "I can't see you, but I remember seeing you."

"Then I can't do magic."

My sister turned her head to the window; sunlight surged out over her face, soaking into her skin, lighting her clearly, as I now see her in my mind.

"I can only see light," she said.

Two days later she died. In a week I came onto the same sickness. I could feel my sight going, but it was like the going had nothing to do with what I saw or what lived outside me. My sight was going from the inside, almost backward, like the memory of the operation of the eyes left out particulars and details, like my head was shoveling the inner light I needed to see into a great mound of expanding and hungry shadows.

I asked my grandfather about magic. "We have none here," he said, "at least not the kind you know, of the eye and memory games. But there are healers among us, men and women of gifts and visions. Some are relatives of light people. Sometimes their gifts can bring people back. Quite a few people have told us not to believe in those gifts, but with all the sickness around us and no cures by the white doctors, some people have returned to these descendants of the original teachers and bringers of light."

Then the old man took me to Jake Seed and he healed me. When I was well I went to Seed again and asked if he could teach me the magic he had. He told me to come every day and he would decide if he could teach me. I went to his place every day for about four years. Then he put me through a ceremony. After days of preparation and explanation of the meaning of the ceremony, he took me way back into the woods behind his place. We walked up a hill. I dug a hole; he prayed over it and put tobacco down. I stepped down into the hole and waited. Once again he prayed. Then he put a ring of tobacco around me and buried me up to my neck.

Darkness swelled out of the earth swallowing shadows, leaving only the light of animal's eyes and distant stars to compose the sights I saw. I was not there long when animals came shining low to the ground. They moved up to my face, scratching the earth, scratching dirt into my eyes. After a while, minutes, hours, a thousand blue blinks of stats, a hundred rustlings in the trees, animals sat in a circle around me, outside the ring of tobacco, growling and moaning. Then I understood their language and I felt fear for all of creation. My thoughts raced in the darkness to find the old man, but my body was still in the hole, nervous, shivering in the cold night dirt. There was no magic to match the feeling; no illusions could pull me from the ground. I waited for power and I sang like I always do when I'm nervous. The first song came out rough, a coarse melody, bent with fear, like a sapling resisting strong wind. The deeper I went into the song the more I felt the fear slacken into a strength of human sound mixing with air and elements. Soon the animals joined in, growling to long musical howls, introspective calls and silences. My own vocals hung on for a long time; note faded into note; song faded into song. There were words and there were no words; there were sounds and there were voices from the once fearful gut, grasping each musical moment. Then, when the songs grew longer, I knew no more of the source of the memorized and invented tones. The animals left. I felt their shadows slink back out of the circle and bolt away, skittering across dirt into the leaves, into the bush. In silence and solitude, I heard footsteps behind me; then laughter careened, in a strange dance. I finally caught sight, out of the corner of my eye, of a small person. At first, I thought he was a child, but as he drew closer I knew he was a little man. He had a small drum in his hand and he sang in laughter.

> Red day coming
> Red boy dreams
> Red day coming
> over the back of clouds
>
> Eye of the Eagle
> Swift and Swallow
> Red day coming Red boy sings

Then the little man stopped, turned his back to me, and he wheeled back around. He held his enormous penis in his hands and pissed on the ground in front of me, close enough that I could see steam rising from the earth and smell and feel the sprinkle of his spray as he snickered. When he finished he abused me with gruff, untranslatable language, and he kicked dirt into my face. He swung his drumstick and struck the back of my neck with a force that astonished me with pain and the little man's power. I felt the sting of the blow vibrate in violent waves down to my feet. I rocked and twisted in the hole. I screamed, wailing anger. I cried "Go away." I called to the spirit of god for mercy. But the little man stayed. He clubbed my ears, he crapped in front of me and danced with joy at my pain and degradation. Then I gave up. "Go ahead," I said, "do what you want, I surrender." Right then, in the middle of a wild raucous dance, in the middle of his ridiculing laughter, he stopped and sang again, a song of sorrow.

> sees the fading stars
> sees the northern lights
> sees the eyes of animals
> all in the face
> all in the face
> the face eats
> the face speaks
> boy and man
> the faces love
> the faces love the stars
> the faces love the ghost lights
> the animal faces
> the faces eat
> the boy and man
> speak and eat
> the faces they love

With that the man trudged off toward a huge stone, and walked around and vanished behind it. There the sky was coming onto day, and light shone red over and through the eastern trees.

Seed came up then, carrying a basket and a piece of red material. He sat down on the ground a short distance in front of me, took out a tobacco pouch and rolled up a smoke. For a long time he said nothing. Then he got up, reached into his basket, and brought out a plate of food. I smelled the boiled potatoes, and my eyes rested on the boiled meat as he set the plate in front of me. Next to the plate he set down a glass of water. "Let the eyes drink for you. Let the eyes eat for you," he said. Then he tied the material to a tree, toward the east, about fifty feet away from where I was buried.

That day the sun burned the memory of thirst and hunger into me. I grew angry at the sun, at Seed, at myself. I tried to sing again but my throat didn't work in the heat, in dryness. Then I cried. I cried for the rest of the day until the sun went down. At night I tried to sleep, but the animals returned, encircling me and keeping me awake. Just before dawn I heard laughter. I thought of the little man again, but I couldn't see anyone or anything in any direction. At last the sun pushed out red light, and I saw out in the east, on the tree where the tobacco was tied, a woodpecker, one of those big ones, pileated. The bird was laughing, driving its beak into the tree in the dawn light. Light streamed out from each place the woodpecker struck, as if the tree held its own sun inside and the bird conducted the light of that sun out. Time and again the bird backed off, lifted away from the tree, and landed on another part of the tree to peck and strike another place from which light flowed out. One final time the bird did this. Then the bird reached into the tree with its beak and extracted the light in a long bending waving string that followed the course of its flight to where it circled me. Then the woodpecker flew down over the hill out of my sight, with the long string of golden light trailing behind it. From there I saw Seed approaching, and after he dug me out I left the hole and the hill.

By the next spring it was clear that Seed had accepted me as his helper. Through him I learned to assist with ceremonials. At the same time, I continued practicing the magic I learned in the city, among the people of the reservation and the people of nearby communities. I ran ads in local news publications, and I posted my card on bulletin boards outside grocery stores, outside the tribal offices, all over. I got a few jobs but the work wasn't steady, so I started working part-time as a janitor at the Original Man School.

Things were going well for me. I was learning and I had work; I was surviving. Then in the fall I did my magic act for a children's birthday party in a town outside the reservation, in Detroit Lakes. I performed my most difficult tricks with the most success I'd ever had. One was a mentalist memory trick through which I heard, and recited back with my eyes closed, the names and details of clothing of every person at the party. For the other most difficult trick I had the birthday child rip up a piece of his parent's most important correspondence and put the ripped pieces into a fishbowl full of water. Then I threw my magic coat over the bowl and sang.

> *Sleep, peels, angles of angels sing of sign, sword of words, elm smells concrete, encore on the corner, a northern ornithologist, jest in case, sends a letter which ends in ways to sway opinion to slice the union onion with a sword of words, without tears.*

After that and the conventional magical smoke, the child retrieved the letter from the family mailbox and returned to show everyone that the ripped-up correspondence was whole and dry. Everyone was impressed; I was impressed; the children were impressed; the parents were impressed.

When I returned to the reservation to see Seed, to tell him about my success, a young woman met me at his door. She told me that she was Seed's daughter, Rose Meskwaa Geeshik, that the old man was sick. She had come to see him after a violent disturbing dream and found him sweating, fevered and weak. "He's been reciting names," she said. "Oskinaway, Minogeshig, Broken Tooth, Kubbemubbe, Shagonawshee, Bwanequay, Nawawzhee, Yellowhead, Abetung, Aishkonance. repeats the names and shivers. I don't know what it means."

In the time I worked with Seed he never mentioned any living family or any children. She took me back to see the old man. I followed her to the back bedroom. Seed slept there, on the bed, wrapped in a star blanket. Sundown named the hour in the window of the room. The songs of faraway crows coruscated into the room in sundown angles. I spoke to him. "Seed," I said, "it's me, Boozhoo. How are you? Seed, wake up; I need to speak to you." For a long time there was no answer. Darkness worked into the room and only an occasional cigarette, the flare of a match, touched off any semblance of sight. After a time Rose asked me to pray with her for Seed. She called on grandfathers, the creator; she spoke of her love for the old man. Her eyes squeezed tight in the intensity of her thought.

> Creator bring him back to us
> he is far away now within the sight of ancestors
> their arms are open across the silver river
> there are giants and abysmal sorrows in the river
> Some of us will float over
> Some of us will find the water solid beneath our feet
> Some will step on the backs of the giants and slide away
> into an angry foam
> Some will sink straight down into a place
> where the river has no bottom.
> O creator do not take the man
> Dear ancestors sing a song that tells it is not time
> turn him back to us with your song
> Let Seed return to earth
> Let the skies drench him again

Let him know again the fragrances of the great mother earth
Let him draw his strength from the love that is here
in my heart.

Rose prayed on and on, crying off and on between the words, at times
screaming out into the darkness of the room, with a voice and a hope
powerful enough to wake the most distant sleeping star. Still Seed didn't
move; his face showed no change. Rose prayed on and on. I wanted to stay
awake to help her, but only fear ever kept me from sleeping and at that time
I felt no fear: maybe it was Rose's voice, maybe it was the strength I'd seen
in Seed in times past, but I felt no fear.

*Somehow I have come to sit on a log. After thinking I am asleep, I
understand I am awake when a yellow dog crosses in front of me. Voices inside
the log tell me I must learn to fly. So I make a man out of tall grass and call him
by my own name. Then I throw him into the air and a whirlwind of leaves and
human voices carries the grass man away.*

Rose woke me at dawn with a gentle hand on my shoulder. "Have some
coffee," she said, offering me a yellow cup. "He'll be okay, now."

I took the coffee cup from her. "Where's the old man?" I said.

"Sleeping still, but he's okay. I think the fever is gone. He woke up for a few
minutes, but he needs rest. You go wash up; I'll fix some breakfast. Then you can
go home and get some rest. Come back later; he said he wants to speak to you."

"No," I said. "I'll stay for a while; I can watch him while you get some
rest. He's been good to me, I'll stay."

Then I got up and went to the washbowl. There was no water, so I
walked outside and worked the pump until water flowed out into the white
bowl. When I came back inside Rose had breakfast ready. The table was set
with eggs and fried potatoes, frybread, strawberry jam and honey. Rose
poured another cup of coffee for me, and we both ate heartily. After breakfast I went out to the front porch to smoke. The sun had cleared the tallest
trees of the reservation by then, and I could hear voices on the road to the
church hall. As I lit a cigarette Rose came out and sat down beside me.

"Go inside," I said. "I'll watch the old man as soon as I'm done here."

She looked out into the trees as wisps of black hair licked the bones of
her chin and grazed the flatness of her cheek. "I don't know if I can sleep,"
she said. "I keep hearing the voices out here, I keep thinking of my father,
this whole place. You know, where we all come from."

1994

THE 1980S: DISASTERS, DIVESTMENT, DIVERSITY

Despite global progress toward democracy, the 1980s can be viewed as a decade when much went wrong. As if to signal the disasters to come, a long inactive volcano, Mount St. Helens, erupted in 1980 in Washington state, killing 57 people, but most of the ensuing disasters of the decade were caused by humans. The senseless murders of two popular music icons—John Lennon in 1980 and Marvin Gaye in 1984—signaled a terrible loss of the potential for humane values in a world consumed by its own mad drive for progress. Lennon had urged his listeners to "Give Peace a Chance" and suggested "All You Need is Love"; Gaye looked around at social and environmental ills in 1969 and asked the musical question "What's Going On?" President Ronald Reagan and Pope John Paul II were also the targets of assassination attempts, both in 1981, and that same year an assassin's bullet felled Egyptian President Anwar Sadat, whose work with Israeli Prime Minister Menachem Begin to achieve peace in the Middle East had earned him the Nobel Peace Prize in 1979.

The murders or attempted murders of world leaders and prominent artists along with the alarming spread of a deadly virus known as AIDS were likely to have caused everyone to ask, "What's going on?" The Chernobyl nuclear disaster in the Soviet Union in 1986 and the explosion of the U.S. space shuttle *Challenger* that same year indicated that the world's superpowers, despite their technological superiority, were far from infallible.

The anxiety that had permeated the Cold War for decades was somewhat diminished in the 1980s as the world started to contemplate the tremors caused by realignments in smaller, less powerful nations than the two global superpowers: the United States and the Soviet Union. The Iran-Iraq war from 1980 to 1988 would have lasting implications for instability in that region of the world. The United States was involved in a number of covert and overt military missions in Central America that either proved disastrous or caused the nation to question its imperialistic aspirations. The Soviet Union was having difficulties of its own in Afghanistan. Britain adamantly defended a tiny vestige of its empire off the coast of Argentina in the Falkland Islands, resulting in a two-month war between those nations. While all this was taking place, a number of nations in Africa and Europe were preparing for a series of revolutions—some peaceful, some not—that were to realign global politics in profound ways.

From an American perspective, the late 1980s are perhaps most remembered as the years when the Soviet Union disintegrated and the Berlin Wall crumbled, but the end of the racist *apartheid* government in South Africa was every bit as dramatic, and it indicated in no uncertain terms that the influence of the United States around the world could be better understood in terms of economics rather than politics (although, of course, the two are closely related). College campuses, which had not been hotbeds of activism since the tragic events at Kent State University in 1970, were suddenly revitalized by student protests calling on their universities to divest themselves of any investments they had in South African corporations in an attempt to pressure the government to reform. Pop musicians, who had begun to discover their potential for humanitarian good deeds through concerts like Live Aid and collaborative benefit songs like "We Are the World" and "Feed the World," refused to play at the South African resort Sun City. In a dramatic reversal of long-standing racist politics, the South African government considered deep and significant changes in its very structure. Longtime political prisoner Nelson Mandela was released, took part in restructuring the new political system, and became South Africa's first black president in the postapartheid era. This change, along with the rise of democracy in eastern Europe, resonated with Americans aware of similar stories in their own history (the struggle to overcome slavery and the war for independence from England, respectively) and made them aware, perhaps more than ever before, of the meaning of global citizenship.

Accompanying this realization in the 1980s was a broadly increasing definition of what racial and ethnic diversity might mean within our own borders. Even a progressive work like Randolph Bourne's 1916 essay "Trans-National America" (in volume D of *The Heath Anthology*) is only concerned with the ethnic diversity resulting from the influx of European immigrants in the late nineteenth and early twentieth centuries; it does not consider the African, Asian, or South American presence in American society. By the 1980s, though, a perspective like Bourne's would have easily accommodated immigrants or descendants of immigrants from around the globe. The literature in the following section clearly reflects this diversity and the global perspective that accompanies it. Many of the selections—including June Jordan's poem "To Free Nelson Mandela," Jamaica Kincaid's withering critique from her book *A Small Place*, Carolyn Forché's poems about fighting in El Salvador such as "Because One is Not Always Forgotten," and Helena Viramontes' immigration story "The Cariboo Café"—demonstrate that diversity, which we have shown to be ubiquitous throughout American literary history, by the 1980s had become fully accepted and expected as part of the American story. The strong emphasis on the individual that had evolved in American literature since the rise of the confessional poets in the early 1960s was cycling back to an emphasis on the collective in the 1980s, though the confessional impulse certainly did not disappear.

The undisputed literary high point of this decade was the publication in 1987 of Toni Morrison's novel *Beloved*, which manages, in tough, original prose, to tell the story of slavery in such a way as to be both personal and collective. This triumph unites the two poles of any national literature, but especially the literature of a nation long conflicted about its official slogan "*E pluribus unum*": "From many (people) one (nation)." That slogan took on new meaning in the 1980s, and the nation that was beginning to realize its own unity was also forced to contemplate its history and its role on the global stage in more sophisticated ways than ever before.

CYNTHIA OZICK
B. 1928

For Cynthia Ozick, literature is seductive: stories "arouse"; they "enchant"; they "transfigure." Ozick describes herself in "early young-womanhood" as "a worshipper of literature," drawn to the world of the imagination "with all the rigor and force and stunned ardor of religious belief." Yet the pleasure of attraction is tempered by danger. Adoration of art can become a form of idolatry—a kind of "aesthetic paganism" that for her is incompatible with Judaism because it betrays the biblical commandment against graven images. Art can also "tear away from humanity," and Ozick worries that the beauty of language can distract from art's moral function of judging and interpreting the world. These tensions—between art and idolatry, between aestheticism and moral seriousness, between the attraction of surfaces and the weight of history—lie at the heart of Ozick's fiction and essays. Indeed, Ozick is often considered a writer of oppositions, many of which are reflected in her efforts to translate what she calls a "Jewish sensibility" into the English language. "I suppose you might say that I am myself an oxymoron," she explains, "but in the life of story-writing, there are no boundaries."

Cynthia Ozick was born in New York City on April 17, 1928, to Russian Jewish immigrants, William and Celia Regelson Ozick. Her childhood was spent in the Pelham Bay section of the Bronx, where her parents worked long hours to maintain a pharmacy during the Depression. She recalls these years as an idyllic time of reading and dreaming of writing; she also remembers being made to feel "hopelessly stupid" at school and being subjected to overt anti-Semitism. After graduating from Hunter High School, Ozick went on to complete a B.A. at New York University and an M.A. in English Literature at Ohio State University, where she wrote a thesis on the late novels of Henry James. James became a kind of obsession for her, both inspiring and inhibiting her burgeoning writing career. For nearly seven years, she struggled to write a long "philosophical" novel titled *Mercy, Pity, Peace, and Love*, which she finally abandoned after writing some 300,000 words. During this time, Ozick moved back to New York, married Bernard Hallote, and began working as an advertising copywriter. She also wrote short stories and labored for six more years on what became her first novel, *Trust*, published soon after the birth of her daughter Rachel in 1965. At this time, she also began the intensive study of Jewish philosophy, history, and literature that eventually transformed her writing.

Although slow to come into her own as a writer, Ozick is now prolific and widely acclaimed. She has been recognized through numerous awards and grants, including a National Endowment for the Arts Fellowship, a Guggenheim Fellowship, the American Academy and Institute of Arts and Letters Strauss Livings grant, and the Jewish Book Council Award. Three of her essays have been republished in the annual collection of *Best American Essays*, five of her stories have been chosen to appear in *Best American Short Stories*, and three have received first prize in the O. Henry Prize Stories competition. Perhaps best known for her fiction and essays, Ozick also writes and translates poetry, and she has recently written a play based on two of her short stories, "The Shawl" (1981) and "Rosa" (1984) (later published together in a single volume).

In characteristically contradictory terms, Ozick has described herself, as a first-generation American Jew, to be "perfectly at home and yet perfectly insecure, perfectly acculturated and yet perfectly marginal." However, unlike many Jewish American writers who were the children of immigrants, Ozick does not write about the sociological experiences of assimilation and subsequent generational conflict. Rather, her sense of being simultaneously inside and outside the dominant culture is manifested in a real faith in "the thesis of American pluralism," a pluralism that accommodates particularist and diverse impulses. Perhaps somewhat paradoxically, one of Ozick's greatest contributions to American literature is her unwavering effort to remain "centrally Jewish" in her concerns, perpetuating the stories and histories of Jewish texts and traditions. "The Shawl," reprinted here, reflects Ozick's commitment to Jewish memory, as well as her long-standing fears about the dangers of artistic representation. Although many of Ozick's works address the historical and psychological consequences of the Holocaust, only in "The Shawl" does she attempt to render life in the concentration camps directly. She has explained her reluctance to write fiction about the events of the Holocaust by insisting instead that "we ought to absorb the documents, the endless, endless data.... I want the documents to be enough; I don't want to tamper or invent or imagine. And yet I have done it. I can't not do it. It comes, it invades." The imaginative origin of "The Shawl" was, in fact, a historical text: the story evolved out of one evocative sentence in William Shirer's *The Rise and Fall of the Third Reich* about babies being thrown against electrified fences.

In an extraordinarily compressed and almost incantatory prose, Ozick depicts such horrifyingly familiar images of Nazi brutality as forced marches, starvation, dehumanization, and murder, while nevertheless managing to convey her ambivalence about using metaphoric language to represent an experience that is nearly unimaginable. The story makes clear that speech itself is dangerous: despite Rosa's desire to hear her child's voice, Magda is safe only as long as she is mute. The consequence of her cry—the only dialogue in the story—is death. Through a series of paradoxical images that combine the fantastical and the realistic, Ozick demonstrates that in writing and thinking about the unnatural world of a death camp, all expectations must be subverted: here, a baby's first tooth is an "elfin tombstone"; a breast is a "dead volcano"; a starved belly is "fat, full and round"; and a shawl can be "magic," sheltering and nourishing a child as an extension of the mother's body. Yet neither motherhood nor magic can save lives here; that which protects is also that which causes death. By overturning the natural order and unsettling the reader's ability to "know," Ozick makes the powerful point that the "reality" of the Holocaust is fundamentally inaccessible and that conventional means of understanding simply do not apply.

Tresa Grauer
University of Pennsylvania

PRIMARY WORKS

Trust, 1966; *The Pagan Rabbi, and Other Stories*, 1971; *Bloodshed and Three Novellas*, 1976; *Levitation: Five Fictions*, 1982; *Art & Ardor: Essays*, 1983; *The Cannibal Galaxy*, 1983; *The Messiah of Stockholm*, 1987; *The Shawl*, 1988; *Metaphor & Memory: Essays*, 1989; *Epodes: First Poems*, 1992; *Blue Light: A Play*, 1994; *Fame & Folly: Essays*, 1996; *Portrait of the Artist as a Bad Character*, 1996; *The Putter-Messer Papers*, 1997; *SHE: Portrait of the Essay as a Warm Body*, 1998; *Quarrel and Quandary: Essays*, 2000; *Heir to the Glimmering World*, 2004; *The Din in the Head: Essays*, 2006; *Dictation: A Quartet*, 2008; *Foreign Bodies*, 2010.

The Shawl

Stella, cold, cold, the coldness of hell. How they walked on the roads together, Rosa with Magda curled up between sore breasts, Magda wound up in the shawl. Sometimes Stella carried Magda. But she was jealous of Magda. A thin girl of fourteen, too small, with thin breasts of her own, Stella wanted to be wrapped in a shawl, hidden away, asleep, rocked by the march, a baby, a round infant in arms. Magda took Rosa's nipple, and Rosa never stopped walking, a walking cradle. There was not enough milk; sometimes Magda sucked air; then she screamed. Stella was ravenous. Her knees were tumors on sticks, her elbows chicken bones.

Rosa did not feel hunger; she felt light, not like someone walking but like someone in a faint, in trance, arrested in a fit, someone who is already a floating angel, alert and seeing everything, but in the air, not there, not touching the road. As if teetering on the tips of her fingernails. She looked into Magda's face through a gap in the shawl: a squirrel in a nest, safe, no one could reach her inside the little house of the shawl's windings. The face, very round, a pocket mirror of a face: but it was not Rosa's bleak complexion, dark like cholera, it was another kind of face altogether, eyes blue as air, smooth feathers of hair nearly as yellow as the Star sewn into Rosa's coat. You could think she was one of *their* babies.

Rosa, floating, dreamed of giving Magda away in one of the villages. She could leave the line for a minute and push Magda into the hands of any woman on the side of the road. But if she moved out of line they might shoot. And even if she fled the line for half a second and pushed the shawl-bundle at a stranger, would the woman take it? She might be surprised, or afraid; she might drop the shawl, and Magda would fall out and strike her head and die. The little round head. Such a good child, she gave up screaming, and sucked now only for the taste of the drying nipple itself. The neat grip of the tiny gums. One mite of a tooth tip sticking up in the bottom gum, how shining, an elfin tombstone of white marble gleaming there. Without complaining, Magda relinquished Rosa's teats, first the left, then the right; both were cracked, not a sniff of milk. The duct-crevice extinct, a dead volcano, blind eye, chill hole, so Magda took the corner of the shawl and milked it instead. She sucked and sucked, flooding threads with wetness. The shawl's good flavor, milk of linen.

It was a magic shawl, it could nourish an infant for three days and three nights. Magda did not die, she stayed alive, although very quiet. A peculiar smell, of cinnamon and almonds, lifted out of her mouth. She held her eyes open every moment, forgetting how to blink or nap, and Rosa and sometimes Stella studied their blueness. On the road they raised one burden of a leg after another and studied Magda's face. "Aryan," Stella said, in a voice grown as thin as a string; and Rosa thought how Stella gazed at Magda like a young cannibal. And the time that Stella said "Aryan," it sounded to Rosa as if Stella had really said "Let us devour her."

But Magda lived to walk. She lived that long, but she did not walk very well, partly because she was only fifteen months old, and partly because the spindles of her legs could not hold up her fat belly. It was fat with air, full and round. Rosa gave almost all her food to Magda, Stella gave nothing; Stella was ravenous, a growing child herself, but not growing much. Stella did not menstruate. Rosa did not menstruate. Rosa was ravenous, but also not; she learned from Magda how to drink the taste of a finger in one's mouth. They were in a place without pity, all pity was annihilated in Rosa, she looked at Stella's bones without pity. She was sure that Stella was waiting for Magda to die so she could put her teeth into the little thighs.

Rosa knew Magda was going to die very soon; she should have been dead already, but she had been buried away deep inside the magic shawl, mistaken there for the shivering mound of Rosa's breasts; Rosa clung to the shawl as if it covered only herself. No one took it away from her. Magda was mute. She never cried. Rosa hid her in the barracks, under the shawl, but she knew that one day someone would inform; or one day someone, not even Stella, would steal Magda to eat her. When Magda began to walk Rosa knew that Magda was going to die very soon, something would happen. She was afraid to fall asleep; she slept with the weight of her thigh on Magda's body; she was afraid she would smother Magda under her thigh. The weight of Rosa was becoming less and less; Rosa and Stella were slowly turning into air.

Magda was quiet, but her eyes were horribly alive, like blue tigers. She watched. Sometimes she laughed—it seemed a laugh, but how could it be? Magda had never seen anyone laugh. Still, Magda laughed at her shawl when the wind blew its corners, the bad wind with pieces of black in it, that made Stella's and Rosa's eyes tear. Magda's eyes were always clear and tearless. She watched like a tiger. She guarded her shawl. No one could touch it; only Rosa could touch it. Stella was not allowed. The shawl was Magda's own baby, her pet, her little sister. She tangled herself up in it and sucked on one of the corners when she wanted to be very still.

Then Stella took the shawl away and made Magda die.

Afterward Stella said: "I was cold."

And afterward she was always cold, always. The cold went into her heart: Rosa saw that Stella's heart was cold. Magda flopped onward with her little pencil legs scribbling this way and that, in search of the shawl; the pencils faltered at the barracks opening, where the light began. Rosa saw and pursued. But already Magda was in the square outside the barracks, in the jolly light. It was the roll-call arena. Every morning Rosa had to conceal Magda under the shawl against a wall of the barracks and go out and stand in the arena with Stella and hundreds of others, sometimes for hours, and Magda, deserted, was quiet under the shawl, sucking on her corner. Every day Magda was silent, and so she did not die. Rosa saw that today Magda was going to die, and at the same time a fearful joy ran in Rosa's two palms, her fingers were on fire, she was astonished, febrile: Magda, in the sunlight, swaying on her pencil legs, was howling. Ever since the drying up of Rosa's nipples, ever since Magda's last scream on the road, Magda had been devoid of any syllable; Magda was a mute. Rosa believed that something had gone wrong with her vocal cords, with her windpipe, with the cave of her larynx; Magda was defective, without a voice; perhaps she was deaf; there might be something amiss with her intelligence; Magda was dumb. Even the laugh that came when the ash-stippled wind made a clown out of Magda's shawl was only the air-blown showing of her teeth. Even when the lice, head lice and body lice, crazed her so that she became as wild as one of the big rats that plundered the barracks at daybreak looking for carrion, she rubbed and scratched and kicked and bit and rolled without a whimper. But now Magda's mouth was spilling a long viscous rope of clamor.

"Maaaa—"

It was the first noise Magda had ever sent out from her throat since the drying up of Rosa's nipples.

"Maaaa . . . aaa!"

Again! Magda was wavering in the perilous sunlight of the arena, scribbling on such pitiful little bent shins. Rosa saw. She saw that Magda was grieving for the loss of her shawl, she saw that Magda was going to die. A tide of commands hammered in Rosa's nipples: Fetch, get, bring! But she did not know which to go after first, Magda or the shawl. If she jumped out into the arena to snatch Magda up, the howling would not stop, because Magda would still not have the shawl; but if she ran back into the barracks to find the shawl, and if she found it, and if she came after Magda holding it and shaking it, then she would get Magda back, Magda would put the shawl in her mouth and turn dumb again.

Rosa entered the dark. It was easy to discover the shawl. Stella was heaped under it, asleep in her thin bones. Rosa tore the shawl free and flew—she could fly, she was only air—into the arena. The sunheat murmured of another life, of butterflies in summer. The light was placid, mellow. On the other side of the steel fence, far away, there were green meadows speckled with dandelions and deep-colored violets; beyond them, even farther, innocent tiger lilies, tall, lifting their orange bonnets. In the barracks they spoke of "flowers," of "rain": excrement, thick turd-braids, and the slow stinking maroon waterfall that slunk down from the upper bunks, the stink mixed with a bitter fatty floating smoke that greased Rosa's skin. She stood for an instant at the margin of the arena. Sometimes the electricity inside the fence would seem to hum; even Stella said it was only an imagining, but Rosa heard real sounds in the wire; grainy sad voices. The farther she was from the fence, the more clearly the voices crowded at her. The lamenting voices strummed so convincingly, so passionately, it was impossible to suspect them of being phantoms. The voices told her to hold up the shawl, high; the voices told her to shake it, to whip with it, to unfurl it like a flag. Rosa lifted, shook, whipped, unfurled. Far off, very far, Magda leaned across her air-fed belly, reaching out with the rods of her arms. She was high up, elevated, riding someone's shoulder. But the shoulder that carried Magda was not coming toward Rosa and the shawl, it was drifting away, the speck of Magda was moving more and more into the smoky distance. Above the shoulder a helmet glinted. The light tapped the helmet and sparkled it into a goblet. Below the helmet a black body like a domino and a pair of black boots hurled themselves in the direction of the electrified fence. The electric voices began to chatter wildly. "Maamaa, maaamaaa," they all hummed together. How far Magda was from Rosa now, across the whole square, past a dozen barracks, all the way on the other side! She was no bigger than a moth.

All at once Magda was swimming through the air. The whole of Magda traveled through loftiness. She looked like a butterfly touching a silver vine. And the moment Magda's feathered round head and her pencil legs and balloonish belly and zigzag arms splashed against the fence, the steel voices went mad in their growling, urging Rosa to run and run to the spot where Magda had fallen from her flight against the electrified fence; but of course Rosa did not obey them. She only stood, because if she ran they would shoot, and if she tried to pick up the sticks of Magda's body they would shoot, and if she let the wolf's screech ascending now through the ladder of her skeleton break out, they would shoot; so she took Magda's shawl and filled her own mouth with it, stuffed it in and stuffed it in, until she was swallowing up the wolf's screech and tasting the cinnamon and almond depth of Magda's saliva; and Rosa drank Magda's shawl until it dried.

1981

JANICE MIRIKITANI
B. 1942

Janice Mirikitani, a Sansei or third-generation Japanese American, was born in Stockton, California, just before World War II, during which she and her family, along with 110,000 other Japanese Americans, were interned in concentration camps. Mirikitani is the editor of several anthologies, including *Third World Women, Time to Greez! Incantations from the Third World*, and *AYUMI, A Japanese American Anthology*, a 320-page bilingual anthology featuring four generations of Japanese American writers, poets, and graphic artists. She has published in many anthologies, textbooks, and periodicals, including *Asian American Heritage*, *The Third Woman: Minority Women Writers of the United States*, *Amerasia*, and *Bridge*.

Mirikitani is a poet, dancer, and teacher, as well as a social and political activist; she has been program director of Glide Church/Urban Center since 1967 and director of the Glide Theater Group. Her commitment to Third World positions against racism and oppression is reflected in the protest content of her major collections, *Awake in the River* (1978) and *Shedding Silence* (1987). George Leong says of her: "From the eye of racist relocation fever which came about and plagued America during World War II, Janice Mirikitani grew/bloomed/ fought as a desert flower behind barbed wire. She grew with that pain, of what it all represented; from the multinational corporations to war from Korea to Vietnam to Latin America to Africa to Hunter's Point and Chinatown" ("Afterword," *Awake in the River*).

Much of her work seeks defiantly to break the stereotypes of Asian Americans prevalent in mainstream American culture. Her voice is often angry, aggressive, blunt, and direct, but it can also be elegiac. Because she is finding new ground, Mirikitani takes the time to explore her family history, and she anchors her identity securely in the details of Asian American experience. In this manner, she manages to escape easy nostalgia and cultural sentimentality. Mirikitani does not separate her writing from a social and political platform and sees the necessity to write out of a political agenda. Identifying her community as Third World, she says, "I don't think that Third World writers can really afford to separate themselves from the ongoing struggles of their people. Nor can we ever not embrace our history."

Shirley Geok-lin Lim
University of California, Santa Barbara

PRIMARY WORKS

Awake in the River, 1978; *Shedding Silence*, 1987; *We the Dangerous*, 1995; *Love Works*, 2000.

For My Father

He came over the ocean
carrying Mt. Fuji
on his back/Tule Lake on his chest
hacked through the brush
of deserts   5
and made them grow
strawberries

     we stole berries
     from the stem
     we could not afford them   10
     for breakfast

his eyes held
nothing
as he whipped us
for stealing.   15

the desert had dried
his soul.

wordless
he sold
the rich,   20
full berries
to hakujines
whose children
pointed at our eyes

     they ate fresh   25
     strawberries
     with cream.
Father,
I wanted to scream
at your silence.   30
Your strength
was a stranger
I could never touch.
iron
in your eyes   35
to shield
the pain
to shield desert-like wind
from patches
of strawberries   40
grown
from
tears.

               1978

Desert Flowers

Flowers
faded
in the desert wind.
No flowers grow
where dust winds blow   5
and rain is like
a dry heave moan.

Mama, did you dream about that
beau who would take you
away from it all,   10
who would show you
in his '41 ford
and tell you how soft
your hands
like the silk kimono   15
you folded for the wedding?
Make you forget
about That place,
the back bending
wind that fell like a wall,   20
drowned all your geraniums
and flooded the shed
where you tried to sleep
away hyenas?
    And mama,   25
    bending in the candlelight,
    after lights out in barracks,
    an ageless shadow
    grows victory flowers
    made from crepe paper,   30
    shaping those petals
    like the tears
    your eyes bled.

Your fingers
knotted at knuckles   35
wounded, winding around wire stems
the tiny, sloganed banner:

    "america for americans".

Did you dream
of the shiny ford   40
(only always a dream)
ride your youth
like the wind
in the headless night?
Flowers   45
2 ¢ a dozen,
flowers for American Legions
worn like a badge
on america's lapel

made in post-concentration camps 50
by candlelight.
Flowers
watered
by the spit
of "no japs wanted here", 55
planted in poverty
of postwar relocations,
plucked by
victory's veterans.
        Mama, do you dream 60
        of the wall of wind
        that falls
        on your limbless desert,
        on stems
        brimming with petals/crushed 65
        crepepaper
        growing
        from the crippled
        mouth of your hand?
Your tears, mama, 70
have nourished us.
Your children
like pollen
scatter in the wind.

1978

Breaking Tradition

for my Daughter

My daughter denies she is like me,
her secretive eyes avoid mine.
    She reveals the hatreds of womanhood
    already veiled behind music and smoke and telephones.
I want to tell her about the empty room 5
    of myself.
    This room we lock ourselves in
    where whispers live like fungus,
    giggles about small breasts and cellulite,
    where we confine ourselves to jealousies, 10
    bedridden by menstruation.
    This waiting room where we feel our hands
    are useless, dead speechless clamps
    that need hospitals and forceps and kitchens
    and plugs and ironing boards to make them useful. 15

I deny I am like my mother. I remember why:
    She kept her room neat with silence,
    defiance smothered in requirements to be otonashii,
    passion and loudness wrapped in an obi,
    her steps confined to ceremony,   20
    the weight of her sacrifice she carried like
    a foetus. Guilt passed on in our bones.
I want to break tradition—unlock this room
    where women dress in the dark
    Discover the lies my mother told me.   25
    The lies that we are small and powerless
    that our possibilities must be compressed
    to the size of pearls, displayed only as
    passive chokers, charms around our neck.
Break Tradition.   30
    I want to tell my daughter of this room
    of myself
    filled with tears of shakuhachi,
    the light in my hands,
    poems about madness,   35
    the music of yellow guitars—
    sounds shaken from barbed wire and
    goodbyes and miracles of survival.
    This room of open window where daring ones escape.

My daughter denies she is like me   40
    her secretive eyes are walls of smoke
    and music and telephones,
    her pouting ruby lips, her skirts
    swaying to salsa, Madonna and the Stones,
    her thighs displayed in carnavals of color.   45
    I do not know the contents of her room.
She mirrors my aging.

She is breaking tradition.

1978

Recipe

Round Eyes

Ingredients: scissors, Scotch magic transparent tape,
                eyeliner—water based, black.
                Optional: false eyelashes.

Cleanse face thoroughly.   5

For best results, powder entire face, including eyelids.
    (lighter shades suited to total effect desired)

With scissors, cut magic tape 1/16″ wide, 3/4″–1/2″ long—
depending on length of eyelid.

Stick firmly onto mid-upper eyelid area   10
    (looking down into handmirror facilitates finding
    adequate surface)

If using false eyelashes, affix first on lid, folding any
excess lid over the base of eyelash with glue.

Paint black eyeliner on tape and entire lid.   15

Do not cry.

                                                 1987

■ LESLIE MARMON SILKO (LAGUNA) ■
B. 1948

Leslie Marmon Silko grew up on the Laguna Pueblo Reservation in the house where her father, Lee H. Marmon, was born. Her mother, Virginia, worked outside the home, and Silko spent most of her preschool years with her great-grandmother, who lived next door.

She attended Bureau of Indian Affairs schools at Laguna until high school in Albuquerque. Then she attended the University of New Mexico, graduating magna cum laude in 1969. She then attended three semesters of law school before deciding to devote herself to writing and to enter graduate school in English.

Silko has taught at Navajo Community College in Many Farms, Arizona, at the University of New Mexico, and at the University of Arizona. Formerly married to attorney John Silko, she has two sons, Robert, born in 1966, and Cazimir, born in 1972. The family lived in Alaska during the mid-seventies when Silko was writing *Ceremony*. Although Alaska is the setting for the title story of her book *Storyteller*, most of her early fiction and poetry is set in the Laguna area.

Many cultures have influenced the history of Laguna. Hopi, Jemez, and Zuni people had married into the pueblo by the time it was established at its present site in the early 1500s. Later Navajos, Spanish settlers, and others of European ancestry intermarried with the Lagunas. The incorporation of rituals and stories from other tribes and cultures into their oral tradition occurred early in Laguna society and became an ongoing practice. Silko's own ancestry is mixed. Her father's people were Laguna and European American. Her mother, born in Montana, was from a Plains tribe. Silko also has Mexican ancestry.

Her first book, *Laguna Woman* (1974), a collection of her poetry, shows an awareness of the interrelationships between the people and the river, mesas, hills, and mountains surrounding Laguna. But this awareness of place is not narrowly regional. For example, "Prayer to the Pacific" affirms the Lagunas' dependence on the rain that the west winds bring from as far as China.

The nearly 500-year existence of present-day Laguna enables Silko to write out of a culture intimately knowledgeable about the natural environment. This culture and its landscape have suffered severe trauma during the past half-century. During World War II, the atomic bomb was developed at nearby Los Alamos, and the first atomic explosion, at the Trinity site, occurred only 150 miles from Laguna. In the early 1950s, the Anaconda company opened a large open-pit uranium mine on Laguna land, and uranium mining became a major source of income for Laguna and neighboring Pueblo and Navajo peoples. Nuclear destruction is a central concern in *Ceremony* (1977), Silko's first novel. An important theme in all of Silko's work is the recurrence of everything that happens. As "old Grandma" in *Ceremony* simply states, "'It seems like I already heard these stories before . . . only thing is, the names sound different.'"

Silko's second novel, *Almanac of the Dead* (1991), sounds an alarm in the face of escalating interpersonal violence and greed threatening to destroy humanity at the end of the twentieth century. A wide-ranging analysis and critique of contemporary American culture, the novel ends with the prophetic vision of a revolution in which the buffalo, the indigenous people, and the poor regain their land. Silko's third novel, *Gardens in the Dunes* (1999), juxtaposes the world of the indigenous peoples of the desert Southwest with that of the European and American upper class during the period between the Ghost Dance era at the end of the nineteenth century and World War I.

The most useful guide to understanding the cultural and social contexts of *Ceremony* and *Almanac of the Dead* is Silko's *Yellow Woman and a Beauty of the Spirit: Essays on Native American Life Today* (1996). Silko models her fiction on the Laguna storytelling tradition, which she describes as patterned like the web of a spider.

Norma C. Wilson
University of South Dakota

PRIMARY WORKS

Laguna Woman, 1974; *Ceremony*, 1977; *Storyteller*, 1981; *Almanac of the Dead*, 1991; *Yellow Woman and a Beauty of the Spirit: Essays on Native American Life Today*, 1996; *Gardens in the Dunes*, 1999; *The Turquoise Ledge*, 2010.

Lullaby

The sun had gone down but the snow in the wind gave off its own light. It came in thick tufts like new wool—washed before the weaver spins it. Ayah reached out for it like her own babies had, and she smiled when she remembered how she had laughed at them. She was an old woman now, and her life had become memories. She sat down with her back against the wide cottonwood tree, feeling the rough bark on her back bones; she faced east and listened to the wind and snow sing a high-pitched Yeibechei[1] song. Out of the wind she felt warmer, and she could watch the wide fluffy snow fill in her tracks, steadily, until the direction she had come from was gone. By the light of the snow she could see the dark outline of the big arroyo a few feet away. She was sitting on the edge of Cebolleta Creek, where in the springtime the thin cows would graze on grass already chewed flat to the ground. In the wide deep creek bed where only a trickle of water flowed in the summer, the skinny cows would wander, looking for new grass along winding paths splashed with manure.

Ayah pulled the old Army blanket over her head like a shawl. Jimmie's blanket—the one he had sent to her. That was a long time ago and the green wool was faded, and it was unraveling on the edges. She did not want to think about Jimmie. So she thought about the weaving and the way her mother had done it. On the tall wooden loom set into the sand under a tamarack tree for shade. She could see it clearly. She had been only a little girl when her grandma gave her the wooden combs to pull the twigs and burrs from the raw, freshly washed wool. And while she combed the wool, her grandma sat beside her, spinning a silvery strand of yarn around the smooth cedar spindle. Her mother worked at the loom with yarns dyed bright yellow and red and gold. She watched them dye the yarn in boiling black pots full of beeweed petals, juniper berries, and sage. The blankets her mother made were soft and woven so tight that rain rolled off them like birds' feathers. Ayah remembered sleeping warm on cold windy nights, wrapped in her mother's blankets on the hogan's[2] sandy floor.

The snow drifted now, with the northwest wind hurling it in gusts. It drifted up around her black overshoes—old ones with little metal buckles. She smiled at the snow which was trying to cover her little by little. She could remember when they had no black rubber overshoes; only the high buckskin leggings that they wrapped over their elkhide moccasins. If the snow was dry or frozen, a person could walk all day and not get wet; and in the evenings the beams of the ceiling would hang with lengths of pale buckskin leggings, drying out slowly.

She felt peaceful remembering. She didn't feel cold any more. Jimmie's blanket seemed warmer than it had ever been. And she could remember the morning he was born. She could remember whispering to her mother, who was sleeping on the other side of the hogan, to tell her it was time now. She did not want to wake the others. The second time she called to her, her mother stood up and pulled on her shoes; she knew. They walked to the old stone hogan together, Ayah walking a step behind her mother. She waited

---

[1] Navajo Night Chant—a song of healing. [2] Traditional six-sided Navajo dwelling, the door of which faces east.

alone, learning the rhythms of the pains while her mother went to call the old woman to help them. The morning was already warm even before dawn and Ayah smelled the bee flowers blooming and the young willow growing at the springs. She could remember that so clearly, but his birth merged into the births of the other children and to her it became all the same birth. They named him for the summer morning and in English they called him Jimmie.

It wasn't like Jimmie died. He just never came back, and one day a dark blue sedan with white writing on its doors pulled up in front of the boxcar shack where the rancher let the Indians live. A man in a khaki uniform trimmed in gold gave them a yellow piece of paper and told them that Jimmie was dead. He said the Army would try to get the body back and then it would be shipped to them; but it wasn't likely because the helicopter had burned after it crashed. All of this was told to Chato because he could understand English. She stood inside the doorway holding the baby while Chato listened. Chato spoke English like a white man and he spoke Spanish too. He was taller than the white man and he stood straighter too. Chato didn't explain why; he just told the military man they could keep the body if they found it. The white man looked bewildered; he nodded his head and he left. Then Chato looked at her and shook his head, and then he told her, "Jimmie isn't coming home anymore," and when he spoke, he used the words to speak of the dead. She didn't cry then, but she hurt inside with anger. And she mourned him as the years passed, when a horse fell with Chato and broke his leg, and the white rancher told them he wouldn't pay Chato until he could work again. She mourned Jimmie because he would have worked for his father then; he would have saddled the big bay horse and ridden the fence lines each day, with wire cutters and heavy gloves, fixing the breaks in the barbed wire and putting the stray cattle back inside again.

She mourned him after the white doctors came to take Danny and Ella away. She was at the shack alone that day they came. It was back in the days before they hired Navajo women to go with them as interpreters. She recognized one of the doctors. She had seen him at the children's clinic at Cañoncito about a month ago. They were wearing khaki uniforms and they waved papers at her and a black ball-point pen, trying to make her understand their English words. She was frightened by the way they looked at the children, like the lizard watches the fly. Danny was swinging on the tire swing on the elm tree behind the rancher's house, and Ella was toddling around the front door, dragging the broomstick horse Chato made for her. Ayah could see they wanted her to sign the papers, and Chato had taught her to sign her name. It was something she was proud of. She only wanted them to go, and to take their eyes away from her children.

She took the pen from the man without looking at his face and she signed the papers in three different places he pointed to. She stared at the ground by their feet and waited for them to leave. But they stood there and began to point and gesture at the children. Danny stopped swinging. Ayah could see his fear. She moved suddenly and grabbed Ella into her arms; the child squirmed, trying to get back to her toys. Ayah ran with the baby toward Danny; she screamed for him to run and then she grabbed him around his chest and carried him too. She ran south into the foothills of juniper trees and black lava rock. Behind her she heard the doctors running, but they had been taken by surprise, and as the hills became steeper and the cholla cactus were thicker, they stopped. When she reached the top of the hill, she stopped to listen in case they were circling around her. But in a few minutes she heard a car engine start and they drove away. The children had been too surprised to cry while she ran with them. Danny was shaking and Ella's little fingers were gripping Ayah's blouse.

She stayed up in the hills for the rest of the day, sitting on a black lava boulder in the sunshine where she could see for miles all around her. The sky was light blue and cloudless, and it was warm for late April. The sun warmth relaxed her and took the fear and anger away. She lay back on the rock and watched the sky. It seemed to her that she could walk into the sky, stepping through clouds endlessly. Danny played with little pebbles and stones, pretending they were birds eggs and then little rabbits. Ella sat at her feet and dropped fistfuls of dirt into the breeze, watching the dust and particles of sand intently. Ayah watched a hawk soar high above them, dark wings gliding; hunting or only watching, she did not know. The hawk was patient and he circled all afternoon before he disappeared around the high volcanic peak the Mexicans called Guadalupe.

Late in the afternoon, Ayah looked down at the gray boxcar shack with the paint all peeled from the wood; the stove pipe on the roof was rusted and crooked. The fire she had built that morning in the oil drum stove had burned out. Ella was asleep in her lap now and Danny sat close to her, complaining that he was hungry; he asked when they would go to the house. "We will stay up here until your father comes," she told him, "because those white men were chasing us." The boy remembered then and he nodded at her silently.

If Jimmie had been there he could have read those papers and explained to her what they said. Ayah would have known then, never to sign them. The doctors came back the next day and they brought a BIA[3] policeman with them. They told Chato they had her signature and that was all they needed. Except for the kids. She listened to Chato sullenly; she hated him when he told her it was the old woman who died in the winter, spitting blood; it was her old grandma who had given the children this disease. "They don't spit blood," she said coldly. "The whites lie." She held Ella and Danny close to her, ready to run to the hills again. "I want a medicine man first," she said to Chato, not looking at him. He shook his head. "It's too late now. The policeman is with them. You signed the paper." His voice was gentle.

It was worse than if they had died: to lose the children and to know that somewhere, in a place called Colorado, in a place full of sick and dying strangers, her children were without her. There had been babies that died soon after they were born, and one that died before he could walk. She had carried them herself, up to the boulders and great pieces of the cliff that

[3]U.S. Bureau of Indian Affairs.

long ago crashed down from Long Mesa; she laid them in the crevices of sandstone and buried them in fine brown sand with round quartz pebbles that washed down the hills in the rain. She had endured it because they had been with her. But she could not bear this pain. She did not sleep for a long time after they took her children. She stayed on the hill where they had fled the first time, and she slept rolled up in the blanket Jimmie had sent her. She carried the pain in her belly and it was fed by everything she saw: the blue sky of their last day together and the dust and pebbles they played with; the swing in the elm tree and broomstick horse choked life from her. The pain filled her stomach and there was no room for food or for her lungs to fill with air. The air and the food would have been theirs.

She hated Chato, not because he let the policeman and doctors put the screaming children in the government car, but because he had taught her to sign her name. Because it was like the old ones always told her about learning their language or any of their ways: it endangered you. She slept alone on the hill until the middle of November when the first snows came. Then she made a bed for herself where the children had slept. She did not lie down beside Chato again until many years later, when he was sick and shivering and only her body could keep him warm. The illness came after the white rancher told Chato he was too old to work for him anymore, and Chato and his old woman should be out of the shack by the next afternoon because the rancher had hired new people to work there. That had satisfied her. To see how the white man repaid Chato's years of loyalty and work. All of Chato's fine-sounding English talk didn't change things.

It snowed steadily and the luminous light from the snow gradually diminished into the darkness. Somewhere in Cebolleta a dog barked and other village dogs joined with it. Ayah looked in the direction she had come, from the bar where Chato was buying the wine. Sometimes he told her to go on ahead and wait; and then he never came. And when she finally went back looking for him, she would find him passed out at the bottom of the wooden steps to Azzie's Bar. All the wine would be gone and most of the money too, from the pale blue check that came to them once a month in a government envelope. It was then that she would look at his face and his hands, scarred by ropes and the barbed wire of all those years, and she would think, this man is a stranger; for forty years she had smiled at him and cooked his food, but he remained a stranger. She stood up again, with the snow almost to her knees, and she walked back to find Chato.

It was hard to walk in the deep snow and she felt the air burn in her lungs. She stopped a short distance from the bar to rest and readjust the blanket. But this time he wasn't waiting for her on the bottom step with his old Stetson hat pulled down and his shoulders hunched up in his long wool overcoat.

She was careful not to slip on the wooden steps. When she pushed the door open, warm air and cigarette smoke hit her face. She looked around slowly and deliberately, in every corner, in every dark place that the old man might find to sleep. The bar owner didn't like Indians in there, especially Navajos, but he let Chato come in because he could talk Spanish like he was one of them. The men at the bar stared at her, and the bartender saw that she left the door open wide. Snowflakes were flying inside like moths and melting into a puddle on the oiled wood floor. He motioned to her to close the door, but she did not see him. She held herself straight and walked across the room slowly, searching the room with every step. The snow in her hair melted and she could feel it on her forehead. At the far corner of the room, she saw red flames at the mica window of the old stove door; she looked behind the stove just to make sure. The bar got quiet except for the Spanish polka music playing on the jukebox. She stood by the stove and shook the snow from her blanket and held it near the stove to dry. The wet wool smell reminded her of new-born goats in early March, brought inside to warm near the fire. She felt calm.

In past years they would have told her to get out. But her hair was white now and her face was wrinkled. They looked at her like she was a spider crawling slowly across the room. They were afraid; she could feel the fear. She looked at their faces steadily. They reminded her of the first time the white people brought her children back to her that winter. Danny had been shy and hid behind the thin white woman who brought them. And the baby had not known her until Ayah took her into her arms, and then Ella had nuzzled close to her as she had when she was nursing. The blonde woman was nervous and kept looking at a dainty gold watch on her wrist. She sat on the bench near the small window and watched the dark snow clouds gather around the mountains; she was worrying about the unpaved road. She was frightened by what she saw inside too: the strips of venison drying on a rope across the ceiling and the children jabbering excitedly in a language she did not know. So they stayed for only a few hours. Ayah watched the government car disappear down the road and she knew they were already being weaned from these lava hills and from this sky. The last time they came was in early June, and Ella stared at her the way the men in the bar were now staring. Ayah did not try to pick her up; she smiled at her instead and spoke cheerfully to Danny. When he tried to answer her, he could not seem to remember and he spoke English words with the Navajo. But he gave her a scrap of paper that he had found somewhere and carried in his pocket; it was folded in half, and he shyly looked up at her and said it was a bird. She asked Chato if they were home for good this time. He spoke to the white woman and she shook her head. "How much longer?" he asked, and she said she didn't know; but Chato saw how she stared at the boxcar shack. Ayah turned away then. She did not say good-bye.

She felt satisfied that the men in the bar feared her. Maybe it was her face and the way she held her mouth with teeth clenched tight, like there was nothing anyone could do to her now. She walked north down the road, searching for the old man. She did this because she had the blanket, and there would be no place for him except with her and the blanket in the old adobe barn near the arroyo. They always slept there when they came to

Cebolleta. If the money and the wine were gone, she would be relieved because then they could go home again; back to the old hogan with a dirt roof and rock walls where she herself had been born. And the next day the old man could go back to the few sheep they still had, to follow along behind them, guiding them, into dry sandy arroyos where sparse grass grew. She knew he did not like walking behind old ewes when for so many years he rode big quarter horses and worked with cattle. But she wasn't sorry for him; he should have known all along what would happen.

There had not been enough rain for their garden in five years; and that was when Chato finally hitched a ride into the town and brought back brown boxes of rice and sugar and big tin cans of welfare peaches. After that, at the first of the month they went to Cebolleta to ask the postmaster for the check; and then Chato would go to the bar and cash it. They did this as they planted the garden every May, not because anything would survive the summer dust, but because it was time to do this. The journey passed the days that smelled silent and dry like the caves above the canyon with yellow painted buffaloes on their walls.

He was walking along the pavement when she found him. He did not stop or turn around when he heard her behind him. She walked beside him and she noticed how slowly he moved now. He smelled strong of woodsmoke and urine. Lately he had been forgetting. Sometimes he called her by his sister's name and she had been gone for a long time. Once she had found him wandering on the road to the white man's ranch, and she asked him why he was going that way; he laughed at her and said, "You know they can't run that ranch without me," and he walked on determined, limping on the leg that had been crushed many years before. Now he looked at her curiously, as if for the first time, but he kept shuffling along, moving slowly along the side of the highway. His gray hair had grown long and spread out on the shoulders of the long overcoat. He wore the old felt hat pulled down over his ears. His boots were worn out at the toes and he had stuffed pieces of an old red shirt in the holes. The rags made his feet look like little animals up to their ears in snow. She laughed at his feet; the snow muffled the sound of her laugh. He stopped and looked at her again. The wind had quit blowing and the snow was falling straight down; the southeast sky was beginning to clear and Ayah could see a star.

"Let's rest awhile," she said to him. They walked away from the road and up the slope to the giant boulders that had tumbled down from the red sandrock mesa throughout the centuries of rainstorms and earth tremors. In a place where the boulders shut out the wind, they sat down with their backs against the rock. She offered half of the blanket to him and they sat wrapped together.

The storm passed swiftly. The clouds moved east. They were massive and full, crowding together across the sky. She watched them with the feeling of horses—steely blue-gray horses startled across the sky. The powerful haunches pushed into the distances and the tail hairs streamed white mist behind them. The sky cleared. Ayah saw that there was nothing between her and the stars. The light was crystalline. There was no shimmer, no distortion through earth haze. She breathed the clarity of the night sky; she smelled the purity of the half moon and the stars. He was lying on his side with his knees pulled up near his belly for warmth. His eyes were closed now, and in the light from the stars and the moon, he looked young again.

She could see it descend out of the night sky: an icy stillness from the edge of the thin moon. She recognized the freezing. It came gradually, sinking snowflake by snowflake until the crust was heavy and deep. It had the strength of the stars in Orion, and its journey was endless. Ayah knew that with the wine he would sleep. He would not feel it. She tucked the blanket around him, remembering how it was when Ella had been with her; and she felt the rush so big inside her heart for the babies. And she sang the only song she knew to sing for babies. She could not remember if she had ever sung it to her children, but she knew that her grandmother had sung it and her mother had sung it:

> The earth is your mother,
>   she holds you.
> The sky is your father,
>   he protects you.
> Sleep,
> sleep.
> Rainbow is your sister,
>   she loves you.
> The winds are your brothers,
>   they sing to you.
> Sleep,
> sleep.
> We are together always
> We are together always
> There never was a time
> when this
> was not so.

1981

RAYMOND CARVER
1938–1988

Raymond Carver's characters have been called diminished and lost. His character studies represent a cold look at the complicated inner lives of the working poor in the United States during the 1970s and 1980s: at any time, anyone might lose everything—not only material position but also trust, love, and truth. Carver may occasionally be naturalistic, but he is never nostalgic or romantic about life near the edge.

Carver lived much of his life in the same desperate straits as his characters. His father was a laborer with grand dreams and a deadly attraction to alcohol. Carver himself was married and raising two children before his twentieth birthday. He worked a variety of jobs that would never be presented as a career path on a résumé—picking tulips, pumping gas, sweeping up, delivering packages. He recalled, "Once I even considered, for a few minutes anyway—the job application form there in front of me—becoming a bill collector!" He and his wife declared bankruptcy several times. He inherited his father's drinking problem.

In 1958, with two small children, he and his wife moved to Chico, California. They borrowed $125 from the druggist who employed him as a delivery man. With that money, Carver enrolled in Chico State and took his first writing class from John Gardner, at that time a young, unknown, and unpublished novelist. Encouraged by Gardner and later by the editor Gordon Lish, Carver began to take himself seriously as a writer. He began to publish regularly in "little magazines," but not until 1968 did his first book, a collection of poems, appear in a limited edition. Eight years later, his first collection of stories, *Will You Please Be Quiet, Please?*, was published. Readers did not realize that Carver had stopped writing a couple of years before the book's publication.

In June 1977, Carver's life changed drastically. He stopped drinking, he was awarded a Guggenheim Fellowship, and he met the poet and short story writer Tess Gallagher, who was to become his companion and eventually his second wife. Carver continued to write poems and stories until his death from lung cancer in 1988 at the age of fifty.

To the consternation of many editors, Carver was a rewriter of his own work. At least one of his stories has appeared with as many as three different titles and a slight rewriting at each publication. In an essay called "On Rewriting," he writes, "I like to mess with my stories. I'd rather tinker with a story after writing it, and then tinker some more, changing this, changing that, than have to write the story in the first place." Even his successful stories were not exempt from his rewriting. "The Bath," a widely praised story from *What We Talk about When We Talk about Love* and winner of the Carlos Fuentes Fiction Award, reappears in a much longer form in *Cathedral* as "A Small, Good Thing." Writing in the *Washington Post*, Jonathan Yardley said, "The first version is beautifully crafted and admirably concise, but lacking in genuine compassion; the mysterious caller is not so much a human being as a mere voice, malign and characterless. But in the second version that voice becomes a person, one whose own losses are, in different ways, as crippling and heartbreaking as the one suffered by the grieving parents." Although many do not agree with Yardley, it is obvious that Carver found a different kind of strength in *Cathedral*.

There is a more recent controversy about Carver's rewriting and his relationship to his editors, particularly Lish. In 2007 *The New Yorker* published the story "Beginners" (which, after extensive editing by Lish, became "What We Talk about When We Talk about Love"), an accompanying article, and an online piece that displays Lish's edits in detail, suggesting that Carver's rewriting may have been an attempt to recover his own stories as well as an enlargement of his earlier minimalist works. As soon as some legal issues are resolved, scholars will be able to take a closer look at Carver's process, intentions, and art and evaluate better the relationship between Carver and Lish.

Paul Jones
University of North Carolina at Chapel Hill

PRIMARY WORKS

Will You Please Be Quiet, Please? 1976; *Furious Seasons,* 1977; *What We Talk about When We Talk about Love,* 1981; *Fires: Essays, Poems, and Stories, 1966–1982,* 1983; *Cathedral,* 1984; *Dostoevsky: The Screenplay,* 1985; *Where Water Comes Together With Other Water,* 1985; *Ultramarine,* 1986; *Saints,* 1987; *Where I'm Calling From: New and Selected Stories,* 1988; *A New Path to the Waterfall,* 1989; *No Heroics, Please: Uncollected Writings,* 1992; *Carnations: A One-Act Play,* 1992; *Short Cuts: Selected Stories,* 1993; *All of Us: The Collected Poems,* 1998; *Call If You Need Me: The Uncollected Fiction & Prose,* 2001.

What We Talk about When We Talk about Love

My friend Mel McGinnis was talking. Mel McGinnis is a cardiologist, and sometimes that gives him the right.

The four of us were sitting around his kitchen table drinking gin. Sunlight filled the kitchen from the big window behind the sink. There were Mel and me and his second wife, Teresa—Terri, we called her—and my wife, Laura. We lived in Albuquerque then. But we were all from somewhere else.

There was an ice bucket on the table. The gin and tonic water kept going around, and we somehow got on the subject of love. Mel thought real love was nothing less than spiritual love. He said he'd spent five years in a seminary before quitting to go to medical school. He said he still looked back on those years in the seminary as the most important years in his life.

Terri said the man she lived with before she lived with Mel loved her so much he tried to kill her. Then Terri said, "He beat me up one night. He dragged me around the living room by my ankles. He kept saying, 'I love you, I love you, you bitch.' He went on dragging me around the living room. My head kept knocking on things." Terri looked around the table. "What do you do with love like that?"

She was a bone-thin woman with a pretty face, dark eyes, and brown hair that hung down her back. She liked necklaces made of turquoise, and long pendant earrings.

"My God, don't be silly. That's not love, and you know it," Mel said. "I don't know what you'd call it, but I sure know you wouldn't call it love."

"Say what you want to, but I know it was," Terri said. "It may sound crazy to you, but it's true just the same. People are different, Mel. Sure, sometimes he may have acted crazy. Okay. But he loved me. In his own way maybe, but he loved me. There was love there, Mel. Don't say there wasn't."

Mel let out his breath. He held the glass and turned to Laura and me. "The man threatened to kill me," Mel said. He finished his drink and reached for the gin bottle. "Terri's a romantic. Terri's of the kick-me-so-I'll-know-you-love-me school. Terri, hon, don't look that way." Mel reached across the table and touched Terri's cheek with his fingers. He grinned at her.

"Now he wants to make up," Terri said.

"Make up what?" Mel said. "What is there to make up? I know what I know. That's all."

"How'd we get started on this subject, anyway?" Terri said. She raised her glass and drank from it. "Mel always has love on his mind," she said. "Don't you, honey?" She smiled, and I thought that was the last of it.

"I just wouldn't call Ed's behavior love. That's all I'm saying, honey," Mel said. "What about you guys?" Mel said to Laura and me. "Does that sound like love to you?"

"I'm the wrong person to ask," I said. "I didn't even know the man. I've only heard his name mentioned in passing. I wouldn't know. You have to know the particulars. But I think what you're saying is that love is an absolute."

Mel said, "The kind of love I'm talking about is. The kind of love I'm talking about, you don't try to kill people."

Laura said, "I don't know anything about Ed, or anything about the situation. But who can judge anyone else's situation?"

I touched the back of Laura's hand. She gave me a quick smile. I picked up Laura's hand. It was warm, the nails polished, perfectly manicured, I encircled the broad wrist with my fingers, and I held her.

"When I left, he drank rat poison," Terri said. She clasped her arms with her hands. "They took him to the hospital in Santa Fe. That's where we lived then, about ten miles out. They saved his life. But his gums went crazy from it. I mean they pulled away from his teeth. After that, his teeth stood out like fangs. My God," Terri said. She waited a minute, then let go of her arms and picked up her glass.

"What people won't do!" Laura said.

"He's out of the action now," Mel said. "He's dead."

Mel handed me the saucer of limes. I took a section, squeezed it over my drink, and stirred the ice cubes with my finger.

"It gets worse," Terri said. "He shot himself in the mouth. But he bungled that too. Poor Ed," she said. Terri shook her head.

"Poor Ed nothing," Mel said. "He was dangerous."

Mel was forty-five years old. He was tall and rangy with curly soft hair. His face and arms were brown from the tennis he played. When he was sober, his gestures, all his movements, were precise, very careful.

"He did love me though, Mel. Grant me that, can't you?"

"What do you mean, he bungled it?" I said.

Laura leaned forward with her glass. She put her elbows on the table and held her glass in both hands. She glanced from Mel to Terri and waited with a look of bewilderment on her open face, as if amazed that such things happened to people you were friendly with.

"How'd he bungle it when he killed himself?" I said.

"I'll tell you what happened," Mel said. "He took this twenty-two pistol he'd bought to threaten Terri and me with. Oh, I'm serious, the man was always threatening. You should have seen the way we lived in those days. Like fugitives. I even bought a gun myself. Can you believe it? A guy like me? But I did. I bought one for self-defense and carried it in the glove compartment. Sometimes I'd have to leave the apartment in the middle of the night. To go to the hospital, you know? Terri and I weren't married then, and my first wife had the house and the kids, the dog, everything, and Terri and I were living in this apartment here. Sometimes, as I say, I'd get a call in the middle of the night and have to go in to the hospital at two or three in the morning. It'd be dark out there in the parking lot, and I'd break into a sweat before I could even get to my car. I never knew if he was going to come up out of the shrubbery or from behind a car and start shooting. I mean, the man was crazy. He was capable of wiring a bomb, anything. He used to call my service at all hours and say he needed to talk to the doctor, and when I'd return the call, he'd say, 'Son of a bitch, your days are numbered.' Little things like that. It was scary, I'm telling you."

"I still feel sorry for him," Terri said.

"It sounds like a nightmare," Laura said. "But what exactly happened after he shot himself?"

Laura is a legal secretary. We'd met in a professional capacity. Before we knew it, it was a courtship. She's thirty-five, three years younger than I am. In addition to being in love, we like each other and enjoy one another's company. She's easy to be with.

"What happened?" Laura said.

Mel said, "He shot himself in the mouth in his room. Someone heard the shot and told the manager. They came in with a passkey, saw what had happened, and called an ambulance. I happened to be there when they brought him in, alive but past recall. The man lived for three days. His head swelled up to twice the size of a normal head. I'd never seen anything like it, and I hope I never do again. Terri wanted to go in and sit with him when she found out about it. We had a fight over it. I didn't think she should see him like that. I didn't think she should see him, and I still don't."

"Who won the fight?" Laura said.

"I was in the room with him when he died," Terri said. "He never came up out of it. But I sat with him. He didn't have anyone else."

"He was dangerous," Mel said. "If you call that love, you can have it."

"It was love," Terri said. "Sure, it's abnormal in most people's eyes. But he was willing to die for it. He did die for it."

"I sure as hell wouldn't call it love," Mel said. "I mean, no one knows what he did it for. I've seen a lot of suicides, and I couldn't say anyone ever knew what they did it for."

Mel put his hands behind his neck and tilted his chair back. "I'm not interested in that kind of love," he said. "If that's love, you can have it."

Terri said, "We were afraid. Mel even made a will out and wrote to his brother in California who used to be a Green Beret. Mel told him who to look for if something happened to him."

Terri drank from her glass. She said, "But Mel's right—we lived like fugitives. We were afraid. Mel was, weren't you, honey? I even called the police at one point, but they were no help. They said they couldn't do anything until Ed actually did something. Isn't that a laugh?" Terri said.

She poured the last of the gin into her glass and waggled the bottle. Mel got up from the table and went to the cupboard. He took down another bottle.

"Well, Nick and I know what love is," Laura said. "For us, I mean," Laura said. She bumped my knee with her knee. "You're supposed to say something now," Laura said, and turned her smile on me.

For an answer, I took Laura's hand and raised it to my lips. I made a big production out of kissing her hand. Everyone was amused.

"We're lucky," I said.

"You guys," Terri said. "Stop that now. You're making me sick. You're still on the honeymoon, for God's sake. You're still gaga, for crying out loud. Just wait. How long have you been together now? How long has it been? A year? Longer than a year?"

"Going on a year and a half," Laura said, flushed and smiling.

"Oh, now," Terri said. "Wait awhile."

She held her drink and gazed at Laura.

"I'm only kidding," Terri said.

Mel opened the gin and went around the table with the bottle.

"Here, you guys," he said. "Let's have a toast. I want to propose a toast. A toast to love. To true love," Mel said.

We touched glasses.

"To love," we said.

Outside in the backyard, one of the dogs began to bark. The leaves of the aspen that leaned past the window ticked against the glass. The afternoon sun was like a presence in this room, the spacious light of ease and generosity. We could have been anywhere, somewhere enchanted. We raised our glasses again and grinned at each other like children who had agreed on something forbidden.

"I'll tell you what real love is," Mel said. "I mean, I'll give you a good example. And then you can draw your own conclusions." He poured more gin into his glass. He added an ice cube and a sliver of lime. We waited and sipped our drinks. Laura and I touched knees again. I put a hand on her warm thigh and left it there.

"What do any of us really know about love?" Mel said. "It seems to me we're just beginners at love. We say we love each other and we do, I don't doubt it. I love Terri and Terri loves me, and you guys love each other too. You know the kind of love I'm talking about now. Physical love, that impulse that drives you to someone special, as well as love of the other person's being, his or her essence, as it were. Carnal love and, well, call it sentimental love, the day-to-day caring about the other person. But sometimes I have a hard time accounting for the fact that I must have loved my first wife too. But I did, I know I did. So I suppose I am like Terri in that regard. Terri and Ed." He thought about it and then he went on. "There was a time when I thought I loved my first wife more than life itself. But now I hate her guts. I do. How do you explain that? What happened to that love? What happened to it, is what I'd like to know. I wish someone could tell me. Then there's Ed. Okay, we're back to Ed. He loves Terri so much he tries to kill her and winds up killing himself." Mel stopped talking and swallowed from his glass. "You guys have been together eighteen months and you love each other. It shows all over you. You glow with it. But you both loved other people before you met each other. You've both been married before, just like us. And you probably loved other people before that too, even. Terri and I have been together five years, been married for four. And the terrible thing, the terrible thing is, but the good thing too, the saving grace, you might say, is that if something happened to one of us—excuse me for saying this—but if something happened to one of us tomorrow, I think the other one, the other person, would grieve for a while, you know, but then the surviving party would go out and love again, have someone else soon enough. All this, all of this love we're talking about, it would just be a memory. Maybe not even a memory. Am I wrong? Am I way off base? Because I want you to set me straight if you think I'm wrong. I want to know. I mean, I don't know anything, and I'm the first one to admit it."

"Mel, for God's sake," Terri said. She reached out and took hold of his wrist. "Are you getting drunk? Honey? Are you drunk?"

"Honey, I'm just talking," Mel said. "All right? I don't have to be drunk to say what I think. I mean, we're all just talking, right?" Mel said. He fixed his eyes on her.

"Sweetie, I'm not criticizing," Terri said.

She picked up her glass.

"I'm not on call today," Mel said. "Let me remind you of that. I am not on call," he said.

"Mel, we love you," Laura said.

Mel looked at Laura. He looked at her as if he could not place her, as if she was not the woman she was.

"Love you too, Laura," Mel said. "And you, Nick, love you too. You know something?" Mel said. "You guys are our pals," Mel said.

He picked up his glass.

Mel said, "I was going to tell you about something. I mean, I was going to prove a point. You see, this happened a few months ago, but it's still going on right now, and it ought to make us feel ashamed when we talk like we know what we're talking about when we talk about love."

"Come on now," Terri said. "Don't talk like you're drunk if you're not drunk."

"Just shut up for once in your life," Mel said very quietly. "Will you do me a favor and do that for a minute? So as I was saying, there's this old couple who had this car wreck out on the interstate. A kid hit them and they were all torn to shit and nobody was giving them much chance to pull through."

Terri looked at us and then back at Mel. She seemed anxious, or maybe that's too strong a word.

Mel was handing the bottle around the table.

"I was on call that night," Mel said. "It was May or maybe it was June. Terri and I had just sat down to dinner when the hospital called. There'd been this thing out on the interstate. Drunk kid, teenager, plowed his dad's pickup into this camper with this old couple in it. They were up in the mid-seventies, that couple. The kid—eighteen, nineteen, something—he was DOA. Taken the steering wheel through his sternum. The old couple, they were alive, you understand. I mean, just barely. But they had everything. Multiple fractures, internal injuries, hemorrhaging, contusions, lacerations, the works, and they each of them had themselves concussions. They were in a bad way, believe me. And, of course, their age was two strikes against them. I'd say she was worse off than he was. Ruptured spleen along with everything else. Both kneecaps broken. But they'd been wearing their seatbelts and, God knows, that's what saved them for the time being."

"Folks, this is an advertisement for the National Safety Council," Terri said. "This is your spokesman, Dr. Melvin R. McGinnis, talking." Terri laughed. "Mel," she said, "sometimes you're just too much. But I love you, hon," she said.

"Honey, I love you," Mel said.

He leaned across the table. Terri met him halfway. They kissed.

"Terri's right," Mel said as he settled himself again. "Get those seatbelts on. But seriously, they were in some shape, those oldsters. By the time I got down there, the kid was dead, as I said. He was off in a corner, laid out on a gurney. I took one look at the old couple and told the ER nurse to get me a neurologist and an orthopedic man and a couple of surgeons down there right away."

He drank from his glass. "I'll try to keep this short," he said. "So we took the two of them up to the OR and worked like fuck on them most of the night. They had these incredible reserves, those two. You see that once in a while. So we did everything that we could be done, and toward morning we're giving them a fifty-fifty chance, maybe less than that for her. So here they are, still alive the next morning. So, okay, we move them into the ICU, which is where they both kept plugging away at it for two weeks, hitting it better and better on all the scopes. So we transfer them out to their own room."

Mel stopped talking. "Here," he said, "let's drink this cheapo gin the hell up. Then we're going to dinner, right? Terri and I know a new place. That's where we'll go to this new place we know about. But we're not going until we finish up this cut-rate, lousy gin."

Terri said, "We haven't actually eaten there yet. But it looks good. From the outside, you know."

"I like food," Mel said. "If I had it to do over again, I'd be a chef, you know? Right, Terri?" Mel said.

He laughed. He fingered the ice in his glass.

"Terri knows," he said. "Terri can tell you. But let me say this. If I could come back again in a different life, a different time and all, you know what? I'd like to come back as a knight. You were pretty safe wearing all that armor. It was all right being a knight until gunpowder and muskets and pistols came along."

"Mel would like to ride a horse and carry a lance," Terri said.

"Carry a woman's scarf with you everywhere," Laura said.

"Or just a woman," Mel said.

"Shame on you," Laura said.

Terri said, "Suppose you came back as a serf. The serfs didn't have it so good in those days," Terri said.

"The serfs never had it good," Mel said. "But I guess even the knights were vessels to someone. Isn't that the way it worked? But then everyone is always a vessel to someone. Isn't that right, Terri? But what I liked about knights, besides their ladies, was that they had that suit of armor, you know, and they couldn't get hurt very easy. No cars in those days, you know? No drunk teenagers to tear into your ass."

"Vassals," Terri said.

"What?" Mel said.

"Vassals," Terri said. "They were called vassals, not vessels."

"Vassals, vessels," Mel said. "what the fuck's the difference? You know what I meant anyway. All right," Mel said, "So I'm not educated. I learned my stuff. I'm a heart surgeon, sure, but I'm just a mechanic. I go in and I fuck around and I fix things. Shit," Mel said.

"Modesty doesn't become you," Terri said.

"He's just a humble sawbones," I said. "But sometimes they suffocated in all that armor, Mel. They'd even have heart attacks if it got too hot and they were too tired and worn out. I read somewhere that they'd fall off their horses and not be able to get up because they were too tired to stand with all that armor on them. They got trampled by their own horses sometimes."

"That's terrible," Mel said. "That's a terrible thing, Nicky. I guess they'd just lay there and wait until somebody came along and made a shish kebab out of them."

"Some other vessel," Terri said.

"That's right," Mel said. "Some vassal would come along and spat the bastard in the name of love. Or whatever the fuck it was they fought over in those days."

"Same things we fight over these days," Terri said.

Laura said, "Nothing's changed."

The color was still high in Laura's cheeks. Her eyes were bright. She brought her glass to her lips.

Mel poured himself another drink. He looked at the label closely as if studying a long row of numbers. Then he slowly put the bottle down on the table and slowly reached for the tonic water.

"What about the old couple?" Laura said. "You didn't finish that story you started."

Laura was having a hard time lighting her cigarette. Her matches kept going out.

The sunshine inside the room was different now, changing, getting thinner. But the leaves outside the window were still shimmering, and I stared at the pattern they made on the panes and on the Formica counter. They weren't the same patterns, of course.

"What about the old couple?" I said.

"Older but wiser," Terri said.

Mel stared at her.

Terri said, "Go on with your story, hon. I was only kidding. Then what happened?"

"Terri, sometimes," Mel said.

"Please, Mel," Terri said. "Don't always be so serious, sweetie. Can't you take a joke?"

"Where's the joke?" Mel said.

He held his glass and gazed steadily at his wife.

"What happened?" Laura said.

Mel fastened his eyes on Laura. He said, "Laura, if I didn't have Terri and if I didn't love her so much, and if Nick wasn't my best friend, I'd fall in love with you. I'd carry you off, honey," he said.

"Tell your story," Terri said. "Then we'll go to that new place, okay?"

"Okay," Mel said. "Where was I?" he said. He stared at the table and then he began again.

"I dropped in to see each of them every day, sometimes twice a day if I was up doing other calls anyway. Casts and bandages, head to foot, the both of them. You know, you've seen it in the movies. That's just the way they looked, just like in the movies. Little eye-holes and nose-holes and mouth-holes. And she had to have her legs slung up on top of it. Well, the husband was very depressed for the longest while. Even after he found out that his wife was going to pull through, he was still very depressed. Not about the accident, though. I mean, the accident was one thing, but it wasn't everything. I'd get up to his mouth-hole, you know, and he'd say no, it wasn't the accident exactly but it was because he couldn't see her through his eye-holes. He said that was what was making him feel so bad. Can you imagine? I'm telling you, the man's heart was breaking because he couldn't turn his goddamn head and *see* his goddamn wife."

Mel looked around the table and shook his head at what he was going to say.

"I mean, it was killing the old fart just because he couldn't *look* at the fucking woman."

We all looked at Mel.

"Do you see what I'm saying?" he said.

Maybe we were a little drunk by then. I know it was hard keeping things in focus. The light was draining out of the room, going back through the window where it had come from. Yet nobody made a move to get up from the table to turn on the overhead light.

"Listen," Mel said. "Let's finish this fucking gin. There's about enough left here for one shooter all around. Then let's go eat. Let's go to the new place."

"He's depressed," Terri said. "Mel, why don't you take a pill?"

Mel shook his head. "I've taken everything there is."

"We all need a pill now and then," I said.

"Some people are born needing them," Terri said.

She was using her finger to rub at something on the table. Then she stopped rubbing.

"I think I want to call my kids," Mel said. "Is that all right with everybody? I'll call my kids," he said.

Terri said, "What if Marjorie answers the phone? You guys, you've heard us on the subject of Marjorie? Honey, you know you don't want to talk to Marjorie. It'll make you feel even worse."

"I don't want to talk to Marjorie," Mel said. "But I want to talk to my kids."

"There isn't a day goes by that Mel doesn't say he wishes she'd get married again. Or else die," Terri said. "For one thing," Terri said, "she's bankrupting us. Mel says it's just to spite him that she won't get married again. She has a boyfriend who lives with her and the kids, so Mel is supporting the boyfriend too."

"She's allergic to bees," Mel said. "If I'm not praying she'll get married again. I'm praying she'll get herself stung to death by a swarm of fucking bees."

"Shame on you," Laura said.

"Bzzzzzzz," Mel said, turning his fingers into bees and buzzin them at Terri's throat. Then he let his hands drop all the way to his sides.

"She's vicious," Mel said. "Sometimes I think I'll go up there dressed like a beekeeper. You know, that hat that's like a helmet with the plate that comes down over your face, the big gloves, and the padded coat? I'll knock on the door and let loose a hive of bees in the house. But first I'd make sure the kids were out, of course."

He crossed one leg over the other. It seemed to take him a lot of time to do it. Then he put both feet on the floor and leaned forward, elbows on the table, his chin cupped in his hands.

"Maybe I won't call the kids, after all. Maybe it isn't such a hot idea. Maybe we'll just go eat. How does that sound?"

"Sounds fine to me," I said. "Eat or not eat. Or keep drinking. I could head right on out into the sunset."

"What does that mean, honey?" Laura said.

"It just means what I said," I said. "It means I could just keep going. That's all it means."

"I could eat something myself," Laura said. "I don't think I've ever been so hungry in my life. Is there something to nibble on?"

"I'll put out some cheese and crackers," Terri said.

But Terri just sat there. She did not get up to get anything.

Mel turned his glass over. He spilled it out on the table.

"Gin's gone," Mel said.

Terri said, "Now what?"

I could hear my heart beating. I could hear everyone's heart. I could hear the human noise we sat there making, not one of us moving, not even when the room went dark.

1981

■   RICHARD FORD   ■

B. 1944

Richard Ford was born in Jackson, Mississippi. This fact, and the fact that his first novel, *A Piece of My Heart* (1976), is set on an island in the Mississippi, immediately led critics to deem him a writer working in the Southern gothic literary tradition. Ford himself has chafed at this identification, and he might more properly be called a peripatetic writer, having lived for a time in twelve states as well as in Mexico and France. His fiction similarly resists being tied down to any particular region; his novels and short stories move restlessly from the expansive landscape of the American West to the crowded suburbs of New Jersey and everywhere between and beyond. Similarly, if Ford was originally dubbed a "neo-Faulknerian," his subsequent work has invited comparison to writers as diverse as Walker Percy, Sinclair Lewis, John Updike, and Ernest Hemingway. Among his contemporaries, he has been identified as part of a group of writers who emerged in the late 1970s and 1980s—Raymond Carver, Andres Dubus, and Jayne Ann Phillips, for instance—whose minimalist aesthetic uses spare, affectless prose to depict characters struggling at the margins of society. The story included here, "Rock Springs," epitomizes the style and concerns of these so-called dirty realists, whose straightforward narratives conveyed through a single perspective can be read against the fragmented, intertextual, and discontinuous narratives of contemporaneous postmodernists such as John Barth, Thomas Pynchon, and Don DeLillo.

Yet Ford might have been a mere footnote in literary history. Disappointed by the reception of his first two novels—the second being *The Ultimate Good Luck* (1981), about a Vietnam veteran and drifter—Ford gave up fiction writing altogether and took a job at the magazine *Inside Sports*. After the magazine folded, Ford returned to fiction with *The Sportswriter* (1986), which would prove to be his breakout novel. *The Sportswriter* also provided the foundation for two more novels, *Independence Day* (1995) and *The Lay of the Land* (2006). It is this trilogy that has arguably secured Ford's place in the canon as a chronicler of late-twentieth-century American experience. On the face of it, these novels' protagonist, Frank Bascombe, could not be more different from the hapless car thief of "Rock Springs"; unlike him and the other drifters who roam throughout Ford's early works, Bascombe ultimately becomes a successful real estate broker, comfortably settled in an affluent New Jersey suburb. Stylistically, this trilogy is also markedly different from both the portentous Southern gothic tone of his first novel and the pared down prose of much of his short fiction. These novels teem with the sights, sounds, and effluvia that bombard Bascombe in his travels up and down the Northeastern corridor. Here, the accumulation of detail calls attention to the human causes of a depleted environment in the same manner that the unadorned narrative mimics the empty landscape of Montana and Wyoming in "Rock Springs."

As wide-ranging as Ford's fiction may seem, his chief concerns have remained the same: whether settled or adrift, the quintessential Ford protagonist is an alienated male who simultaneously seeks and runs from human connection in his nostalgic quest for an imagined past that might foretell a brighter future. In Ford's handling, these are not abstract existential crises that his characters suffer but circumstances stubbornly rooted in time and place. Whether we are following Earl's luckless journey in "Rock Springs" as he reverses the iconic trajectory by heading east rather than west in order to reinvent himself, tracing Frank Bascombe's course as he makes his way through I-95 traffic on an ill-conceived father-son road trip to Cooperstown and the Baseball Hall of Fame in *Independence Day*; or eavesdropping on a couple of drunks as they argue over the contested presidential race of 2000 in *The Lay of the Land*, it is clear that Ford's fiction is preoccupied with teasing out the various strains of American mythology, the burden of its history, and the fractiousness of its politics.

But Ford's fiction is not mere scaffolding meant to support the author's meditations on history, politics, and national belonging. Ford maintains in an essay titled "How Does Being American Inform What I Write?" that while his fiction may indeed grapple with the vast, diverse terrain of American identity in order to ask "how we can be so different yet so alike," it does so by attending what he calls "the intimate, ground-level lives of its human participants." In other words, Ford's realist fiction aims to provide the moment of recognition for which Earl, and so many of Ford's characters, yearn.

Kathy Knapp
University of Connecticut, Torrington

PRIMARY WORKS

A Piece of My Heart, 1976; *The Ultimate Good Luck,* 1981; *The Sportswriter,* 1986; *Rock Springs,* 1987; *Wildlife,* 1990; *Independence Day,* 1995; *Women with Men: Three Stories,* 1997; *A Multitude of Sins,* 2002; *The Lay of the Land,* 2006.

Rock Springs

Edna and I had started down from Kalispell, heading for Tampa-St. Pete where I still had some friends from the old glory days who wouldn't turn me in to the police. I had managed to scrape with the law in Kalispell over several bad checks—which is a prison crime in Montana. And I knew Edna was already looking at her cards and thinking about a move, since it wasn't the first time I'd been in law scrapes in my life. She herself had already had her own troubles, losing her kids and keeping her ex-husband, Danny, from breaking in her house and stealing her things while she was at work, which was really why I had moved in in the first place, that and needing to give my little daughter, Cheryl, a better shake in things.

I don't know what was between Edna and me, just beached by the same tides when you got down to it. Though love has been built on frailer ground than that, as I well know. And when I came in the house that afternoon, I just asked her if she wanted to go to Florida with me, leave things where they sat, and she said, "Why not? My datebook's not that full."

Edna and I had been a pair eight months, more or less man and wife, some of which time I had been out of work, and some when I'd worked at the dog track as a lead-out and could help with the rent and talk sense to Danny when he came around. Danny was afraid of me because Edna had told him I'd been in prison in Florida for killing a man, though that wasn't true. I had once been in jail in Tallahassee for stealing tires and had gotten into a fight on the county farm where a man had lost his eye. But I hadn't done the hurting, and Edna just wanted the story worse than it was so Danny wouldn't act crazy and make her have to take her kids back, since she had made a good adjustment to not having them, and I already had Cheryl with me. I'm not a violent person and would never put a man's eye out, much less kill someone. My former wife, Helen, would come all the way from Waikiki Beach to testify to that. We never had violence, and I believe in crossing the street to stay out of trouble's way. Though Danny didn't know that.

But we were half down through Wyoming, going toward I-80 and feeling good about things, when the oil light flashed on in the car I'd stolen, a sign I knew to be a bad one.

I'd gotten us a good car, a cranberry Mercedes I'd stolen out of an ophthalmologist's lot in Whitefish, Montana. I stole it because I thought it would be comfortable over a long haul, because I thought it got good mileage, which it didn't, and because I'd never had a good car in my life, just old Chevy junkers and used trucks back from when I was a kid swamping citrus with Cubans.

The car made us all high that day. I ran the windows up and down, and Edna told us some jokes and made faces. She could be lively. Her features would light up like a beacon and you could see her beauty, which wasn't ordinary. It all made me giddy, and I drove clear down to Bozeman, then straight on through the park to Jackson Hole. I rented us the bridal suite in the Quality Court in Jackson and left Cheryl and her little dog, Duke, sleeping while Edna and I drove to a rib barn and drank beer and laughed till after midnight.

It felt like a whole new beginning for us, bad memories left behind and a new horizon to build on. I got so worked up, I had a tattoo done on my arm that said FAMOUS TIMES, and Edna bought a Bailey hat with an Indian feather band and a little turquoise-and-silver bracelet for Cheryl, and we made love on the seat of the car in the Quality Court parking lot just as the sun was burning up on the Snake River, and everything seemed then like the end of the rainbow.

It was that very enthusiasm, in fact, that made me keep the car one day longer instead of driving it into the river and stealing another one, like I should've done and *had* done before.

Where the car went bad there wasn't a town in sight or even a house, just some low mountains maybe fifty miles away or maybe a hundred, a barbed-wire fence in both directions, hardpan prairie, and some hawks riding the evening air seizing insects.

I got out to look at the motor, and Edna got out with Cheryl and the dog to let them have a pee by the car. I checked the water and checked the oil stick, and both of them said perfect.

"What's that light mean, Earl?" Edna said. She had come and stood by the car with her hat on. She was just sizing things up for herself.

"We shouldn't run it," I said. "Something's not right in the oil."

She looked around at Cheryl and Little Duke, who were peeing on the hardtop side-by-side like two little dolls, then out at the mountains, which were becoming black and lost in the distance. "What're we doing?" she said. She wasn't worried yet, but she wanted to know what I was thinking about.

"Let me try it again."

"That's a good idea," she said, and we all got back in the car.

When I turned the motor over, it started right away and the red light stayed off and there weren't any noises to make you think something was wrong. I let it idle a minute, then pushed the accelerator down and watched the red bulb. But there wasn't any light on, and I started wondering if maybe I hadn't dreamed I saw it, or that it had been the sun catching an angle off the window chrome, or maybe I was scared of something and didn't know it.

"What's the matter with it, Daddy?" Cheryl said from the backseat. I looked back at her, and she had on her turquoise bracelet and Edna's hat set back on the back of her head and that little black-and-white Heinz dog on her lap. She looked like a little cowgirl in the movies.

"Nothing, honey, everything's fine now," I said.

"Little Duke tinkled where I tinkled," Cheryl said, and laughed.

"You're two of a kind," Edna said, not looking back. Edna was usually good with Cheryl, but I knew she was tired now. We hadn't had much sleep, and she had a tendency to get cranky when she didn't sleep. "We oughta ditch this damn car first chance we get," she said.

"What's the first chance we got?" I asked, because I knew she'd been at the map.

"Rock Springs, Wyoming," Edna said with conviction. "Thirty miles down this road." She pointed out ahead.

I had wanted all along to drive the car into Florida like a big success story. But I knew Edna was right about it, that we shouldn't take crazy chances. I had kept thinking of it as my car and not the ophthalmologist's, and that was how you got caught in these things.

"Then my belief is we ought to go to Rock Springs and negotiate ourselves a new car," I said. I wanted to stay upbeat, like everything was panning out right.

"That's a great idea," Edna said, and she leaned over and kissed me hard on the mouth.

"That's a great idea," Cheryl said. "Let's pull on out of here right now."

The sunset that day I remember as being the prettiest I'd ever seen. Just as it touched the rim of the horizon, it all at once fired the air into jewels and red sequins the precise likes of which I had never seen before and haven't seen since. The West has it all over everywhere for sunsets, even Florida, where it's supposedly flat but where half the time trees block your view.

"It's cocktail hour," Edna said after we'd driven awhile. "We ought to have a drink and celebrate something." She felt better thinking we were going to get rid of the car. It certainly had dark troubles and was something you'd want to put behind you.

Edna had out a whiskey bottle and some plastic cups and was measuring levels on the glove-box lid. She liked drinking, and she liked drinking in the car, which was something you got used to in Montana, where it wasn't against the law, but where, strangely enough, a bad check would land you in Deer Lodge Prison for a year.

"Did I ever tell you I once had a monkey?" Edna said, setting my drink on the dashboard where I could reach it when I was ready. Her spirits were already picked up. She was like that, up one minute and down the next.

"I don't think you ever did tell me that," I said. "Where were you then?"

"Missoula," she said. She put her bare feet on the dash and rested the cup on her breasts. "I was waitressing at the AmVets. This was before I met you. Some guy came in one day with a monkey. A spider monkey. And I said, just to be joking, 'I'll roll you for that monkey.' And the guy said, 'Just one roll?' And I said, 'Sure.' He put the monkey down on the bar, picked up the cup, and rolled out boxcars. I picked it up and rolled out three fives. And I just stood there looking at the guy. He was just some guy passing through, I guess a vet. He got a strange look on his face—I'm sure not as strange as the one I had—but he looked kind of sad and surprised and satisfied all at once. I said, 'We can roll again.' But he said, 'No, I never roll twice for anything.' And he sat and drank a beer and talked about one thing and another for a while, about nuclear war and building a stronghold somewhere up in the Bitterroot, whatever it was, while I just watched the monkey, wondering what I was going to do with it when the guy left. And pretty soon he got up and said, 'Well, good-bye, Chipper'—that was this monkey's name, of course. And then he left before I could say anything. And the monkey just sat on the bar all that night. I don't know what made me think of that, Earl. Just something weird. I'm letting my mind wander."

"That's perfectly fine," I said. I took a drink of my drink. "I'd never own a monkey," I said after a minute. "They're too nasty. I'm sure Cheryl would like a monkey, though, wouldn't you, honey?" Cheryl was down on the seat playing with Little Duke. She used to talk about monkeys all the time then. "What'd you ever do with that monkey?" I said, watching the speedometer. We were having to go slower now because the red light kept fluttering on. And all I could do to keep it off was go slower. We were going maybe thirty-five and it was an hour before dark, and I was hoping Rock Springs wasn't far away.

"You really want to know?" Edna said. She gave me a quick glance, then looked back at the empty desert as if she was brooding over it.

"Sure," I said. I was still upbeat. I figured I could worry about breaking down and let other people be happy for a change.

"I kept it a week." And she seemed gloomy all of a sudden, as if she saw some aspect of the story she had never seen before. "I took it home and back and forth to the AmVets on my shifts. And it didn't cause any trouble. I fixed a chair up for it to sit on, back of the bar, and people liked it. It made a nice little clicking noise. We changed its name to Mary because the bartender figured out it was a girl. Though I was never really comfortable with it at home. I felt like it watched me too much. Then one day a guy came in, some guy who'd been in Vietnam, still wore a fatigue coat. And he said to me, 'Don't you know that a monkey'll kill you? It's got more strength in its fingers than you got in your whole body.' He said people had been killed in Vietnam by monkeys, bunches of them marauding while you were asleep, killing you and covering you with leaves. I didn't believe a word of it, except that when I got home and got undressed I started looking over across the room at Mary on her chair in the dark watching me. And I got the creeps. And after a while I got up and went out to the car, got a length of clothesline wire, and came back in and wired her to the doorknob through her little silver collar, then went back and tried to sleep. And I guess I must've slept the sleep of the dead—though I don't remember it—because when I got up I found Mary had tipped off her chair-back and hanged herself on the wire line. I'd made it too short."

Edna seemed badly affected by that story and slid low in the seat so she couldn't see out over the dash. "Isn't that a shameful story, Earl, what happened to that poor little monkey?"

"I see a town! I see a town!" Cheryl started yelling from the back seat, and right up Little Duke started yapping and the whole car fell into a racket. And sure enough she had seen something I hadn't, which was Rock Springs, Wyoming, at the bottom of a long hill, a little glowing jewel in the desert with I-80 running on the north side and the black desert spread out behind.

"That's it, honey," I said. "That's where we're going. You saw it first."

"We're hungry," Cheryl said. "Little Duke wants some fish, and I want spaghetti." She put her arms around my neck and hugged me.

"Then you'll just get it," I said. "You can have anything you want. And so can Edna and so can Little Duke." I looked over at Edna, smiling, but she was staring at me with eyes that were fierce with anger. "What's wrong?" I said.

"Don't you care anything about that awful thing that happened to me?" Her mouth was drawn tight, and her eyes kept cutting back at Cheryl and Little Duke, as if they had been tormenting her.

"Of course I do," I said. "I thought that was an awful thing." I didn't want her to be unhappy. We were almost there, and pretty soon we could sit down and have a real meal without thinking somebody might be hurting us.

"You want to know what I did with that monkey?" Edna said.

"Sure I do," I said.

"I put her in a green garbage bag, put it in the trunk of my car, drove to the dump, and threw her in the trash." She was staring at me darkly, as if the story meant something to her that was real important but that only she could see and that the rest of the world was a fool for.

"Well, that's horrible," I said. "But I don't see what else you could do. You didn't mean to kill it. You'd have done it differently if you had. And then you had to get rid of it, and I don't know what else you could have done. Throwing it away might seem unsympathetic to somebody, probably, but not to me. Sometimes that's all you can do, and you can't worry about what somebody else thinks." I tried to smile at her, but the red light was staying on if I pushed the accelerator at all, and I was trying to gauge if we could coast to Rock Springs before the car gave out completely. I looked at Edna again. "What else can I say?" I said.

"Nothing," she said, and stared back at the dark highway. "I should've known that's what you'd think. You've got a character that leaves something out, Earl. I've known that a long time."

"And yet here you are," I said. "And you're not doing so bad. Things could be a lot worse. At least we're all together here."

"Things could always be worse," Edna said. "You could go to the electric chair tomorrow."

"That's right," I said. "And somewhere somebody probably will. Only it won't be you."

"I'm hungry," said Cheryl. "When're we gonna eat? Let's find a motel. I'm tired of this. Little Duke's tired of it too."

Where the car stopped rolling was some distance from the town, though you could see the clear outline of the interstate in the dark with Rock Springs lighting up the sky behind. You could hear the big tractors hitting the spacers in the overpass, revving up for the climb to the mountains.

I shut off the lights.

"What're we going to do now?" Edna said irritably, giving me a bitter look.

"I'm figuring it," I said. "It won't be hard, whatever it is. You won't have to do anything."

"I'd hope not," she said and looked the other way.

Across the road and across a dry wash a hundred yards was what looked like a huge mobile-home town, with a factory or a refinery of some kind lit up behind it and in full swing. There were lights on in a lot of the mobile homes, and there were cars moving along an access road that ended near the freeway overpass a mile the other way. The lights in the mobile homes seemed friendly to me, and I knew right then what I should do.

"Get out," I said, opening my door.

"Are we walking?" Edna said.

"We're pushing."

"I'm not pushing." Edna reached up and locked her door.

"All right," I said. "Then you just steer."

"You're pushing us to Rock Springs, are you, Earl? It doesn't look like it's more than about three miles."

"I'll push," Cheryl said from the back.

"No, hon. Daddy'll push. You just get out with Little Duke and move out of the way."

Edna gave me a threatening look, just as if I'd tried to hit her. But when I got out she slid into my seat and took the wheel, staring angrily ahead straight into the cottonwood scrub.

"Edna can't drive that car," Cheryl said from out in the dark. "She'll run it in the ditch."

"Yes, she can, hon. Edna can drive it as good as I can. Probably better."

"No she can't," Cheryl said. "No she can't either." And I thought she was about to cry, but she didn't.

I told Edna to keep the ignition on so it wouldn't lock up and to steer into the cottonwoods with the parking lights on so she could see. And when I started, she steered it straight off into the trees, and I kept pushing until we were twenty yards into the cover and the tires sank in the soft sand and nothing at all could be seen from the road.

"Now where are we?" she said, sitting at the wheel. Her voice was tired and hard, and I knew she could have put a good meal to use. She had a sweet nature, and I recognized that this wasn't her fault but mine. Only I wished she could be more hopeful.

"You stay right here, and I'll go over to that trailer park and call us a cab," I said.

"What cab?" Edna said, her mouth wrinkled as if she'd never heard anything like that in her life.

"There'll be cabs," I said, and tried to smile at her. "There's cabs everywhere."

"What're you going to tell him when he gets here? Our stolen car broke down and we need a ride to where we can steal another one? That'll be a big hit, Earl."

"I'll talk," I said. "You just listen to the radio for ten minutes and then walk on out to the shoulder like nothing was suspicious. And you and Cheryl act nice. She doesn't need to know about this car."

"Like we're not suspicious enough already, right?" Edna looked up at me out of the lighted car. "You don't think right, did you know that, Earl? You think the world's stupid and you're smart. But that's not how it is. I feel sorry for you. You might've *been* something, but things just went crazy someplace."

I had a thought about poor Danny. He was a vet and crazy as a shithouse mouse, and I was glad he wasn't in for all this. "Just get the baby in the car," I said, trying to be patient.

"I'm hungry like you are."

"I'm tired of this," Edna said. "I wish I'd stayed in Montana."

"Then you can go back in the morning," I said. "I'll buy the ticket and put you on the bus. But not till then."

"Just get on with it, Earl." She slumped down in the seat, turning off the parking lights with one foot and the radio on with the other.

The mobile-home community was as big as any I'd ever seen. It was attached in some way to the plant that was lighted up behind it, because I could see a car once in a while leave one of the trailer streets, turn in the direction of the plant, then go slowly into it. Everything in the plant was white, and you could see that all the trailers were painted white and looked exactly alike. A deep hum came out of the plant, and I thought as I got closer that it wouldn't be a location I'd ever want to work in.

I went right to the first trailer where there was a light, and knocked on the metal door. Kids' toys were lying in the gravel around the little wood steps, and I could hear talking on TV that suddenly went off. I heard a woman's voice talking, and then the door opened wide.

A large Negro woman with a wide, friendly face stood in the doorway. She smiled at me and moved forward as if she was going to come out, but she stopped at the top step. There was a little Negro boy behind her peeping out from behind her legs, watching me with his eyes half closed. The trailer had that feeling that no one else was inside, which was a feeling I knew something about.

"I'm sorry to intrude," I said. "But I've run up on a little bad luck tonight. My name's Earl Middleton."

The woman looked at me, then out into the night toward the freeway as if what I had said was something she was going to be able to see. "What kind of bad luck?" she said, looking down at me again.

"My car broke down out on the highway," I said. "I can't fix it myself, and I wondered if I could use your phone to call for help."

The woman smiled down at me knowingly. "We can't live without cars, can we?"

"That's the honest truth," I said.

"They're like our hearts," she said, her face shining in the little bulb light that burned beside the door. "Where's your car situated?"

I turned and looked over into the dark, but I couldn't see anything because of where we'd put it. "It's over there," I said. "You can't see it in the dark."

"Who all's with you now?" the woman said. "Have you got your wife with you?"

"She's with my little girl and our dog in the car," I said. "My daughter's asleep or I would have brought them."

"They shouldn't be left in the dark by themselves," the woman said and frowned. "There's too much unsavoriness out there."

"The best I can do is hurry back." I tried to look sincere, since everything except Cheryl being asleep and Edna being my wife was the truth. The truth is meant to serve you if you'll let it, and I wanted it to serve me. "I'll pay for the phone call," I said. "If you'll bring the phone to the door I'll call from right here."

The woman looked at me again as if she was searching for a truth of her own, then back out into the night. She was maybe in her sixties, but I couldn't say for sure. "You're not going to rob me, are you, Mr. Middleton?" She smiled like it was a joke between us.

"Not tonight," I said, and smiled a genuine smile. "I'm not up to it tonight. Maybe another time."

"Then I guess Terrel and I can let you use our phone with Daddy not here, can't we, Terrel? This is my grandson, Terrel Junior, Mr. Middleton." She put her hand on the boy's head and looked down at him. "Terrel won't talk. Though if he did he'd tell you to use our phone. He's a sweet boy." She opened the screen for me to come in.

The trailer was a big one with a new rug and a new couch and a living room that expanded to give the space of a real house. Something good and sweet was cooking in the kitchen, and the trailer felt like it was somebody's comfortable new home instead of just temporary. I've lived in trailers, but they were just snailbacks with one room and no toilet, and they always felt cramped and unhappy—though I've thought maybe it might've been me that was unhappy in them.

There was a big Sony TV and a lot of kids' toys scattered on the floor. I recognized a Greyhound bus I'd gotten for Cheryl. The phone was beside a new leather recliner, and the Negro woman pointed for me to sit down and call and gave me the phone book. Terrel began fingering his toys and the woman sat on the couch while I called, watching me and smiling.

There were three listings for cab companies, all with one number different. I called the numbers in order and didn't get an answer until the last one, which answered with the name of the second company. I said I was on the highway beyond the interstate and that my wife and family needed to be taken to town and I would arrange for a tow later. While I was giving the location, I looked up the name of a tow service to tell the driver in case he asked.

When I hung up, the Negro woman was sitting looking at me with the same look she had been staring with into the dark, a look that seemed to want truth. She was smiling, though. Something pleased her and I reminded her of it.

"This is a very nice home," I said, resting in the recliner, which felt like the driver's seat of the Mercedes, and where I'd have been happy to stay.

"This isn't *our* house, Mr. Middleton," the Negro woman said. "The company owns these. They give them to us for nothing. We have our own home in Rockford, Illinois."

"That's wonderful," I said.

"It's never wonderful when you have to be away from home, Mr. Middleton, though we're only here three months, and it'll be easier when Terrel Junior begins his special school. You see, our son was killed in the war, and his wife ran off without Terrel Junior. Though you shouldn't worry. He can't understand us. His little feelings can't be hurt." The woman folded her hands in her lap and smiled in a satisfied way. She was an attractive woman, and had on a blue-and-pink floral dress that made her seem bigger than she could've been, just the right woman to sit on the couch she was sitting on. She was good nature's picture, and I was glad she could be, with her little brain-damaged boy, living in a place where no one in his right mind would want to live a minute. "Where do *you* live, Mr. Middleton?" she said politely, smiling in the same sympathetic way.

"My family and I are in transit," I said. "I'm an ophthalmologist, and we're moving back to Florida, where I'm from. I'm setting up practice in some little town where it's warm year-round. I haven't decided where."

"Florida's a wonderful place," the woman said. "I think Terrel would like it there."

"Could I ask you something?" I said.

"You certainly may," the woman said. Terrel had begun pushing his Greyhound across the front of the TV screen, making a scratch that no one watching the set could miss. "Stop that, Terrel Junior," the woman said quietly. But Terrel kept pushing his bus on the glass, and she smiled at me again as if we both understood something sad. Except I knew Cheryl would never damage a television set. She had respect for nice things, and I was sorry for the lady that Terrel didn't. "What did you want to ask?" the woman said.

"What goes on in that plant or whatever it is back there beyond these trailers, where all the lights are on?"

"Gold," the woman said and smiled.

"It's what?" I said.

"Gold," the Negro woman said, smiling as she had for almost all the time I'd been there. "It's a gold mine."

"They're mining gold back there?" I said, pointing.

"Every night and every day." She smiled in a pleased way.

"Does your husband work there?" I said.

"He's the assayer," she said. "He controls the quality. He works three months a year, and we live the rest of the time at home in Rockford. We've waited a long time for this. We've been happy to have our grandson, but I won't say I'll be sorry to have him go. We're ready to start our lives over." She smiled broadly at me and then at Terrel, who was giving her a spiteful look from the floor. "You said you had a daughter," the Negro woman said. "And what's her name?"

"Irma Cheryl," I said. "She's named for my mother."

"That's nice. And she's healthy, too. I can see it in your face." She looked at Terrel Junior with pity.

"I guess I'm lucky," I said.

"So far you are. But children bring you grief, the same way they bring you joy. We were unhappy for a long time before my husband got his job in the gold mine. Now, when Terrel starts to school, we'll be kids again." She stood up. "You might miss your cab, Mr. Middleton," she said, walking toward the door, though not to be forcing me out. She was too polite. "If *we* can't see your car, the cab surely won't be able to."

"That's true." I got up off the recliner, where I'd been so comfortable. "None of us have eaten yet, and your food makes me know how hungry we probably all are."

"There are fine restaurants in town, and you'll find them," the Negro woman said. "I'm sorry you didn't meet my husband. He's a wonderful man. He's everything to me."

"Tell him I appreciate the phone," I said. "You saved me."

"You weren't hard to save," the woman said. "Saving people is what we were all put on earth to do. I just passed you on to whatever's coming to you."

"Let's hope it's good," I said, stepping back into the dark.

"I'll be hoping, Mr. Middleton. Terrel and I will both be hoping."

I waved to her as I walked out into the darkness toward the car where it was hidden in the night.

The cab had already arrived when I got there. I could see its little red-and-green roof lights all the way across the dry wash, and it made me worry that Edna was already saying something to get us in trouble, something about the car or where we'd come from, something that would cast suspicion on us. I thought, then, how I never planned things well enough. There was always a gap between my plan and what happened, and I only responded to things as they came along and hoped I wouldn't get in trouble. I was an offender in the law's eyes. But I always *thought* differently, as if I weren't an offender and had no intention of being one, which was the truth. But as I read on a napkin once, between the idea and the act a whole kingdom lies. And I had a hard time with my acts, which were oftentimes offender's acts, and my ideas, which were as good as the gold they mined there where the bright lights were blazing.

"We're waiting for you, Daddy," Cheryl said when I crossed the road. "The taxicab's already here."

"I see, hon," I said, and gave Cheryl a big hug. The cabdriver was sitting in the driver's seat having a smoke with the lights on inside. Edna was leaning against the back of the cab between the taillights, wearing her Bailey hat. "What'd you tell him?" I said when I got close.

"Nothing," she said. "What's there to tell?"

"Did he see the car?"

She glanced over in the direction of the trees where we had hid the Mercedes. Nothing was visible in the darkness, though I could hear Little

Duke combing around in the underbrush tracking something, his little collar tinkling. "Where're we going?" she said. "I'm so hungry I could pass out."

"Edna's in a terrible mood," Cheryl said. "She already snapped at me."

"We're tired, honey," I said. "So try to be nicer."

"She's never nice," Cheryl said.

"Run go get Little Duke," I said. "And hurry back."

"I guess *my* questions come last here, right?" Edna said.

I put my arm around her. "That's not true."

"Did you find somebody over there in the trailers you'd rather stay with? You were gone long enough."

"That's not a thing to say," I said. "I was just trying to make things look right, so we don't get put in jail."

"So *you* don't, you mean." Edna laughed a little laugh I didn't like hearing.

"That's right. So I don't," I said. "I'd be the one in Dutch." I stared out at the big, lighted assemblage of white buildings and white lights beyond the trailer community, plumes of white smoke escaping up into the heartless Wyoming sky, the whole company of buildings looking like some unbelievable castle, humming away in a distorted dream. "You know what all those buildings are there?" I said to Edna, who hadn't moved and who didn't really seem to care if she ever moved anymore ever.

"No. But I can't say it matters, because it isn't a motel and it isn't a restaurant."

"It's a gold mine," I said, staring at the gold mine, which, I knew now, was a greater distance from us than it seemed, though it seemed huge and near, up against the cold sky. I thought there should've been a wall around it with guards instead of just the lights and no fence. It seemed as if anyone could go in and take what they wanted, just the way I had gone up to that woman's trailer and used the telephone, though that obviously wasn't true.

Edna began to laugh then. Not the mean laugh I didn't like, but a laugh that had something caring behind it, a full laugh that enjoyed a joke, a laugh she was laughing the first time I laid eyes on her, in Missoula in the East Gate Bar in 1979, a laugh we used to laugh together when Cheryl was still with her mother and I was working steady at the track and not stealing cars or passing bogus checks to merchants. A better time all around. And for some reason it made me laugh just hearing her, and we both stood there behind the cab in the dark, laughing at the gold mine in the desert, me with my arm around her and Cheryl out rustling up Little Duke and the cabdriver smoking in the cab and our stolen Mercedes-Benz, which I'd had such hopes for in Florida, stuck up to its axle in sand, where I'd never get to see it again.

"I always wondered what a gold mine would look like when I saw it," Edna said, still laughing, wiping a tear from her eye.

"Me too," I said. "I was always curious about it."

"We're a couple of fools, aren't we, Earl?" she said, unable to quit laughing completely. "We're two of a kind."

"It might be a good sign, though," I said.

"How could it be? It's not our gold mine. There aren't any drive-up windows." She was still laughing.

"We've seen it," I said, pointing. "That's it right there. It may mean we're getting closer. Some people never see it at all."

"In a pig's eye, Earl," she said. "You and me see it in a pig's eye."

And she turned and got in the cab to go.

The cabdriver didn't ask anything about our car or where it was, to mean he'd noticed something queer. All of which made me feel like we had made a clean break from the car and couldn't be connected with it until it was too late, if ever. The driver told us a lot about Rock Springs while he drove, that because of the gold mine a lot of people had moved there in just six months, people from all over, including New York, and that most of them lived out in the trailers. Prostitutes from New York City, who he called "B-girls," had come into town, he said, on the prosperity tide, and Cadillacs with New York plates cruised the little streets every night, full of Negroes with big hats who ran the women. He told us that everybody who got in his cab now wanted to know where the women were, and when he got our call he almost didn't come because some of the trailers were brothels operated by the mine for engineers and computer people away from home. He said he got tired of running back and forth out there just for vile business. He said that *60 Minutes* had even done a program about Rock Springs and that a blow-up had resulted in Cheyenne, though nothing could be done unless the boom left town. "It's prosperity's fruit," the driver said. "I'd rather be poor, which is lucky for me."

He said all the motels were sky-high, but since we were a family he could show us a nice one that was affordable. But I told him we wanted a first-rate place where they took animals, and the money didn't matter because we had had a hard day and wanted to finish on a high note. I also knew that it was in the little nowhere places that the police look for you and find you. People I'd known were always being arrested in cheap hotels and tourist courts with names you'd never heard of before. Never in Holiday Inns or TraveLodges.

I asked him to drive us to the middle of town and back out again so Cheryl could see the train station, and while we were there I saw a pink Cadillac with New York plates and a TV aerial being driven slowly by a Negro in a big hat down a narrow street where there were just bars and a Chinese restaurant. It was an odd sight, nothing you could ever expect.

"There's your pure criminal element," the cabdriver said and seemed sad. "I'm sorry for people like you to see a thing like that. We've got a nice town here, but there're some that want to ruin it for everybody. There used to be a way to deal with trash and criminals, but those days are gone forever."

"You said it," Edna said.

"You shouldn't let it get *you* down," I said to him. "There's more of you than them. And there always will be. You're the best advertisement this town has. I know Cheryl will remember you and not *that* man, won't you, honey?" But Cheryl was alseep by then, holding Little Duke in her arms on the taxi seat.

The driver took us to the Ramada Inn on the interstate, not far from where we'd broken down. I had a small pain of regret as we drove under the Ramada awning that we hadn't driven up in a cranberry-colored Mercedes but instead in a beat-up old Chrysler taxi driven by an old man full of complaints. Though I knew it was for the best. We were better off without that car; better, really, in any other car but that one, where the signs had turned bad.

I registered under another name and paid for the room in cash so there wouldn't be any questions. On the line where it said "Representing" I wrote "Ophthalmologist" and put "M.D." after the name. It had a nice look to it, even though it wasn't my name.

When we got to the room, which was in the back where I'd asked for it, I put Cheryl on one of the beds and Little Duke beside her so they'd sleep. She'd missed dinner, but it only meant she'd be hungry in the morning, when she could have anything she wanted. A few missed meals don't make a kid bad. I'd missed a lot of them myself and haven't turned out completely bad.

"Let's have some fried chicken," I said to Edna when she came out of the bathroom. "They have good fried chicken at Ramadas, and I noticed the buffet was still up. Cheryl can stay right here, where it's safe, till we're back."

"I guess I'm not hungry anymore," Edna said. She stood at the window staring out into the dark. I could see out the window past her some yellowish foggy glow in the sky. For a moment I thought it was the gold mine out in the distance lighting the night, though it was only the interstate.

"We could order up," I said. "Whatever you want. There's a menu on the phone book. You could just have a salad."

"You go ahead," she said. "I've lost my hungry spirit." She sat on the bed beside Cheryl and Little Duke and looked at them in a sweet way and put her hand on Cheryl's cheek just as if she'd had a fever. "Sweet little girl," she said. "Everybody loves you."

"What do you want to do?" I said. "I'd like to eat. Maybe *I'll* order up some chicken."

"Why don't you do that?" she said. "It's your favorite." And she smiled at me from the bed.

I sat on the other bed and dialed room service. I asked for chicken, garden salad, potato and a roll, plus a piece of hot apple pie and iced tea. I realized I hadn't eaten all day. When I put down the phone I saw that Edna was watching me, not in a hateful way or a loving way, just in a way that seemed to say she didn't understand something and was going to ask me about it.

"When did watching me get so entertaining?" I said and smiled at her. I was trying to be friendly. I knew how tired she must be. It was after nine o'clock.

"I was just thinking how much I hated being in a motel without a car that was mine to drive. Isn't that funny? I started feeling like that last night when that purple car wasn't mine. That purple car just gave me the willies, I guess, Earl."

"One of those cars *outside* is yours," I said. "Just stand right there and pick it out."

"I know," she said. "But that's different, isn't it?" She reached and got her blue Bailey hat, put it on her head, and set it way back like Dale Evans. She looked sweet. "I used to like to go to motels, you know," she said. "There's something secret about them and free—I was never paying, of course. But you felt safe from everything and free to do what you wanted because you'd made the decision to be there and paid that price, and all the rest was the good part. Fucking and everything, you know." She smiled at me in a good-natured way.

"Isn't that the way this is?" I was sitting on the bed, watching her, not knowing what to expect her to say next.

"I don't guess it is, Earl," she said and stared out the window. "I'm thirty-two and I'm going to have to give up on motels. I can't keep that fantasy going anymore."

"Don't you like this place?" I said and looked around at the room. I appreciated the modern paintings and the lowboy bureau and the big TV. It seemed like a plenty nice enough place to me, considering where we'd been.

"No, I don't," Edna said with real conviction. "There's no use in my getting mad at you about it. It isn't your fault. You do the best you can for everybody. But every trip teaches you something. And I've learned I need to give up on motels before some bad thing happens to me. I'm sorry."

"What does that mean?" I said, because I really didn't know what she had in mind to do, though I should've guessed.

"I guess I'll take that ticket you mentioned," she said, and got up and faced the window. "Tomorrow's soon enough. We haven't got a car to take me anyhow."

"Well, that's a fine thing," I said, sitting on the bed, feeling like I was in shock. I wanted to say something to her, to argue with her, but I couldn't think what to say that seemed right. I didn't want to be mad at her, but it made me mad.

"You've got a right to be mad at me, Earl," she said, "but I don't think you can really blame me." She turned around and faced me and sat on the windowsill, her hands on her knees. Someone knocked on the door, and I just yelled for them to set the tray down and put it on the bill.

"I guess I *do* blame you," I said, and I was angry. I thought about how I could've disappeared into that trailer community and hadn't, had come back to keep things going, had tried to take control of things for everybody when they looked bad.

"Don't. I wish you wouldn't," Edna said and smiled at me like she wanted me to hug her. "Anybody ought to have their choice in things if they can. Don't you believe that, Earl? Here I am out here in the desert where I don't know anything, in a stolen car, in a motel room under an assumed name, with no money of my own, a kid that's not mine, and the law after me. And I have a choice to get out of all of it by getting on a bus. What would you do? I know exactly what you'd do."

"You think you do," I said. But I didn't want to get into an argument about it and tell her all I could've done and didn't do. Because it wouldn't have done any good. When you get to the point of arguing, you're past the point of changing anybody's mind, even though it's supposed to be the other way, and maybe for some classes of people it is, just never mine.

Edna smiled at me and came across the room and put her arms around me where I was sitting on the bed. Cheryl rolled over and looked at us and smiled, then closed her eyes, and the room was quiet. I was beginning to think of Rock Springs in a way I knew I would always think of it, a lowdown city full of crimes and whores and disappointments, a place where a woman left me, instead of a place where I got things on the straight track once and for all, a place I saw a gold mine.

"Eat your chicken, Earl," Edna said. "Then we can go to bed. I'm tired, but I'd like to make love to you anyway. None of this is a matter of not loving you, you know that."

Sometime late in the night, after Edna was asleep, I got up and walked outside into the parking lot. It could've been anytime because there was still the light from the interstate frosting the low sky and the big red Ramada sign humming motionlessly in the night and no light at all in the east to indicate it might be morning. The lot was full of cars all nosed in, a couple of them with suitcases strapped to their roofs and their trunks weighed down with belongings the people were taking someplace, to a new home or a vacation resort in the mountains. I had laid in bed a long time after Edna was asleep, watching the Atlanta Braves on television, trying to get my mind off how I'd feel when I saw that bus pull away the next day, and how I'd feel when I turned around and there stood Cheryl and Little Duke and no one to see about them but me alone, and that the first thing I had to do was get hold of some automobile and get the plates switched, then get them some breakfast and get us all on the road to Florida, all in the space of probably two hours, since that Mercedes would certainly look less hid in the daytime than the night, and word travels fast. I've always taken care of Cheryl myself as long as I've had her with me. None of the women ever did. Most of them didn't even seem to like her, though they took care of me in a way so that I could take care of her. And I knew that once Edna left, all that was going to get harder. Though what I wanted most to do was not think about it just for a little while, try to let my mind go limp so it could be strong for the rest of what there was. I thought that the difference between a successful life and an unsuccessful one, between me at that moment and all the people who owned the cars that were nosed into their proper places in the lot, maybe between me and that woman out in the trailers by the gold mine, was how well you were able to put things like this out of your mind and not be bothered by them, and maybe, too, by how many troubles like this one you had to face in a lifetime. Through luck or design they had all faced fewer troubles, and by their own characters, they forgot them faster. And that's what I wanted for me. Fewer troubles, fewer memories of trouble.

I walked over to a car, a Pontiac with Ohio tags, one of the ones with bundles and suitcases strapped to the top and a lot more in the trunk, by the way it was riding. I looked inside the driver's window. There were maps and paperback books and sunglasses and the little plastic holders for cans that hang on the window wells. And in the back there were kids' toys and some pillows and a cat box with a cat sitting in it staring up at me like I was the face of the moon. It all looked familiar to me, the very same things I would have in my car if I had a car. Nothing seemed surprising, nothing different. Though I had a funny sensation at that moment and turned and looked up at the windows along the back of the motel. All were dark except two. Mine and another one. And I wondered, because it seemed funny, what would you think a man was doing if you saw him in the middle of the night looking in the windows of cars in the parking lot of the Ramada Inn? Would you think he was trying to get his head cleared? Would you think he was trying to get ready for a day when trouble would come down on him? Would you think his girlfriend was leaving him? Would you think he had a daughter? Would you think he was anybody like you?

1987

■ # PHILIP LEVINE ■
B. 1928

A self-described anarchist, Philip Levine considers himself "an intensely political person, but a man without a party." He was born in Detroit in 1928 and remembers the "very strong familial setting" of his youth. In his early years, he was unaware of the world outside his home. He lived with his Russian-born Jewish parents and two brothers; his grandparents lived downstairs, and his aunt lived nearby. In 1933 (the year is the title of one of Levine's most powerful collections), when he was five, his father died, and the family's relatively comfortable existence ended.

Part of his upbringing involved a sense of persecution in a period when fascism was gaining strength in Europe and Father Charles Coughlin was broadcasting weekly anti-Semitic radio programs in Detroit. The Spanish Civil War, which began when Levine was eight, is a recurrent topic in his work. When he was a junior in high school, he read Wilfred Owen, a poet who chronicled World War I and whose writings confirmed Levine's beliefs about the insanity of war. Levine worked in a number of blue-collar jobs in the automobile industry. He began to write poetry while attending Wayne State University at night, and his early work is influenced by his modernist predecessors.

Levine left Detroit for California in 1957 and does not romanticize his native city, which fell on hard times in the late twentieth century as trends in car manufacturing changed. Yet he has remained an urban poet with a strong affection for people, especially the working class. He regards storytelling as one of the primary motivators in his work. His verse stories tend to reflect the dignity of working-class characters and the realities of their lives. He is careful to draw a distinction between anarchy and antigovernment terrorism. The government is "the enemy" in his work because of its potential to oppress powerless individuals and rob them of their agency. He writes, "I don't believe in the validity of governments, laws, charters, all that hide us from our essential oneness."

Levine has published sixteen volumes of poetry since his first in 1963 and is the recipient of major awards, including two Guggenheim Fellowships and a Pulitzer Prize. Occasionally referred to as America's "proletariat poet" because of his focus on working-class subjects and his belief that property is theft, Levine has been a consistent and important voice on the American literary scene for nearly half a century. He regards poetry not as something mystical so much as the product of work. As he puts it, "I'm not a 'special case.' I'm a man who is more articulate than most people and one who found something called poetry quite early in life, grew to it, determined to make it, and because of his stubbornness is ... still trying."

D. Quentin Miller
Suffolk University

PRIMARY WORKS

On the Edge, 1963; *Not This Pig*, 1968; *Pili's Wall*, 1971; *Red Dust*, 1971; *They Feed They Lion*, 1972; *1933*, 1974; *The Names of the Lost*, 1976; *Ashes: Poems New and Old*, 1979; *Seven Years from Somewhere*, 1979; *One for the Rose*, 1981; *Selected Poems*, 1984; *Sweet Will*, 1985; *A Walk with Tom Jefferson*, 1988; *New Selected Poems*, 1991; *What Work Is*, 1991; *The Simple Truth*, 1994; *Unselected Poems*, 1997; *The Mercy*, 2000; *Breath*, 2004; *News of the World*, 2009.

Coming Home, *Detroit*, 1968

A winter Tuesday, the city pouring fire,
Ford Rouge sulfurs the sun, Cadillac, Lincoln,
Chevy gray. The fat stacks
of breweries hold their tongues. Rags,
papers, hands, the stems of birches   5
dirtied with words.
               Near the freeway
you stop and wonder what came off,
recall the snowstorm where you lost it all,
the wolverine, the northern bear, the wolf   10
caught out, ice and steel raining

from the foundries in a shower
of human breath. On sleds in the false sun
the new material rests. One brown child
stares and stares into your frozen eyes   15
until the lights change and you go
forward to work. The charred faces, the eyes
boarded up, the rubble of innards, the cry
of wet smoke hanging in your throat,
the twisted river stopped at the color of iron.   20
We burn this city every day.

                                                          1972

The Rats

Because of the great press
of steel on steel
I cannot hear the shadows hunched
under the machines. When the power
fails, the machines stop,   5
and the lights go out
I am listening to myself,
to my breathing and to
the noise my breathing makes.

They are moving, the shadows,   10
out of time, out
of sight, somewhere out
there in the darkness, and
when the lights
come back they are no longer   15
where they were.

Someone who never stood
next to me has poisoned
the shadows. They are dead
in the stairwell or under   20
the floorboards, darker
than ever and more compact
and moving in the sweet air
sweetening the air I breathe.

Later I will be in   25
the parking lot looking
for my car or I will remember
I have no car and it

will be tomorrow or years
from then.　　　　　　　　　　　　　　　　　　　　　　30

　　　　　　　　　　　It will be now.
I will have been talking
sitting across from where
you sit at ease on
the outrageous, impeccable sofa　　　　　　　　　35
I have admired,
and in that quiet that comes
in speech I will hear them
moving at last and see them
moving toward you in the light　　　　　　　　　40
bringing their great sweetness.

　　　　　　　　　　　　　　　　　　　　　　　　1980

The Everlasting Sunday

Waiting for it
in line to punch out
or punch in.
Bowed my head
into the cold grey　　　　　　　　　　　　　　　　5
soup of the wash trough,
talked with men
who couldn't talk, marked
my bread with the black
print of my thumb　　　　　　　　　　　　　　　10
and ate it.

Nine-foot lengths
of alloy tubing between
my gloved hands
sliding, and the plop　　　　　　　　　　　　　　15
of the cutter, and again
the tube drawing. Above
like swords, bundles
of steel sliding
in the blackened vaults,　　　　　　　　　　　　20
and I, a lone child,
counting out.
Now to awaken,
pace the wood floor.
Through the torn shade　　　　　　　　　　　　25
the moon between

the poplars riding
toward morning. My
dark suit, my stiffened
shirt stained   30
with God knows what,
my tie, my silvered
underwear guarding
the sad bed.

Naked, my hard arms   35
are thin as a girl's,
my body's hairs tipped
with frost. This house,
this ark of sleeping men,
bobs in the silence. I feel   40
my fingers curl
but not in anger,
the floor warms,
my eyes fill with light.
When was I young?   45

                                                               1980

The Simple Truth

I bought a dollar and a half's worth of small red potatoes,
took them home, boiled them in their jackets
and ate them for dinner with a little butter and salt.
Then I walked through the dried fields
on the edge of town. In middle June the light   5
hung on in the dark furrows at my feet,
and in the mountain oaks overhead the birds
were gathering for the night, the jays and mockers
squawking back and forth, the finches still darting
into the dusty light. The woman who sold me   10
the potatoes was from Poland; she was someone
out of my childhood in a pink spangled sweater and sunglasses
praising the perfection of all her fruits and vegetables
at the road-side stand and urging me to taste
even the pale, raw sweet corn trucked all the way,   15
she swore, from New Jersey. "Eat, eat," she said,
"Even if you don't I'll say you did."
                              Some things
you know all your life. They are so simple and true
they must be said without elegance, meter and rhyme,   20
they must be laid on the table beside the salt shaker,

the glass of water, the absence of light gathering
in the shadows of picture frames, they must be
naked and alone, they must stand for themselves.
My friend Henri and I arrived at this together in 1965   25
before I went away, before he began to kill himself,
and the two of us to betray our love. Can you taste
what I'm saying? It is onions or potatoes, a pinch
of simple salt, the wealth of melting butter, it is obvious,
it stays in the back of your throat like a truth   30
you never uttered because the time was always wrong,
it stays there for the rest of your life, unspoken,
made of that dirt we call earth, the metal we call salt,
in a form we have no words for, and you live on it.

     1995

The Lesson

Early in the final industrial century
on the street where I was born lived
a doctor who smoked black shag
and walked his dog each morning
as he muttered to himself in a language   5
only the dog knew. The doctor had saved
my brother's life, the story went, reached
two stained fingers down his throat
to extract a chicken bone and then
bowed to kiss the ring-encrusted hand   10
of my beautiful mother, a young widow
on the lookout for a professional.
Years before, before the invention of smog,
before Fluid Drive, the eight-hour day,
the iron lung, I'd come into the world   15
in a shower of industrial filth raining
from the bruised sky above Detroit.
Time did not stop. Mother married
a bland wizard in clutch plates
and drive shafts. My uncles went off   20
to their world wars, and I began a career
in root vegetables. Each morning,
just as the dark expired, the corner church
tolled its bells. Beyond the church
an oily river ran both day and night   25
and there along its banks I first conversed
with the doctor and Waldo, his dog.
"Young man," he said in words

resembling English, "you would dress
heavy for autumn, scarf, hat, gloves.   30
Not to smoke," he added, "as I do."
Eleven, small for my age but ambitious,
I took whatever good advice I got,
though I knew then what I know
now: the past, not the future, was mine.   35
If I told you he and I became pals
even though I barely understood him,
would you doubt me? Wakened before dawn
by the Catholic bells, I would dress
in the dark—remembering scarf, hat, gloves—   40
to make my way into the deserted streets
to where Waldo and his master ambled
the riverbank. Sixty-four years ago,
and each morning is frozen in memory,
each a lesson in what was to come.   45
What was to come? you ask. This world
as we have it, utterly unknowable,
utterly unacceptable, utterly unlovable,
the world we waken to each day
with or without bells. The lesson was   50
in his hands, one holding a cigarette,
the other buried in blond dog fur, and in
his words thick with laughter, hushed,
incomprehensible, words that were sound
only without sense, just as these must be.   55
Staring into the moist eyes of my maestro,
I heard the lost voices of creation running
over stones as the last darkness sifted upward,
voices saddened by the milky residue
of machine shops and spangled with first light,   60
discordant, harsh, but voices nonetheless.

2004

■   # VÍCTOR HERNÁNDEZ CRUZ   ■
B. 1949

Born in Aguas Buenas, a small mountain town in Puerto Rico, Víctor Hernández
Cruz moved with his family to the States when he was five. He attended Benjamin Franklin High School in New York City and was associated with The Gut

Theater on East 104th Street. He published *Snaps*, his first collection of poetry, when he was twenty. From the early 1970s, Hernández Cruz lived in San Francisco; in 1990 he returned to Aguas Buenas, where he continues to write in both English and Spanish.

His poetry has been described as "the most conscious of literary forms, and the most influenced by present tendencies in American literature" among Puerto Rican writers in the United States. It is highly introspective and abstract, preoccupied with form, rhythm, and language. His poems lack the referential context of popular culture and life in El Barrio that characterizes the work of Tato Laviera and Miguel Algarín, for example. Rather, his intellectualizing voice exhibits influences of various literary movements, such as minimalism and concrete poetry. Nonetheless, his poems and prose pieces capture Hispanic images and symbols in the urban milieu.

One distinguishing feature of Hernández Cruz's poetry is its conscious language choices. The poet plays with both English and Spanish words, with spelling and phonetics, suggesting at times simultaneous American and Puerto Rican readings. The title of his book *By Lingual Wholes* illustrates his playful and witty use of language. *By Lingual* echoes the word *bilingual*, and the concept of *wholes*, which implies both totality and absence—(w)holes—unifies the poems in this collection. The book itself is a collage in which spatial and visual signs are part of the poem's meaning, as they are in the work of the Brazilian concrete poets. Poetry and prose are intertwined with one-word poems, haikus, short stories, prose poems, and an empty appendix. The epigraph to the book signals this playful yet serious hybridization: "Speech changing within space."

Hernández Cruz's vision of the transformation of literary English because of its contact with Spanish is his unique contribution to American literature. Just as Spanish in the United States has been transforming itself into the distinct dialects of the various Hispanic groups who live here, English has also been affected by Hispanic writers. Hernández Cruz believes that English syntax is being changed through the Spanish influence. His work is substantially enriched by the mixture and interplay of the two languages and by the meaningful intersections between English and Spanish. However, in *Panoramas*, he proposes that English and Spanish not be mixed.

His poetry has evolved from the fragmented and often violent images of urban life, experiences with drugs, and existential beliefs during his youth—as in *Snaps*—to a dynamic and sometimes profound expression of biculturalism and bilingualism. Cosmopolitan and urban, his poetry stands without sacrificing images of Hispanic origin, culture, and tradition. His is the language of the urban, intellectual Latino who nevertheless cannot survive without transforming the past into the present.

Frances R. Aparicio
University of Illinois at Chicago

PRIMARY WORKS

Snaps, 1969; *Mainland*, 1973; *Tropicalization*, 1976; *By Lingual Wholes*, 1982; *Rhythm, Content and Flavor*, 1989; *Red Beans*, 1991; *Panoramas*, 1997; *Maraca*, 2001; *The Mountain in the Sea*, 2006.

urban dream

1

there was fire & the people were yelling.   running crazing.
screaming & falling.   moving up side down.   there was fire.
fires.   & more fires.   & walls caving to the ground.   & mercy
mercy.   death.   bodies falling down.   under bottles flying in the
air. garbage cans going up against windows.   a car singing   5
brightly a blue flame.   a snatch. a snag.   sounds of bombs.   &
other things blowing up.
times square
electrified.   burned.   smashed. stomped
hey over here   10
hey you.   where you going.
no walking.   no running.   no standing.
STOP
you crazy.   running.   stick
this stick up your eyes.   pull your heart out.   15
hey.

2

after noise.   comes silence.   after brightness (or great big flames)
comes darkness.   goes with whispering.   (even soft music can be heard)
even lips smacking.   foots stepping all over bones & ashes, all over
blood & broken lips that left their head somewhere else, all over   20
livers, & bright white skulls with hair on them. standing over a river
watching hamburgers floating by.   steak with teeth in them.
flags.   & chairs.   & beds.   & golf sets.   & mickeymouse broken
   in
half.   25
governors & mayors step out the show.   they split.

3

dancing arrives.

1969

Mountain Building

The mountains have changed to buildings
Is this hallway the inside of a stem
That has a rattling flower for a head,
Immense tree bark with roots made out of

Mailboxes? 5
In the vertical village moons fly out of
Apartment windows and though what you
See is a modern city
The mountain's guitars pluck inside
It's agriculture taking an elevator 10
Through urban caves which lead to
Paths underground They say Camuy
To Hutuado[1]
Taino subground like the IRT in
constant motion 15

The streets take walks in your dark eyes
Seashell necklaces make music in the
Origin of silence
What are we stepping on? Pineapple
Fields frozen with snow 20
Concrete dirt later the rocks of the
Atlantic
The sculpture of the inner earth
Down there where you thought only worms
and unnamed crocodiles parade 25
Lefty stands on a corner
Analyzing every seed
Squeezing the walls as he passes
Through at the bottom of the basement
Where the boiler makes heat 30

The flesh arrives out of a hole
In the mountain that goes up like a
Green wall
Bodies come in making *maraca*[2] sounds
An invisible map out of the flora 35
Bees arrive in the vicinity and sing
Chorus while woody woodpeckers make
Women out of trees and place flowers
On their heads
Waterfalls like Hurakan's faucets 40
Caress the back of Yuquiyu[3]
Arawak's echoes

Hallway of graffiti like the master
Cave drawings made by owls when they

---

[1]Refers to the underground caves at Camuy, Puerto Rico.
[2]Rattle—musical instrument of Taíno origin.
[3]Hurakan and Yuquiyu: Indian deities (Taíno).

Had hands   45
You see the fish with pyramids inside
Their stomachs
Hanging near the doorways where
San Lazaro[4] turns the keys
Villa Manhattan   50
Breeze of saint juice made from
Coconuts
Slide down the stairs to your
Belly and like a hypnotized *guanábana*[5]
You float down the street   55
And win all your hands at dominoes

The Moros live on the top floor eating
Roots and have a rooster on the roof
Africans import okra from the bodega
The Indians make a base of *guava*   60
On the first floor
The building is spinning itself into
a spiral of *salsa*
Heaven must be calling or the
Residents know the direction   65
Because there is an upward pull
If you rise too quickly from your seat
You might have to comb a spirit's
Hair
They float over the chimneys   70
Arrive through the smog
Appear through the plaster of Paris
It is the same people in the windowed
Mountains.

                                                                   1982

Table of Contents

Your tablet is your inner workings, your grasp on the board, which is shifting, trying to knock the items balanced on the table kitchen or desk, motion
contestivis of accumulated objects. Objectivity too is matter of this piece of
wood. A *tabla* is in the dictionary, transporting itself like: *tabla* (1) *(de
madera)* of wood: if you lose this you lose grip as implied in conversation
somewhere like Rio Piedras, Puerto Rico; (2) *(de metal)* sheets: moments
among buildings, big structures, boats, autos, irons ironing your skull base
for greater irony; (3) *(de piedra)* slab: also chunk of reality, let's say a piece
of voice not knowing its pretty qualities are being used beyond its own life;

---

[4]Saint Lazarus.   [5]Soursop, a tropical fruit.

(4) *(de tierra)* strip: episode which should be recalled right in the strip; this feels like going through distance back to a time that was slowly being eaten by this moment when it is still trying to hold onto the table; (5) *(cuadro pintado en una tabla):* situation which has been thoroughly explained into your metabolism or a framework, something that works within a frame of four sides painted clearly so you can distinguish shapes, and *contenido* reversed means *nest contained*. This is a list of tables. Broken legs will lose the tablet, and you will place your fingers on the wrong weather. Whether you at the time thought perfect your box of index, this tablature will accurately give you all the stops on a road for which you have an unsecured map with inscriptions and designs.

Let us not lose our table as we praise the importance of its acquisition. So the flow goes that it is also a catalogue *catalogo*—*cadaloco* means each crazy one of all the material involved. Such a list is the one you have to have faith in to maintain your tables analogous to your mind health. This wealth leads to a Spanish *(table de lavar)* wash table where the surgeons reconstruct dilapidated jungles inside of your vision from which they (this) move you (to a *tabla de planchar*) and stretch you out (to *tabla de salvación*), at which point you might have capreached and you would *(tener tablas)* to present your presence on a stage to the world and bad light would not harm you. Tablear cuts you into pieces, separates you into patches / streams / numbers / notes till you level to approachable grade for tabletear signifies to rattle, ultimately, realizations that a table has four legs and within it contains space, unless it is the table of multiplication, whereupon you will see everything in doubles or substance folded. Tabloid stretched out has many stories that are placed one by the other into pictures and features done so you can continue to follow your interests and arrange them in your pocket neatly like a well-versed drum alphabetizing names of peoples and whereabouts of mountains visible and under earth. Figures pop into your *tabula rasa*, empty where there is no grease or *grasa*, a simple search for *gracia* gracing this directory which has given deep tales and details of detours so we may come to a *principio* or principles. Let us now table this tablederia of context tabled.

1982

SIMON ORTIZ (ACOMA PUEBLO)

B. 1941

Simon Ortiz was born in Albuquerque, New Mexico. After an elementary education in Indian schools, high school, and a stint in the army, he enrolled at the University of New Mexico, where he became aware of N. Scott Momaday, James Welch, and others among the first voices in Native American literature in the late 1960s. Although he was always interested in writing, under the pressures of contemporary experience Ortiz found that his motive for writing changed from self-expression to the desire to "express a Native American nationalistic (some may call it a tribalistic) literary voice."

Ortiz is a member of the Acoma Pueblo tribe, and his experiences in that community endowed him with several passionate concerns. From his father he learned to reverence the power and integrity of language. By choice, his poetry is fundamentally oral and frequently narrative, because he believes that one experiences life through poetry or, in the oral tradition, song. "Song as language," he has written, "is a way of touching." A second recurrent theme of Ortiz is that we establish our identity, individually and communally, in relation to a sense of place. For the most part, he argues, Anglo-Americans have been alienated from the land, a dislocation they try to valorize with an expansionist frontier ideology. It is no wonder, then, that Ortiz is also deeply concerned with the political consequences of his writing. He grew up in the uranium mining area of northwest New Mexico, where laborers daily compromised their health and lives in the ruthless exploitation of the natural environment. Ortiz himself worked in such mines, and his identification with workers and the dehumanizing conditions under which they struggle, highlighted in his short story "To Change in a Good Way," permeates his work. Arguments that literature ought to be above politics, be concerned only with beauty and universal significance, do not sway him. Such a position, he argues, is taken by those who want to obscure the political consequences of their own work, "who do not want to hear the truth spoken by those who defend the earth."

Ortiz's interest in the transformative power of compelling language, a historical sense of place, and the political dimensions of poetry are especially evident in his cycle of poems titled *from Sand Creek*. Based on his experiences as a veteran recovering at a VA hospital, the poems offer a series of discrete but tonally unified moments of reflection that contemplate the present condition of the speaker and his nation in view of each's past. Though the book is full of anger, grief, and pain, its dominant theme is compassion. "Love," he writes, "should be answerable for." Only by claiming responsibility for ourselves and our nation, present and past, can we create the possibility of hope.

Andrew O. Wiget
New Mexico State University

PRIMARY WORKS

Going for the Rain, 1976; *A Good Journey,* 1977; *Howbah Indians,* 1978; *Fight Back: For the Sake of the People, For the Sake of the Land,* 1980; *from Sand Creek,* 1981; *Fightin': New and Selected Short Stories,* 1983; *Woven Stone,* 1992; *After and before the Lightning,* 1994; *Men on the Moon,* 1999; *Out There Somewhere,* 2002; *The Good Rainbow Road,* 2004.

from **Sand Creek**

November 29, 1864: On that cold dawn, about 600 Southern Cheyenne and Arapaho People, two-thirds of them women and children, were camped on a bend of Sand Creek in southeastern Colorado. The People were at peace. This was expressed two months before by Black Kettle, one of the principal elders of the Cheyennes, in Denver to Governor John Evans and Colonel John W. Chivington, head of the Colorado Volunteers. "I want you to give all these chiefs of the soldiers here to understand that we are for peace, and that we have made peace, that we may not be mistaken for enemies." The reverend Colonel Chivington and his Volunteers and Fort Lyon troops, numbering more than 700 heavily armed men, slaughtered 105 women and children and 28 men.

A U.S. flag presented by President Lincoln in 1863 to Black Kettle in Washington, D.C. flew from a pole above the elder's lodge on that gray dawn. The People had been assured they would be protected by the flag. By mid-1865, the Cheyenne and Arapaho People had been driven out of Colorado Territory.

This America
has been a burden
of steel and mad
death,
but, look now,   5
there are flowers
and new grass
and a spring wind
rising
from Sand Creek.   10

It was a national quest, dictated by economic motives. Europe was hungry for raw material, and America was abundant forest, rivers, land.

Many of them
built their sod houses
without windows.
Without madness.

But fierce, o   5
with a just determination.

Consulting axioms
and the dream called America.

Cotton Mather[1] was no fool.

A few remembered   10
Andrew Jackson,
knew who he was,

---

[1]Cotton Mather (1663–1728) was a Puritan minister and author whose writings were influential during the Salem witch trials of 1692–1693.

ruminating, savoring
fresh Indian blood.

Style is a matter   15
of preference,
performance,
judgement yearning
to be settled quickly.

The axiom   20
would be the glory of America
at last,
          no wastelands,
no forgiveness.

The child would be sublime.   25

There are ghost towns all over the West; some are profitable tourist attractions
of the "frontier," others are merely sad and unknown.

What should have been
important and fruitful
became bitter.
          Wasted.
          Spots appeared on their lungs.   5
          Marrow dried
                    in their bones.
          They ranted.
Pointless utterances.
Truth did not speak for them.   10

It is a wonder
they even made it to California.

But, of course,
they did,
and they named it success.   15
Conquest.
Destiny.

Frontiers ended for them
and a dread settled upon them
and became remorseless   20
          nameless
          namelessness.

                    *   *   *

Colonel Chivington was a moral man, believed he was made in the image of God, and he carried out the orders of his nation's law; Kit Carson didn't mind stealing and killing either.

> At the Salvation Army
> a clerk
> caught me
> wandering
> among old spoons   5
> > and knives,
> > sweaters and shoes.
>
> I couldn't have stolen anything;
> my life was stolen already.
>
> In protest though,   10
> I should have stolen.
> My life. My life.
>
> She caught me;
> Carson caught Indians,
> secured them with his lies.   15
> Bound them with his belief.
>
> After winter,
> our own lives fled.
>
> I reassured her
> what she believed.   20
> Bought a sweater.
>
> And fled.
>
> I should have stolen.
> My life. My life.

There is a revolution going on; it is very spiritual and its manifestation is economic, political, and social. Look to the horizon and listen.

> The mind is stunned stark.
>
> At night,
> Africa is the horizon.

The cots of the hospital
are not part of the dream.   5

Lie awake, afraid.
Thinned breath.

Was it a scream again.
                        Far
below, far below,   10
the basement speaks
for Africa, Saigon, Sand Creek.
Souls gather
around campfires.
Hills protect them.   15

Mercenaries gamble
for odds.
            They'll never know.
Indians stalk beyond the dike,
carefully measure the distance,   20
count their bullets.

Stark, I said,
stunned night in the VAH.

The blood poured unto the plains, steaming like breath on winter mornings; the
breath rose into the clouds and became the rain and replenishment.

They were amazed
at so much blood.
                    Spurting,
                    sparkling,
splashing, bubbling, steady   5
hot arcing streams.
                    Red
and bright and vivid
unto the grassed plains.
                                    Steaming.   10
So brightly and amazing.
They were awed.

It almost seemed magical
that they had so much blood.
It just kept pouring,   15
like rivers,

like endless floods from the sky,
thunder that had become liquid,
and the thunder surged forever
into their minds.   20
                    Indeed,
they must have felt
they should get on their knees
and drink the red rare blood,
drink to replenish   25
their own vivid loss.
Their helpless hands
were like sieves.

*The land and Black Kettle took them in like lost children, and by 1876 land allot-
ment and reservations and private property were established.*

They must have known.

                    Surely,
they must have.
                    Black Kettle
met them at the open door   5
of the plains.

                    He swept his hand
all about them.
The vista of the mountains
was at his shoulder.   10
                    The rivers
run from the sky.
                    Stone soothes
every ache.
                    Dirt feeds us.   15
Spirit is nutrition.
                    Like a soul, the land
was open to them, like a child's heart.
There was no paradise,
but it would have gently and willingly   20
and longingly given them food and air
and substance for every comfort.
If they had only acknowledged
even their smallest conceit.

                    *   *   *

That dream
shall have a name
after all,
and it will not be vengeful
but wealthy with love   5
and compassion
and knowledge.
And it will rise
in this heart
which is our America.   10

1981

GARRETT KAORU HONGO
B. 1951

Garrett Kaoru Hongo is a prolific and accomplished Asian American poet. His poetry is characterized by striking images and unexpected, luminous lines. He has a special talent for close observation, an eye for the telling detail, and an ability to make the mundane beautiful, as in the vivid food images of "Who among You Knows the Essence of Garlic?" In dramatic monologues, such as "The Unreal Dwelling: My Years in Volcano," he gives voice to figures from his familial past or from a communal past. Hongo has written of himself, "My project as a poet has been motivated by a search for origins of various kinds— quests for ethnic and familial roots, cultural identities, and poetic inspiration.... I find the landscapes, folkways, and societies of Japan, Hawaii, and even Southern California to continually charm and compel me to write about them and inform myself of their specificities."

Born in Volcano, Hawaii, Hongo moved as a child to Laie, to Kahuku, and then to California—the San Fernando Valley—where he and his brother were the only Japanese in the public school. His family finally settled in Gardena, a Japanese American community in South Los Angeles adjoining the black community of Watts and the white community of Torrance. Hongo graduated from Pomona College, then traveled in Japan on a Thomas J. Watson Fellowship. He returned for graduate work at the University of Michigan, where he won the Hopwood poetry prize and studied with poet-professors Bert Meyers, Donald Hall, and Philip Levine. Later he earned an M.F.A. from the University of California at Irvine. He has taught at various universities, including the University of Missouri, where he was poetry editor of the *Missouri Review*. He is presently professor of English and creative writing at the University of Oregon.

Hongo has produced three volumes of poetry. The first, a joint publication with fellow poets Lawson Fusao Inada and Alan Chong Lau called *The Buddha Bandits down Highway 99* (1978), is a tripartite work of youthful exuberance.

Hongo's contribution to that first volume, "Cruising 99," is included in his second book, *Yellow Light* (1982), from which most of the poems in this selection were taken. *Yellow Light* won the Wesleyan Poetry Prize. *The River of Heaven* (1988), his third book of poetry, was awarded the Lamont Poetry Selection for 1987 by the Academy of American Poets and two years later was a finalist for the Pulitzer Prize in Poetry. "The Unreal Dwelling: My Years in Volcano" comes from this collection. In 1995, Hongo published *Volcano*, a poetic memoir exploring in greater depth some of the themes he had introduced in his poetry: his continuing search for family history and his rediscovery of the land of his childhood.

Hongo has also contributed to the Asian American literary/historical/critical opus by compiling and editing three significant anthologies. *The Open Boat* (1993) showcases the poetry of thirty-one Asian American poets; *Songs My Mother Taught Me* (1994) collects stories, plays, and memoirs of Wakako Yamauchi; *Under Western Eyes* (1995) assembles personal narratives by Asian American writers. Hongo's description of the Asian American poets he has gathered together in *The Open Boat* applies equally to his own poetry: "We come to consciousness aware of the history of immigration and the Asian diaspora, singing from the fissures and fragmentations of culture in order to bring about their momentary unity in the kind of evanescent beauty that the figure of a poem makes."

Amy Ling
University of Wisconsin at Madison
King-Kok Cheung
University of California, Los Angeles

PRIMARY WORKS

The Buddha Bandits down Highway 99 (with Alan Chong Lau and Lawson Fusao Inada), 1978; *Yellow Light*, 1982; *The River of Heaven*, 1988; *Volcano: A Memoir of Hawaii*, 1995; *Coral Road*, 2011.

Yellow Light

One arm hooked around the frayed strap
of a tar-black patent-leather purse,
the other cradling something for dinner:
fresh bunches of spinach from a J-Town *yaoya*,
sides of split Spanish mackerel from Alviso's,   5
maybe a loaf of Langendorf; she steps
off the hissing bus at Olympic and Fig,
begins the three-block climb up the hill,
passing gangs of schoolboys playing war,
Japs against Japs, Chicanas chalking sidewalks   10
with the holy double-yoked crosses of hopscotch,
and the Korean grocer's wife out for a stroll
around this neighborhood of Hawaiian apartments

just starting to steam with cooking
and the anger of young couples coming home   15
from work, yelling at kids, flicking on
TV sets for the Wednesday Night Fights.

If it were May, hydrangeas and jacaranda
flowers in the streetside trees would be
blooming through the smog of late spring.   20
Wisteria in Masuda's front yard would be
shaking out the long tresses of its purple hair.
Maybe mosquitoes, moths, a few orange butterflies
settling on the lattice of monkey flowers
tangled in chain-link fences by the trash.   25

But this is October, and Los Angeles
seethes like a billboard under twilight.
From used-car lots and the movie houses uptown,
long silver sticks of light probe the sky.
From the Miracle Mile, whole freeways away,   30
a brilliant fluorescence breaks out
and makes war with the dim squares
of yellow kitchen light winking on
in all the side streets of the Barrio.

She climbs up the two flights of flagstone   35
stairs to 201-B, the spikes of her high heels
clicking like kitchen knives on a cutting board,
props the groceries against the door,
fishes through memo pads, a compact,
empty packs of chewing gum, and finds her keys.   40

The moon then, cruising from behind
a screen of eucalyptus across the street,
covers everything, everything in sight,
in a heavy light like yellow onions.

                                                    1982

Off from Swing Shift

Late, just past midnight,
freeway noise from the Harbor
and San Diego leaking in
from the vent over the stove,
and he's off from swing shift at Lear's.   5
Eight hours of twisting circuitry,

charting ohms and maximum gains
while transformers hum
and helicopters swirl
on the roofs above the small factory.   10
He hails me with a head-fake,
then the bob and weave
of a weekend middleweight
learned at the Y on Kapiolani
ten years before I was born.   15

The shoes and gold London Fogger
come off first, then the easy grin
saying he's lucky as they come.
He gets into the slippers
my brother gives him every Christmas,   20
carries his Thermos over to the sink,
and slides into the one chair at the table
that's made of wood and not yellow plastic.
He pushes aside stacks
of *Sporting News* and *Outdoor Life*,   25
big round tins of Holland butter cookies,
and clears a space for his elbows, his pens,
and the *Racing Form's* Late Evening Final.

His left hand reaches out,
flicks on the Sony transistor   30
we bought for his birthday
when I was fifteen.
The right ferries in the earphone,
a small, flesh-colored star,
like a tiny miracle of hearing,   35
and fits it into place.
I see him plot black constellations
of figures and calculations
on the magazine's margins,
alternately squint and frown   40
as he fingers the knob of the tuner
searching for the one band
that will call out today's results.

There are whole cosmologies
in a single handicap,   45
a lifetime of two-dollar losing
in one pick of the Daily Double.

Maybe tonight is his night
for winning, his night
for beating the odds   50
of going deaf from a shell
at Anzio still echoing
in the cave of his inner ear,
his night for cashing in
the blue chips of shrapnel still grinding   55
at the thickening joints of his legs.

But no one calls
the horse's name, no one
says Shackles, Rebate, or Pouring Rain.
No one speaks a word.   60

1982

Who among You Knows the Essence of Garlic?

Can your foreigner's nose smell mullets
roasting in a glaze of brown bean paste
and sprinkled with novas of sea salt?

Can you hear my grandmother
chant the mushroom's sutra?   5

Can you hear the papayas crying
as they bleed in porcelain plates?

I'm telling you that the bamboo
slips the long pliant shoots
of its myriad soft tongues   10
into your mouth that is full of oranges.

I'm saying that the silver waterfalls
of bean threads will burst in hot oil
and stain your lips like zinc.

The marbled skin of the blue mackerel   15
works good for men. The purple oils
from its flesh perfume the tongues of women.

If you swallow them whole, the rice cakes
soaking in a broth of coconut milk and brown sugar
will never leave the bottom of your stomach.   20

Flukes of giant black mushrooms
leap from their murky tubs
and strangle the toes of young carrots.

Broiling chickens ooze grease,
yellow tears of fat collect   25
and spatter in the smoking pot.

Soft ripe pears, blushing
on the kitchen window sill,
kneel like plump women
taking a long luxurious shampoo,   30
and invite you to bite their hips.

Why not grab basketfuls of steaming noodles,
lush and slick as the hair of a fine lady,
and squeeze?

The shrimps, big as Portuguese thumbs,   35
stew among cut guavas, red onions,
ginger root, and rosemary in lemon juice,
the palm oil bubbling to the top,
breaking through layers and layers
of shredded coconut and sliced cashews.   40

Who among you knows the essence
of garlic and black lotus root,
of red and green peppers sizzling
among squads of oysters in the skillet,
of crushed ginger, fresh green onions,   45
and pale-blue rice wine simmering
in the stomach of a big red fish?

                                                              1982

And Your Soul Shall Dance

for Wakako Yamauchi

Walking to school beside fields
of tomatoes and summer squash,
alone and humming a Japanese love song,
you've concealed a copy of *Photoplay*
between your algebra and English texts.   5
Your knee socks, saddle shoes, plaid dress,
and blouse, long-sleeved and white

with ruffles down the front,
come from a Sears catalogue
and neatly complement your new Toni curls. 10
All of this sets you apart from the landscape:
flat valley grooved with irrigation ditches,
a tractor grinding through alkaline earth,
the short stands of windbreak eucalyptus
shuttering the desert wind 15
from a small cluster of wooden shacks
where your mother hangs the wash.
You want to go somewhere.
Somewhere far away from all the dust
and sorting machines and acres of lettuce. 20
Someplace where you might be kissed
by someone with smooth, artistic hands.
When you turn into the schoolyard,
the flagpole gleams like a knife blade in the sun,
and classmates scatter like chickens, 25
shooed by the storm brooding on your horizon.

1982

The Unreal Dwelling: My Years in Volcano

What I did, I won't excuse,
except to say it was a way to change,
the way new flows add to the land,
making things new, clearing the garden.
I left two sons, a wife behind— 5
and does it matter? The sons grew,
became their own kinds of men,
lost in the swirl of robes, cries
behind a screen of mist and fire
I drew between us, gambles I lost 10
and walked away from like any bad job.
I drove a cab and didn't care,
let the wife run off too, her combs
loose in some shopkeeper's bed.
When hope blazed up in my heart for the fresh start, 15
I took my daughters with me to keep house,
order my living as I was taught and came to expect.
They swept up, cooked, arranged flowers,
practiced tea and *buyō*, the classical dance.
I knew how because I could read and ordered books, 20
let all movements be disciplined and objects arranged
by an idea of order, the precise sequence of images

which conjure up the abstract I might call
yūgen, or Mystery, *chikara*, . . . Power.
The principles were in the swordsmanship   25
I practiced, in the package of loans
and small thefts I'd managed since coming here.
I could count, keep books, speak English
as well as any white, and I had false papers
recommending me, celebrating the fiction   30
of my long tenure with Hata Shōten of Honolulu.
And my luck was they bothered to check
only those I'd bribed or made love to.
Charm was my collateral, a willingness to move
and live on the frontier my strongest selling point.   35
So they staked me, a small-time hustler
good with cars, odds, and women,
and I tossed some boards together,
dug ponds and a cesspool,
figured water needed tanks, pipes,   40
and guttering on the eaves
to catch the light-falling rain,
and I had it—a store and a house out-back
carved out of rainforests and lava land
beside this mountain road seven leagues from Hilo.   45
I never worried they'd come this far—
the banks, courts, and police—
mists and sulphur clouds from the crater
drenching the land, washing clean my tracks,
bleaching my spotted skin the pallor of long-time residents.   50
I regularized my life and raised my girls,
put in gas pumps out front, stocked varieties of goods
and took in local fruit, flowers on consignment.
And I had liquor—plum wine and *saké*
from Japan, whiskey from Tennessee—   55
which meant I kept a pistol as well.
My girls learned to shoot, and would have
only no one bothered to test us.
It was known I'd shot cats and wild pigs
from across the road rummaging through garbage.   60
I never thought of my boys,
or of women too much
until my oldest bloomed,
suddenly, vanda-like, from spike
to scented flower almost overnight.   65
Young men in Model A's came up from town.
One even bussed, and a Marine from Georgia
stole a Jeep to try taking her

to the coast, or, more simply,
down a mountain road for the night.   70
The Shore Patrol found him.
And I got married again, to a country girl
from Kona who answered my ad.
I approved of her because,
though she was rough-spoken and squat-legged,   75
and, I discovered, her hair
slightly red in the groin,
she could carry 50-lbs. sacks of California Rose
without strain or grunting.
As postmaster and Territorial official,   80
I married us myself, sent announcements
and champagne in medicine vials
to the villagers and my "guarantors" in town.
The toasts tasted of vitamin-B and cough syrup.
My oldest moved away, herself married   85
to a dapper Okinawan who sold Oldsmobiles
and had the leisure to play golf on weekends.
I heard from my boy then, my oldest son,
back from the war and writing to us,
curious, formal, and not a little proud   90
he'd done his part. What impressed me
was his script—florid but under control,
penmanship like pipers at the tideline
lifting and settling on the sand-colored paper.
He wrote first from Europe, then New York,   95
finally from Honolulu. He'd fought,
mustered out near the Madison Square Garden
in time to see LaMotta smash the pretty one,
and then came home to a girl he'd met in night school.
He said he won out over a cop because he danced better,   100
knew from the service how to show up in a tie,
bring flowers and silk in nice wrappings.
I flew the Island Clipper to the wedding,
the first time I'd seen the boy in twenty years,
gave him a hundred cash and a wink   105
since the girl was pretty,
told him to buy, not rent his suits,
and came home the next day, hungover,
a raw ache in my throat.
I sobered up, but the ache   110
stayed and doctors tell me
it's this sickness they can't get rid of,
pain all through my blood and nerve cells.
I cough too much, can't smoke or drink

or tend to things. Mornings, I roll   115
myself off the damp bed, wrap
a blanket on, slip into the wooden clogs,
and take a walk around my pond and gardens.
On this half-acre, calla lilies in bloom,
cream-white cups swollen with milk,   120
heavy on their stems, and rocking in the slight wind,
cranes coming to rest on the wet, coppery soil.
The lotuses ride, tiny flamingoes, sapphired
pavilions buoyed on their green keels on the pond.
My fish follow me, snorting to be fed,   125
gold flashes and streaks of color
like blood satin and brocade in the algaed waters.
And when the sky empties of its many lights,
I see the quarter moon, horned junk,
sailing over the Ka'u and the crater rim.   130
This is the River of Heaven....
Before I cross, I know I must bow down,
call to my oldest son, say what I must
to bring him, and all the past, back to me.

1985

■ ## GARY SOTO ■
B. 1952

Gary Soto was born in Fresno, California, in the heart of the San Joaquin Valley, one of the world's richest agricultural regions. Raised in a working-class family, Soto attended parochial and public schools before enrolling in Fresno State College, intending to study geography and urban planning. His interests soon shifted to literature, however, especially after studying with the prominent poet Philip Levine. Soto published his first poem in 1973 in the *Iowa Review* as a college senior. After graduation, he entered the creative writing program at the University of California, Irvine, where he earned a master of fine arts degree in 1976. Soto then resided briefly in Mexico. His first book of poetry, *The Elements of San Joaquin*, appeared in 1977 to much critical acclaim. That same year, Soto began teaching at the University of California, Berkeley, where he remains. In addition to eleven volumes of poetry, Soto has published widely in many genres, including fiction for young adults, autobiographical sketches, and essays. He is the winner of various prestigious prizes including a Guggenheim Fellowship and the Academy of American Poets Award.

Like much contemporary American verse, Soto's poetry is largely autobiographical, recalling childhood and adolescent incidents and delineating family experience. Soto possesses the skill of converting ordinary, even banal, events into poetic occasions; much of his power and appeal as a poet derives precisely from the accessibility and familiarity of his subjects: a grandmother's courage, a youthful failure as an athlete, a father's relationship with his curious, energetic daughter. Soto's preference for clear, uncomplicated language and concrete images also enhances his work's accessibility. In terms of technique, the most striking feature of Soto's poetry is enjambment, the device of carrying meaning without pause from one line to the next.

Soto's ethnic consciousness—his sense of himself as a Mexican American—animates much of his work without delimiting it. Soto moves easily between the United States and Mexico to find his settings, his themes, and his protagonists. He often focuses on peculiarly Mexican American issues, and he frequently delineates, especially in poems recalling his childhood, the Mexican Americans' sense of community. But Soto presents Mexican American experience and culture as they fit within a broader context of human events and values. It is fair to say that Soto's largest concern as a poet is the plight of that segment of humanity that is exploited, ignored, unheard. Soto lifts his voice in their behalf; as he once wrote, "I believe in the culture of the poor."

Raymund Paredes
University of California, Los Angeles

PRIMARY WORKS

The Elements of San Joaquin, 1977; *The Tale of Sunlight*, 1978; *Where Sparrows Work Hard*, 1981; *Black Hair*, 1985; *Living up the Street*, 1985; *Small Faces*, 1986; *Lesser Evils: Ten Quartets*, 1988; *Who Will Know Us?: New Poems*, 1990; *A SummerLife*, 1990; *A Fire in My Hands: A Book of Poems*, 1990; *Baseball in April and Other Stories*, 1990; *Home Course in Religion: New Poems*, 1991; *Pacific Crossing*, 1992; *Neighborhood Odes*, 1992; *Local News*, 1993; *Crazy Weekend*, 1994; *Jesse*, 1994; *New and Selected Poems*, 1995; *Petty Crimes*, 1998; *Nerdlandia: A Play*, 1999; *A Natural Man*, 1999; *Buried Onions*, 1999; *Nickel and Dime*, 2000; *The Effects of Knut Hamsun on a Fresno Boy: Recollections and Short Essays*, 2000; *Poetry Lover*, 2001; *Baseball in April and Other Stories*, 2000; *A Simple Plan*, 2006; *Accidental Love*, 2007; *Partly Cloudy: Poems of Love and Longing*, 2009; *Human Nature*, 2010.

Braly Street

Every summer
The asphalt softens
Giving under the edge
Of boot heels and the trucks
That caught radiators   5
Of butterflies.
Bottle caps and glass
Of the '40s and '50s
Hold their breath
Under the black earth   10
Of asphalt and are silent

Like the dead whose mouths
Have eaten dirt and bermuda.
Every summer I come
To this street   15
Where I discovered ants bit,
Matches flare,
And pinto beans unraveled
Into plants; discovered
Aspirin will not cure a dog   20
Whose fur twiches.
It's 16 years
Since our house
Was bulldozed and my father
Stunned into a coma . . .   25
Where it was,
An oasis of chickweed
And foxtails.
Where the almond tree stood
There are wine bottles   30
Whose history
Is a liver. The long caravan
Of my uncle's footprints
Has been paved
With dirt. Where my father   35
Cemented a pond
There is a cavern of red ants
Living on the seeds
The wind brings
And cats that come here   40
To die among
The browning sage.

It's 16 years
Since bottle collectors
Shoveled around   45
The foundation
And the almond tree
Opened its last fruit
To the summer.
The houses are gone,   50
The Molinas, Morenos,
The Japanese families
Are gone, the Okies gone
Who moved out at night
Under a canopy of   55
Moving stars.

In '57 I sat
On the porch, salting
Slugs that came out
After the rain,
While inside my uncle   60
Weakened with cancer
And the blurred vision
Of his hands
Darkening to earth.
In '58 I knelt   65
Before my father
Whose spine was pulled loose.
Before his face still
Growing a chin of hair,
Before the procession   70
Of stitches behind
His neck, I knelt
And did not understand.

Braly Street is now   75
Tin ventilators
On the warehouses, turning
Our sweat
Towards the yellowing sky;
Acetylene welders   80
Beading manifolds,
Stinging the half-globes
Of retinas. When I come
To where our house was,
I come to weeds   85
And a sewer line tied off
Like an umbilical cord;
To the chinaberry
Not pulled down
And to its rings   90
My father and uncle
Would equal, if alive.

                                              1977

The Cellar

I entered the cellar's cold,
Tapping my way deeper
Than light reaches,
And stood in a place

Where the good lumber 5
Ticked from its breathing
And slept in a weather
Of fine dust.
Looking for what we
Discarded some time back, 10
I struck a small fire
And stepped back
From its ladder of smoke,
Watching the light
Pull a chair 15
And a portion of the wall
From where they crouched
In the dark.
I saw small things—
Hat rack and suitcase, 20
Tire iron and umbrella
That closed on a great wind—
Step slowly, as if shy,
From their kingdom of mold
Into a new light. 25

Above, in the rented rooms,
In the lives
I would never know again,
Footsteps circled
A bed, the radio said 30
What was already forgotten.
I imagined the sun
And how a worker
Home from the fields
Might glimpse at it 35
Through the window's true lens
And ask it not to come back.
And because I stood
In this place for hours,
I imagined I could climb 40
From this promise of old air
And enter a street
Stunned gray with evening
Where, if someone
Moved, I could turn, 45
And seeing through the years,
Call him brother, call him Molina.

1978

Mexicans Begin Jogging

At the factory I worked
In the fleck of rubber, under the press
Of an oven yellow with flame,
Until the border patrol opened
Their vans and my boss waved for us to run.   5
"Over the fence, Soto," he shouted,
And I shouted that I was American.
"No time for lies," he said, and pressed
A dollar in my palm, hurrying me
Through the back door.   10

Since I was on his time, I ran
And became the wag to a short tail of Mexicans—
Ran past the amazed crowds that lined
The street and blurred like photographs, in rain.
I ran from that industrial road to the soft   15
Houses where people paled at the turn of an autumn sky.
What could I do but yell *vivas*
To baseball, milkshakes, and those sociologists
Who would clock me
As I jog into the next century   20
On the power of a great, silly grin.

                                                   1981

Black Hair

At eight I was brilliant with my body.
In July, that ring of heat
We all jumped through, I sat in the bleachers
Of Romain Playground, in the lengthening
Shade that rose from our dirty feet.   5
The game before us was more than baseball.
It was a figure—Hector Moreno
Quick and hard with turned muscles,
His crouch the one I assumed before an altar
Of worn baseball cards, in my room.   10

I came here because I was Mexican, a stick
Of brown light in love with those
Who could do it—the triple and hard slide,
The gloves eating balls into double plays.
What could I do with 50 pounds, my shyness,   15

My black torch of hair, about to go out?
Father was dead, his face no longer
Hanging over the table or our sleep,
And mother was the terror of mouths
Twisting hurt by butter knives.   20
In the bleachers I was brilliant my body,
Waving players in and stomping my feet,
Growing sweaty in the presence of white shirts.
I chewed sunflower seeds. I drank water
And bit my arm through the late innings.   25
When Hector lined balls into deep
Center, in my mind I rounded the bases
With him, my face flared, my hair lifting
Beautifully, because we were coming home
To the arms of brown people.   30

                                                                 1985

Kearney Park

True Mexicans or not, let's open our shirts
And dance, a spark of heels
Chipping at the dusty cement. The people
Are shiny like the sea, turning
To the clockwork of rancheras,   5
The accordion wheezing, the drum-tap
Of work rising and falling.
Let's dance with our hats in hand.
The sun is behind the trees,
Behind my stutter of awkward steps   10
With a woman who is a brilliant arc of smiles,
An armful of falling water. Her skirt
Opens and closes. My arms
Know no better but to flop
On their own, and we spin, dip   15
And laugh into each other's faces—
Faces that could be famous
On the coffee table of my abuelita.
But grandma is here, at the park, with a beer
At her feet, clapping   20
And shouting, "Dance, hijo, dance!"
Laughing, I bend, slide, and throw up
A great cloud of dust,
Until the girl and I are no more.

                                                                 1985

SONIA SANCHEZ

B. 1934

Born in Birmingham, Alabama, Sanchez has taught creative writing and African American literature in at least eight universities across the United States. A professor emerita of English at Temple University, where she taught for more than twenty years, she has performed her poems and given poetry workshops in Australia, England, Cuba, Nicaragua, and Africa, as well as the United States. No other American figure blends the roles of mother, teacher, poet, and political activist more sincerely and energetically than Sanchez.

Her poems manifest the spiritual link between art and politics. If her earlier poems are to be appreciated, the reader must forget all conceptions of what a poem is and listen attentively to Sanchez's attacks on the Euro-American political, social, and aesthetic establishments. Her work is intentionally nonintellectual, unacademic, and anti–middle class. "To blk/record/buyers" is characteristic of her work, which aims at teaching blacks to know themselves, to be self-reliant and strong. In this poem, she attacks the Righteous Brothers for aping a style that originated with black performers such as James Brown. What appears to be a list of the activities in the black urban community contains more than three hundred years of black history. Sex, language and retorts, drinking, mocking war materials, crime, and religion are the placebos blacks have used for comfort. Sanchez's poem ends with the "AAAH, AAAH, AAAH, yeah" that both affirms her point and echoes the style of popular artists like Aretha Franklin and James Brown.

Sanchez's language comes out of her immediate surroundings and accents her characters' lifestyles. Her refusal to use standard academic English is a part of a political statement that undermines the use of language as a tool for oppression.

Two of her more important thematic concerns are the relationship between black men and black women and her interest in black children. Two of her books are written for the young: *It's a New Day* and *A Sound Investment*. In these texts, too, Sanchez's purpose is to teach black people to know themselves, to be themselves, and to love themselves.

By the time of the publication of *It's a New Day*, Sanchez had become a member of Elijah Muhammad's Muslim community. Her Islamic ideology infuses her fourth and fifth books of poetry, *Love Poems* and *A Blues Book for Blue Black Magical Women;* in them she expresses her spiritual nature through poetry that is more mystical, more suggestive and abstract. Although she experiments with the spatial possibilities in her earlier collections, *Homegirls & Handgrenades* introduces several prose-poems, such as the very moving "Just Don't Never Give Up on Love," that look like prose but have many of the characteristics of poetry. Her next collection, *Under a Soprano Sky*, demonstrates her perfectly honed skills of repetition, hyperbole, and invective and her growing captivation by the sounds of language and the use of metaphor and imagery. Following these early works, she has continued to hone her aesthetic and to experiment with new forms and genres.

Joyce Ann Joyce
Chicago State University

PRIMARY WORKS

Homecoming, 1969; *Liberation Poem*, 1970; *We a BaddDDD People*, 1970; *Ima Talken bout the Nation of Islam*, 1972; *A Blues Book for Blue Black Magical Women*, 1973; *Love Poems*, 1973; *I've Been a Woman: New and Selected Poems*, 1981; *Homegirls & Handgrenades*, 1984; *Under a Soprano Sky*, 1987; *Wounded in the House of a Friend*, 1995; *Does Your House Have Lions?*, 1997; *Like Singing Coming off the Drums: Love Poems*, 1998; *Shake Loose My Skin: New and Selected Poems*, 1999; *Ash*, 2001; *Morning Haiku*, 2010; *I'm Black When I'm Singing, I'm Blue When I Ain't and Other Plays*, 2010.

to blk/record/buyers

don't play me no
righteous bros.
    white people
ain't rt bout nothing
no mo.   5
   don't tell me bout
foreign dudes
      cuz no blk/
people are grooving on a
sunday afternoon.   10
    they either
making out/
   signifying/
      drinking/
making molotov cocktails/   15
     stealing
or rather more taking their goods
from the honky thieves who
ain't hung up
     on no pacifist/jesus/ 20
      cross/   but.
play blk/songs
   to drown out the
shit/screams of honkies. AAAH.
AAAH AAAH yeah.   brothers. 25
andmanymoretogo.

           1969

Masks

(blacks don't have the intellectual capacity to succeed.)

—WILLIAM COORS

the river runs toward day
and never stops.

so life receives the lakes
patrolled by one-eyed pimps
who wash their feet in our blue whoredom   5

the river floods
the days grow short
we wait to change our masks with
we wait for warmer days and
fountains without force   10
we wait for seasons without power.

today
ah today
only the shrill sparrow seeks the sky
our days are edifice.   15
we look toward temples that give birth to sanctioned flesh.

          o bring the white mask
            full of the chalk sky.

entering the temple
on this day of sundays   20
i hear the word spoken
by the unhurried speaker
who speaks of unveiled eyes.

          o bring the chalk mask
            full of altitudes.   25

straight in this chair
tall in an unrehearsed role
i rejoice
and the spirit sinks in twilight of
distant smells.   30

          o bring the mask
            full of drying blood.

fee, fie, fo, fum,
i smell the blood
of an englishman   35

o my people
wear the white masks
for they speak without speaking
and hear words of forgetfulness.
o my people.   40

                1984

Just Don't Never Give Up on Love

Feeling tired that day, I came to the park with the children. I saw her as I rounded the corner, sitting old as stale beer on the bench, ruminating on some uneventful past. And I thought, "Hell. No rap from the roots today. I need the present. On this day. This Monday. This July day buckling me under her summer wings, I need more than old words for my body to squeeze into."

I sat down at the far end of the bench, draping my legs over the edge, baring my back to time and time unwell spent. I screamed to the children to watch those curves threatening their youth as they rode their 10-speed bikes against mid-western rhythms.

I opened my book and began to write. They were coming again, those words insistent as his hands had been, pounding inside me, demanding their time and place. I relaxed as my hands moved across the paper like one possessed.

I wasn't sure just what it was I heard. At first I thought it was one of the boys calling me so I kept on writing. They knew the routine by now. Emergencies demanded a presence. A facial confrontation. No long distance screams across trees and space and other children's screams. But the sound pierced the pages and I looked around, and there she was inching her bamboo-creased body toward my back, coughing a beaded sentence off her tongue.

"Guess you think I ain't never loved, huh girl? Hee. Hee. Guess that what you be thinking, huh?"

I turned. Startled by her closeness and impropriety, I stuttered, "I, I, I, Whhhaat dooooo you mean?"

"Hee. Hee. Guess you think I been old like this fo'ever, huh?" She leaned toward me, "Huh? I was so pretty that mens brought me breakfast in bed. Wouldn't let me hardly do no work at all."

"That's nice ma'am. I'm glad to hear that." I returned to my book. I didn't want to hear about some ancient love that she carried inside her. I had to finish a review for the journal. I was already late. I hoped she would get the hint and just sit still. I looked at her out of the corner of my eyes.

"He could barely keep hisself in changing clothes. But he was pretty. My first husband looked like the sun. I used to say his name over and over again 'til it hung from my ears like diamonds. Has you ever loved a pretty man, girl?"

I raised my eyes, determined to keep a distance from this woman disturbing my day.

"No ma'am. But I've seen many a pretty man. I don't like them though cuz they keep their love up high in a linen closet and I'm too short to reach it."

Her skin shook with laughter.

"Girl you gots some spunk about you after all. C'mon over here next to me. I wants to see yo' eyes up close. You looks so uneven sittin' over there."

Did she say uneven? Did this old buddah splintering death say uneven? Couldn't she see that I had one eye shorter than the other; that my breath was painted on porcelain; that one breast crocheted keloids under this white blouse?

I moved toward her though. I scooped up the years that had stripped me to the waist and moved toward her. And she called to me to come out, come out wherever you are young woman, playing hide and go seek with scarecrow men. I gathered myself up at the gateway of her confessionals.

"Do you know what it mean to love a pretty man, girl?" She crooned in my ear. "You always running behind a man like that girl while he cradles his privates. Ain't no joy in a pretty yellow man, cuz he always out pleasurin' and givin' pleasure."

I nodded my head as her words sailed in my ears. Here was the pulse of a woman whose black ass shook the world once.

She continued. "A woman crying all the time is pitiful. Pitiful I says. I wuz pitiful sitting by the window every night like a cow in the fields chewin' on cud. I wanted to cry out, but not even God hisself could hear me. I tried to cry out til my mouth wuz split open at the throat. I 'spoze there is a time all womens has to visit the slaughter house. My visit lasted five years."

Touching her hands, I felt the summer splintering in prayer, touching her hands, I felt my bones migrating in red noise. I asked, "When did you see the butterflies again?"

Her eyes wandered like quicksand over my face. Then she smiled, "Girl don't you know yet that you don't never give up on love? Don't you know you has in you the pulse of winds? The noise of dragon flies?" Her eyes squinted close and she said, "One of them mornings he woke up callin' me and I wuz gone. I wuz gone running with the moon over my shoulders. I looked no which way at all. I had inside me 'nough knives and spoons to cut/scoop out the night. I wuz a tremblin' as I met the mornin'."

She stirred in her 84-year-old memory. She stirred up her body as she talked. "They's men and mens. Some good. Some bad. Some breathing death. Some breathing life. William wuz my beginnin'. I come to my second husband spittin' metal and he just pick me up and fold me inside him. I wuz christen' with his love."

She began to hum. I didn't recognize the song; it was a prayer. I leaned back and listened to her voice rustling like silk. I heard cathedrals and sonnets; I heard tents and revivals and a black woman spilling black juice among her ruins.

"We all gotta salute death one time or 'nother girl. Death be waitin' out doors trying to get inside. William died at his job. Death just turned 'round and snatched him right off the street."

Her humming became the only sound in the park. Her voice moved across the bench like a mutilated child. And I cried. For myself. For this woman talkin' about love. For all the women who have ever stretched their bodies out anticipating civilization and finding ruins.

The crashing of the bikes was anticlimactic. I jumped up, rushed toward the accident. Man. Little man. Where you bicycling to so very fast? Man. Second little man. Take it slow. It all passes so fast any how.

As I walked the boys and their bikes toward the bench, I smiled at this old woman waiting for our return.

"I want you to meet a great lady, boys."

"Is she a writer, too, ma?"

"No honey. She's a lady who has lived life instead of writing about it."

"After we say hello can we ride a little while longer? Please!"

"Ok. But watch your manners now and your bones afterwards."

"These are my sons, Ma'am."

"How you do sons? I'm Mrs. Rosalie Johnson. Glad to meet you."

The boys shook her hand and listened for a minute to her words. Then they rode off, spinning their wheels on a city neutral with pain.

As I stood watching them race the morning, Mrs. Johnson got up.

"Don't go," I cried. "You didn't finish your story."

"We'll talk by-and-by. I comes out here almost everyday. I sits here on the same bench everyday. I'll probably die sittin' here one day. As good a place as any I 'magine."

"May I hug you, ma'am? You've helped me so much today. You've given me strength to keep on looking."

"No. Don't never go looking for love girl. Just wait. It'll come. Like the rain fallin' from the heaven, it'll come. Just don't never give up on love."

We hugged; then she walked her 84-year-old walk down the street. A black woman. Echoing gold. Carrying couplets from the sky to crease the ground.

1984

A Letter to Dr. Martin Luther King

Dear Martin,

Great God, what a morning, Martin!

The sun is rolling in from faraway places. I watch it reaching out, circling these bare trees like some reverent lover. I have been standing still listening to the morning, and I hear your voice crouched near hills, rising from the mountain tops, breaking the circle of dawn.

You would have been 54 today.

As I point my face toward a new decade, Martin, I want you to know that the country still crowds the spirit. I want you to know that we still hear your footsteps setting out on a road cemented with black bones. I want you to know that the stuttering of guns could not stop your light from crashing against cathedrals chanting piety while hustling the world.

Great God, what a country, Martin!

The decade after your death docked like a spaceship on a new planet. Voyagers all we were. We were the aliens walking up the '70s, a holocaust people on the move looking out from dark eyes. A thirsty generation, circling the peaks of our country for more than a Pepsi taste. We were young-bloods, spinning hip syllables while saluting death in a country neutral with pain.

And our children saw the mirage of plenty spilling from capitalistic sands.

And they ran toward the desert.

And the gods of sand made them immune to words that strengthen the breast.

And they became scavengers walking on the earth.

And you can see them playing. Hide-and-go-seek robbers. Native sons. Running on their knees. Reinventing slavery on asphalt. Peeling their umbilical cords for a gold chain.

And you can see them on Times Square, in N.Y.C., Martin, selling their 11-, 12-year-old, 13-, 14-year-old bodies to suburban forefathers.

And you can see them on Market Street in Philadelphia bobbing up bellywise, young fishes for old sharks.

And no cocks are crowing on those mean streets.

Great God, what a morning it'll be someday, Martin!

That decade fell like a stone on our eyes. Our movements. Rhythms. Loves. Books. Delivered us from the night, drove out the fears keeping some of us hoarse. New births knocking at the womb kept us walking.

We crossed the cities while a backlash of judges tried to turn us into moles with blackrobed words of reverse racism. But we knew. And our knowing was like a sister's embrace. We crossed the land where famine was fed in public. Where black stomachs exploded on the world's dais while men embalmed their eyes and tongues in gold. But we knew. And our knowing squatted from memory.

Sitting on our past, we watch the new decade dawning. These are strange days, Martin, when the color of freedom becomes disco fever; when soap operas populate our Zulu braids; as the world turns to the conservative right and general hospitals are closing in Black neighborhoods and the young and the restless are drugged by early morning reefer butts. And houses tremble.

These are dangerous days, Martin, when cowboy-riding presidents corral Blacks (and others) in a common crown of thorns; when nuclear-toting generals recite an alphabet of blood; when multinational corporations assassinate ancient cultures while inaugurating new civilizations. Comeout comeout wherever you are. Black country. Waiting to be born . . .

But, Martin, on this, your 54th birthday—with all the reversals—we have learned that black is the beginning of everything.

> it was black in the universe before the sun;
> it was black in the mind before we opened our eyes;
> it was black in the womb of our mother;
> black is the beginning,
> and if we are the beginning we will be forever.

Martin. I have learned too that fear is not a Black man or woman. Fear cannot disturb the length of those who struggle against material gains for self-aggrandizement. Fear cannot disturb the good of people who have moved to a meeting place where the pulse pounds out freedom and justice for the universe.

Now is the changing of the tides, Martin. You forecast it where leaves
dance on the wings of man. Martin. Listen. On this your 54th year, listen
and you will hear the earth delivering up curfews to the missionaries and
assassins. Listen. And you will hear the tribal songs:

Ayeeee	Ayooooo	Ayeee
Ayeeee	Ayooooo	Ayeee

        Malcolm ...
        Robeson ...
        Lumumba ...
        Fannie Lou ...
        Garvey ...
        Johnbrown ...
        Tubman ...
        Mandela ...
          (free Mandela,
          free Mandela)
        Assata ...
        Ke wa rona[1]
        Ke wa rona
        Ke wa rona
        Ke wa rona
        Ke wa rona
        Ke wa rona
        Ke wa rona
        Ke wa rona
As we go with you to the sun,
as we walk in the dawn, turn our eyes
Eastward and let the prophecy come true
and let the prophecy come true.
    Great God, Martin, what a morning it will be!

                                1984

Father and Daughter

we talk of light things you and I in this
small house. no winds stir here among
flame orange drapes that drape our genesis
And snow melts into rivers. The young
grandchild reviews her impudence that
makes you laugh and clap for more allure.
Ah, how she twirls the emerald lariat.
When evening comes your eyes transfer

                                              5

[1] He is ours.

to space you have not known and taste the blood
breath of a final flower. Past equal birth,   10
the smell of salt begins another flood:
your land is in the ashes of the South.
perhaps the color of our losses:
perhaps the memory that dreams nurse:
old man, we do not speak of crosses.   15

1985

LUCILLE CLIFTON
1936–2010

Thelma Lucille Sayles Clifton was born in Depew, New York, and educated at
Fredonia State Teachers College in Fredonia, New York, and at Howard University. Although she began writing at a young age, Clifton devoted her early
adult life to raising her family. In the midst of her life with her husband, Fred,
and six children under the age of ten, she published her first collection of
poetry, *Good Times*, in 1969. She subsequently published eight more books of
poetry, a memoir, a compilation of her early work, and more than sixteen
books for young readers—including the popular Everett Anderson series.
Toward the end of her life she was Distinguished Professor of Humanities at
St. Mary's College in Maryland, having also taught at Coppin State College,
Goucher College, American University, and the University of California at Santa
Cruz, among other colleges and universities. Her awards and distinctions include
the University of Massachusetts Press Juniper Prize for Poetry, two National
Endowment for the Arts Fellowships for creative writing, a nomination for the
Pulitzer Prize for Poetry for *Two-Headed Woman*, a second Pulitzer Prize nomination for both *Good Woman: Poems and a Memoir 1969–1980* and *Next: New
Poems*, an Emmy Award from the American Academy of Television Arts and Sciences, Poet Laureate of the State of Maryland, and a 1996 Lannan Literary
Award for Poetry.

The themes and language of Clifton's poetry are shaped by her concern with
family history and relationships, with community, with racial history, and with
the possibilities of reconciliation and transcendence. In *Good Times*, she uses
direct, unadorned language to capture the rhythms and values of urban African
American working-class life. Throughout this collection, Clifton consciously pits
her spare, economical language against the pervasive and negative images of
black urban life, insistently reminding her readers of the humanity concealed
behind social and economic statistics. Like Langston Hughes and Gwendolyn
Brooks, she sees virtue and dignity in the lives of ordinary African Americans,
giving them faces, names, and histories and validating their existence. In the
face of the daily realities of urban life, Clifton records both the adversity and

the small triumphs, always maintaining a strong-willed sense of optimism and spiritual resilience.

One source of this equanimity, of this poise in the face of adversity and tragedy, is Clifton's strong sense of rootedness in the legacy of her family history—particularly of her great-great-grandmother Caroline, a woman kidnapped to America from Dahomey, and Caroline's daughter, Lucille, who bore the distinction of being the first black woman lynched in Virginia. These two women in particular conjure up images of survival and endurance, on the one hand, and avenging spirits, on the other. By locating herself within this family history, Clifton not only lays claim to an African past—a recurrent feature of many of her poems—she also defines herself as a poet whose task is to keep historical memory alive. At the same time that Clifton accepts the weight of this history, however, she refuses to be trapped or defeated by it. Like a blues singer's lyrics, Clifton's poems confront the chaos, disorder, and pain of human experience to transcend these conditions and to reaffirm her humanity.

The optimism that shapes Clifton's poetry is nourished by her deep spiritual beliefs. While she often invokes Christian motifs and biblical references in her poems, she draws freely upon other values and beliefs as well. "The black God, Kali/a woman God and terrible/with her skulls and breasts" often appears in her poems, as do references to African goddesses like Yemoja, the Yoruba water deity, and to Native American beliefs. More specifically, Clifton's invocation of the "two-headed woman" of African American folk belief, with its overtones of Hoodoo and conjure, makes plain her commitment to other ways of knowing and understanding the world. The spiritual dimension of her poetry deepened after the death of her husband, Fred Clifton, in 1984. Whether her poetry is exploring the biological changes within her own body or imagining the death of the Sioux chief Crazy Horse, Lucille Clifton's world is both earthy and spiritual. In her capacity as both witness and seer, she looks through the madness and sorrow of the world, locating moments of epiphany in the mundane and ordinary. Her poetry invariably moves toward those moments of calm and tranquillity, of grace, that speak to the continuity of the human spirit.

James A. Miller
George Washington University

PRIMARY WORKS

Good Times, 1969; *Good News about the Earth*, 1972; *An Ordinary Woman*, 1974; *Generations*, 1976; *Two-Headed Woman*, 1980; *Next: New Poems*, 1987; *Good Woman: Poems and a Memoir 1969–1980*, 1987; *Quilting: Poems 1987–1990*, 1991; *The Book of Light*, 1993; *The Terrible Stories: Poems*, 1996; *Blessing the Boats: New and Collected Poems, 1998–2000*, 2000; *Mercy*, 2004; *Voices*, 2008; also children's books.

the thirty eighth year

the thirty eighth year
of my life,
plain as bread

round as a cake
an ordinary woman.   5

an ordinary woman.

i had expected to be
smaller than this,
more beautiful,
wiser in afrikan ways,   10
more confident,
i had expected
more than this.

i will be forty soon.
my mother once was forty.   15

my mother died at forty four,
a woman of sad countenance
leaving behind a girl
awkward as a stork.
my mother was thick,   20
her hair was a jungle and
she was very wise
and beautiful
and sad.

i have dreamed dreams   25
for you mama
more than once.
i have wrapped me
in your skin
and made you live again   30
more than once.
i have taken the bones you hardened
and built daughters
and they blossom and promise fruit
like afrikan trees.   35
i am a woman now.
an ordinary woman.

in the thirty eighth
year of my life,
surrounded by life,   40
a perfect picture of
blackness blessed,
i had not expected this
loneliness.

if it is western,   45
if it is the final
europe in my mind,
if in the middle of my life
i am turning the final turn
into the shining dark   50
let me come to it whole
and holy
not afraid
not lonely
out of my mother's life   55
into my own.
into my own.

i had expected more than this.
i had not expected to be
an ordinary woman.   60

                                                                     1974

i am accused of tending to the past

i am accused of tending to the past
as if i made it,
as if i sculpted it
with my own hands. i did not.
this past was waiting for me   5
when i came,
a monstrous unnamed baby,
and i with my mother's itch
took it to breast
and named it   10
History.
she is more human now,
learning language everyday,
remembering faces, names and dates.
when she is strong enough to travel   15
on her own, beware, she will.

                                                                     1991

at the cemetery, walnut grove plantation,
south carolina, 1989

among the rocks
at walnut grove

your silence drumming
in my bones,
tell me your names.   5

nobody mentioned slaves
and yet the curious tools
shine with your fingerprints.
nobody mentioned slaves
but somebody did this work   10
who had no guide, no stone,
who moulders under rock.

tell me your names,
tell me your bashful names
and i will testify.   15
the inventory lists ten slaves
but only men were recognized.

among the rocks
at walnut grove
some of these honored dead   20
were dark
some of these dark
were slaves
some of these slaves
were women   25
some of them did this
honored work.
tell me your names
foremothers, brothers,
tell me your dishonored names.   30
here lies
here lies
here lies
here lies
hear   35

                                                          1991

reply

[from a letter written to Dr. W.E.B. Dubois by Alvin Borgquest of Clark
University in Massachusetts and dated April 3, 1905:

   "We are pursuing an investigation here on the subject of crying as an
expression of the emotions, and should like very much to learn about its
peculiarities among the colored people. We have been referred to you as a

person competent to give us information on the subject. We desire
especially to know about the following salient aspects: 1. Whether the Negro
sheds tears ..."]

reply

he do
she do
they live
they love   5
they try
they tire
they flee
they fight
they bleed   10
they break
they moan
they mourn
they weep
they die   15
they do
they do
they do

                                                             1991

in white america

1   i come to read them poems

i come to read them poems,
a fancy trick i do
like juggling with balls of light.
i stand, a dark spinner,
in the grange hall,   5
in the library, in the
smaller conference room,
and toss and catch as if by magic,
my eyes bright, my mouth smiling,
my singed hands burning.   10

2   the history

1800's in this town
fourteen longhouses were destroyed
by not these people here.
not these people
burned the crops and chopped down   15

all the peach trees.
not these people. these people
preserve peaches, even now.

3   the tour

"this was a female school.
my mother's mother graduated   20
second in her class.
they were taught embroidery,
and chenille and filigree,
ladies' learning. yes,
we have a liberal history here."   25
smiling she pats my darky hand.

4   the hall

in this hall
dark women
scrubbed the aisles
between the pews   30
on their knees.
they could not rise
to worship.
in this hall
dark women   35
my sisters and mothers

though i speak with the tongues
of men and of angels and
have not charity . . .

in this hall   40
dark women,
my sisters and mothers,
i stand
and let the church say
let the church say   45
let the church say
AMEN.

5   the reading

i look into none of my faces
and do the best i can.
the human hair between us   50

stretches but does not break.
i slide myself along it and
love them, love them all.

6 it is late

it is late
in white america.   55
i stand
in the light of the
7–11
looking out toward
the church   60
and for a moment only
i feel the reverberation
of myself
in white america
a black cat   65
in the belfry
hanging
and
ringing.

1987

■   JUNE JORDAN   ■
                1936–2002

Born July 9, 1936, in Harlem, June Jordan began writing poetry at the age of
seven after her family had moved into a brownstone in Brooklyn's now well-
known Bedford-Stuyvesant area. Like many of the finest writers in the African
American literary tradition, Jordan proved her skill in several genres. Poet,
essayist, playwright, novelist, and composer, she was also a seasoned political activist and teacher. A professor of African American studies and women's studies
at the University of California at Berkeley toward the end of her life, she also
taught at City College of New York, Sarah Lawrence College, and Yale University.

Although her parents, particularly her father, introduced her to the poetry
of Shakespeare, Edgar Allan Poe, and Paul Laurence Dunbar, and although the
writing of T. S. Eliot and Emily Dickinson is also reflected in her work, she later
studied the poetry of Langston Hughes, Margaret Walker, and Robert Hayden.
Jordan's poetry is unique. Because of the diversity of these early influences and
because of the ingenious way in which she weaves her political activism and her

personal experiences as a black bisexual woman into the fabric of her art, her poetry defines its own place in African American literary history, despite the commonalities she shares with Audre Lorde and Alexis Deveaux.

Jordan's work is heavily influenced by important and sometimes devastating events from her life: her father's disappointment that she was not a boy, his extreme discipline while she was growing up, her mother's suicide, an early marriage that failed, and her having been raped. Jordan's essays and poetry chart the connections she finds among the personal, the literary, the political, and the global. In a 1981 *Essence* interview with Alexis Deveaux, Jordan said of "Poem about My Rights," which she wrote in response to the rape, "I tried to show as clearly as I could that the difference between South Africa and rape and my mother trying to change my face and my father wanting me to be a boy was not an important difference to me. *It all violates self-determination.*"

The relationship that Jordan addresses between her personal experiences and those of others throughout the world, particularly those in oppressed cultures, defines the depth and range of her art. The titles of her essay collections—*Civil Wars* (1981), *On Call: Political Essays* (1985), *Moving towards Home: Political Essays* (1989), and *Technical Difficulties: African-American Notes on the State of the Union* (1992)—suggest the connection she makes between the personal, the global, and the political. Her essays as well as her poetry are rooted in her blackness, her bisexuality, and the honest, fearless way in which she attacks racism and all its related illnesses.

Her travels to Nicaragua, her teaching experience (including children's writing workshops), her work as a freelance journalist, her work as a research associate and writer for Mobilization for Youth, and her study of architecture at the Donnell Library in Manhattan are all manifest in her poems. In 1969 Jordan won the Prix de Rome in Environmental Design for the way in which she transformed architectural design into fiction in her novel for adolescents *His Own Where*, later published in 1971. She also wrote three other books primarily for children.

Although Jordan published three early collections of poetry—*Who Look at Me* (1969), *Some Changes* (1971), and *New Days: Poems of Exile and Return* (1974)—the 1977 *Things That I Do in the Dark: Selected Poetry* contains most of this early work. Prefaced by the poem "These poems they are things that I do in the dark," this rich collection addresses everything and everybody from her son Christopher to her father, Granville Ivanhoe Jordan, her mother, marriage, former President Lyndon Johnson, Malcolm X, bisexuality, and Senator Daniel Patrick Moynihan. Both *Living Room: New Poems* (1985) and *Naming Our Own Destiny* (1989), Jordan's later collections, show her skill at using titles to illuminate her purpose. The poems in both books address the physical/emotional/spiritual space the oppressed in the United States, Lebanon, Nicaragua, and South Africa need in order to become self-determining. "Moving towards Home," the last poem in *Living Room*, captures the essence of Jordan's irony and repetition, her ability to use a word seemingly out of context, such as her use of *redeem* near the end of this poem. Translated into Arabic, Spanish, French, Swedish, German, and Japanese, "Moving towards Home" affirms the international status of Jordan's poetry.

Joyce Ann Joyce
Chicago State University

PRIMARY WORKS

Who Look at Me, 1969; *Some Changes*, 1971; *New Days: Poems of Exile and Return*, 1974; *Things That I Do in the Dark: Selected Poetry*, 1977; *Passion: New Poems, 1977–1980*, 1980; *Civil Wars*, 1981; *On Call: Political Essays*, 1985; *Living Room: New Poems*, 1985; *Lyrical Campaigns: Selected Poems*, 1989; *Naming Our Destiny: New and Selected Poems*, 1989; *Moving towards Home: Political Essays*, 1989; *Technical Difficulties: African-American Notes on the State of the Union*, 1992; *Haruko: Love Poems*, 1994; *Kissing God Goodbye: Poems 1991–1997*, 1997; *Affirmative Acts: Political Essays*, 1998; *Soldier: A Poet's Childhood*, 2000; *Some of Us Did Not Die: New and Selected Essays*, 2002.

Poem about My Rights

Even tonight and I need to take a walk and clear
my head about this poem about why I can't
go out without changing my clothes my shoes
my body posture my gender identity my age
my status as a woman alone in the evening/   5
alone on the streets/alone not being the point/
the point being that I can't do what I want
to do with my own body because I am the wrong
sex the wrong age the wrong skin and
suppose it was not here in the city but down on the beach/   10
or far into the woods and I wanted to go
there by myself thinking about God/or thinking
about children or thinking about the world/all of it
disclosed by the stars and the silence:
I could not go and I could not think and I could not   15
stay there
alone
as I need to be
alone because I can't do what I want to do with my own
body and   20
who in the hell set things up
like this
and in France they say if the guy penetrates
but does not ejaculate then he did not rape me
and if after stabbing him if after screams if   25
after begging the bastard and if even after smashing
a hammer to his head if even after that if he
and his buddies fuck me after that
then I consented and there was
no rape because finally you understand finally   30
they fucked me over because I was wrong I was
wrong again to be me being me where I was/wrong
to be who I am

which is exactly like South Africa
penetrating into Namibia penetrating into   35
Angola and does that mean I mean how do you know if
Pretoria ejaculates what will the evidence look like the
proof of the monster jackboot ejaculation on Blackland
and if
after Namibia and if after Angola and if after Zimbabwe   40
and if after all of my kinsmen and women resist even to
self-immolation of the villages and if after that
we lose nevertheless what will the big boys say will they
claim my consent:
Do You Follow Me: We are the wrong people of   45
the wrong skin on the wrong continent and what
in the hell is everybody being reasonable about
and according to the *Times* this week
back in 1966 the C.I.A. decided that they had this problem
and the problem was a man named Nkrumah so they   50
killed him and before that it was Patrice Lumumba
and before that it was my father on the campus
of my Ivy League school and my father afraid
to walk into the cafeteria because he said he
was wrong the wrong age the wrong skin the wrong   55
gender identity and he was paying my tuition and
before that
it was my father saying I was wrong saying that
I should have been a boy because he wanted one/a
boy and that I should have been lighter skinned and   60
that I should have had straighter hair and that
I should not be so boy crazy but instead I should
just be one/a boy and before that
it was my mother pleading plastic surgery for
my nose and braces for my teeth and telling me   65
to let the books loose to let them loose in other
words
I am very familiar with the problems of the C.I.A.
and the problems of South Africa and the problems
of Exxon Corporation and the problems of white   70
America in general and the problems of the teachers
and the preachers and the F.B.I. and the social
workers and my particular Mom and Dad/I am very
familiar with the problems because the problems
turn out to be   75
me
I am the history of rape
I am the history of the rejection of who I am
I am the history of the terrorized incarceration of

my self   80
I am the history of battery assault and limitless
armies against whatever I want to do with my mind
and my body and my soul and
whether it's about walking out at night
or whether it's about the love that I feel or   85
whether it's about the sanctity of my vagina or
the sanctity of my national boundaries
or the sanctity of my leaders or the sanctity
of each and every desire
that I know from my personal and idiosyncratic   90
and indisputably single and singular heart
I have been raped
be-
cause I have been wrong the wrong sex the wrong age
the wrong skin the wrong nose the wrong hair the   95
wrong need the wrong dream the wrong geographic
the wrong sartorial I
I have been the meaning of rape
I have been the problem everyone seeks to
eliminate by forced   100
penetration with or without the evidence of slime and/
but let this be unmistakable this poem
is not consent I do not consent
to my mother to my father to the teachers to
the F.B.I. to South Africa to Bedford-Stuy   105
to Park Avenue to American Airlines to the hardon
idlers on the corners to the sneaky creeps in
cars
I am not wrong: Wrong is not my name
My name is my own my own my own   110
and I can't tell you who the hell set things up like this
but I can tell you that from now on my resistance
my simple and daily and nightly self-determination
may very well cost you your life

                                                                                          1989

To Free Nelson Mandela

Every night Winnie Mandela
Every night the waters of the world
turn to the softly burning
light of the moon

Every night Winnie Mandela   5
Every night

Have they killed the twelve-year-old girl?
Have they hung the poet?
Have they shot down the students?
Have they splashed the clinic the house   10
and the faces of the children
with blood?

Every night Winnie Mandela
Every night the waters of the world
turn to the softly burning   15
light of the moon

They have murdered Victoria Mxenge
They have murdered her
victorious now
that the earth recoils from that crime   20
of her murder now
that the very dirt shudders from the falling blood
the thud of bodies fallen
into the sickening
into the thickening   25
crimes of apartheid

Every night
Every night Winnie Mandela

Every night Winnie Mandela
Every night the waters of the world   30
turn to the softly burning
light of the moon

At last the bullets boomerang
At last the artifice of exile explodes
At last no one obeys the bossman of atrocities   35

At last the carpenters the midwives

the miners the weavers the anonymous
housekeepers the anonymous
street sweepers
the diggers of the ditch   40
the sentries the scouts the ministers
the mob the pallbearers the practical

nurse
the diggers of the ditch
the banned   45
the tortured
the detained
the everlastingly insulted
the twelve-year-old girl and her brothers at last
the diggers of the ditch   50
despise the meal without grace
      the water without wine
      the trial without rights
      the work without rest
at last the diggers of the ditch   55
begin the living funeral
for death

Every night Winnie Mandela
Every night

Every night Winnie Mandela   60
Every night the waters of the world
turn to the softly burning
light of the moon

Every night Winnie Mandela
Every night   65

1989

Moving towards Home

"Where is Abu Fadi," she wailed.
"Who will bring me my loved one?"

—*NEW YORK TIMES 9/20/82*

I do not wish to speak about the bulldozer and the
red dirt
not quite covering all of the arms and legs
Nor do I wish to speak about the nightlong screams
that reached   5
the observation posts where soldiers lounged about
Nor do I wish to speak about the woman who shoved
her baby
into the stranger's hands before she was led away
Nor do I wish to speak about the father whose sons   10
were shot
through the head while they slit his own throat before

the eyes
of his wife
Nor do I wish to speak about the army that lit continuous   15
flares into the darkness so that the others could see
the backs of their victims lined against the wall
Nor do I wish to speak about the piled up bodies and
the stench
that will not float   20
Nor do I wish to speak about the nurse again and
again raped
before they murdered her on the hospital floor
Nor do I wish to speak about the rattling bullets that
did not   25
halt on that keening trajectory
Nor do I wish to speak about the pounding on the
doors and
the breaking of windows and the hauling of families into
the world of the dead   30
I do not wish to speak about the bulldozer and the
red dirt
not quite covering all of the arms and legs
because I do not wish to speak about unspeakable events
that must follow from those who dare   35
"to purify" a people
those who dare
"to exterminate" a people
those who dare
to describe human beings as "beasts with two legs"   40
those who dare
"to mop up"
"to tighten the noose"
"to step up the military pressure"
"to ring around" civilian streets with tanks   45
those who dare
to close the universities
to abolish the press
to kill the elected representatives
of the people who refuse to be purified   50
those are the ones from whom we must redeem
the words of our beginning
because I need to speak about home
I need to speak about living room
where the land is not bullied and beaten into   55
a tombstone
I need to speak about living room
where the talk will take place in my language

I need to speak about living room
where my children will grow without horror   60
I need to speak about living room where the men
of my family between the ages of six and sixty-five
are not
marched into a roundup that leads to the grave
I need to talk about living room   65
where I can sit without grief without wailing aloud
for my loved ones
where I must not ask where is Abu Fadi
because he will be there beside me
I need to talk about living room   70
because I need to talk about home

I was born a Black woman
and now
I am become a Palestinian
against the relentless laughter of evil   75
there is less and less living room
and where are my loved ones?

It is time to make our way home.

                                                                        1985

TONI MORRISON

B. 1931

The only living American recipient of the Nobel Prize for Literature, Toni Morrison has been designated everything from "Word Wizard" to "Living Legend,"
both because of her exquisite signature use of language and because of her prodigious and multifaceted literary production. As an author, teacher, editor, and
critic, Morrison has embraced not only the novels for which she is most famous
but also social analysis and critique, literary criticism, lyrics for both opera and
musical, dramatic plays, stories for children, and the one short story anthologized here. She is not only a prolific writer but also an engaging speaker and an
intellectually commanding figure on the public scene. When Toni Morrison
writes or speaks, people sit up and listen.

    Born in Lorain, Ohio, to Ramah and George Wofford, both migrants from
the deep South, Morrison grew up in a working-class family that provided not
only a loving, stable environment but also the basis for her lifelong commitment to intellectual development and honesty. Steeped in the stories and

folklore of her own black community, the future author learned from an early age that her identity was never contingent on what others thought. To this end, she credits her father's guidance and strong sense of self. After teaching appointments at both Texas Southern University and Howard, she moved to New York, where, as an editor for Random House, she ushered into print a number of outstanding black writers, including Angela Davis, Toni Cade Bambara, Leon Forest, and Gayle Jones. At Random House, she also worked assiduously with the editors on compiling *The Black Book* (1974), a collection of memorabilia from the history of African Americans from which she would eventually take the premises for each novel of her trilogy. She held the Robert F. Goheen Chair in the Humanities at Princeton University until her retirement in 2006.

Morrison has stated that she wanted to write stories that she wanted to read and that she often begins a novel with a question for which she has no answer. Indeed, far from closing down her stories with easy resolutions, the author is much more given to posing questions than to answering them. Throughout her career, no matter what format she has chosen, she has been politically engaged with her era. She is adamant about her service to the black community, which makes her writing political, but equally adamant about making her language "irrevocably beautiful," never sacrificing the writing to political correctness. Her ten novels span the entirety of the "Africanist presence" in what is now the United States, so that some critics recommend reading her novels not in the order of their publication but in the chronological order of the historical moments with which they deal. This history begins with *A Mercy* (2008), which examines colonial America before slavery became equated with blackness, and continues through *Love* (2003), which evaluates both the gains and losses of the civil rights movement through the 1990s. Reading her novels this way, however, runs the risk of missing the author's engagement with the most pressing issues of each moment. Although *A Mercy* deals with a "preracial" conception of slavery, it equally addresses the excesses of religious fanaticism so overtly present in the very founding of the country and warns of the dangers of returning to such fanaticism in a post-9/11 world order.

By the author's own admission, her first novel, *The Bluest Eye* (1970), though set in the 1940s, was written as a direct response to the popular "Black is beautiful" of the late 1960s. She was concerned that there was a story that was missing, that the trauma of growing up poor, black, and female was not going to be erased by easy slogans. The "invisibility" of Pecola Breedlove and her subsequent descent into madness belies the beauty of her blackness as she comes to assume that it is a sign of her ugliness. In 1974 Morrison published *Sula*, the story of a friendship between two black girls as they grow into adulthood; it arrived on the scene during the rebirth of the women's movement at a time when the movement was still much criticized for its racial and class exclusivity.

Song of Solomon (1977) takes the form of a quest by its male protagonist to discover his history, his roots, and his identity as a black man. Milkman Dead's search contrasts the thoughtless ease of an aspiring middle class of blacks with the militancy of the Seven Days, who would exact retribution for each African American killed with impunity in the United States. Morrison turns her "unflinching eye" on both the misogynist attitudes of the late 1960s in the black power movement and the struggle for reclaiming a mythic history of slavery in the empowerment of black masculinity. *Tar Baby* (1981) draws on the old folktale to problematize both the cultural assimilation of blacks into the mainstream and the cultural legacy of the African American past.

Although *Beloved* (1987) would be second in line in the historical chronology (its present is the post-Reconstruction era of the 1870s), the novel appeared within the context of a postmodern reevaluation of historical memory. It was initially passed over for both the American Book Critics Award and the Pulitzer Prize, but after an open letter of protest signed by more than 40 black novelists and intellectuals was published in the *New York Times*, the novel went on to win not only the Pulitzer for 1988 but also the best novel of the previous 25 years in the *Times* informal survey of 2006. Though censored in certain school districts (a fact that for the author validates its importance), the challenging and multilayered novel is now required reading in college courses around the world and has been the subject of hundreds of scholarly articles as well as dissertations.

Second and third in the Morrison trilogy, *Jazz* (1992) and *Paradise* (1998), set in the 1920s and the 1970s, respectively, continue to address postmodern concerns with language, stories, and the production of history even as they reach back to the 1870s, thus providing an overview of one hundred years of black presence in the United States in its rural, urban, and small town locations. Morrison's Nobel Prize for Literature in 1993 catapulted her into worldwide prominence. Following *Love* and *A Mercy*, the author's latest novel, *Home* (2012), is set in the 1950s, an era she calls "my time"; it concerns the return of a medic from the Korean War and his effort to negotiate his return to Georgia after his arrival on the West Coast.

Engaging these historical periods through fiction has not detracted from Morrison's direct involvement in crucial issues affecting African Americans, particularly in the 1990s. Indeed, her perceptive introductions to two edited volumes, *Race-ing Justice and En-Gendering Power: Essays on Anita Hill, Clarence Thomas and the Construction of Social Reality* (1992) and *Birth of a Nation'hood: Gaze, Script and Spectacle in the O.J. Simpson Case* (1997), both use canonical literary works to explain the nature of the critique—Defoe's *Robinson Crusoe* in the former, and Melville's *Benito Cereno* in the latter. Morrison's contribution to her edited volume of essays, *Burn This Book* (2009), reiterates the crucial role that literature must play in the understanding of our lives and our environment. Her dramatic works also draw on history (*Dreaming Emmett*, 1986) and classical literature (*Desdemona*, 2011), providing new twists on conventional readings. The libretto to the opera *Margaret Garner* (2005) returns to the story that inspired *Beloved*, again giving voice and pathos to the historical figure; the lyrics to *District Storeyville* (1982) bring to life the New Orleans quarter credited with being the birthplace of *Jazz*. In *Playing in the Dark* (1992), her challenging new analyses of canonical American works have altered paradigms not just in literary criticism but in law, sociology, philosophy, and psychology. Even the author's children's books (written with her son Slade Morrison), *The Big Box* (1999) and *The Book of Mean People* (2002), rewrite conventional stories from a child's point of view, providing challenging interpretations of adult versions of "model" behavior, particularly in the rewriting of Aesop's fables.

"Recitatif" is Toni Morrison's only published short story. The narrative of an ongoing yet sometimes strained friendship between two preadolescent girls left in a shelter at a young age, it is an experimental piece that conscientiously eliminates reference to the race of each of these two characters while presenting characteristics of racial stereotyping indiscriminately assigned. Neither "racial" nor class distinctions are overly expressed, leaving the reader to come to terms with his or her own preconceptions. Critics have also factored in the historical circumstances that might help to discern the background of each protagonist, and some have pointed out that the racial affiliation of the reader is often determinant in understanding the girls. Over their thirty-year friendship, both Twyla and Roberta must come to terms with their dark desire to hurt the mute, "lopsided" Maggie, of unspecified identity, and with their own psychic trauma as children. In a very real sense, the way in which the story is deciphered ultimately reflects as much on readers' cultural background as on their intellectual acuity. And ultimately, as in the case of the "white girl" of *Paradise*, why does it really matter?

Justine Tally
Universidad de La Laguna

PRIMARY WORKS

The Bluest Eye, 1970; *Sula*, 1974; *The Black Book* (with Middleton Harris), 1974; *Song of Solomon*, 1977; *Tar Baby*, 1981; *Beloved*, 1987; *Playing in the Dark: Whiteness and the Literary Imagination*, 1992; *Jazz*, 1992; *Paradise*, 1998; *Love*, 2003; *A Mercy*, 2008; *What Moves at the Margin: Selected Nonfiction*, 2008; *Home*, 2012.

Recitatif

My mother danced all night and Roberta's was sick. That's why we were taken to St. Bonny's. People want to put their arms around you when you tell them you were in a shelter, but it really wasn't bad. No big long room with one hundred beds like Bellevue. There were four to a room, and when Roberta and me came, there was a shortage of state kids, so we were the only ones assigned to 406 and could go from bed to bed if we wanted to. And we wanted to, too. We changed beds every night and for the whole four months we were there we never picked one out as our own permanent bed.

It didn't start out that way. The minute I walked in and the Big Bozo introduced us, I got sick to my stomach. It was one thing to be taken out of your own bed early in the morning—it was something else to be stuck in a strange place with a girl from a whole other race. And Mary, that's my mother, she was right. Every now and then she would stop dancing long enough to tell me something important and one of the things she said was that they never washed their hair and they smelled funny. Roberta sure did. Smell funny, I mean. So when the Big Bozo (nobody ever called her Mrs. Itkin, just like nobody ever said St. Bonaventure)—when she said, "Twyla, this is Roberta. Roberta, this is Twyla. Make each other welcome." I said, "My mother won't like you putting me in here."

"Good," said Bozo. "Maybe then she'll come and take you home."

How's that for mean? If Roberta had laughed I would have killed her, but she didn't. She just walked over to the window and stood with her back to us.

"Turn around," said Bozo. "Don't be rude. Now Twyla. Roberta. When you hear a loud buzzer, that's the call for dinner. Come down to the first floor. Any fights and no movie." And then, just to make sure we knew what we would be missing: "*The Wizard of Oz.*"

Roberta must have thought I meant that my mother would be mad about my being put in a shelter. Not about rooming with her, because as soon as Bozo left she came over to me and said, "Is your mother sick too?"

"No," I said. "She just likes to dance all night."

"Oh." She nodded her head and I liked the way she understood things so fast. So for the moment it didn't matter that we looked like salt and pepper standing there and that's what the other kids called us sometimes. We were eight years old and got F's all the time. Me because I couldn't remember what I read or what the teacher said. And Roberta because she couldn't read at all and didn't even listen to the teacher. She wasn't good at anything except jacks, at which she was a killer: pow scoop pow scoop pow scoop.

We didn't like each other all that much at first, but nobody else wanted to play with us because we weren't real orphans with beautiful dead parents in the sky. We were dumped. Even the New York City Puerto Ricans and the upstate Indians ignored us. All kinds of kids were in there, black ones, white ones, even two Koreans. The food was good, though. At least I thought so. Roberta hated it and left whole pieces of things on her plate: Spam, Salisbury steak—even Jell-O with fruit cocktail in it, and she didn't care if I ate what she wouldn't. Mary's idea of supper was popcorn and a can of Yoo-Hoo. Hot mashed potatoes and two weenies was like Thanksgiving for me.

It really wasn't bad, St. Bonny's. The big girls on the second floor pushed us around now and then. But that was all. They wore lipstick and eyebrow pencil and wobbled their knees while they watched TV. Fifteen, sixteen, even, some of them were. They were put-out girls, scared runaways most of them. Poor little girls who fought their uncles off but looked tough to us, and mean. God, did they look mean. The staff tried to keep them separate from the younger children, but sometimes they caught us watching them in the orchard where they played radios and danced with each other. They'd light out after us and pull our hair or twist our arms. We were scared of them, Roberta and me, but neither of us wanted the other one to know it. So we got a good list of dirty names we could shout back when we ran from them through the orchard. I used to dream a lot and almost always the orchard was there. Two acres, four maybe, of these little apple trees. Hundreds of them. Empty and crooked like beggar women when I first came to St. Bonny's but fat with flowers when I left. I don't know why I dreamt about that orchard so much. Nothing really happened there. Nothing all that important, I mean. Just the big girls dancing and playing the radio. Roberta and me watching. Maggie fell down there once. The kitchen woman with legs like parentheses. And the big girls laughed at her. We should have helped her up, I know, but we were scared of those girls with lipstick and eyebrow pencil. Maggie couldn't talk. The kids said she had her tongue cut out, but I think she was just born that way: mute. She was old and sandy-colored and she worked in the kitchen. I don't know if she was nice or not. I just remember her legs like parentheses and how she rocked when she walked. She worked from early in the morning till two o'clock, and if she was late, if she had too much cleaning and didn't get out till two-fifteen or so, she'd cut through the orchard so she wouldn't miss her bus and have to wait another hour. She wore this really stupid little hat—a kid's hat with ear flaps—and she wasn't much taller than we were. A really awful little hat. Even for a mute, it was dumb—dressing like a kid and never saying anything at all.

"But what about if somebody tries to kill her?" I used to wonder about that. "Or what if she wants to cry? Can she cry?"

"Sure," Roberta said. "But just tears. No sounds come out."

"She can't scream?"

"Nope. Nothing."

"Can she hear?"

"I guess."

"Let's call her," I said. And we did.

"Dummy! Dummy!" She never turned her head.

"Bow legs! Bow legs!" Nothing. She just rocked on, the chin straps of her baby-boy hat swaying from side to side. I think we were wrong. I think she could hear and didn't let on. And it shames me even now to think there was somebody in there after all who heard us call her those names and couldn't tell on us.

We got along all right, Roberta and me. Changed beds every night, got F's in civics and communication skills and gym. The Bozo was disappointed in us, she said. Out of 130 of us state cases, 90 were under twelve. Almost all were real orphans with beautiful dead parents in the sky. We were the only ones dumped and the only ones with F's in three classes including gym. So we got along—what with her leaving whole pieces of things on her plate and being nice about not asking questions.

I think it was the day before Maggie fell down that we found out our mothers were coming to visit us on the same Sunday. We had been at the shelter twenty-eight days (Roberta twenty-eight and a half) and this was their first visit with us. Our mothers would come at ten o'clock in time for chapel, then lunch with us in the teacher's lounge. I thought if my dancing mother met her sick mother it might be good for her. And Roberta thought her sick mother would get a bang out of a dancing one. We got excited about it and curled each other's hair. After breakfast we sat on the bed watching the road from the window. Roberta's socks were still wet. She washed them the night before and put them on the radiator to dry. They hadn't, but she put them on anyway because their tops were so pretty—scalloped in pink. Each of us had a purple construction-paper basket that we had made in craft class. Mine had a yellow crayon rabbit on it. Roberta's had eggs with wiggly lines of color. Inside were cellophane grass and just the jelly beans because I'd eaten the two marshmallow eggs they gave us. The Big Bozo came herself to get us. Smiling she told us we looked very nice and to come downstairs. We were so surprised by the smile we'd never seen before, neither of us moved.

"Don't you want to see your mommies?"

I stood up first and spilled the jelly beans all over the floor. Bozo's smile disappeared while we scrambled to get the candy up off the floor and put it back in the grass.

She escorted us downstairs to the first floor, where the other girls were lining up to file into the chapel. A bunch of grown-ups stood to one side. Viewers mostly. The old biddies who wanted servants and the fags who wanted company looking for children they might want to adopt. Once in a while a grandmother. Almost never anybody young or anybody whose face wouldn't scare you in the night. Because if any of the real orphans had young relatives they wouldn't be real orphans. I saw Mary right away. She had on those green slacks I hated and hated even more now because didn't she know we were going to chapel? And that fur jacket with the pocket linings so ripped she had to pull to get her hands out of them. But her face was pretty—like always—and she smiled and waved like she was the little girl looking for her mother, not me.

I walked slowly, trying not to drop the jelly beans and hoping the paper handle would hold. I had to use my last Chiclet because by the time I finished cutting everything out, all the Elmer's was gone. I am left-handed and the scissors never worked for me. It didn't matter, though; I might just as well have chewed the gum. Mary dropped to her knees and grabbed me, mashing the basket, the jelly beans, and the grass into her ratty fur jacket.

"Twyla, baby. Twyla, baby!"

I could have killed her. Already I heard the big girls in the orchard the next time saying, "Twyyyyla, baby!" But I couldn't stay mad at Mary while she was smiling and hugging me and smelling of Lady Esther dusting powder. I wanted to stay buried in her fur all day.

To tell the truth I forgot about Roberta. Mary and I got in line for the traipse into chapel and I was feeling proud because she looked so beautiful even in those ugly green slacks that made her behind stick out. A pretty mother on earth is better than a beautiful dead one in the sky even if she did leave you all alone to go dancing.

I felt a tap on my shoulder, turned, and saw Roberta smiling. I smiled back, but not too much lest somebody think this visit was the biggest thing that ever happened in my life. Then Roberta said, "Mother, I want you to meet my roommate, Twyla. And that's Twyla's mother."

I looked up it seemed for miles. She was big. Bigger than any man and on her chest was the biggest cross I'd ever seen. I swear it was six inches long each way. And in the crook of her arm was the biggest Bible ever made.

Mary, simpleminded as ever, grinned and tried to yank her hand out of the pocket with the raggedy lining—to shake hands, I guess. Roberta's mother looked down at me and then looked down at Mary too. She didn't say anything, just grabbed Roberta with her Bible-free hand and stepped out of line, walking quickly to the rear of it. Mary was still grinning because she's not too swift when it comes to what's really going on. Then this light bulb goes off in her head and she says "That bitch!" really loud and us almost in the chapel now. Organ music whining; the Bonny Angels singing sweetly. Everybody in the world turned around to look. And Mary would have kept it up—kept calling names if I hadn't squeezed her hand as hard as I could. That helped a little, but she still twitched and crossed and uncrossed her legs all through service. Even groaned a couple of times. Why did I think she would come there and act right? Slacks. No hat like the grandmothers and viewers, and groaning all the while. When we stood for hymns she kept her mouth shut. Wouldn't even look at the words on the page. She actually reached in her purse for a mirror to check her lipstick. All I could think of was that she really needed to be killed. The sermon lasted a year, and I knew the real orphans were looking smug again.

We were supposed to have lunch in the teachers' lounge, but Mary didn't bring anything, so we picked fur and cellophane grass off the mashed jelly beans and ate them. I could have killed her. I sneaked a look at Roberta. Her mother had brought chicken legs and ham sandwiches and oranges and a whole box of chocolate-covered grahams. Roberta drank milk from a thermos while her mother read the Bible to her.

Things are not right. The wrong food is always with the wrong people. Maybe that's why I got into waitress work later—to match up the right people with the right food. Roberta just let those chicken legs sit there, but she did bring a stack of grahams up to me later when the visit was over. I think she was sorry that her mother would not shake my mother's hand. And I liked that and I liked the fact that she didn't say a word about Mary groaning all the way through the service and not bringing any lunch.

Roberta left in May when the apple trees were heavy and white. On her last day we went to the orchard to watch the big girls smoke and dance by the radio. It didn't matter that they said, "Twyyyyla, baby." We sat on the ground and breathed. Lady Esther. Apple blossoms. I still go soft when I smell one or the other. Roberta was going home. The big cross and the big Bible was coming to get her and she seemed sort of glad and sort of not. I thought I would die in that room of four beds without her and I knew Bozo had plans to move some other dumped kid in there with me. Roberta promised to write every day, which was really sweet of her because she couldn't read a lick so how could she write anybody? I would have drawn pictures and sent them to her but she never gave me her address. Little by little she faded. Her wet socks with the pink scalloped tops and her big serious-looking eyes—that's all I could catch when I tried to bring her to mind.

I was working behind the counter at the Howard Johnson's on the Thruway just before the Kingston exit. Not a bad job. Kind of a long ride from

Newburgh, but okay once I got there. Mine was the second shift, eleven to seven. Very light until a Greyhound checked in for breakfast around six-thirty. At that hour the sun was all the way clear of the hills behind the restaurant. The place looked better at night—more like shelter—but I loved it when the sun broke in, even if it did show all the cracks in the vinyl and the speckled floor looked dirty no matter what the mop boy did.

It was August and a bus crowd was just unloading. They would stand around a long while: going to the john, and looking at gifts and junk-for-sale machines, reluctant to sit down so soon. Even to eat. I was trying to fill the cof-feepots and get them all situated on the electric burners when I saw her. She was sitting in a booth smoking a cigarette with two guys smothered in head and facial hair. Her own hair was so big and wild I could hardly see her face. But the eyes. I would know them anywhere. She had on a powder-blue halter and shorts outfit and earrings the size of bracelets. Talk about lipstick and eye-brow pencil. She made the big girls look like nuns. I couldn't get off the counter until seven o'clock but I kept watching the booth in case they got up to leave before that. My replacement was on time for a change, so I counted and stacked my receipts as fast as I could and signed off. I walked over to the booth, smiling and wondering if she would remember me. Or even if she wanted to remember me. Maybe she didn't want to be reminded of St. Bonny's or have anybody know she was ever there. I know I never talked about it to anybody.

I put my hands in my apron pockets and leaned against the back of the booth facing them.

"Roberta? Roberta Fisk?"

She looked up. "Yeah?"

"Twyla."

She squinted for a second and then said, "Wow."

"Remember me?"

"Sure. Hey. Wow."

"It's been awhile," I said, and gave a smile to the two hairy guys.

"Yeah. Wow. You work here?"

"Yeah," I said. "I live in Newburgh."

"Newburgh? No kidding?" She laughed then, a private laugh that included the guys, and they laughed with her. What could I do but laugh too and wonder why I was standing there with my knees showing out from under that uniform. Without looking I could see the blue-and-white triangle on my head, my hair shapeless in a net, my ankles thick in white oxfords. Nothing could have been less sheer than my stockings. There was this silence that came down right after I laughed. A silence it was her turn to fill up. With introductions, maybe, to her boyfriends or an invitation to sit down and have a Coke. Instead she lit a cigarette off the one she'd just fin-ished and said, "We're on our way to the Coast. He's got an appointment with Hendrix." She gestured casually toward the boy next to her.

"Hendrix? Fantastic," I said. "Really fantastic. What's she doing now?"

Roberta coughed on her cigarette and the two guys rolled their eyes up at the ceiling.

"Hendrix. Jimi Hendrix, asshole. He's only the biggest—Oh, wow. Forget it."

I was dismissed without anyone saying good-bye, so I thought I would do it for her.

"How's your mother?" I asked. Her grin cracked her whole face. She swallowed. "Fine," she said. "How's yours?"

"Pretty as a picture," I said and turned away. The backs of my knees were damp. Howard Johnson's really was a dump in the sunlight.

James is as comfortable as a house slipper. He liked my cooking and I liked his big loud family. They have lived in Newburgh all of their lives and talk about it the way people do who have always known a home. His grandmother has a porch swing older than his father and when they talk about streets and avenues and buildings they call them names they no longer have. They still call the A&P Rico's because it stands on property once a mom-and-pop store owned by Mr. Rico. And they call the new community college Town Hall because it once was. My mother-in-law puts up jelly and cucumbers and buys butter wrapped in cloth from a dairy. James and his father talk about fishing and baseball and I can see them all together on the Hudson in a raggedy skiff. Half the population of Newburgh is on welfare now, but to my husband's family it was still some upstate paradise of a time long past. A time of ice houses and vegetable wagons, coal furnaces and children weeding gardens. When our son was born my mother-in-law gave me the crib blanket that had been hers.

But the town they remembered had changed. Something quick was in the air. Magnificent old houses, so ruined they had become shelter for squatters and rent risks, were bought and renovated. Smart IBM people moved out of their suburbs back into the city and put shutters up and herb gardens in their backyards. A brochure came in the mail announcing the opening of a Food Emporium. Gourmet food, it said—and listed items the rich IBM crowd would want. It was located in a new mall at the edge of town and I drove out to shop there one day—just to see. It was late in June. After the tulips were gone and the Queen Elizabeth roses were open everywhere. I trailed my cart along the aisle tossing in smoked oysters and Robert's sauce and things I knew would sit in my cupboard for years. Only when I found some Klondike ice cream bars did I feel less guilty about spending Jame's fireman's salary so foolishly. My father-in-law ate them with the same gusto little Joseph did.

Waiting in the checkout line I heard a voice say, "Twyla!"

The classical music piped over the aisles had affected me and the woman leaning toward me was dressed to kill. Diamonds on her hands, a smart white summer dress. "I'm Mrs. Benson," I said.

"Ho. Ho. The Big Bozo," she sang.

For a split second I didn't know what she was talking about. She had a bunch of asparagus and two cartons of fancy water.

"Roberta!"

"Right."

"For heaven's sake. Roberta."

"You look great," she said.

"So do you. Where are you? Here? In Newburgh?"

"Yes. Over in Annandale."

I was opening my mouth to say more when the cashier called my attention to her empty counter.

"Meet you outside." Roberta pointed her finger and went into the express line.

I placed the groceries and kept myself from glancing around to check Roberta's progress. I remembered Howard Johnson's and looking for a chance to speak only to be greeted with a stingy "wow." But she was waiting for me and her huge hair was sleek now, smooth around a small, nicely shaped head. Shoes, dress, everything lovely and summery and rich. I was dying to know what happened to her, how she got from Jimi Hendrix to Annandale, a neighborhood full of doctors and IBM executives. Easy, I thought. Everything is so easy for them. They think they own the world.

"How long," I asked her. "How long have you been here?"

"A year. I got married to a man who lives here. And you, you're married too, right? Benson, you said."

"Yeah. James Benson."

"And is he nice?"

"Oh, is he nice?"

"Well, is he?" Roberta's eyes were steady as though she really meant the question and wanted an answer.

"He's wonderful, Roberta. Wonderful."

"So you're happy."

"Very."

"That's good," she said and nodded her head. "I always hoped you'd be happy. Any kids? I know you have kids."

"One. A boy. How about you?"

"Four."

"Four?"

She laughed. "Step kids. He's a widower."

"Oh."

"Got a minute? Let's have coffee."

I thought about the Klondikes melting and the inconvenience of going all the way to my car and putting the bags in the trunk. Served me right for buying all that stuff I didn't need. Roberta was ahead of me.

"Put them in my car. It's right here."

And then I saw the dark blue limousine.

"You married a Chinaman?"

"No." She laughed. "He's the driver."

"Oh, my. If the Big Bozo could see you now."

We both giggled. Really giggled. Suddenly, in just a pulse beat, twenty years disappeared and all of it came rushing back. The big girls (whom we called gar girls—Roberta's misheard word for the evil stone faces described in a civics class) there dancing in the orchard, the ploppy mashed potatoes, the double weenies, the Spam with pineapple. We went into the coffee shop holding on to one another and I tried to think why we were glad to see each other this time and not before. Once, twelve years ago, we passed like strangers. A black girl and white girl meeting in a Howard Johnson's on the road and having nothing to say. One in a blue-and-white triangle waitress hat, the other on her way to see Hendrix. Now we were behaving like sisters separated for much too long. Those four short months were nothing in time. Maybe it was the thing itself. Just being there, together. Two little girls who knew what nobody else in the world knew—how not to ask questions. How to believe what had to be believed. There was politeness in that reluctance and generosity as well. Is your mother sick too? No, she dances all night. Oh—and an understanding nod.

We sat in a booth by the window and fell into recollection like veterans.

"Did you ever learn to read?"

"Watch." She picked up the menu. "Special of the day. Cream of corn soup. Entrées. Two dots and a wiggly line. Quiche. Chef salad, scallops. . . ."

I was laughing and applauding when the waitress came up.

"Remember the Easter baskets?"

"And how we tried to *introduce* them?"

"Your mother with that cross like two telephone poles."

"And yours with those tight slacks."

We laughed so loudly heads turned and made the laughter hard to suppress.

"What happened to the Jimi Hendrix date?"

Roberta made a blow-out sound with her lips.

"When he died I thought about you."

"Oh, you heard about him finally?"

"Finally. Come on. I was a small-town waitress."

"And I was a small-town country dropout. God, were we wild. I still don't know how I got out of there alive."

"But you did."

"I did. I really did. Now I'm Mrs. Kenneth Norton."

"Sounds like a mouthful."

"It is."

"Servants and all?"

Roberta held up two fingers.

"Ow! What does he do?"

"Computers and stuff. What do I know?"

"I don't remember a hell of a lot from those days, but Lord, St. Bonny's is as clear as daylight. Remember Maggie? The day she fell down and those gar girls laughed at her?"

Roberta looked up from her salad and stared at me. "Maggie didn't fall," she said.

"Yes, she did. You remember."

"No, Twyla. They knocked her down. Those girls pushed her down and tore her clothes. In the orchard."

"I don't—that's not what happened."

"Sure it is. In the orchard. Remember how scared we were?"

"Wait a minute. I don't remember any of that."

"And Bozo was fired."

"You're crazy. She was there when I left. You left before me."

"I went back. You weren't there when they fired Bozo."

"What?"

"Twice. Once for a year when I was about ten, another for two months when I was fourteen. That's when I ran away."

"You ran away from St. Bonny's?"

"I had to. What do you want? Me dancing in that orchard?"

"Are you sure about Maggie?"

"Of course I'm sure. You've blocked it, Twyla. It happened. Those girls had behavior problems, you know."

"Didn't they, though. But why can't I remember the Maggie thing?"

"Believe me. It happened. And we were there."

"Who did you room with when you went back?" I asked her as if I would know her. The Maggie thing was troubling me.

"Creeps. They tickled themselves in the night."

My ears were itching and I wanted to go home suddenly. This was all very well but she couldn't just comb her hair, wash her face, and pretend everything was hunky-dory. After the Howard Johnson's snub. And no apology. Nothing.

"Were you on dope or what that time at Howard Johnson's?" I tried to make my voice sound friendlier than I felt.

"Maybe, a little. I never did drugs much. Why?"

"I don't know, you acted sort of like you didn't want to know me then."

"Oh, Twyla, you know how it was in those days: black—white. You know how everything was."

But I didn't know. I thought it was just the opposite. Busloads of blacks and whites came into Howard Johnson's together. They roamed together then: students, musicians, lovers, protesters. You got to see everything at Howard Johnson's, and blacks were very friendly with whites in those days. But sitting there with nothing on my plate but two hard tomato wedges wondering about the melting Klondikes it seemed childish remembering the slight. We went to her car and, with the help of the driver, got my stuff into my station wagon.

"We'll keep in touch this time," she said.

"Sure," I said. "Sure. Give me a call."

"I will," she said, and then, just as I was sliding behind the wheel, she leaned into the window. "By the way. Your mother. Did she ever stop dancing?"

I shook my head. "No. Never."

Roberta nodded.

"And yours? Did she ever get well?"

She smiled a tiny sad smile. "No. She never did. Look, call me, okay?"

"Okay," I said, but I knew I wouldn't. Roberta had messed up my past somehow with that business about Maggie. I wouldn't forget a thing like that. Would I?

Strife came to us that fall. At least that's what the paper called it. Strife. Racial strife. The word made me think of a bird—a big shrieking bird out of 1,000,000,000 B.C. Flapping its wings and cawing. Its eye with no lid always bearing down on you. All day it screeched and at night it slept on the rooftops. It woke you in the morning, and from the Today show to the eleven o'clock news it kept you an awful company. I couldn't figure it out from one day to the next. I knew I was supposed to feel something strong, but I didn't know what, and James wasn't any help. Joseph was on the list of kids to be transferred from the junior high school to another one at some far-out-of-the-way place and I thought it was a good thing until I heard it was a bad thing. I mean I didn't know. All the schools seemed dumps to me, and the fact that one was nicer looking didn't hold much weight. But the papers were full of it and then the kids began to get jumpy. In August, mind you. Schools weren't even open yet. I thought Joseph might be frightened to go over there, but he didn't seem scared so I forgot about it, until I found myself driving along Hudson Street out there by the school they were trying to integrate and saw a line of women marching. And who do you suppose was in line, big as life, holding a sign in front of her bigger than her mother's cross. MOTHERS HAVE RIGHTS TOO! it said.

I drove on and then changed my mind. I circled the block, slowed down, and honked my horn.

Roberta looked over and when she saw me she waved. I didn't wave back, but I didn't move either. She handed her sign to another woman and came over to where I was parked.

"Hi."

"What are you doing?"

"Picketing. What's it look like?"

"What for?"

"What do you mean. 'What for?' They want to take my kids and send them out of the neighborhood. They don't want to go."

"So what if they go to another school? My boy's being bussed too, and I don't mind. Why should you?"

"It's not about us, Twyla. Me and you. It's about our kids."

"What's more *us* than that?"

"Well, it is a free country."

"Not yet, but it will be."

"What the hell does that mean? I'm not doing anything to you."

"You really think that?"

"I know it."

"I wonder what made me think you were different."

"I wonder what made me think you were different."

"Look at them," I said. "Just look. Who do they think they are? Swarming all over the place like they own it. And now they think they can decide where my child goes to school. Look at them, Roberta. They're Bozos."

Roberta turned around and looked at the women. Almost all of them were standing still now, waiting. Some were even edging toward us. Roberta looked at me out of some refrigerator behind her eyes. "No, they're not. They're just mothers."

"And what am I? Swiss cheese?"

"I used to curl your hair."

"I hated your hands in my hair."

The women were moving. Our faces looked mean to them of course and they looked as though they could not wait to throw themselves in front of a police car or, better yet, into my car and drag me away by my ankles. Now they surrounded my car and gently, gently began to rock it. I swayed back and forth like a sideways yo-yo. Automatically I reached for Roberta, like the old days in the orchard when they saw us watching them and we had to get out of there, and if one of us fell the other pulled her up and if one of us was caught the other stayed to kick and scratch, and neither would leave the other behind. My arm shot out of the car window but no receiving hand was there. Roberta was looking at me sway from side to side in the car and her face was still. My purse slid from the car seat down under the dashboard. The four policemen who had been drinking Tab in their car finally got the message and strolled over, forcing their way through the women. Quietly, firmly they spoke, "Okay, ladies. Back in line off the streets."

Some of them went away willingly; others had to be urged away from the car doors and the hood. Roberta didn't move. She was looking steadily at me. I was fumbling to turn on the ignition, which wouldn't catch because the gearshift was still in drive. The seats of the car were a mess because the swaying had thrown my grocery coupons all over and my purse was sprawled on the floor.

"Maybe I am different now, Twyla. But you're not. You're the same little state kid who kicked a poor old black lady when she was down on the ground. You kicked a black lady and you have the nerve to call me a bigot."

The coupons were everywhere and the guts of my purse were bunched under the dashboard. What was she saying? Black? Maggie wasn't black.

"She wasn't black," I said.

"Like hell she wasn't, and you kicked her. We both did. You kicked a black lady who couldn't even scream."

"Liar!"

"You're the liar! Why don't you just go on home and leave us alone, huh?"

She turned away and I skidded away from the curb.

The next morning I went into the garage and cut the side out of the carton our portable TV had come in. It wasn't nearly big enough, but after a while I had a decent sign: red spray-painted letters on a white background— AND SO DO CHILDREN****. I meant just to go down to the school and tack it up somewhere so those cows on the picket line across the street could see it, but when I got there, some ten or so others had assembled—protesting the cows across the street. Police permits and everything. I got in line and we strutted in time on our side while Roberta's group strutted on theirs. That first day we were all dignified, pretending the other side didn't exist. The second day there was name calling and finger gestures. But that was about all. People changed signs from time to time, but Roberta never did and neither did I. Actually my sign didn't make sense without Roberta's. "And so do children what?" one of the women on my side asked me. Have rights, I said, as though it was obvious.

Roberta didn't acknowledge my presence in any way, and I got to thinking maybe she didn't know I was there. I began to pace myself in line, jostling people one minute and lagging behind the next, so Roberta and I could reach the end of our respective lines at the same time and there would be a moment in our turn when we would face each other. Still, I couldn't tell whether she saw me and knew my sign was for her. The next day I went early before we were scheduled to assemble. I waited until she got there before I exposed my new creation. As soon as she hoisted her MOTHERS HAVE RIGHTS TOO I began to wave my new one, which said, HOW WOULD YOU KNOW? I know she saw that one, but I had gotten addicted now. My signs got crazier each day, and the women on my side decided that I was a kook. They couldn't make heads or tails out of my brilliant screaming posters.

I brought a painted sign in queenly red with huge black letters that said, IS YOUR MOTHER WELL? Roberta took her lunch break and didn't come back for the rest of the day or any day after. Two days later I stopped going too and couldn't have been missed because nobody understood my signs anyway.

It was a nasty six weeks. Classes were suspended and Joseph didn't go to anybody's school until October. The children—everybody's children—soon got bored with that extended vacation they thought was going to be so great. They looked at TV until their eyes flattened. I spent a couple of mornings tutoring my son, as the other mothers said we should. Twice I opened a text from last year that he had never turned in. Twice he yawned in my face. Other mothers organized living room sessions so the kids would keep up. None of the kids could concentrate, so they drifted back to The Price Is Right and The Brady Bunch. When the school finally opened there were fights once or twice and some sirens roared through the streets every once in a while. There were a lot of photographers from Albany. And just when ABC was about to send up a news crew, the kids settled down like nothing in the world had happened. Joseph hung my HOW WOULD YOU KNOW? sign in his bedroom. I don't know what became of AND SO DO CHILDREN****. I think my father-in-law cleaned some fish on it. He was always puttering around in our garage. Each of his five children lived in Newburgh, and he acted as though he had five extra homes.

I couldn't help looking for Roberta when Joseph graduated from high school, but I didn't see her. It didn't trouble me much what she had said to me in the car. I mean the kicking part. I know I didn't do that, I couldn't do that. But I was puzzled by her telling me Maggie was black. When I thought about it I actually couldn't be certain. She wasn't pitch-black, I knew, or I would have remembered that. What I remember was the kiddie hat and the semicircle legs. I tried to reassure myself about the race thing for a long time until it dawned on me that the truth was already there, and Roberta knew it. I didn't kick her; I didn't join in with the gar girls and kick that lady, but I sure did want to. We watched and never tried to help her and never called for help. Maggie was my dancing mother. Deaf, I thought, and dumb. Nobody inside. Nobody who would hear you if you cried in the night. Nobody who could tell you anything important that you could use. Rocking, dancing, swaying as she walked. And when the gar girls pushed her down and started roughhousing, I knew she wouldn't scream, couldn't—just like me—and I was glad about that.

We decided not to have a tree, because Christmas would be at my mother-in-law's house, so why have a tree at both places? Joseph was at SUNY New Paltz and we had to economize, we said. But at the last minute, I changed my mind. Nothing could be that bad. So I rushed around town looking for a tree, something small but wide. By the time I found a place, it was snowing and very late. I dawdled like it was the most important purchase in the world and the tree man was fed up with me. Finally I chose one and had it tied onto the trunk of the car. I drove away slowly because the sand trucks were not out yet and the streets could be murder at the beginning of a snowfall. Downtown the streets were wide and rather empty except for a cluster of people coming out of the Newburgh Hotel. The one hotel in town that wasn't built out of cardboard and Plexiglas. A party, probably. The men huddled in the snow were dressed in tails and the women had on furs. Shiny things glittered from underneath their coats. It made me tired to look at them. Tired, tired, tired. On the next corner was a small diner with loops and loops of paper bells in the window. I stopped the car and went in. Just for a cup of coffee and twenty minutes of peace before I went home and tried to finish everything before Christmas Eve.

"Twyla?"

There she was. In a silvery evening gown and dark fur coat. A man and another woman were with her, the man fumbling for change to put in the cigarette machine. The woman was humming and tapping the counter with her fingernails. They all looked a little bit drunk.

"Well. It's you."

"How are you?"

I shrugged. "Pretty good. Frazzled. Christmas and all."

"Regular?" called the woman from the counter.

"Fine," Roberta called back and then, "Wait for me in the car."

She slipped into the booth beside me. "I have to tell you something, Twyla. I made up my mind if I ever saw you again, I'd tell you."

"I'd just as soon not hear anything, Roberta. It doesn't matter now, anyway."

"No," she said. "Not about that."

"Don't be long," said the woman. She carried two regulars to go and the man peeled his cigarette pack as they left.

"It's about St. Bonny's and Maggie."

"Oh, please."

"Listen to me. I really did think she was black. I didn't make that up. I really thought so. But now I can't be sure. I just remember her as old, so old. And because she couldn't talk—well, you know, I thought she was crazy. She'd been brought up in an institution like my mother was and like I thought I would be too. And you were right. We didn't kick her. It was the gar girls. Only them. But, well, I wanted to. I really wanted them to hurt her. I said we did it, too. You and me, but that's not true. And I don't want you to carry that around. It was just that I wanted to do it so bad that day—wanting to is doing it."

Her eyes were watery from the drinks she'd had, I guess. I know it's that way with me. One glass of wine and I start bawling over the littlest thing.

"We were kids, Roberta."

"Yeah. Yeah. I know, just kids."

"Eight."

"Eight."

"And lonely."

"Scared, too."

She wiped her cheeks with the heel of her hand and smiled. "Well, that's all I wanted to say."

I nodded and couldn't think of any way to fill the silence that went from the diner past the paper bells on out into the snow. It was heavy now. I thought I'd better wait for the sand trucks before starting home.

"Thanks, Roberta."

"Sure."

"Did I tell you? My mother, she never did stop dancing."

"Yes. You told me. And mine, she never got well." Roberta lifted her hands from the tabletop and covered her face with her palms. When she took them away she really was crying. "Oh, shit, Twyla. Shit, shit, shit. What the hell happened to Maggie?"

1983

NICHOLASA MOHR

B. 1938

Nicholasa Mohr is one of the most widely published Puerto Rican writers in the United States. Born to parents who came to New York City with the massive migration during World War II, Mohr grew up in the Bronx, studied art at the Students' Art League, and became a well-known graphic artist. Her art agent asked her to write about growing up Puerto Rican and female in the Bronx, perhaps expecting sensationalist tales of crime, drugs, and gang activity. The stories Mohr wrote were quite different, and she had difficulty getting editors interested in publishing her work. *Nilda*, her first novel, appeared in 1974.

Somewhat autobiographical, *Nilda* relates life in the Bronx through the eyes of a ten-year-old girl who is a second-generation Puerto Rican American. Mohr's protagonist uses her imagination and her fantasies to sustain herself through the hardships of her cultural and economic circumstances. As in this book, Mohr chooses to use a child's perspective for much of her writing. *Felita* and *Going Home* are, in fact, aimed at an adolescent audience. They relate Felita's experiences growing up in El Barrio and on a return trip to Puerto Rico, where she discovers differences between the values of her family and community in New York and the values of her relatives and society at large in Puerto Rico.

Rituals of Survival: A Woman's Portfolio is one of Mohr's most interesting publications. It consists of six vignettes about adult Puerto Rican women, representing various lifestyles, ages, and circumstances. Their common bond is their need to survive as individuals and as women free from restrictive social and cultural expectations. In "A Thanksgiving Celebration," reproduced here, Amy, a young widowed mother of four, uses her ingenuity and storytelling traditions inherited from her grandmother to give meaning to Thanksgiving Day. All of Mohr's characters have to struggle with the gender roles imposed on them by the Hispanic culture, with the *machista* attitudes of the men in their lives, and with the expectations assigned to them by their families.

Although Nicholasa Mohr has been called a "meat-and-potatoes" writer because of her simple style and the emphasis she places on the humanity of her characters, everyday people with everyday conflicts to surmount, her storytelling is clear, direct, and powerful. That it found publication in the adolescent reader market does not detract from its importance as a voice of a people sometimes marginalized by economic and social stratifications. Mohr's work is important because it has, often for the first time in English, presented and preserved family and household rituals from the Puerto Rican culture. It has also recorded the conflicts and ambivalences of a young Puerto Rican girl growing up in El Barrio of New York. As Mohr once said, "In American literature, I, as a Puerto Rican child, did not exist ... and I as a Puerto Rican woman do not exist now." Her prose has established a precedent for young Puerto Rican women writers to continue to explore, question, and critique their lives in a bicultural world. Most important, Mohr has rescued readers' images of Barrio life from stereotypes of *puertorriqueños* as gang members or criminals. Her work has received several prizes, among them the 1974 Jane Addams Children's Book Award and *The New York Times* Outstanding Book of the Year. She was also a National Book Award finalist.

Frances R. Aparicio
University of Illinois at Chicago

PRIMARY WORKS

Nilda, 1974; *El Bronx Remembered*, 1976; *In Nueva York*, 1977; *Felita*, 1979; *Rituals of Survival: A Woman's Portfolio*, 1985; *Going Home*, 1986; *All for the Better: A Story of El Barrio*, 1993; *The Song of El Coqui and Other Tales of Puerto Rico*, 1995; *The Magic Shell*, 1995; *A Matter of Pride and Other Stories*, 1997.

from **Rituals of Survival**

A Thanksgiving Celebration (Amy)

Amy sat on her bed thinking. Gary napped soundly in his crib, which was placed right next to her bed. The sucking sound he made as he chewed on his thumb interrupted her thoughts from time to time. Amy glanced at Gary and smiled. He was her constant companion now; he shared her bedroom and was with her during those frightening moments when, late into the night and early morning, she wondered if she could face another day just like the one she had safely survived. Amy looked at the small alarm clock on the bedside table. In another hour or so it would be time to wake Gary and give him his milk, then she had just enough time to shop and pick up the others, after school.

She heard the plopping sound of water dropping into a full pail. Amy hurried into the bathroom, emptied the pail into the toilet, then replaced it so that the floor remained dry. Last week she had forgotten, and the water had overflowed out of the pail and onto the floor, leaking down into Mrs. Wynn's bathroom. Now, Mrs. Wynn was threatening to take her to small claims court, if the landlord refused to fix the damage done to her bathroom ceiling and wallpaper. All right, Amy shrugged, she would try calling the landlord once more. She was tired of the countless phone calls to plead with them to come and fix the leak in the roof.

"Yes, Mrs. Guzman, we got your message and we'll send somebody over. Yes, just as soon as we can ... we got other tenants with bigger problems, you know. We are doing our best, we'll get somebody over; you gotta be patient ..."

Time and again they had promised, but no one had ever showed up. And it was now more than four months that she had been forced to live like this. Damn, Amy walked into her kitchen, they never refuse the rent for that, there's somebody ready any time! Right now, this was the best she could do. The building was still under rent control and she had enough room. Where else could she go? No one in a better neighborhood would rent to her, not the way things were.

She stood by the window, leaning her side against the molding, and looked out. It was a crisp sunny autumn day, mild for the end of November. She remembered it was the eve of Thanksgiving and felt a tightness in her chest. Amy took a deep breath, deciding not to worry about that right now.

Rows and rows of endless streets scattered with abandoned buildings and small houses stretched out for miles. Some of the blocks were almost entirely leveled, except for clumps of partial structures charred and blackened by fire. From a distance they looked like organic masses pushing their way out of the earth. Garbage, debris, shattered glass, bricks and broken, discarded furniture covered the ground. Rusting carcasses of cars that had been stripped down to the shell shone and glistened a bright orange under the afternoon sun.

There were no people to be seen nor traffic, save for a group of children jumping on an old filthy mattress that had been ripped open. They were busy pulling the stuffing out of the mattress and tossing it about playfully. Nearby, several stray dogs searched the garbage for food. One of the boys picked up a brick, then threw it at the dogs, barely missing them. Reluctantly, the dogs moved on.

Amy sighed and swallowed, it was all getting closer and closer. It seemed as if only last month, when she had looked out of this very window, all of that was much further away; in fact, she recalled feeling somewhat removed and safe. Now the decay was creeping up to this area. The fire engine sirens screeching and screaming in the night reminded her that the devastation was constant, never stopping even for a night's rest. Amy was fearful of living on the top floor. Going down four flights to safety with the kids in case of a fire was another source of worry for her. She remembered how she had argued with Charlie when they had first moved in.

"All them steps to climb with Michele and Carlito, plus carrying the carriage for Carlito, is too much."

"Come on baby," Charlie had insisted "it's only temporary. The rent's cheaper and we can save something towards buying our own place. Come on ..."

That was seven years ago. There were two more children now, Lisabeth and Gary; and she was still here, without Charlie.

"Soon it'll come right to this street and to my doorstep. God Almighty!" Amy whispered. It was like a plague: a disease for which there seemed to be no cure, no prevention. Gangs of youngsters occupied empty store fronts and basements; derelicts, drunk or wasted on drugs, positioned themselves on street corners and in empty doorways. Every day she saw more abandoned and burned-out sections.

As Amy continued to look out, a feeling that she had been in this same situation before, a long time ago, startled her. The feeling of deja vu so real to her, reminded Amy quite vividly of the dream she had had last night. In that dream, she had been standing in the center of a circle of little girls. She herself was very young and they were all singing a rhyme. In a soft whisper, Amy sang the rhyme: "London Bridge is falling down, falling down, falling down, London Bridge is falling down, my fair lady ..." She stopped and saw herself once again in her dream, picking up her arms and chanting, "wave your arms and fly away, fly away, fly away ..."

She stood in the middle of the circle waving her arms, first gently, then more forcefully, until she was flapping them. The other girls stared silently at her. Slowly, Amy had felt herself elevated above the circle, higher and higher until she could barely make out the human figures below. Waving her arms like the wings of a bird, she began to fly. A pleasant breeze pushed her gently, and she glided along, passing through soft white clouds into an intense silence. Then she saw it. Beneath her, huge areas were filled with crumbling buildings and large caverns; miles of destruction spread out in every direction. Amy had felt herself suspended in this silence for a moment and then she began to fall. She flapped her arms and legs furiously, trying to clutch at the air, hoping for a breeze, something to get her going again, but there was nothing. Quickly she fell, faster and faster, as the ground below her swirled and turned, coming closer and closer, revealing destroyed, burned buildings, rubble and a huge dark cavern. In a state of hysteria, Amy had fought against the loss of control and helplessness, as her body descended into the large black hole and had woken up with a start just before she hit bottom.

Amy stepped away from the window for a moment, almost out of breath as she recollected the fear she had felt in her dream. She walked over to the sink and poured herself a glass of water.

"That's it, Europe and the war," she said aloud. "In the movies, just like my dream."

Amy clearly remembered how she had sat as a very little girl in a local movie theatre with her mother and watched horrified at the scenes on the screen. Newsreels showed entire cities almost totally devastated. Exactly as it had been in her dream, she recalled seeing all the destruction caused by warfare. Names like "Munich, Nuremburg, Berlin" and "the German people" identified the areas. Most of the streets were empty, except for the occasional small groups of people who rummaged about, searching among the ruins and huge piles of debris, sharing the spoils with packs of rats who scavenged at a safe distance. Some people pulled wagons and baby carriages loaded with bundles and household goods. Others carried what they owned on their backs.

Amy remembered turning to her mother, asking, "What was going on? Mami, who did this? Why did they do it? Who are those people living there?"

"The enemy, that's who," her mother had whispered emphatically. "Bad people who started the war against our country and did terrible things to other people and to us. That's where your papa was for so long, fighting in the army. Don't you remember, Amy?"

"What kinds of things, Mami? Who were the other people they did bad things to?"

"Don't worry about them things. These people got what they deserved. Besides, they are getting help from us, now that we won the war. There's a plan to help them, even though they don't deserve no help from us."

Amy had persisted, "Are there any little kids there? Do they go to school? Do they live in them holes?"

"Shh . . . let me hear the rest of the news . . ." her mother had responded, annoyed. Amy had sat during the remainder of the double feature, wondering where those people lived and all about the kids there. And she continued to wonder and worry for several days, until one day she forgot all about it.

Amy sipped from the glass she held, then emptied most of the water back into the sink. She sat and looked around at her small kitchen. The ceiling was peeling and flakes of paint had fallen on the kitchen table. The entire apartment was in urgent need of a thorough plastering and paint job. She blinked and shook her head, and now? Who are we now? What have I done? Who is the enemy? Is there a war? Are we at war? Amy suppressed a loud chuckle.

"Nobody answered my questions then, and nobody's gonna answer them now," she spoke out loud.

Amy still wondered and groped for answers about Charlie. No one could tell her what had really happened ... how he had felt and what he was thinking before he died. Almost two years had gone by, but she was still filled with an overwhelming sense of loneliness. That day was just like so many other days; they were together, planning about the kids, living from one crisis to the next, fighting, barely finding the time to make love without being exhausted; then late that night, it was all over. Charlie's late again, Amy had thought, and didn't even call me. She was angry when she heard the doorbell. He forgot the key again. Dammit, Charlie! You would forget your head if it weren't attached to you!

They had stood there before her; both had shown her their badges, but only one had spoken.

"Come in ... sit down, won't you."

"You better sit down, miss." The stranger told her very calmly and soberly that Charlie was dead.

"On the Bruckner Boulevard Expressway ... head on collision ... dead on arrival ... didn't suffer too long ... nobody was with him, but we found his wallet."

Amy had protested and argued—No way! They were lying to her. But after a while she knew they brought the truth to her, and Charlie wasn't coming back.

Tomorrow would be the second Thanksgiving without him and one she could not celebrate. Celebrate with what? Amy stood and walked over and opened the refrigerator door. She had enough bread, a large pitcher of powdered milk which she had flavored with Hershey's cocoa and powdered sugar. There was plenty of peanut butter and some graham crackers she had kept fresh by sealing them in a plastic bag. For tonight she had enough chopped meat and macaroni. But tomorrow? What could she buy for tomorrow?

Amy shut the refrigerator door and reached over to the money tin set way back on one of the shelves. Carefully she took out the money and counted every cent. There was no way she could buy a turkey, even a small one. She still had to manage until the first; she needed every penny just to make it to the next check. Things were bad, worse than they had ever been. In the past, when things were rough, she had turned to Charlie and sharing had made it all easier. Now there was no one. She resealed the money tin and put it away.

Amy had thought of calling the lawyers once more. What good would that do? What can they do for me? Right now ... today!

"These cases take time before we get to trial. We don't want to take the first settlement they offer. That wouldn't do you or the children any good. You have a good case, the other driver was at fault. He didn't have his license or the registration, and we have proof he was drinking. His father is a prominent judge who doesn't want that kind of publicity. I know ... yes, things are rough, but just hold on a little longer. We don't want to accept a poor settlement and risk your future and the future of your children, do we?" Mr. Silverman of Silverman, Knapp and Ullman was handling the case personally. "By early Spring we should be making a date for trial ... just hang in there a bit longer ..." And so it went every time she called: the promise that in just a few more months she could hope for relief, some money, enough to live like people.

Survivor benefits had not been sufficient, and since they had not kept up premium payments on Charlie's G.I. insurance policy, she had no other income. Amy was given a little more assistance from the Aid to Dependent Children agency. Somehow she had managed so far.

The two food stores that extended her credit were still waiting for Amy to settle overdue accounts. In an emergency she could count on a few friends; they would lend her something, but not for this, not for Thanksgiving dinner.

She didn't want to go to Papo and Mary's again. She knew her brother meant well, and that she always had an open invitation. They're good people, but we are five more mouths to feed, plus they've been taking care of Papa all these years, ever since Mami died. Enough is enough. Amy shut her eyes. I want my own dinner this year, just for my family, for me and the kids.

If I had the money, I'd make a dinner tomorrow and invite Papa and Lou Ann from downstairs and her kids. She's been such a good friend to us. I'd get a gallon of cider and a bottle of wine ... a large cake at the bakery by Alexander's, some dried fruits and nuts ... even a holiday centerpiece for the table. Yes, it would be my dinner for us and my friends. I might even invite Jimmy. She hadn't seen Jimmy for a long time. Must be over six months ... almost a year? He worked with Charlie at the plant. After Charlie's death, Jimmy had come by often, but Amy was not ready to see another man, not just then, so she discouraged him. From time to time, she thought of Jimmy and hoped he would visit her again.

Amy opened her eyes and a sinking feeling flowed through her, as she looked down at the chips of paint spread out on the kitchen table. Slowly, Amy brushed them with her hand, making a neat pile.

These past few months, she had seriously thought of going out to work. Before she had Michele, she had worked as a clerk-typist for a large insurance company, but that was almost ten years ago. She would have to brush up on her typing and math. Besides, she didn't know if she could earn enough to pay for a sitter. She couldn't leave the kids alone; Gary wasn't even three and Michele had just turned nine. Amy had applied for part-time work as a teacher's aide, but when she learned that her check from Aid to Dependent Children could be discontinued, she withdrew her application. Better to go on like this until the case comes to trial.

Amy choked back the tears. I can't let myself get like this. I just can't! Lately, she had begun to find comfort at the thought of never waking up again. What about my kids, then? I must do something. I have to. Tomorrow is going to be for us, just us, our day.

Her thoughts went back to her own childhood and the holiday dinners with her family. They had been poor, but there was always food. We used to have such good times. Amy remembered the many stories her grandmother used to tell them. She spoke about her own childhood on a farm in a rural area of Puerto Rico. Her grandmother's stories were about the animals, whom she claimed to know personally and very well. Amy laughed, recalling that most of the stories her grandmother related were too impossible to be true, such as a talking goat who saved the town from a flood, and the handsome mouse and beautiful lady beetle who fell in love, got married and had the biggest and fanciest wedding her grandmother had ever attended. Her grandmother was very old and had died before Amy was ten. Amy had loved her best, more than her own parents, and she still remembered the old woman quite clearly.

"Abuelita,[1] did them things really happen? How come them animals talked? Animals don't talk. Everybody knows that."

"Oh, but they do talk! And yes, everything I tell you is absolutely the truth. I believe it and you must believe it too." The old woman had been completely convincing. And for many years Amy had secretly believed that when her grandmother was a little girl, somewhere in a special place, animals talked, got married and were heroes.

"Abuelita," Amy whispered, "I wish you were here and could help me now." And then she thought of it. Something special for tomorrow. Quickly, Amy took out the money tin, counting out just the right amount of money she needed. She hesitated for a moment. What if it won't work and I can't convince them? Amy took a deep breath. Never mind, I have to try, I must. She counted out a few more dollars. I'll work it all out somehow. Then she warmed up Gary's milk and got ready to leave.

Amy heard the voices of her children with delight. Shouts and squeals of laughter bounced into the kitchen as they played in the living room. Today they were all happy, anticipating their mother's promise of a celebration. Recently, her frequent moods of depression and short temper had frightened them. Privately, the children had blamed themselves for their mother's unhappiness, fighting with each other in helpless confusion. The children welcomed their mother's energy and good mood with relief.

Lately Amy had begun to realize that Michele and Carlito were constantly fighting. Carlito was always angry and would pick on Lisabeth. Poor Lisabeth, she's always so sad. I never have time for her and she's not really much older than Gary. This way of life has been affecting us all ... but not today. Amy worked quickly. The apartment was filled with an air of festivity. She had set the kitchen table with a paper tablecloth, napkins and paper cups to match. These were decorated with turkeys, pilgrims, Indian corn and all the symbols of the Thanksgiving holiday. Amy had also bought a roll

[1]Abuelita, grandmother in Spanish. The diminutive form expresses warmth and affection.

of orange paper streamers and decorated the kitchen chairs. Each setting had a name-card printed with bright magic markers. She had even managed to purchase a small holiday cake for dessert.

As she worked, Amy fought moments of anxiety and fear that threatened to weaken her sense of self-confidence. What if they laugh at me? Dear God in heaven, will my children think I'm a fool? But she had already spent the money, cooked and arranged everything; she had to go ahead. If I make it through this day, Amy nodded, I'll be all right.

She set the food platter in the center of the table and stepped back. A mound of bright yellow rice, flavored with a few spices and bits of fatback, was surrounded by a dozen hardboiled eggs that had been colored a bright orange. Smiling, Amy felt it was all truly beautiful; she was ready for the party.

"All right," Amy walked into the living room. "We're ready!" The children quickly followed her into the kitchen.

"Oooh, Mommy," Lisabeth shouted, "everything looks so pretty."

"Each place has got a card with your own name, so find the right seat." Amy took Gary and sat him down on his special chair next to her.

"Mommy," Michele spoke, "is this the whole surprise?"

"Yes," Amy answered, "just a minute, we also have some cider." Amy brought a small bottle of cider to the table.

"Easter eggs for Thanksgiving?" Carlito asked.

"Is that what you think they are, Carlito?" Amy asked. "Because they are not Easter eggs."

The children silently turned to one another, exchanging bewildered looks.

"What are they?" Lisabeth asked.

"Well," Amy said, "these are ... turkey eggs, that's what. What's better than a turkey on Thanksgiving day? Her eggs, right?" Amy continued as all of them watched her. "You see, it's not easy to get these eggs. They're what you call a delicacy. But I found a special store that sells them, and they agreed to sell me a whole dozen for today."

"What store is that, Mommy?" Michele asked. "Is it around here?"

"No. They don't have stores like that here. It's special, way downtown."

"Did the turkey lay them eggs like that? That color?" Carlito asked.

"I want an egg," Gary said pointing to the platter.

"No, no ... I just colored them that way for today, so everything goes together nicely, you know ..." Amy began to serve the food. "All right, you can start eating."

"Well then, what's so special about these eggs? What's the difference between a turkey egg and an egg from a chicken?" Carlito asked.

"Ah, the taste, Carlito, just wait until you have some." Amy quickly finished serving everyone. "You see, these eggs are hard to find because they taste so fantastic." She chewed a mouthful of egg. "Ummm ... fantastic, isn't it?" She nodded at them.

"Wonderful, Mommy," said Lisabeth. "It tastes real different."

"Oh yeah," Carlito said, "you can taste it right away. Really good."

Everyone was busy eating and commenting on how special the eggs tasted. As Amy watched her children, a sense of joy filled her, and she knew it had been a very long time since they had been together like this, close and loving.

"Mommy, did you ever eat these kinds of eggs before?" asked Michele.

"Yes, when I was little" she answered. "My grandmother got them for me. You know, I talked about my abuelita before. When I first ate them, I couldn't get over how good they tasted, just like you." Amy spoke with assurance, as they listened to every word she said. "Abuelita lived on a farm when she was very little. That's how come she knew all about turkey eggs. She used to tell me the most wonderful stories about her life there."

"Tell us!"

"Yeah, please Mommy, please tell us."

"All right, I'll tell you one about a hero who saved her whole village from a big flood. He was ... a billy goat."

"Mommy," Michele interrupted, "a billy goat?"

"That's right, and you have to believe what I'm going to tell you. All of you have to believe me. Because everything I'm going to say is absolutely the truth. Promise? All right, then, in the olden days, when my grandmother was very little, far away in a small town in Puerto Rico ..."

Amy continued, remembering stories that she had long since forgotten. The children listened, intrigued by what their mother had to say. She felt a calmness within. Yes, Amy told herself, today's for us, for me and the kids.

1985

HELENA MARÍA VIRAMONTES
B. 1954

Chronicler of the West Coast urban barrios, Helena María Viramontes was born, raised, and educated in East Los Angeles, California. Daughter of working-class parents, she and her nine brothers and sisters grew up surrounded by the family friends and relatives who found temporary sanctuary in the Viramontes household as they made the crossing from Mexico to the United States. Her writings reveal the political and aesthetic significance of the contemporary Chicana feminist's entrance into the publishing world. Viramontes's aesthetics are a practice of political intervention carried out in literary form. Her tales of the urban barrios, of the border cities, of the Third World metropolises that cities such as Los Angeles have become, record the previously silenced experiences of life on the border for Chicanas and Latinas. Viramontes remains an exemplar of the organic intellectual: she organizes the community to protest the closing of local public libraries in areas populated with Chicanos and Latinos; she gives readings and literary presentations to a population that is represented by the media as gang-infested and whose young men are more represented in the prison system than in the education system.

Viramontes's first short story collection, *The Moths and Other Stories* (1985), is a feminist statement on the status of the family in the Chicana/o community. In many of the stories, she transforms the concept of *familia* as the community itself changes with the infusion of refugees from war-torn countries in Central America: what were once predominantly Mexican American areas are now international Latina/o communities within the borders of the United States. The new immigrants bring with them specific histories, producing new stories that further emphasize the resemblances between Chicanas/os and *los otros Americanos*—people Cherríe Moraga calls "refugees of a world on fire."

Viramontes's short stories also give historical context and voice to the women whom many Chicano writers have silenced through their appropriation of female historicity. As she challenges an uncritical view of the traditional Chicano family, she presents an altered version of *familia* that makes more sense in a world where governments continue to exert power over women's bodies by hiding behind the rhetoric of the sacred family as they simultaneously exploit and destroy members of families who do not conform to a specific political agenda or whose class position or race automatically disqualifies them from inclusion.

In "The Cariboo Cafe," Viramontes makes explicit the connection between Chicanas and refugees from Central America. Written in early 1984 after Viramontes learned of the atrocities that U.S. policies in countries such as El Salvador had enabled, this story embodies a Chicana feminist's critique of the political and economic policies of the United States government and its collaborators south of its border. Viramontes presents the oppression and exploitation of the reserve army of laborers that such policies create and then designate as "other," the "illegal" immigrants. Combining feminism with race and class consciousness, Viramontes commits herself, in this Chicana political discourse, to a transnational solidarity with the working-class political refugee seeking asylum from right-wing death squads in countries such as El Salvador.

The narrative structure of "The Cariboo Cafe" connects Chicana aesthetics to the literary traditions of Latin American political writers such as Gabriel García Márquez and Isabel Allende. The fractured narrative employed in this story reflects the disorientation that the immigrant workers feel when they are subjected to life in a country that controls their labor but does not value their existence as human beings. This narrative structure shoots the reader, an alien to this refugee culture, into a world where she or he is as disoriented as the story's characters: two lost Mexican children; a refugee woman, possibly from El Salvador, whose mental state reflects the trauma of losing her five-year-old son to the labyrinth of the disappeared in Latin American countries ruled by armies and dictators the United States trains and supports; and a working-class man, an ironic representative of dominant Anglo-American culture, who runs the "double zero" cafe. The reader, particularly one unfamiliar with life in the border regions of that other America, must work to decipher the signs in much the same way as the characters do. Through the artistry of her narrative, Helena

María Viramontes shows how a Chicana oppositional art form also becomes an arena that reflects politics.

Sonia Saldívar-Hull
University of California, Los Angeles

PRIMARY WORKS

The Moths and Other Stories, 1985; *Paris Rats in E. L. A.*, 1993; *Under the Feet of Jesus*, 1995; *Their Dogs Came with Them*, 2007.

The Cariboo Cafe

I

They arrived in the secrecy of night, as displaced people often do, stopping over for a week, a month, eventually staying a lifetime. The plan was simple. Mother would work too until they saved enough to move into a finer future where the toilet was one's own and the children needn't be frightened. In the meantime, they played in the back alleys, among the broken glass, wise to the ways of the streets. Rule one: never talk to strangers, not even the neighbor who paced up and down the hallways talking to himself. Rule two: the police, or "polie" as Sonya's popi pronounced the word, was La Migra in disguise and thus should always be avoided. Rule three: keep your key with you at all times—the four walls of the apartment were the only protection against the streets until Popi returned home.

Sonya considered her key a guardian saint and she wore it around her neck as such until this afternoon. Gone was the string with the big knot. Gone was the key. She hadn't noticed its disappearance until she picked up Macky from Mrs. Avila's house and walked home. She remembered playing with it as Amá walked her to school. But lunch break came, and Lalo wrestled her down so that he could see her underwear, and it probably fell somewhere between the iron rings and sandbox. Sitting on the front steps of the apartment building, she considered how to explain the missing key without having to reveal what Lalo had seen, for she wasn't quite sure which offense carried the worse penalty.

She watched people piling in and spilling out of the buses, watched an old man asleep on the bus bench across the street. He resembled a crumbled ball of paper, huddled up in the security of a tattered coat. She became aware of their mutual loneliness and she rested her head against her knees blackened by the soot of the playground asphalt.

The old man eventually awoke, yawned like a lion's roar, unfolded his limbs and staggered to the alley where he urinated between two trash bins. (She wanted to peek, but it was Macky who turned to look.) He zipped up, drank from a paper bag and she watched him until he disappeared around the corner. As time passed, buses came less frequently, and every other person seemed to resemble Popi. Macky became bored. He picked through the trash barrel; later, and to Sonya's fright, he ran into the street after a pigeon. She understood his restlessness for waiting was as relentless as long lines to the bathroom. When a small boy walked by, licking away at a scoop of vanilla ice cream, Macky ran after him. In his haste to outrun Sonya's grasp, he fell and tore the knee of his denim jeans. He began to cry, wiping snot against his sweater sleeve.

"See?" She asked, dragging him back to the porch steps by his wrist. "See? God punished you!" It was a thing she always said because it seemed to work. Terrified by the scrawny tortured man on the cross, Macky wanted to avoid his wrath as much as possible. She sat him on the steps in one gruff jerk. Seeing his torn jeans, and her own scraped knees, she wanted to join in his sorrow, and cry. Instead she snuggled so close to him, she could hear his stomach growling.

"Coke," he asked. Mrs. Avila gave him an afternoon snack which usually held him over until dinner. But sometimes Macky got lost in the midst of her own six children and . . .

Mrs. Avila! It took Sonya a few moments to realize the depth of her idea. They could wait there, at Mrs. Avila's. And she'd probably have a stack of flour tortillas, fresh off the comal, ready to eat with butter and salt. She grabbed his hand. "Mrs. Avila has Coke."

"Coke!" He jumped up to follow his sister. "Coke," he cooed.

At the major intersection, Sonya quietly calculated their next move while the scores of adults hurried to their own destinations. She scratched one knee as she tried retracing her journey home in the labyrinth of her memory. Things never looked the same when backwards and she searched for familiar scenes. She looked for the newspaperman who sat in a little house with a little T.V. on and selling magazines with naked girls holding beach balls. But he was gone. What remained was a little closet-like shed with chains and locks, and she wondered what happened to him, for she thought he lived there with the naked ladies.

They finally crossed the street at a cautious pace, the colors of the street lights brighter as darkness descended, a stereo store blaring music from two huge, blasting speakers. She thought it was the disco store she passed, but she didn't remember if the sign was green or red. And she didn't remember it flashing like it was now. Studying the neon light, she bumped into a tall, lanky dark man. Maybe it was Raoul's Popi. Raoul was a dark boy in her class that she felt sorry for because everyone called him sponge head. Maybe she could ask Raoul's Popi where Mrs. Avila lived, but before she could think it all out, red sirens flashed in their faces and she shielded her eyes to see the polie.

The polie is men in black who get kids and send them to Tijuana, says Popi. Whenever you see them, run, because they hate you, says Popi. She grabs Macky by his sleeve and they crawl under a table of bargain cassettes. Macky's nose is running, and when he sniffles, she puts her finger to her lips. She peeks from behind the poster of Vincente Fernandez to see Raoul's father putting keys and stuff from his pockets onto the hood of the polie car. And it's true, they're putting him in the car and taking him to Tijuana. Popi, she murmured to herself. Mamá.

"Coke." Macky whispered, as if she had failed to remember.

"Ssssh. Mi'jo, when I say run, you run, okay?" She waited for the tires to turn out, and as the black and white drove off, she whispered "Now," and they scurried out from under the table and ran across the street, oblivious to the horns.

They entered a maze of allies and dead ends, the long, abandoned warehouses shadowing any light. Macky stumbled and she continued to drag him until his crying, his untied sneakers, and his raspy breathing finally forced her to stop. She scanned the boarded up boxcars, the rows of rusted rails to make sure the polie wasn't following them. Tired, her heart bursting, she leaned him against a tall, chainlink fence. Except for the rambling of some railcars, silence prevailed, and she could hear Macky sniffling in the darkness. Her mouth was parched and she swallowed to rid herself of the metallic taste of fear. The shadows stalked them, hovering like nightmares. Across the tracks, in the distance, was a room with a yellow glow, like a beacon light at the end of a dark sea. She pinched Macky's nose with the corner of her dress, took hold of his sleeve. At least the shadows will be gone, she concluded, at the zero zero place.

II

Don't look at me. I didn't give it the name. It was passed on. Didn't even know what it meant until I looked it up in some library dictionary. But I kinda liked the name. It's, well, romantic, almost like the name of a song, you know, so I kept it. That was before JoJo turned fourteen even. But now if you take a look at the sign, the paint's peeled off 'cept for the two O's. The double zero cafe. Story of my life. But who cares, right? As long as everyone 'round the factories know I run an honest business.

The place is clean. That's more than I can say for some people who walk through that door. And I offer the best prices on double burger deluxes this side of Main Street. Okay, so its not pure beef. Big deal, most meat markets do the same. But I make no bones 'bout it. I tell them up front, 'yeah, it ain't dogmeat, but it ain't sirloin either.' Cause that's the sort of guy I am. Honest.

That's the trouble. It never pays to be honest. I tried scrubbing the stains off the floor, so that my customers won't be reminded of what happened. But they keep walking as if my cafe ain't fit for lepers. And that's the thanks I get for being a fair guy.

Not once did I hang up all those stupid signs. You know, like 'We reserve the right to refuse service to anyone,' or 'No shirt, no shoes, no service.' To tell you the truth—which is what I always do though it don't pay—I wouldn't have nobody walking through that door. The streets are full of scum, but scum gotta eat too is the way I see it. Now, listen. I ain't talkin 'bout out-of-luckers, weirdos, whores, you know. I'm talking 'bout five-to-lifers out of some tech. I'm talking Paulie.

I swear Paulie is thirty-five, or six. JoJo's age if he were still alive, but he don't look a day over ninety. Maybe why I let him hang out 'cause he's JoJo's age. Shit, he's okay as long as he don't bring his wigged out friends whose voices sound like a record at low speed. Paulie's got too many stories and they all get jammed up in his mouth so I can't make out what he's saying. He scares the other customers too, acting like he is shadow boxing, or like a monkey hopping on a frying pan. You know, nervous, jumpy, his jaw all falling and his eyes bulgy and dirt yellow. I give him the last booth, coffee and yesterday's donut holes to keep him quiet. After a few minutes, out he goes, before lunch. I'm too old, you know, too busy making ends meet to be nursing the kid. And so is Delia.

That Delia's got these unique titties. One is bigger than another. Like an orange and grapefruit. I kid you not. They're like that on account of when she was real young she had some babies, and they all sucked only one favorite tittie. So one is bigger than the other, and when she used to walk in with Paulie, huggy huggy and wearing those tight leotard blouses that show the nipple dots, you could see the difference. You could tell right off that Paulie was proud of them, the way he'd hang his arm over her shoulder and squeeze the grapefruit. They kill me, her knockers. She'd come in real queen-like, smacking gum and chewing the fat with the illegals who work in that garment warehouse. They come in real queen-like too, sitting in the best booth near the window, and order cokes. That's all. Cokes. Hey, but I'm a nice guy, so what if they mess up my table, bring their own lunches and only order small cokes, leaving a dime as tip? So sometimes the place ain't crawling with people, you comprende buddy? A dime's a dime as long as its in my pocket.

Like I gotta pay my bills too, I gotta eat. So like I serve anybody whose got the greens, including that crazy lady and the two kids that started all the trouble. If only I had closed early. But I had to wash the dinner dishes on account of I can't afford a dishwasher. I was scraping off some birdshit glue stuck to this plate, see, when I hear the bells jingle against the door. I hate those fucking bells. That was Nell's idea. Nell's my wife; my ex-wife. So people won't sneak up on you, says my ex. Anyway, I'm standing behind the counter staring at this short woman. Already I know that she's bad news because she looks street to me. Round face, burnt toast color, black hair that hangs like straight ropes. Weirdo, I've had enough to last me a lifetime. She's wearing a shawl and a dirty slip is hanging out. Shit if I have to dish out a free meal. Funny thing, but I didn't see the two kids 'til I got to the booth. All of a sudden I see these big eyes looking over the table's edge at me. It shook me up, the way they kinda appeared. Aw, maybe they were there all the time.

The boy's a sweetheart. Short Order don't look nothing like his mom. He's got dried snot all over his dirty cheeks and his hair ain't seen a comb for years. She can't take care of herself, much less him or the doggie of a sister. But he's a tough one, and I pinch his nose 'cause he's a real sweetheart like JoJo. You know, my boy.

It's his sister I don't like. She's got these poking eyes that follow you 'round 'cause she don't trust no one. Like when I reach for Short Order, she flinches like I'm 'bout to tear his nose off, gives me a nasty, squinty look. She's maybe five, maybe six, I don't know, and she acts like she owns him. Even when I bring the burgers, she doesn't let go of his hand. Finally, the fellow bites it and I wink at him. A real sweetheart.

In the next booth, I'm twisting the black crud off the top of the ketchup bottle when I hear the lady saying something in Spanish. Right off I know she's illegal, which explains why she looks like a weirdo. Anyway, she says something nice to them 'cause it's in the same tone that Nell used when I'd rest my head on her lap. I'm surprised the illegal's got a fiver to pay, but she and her tail leave no tip. I see Short Order's small bites on the bun.

You know, a cafe's the kinda business that moves. You get some regulars but most of them are on the move, so I don't pay much attention to them. But this lady's face sticks like egg yolk on a plate. It ain't 'til I open a beer and sit in front of the B & W to check out the wrestling matches that I see this news bulletin 'bout two missing kids. I recognize the mugs right away. Short Order and his doggie sister. And all of a sudden her face is out of my mind. Aw fuck, I say, and put my beer down so hard that the foam spills onto last months Hustler. Aw fuck.

See, if Nell was here, she'd know what to do: call the cops. But I don't know. Cops ain't exactly my friends, and all I need is for bacon to be crawling all over my place. And seeing how her face is vague now, I decide to wait 'til the late news. Short Order don't look right neither. I'll have another beer and wait for the late news.

The alarm rings at four and I have this headache, see, from the sixpak, and I gotta get up. I was supposed to do something, but I got all suck-faced and forgot. Turn off the T.V., take a shower, but that don't help my memory any.

Hear sirens near the railroad tracks. Cops. I'm supposed to call the cops. I'll do it after I make the coffee, put away the eggs, get the donuts out. But Paulie strolls in looking partied out. We actually talk 'bout last night's wrestling match between BoBo Brazil and the Crusher. I slept through it, you see. Paulie orders an O.J. on account of he's catching a cold. I open up my big mouth and ask about De. Drinks the rest of his O.J., says real calm like, that he caught her eaglespread with the Vegetable fatso down the block. Then, very polite like, Paulie excuses himself. That's one thing I gotta say about Paulie. He may be one big Fuck-up, but he's got manners. Juice gave him shit cramps, he says.

Well, leave it to Paulie. Good ole Mr. Fuck-Up himself to help me with the cops. The prick O.D.'s in my crapper; vomits and shits are all over—I mean all over the fuckin' walls. That's the thanks I get for being Mr. Nice Guy. I had the cops looking up my ass for the stash; says one, the one wearing a mortician's suit, We'll be back, we'll be back when you ain't looking. If I was pushing, would I be burning my goddamn balls off with spitting grease? So fuck 'em, I think. I ain't gonna tell you nothing 'bout the lady. Fuck you, I say to them as they drive away. Fuck your mother.

That's why Nell was good to have 'round. She could be a pain in the ass, you know, like making me hang those stupid bells, but mostly she knew what to do. See, I go bananas. Like my mind fries with the potatoes and by the end of the day, I'm deader than dogshit. Let me tell you what I mean. A few hours later, after I swore I wouldn't give the fuckin' pigs the time of day, the green vans roll up across the street. While I'm stirring the chili con carne I see all these illegals running out of the factory to hide, like roaches when the lightswitch goes on. I taste the chile, but I really can't taste nothing on account of I've lost my appetite after cleaning out the crapper, when three of them run into the Cariboo. They look at me as if I'm gonna stop them, but when I go on stirring the chile, they run to the bathroom. Now look, I'm a nice guy, but I don't like to be used, you know? Just 'cause they're regulars don't mean jackshit. I run an honest business. And that's what I told them Agents. See, by that time, my stomach being all dizzy, and the cops all over the place, and the three illegals running in here, I was all confused, you know. That's how it was, and well, I haven't seen Nell for years, and I guess that's why I pointed to the bathroom.

I don't know. I didn't expect handcuffs and them agents putting their hands up and down their thighs. When they walked passed me, they didn't look at me. That is the two young ones. The older one, the one that looked silly in the handcuffs on account of she's old enough to be my grandma's grandma, looks straight at my face with the same eyes Short Order's sister gave me yesterday. What a day. Then, to top off the potatoes with the gravy, the bells jingle against the door and in enters the lady again with the two kids.

III

He's got lice. Probably from living in the detainers. Those are the rooms where they round up the children and make them work for their food. I saw them from the window. Their eyes are cut glass, and no one looks for sympathy. They take turns, sorting out the arms from the legs, heads from the torsos. Is that one your mother? one guard asks, holding a mummified head with eyes shut tighter than coffins. But the children no longer cry. They just continue sorting as if they were salvaging cans from a heap of trash. They do this until time is up and they drift into a tunnel, back to the womb of sleep, while a new group comes in. It is all very organized. I bite my fist to keep from retching. Please God, please don't let Geraldo be there.

For you see, they took Geraldo. By mistake, of course. It was my fault. I shouldn't have sent him out to fetch me a mango. But it was just to the corner. I didn't even bother to put his sweater on. I hear his sandals flapping against the gravel. I follow him with my eyes, see him scratching his buttocks when the wind picks up swiftly, as it often does at such unstable times, and I have to close the door.

The darkness becomes a serpent's tongue, swallowing us whole. It is the night of La Llorona. The women come up from the depths of sorrow to search for their children. I join them, frantic, desperate, and our eyes become scrutinizers, our bodies opiated with the scent of their smiles. Descending from door to door, the wind whips our faces. I hear the wailing of the women and know it to be my own. Geraldo is nowhere to be found.

Dawn is not welcomed. It is a drunkard wavering between consciousness and sleep. My life is fleeing, moving south towards the sea. My tears are now hushed and faint.

The boy, barely a few years older than Geraldo, lights a cigarette, rests it on the edge of his desk, next to all the other cigarette burns. The blinds are down to keep the room cool. Above him hangs a single bulb that shades and shadows his face in such a way as to mask his expressions. He is not to be trusted. He fills in the information, for I cannot write. Statements delivered, we discuss motives.

"Spies," says he, flicking a long burning ash from the cigarette onto the floor, then wolfing the smoke in as if his lungs had an unquenchable thirst for nicotine. "We arrest spies. Criminals." He says this with cigarette smoke spurting out from his nostrils like a nose bleed.

"Spies? Criminal?" My shawl falls to the ground. "He is only five and a half years old." I plead for logic with my hands. "What kind of crimes could a five year old commit?"

"Anyone who so willfully supports the contras in any form must be arrested and punished without delay." He knows the line by heart.

I think about moths and their stupidity. Always attracted by light, they fly into fires, or singe their wings with the heat of the single bulb and fall on his desk, writhing in pain. I don't understand why nature has been so cruel as to prevent them from feeling warmth. He dismisses them with a sweep of a hand. "This," he continues, "is what we plan to do with the contras, and those who aid them." He inhales again.

"But, Señor, he's just a baby."

"Contras are tricksters. They exploit the ignorance of people like you. Perhaps they convinced your son to circulate pamphlets. You should be talking to them, not us." The cigarette is down to his yellow finger tips, to where he can no longer continue to hold it without burning himself. He throws the stub on the floor, crushes it under his boot. "This," he says, screwing his boot into the ground, "is what the contras do to people like you."

"Señor. I am a washer woman. You yourself see I cannot read or write. There is my X. Do you think my son can read?" How can I explain to this man that we are poor, that we live as best we can? "If such a thing has happened, perhaps he wanted to make a few centavos for his mamá. He's just a baby."

"So you are admitting his guilt?"

"So you are admitting he is here?" I promise, once I see him, hold him in my arms again, I will never, never scold him for wanting more than I can give. "You see, he needs his sweater ..." The sweater lies limp on my lap.

"Your assumption is incorrect."

"May I check the detainers for myself?"

"In time."

"And what about my Geraldo?"

"In time." He dismisses me, placing the forms in a big envelope crinkled by the day's humidity.

"When?" I am wringing the sweater with my hands.

"Don't be foolish, woman. Now off with your nonsense. We will try to locate your Pedro."

"Geraldo."

Maria came by today with a bowl of hot soup. She reports in her usual excited way, that the soldiers are now eating the brains of their victims. It is unlike her to be so scandalous. So insane. Geraldo must be cold without his sweater.

"Why?" I ask as the soup gets cold. I will write Tavo tonight.

At the plaza a group of people are whispering. They are quiet when I pass, turn to one another and put their finger to their lips to cage their voices. They continue as I reach the church steps. To be associated with me is condemnation.

Today I felt like killing myself, Lord. But I am too much of a coward. I am a washer woman, Lord. My mother was one, and hers too. We have lived as best we can, washing other people's laundry, rinsing off other people's dirt until our hands crust and chap. When my son wanted to hold my hand, I held soap instead. When he wanted to play, my feet were in pools of water. It takes such little courage, being a washer woman. Give me strength, Lord.

What have I done to deserve this, Lord? Raising a child is like building a kite. You must bend the twigs enough, but not too much, for you might break them. You must find paper that is delicate and light enough to wave on the breath of the wind, yet must withstand the ravages of a storm. You must tie the strings gently but firmly so that it may not fall apart. You must let the string go, eventually, so that the kite will stretch its ambition. It is such delicate work, Lord, being a mother. This I understand, Lord, because I am, but you have snapped the cord, Lord. It was only a matter of minutes and my life is lost somewhere in the clouds. I don't know, I don't know what games you play, Lord.

These four walls are no longer my house, the earth beneath it, no longer my home. Weeds have replaced all good crops. The irrigation ditches are clodded with bodies. No matter where we turn, there are rumors facing us and we try to live as best we can, under the rule of men who rape women, then rip their fetuses from their bellies. Is this our home? Is this our country? I ask Maria. Don't these men have mothers, lovers, babies, sisters? Don't they see what they are doing? Later, Maria says, these men are babes farted out from the Devil's ass. We check to make sure no one has heard her say this.

Without Geraldo, this is not my home, the earth beneath it, not my country. This is why I have to leave. Maria begins to cry. Not because I am going, but because she is staying.

Tavo. Sweet Tavo. He has sold his car to send me the money. He has just married and he sold his car for me. Thank you, Tavo. Not just for the

money. But also for making me believe in the goodness of people again ...
The money is enough to buy off the border soldiers. The rest will come from
the can. I have saved for Geraldo's schooling and it is enough for a bus ticket
to Juarez. I am to wait for Tavo there.

I spit. I do not turn back.

Perhaps I am wrong in coming. I worry that Geraldo will not have a home
to return to, no mother to cradle his nightmares away, soothe the scars, stop
the hemorrhaging of his heart. Tavo is happy I am here, but it is crowded, the
three of us, and I hear them arguing behind their closed door. There is only so
much a nephew can provide. I must find work. I have two hands willing to work.
But the heart. The heart wills only to watch the children playing in the street.

The machines, their speed and dust, make me ill. But I can clean. I clean
toilets, dump trash cans, sweep. Disinfect the sinks. I will gladly do whatever is necessary to repay Tavo. The baby is due any time and money is
tight. I volunteer for odd hours, weekends, since I really have very little to
do. When the baby comes I know Tavo's wife will not let me hold it, for she
thinks I am a bad omen. I know it.

Why would God play such a cruel joke, if he isn't my son? I jumped the
curb, dashed out into the street, but the street is becoming wider and wider.
I've lost him once and can't lose him again and to hell with the screeching tires
and the horns and the headlights barely touching my hips. I can't take my eyes
off him because, you see, they are swift and cunning and can take your life with
a snap of a finger. But God is a just man and His mistakes can be undone.

My heart pounds in my head like a sledge hammer against the asphalt.
What if it isn't Geraldo? What if he is still in the detainer waiting for me? A
million questions, one answer: Yes. Geraldo, yes. I want to touch his hand
first, have it disappear in my own because it is so small. His eyes look at me
in total bewilderment. I grab him because the earth is crumbling beneath us
and I must save him. We both fall to the ground.

A hot meal is in store. A festival. The cook, a man with shrunken cheeks
and the hands of a car mechanic, takes a liking to Geraldo. Its like birthing
you again, mi'jo. My baby.

I bathe him. He flutters in excitement, the water grey around him. I
scrub his head with lye to kill off the lice, comb his hair out with a fine
tooth comb. I wash his rubbery penis, wrap him in a towel and he stands in
front of the window, shriveling and sucking milk from a carton, his hair
shiny from the dampness.

He finally sleeps. So easily, she thinks. On her bed next to the open window he coos in the night. Below the sounds of the city become as monoto-
nous as the ocean waves. She rubs his back with warm oil, each stroke
making up for the days of his absence. She hums to him softly so that her
breath brushes against his face, tunes that are rusted and crack in her
throat. The hotel neon shines on his back and she covers him.

All the while the young girl watches her brother sleeping. She removes
her sneakers, climbs into the bed, snuggles up to her brother, and soon her
breathing is raspy, her arms under her stomach.

The couch is her bed tonight. Before switching the light off, she checks once more to make sure this is not a joke. Tomorrow she will make arrangements to go home. Maria will be the same, the mango stand on the corner next to the church plaza will be the same. It will all be the way it was before. But enough excitement. For the first time in years, her mind is quiet of all noise and she has the desire to sleep.

The bells jingle when the screen door slaps shut behind them. The cook wrings his hands in his apron, looking at them. Geraldo is in the middle, and they sit in the booth farthest away from the window, near the hall where the toilets are, and right away the small boy, his hair now neatly combed and split to the side like an adult, wrinkles his nose at the peculiar smell. The cook wipes perspiration off his forehead with the corner of his apron, finally comes over to the table.

She looks so different, so young. Her hair is combed slick back into one thick braid and her earrings hang like baskets of golden pears on her finely sculptured ears. He can't believe how different she looks. Almost beautiful. She points to what she wants on the menu with a white, clean fingernail. Although confused, the cook is sure of one thing—it's Short Order all right, pointing to him with a commanding finger, saying his only English word: coke.

His hands tremble as he slaps the meat on the grill; the patties hiss instantly. He feels like vomiting. The chile overboils and singes the fires, deep red trail of chile crawling to the floor and puddling there. He grabs the handles, burns himself, drops the pot on the wooden racks of the floor. He sucks his fingers, the patties blackening and sputtering grease. He flips them, and the burgers hiss anew. In some strange way he hopes they have disappeared, and he takes a quick look only to see Short Order's sister, still in the same dress, still holding her brother's hand. She is craning her neck to peek at what is going on in the kitchen.

Aw, fuck, he says, in a fog of smoke his eyes burning tears. He can't believe it, but he's crying. For the first time since JoJo's death, he's crying. He becomes angry at the lady for returning. At JoJo. At Nell for leaving him. He wishes Nell here, but doesn't know where she's at or what part of Vietnam JoJo is all crumbled up in. Children gotta be with their parents, family gotta be together, he thinks. It's only right. The emergency line is ringing.

Two black and whites roll up and skid the front tires against the curb. The flashing lights carousel inside the cafe. She sees them opening the screen door, their guns taut and cold like steel erections. Something is wrong, and she looks to the cowering cook. She has been betrayed, and her heart is pounding like footsteps running, faster, louder, faster and she can't hear what they are saying to her. She jumps up from the table, grabs Geraldo by the wrist, his sister dragged along because, like her, she refuses to release his hand. Their lips are mouthing words she can't hear, can't comprehend. Run, Run is all she can think of to do, Run through the hallway, out to the alley, Run because they will never take him away again.

But her legs are heavy and she crushes Geraldo against her, so tight, as if she wants to conceal him in her body again, return him to her belly so that they will not castrate him and hang his small, blue penis on her door, not crush his face so that he is unrecognizable, not bury him among the heaps of bones, and ears, and teeth, and jaws, because no one, but she, cared to know that he cried. For years he cried and she could hear him day and night. Screaming, howling, sobbing, shriveling and crying because he is only five years old, and all she wanted was a mango.

But the crying begins all over again. In the distance, she hears crying.

She refuses to let go. For they will have to cut her arms off to take him, rip her mouth off to keep her from screaming for help. Without thinking, she reaches over to where two pots of coffee are brewing and throws the streaming coffee into their faces. Outside, people begin to gather, pressing their faces against the window glass to get a good view. The cook huddles behind the counter, frightened, trembling. Their faces become distorted and she doesn't see the huge hand that takes hold of Geraldo and she begins screaming all over again, screaming so that the walls shake, screaming enough for all the women of murdered children, screaming, pleading for help from the people outside, and she pushes an open hand against an officer's nose, because no one will stop them and he pushes the gun barrel to her face.

And I laugh at his ignorance. How stupid of him to think that I will let them take my Geraldo away, just because he waves that gun like a flag. Well, to hell with you, you pieces of shit, do you hear me? Stupid, cruel pigs. To hell with you all, because you can no longer frighten me. I will fight you for my son until I have no hands left to hold a knife. I will fight you all because you're all farted out of the Devil's ass, and you'll not take us with you. I am laughing, howling at their stupidity. Because they should know by now that I will never let my son go and then I hear something crunching like broken glass against my forehead and I am blinded by the liquid darkness. But I hold onto his hand. That I can feel, you see, I'll never let go. Because we are going home. My son and I.

1984

GRACE PALEY
1922–2007

Grace Paley was born to Isaac and Mary Goodside, Russian Jewish immigrants full of secular and socialist ideas gleaned from the intellectual ferment that preceded the Russian Revolution of 1917. Although her father, a doctor, influenced her love of Russian literature, both parents encouraged her intellectual precocity and political activism.

For a while Paley attended Hunter College and New York University, but a consuming interest in ordinary lives and a resistance to institutional authority caused her to drop out. In 1942, at the age of twenty, she married Jess Paley, a photographer, with whom she had a son and a daughter. After they were divorced, Paley married Robert Nichols, a poet and playwright. Despite the vicissitudes inherent in raising children and working at marginal jobs, she found time to perfect her writing craft. Three small short story collections— *The Little Disturbances of Man* (1959), *Enormous Changes at the Last Minute* (1974), and *Later the Same Day* (1985)—established her reputation as a unique, virtually inimitable contemporary writer. In 1961 she was awarded a Guggenheim Fellowship in Fiction, and in 1970 she received both a National Council on the Arts grant and a National Institute of Arts and Letters award for short story writing.

The titles of Paley's collections suggest the stories' themes: the irrepressible life force underlying the daily lives of New York working-class men and women; human courage in the face of aging and loss; the willingness to take risks that ensure the possibility of change within their lifetimes. Paley's readers will discover more: loose vignettes artfully fragmented; the precise metaphors of a poet; characters created through conversations articulated with an impeccable ear for the varied tones, rhythms, and cadences of New York speech. Paley's style creates small worlds, allowing readers to see what William Blake in another context called "the world in a grain of sand." Above all, Paley's is an extraordinary narrative voice, sassy, ironic, always authoritative, insistently faithful to pacifist and feminist ideals.

Paley's abiding love for independent-minded children extended later to include their feisty mothers resisting boorish husbands and involving themselves in love affairs, playground politics, and an activism ranging from the fight for drug-free schools to vehement opposition to the Vietnam War and the ongoing resistance to nuclear proliferation. Until her death, she remained engaged politically and personally, an iconoclast loudly debunking patriarchal institutions denying life-affirming choice. All of her stories embody this engagement.

"The Expensive Moment," reprinted here, is best characterized as expansive, including as it does women beyond the confines of Vesey Street—namely, Xie Feng, sent as a delegate to a woman's convention from mainland China during a lull in the Cold War and after the Cultural Revolution. Ruthie has been to China, where she met Xie Feng; the latter understands her fears about Rachel because Xie Feng's children were left against her will with harsh grandparents. As Faith and Xie Feng wander throughout the urban ethnic neighborhood, where Faith recapitulates for her friend's benefit the places where she has come of age, loved, married, divorced, and fought to make life safer and saner for her children, they are joined by Ruthie. The three women bond in mutual concern over their children and are united by the nagging question of whether in violent and dangerous times they have raised them to be resilient, compassionate, and responsible human beings.

Rose Yalow Kamel
Philadelphia College of Pharmacy and Science

PRIMARY WORKS

The Little Disturbances of Man: Stories of Men and Women at Love, 1959; *Enormous Changes at the Last Minute*, 1974; *Later the Same Day*, 1985; *Leaning Forward*, 1985; *Long Walks and Intimate Talks*, 1991; *New and Collected Poems*, 1992; *Collected Stories*, 1994; *Just as I Thought*, 1998; *Begin Again: The Collected Poems of Grace Paley*, 2000; *Fidelity*, 2008.

The Expensive Moment

Faith did not tell Jack.

At about two in the afternoon she went to visit Nick Hegstraw, the famous sinologist.[1] He was not famous in the whole world. He was famous in their neighborhood and in the adjoining neighborhoods, north, south, and east. He was studying China, he said, in order to free us all of distance and mystery. But because of foolish remarks that were immediately published, he had been excluded from wonderful visits to China's new green parlor. He sometimes felt insufficiently informed. Hundreds of people who knew nothing about Han and Da tung visited, returned, wrote articles; one friend with about seventy-five Chinese words had made a three-hour documentary. Well, sometimes he did believe in socialism and sometimes only in the Late T'ang. It's hard to stand behind a people and culture in revolutionary transition when you are constantly worried about their irreplaceable and breakable artifacts.

He was noticeably handsome, the way men are every now and then, with a face full of good architectural planning. (Good use of face space, Jack said.) In the hardware store or in line at the local movie, women and men would look at him. They might turn away saying, Not my type, or, Where have I seen him before? TV? Actually they had seen him at the vegetable market. As an unmarried vegetarian sinologist he bought bagfuls of broccoli and waited with other eaters for snow peas from California at $4.79 a pound.

Are you lovers? Ruth asked.

Oh God, no. I'm pretty monogamous when I'm monogamous. Why are you laughing?

You're lying. Really, Faith, why did you describe him at such length? You don't usually do that.

But the fun of talking, Ruthy. What about that? It's as good as fucking lots of times. Isn't it?

Oh boy, Ruth said, if it's that good, then it's got to be that bad.

At lunch Jack said, Ruth is not a Chinese cook. She doesn't mince words. She doesn't sauté a lot of imperial verbs and docile predicates like some women.

Faith left the room. Someday, she said, I'm never coming back.

---

[1]One who makes a study of the Chinese language and its civilization.

But I love the way Jack talks, said Ruth. He's a true gossip like us. And another thing, he's the only one who ever asks me anymore about Rachel.

Don't trust him, said Faith.

After Faith slammed the door, Jack decided to buy a pipe so he could smoke thoughtfully in the evening. He wished he had a new dog or a new child or a new wife. He had none of these things because he only thought about them once in ten days and then only for about five minutes. The interest in sustained shopping or courtship had left him. He was a busy man selling discount furniture in a rough neighborhood during the day, and reading reading reading, thinking writing grieving all night the bad world-ending politics which were using up the last years of his life. Oh, come back, come back, he cried. Faith! At least for supper.

On this particular afternoon, Nick (the sinologist) said, How are your children? Fine, she said. Tonto is in love and Richard has officially joined the League for Revolutionary Youth.

Ah, said Nick. L.R.Y. I spoke at one of their meetings last month. They threw half a pizza pie at me.

Why? What'd you say? Did you say something terrible? Maybe it's an anti-agist coalition of New Left pie throwers and Old Left tomato throwers.

It's not a joke, he said. And it's not funny. And besides, that's not what I want to talk about. He then expressed opposition to the Great Leap Forward[2] and the Cultural Revolution.[3] He did this by walking back and forth muttering, Wrong. Wrong. Wrong.

Faith, who had just read *Fanshen* at his suggestion, accepted both. But he worried about great art and literature, its way of rising out of the already risen. Faith, sit down, he said. Where were the already risen nowadays? Driven away from their typewriters and calligraphy pens by the Young Guards—like all the young, wild with a dream of wildness.

Faith said, Maybe it's the right now rising. Maybe the already risen don't need anything more. They just sit there in their lawn chairs and appreciate the culture of the just rising. They may even like to do that. The work of creation is probably too hard when you are required because of having already risen to be always distinguishing good from bad, great from good . . .

Nick would not even laugh at serious jokes. He decided to show Faith with mocking examples how wrong she was. None of the examples convinced her. In fact, they seemed to support an opposing position. Faith wondered if his acquisitive mind was not sometimes betrayed by a poor filing system.

---

[2]Under Chairman Mao Tse Tung's leadership, the Chinese Communist Party from 1958–1960 forcibly decentralized and collectivized the peasantry. Using manpower, not machinery, to irrigate channels and build dikes, the Great Leap Forward caused mass starvation.

[3]The decade 1966–1976 saw a split with the Communist Party between Mao and intellectual reformers called revisionists. Mao's Red Guards rampaged through cities and villages, seized power, and destroyed old ideas, customs, and habits. Those perceived as intellectuals or middle-class were publicly humiliated; some were killed or driven to commit suicide, others forced to become manual laborers.

Here they are anyway:

Working hard in the fields of Shanxi is John Keats,[4] brilliant and tubercular. The sun beats on his pale flesh. The water in which he is ankle-deep is colder than he likes. The little green shoots are no comfort to him despite their light-green beauty. He is thinking about last night—this lunar beauty, etc. When he gets back to the commune he learns that they have been requested by the province to write poems. Keats is discouraged. He's thinking, This lunar beauty, this lunar beauty ... The head communard, a bourgeois leftover, says, Oh, what can ail thee, pale individualist?[5] He laughs, then says, Relax, comrade. Just let politics take command. Keats does this, and soon, smiling his sad intelligent smile, he says, Ah ...

> *This lunar beauty*
> > *touches Shanxi province*
> *in the year of the bumper crops*
> > *the peasants free of the landlords*
> *stand in the fields*
> > *they talk of this and that*
> > *and admire*
> *the harvest moon.*

Meanwhile, all around him peasants are dampening the dry lead pencil points with their tongues.

Faith interrupted. She hoped someone would tell them how dangerous lead was. And industrial pollution.

For godsakes, said Nick, and continued. One peasant writes:

> *This morning the paddy*
> > *looked like the sea*
> *At high tide we will*
> > *harvest the rice*
> *This is because of Mao Zedong*
> > *whose love for the peasants*
> *has fed the urban proletariat.*

That's enough. Do you get it? Yes, Faith said. Something like this? And sang.

> *On the highway to Communism*
> *the little children put plum blossoms*
> *in their hair and dance*
> *on the new-harvested wheat*

---

[4]English Romantic poet (1795–1821) who died of tuberculosis. Keat's "Ode to Psyche" focused on his inner life and imaginative power, which the Maoist Cultural Revolution would have considered decadent.

[5]Paley parodies the Maoist rejection of Keats's "La Belle Dame sans Merci."

She was about to remember another poem from her newly invented memory, but Nick said, Faith, it's already 3:30, so—full of the play of poems they unfolded his narrow daybed to a comfortable three-quarter width. Their lovemaking was ordinary but satisfactory. Its difference lay only in difference. Of course, if one is living a whole life in passionate affection with another, this differentness on occasional afternoons is often enough.

And besides that, almost at once on rising to tea or coffee, Faith asked, Nick, why do they have such a rotten foreign policy? The question had settled in her mind earlier, resting just under the light inflammation of desire.

It was not the first time she had asked this question, nor was Nick the last person who answered.

Nick: For godsakes, don't you understand anything about politics?

Richard: Yeah, and why does Israel trade probably every day with South Africa?

Ruth (*Although her remarks actually came a couple of years later*): Cuba carries on commercial negotiations with Argentina. No?

The boys at supper: Tonto (*Softly, with narrowed eyes*): Why did China recognize Pinochet[6] just about ten minutes after the coup in Chile?

Richard (*Tolerantly explaining*): Asshole, because Allende didn't know how to run a revolution, that's why.

Jack reminded them that the U.S.S.R. may have had to overcome intense ideological repugnance in order to satisfy her old longing for South African industrial diamonds.

Faith thought, But if you think like that forever you can be sad forever. You can be cynical, you can go around saying no hope, you can say import-export, you can mumble all day, World Bank. So she tried thinking: The beauty of trade, the caravans crossing Africa and Asia, the roads to Peru through the terrible forests of Guatemala, and then especially the village markets of underdeveloped countries, plazas behind churches under awnings and tents, not to mention the Orlando Market around the corner; also the Free Market, which costs so much in the world, and what about the discount house of Jack, Son of Jake.

Oh sure, Richard said, the beauty of trade. I'm surprised at you, Ma, the beauty of trade—those Indians going through Guatemala with leather thongs cutting into their foreheads holding about a ton of beauty on their backs. Beauty, he said.

He rested for about an hour. Then he continued. I'm surprised at you Faith, really surprised. He blinked his eyes a couple of times. Mother, he said, have you ever read any political theory? No. All those dumb peace meetings you go to. Don't they ever talk about anything but melting up a couple of really great swords?

[6]Augusto Pinochet (1915–2006), a right-wing Chilean army general who seized power from the democratically elected Salvadore Allende, president of Chile from 1970 to 1973.

He'd become so pale.

Richard, she said. You're absolutely white. You seem to have quit drinking orange juice.

This simple remark made him leave home for three days.

But first he looked at her with either contempt or despair.

Then, because the brain at work pays no attention to time and speedily connects and chooses, she thought: Oh, long ago I looked at my father. What kind of face is that? he had asked. She was leaning against their bedroom wall. She was about fourteen. Fifteen? A lot you care, she said. A giant war is coming out of Germany[7] and all you say is Russia. Bad old Russia. I'm the one that's gonna get killed. You? he answered. Ha ha! A little girl sitting in safe America is going to be killed. Ha ha!

And what about the looks those other boys half a generation ago had made her accept. Ruth had called them put-up-or-shut-up looks. She and her friends had walked round and round the draft boards with signs that said I COUNSEL DRAFT REFUSAL. Some of those young fellows were calm and holy, and some were fierce and grouchy. But not one of them was trivial, and neither was Richard.

Still, Faith thought, what if history should seize him as it had actually taken Ruth's daughter Rachel when her face was still as round as an apple; a moment in history, the expensive moment when everyone his age is called but just a few are chosen by conscience or passion or even only love of one's own agemates, and they are the ones who smash an important nosecone (as has been recently done) or blow up some building full of oppressive money or murderous military plans; but, oh, what if a human creature (maybe rotten to the core but a living person still) is in it? What if they disappear then to live in exile or in the deepest underground and you don't see them for ten years or have to travel to Cuba or Canada or farther to look at their changed faces? Then you think sadly, I could have worked harder at raising that child, the one that was once mine. I could have raised him to become a brilliant economist or finish graduate school and be a lawyer or a doctor maybe. He could have done a lot of good, just as much *that* way, healing or defending the underdog.

But Richard had slipped a note under the door before he left. In his neat handwriting it said: "Trade. Shit. It's production that's beautiful. That's what's beautiful. And the producers. They're beautiful."

What's the use, said Ruth when she and Faith sat eating barley soup in the Art Foods Deli. You're always wrong. She looked into the light beyond the plate-glass window. It was unusual for her to allow sadness. Faith took her hand and kissed it. She said, Ruthy darling. Ruth leaned across the table to hug her. The soup spoon fell to the floor, mixing barley and sawdust.

But look, Ruth said, Joe got this news clipping at the office from some place in Minnesota. "Red and green acrylic circles were painted around telephone

---

[7]The adolescent Faith is referring to World War II.

poles and trees ringing the Dakota State Prison last night. It was assumed that the Red and the Green were planning some destructive act. These circles were last seen in Arizona. Two convicts escaped from that prison within a week. Red and green circles were stenciled on the walls of their cells. The cost for removing these signatures will probably go as high as $4,300."

What for? said Faith.

For? asked Ruth. They were political prisoners. Someone has to not forget them. The green is for ecology.

Nobody leaves that out nowadays.

Well, they shouldn't, said Ruth.

This Rachel of Ruth and Joe's had grown from girl to woman in far absence, making little personal waves from time to time in the newspapers or in rumor which would finally reach her parents on the shores of their always waiting—that is, the office mailbox or the eleven o'clock news.

One day Ruth and Joe were invited to a cultural event. This was because Joe was a cultural worker. He had in fact edited *The Social Ordure*, a periodical which published everything Jack wrote. He and Ruth had also visited China and connected themselves in print to some indulgent views of the Gang of Four, from which it had been hard to disengage. Ruth was still certain that the bad politics and free life of Jiang Qing would be used for at least a generation to punish ALL Chinese women.

But isn't that true everywhere, said Faith. If you say a simple thing like, "There are only eight women in Congress," or if you say the word "patriarchy," someone always says, Yeah? look at Margaret Thatcher, or look at Golda Meir.[8]

I love Golda Meir.

You do? Oh! said Faith.

But the evening belonged to the Chinese artists and writers who had been rehabilitated while still alive. All sorts of American cultural workers were invited. Some laughed to hear themselves described in this way. They were accustomed to being called "dreamer poet realist postmodernist." They might have liked being called "cultural dreamer," but no one had thought of that yet.

Many of these Chinese artists (mostly men and some women) flew back and forth from American coast to coast so often (sometimes stopping in Iowa City) that they were no longer interested in window seats but slept on the aisle or across the fat center where the armrests can be adjusted ... while the great deep dipping Rockies, the Indian Black Hills, the Badlands, the good and endless plains moved slowly west under the gently trembling jet. They never bother anymore to dash to the windows at the circling of New York as the pattern holds and the lights of our city engage and eliminate the sky.

Ruth said she would personally bring Nick to the party since China was still too annoyed to have invited him. It wasn't fair for a superficial visitor

[8]Margaret Thatcher (b. 1925) was British prime minister from 1979 to 1990; Golda Meir (1898–1978) was Israeli premier from 1969 to 1974.

like herself to be present when a person like Nick, with whole verses of his obsession falling out of his pockets, was excluded.

That's O.K., Ruth. You don't have to ask him, Faith said. Don't bother on my account. I don't even see him much anymore.

How come?

I don't know. Whenever I got to like one of his opinions he'd change it, and he never liked any of mine. Also, I couldn't talk to you about it, so it never got thick enough. I mean woofed and warped. Anyway, it hadn't been Nick, she realized. He was all right, but it was travel she longed for—somewhere else—the sexiness of the unknown parts of far imaginable places.

Sex? Ruth said. She bit her lips. Wouldn't it be interesting if way out there Rachel was having a baby?

God, yes, of course! Wonderful! Oh, Ruthy, Faith said, remembering babies, those round, staring, day-in day-out companions of her youth.

Well, Faith asked, what was he like, Nick—the poet Ai Qing? What'd he say?

He has a very large head, Nick said. The great poet raised from exile.

Was Ding Ling there? The amazing woman, the storyteller, Ding Ling?

They're not up to her yet, Nick said. Maybe next year.

Well, what did Bien Tselin say? Faith asked. Nick, tell me.

Well, he's very tiny. He looks like my father did when he was old.

Yes, but what did they say?

Do you have any other questions? he asked. I'm thinking about something right now. He was writing in his little book—thoughts, comments, maybe even new songs for Chinese modernization—which he planned to publish as soon as possible. He thought Faith could read them then.

Finally he said, They showed me their muscles. There were other poets there. They told some jokes but not against us. They laughed and nudged each other. They talked Chinese, you know. I don't know why they were so jolly. They kept saying, Do not think that we have ceased to be Communists. We are Communists. They weren't bitter. They acted interested and happy.

Ruthy, Faith said, please tell me what they said.

Well, one of the women, Faith, about our age, she said the same thing. She also said the peasants were good to her. But the soldiers were bad. She said the peasants in the countryside helped her. They knew she felt lonely and frightened. She said she loved the Chinese peasant. That's exactly the way she said it, like a little speech: I'll never forget and I will always love the Chinese peasant. It's the one thing Mao was right about—of course he was also a good poet. But she said, well, you can imagine—she said, the children ... When the entire working office was sent down to the countryside to dig up stones, she left her daughters with her mother. Her mother was old-fashioned, especially about girls. It's not so hard to be strong about oneself.

Some months later, at a meeting of women's governmental organizations sponsored by the UN, Faith met the very same Chinese woman who'd talked to Ruth. She remembered Ruth well. Yes, the lady who hasn't seen her daughter in eight years. Oh, what a sadness. Who would forget that woman. I have known a few. My name is Xie Feng, she said. Now you say it.

The two women said each other's strange name and laughed. The Chinese woman said, Faith in what? Then she gathered whatever strength and aggression she'd needed to reach this country; she added the courtesy of shyness, breathed deep, and said, Now I would like to see how you live. I have been to meetings, one after another and day after day. But what is a person's home like? How do you live?

Faith said, Me? My house? You want to see my house? In the mirror that evening brushing her teeth, she smiled at her smiling face. She had been invited to be hospitable to a woman from half the world away who'd lived a life beyond foreignness and had experienced extreme history.

The next day they drank tea in Faith's kitchen out of Chinese cups that Ruth had brought from her travels. Misty terraced hills were painted on these cups and a little oil derrick inserted among them.

Faith showed her the boys' bedroom. The Chinese woman took a little camera out of her pocket. You don't mind? she asked. This is the front room, said Faith. It's called the living room. This is our bedroom. That's a picture of Jack giving a paper at the Other Historian meeting and that picture is Jack with two guys who've worked in his store since they were all young. The skinny one just led a strike against Jack and won. Jack says they were right.

I see—both principled men, said the Chinese woman.

They walked around the block a couple of times to get the feel of a neighborhood. They stopped for strudel at the Art Foods. It was half past two and just in time to see the children fly out of the school around the corner. The littlest ones banged against the legs of teachers and mothers. Here and there a father rested his length against somebody's illegally parked car. They stopped to buy a couple of apples. This is my Chinese friend from China, Faith said to Eddie the butcher, who was smoking a cigar, spitting and smiling at the sunlight of an afternoon break. So many peaches, so many oranges, the woman said admiringly to Eddie.

They walked west to the Hudson River. It's called the North River but it's really our Lordly Hudson. This is a good river, but very quiet, said the Chinese woman as they stepped onto the beautiful, green, rusting, slightly crumpled, totally unused pier and looked at New Jersey. They returned along a street of small houses and Faith pointed up to the second-floor apartment where she and Jack had first made love. Ah, the woman said, do you notice that in time you love the children more and the man less? Faith said, Yes! but as soon as she said it, she wanted to run home and find Jack and kiss his pink ears and his 243 last hairs, to call out, Old friend, don't worry, you are loved. But before she could speak of this, Tonto flew by on his financially rewarding messenger's bike, screaming, Hi, Mom, *nee hau, nee hau*. He has a Chinese girlfriend this week. He says that means hello. My other son is at a meeting. She didn't say it was the L.R.Y.'s regular beep-the-horn-if-you-support-Mao meeting. She showed her the church basement where she and Ruth and Ann and Louise and their group of mostly women and some men had made leaflets, offered sanctuary to draft resisters. They would probably do so soon again. Some young people looked up from a light board, saw a representative of the Third World, and smiled peacefully. They walked east and south to neighborhoods where our city, in fields of garbage and broken brick, stands desolate, her windows burnt and blind. Here, Faith said, the people suffer and struggle, their children turn round and round in one place, growing first in beauty, then in rage.

Now we are home again. And I will tell you about my life, the Chinese woman said. Oh yes, please, said Faith, very embarrassed. Of course the desire to share the facts and places of her life had come from generosity, but it had come from self–centeredness too.

Yes, the Chinese woman said. Things are a little better now. They get good at home, they get a little bad, then improve. And the men, you know, they were very bad. But now they are a little better, not all, but some, a few. May I ask you, do you worry that your older boy is in a political group that isn't liked? What will be his trade? Will he go to university? My eldest is without skills to this day. Her school years happened in the time of great confusion and running about. My youngest studies well. Ah, she said, rising. Hello. Good afternoon.

Ruth stood in the doorway. Faith's friend, the listener and the answerer, listening.

We were speaking, the Chinese woman said. About the children, how to raise them. My youngest sister is permitted to have a child this year, so we often talk thoughtfully. This is what we think: Shall we teach them to be straightforward, honorable, kind, brave, maybe shrewd, self-serving a little? What is the best way to help them in the real world? We don't know the best way. You don't want them to be cruel, but you want them to take care of themselves wisely. Now my own children are nearly grown. Perhaps it's too late. Was I foolish? I didn't know in those years how to do it.

Yes, yes, said Faith. I know what you mean. Ruthy?

Ruth remained quiet.

Faith waited a couple of seconds. Then she turned to the Chinese woman. Oh, Xie Feng, she said. Neither did I.

1985

WENDY ROSE (HOPI)
B. 1948

Wendy Rose, born in Oakland, California, is of Hopi, Miwok, English, Scottish, Irish, and German extraction. She spent her childhood in the Bay Area just as that region experienced its postwar boom and urban sprawl. She grew up coming to terms with her ethnicity, her gender, and with an Indian's place (or lack of it) in an urban setting. In 1976 she married Arthur Murata while she was an anthropology student at the University of California, Berkeley; she received her master's degree there in cultural anthropology in 1978. From 1979 to 1983, she taught at Berkeley in both ethnic studies and Native American studies, then spent a year teaching at Fresno State University, and in 1984 became coordinator of the American Indian Studies Program at Fresno City College, California. She has also served on the Modern Language Association Commission on Languages and Literatures of America and is active in a wide array of American Indian community affairs.

Wendy Rose is best known as an American Indian poet, and her work is widely anthologized in American literary titles. Her poems show a persistent evolution and understanding of her own voice as an Indian, as a woman, and as a poet, serving as a bridge between ancient storytellers and singers and the modern analyst of literature and culture. She sees American culture critically from the inside as well as from the outside. Her poems project the defiance of indigenous peoples in this century, the poignancy of a precarious survival in an occupied land, and a challenge to the Eurocentric poetic tradition while at the same time using its medium to convey her images. Her verse combines pieces from her own background, glimpses of modern American life, and bits from Indian tradition to weave a tapestry of contemporary indigenous poetry that is unsurpassed in its realism and beauty. Wendy Rose's poetry also carries the rage of a mixed-blood American Indian and that of a woman in a male-dominated academic environment, as seen in her 1977 *Academic Squaw*. Her poems present the tragedy of the loss of millions of native lives under the onslaught of Europeans coming to the New World, yet also preserve the strength for survival of the remaining Indian women of the hemisphere. This sense of poignancy is captured in her poem "To the Hopi in Richmond." Rose's poetry offers a slice of contemporary American Indian existence in the United States, bringing to the late twentieth century the sacredness and balance of the ancients.

C. B. Clark
Oklahoma City University

PRIMARY WORKS

Hopi Roadrunner Dancing, 1973; *Long Division: A Tribal History*, 1977; *Academic Squaw: Reports to the World from the Ivory Tower*, 1977; *Poetry of the American Indian Series*, 1978; *Builder Kachina: A Home-Going Cycle*, 1979; *Lost Copper*, 1980; *What Happened When the Hopi Hit New York*, 1982; *Halfbreed Chronicles*, 1985; *Great Pretenders: Further Reflections on Whiteshamanism*, 1992; *Going to War with All My Relations*, 1993; *Now Proof She Is Gone*, 1994; *Bone Dance: New and Selected Poems, 1965–1993*, 1994; *Itch Like Crazy*, 2002.

Throat Song: The Rotating Earth

"Eskimo throat singers imitate the sounds the women hear . . .
listening to the sound of wind going through the cracks of an igloo
. . . the sound of the sea shore, a river of geese, the sound of the
northern lights while the lights are coming closer . . . in the old days

*the people used to think the world was flat, but when they learned
the world was turning, they made a throat-singing song about it."*

—INUKTITUT MAGAZINE, DECEMBER 1980

I always knew you were singing!

As my fingers have pulled your clay,
as your mountains have pulled the clay of me;
as my knees have deeply printed your mud,
as your winds have drawn me down and dried the mud of me;   5
around me always the drone and scrape of stone,
small movements atom by atom I heard like tiny drums;
I heard flutes and reeds that whine in the wind,
the bongo scratch of beetles in redwood bark,

the constant rattle that made of this land   10
a great gourd!

Oh I always knew you were singing!

1982

Loo-wit[1]

The way they do
this old woman
no longer cares
what others think
but spits her black tobacco   5
any which way
stretching full length
from her bumpy bed.
Finally up
she sprinkles ash on the snow,   10
cold and rocky buttes
that promise nothing
but winter is going at last.
Centuries of cedar
have bound her to earth,   15
huckleberry ropes
lay prickly about her neck.
Her children play games
(no sense of tomorrow);
her eyes are covered   20

---

[1]Loo-wit: "Lady of Fire," Mt. St. Helens.

with bark and she wakes
at night, fears
she is blind.
Nothing but tricks
left in this world,   25
nothing to keep
an old woman home.
Around her
machinery growls,
snarls and ploughs   30
great patches of her skin.
She crouches
in the north,
the source
of her trembling—   35
dawn appearing
with the shudder
of her slopes.
Blackberries unravel,
stones dislodge;   40
it's not as if
they weren't warned.

She was sleeping
but she heard the boot scrape;
the creaking floor;   45
felt the pull of the blanket
from her thin shoulder.
With one free heand
she finds her weapons
and raises them high;   50
clearing the twigs from her throat
she sings, she sings,
shaking the sky like a blanket about her
Loo-wit sings and sings and sings!

                                                                    1983

To the Hopi in Richmond[1] (Santa Fe Indian Village)

My people in boxcars
my people   my pain
united by the window steam

[1]A small colony of Hopi were brought to the
San Francisco Bay area to build railroads and
remained.

of lamb stew cooking
and the metal   5
of your walls,
your floors with cracks and crickets,
your tin roofs
full of holes;

that rain you prayed for   10
thousands of years
comes now
when you live
in a world
of water.   15

So remember
the sun
remember it was not easy
the gentle sun
of August mornings   20
remember it

as you pray today
for the rain
below the mesas;
the moisture   25
in your fields.

                                                        1985

If I Am Too Brown or Too White for You

remember I am a garnet woman
whirling into precision
as a crystal arithmetic
or a cluster and so

why the dream   5
in my mouth,
the flutter of blackbirds
at my wrists?

In the morning
there you are
at the edge of the river   10
on one knee

and you are selecting me
from among polished stones
more definitely red or white   15
between which tiny serpents swim

and you see that my body
is blood frozen
into giving birth
over and over in a single motion   20

and you touch the matrix
shattered in winter
and begin to piece together
the shape of me

wanting the fit in your palm   25
to be perfect
and the image less
clouded, less mixed

but you always see
just in time   30
working me around
in the evening sun

there is a small light
in the smoke, a tiny sun
in the blood, so deep   35
it is there and not there,

so pure
it is singing.

                                                                1985

Story Keeper

The stories would be braided in my hair
between the plastic combs and blue wing tips
but as the rattles would spit,
the drums begin,
along would come someone   5
to stifle and stop the sound
and the story keeper I would have been
must melt into the cave
of artifacts discarded

and this is a wound   10
to be healed
in the spin of winter,
the spiral
of beginning.
This is the task: 15
to find the stories now
and to heave at the rocks,
dig at the moss
with my fingernails,
let moisture seep along my skin   20
and fall within
soft and dark
to the blood

and I promise
I will find them   25
even after so long: where underground
they are albino
and they listen, they shine,
and they wait
with tongues shriveled like leaves   30
and fearful of their names
that would crystallize them,
make them fossils
with the feathers on their backs
frozen hard   35
like beetle wings.

ΔΔΔΔ   ΔΔΔΔ

But spring is floating
to the canyon rim;
needles burst yellow
from the pine branch   40
and the stories have built a new house.
Oh they make us dance
the old animal dances
that go a winding way
back and back   45
to the red clouds
of our first
Hopi morning.
Where I saw them last
they are still: antelope and bear   50
dancing in the dust,

prairie dog and lizard
whirling just whirling,
pinyon and willow
bending, twisting,   55
we women
rooting into the earth
our feet becoming water
and our hair pushing up
like tumbleweed   60

and the spirits should have noticed
how our thoughts wandered those first days,
how we closed our eyes against them
and forgot the signs;
the spirits were never smart about this   65
but trusted us to remember it right
and we were distracted,
we were new.
We mapped the trails
the spirits had walked   70
as if the footprints had more meaning
than the feet.
color after color,
designs that spin and sprout
were painted on the sky   75
but we were only confused
and turned our backs
and now we are trapped
inside our songlessness.

We are that kind of thing   80
that pushes away
the very song
keeping us alive
so the stories have been strong
and tell themselves   85
to this very day,
with or without us
it no longer matters.
The flower merges with the mud,
songs are hammered onto spirits   90
and spirits onto people;
every song is danced out loud
for we are the spirits,
we are the people,
descended from the ones   95

who circled the underworld
and return to circle again.

I feel the stories
rattle under my hand
like sun-dried greasy   100
gambling bones.

                                                          1985

Julia

[Julia Pastrana was a mid-nineteenth-century singer and dancer in the
circus who was billed as "The Ugliest Woman in the World," or sometimes
"The Lion Lady." She was a Mexican Indian who had been born with facial
deformities and with long hair growing from all over her body, including
her face. In an effort to maintain control over her professional life, her
manager persuaded her to marry him, and she expressed her belief that he
was actually in love with her. She bore him a son, who lived for only six
hours and had inherited his mother's physical appearance. She died three
days later. Her husband, unwilling to forfeit his financial investment, had
Julia and her infant boy stuffed, mounted, and put on display in a case
made of wood and glass. As recently as 1975, Julia Pastrana and her baby
were exhibited in Europe and in the United States.]

Tell me it was just a dream,
my husband, a clever trick
made by some tin-faced village god
or ghost coyote, to frighten me
with his claim that our marriage is made   5
of malice and money.
Oh tell me again
how you admire my hands,
how my jasmine tea is rich and strong,
my singing sweet, my eyes so dark   10
you would lose yourself swimming
man into fish
as you mapped the pond
you would own.
That was not all.   15
The room grew cold
as if to joke
with these warm days;
the curtains blew out
and fell back   20
against the moon-painted sill.

I rose from my bed like a spirit
and, not a spirit at all, floated slowly
to my great glass oval
to see myself reflected   25
as the burnished bronze woman
skin smooth and tender
I know myself to be
in the dark
above the confusion   30
of French perfumes
and I was there in the mirror
and I was not.

I had become hard
as the temple stones   35
of O'tomi,[1] hair grown over my ancient face
like black moss, gray as jungle fog
soaking green the tallest tree tops.
I was frail
as the breaking dry branches   40
of my winter sand canyons,
standing so still as if
to stand forever.

Oh such a small room!
No bigger than my elbows outstretched   45
and just as tall as my head.
A small room from which to sing
open the doors
with my cold graceful mouth,
my rigid lips, my silences   50
dead as yesterday,
cruel as the children
and cold as the coins
that glitter
in your pink fist.   55

And another magic
in the cold
of that small room:
in my arms
or standing near me   60
on a tall table
by my right side:

---

[1]An Indian tribe in east central Mexico.

a tiny doll
that looked
like me.   65

Oh my husband
tell me again
this is only a dream
I wake from warm
and today is still today,   70
summer sun and quick rain;
tell me, husband, how you love me
for my self one more time.
It scares me so
to be with child,   75
lioness
with cub.

                                                             1985

George C. Wolfe
b. 1954

George C. Wolfe's career as a playwright, producer, and director has significantly redefined American theater by introducing more complex representations of African Americans to the stage. He was born in Frankfort, Kentucky, and raised in a middle-class home with a father who worked as a clerk at Kentucky State University and a mother who was a schoolteacher (with a doctorate from Miami University). Although he lived in a segregated community, it was full of committed adults who, along with his family, instilled in him a deep sense of pride about African American history and culture. Although Wolfe enjoyed a charmed childhood, he insists that his neighborhood and school trained his generation to be "integration warriors" prepared for battle. Much of his work considers the peculiar way in which black culture is central to, yet outside of, American culture.

Wolfe moved to Claremont, California, to attend Pomona College. After graduation he staged his own plays at the Inner City Cultural Center with the support of founders Bernard Jackson and Josie Dotson. Wolfe eventually moved to New York, where he enrolled in New York University and earned an MFA in musical theater.

Wolfe's groundbreaking play *The Colored Museum*, first produced at the Crossroads Theatre in New Brunswick, New Jersey, in 1986, examines the joys, contradictions, and pains of African American history, identity, and culture. The show, composed of witty and humorous vignettes, examines solemn topics such as slavery, integration, teen pregnancy, homosexuality, and racial stereotypes.

The Colored Museum also ruthlessly parodies two African American theatrical icons: Lorriane Hansberry's *A Raisin in the Sun* and Ntozake Shange's *For Colored Girls Who Have Considered Suicide When the Rainbow Is Enuf*. It was clear to audiences and critics alike that Wolfe possessed a bold theatrical sensibility and a fondness for questioning the sacred elements of black culture as well as the cruelties of American racism. The father of contemporary African American satirical theater, Wolfe is credited with influencing the work of a younger generation of irreverent provocative playwrights such as Robert O'Hara, Branden-Jacobs Jenkins, and Young Jean Lee.

Wolfe has collaborated with the most innovative dramatists working on Broadway and has had a hand in some of the most significant productions for more than two decades. His credits include directing Tony Kushner's *Angels in America: Millennium Approaches* and *Perestroika*, considered the most significant play about the AIDS crisis (Tony Award, Drama Desk Award, Pulitzer Prize), as well as Kushner's musical *Caroline, or Change*, which explores the relationship between blacks and Jews in the segregated South. Wolfe also directed the Pulitzer Prize–winning production of Suzan-Lori Parks's enigmatic *Topdog/Underdog*, as well as award-winning one-woman shows by Anna Deavere Smith (*Twilight Los Angeles, 1992*) and Elaine Stritch (*Elaine Stritch: At Liberty*).

Although Wolfe has directed some of the most critically acclaimed shows on Broadway, he continues to create his own work. He wrote the book for and directed *Jelly's Last Jam*, a musical about ragtime pianist Jelly Roll Morton, which garnered eleven Tony Awards nominations and won three. He also conceived the musical *Bring in da Noise, Bring in da Funk*, which renders the black experience from the middle passage to the present in music and dance; it earned Wolfe another Tony Award for best direction. Both shows possess Wolfe's resplendent energy and narrative focus on the profound contributions African American have made to American culture.

As the producer of the Public Theater/New York Shakespeare Festival from 1993 to 2005, Wolfe was responsible for several critically acclaimed productions, including *Mother Courage and Her Children*, *The Caucasian Chalk Circle*, *This Is How It Goes*, and *Radiant Baby*, a musical about the life of artist Keith Haring. Besides his substantial contributions to American theater, Wolfe has directed for film and television, including the adaptation of *The Colored Museum* and Anna Deavere Smith's *Fires in the Mirror*, as well as Ruben Santiago Hudson's *Lackawanna Blues* and the feature film *Nights in Rodanthe*.

Despite his prolific career, *The Colored Museum* continues to be Wolfe's signature piece. When asked in 2011 if he ever wanted to quit working in theater, Wolfe replied that no because theater is "a place where intellect and passion and heart can live for me and there are not a lot of places where that can happen."

Lisa B. Thompson
State University of New York at Albany

PRIMARY WORKS

The Colored Museum, 1986; *Spunk* (adaptation of Zora Neale Hurston stories), 1989; *Jelly's Last Jam*, 1991; *Bring in da Noise, Bring in da Funk*, 1996; *The Wild Party* (coauthor of musical's book), 2000; *Harlem Song*, 2002.

The Colored Museum

THE CAST: *An ensemble of five, two men and three women, all black, who perform all the characters that inhabit the exhibits.**

THE STAGE: *White walls and recessed lighting. A starkness befitting a museum where the myths and madness of black/Negro/colored Americans are stored.*

Built into the walls are a series of small panels, doors, revolving walls, and compartments from which actors can retrieve key props and make quick entrances.

A revolve is used, which allows for quick transitions from one exhibit to the next.

MUSIC: *All of the music for the show should be pre-recorded. Only the drummer, who is used in* Git on Board, *and then later in* Permutations *and* The Party, *is live.*

THERE IS NO INTERMISSION

THE EXHIBITS

Git on Board
Cookin' with Aunt Ethel
The Photo Session
Soldier with a Secret
The Gospel according to Miss Roj
The Hairpiece
The Last Mama-on-the-Couch Play
Symbiosis
Lala's Opening
Permutations
The Party

CHARACTERS

Git on Board
  MISS PAT

Cookin' with Aunt Ethel
  AUNT ETHEL

The Photo Session
  GIRL
  GUY

Soldier with a Secret
  JUNIE ROBINSON

---

*A LITTLE GIRL, seven to twelve years old, is needed for a walk-on part in *Lala's Opening*.

The Gospel According to Miss Roj
   MISS ROJ
   WAITER

The Hairpiece
   THE WOMAN
   JANINE
   LA WANDA

The Last Mama-on-the-Couch Play
   NARRATOR
   MAMA
   WALTER-LEE-BEAU-WILLIE-JONES
   LADY IN PLAID
   MEDEA JONES

Symbiosis
   THE MAN
   THE KID

Lala's Opening
   LALA LAMAZING GRACE
   ADMONIA
   FLO'RANCE
   THE LITTLE GIRL

Permutations
   NORMAL JEAN REYNOLDS

The Party
   TOPSY WASHINGTON
   MISS PAT
   MISS ROJ
   LALA LAMAZING GRACE
   THE MAN (*from Symbiosis*)

Git on Board

(*Blackness. Cut by drums pounding. Then slides, rapidly flashing before us. Images we've all seen before, of African slaves being captured, loaded onto ships, tortured. The images flash, flash, flash. The drums crescendo. Blackout. And then lights reveal* MISS PAT, *frozen. She is black, pert, and cute. She has a flip to her hair and wears a hot pink mini-skirt stewardess uniform.*)

(She stands in front of a curtain which separates her from an offstage cockpit.)
(An electronic bell goes "ding" and MISS PAT *comes to life, presenting herself in a friendly but rehearsed manner, smiling and speaking as she has done so many times before.)*

MISS PAT: Welcome aboard Celebrity Slaveship, departing the Gold Coast and making short stops at Bahia, Port Au Prince, and Havana, before our final destination of Savannah.

Hi. I'm Miss Pat and I'll be serving you here in Cabin A. We will be crossing the Atlantic at an altitude that's pretty high, so you must wear your shackles at all times.

(She removes a shackle from the overhead compartment and demonstrates.)

To put on your shackle, take the right hand and close the metal ring around your left hand like so. Repeat the action using your left hand to secure the right. If you have any trouble bonding yourself, I'd be more than glad to assist.

Once we reach the desired altitude, the captain will turn off the "Fasten Your Shackle" sign ... (she efficiently points out the "FASTEN YOUR SHACKLE" signs on either side of her, which light up.) ... allowing you a chance to stretch and dance in the aisles a bit. But otherwise, shackles must be worn at all times.

(The "Fasten Your Shackles" signs go off.)

MISS PAT: Also, we ask that you please refrain from call-and-response singing between cabins as that sort of thing can lead to rebellion. And, of course, no drums are allowed on board. Can you repeat after me, "No drums." *(She gets the audience to repeat.)* With a little more enthusiasm, please. "No drums." *(After the audience repeats it.)* That was great!

Once we're airborn, I'll be by with magazines, and earphones can be purchased for the price of your first-born male.

If there's anything I can do to make this middle passage more pleasant, press the little button overhead and I'll be with you faster than you can say, "Go down, Moses." *(She laughs at her "little joke.")* Thanks for flying Celebrity and here's hoping you have a pleasant takeoff.

(The engines surge, the "Fasten Your Shackle" signs go on, and over-articulate Muzak voices are heard singing as MISS PAT *pulls down a bucket seat and "shackles-up" for takeoff.)*

VOICES:
> *GET ON BOARD CELEBRITY SLAVESHIP*
> *GET ON BOARD CELEBRITY SLAVESHIP*
> *GET ON BOARD CELEBRITY SLAVESHIP*
> *THERE'S ROOM FOR MANY A MORE*

(The engines reach an even, steady hum. Just as MISS PAT *rises and replaces the shackles in the overhead compartment, the faint sound of African drumming is heard.)*

MISS PAT: Hi. Miss Pat again. I'm sorry to disturb you, but someone is playing drums. And what did we just say . . . "No drums." It must be someone in coach. But we here in cabin A are not going to respond to those drums. As a matter of fact, we don't even hear them. Repeat after me. "I don't hear any drums." (*The audience repeats.*) And "I will not rebel."

(*The audience repeats. The drumming grows.*)

MISS PAT: (*Placating*) OK, now I realize some of us are a bit edgy after hearing about the tragedy on board The Laughing Mary, but let me assure you Celebrity has no intention of throwing you overboard and collecting the insurance. We value you!

(*She proceeds to single out individual passengers/audience members.*)

Why the songs *you* are going to sing in the cotton fields, under the burning heat and stinging lash, will metamorphose and give birth to the likes of James Brown and the Fabulous Flames. And you, yes *you*, are going to come up with some of the best dances. The best dances! The Watusi! The Funky Chicken! And just think of what *you* are going to mean to William Faulkner.

All right, so you're gonna have to suffer for a few hundred years, but from your pain will come a culture so complex. *And*, with this little item here . . . (*She removes a basketball from the overhead compartment.*) . . . you'll become millionares!

(*There is a roar of thunder. The lights quiver and the "Fasten Your Shackle" signs begin to flash.* MISS PAT *quickly replaces the basketball in the overhead compartment and speaks very reassuringly.*)

MISS PAT: No, don't panic. We're just caught in a little thunder storm. Now the only way you're going to make it through is if you abandon your God and worship a new one. So, on the count of three, let's all sing. One, two, three . . .

> *NOBODY KNOWS DE TROUBLE I SEEN*

Oh, I forgot to mention, when singing, omit the T-H sound. "The" becomes "de." "They" becomes "dey." Got it? Good!

> *NOBODY KNOWS . . .*
> *NOBODY KNOWS . . .*

Oh, so you don't like that one? Well then let's try another—

> *SUMMER TIME*
> *AND DE LIVIN' IS EASY*

Gershwin. He comes from another oppressed people so he understands.

> *FISH ARE JUMPIN' . . . come on.*
> *AND DE COTTON IS HIGH.*
> *AND DE COTTON IS . . . Sing, damnit!*

(*Lights begin to flash, the engines surge, and there is wild drumming.* MISS PAT *sticks her head through the curtain and speaks with an offstage* CAPTAIN.)

MISS PAT: What?

VOICE OF CAPTAIN (O.S.): Time warp!

MISS PAT: Time warp! (*She turns to the audience and puts on a pleasant face.*) The Captain has assured me everything is fine. We're just caught in a little time warp. (*Trying to fight her growing hysteria.*) On your right you will see the American Revolution, which will give the U.S. of A. exclusive rights to your life. And on your left, the Civil War, which means you will vote Republican until F.D.R. comes along. And now we're passing over the Great Depression, which means everybody gets to live the way you've been living. (*There is a blinding flash of light, and an explosion. She screams.*) Ahhhhhhhh! That was World War I, which is not to be confused with World War II . . . (*There is a larger flash of light, and another explosion.*) . . . Ahhhhh! Which is not to be confused with the Korean War or the Vietnam War, all of which you will play a major role in.

Oh, look, now we're passing over the sixties. Martha and the Vandellas . . . "Julia" with Miss Diahann Carroll . . . Malcom X . . . those five little girls in Alabama . . . Martin Luther King . . . Oh no! The Supremes broke up! (*The drumming intensifies.*) Stop playing those drums! Those drums will be confiscated once we reach Savannah. You can't change history! You can't turn back the clock! (*To the audience.*) Repeat after me, I don't hear any drums! I will not rebel! I will not rebel! I will not re—

(*The lights go out, she screams, and the sound of a plane landing and screeching to a halt is heard. After a beat, lights reveal a wasted, disheveled MISS PAT, but perky nonetheless.*)

MISS PAT: Hi. Miss Pat here. Things got a bit jumpy back there, but the Captain has just informed me we have safely landed in Savannah. Please check the overhead before exiting as any baggage you don't claim, we trash.

It's been fun, and we hope the next time you consider travel, it's with Celebrity.

(*Luggage begins to revolve onstage from offstage left, going past MISS PAT and revolving offstage right. Mixed in with the luggage are two male slaves and a woman slave, complete with luggage and I.D. tags around their necks.*)

MISS PAT: (*With routine, rehearsed pleasantness.*)
Have a nice day. Bye bye.
Button up that coat, it's kind of chilly.
Have a nice day. Bye bye.
You take care now.
See you.
Have a nice day.
Have a nice day.
Have a nice day.

Cookin' with Aunt Ethel

(As the slaves begin to revolve off, a low-down gut-bucket blues is heard. AUNT
ETHEL, *a down-home black woman with a bandana on her head, revolves to center stage. She stands behind a big black pot and wears a reassuring grin.)*

AUNT ETHEL: Welcome to "Aunt Ethel's Down-Home Cookin' Show," where we
explores the magic and mysteries of colored cuisine.

Today, we gonna be servin' ourselves up some … *(She laughs.)* I'm not
gonna tell you. That's right! I'm not gonna tell you what it is till after you
done cooked it. Child, on "The Aunt Ethel Show" we loves to have ourselves some fun. Well, are you ready? Here goes.

*(She belts out a hard-drivin' blues and throws invisible ingredients into the big,
black pot.)*

>   FIRST YA ADD A PINCH OF STYLE
>   AND THEN A DASH OF FLAIR
>   NOW YA STIR IN SOME PREOCCUPATION
>   WITH THE TEXTURE OF YOUR HAIR
>   NEXT YA ADD ALL KINDS OF RHYTHMS
>   LOTS OF FEELINGS AND PIZAZZ
>   THEN HUNNY THROW IN SOME RAGE
>   TILL IT CONGEALS AND TURNS TO JAZZ
>   NOW YOU COOKIN'
>   COOKIN' WITH AUNT ETHEL
>   YOU REALLY COOKIN'
>   COOKIN' WITH AUNT ETHEL, OH YEAH
>   NOW YA ADD A HEAP OF SURVIVAL
>   AND HUMILITY, JUST A TOUCH
>   ADD SOME ATTITUDE
>   OOPS! I PUT TOO MUCH
>   AND NOW A WHOLE LOT OF HUMOR
>   SALTY LANGUAGE, MIXED WITH SADNESS
>   THEN THROW IN A BOX OF BLUES
>   AND SIMMER TO MADNESS
>   NOW YOU COOKIN'
>   COOKIN' WITH AUNT ETHEL, OH YEAH!
>   NOW YOU BEAT IT—REALLY WORK IT
>   DISCARD AND DISOWN
>   AND IN A FEW HUNDRED YEARS
>   ONCE IT'S AGED AND FULLY GROWN
>   YA PUT IT IN THE OVEN
>   TILL IT'S BLACK
>   AND HAS A SHEEN
>   OR TILL IT'S NICE AND YELLA
>   OR ANY SHADE IN BETWEEN

> *NEXT YA TAKE 'EM OUT AND COOL 'EM*
> *'CAUSE THEY NO FUN WHEN THEY HOT*
> *AND WON'T YOU BE SURPRISED*
> *AT THE CONCOCTION YOU GOT*
> *YOU HAVE BAKED*
> *BAKED YOURSELF A BATCH OF NEGROES*
> *YES YOU HAVE BAKED YOURSELF*
> *BAKED YOURSELF A BATCH OF NEGROES*

(*She pulls from the pot a handful of Negroes, black dolls.*)

But don't ask me what to do with 'em now that you got 'em, 'cause child, that's your problem. (*She throws the dolls back into the pot.*) But in any case, yaw be sure to join Aunt Ethel next week, when we gonna be servin' ourselves up some chitlin quiche ... some grits-under-glass,

> *AND A SWEET POTATO PIE*
> *AND YOU'LL BE COOKIN'*
> *COOKIN' WITH AUNT ETHEL*
> *OH YEAH!*

(*On* AUNT ETHEL'S *final rift, lights reveal ...*)

The Photo Session

(*... a very glamorous, gorgeous, black couple, wearing the best of everything and perfect smiles. The stage is bathed in color and bright white light. Disco music with the chant: "We're fabulous" plays in the background. As they pose, larger-than-life images of their perfection are projected on the museum walls. The music quiets and the images fade away as they begin to speak and pose.*)

GIRL: The world was becoming too much for us.

GUY: We couldn't resolve the contradictions of our existence.

GIRL: And we couldn't resolve yesterday's pain.

GUY: So we gave away our life and we now live inside *Ebony Magazine*.

GIRL: Yes, we live inside a world where everyone is beautiful, and wears fabulous clothes.

GUY: And no one says anything profound.

GIRL: Or meaningful.

GUY: Or contradictory.

GIRL: Because no one talks. Everyone just smiles and shows off their cheekbones.

(*They adopt a profile pose.*)

GUY: Last month I was black and fabulous while holding up a bottle of vodka.

GIRL: This month we get to be black and fabulous together.

(*They dance/pose. The "We're fabulous" chant builds and then fades as they start to speak again.*)

GIRL: There are of course setbacks.

GUY: We have to smile like this for a whole month.

GIRL: And we have no social life.

GUY: And no sex.

GIRL: And at times it feels like we're suffocating, like we're not human anymore.

GUY: And everything is rehearsed, including this other kind of pain we're starting to feel.

GIRL: The kind of pain that comes from feeling no pain at all.

(*They then speak and pose with a sudden burst of energy.*)

GUY: But one can't have everything.

GIRL: Can one?

GUY: So if the world is becoming too much for you, do like we did.

GIRL: Give away your life and come be beautiful with us.

GUY: We guarantee, no contradictions.

GIRL/GUY: Smile/click, smile/click, smile/click.

GIRL: And no pain.

(*They adopt a final pose and revolve off as the "We're fabulous" chant plays and fades into the background.*)

A Soldier with a Secret

(*Projected onto the museum walls are the faces of black soldiers—from the Spanish-American thru to the Vietnam War. Lights slowly reveal* JUNIE ROBINSON, *a black combat soldier, posed on an onyx plinth. He comes to life and smiles at the audience. Somewhat dim-witted, he has an easy-going charm about him.*)

JUNIE: Pst. Pst. Guess what? I know the secret. The secret to your pain. 'Course, I didn't always know. First I had to die, then come back to life, 'fore I had the gift.

Ya see the Cappin sent me off up ahead to scout for screamin' yella bastards. 'Course, for the life of me I couldn't understand why they'd be screamin', seein' as how we was tryin' to kill them and they us.

But anyway, I'm off lookin', when all of a sudden I find myself caught smack dead in the middle of this explosion. This blindin', burnin', scaldin' explosion. Musta been a booby trap or something, 'cause all around me is fire. Hell, I'm on fire. Like a piece of chicken dropped in a skillet of cracklin' grease. Why, my flesh was justa peelin' off of my bones.

But then I says to myself, "Junie, if yo' flesh is on fire, how come you don't feel no pain!" And I didn't. I swear as I'm standin' here, I felt nuthin'. That's when I sort of put two and two together and realized I didn't feel no whole lot of hurtin' cause I done died.

Well I just picked myself up and walked right on out of that explosion. Hell, once you know you dead, why keep on dyin', ya know?

So, like I say, I walk right outta that explosion, fully expectin' to see white clouds, Jesus, and my Mama, only all I saw was more war. Shootin' goin' on way off in this direction and that direction. And there, standin' around, was all the guys. Hubert, J.F., the Cappin. I guess the sound of the explosion must of attracted 'em, and they all starin' at me like I'm some kind of ghost.

So I yells to 'em, "Hey there Hubert! Hey there Cappin!" But they just stare. So I tells 'em how I'd died and how I guess it wasn't my time 'cause here I am, "Fully in the flesh and not a scratch to my bones." And they still just stare. So I took to starin' back.

(*The expression on* JUNIE'S *face slowly turns to horror and disbelief.*)

Only what I saw ... well I can't exactly to this day describe it. But I swear, as sure as they was wearin' green and holdin' guns, they was each wearin' a piece of the future on their faces.

Yeah. All the hurt that was gonna get done to them and they was gonna do to folks was right there clear as day.

I saw how J.F., once he got back to Chicago, was gonna get shot dead by this po-lice, and I saw how Hubert was gonna start beatin' up on his old lady which I didn't understand, 'cause all he could do was talk on and on about how much he loved her. Each and every one of 'em had pain in his future and blood on his path. And God or the Devil one spoke to me and said, "Junie, these colored boys ain't gonna be the same after this war. They ain't gonna have no kind of happiness."

Well right then and there it come to me. The secret to their pain.

Late that night, after the medics done checked me over and found me fit for fightin', after everybody done settle down for the night, I sneaked over to where Hubert was sleepin', and with a needle I stole from the medics ... pst, pst ... I shot a little air into his veins. The second he died, all the hurtin-to-come just left his face.

Two weeks later I got J.F. and after that Woodrow ... Jimmy Joe ... I even spent all night waitin' by the latrine 'cause I knew the Cappin always made a late night visit and pst ... pst ... I got him.

(*Smiling, quite proud of himself.*) That's how come I died and come back to life. 'Cause just like Jesus went around healin' the sick, I'm supposed to go around healin' the hurtin' all these colored boys wearin' from the war.

Pst, pst. I know the secret. The secret to your pain. The secret to yours, and yours. Pst. Pst. Pst. Pst.

(*The lights slowly fade.*)

The Gospel According to Miss Roj

(*The darkness is cut by electronic music. Cold, pounding, unrelenting. A neon sign which spells out* THE BOTTOMLESS PIT *clicks on. There is a lone bar stool. Lights flash on and off, pulsating to the beat. There is a blast of smoke and, from the haze,* MISS ROJ *appears. He is dressed in striped patio pants, white go-go boots, a halter, and cat-shaped sunglasses. What would seem ridiculous on any-one else,* MISS ROJ *wears as if it were high fashion. He carries himself with total elegance and absolute arrogance.)*

MISS ROJ: God created black people and black people created style. The name's Miss Roj ... that's R.O.J. thank you and you can find me every Wednes-day, Friday and Saturday nights at "The Bottomless Pit," the watering hole for the wild and weary which asks the question, "Is there life after Jherri-curl?"

(A waiter enters, hands MISS ROJ *a drink, and then exits.)*

Thanks, doll. *Yes,* if they be black and swish, the B.P. has seen them, which is not to suggest the Pit is lacking in cultural diversity. Oh no. There are your dinge queens, white men who like their chicken legs dark. *(He winks/flirts with a man in the audience.)* And let's not forget, "Los Muchachos de la Neighborhood." But the speciality of the house is The Snap Queens. *(He snaps his fingers.)* We are a rare breed.

For, you see, when something strikes our fancy, when the truth comes piercing through the dark, well you just can't let it pass unnoticed. No darling. You must pronounce it with a snap. *(He snaps.)*

Snapping comes from another galaxy, as do all snap queens. That's right. I ain't just your regular oppressed American Negro. No-no-no! I am an extra-terrestial. And I ain't talkin' none of that shit you seen in the movies! I have real power.

(The waiter enters. MISS ROJ *stops him.)*

Speaking of no power, will you please tell Miss Stingy-with-the-rum, that if MISS ROJ had wanted to remain sober, she could have stayed home and drank Kool-aid. *(He snaps.)* Thank you.

(The waiter exits. MISS ROJ *crosses and sits on bar stool.)*

Yes, I was placed here on Earth to study the life habits of a deteriorating society, and child when we talkin' New York City, we are discussing the Queen of Deterioration. Miss New York is doing a slow dance with death, and I am here to warn you all, but before I do, I must know ... don't you just love my patio pants? Annette Funicello immortalized them in "Beach Blanket Bingo," and I have continued the legacy. And my go-gos? I realize white after Labor Day is very gauche, but as the saying goes, if you've got it flaunt it, if you don't, front it and snap to death any bastard who dares to defy you. *(Laughing)* Oh ho! My demons are showing. Yes, my demons live at the bottom of my Bacardi and Coke.

Let's just hope for all concerned I dance my demons out before I drink them out 'cause child, dancing demons take you on a ride, but those drin-kin' demons just take you, and you find yourself doing the strangest things. Like the time I locked my father in the broom closet. Seems the liquor made his tongue real liberal and he decided he was gonna baptize me with the word "faggot" over and over. Well, he's just going on and on with "faggot this" and "faggot that," all the while walking toward the broom closet to piss. So the demons just took hold of my wedges and forced me to kick the drunk son-of-a-bitch into the closet and lock the door. (*Laughter*) Three days later I remembered he was there. (*He snaps.*)

(*The waiter enters.* MISS ROJ *takes a drink and downs it.*)

Another!

(*The waiter exits.*)

(*Dancing about*) Oh yes-yes-yes! Miss Roj is quintessential style. I corn row the hairs on my legs so that they spell out M.I.S.S. R.O.J. And I dare any bastard to fuck with me because I will snap your ass into oblivion.

I have the power, you know. Everytime I snap, I steal one beat of your heart. So if you find yourself gasping for air in the middle of the night, chances are you fucked with Miss Roj and she didn't like it.

Like the time this asshole at Jones Beach decided to take issue with my coulotte-sailor ensemble. This child, this muscle-bound Brooklyn thug in a skin-tight bikini, very skin-tight so the whole world can see that instead of a brain, God gave him an extra thick piece of sausage. You know the kind who beat up on their wives for breakfast. Snap your fingers if you know what I'm talking about ... come on and snap, child. (*He gets the audience to snap.*) Well, he decided to blurt out when I walked by, "Hey look at da monkey coon in da faggit suit." Well, I walked up to the poor dear, very calmly lifted my hand, and.... (*He snaps in rapid succession.*) A heart attack, right there on the beach. (*He singles out someone in the audience.*) You don't believe it? Cross me! Come on! Come on!

(*The waiter enters, hands* MISS ROJ *a drink.* MISS ROJ *downs it. The waiter exits.*)

(*Looking around.*) If this place is the answer, we're asking all the wrong questions. The only reason I come here is to communicate with my origins. The flashing lights are signals from my planet way out there. Yes, girl, even further than Flatbush. We're talking another galaxy. The flashing lights tell me how much time is left before the end.

(*Very drunk and loud by now.*) I hate the people here. I hate the drinks. But most of all I hate this goddamn music. That ain't music. Give me Aretha Franklin any day. (*Singing*) "Just a little respect. R.E.S.P.E.C.T." Yeah! Yeah!

Come on and dance your last dance with Miss Roj. Last call is but a drink away and each snap puts you one step closer to the end.

A high-rise goes up. You can't get no job. Come on everybody and dance. A whole race of people gets trashed and debased. Snap those fingers and dance. Some sick bitch throws her baby out the window 'cause she thinks it's the Devil. Everybody snap! *The New York Post.* Snap!

Snap for every time you walk past someone lying in the street, smelling like frozen piss and shit and you don't see it. Snap for every crazed bastard who kills himself so as to get the jump on being killed. And snap for every sick muthafucker who, bored with carrying around his fear, takes to shooting up other people.

Yeah, snap your fingers and dance with Miss Roj. But don't be fooled by the banners and balloons 'cause, child, this ain't no party going on. Hell no! It's a wake. And the casket's made out of stone, steel, and glass and the people are racing all over the pavement like maggots on a dead piece of meat.

Yeah, dance! But don't be surprised if there ain't no beat holding you together 'cause we traded in our drums for respectability. So now it's just words. Words rappin'. Words screechin'. Words flowin' instead of blood 'cause you know that don't work. Words cracklin' instead of fire 'cause by the time a match is struck on 125th Street and you run to mid-town, the flame has been blown away.

So come on and dance with Miss Roj and her demons. We don't ask for acceptance. We don't ask for approval. We know who we are and we move on it!

I guarantee you will never hear two fingers put together in a snap and not think of Miss Roj. That's power, baby. Patio pants and all.

(*The lights begin to flash in rapid succession.*)

So let's dance! And snap! And dance! And snap!

(MISS ROJ *begins to dance as if driven by his demons. There is a blast of smoke and when the haze settles,* MISS ROJ *has revolved off and in place of him is a recording of Aretha Franklin singing "Respect."*)

The Hairpiece

(*As "Respect" fades into the background, a vanity revolves to center stage. On this vanity are two wigs, an Afro wig, circa 1968, and a long, flowing wig, both resting on wig stands. A black* WOMAN *enters, her head and body wrapped in towels. She picks up a framed picture and after a few moments of hesitation, throws it into a small trash can. She then removes one of her towels to reveal a totally bald head. Looking into a mirror on the "fourth wall," she begins applying makeup.*)

(*The wig stand holding the Afro wig opens her eyes. Her name is* JANINE. *She stares in disbelief at the bald woman.*)

JANINE: (*Calling to the other wig stand.*) LaWanda. LaWanda girl, wake up.

(*The other wig stand, the one with the long, flowing wig, opens her eyes. Her name is* LAWANDA.)

LAWANDA: What? What is it?

JANINE: Check out girlfriend.

LAWANDA: Oh, girl, I don't believe it.

JANINE: (*Laughing*) Just look at the poor thing, trying to paint some life onto that face of hers. You'd think by now she'd realize it's the hair. It's all about the hair.

LAWANDA: What hair! She ain't go no hair! She done fried, dyed, de-chemical-ized her shit to death.

JANINE: And all that's left is that buck-naked scalp of hers, sittin' up there apologizin' for being odd-shaped and ugly.

LAWANDA: (*Laughing with* JANINE.) Girl, stop!

JANINE: I ain't sayin' nuthin' but the truth.

LAWANDA/JANINE: The bitch is bald! (*They laugh.*)

JANINE: And all over some man.

LAWANDA: I tell ya, girl, I just don't understand it. I mean, look at her. She's got a right nice face, a good head on her shoulders. A good job even. And she's got to go fall in love with that fool.

JANINE: That political quick-change artist. Everytime the nigga went and changed his ideology, she went and changed her hair to fit the occasion.

LAWANDA: Well at least she's breaking up with him.

JANINE: Hunny, no!

LAWANDA: Yes child.

JANINE: Oh, girl, dish me the dirt!

LAWANDA: Well, you see, I heard her on the phone, talking to one of her girl-friends, and she's meeting him for lunch today to give him the ax.

JANINE: Well it's about time.

LAWANDA: I hear ya. But don't you worry 'bout a thing, girlfriend. I'm gonna tell you all about it.

JANINE: Hunny, you won't have to tell me a damn thing 'cause I'm gonna be there, front row, center.

LAWANDA: You?

JANINE: Yes, child, she's wearing me to lunch.

LAWANDA: (*Outraged*) I don't think so!

JANINE: (*With an attitude*) What do you mean, you don't think so?

LAWANDA: Exactly what I said, "I don't think so." Damn, Janine, get real. How the hell she gonna wear both of us?

JANINE: She ain't wearing both of us. She's wearing me.

LAWANDA: Says who?

JANINE: Says me! Says her! Ain't that right, girlfriend?

(*The* WOMAN *stops putting on makeup, looks around, sees no one, and goes back to her makeup.*)

JANINE: I said, ain't that right!

(*The* WOMAN *picks up the phone.*)

WOMAN: Hello ... hello ...

JANINE: Did you hear the damn phone ring?

WOMAN: No.

JANINE: Then put the damn phone down and talk to me.

WOMAN: I ah ... don't understand.

JANINE: It ain't deep so don't panic. Now, you're having lunch with your boyfriend, right?

WOMAN: (*Breaking into tears.*) I think I'm having a nervous breakdown.

JANINE: (*Impatient*) I said you're having lunch with your boyfriend, right!

WOMAN: (*Scared, pulling herself together.*) Yes, right ... right.

JANINE: To break up with him.

WOMAN: How did you know that?

LAWANDA: I told her.

WOMAN: (*Stands and screams.*) Help! Help!

JANINE: Sit down. I said sit your ass down!

(*The* WOMAN *does.*)

JANINE: Now set her straight and tell her you're wearing me.

LAWANDA: She's the one that needs to be set straight, so go on and tell her you're wearing me.

JANINE: No, tell her you're wearing me.

(*There is a pause.*)

LAWANDA: Well?

JANINE: Well?

WOMAN: I ah ... actually hadn't made up my mind.

JANINE: (*Going off*) What do you mean you ain't made up you mind! After all that fool has put you through, you gonna need all the attitude you can get and there is nothing like attitude and a healthy head of kinks to make his shit shrivel like it should!

That's right! When you wearin' me, you lettin' him know he ain't gonna get no sweet-talkin' comb through your love without some serious resistance. No-no! The kink of my head is like the kink of your heart and neither is about to be hot-pressed into surrender.

LAWANDA: That shit is so tired. The last time attitude worked on anybody was 1968. Janine girl, you need to get over it and get on with it. (*To the* WOMAN.) And you need to give the nigga a goodbye he will never forget.

I say give him hysteria! Give him emotion! Give him rage! And there is nothing like a toss of the tresses to make your emotional outburst shine with emotional flair.

You can toss me back, shake me from side to side, all the while screaming, "I want you out of my life forever!!!" And not only will I come bouncing back for more, but you just might win an Academy Award for best performance by a head of hair in a dramatic role.

JANINE: Miss hunny, please! She don't need no Barbie doll dipped in chocolate telling her what to do. She needs a head of hair that's coming from a fo' real place.

LAWANDA: Don't you dare talk about nobody coming from a "fo' real place," Miss Made-in-Taiwan!

JANINE: Hey! I ain't ashamed of where I come from. Besides, it don't matter where you come from as long as you end up in the right place.

LAWANDA: And it don't matter the grade as long as the point gets made. So go on and tell her you're wearing me.

JANINE: No, tell her you're wearing me.

(*The* WOMAN, *unable to take it, begins to bite off her fake nails, as* LAWANDA *and* JANINE *go at each other.*)

LA WANDA:

Set the bitch straight. Let her know there is no way she could even begin to compete with me. I am quality. She is kink. I am exotic. She is common. I am class and she is trash. That's right. T.R.A.S.H. We're talking three strikes and you're out. So go on and tell her you're wearing me. Go on, tell her! Tell her! Tell her!

JANINE:

Who you callin' a bitch? Why, if I had hands I'd knock you clear into next week. You think you cute. She thinks she's cute just 'cause that synthetic mop of hers blows in the wind. She looks like a fool and you look like an even bigger fool when you wear her, so go on and tell her you're wearing me. Go on, tell her! Tell her! Tell her!

(*The* WOMAN *screams and pulls the two wigs off the wig stands as the lights go to black on three bald heads.*)

The Last Mama-on-the-Couch Play

(*A* NARRATOR, *dressed in a black tuxedo, enters through the audience and stands center stage. He is totally solemn.*)

NARRATOR: We are pleased to bring you yet another Mama-on-the-Couch play. A searing domestic drama that tears at the very fabric of racist America. (*He crosses upstage center and sits on a stool and reads from a playscript.*) Act One. Scene One.

(MAMA *revolves on stage left, sitting on a couch reading a large, oversized Bible. A window is placed stage right.* MAMA'S *dress, the couch, and drapes are made from the same material. A doormat lays down center.*)

NARRATOR: Lights up on a dreary, depressing, but with middle-class aspirations tenement slum. There is a couch, with a Mama on it. Both are well worn. There is a picture of Jesus on the wall ... (*A picture of Jesus is instantly revealed*) ... and a window which looks onto an abandoned tenement. It is late spring.

Enter Walter-Lee-Beau-Willie-Jones (SON *enters through the audience.*) He is Mama's thirty-year-old son. His brow is heavy from three hundred years of oppression.

MAMA: (*Looking up from her Bible, speaking in a slow manner.*) Son, did you wipe your feet?

SON: (*An ever-erupting volcano.*) No, Mama, I didn't wipe my feet! Out there, every day, Mama is the Man. The Man Mama. Mr. Charlie! Mr. Bossman! And he's wipin' his feet on me. On me, Mama, every damn day of my life. Ain't that enough for me to deal with? Ain't that enough?

MAMA: Son, wipe your feet.

SON: I wanna dream. I wanna be somebody. I wanna take charge of my life.

MAMA: You can do all of that, but first you got to wipe your feet.

SON: (*As he crosses to the mat, mumbling and wiping his feet.*) Wipe my feet ... wipe my feet.... wipe my feet ...

MAMA: That's a good boy.

SON: (*Exploding*) Boy! Boy! I don't wanna be nobody's good boy, Mama. I wanna be my own man!

MAMA: I know son, I know. God will show the way.

SON: God, Mama! Since when did your God ever do a damn thing for the black man. Huh, Mama, huh? You tell me. When did your God ever help me?

MAMA: (*Removing her wire-rim glasses.*) Son, come here.

(SON *crosses to* MAMA, *who slowly stands and in a exaggerated stage slap, backhands* SON *clear across the stage. The* NARRATOR *claps his hands to create the sound for the slap.* MAMA *then lifts her clinched fists to the heavens.*)

MAMA: Not in my house, my house, will you ever talk that way again!

(*The* NARRATOR, *so moved by her performance, erupts in applause and encourages the audience to do so.*)

NARRATOR: Beautiful. Just stunning.

(*He reaches into one of the secret compartments of the set and gets an award which he ceremoniously gives to* MAMA *for her performance. She bows and then returns to the couch.*)

NARRATOR: Enter Walter-Lee-Beau-Willie's wife, The Lady in Plaid.

(*Music from nowhere is heard, a jazzy pseudo-abstract intro as the* LADY IN PLAID *dances in through the audience, wipes her feet, and then twirls about.*)

LADY:

> She was a creature of regal beauty
> who in ancient time graced the temples of the Nile
> with her womanliness
> But here she was, stuck being colored
> and a woman in a world that valued neither.

SON: You cooked my dinner?

LADY: (*Oblivious to* SON.)

> Feet flat, back broke,
> she looked at the man who, though he be thirty,
> still ain't got his own apartment.
> Yeah, he's still livin' with his Mama!
> And she asked herself, was this the life
> for a Princess Colored, who by the
> translucence of her skin, knew the
> universe was her sister.

(*The* LADY IN PLAID *twirls and dances.*)

SON: (*Becoming irate.*) I've had a hard day of dealin' with the Man. Where's my damn dinner? Woman, stand still when I'm talkin' to you!

LADY:
> And she cried for her sisters in Detroit
> Who knew, as she, that their souls belonged
> in ancient temples on the Nile.
> And she cried for her sisters in Chicago
> who, like her, their life has become
> one colored hell.

SON: There's only one thing gonna get through to you.

LADY:
> And she cried for her sisters in New Orleans
> And her sisters in Trenton and Birmingham,
> and
> Poughkeepsie and Orlando and Miami Beach
> and
> Las Vegas, Palm Springs.

(*As she continues to call out cities, he crosses offstage and returns with two black dolls and then crosses to the window.*)

SON: Now are you gonna cook me dinner?

LADY: Walter-Lee-Beau-Willie-Jones, no! Not my babies.

(SON *throws them out the window. The* LADY IN PLAID *then lets out a primal scream.*)

LADY: He dropped them!!!!

(*The* NARRATOR *breaks into applause.*)

NARRATOR: Just splendid. Shattering.

(*He thens crosses and after an intense struggle with* MAMA, *he takes the award from her and gives it to the* LADY IN PLAID, *who is still suffering primal pain.*)

LADY: Not my babies ... not my ... (*Upon receiving the award, she instantly recovers.*) Help me up, sugar. (*She then bows and crosses and stands behind the couch.*)

NARRATOR: Enter Medea Jones, Walter-Lee-Beau-Willie's sister.

(MEDEA *moves very ceremoniously, wiping her feet and then speaking and gesturing as if she just escaped from a Greek tragedy.*)

MEDEA:

Ah, see how the sun kneels to speak
her evening vespers, exaulting all
in her vision, even lowly tenement
long abandoned.
Mother, wife of brother, I trust
the approaching darkness finds you
safe in Hestia's busom.
Brother, why wear the face of a man
in anguish. Can the garment of thine
feelings cause the shape of your
countenance to disfigure so?

SON: (*At the end of his rope.*) Leave me alone, Medea.

MEDEA: (*To* MAMA)

Is good brother still going on and on and on
about He and The Man.

MAMA/LADY: What else?

MEDEA:

Ah brother, if with our thoughts and
words we could cast thine oppressors
into the lowest bowels of wretched
hell, would that make us more like the
gods or more like our oppressors.
No, brother, no, do not let thy rage
choke the blood which anoints thy
heart with love. Forgo thine darkened
humor and let love shine on your
soul, like a jewel on a young maiden's hand.
(Dropping to her knees.)
I beseech thee, forgo thine
anger and leave wrath to the gods!

SON: Girl, what has gotten into you.

MEDEA:

Juliard, good brother. For I am no
longer bound by rhythms of race or
region. Oh, no. My speech, like my
pain and suffering, have become
classical and therefore universal.

LADY: I didn't understand a damn thing she said, but girl you usin' them words.

(LADY IN PLAID *crosses and gives* MEDEA *the award and everyone applauds.*)

SON: (*Trying to stop the applause.*) Wait one damn minute! This my play. It's about me and the Man. It ain't got nuthin' to do with no ancient temples on the Nile and it ain't got nuthin' to do with Hestia's busom. And it ain't got nuthin' to do with you slappin' me across no room. (*His gut-wrenching best.*) It's about me. Me and my pain! My pain!

THE VOICE OF THE MAN: Walter-Lee-Beau-Willie, this is the Man. You have been convicted of overacting. Come out with your hands up.

(SON *starts to cross to the window.*)

SON: Well now that does it.

MAMA: Son, no, don't go near that window. Son, no!

(*Gun shots ring out and* SON *falls dead.*)

MAMA: (*Crossing to the body, too emotional for words.*) My son, he was a good boy. Confused. Angry. Just like his father. And his father's father. And his father's father's father. And now he's dead.

(*Seeing she's about to drop to her knees, the* NARRATOR *rushes and places a pillow underneath her just in time.*)

If only he had been born into a world better than this. A world where there are no well-worn couches and no well-worn Mamas and nobody overemotes.

If only he had been born into an all-black musical.

(*A song intro begins.*)

Nobody ever dies in an all-black musical.

(MEDEA *and* LADY IN PLAID *pull out church fans and begin to fan themselves.*)

MAMA: (*Singing a soul-stirring gospel.*)
　　OH WHY COULDN'T HE
　　BE BORN
　　INTO A SHOW WITH LOTS OF SINGING
　　AND DANCING
　　I SAY WHY
　　COULDN'T HE
　　BE BORN

LADY: Go ahead hunny. Take your time.

MAMA:
　　INTO A SHOW WHERE EVERYBODY
　　IS HAPPY

NARRATOR/MEDEA: Preach! Preach!

MAMA:
　　OH WHY COULDN'T HE BE BORN WITH THE CHANCE
　　TO SMILE A LOT AND SING AND DANCE
　　OH WHY

OH WHY
OH WHY
COULDN'T HE
BE BORN
INTO AN ALL-BLACK SHOW
WOAH-WOAH

(*The* CAST *joins in, singing do-wop gospel background to* MAMA'S *lament.*)

OH WHY
COULDN'T HE
BE BORN
(HE BE BORN)
INTO A SHOW WHERE EVERYBODY
IS HAPPY
WHY COULDN'T HE BE BORN WITH THE CHANCE
TO SMILE A LOT AND SING AND DANCE
WANNA KNOW WHY
WANNA KNOW WHY
OH WHY
COULDN'T HE
BE BORN
INTO AN ALL-BLACK SHOW
A-MEN

(*A singing/dancing, spirit-raising revival begins.*)

OH, SON, GET UP
GET UP AND DANCE
WE SAY GET UP
THIS IS YOUR SECOND CHANCE
DON'T SHAKE A FIST
JUST SHAKE A LEG
AND DO THE TWIST
DON'T SCREAM AND BEG
SON SON SON
GET UP AND DANCE
GET
GET UP
GET UP AND
GET UP AND DANCE — ALL RIGHT!
GET UP AND DANCE — ALL RIGHT!
GET UP AND DANCE!

(WALTER-LEE-BEAU-WILLIE *springs to life and joins in the dancing. A foot-stomping, hand-clapping production number takes off, which encompasses a myriad of black-Broadwayesque dancing styles—shifting speeds and styles with exuberant abandonment.*)

MAMA: (*Bluesy*)
> WHY COULDN'T HE BE BORN INTO AN ALL-BLACK SHOW

CAST:
> WITH SINGING AND DANCING

MAMA:
> BLACK SHOW

(MAMA *scats and the dancing becomes manic and just a little too desperate to please.*)

CAST:
> WE GOTTA DANCE
> WE GOTTA DANCE
> GET UP GET UP GET UP AND DANCE
> WE GOTTA DANCE
> WE GOTTA DANCE
> GOTTA DANCE!

(*Just at the point the dancing is about to become violent, the cast freezes and pointedly, simply sings:*)

> IF WE WANT TO LIVE
> WE HAVE GOT TO
> WE HAVE GOT TO
> DANCE . . . AND DANCE . . . AND DANCE . . .

(*As they continue to dance with zombie-like frozen smiles and faces, around them images of coon performers flash as the lights slowly fade.*)

Symbiosis

(*The Temptations singing "My Girl" are heard as lights reveal a* BLACK MAN *in corporate dress standing before a large trash can throwing objects from a Saks Fifth Avenue bag into it. Circling around him with his every emotion on his face is* THE KID, *who is dressed in a late-sixties street style. His moves are slightly heightened. As the scene begins the music fades.*)

MAN: (*With contained emotions.*)
> My first pair of Converse All-stars. Gone.
> My first Afro-comb. Gone.
> My first dashiki. Gone.
> My autographed pictures of Stokley Carmichael, Jomo Kenyatta and Donna Summer. Gone.

KID: (*Near tears, totally upset.*) This shit's not fair man.
> Damn! Hell! Shit! Shit! It's not fair!

MAN: My first jar of Murray's Pomade.

My first can of Afro-sheen.

My first box of curl relaxer. Gone! Gone! Gone!

Eldridge Cleaver's *Soul on Ice.*

KID: Not *Soul on Ice!*

MAN: It's been replaced on my bookshelf by *The Color Purple.*

KID: (*Horrified*) No!

MAN: Gone!

KID: But—

MAN: Jimi Hendrix's "Purple Haze." Gone.

Sly Stone's "There's A Riot Goin' On." Gone.

The Jackson Five's "I Want You Back."

KID: Man, you can't throw that away. It's living proof Michael had a black nose.

MAN: It's all going. Anything and everything that connects me to you, to who I was, to what we were, is out of my life.

KID: You've got to give me another chance.

MAN: *Fingertips Part 2.*

KID: Man, how can you do that? That's vintage Stevie Wonder.

MAN: You want to know how, Kid? You want to know how? Because my survival depends on it. Whether you know it or not, the Ice Age is upon us.

KID: (*Jokingly*) Man, what the hell you talkin' about. It's 95 damn degrees.

MAN: The climate is changing, Kid, and either you adjust or you end up extinct. A sociological dinosaur. Do you understand what I'm trying to tell you? King Kong would have made it to the top if only he had taken the elevator. Instead he brought attention to his struggle and ended up dead.

KID: (*Pleading*) I'll change. I swear I'll change. I'll maintain a low profile. You won't even know I'm around.

MAN: If I'm to become what I'm to become then you've got to go.... I have no history. I have no past.

KID: Just like that?

MAN: (*Throwing away a series of buttons.*) Free Angela! Free Bobby! Free Huey, Duey, and Louie! U.S. out of Viet Nam. U.S. out of Cambodia. U.S. out of Harlem, Detroit, and Newark. Gone! . . . The Temptations Greatest Hits!

KID: (*Grabbing the album.*) No!!!

MAN: Give it back, Kid.

KID: No.

MAN: I said give it back!

KID: No. I can't let you trash this. Johnny man, it contains fourteen classic cuts by the tempting Temptations. We're talking, "Ain't Too Proud to Beg," "Papa Was a Rolling Stone," "My Girl."

MAN: (*Warning*) I don't have all day.

KID: For God's sake, Johnny man, "My Girl" is the jam to end all jams. It's what we are. Who we are. It's a way of life. Come on, man, for old times sake. (*Singing*)

I GOT SUNSHINE ON A CLOUDY DAY
BUM-DA-DUM-DA-DUM-DA-BUM
AND WHEN IT'S COLD OUTSIDE

Come on, Johnny man, you ain't "bummin'," man.

I GOT THE MONTH OF MAY

Here comes your favorite part. Come on, Johnny man, sing.

I GUESS YOU SAY
WHAT CAN MAKE ME FEEL THIS WAY
MY GIRL, MY GIRL, MY GIRL
TALKIN' 'BOUT

MAN: (*Exploding*) I said give it back!

KID: (*Angry*) I ain't givin' you a muthafuckin' thing!

MAN: Now you listen to me!

KID: No, you listen to me. This is the kid you're dealin' with, so don't fuck with me!

(*He hits his fist into his hand, and* THE MAN *grabs for his heart.* THE KID *repeats with two more hits, which causes the man to drop to the ground, grabbing his heart.*)

KID: Jai! Jai! Jai!

MAN: Kid, please.

KID: Yeah. Yeah. Now who's begging who.... Well, well, well, look at Mr. Cream-of-the-Crop, Mr. Colored-Man-on-Top. Now that he's making it, he no longer wants anything to do with the Kid. Well, you may put all kinds of silk ties 'round your neck and white lines up your nose, but the Kid is here to stay. You may change your women as often as you change your underwear, but the Kid is here to stay. And regardless of how much of your past that you trash, I ain't goin' no damn where. Is that clear? Is that clear?

MAN: (*Regaining his strength, beginning to stand.*) Yeah.

KID: Good. (*After a beat.*) You all right man? You all right? I don't want to hurt you, but when you start all that talk about getting rid of me, well, it gets me kind of crazy. We need each other. We are one ...

(*Before* THE KID *can complete his sentence,* THE MAN *grabs him around his neck and starts to choke him violently.*)

MAN: (*As he strangles him.*) The ... Ice ... Age ... is ... upon us ... and either we adjust ... or we end up ... extinct.

(THE KID *hangs limp in* THE MAN'S *arms.*)

MAN: (*Laughing*) Man kills his own rage. Film at eleven. (*He then dumps* THE KID *into the trash can, and closes the lid. He speaks in a contained voice.*) I have no history. I have no past. I can't. It's too much. It's much too much.

I must be able to smile on cue. And watch the news with an impersonal eye. I have no stake in the madness.

Being black is too emotionally taxing; therefore I will be black only on weekends and holidays.

(*He then turns to go, but sees the Temptations album lying on the ground. He picks it up and sings quietly to himself.*)

> I GUESS YOU SAY
> WHAT CAN MAKE ME FEEL THIS WAY

(*He pauses, but then crosses to the trash can, lifts the lid, and just as he is about to toss the album in, a hand reaches from inside the can and grabs hold of* THE MAN's *arm.* THE KID *then emerges from the can with a death grip on* THE MAN's *arm.*)

KID: (*Smiling*) What's happenin'?

BLACKOUT

Lala's Opening

(*Roving follow spots. A timpani drum roll. As we hear the voice of the* AN-NOUNCER, *outrageously glamorous images of* LALA *are projected onto the museum walls.*)

VOICE OF ANNOUNCER: From Rome to Rangoon! Paris to Prague! We are pleased to present the American debut of the one! The only! The breathtaking! The astounding! The stupendous! The incredible! The magnificient! Lala Lamazing Grace!

(*Thunderous applause as* LALA *struts on, the definitive black diva. She has long, flowing hair, an outrageous lamé dress, and an affected French accent which she loses when she's upset.*)

LALA:

> EVERYBODY LOVES LALA
> EVERYBODY LOVES ME
> PARIS! BELIN! LONDON! ROME!
> NO MATTER WHERE I GO
> I ALWAYS FEEL AT HOME
> OHHHH
> EVERYBODY LOVES LALA
> EVERYBODY LOVES ME
> I'M TRES MAGNIFIQUE
> AND OH SO UNIQUE
> AND WHEN IT COMES TO GLAMOUR

I'M CHIC-ER THAN CHIC

(She giggles)

THAT'S WHY EVERYBODY
EVERYBODY
EVERYBODY-EVERYBODY-EVERYBODY
LOVES ME

(She begins to vocally reach for higher and higher notes, until she has to point to her final note. She ends the number with a grand flourish and bows to thunderous applause.)

LALA: Yes, it's me! Lala Lamazing Grace and I have come home. Home to the home I never knew as home. Home to you, my people, my blood, my guts.

My story is a simple one, full of fire, passion, magique. You may ask how did I, a humble girl from the backwoods of Mississippi, come to be the ninth wonder of the modern world. Well, I can't take all of the credit. Part of it goes to him. (She points toward the heavens)

No, not the light man, darling, but God, For, you see, Lala is a star. A very big star. Let us not mince words, I'm a fucking meteorite. (She laughs.) But He is the universe and just like my sister, Aretha la Franklin, Lala's roots are in the black church. (She sings in a showy gospel styled:)

THAT'S WHY EVERYBODY LOVES
SWING LOW SWEET CHARIOT
THAT'S WHY EVERYBODY LOVES
GO DOWN MOSES WAY DOWN IN EGYPT LAND
THAT'S WHY EVERYBODY EVERYBODY LOVES
ME!!!

(Once again she points to her final note and then basks in applause.)

I love that note. I just can't hit it.

Now, before I dazzle you with more of my limitless talent, tell me something, America. (Musical underscoring) Why has it taken you so long to recognize my artistry? Mother France opened her loving arms and Lala came running. All over the world Lala was embraced. But here, ha! You spat at Lala. Was I too exotic? Too much woman, or what?

Diana Ross you embrace. A two-bit nobody from Detroit, of all places. Now, I'm not knocking la Ross.

She does the best she can with the little she has. (She laughs.) But the Paul la Robesons, the James la Baldwins, the Josephine la Bakers, who was my godmother you know. The Lala Lamazing Graces you kick out. You drive . . .

AWAY
I AM GOING AWAY

> *HOPING TO FIND A BETTER DAY*
> *WHAT DO YOU SAY*
> *HEY HEY*
> *I AM GOING AWAY*
> *AWAY*

(LALA, *caught up in the drama of the song, doesn't see* ADMONIA, *her maid, stick her head out from offstage.*)

(*Once she is sure* LALA *isn't looking, she wheels onto stage right* FLO'RANCE, LALA'S *lover, who wears a white mask/blonde hair. He is gagged and tied to a chair.* ADMONIA *places him on stage and then quickly exits.*)

LALA:

> *AU REVOIR—JE VAIS PARTIR MAINTENANT*
> *JE VEUX DIRE MAINTENANT*
> *AU REVOIR*
> *AU REVOIR*
> *AU REVOIR*
> *AU REVOIR*
> *A-MA-VIE*

(*On her last note, she see* FLO'RANCE *and, in total shock, crosses to him.*)

LALA: Flo'rance, what the hell are you doing out here looking like that. I haven't seen you for three days and you decide to show up now?

(*He mumbles.*)

I don't want to hear it!

(*He mumbles.*)

I said shut up!

(ADMONIA *enters from stage right and has a letter opener on a silver tray.*)

ADMONIA: Pst!

(LALA, *embarrassed by the presence of* ADMONIA *on stage, smiles apologetically at the audience.*)

LALA: Un momento.

(*She then pulls* ADMONIA *to the side.*)

LALA: Darling, have you lost your mind coming onstage while I'm performing. And what have you done to Flo'rance? When I asked you to keep him tied up, I didn't mean to tie him up.

(ADMONIA *gives her the letter opener.*)

LALA: Why are you giving me this? I have no letters to open. I'm in the middle of my American debut. Admonia, take Flo'rance off this stage with you! Admonia!

(ADMONIA *is gone.* LALA *turns to the audience and tries to make the best of it.*)

LALA: That was Admonia, my slightly overweight black maid, and this is Flo'rance, my amour. I remember how we met, don't you Flo'rance. I was sitting in a cafe on the Left Bank, when I looked up and saw the most beautiful man staring down at me.

"Who are you," he asked. I told him my name ... whatever my name was back then. And he said, "No, that cannot be your name. Your name should fly, like Lala." And the rest is la history.

Flo'rance molded me into the woman I am today. He is my Svengali, my reality, my all. And I thought I was all to him, until we came here to America, and he fucked that bitch. Yeah, you fucked 'em all. Anything black and breathing. And all this time, I thought you loved me for being me. (*She holds the letter opener to his neck.*)

You may think you made me, but I'll have you know I was who I was, whoever that was, long before you made me what I am. So there! (*She stabs him and breaks into song.*)

> OH, LOVE CAN DRIVE A WOMAN TO MADNESS
> TO PAIN AND SADNESS
> I KNOW
> BELIEVE ME I KNOW
> I KNOW
> I KNOW

(LALA *sees what she's done and is about to scream but catches herself and tries to play it off.*)

LALA: Moving right along.

(ADMONIA *enters with a telegram on a tray.*)

ADMONIA: Pst.

LALA: (*Anxious/hostile*) What is it now?

(ADMONIA *hands* LALA *a telegram.*)

LALA: (*Excited*) Oh, la telegram from one of my fans and the concert isn't even over yet. Get me the letter opener. It's in Flo'rance.

(ADMONIA *hands* LALA *the letter opener.*)

LALA: Next I am going to do for you my immortal hit song, "The Girl Inside." But first we open the telegram. (*She quickly reads it and is outraged.*) What! Which pig in la audience wrote this trash? (*Reading*) "Dear Sadie, I'm so proud. The show's wonderful, but talk less and sing more. Love, Mama."

First off, no one calls me Sadie. Sadie died the day Lala was born. And secondly, my Mama's dead. Anyone who knows anything about Lala Lamazing Grace knows that my mother and Josephine Baker were French patriots together. They infiltrated a carnival rumored to be the center of Nazi intelligence, disguised as Hottentot Siamese twins. You may laugh but it's true. Mama died a heroine. It's all in my autobiography, "Voilá Lala!" So whoever sent this telegram is a liar!

(ADMONIA *promptly presents her with another telegram.*)

LALA: This had better be an apology. (*To* ADMONIA.) Back up, darling. (*Reading*) "Dear Sadie, I'm not dead. P.S. Your child misses you." What? (*She squares off at the audience.*) Well, now, that does it! If you are my mother, which you are not. And this alleged child is my child, then that would mean I am a mother and I have never given birth. I don't know nothin' 'bout birthin' no babies! (*She laughs.*) Lala made a funny.

So whoever sent this, show me the child! Show me!

(ADMONIA *offers another telegram.*)

LALA: (*To* ADMONIA) You know you're gonna get fired! (*She reluctantly opens it.*) "The child is in the closet." What closet?

ADMONIA: Pst.

(ADMONIA *pushes a button and the center wall unit revolves around to reveal a large black door.* ADMONIA *exits, taking* FLO'RANCE *with her, leaving* LALA *alone.*)

LALA: (*Laughing*) I get it. It's a plot, isn't it. A nasty little CIA, FBI kind of plot. Well let me tell you mutha-fuckers one thing, there is nothing in that closet, real or manufactured, that will be a dimmer to the glimmer of Lamé the star. You may have gotten Billie and Bessie and a little piece of everyone else who's come along since, but you won't get Lala. My clothes are too fabulous! My hair is too long! My accent too French. That's why I came home to America. To prove you ain't got nothing on me!

(*The music for her next song starts, but* LALA *is caught up in her tirade, and talks/screams over the music.*)

My mother and Josephine Baker were French patriots together! I've had brunch with the Pope! I've dined with the Queen! Everywhere I go I cause riots! Hunny, I am a star! I have transcended pain! So there! (*Yelling*) Stop the music! Stop that goddamn music.

(*The music stops.* LALA *slowly walks downstage and singles out someone in the audience.*)

Darling, you're not looking at me. You're staring at that damn door. Did you pay to stare at some fucking door or be mesmerized by my talent?

(*To the whole audience*)

Very well! I guess I am going to have to go to the closet door, fling it open, in order to dispell all the nasty little thoughts these nasty little telegrams have planted in your nasty little minds. (*Speaking directly to someone in the audience.*) Do you want me to open the closet door? Speak up, darling, this is live. (*Once she gets the person to say "yes."*) I will open the door, but before I do, let me tell you bastards one last thing. To hell with coming home and to hell with lies and insinuations!

(LALA *goes into the closet and after a short pause comes running out, ready to scream, and slams the door. Traumatized to the point of no return, she tells the following story as if it were a jazz solo of rushing, shifting emotions.*)

LALA: I must tell you this dream I had last night. Simply magnifique. In this dream, I'm running naked in Sammy Davis Junior's hair. (*Crazed laughter*)

Yes! I'm caught in this larger than life, deep, dark forest of savage, nappy-nappy hair. The kinky-kinks are choking me, wrapped around my naked arms, thighs, breast, face. I can't breath. And there was nothing in that closet!

And I'm thinking if only I had a machete, I could cut away the kinks. Remove once and for all the roughness. But then I look up and it's coming toward me. Flowing like lava. It's pomade! Ohhh, Sammy!

Yes, cakes and cakes of pomade. Making everything nice and white and smooth and shiny, like my black/white/black/white/black behiney.

Mama no!

And then spikes start cutting through the pomade. Combing the coated kink. Cutting through the kink, into me. There are bloodlines on my back. On my thighs.

It's all over. All over . . . all over me. All over for me.

(LALA *accidentally pulls off her wig to reveal her real hair. Stripped of her "disguise" she recoils like a scared little girl and sings.*)

> *MOMMY AND DADDY*
> *MEET AND MATE*
> *THE CHILD THAT'S BORN*
> *IS TORN WITH LOVE AND WITH HATE*
> *SHE RUNS AWAY TO FIND HER OWN*
> *AND TRIES TO DENY*
> *WHAT SHE'S ALWAYS KNOWN*
> *THE GIRL INSIDE*

(*The closet door opens.* LALA *runs away, and a* LITTLE BLACK GIRL *emerges from the closet. Standing behind her is* ADMONIA.)
(*The* LITTLE GIRL *and* LALA *are in two isolated pools of light, and mirror each other's moves until* LALA *reaches past her reflection and the* LITTLE GIRL *comes to* LALA *and they hug.* ADMONIA *then joins them as* LALA *sings. Music underscored.*)

LALA:

>WHAT'S LEFT IS THE GIRL INSIDE
>THE GIRL WHO DIED
>SO A NEW GIRL COULD BE BORN

SLOW FADE TO BLACK

Permutations

(*Lights up on* NORMAL JEAN REYNOLDS. *She is very Southern/country and very young. She wears a simple faded print dress and her hair, slightly mussed, is in plaits. She sits, her dress covering a large oval object.*)

NORMAL: My mama used to say, God made the exceptional, then God made the special and when God got bored, he made me. 'Course she don't say too much of nuthin' no more, not since I lay me this egg.

(*She lifts her dress to uncover a large, white egg laying between her legs.*)

Ya see it all got started when I had me sexual relations with the garbage man. Ooowee, did he smell.

No, not bad. No! He smelled of all the good things folks never shoulda thrown away. His sweat was like cantaloupe juice. His neck was like a ripe-red strawberry. And the water that fell from his eyes was like a deep, dark, juicy-juicy grape. I tell ya, it was like fuckin' a fruit salad, only I didn't spit out the seeds. I kept them here, deep inside. And three days later, my belly commence to swell, real big like.

Well my mama locked me off in some dark room, refusin' to let me see light of day 'cause, "What would the neighbors think." At first I cried a lot, but then I grew used to livin' my days in the dark, and my nights in the dark.... (*She hums.*) And then it wasn't but a week or so later, my mama off at church, that I got this hurtin' feelin' down here. Worse than anything I'd ever known. And then I started bleedin', real bad. I mean there was blood everywhere. And the pain had me howlin' like a near-dead dog. I tell ya, I was yellin' so loud, I couldn't even hear myself. Noooooooo! Noooooo! carrying on something like that.

And I guess it was just too much for the body to take, 'cause the next thing I remember ... is me coming to and there's this big white egg layin' 'tween my legs. First I thought somebody musta put it there as some kind of joke. But then I noticed that all 'round this egg were thin lines of blood that I could trace to back between my legs.

(*Laughing*) Well, when my mama come home from church she just about died. "Normal Jean, what's that thing 'tween your legs? Normal Jean, you answer me, girl!" It's not a thing, Mama. It's an egg. And I laid it.

She tried separatin' me from it, but I wasn't havin' it. I stayed in that dark room, huggin', holdin' onto it.

And then I heard it. It wasn't anything that coulda been heard 'round the world, or even in the next room. It was kinda like layin' back in the bath tub, ya know, the water just coverin' your ears ... and if you lay real still and listen real close, you can hear the sound of your heart movin' the water. You ever done that? Well that's what it sounded like. A heart movin' water. And it was happenin' inside here.

Why, I'm the only person I know who ever lay themselves an egg before so that makes me special. You hear that, Mama? I'm special and so's my egg! And special things supposed to be treated like they matter. That's why every night I count to it, so it knows nuthin' never really ends. And I sing it every song I know so that when it comes out, it's full of all kinds of feelings. And I tell it secrets and laugh with it and ...

(*She suddenly stops and puts her ear to the egg and listens intently.*)

Oh! I don't believe it! I thought I heard ... yes! (*Excited*) Can you hear it? Instead of one heart, there's two. Two little hearts just pattering away. Boom-boom-boom. Boom-boom-boom. Talkin to each other like old friends. Racin' toward the beginnin' of their lives.

(*Listening*) Oh, no, now there's three ... four ... five, six. More hearts than I can count. And they're all alive, beatin' out life inside my egg.

(*We begin to hear the heartbeats, drums, alive inside* NORMAL'S *egg.*)

Any day now, this egg is gonna crack open and what's gonna come out a be the likes of which nobody has ever seen. My babies! And their skin is gonna turn all kinds of shades in the sun and their hair a be growin' every which-a-way. And it won't matter and they won't care 'cause they know they are so rare and so special 'cause it's not everyday a bunch of babies break outta a white egg and start to live.

And nobody better not try and hurt my babies 'cause if they do, they gonna have to deal with me.

Yes, any day now, this shell's gonna crack and my babies are gonna fly. Fly! Fly!

(*She laughs at the thought, but then stops and says the word as if it's the most natural thing in the world.*)

Fly.

BLACKOUT

The Party

(*Before we know what's hit us, a hurricane of energy comes bounding into the space. It is* TOPSY WASHINGTON. *Her hair and dress are a series of stylistic contradictions which are hip, black, and unencumbered.*)
(*Music, spiritual and funky, underscores.*)

TOPSY: (*Dancing about.*) Yoho! Party! Party! Turn up the music! Turn up the music!

Have yaw ever been to a party where there was one fool in the middle of the room, dancing harder and yelling louder than everybody in the entire place? Well, hunny, that fool was me!

Yes, child! The name is Topsy Washington and I love to party. As a matter of fact, when God created the world, on the seventh day, he didn't rest. No child, he P-A-R-T-I-E-D. Partied!

But now let me tell you 'bout this function I went to the other night, way uptown. And baby when I say way uptown, I mean way-way-way-way-way-way-way-way uptown. Somewhere's between 125th Street and infinity.

Inside was the largest gathering of black/Negro/colored Americans you'd ever want to see. Over in one corner you got Nat Turner sippin' champagne out of Eartha Kitt's slipper. And over in another corner, Bert Williams and Malcom X was discussing existentialism as it relates to the shuffle-ball-change. Girl, Aunt Jemima and Angela Davis was in the kitchen sharing a plate of greens and just goin' off about South Africa.

And then Fats sat down and started to work them eighty-eights. And then Stevie joined in. And then Miles and Duke and Ella and Jimi and Charlie and Sly and Lightin' and Count and Louie! And then everybody joined in. I tell you all the children was just all up in there, dancing to the rhythm of one beat. Dancing to the rhythm of their own definition. Celebrating in their cultural madness.

And then the floor started to shake. And the walls started to move. And before anybody knew what was happening, the entire room lifted up off the ground. The whole place just took off and went flying through space—defying logic and limitations. Just a spinning and a spinning and a spinning until it disappeared inside of my head.

(TOPSY *stops dancing and regains her balance and begins to listen to the music in her head. Slowly we begin to hear it, too.*)

That's right, girl, there's a party goin' on inside of here. That's why when I walk down the street my hips just sashay all over the place. 'Cause I'm dancing to the music of the madness in me.

And whereas I used to jump into a rage anytime anybody tried to deny who I was, now all I got to do is give attitude, quicker than light, and then go on about the business of being me. 'Cause I'm dancing to the music of the madness in me.

(*As* TOPSY *continues to speak,* MISS ROJ, LALA, MISS PAT, *and* THE MAN *from* SYMBIOSIS *revolve on, frozen like soft sculptures.*)

TOPSY: And here, all this time I been thinking we gave up our drums. But, naw, we still got 'em. I know I got mine. They're here, in my speech, my walk, my hair, my God, my style, my smile, and my eyes. And everything I need to get over in this world, is inside here, connecting me to everybody and everything that's ever been.

So, hunny, don't waste your time trying to label or define me.

(*The sculptures slowly begin to come to "life" and they mirror/echo* TOPSY'S *words.*)

TOPSY/EVERYBODY: . . . 'cause I'm not what I was ten years ago or ten minutes ago. I'm all of that and then some. And whereas I can't live inside yesterday's pain, I can't live without it.

(*All of a sudden, madness erupts on the stage. The sculptures begin to speak all at once. Images of black/Negro/colored Americans begin to flash—images of them dancing past the madness, caught up in the madness, being lynched, rioting, partying, surviving. Mixed in with these images are all the characters from the exhibits. Through all of this* TOPSY *sings. It is a vocal and visual cacophony which builds and builds.*)

LALA:

I must tell you about this dream I had last night. Simply magnifique. In this dream I'm running naked in Sammy Davis Junior's hair. Yes. I'm caught in this larger-than-life, deep, dark tangled forest of savage, nappy-nappy hair. Yes, the kinky kinks are choking me, are wrapped around my naked arms, my naked thighs, breast, and face, and I can't breath and there was nothing in that closet.

MISS ROJ:

Snap for every time you walk past someone lying in the street smelling like frozen piss and shit and you don't see it. Snap for every crazed bastard who kills himself so as to get the jump on being killed. And snap for every sick muthafucker who, bored with carrying about his fear, takes to shooting up other people.

THE MAN:

I have no history. I have no past. I can't. It's too much. It's much too much. I must be able to smile on cue and watch the news with an impersonal eye. I have no stake in the madness. Being black is too emotionally taxing, therefore I will be black only on weekends and holidays.

MISS PAT:

Stop playing those drums. I said stop playing those damn drums. You can't stop history. You can't stop time. Those drums will be confiscated once we reach Savannah, so give them up now. Repeat after me: I don't hear any drums and I will not rebel. I will not rebel!

TOPSY: (*Singing*)

THERE'S MADNESS IN ME
AND THAT MADNESS SETS ME FREE
THERE'S MADNESS IN ME
AND THAT MADNESS SETS ME FREE
THERE'S MADNESS IN ME

AND THAT MADNESS SETS ME FREE
THERE'S MADNESS IN ME
AND THAT MADNESS SETS ME FREE
THERE'S MADNESS IN ME
AND THAT MADNESS SETS ME FREE

TOPSY: My power is in my . . .
EVERYBODY: *Madness!*
TOPSY: And my colored contradictions.

(*The sculptures freeze with a smile on their faces as we hear the voice of* MISS PAT.)

VOICE OF MISS PAT: Before exiting, check the overhead as any baggage you don't claim, we trash.

BLACKOUT

1986

PAT MORA
B. 1942

A Chicana from El Paso, Texas, Pat Mora has written three books of poetry, a children's book, and a collection of essays. She earned both a B.A. and an M.A. in English from the University of Texas at El Paso while she raised three children, all of whom attended universities. She lives and writes in Cincinnati, Ohio.

The poem "University Avenue" presents Chicanas, working-class women, who only recently gained front-door entry to universities, particularly in traditionally racist institutions in Texas that historically relegated Mexican women to roles as faceless workers pushing the broomcarts, mopping the corridors of academia, and cleaning the departments' bathrooms. Mora's poem recognizes that the "first of our people" to attend universities as students, administrators, and faculty, however, need not sacrifice Mexican indigenous traditions that inform Chicana/Chicano identity. Implicit in her use of Spanish words is the succor that bilingualism offers, the richness that biculturalism should evoke. The lessons whispered in Spanish are also the stories, the rich oral traditions that we carry with us to seminars, meetings, and lectures.

In "Unnatural Speech," Mora explores the dual voices of this bilingual, bicultural student. She speaks to the pain that the Chicana confronts as she makes the transition from Spanish speaker to English-dominant speaker. Must the Spanish oral tradition of childhood nursery rhymes remain in the past, hidden in the memory of carefree childhood? Is there danger in learning and internalizing the "new rules" of the dominant language too well? The dilemma remains:

will accommodating the dominant culture in the United States erase the songs of the other, the indigenous Mexican culture?

"Border Town: 1938" presents the other side of the bicultural dilemma. While we can now assert the importance of keeping both the Mexican and the American languages and traditions, Mora's poetry urges us to remember the specificities of Chicana history in the United States, a history of separate and unequal educational systems. Evoking that memory of segregated "Mexican schools" in Texas of the recent past, Mora does not allow the reader to romanticize that history. The problem she presents in these poems, from her collection *Borders*, is that Mexican Americans on the border too often are forced to choose one side or the other, one language or the other, one culture or the other. Struggling to gain a foothold in the land of their ancestors, Chicanas must learn to gain power from a constantly shifting, ambiguous, multiple identity. As Mora asserts in a poem from *Chants*, "Legal Alien," "an American to Mexicans / a Mexican to Americans / a handy token / sliding back and forth / between the fringes of both worlds / by smiling / by masking the discomfort / of being prejudged / Bi-laterally."

Sonia Saldívar-Hull
University of California, Los Angeles

PRIMARY WORKS

Chants, 1984; *Borders*, 1986; *Communion*, 1991; *Nepantla: Essays from the Land in the Middle*, 1993; *Agua Santa/Holy Water*, 1995; *House of Houses*, 1997; *Aunt Carmen's Book of Practical Saints*, 1997; *Adobe Odes*, 2006.

Border Town: 1938

She counts cement cracks
little Esperanza with the long brown braids,
counts so as not to hear
the girls in the playground singing,
    "the farmer's in the dell   5
        the farmer's in the dell"
laughing and running round-round
while little Esperanza walks head down
eyes full of tears.
    "The nurse takes the child"   10
but Esperanza walks alone across the loud
street, through the graveyard gates
down the dirt path, walks faster,
faster ... away
from ghosts with long arms,   15
no "hi-ho the dairy-o" here,
runs to that other school
for Mexicans
every day wanting to stay close to home,

every day wanting to be the farmer in the dell,   20
little Esperanza in the long brown braids
counts cement cracks

ocho, nueve, diez.

1986

Unnatural Speech

The game has changed
girl/child, no humming
or singing in these halls,
long, dark, ending at the desk
you want, where you'd sit   5
adding numbers one by one,
a C.P.A., daisies on your desk.

                    I study hard

you say, your smile true,
like dawn is, fresh, vulnerable,   10
but my English language scares
you, makes your palms sweat
when you speak before a class

                    I say my speeches
                    to my dolls   15

you say. Dolls? The game
has changed, girl/child.
I hear you once singing
to those unblinking eyes
lined up on your bed   20

                    Víbora, víbora de la mar,
your words light in your mouth.

Now at twenty
you stand before
those dolls tense,   25
feet together,
tongue thick, dry,
pushing heavy English
words out.

                    In class I hide   30
                    my hands behind
                    my back. They shake.
                    My voice too.

I know the new rules,
girl/child, one by one,   35
víboras I've lived with

all my life, learned to hold
firmly behind the head.
If I teach you, will your songs
evaporate, like dawn?   40

1986

University Avenue

We are the first
of our people to walk this path.
We move cautiously
unfamiliar with the sounds,
guides for those who follow.   5
Our people prepared us
with gifts from the land
      fire
          herbs and song
          hierbabuena soothes us into morning   10
          rhythms hum in our blood
          abrazos linger round our bodies
          cuentos whisper lessons *en español*.
We do not travel alone.
Our people burn deep within us.   15

1986

JUDITH ORTIZ COFER
B. 1952

The daughter of a teenage mother and a career Navy father, Judith Ortiz Cofer spent her childhood traveling back and forth between the U.S. mainland and Puerto Rico, her birthplace, experiencing schools and neighborhoods in both Spanish and English and adjusting and readjusting to different cultural environments. After retirement, her father settled the family in Georgia, which stabilized Judith's education. During college she married and, with husband and daughter, moved to Florida, where she finished an M.A. in English. A fellowship allowed her to pursue graduate work at Oxford, after which she returned to Florida and simultaneously began teaching English and writing poetry. In 1981 and 1982, she received scholarships to the Bread Loaf Writers' Conference, and she continued on the program's staff until 1985. *Peregrina* won first place in the Riverstone International Poetry Chapbook Competition in 1985. *Reaching for the*

Mainland and *Terms of Survival* appeared in 1987. After that she began publishing prose, including *The Line of the Sun* (1989), a novel; *Silent Dancing* (1990), autobiographical essays; and *The Latin Deli* (1993) and *An Island Like You* (1995), short stories. Her most recent poetry collection is *A Love Story Beginning in Spanish*.

When Ortiz Cofer was a child, living amid the violence and racial tensions of the Paterson, New Jersey, slums, the library became her refuge and books her English teachers; on the island, the written word gave way to the oral tradition of her Spanish-speaking grandmother. Though strongly determined by the English language and literary tradition of her academic training, her writing still reflects the tension of that dynamic intercultural background. Spanish lingers, filtering through in emotion-packed words or phrases that remind us we are reading something other than a monolingual text. Her poems offer continual overlays and blends of cultures and languages that refuse to settle completely into either side, hence defining their ever-shifting, never-ending synthesis as authentic Puerto Rican life. She calls it the "habit of movement," a state of instability that informs and stimulates her creativity.

One pattern her exploration takes is that of gathering, like an anthropologist, sayings, expressions, or words from Puerto Rican Spanish and recasting them into English poems in which the essence is conveyed across linguistic borders. In the process, she charts the experience of intercultural life, exposing readers to alternative perspectives on everyday matters that can seem so common and simple when safely encapsulated in the familiar words of one's own language. That is, Ortiz Cofer achieves what many claim to be the function of poetry: she rarifies language and experience to an intensity that enables it to stir the reader's otherwise callous sensibilities. At a more pedestrian level, this experience is and has been fundamental to the development of the U.S. idiom and culture, themselves a product of the continual intercultural synthesis that makes them so rich and dynamic. Thus, beyond displaying the particularities of Puerto Rican experience, Ortiz Cofer reminds us of our common national character.

While much of her poetry and prose displays the texture of her interwoven cultures, the underlying preoccupation is more sexual than cultural. More than languages and geographic locations, the figures gripped in an unstable embrace are men and women, with the former more an ever-absent presence and the latter a long-suffering presence longing for that absence. Perhaps her works document the disintegration of the traditional family resulting from the pressures of migratory life, but even in the pieces that recall prior lives in more settled times, stable relationships are illusions. Ortiz Cofer's concern is not simply ethnic, but profoundly sexual: the key to any stable culture is the viability of the male-female relationship. Her basic question is the essential one of desire and its fulfillment. Everything else—ethnic strife, social injustice, gender conflict, religion, tradition, language itself—becomes mere incarnation of frustrated desire. *Silent Dancing* plays with memory and the power of media to document events, despite its inability to convey the emotive value of images. A powerful commentary on lost moments, it is equally forceful as a recovery of the ephemeral quality of experience.

Juan Bruce-Novoa
University of California, Irvine

PRIMARY WORKS

Latin Women Pray, 1980; *The Native Dancer*, 1981; *Among the Ancestors*, 1981; *Peregrina*, 1986; *Reaching for the Mainland*, 1987; *Terms of Survival*, 1987; *The Line of the Sun*, 1989; *Silent Dancing*, 1990; *The Latin Deli*, 1993; *An Island Like You*, 1995; *Reaching for the Mainland*, 1995; *The Year of Our Revolution*, 1998; *Sleeping with One Eye Open*, 1999; *Woman in Front of the Sun*, 2000; *The Meaning of Consuelo*, 2003; *Call Me Maria*, 2004; *A Love Story Beginning in Spanish: Poems*, 2005.

Claims

Last time I saw her, Grandmother
had grown seamed as a Bedouin tent.
She had claimed the right
to sleep alone, to own
her nights, to never bear   5
the weight of sex again nor to accept
its gift of comfort, for the luxury
of stretching her bones.
She'd carried eight children,
three had sunk in her belly, *náufragos*[1]   10
she called them, shipwrecked babies
drowned in her black waters.
Children are made in the night and
steal your days
for the rest of your life, amen. She said this   15
to each of her daughters in turn. Once she had made a pact
with man and nature and kept it. Now like the sea,
she is claiming back her territory.

                                                                          1987

The Woman Who Was Left at the Altar

She calls her shadow Juan,
looking back often as she walks.
She has grown fat, her breasts huge
as reservoirs. She once opened her blouse
in church to show the silent town   5
what a plentiful mother she could be.
Since her old mother died, buried in black,
she lives alone.
Out of the lace she made curtains for her room,
doilies out of the veil. They are now   10
yellow as malaria.

[1]Spanish: victims of shipwrecks.

She hangs live chickens from her waist to sell,
walks to the town swinging her skirts of flesh.
She doesn't speak to anyone. Dogs follow
the scent of blood to be shed. In their hungry,   15
yellow eyes she sees his face. She takes him
to the knife time after time.

                                                                   1987

My Father in the Navy: A Childhood Memory

Stiff and immaculate
in the white cloth of his uniform
and a round cap on his head like a halo,
he was an apparition on leave from a shadow-world
and only flesh and blood when he rose from below   5
the waterline where he kept watch over the engines
and dials making sure the ship parted the waters
on a straight course.
Mother, brother and I kept vigil
on the nights and dawns of his arrivals,   10
watching the corner beyond the neon sign of a quasar
for the flash of white our father like an angel
heralding a new day.
His homecomings were the verses
we composed over the years making up   15
the siren's song that kept him coming back
from the bellies of iron whales
and into our nights
like the evening prayer.

                                                                   1987

En Mis Ojos No Hay Días[1]

from Borges'[2] poem "The Keeper of the Books"

Back before the fire burned in his eyes,
in the blast furnace which finally consumed him,
Father told us about the reign of little terrors
of his childhood beginning
    at birth with a father who cursed him   5
    for being the twelfth and the fairest
    too blond and pretty to be from his loins,

---

[1]Spanish: In My Eyes There Are No Days.   [2]Jorge Luis Borges (1899–1986), Argentine
                                              writer.

so he named him the priest's pauper son.
He said the old man kept:
a mule for labor   10
a horse for sport
wine in his cellar
a mistress in town
and a wife to bear him daughters,
to send to church   15
to pray for his soul.
And sons,
to send to the fields
to cut the cane
and raise the money   20
to buy his rum.
He was only ten when he saw his father
split a man in two with his machete
and walk away proud to have rescued his honor
like a true "hombre."   25

Father always wrapped these tales
in the tissue paper of his humor
and we'd listen at his knees rapt,
warm and safe,
by the blanket of his caring,   30
but he himself could not be saved,
"What on earth drove him mad?"
his friends still ask,
remembering Prince Hamlet, I reply,
"Nothing on earth,"   35
but no one listens to ghost stories anymore.

                                                          1987

Latin Women Pray

Latin women pray
In incense sweet churches
They pray in Spanish to an Anglo God
With a Jewish heritage.
And this Great White Father   5
Imperturbable in his marble pedestal
Looks down upon his brown daughters
Votive candles shining like lust
In his all seeing eyes
Unmoved by their persistent prayers.   10

Yet year after year
Before his image they kneel

Margarita Josefina Maria and Isabel
All fervently hoping
That if not omnipotent   15
At least he be bilingual.

                                                              1987

TATO LAVIERA

B. 1951

Tato Laviera was born in Puerto Rico and has lived in New York City since 1960. A second-generation Puerto Rican writer, a poet and playwright, he is deeply committed to the social and cultural development of Puerto Ricans in New York. In addition, he has taught creative writing at Rutgers and other universities on the East Coast.

His poetry and plays are linguistic and artistic celebrations of Puerto Rican culture, African Caribbean traditions, the fast rhythms of life in New York City, and life in general. Laviera writes in English, Spanish, and Spanglish, a mixture of the two. His superior command of both languages and the playful yet serious value he imparts to Spanglish distinguish him from other writers of his generation. For example, the titles of two of his books, *Enclave* and *AmeRícan*, suggest double readings in Spanish and English. Laviera's poetry is highly relevant to the study of bilingual and bicultural issues, for in it he documents, examines, and questions what it means to be a Puerto Rican in the United States. His texts reflect the changes and transitions that his community has undergone since the major migrations of the 1940s and offer a paradigm of what pluralistic America should really be all about.

In *La Carreta Made a U-Turn*, one finds forceful poems denouncing the hardships, injustices, and social problems that the poor Puerto Rican confronts in New York City: cold, hunger, high rents, eviction, drug addiction, linguistic alienation, unemployment. The second part of this collection, titled "Loisaida (Lower East Side) Streets: Latinas Sing," examines the issues and problems affecting today's Latina women—one of the few instances in which a Hispanic male writer conscientiously and sympathetically addresses the conflicts of bicultural Hispanic women. Laviera concludes this book with a series of poems that celebrate African Caribbean music, both in its traditional functions and in its resurgence within the contemporary urban context of New York City.

Laviera has been called a "chronicler of life in El Barrio" and rightly so. His poetic language is not influenced by the written, academic tradition of poetry but is instead informed by popular culture, by the oral tradition of Puerto Rico and the Caribbean, and by the particular voices spoken and heard in El Barrio. Gossip, refrains, street language, idiomatic expressions, interjections, poetic declamation, and African Caribbean music such as *salsa*, rhumbas, *mambos*, *sones*, and *música jíbara* (mountain music) are but some of the raw materials from which Laviera constructs his poems. Though published in a written format, Laviera's poetry is meant to be sung and recited.

A central tenet of Laviera's work is his identification with the African American community in this country. He reinforces the unity and common roots of blacks and Puerto Ricans—"it is called Africa in all of us"—reflecting the new multiethnic constitution of America that has supplanted the old myth of the melting pot. In this context, Laviera's poems are reaffirmations of his Puetrori-canness and of his community's new national identity, which diverges from that of the insular Puerto Rican. He proposes a new ethnic identity that includes other minority groups in the United States. New York City becomes the space where this convergence and cultural *mestizaje* (mixing) take place. While maintaining a denunciative stance through the use of irony and tongue-in-cheek humor, Laviera's work flourishes with a contagious optimism, and his poems are true songs to the joy of living that Puerto Ricans feel despite the harsh circumstances in which they live.

Frances R. Aparicio
University of Illinois at Chicago

PRIMARY WORKS

La Carreta Made a U-Turn, 1976; *Olú Clemente* (theater), 1979; *Enclave*, 1981; *AmeRí-can*, 1985; *Mainstream Ethics*, 1988; *Mixturao and Other Poems*, 2008.

frío[1]

35 mph winds
& the 10 degree
weather
penetrated the pores
of our windows   5
mr. steam rested for
the night
the night we most
needed him
everybody arropándose[2]   10
on their skin blankets
curled-up like the embryo
in my mother's womb
a second death birth
called nothingness   15

& the frío made more

[1]Spanish: the cold.
[2]Spanish: covering themselves.

asustos[3] in our empty
stomachs

   the toilet has not
   been flushed for   20
   three days

              1976

AmeRícan

we gave birth to a new generation,
AmeRícan, broader than lost gold
never touched, hidden inside the
puerto rican mountains.

we gave birth to a new generation,   5
AmeRícan, it includes everything
imaginable you-name-it-we-got-it
society.

we gave birth to a new generation,
AmeRícan salutes all folklores,   10
european, indian, black, spanish,
and anything else compatible:

AmeRícan,   singing to composer pedro flores'[1] palm
      trees high up in the universal sky!

AmeRícan,   sweet soft spanish danzas gypsies   15
      moving lyrics la española[2] cascabelling
      presence always singing at our side!

AmeRícan,   beating jíbaro[3'] modern troubadours
      crying guitars romantic continental
      bolero love songs!   20

AmeRícan,   across forth and across back
      back across and forth back
      forth across and back and forth
      our trips are walking bridges!

---

[3]Spanish: frightening.
[1]Pedro Flores, Puerto Rican composer of popular romantic songs.
[2]"Spanish" (feminine).

[3']Term referring to the Puerto Rican farmer who lives in the mountains. The jíbaros have a particular musical style.

it all dissolved into itself, the attempt   25
was truly made, the attempt was truly
absorbed, digested, we spit out
the poison, we spit out the malice,
we stand, affirmative in action,
to reproduce a broader answer to the   30
marginality that gobbled us up abruptly!

AmeRícan,   walking plena-[4]rhythms in new york,
strutting beautifully alert, alive,
many turning eyes wondering,
admiring!   35

AmeRícan,   defining myself my own way any way many
ways Am e Rícan, with the big R and the
accent on the í!

AmeRícan,   like the soul gliding talk of gospel
boogie music!   40

AmeRícan,   speaking new words in spanglish tenements,
fast tongue moving street corner *"que
corta"*[5] talk being invented at the insistence
of a smile!

AmeRícan,   abounding inside so many ethnic english   45
people, and out of humanity, we blend
and mix all that is good!

AmeRícan,   integrating in new york and defining our
own *destino*,[6] our own way of life,

AmeRícan,   defining the new america, humane america,   50
admired america, loved america, harmonious
america, the world in peace, our energies
collectively invested to find other civilizations, to touch God, further and further,
to dwell in the spirit of divinity!   55

AmeRícan,   yes, for now, for i love this, my second
land, and i dream to take the accent from
the altercation, and be proud to call
myself american, in the u.s. sense of the
word, AmeRícan, America!   60

1985

---

[4]African Puerto Rican folklore.   [6]Spanish: destiny.
[5]Spanish: that cuts.

Latero[1] Story

i am a twentieth-century welfare recipient
moonlighting in the sun as a latero
a job invented by national state laws
designed to re-cycle aluminum cans
returned to consumer's acid laden   5
gastric inflammation pituitary glands
coca diet rites low cal godsons
of artificially flavored malignant
indigestions somewhere down the line
of a cancerous cell   10

i collect garbage cans in outdoor facilities
congested with putrid residues
my hands shelving themselves
opening plastic bags never knowing
what they'll encounter   15

several times a day i touch evil rituals
cut throats of chickens
tongues of poisoned rats
salivating my index finger
smells of month old rotten foods   20
next to pamper's diarrhea
        dry blood infectious diseases
hypodermic needles tissued with
heroin water drops pilfered in
slimy greases hazardous waste materials   25
but i cannot use rubber gloves
they undermine my daily profits

i am a twentieth-century welfare recipient
moonlighting in the day as a latero
that is the only opportunity i have   30
to make it big in america
some day i might become experienced enough
to offer technical assistance
to other lateros
i am thinking of publishing   35
my own guide to latero's collection
and founding a latero's union offering
medical dental benefits

[1]From Spanish *lata*: can. A man who picks up
cans from garbage containers and the streets.

i am a twentieth-century welfare recipient
moonlighting in the night as a latero   40
i am considered some kind of expert
at collecting cans during fifth avenue parades
i can now hire workers at twenty
five cents an hour guaranteed salary
and fifty per cent of two and one half cents   45
profit on each can collected

i am a twentieth-century welfare recipient
moonlighting in midnight as a latero
i am becoming an entrepreneur
an american success story   50
i have hired bag ladies to keep peddlers
from my territories
i have read in some guide to success
that in order to get rich
to make it big   55
i have to sacrifice myself
moonlighting until dawn by digging
deeper into the extra can
margin of profit
i am on my way up the opportunistic   60
ladder of success
in ten years i will quit welfare
to become a legitimate businessman
i'll soon become a latero executive
with corporate conglomerate intents   65
god bless america

1988

GLORIA ANZALDÚA
1942–2004

When Gloria Anzaldúa described the United States–Mexico border as "una her-ida abierta" (an open wound), she spoke from her lived experience as a native border dweller. Born in the ranch settlement of Jesus Maria in south Texas, Anzaldúa grew up in the small town of Hargill, Texas, and later wrote and taught in northern California. In her poetry, fiction, essays, and autobiography, she wrote eloquently of the indignities a Chicana lesbian feminist overcomes as she escapes the strictures of patriarchal Chicano traditions and confronts the injustices of dominant culture.

Her highly acclaimed text, *Borderlands/La Frontera: The New Mestiza*, interweaves autobiography, history of the Chicana/o Southwest, essay, and poetry in a manner that defies traditional categorization. Chicana *mestizaje* in the late twentieth century can be seen as a new genre that describes the cultural and linguistic connections between Chicana writers and other writers of the Americas. The bilingual title of her book illustrates the transcultural experience of border dwellers and border consciousness. English and Spanish coexist for Mexican-descent people of the borderlands. In Anzaldúa's text, the preconquest language, Nahuatl, mixes with English and Spanish. The language that Anzaldúa deploys in this text can be said to be a new Chicana language, one that legitimizes the intermingling of English and Spanish with indigenous Nahuatl.

In *Borderlands*, Anzaldúa presents multiple issues that inform a radical political awareness, culminating in what she called a new consciousness for the women who examine and question the restrictions placed on them in the borderlands of the United States. In Anzaldúa's political manifesto, a "new mestiza" emerges only after her oppositional consciousness develops.

The chapter "Entering into the Serpent" presents some *cuentos* (stories) that border families tell their children. For Prieta, the narrator of this section, the story of the snake that slithers into a woman's uterus and impregnates her provides the link to Anzaldúa's "serpentine" feminist theory. The new mestiza's task is to "winnow out the lies" as a Chicana feminist historian. She also provides alternative metaphors to the ones promoted by androcentric psychologists and priests. Anzaldúa's new mestiza invokes Olmec myth when she asserts that "Earth is a coiled Serpent" and rewrites the origin of the Catholic Guadalupe, empowering her as a pre-Columbian "*Coatlalopeuh*, She Who Has Dominion over Serpents."

Like the constantly shifting identities of the Chicana in the contemporary world, the deities that Anzaldúa unearths and names become a pantheon of possible feminist icons. Through these icons mestizas can unlearn the masculinist versions of history, religion, and myth. She methodically shows how both the "male-dominated Azteca-Mexica culture" and the postconquest church established the binary of the *virgen/puta* (Virgin/whore) when they split Coatlalopeuh/Coatlicue/Tonantsi/Tlazolteotl/Cihuacoatl into good and evil, light and dark, sexual and asexual beings. Guadalupe, then, is Coatlalopeuh with "the serpent/sexuality out of her."

Anzaldúa revises androcentric myths of the Chicano homeland, Aztlán, and of *La Llorona* (the Weeping Woman). She intertwines the familiar stories with new feminist threads so that her insistence on the recuperation of the feminist—the serpent—produces a tapestry at once familiar and radically different. While "la facultad" can be interpreted as a spiritual extrasensory perception, what Anzaldúa has in fact developed is the ability to rupture dominating belief systems that have been presented as ancient truths and accurate histories.

The second excerpt, "*La conciencia de la mestiza*: Towards a New Consciousness," is the final chapter of the prose section of the book. In this essay, Anzaldúa summarizes her mestiza methodology, which offers strategies for unearthing a razed indigenous history as a process of coming to consciousness as political agents of change. Mestizas can turn to preconquest history and historical sites such as the Aztec temples to recover women's place in a past that has been satanized. With this new knowledge, they learn of the central importance of

female deities rendered passive by Western androcentric ideology. The mestiza/
mestizo Aztec legacy focuses only on the blood sacrifices of this military power
and further obscures the other indigenous tribal traditions that Aztec hegemony
absorbed. Anzaldúa's reclamation of Aztec deities and traditions begins a reformu-
lation of Aztlán from a male nation-state to a feminist site of resistance.

For Anzaldúa, Chicana feminism and lesbian politics emerged as forces that
gave voice to her political agenda as a new mestiza, an identity that claims much
more than the simple definition of *mestizo* (mixed blood) allows. In this section,
Anzaldúa clearly presents her political ideology, which is historically grounded
in the colonial legacy of the American Southwest in its relation to larger hemispheric events. In *Borderlands*, American and Mexican history and American and
Mexican culture are contested fields.

Sonia Saldívar-Hull
University of California, Los Angeles

PRIMARY WORKS

This Bridge Called My Back: Writing by Radical Women of Color (ed. with Cherríe Moraga), 1981; *Borderlands/La Frontera: The New Mestiza*, 1987; *Interviews/Entrevistas*,
2000; *This Bridge We Call Home*, 2002.

from **Borderlands/La Frontera**

3

Entering into the Serpent

Sueño con serpientes, con serpientes del mar,
Con cierto mar, ay de serpientes sueño yo.
Largas, transparentes, en sus barrigas llevan
Lo que pueden arebatarle al amor.
Oh, oh, oh, la mató y aparese una mayor.
Oh, con mucho más infierno en digestión.

I dream of serpents, serpents of the sea,
A certain sea, oh, of serpents I dream.
Long, transparent, in their bellies they carry
All that they can snatch away from love.
Oh, oh, oh, I kill one and a larger one appears.
Oh, with more hellfire burning inside!

—Silvio Rodríguez, "*Sueño Con Serpientes*"[1]

In the predawn orange haze, the sleepy crowing of roosters atop the trees.
No vayas al escusado en lo oscuro. Don't go to the outhouse at night, Prieta,
my mother would say. *No se te vaya a meter algo por allá.* A snake will crawl

---

[1]From the song "*Sueño Con Serpientes*" by Silvio Rodríguez, from the album *Días y flores.*
Translated by Barbara Dane with the collaboration of Rina Benmauor and Juan Flores.
[All notes are Anzaldúa's—*Ed.*]

into your *nalgas*,[2] make you pregnant. They seek warmth in the cold. *Dicen que las culebras* like to suck *chiches*,[3] can draw milk out of you.

En el escusado in the half-light spiders hang like gliders. Under my bare buttocks and the rough planks the deep yawning tugs at me. I can see my legs fly up to my face as my body falls through the round hole into the sheen of swarming maggots below. Avoiding the snakes under the porch I walk back into the kitchen, step on a big black one slithering across the floor.

Ella tiene su tono[4]

Once we were chopping cotton in the fields of Jesus Maria Ranch. All around us the woods. *Quelite*[5] towered above me, choking the stubby cotton that had outlived the deer's teeth.

I swung *el azadón*[6] hard. *El quelite* barely shook, showered nettles on my arms and face. When I heard the rattle the world froze.

I barely felt its fangs. Boot got all the *veneno*.[7] My mother came shrieking, swinging her hoe high, cutting the earth, the writhing body.

I stood still, the sun beat down. Afterwards I smelled where fear had been: back of neck, under arms, between my legs; I felt its heat slide down my body. I swallowed the rock it had hardened into.

When Mama had gone down the row and was out of sight, I took out my pocketknife. I made an X over each prick. My body followed the blood, fell onto the soft ground. I put my mouth over the red and sucked and spit between the rows of cotton.

I picked up the pieces, placed them end on end. *Culebra de cascabel*.[8] I counted the rattlers: twelve. It would shed no more. I buried the pieces between the rows of cotton.

That night I watched the window sill, watched the moon dry the blood on the tail, dreamed rattler fangs filled my mouth, scales covered my body. In the morning I saw through snake eyes, felt snake blood course through my body. The serpent, *mi tono*, my animal counterpart. I immune to its venom. Forever immune.

Snakes, *víboras*: since that day I've sought and shunned them. Always when they cross my path, fear and elation flood my body. I know things older than Freud, older than gender. She—that's how I think of *la Víbora*, Snake Woman. Like the ancient Olmecs, I know Earth is a coiled Serpent. Forty years it's taken me to enter into the Serpent, to acknowledge that I have a body, that I am a body and to assimilate the animal body, the animal soul.

---

[2] Vagina, buttocks.
[3] They say snakes like to suck women's teats.
[4] She has supernatural power from her animal soul, the *tono*.

[5] Weed.
[6] The hoe.
[7] Venom, poison.
[8] Rattlesnake.

Coatlalopeuh, She Who Has Dominion over Serpents

Mi mamagrande Ramona toda su vida mantuvo un altar pequeño en la esquina del comedor. Siempre tenía las velas prendidas. Allí hacía promesas a la Virgen de Guadalupe. My family, like most Chicanos, did not practice Roman Catholicism but a folk Catholicism with many pagan elements. *La Virgen de Guadalupe*'s Indian name is *Coatlalopeuh*. She is the central deity connecting us to our Indian ancestry.

Coatlalopeuh is descended from, or is an aspect of, earlier Mesoamerican fertility and Earth goddesses. The earliest is *Coatlicue*, or "Serpent Skirt." She had a human skull or serpent for a head, a necklace of human hearts, a skirt of twisted serpents and taloned feet. As creator goddess, she was mother of the celestial deities, and of *Huitzilopochtli* and his sister, *Coyolxauhqui*, She With Golden Bells, Goddess of the Moon, who was decapitated by her brother. Another aspect of *Coatlicue* is *Tonantsi*.[9] The Totonacs, tired of the Aztec human sacrifices to the male god, *Huitzilopochtli*, renewed their reverence for *Tonantsi* who preferred the sacrifice of birds and small animals.[10]

The male-dominated Azteca-Mexica culture drove the powerful female deities underground by giving them monstrous attributes and by substituting male deities in their place, thus splitting the female Self and the female deities. They divided her who had been complete, who possessed both upper (light) and underworld (dark) aspects. *Coatlicue*, the Serpent goddess, and her more sinister aspects, *Tlazolteotl* and *Cihuacoatl*, were "darkened" and disempowered much in the same manner as the Indian *Kali*.

Tonantsi—split from her dark guises, *Coatlicue, Tlazolteotl,* and *Cihuacoatl*,—became the good mother. The Nahuas, through ritual and prayer, sought to oblige *Tonantsi* to ensure their health and the growth of their crops. It was she who gave *México* the cactus plant to provide her people with milk and pulque. It was she who defended her children against the wrath of the Christian God by challenging God, her son, to produce mother's milk (as she had done) to prove that his benevolence equalled his disciplinary harshness.[11]

After the Conquest, the Spaniards and their Church continued to split *Tonantsi/Guadalupe*. They desexed *Guadalupe*, taking *Coatlalopeuh*, the serpent/sexuality, out of her. They completed the split begun by the Nahuas by making *la Virgen de Guadalupe/Virgen María* into chaste virgins and

---

[9]In some Nahuatl dialects *Tonantsi* is called *Tonatzin*, literally "Our Holy Mother." "*Tonan* was a name given in Nahuatl to several mountains, these being the congelations of the Earth Mother at spots convenient for her worship." The Mexica considered the mountain mass southwest of Chapultepec to be their mother. Burr Cartwright Brundage, *The Fifth Sun: Aztec Gods, Aztec World* (Austin, TX: University of Texas Press, 1979), 154, 242.

[10]Ena Campbell, "The Virgin of Guadalupe and the Female Self-Image: A Mexican Case History," *Mother Worship: Themes and Variations*, James J. Preston, ed. (Chapel Hill, NC: University of North Carolina Press, 1982), 22.

[11]Alan R. Sandstrom, "The Tonantsi Cult of the Eastern Nahuas," *Mother Worship: Themes and Variations*, James J. Preston, ed.

Tlazolteotl/Coatlicue/la Chingada into *putas*; into the Beauties and the Beasts. They went even further; they made all Indian deities and religious practices the work of the devil.

Thus *Tonantsi* became *Guadalupe*, the chaste protective mother, the defender of the Mexican people.

> *El nueve de diciembre del año 1531*
> *a las cuatro de la madrugada*
> *un pobre indio que se llamaba Juan Diego*
> *iba cruzando el cerro de Tepeyác*
> *cuando oyó un cantó de pájaro.*
> *Alzó al cabeza vío que en la cima del cerro*
> *estaba cubierta con una brillante nube blanca.*
> *Parada en frente del sol*
> *sobre una luna creciente*
> *sostenida por un ángel*
> *estaba una azteca*
> *vestida en ropa de india.*
> *Nuestra Señora María de Coatlalopeuh*
> *se le apareció.*
> *"Juan Diegito, El-que-habla-como-un-águila,"*
> *la Virgen le dijo en el lenguaje azteca.*
> *"Para hacer mi altar este cerro eligo.*
> *Dile a tu gente que yo soy la madre de Dios,*
> *a los indios yo les ayudaré."*
> *Estó se lo contó a Juan Zumarraga*
> *pero el obispo no le creyo.*
> *Juan Diego volvió, lleño su tilma[12]*
> *con rosas de castilla*
> *creciendo milagrosamente en la nieve.*
> *Se las llevó al obispo,*
> *y cuando abrío su tilma*
> *el retrato de la Virgen*
> *ahí estaba pintado.*

Guadalupe appeared on December 9, 1531, on the spot where the Aztec goddess, *Tonantsi* ("Our Lady Mother"), had been worshipped by the Nahuas and where a temple to her had stood. Speaking Nahua, she told Juan Diego, a poor Indian crossing Tepeyac Hill, whose Indian name was *Cuautlaohuac* and who belonged to the *mazehual* class, the humblest within the Chichimeca tribe, that her name was *María Coatlalopeuh*. *Coatl* is the Nahuatl word for serpent. *Lopeuh* means "the one who has dominion over serpents." I interpret this as "the one who is at one with the beasts." Some spell her name *Coatlaxopeuh* (pronounced "Cuatlashupe" in Nahuatl) and say that "*xopeuh*" means

---

[12]An oblong cloth that hangs over the back and ties together across the shoulders.

"crushed or stepped on with disdain." Some say it means "she who crushed the serpent," with the serpent as the symbol of the indigenous religion, meaning that her religion was to take the place of the Aztec religion.[13] Because *Coatlalopeuh* was homophonous to the Spanish *Guadalupe*, the Spanish identified her with the dark Virgin, *Guadalupe*, patroness of West Central Spain.[14]

From that meeting, Juan Diego walked away with the image of *la Virgen* painted on his cloak. Soon after, Mexico ceased to belong to Spain, and *la Virgen de Guadalupe* began to eclipse all the other male and female religious figures in Mexico, Central America and parts of the U.S. Southwest. "*Desde entonces para el mexicano ser Guadalupano es algo esencial*/Since then for the Mexican, to be a *Guadalupano* is something essential."[15]

Mi Virgen Morena	My brown virgin
Mi Virgen Ranchera	my country virgin
Eres nuestra Reina	you are our queen
México es tu tierra	Mexico is your land
Y tú su bandera.	and you its flag.

—*"La Virgen Ranchera"*[16]

In 1660 the Roman Catholic Church named her Mother of God, considering her synonymous with *la Virgen María*; she became *la Santa Patrona de los mexicanos*. The role of defender (or patron) has traditionally been assigned to male gods. During the Mexican Revolution, Emiliano Zapata and Miguel Hidalgo used her image to move *el pueblo mexicano* toward freedom. During the 1965 grape strike in Delano, California, and in subsequent Chicano farmworkers' marches in Texas and other parts of the Southwest, her image on banners heralded and united the farmworkers. *Pachucos* (zoot suiters) tattoo her image on their bodies. Today, in Texas and Mexico she is more venerated than Jesus or God the Father. In the Lower Rio Grande Valley of south Texas it is *la Virgen de San Juan de los Lagos* (an aspect of *Guadalupe*) that is worshipped by thousands every day at her shrine in San Juan. In Texas she is considered the patron saint of Chicanos. *Cuando Carito, mi hermanito*, was missing in action and, later, wounded in Viet Nam, *mi mamá* got on her knees *y le prometío a Ella que si su hijito volvía vivo* she would crawl on her knees and light novenas in her honor.

Today, *la Virgen de Guadalupe* is the single most potent religious, political and cultural image of the Chicano/*mexicano*. She, like my race, is a synthesis of the old world and the new, of the religion and culture of the

[13]Andres Gonzales Guerrero, Jr., *The Significance of* Nuestra Señora de Gualdalupe *and* La Raza Cósmica *in the Development of a Chicano Theology of Liberation* (Ann Arbor, MI: University Microfilms International, 1984), 122.

[14]*Algunos dicen que Guadalupe es una palabra derivada del lenguaje árabe que significa "Río Oculto."* Tomie de Paola, *The Lady of Guadalupe* (New York: Holiday House, 1980), 44.

[15]*"Desde el cielo una hermosa mañana,"* from *Propios de la misa de Nuestra Señora de Guadalupe*, Guerrero, 124.

[16]From *"La Virgen Ranchera,"* Guerrero, 127.

two races in our psyche, the conquerors and the conquered. She is the symbol of the *mestizo* true to his or her Indian values. *La cultura chicana* identifies with the mother (Indian) rather than with the father (Spanish). Our faith is rooted in indigenous attributes, images, symbols, magic and myth. Because *Guadalupe* took upon herself the psychological and physical devastation of the conquered and oppressed *indio*, she is our spiritual, political and psychological symbol. As a symbol of hope and faith, she sustains and insures our survival. The Indian, despite extreme despair, suffering and near genocide, has survived. To Mexicans on both sides of the border, *Guadalupe* is the symbol of our rebellion against the rich, upper and middleclass; against their subjugation of the poor and the *indio*.

Guadalupe unites people of different races, religions, languages: Chicano protestants, American Indians and whites. "*Nuestra abogada siempre serás/* Our *mediatrix* you will always be." She mediates between the Spanish and the Indian cultures (or three cultures as in the case of *mexicanos* of African or other ancestry) and between Chicanos and the white world. She mediates between humans and the divine, between this reality and the reality of spirit entities. *La Virgen de Guadalupe* is the symbol of ethnic identity and of the tolerance for ambiguity that Chicanos-*mexicanos*, people of mixed race, people who have Indian blood, people who cross cultures, by necessity possess.

La gente Chicana tiene tres madres. All three are mediators: *Guadalupe,* the virgin mother who has not abandoned us, *la Chingada (Malinche),* the raped mother whom we have abandoned, and *la Llorona,* the mother who seeks her lost children and is a combination of the other two.

Ambiguity surrounds the symbols of these three "Our Mothers." *Guadalupe* has been used by the Church to mete out institutionalized oppression: to placate the Indians and *mexicanos* and Chicanos. In part, the true identity of all three has been subverted—*Guadalupe* to make us docile and enduring, *la Chingada* to make us ashamed of our Indian side, and *la Llorona* to make us long-suffering people. This obscuring has encouraged the *virgen/puta* (whore) dichotomy.

Yet we have not all embraced this dichotomy. In the U.S. Southwest, Mexico, Central and South America the *indio* and the *mestizo* continue to worship the old spirit entities (including *Guadalupe*) and their supernatural power, under the guise of Christian saints.[17]

> *Las invoco diosas mías, ustedes las indias*
> *sumergidas en mi carne que son mis sombras.*
> *Ustedes que persisten mudas en sus cuevas.*
> *Ustedes Señoras que ahora, como yo,*
> *   están en desgracia.*

---

[17]*La Virgen María* is often equated with the Aztec *Teleoinam*, the Maya *Ixchel*, the Inca *Mamacocha* and the Yuroba *Yemayá*.

For Waging War Is My Cosmic Duty: The Loss of the Balanced Oppositions and the Change to Male Dominance

Therefore I decided to leave
The country (Aztlán),
Therefore I have come as one charged with a
    special duty,
Because I have been given arrows and shields,
For waging war is my duty,
And on my expeditions I
Shall see all the lands,
I shall wait for the people and meet them
In all four quarters and I shall give them
Food to eat and drinks to quench their thirst,
For here I shall unite all the different peoples!

—*Huitzilopochtli* speaking to the Azteca-Mexica[18]

Before the Aztecs became a militaristic, bureaucratic state where male predatory warfare and conquest were based on patrilineal nobility, the principle of balanced opposition between the sexes existed.[19] The people worshipped the Lord and Lady of Duality, *Ometecuhtli* and *Omecihuatl*. Before the change to male dominance, *Coatlicue*, Lady of the Serpent Skirt, contained and balanced the dualities of male and female, light and dark, life and death.

The changes that led to the loss of the balanced oppositions began when the Azteca, one of the twenty Toltec tribes, made the last pilgrimage from a place called Aztlán. The migration south began about the year A.D. 820. Three hundred years later the advance guard arrived near Tula, the capital of the declining Toltec empire. By the 11th century, they had joined with the Chichimec tribe of Mexitin (afterwards called Mexica) into one religious and administrative organization within Aztlán, the Aztec territory. The Mexitin, with their tribal god *Tetzauhteotl Huitzilopochtli* (Magnificent Humming Bird on the Left), gained control of the religious system.[20] (In some stories *Huitzilopochtli* killed his sister, the moon goddess *Malinalxoch*, who used her supernatural power over animals to control the tribe rather than wage war.)

Huitzilopochtli assigned the Azteca-Mexica the task of keeping the human race (the present cosmic age called the Fifth Sun, *El Quinto Sol*) alive. They were to guarantee the harmonious preservation of the human race by unifying all the people on earth into one social, religious and administrative organ. The Aztec people considered themselves in charge of regulating all

---

[18]Geoffrey Parrinder, ed., *World Religions: From Ancient History to the Present* (New York, NY: Facts on File Publications, 1971), 72.

[19]Levi-Stauss's paradigm which opposes nature to culture and female to male has no

such validity in the early history of our Indian forebears. June Nash, "The Aztecs and the Ideology of Male Dominance," *Signs* (Winter, 1978), 349.

[20]Parrinder, 72.

earthly matters.[21] Their instrument: controlled or regulated war to gain and exercise power.

After 100 years in the central plateau, the Azteca-Mexica went to Chapultepec, where they settled in 1248 (the present site of the park on the outskirts of Mexico City). There, in 1345, the Aztec-Mexica chose the site of their capital, Tenochtitlan.[22] By 1428, they dominated the Central Mexican lake area.

The Aztec ruler, *Itzcoatl*, destroyed all the painted documents (books called codices) and rewrote a mythology that validated the wars of conquest and thus continued the shift from a tribe based on clans to one based on classes. From 1429 to 1440, the Aztecs emerged as a militaristic state that preyed on neighboring tribes for tribute and captives.[23] The "wars of flowers" were encounters between local armies with a fixed number of warriors, operating within the Aztec World, and, according to set rules, fighting ritual battles at fixed times and on predetermined battlefields. The religious purpose of these wars was to procure prisoners of war who could be sacrificed to the deities of the capturing party. For if one "fed" the gods, the human race would be saved from total extinction. The social purpose was to enable males of noble families and warriors of low descent to win honor, fame and administrative offices, and to prevent social and cultural decadence of the elite. The Aztec people were free to have their own religious faith, provided it did not conflict too much with the three fundamental principles of state ideology: to fulfill the special duty set forth by *Huitzilopochtli* of unifying all peoples, to participate in the wars of flowers, and to bring ritual offerings and do penance for the purpose of preventing decadence.[24]

Matrilineal descent characterized the Toltecs and perhaps early Aztec society. Women possessed property, and were curers as well as priestesses. According to the codices, women in former times had the supreme power in Tula, and in the beginning of the Aztec dynasty, the royal blood ran through the female line. A council of elders of the Calpul headed by a supreme leader, or *tlactlo*, called the father and mother of the people, governed the tribe. The supreme leader's vice-emperor occupied the position of "Snake Woman" or *Cihuacoatl*, a goddess.[25] Although the high posts were occupied by men, the terms referred to females, evidence of the exalted role of women before the Aztec nation became centralized. The final break with the democratic Calpul came when the four Aztec lords of royal lineage picked the king's successor from his siblings or male descendants.[26]

La Llorona's wailing in the night for her lost children has an echoing note in the wailing or mourning rites performed by women as they bid their sons, brothers and husbands good-bye before they left to go to the "flowery

[21]Parrinder, 77.
[22]Nash, 352
[23]Nash, 350, 355.
[24]Parrinder, 355.
[25]Jacques Soustelle, *The Daily Life of the Aztecs on the Eve of the Spanish Conquest*

(New York, NY: Macmillan Publishing Company, 1962). Soustelle and most other historians got their information from the Franciscan father Bernardino de Sahagún, chief chronicler of Indian religious life.
[26]Nash, 252–253.

wars." Wailing is the Indian, Mexican and Chicana woman's feeble protest when she has no other recourse. These collective wailing rites may have been a sign of resistance in a society which glorified the warrior and war and for whom the women of the conquered tribes were booty.[27]

In defiance of the Aztec rulers, the *macehuales* (the common people) continued to worship fertility, nourishment and agricultural female deities, those of crops and rain. They venerated *Chalchiuhtlicue* (goddess of sweet or inland water), *Chicomecoatl* (goddess of food) and *Huixtocihuatl* (goddess of salt).

Nevertheless, it took less than three centuries for Aztec society to change from the balanced duality of their earlier times and from the egalitarian traditions of a wandering tribe to those of a predatory state. The nobility kept the tribute, the commoner got nothing, resulting in a class split. The conquered tribes hated the Aztecs because of the rape of their women and the heavy taxes levied on them. The *Tlaxcalans* were the Aztec's bitter enemies and it was they who helped the Spanish defeat the Aztec rulers, who were by this time so unpopular with their own common people that they could not even mobilize the populace to defend the city. Thus the Aztec nation fell not because *Malinali* (*la Chingada*) interpreted for and slept with Cortés, but because the ruling elite had subverted the solidarity between men and women and between noble and commoner.[28]

Sueño con serpientes

Coatl. In pre-Columbian America the most notable symbol was the serpent. The Olmecs associated womanhood with the Serpent's mouth which was guarded by rows of dangerous teeth, a sort of *vagina dentate*. They considered it the most sacred place on earth, a place of refuge, the creative womb from which all things were born and to which all things returned. Snake people had holes, entrances to the body of the Earth Serpent; they followed the Serpent's way, identified with the Serpent deity, with the mouth, both the eater and the eaten. The destiny of humankind is to be devoured by the Serpent.[29]

> Dead,
> the doctor by the operating table said.
> I passed between the two fangs,
> the flickering tongue.
> Having come through the mouth of the serpent,
> swallowed,
> I found myself suddenly in the dark,
> sliding down a smooth wet surface
> down down into an even darker darkness.

[27]Nash, 358.
[28]Nash, 361–362.
[29]Karl W. Luckert, *Olmec Religion: A Key to Middle America and Beyond* (Norman, OK:

University of Oklahoma Press, 1976), 68, 69, 87, 109.

Having crossed the portal, the raised hinged mouth,
    having entered the serpent's belly,
    now there was no looking back, no going back.

    Why do I cast no shadow?
Are there lights from all sides shining on me?
    Ahead, ahead.
    curled up inside the serpent's coils,
    the damp breath of death on my face.
I knew at that instant: something must change
        or I'd die.
    Algo tenía que cambiar.

After each of my four bouts with death I'd catch glimpses of an other-world Serpent. Once, in my bedroom, I saw a cobra the size of the room, her hood expanding over me. When I blinked she was gone. I realized she was, in my psyche, the mental picture and symbol of the instinctual in its collective impersonal, prehuman. She, the symbol of the dark sexual drive, the chthonic (underworld), the feminine, the serpentine movement of sexuality, of creativity, the basis of all energy and life.

The Presences

She appeared in white, garbed in white,
standing white, pure white.

—*Bernardino de Sahagún*[30]

On the gulf where I was raised, *en el Valle del Río Grande* in South Texas—that triangular piece of land wedged between the river *y el golfo* which serves as the Texas-U.S./Mexican border—is a Mexican *pueblito* called Hargill (at one time in the history of this one-grocery-store, two-service-stations town there were thirteen churches and thirteen *cantinas*). Down the road, a little ways from our house, was a deserted church. It was known among the *mexicanos* that if you walked down the road late at night you would see a woman dressed in white floating about, peering out the church window. She would follow those who had done something bad or who were afraid. *Los mexicanos* called her *la Jila*. Some thought she was *la Llorona*. She was, I think, *Cihuacoatl*, Serpent Woman, ancient Aztec goddess of the earth, of war and birth, patron of midwives, and antecedent of *la Llorona*. Covered with chalk, *Cihuacoatl* wears a white dress with a decoration half red and half black. Her hair forms two little horns (which the Aztecs depicted as knives) crossed on her forehead. The lower part of her face is a

[30]Bernardino de Sahagún, *General History of the Things of New Spain* (Florentine Codex), Vol. I Revised, trans. Arthur Anderson and Charles Dibble (Sante Fe, NM: School of American Research, 1950), 11.

bare jawbone, signifying death. On her back she carries a cradle, the knife of sacrifice swaddled as if it were her papoose, her child.[31] Like *la Llorona*, *Cihuacoatl* howls and weeps in the night, screams as if demented. She brings mental depression and sorrow. Long before it takes place, she is the first to predict something is to happen.

Back then, I, an unbeliever, scoffed at these Mexican superstitions as I was taught in Anglo school. Now, I wonder if this story and similar ones were the culture's attempts to "protect" members of the family, especially girls, from "wandering." Stories of the devil luring young girls away and having his way with them discouraged us from going out. There's an ancient Indian tradition of burning the umbilical cord of an infant girl under the house so she will never stray from it and her domestic role.

> *A mis ancas caen los cueros de culebra,*
> *cuatro veces por año los arrastro,*
> *me tropiezo y me caigo*
> *y cada vez que miro una culebra le pregunto*
> *¿Qué traes conmigo?*

Four years ago a red snake crossed my path as I walked through the woods. The direction of its movement, its pace, its colors, the "mood" of the trees and the wind and the snake—they all "spoke" to me, told me things. I look for omens everywhere, everywhere catch glimpses of the patterns and cycles of my life. Stones "speak" to Luisah Teish, a Santera; trees whisper their secrets to Chrystos, a Native American. I remember listening to the voices of the wind as a child and understanding its messages. *Los espíritus* that ride the back of the south wind. I remember their exhalation blowing in through the slits in the door during those hot Texas afternoons. A gust of wind raising the linoleum under my feet, buffeting the house. Everything trembling.

We're not supposed to remember such otherworldly events. We're supposed to ignore, forget, kill those fleeting images of the soul's presence and of the spirit's presence. We've been taught that the spirit is outside our bodies or above our heads somewhere up in the sky with God. We're supposed to forget that every cell in our bodies, every bone and bird and worm has spirit in it.

Like many Indians and Mexicans, I did not deem my psychic experiences real. I denied their occurrences and let my inner senses atrophy. I allowed white rationality to tell me that the existence of the "other world" was mere pagan superstition. I accepted their reality, the "official" reality of the

---

[31]The Aztecs muted Snake Woman's patronage of childbirth and vegetation by placing a sacrificial knife in the empty cradle she carried on her back (signifying a child who died in childbirth), thereby making her a devourer of sacrificial victims. Snake Woman had the ability to change herself into a serpent or into a lovely young woman to entice young men who withered away and died after intercourse with her. She was known as a witch and a shape-shifter. Brundage, 168–171.

rational, reasoning mode which is connected with external reality, the upper world, and is considered the most developed consciousness—the consciousness of duality.

The other mode of consciousness facilitates images from the soul and the unconscious through dreams and the imagination. Its work is labeled "fiction," make-believe, wish-fulfillment. White anthropologists claim that Indians have "primitive" and therefore deficient minds, that we cannot think in the higher mode of consciousness—rationality. They are fascinated by what they call the "magical" mind, the "savage" mind, the *participation mystique* of the mind that says the world of the imagination—the world of the soul—and of the spirit is just as real as physical reality.[32] In trying to become "objective," Western culture made "objects" of things and people when it distanced itself from them, thereby losing "touch" with them. This dichotomy is the root of all violence.

Not only was the brain split into two functions but so was reality. Thus people who inhabit both realities are forced to live in the interface between the two, forced to become adept at switching modes. Such is the case with the *india* and the *mestiza*.

Institutionalized religion fears trafficking with the spirit world and stigmatizes it as witchcraft. It has strict taboos against this kind of inner knowledge. It fears what Jung calls the Shadow, the unsavory aspects of ourselves. But even more it fears the supra-human, the god in ourselves.

"The purpose of any established religion ... is to glorify, sanction and bless with a superpersonal meaning all personal and interpersonal activities. This occurs through the 'sacraments,' and indeed through most religious rites."[33] But it sanctions only its own sacraments and rites. Voodoo, Santeria, Shamanism and other native religions are called cults and their beliefs are called mythologies. In my own life, the Catholic Church fails to give meaning to my daily acts, to my continuing encounters with the "other world." It and other institutionalized religions impoverish all life, beauty, pleasure.

The Catholic and Protestant religions encourage fear and distrust of life and of the body; they encourage a split between the body and the spirit and totally ignore the soul; they encourage us to kill off parts of ourselves. We are taught that the body is an ignorant animal; intelligence dwells only in the head. But the body is smart. It does not discern between external stimuli and stimuli from the imagination. It reacts equally viscerally to events from the imagination as it does to "real" events.

[32]Anthropologist Lucien Levy-Bruhl coined the word *participation mystique*. According to Jung, "It denotes a peculiar kind of psychological connection . . . (in which) the subject cannot clearly distinguish himself from the object but is bound to it by a direct relationship which amounts to partial identity."

Carl Jung, "Definitions," in *Psychological Types, The Collected Works of C. G. Jung*, Vol. 6 (Princeton, NJ: Princeton University Press, 1953), par. 781.

[33]I have lost the source of this quote. If anyone knows what it is, please let the publisher know.

So I grew up in the interface trying not to give countenance to *el mal aigre*,[34] evil non-human, non-corporeal entities riding the wind, that could come in through the window, through my nose with my breath. I was not supposed to believe in *susto*, a sudden shock or fall that frightens the soul out of the body. And growing up between such opposing spiritualities how could I reconcile the two, the pagan and the Christian?

No matter to what use my people put the supranatural world, it is evident to me now that the spirit world, whose existence the whites are so adamant in denying, does in fact exist. This very minute I sense the presence of the spirits of my ancestors in my room. And I think *la Jila* is *Cihuacoatl*, Snake Woman; she is *la Llorona*, Daughter of Night, traveling the dark terrains of the unknown searching for the lost parts of herself. I remember *la Jila* following me once, remember her eerie lament. I'd like to think that she was crying for her lost children, *los* Chicanos/*mexicanos*.

La facultad

La facultad is the capacity to see in surface phenomena the meaning of deeper realities, to see the deep structure below the surface. It is an instant "sensing," a quick perception arrived at without conscious reasoning. It is an acute awareness mediated by the part of the psyche that does not speak, that communicates in images and symbols which are the faces of feelings, that is, behind which feelings reside/hide. The one possessing this sensitivity is excruciatingly alive to the world.

Those who are pushed out of the tribe for being different are likely to become more sensitized (when not brutalized into insensitivity). Those who do not feel psychologically or physically safe in the world are more apt to develop this sense. Those who are pounced on the most have it the strongest—the females, the homosexuals of all races, the darkskinned, the outcast, the persecuted, the marginalized, the foreign.

When we're up against the wall, when we have all sorts of oppressions coming at us, we are forced to develop this faculty so that we'll know when the next person is going to slap us or lock us away. We'll sense the rapist when he's five blocks down the street. Pain makes us acutely anxious to avoid more of it, so we hone that radar. It's a kind of survival tactic that people, caught between the worlds, unknowingly cultivate. It is latent in all of us.

I walk into a house and I know whether it is empty or occupied. I feel the lingering charge in the air of a recent fight or lovemaking or depression. I sense the emotions someone near is emitting—whether friendly or threatening. Hate and fear—the more intense the emotion, the greater my reception of it. I feel a tingling on my skin when someone is staring at me or thinking about me. I can tell how others feel by the way they smell, where

---

[34]Some *mexicanos* and Chicanos distinguish between *aire*, air, and *mala aigre*, the evil spirits which reside in the air.

others are by the air pressure on my skin. I can spot the love or greed or generosity lodged in the tissues of another. Often I sense the direction of and my distance from people or objects—in the dark, or with my eyes closed, without looking. It must be a vestige of a proximity sense, a sixth sense that's lain dormant from long-ago times.

Fear develops the proximity sense aspect of *la facultad*. But there is a deeper sensing that is another aspect of this faculty. It is anything that breaks into one's everyday mode of perception, that causes a break in one's defenses and resistance, anything that takes one from one's habitual grounding, causes the depths to open up, causes a shift in perception. This shift in perception deepens the way we see concrete objects and people; the senses become so acute and piercing that we can see through things, view events in depth, a piercing that reaches the underworld (the realm of the soul). As we plunge vertically, the break, with its accompanying new seeing, makes us pay attention to the soul, and we are thus carried into awareness—an experiencing of soul (Self).

We lose something in this mode of initiation, something is taken from us: our innocence, our unknowing ways, our safe and easy ignorance. There is a prejudice and a fear of the dark, chthonic (underworld), material such as depression, illness, death and the violations that can bring on this break. Confronting anything that tears the fabric of our everyday mode of consciousness and that thrusts us into a less literal and more psychic sense of reality increases awareness and *la facultad*.

7

La conciencia de la mestiza/Towards a New Consciousness

> *Por la mujer de mi raza*
> *hablará el espíritu.*[35]

Jose Vasconcelos, Mexican philosopher, envisaged *una raza mestiza, una mezcla de razas afines, una raca de color—la primera raza síntesis del globo.* He called it a cosmic race, *la raza cósmica*, a fifth race embracing the four major races of the world.[36] Opposite to the theory of the pure Aryan, and to the policy of racial purity that white America practices, his theory is one of inclusivity. At the confluence of two or more genetic streams, with chromosomes constantly "crossing over," this mixture of races, rather than resulting in an inferior being, provides hybrid progeny, a mutable, more malleable species with a rich gene pool. From this racial, ideological, cultural and biological cross-pollination, an "alien" consciousness is presently in the making—a new *mestiza* consciousness, *una conciencia de mujer*. It is a consciousness of the Borderlands.

[35]This is my own "take off" on Jose Vasconcelos's idea. Jose Vasconcelos, *La Raza Cósmica: Misión de la Raza Ibero-Americana* (México: Aguilar S.A. de Ediciones, 1961).

[36]Vasconcelos.

Una lucha de fronteras/A Struggle of Borders

Because I, a *mestiza,*
continually walk out of one culture
and into another,
because I am in all cultures at the same time,
alma entre dos mundos, tres, cuatro,
me zumba la cabeza con lo contradictorio.
Estoy norteada por todas las voces que me hablan
simultáneamente.

The ambivalence from the clash of voices results in mental and emotional states of perplexity. Internal strife results in insecurity and indecisiveness. The mestiza's dual or multiple personality is plagued by psychic restlessness.

In a constant state of mental nepantilism, an Aztec word meaning torn between ways, *la mestiza* is a product of the transfer of the cultural and spiritual values of one group to another. Being tricultural, monolingual, bilingual, or multilingual, speaking a patois, and in a state of perpetual transition, the *mestiza* faces the dilemma of the mixed breed: which collectivity does the daughter of a darkskinned mother listen to?

El choque de un alma atrapado entre el mundo del espíritu y el mundo de la técnica a veces la deja entullada. Cradled in one culture, sandwiched between two cultures, straddling all three cultures and their value systems, *la mestiza* undergoes a struggle of flesh, a struggle of borders, an inner war. Like all people, we perceive the version of reality that our culture communicates. Like others having or living in more than one culture, we get multiple, often opposing messages. The coming together of two self-consistent but habitually incompatible frames of reference[37] causes *un choque,* a cultural collision.

Within us and within *la cultura chicana,* commonly held beliefs of the white culture attack commonly held beliefs of the Mexican culture, and both attack commonly held beliefs of the indigenous culture. Subconsciously, we see an attack on ourselves and our beliefs as a threat and we attempt to block with a counterstance.

But it is not enough to stand on the opposite river bank, shouting questions, challenging patriarchal, white conventions. A counterstance locks one into a duel of oppressor and oppressed; locked in mortal combat, like the cop and the criminal, both are reduced to a common denominator of violence. The counterstance refutes the dominant culture's views and beliefs, and, for this, it is proudly defiant. All reaction is limited by, and dependent on, what it is reacting against. Because the counterstance stems from a problem with authority—outer as well as inner—it's a step towards liberation from cultural domination. But it is not a way of life. At some point, on our way to a new consciousness, we will have to leave the opposite bank, the split between the two mortal combatants somehow healed so that we

[37]Arthur Koestler termed this "bisociation." Albert Rothenberg, *The Creative Process in* *Art, Science, and Other Fields* (Chicago, IL: University of Chicago Press, 1979), 12.

are on both shores at once and, at once, see through serpent and eagle eyes. Or perhaps we will decide to disengage from the dominant culture, write it off altogether as a lost cause, and cross the border into a wholly new and separate territory. Or we might go another route. The possibilities are numerous once we decide to act and not react.

A Tolerance for Ambiguity

These numerous possibilities leave *la mestiza* floundering in uncharted seas. In perceiving conflicting information and points of view, she is subjected to a swamping of her psychological borders. She has discovered that she can't hold concepts or ideas in rigid boundaries. The borders and walls that are supposed to keep the undesirable ideas out are entrenched habits and patterns of behavior; these habits and patterns are the enemy within. Rigidity means death. Only by remaining flexible is she able to stretch the psyche horizontally and vertically. *La mestiza* constantly has to shift out of habitual formations; from convergent thinking, analytical reasoning that tends to use rationality to move toward a single goal (a Western mode), to divergent thinking,[38] characterized by movement away from set patterns and goals and toward a more whole perspective, one that includes rather than excludes.

The new *mestiza* copes by developing a tolerance for contradictions, a tolerance for ambiguity. She learns to be an Indian in Mexican culture, to be Mexican from an Anglo point of view. She learns to juggle cultures. She has a plural personality, she operates in a pluralistic mode—nothing is thrust out, the good the bad and the ugly, nothing rejected, nothing abandoned. Not only does she sustain contradictions, she turns the ambivalence into something else.

She can be jarred out of ambivalence by an intense, and often painful, emotional event which inverts or resolves the ambivalence. I'm not sure exactly how. The work takes place underground—subconsciously. It is work that the soul performs. That focal point or fulcrum, that juncture where the mestiza stands, is where phenomena tend to collide. It is where the possibility of uniting all that is separate occurs. This assembly is not one where severed or separated pieces merely come together. Nor is it a balancing of opposing powers. In attempting to work out a synthesis, the self has added a third element which is greater than the sum of its severed parts. That third element is a new consciousness—a mestiza consciousness—and though it is a source of intense pain, its energy comes from continual creative motion that keeps breaking down the unitary aspect of each new paradigm.

En unas pocas centurias, the future will belong to the mestiza. Because the future depends on the breaking down of paradigms, it depends on the straddling of two or more cultures. By creating a new mythos—that is, a

---

[38]In part, I derive my definitions for "convergent" and "divergent" thinking from Rothenberg, 12–13.

change in the way we perceive reality, the way we see ourselves, and the ways we behave—*la mestiza* creates a new consciousness.

The work of *mestiza* consciousness is to break down the subject-object duality that keeps her a prisoner and to show in the flesh and through the images in her work how duality is transcended. The answer to the problem between the white race and the colored, between males and females, lies in healing the split that originates in the very foundation of our lives, our culture, our languages, our thoughts. A massive uprooting of dualistic thinking in the individual and collective consciousness is the beginning of a long struggle, but one that could, in our best hopes, bring us to the end of rape, of violence, of war.

La encrucijada/The Crossroads

> A chicken is being sacrificed
> at a crossroads, a simple mound of earth
> a mud shrine for *Eshu*,
> *Yoruba* god of indeterminacy,
> who blesses her choice of path.
> She begins her journey.

Su cuerpo es una bocacalle. La mestiza has gone from being the sacrificial goat to becoming the officiating priestess at the crossroads.

As a *mestiza* I have no country, my homeland cast me out; yet all countries are mine because I am every woman's sister or potential lover. (As a lesbian I have no race, my own people disclaim me; but I am all races because there is the queer of me in all races.) I am cultureless because, as a feminist, I challenge the collective cultural/religious male-derived beliefs of Indo-Hispanics and Anglos; yet I am cultured because I am participating in the creation of yet another culture, a new story to explain the world and our participation in it, a new value system with images and symbols that connect us to each other and to the planet. *Soy un amasamiento*, I am an act of kneading, of uniting and joining that not only has produced both a creature of darkness and a creature of light, but also a creature that questions the definitions of light and dark and gives them new meanings.

We are the people who leap in the dark, we are the people on the knees of the gods. In our very flesh, (r)evolution works out the clash of cultures. It makes us crazy constantly, but if the center holds, we've made some kind of evolutionary step forward. *Nuestra alma el trabajo*, the opus, the great alchemical work; spiritual *mestizaje*, a "morphogenesis,"[39] an inevitable unfolding. We have become the quickening serpent movement.

---

[39]To borrow chemist Ilya Prigogine's theory of "dissipative structures." Prigogine discovered that substances interact not in predictable ways as it was taught in science, but in different and fluctuating ways to produce new and more complex structures, a kind of birth he called "morphogenesis," which created unpredictable innovations. Harold Gilliam, "Searching for a New World View," *This World* (January, 1981), 23.

Indigenous like corn, like corn, the *mestiza* is a product of crossbreeding, designed for preservation under a variety of conditions. Like an ear of corn—a female seed-bearing organ—the *mestiza* is tenacious, tightly wrapped in the husks of her culture. Like kernels she clings to the cob; with thick stalks and strong race roots, she holds tight to the earth—she will survive the crossroads.

Lavando y remojando el maíz en agua de cal, despojando el pellejo. Moliendo, mixteando, amasando, haciendo tortillas de masa.[40] She steeps the corn in lime, it swells, softens. With stone roller on *metate*, she grinds the corn, then grinds again. She kneads and moulds the dough, pats the round balls into *tortillas*.

> We are the porous rock in the stone *metate*
> squatting on the ground.
> We are the rolling pin, *el maíz y agua,*
> *la masa harina. Somos e amasijo.*
> *Somos lo molido en el metate.*
> We are the *comal* sizzling hot,
> the hot *tortilla*, the hungry mouth.
> We are the coarse rock.
> We are the grinding motion,
> the mixed potion, *somos el molcajete.*
> We are the pestle, the *comino, ajo, pimienta,*
> We are the *chile colorado,*
> the green shoot that cracks the rock.
> We will abide.

El camino de la mestiza/The Mestiza Way

Caught between the sudden contraction, the breath sucked in and the endless space, the brown woman stands still, looks at the sky. She decides to go down, digging her way along the roots of trees. Sifting through the bones, she shakes them to see if there is any marrow in them. Then, touching the dirt to her forehead, to her tongue, she takes a few bones, leaves the rest in their burial place.

She goes through her backpack, keeps her journal and address book, throws away the muni-bart metromaps. The coins are heavy and they go next, then the greenbacks flutter through the air. She keeps her knife, can opener and eyebrow pencil. She puts bones, pieces of bark, hierbas, eagle feather, snakeskin, tape recorder, the rattle and drum in her pack and she sets out to become the complete tolteca.[41]

Her first step is to take inventory. *Despojando, desgranando, quitando paja.* Just what did she inherit from her ancestors? This weight on her back—

---

[40]Corn tortillas are of two types, the smooth uniform ones made in a tortilla press and usually bought at a tortilla factory or supermarket, and *gorditas*, made by mixing *masa* with lard or shortening or butter (my mother sometimes puts in bits of bacon or *chicharrones*).

[41]Gina Valdés, *Puentes y Fronteras: Coplas Chi* (Los Angeles: Castle Lithograph, 1982), 2.

which is the baggage from the Indian mother, which the baggage from the Spanish father, which the baggage from the Anglo?

Pero es difícil differentiating between *lo heredado, lo adquirido, lo impuesto.* She puts history through a sieve, winnows out the lies, looks at the forces that we as a race, as women, have been a part of. *Luego bota lo que no vale, los desmientos, los desencuentros, el embrutecimiento. Aguarda el juicio, hondo y enraízado, de la gente antigua.* This step is a conscious rupture with all oppressive traditions of all cultures and religions. She communicates that rupture, documents the struggle. She reinterprets history and, using new symbols, she shapes new myths. She adopts new perspectives toward the darkskinned, women and queers. She strengthens her tolerance (and intolerance) for ambiguity. She is willing to share, to make herself vulnerable to foreign ways of seeing and thinking. She surrenders all notions of safety, of the familiar. Deconstruct, construct. She becomes a *nahual*, able to transform herself into a tree, a coyote, into another person. She learns to transform the small "I" into the total Self. *Se hace moldeadora de su alma. Según la concepción que tiene de sí misma, así será.*

Que no se nos olvide los hombres

"Tú no sirves pa' nada—
you're good for nothing.
Eres pura vieja."

"You're nothing but a woman" means you are defective. Its opposite is to be *un macho.* The modern meaning of the word "machismo," as well as the concept, is actually an Anglo invention. For men like my father, being "macho" meant being strong enough to protect and support my mother and us, yet being able to show love. Today's macho has doubts about his ability to feed and protect his family. His "machismo" is an adaptation to oppression and poverty and low self-esteem. It is the result of hierarchical male dominance. The Anglo, feeling inadequate and inferior and powerless, displaces or transfers these feelings to the Chicano by shaming him. In the Gringo world, the Chicano suffers from excessive humility and self-effacement, shame of self and self-deprecation. Around Latinos he suffers from a sense of language inadequacy and its accompanying discomfort; with Native Americans he suffers from a racial amnesia which ignores our common blood, and from guilt because the Spanish part of him took their land and oppressed them. He has an excessive compensatory hubris when around Mexicans from the other side. It overlays a deep sense of racial shame.

The loss of a sense of dignity and respect in the macho breeds a false machismo which leads him to put down women and even to brutalize them. Coexisting with his sexist behavior is a love for the mother which takes precedence over that of all others. Devoted son, macho pig. To wash down the shame of his fears, of his very being, and to handle the brute in the mirror, he takes to the bottle, the snort, the needle, and the fist.

*   *   *

Though we "understand" the root causes of male hatred and fear, and the subsequent wounding of women, we do not excuse, we do not condone, and we will no longer put up with it. From the men of our race, we demand the admission/acknowledgment/disclosure/testimony that they wound us, violate us, are afraid of us and of our power. We need them to say they will begin to eliminate their hurtful put-down ways. But more than the words, we demand acts. We say to them: We will develop equal power with you and those who have shamed us.

It is imperative that mestizas support each other in changing the sexist elements in the Mexican-Indian culture. As long as woman is put down, the Indian and the Black in all of us is put down. The struggle of the mestiza is above all a feminist one. As long as *los hombres* think they have to *chingar mujeres* and each other to be men, as long as men are taught that they are superior and therefore culturally favored over *la mujer*, as long as to be a *vieja* is a thing of derision, there can be no real healing of our psyches. We're halfway there—we have such love of the Mother, the good mother. The first step is to unlearn the *puta/virgen* dichotomy and to see *Coatlapopeuh-Coatlicue* in the Mother, *Guadalupe*.

Tenderness, a sign of vulnerability, is so feared that it is showered on women with verbal abuse and blows. Men, even more than women, are fettered to gender roles. Women at least have had the guts to break out of bondage. Only gay men have had the courage to expose themselves to the woman inside them and to challenge the current masculinity. I've encountered a few scattered and isolated gentle straight men, the beginnings of a new breed, but they are confused, and entangled with sexist behaviors that they have not been able to eradicate. We need a new masculinity and the new man needs a movement.

Lumping the males who deviate from the general norm with man, the oppressor, is a gross injustice. *Asombra pensar que nos hemos quedado en ese pozo oscuro donde el mundo encierra a las lesbianas. Asombra pensar que hemos, como femenistas y lesbianas, cerrado nuestros corazónes a los hombres, a nuestros hermanos los jotos, desheredados y marginales como nosotros.* Being the supreme crossers of cultures, homosexuals have strong bonds with the queer white, Black, Asian, Native American, Latino, and with the queer in Italy, Australia and the rest of the planet. We come from all colors, all classes, all races, all time periods. Our role is to link people with each other—the Blacks with Jews with Indians with Asians with whites with extraterrestrials. It is to transfer ideas and information from one culture to another. Colored homosexuals have more knowledge of other cultures; have always been at the forefront (although sometimes the closet) of all liberation struggles in this country; have suffered more injustices and have survived them despite all odds. Chicanos need to acknowledge the political and artistic contributions of their queer. People, listen to what your *jotería* is saying.

The mestizo and the queer exist at this time and point on the evolutionary continuum for a purpose. We are a blending that proves that all blood is intricately woven together, and that we are spawned out of similar souls.

Somos una gente

Hay tantísimas fronteras
que dividen a la gente,
pero por cada frontera
existe también un puente

—Gina Valdés[42]

Divided Loyalties. Many women and men of color do not want to have any dealings with white people. It takes too much time and energy to explain to the downwardly mobile, white middle-class women that it's okay for us to want to own "possessions," never having had any nice furniture on our dirt floors or "luxuries" like washing machines. Many feel that whites should help their own people rid themselves of race hatred and fear first. I, for one, choose to use some of my energy to serve as mediator. I think we need to allow whites to be our allies. Through our literature, art, *corridos*, and folktales we must share our history with them so when they set up committees to help Big Mountain Navajos or the Chicano farmworkers or *los Nicaragüenses* they won't turn people away because of their racial fears and ignorances. They will come to see that they are not helping us but following our lead.

Individually, but also as a racial entity, we need to voice our needs. We need to say to white society: We need you to accept the fact that Chicanos are different, to acknowledge your rejection and negation of us. We need you to own the fact that you looked upon us as less than human, that you stole our lands, our personhood, our self-respect. We need you to make public restitution: to say that, to compensate for your own sense of defectiveness, you strive for power over us, you erase our history and our experience because it makes you feel guilty—you'd rather forget your brutish acts. To say you've split yourself from minority groups, that you disown us, that your dual consciousness splits off parts of yourself, transferring the "negative" parts onto us. (Where there is persecution of minorities, there is shadow projection. Where there is violence and war, there is repression of shadow.) To say that you are afraid of us, that to put distance between us, you wear the mask of contempt. Admit that Mexico is your double, that she exists in the shadow of this country, that we are irrevocably tied to her. Gringo, accept the doppelganger in your psyche. By taking back your collective shadow the intracultural split will heal. And finally, tell us what you need from us.

By Your True Faces We Will Know You

I am visible—see this Indian face—yet I am invisible. I both blind them with my beak nose and am their blind spot. But I exist, we exist. They'd like to think I have melted in the pot. But I haven't, we haven't.

* * *

[42]Richard Wilhelm, *The I Ching or Book of Changes*, trans. Cary F. Baynes (Princeton, NJ: Princeton University Press, 1950), 98.

The dominant white culture is killing us slowly with its ignorance. By taking away our self-determination, it has made us weak and empty. As a people we have resisted and we have taken expedient positions, but we have never been allowed to develop unencumbered—we have never been allowed to be fully ourselves. The whites in power want us people of color to barricade ourselves behind our separate tribal walls so they can pick us off one at a time with their hidden weapons; so they can whitewash and distort history. Ignorance splits people, creates prejudices. A misinformed people is a subjugated people.

Before the Chicano and the undocumented worker and the Mexican from the other side can come together, before the Chicano can have unity with Native Americans and other groups, we need to know the history of their struggle and they need to know ours. Our mothers, our sisters and brothers, the guys who hang out on street corners, the children in the playgrounds, each of us must know our Indian lineage, our afro-*mestizaje*, our history of resistance.

To the immigrant *mexicano* and the recent arrivals we must teach our history. The 80 million *mexicanos* and the Latinos from Central and South America must know of our struggles. Each one of us must know basic facts about Nicaragua, Chile and the rest of Latin America. The Latinoist movement (Chicanos, Puerto Ricans, Cubans and other Spanish-speaking people working together to combat racial discrimination in the market place) is good but it is not enough. Other than a common culture we will have nothing to hold us together. We need to meet on a broader communal ground.

The struggle is inner: Chicano, *indio*, American Indian, *mojado, mexicano*, immigrant Latino, Anglo in power, working class Anglo, Black, Asian—our psyches resemble the bordertowns and are populated by the same people. The struggle has always been inner, and is played out in the outer terrains. Awareness of our situation must come before inner changes, which in turn come before changes in society. Nothing happens in the "real" world unless it first happens in the images in our heads.

El día de la Chicana

> I will not be shamed again
> Nor will I shame myself.

I am possessed by a vision: that we Chicanas and Chicanos have taken back or uncovered our true faces, our dignity and self-respect. It's a validation vision.

Seeing the Chicana anew in light of her history. I seek an exoneration, a seeing through the fictions of white supremacy, a seeing of ourselves in our true guises and not as the false racial personality that has been given to us and that we have given to ourselves. I seek our woman's face, our true features, the positive and the negative seen clearly, free of the tainted biases of male dominance. I seek new images of identity, new beliefs about ourselves, our humanity and worth no longer in question.

Estamos viviendo en la noche de la Raza, un tiempo cuando el trabajo se hace a lo quieto, en el oscuro. El día cuando aceptamos tal y como somos y para en donde vamos y porque—ese día será el día de la Raza. Yo tengo el compromiso de

*expresar mi visión, mi sensibilidad, mi percepción de la revalidación de la gente
mexicana, su mérito, estimación, honra, aprecio, y validez.*

On December 2nd when my sun goes into my first house, I celebrate *el
día de la Chicana y el Chicano.* On that day I clean my altars, light my *Coatlalopeuh* candle, burn sage and copal, take *el baño para espantar basura,* sweep
my house. On that day I bare my soul, make myself vulnerable to friends
and family by expressing my feelings. On that day I affirm who we are.

On that day I look inside our conflicts and our basic introverted racial temperament. I identify our needs, voice them. I acknowledge that the self and the
race have been wounded. I recognize the need to take care of our personhood,
of our racial self. On that day I gather the splintered and disowned parts of *la
gente mexicana* and hold them in my arms. *Todas las partes de nosotros valen.*

On that day I say, "Yes, all you people wound us when you reject us.
Rejection strips us of self-worth; our vulnerability exposes us to shame. It is
our innate identity you find wanting. We are ashamed that we need your
good opinion, that we need your acceptance. We can no longer camouflage
our needs, can no longer let defenses and fences sprout around us. We can no
longer withdraw. To rage and look upon you with contempt is to rage and be
contemptuous of ourselves. We can no longer blame you, nor disown the
white parts, the male parts, the pathological parts, the queer parts, the vulnerable parts. Here we are weaponless with open arms, with only our magic.
Let's try it our way, the mestiza way, the Chicana way, the woman way."

On that day, I search for our essential dignity as a people, a people with
a sense of purpose—to belong and contribute to something greater than
our *pueblo.* On that day I seek to recover and reshape my spiritual identity.
¡Anímate! Raza, a celebrar el día de la Chicana.

El retorno

All movements are accomplished in six stages,
and the seventh brings return.

—I Ching

*Tanto tiempo sin verte casa mía,
mi cuna, mi hondo nido de la huerta.*

—"Soledad"[43]

I stand at the river, watch the curving, twisting serpent, a serpent nailed to
the fence where the mouth of the Rio Grande empties into the Gulf.

I have come back. *Tanto dolor me costó el alejamiento.* I shade my eyes and
look up. The bone beak of a hawk slowly circling over me, checking me out as
potential carrion. In its wake a little bird flickering its wings, swimming spor-
adically like a fish. In the distance the expressway and the slough of traffic like
an irritated sow. The sudden pull in my gut, *la tierra, los aguacerros.* My land, *el
viento soplando la arena, el lagartijo debajo de un nopalito. Me acuerdo como era
antes. Una región desértica de vasta llanuras, costeras de baja altura, de escasa*

---

[43]*"Soledad"* is sung by the group, Haciendo
Punto en Otro Son.

lluvia, de chaparrales formados por mesquites y huizaches. If I look real hard I can almost see the Spanish fathers who were called "the cavalry of Christ" enter this valley riding their burros, see the clash of cultures commence.

Tierra natal. This is home, the small towns in the Valley, *los pueblitos* with chicken pens and goats picketed to mesquite shrubs. *En las colonias* on the other side of the tracks, junk cars line the front yards of hot pink and lavender-trimmed houses—Chicano architecture we call it, self-consciously. I have missed the TV shows where hosts speak in half and half, and where awards are given in the category of Tex-Mex music. I have missed the Mexican cemeteries blooming with artificial flowers, the fields of aloe vera and red pepper, rows of sugar cane, of corn hanging on the stalks, the cloud of *polvareda* in the dirt roads behind a speeding pickup truck, *el sabor de tamales de rez y venado.* I have missed *la yegua colorada* gnawing the wooden gate of her stall, the smell of horse flesh from Carito's corrals. *He hecho menos las noches calientes sin aire, noches de linternas y lechuzas* making holes in the night.

I still feel the old despair when I look at the unpainted, dilapidated, scrap lumber houses consisting mostly of corrugated aluminum. Some of the poorest people in the U.S. live in the Lower Rio Grande Valley, an arid and semi-arid land of irrigated farming, intense sunlight and heat, citrus groves next to chaparral and cactus. I walk through the elementary school I attended so long ago, that remained segregated until recently. I remember how the white teachers used to punish us for being Mexican.

How I love this tragic valley of South Texas, as Ricardo Sánchez calls it; this borderland between the Nueces and the Rio Grande. This land has survived possession and ill-use by five countries: Spain, Mexico, the Republic of Texas, the U.S., the Confederacy, and the U.S. again. It has survived Anglo-Mexican blood feuds, lynchings, burnings, rapes, pillage.

Today I see the Valley still struggling to survive. Whether it does or not, it will never be as I remember it. The borderlands depression that was set off by the 1982 peso devaluation in Mexico resulted in the closure of hundreds of Valley businesses. Many people lost their homes, cars, land. Prior to 1982, U.S. store owners thrived on retail sales to Mexicans who came across the border for groceries and clothes and appliances. While goods on the U.S. side have become 10, 100, 1000 times more expensive for Mexican buyers, goods on the Mexican side have become 10, 100, 1000 times cheaper for Americans. Because the Valley is heavily dependent on agriculture and Mexican retail trade, it has the highest unemployment rates along the entire border region; it is the Valley that has been hardest hit.[44]

* * *

[44]Out of the twenty-two border counties in the four border states, Hidalgo County (named for Father Hidalgo who was shot in 1810 after instigating Mexico's revolt against Spanish rule under the banner of *la Virgen de Guadalupe*) is the most poverty-stricken county in the nation as well as the largest home base (along with Imperial in California) for migrant farmworkers. It was here that I was born and raised. I am amazed that both it and I have survived.

"It's been a bad year for corn," my brother, Nune, says. As he talks, I remember my father scanning the sky for a rain that would end the drought, looking up into the sky, day after day, while the corn withered on its stalk. My father has been dead for 29 years, having worked himself to death. The life span of a Mexican farm laborer is 56—he lived to be 38. It shocks me that I am older than he. I, too, search the sky for rain. Like the ancients, I worship the rain god and the maize goddess, but unlike my father I have recovered their names. Now for rain (irrigation) one offers not a sacrifice of blood, but of money.

"Farming is in a bad way," my brother says. "Two to three thousand small and big farmers went bankrupt in this country last year. Six years ago the price of corn was $8.00 per hundred pounds," he goes on. "This year it is $3.90 per hundred pounds." And, I think to myself, after taking inflation into account, not planting anything puts you ahead.

I walk out to the back yard, stare at *los rosales de mamá*. She wants me to help her prune the rose bushes, dig out the carpet grass that is choking them. *Mamagrande Ramona también tenía rosales.* Here every Mexican grows flowers. If they don't have a piece of dirt, they use car tires, jars, cans, shoe boxes. Roses are the Mexican's favorite flower. I think, how symbolic—thorns and all.

Yes, the Chicano and Chicana have always taken care of growing things and the land. Again I see the four of us kids getting off the school bus, changing into our work clothes, walking into the field with Papí and Mamí, all six of us bending to the ground. Below our feet, under the earth lie the watermelon seeds. We cover them with paper plates, putting *terremotes* on top of the plates to keep them from being blown away by the wind. The paper plates keep the freeze away. Next day or the next, we remove the plates, bare the tiny green shoots to the elements. They survive and grow, give fruit hundreds of times the size of the seed. We water them and hoe them. We harvest them. The vines dry, rot, are plowed under. Growth, death, decay, birth. The soil prepared again and again, impregnated, worked on. A constant changing of forms, *renacimientos de la tierra madre*.

> This land was Mexican once
> was Indian always
> and is.
> And will be again.

1987

■   **ANN BEATTIE**   ■
B. 1947

Frequently associated with the literary minimalism of the 1970s and 1980s (along with writers such as Raymond Carver, Richard Ford, and Bobbie Ann Mason),

Ann Beattie has been a consistent presence on the American literary scene since the early 1970s. Chiefly a practitioner of the short story, many of which appeared in *The New Yorker*, Beattie might be paired with T. C. Boyle as a writer who focuses on post-1960s idealism gone flat, though in interviews Beattie bristles both at the term *minimalism* and at the notion that she was the chronicler of her peer group. There was even talk of a "Beattie generation" when she rose to prominence in the 1970s as disaffected Baby Boomers searched for reflections of bourgeois posthippie life in fiction and found it in Beattie's spare stories. Although she has demonstrated her range in a series of successful novels since her early years, she remains associated with that period. As is often true of stories published in the 1970s and 1980s, Beattie's characters tend to be sad or somewhat bored with their lives. The title of her first novel, *Chilly Scenes of Winter*, indicates this emotional and social emptiness. Her work, with an emphasis on details and/or stylized conversations that say little and suggest much, is capable of evoking stubborn moods and raising lingering questions in the minds of her readers.

Raised in the suburbs of Washington, D.C., Beattie earned her undergraduate degree at American University and a master's degree at the University of Connecticut. She currently teaches at the University of Virginia and is married to the painter Lincoln Perry. Perry's emphasis on literary motifs and Beattie's visually precise prose have led to fruitful collaborations. In a recent tribute to John Updike, Beattie said, "Writers distrust words" and explains further, of Updike, that he instead "trusts the visuals ... nonverbal forms of communication." This assessment could easily be applied to Beattie's fiction as well: most of what is being communicated is not said outright, but deeply felt. The central symbol of the bowl in the following story, "Janus," with its aesthetic perfection and its emptiness, is an excellent example of the way objects communicate more than words in her fiction.

D. Quentin Miller
Suffolk University

PRIMARY WORKS

Distortions, 1976; *Chilly Scenes of Winter*, 1976; *Secrets and Surprises*, 1978; *Falling in Place*, 1981; *The Burning House*, 1982; *Love Always*, 1986; *Where You'll Find Me and Other Stories*, 1986; *Picturing Will*, 1989; *What Was Mine*, 1991; *Another You*, 1995; *My Life, Starring Dara Falcon*, 1997; *Park City*, 1998; *Perfect Recall*, 2000; *The Doctor's House*, 2002; *Follies: New Stories*, 2005; *Walks with Men*, 2010.

Janus

The bowl was perfect. Perhaps it was not what you'd select if you faced a shelf of bowls, and not the sort of thing that would inevitably attract a lot of attention at a crafts fair, yet it had real presence. It was as predictably admired as a mutt who has no reason to suspect he might be funny. Just such a dog, in fact, was often brought out (and in) along with the bowl.

Andrea was a real estate agent, and when she thought that some prospective buyers might be dog lovers, she would drop off her dog at the same time she placed the bowl in the house that was up for sale. She would put a dish of water in the kitchen for Mondo, take his squeaking plastic frog out of her purse and drop it on the floor. He would pounce delightedly, just as he did every day at home, batting around his favorite toy. The bowl usually sat on a coffee table, though recently she had displayed it on top of a pine blanket chest and on a lacquered table. It was once placed on a cherry table beneath a Bonnard still life, where it held its own.

Everyone who has purchased a house or who has wanted to sell a house must be familiar with some of the tricks used to convince a buyer that the house is quite special: a fire in the fireplace in early evening; jonquils in a pitcher on the kitchen counter, where no one ordinarily has space to put flowers; perhaps the slight aroma of spring, made by a single drop of scent vaporizing from a lamp bulb.

The wonderful thing about the bowl, Andrea thought, was that it was both subtle and noticeable—a paradox of a bowl. Its glaze was the color of cream and seemed to glow no matter what light it was placed in. There were a few bits of color in it—tiny geometric flashes—and some of these were tinged with flecks of silver. They were as mysterious as cells seen under a microscope; it was difficult not to study them, because they shimmered, flashing for a split second, and then resumed their shape. Something about the colors and their random placement suggested motion. People who liked country furniture always commented on the bowl, but then it turned out that people who felt comfortable with Biedermeier loved it just as much. But the bowl was not at all ostentatious, or even so noticeable that anyone would suspect that it had been put in place deliberately. They might notice the height of the ceiling on first entering a room, and only when their eye moved down from that, or away from the refraction of sunlight on a pale wall, would they see the bowl. Then they would go immediately to it and comment. Yet they always faltered when they tried to say something. Perhaps it was because they were in the house for a serious reason, not to notice some object.

Once, Andrea got a call from a woman who had not put in an offer on a house she had shown her. That bowl, she said—would it be possible to find out where the owners had bought that beautiful bowl? Andrea pretended that she did not know what the woman was referring to. A bowl, somewhere in the house? Oh, on a table under the window. Yes, she would ask, of course. She let a couple of days pass, then called back to say that the bowl had been a present and the people did not know where it had been purchased.

When the bowl was not being taken from house to house, it sat on Andrea's coffee table at home. She didn't keep it carefully wrapped (although she transported it that way, in a box); she kept it on the table, because she liked to see it. It was large enough so that it didn't seem fragile, or particularly vulnerable if anyone sideswiped the table or Mondo blundered into it at play. She had asked her husband to please not drop his house key in it. It was meant to be empty.

When her husband first noticed the bowl, he had peered into it and smiled briefly. He always urged her to buy things she liked. In recent years, both of them had acquired many things to make up for all the lean years when they were graduate students, but now that they had been comfortable for quite a while, the pleasure of new possessions dwindled. Her husband had pronounced the bowl "pretty," and he had turned away without picking it up to examine it. He had no more interest in the bowl than she had in his new Leica.

She was sure that the bowl brought her luck. Bids were often put in on houses where she had displayed the bowl. Sometimes the owners, who were always asked to be away or to step outside when the house was being shown, didn't even know that the bowl had been in their house. Once—she could not imagine how—she left it behind, and then she was so afraid that something might have happened to it that she rushed back to the house and sighed with relief when the woman owner opened the door. The bowl, Andrea explained—she had purchased a bowl and set it on the chest for safekeeping while she toured the house with the prospective buyers, and she ... She felt like rushing past the frowning woman and seizing her bowl. The owner stepped aside, and it was only when Andrea ran to the chest that the lady glanced at her a little strangely. In the few seconds before Andrea picked up the bowl, she realized that the owner must have just seen that it had been perfectly placed, that the sunlight struck the bluer part of it. Her pitcher had been moved to the far side of the chest, and the bowl predominated. All the way home, Andrea wondered how she could have left the bowl behind. It was like leaving a friend at an outing—just walking off. Sometimes there were stories in the paper about families forgetting a child somewhere and driving to the next city. Andrea had only gone a mile down the road before she remembered.

In time, she dreamed of the bowl. Twice, in a waking dream—early in the morning, between sleep and a last nap before rising—she had a clear vision of it. It came into sharp focus and startled her for a moment—the same bowl she looked at every day.

She had a very profitable year selling real estate. Word spread, and she had more clients than she felt comfortable with. She had the foolish thought that if only the bowl were an animate object she could thank it. There were times when she wanted to talk to her husband about the bowl. He was a stockbroker, and sometimes told people that he was fortunate to be married to a woman who had such a fine aesthetic sense and yet could also function in the real world. They were a lot alike, really—they had agreed on that. They were both quiet people—reflective, slow to make value judgments, but almost intractable once they had come to a conclusion. They both liked details, but while ironies attracted her, he was more impatient and dismissive when matters became many sided or unclear. But they both knew this; it was the kind of thing they could talk about when they were alone in the car together, coming home from a party or after a weekend with friends. But she never talked to him about the bowl. When they were at dinner, exchanging their news of the day, or while they lay in bed at night listening to the stereo and murmuring sleepy disconnections, she was often tempted to come right out and say that she thought that the bowl in the living room, the cream-colored bowl, was responsible for her success. But she didn't say it. She couldn't begin to explain it. Sometimes in the morning, she would look at him and feel guilty that she had such a constant secret.

Could it be that she had some deeper connection with the bowl—a relationship of some kind? She corrected her thinking: how could she imagine such a thing, when she was a human being and it was a bowl? It was ridiculous. Just think of how people lived together and loved each other ... But was that always so clear, always a relationship? She was confused by these thoughts, but they remained in her mind. There was something within her now, something real, that she never talked about.

The bowl was a mystery, even to her. It was frustrating, because her involvement with the bowl contained a steady sense of unrequited good fortune; it would have been easier to respond if some sort of demand were made in return. But that only happened in fairy tales. The bowl was just a bowl. She did not believe that for one second. What she believed was that it was something she loved.

In the past, she had sometimes talked to her husband about a new property she was about to buy or sell—confiding some clever strategy she had devised to persuade owners who seemed ready to sell. Now she stopped doing that, for all her strategies involved the bowl. She became more deliberate with the bowl, and more possessive. She put it in houses only when no one was there, and removed it when she left the house. Instead of just moving a pitcher or a dish, she would remove all the other objects from a table. She had to force herself to handle them carefully, because she didn't really care about them. She just wanted them out of sight.

She wondered how the situation would end. As with a lover, there was no exact scenario of how matters would come to a close. Anxiety became the operative force. It would be irrelevant if the lover rushed into someone else's arms, or wrote her a note and departed to another city. The horror was the possibility of the disappearance. That was what mattered.

She would get up at night and look at the bowl. It never occurred to her that she might break it. She washed and dried it without anxiety, and she moved it often, from coffee table to mahogany corner table or wherever, without fearing an accident. It was clear that she would not be the one who would do anything to the bowl. The bowl was only handled by her, set safely on one surface or another; it was not very likely that anyone would break it. A bowl was a poor conductor of electricity: it would not be hit by lightning. Yet the idea of damage persisted. She did not think beyond that—to what her life would be without the bowl. She only continued to fear that some accident would happen. Why not, in a world where people set plants where they did not belong, so that visitors touring a house would be fooled into thinking that dark corners got sunlight—a world full of tricks?

She had first seen the bowl several years earlier, at a crafts fair she had visited half in secret, with her lover. He had urged her to buy the bowl. She didn't *need* any more things, she told him. But she had been drawn to the bowl, and they had lingered near it. Then she went on to the next booth, and he came up behind her, tapping the rim against her shoulder as she ran her fingers over a wood carving. "You're still insisting that I buy that?" she said. "No," he said. "I bought it for you." He had bought her other things before this—things she liked more, at first—the child's ebony-and-turquoise ring that fitted her little finger; the wooden box, long and thin, beautifully dovetailed, that she used to hold paper clips; the soft gray sweater with a pouch pocket. It was his idea that when he could not be there to hold her hand she could hold her own—clasp her hands inside the lone pocket that stretched across the front. But in time she became more attached to the bowl than to any of his other presents. She tried to talk herself out of it. She owned other things that were more striking or valuable. It wasn't an object whose beauty jumped out at you; a lot of people must have passed it by before the two of them saw it that day.

Her lover had said that she was always too slow to know what she really loved. Why continue with her life the way it was? Why be two-faced, he asked her. He had made the first move toward her. When she would not decide in his favor, would not change her life and come to him, he asked her what made her think she could have it both ways. And then he made the last move and left. It was a decision meant to break her will, to shatter her intransigent ideas about honoring previous commitments.

Time passed. Alone in the living room at night, she often looked at the bowl sitting on the table, still and safe, unilluminated. In its way, it was perfect: the world cut in half, deep and smoothly empty. Near the rim, even in dim light, the eye moved toward one small flash of blue, a vanishing point on the horizon.

1986

JOY HARJO (CREEK)
B. 1951

Joy Harjo is a Creek Indian, born in the heart of the Creek Nation in Tulsa, Oklahoma. After graduating from the Institute of American Indian Arts in Santa Fe, New Mexico, she taught there from 1978 to 1979 and again from 1983 to 1984. In 1978 she earned an M.F.A. after studying at the University of Iowa Writers' Workshop. She now teaches at the University of New Mexico. Along with her continuing poetry, other projects have included screenplays and a book of prose poems written in collaboration with an astronomer.

Joy Harjo's poetry is widely praised and recognized. She has seen her work published in many literary reviews in the United States, as well as in magazines and anthologies. A cadence marks her work that is reminiscent of the repetitions of the Indian ceremonial drum, exemplified in the energy and motion of "She Had Some Horses." Her poetic voice and imagery have steadily developed as she resurrects the carnage of the early conflict between native and European, "the fantastic and terrible story of our survival" ("Anchorage"), and the rejoicing experienced by those who carry on Indian traditions and culture. Her work provides a unique perspective and a piquant examination of American culture from a native point of view. Her verse cries out for the lost, the dispossessed, and the forgotten of reservation, rural, and urban America. Her rigorous words pronounce an awakening for those left voiceless in the past. She relentlessly pursues in print tensions surrounding gender and ethnicity. She explores the pain of existence and the dream fusion of the individual with the landscape, especially the mesa-strewn Southwest. Like so many other Native Americans, Joy Harjo has traveled across the nation, and her poetry reflects the exuberance for sight and sound of the Indian powwow circuit, moving through the culture of pan-Indian America, and participation in Indian-related conferences. Her lyricism mirrors the lushness of feel for the countryside and rich images of the people she encounters. Her work mingles realism and the philosophy of American Indian spirituality. She recalls the wounds of the past, the agony of the Indian present, and dream visions of a better future for indigenous peoples. Her work continues to deal with themes that call forth rage and elation at the same time. The multiplicity of emotions she touches is encompassed in the title poem of her 1983 *She Had Some Horses*: "She had some horses she loved. / She had some horses she hated. / These were the same horses."

C. B. Clark
Oklahoma City University

PRIMARY WORKS

The Last Song, 1975; *What Moon Drove Me to This*, 1979; *She Had Some Horses*, 1983; *Secrets from the Center of the World* (with Steven Strom), 1989; *In Mad Love and War*, 1990; *The Woman Who Fell from the Sky*, 1994; *Letter from the End of the Twentieth Century* (CD), 1996; *The Spiral of Memory: Interviews*, 1996; *A Map to the Next World: Poetry and Tales*, 2000; *How We Became Human*, 2002.

The Woman Hanging from the Thirteenth Floor Window

She is the woman hanging from the 13th floor
window. Her hands are pressed white against the
concrete moulding of the tenement building. She
hangs from the 13th floor window in east Chicago,
with a swirl of birds over her head. They could   5
be a halo, or a storm of glass waiting to crush her.

She thinks she will be set free.

The woman hanging from the 13th floor window
on the east side of Chicago is not alone.
She is a woman of children, of the baby, Carlos,   10
and of Margaret, and of Jimmy who is the oldest.
She is her mother's daughter and her father's son.
She is several pieces between the two husbands
she has had. She is all the women of the apartment
building who stand watching her, watching themselves.   15

When she was young she ate wild rice on scraped down
plates in warm wood rooms. It was in the farther
north and she was the baby then. They rocked her.

She sees Lake Michigan lapping at the shores of
herself. It is a dizzy hole of water and the rich   20
live in tall glass houses at the edge of it. In some
places Lake Michigan speaks softly, here, it just sputters
and butts itself against the asphalt. She sees
other buildings just like hers. She sees other
women hanging from many-floored windows   25
counting their lives in the palms of their hands
and in the palms of their children's hands.

She is the woman hanging from the 13th floor window
on the Indian side of town. Her belly is soft from
her children's births, her worn levis swing down below   30
her waist, and then her feet, and then her heart.
She is dangling.

The woman hanging from the 13th floor hears voices.
They come to her in the night when the lights have gone
dim. Sometimes they are little cats mewing and scratching   35
at the door, sometimes they are her grandmother's voice,
and sometimes they are gigantic men of light whispering
to her to get up, to get up, to get up. That's when she wants
to have another child to hold onto in the night, to be able
to fall back into dreams.   40

And the woman hanging from the 13th floor window
hears other voices. Some of them scream out from below
for her to jump, they would push her over. Others cry softly
from the sidewalks, pull their children up like flowers and gather
them into their arms. They would help her, like themselves.   45

But she is the woman hanging from the 13th floor window,
and she knows she is hanging by her own fingers, her
own skin, her own thread of indecision.

She thinks of Carlos, of Margaret, of Jimmy.
She thinks of her father, and of her mother.   50
She thinks of all the women she has been, of all
the men. She thinks of the color of her skin, and
of Chicago streets, and of waterfalls and pines.
She thinks of moonlight nights, and of cool spring storms.
Her mind chatters like neon and northside bars.   55
She thinks of the 4 A.M. lonelinesses that have folded
her up like death, discordant, without logical and
beautiful conclusion. Her teeth break off at the edges.
She would speak.

The woman hangs from the 13th floor window crying for   60
the lost beauty of her own life. She sees the
sun falling west over the grey plane of Chicago.
She thinks she remembers listening to her own life
break loose, as she falls from the 13th floor
window on the east side of Chicago, or as she   65
climbs back up to claim herself again.

                                                                       1983

New Orleans

This is the south. I look for evidence
of other Creeks, for remnants of voices,
or for tobacco brown bones to come wandering
down Conti Street, Royale, or Decatur.
Near the French Market I see a blue horse   5
caught frozen in stone in the middle of
a square. Brought in by the Spanish on
an endless ocean voyage he became mad
and crazy. They caught him in blue
rock, said   10
            don't talk.

I know it wasn't just a horse
                    that went crazy.

Nearby is a shop with ivory and knives.
There are red rocks. The man behind the   15
counter has no idea that he is inside
magic stones. He should find out before
they destroy him. These things
have memory,
                you know.   20

I have a memory.
                    It swims deep in blood,
a delta in the skin. It swims out of Oklahoma,
deep the Mississippi River. It carries my
feet to these places: the French Quarter,   25
stale rooms, the sun behind thick and moist
clouds, and I hear boats hauling themselves up
and down the river.

My spirit comes here to drink.
My spirit comes here to drink.   30
Blood is the undercurrent.

There are voices buried in the Mississippi
mud. There are ancestors and future children
buried beneath the currents stirred up by
pleasure boats going up and down.   35
There are stories here made of memory.

I remember DeSoto. He is buried somewhere in
this river, his bones sunk like the golden
treasure he traveled half the earth to find,
came looking for gold cities, for shining streets   40
of beaten gold to dance on with silk ladies.

He should have stayed home.

                    (Creeks knew of him for miles
                    before he came into town.
                        Dreamed of silver blades   45
                        and crosses.)
And knew he was one of the ones who yearned
for something his heart wasn't big enough
to handle.
                    (And DeSoto thought it was gold.)   50

The Creeks lived in earth towns,
                              not gold,
          spun children, not gold.
That's not what DeSoto thought he wanted to see
The Creeks knew it, and drowned him in   55
          the Mississippi River
              so he wouldn't have to drown himself.

Maybe his body is what I am looking for
as evidence. To know in another way

that my memory is alive.   60
But he must have got away, somehow,
because I have seen New Orleans,
the lace and silk buildings,
trolley cars on beaten silver paths,
graves that rise up out of soft earth in the rain,   65
shops that sell black mammy dolls
holding white babies.

And I know I have seen DeSoto,
                    having a drink on Bourbon Street,
                    mad and crazy   70
                    dancing with a woman as gold
                    as the river bottom.

                                                                    1983

Remember

Remember the sky that you were born under,
know each of the star's stories.
Remember the moon, know who she is.
Remember the sun's birth at dawn, that is the
strongest point of time. Remember sundown   5
and the giving away to night.
Remember your birth, how your mother struggled
to give you form and breath. You are evidence of
her life, and her mother's, and hers.
Remember your father. He is your life, also.   10
Remember the earth whose skin you are:
red earth, black earth, yellow earth, white earth
brown earth, we are earth.
Remember the plants, trees, animal life who all have their
tribes, their families, their histories, too. Talk to them,   15
listen to them. They are alive poems.
Remember the wind. Remember her voice. She knows the
origin of this universe.
Remember you are all people and all people are you.
Remember you are this universe and this   20
universe is you.
Remember all is in motion, is growing, is you.
Remember language comes from this.
Remember the dance language is, that life is.
Remember.   25

                                                                    1983

Vision

The rainbow touched down
"somewhere in the Rio Grande,"
we said. And saw the light of it
from your mother's house in Isleta.[1]
How it curved down between earth   5
and the deepest sky to give us horses
of color
      horses that were within us all of this time
but we didn't see them because
we wait for the easiest vision   10
      to save us.
In Isleta the rainbow was a crack
in the universe. We saw the barest
of all life that is possible.
Bright horses rolled over   15
and over the dusking sky.
I heard the thunder of their beating
hearts. Their lungs hit air
and sang. All the colors of horses
formed the rainbow,   20
      and formed us
watching them.

      1983

Anchorage

    for Audre Lorde

This city is made of stone, of blood, and fish.
There are Chugatch Mountains[1'] to the east
and whale and seal to the west.
It hasn't always been this way, because glaciers
who are ice ghosts create oceans, carve earth   5
and shape this city here, by the sound.
They swim backwards in time.

Once a storm of boiling earth cracked open
the streets, threw open the town.
It's quiet now, but underneath the concrete   10
is the cooking earth,
     and above that, air

---

[1] An Indian pueblo in New Mexico.

[1'] A range extending about 280 miles along the coast of south Alaska just above the panhandle. Chugach Eskimo (Ahtnas) reside there.

which is another ocean, where spirits we can't see
are dancing   joking   getting full
on roasted caribou, and the praying   15
goes on, extends out.

Nora and I go walking down 4th Avenue
and know it is all happening.
On a park bench we see someone's Athabascan[2]
grandmother, folded up, smelling like 200 years   20
of blood and piss, her eyes closed against some
unimagined darkness, where she is buried in an ache
in which nothing makes
                         sense.

We keep on breathing, walking, but softer now,   25
the clouds whirling in the air above us.
What can we say that would make us understand
better than we do already?
Except to speak of her home and claim her
as our own history, and know that our dreams   30
don't end here, two blocks away from the ocean
where our hearts still batter away at the muddy shore.

And I think of the 6th Avenue jail, of mostly Native
and Black men, where Henry told about being shot at
eight times outside a liquor store in L.A., but when   35
the car sped away he was surprised he was alive,

no bullet holes, man, and eight cartridges strewn
on the sidewalk
                 all around him.

Everyone laughed at the impossibility of it,   40
but also the truth. Because who would believe
the fantastic and terrible story of all of our survival
those who were never meant
                         to survive?

                                                                       1983

---

[2]Athabascan is a complicated but widespread Indian language, part of the Na-Dene Indian language superstock of North America. Indians speak Athabascan in the sub-Arctic interior of Alaska, along the Pacific Northwest Coast (Tlingit of Alaska panhandle, Tolowa of Oregon, and Hupa of California), and in the American Southwest (Apache and Navajo).

Deer Dancer

Nearly everyone had left that bar in the middle of winter except the
hardcore. It was the coldest night of the year, every place shut down,
but not us. Of course we noticed when she came in. We were Indian
ruins. She was the end of beauty. No one knew her, the stranger
whose tribe we recognized, her family related to deer, if that's who she   5
was, a people accustomed to hearing songs in pine trees, and making
them hearts.

The woman inside the woman who was to dance naked in the bar of
misfits blew deer magic. Henry Jack, who could not survive a sober
day, thought she was Buffalo Calf Woman[1] come back, passed out, his 10
head by the toilet. All night he dreamed a dream he could not say.
The next day he borrowed money, went home, and sent back the
money I lent. Now that's a miracle. Some people see vision in a
burned tortilla, some in the face of a woman.

This is the bar of broken survivors, the club of shotgun, knife wound, 15
of poison by culture. We who were taught not to stare drank our beer.
The players gossiped down their cues. Someone put a quarter in the
jukebox to relive despair. Richard's wife dove to kill her. We had to
hold her back, empty her pockets of knives and diaper pins, buy her
two beers to keep her still, while Richard secretly bought the beauty a 20
drink.

How do I say it? In this language there are no words for how the real
world collapses. I could say it in my own and the sacred mounds
would come into focus, but I couldn't take it in this dingy envelope.

So I look at the stars in this strange city, frozen to the back of the sky, 25
the only promises that ever make sense.

My brother-in-law hung out with white people, went to law school
with a perfect record, quit. Says you can keep your laws, your words.
And practiced law on the street with his hands. He jimmied to the
proverbial dream girl, the face of the moon, while the players racked a 30
new game. He bragged to us, he told her magic words and that's
when she broke, became human. But we all heard his bar voice crack:

What's a girl like you doing in a place like this?

That's what I'd like to know, what are we all doing in a place like this?

---

[1]The culture heroine of the Lakota, who
brought them the sacred pipe and the seven
central rites of the Sioux. In myth she is
remarkably beautiful and stirs the desire of
the men who first meet her. See "Wohpe and
the Gift of the Pipe" in Volume A.

You would know she could hear only what she wanted to; don't we   35
all? Left the drink of betrayal Richard bought her, at the bar. What
was she on? We all wanted some. Put a quarter in the juke. We all
take risks stepping into thin air. Our ceremonies didn't predict this.
Or we expected more.

I had to tell you this, for the baby inside the girl sealed up with a lick   40
of hope and swimming into praise of nations. This is not a rooming
house, but a dream of winter falls and the deer who portrayed the
relatives of strangers. The way back is deer breath on icy windows.

The next dance none of us predicted. She borrowed a chair for the
stairway to heaven and stood on a table of names. And danced in the   45
room of children without shoes.

You picked a fine time to leave me, Lucille.
With four hungry children and a crop in the field.

And then she took off her clothes. She shook loose memory, waltzed
with the empty lover we'd all become.   50

She was the myth slipped down through dreamtime. The promise of
feast we all knew was coming. The deer who crossed through knots of
a curse to find us. She was no slouch, and neither were we, watching.

The music ended. And so does the story. I wasn't there. But I
imagined her like this, not a stained red dress with tape on her heels   55
but the deer who entered our dream in white dawn, breathed mist into
pine trees, her fawn a blessing of meat, the ancestors who never left.

1990

We Must Call a Meeting

I am fragile, a piece of pottery smoked from fire
                                            made of dung,
the design drawn from nightmares. I am an arrow, painted
                                            with lightning
to seek the way to the name of the enemy,   5
                        but the arrow has now created
its own language.
                It is a language of lizards and storms, and we have
begun to hold conversations
                        long into the night.   10
                                I forget to eat.
I don't work. My children are hungry and the animals who live

in the backyard are starving.
                                    I begin to draw maps of stars.
The spirits of old and new ancestors perch on my shoulders.   15
I make prayers of clear stone
                            of feathers from birds
                                    who live closest to the gods.
The voice of the stone is born
                            of a meeting of yellow birds   20
who circle the ashes of a smoldering volcano.
                                    The feathers sweep the prayers up
and away.
                I, too, try to fly but get caught in the cross fire of signals
                            and my spirit drops back down to earth.   25
I am lost; I am looking for you
                who can help me walk this thin line between the breathing
                                    and the dead.
You are the curled serpent in the pottery of nightmares.
You are the dreaming animal who paces back and forth in my head. 30
We must call a meeting.
                            Give me back my language and build a house
Inside it.
            A house of madness.
                    A house for the dead who are not dead.   35
And the spiral of the sky above it.
And the sun
                and the moon.
                            And the stars to guide us called promise.

                                                                1990

BOBBIE ANN MASON
B. 1940

Bobbie Ann Mason's parents chose her masculine-sounding first name because they were certain that she would be a boy. Questions surrounding gender identity are prominent throughout her work, but they serve to highlight a broader theme illustrated by this anecdote: the difficulty of accepting change or difference. Although young women tend to be the protagonists of her fiction, Mason's subjects are consistently rural, working-class Americans who are facing or evading the rapidly changing late twentieth century.

Born in Mayfield, Kentucky, she grew up on a farm that had been in her father's family for generations. In the aftermath of the Great Depression, farming was a difficult way to earn a living, yet her father's stint in the army during World War II was for him a mystifying departure from the world that he had always known rather than a glimpse of the possibilities available in the wider world. Like many young people destined to become writers, Mason escaped from her rural surroundings through books. She graduated from the University of Kentucky and went immediately to New York, the best place to begin a writing career. After writing fan magazine features about teen stars, she longed to return to more substantial literature and earned a Ph.D. at the University of Connecticut, where her childhood passion for detective stories developed into a fascination with Nabokov, the subject of her dissertation and her first book. After a half-dozen years of teaching at Mansfield State College in Pennsylvania, Mason began her career as a fiction writer.

Mason has published four collections of short stories, *Shiloh and Other Stories* (1982), *Love Life* (1989), *Zigzagging down a Wild Trail* (2001), and *Nancy Culpepper* (2006). These stories, many originally published in the *New Yorker*, earned Mason the title of "regional writer," yet her regionalism is tempered to a large degree by her tendency to saturate her stories with references to contemporary popular culture, especially allusions to television and rock music. Virtually all of her fiction takes place in her native Kentucky, and her main characters tend to be people who both desire and are mystified by change. The potent forces of accelerated change war against the conservative values of rural America in her fiction, and the battleground is often the flickering television screen in living rooms. Mason refuses to judge or romanticize the lives of her characters; she is more interested in allowing them to enact their dramas, occasionally experiencing moments of realization but unaware of what to do with them.

Of her five novels, the one that has gained the most attention is *In Country* (1985), the story of a teenager's quest to learn the truth about her father, who died in the Vietnam War. The story reprinted here, "Airwaves," contains many of the same elements as *In Country*: confusion about appropriate gender roles, a female main character who longs to empower herself, and an almost spiritual turning to radio and television for insight into the mysteries of the contemporary world.

D. Quentin Miller
Suffolk University

PRIMARY WORKS

Shiloh and Other Stories, 1982; *In Country*, 1985; *Spence + Lila*, 1988; *Love Life*, 1989; *Feather Crowns*, 1993; *Midnight Magic*, 1998; *Clear Springs*, 1999; *Zigzagging down a Wild Trail*, 2001; *An Atomic Romance: A Novel*, 2005; *Nancy Culpepper: Stories*, 2006; *The Girl in the Blue Beret*, 2011.

Airwaves

When Jane lived with Coy Wilson, he couldn't listen to rock music before noon or after supper. In the morning, it was too jarring; at night, the vibrations lingered in his head and interfered with his sleep. But now that they

are apart, Jane listens to Rock-95 all the time. Rock-95 is a college station—
"your station for kick-ass rock and roll." She sets the radio alarm every night
for 8 A.M., and when it goes off she dozes and dreams while the music blasts
in her ears for an hour or more. Women rock singers snarl and scream their
independence. The sounds are numbing. Jane figures if she can listen to
hard rock in her sleep, she won't care that Coy has gone.

Jane stands in the window in pink shortie pajamas, watching her landlady, Mrs. Bush, hang out her wash. Today is white things: sheets, socks,
underwear, towels. Jane's mother used to say, "Always separate your colored
things from your white things!" as though there were something morally
significant about the way you do laundry. Jane never follows the rules. All
her sheets have flowers on them, and her underwear is bright colors. Anything white is outnumbered. The men's shorts on Mrs. Bush's wash line flap
in the breeze like flags of surrender.

The coffee is bitter. She bought the store brand, because Mrs. Bush gave
her a fifty-cent coupon and the store paid double coupons. Mrs. Bush, who
is a waitress at the Villa Romano, keeps asking Jane when she is going to
get a job. When Coy lived there, Mrs. Bush was always asking him when he
was going to marry Jane. Six weeks ago, not long after she split up with
Coy, Jane was laid off from the Holiday Clothing Company. First she was a
folder, then a presser. Folding was more satisfying than pressing—the heat
from the presser took the curl out of her hair—but when she was switched
to the pressing room, she got a fifty-cents-an-hour raise. She was hoping to
go to the Villa Romano that night with Coy and have a spaghetti supper to
celebrate, but he chose that day to move back home with his mother. His
unemployment had run out two weeks before, and he had been at loose
ends. He thought he was getting an ulcer. When Jane got home, he had
lined up their joint possessions on the floor—the toaster, the blender, the
records, the TV tables, a whatnot, even the kitchen utensils.

"The TV's mine," he said apologetically. "I had it when we started out."

"I told you I'd pay the rent," she said, as he punched his jeans into a duf-
fle bag. When he wouldn't answer, she set the coffeepot in the cabinet and
shut the door. "I got the coffeepot with Green Stamps," she said.

"I'm going to cut out coffee anyway."

"Good. It makes you irritable."

Coy set the toaster in a grocery box with some shaving cream and
socks—all his mateless socks from what Jane called his Lonely Sock Drawer.
Jane tried to keep from crying as she pleaded with him to stay.

"I can't let you go on supporting me," he said. "I wasn't raised that
way."

"What's the difference? Your mother will support you. You could even
watch her TV."

He divided the record albums as though he were dealing out cards. "One
for you and one for me." He left his favorite Willie Nelson record on her pile.

When he left, she said, "You just let me know when you get yourself
straightened out, and we'll take it from there."

"That's my whole point," said Coy. "I have to work things out."

Jane knew she should have been more understanding. He was appreciative of delicate, fine things most men wouldn't notice, such as flowers and pretty dishes. Coy was tender in his lovemaking, with more sensitivity than men were usually given credit for. On Phil Donahue's show, when the topic was sex, the women in the audience always said they wanted men who were gentle and considerate and involved in a lot of touching during the day instead of "wham-bam-thank-you-ma'am" at the end of the day. Coy was the answer to those women's prayers, but he went too far. He was so fragile, with his nervous stomach. He couldn't watch meat being cut up. Jane still finds broken rolls of Tums stashed around the apartment.

Unemployed, Jane is adrift. She watches a lot of TV. She managed to buy a TV on sale before she lost her job. She has had to stop smoking (not a serious problem) and eating out so that she can keep up her car and TV payments. She canceled her subscription to a cosmetics club. She has accumulated a lot of bizarre eye shadows and creams that she doesn't use. When she goes out to a job interview, she paints her face and feels silly. Job-hunting is like going to church—a pointless ritual of dressing up. At the factory, she had to wear a blue smock over a dark skirt. Pants weren't allowed. "I wish I could get on at the Villa Romano," she tells Mrs. Bush. "The uniform is nice, and I could wear pants."

Coy used to go to Kentucky Lake alone sometimes, for the whole weekend, to meditate and restore himself. She once thought his desire to be alone was peculiar, but now she appreciates it. Being alone is incredibly easy. Her mind sails off into unexpected trances. Sometimes she pretends she is an invalid recovering from a coma, and she rediscovers everything around her—simple things, like the noise the rotary antenna makes, a sound she never heard when the TV volume was loud. Or she pretends she is in a wheelchair, viewing the world from one certain level. She likes to see things suddenly, from new angles. Once when Coy lived there, she stepped up on a crate to dust the top of a shelf, and Coy suddenly appeared and caught her in an embrace. On the crate, she was exactly his height. The dusty shelf was at eye level. For a day or two, she went around noticing the spaces that would be in his line of vision—the top of the refrigerator, the top of an old cardboard wardrobe her father had given her, curtain rods, moldings.

Today, when Jane leaves the apartment to pick up her unemployment check, Mrs. Bush is outside, watering her petunias. She pulls a letter from her pocket and waves it at Jane.

"My boy's in California," she says. "They're going to let him have a furlough, but he likes it so much out there he won't come home."

"I don't blame him," says Jane. "It's too far, and California must be a lot more fun than here."

"They start him out on heavy-duty equipment, but that didn't suit him and they've switched him to electronics. They take a hundred dollars out of his pay every month, and then when he gets out they'll double it and give him a bonus so he can go to school."

Mrs. Bush fires water at a border of hollyhocks. Jane steps over the coiled hose and casually thinks of evil serpents. She says, "My brother couldn't get in the Army because he had high arches, so he became a Holy Roller preacher instead. He used to cuss like the devil, but now he's preaching up a storm." Jane looks Mrs. Bush straight in the eyes. She's not old but looks old. If she died, maybe Jane could get her job.

"My cousin was a Holy Roller," says Mrs. Bush. "He got sanctified and then got hit by a truck the next day."

Nervously, Mrs. Bush tears off the edging of paper where she has ripped open the letter from her son. She balls the bit of paper and drops it into a pot of hen and chickens.

Jane's mother died when she was fifteen, and her father, Vernon Motherall, has never learned to cook for himself. "What's in this?" he asks suspiciously that weekend, when she takes him a tuna casserole.

"Macaroni. Tuna fish. Mushroom soup."

"I don't like mushrooms. Mushrooms is poison."

"This isn't poison. It's Campbell's." Jane has brought him this same kind of casserole dozens of times, and he always argues against mushrooms. He's convinced that someday a mushroom is going to get him.

Vernon rents the bottom of a dilapidated clapboard house. He has two dump trucks in the backyard. He hauls rock and sand and asphalt—"whatever needs hauling," his ad in the yellow pages says. His dingy office is filled with greasy papers on spikes and piles of *Field and Stream* magazines. In a ray of sunlight, the dust whirls and sparkles. Jane sweeps her hand through it.

"I wish I had some money," she says. "I'd buy one of those things that takes the negative ions out of the air."

"What good's that do?" Vernon is swigging a Pabst, though it's still morning.

"It knocks the dust out of the air."

"What for?" The way Jane's father speaks is more like an extended grunt than conversation. He sits in a large stuffed chair that seems to be part of his own big lumpy body.

"I don't know. I think the dust just falls down instead of circulating. If you had one of those, your sinuses wouldn't be so bad."

"They ain't been bothering me none lately."

"Those ionizers make you feel good, too. They do something to your mood."

"I've got all I need for my mood," he says, lifting his bottle of beer.

"You drink too much."

"Don't look at my beer belly."

"I will if I want to," Jane says, playfully thumping his belt buckle. "You get loaded and go out and have wrecks. You're going to get yourself killed."

Vernon grins at her mockingly. They always have this conversation, and he never takes her seriously.

"Here, eat this," Jane says, plopping a scoop of casserole on a melamine plate that has discoloration on it.

Vernon plucks another beer from the refrigerator and sits down at the card table in his dirty kitchen. He eats without comment, then mops his plate with a bread heel. When he finishes, he says, "I went to hear Joe preach at his new church the other Sunday. How did I turn out a boy like that? He's bound and determined to make a fool out of himself. His wife runs out on him, and he turns around and starts preaching Holy Roller. Did you know he talks in tongues now? What will he think of next?"

"Well, Joe goes at anything like killing snakes," says Jane. "It's all or nothing."

Vernon laughs. "His text for the day was the Twenty-third Psalm, and he comes to the part where the Lord maketh me lie down in green pastures and restoreth my soul? And he reads it 'he *storeth* my soul,' and starts preaching on the Lord's storehouses." Vernon doubles over laughing. "He thinks the Lord stores souls—like corn in a grain elevator!"

"I wonder what ever happened to all those grain-elevator explosions we used to hear about," Jane says, giggling.

"If the Lord stores some of those pitiful souls Joe's dragged in, his storehouse is liable to explode!" Vernon laughs, and beer sprays out of his mouth.

"Have some more tuna casserole," Jane says affectionately. When it comes to her brother, who was always in trouble, she and her father are in cahoots.

"You should have a good man to cook for. Not Coy Wilson. He's too prissy, and he took advantage of you, living with you with no intention of marrying."

"You're still feeling guilty 'cause you ran out on me and Joe and Mother that time," says Jane, shifting the subject.

"The trouble is, too many women are working and the men can't get jobs," her father says. "Women should stay home."

"Don't start in," Jane says in a warning voice. "I've got enough trouble."

"You could move back home with me," Vernon says plaintively. "Parents always used to take care of their kids till they married."

"I guess that's why Coy ran home to his mama."

"You can come home to your old daddy anytime," Vernon says, moving back to his easy chair. The vinyl upholstery makes obscene noises when he lands.

"It would never work," Jane says. "We don't like the same TV shows anymore."

Waiting in the unemployment line the next afternoon is tedious, and all the faces have deadpan expressions, but Jane is feeling elated, almost euphoric, though for no substantial reason. In the car, driving past a local radio transmitter, she suddenly realized that she had no idea how sound got from the transmitter to the radio. She felt so ignorant. The idea of sound waves seemed farfetched. She went to the library and asked for a book about radio. The librarian showed her a pamphlet about Nathan Stubblefield.

"He invented radio," the woman said. "They say it was Marconi, but Stubblefield was really the first, and he was from right around here. He lived about five miles from my house."

"I always heard radio was invented in Kentucky," Jane said.

"He just never got credit for it." The woman reminded Jane of a bouncy game-show contestant. "Kentucky never gets enough credit, if you ask me. We've go so much here to be proud of. Kentucky even has a Golden Pond, like in the movie."

Reading the pamphlet in the unemployment line, Jane feels strangely connected to something historically important. It is a miracle that sound can travel long distances through the air and then appear instantaneously, like a genie from a bottle, and that a man from Kentucky was the first to make it happen. Who can she tell? Who would care? This is the sort of thing that wouldn't register on her father, and Coy would think she was crazy. Her brother, though, would recognize the feeling. It occurs to Jane that he probably hears voices from heaven every day, just as though he were tuned in to heaven's airways. She wonders if he can really talk in tongues. Her brother is a radio! Jane feels like dancing. In her mind, the unemployment line suddenly turns into a chorus line, a movie scene. For a moment, she's afraid she's going nuts. The line inches forward.

After collecting her check, she cashes it at the bank's drive-in window, talking to the teller through a speaker, then goes to Jerry's Drive-In and orders a Coke through another speaker. A voice confirms her order, and in the background behind the voice, Jane hears a radio playing—Rock-95, the same station she is hearing on her car radio.

Coy calls up during a "Mary Tyler Moore" rerun that week, one Jane hasn't seen before. Jane is eating canned ravioli. The clarity of his voice startles her. He could be in the same room.

"I got a job! Floorwalking at Wal-Mart."

"Oh, I'm glad." Jane spears a pillow of ravioli and listens while Coy describes his hours and his duties and the amount of take-home pay he gets—less than he made at the plant before his layoff, but with more security. The job sounds incredibly boring.

"When I get on my feet, maybe we can reconsider some things," he says.

"If you're floorwalking, you're already on your feet," she says. "That's a joke," she says, when he doesn't respond. "I don't want to get back together if money's the issue."

"I thought we went through all that."

"I've been thinking, and I can't let you support me."

"Well, I've got a job now, and you don't."

"You wouldn't let *me* support *you*," Jane says. Why should I let you support me?"

"If we got back together, you could go to school part-time."

"I have to find a job first. I'd go to school now if I could go and still draw unemployment, but they won't let you draw and go to school too. Let's change the subject. How's your stomach?"

Coy tells Jane that on the news he saw pictures of starving children in Africa, and managed to watch without getting queasy. Jane always told him he was too sensitive to misfortunes that had nothing to do with him.

An awkward silence follows. Finally, Jane says, "My brother's got a Holy Roller church. He's preaching."

"That sounds about like him," Coy says, without surprise.

"I think I'll go Sunday. I need some religion. Do you want to go?"

"Hell, no. I don't want to invite a migraine."

"I thought your nerves were getting better."

"They are, but they're not that good yet."

After Coy hangs up, Jane feels lonely, wishing Coy were there touching her lightly with promising caresses, like the women on "Donahue" always wanted. Once, Rita Jenrette, whose husband was involved in a political scandal, was on Donahue's show, and during the program her husband called up. Coy's job sounds so depressing. Jane wishes he were the host of a radio call-in show. She could call him up and talk to him, pretending there was nothing personal between them. She would ask him about love. She'd ask whether he thought the magic of love worked anything at all like radio waves. Her ravioli grows cold.

Joe's church is called the Foremost Evangelical Assembly. The church is a converted house trailer, with a perpendicular extension. There is a Coke machine in the corridor. People sit around drinking Cokes and 7-Ups. No one is dressed up.

"Can you believe it!" cries Joe, clasping both of Jane's hands and jerking her forward as though about to swing her around in a game children play.

"Can you pray for me to find a job?" Jane says, grinning. "Daddy says you could talk in tongues, and I thought that might help."

"Was Daddy drinking when you saw him last?" Joe asks anxiously.

"Of course. Is the Pope Catholic?"

"I told him I could stop him from that if he'd just get his tail down here every Sunday." Joe has on a pin-striped double-knit suit with an artificial daisy in the lapel. He looks the part.

"Are you going to talk in tongues today?" Jane asks. "I want to see how you do it."

"Watch close," he says with a wink. "But I'm not allowed to give away the secret."

"Is it like being a magician?"

Her brother only grins mysteriously.

Jane sits cross-legged on the floor behind the folding chairs. People turn around and stare at her, probably wondering if she is Joe's girlfriend. The congregation loves Joe. He is a large man, and his size makes him seem powerful and authoritative, like an Army general. He has always been a goof-off, calling attention to himself, staging some kind of show. If Alexander Haig became a stand-up comedian, he would be just like Joe. He stands behind a card table with two overturned plastic milk crates stacked on it. On his right, a TV set stares at the congregation.

The service is long and peculiar and filled with individual testimonials that seem to come randomly, interrupting Joe's talk. It's not really a sermon. It's just Joe telling stories about how bad he used to be before he found Christ. He always had the gift of the gab, Vernon used to say. Joe tells a long anecdote about how his wife's infidelity made him turn to the Lord. He exaggerates parts of the story that Jane recognizes. (He *never* gave his wife a beautiful house with a custom-built kitchen and a two-car garage. It was a dumpy old house that they rented.) She almost giggles aloud when he opens the Bible and reads from "the Philippines," and she makes a mental note to tell her father. A woman takes a crying baby into the corridor and tries to make it drink some Coke. Jane wishes she had a cigarette. In this crazy setting, if Joe talked in tongues, nobody would notice it as anything odd.

When a young couple brings forth a walleyed child to be healed, Joe cries out in astonishment, "Who, me? I can't heal nobody!" He paces around in front of the TV set. "But I can guarantee that if you just let the spirit in, miracles have been known to happen." He rambles along on this point, and the little girl's head droops indifferently. "Just open up your heart and let him in!" Joe shouts. "Let the spirit in, and the Lord will shake up the alignment of them eyes." A song from *Hair*, "Let the Sunshine In," starts going through Jane's head. The child's eye shoots out across the room. While Joe is ranting, Jane gets a Coke and stands in the doorway.

"Icky-bick-eye-bo!" Joe cries suddenly. He looks embarrassed and bows his head. "Freema-di-kibbi-frida," he says softly.

Jane has been thinking of talking in tongues as an involuntary expression—a kind of gibberish that pours forth when people are possessed by the spirit of God. But now, in amazement, she watches her brother, his hands folded and eyes closed, as though bowing his head for a moment of prayer, chanting strange words slowly and carefully, as methodically as Mrs. Bush hangs out her wash. He is speaking a singsong language made of hard, disturbing sounds. "Shecky-beck-be-floyt-I-shecky-tibby-libby. Dat-cree-la-croo-la-crow." He seems to be trying hard not to say "abracadabra" or any other familiar words. Jane, disappointed, doubts that these words are messages from heaven. Joe seems afraid that some repressed obscenity might rush out. He used to cuss freely. Now he probably really believes he is tuned in to heaven.

"Where's Coy?" he asks her after the service. He has failed to correct the child's eyes but won't admit it.

"We don't get along so good. After he lost his job, he couldn't handle it."

"Well, get him on down here! We'll help him."

He tries to talk Jane into bringing Coy for Wednesday-night prayer meeting. "There's two kinds of men," Joe says. "Them that goes to church and them that don't. You should never get mixed up with some boy who won't take you to church."

"I know."

Joe says goodbye, with his arms around her like a lover's. Jane can smell the Tic Tacs on his breath.

*   *   *

"Do you want one hamburger patty or two?" Jane asks her father.

"One. No, two." Vernon looks confused. "No, make it one."

They ate at the lake, in a trailer belonging to Jane's former boss, who had promised to let her use it some weekend. Jane, wanting a change of scene for her father, brought a cooler of supplies, and Vernon brought his dog, Buford. He grumbled because Jane wouldn't let him bring any beer, but he sneaked along a quart of Heaven Hill, and he is already drunk. Jane is furious.

"How can you watch 'Hogan's Heroes' on that cruddy TV?" she asks. "The reception's awful."

"I've seen this one so many times I know what's going on. See that machine gun? Watch that guy in the tower. He's going to shoot."

"That's a tower? I thought it was a giraffe."

When they sit down to eat at the picnic table outside, Buford tries to get in Jane's lap. He has the broad shoulders of a bulldog and the fine facial features of a chihuahua. He goes around in a little cloud of gnats.

"I can't eat with a dog in my lap," Jane says, pushing the dog away. "Coy wants to come back to me," she tells her father. "He's got his pride again."

"Don't let him."

"He's more of a man than you think." Jane laughs. "Joe says he can help us work things out. He wants us to come to Wednesday-night prayer meetings."

"How did I go wrong?" Vernon asks helplessly, addressing a tree. "One kid starts preaching just to stay out of jail, and the other one wants to live in sin and ruin her reputation." Vernon turns to the dog and says, "It's all my fault. Children always hurt you."

"And what about you?" Jane shouts at him. "You worry us half to death with your drinking and then expect us to be little angels."

She takes her plate indoors and turns on "M*A*S*H." The reception is so poor without a cable that the figures undulate on the screen. Hawkeye and B.J. turn into wavy lines, staggering drunks.

That night, Vernon's drunken sleep on the couch is loud and unrestrained. Jane thinks of his sleep as slumber. She always thought of Coy's sleep as catnapping. She misses Coy, but wonders if she can ever get along with any man. In all her relationships with people, she has to deal with one or another intolerable habit. Jane is not sure the hard-rock music has hardened her to pain and distraction. Her father is hopeless. He used to get drunk and throw her mother's good dishes against the wall. He lined them up on the table and broke them one by one until her mother relented and gave him the keys to the car. He had accidents. He was always apologetic afterward, and he made it up to them in lavish ways, bringing home absurd presents, such as a bushel of peaches or a pint of oysters in a little white fold-together cardboard container like the ones goldfish come in. Once, he brought goldfish, but Jane's mother had expected oysters. Her disappointment hurt him, and he went back and bought oysters. One year, he ran away to Detroit. When he came back months later, Jane's mother forgave him. By then, she was dying of cancer, and Jane suspects that he never really forgave himself for being there too late to make it up to her.

Buford paces around the trailer fretfully. Jane can't sleep. The bed is musty and lumpy. She recalls a story her mother once told her about a woman who was trapped in a lion cage by a lion who tried to mate with her. From outside the cage, the lion's trainer yelled instructions to her—how she had to stroke the lion until he was satisfied. Pinned under the lion, the woman saved her life by obeying the man's instructions. That was more or less how her mother always told her she had to be with a husband, or a rapist. She thinks of her mother as the woman in the cage, listening to the lion tamer shouting instructions—do anything to keep from being murdered. As Jane recalls her mother telling it, the lion's eyes went all dreamy, and he rolled over on his back and went to sleep.

Jane suspects that what she really wants is a man something like the lion. She loves Coy's gentleness, but she wants him to be aggressive at times. The women on "Donahue" said they wanted that, too. Someone in the audience said women can't have it both ways.

During the weekend, Jane tries to get Vernon to go fishing, but he hasn't renewed his fishing license since the price went up. He complains about the snack cakes she brought, and he sits around drinking. Jane listens to the radio and reads a book called *Working*, about people's jobs. "It takes all kinds," she tells her father when he asks about the book. She has given up trying to entertain him, but by Sunday evening he seems mellow and talkative.

At the picnic table, Jane watches the sun setting behind the oak trees. "Look how pretty it is. The light on the water looks like a melted orange Popsicle."

Vernon grunts, acknowledging the sunset.

"I want you to enjoy yourself," Jane says calmly.

"I'm an old fool," he says, sloshing his drink. "I never amounted to anything. This country is taking away every chance the little man ever had. If it weren't for the Republicans and the Democrats, we'd be better off."

"Don't we have to have one or the other?"

"Throw 'em all out. They cancel each other out anyway." Vernon snatches at a mosquito. "The minorities rule this country. They've meddled with the Constitution till it's all out of shape."

The sun disappears, and the mosquitoes come out. Jane slaps her arms. Her toes are under the dog, warming like buns in a toaster oven. She nudges him away, and he pads across the porch, taking his gnat cloud with him.

"Tell me something," Jane asks later, as they are eating. "What did you do in Detroit that time when you ran off and left Mom with Joe and me?"

Vernon shrugs and drinks from a fresh drink. "Worked a Chrysler."

"Why did you leave us?"

"Your mother couldn't put up with me."

Jane can't see her father's face in the growing dark, so she feels bolder. Taking a deep breath, she says, "I guess for a long time I felt guilty after you left—not because you left but because I wanted you to leave. Mom and Joe and me got along just fine without you. I liked moving into that restaurant, living upstairs with Mom, and her going downstairs to cook hamburgers for people. I think I liked it so much not just because I could have all the hamburgers and milk shakes I wanted but because *she* loved it. She loved waiting on people and cooking food for the public. But we were glad when you came back and we moved back home."

Vernon nods and nods, about to say something. Jane gets up and turns on the bug light on the porch. She says, "That's how I've been feeling, living by myself. If I found something I liked as much as Mom liked cooking for the public, I'd be happy."

Vernon pours some more bourbon into his Yosemite Sam jelly glass and nods thoughtfully. He sips his drink and looks out on the darkening lake for so long that Jane thinks he must be working up to a spectacular confession or apology. Finally, he says "The Constitution is damaged all to hell." He sets his plate on the ground for the dog to lick.

The next morning is work-pants day. On Mrs. Bush's line is a row of dark green work pants and matching shirts. The pants are heavy and wrinkled. The sun comes out, and by afternoon, when Jane returns from shopping, the wrinkles are gone and the pants look fluffy. Jane reaches into the back seat of her car for her sack of groceries—soup, milk, cereal, and a Sara Lee cheesecake, marked down.

"Faired up nice, didn't it?" cries Mrs. Bush, appearing with her laundry basket. "They say another front's coming through and we'll have a storm."

"I hope so," says Jane, wishing it would be a tornado.

"I've got some news for you," Mrs. Bush says, as she drops clothespins into a plastic bucket. "A girl I work with is pregnant, and she's quitting work next week."

"I thought I wanted to work at the Villa Romano more than anything, but now I'm not sure," Jane says. What would it be like, waiting on tables with Mrs. Bush?

"It's a good job, and they feed you all you can eat. They've got the *best* ambrosia!"

She drops a clothespin and Jane picks it up. Jane says, "I think I'll join the Army."

Mrs. Bush laughs. "Jimmy's still in California. They would have flown him here and back, but he wouldn't come home. Is that any way for a boy to do his mama?" She tests a pant leg for dampness, and frowns. "I've got to go. Could you bring in these britches for me later?" she asks. "If I'm late to work, my boss will shoot me."

When Jane puts her groceries away, the cereal tumbles to the floor. The milk carton is leaking. She turns on Rock-95 full blast, then rips the cover off the cheesecake and starts eating from the middle. Jane feels strange, quivery. One simple idea could suddenly change everything, the same way a tornado could. Everything in her life is converging, narrowing, like a multitude of tiny lines trying to get through one pinhole. She imagines straightening out a rainbow and rolling it up in a tube. The sound waves travel on rainbows. She can't explain these notions to Coy. They don't even make sense to her. Today, he looked worried about her when she stopped in at Wal-Mart. It has been a crazy day, a stupid weekend. After picking up her unemployment check, she applied for a job at Betty's Boutique, but the opening had been filled five minutes earlier. At Wal-Mart, Coy was patrolling the pet department. In his brown plaid pants, blue shirt, and yellow tie, he looked stylish and comfortable, as though he had finally found a place where he belonged. He seemed like a man whose ambition was to get a service award so he could have his picture in the paper, shaking hands with his boss.

"I hope you're warming a place in bed for me," he whispered to her, within earshot of customers. He touched her elbow, and his thumb poked surreptitiously at her waist. "I have to work tonight," he went on. "We're doing inventory. But we've got to talk."

"O.K.," she said, her eyes fixing on a fish tank in which some remarkably blue fish were darting around like darning-needle flies.

On her way out of the store, without thinking, she stopped and bought a travel kit for her cosmetics, with plastic cases inside for her toothbrush, lotion, and soap. She wasn't sure where she was going. Driving out of the parking lot, she thought how proudly Coy had said, "We're taking inventory," as though he were in thick with Wal-Mart executives. It didn't seem like him. She had deluded herself, expecting more of him just because he was such a sweet lover. She had thought he was an ideal man, like the new contemporary man described in the woman's magazines, but he was just a floorwalker. There was not future in that. Women had been walking the floors for years. She remembered her mother walking the floor with worry, when her father was out late, drinking.

At the Army recruiting station, Jane stuffed the literature into her purse. She took one of everything. On a bulletin board, she read down a list of career-management fields, strange-sounding phrases like Air Defense Artillery, Missile Maintenance, Ballistic Maintenance, Cryptologic Operations, Topographic Engineering. The words stirred her, filled her with awe.

"Here's what I want," she said to the recruiter. "Communications and Electronics Operations."

"That's our top field," said the man, who was wearing a beautiful uniform trimmed with bright ribbons. "You join that and you'll get somewhere."

Later, in her kitchen, her mouth full of cheesecake, Jane reads the electronics brochure, pausing over the phrases "field radio," "teletype," and "radio relay equipment." Special security clearance is required for some electronics operations. She pictures herself someplace remote, in a control booth, sending signals for war, like an engineer in charge of a sports special on TV. She doesn't want to go to war, but if there is one, women should go. She imagines herself in a war, crouching in the jungle, sweating, on the lookout for something to happen. The sounds of warfare would be like the sounds of rock and roll, hard-driving and satisfying.

She sleeps so soundly that when Coy calls the next morning, the telephone rings several times. Rock-95 is already blasting away, and she wonders groggily if it is loud enough over the telephone to upset his equilibrium.

"I'm trying to remember what you used to say about waking up," she says sleepily.

"You know I could never talk till I had my coffee."

"I thought you were giving up coffee. Does your mama make you coffee?"

"Yeah."

"I knew she would." Jane sits up and turns down the radio. "Oh, now I remember what you said. You said it was like being born."

Coy had said that the relaxation of sleep left him defenseless and shattered, so that the daytime was spent restructuring himself, rebuilding defenses. Sleep was a forgetting, and in the daylight he had to gather his strength, remember who he was. For him, the music was an intrusion on a fragile life, and now it makes Jane sad that she hasn't been fair to him.

"Can I come for breakfast?" he asks.

"You took the toaster, and I can't make toast the way you like it."

"Let's go to the Dairy Barn and have some country ham and biscuits."

Jane's sheets are dirty. She was going to wash them at the laundromat and bring them home to dry—to save money and to score a point with her landlady. She says, "I'll meet you as soon as I drop off my laundry at the Washeteria. I've got something to tell you."

"I hope it's good."

"It's not what you think." On the radio, Rod Stewart is bouncing blithely away on "Young Turks." Jane feels older, too old for her and Coy to be young hearts together, free tonight, as the song directs. Jane says, "Red-eye gravy. That's what I want. Do you think they'll have red-eye gravy?"

"Of course they'll have red-eye gravy. Who ever heard of country ham without red-eye gravy?"

After hanging up, Jane lays the sheets on the living-room rug, and in the center she tosses her underwear and blouses and slacks. The colors clash. A tornado in a flower garden. After throwing in her jeans, she ties the corners of the sheets and sets the bundle by the door. As she puts on her makeup, she rehearses what she has to tell Coy. She has imagined his stunned silence. She imagines gathering everyone she knows in the same room, so she can make her announcement as if she were holding a press conference. It would be so much more official.

With her bundle of laundry, she goes bumping down the stairs. A stalk of light from a window on the landing shoots down the stairway. Jane floats through the light, with the dust motes shining all around her, penetrating silently, and then she remembers a dirty T-shirt in the bathroom. Letting the bundle slide to the bottom of the stairs, she turns back to her apartment. She has left the radio on, and for a moment on the landing she thinks that someone must be home.

1987

LORNA DEE CERVANTES
B. 1954

A northern California native, Lorna Dee Cervantes typifies the young Chicano writers who began appearing in the mid-1970s, ten years after the Chicano movement began. Younger authors, having access to Chicano literature in school and in the community, could recast and adjust images and concepts that earlier Chicano movement writers offered as self-defining, as well as the forms they used. The new writers, without rejecting the importance of cultural identity, emphasized questions of style and form, bringing polish and control to the ideologically overloaded earlier poetry. Age, however, was not the only difference. Women, excluded from the first decade of Chicano publishing, found outlets for their work. A new female, often feminist, voice forced the Chicano image into a more balanced perspective, with a mixture of cultural concern and gender-based criticism. Although Cervantes resisted academics for a number of years during which she attempted to survive strictly as a writer and publisher—she founded her own press and poetry magazine, *Mango*—from 1988 to 2007 she taught in the Creative Writing Program of the University of Colorado, Boulder. She has since moved back to the San Francisco Bay area and, during the academic year 2011–2012, is the Regents Lecturer at the University of California, Berkeley.

Influenced by Carlos Castaneda, Cervantes sees life as a struggle with the enemy/guide—incarnations of the spiritual forces in Nature that can destroy if not brought into harmony and control but, once mastered, help one reach fulfillment. At the personal level, men are the enemy; at the ethnic level, machismo and male dominance threaten family unity; at the social level, it is Anglo-American society and racial prejudice; and at the artistic level, English and words themselves must be mastered. Cervantes defines her terms through poems about male-female struggle within the context of class and cultural struggle. Men are trained to exploit their environment, which leads them to abuse women, a situation that forces women to become self-reliant. Cervantes' feminism seems to culminate in "Beneath the Shadow of the Freeway" with its image of the multigeneration, all-women family surviving in the midst of social alienation and menaced by the male adversary.

Yet ethnic unity, necessary to combat anti-Chicano prejudice, demands sexual harmony, so the author synthesizes from older generations the wisdom of female oral tradition: a balance of strength and tenderness, of openness and caution, of sincerity and reserve. Castaneda's lesson—struggle with the enemy to turn it into your assistant—is applied to men and to nature. She learns to live with them, although never completely at ease. Survival depends on constant vigilance against betrayal because, despite the façade of peace, society and nature are essentially a battle.

Cervantes' manner of self-defense is to develop a harmonious identity through personal symbols in nature—birds—related to a chosen cultural emphasis—the Native American element in her Mexican American past. She blends these elements into the image of her art in the metaphor of the pen through an interlingual play on words: *pluma* in Spanish means both pen and feather, so to be *emplumada* is to be feathered like a bird or an Indian, or to be armed with a pen like a writer. That she can also rework the rhetoric of warrior-like struggle is clear in "Poem for the Young White Man," reminiscent of the stringent Chicano movement poetry. However, she is most successful when she eschews the easy clichés of political rhetoric to pursue her vision of the spirit of nature hidden under the surface of everyday existence, one that struggles to express itself through the tenuous harmony of lovers and writers. The last half of *Emplumada* and her entire second book, *From the Cables of Genocide*, explore and construct female-male relationships to feed a society starved for love.

Juan Bruce-Novoa
University of California, Irvine

PRIMARY WORKS

Emplumada, 1981; *From the Cables of Genocide: Poems of Love and Hunger*, 1991; *Drive: The First Quartet*, 2006; *Ciento: 100 100-word Love Poems*, 2011.

Beneath the Shadow of the Freeway

1

Across the street—the freeway,
blind worm, wrapping the valley up
from Los Altos[1] to Sal Si Puedes.[2]
I watched it from my porch
unwinding. Every day at dusk   5
as Grandma watered geraniums
the shadow of the freeway lengthened.

2

We were a woman family:
Grandma, our innocent Queen;
Mama, the Swift Knight, Fearless Warrior.   10

---

[1]Spanish: The Heights.   [2]Spanish: Escape If You Can.

Mama wanted to be Princess instead.
I know that. Even now she dreams of taffeta
and foot-high tiaras.

Myself: I could never decide.
So I turned to books, those staunch, upright men.   15
I became Scribe: Translator of Foreign Mail,
interpreting letters from the government, notices
of dissolved marriages and Welfare stipulations.
I paid the bills, did light man-work, fixed faucets,
insured everything   20
against all leaks.

3

Before rain I notice seagulls.
They walk in flocks,
cautious across lawns: splayed toes,
indecisive beaks. Grandma says   25
seagulls mean storm.
In California in the summer,
mockingbirds sing all night.
Grandma says they are singing for their nesting wives.
"They don't leave their families   30
borrachando."³

She likes the ways of birds,
respects how they show themselves
for toast and a whistle.

She believes in myths and birds.   35
She trusts only what she builds
with her own hands.

4

She built her house,
cocky, disheveled carpentry,
after living twenty-five years   40
with a man who tried to kill her.

Grandma, from the hills of Santa Barbara,
I would open my eyes to see her stir mush

³Spanish: getting drunk.

in the morning, her hair in loose braids,
tucked close around her head   45
with a yellow scarf.

Mama said, "It's her own fault,
getting screwed by a man for that long.
Sure as shit wasn't hard."
soft she was soft   50

5

in the night I would hear it
glass bottles shattering the street
words cracked into shrill screams
inside my throat   a cold fear
as it entered the house in hard   55
unsteady steps   stopping at my door
my name   bathrobe   slippers
outside a 3 A.M. mist heavy
as a breath full of whiskey
stop it   go home   come inside   60
mama if he comes here again
I'll call the police

inside
a gray kitten   a touchstone
purring beneath the quilts   65
grandma stitched
from his suits
the patchwork singing
of mockingbirds

6

"You're too soft ... always were.   70
You'll get nothing but shit.
Baby, don't count on nobody."

—a mother's wisdom.
Soft. I haven't changed,
maybe grown more silent, cynical   75
on the outside.

"O Mama, with what's inside of me
I could wash that all away. I could."

"But Mama, if you're good to them
they'll be good to you back."   80

Back. The freeway is across the street.
It's summer now. Every night I sleep with a gentle man
to the hymn of mockingbirds,

and in time, I plant geraniums.
I tie up my hair into loose braids,   85
and trust only what I have built
with my own hands.

1981

Poem for the Young White Man Who Asked Me How I, an Intelligent, Well-Read Person, Could Believe in the War between Races

In my land there are no distinctions.
The barbed wire politics of oppression
have been torn down long ago. The only reminder
of past battles, lost or won, is a slight
rutting in the fertile fields.   5

In my land
people write poems about love,
full of nothing but contented childlike syllables.
Everyone reads Russian short stories and weeps.
There are no boundaries.   10
There is no hunger, no
complicated famine or greed.

I am not a revolutionary.
I don't even like political poems.
Do you think I can believe in a war between races?   15

I can deny it. I can forget about it
when I'm safe,
living on my own continent of harmony
and home, but I am not
there.   20

I believe in revolution
because everywhere the crosses are burning,
sharp-shooting goose-steppers round every corner,
there are snipers in the schools . . .

(I know you don't believe this.   25
You think this is nothing
but faddish exaggeration. But they
are not shooting at you.)

I'm marked by the color of my skin.
The bullets are discrete and designed to kill slowly.   30
They are aiming at my children.
These are facts.
Let me show you my wounds: my stumbling mind, my
"excuse me" tongue, and this
nagging preoccupation   35
with the feeling of not being good enough.

These bullets bury deeper than logic.
Racism is not intellectual.
I can not reason these scars away.

Outside my door   40
there is a real enemy
who hates me.

I am a poet
who yearns to dance on rooftops,
to whisper delicate lines about joy   45
and the blessings of human understanding.
I try. I go to my land, my tower of words and
bolt the door, but the typewriter doesn't fade out
the sounds of blasting and muffled outrage.
My own days bring me slaps on the face.   50
Every day I am deluged with reminders
that this is not
my land

and this is my land.

I do not believe in the war between races   55
but in this country
there is war.

                                                            1981

Macho

Slender, you are, secret as rail
under a stairwell of snow, slim
as my lips in the shallow hips.

I had a man of gristle and flint,
fingered the fine lineament of flexed   5
talons under his artifice of grit.

Every perfect body houses force
or deception. Every calculated figure
fears the summing up of age.

You're a beautiful mess of thread and silk,   10
a famous web of work and waiting, an
angular stylus with the patience of lead.

Your potent lure links hunger to flesh
as a frail eagle alights on my chest,
remember: the word for *machismo* is *real*.   15

1991

JAMAICA KINCAID
B. 1949

Jamaica Kincaid began life as Elaine Potter Richardson, the oldest daughter of a determined Dominican woman, descended from Carib Indians, who had fled a tyrannical father for the tiny island of Antigua. The largest and most developed of the Leeward Islands in the West Indies, this "small place" (about the size of Staten Island) had an indigenous population of Arawak Indians who were nearly exterminated by contact with Europeans. In the seventeenth century, Antigua was occupied by English colonists, who started tobacco cultivation and later sugar production, importing slave labor from Africa to plant and tend the sugarcane. Antigua remained a British colony, became a self-governing state associated with the United Kingdom in 1967, and finally gained full independence in 1981.

After an Anglophilic upbringing in colonial schools, Kincaid left her powerful mother and her island home in 1965 for New York City. In the heady atmosphere of the women's movement and sexual revolution, she worked as an au pair, studied photography, and in 1973 reinvented herself with a name that alludes to her island origins. At this time, she was writing for magazines like *Ingenue* and *Rolling Stone*. She did not return to Antiqua until 1985, when her brother was dying of AIDS.

Her break came when she met William Shawn, the exacting editor of the *New Yorker*, who became her mentor. She worked at the magazine as a staff writer until 1995. Most of the stories and essays that form her books were published and continue to appear in its pages. They focus almost obsessively on her West Indian background.

In 1979 Kincaid married Shawn's son Allen, a composer and professor of music at Bennington College, and moved to Vermont, where she had two children, converted to Judaism, divorced, and still lives, gardens, and writes.

Kincaid's books have been both popular successes as coming-of-age tales and critically acclaimed chronicles of the immigrant experience. Stylistically, she uses powerful rhythms, repetition, mimicry, satire, and deceptively simple sentences to push beyond the "rationality" of canonical and masculinist prose. Her works interrogate gender relations, sexuality, family, colonial history, and diasporic identities. Her first collection of stories, *At the Bottom of the River* (1983), uses an incantatory style to evoke West Indian speech and surreal poetic imagery to express the harrowing power struggles and fierce attachment between mothers and daughters.

This theme also defines her next book, *Annie John* (1985), the story of an Antiguan girl whose growing maturity forces a separation from her mother and father. Readers found this book charming and universal because its critique of postcolonial privilege was largely inferential. Kincaid dropped this indirection in her next book, *A Small Place* (1988), from which the excerpt included here is taken; it is a bitter indictment of the legacy of British colonialism in Antigua.

Since this breakthrough, Kincaid's work has looked unsparingly at the effects of colonization on individuals and families in a series of novels and memoirs: *Lucy* (1990), about a young Antiguan au pair in freewheeling New York; *The Autobiography of My Mother* (1995), a despairing portrait of lives enmeshed in the colonial past; *My Brother* (1997), a poignant account of her younger brother's death from AIDS; *Mr. Potter: A Novel* (2002), episodes in the life of an ordinary Antiguan man.

In 1999 Kincaid published *My Garden [Book]*, essays that connect the pleasures of gardening to Europe's botanical theft of the Americas and to Kincaid's familiar themes of power, conquest, and betrayal. More recently, *Among Flowers: A Walk in the Himalayas* (2005) describes a trek through the Himalayas to gather the seeds of rare plants in which Kincaid seems to enact the role of thief.

In an interview, Kincaid said about *A Small Place*, "I realized in writing that book that the first step to claiming yourself is anger." In acidic prose, Kincaid indicts the legacy of British colonialism and the tourism industry as the sources of the corruption of the Antiguan government and the suffering of the Antiguan people. This quasi-memoir was so incendiary that the *New Yorker* refused to publish it. Parts of it form the narrative for the 2001 documentary film *Life and Debt*, about the economic decline of Jamaica and other small nations despoiled by globalism.

Ivy Schweitzer
Dartmouth College

PRIMARY WORKS

At the Bottom of the River, 1983; *Annie John*, 1985; *A Small Place*, 1988; *Annie, Gwen, Lilly, Pam, and Tulip*, 1989; *Lucy*, 1990; *Biography of a Dress*, 1990; *The Autobiography of My Mother*, 1995; *My Brother*, 1997; *My Favorite Plant: Writers and Gardeners on the Plants They Love* (editor), 1998; *My Garden [Book:]*, 1999; *Talk Stories*, 2000; *Life and Debt* (film narrator), 2001; *Mr. Potter: A Novel*, 2002; *Among Flowers: A Walk in the Himalayas*, 2005.

from **A Small Place**

The Antigua that I knew, the Antigua in which I grew up, is not the Antigua you, a tourist, would see now. That Antigua no longer exists. That Antigua no longer exists partly for the usual reason, the passing of time, and partly because the bad-minded people who used to rule over it, the English, no longer do so. (But the English have become such a pitiful lot these days, with hardly any idea what to do with themselves now that they no longer have one quarter of the earth's human population bowing and scraping before them. They don't seem to know that this empire business was all wrong and they should, at least, be wearing sackcloth and ashes in token penance of the wrongs committed, the irrevocableness of their bad deeds, for no natural disaster imaginable could equal the harm they did. Actual death might have been better. And so all this fuss over empire—what went wrong here, what went wrong there—always makes me quite crazy, for I can say to them what went wrong: they should never have left their home, their precious England, a place they loved so much, a place they had to leave but could never forget. And so everywhere they went they turned it into England; and everybody they met turned English. But no place could ever really be England, and nobody who did not look exactly like them would ever be English, so you can imagine the destruction of people and land that came from that. The English hate each other and they hate England, and the reason they are so miserable now is that they have no place else to go and nobody else to feel better than.) But let me show you the Antigua that I used to know.

In the Antigua that I knew, we lived on a street named after an English maritime criminal, Horatio Nelson, and all the other streets around us were named after some other English maritime criminals. There was Rodney Street, there was Hood Street, there was Hawkins Street, and there was Drake Street. There were flamboyant trees and mahogany trees lining East Street. Government House, the place where the Governor, the person standing in for the Queen, lived, was on East Street. Government House was surrounded by a high white wall—and to show how cowed we must have been, no one ever wrote bad things on it; it remained clean and white and high. (I once stood in hot sun for hours so that I could see a putty-faced Princess from England disappear behind these walls. I was seven years old at the time, and I thought, She has a putty face.) There was the library on lower High Street, above the Department of the Treasury, and it was in the part of High Street that all colonial government business took place. In that part of High Street, you could cash a cheque at the Treasury, read a book in the library, post a letter at the post office, appear before a magistrate in court. (Since we were ruled by the English, we also had their laws. There was a law against using abusive language. Can you imagine such a law among people for whom making a spectacle of yourself through speech is everything? When West Indians went to England, the police there had to get a glossary of bad West Indian words so they could understand whether they were hearing abusive language or not.) It was in the same part of High Street that you could get a passport in another government office. In the middle of High Street was the Barclays Bank. The Barclay brothers, who started Barclays Bank, were slave-traders. That is how they made their money. When the English outlawed the slave trade, the Barclay brothers went into banking. It made them even richer. It's possible that when they saw how rich banking made them, they gave themselves a good beating for opposing an end to slave trading (for surely they would have opposed that), but then again, they may have been visionaries and agitated for an end to slavery, for look at how rich they became with their banks borrowing from (through their savings) the descendants of the slaves and then lending back to them. But people just a little older than I am can recite the name of and the day the first black person was hired as a cashier at this very same Barclays Bank in Antigua. Do you ever wonder why some people blow things up? I can imagine that if my life had taken a certain turn, there would be the Barclays Bank, and there I would be, both of us in ashes. Do you ever try to understand why people like me cannot get over the past, cannot forgive and cannot forget? There is the Barclays Bank. The Barclay brothers are dead. The human beings they traded, the human beings who to them were only commodities, are dead. It should not have been that they came to the same end, and heaven is not enough of a reward for one or hell enough of a punishment for the other. People who think about these things believe that every bad deed, even every bad thought, carries with it its own retribution. So do you see the queer thing about people like me? Sometimes we hold your retribution. . . .

And what were these people from North America, these people from England, these people from Europe, with their bad behaviour, doing on this little island? For they so enjoyed behaving badly, as if there was pleasure immeasurable to be had from not acting like a human being. Let me tell you about a man; trained as a dentist, he took it on himself to say he was a doctor, specialising in treating children's illnesses. No one objected—certainly not us. He came to Antigua as a refugee (running away from Hitler) from Czechoslovakia. This man hated us so much that he would send his wife to inspect us before we were admitted into his presence, and she would make sure that we didn't smell, that we didn't have dirt under our fingernails, and that nothing else about us—apart from the colour of our skin—would offend the doctor. (I can remember once, when I had whooping cough and I took a turn for the worse, that my mother, before bundling me up and taking me off to see this man, examined me carefully to see that I had no bad smells or dirt in the crease of my neck, behind my ears, or anywhere else. Every horrible thing that a housefly could do was known by heart to my mother, and in her innocence she thought that she and the doctor shared the same crazy obsession—germs.) Then there was a headmistress of a girls' school, hired through the colonial office in England and sent to Antigua to run this school which only in my lifetime began to accept girls who were born outside a marriage; in Antigua it had never dawned on anyone that this was a way of keeping black children out of this school. This woman was twenty-six years old, not too long out of university, from Northern Ireland, and she told these girls over and over again to stop behaving as if they were monkeys just out of trees. No one ever dreamed that the word for any of this was racism. We thought these people were so ill-mannered and we were so surprised by this, for they were far away from their home, and we believed that the farther away you were from your home the better you should behave. (This is because if your bad behaviour gets you in trouble you have your family not too far off to help defend you.) We thought they were un-Christian-like; we thought they were small-minded; we thought they were like animals, a bit below human standards as we understood those standards to be. We felt superior to all these people; we thought that perhaps the English among them who behaved this way weren't English at all, for the English were supposed to be civilised, and this behaviour was so much like that of an animal, the thing we were before the English rescued us, that maybe they weren't from the real England at all but from another England, one we were not familiar with, not at all from the England we were told about, not at all from the England we could never be from, the England that was so far away, the England that not even a boat could take us to, the England that, no matter what we did, we could never be of. We felt superior, for we were so much better behaved and we were full of grace, and these people were so badly behaved and they were so completely empty of grace. (Of course, I now see that good behaviour is the proper posture of the weak, of children.) We were taught the names of the Kings of England. In Antigua, the twenty-fourth of May was a holiday—Queen Victoria's official birthday. We didn't say to ourselves, Hasn't this extremely unappealing person been dead for years and years? Instead, we were glad for a holiday. Once, at dinner (this happened in my present life), I was sitting across from an Englishman, one of those smart people who know how to run things that England still turns out but who now, since the demise of the empire, have nothing to do; they look so sad, sitting on the rubbish heap of history. I was reciting my usual litany of things I hold against England and the English, and to round things off I said, "And do you know that we had to celebrate Queen Victoria's birthday?" So he said that every year, at the school he attended in England, they marked the day she died. I said, "Well, apart from the fact that she belonged to you and so anything you did about her was proper, at least you know she died." So that was England to us—Queen Victoria and the glorious day of her coming into the world, a beautiful place, a blessed place, a living and blessed thing, not the ugly, piggish individuals we met. I cannot tell you how angry it makes me to hear people from North America tell me how much they love England, how beautiful England is, with its traditions. All they see is some frumpy, wrinkled-up person passing by in a carriage waving at a crowd. But what I see is the millions of people, of whom I am just one, made orphans: no motherland, no fatherland, no gods, no mounds of earth for holy ground, no excess of love which might lead to the things that an excess of love sometimes brings, and worst and most painful of all, no tongue. (For isn't it odd that the only language I have in which to speak of this crime is the language of the criminal who committed the crime? And what can that really mean? For the language of the criminal can contain only the goodness of the criminal's deed. The language of the criminal can explain and express the deed only from the criminal's point of view. It cannot contain the horror of the deed, the injustice of the deed, the agony, the humiliation inflicted on me. When I say to the criminal, "This is wrong, this is wrong, this is wrong," or, "This deed is bad, and this other deed is bad, and this one is also very, very bad," the criminal understands the word "wrong" in this way: It is wrong when "he" doesn't get his fair share of profits from the crime just committed; he understand the word "bad" in this way: a fellow criminal betrayed a trust. That must be why, when I say, "I am filled with rage," the criminal says, "But why?" And when I blow things up and make life generally unlivable for the criminal (is my life not unlivable, too?) the criminal is shocked, surprised. But nothing can erase my rage—not an apology, not a large sum of money, not the death of the criminal—for this wrong can never be made right, and only the impossible can make me still: can a way be found to make what happened not have happened? And so look at this prolonged visit to the bile duct that I am making, look at how bitter, how dyspeptic just to sit and think about these things makes me. . . . Have I given you the impression that the Antigua I grew up in revolved almost completely around England? Well, that was so. I met the world through England, and if the world wanted to meet me it would have to do so through England.

Are you saying to yourself, "Can't she get beyond all that, everything happened so long ago, and how does she know that if things had been the other way around her ancestors wouldn't have behaved just as badly, because, after all, doesn't everybody behave badly given the opportunity?"

Our perception of this Antigua—the perception we had of this place ruled by these bad-minded people—was not a political perception. The English were ill-mannered, not racists; the school headmistress was especially ill-mannered, not a racist; the doctor was crazy—he didn't even speak English properly, and he came from a strangely named place, he also was not a racist; the people at the Mill Reef Club were puzzling (why go and live in a place populated mostly by people you cannot stand), not racists.

Have you ever wondered to yourself why it is that all people like me seem to have learned from you is how to imprison and murder each other, how to govern badly, and how to take the wealth of our country and place it in Swiss bank accounts? Have you ever wondered why it is that all we seem to have learned from you is how to corrupt our societies and how to be tyrants? You will have to accept that this is mostly your fault. Let me just show you how you looked to us. You came. You took things that were not yours, and you did not even, for appearances' sake, ask first. You could have said, "May I have this, please?" and even though it would have been

clear to everybody that a yes or no from us would have been of no consequence you might have looked so much better. Believe me, it would have
gone a long way. I would have had to admit that at least you were polite.
You murdered people. You imprisoned people. You robbed people. You
opened your own banks and you put our money in them. The accounts
were in your name. The banks were in your name. There must have been
some good people among you, but they stayed home. And that is the point.
That is why they are good. They stayed home. But still, when you think
about it, you must be a little sad. The people like me, finally, after years
and years of agitation, made deeply moving and eloquent speeches against
the wrongness of your domination over us, and then finally, after the mutilated bodies of you, your wife, and your children were found in your beautiful and spacious bungalow at the edge of your rubber plantation—found by
one of your many house servants (none of it was ever yours; it was never,
ever yours)—you say to me, "Well, I wash my hands of all of you, I am
leaving now," and you leave, and from afar you watch as we do to ourselves
the very things you used to do to us. And you might feel that there was
more to you than that, you might feel that you had understood the meaning of the Age of Enlightenment (though, as far as I can see, it had done
you very little good); you loved knowledge, and wherever you went you
made sure to build a school, a library (yes, and in both of these places you
distorted or erased my history and glorified your own). But then again, perhaps as you observe the debacle in which I now exist, the utter ruin that I
say is my life, perhaps you are remembering that you had always felt people
like me cannot run things, people like me will never grasp the idea of Gross
National Product, people like me will never be able to take command of the
thing the most simple-minded among you can master, people like me will
never understand the notion of rule by law, people like me cannot really
think in abstractions, people like me cannot be objective, we make everything
so personal. You will forget your part in the whole setup, that bureaucracy is
one of your inventions, that Gross National Product is one of your inventions, and all the laws that you know mysteriously favour you. Do you know
why people like me are shy about being capitalists? Well, it's because we, for
as long as we have known you, *were* capital, like bales of cotton and sacks of
sugar, and you were the commanding, cruel capitalists, and the memory of
this is so strong, the experience so recent, that we can't quite bring ourselves
to embrace this idea that you think so much of. As for what we were like
before we met you, I no longer care. No periods of time over which my
ancestors held sway, no documentation of complex civilisations, is any comfort to me. Even if I really came from people who were living like monkeys
in trees, it was better to be that than what happened to me, what I became
after I met you.

1988

BHARATI MUKHERJEE
B. 1940

Bharati Mukherjee is one of the best-known South Asian American woman writers. She has stated that she wants to be viewed not as a hyphenated South Asian–American writer but as an American writer. In an interview with Bill Moyers, she commented, "I feel very American ... I knew the moment I landed as a student in 1961 ... that this is where I belonged. It was an instant kind of love."

One wonders, however, if one can really discard a part of one's personal/political history even in the process of transformation, especially since the past displays a tenacious, trickster-like ability to appear at the oddest times and in the most astonishing disguises. The insistence on being known as an American, without acknowledging one's Asian heritage, may grate on those who see the term *American* as denoting the Euro-American sociopolitically dominant group only. For those of us who feel that it is absolutely necessary to continue emphasizing our essentially non-European American identities until we are truly acknowledged as Americans with our own distinctive American presence, Mukherjee's stance may seem simplistic. Yet, as many of her stories show, she is neither ignorant of nor insensitive to racism and oppression in the United States. In the interview with Moyers, she also said that "Multiculturalism, in a sense, is well intentioned, but it ends up marginalizing the person."

Mukherjee's ease with discovering her identity as a mainstream American, her skill with the dialogues and incidents familiar to the dominant society, her refusal to be marginalized, and her absolute mastery of English are not surprising when one looks at her biography. She was born in 1940 to an upper-middle-class Brahmin family in Calcutta. Her education in India was at a convent school run by Irish nuns. She was also educated in England and Switzerland. She came to the United States in 1961 to attend the Writer's Workshop at the University of Iowa, where she received an M.F.A. in creative writing and a Ph.D. in English and comparative literature. She and her husband, the Canadian writer Clark Blaise, lived in Canada from 1966 until 1980, when they emigrated to the United States. Mukherjee is a professor of English at the University of California, Berkeley.

Mukherjee's first novel, *The Tiger's Daughter*, portrays Tara Banerjee Cartwright, a Western-educated, well-to-do Bengali woman married to an American. Her second novel, *Wife*, begins in Bengal with an opening sentence that would do credit to Jane Austen: "Dimple Dasgupta had set her heart on marrying a neuro-surgeon, but her father was looking for engineers in the matrimonial ads." Her novels *Holder of the World*, *Jasmine*, and *Leave It to Me* and her brilliantly written collections of short stories, *Darkness* and *Middleman and Other Stories*, extend Mukherjee's discussion into the more violent and grotesque yet very real aspects of collisions between cultures at different times in the histories of India and the United States.

"A Wife's Story" is a carefully crafted narrative with an interesting twist: the wife comes to America to study, and the husband comes to visit her. The story begins with Panna watching a play that insults Indian men and women. It ends with Panna waiting for her husband, who is leaving for India the next morning without her, to make love to her: "The water is running in the bathroom. In the ten days he has been here he has learned American rites: deodorants, fragrances." Panna ends her narrative with "I am free, afloat, watching somebody else." One hears echoes of Mukherjee's statement about America being a place where one can choose "to discard . . . history . . . and invent a whole new history for myself." As Panna glories in her beautiful body and her freedom, one is haunted by the question of the price and texture of her freedom. "A Wife's Story," like many of Mukherjee's other stories, leaves the narrative unresolved and open for discussion. It also raises important questions about the forging of cultural, national, and sexual alliances in a United States that glorifies individual freedom and urges the loss of a racial and ethnic memory that is not Eurocentric.

Roshni Rustomji-Kerns
Sonoma State University

PRIMARY WORKS

The Tiger's Daughter, 1971; *Wife*, 1975; *Days and Nights in Calcutta* (coauthored with Clark Blaise), 1977; *Darkness*, 1985; *The Sorrow and the Terror: The Haunting Legacy of the Air India Tragedy*, 1987; *The Middleman and Other Stories*, 1988; *Jasmine*, 1989; *Holder of the World*, 1993; *Leave It to Me*, 1997; *Desirable Daughters*, 2002; *The Tree Bride*, 2004.

A Wife's Story

Imre says forget it, but I'm going to write David Mamet.[1] So Patels are hard to sell real estate to. You buy them a beer, whisper Glengarry Glen Ross, and they smell swamp instead of sun and surf. They work hard, eat cheap, live ten to a room, stash their savings under futons in Queens, and before you know it they own half of Hoboken. You say, where's the sweet gullibility that made this nation great?

Polish jokes, Patel jokes: that's not why I want to write Mamet.

Seen their women?

Everybody laughs. Imre laughs. The dozing fat man with the Barnes & Noble sack between his legs, the woman next to him, the usher, everybody. The theater isn't so dark that they can't see me. In my red silk sari I'm conspicuous. Plump, gold paisleys sparkle on my chest.

The actor is just warming up. *Seen their women?* He plays a salesman, he's had a bad day and now he's in a Chinese restaurant trying to loosen up. His face is pink. His wool-blend slacks are creased at the crotch. We bought our tickets at half-price, we're sitting in the front row, but at the edge, and

---

[1]David Mamet (b. 1947) is an American playwright, essayist, and film director. The narrator is referring to his 1984 play *Glengarry Glen Ross*, which is about the ethics of real estate salesmen. "Patel" is an Indian title (also a surname) that refers generally to a landowning caste.

we see things we shouldn't be seeing. At least I do, or think I do. Spittle, actors goosing each other, little winks, streaks of makeup.

Maybe they're improvising dialogue too. Maybe Mamet's provided them with insult kits, Thursdays for Chinese, Wednesdays for Hispanics, today for Indians. Maybe they get together before curtain time, see an Indian woman settling in the front row off to the side, and say to each other: "Hey, forget Friday. Let's get *her* today. See if she cries. See if she walks out." Maybe, like the salesmen they play, they have a little bet on.

Maybe I shouldn't feel betrayed.

Their women, he goes again. *They look like they've just been fucked by a dead cat.*

The fat man hoots so hard he nudges my elbow off our shared armrest.

"Imre. I'm going home." But Imre's hunched so far forward he doesn't hear. English isn't his best language. A refugee from Budapest, he has to listen hard. "I didn't pay eighteen dollars to be insulted."

I don't hate Mamet. It's the tyranny of the American dream that scares me. First, you don't exist. Then you're invisible. Then you're funny. Then you're disgusting. Insult, my American friends will tell me, is a kind of acceptance. No instant dignity here. A play like this, back home, would cause riots. Communal, racist, and antisocial. The actors wouldn't make it off stage. This play, and all these awful feelings, would be safely locked up.

I long, at times, for clear-cut answers. Offer me instant dignity, today, and I'll take it.

"What?" Imre moves toward me without taking his eyes off the actor. "Come again?"

Tears come. I want to stand, scream, make an awful scene. I long for ugly, nasty rage.

The actor is ranting, flinging spittle. *Give me a chance. I'm not finished, I can get back on the board. I tell that asshole, give me a real lead. And what does that asshole give me? Patels. Nothing but Patels.*

This time Imre works an arm around my shoulders. "Panna, what is Patel? Why are you taking it all so personally?"

I shrink from his touch, but I don't walk out. Expensive girls' schools in Lausanne and Bombay have trained me to behave well. My manners are exquisite, my feelings are delicate, my gestures refined, my moods undetectable. They have seen me through riots, uprootings, separation, my son's death.

"I'm not taking it personally."

The fat man looks at us. The woman looks too, and shushes.

I stare back at the two of them. Then I stare, mean and cool, at the man's elbow. Under the bright blue polyester Hawaiian shirt sleeve, the elbow looks soft and runny. "Excuse me," I say. My voice has the effortless meanness of well-bred displaced Third World women, though my rhetoric has been learned elsewhere. "You're exploiting my space."

Startled, the man snatches his arm away from me. He cradles it against his breast. By the time he's ready with comebacks, I've turned my back on him. I've probably ruined the first act for him. I know I've ruined it for Imre.

It's not my fault; it's the *situation*. Old colonies wear down. Patels—the new pioneers—have to be suspicious. Idi Amin's lesson is permanent. AT&T wires move good advice from continent to continent. Keep all assets liquid. Get into 7-11s, get out of condos and motels. I know how both sides feel, that's the trouble. The Patel sniffing out scams, the sad salesmen on the stage: postcolonialism has made me their referee. It's hate I long for; simple, brutish, partisan hate.

After the show Imre and I make our way toward Broadway. Sometimes he holds my hand; it doesn't mean anything more than that crazies and drunks are crouched in doorways. Imre's been here over two years, but he's stayed very old-world, very courtly, openly protective of women. I met him in a seminar on special ed. last semester. His wife is a nurse somewhere in the Hungarian countryside. There are two sons, and miles of petitions for their emigration. My husband manages a mill two hundred miles north of Bombay. There are no children.

"You make things tough on yourself," Imre says. He assumed Patel was a Jewish name or maybe Hispanic; everything makes equal sense to him. He found the play tasteless, he worried about the effect of vulgar language on my sensitive ears. "You have to let go a bit." And as though to show me how to let go, he breaks away from me, bounds ahead with his head ducked tight, then dances on amazingly jerky legs. He's a Magyar, he often tells me, and deep down, he's an Asian too. I catch glimpses of it, knife-blade Attila cheekbones, despite the blondish hair. In his faded jeans and leather jacket, he's a rock video star. I watch MTV for hours in the apartment when Charity's working the evening shift at Macy's. I listen to WPLJ on Charity's earphones. Why should I be ashamed? Television in India is so uplifting.

Imre stops as suddenly as he'd started. People walk around us. The summer sidewalk is full of theatergoers in seersucker suits; Imre's year-round jacket is out of place. European. Cops in twos and threes huddle, lightly tap their thighs with night sticks and smile at me with benevolence. I want to wink at them, get us all in trouble, tell them the crazy dancing man is from the Warsaw Pact. I'm too shy to break into dance on Broadway. So I hug Imre instead.

The hug takes him by surprise. He wants me to let go, but he doesn't really expect me to let go. He staggers, though I weigh no more than 104 pounds, and with him, I pitch forward slightly. Then he catches me, and we walk arm in arm to the bus stop. My husband would never dance or hug a woman on Broadway. Nor would my brothers. They aren't stuffy people, but they went to Anglican boarding schools and they have a well-developed sense of what's silly.

"Imre." I squeeze his big, rough hand. "I'm sorry I ruined the evening for you."

"You did nothing of the kind." He sounds tired. "Let's not wait for the bus. Let's splurge and take a cab instead."

Imre always has unexpected funds. The Network, he calls it, Class of '56.

In the back of the cab, without even trying, I feel light, almost free. Memories of Indian destitutes mix with the hordes of New York street people, and they float free, like astronauts, inside my head. I've made it. I'm making something of my life. I've left home, my husband, to get a Ph.D. in special ed. I have a multiple-entry visa and a small scholarship for two years. After that, we'll see. My mother was beaten by her mother-in-law, my grandmother, when she'd registered for French lessons at the Alliance Française. My grandmother, the eldest daughter of a rich zamindar, was illiterate.

Imre and the cabdriver talk away in Russian. I keep my eyes closed. That way I can feel the floaters better. I'll write Mamet tonight. I feel strong, reckless. Maybe I'll write Steven Spielberg too; tell him that Indians don't eat monkey brains.

We've made it. Patels must have made it. Mamet, Spielberg: they're not condescending to us. Maybe they're a little bit afraid.

Charity Chin, my roommate, is sitting on the floor drinking Chablis out of a plastic wineglass. She is five foot six, three inches taller than me, but weighs a kilo and a half less than I do. She is a "hands" model. Orientals are supposed to have a monopoly in the hands-modelling business, she says. She had her eyes fixed eight or nine months ago and out of gratitude sleeps with her plastic surgeon every third Wednesday.

"Oh, good," Charity says. "I'm glad you're back early. I need to talk."

She's been writing checks. MCI, Con Ed, Bonwit Teller. Envelopes, already stamped and sealed, form a pyramid between her shapely, knee-socked legs. The checkbook's cover is brown plastic, grained to look like cowhide. Each time Charity flips back the cover, white geese fly over sky-colored checks. She makes good money, but she's extravagant. The difference adds up to this shared, rent-controlled Chelsea one-bedroom.

"All right. Talk."

When I first moved in, she was seeing an analyst. Now she sees a nutritionist.

"Eric called. From Oregon."

"What did he want?"

"He wants me to pay half the rent on his loft for last spring. He asked me to move back, remember? He *begged* me."

Eric is Charity's estranged husband.

"What does your nutritionist say?" Eric now wears a red jumpsuit and tills the soil in Rajneeshpuram.

"You think Phil's a creep too, don't you? What else can he be when creeps are all I attract?"

Phil is a flutist with thinning hair. He's very touchy on the subject of *flautists* versus *flutists*. He's touchy on every subject, from music to books to foods to clothes. He teaches at a small college upstate, and Charity bought a used blue Datsun ("Nissan," Phil insists) last month so she could spend weekends with him. She returns every Sunday night, exhausted and exasperated. Phil and I don't have much to say to each other—he's the only musician I know; the men in my family are lawyers, engineers, or in business—but I like him. Around me, he loosens up. When he visits, he bakes us loaves of pumpernickel bread. He waxes our kitchen floor. Like many men in this country, he seems to me a displaced child, or even a woman, looking for something that passed him by, or for something that he can never have. If he thinks I'm not looking, he sneaks his hands under Charity's sweater, but there isn't too much there. Here, she's a model with high ambitions. In India, she'd be a flat-chested old maid.

I'm shy in front of the lovers. A darkness comes over me when I see them horsing around.

"It isn't the money," Charity says. Oh? I think. "He says he still loves me. Then he turns around and asks me for five hundred."

What's so strange about that, I want to ask. She still loves Eric, and Eric, red jump suit and all, is smart enough to know it. Love is a commodity, hoarded like any other. Mamet knows. But I say, "I'm not the person to ask about love." Charity knows that mine was a traditional Hindu marriage. My parents, with the help of a marriage broker, who was my mother's cousin, picked out a groom. All I had to do was get to know his taste in food.

It'll be a long evening, I'm afraid. Charity likes to confess. I unpleat my silk sari—it no longer looks too showy—wrap it in muslin cloth and put it away in a dresser drawer. Saris are hard to have laundered in Manhattan, though there's a good man in Jackson Heights. My next step will be to brew us a pot of chrysanthemum tea. It's a very special tea from the mainland. Charity's uncle gave it to us. I like him. He's a humpbacked, awkward, terrified man. He runs a gift store on Mott Street, and though he doesn't speak much English, he seems to have done well. Once upon a time he worked for the railways in Chengdu, Szechwan Province, and during the Wuchang Uprising, he was shot at. When I'm down, when I'm lonely for my husband, when I think of our son, or when I need to be held, I think of Charity's uncle. If I hadn't left home, I'd never have heard of the Wuchang Uprising. I've broadened my horizons.

Very late that night my husband calls me from Ahmadabad, a town of textile mills north of Bombay. My husband is a vice president at Lakshmi Cotton Mills. Lakshmi is the goddess of wealth, but LCM (Priv.), Ltd., is doing poorly. Lockouts, strikes, rock-throwings. My husband lives on digitalis, which he calls the food for our *yuga* of discontent.

"We had a bad mishap at the mill today." Then he says nothing for seconds.

The operator comes on. "Do you have the right party, sir? We're trying to reach Mrs. Butt."

"Bhatt," I insist. "*B* for Bombay, *H* for Haryana, *A* for Ahmadabad, double *T* for Tamil Nadu." It's a litany. "This is she."

"One of our lorries was firebombed today. Resulting in three deaths. The driver, old Karamchand, and his two children."

I know how my husband's eyes look this minute, how the eye rims sag and the yellow corneas shine and bulge with pain. He is not an emotional man—the Ahmadabad Institute of Management has trained him to cut losses, to look on the bright side of economic catastrophes—but tonight he's feeling low. I try to remember a driver named Karamchand, but can't. That part of my life is over, the way *trucks* have replaced *lorries* in my vocabulary, the way Charity Chin and her lurid love life have replaced inherited notions of marital duty. Tomorrow he'll come out of it. Soon he'll be eating again. He'll sleep like a baby. He's been trained to believe in turnovers. Every morning he rubs his scalp with cantharidine oil so his hair will grow back again.

"It could be your car next." Affection, love. Who can tell the difference in a traditional marriage in which a wife still doesn't call her husband by his first name?

"No. They know I'm a flunky, just like them. Well paid, maybe. No need for undue anxiety, please."

Then his voice breaks. He says he needs me, he misses me, he wants me to come to him damp from my evening shower, smelling of sandalwood soap, my braid decorated with jasmines.

"I need you too."

"Not to worry, please," he says. "I am coming in a fortnight's time. I have already made arrangements."

Outside my window, fire trucks whine, up Eighth Avenue. I wonder if he can hear them, what he thinks of a life like mine, led amid disorder.

"I am thinking it'll be like a honeymoon. More or less."

When I was in college, waiting to be married, I imagined honeymoons were only for the more fashionable girls, the girls who came from slightly racy families, smoked Sobranies in the dorm lavatories and put up posters of Kabir Bedi, who was supposed to have made it as a big star in the West. My husband wants us to go to Niagara. I'm not to worry about foreign exchange. He's arranged for extra dollars through the Gujarati Network, with a cousin in San Jose. And he's bought four hundred more on the black market. "Tell me you need me. Panna, please tell me again."

I change out of the cotton pants and shirt I've been wearing all day and put on a sari to meet my husband at JFK. I don't forget the jewelry; the marriage necklace of mangalsutra, gold drop earrings, heavy gold bangles. I don't wear them every day. In this borough of vice and greed, who knows when, or whom, desire will overwhelm.

My husband spots me in the crowd and waves. He has lost weight, and changed his glasses. The arm, uplifted in a cheery wave, is bony, frail, almost opalescent.

In the Carey Coach, we hold hands. He strokes my fingers one by one. "How come you aren't wearing my mother's ring?"

"Because muggers know about Indian women," I say. They know with us it's 24-karat. His mother's ring is showy, in ghastly taste anywhere but

India: a blood-red Burma ruby set in a gold frame of floral sprays. My mother-in-law got her guru to bless the ring before I left for the States.

He looks disconcerted. He's used to a different role. He's the knowing, suspicious one in the family. He seems to be sulking, and finally he comes out with it. "You've said nothing about my new glasses." I compliment him on the glasses, how chic and Western-executive they make him look. But I can't help the other things, necessities until he learns the ropes. I handle the money, buy the tickets. I don't know if this makes me unhappy.

Charity drives her Nissan upstate, so for two weeks we are to have the apartment to ourselves. This is more privacy than we ever had in India. No parents, no servants, to keep us modest. We play at housekeeping. Imre has lent us a hibachi, and I grill saffron chicken breasts. My husband marvels at the size of the Perdue hens. "They're big like peacocks, no? These Americans, they're really something!" He tries out pizzas, burgers, McNuggets. He chews. He explores. He judges. He loves it all, fears nothing, feels at home in the summer odors, the clutter of Manhattan streets. Since he thinks that the American palate is bland, he carries a bottle of red peppers in his pocket. I wheel a shopping cart down the aisles of the neighborhood Grand Union, and he follows, swiftly, greedily. He picks up hair rinses and high-protein diet powders. There's so much I already take for granted.

One night, Imre stops by. He wants us to go with him to a movie. In his work shirt and red leather tie, he looks arty or strung out. It's only been a week, but I feel as though I am really seeing him for the first time. The yellow hair worn very short at the sides, the wide, narrow lips. He's a good-looking man, but self-conscious, almost arrogant. He's picked the movie we should see. He always tells me what to see, what to read. He buys the *Voice*. He's a natural avant-gardist. For tonight he's chosen *Numéro Deux*.

"Is it a musical?" my husband asks. The Radio City Music Hall is on his list of sights to see. He's read up on the history of the Rockettes. He doesn't catch Imre's sympathetic wink.

Guilt, shame, loyalty. I long to be ungracious, not ingratiate myself with both men.

That night my husband calculates in rupees the money we've wasted on Godard. "That refugee fellow, Nagy, must have a screw loose in his head. I paid very steep price for dollars on the black market."

Some afternoons we go shopping. Back home we hated shopping, but now it is a lovers' project. My husband's shopping list startles me. I feel I am just getting to know him. Maybe, like Imre, freed from the dignities of old-world culture, he too could get drunk and squirt Cheez Whiz on a guest. I watch him dart into stores in his gleaming leather shoes. Jockey shorts on sale in outdoor bins on Broadway entrance him. White tube socks with different bands of color delight him. He looks for microcassettes, for anything small and electronic and smuggleable. He needs a garment bag. He calls it a "wardrobe," and I have to translate.

"All of New York is having sales, no?"

My heart speeds watching him this happy. It's the third week in August, almost the end of summer, and the city smells ripe, it cannot bear more heat, more money, more energy.

"This is so smashing! The prices are so excellent!" Recklessly, my prudent husband signs away traveller's checks. How he intends to smuggle it all back I don't dare ask. With a microwave, he calculates, we could get rid of our cook.

This has to be love, I think. Charity, Eric, Phil: they may be experts on sex. My husband doesn't chase me around the sofa, but he pushes me down on Charity's battered cushions, and the man who has never entered the kitchen of our Ahmadabad house now comes toward me with a dish tub of steamy water to massage away the pavement heat.

Ten days into his vacation my husband checks out brochures for sightseeing tours. Shortline, Grayline, Crossroads: his new vinyl briefcase is full of schedules and pamphlets. While I make pancakes out of a mix, he comparison-shops. Tour number one costs $10.95 and will give us the World Trade Center, Chinatown, and the United Nations. Tour number three would take us both uptown *and* downtown for $14.95, but my husband is absolutely sure he doesn't want to see Harlem. We settle for tour number four: Downtown and the Dame. It's offered by a new tour company with a small, dirty office at Eighth and Forty-eighth.

The sidewalk outside the office is colorful with tourists. My husband sends me in to buy the tickets because he has come to feel Americans don't understand his accent.

The dark man, Lebanese probably, behind the counter comes on too friendly. "Come on, doll, make my day!" He won't say which tour is his. "Number four? Honey, no! Look, you've wrecked me! Say you'll change your mind." He takes two twenties and gives back change. He holds the tickets, forcing me to pull. He leans closer. "I'm off after lunch."

My husband must have been watching me from the sidewalk. "What was the chap saying?" he demands. "I told you not to wear pants. He thinks you are Puerto Rican. He thinks he can treat you with disrespect."

The bus is crowded and we have to sit across the aisle from each other. The tour guide begins his patter on Forty-sixth. He looks like an actor, his hair bleached and blow-dried. Up close he must look middle-aged, but from where I sit his skin is smooth and his cheeks faintly red.

"Welcome to the Big Apple, folks." The guide uses a microphone. "Big Apple. That's what we native Manhattan degenerates call our city. Today we have guests from fifteen foreign countries and six states from this U.S. of A. That makes the Tourist Bureau real happy. And let me assure you that while we may be the richest city in the richest country in the world, it's okay to tip your charming and talented attendant." He laughs. Then he swings his hip out into the aisle and sings a song.

"And it's mighty fancy on old Delancey Street, you know...."

My husband looks irritable. The guide is, as expected, a good singer. "The bloody man should be giving us histories of buildings we are passing, no?" I pat his hand, the mood passes. He cranes his neck. Our window seats have both gone to Japanese. It's the tour of his life. Next to this, the quick business trips to Manchester and Glasgow pale.

"And tell me what street compares to Mott Street, in July...."

The guide wants applause. He manages a derisive laugh from the Americans up front. He's working the aisles now. "I coulda been somebody, right? I coulda been a star!" Two or three of us smile, those of us who recognize the parody. He catches my smile. The sun is on his harsh, bleached hair. "Right, your highness? Look, we gotta maharani with us! Couldn't I have been a star?"

"Right!" I say, my voice coming out a squeal. I've been trained to adapt; what else can I say?

We drive through traffic past landmark office buildings and churches. The guide flips his hands. "Art deco," he keeps saying. I hear him confide to one of the Americans: "Beats me. I went to a cheap guide's school." My husband wants to know more about this Art Deco, but the guide sings another song.

"We made a foolish choice," my husband grumbles. "We are sitting in the bus only. We're not going into famous buildings." He scrutinizes the pamphlets in his jacket pocket. I think, at least it's air-conditioned in here. I could sit here in the cool shadows of the city forever.

Only five of us appear to have opted for the "Downtown and the Dame" tour. The others will ride back uptown past the United Nations after we've been dropped off at the pier for the ferry to the Statue of Liberty.

An elderly European pulls a camera out of his wife's designer tote bag. He takes pictures of the boats in the harbor, the Japanese in kimonos eating popcorn, scavenging pigeons, me. Then, pushing his wife ahead of him, he climbs back on the bus and waves to us. For a second I feel terribly lost. I wish we were on the bus going back to the apartment. I know I'll not be able to describe any of this to Charity, or to Imre. I'm too proud to admit I went on a guided tour.

The view of the city from the Circle Line ferry is seductive, unreal. The skyline wavers out of reach, but never quite vanishes. The summer sun pushes through fluffy clouds and dapples the glass of office towers. My husband looks thrilled, even more than he had on the shopping trips down Broadway. Tourists and dreamers, we have spent our life's savings to see this skyline, this statue.

"Quick, take a picture of me!" my husband yells as he moves toward a gap of railings. A Japanese matron has given up her position in order to change film. "Before the Twin Towers disappear!"

I focus, I wait for a large Oriental family to walk out of my range. My husband holds his pose tight against the railing. He wants to look relaxed, an international businessman at home in all the financial markets.

A bearded man slides across the bench toward me. "Like this," he says and helps me get my husband in focus. "You want me to take the photo for you?" His name, he says, is Goran. He is Goran from Yugoslavia, as though that were enough for tracking him down. Imre from Hungary. Panna from

India. He pulls the old Leica out of my hand, signaling the Orientals to beat it, and clicks away. "I'm a photographer," he says. He could have been a camera thief. That's what my husband would have assumed. Somehow, I trusted. "Get you a beer?" he asks.

"I don't. Drink, I mean. Thank you very much." I say those last words very loud, for everyone's benefit. The odd bottles of Soave with Imre don't count.

"Too bad." Goran gives back the camera.

"Take one more!" my husband shouts from the railing. "Just to be sure!"

The island itself disappoints. The Lady has brutal scaffolding holding her in. The museum is closed. The snack bar is dirty and expensive. My husband reads out the prices to me. He orders two french fries and two Cokes. We sit at picnic tables and wait for the ferry to take us back.

"What was that hippie chap saying?"

As if I could say. A day-care center has brought its kids, at least forty of them, to the island for the day. The kids, all wearing name tags, run around us. I can't help noticing how many are Indian. Even a Patel, probably a Bhatt if I looked hard enough. They toss hamburger bits at pigeons. They kick styrofoam cups. The pigeons are slow, greedy, persistent. I have to shoo one off the table top. I don't think my husband thinks about our son.

"What hippie?"

"The one on the boat. With the beard and the hair."

My husband doesn't look at me. He shakes out his paper napkin and tries to protect his french fries from pigeon feathers.

"Oh, him. He said he was from Dubrovnik." It isn't true, but I don't want trouble.

"What did he say about Dubrovnik?"

I know enough about Dubrovnik to get by. Imre's told me about it. And about Mostar and Zagreb. In Mostar white Muslims sing the call to prayer. I would like to see that before I die: white Muslims. Whole peoples have moved before me; they've adapted. The night Imre told me about Mostar was also the night I saw my first snow in Manhattan. We'd walked down to Chelsea from Columbia. We'd walked and talked and I hadn't felt tired at all.

"You're too innocent," my husband says. He reaches for my hand. "Panna," he cries with pain in his voice, and I am brought back from perfect, floating memories of snow, "I've come to take you back. I have seen how men watch you."

"What?"

"Come back, now. I have tickets. We have all the things we will ever need. I can't live without you."

A little girl with wiry braids kicks a bottle cap at his shoes. The pigeons wheel and scuttle around us. My husband covers his fries with spread-out fingers. "No kicking," he tells the girl. Her name, Beulah, is printed in green ink on a heart-shaped name tag. He forces a smile, and Beulah smiles back. Then she starts to flap her arms. She flaps, she hops. The pigeons go crazy for fries and scraps.

"Special ed. course is two years," I remind him. "I can't go back."

My husband picks up our trays and throws them into the garbage before I can stop him. He's carried disposability a little too far. "We've been taken," he says, moving toward the dock, though the ferry will not arrive for another twenty minutes. "The ferry costs only two dollars round-trip per person. We should have chosen tour number one for $10.95 instead of tour number four for $14.95."

With my Lebanese friend, I think. "But this way we don't have to worry about cabs. The bus will pick us up at the pier and take us back to midtown. Then we can walk home."

"New York is full of cheats and whatnot. Just like Bombay." He is not accusing me of infidelity. I feel dread all the same.

That night, after we've gone to bed, the phone rings. My husband listens, then hands the phone to me. "What is this woman saying?" He turns on the pink Macy's lamp by the bed. "I am not understanding these Negro people's accents."

The operator repeats the message. It's a cable from one of the directors of Lakshmi Cotton Mills. "Massive violent labor confrontation anticipated. Stop. Return posthaste. Stop. Cable flight details. Signed Kantilal Shah."

"It's not your factory," I say. "You're supposed to be on vacation."

"So, you are worrying about me? Yes? You reject my heartfelt wishes but you worry about me?" He pulls me close, slips the straps of my nightdress off my shoulder. "Wait a minute."

I wait, unclothed, for my husband to come back to me. The water is running in the bathroom. In the ten days he has been here he has learned American rites: deodorants, fragrances. Tomorrow morning he'll call Air India; tomorrow evening he'll be on his way back to Bombay. Tonight I should make up to him for my years away, the gutted trucks, the degree I'll never use in India. I want to pretend with him that nothing has changed.

In the mirror that hangs on the bathroom door, I watch my naked body turn, the breasts, the thighs glow. The body's beauty amazes. I stand here shameless, in ways he has never seen me. I am free, afloat, watching somebody else.

1988

■ CAROLYN FORCHÉ ■

B. 1950

Carolyn Forché's spirited paternal grandmother, Anna, a Slovak immigrant, spoke "a funny English," in the poet's words, partly to display her resistance to American culture. Forché's life and poetry have responded to the challenge in Anna's declaration, "in your country / you have nothing" ("Endurance"). Anna nicknamed Carolyn *Piskata*, "Chatterbox," and passed on to her granddaughter an old homily: "Eat Bread and Salt and Speak the Truth" ("Burning the Tomato Worms"). Forché was born in Detroit; her father, Michael Sidlosky, labored as a tool and die maker ten and twelve hours a day, six and sometimes seven days a week. Her mother, Louise, bore seven children before attending college.

Forché was educated in Catholic schools and then graduated from Michigan State University. She has an M.F.A. from Bowling Green State University (1975) and an honorary doctorate from Russell Sage College (1985).

Her first book of poems, *Gathering the Tribes*, received the Yale Series of Younger Poets Award in 1975. These poems derived partly from Forché's alternately living among Pueblo Indians near Taos, New Mexico, and backpacking in the desert regions of Utah, on the Pacific Crest Trail, and in the Okanogan region of British Columbia. As its title suggests, this volume is characterized not by the self-absorption of much twentieth-century American verse but by a desire for community—incorporating, among other voices, those of the "silenced" Pueblo Indians and her own Slovak ancestors.

From January 1978 to March 1980, Forché made a number of trips to El Salvador; during this period, she documented human rights violations for Amnesty International, verifying information and evaluating the organization's reports on El Salvador. While living in El Salvador, she also wrote seven of the twenty-two poems included in *The Country between Us*, her second collection and the Academy of American Poets' 1981 Lamont Poetry Selection. In 1980 Forché worked closely with Monsignor Oscar Romero, the beloved Archbishop of San Salvador who was assassinated that year by a right-wing death squad; after several attempts had been made on Forché's life, Monsignor Romero asked that she return to the United States to "tell the American people what is happening." She has said that her El Salvador experience transformed her life and work: it "prevent[s] me from ever viewing myself or my country again through precisely the same fog of unwitting connivance" ("El Salvador: An Aide Memoire").

Forché has continued to travel and to act on her beliefs. In 1983 she accompanied a congressional fact-finding delegation to Israel; in 1984 she contributed to the program *All Things Considered* on National Public Radio from Beirut, Lebanon; from December 1985 to March 1986 she lived in South Africa. She has held numerous teaching positions at American universities.

Denise Levertov's praise for *The Country between Us* suggests what Forché accomplishes: a seamless merging of the "personal and political, lyrical and engaged." Her important anthology, *Against Forgetting: Twentieth Century Poetry of Witness*, and her 1994 collection of poems, *The Angel of History*, a consummate book of fragmented images and characters who voice the largely untold narratives of modern wars, brought her the Swedish Edita and Ira Morris Award for Peace and Culture in 1998.

Constance Coiner
State University of New York at Binghamton
Linda Wagner-Martin
University of North Carolina at Chapel Hill

PRIMARY WORKS

Gathering the Tribes, 1976; *The Country between Us*, 1982; *Flowers from the Volcano* (translations of the poetry of Claribel Alegría), 1982; *El Salvador: Work of Thirty Photographers*, 1983; *The Angel of History*, 1994; *Sorrow*, 1999; *Blue Hour*, 2003.

from **The Country between Us**

The Colonel

What you have heard is true. I was in his house. His wife carried a tray of coffee and sugar. His daughter filed her nails, his son went out for the night. There were daily papers, pet dogs, a pistol on the cushion beside him. The moon swung bare on its black cord over the house. On the television was a cop show. It was in English. Broken bottles were embedded in the walls around the house to scoop the kneecaps from a man's legs or cut his hands to lace. On the windows there were gratings like those in liquor stores. We had dinner, rack of lamb, good wine, a gold bell was on the table for calling the maid. The maid brought green mangoes, salt, a type of bread. I was asked how I enjoyed the country. There was a brief commercial in Spanish. His wife took everything away. There was some talk then of how difficult it had become to govern. The parrot said hello on the terrace. The colonel told it to shut up, and pushed himself from the table. My friend said to me with his eyes: say nothing. The colonel returned with a sack used to bring groceries home. He spilled many human ears on the table. They were like dried peach halves. There is no other way to say this. He took one of them in his hands, shook it in our faces, dropped it into a water glass. It came alive there. I am tired of fooling around he said. As for the rights of anyone, tell your people they can go fuck themselves. He swept the ears to the floor with his arm and held the last of his wine in the air. Something for your poetry, no? he said. Some of the ears on the floor caught this scrap of his voice. Some of the ears on the floor were pressed to the ground.

1981

Because One Is Always Forgotten

In Memoriam, José Rudolfo Viera[1] *1939–1981: El Salvador*

When Viera was buried we knew it had come to an end,
his coffin rocking into the ground like a boat or a cradle.

I could take my heart, he said, and give it to a *campesino*[2]
and he would cut it up and give it back:

---

[1] Labor activist and director of El Salvador's Institute of Agrarian Reform from October 1979 until his death in January 1981. Along with two U.S. agrarian reform specialists, Michael Hammer and Mark Pearlman, Viera was gunned down in the Sheraton Hotel coffee shop in San Salvador. As Forché reports in *El Salvador: Work of Thirty Photographers*,

"Shortly before his murder, Viera appeared on television demanding an investigation of a $40 million fraud by the former military administrators of [El Salvador's] Institute of Agrarian Transformation." U.S. newspapers reported Hammer and Pearlman's deaths but failed to report Viera's.
[2] Peasant, farmer, one who works the land.

you can't eat heart in those four dark   5
chambers where a man can be kept years.

A boy soldier in the bone-hot sun works his knife
to peel the face from a dead man

and hang it from the branch of a tree
flowering with such faces.   10

The heart is the toughest part of the body.
Tenderness is in the hands.

                                                                    1981

As Children Together

Under the sloped snow
pinned all winter with Christmas
lights, we waited for your father
to whittle his soap cakes
away, finish the whisky,   5
your mother to carry her coffee
from room to room closing lights
cubed in the snow at our feet.
Holding each other's
coat sleeves we slid down   10
the roads in our tight
black dresses, past
crystal swamps and the death
face of each dark house,
over the golden ice   15
of tobacco spit, the blue
quiet of ponds, with town
glowing behind the blind
white hills and a scant
snow ticking in the stars.   20
You hummed *blanche comme
la neige*[1] and spoke of Montreal
where a *quebeçoise*[2] could sing,
take any man's face
to her unfastened blouse   25
and wake to wine
on the bedside table.

[1]French for "white as the snow," this is the   [2]A female native of Quebec.
title of a traditional song of Quebec.

I always believed this,
Victoria, that there might
be a way to get out.   30

You were ashamed of that house,
its round tins of surplus flour,
chipped beef and white beans,
relief checks and winter trips
that always ended in deer   35
tied stiff to the car rack,
the accordion breath of your uncles
down from the north, and what
you called the stupidity
of the Michigan French.   40

Your mirror grew ringed
with photos of servicemen
who had taken your breasts
in their hands, the buttons
of your blouses in their teeth,   45
who had given you the silk
tassles of their graduation,
jackets embroidered with dragons
from the Far East. You kept
the corks that had fired   50
from bottles over their beds,
their letters with each city
blackened, envelopes of hair
from their shaved heads.
I am going to have it, you said.   55
Flowers wrapped in paper from carts
in Montreal, a plane lifting out
of Detroit, a satin bed, a table
cluttered with bottles of scent.

So standing in a platter of ice   60
outside a Catholic dance hall
you took their collars
in your fine chilled hands
and lied your age to adulthood.

I did not then have breasts of my own,   65
nor any letters from bootcamp
and when one of the men who had
gathered around you took my mouth
to his own there was nothing

other than the dance hall music   70
rising to the arms of iced trees.

I don't know where you are now, Victoria.
They say you have children, a trailer
in the snow near our town,
and the husband you found as a girl   75
returned from the Far East broken
cursing holy blood at the table
where nightly a pile of white shavings
is paid from the edge of his knife.

If you read this poem, write to me.   80
I have been to Paris since we parted.

                                                                     1981

from **The Recording Angel**

I

Memory insists she stood there, able to go neither forward nor back,
    and in that
Unanimous night, time slowed, in light pulsing through ash, light of
    which the coat was made
Light of their brick houses   5
In matter's choreography of light, time slowed, then reversed until
    memory
Held her, able to go neither forward nor back
They were alone where once hundreds of thousands lived

Doves, or rather their wings, heard above the roof and the linens   10
    floating
Above a comic wedding in which corpses exchange vows. A grand
    funeral celebration
Everyone has died at once
Walking home always, always on this same blue road, cold through   15
    the black-and-white trees
Unless the film were reversed, she wouldn't reach the house
As she doesn't in her memory, or in her dream
Often she hears him calling out, half her name, his own, behind her in
    a room until she turns   20
Standing forever, where often she hears him calling out

He is there, hidden in the blue winter fields and the burnt acreage of
    summer

As if, in reflecting the ruins, the river were filming what their city had
    been   25
And *had it not been for this* lines up behind *if it weren't for that*
Until the past is something of a regiment
Yet looking back down the row of marching faces one sees one face
Before the shelling, these balconies were for geraniums and children
The slate roofs for morning   30

Market flowers in a jar, a string of tied garlic, and a voice moving off
    as if fearing itself
Under the leprous trees a white siren of light searches
Under the leprous trees a white siren of sun

II

A row of cabanas with white towels near restorative waters where   35
    once it was possible to be cured
A town of vacant summer houses
Mists burning the slightest lapse of sea
The child has gone to the window filled with desire, a glass light
    passing through its hand   40
There are tide tables by which the sea had been predictable, as were
    the heavens
As sickness chose from among us we grew fewer
There were jetty lights where there was no jetty
What the rain forests had been became our difficult breath   45

At the moment when the snow geese lifted, thousands at once after
    days of crying in the wetlands
At once they lifted in a single ascent, acres of wind in their wingbones
Wetlands of morning light in their lift moving as one over the
    continent   50
As a white front, one in their radiance, in their crying, a cloud of one
    desire

The child plays with its dead telephone. The father blows a kiss. The
    child laughs
The fire of his few years is carried toward the child on a cake   55
The child can't help itself. Would each day be like this?

And the geese, rising and falling in the rain on a surf of black hands
Sheets of rain and geese invisible or gone

Someone was supposed to have come
Waves turning black with the beach weed called dead men's hands   60
The sea strikes a bottle against a rock

III

The photographs were found at first by mistake in the drawer. After
    that I went to them often
She was standing on her toes in a silk *yukata*, her arms raised
Wearing a girl's white socks and near her feet a vase of calla lilies: 65
Otherwise she wore nothing
And in this one, her long hair is gathered into a white towel
Or tied back not to interfere
She had been wounded by so many men, abused by them
From behind in a silk *yukata*, then like this   70
One morning they were gone and I searched his belongings for them
    like a madwoman
In every direction, melted railyards, felled telegraph poles
For two months to find some trace of her
Footsteps on the floor above. More birds   75
It might have been less painful had it not been for the photographs
And beyond the paper walls, the red maple
Shirt in the wind of what the past meant
The fresh claw of a swastika on Rue Boulard
A man walking until he can no longer be seen   80
Don't say I was there. Always say I was never there.

    1994

Elegy

The page opens to snow on a field: boot-holed month, black hour
the bottle in your coat half vodka half winter light.
To what and to whom does one say *yes*?
If God were the uncertain, would you cling to him?

Beneath a tattoo of stars the gate opens, so silent so like a tomb.   5
This is the city you most loved, an empty stairwell
where the next rain lifts invisibly from the Seine.

With solitude, your coat open, you walk
steadily as if the railings were there and your hands weren't passing
    through them.   10

"When things were ready, they poured on fuel and touched off the
    fire.
They waited for a high wind. It was very fine, that powdered bone.
It was put into sacks, and when there were enough we went to a
    bridge on the Narew River."   15

And even less explicit phrases survived:
"To make charcoal.
For laundry irons."
And so we revolt against silence with a bit of speaking.
The page is a charred field where the dead would have written   20
We went on. And it was like living through something again one could
   not live through again.

The soul behind you no longer inhabits your life: the unlit house
with its breathless windows and a chimney of ruined wings
where wind becomes an aria, your name, voices from a field,   25
And you, smoke, dissonance, a psalm, a stairwell.

                                                   1994

■ DOROTHY ALLISON ■
B. 1949

Born in Greenville, South Carolina, to a fourteen-year-old mother, Dorothy Allison was raised near her large extended family. After her mother married, her aunts provided occasional refuge from an abusive stepfather. The violence and chaos of her upbringing, stemming largely from her family's poverty, fuel Allison's writing, as does the strength she saw in her relatives' survival despite such hopeless conditions. Her chance to escape came when a National Merit Scholarship paid for her to attend Florida Presbyterian College. She later earned a master's degree in anthropology from the New School for Social Research in New York.

Allison became active in the women's movement in the early 1970s, working for several feminist publications and helping establish Herstore, a feminist bookstore in Tallahassee, Florida. She credits feminism for enabling her to become a writer. Although she had begun writing as a child, she viewed writing the truth as such a dangerous activity that she burned everything she wrote. In 1973 friends in the lesbian feminist collective where she was living convinced her to stop destroying her work.

Her first book, *The Women Who Hate Me,* was a collection of poems, most written in reaction to the protest surrounding the 1982 Barnard College conference Towards a Politics of Sexuality. The intent of that feminist conference was to discuss sexuality in all its complexity, but antipornography protesters effectively shut down the event by appealing to university administrators and personally attacking conference participants. Allison's poems, which are frequently angry, focus on women's relationships and lesbian sexuality. An expanded version of the book was published in 1991 with the subtitle *Poetry 1980–1990.*

In 1988 Allison published *Trash*, a collection of emotionally intense, frequently violent, and often comic short stories. Class difference is a predominant theme, as many of her characters confront others' stereotypical expectations of rural Southerners. The misunderstandings created by often romantic stereotypes are particularly poignant in stories depicting lesbian relationships. Given Allison's subject matter, it is not surprising that among the writers she credits as influences are Flannery O'Connor, James Baldwin, Eudora Welty, Tennessee Williams, Carson McCullers, Muriel Rukeyser, and Toni Morrison.

Allison's earliest published work established her audience and reputation primarily in the lesbian community. Her first novel, *Bastard out of Carolina* (1992), gained her national attention. It won the Lambda Award and was a finalist for the National Book Award. Loosely autobiographical, the compelling first-person narrative follows Bone Boatwright's survival of her stepfather's sexual abuse. In 1996 the novel became a film directed by Anjelica Huston.

Two or Three Things I Know for Sure, composed after Allison completed the novel, debuted as a performance piece at The Lab in San Francisco in August 1991. Revised for publication in 1995, the work, which traces Allison's family history by describing family photographs, explores the paradoxical power of stories to both support and delude. While Allison writes of her need to tell stories as part of her own survival, she also describes the "meanest" ones as those "the women [she] loved told themselves in secret—the stories that sustained and broke them." A short documentary based on the work, *Two or Three Things but Nothing for Sure*, by Tina DiFeliciantonio and Jane Wagner, won prizes at both the Aspen and Toronto film festivals and aired on PBS in 1998.

In 1994 Allison published a collection of critical and political essays under the descriptive title *Skin: Talking about Sex, Class, and Literature*. Her second novel appeared in 1998. *Cavedweller*, a *New York Times* best seller, portrays the relationships between a woman and her three daughters, two of whom she abandoned when she fled from their father. Reviews praised the language, characterization, and emotional power of the story but noted that the novel's structure weakens in the second half. Allison currently lives in northern California with her partner Alix and her son Wolf.

Kelly Lynch Reames
Oklahoma State University

PRIMARY WORKS

The Women Who Hate Me, 1983; *Trash*, 1988; *The Women Who Hate Me: Poetry 1980–1990*, 1991; *Bastard out of Carolina*, 1992; *Skin: Talking about Sex, Class, and Literature*, 1994; *Two or Three Things I Know for Sure*, 1995; *Cavedweller*, 1998.

Don't Tell Me You Don't Know

I came out of the bathroom with my hair down wet on my shoulders. My Aunt Alma, my mama's oldest sister, was standing in the middle of Casey's dusty hooked rug looking like she had just flown in on it, her grey hair straggling out of its misshapen bun. For a moment I was so startled I couldn't move. Aunt Alma just stood there looking around at the big bare room with its two church pews bracketing the only other furniture—a massive pool table. I froze while the water ran down from my hair to dampen the collar of the oversized tuxedo shirt I used for a bathrobe.

"Aunt Alma," I stammered, "well . . . welcome. . . ."

"You really live here?" she breathed, as if, even for me, such a situation was quite past her ability to believe. "Like this?"

I looked around as if I were seeing it for the first time myself, shrugged and tried to grin. "It's big," I offered, "lots of space, four porches, all these windows. We get along well here, might not in a smaller place." I looked back through the kitchen to Terry's room with its thick dark curtains covering a wall of windows. Empty. So was Casey's room on the other side of the kitchen. It was quiet and still, with no one even walking through the rooms overhead.

"Thank God," I whispered to myself. Nobody else was home.

Aunt Alma turned around slowly and stepped over to the mantel with the old fly-spotted mirror over it. She pushed a few of her loose hairs back and then laid her big rattan purse up by a stack of fliers Terry had left there, brushing some of the dust away first.

"My God," she echoed, "dirtier than we ever lived. Didn't think you'd turn out like this."

I shrugged again, embarrassed and angry and trying not to show it. Well hell, what could I do? I hadn't seen her in so long. She hadn't even been around that last year I'd lived with Mama, and I wasn't sure I particularly wanted to see her now. But why was she here anyway? How had she found me?

I closed the last two buttons on my shirt and tried to shake some of the water out of my hair. Aunt Alma watched me through the dark spots of the mirror, her mouth set in an old familiar line. "Well," I said, "I didn't expect to see you." I reached up to push hair back out of my eyes. "You want to sit down?"

Aunt Alma turned around and bumped her hip against the pool table. "Where?" One disdainful glance rendered the pews for what they were—exquisitely uncomfortable even for my hips. Her expression reminded me of my Uncle Jack's jokes about her, about how she refused to go back to church till they put in rocking chairs.

"No rocking chairs here," I laughed, hoping she'd laugh with me. Aunt Alma just leaned forward and rocked one of the balls on the table against another. Her mouth kept its flat, impartial expression. I tried gesturing across the pool table to my room and the big waterbed outlined in sunlight and tree shade from the three windows overlooking it.

"It's cleaner in there," I offered, "it's my room. This is our collective space." I gestured around.

"Collective," my aunt echoed me again, but the way she said the word expressed clearly her opinion of such arrangements. She looked toward my room with its narrow cluttered desk and stacks of books, then turned back to the pool table as by far the more interesting view. She rocked the balls again so that the hollow noise of the thump resounded against the high, dim ceiling.

"Pitiful," she sighed, and gave me a sharp look, her washed-out blue eyes almost angry. Two balls broke loose from the others and rolled idly across the matted green surface of the table. The sunlight reflecting through the oak leaves outside made Aunt Alma's face seem younger than I remembered it, some of the hard edge eased off the square jaw.

"Your mama is worried about you."

"I don't know why." I turned my jaw to her, knowing it would remind her of how much alike we had always been, the people who had said I was more her child than my mama's. "I'm fine. Mama should know that. I spoke to her not too long ago."

"How long ago?"

I frowned, mopped at my head some more. Two months, three, last month? "I'm not sure ... Reese's birthday. I think it was Reese's birthday."

"Three months." My aunt rocked one ball back and forth across her palm, a yellow nine ball. The light filtering into the room went a shade darker. The -9- gleamed pale through her fingers. I looked more closely at her. She looked just as she had when I was thirteen, her hair grey in that loose bun, her hands large and swollen, her body straining the seams of the faded print dress. She'd worn her hair short for a while, but it was grown long again now, and the print dress under her coat could have been any dress she'd worn in the last twenty years. She'd gotten old, suddenly, after the birth of her eighth child, but since then she seemed not to change at all. She looked now as if she would go on forever—a worn stubborn woman who didn't care what you saw when you looked at her.

I drew breath in slowly, carefully. I knew from old experience to use caution in dealing with any of my aunts, and this was the oldest and most formidable. I'd seen grown men break down and cry when she'd kept that look on them too long; little children repent and swear to change their ways. But I'd also seen my other aunts stare her right back, and like them I was a grown woman minding my own business. I had a right to look her in the eye, I told myself. I was no wayward child, no half-drunk, silly man. I was her namesake, my mama's daughter. I had to be able to look her in the eye. If I couldn't, I was in trouble, and I didn't want that kind of trouble here, 500 miles and half a lifetime away from my aunts and the power of their eyes.

Slow, slow, the balls rocked one against the other. Aunt Alma looked over at me levelly. I let the water run down between my breasts, looked back at her. My mama's sister. I could feel the tears pushing behind my eyes. It had been so long since I'd seen her or any of them! The last time I'd been to Old Henderson Road had been years back. Aunt Alma had stood on that sagging porch and looked at me, memorizing me, both of us knowing we might not see each other again. She'd moved her mouth and I'd seen the pain there, the shadow of the nephew behind her—yet another one she was raising since her youngest son, another cousin of mine, had run off and left the girl who'd birthed that boy. The pain in her eyes was achingly clear to me, the certain awful knowledge that measured all her children and wrenched her heart.

Something wrong with that boy, my uncles had laughed.

Yeah, something. Dropped on his head one too many times, you think?

I think.

My aunt, like my mama, understood everything, expected nothing, and watched her own life like a terrible fable from a Sunday morning sermon. It was the perspective that all those women shared, the view that I could not, for my life, accept. I believed, I believed with all my soul that death was behind it, that death was the seed and the fruit of that numbed and numbing attitude. More than anything else, it was my anger that had driven me away from them, driven them away from me—my unpredictable, automatic anger. Their anger, their hatred, always seemed shielded, banked and secret, and because of that—shameful. My uncles were sudden, violent, and daunting. My aunts wore you down without ever seeming to fight at all. It was my anger that my aunts thought queer, my wild raging temper they respected in a boy and discouraged in a girl. That I slept with girls was curious, but not dangerous. That I slept with a knife under my pillow and refused to step aside for my uncles was more than queer. It was crazy.

Aunt Alma's left eye twitched, and I swallowed my tears, straightened my head, and looked her full in the face. I could barely hold myself still, barely return her look. Again those twin emotions, the love and the outrage that I'd always felt for my aunt, warred in me. I wanted to put out my hand and close my fingers on her hunched, stubborn shoulder. I wanted to lay my head there and pull tight to her, but I also wanted to hit her, to scream and kick and make her ashamed of herself. Nothing was clean between us, especially not our love.

Between my mama and Aunt Alma there were five other sisters. The most terrible and loved was Bess, the one they swore had always been so smart. From the time I was eight Aunt Bess had a dent in the left side of her head—a shadowed dent that emphasized the twitch of that eye, just like the twitch Aunt Alma has, just like the twitch I sometimes get, the one they tell me is nerves. But Aunt Bess wasn't born with that twitch as we were, just as she wasn't born with that dent. My uncle, her husband, had come up from the deep dust on the road, his boots damp from the river, picking up clumps of dust and making mud, knocking it off on her steps, her screen door, her rug, the back rung of a kitchen chair. She'd shouted at him, "Not on my clean floor!" and he'd swung the bucket, river-stained and heavy with crawfish. He'd hit her in the side of the head—dented her into a lifetime of stupidity and half-blindness. Son of a bitch never even said he was sorry, and all my childhood he'd laughed at her, the way she'd sometimes stop in the middle of a sentence and grope painfully for a word.

None of *them* had told me that story. I had been grown and out of the house before one of the Greenwood cousins had told it so I understood, and as much as I'd hated him then, I'd raged at them more.

"You let him live?" I'd screamed at them. "He did that to her and you did nothing! You did nothing to him, nothing for her."

"What'd you want us to do?"

My Aunt Grace had laughed at me. "You want us to cut him up and feed him to the river? What good would that have done her or her children?"

She'd shaken her head, and they had all stared at me as if I were still a child and didn't understand the way the world was. The cold had gone through me then, as if the river were running up from my bowels. I'd felt my hands curl up and reach, but there was nothing to reach for. I'd taken hold of myself, my insides, and tried desperately to voice the terror that was tearing at me.

"But to leave her with him after he did that, to just let it stand, to let him get away with it." I'd reached and reached, trying to get to them, to make them feel the wave moving up and through me. "It's like all of it, all you let them get away with."

"Them?" My mama had watched my face as if afraid of what she might find there. "Who do you mean? And what do you think we could do?"

I couldn't say it. I'd stared into mama's face, and looked from her to all of them, to those wide, sturdy cheekbones, those high, proud eyebrows, those set and terrible mouths. I had always thought of them as mountains, mountains that everything conspired to grind but never actually broke. The women of my family were all I had ever believed in. What was I if they were not what I had shaped them in my own mind? All I had known was that I had to get away from them—all of them—the men who could do those terrible things and the women who would let it happen to you. I'd never forgiven any of them.

It might have been more than three months since I had talked to Mama on the telephone. It had been far longer than that since I had been able to really talk to any of them. The deepest part of me didn't believe that I would ever be able to do so. I dropped my eyes and pulled myself away from Aunt Alma's steady gaze. I wanted to reach for her, touch her, maybe cry with her, if she'd let me.

"People will hurt you more with pity than with hate," she'd always told me. "I can hate back, or laugh at them, but goddamn the son of a bitch that hands me pity."

No pity. Not allowed. I reached to rock a ball myself.

"Want to play?" I tried looking up into her eyes again. It was too close. Both of us looked away.

"I'll play myself." She set about racking up the balls. Her mouth was still set in that tight line. I dragged a kitchen stool in and sat in the doorway out of her way, telling myself I had to play this casually, play this as family, and wait and see what the point was.

"Where's Uncle Bill?" I was rubbing my head again and trying to make conversation.

"What do you care? I don't think Bill said ten words to you in your whole life." She rolled the rack forward and back, positioning it perfectly for the break. "'Course he didn't say many more to anybody else either." She grinned, not looking at me, talking as if she were pouring tea at her own kitchen table. "Nobody can say I married that man for his conversation."

She leaned into her opening shot, and I leaned forward in appreciation. She had a great stance, her weight centered over her massive thighs. My family runs to heavy women, gravy-fed working women, the kind usually seen in pictures taken at mining disasters. Big women, all of my aunts move under their own power and stalk around telling everybody else what to do. But Aunt Alma was the prototype, the one I had loved most, starting back when she had given us free meals in the roadhouse she'd run for a while. It had been one of those bad times when my stepfather had been out of work and he and Mama were always fighting. Mama would load us all in the Pontiac and crank it up on seventy-five cents worth of gas, just enough to get to Aunt Alma's place on the Eustis Highway. Once there, we'd be fed on chicken gravy and biscuits, and Mama would be fed from the well of her sister's love and outrage.

You tell that bastard to get his ass out on the street. Whining don't make money. Cursing don't get a job . . .

Bitching don't make the beds and screaming don't get the tomatoes planted. They had laughed together then, speaking a language of old stories and older jokes.

You tell him.

I said.

Now girl, you listen to me.

The power in them, the strength and the heat! How could anybody not love my mama, my aunts? How could my daddy, my uncles, ever stand up to them, dare to raise hand or voice to them? They were a power on the earth.

I breathed deep, watching my aunt rock on her stance, settling her eye on the balls, while I smelled chicken gravy and hot grease, the close thick scent of love and understanding. I used to love to eat at Aunt Alma's house, all those home-cooked dinners at the roadhouse; pinto beans with peppers for fifteen, nine of them hers. Chow-chow on a clean white plate passed around the table while the biscuits passed the other way. My aunt always made biscuits. What else stretched so well? Now those starch meals shadowed her loose shoulders and dimpled her fat white elbows.

She gave me one quick glance and loosed her stroke. The white ball punched the center of the table. The balls flew to the edges. My sixty-year-old aunt gave a grin that would have scared piss out of my Uncle Bill, a grin of pure, fierce enjoyment. She rolled the stick in fingers loose as butter on a biscuit, laughed again, and slid her palms down the sides of polished wood, while the anger in her face melted into skill and concentration.

I rocked back on my stool and covered my smile with my wet hair. Goddamn! Aunt Alma pushed back on one ankle, swung the stick to follow one ball, another, dropping them as easily as peas on potatoes. Goddamn! She went after those balls like kids on a dirt yard, catching each lightly and dropping them lovingly. Into the holes, move it! Turning and bracing on ankles thickened with too many years of flour and babies, Aunt Alma blitzed that table like a twenty-year-old hustler, not sparing me another glance.

Not till the eighth stroke did she pause and stop to catch her breath.

"You living like this—not for a man, huh?" she asked, one eyebrow arched and curious.

"No," I shrugged, feeling more friendly and relaxed. Moving like that, aunt of mine I wanted to say, don't tell me you don't understand.

"Your mama said you were working in some photo shop, doing shit work for shit money. Not much to show for that college degree, is that?"

"Work is work. It pays the rent."

"Which ought not to be much here."

"No," I agreed, "not much. I know," I waved my hands lightly, "it's a wreck of a place, but it's home. I'm happy here. Terry, Casey and everybody—they're family."

"Family." Her mouth hardened again. "You have a family, don't you remember? These girls might be close, might be important to you, but they're not family. You know that." Her eyes said more, much more. Her eyes threw the word *family* at me like a spear. All her longing, all her resentment of my abandonment was in that word, and not only hers, but Mama's and my sisters' and all the cousins' I had carefully not given my new address.

"How about a beer?" I asked. I wanted one myself. "I've got a can of Pabst in the icebox."

"A glass of water," she said. She leaned over the table to line up her closing shots.

I brought her a glass of water. "You're good," I told her, wanting her to talk to me about how she had learned to play pool, anything but family and all this stuff I so much did not want to think about.

"Children," she stared at me again. "What about children?" There was something in her face then that waited, as if no question were more important, as if she knew the only answer I could give.

Enough, I told myself, and got up without a word to get myself that can of Pabst. I did not look in her eyes. I walked into the kitchen on feet that felt suddenly unsteady and tender. Behind me, I heard her slide the cue stick along the rim of the table and then draw it back to set up another shot.

Play it out, I cursed to myself, just play it out and leave me alone. Everything is so simple for you, so settled. Make babies. Grow a garden. Handle some man like he's just another child. Let everything come that comes, die that dies; let everything go where it goes. I drank straight from the can and watched her through the doorway. All my uncles were drunks, and I was more like them than I had ever been like my aunts.

Aunt Alma started talking again, walking around the table, measuring shots and not even looking in my direction. "You remember when ya'll lived out on Greenlake Road? Out on that dirt road where that man kept that old egg-busting dog? Your mama couldn't keep a hen to save her life till she emptied a shell and filled it again with chicken shit and baby piss. Took that dog right out of himself when he ate it. Took him right out of the taste for hens and eggs." She stopped to take a deep breath, sweat glittering on her lip. With one hand she wiped it away, the other going white on the pool cue.

"I still had Annie then. Lord, I never think about her anymore."

I remembered then the last child she had borne, a tiny girl with a heart that fluttered with every breath, a baby for whom the doctors said nothing could be done, a baby they swore wouldn't see six months. Aunt Alma had kept her in an okra basket and carried her everywhere, talking to her one minute like a kitten or a doll and the next minute like a grown woman. Annie had lived to be four, never outgrowing the vegetable basket, never talking back, just lying there and smiling like a wise old woman, dying between a smile and a laugh while Aunt Alma never interrupted the story that had almost made Annie laugh.

I sipped my beer and watched my aunt's unchanging face. Very slowly she swung the pool cue up and down, not quite touching the table. After a moment she stepped in again and leaned half her weight on the table. The 5-ball became a bird murdered in flight, dropping suddenly into the far right pocket.

Aunt Alma laughed out loud, delighted. "Never lost it," she crowed. "Four years in the roadhouse with that table set up in the back. Every one of them sons of mine thought he was going to make money on it. Lord those boys! Never made a cent." She swallowed the rest of her glass of water.

"But me," she wiped the sweat away again. "I never would have done it for money. I just loved it. Never went home without playing myself three or four games. Sometimes I'd set Annie up on the side and we'd pretend we was playing. I'd tell her when I was taking her shots. And she'd shout when I'd sink 'em. I let her win most every time."

She stopped, put both hands on the table, closed her eyes.

"'Course, just after we lost her, we lost the roadhouse." She shook her head, eyes still closed. "Never did have anything fine that I didn't lose."

The room was still, dust glinted in the sunlight past her ears. She opened her eyes and looked directly at me.

"I don't care," she began slowly, softly. "I don't care if you're queer or not. I don't care if you take puppydogs to bed, for that matter, but your mother was all my heart for twenty years when nobody else cared what happened to me. She stood by me. I've stood by her and I always thought to do the same for you and yours. But she's sitting there, did you know that? She's sitting there like nothing's left of her life, like ... like she hates her life and won't say shit to nobody about it. She wouldn't tell me. She won't tell me what it is, what has happened."

I sat the can down on the stool, closed my own eyes, dropped my head. I didn't want to see her. I didn't want her to be there. I wanted her to go away, disappear out of my life the way I'd run out of hers. Go away, old woman. Leave me alone. Don't talk to me. Don't tell me your stories. I an't a baby in a basket, and I can't lie still for it.

"You know. You know what it is. The way she is about you. I know it has to be you—something about you. I want to know what it is, and you're going to tell me. Then you're going to come home with me and straighten this out. There's a lot I an't never been able to fix, but this time, this thing, I'm going to see it out. I'm going to see it fixed."

I opened my eyes and she was still standing there, the cue stick shiny in her hand, her face all flushed and tight.

"Go," I said and heard my voice, a scratchy, strangling cry in the big room. "Get out of here."

"What did you tell her? What did you say to your mama?"

"Ask her. Don't ask me. I don't have nothing to say to you."

The pool cue rose slowly, slowly till it touched the right cheek, the fine lines of broken blood vessels, freckles, and patchy skin. She shook her head slowly. My throat pulled tighter and tighter until it drew my mouth down and open. Like a shot the cue swung. The table vibrated with the blow. Her cheeks pulled tight, the teeth all a grimace. The cue split and broke. White dust rose in a cloud. The echo hurt my ears while her hands rose up as fists, the broken cue in her right hand as jagged as the pain in her face.

"Don't you say that to me. Don't you treat me like that. Don't you know who I am, what I am to you? I didn't have to come up here after you. I could have let it run itself out, let it rest on your head the rest of your life, just let you carry it—your mama's life. YOUR MAMA'S LIFE, GIRL. Don't you understand me? I'm talking about your mama's life."

She threw the stick down, turned away from me, her shoulders heaving and shaking, her hands clutching nothing. "I an't talking about your stepfather. I an't talking about no man at all. I'm talking about your mama sitting at her kitchen table, won't talk to nobody, won't eat, won't listen to nothing. What'd she ever ask from you? Nothing. Just gave you your life and everything she had. Worked herself ugly for you and your sister. Only thing she ever hoped for was to do the same for your children, someday to sit herself back and hold her grandchildren on her lap...."

It was too much. I couldn't stand it.

"GODDAMN YOU!" I was shaking all over. "CHILDREN! All you ever talk about—you and her and all of you. Like that was the end-all and be-all of everything. Never mind what happens to them once they're made. That don't matter. It's only the getting of them. Like some goddamned crazy religion. Get your mother a grandchild and solve all her problems. Get yourself a baby and forget everything else. It's what you were born for, the one thing you can do with no thinking about it at all. Only I can't. To get her a grandchild, I'd have to steal one!"

I was wringing my own hands, twisting them together and pulling them apart. Now I swung them open and slapped down at my belly, making my own hollow noise in the room.

"No babies in there, aunt of mine, and never going to be. I'm sterile as a clean tin can. That's what I told Mama, and not to hurt her. I told her because she wouldn't leave me alone about it. Like you, like all of you, always talking about children, never able to leave it alone." I was walking back and forth now, unable to stop myself from talking. "Never able to hear me when I warned her to leave it be. Going on and on till I thought I'd lose my mind."

I looked her in the eye, loving her and hating her, and not wanting to speak, but hearing the words come out anyway. "Some people never do have babies, you know. Some people get raped at eleven by a stepfather their mama half-hates but can't afford to leave. Some people then have to lie and hide it 'cause it would make so much trouble. So nobody will know, not the law and not the rest of the family. Nobody but the women supposed to be the ones who take care of everything, who know what to do and how to do it, the women who make children who believe in them and trust in them, and sometimes die for it. Some people never go to a doctor and don't find out for ten years that the son of a bitch gave them some goddamned disease."

I looked away, unable to stand how grey her face had gone.

"You know what it does to you when the people you love most in the world, the people you believe in—cannot survive without believing in—when those people do nothing, don't even know something needs to be done? When you cannot hate them but cannot help yourself? The hatred grows. It just takes over everything, eats you up and makes you somebody full of hate."

I stopped. The roar that had been all around me stopped, too. The cold was all through me now. I felt like it would never leave me. I heard her move. I heard her hip bump the pool table and make the balls rock. I heard her turn and gather up her purse. I opened my eyes to see her moving toward the front door. That cold cut me then like a knife in fresh slaughter. I knew certainly that she'd go back and take care of Mama, that she'd never say a word, probably never tell anybody she'd been here. 'Cause then she'd have to talk about the other thing, and I knew as well as she that however much she tried to forget it, she'd really always known. She'd done nothing then. She'd do nothing now. There was no justice. There was no justice in the world.

When I started to cry it wasn't because of that. It wasn't because of babies or no babies, or pain that was so far past I'd made it a source of strength. It wasn't even that I'd hurt her so bad, hurt Mama when I didn't want to. I cried because of the things I hadn't said, didn't know how to say, cried most of all because behind everything else there was no justice for my aunts or my mama. Because each of them to save their lives had tried to be strong, had become, in fact, as strong and determined as life would let them. I and all their children had believed in that strength, had believed in them and their ability to do anything, fix anything, survive anything. None of us had ever been able to forgive ourselves that we and they were not strong enough, that strength itself was not enough.

Who can say where that strength ended, where the world took over and rolled us all around like balls on a pool table? None of us ever would. I brought my hands up to my neck and pulled my hair around until I clenched it in my fists, remembering how my aunt used to pick up Annie to rub that baby's belly beneath her chin—Annie bouncing against her in perfect trust. Annie had never had to forgive her mama anything.

"Aunt Alma, wait. Wait!"

She stopped in the doorway, her back trembling, her hands gripping the doorposts. I could see the veins raised over her knuckles, the cords that stood out in her neck, the flesh as translucent as butter beans cooked until the skins come loose. Talking to my mama over the phone, I had not been able to see her face, her skin, her stunned and haunted eyes. If I had been able to see her, would I have ever said those things to her?

"I'm sorry."

She did not look back. I let my head fall back, rolled my shoulders to ease the painful clutch of my own muscles. My teeth hurt. My ears stung. My breasts felt hot and swollen. I watched the light as it moved on her hair.

"I'm sorry. I would ... I would ... anything. If I could change things, if I could help. . . ."

I stopped. Tears were running down my face. My aunt turned to me, her wide pale face as wet as mine. "Just come home with me. Come home for a little while. Be with your mama a little while. You don't have to forgive her. You don't have to forgive anybody. You just have to love her the way she loves you. Like I love you. Oh girl, don't you know how we love you!"

I put my hands out, let them fall apart on the pool table. My aunt was suddenly across from me, reaching across the table, taking my hands, sobbing into the cold dirty stillness—an ugly sound, not softened by the least self-consciousness. When I leaned forward, she leaned to me and our heads met, her grey hair against my temple brightened by the sunlight pouring in the windows.

"Oh, girl! Girl, you are our precious girl."

I cried against her cheek, and it was like being five years old again in the roadhouse, with Annie's basket against my hip, the warmth in the room purely a product of the love that breathed out from my aunt and my mama. If they were not mine, if I was not theirs, who was I? I opened my mouth, put my tongue out, and tasted my aunt's cheek and my own. Butter and salt, dust and beer, sweat and stink, flesh of my flesh.

"Precious," I breathed back to her.

"Precious."

1988

FRANK CHIN
B. 1940

Frank Chin was born in Berkeley, California. His father was an immigrant and his mother a fourth-generation resident of Oakland Chinatown, where Chin spent much of his childhood. He attended the University of California at Berkeley and at Santa Barbara and participated in the Program in Creative Writing at the University of Iowa. Chin is a tireless and influential promoter of Asian American literature, though his vision of it has often been criticized for its exclusionary tendencies. He has written novels, short stories, plays, comic books, and numerous essays; produced documentaries; worked as a script consultant in Hollywood; taught college courses in Asian American literature; and helped form the Asian American Theatre Workshop in San Francisco.

He coedited (with Jeffery Paul Chan, Lawson Fusao Inada, and Shawn Wong) a foundational anthology of Asian American writings titled *Aiiieeeee!* (1974). A second volume, *The Big Aiiieeeee!*, was published in 1991. Much of Chin's notoriety stems from the positions he and his colleagues take in the introductory essays in those collections. One of their central concerns is the emasculating effect of anti-Asian racism as epitomized by stereotypical figures like Charlie Chan and Fu Manchu. Another controversial aspect of Chin's nonfiction writing has been his relentless criticism of writers such as David Henry Hwang, Maxine Hong Kingston, and Amy Tan; in his view, these writers falsify Asian and Asian American culture. Critics point out the misogyny and homophobia that propel Chin's polemics, but they also acknowledge the significance of his pioneering work as a literary historian. Indeed, many of the writers that Chin and his colleagues champion—such as Louis Chu, John Okada, and Hisaye Yamamoto—have been accorded a privileged place in Asia American literary studies.

The controversy generated by Chin's polemics has tended to overshadow his fictional and dramatic works. First staged in 1972, *The Chickencoop Chinaman* was one of the first plays written by an Asian American to be produced in New York. A second play, *The Year of the Dragon*, premiered two years later. Many of Chin's early writings contain an autobiographical element. They often revolve around a male protagonist—usually a would-be writer—alienated from his family or from his Chinatown community. This is the predicament shared by Johnny in Chin's first published short story, "Food for All His Dead" (1962), and Fred in *The Year of the Dragon*. Much of Chin's early fiction was published in *The Chinaman Pacific & Frisco R.R. Co.* (1988), which won the National Book Award and from which "Railroad Standard Time" has been excerpted. The writings from this period tend to revel in masochistic self-loathing. The male heroes find only momentary relief when they are able to articulate their agony in elaborate monologues and when they gain tenuous access to a Chinese American history of mythical dimensions—a history usually associated with the railroad.

A shift can be detected in Chin's writings around the mid-1980s: he begins to forge a new vision of literary and racial authenticity based on a selective reading of classic Chinese texts, including *Romance of the Three Kingdoms*, *Water Margin*, and Sun Tzu's *The Art of War*. At the heart of the Chinese "real," Chin asserts, is an essentially martial view of the world: Life is war. His later works feature protagonists who embrace these values; furthermore, they frequently allude to the figure of Kwan Kung, a warrior deified in Chinese folklore. The novel *Donald Duk* (1991) recounts the coming of age of its eponymous twelve-year-old protagonist. Unlike the antiheroes of Chin's earlier fiction, Donald is able to move beyond racial self-loathing by discovering the history of the Chinese American laborers who built the railroad and the world of Chinese mythology. The novel *Gunga Din Highway* (1994) features characters who are more exuberant and virile versions of the tortured protagonists of Chin's early writings; the male heroes of this later work have access to the heroic tradition that Chin identifies with Kwan Kung. In *Bulletproof Buddhists and Other Essays* (1998), Chin finds evidence for the persistence of "real" Chinese values in a wide range of cultural locations: in the rituals of Southeast Asian youth gangs in southern California, in the Chinese American communities along the California-Mexico border, and in the works of dissident writers in Singapore.

Daniel Y. Kim
Brown University

PRIMARY WORKS

The Chickencoop Chinaman and The Year of the Dragon: Two Plays by Frank Chin, 1981; *The Chinaman Pacific & Frisco R.R. Co.*, 1988; *Donald Duk*, 1991; *Gunga Din Highway*, 1994; *Bulletproof Buddhists and Other Essays*, 1998; *Born in the USA: A Story of Japanese America*, 2002.

Railroad Standard Time

"This was your grandfather's," Ma said. I was twelve, maybe fourteen years old when Grandma died. Ma put it on the table. The big railroad watch, Elgin. Nineteen-jewel movement. American made. Lever set. Stem wound. Class facecover. Railroad standard all the way. It ticked on the table between stacks of dirty dishes and cold food. She brought me in here to the kitchen, always to the kitchen to loose her thrills and secrets, as if the sound of running water and breathing the warm soggy ghosts of stale food, floating grease, old spices, ever comforted her, as if the kitchen was a paradise for conspiracy, sanctuary for us *juk sing* Chinamen from the royalty of pure-talking China-born Chinese, old, mourning, and belching in the other rooms of my dead grandmother's last house. Here, private, to say in Chinese, "This was your grandfather's," as if now that her mother had died and she'd been up all night long, not weeping, tough and lank, making coffee and tea and little foods for the brokenhearted family in her mother's kitchen, Chinese would be easier for me to understand. As if my mother would say all the important things of the soul and blood to her son, me, only in Chinese from now on. Very few people spoke the language at me the way she did. She chanted a spell up over me that conjured the meaning of what she was saying in the shape of old memories come to call. Words I'd never heard before set me at play in familiar scenes new to me, and ancient.

She lay the watch on the table, eased it slowly off her fingertips down to the tabletop without a sound. She didn't touch me, but put it down and held her hands in front of her like a bridesmaid holding an invisible bouquet and stared at the watch. As if it were talking to her, she looked hard at it, made faces at it, and did not move or answer the voices of the old, calling her from other rooms, until I picked it up.

A two-driver, high stepping locomotive ahead of a coal tender and baggage car, on double track between two semaphores showing a stop signal was engraved on the back.

"Your grandfather collected railroad watches," Ma said. "This one is the best." I held it in one hand and then the other, hefted it, felt out the meaning of "the best," words that rang of meat and vegetables, oils, things we touched, smelled, squeezed, washed, and ate, and I turned the big cased thing over several times. "Grandma gives it to you now," she said. It was big in my hand. Gold. A little greasy. Warm.

I asked her what her father's name had been, and the manic heat of her all-night burnout seemed to go cold and congeal. "Oh," she finally said, "it's one of those Chinese names I . . ." in English, faintly from another world, woozy and her throat and nostrils full of bubbly sniffles, the solemnity of the moment gone, the watch in my hand turned to cheap with the mumbling of a few awful English words. She giggled herself down to nothing but breath and moving lips. She shuffled backward, one step at a time, fox-trotting dreamily backwards, one hand dragging on the edge of the table, wobbling the table, rattling the dishes, spilling cold soup. Back down one side of the table, she dropped her butt a little with each step then muscled it back up. There were no chairs in the kitchen tonight. She knew, but still she looked. So this dance and groggy mumbling about the watch being no good, in strange English, like an Indian medicine man in a movie.

I wouldn't give it back or trade it for another out of the collection. This one was mine. No other. It had belonged to my grandfather. I wore it braking on the Southern Pacific, though it was two jewels short of new railroad standard and an outlaw watch that could get me fired. I kept it on me, arrived at my day-off courthouse wedding to its time, wore it as a railroad relic/family heirloom/grin-bringing affectation when I was writing background news in Seattle, reporting from the shadows of race riots, grabbing snaps for the 11:00 P.M., timing today's happenings with a nineteenth-century escapement. (Ride with me, Grandmother.) I was wearing it on my twenty-seventh birthday, the Saturday I came home to see my son asleep in the back of a strange station wagon, and Sarah inside, waving, shouting through an open window, "Goodbye Daddy," over and over.

I stood it. Still and expressionless as some good Chink, I watched Barbara drive off, leave me, like some blonde white goddess going home from the jungle with her leather patches and briar pipe sweetheart writer and my kids. I'll learn to be a sore loser. I'll learn to hit people in the face. I'll learn to cry when I'm hurt and go for the throat instead of being polite and worrying about being obnoxious to people walking out of my house with my things, taking my kids away. I'll be more than quiet, embarrassed. I won't be likable anymore.

I hate my novel about a Chinatown mother like mine dying, now that Ma's dead. But I'll keep it. I hated after reading *Father and Glorious Descendant, Fifth Chinese Daughter, The House That Tai Ming Built*. Books scribbled up by a sad legion of snobby autobiographical Chinatown saps all on their own. Christians who never heard of each other, hardworking people who sweat out the exact same Chinatown book, the same cunning "Confucius says" joke, just like me. I kept it then and I'll still keep it. Part cookbook, memories of Mother in the kitchen slicing meat paper-thin with a cleaver. Mumbo jumbo about spices and steaming. The secret of Chinatown rice. The hands come down toward the food. The food crawls with culture. The thousand-year-old living Chinese meat makes dinner a safari into the unknown, a blood ritual. Food pornography. Black magic. Between the lines, I read a madman's detailed description of the preparation of shrunken heads. I never wrote to mean anything more than word fun with the food Grandma cooked at home. Chinese food. I read a list of what I remembered eating at my grandmother's table and knew I'd always be known by what I ate, that we come from a hungry tradition. Slop eaters following the wars on all fours. Weed cuisine and mud gravy in the shadow of corpses. We plundered the dust for fungus. Buried things. Seeds plucked out of the wind to feed a race of lace-boned skinnys, in high-school English, become transcendental Oriental art to make the dyke-ish spinster teacher cry. We always come to fake art and write the Chinatown book like bugs come to fly in the light. I hate my book now that ma's dead, but I'll keep it. I know she's not the woman I wrote up like my mother, and dead, in a book that was like everybody else's Chinatown book. Part word map of Chinatown San Francisco, shop to shop down Grant Avenue. Food again. The wind sucks the shops out and you breathe warm roast ducks dripping fat, hooks into the neck, through the head, out an eye. Stacks of iced fish, blue and fluorescent pink in the neon. The air is thin soup, sharp up the nostrils.

All mention escape from Chinatown into the movies. But we all forgot to mention how stepping off the streets into a faceful of Charlie Chaplin or a Western on a ripped and stained screen that became caught in the grip of winos breathing in unison in their sleep and billowed in and out, that shuddered when cars went by . . . we all of us Chinamans watched our own MOVIE ABOUT ME! I learned how to box watching movies shot by James Wong Howe. Cartoons were our nursery rhymes. Summers inside those neon-and-stucco downtown hole-in-the-wall Market Street Frisco movie houses blowing three solid hours of full-color seven-minute cartoons was school, was rows and rows of Chinamans learning English in a hurry from Daffy Duck.

When we ate in the dark and recited the dialogue of cartoon mice and cats out loud in various tones of voice with our mouths full, we looked like people singing hymns in church. We learned to talk like everybody in America. Learned to need to be afraid to stay alive, keep moving. We learned to run, to be cheerful losers, to take a sudden pie in the face, talk American with a lot of giggles. To us a cartoon is a desperate situation. Of the movies, cartoons were the high art of our claustrophobia. They understood us living too close to each other. How, when you're living too close to too many people, you can't wait for one thing more without losing your mind. Cartoons were a fine way out of waiting in Chinatown around the rooms. Those of our Chinamans who every now and then break a reverie with, "Thank you, Mighty Mouse," mean it. Other folks thank Porky Pig, Snuffy Smith, Woody Woodpecker.

The day my mother told me I was to stay home from Chinese school one day a week starting today, to read to my father and teach him English while he was captured in total paralysis from a vertebra in the neck on down, I stayed away from cartoons. I went to a matinee in a white neighborhood looking for the MOVIE ABOUT ME and was the only Chinaman in the house. I liked the way Peter Lorre ran along non-stop routine hysterical. I came back home with Peter Lorre. I turned out the lights in Pa's room. I put a candle on the dresser and wheeled Pa around in his chair to see me in front of the dresser mirror, reading Edgar Allan Poe out loud to him in the voice of Peter Lorre by candlelight.

The old men in the Chinatown books are all Muses for Chinese ceremonies. All the same. Loyal filial children kowtow to the old and whiff food laid out for the dead. The dead eat the same as the living but without the sauces. White food. Steamed chicken. Rice we all remember as children scrambling down to the ground, to all fours and bonking our heads on the floor, kowtowing to a dead chicken.

My mother and aunts said nothing about the men of the family except they were weak. I like to think my grandfather was a good man. Even the kiss-ass steward service, I like to think he was tough, had a few laughs and ran off with his pockets full of engraved watches. Because I never knew him, not his name, nor anything about him, except a photograph of him as a young man with something of my mother's face in his face, and a watch chain across his vest. I kept his watch in good repair and told everyone it would pass to my son someday, until the day the boy was gone. Then I kept it like something of his he'd loved and had left behind, saving it for him maybe, to give to him when he was a man. But I haven't felt that in a long time.

The watch ticked against my heart and pounded my chest as I went too fast over bumps in the night and the radio on, on an all-night run downcoast, down country, down old Highway 99, Interstate 5, I ran my grandfather's time down past road signs that caught a gleam in my headlights and came at me out of the night with the names of forgotten high school girlfriends, BELLEVUE KIRKLAND, ROBERTA GERBER, AURORA CANBY, and sang with the radio to Jonah and Sarah in Berkeley, my Chinatown in Oakland and Frisco, to raise the dead. Ride with me, Grandfather, this is your grandson the ragmouth, called Tampax, the burned scarred boy, called Barbecue, going to San Francisco to bury my mother, your daughter, and spend Chinese New Year's at home. When we were sitting down and into our dinner after Grandma's funeral, and ate in front of the table set with white food for the dead, Ma said she wanted no white food and money burning after her funeral. Her sisters were there. Her sisters took charge of her funeral and the dinner afterwards. The dinner would most likely be in a Chinese restaurant in Frisco. Nobody had these dinners at home anymore. I wouldn't mind people having dinner at my place after my funeral, but no white food.

The whiz goes out of the tires as their roll bites into the steel grating of the Carquinez Bridge. The noise of the engine groans and echoes like a bomber in flight through the steel roadway. Light from the water far below shines through the grate, and I'm driving high, above a glow. The voice of the tires hums a shrill rubber screechy mosquito hum that vibrates through the chassis and frame of the car into my meatless butt, into my tender asshole, my pelvic bones, the roots of my teeth. Over the Carquinez Bridge to CROCK-ETT MARTINEZ closer to home, roll the tires of Ma's Chevy, my car now, carrying me up over the water southwest toward rolls of fog. The fat man's coming home on a sneaky breeze. Dusk comes a drooly mess of sunlight, a slobber of cheap pawnshop gold, a slow building heat across the water, all through the milky air through the glass of the window into the closed atmosphere of a driven car, into one side of my bomber's face. A bomber, flying my mother's car into the unknown charted by the stars and the radio, feels the coming of some old night song climbing hand over hand, bass notes plunking as steady and shady as reminiscence to get on my nerves one stupid beat after the other crossing the high rhythm six-step of the engine. I drive through the shadows of the bridge's steel structure all over the road. Fine day. I've been on the road for sixteen hours straight down the music of Seattle, Spokane, Salt Lake, Sacramento, Los Angeles, and Wolfman Jack lurking in odd hours of darkness, at peculiar altitudes of darkness, favoring the depths of certain Oregon valleys and heat and moonlight of my miles. And I'm still alive. Country 'n' western music for the night road. It's pure white music. Like "The Star-Spangled Banner," it was the first official American music out of school into my jingling earbones sung by sighing white big tits in front of the climbing promise of FACE and Every Good Boy Does Fine chalked on the blackboard.

She stood up singing, one hand cupped in the other as if to catch drool slipping off her lower lip. Our eyes scouted through her blouse to elastic straps, lacy stuff, circular stitching, buckles, and in the distance, finally some skin. The color of her skin spread through the stuff of her blouse like melted butter through bread nicely to our tongues and was warm there. She sat flopping them on the keyboard as she breathed, singing "Home on the Range" over her shoulder, and pounded the tune out with her palms. The lonesome prairie was nothing but her voice, some hearsay country she stood up to sing *a capella* out of her. Simple music you can count. You can hear the words clear. The music's run through Clorox and Simonized, beating so insistently right and regular that you feel to sing it will deodorize you, make you clean. The hardhat hit parade. I listen to it a lot on the road. It's that get-outta-town beat and tune that makes me go.

Mrs. Morales was her name. Aurora Morales. The music teacher us boys liked to con into singing for us. Come-on opera, we wanted from her, not them Shirley Temple tunes the girls wanted to learn, but big notes, high long ones up from the navel that drilled through plaster and steel and skin and meat for bone marrow and electric wires on one long titpopping breath.

This is how I come home, riding a mass of spasms and death throes, warm and screechy inside, itchy, full of ghostpiss, as I drive right past what's left of Oakland's dark wooden Chinatown and dark streets full of dead lettuce and trampled carrot tops parallel all the time in line with the tracks of the Western Pacific and Southern Pacific railroads.

1988

JOHN EDGAR WIDEMAN
B. 1941

John Edgar Wideman was born in Washington, D.C., and grew up in the black Homewood section of Pittsburgh, Pennsylvania. Wideman's parents struggled financially but managed a decent standard of living for their family. During Wideman's high school years, circumstances allowed the family to move out of Homewood to Shadyside, a more economically prosperous neighborhood; Wideman attended the integrated Peabody High School in Shadyside, starred on the basketball team, became senior class president, and earned the honor of valedictorian.

It was at Peabody High School that Wideman's remarkable intellectual and creative career started to emerge clearly. In these early years, he began to immerse himself in white, Western intellectual influences and traditions, which caused some estrangement from black cultural traditions and psychological separation from black people. After high school, he went on to the University of Pennsylvania to major in English, study the traditional curriculum, and develop his creative writing skills. He also became an All Ivy League basketball player. These impressive credentials earned Wideman a Rhodes Scholarship at his graduation in 1963. Wideman went to Oxford and was one of the first two black Rhodes Scholars in more than fifty years to complete the term. After Oxford, Wideman returned to the University of Pennsylvania to become that school's first black tenured professor. His first novel was published in 1967, when he was twenty-six,

In order to raise their children in a different environment, Wideman and his wife, Judy, moved to Laramie, Wyoming, where he taught at the University of Wyoming. Wideman's distance from Homewood ironically drew him back to the African American experience. Listening to family stories while visiting Homewood for his grandmother's funeral in 1973, he began to incorporate influences from the black cultural tradition into his writing and to move psychologically closer to his family and to black people in his personal life. Wideman spent the years between 1973 and 1981, during which he published none of what he wrote, studying African American cultural influences. He read a wide range of books about the black experience and also studied the culture firsthand, making his family in Homewood his main source. Wideman and his family left Laramie in the late 1980s; he taught at the University of Massachusetts at Amherst and is now a professor at Brown University.

Wideman's first three novels, the third of which appeared in 1973, show strong influences from the mainstream modernist tradition that he studied and knew so thoroughly. These works have black settings and mostly black characters, but Wideman makes the bleak, pessimistic modernist voice dominant over a black cultural voice. These novels often show Wideman as a virtuoso craftsman and writer of great power; however, he did not feel satisfied with what he had done. His writing after 1981, when he refocused his fiction and himself toward blackness, displays very strong postmodernist influences, but postmodernism serves the needs of articulating African American racial concerns and cultural traditions. Wideman has published prolifically since 1981, including novels, short story collections, and memoirs. The quality and volume of his work place him in the first rank of contemporary American writers.

James W. Coleman
University of North Carolina at Chapel Hill

PRIMARY WORKS

A Glance Away, 1967; *Hurry Home*, 1970; *The Lynchers*, 1973; *Hiding Place*, 1981; *Damballah*, 1981; *Sent for You Yesterday*, 1983; *Brothers and Keepers*, 1984; *The Homeward Trilogy*, 1985; *Reuben*, 1987; *Fever*, 1989; *Philadelphia Fire*, 1990; *All Stories Are True*, 1993; *Fatheralong: A Meditation on Fathers and Sons, Race and Society*, 1994; *The Cattle Killing*, 1996; *Two Cities*, 1998; *Hoop Roots*, 2001; *The Island: Martinique*, 2003; *God's Gym*, 2005; *Fanon*, 2008.

Valaida[1]

Whither shall I go from thy spirit?
Or whither shall I flee from thy presence?

Bobby tell the man what he wants to hear. Bobby lights a cigarette. Blows smoke and it rises and rises to where I sit on my cloud overhearing everything. Singing to no one. Golden trumpet from the Queen of Denmark across my knees. In my solitude. Dead thirty years now and meeting people still. Primping loose ends of my hair. Worried how I look. How I sound. Silly. Because things don't change. Bobby with your lashes a woman would kill for, all cheekbones, bushy brows and bushy upper lip, ivory when you smile. As you pretend to contemplate his jive questions behind your screen of smoke and summon me by rolling your big, brown-eyed-handsome-man eyeballs to the ceiling where smoke pauses not one instant, but scoots through and warms me where I am, tell him, Bobby, about "fabled Valaida Snow who traveled in an orchid-colored Mercedes-Benz, dressed in an orchid suit, her pet monkey rigged out in an orchid jacket and cap, with the chauffeur in orchid as well." If you need to, lie like a rug, Bobby. But don't waste the truth, either. They can't take that away from me. Just be cool. As always. Recite those countries and cities we played. Continents we conquered. Roll those faraway places with strange-sounding names around in your sweet mouth. Tell him they loved me at home too, a down-home girl from Chattanooga, Tennessee, who turned out the Apollo, not a mumbling word from wino heaven till they were on their feet hollering and clapping for more with the rest of the audience. Reveries of days gone by, yes, yes, they haunt me, baby, I can taste it. Yesteryears, yesterhours. Bobby, do you also remember what you're not telling him? Blues lick in the middle of a blind flamenco singer's moan. Mother Africa stretching her crusty, dusky hands forth, calling back her far-flung children. Later that same

---

[1]Valaida Snow (c. 1900–1956) was a jazz trumpeter, singer, and dancer of considerable talent whose life inspired this story.

night both of us bad on bad red wine wheeling round and round a dark gypsy cave. Olé. Olé.

Don't try too hard to get it right, he'll never understand. He's watching your cuff links twinkle. Wondering if they're real gold and the studs real diamonds. You called me Minnie Mouse. But you never saw me melted down to sixty-eight pounds soaking wet. They beat me, and fucked me in every hole I had. I was their whore. Their maid. A stool they stood on when they wanted to reach a little higher. But I never sang in their cage, Bobby. Not one note. Cost me a tooth once, but not a note. Tell him that one day I decided I'd had enough and walked away from their hell. Walked across Europe, the Atlantic Ocean, the whole U.S. of A. till I found a quiet spot to put peace back in my soul, and then I began performing again. My tunes. In my solitude. And yes. There was a pitiful little stomped-down white boy in the camp I tried to keep the guards from killing, but if he lived or died I never knew. Then or now. Monkey and chauffeur and limo and champagne and cigars and outrageous dresses with rhinestones, fringe and peekaboo slits. That's the fool-ishness the reporter's after. Stuff him with your MC b.s., and if he's still curious when you're finished, if he seems a halfway decent sort in spite of himself, you might suggest listening to the trumpet solo in My Heart Belongs to Daddy, *hip him to* Hot Snow, *the next to last cut, my voice and Lady Day's figure and ground, ground and figure* Dear Lord *above, send back my love.*

He heard her in the bathroom, faucets on and off, on and off, spurting into the sink bowl, the tub. Quick burst of shower spray, rain sound spattering plastic curtain. Now in the quiet she'll be polishing. Every fixture will gleam. *Shine's what people see. See something shiny, don't look no further, most people don't.* If she's rushed she'll wipe and polish faucets, mirrors, metal collars around drains. Learned that trick when she first came to the city and worked with gangs of girls in big downtown hotels. *Told me, said, Don't be fussing around behind in there or dusting under them things, child. Give that mirror a lick. Rub them faucets. Twenty more rooms like this one here still to do before noon.* He lowers the newspaper just enough so he'll see her when she passes through the living room, so she won't see him looking unless she stops and stares, something she never does. She knows he watches. Let him know just how much was enough once upon a time when she first started coming to clean the apartment. Back when he was still leaving for work some mornings. Before they understood each other, when suspicions were mutual and thick as the dust first time she bolted through his doorway, into his rooms, out of breath and wary eyed like someone was chasing her and it might be him.

She'd burst in his door and he'd felt crowded. Retreated, let her stake out the space she required. She didn't bully him but demanded in the language of her brisk, efficient movements that he accustom himself to certain accommodations. They developed an etiquette that spelled out precisely how close, how distant the two of them could be once a week while she cleaned his apartment.

Odd that it took him years to realize how small she was. Shorter than him and no one in his family ever stood higher than five foot plus an inch or so of that thick, straight, black hair. America a land of giants and early on he'd learned to ignore height. You couldn't spend your days like a country lout gawking at the skyscraper heads of your new countrymen. No one had asked him so he'd never needed to describe his cleaning woman. Took no notice of her height. Her name was Clara Jackson and when she arrived he was overwhelmed by the busyness of her presence. How much she seemed to be doing all at once. Noises she'd manufacture with the cleaning paraphernalia, her humming and singing, the gum she popped, heavy thump of her heels even though she changed into tennis sneakers as soon as she crossed the threshold of his apartment, her troubled breathing, asthmatic wheezes and snorts of wrecked sinuses getting worse and worse over the years, her creaking knees, layers of dresses, dusters, slips whispering, the sighs and moans and wincing ejaculations, addresses to invisible presences she smuggled with her into his domain. *Yes, Lord. Save me, Jesus. Thank you, Father.* He backed away from the onslaught, the clamorous weight of it, avoided her systematically. Seldom were they both in the same room at the same time more than a few minutes because clearly none was large enough to contain them and the distance they needed.

She was bent over, replacing a scrubbed rack in the oven when he'd discovered the creases in her skull. She wore a net over her hair like serving girls in Horn and Hardart's. Under the webbing were clumps of hair, defined by furrows exposing her bare scalp. A ribbed yarmulke of hair pressed down on top of her head. Hair he'd never imagined. Like balled yarn in his grandmother's lap. Like a nursery rhyme. *Black sheep. Black sheep, have you any wool?* So different from what grew on his head, the heads of his brothers and sisters and mother and father and cousins and everyone in the doomed village where he was born, so different that he could not truly consider it hair, but some ersatz substitute used the evening of creation when hair ran out. Easier to think of her as bald. Bald and wearing a funny cap fashioned from the fur of some swarthy beast. Springy wires of it jutted from the netting. One dark strand left behind, shocking him when he discovered it marooned in the tub's gleaming, white belly, curled like a question mark at the end of the sentence he was always asking himself. He'd pinched it up in a wad of toilet paper, flushed it away.

Her bag of fleece had grayed and emptied over the years. Less of it now. He'd been tempted countless times to touch it. Poke his finger through the netting into one of the mounds. He'd wondered if she freed it from the veil when she went to bed. If it relaxed and spread against her pillow or if she slept all night like a soldier in a helmet.

When he stood beside her or behind her he could spy on the design of creases, observe how the darkness was cultivated into symmetrical plots and that meant he was taller than Clara Jackson, that he was looking down at her. But those facts did not calm the storm of motion and noise, did not undermine her power any more than the accident of growth, the half inch he'd attained over his next tallest brother, the inch eclipsing the height of his father, would have diminished his father's authority over the family, if there had been a family, the summer after he'd shot up past everyone, at thirteen the tallest, the height he remained today.

Mrs. Clara. Did you know a colored woman once saved my life?

Why is she staring at him as if he's said, Did you know I slept with a colored woman once? He didn't say that. Her silence fusses at him as if he did, as if he'd blurted out something unseemly, ungentlemanly, some insult forcing her to tighten her jaw and push her tongue into her cheek, and taste the bitterness of the hard lump inside her mouth. Why is she ready to cry, or call him a liar, throw something at him or demand an apology or look right through him, past him, the way his mother stared at him on endless October afternoons, gray slants of rain falling so everybody's trapped indoors and she's cleaning, cooking, tending a skeletal fire in the hearth and he's misbehaving, teasing his little sister till he gets his mother's attention and then he shrivels in the weariness of those sad eyes catching him in the act, piercing him, ignoring him, the hurt, iron and distance in them accusing him. Telling him for this moment, and perhaps forever, for this cruel, selfish trespass, you do not exist.

No, Mistah Cohen. That's one thing I definitely did not know.

His fingers fumble with a button, unfastening the cuff of his white shirt. He's rolling up one sleeve. Preparing himself for the work of storytelling. She has laundered the shirt how many times. It's held together by cleanliness and starch. A shirt that ought to be thrown away but she scrubs and sprays and irons it; he knows the routine, the noises. She saves it how many times, patching, mending, snipping errant threads, the frayed edges of cuff and collar hardened again so he is decent, safe within them, the blazing white breast he puffs out like a penguin when it's spring and he descends from the twelfth floor and conquers the park again, shoes shined, the remnants of that glorious head of hair slicked back, freshly shaved cheeks raw as a baby's in the brisk sunshine of those first days welcoming life back and yes he's out there in it again, his splay-foot penguin walk and gentleman's attire, shirt like a pledge, a promise, a declaration framing muted stripes of his dark tie. Numbers stamped inside the collar. Mark of the dry cleaners from a decade ago, before Clara Jackson began coming to clean. Traces still visible inside the neck of some of his shirts she's maintained impossibly long past their prime, a row of faded numerals like those he's pushing up his sleeve to show her on his skin.

The humped hairs on the back of his forearm are pressed down like grass in the woods where a hunted animal has slept. Gray hairs the color of his flesh, except inside his forearm, just above his wrist, the skin is whiter, blue veined. All of it, what's gray, what's pale, what's mottled with dark spots is meat that turns to lard and stinks a sweet sick stink to high heaven if you cook it.

Would you wish to stop now? Sit down a few minutes, please. I will make a coffee for you and my tea. I tell you a story. It is Christmas soon, no?

She is stopped in her tracks. A tiny woman, no doubt about it. Lumpy now. Perhaps she steals and hides things under her dress. Lumpy, not fat.

Her shoulders round and padded. Like the derelict women who live in the streets and wear their whole wardrobes winter spring summer fall. She has put on flesh for protection. To soften blows. To ease around corners. Something cushioned to lean against. Something to muffle the sound of bones breaking when she falls. A pillow for all the heads gone and gone to dust who still find ways at night to come to her and seek a resting place. He could find uses for it. Extra flesh on her bones was not excess, was a gift. The female abundance, her thickness, her bulk reassuring as his hams shrink, his fingers become claws, the chicken neck frets away inside those razor-edged collars she scrubs and irons.

Oh you scarecrow. Death's-head stuck on a stick. Another stick lashed crossways for arms. First time you see yourself dead you giggle. You are a survivor, a lucky one. You grin, stick out your tongue at the image in the shard of smoky glass because the others must be laughing, can't help themselves, the ring of them behind your back, peeking over your scrawny shoulders, watching as you discover in the mirror what they've been seeing since they stormed the gates and kicked open the sealed barracks door and rescued you from the piles of live kindling that were to be your funeral pyre. Your fellow men. Allies. Victors. Survivors. Who stare at you when they think you're not looking, whose eyes are full of shame, as if they've been on duty here, in this pit, this stewpot cooking the meat from your bones. They cannot help themselves. You laugh to help them forget what they see. What you see. When they herded your keepers past you, their grand uniforms shorn of buttons, braid, ribbons, medals, the twin bolts of frozen lightning, golden skulls, eagles' wings, their jackboots gone, feet bare or in peasant clogs, heads bowed and hatless, iron faces unshaven, the butchers still outweighed you a hundred pounds a man. You could not conjure up the spit to mark them. You dropped your eyes in embarrassment, pretended to nod off because your body was too weak to manufacture a string of spittle, and if you could have, you'd have saved it, hoarded and tasted it a hundred times before you swallowed the precious bile.

A parade of shambling, ox-eyed animals. They are marched past you, marched past open trenches that are sewers brimming with naked, rotting flesh, past barbed-wire compounds where the living sift slow and insubstantial as fog among the heaps of dead. No one believes any of it. Ovens and gas chambers. Gallows and whipping posts. Shoes, shoes, shoes, a mountain of shoes in a warehouse. Shit. Teeth. Bones. Sacks of hair. The undead who huddle into themselves like bats and settle down on a patch of filthy earth mourning their own passing. No one believes the enemy. He is not these harmless farmers filing past in pillaged uniforms to do the work of cleaning up this mess someone's made. No one has ever seen a ghost trying to double itself in a mirror so they laugh behind its back, as if, as if the laughter is a game and the dead one could muster up the energy to join in and be made whole again. I giggle. I say, Who in God's name would steal a boy's face and leave this thing?

Nearly a half century of rich meals with seldom one missed but you cannot fill the emptiness, cannot quiet the clamor of those lost souls starving, the child you were, weeping from hunger, those selves, those stomachs you watched swelling, bloating, unburied for days and you dreamed of opening them, of taking a spoon to whatever was growing inside because you were so empty inside and nothing could be worse than that gnawing emptiness. Why should the dead be ashamed to eat the dead? Who are their brothers, sisters, themselves? You hear the boy talking to himself, hallucinating milk, bread, honey. Sick when the spoiled meat is finally carted away.

Mistah Cohen, I'm feeling kinda poorly today. If you don min I'ma work straight through and gwan home early. Got all my Christmas still to do and I'm tired.

She wags her head. Mumbles more he can't decipher. As if he'd offered many times before, as if there is nothing strange or special this morning at 10:47, him standing at the china cupboard prepared to open it and bring down sugar bowl, a silver cream pitcher, cups and saucers for the two of them, ready to fetch instant coffee, a tea bag, boil water and sit down across the table from her. As if it happens each day she comes, as if this once is not the first time, the only time he's invited this woman to sit with him and she can wag her old head, stare at him moon eyed as an owl and refuse what's never been offered before.

The tattoo is faint. From where she's standing, fussing with the vacuum cleaner, she won't see a thing. Her eyes, in spite of thick spectacles, watery and weak as his. They have grown old together, avoiding each other in these musty rooms where soon, soon, no way round it, he will wake up dead one morning and no one will know till she knocks Thursday, and knocks again, then rings, pounds, hollers, but no one answers and she thumps away to rouse the super with his burly ring of keys.

He requires less sleep as he ages. Time weighs more on him as time slips away, less and less time as each second passes but also more of it, the past accumulating in vast drifts like snow in the darkness outside his window. In the wolf hours before dawn this strange city sleeps as uneasily as he does, turning, twisting, groaning. He finds himself listening intently for a sign that the night knows he's listening, but what he hears is his absence. The night busy with itself, denying him. And if he is not out there, if he can hear plainly his absence in the night pulse of the city, where is he now, where was he before his eyes opened, where will he be when the flutter of breath and heart stop?

They killed everyone in the camps. The whole world was dying there. Not only Jews. People forget. All kinds locked in the camps. Yes. Even Germans who were not Jews. Even a black woman. Not gypsy. Not African. American like you, Mrs. Clara.

They said she was a dancer and could play any instrument. Said she could line up shoes from many countries and hop from one pair to the next, performing the dances of the world. They said the Queen of Denmark had honored her with a gold trumpet. But she was there, in hell with the rest of us.

A woman like you. Many years ago. A lifetime ago. Young then as you would have been. And beautiful. As I believe you must have been,

Mrs. Clara. Yes. Before America entered the war. Already camps had begun devouring people. All kinds of people. Yet she was rare. Only woman like her I ever saw until I came here, to this country, this city. And she saved my life.

Poor thing.

I was just a boy. Thirteen years old. The guards were beating me. I did not know why. Why? They didn't need a why. They just beat. And sometimes the beating ended in death because there was no reason to stop, just as there was no reason to begin. A boy. But I'd seen it many times. In the camp long enough to forget why I was alive, why anyone would want to live for long. They were hurting me, beating the life out of me but I was not surprised, expected no explanation. I remember curling up as I had seen a dog once cowering from the blows of a rolled newspaper. In the old country lifetimes ago. A boy in my village staring at a dog curled and rolling on its back in the dust outside the baker's shop and our baker in his white apron and tall white hat striking this mutt again and again. I didn't know what mischief the dog had done. I didn't understand why the fat man with flour on his apron was whipping it unmercifully. I simply saw it and hated the man, felt sorry for the animal, but already the child in me understood it could be no other way so I rolled and curled myself against the blows as I'd remembered that spotted dog in the dusty village street because that's the way it had to be.

Then a woman's voice in a language I did not comprehend reached me. A woman angry, screeching. I heard her before I saw her. She must have been screaming at them to stop. She must have decided it was better to risk dying than watch the guards pound a boy to death. First I heard her voice, then she rushed in, fell on me, wrapped herself around me. The guards shouted at her. One tried to snatch her away. She wouldn't let go of me and they began to beat her too. I heard the thud of clubs on her back, felt her shudder each time a blow was struck.

She fought to her feet, dragging me with her. Shielding me as we stumbled and slammed into a wall.

My head was buried in her smock. In the smell of her, the smell of dust, of blood. I was surprised how tiny she was, barely my size, but strong, very strong. Her fingers dug into my shoulders, squeezing, gripping hard enough to hurt me if I hadn't been past the point of feeling pain. Her hands were strong, her legs alive and warm, churning, churning as she pressed me against herself, into her. Somehow she'd pulled me up and back to the barracks wall, propping herself, supporting me, sheltering me. Then she screamed at them in this language I use now but did not know one word of then, cursing them, I'm sure, in her mother tongue, a stream of spit and sputtering sounds as if she could build a wall of words they could not cross.

The kapos hesitated, astounded by what she'd dared. Was this black one a madwoman, a witch? Then they tore me from her grasp, pushed me down and I crumpled there in the stinking mud of the compound. One more kick, a numbing, blinding smash that took my breath away. Blood flooded my eyes. I lost consciousness. Last I saw of her she was still fighting, slim, beautiful legs kicking at them as they dragged and punched her across the yard.

You say she was colored?

Yes. Yes. A dark angel who fell from the sky and saved me.

Always thought it was just you people over there doing those terrible things to each other.

He closes the china cupboard. Her back is turned. She mutters something at the metal vacuum tubes she's unclamping. He realizes he's finished his story anyway. Doesn't know how to say the rest. She's humming, folding rags, stacking them on the bottom pantry shelf. Lost in the cloud of her own noise. Much more to his story, but she's not waiting around to hear it. This is her last day before the holidays. He'd sealed her bonus in an envelope, placed the envelope where he always does on the kitchen counter. The kitchen cabinet doors have magnetic fasteners for a tight fit. After a volley of doors clicking, she'll be gone. When he's alone preparing his evening meal, he depends on those clicks for company. He pushes so they strike not too loud, not too soft. They punctuate the silence, reassure him like the solid slamming of doors in big sedans he used to ferry from customer to customer. How long since he'd been behind the wheel of a car? Years, and now another year almost gone. In every corner of the city they'd be welcoming their Christ, their New Year with extravagant displays of joy. He thinks of Clara Jackson in the midst of her family. She's little but the others are brown and large, with lips like spoons for serving the sugary babble of their speech. He tries to picture them, eating and drinking, huge people crammed in a tiny, shabby room. Unimaginable, really. The faces of her relatives become his. Everyone's hair is thick and straight and black.

1989

THE 1990S: NEW WORLD DISORDER

After the disintegration of the Soviet Union realigned the globe in 1989 and 1990, then-president George Herbert Walker Bush described a "new world order" in a 1991 speech while the United States was facing off with Iraq in the Persian Gulf War. (Ironically, the speech took place on September 11, 1991, ten years to the day before the 9/11 attacks.) Bush's speech marked the definitive end of the Cold War: what had been an even competition with a powerful adversary—the Soviet Union—had turned into a lopsided game. As the former Soviet Union attempted to understand its new identity as a collection of smaller nations, the United States had to understand its role as the only remaining superpower, a distinction that did not necessarily make Americans comfortable. Yet the national mood was undeniably positive. Dictators fell and democracies took their place. The New World—once a nickname for America—was now global, connected by the Internet. The years of the Clinton presidency (essentially the 1990s) secured that sense of a new world order as venture capitalists and even modest middle-class investors became rich. Clinton chose as his campaign song the Fleetwood Mac hit "Don't Stop (Thinking about Tomorrow)," and the emphasis on a bright future ("It'll be better than before/Yesterday's gone") could not have been clearer.

Just beneath the surface, though, a sense of disorder clutched the 1990s. A series of armed standoffs between government agencies and antigovernment forces—militias, cults, or rogue individuals—marred the ebullient mood of prosperity and forward-thinking innovation. In 1992 a man named Randy Weaver and his family engaged in a firefight at Ruby Ridge, Idaho, resulting in the death of Weaver's wife and son. The following year saw an even more violent confrontation between some of the same government agencies—notably the Federal Bureau of Investigation and the Bureau of Alcohol, Firearms, and Tobacco—and a Christian sect (most would say "cult") known as the Branch Davidians in Waco, Texas. After a prolonged standoff and firefight, the government set fire to the compound, resulting in 76 deaths. These two incidents catalyzed a widespread antigovernment militia movement across the country, culminating in the most destructive act of terrorism on American soil to date in 1995. Timing his attack to correspond with the anniversary of the Waco incident, former soldier Timothy McVeigh drove a rental truck full of explosive materials up to a federal building in Oklahoma City, killing 168 people (including 19 children under the age of six). In 1999, observing the same anniversary, two high school students named Eric Harris and Dylan Klebold went on a shooting rampage at Columbine High School in Littleton, Colorado, killing twelve students and one teacher, the deadliest of a series of school shootings that decade. The benefits of American-style democracy were flourishing around the globe, but at home the rights guaranteed by the Constitution and Bill of Rights were being subjected to gross misinterpretation, giving rise to an unpredictable series of violent events. The world had changed, but the strife Americans had to deal with largely took place on the home front.

Literature of the 1990s, like these instances of strife and terrorism, tends toward the domestic. The dysfunctional family—at the center of many of the works included here—can perhaps be seen as a metaphor for the dysfunctional American citizenry, though none of the events chronicled in the literature included here is violent. One prominent theme of 1990s literature, glimpsed in earlier decades by writers like Maxine Hong Kingston and Amy Tan, is the intense need for the sons or daughters of immigrants to understand and appreciate their parents, who made the difficult decision to leave behind their homelands, but also to help negotiate between their stories and the somewhat intransigent American story. Poems by Li-Young Lee, Kimiko Hahn, and Naomi Shihab Nye and stories by Edwidge Danticat and Gish Jen in this section all explore this theme. Other writers included in this section, such as Lawson Inada, Chang-Rae Lee, Rane Arroyo, and Sandra Cisneros, are equally concerned with the family and the self within this same context.

Questions of gender identity are also related to the expectations of one's family, often a favorite subject of ethnic writers. One consistent motif in women's writing during this period is an examination of the circumstances and meaning of one's sexual awakening—as in the play *How I Learned to Drive* by Paula Vogel—and a curiosity about how one's sexual experiences connect or fail to connect to one's public gender identity. Vogel's play is an excellent example of a common motif of twentieth-century drama—hiding and disclosing family secrets on stage—set against a broader background of cultural history.

One of the more striking aspects of 1990s literature is its willingness to accommodate the predominantly visual aspects of American popular culture. The rise of the graphic narrative in the 1990s reflects the desire of writers and readers to consider the way literature has changed as Americans became more comfortable "reading" images, perhaps due to the rise of the Internet. In the early 1990s, postmodern writers such as Robert Coover began experimenting with hypertext, which was a way to make the reading experience more interactive by enabling readers to click on links within stories to pursue various narrative paths. Although hypertext was short-lived (and Coover, one of its most vocal proponents, publicly gave up on it), it was clear that writers were willing to embrace technological change in the 1990s. Even traditional printed books were packaged with high visual appeal: Douglas Coupland's *zeitgeist*-defining *Generation X* (1991), Kathy Acker's punk-influenced neofeminist novels, and Mark Danielewski's kaleidoscopic art novel *House of Leaves* (2000) demonstrated publishers' willingness to appeal to a new generation of readers attuned to visual elements as they relate to literary culture. The graphic narratives included here by three of the most prominent practitioners of that genre—Art Spiegelman, Chris Ware, and Lynda Barry—challenge readers to break down preconceived notions of the "serious" (print literature) and the merely entertaining ("comics").

One of the most ambitious and most challenging publications of the 1990s was David Foster Wallace's 1996 gargantuan novel *Infinite Jest*. With this massive volume containing hundreds of footnotes, Wallace was, like his graphic narrative counterparts, deliberately attempting to disrupt his readers' preconceived notions of linearity. (A much shorter work by Wallace is included here.) Wallace may have been more in touch with the violent subtext of the decade than anyone knew: the life-robbing destruction of the incidents described may have affected the writer, who took his own life in 2008. Viewed from the twenty-first century, *Infinite Jest* reads like one fragile man's attempt to organize the disorder of the contemporary world.

A final instance of 1990s disorder worth mentioning is the so-called Rodney King riots that took place in South Central Los Angeles in 1992. King was a motorist who was, based on widely circulated and publicized amateur video footage, brutally and excessively beaten by four police officers. When the officers were acquitted, the city erupted in widespread arson, looting, and violence, leaving more than fifty people dead and the nation's second-largest city severely damaged. This explosive reaction demonstrated the long-simmering resentment of a disenfranchised population toward its judicial and penal systems. The U.S. prison population increased dramatically in the final decades of the twentieth century, and the trend has not abated in the twenty-first. Our "In Focus" feature in this section presents some voices from the other side of the walls that divide the incarcerated citizens of this nation from the free. Although most of these writings were published in the 1990s, they span the period from the late 1960s through the early 2000s, reflecting an ongoing trend in our nation's response to crime and in publishing: for better or worse, prison literature is a rapidly growing field.

LI-YOUNG LEE
B. 1957

Li-Young Lee has been praised for his passionate poetry and its deceptively simple style. His poems are unique in their emotional intensity and metaphysical abstraction, particularly at a time when many contemporary American poets are breaking away from the "lyric I" to articulate an unstable and plural "I." Lee's three prize-winning books, *Rose* (1986), *The City in Which I Love You* (1990), and *The Winged Seed: A Remembrance* (1995), share recurrent themes of love, exile, and mortality. Haunted by memories, Lee's poems are exploratory, showing a relentless search for understanding and for the right language to give form to what is invisible and evanescent. He once said, "When I write, I'm trying to make that which is *visible*—this face, this body, this person—*invisible*, and at the same time, make what is *invisible*—that which exists at the level of pure *being*—completely visible." Critics who celebrate the disappearance of the "lyric I" from postmodern poetry as the only possible way of opening the poetic to the historical and political might take issue with Lee's poetics. Yet for minority American poets like Lee to explore the interior and the abstract may not be as escapist or politically inconsequential as some critics might think.

Lee was born in 1957 in Indonesia of Chinese parents. His mother, a granddaughter of Yuan Shi-kai, China's first president (1912–1916), married the son of a gangster and an entrepreneur. His parents' marriage in Communist China was much frowned upon, and they eventually fled to Indonesia, where Lee's father taught medicine and philosophy at Gamliel University in Jakarta and served as President Sukarno's medical adviser. In 1959, when Sukarno launched a violent ethnic purge of the Chinese, Lee's father was incarcerated for his interest in Western culture and ideas; he loved Shakespeare, opera, and Kierkegaard, and he taught the King James version of the Bible. After nineteen months of imprisonment, he escaped; with his family, he traveled to Macao, Japan, and Singapore before settling in Hong Kong, where he became a revered evangelist minister. In 1964, the family emigrated to the United States. Lee's father studied at the Pittsburgh Theological Seminary and later became a Presbyterian minister. Lee went to the University of Pittsburgh, where he took Gerald Stern's poetry writing class and earned his B.A. in 1979; he continued to study creative writing at the University of Arizona and the State University of New York at Brockport. He lives in Chicago with his wife and their two sons.

Lee's father and his family's experience of exile have had a significant impact on Lee's poetry. As a child, he learned to recite Chinese poems from the Tang dynasty (618–907) and was often enchanted by his father's poetic preaching and reading of the Psalms. Many of his poems recall his father, who is portrayed as strict and tender, powerful and vulnerable, godlike and human.

Breaking away from linear, rhetorical structure, Lee's poems unfold and expand from a central image, which holds together the discontinuous narratives and fragmentary scenes. Similar to the functions of imagery in classical Chinese poetry, his composition method gives him greater freedom in making leaps from narrative to lyricism and from the concrete to the abstract. Lee's poems bring together Eastern and Western ideas and traditions. Among the literary influences that Lee has acknowledged are the biblical Song of Songs, Gerald Stern's *Lucky Life*, Kierkegaard's *Fear and Trembling*, Meister Eckhart's sermons, and Rainer Maria Rilke's "Duino Elegies." The spiritual and emotional experience of the poems is accompanied by a down-to-earth sensualness that Lee says "comes from my obsession with the body, man-body, earth-body, woman-body, father-body, mother-body, mind-body (for I experience the mind as another body) and the poem body." This vision may suggest the influence of Whitman, but it is also rooted in Daoism. Lee is familiar with Daoist texts and admires Lao Zi, Lie Zi, and Zhuang Zi, whose sense of wonder and mystery and whose paradoxical and skeptical characteristics are evident in Lee's poems and prose-poem memoir.

Xiaojing Zhou
State University of New York at Buffalo

PRIMARY WORKS

Rose, 1986; *The City in Which I Love You*, 1990; *The Winged Seed*, 1995; *Book of My Nights*, 2001; *Behind My Eyes*, 2008.

I Ask My Mother to Sing

She begins, and my grandmother joins her.
Mother and daughter sing like young girls.
If my father were alive, he would play
his accordion and sway like a boat.

I've never been in Peking, or the Summer Palace,   5
nor stood on the great Stone Boat to watch
the rain begin on Kuen Ming Lake, the picnickers
running away in the grass.

But I love to hear it sung;
how the waterlilies fill with rain until   10
they overturn, spilling water into water,
then rock back, and fill with more.

Both women have begun to cry.
But neither stops her song.

                                                                1986

My Father, in Heaven, Is Reading Out Loud

My father, in heaven, is reading out loud
to himself Psalms or news. Now he ponders what
he's read. No. He is listening for the sound
of children in the yard. Was that laughing
or crying? So much depends upon the   5
answer, for either he will go on reading,
or he'll run to save a child's day from grief.
As it is in heaven, so it was on earth.

Because my father walked the earth with a grave,
determined rhythm, my shoulders ached   10
from his gaze. Because my father's shoulders
ached from the pulling of oars, my life now moves
with a powerful back-and-forth rhythm:
nostalgia, speculation. Because he
made me recite a book a month, I forget   15
everything as soon as I read it. And knowledge
never comes but while I'm mid-stride a flight
of stairs, or lost a moment on some avenue.

A remarkable disappointment to him,
I am like anyone who arrives late   20

in the millennium and is unable
to stay to the end of days. The world's
beginnings are obscure to me, its outcomes
inaccessible. I don't understand
the source of starlight, or starlight's destinations.   25
And already another year slides out
of balance. But I don't disparage scholars;
my father was one and I loved him,
who packed his books once, and all of our belongings,
then sat down to await instruction   30
from his god, yes, but also from a radio.
At the doorway, I watched, and I suddenly
knew he was one like me, who got my learning
under a lintel; he was one of the powerless,
to whom knowledge came while he sat among   35
suitcases, boxes, old newspapers, string.

He did not decide peace or war, home or exile,
escape by land or escape by sea.
He waited merely, as always someone
waits, far, near, here, hereafter, to find out: 40
is it praise or lament hidden in the next moment?

                                                            1990

With Ruins

Choose a quiet
place, a ruins, a house no more
a house,
under whose stone archway I stood
one day to duck the rain.   5

The roofless floor, vertical
studs, eight wood columns
supporting nothing,
two staircases careening to nowhere, all
make it seem   10

a sketch, notes to a house, a three-
dimensional grid negotiating
absences,
an idea
receding into indefinite rain,   15

or else that idea
emerging, skeletal

against the hammered sky, a
human thing, scoured, seen clean
through from here to an iron heaven.   20

A place where things
were said and done,
there you can remember
what you need to
remember. Melancholy is useful. Bring yours.   25

1990

This Room and Everything in It

Lie still now
while I prepare for my future,
certain hard days ahead,
when I'll need what I know so clearly this moment.

I am making use   5
of the one thing I learned
of all the things my father tried to teach me:
the art of memory.

I am letting this room
and everything in it   10
stand for my ideas about love
and its difficulties.

I'll let your love-cries,
those spacious notes
of a moment ago,   15
stand for distance.

Your scent,
that scent
of spice and a wound,
I'll let stand for mystery.   20

Your sunken belly
is the daily cup
of milk I drank
as a boy before morning prayer.

The sun on the face   25
of the wall

is God, the face
I can't see, my soul,

and so on, each thing
standing for a separate idea,   30
and those ideas forming the constellation
of my greater idea.
And one day, when I need
to tell myself something intelligent
about love,   35

I'll close my eyes
and recall this room and everything in it:
My body is estrangement.
This desire, perfection.
Your closed eyes my extinction.   40
Now I've forgotten my
idea. The book
on the windowsill, riffled by wind . . .
the even-numbered pages are
the past, the odd-   45
numbered pages, the future.
The sun is
God, your body is milk . . .

useless, useless . . .
your cries are song, my body's not me . . .   50
no good . . . my idea
has evaporated . . . your hair is time, your thighs are song . . .
it had something to do
with death . . . it had something
to do with love.   55

                                                      1990

ART SPIEGELMAN
B. 1948

Art Spiegelman, arguably the world's most influential living progenitor of the idea that comic books can be literature, is a material and cultural blacksmith, as he puts it, and he is important to any study of today's narrative forms. As a conceptual thinker and as an author, Spiegelman enlivens any inquiry into comics, and the publication of his book *Maus: A Survivor's Tale* in 1986 marked a transformative moment in the field of contemporary literature.

Spiegelman was born in Sweden in 1948 to Anja and Vladek Spiegelman, Polish Jews who had survived Auschwitz. His older brother, Richieu, was a child when he died during the war. Spiegelman grew up in Rego Park, Queens, where his love for comics began at an early age. After dropping out of Harpur College (now the State University of New York at Binghamton), Spiegelman moved to San Francisco, where in the early 1970s he produced work in the underground comix community that led directly to the serious, textured, rigorous work that today is known as the graphic novel.

Spiegelman's influential underground pieces (collected in his large-format book *Breakdowns* in 1977) include experimental works like "Ace Hole: Midget Detective" and "Don't Get Around Much Anymore" but also two autobiographical strips, "Prisoner on the Hell Planet: A Case Study" and "Maus," the prototype for the book-length version. "Don't Get Around Much Anymore," a dense, compact, one-page strip from 1973 that looks both cubist and art deco–inspired, is a vigorous exploration of how comics present time and space. Here Spiegelman unmoors the two from each other. Although nothing much happens in the strip, its modernist exploration of the medium's formal capacities pointed the way to the rich formal capacities of comics and has had an enduring influence.

Spiegelman has said that he had to subsume his more formal interests to produce *Maus*, but *Maus* (which was published in two volumes; the second appeared in 1991) shows the same kinds of aesthetic concerns as his underground work, expanded and enriched by a postmodern emphasis on narrative. The seemingly disparate strands of Spiegelman's underground-era comic strips finally coalesce in *Maus*, his novel-length, career-defining work that is engaged with form and the power of narrative.

Maus changed the way that the public at large—as well as academic audiences—think about comics. Thirteen years in the making, *Maus* is a black-and-white text that is driven by Vladek Spiegelman's Holocaust testimony. It represents Jews as mice and Nazis as cats, inhabiting and reversing stereotypes created by Nazi propaganda. It is also self-reflexive, meditating on and rupturing its own established frameworks, including its animal metaphor and its past-and-present narrative structure. It has won numerous awards, including a special Pulitzer Prize in 1992 that celebrated its achievement and marked its challenge to traditional classification (a comic book about the Holocaust was at that time an utterly foreign phenomenon). Translated into more than twenty languages, *Maus* is probably the most famous graphic narrative ever produced in the United States.

Spiegelman was a contributor to *The New Yorker* for more than ten years. His book on 9/11, *In the Shadow of No Towers*, came out in 2004. A reprint of his now classic *Breakdowns*, with a new comics introduction titled "Portrait of the Artist as a Young %@?*!," was published by Pantheon in 2008. He is preparing a book titled *Meta Maus*, about the making of *Maus*.

Hillary Chute
Harvard University

PRIMARY WORKS

Maus, 1986; *Maus II*, 1991; *Jack Cole and Plastic Man: Forms Stretched to Their Limits*, 2001; *In the Shadow of No Tower*, 2002; *Breakdowns: Portraits of the Artist as a Young %&@*!*, 2008.

Don't Get Around Much Anymore

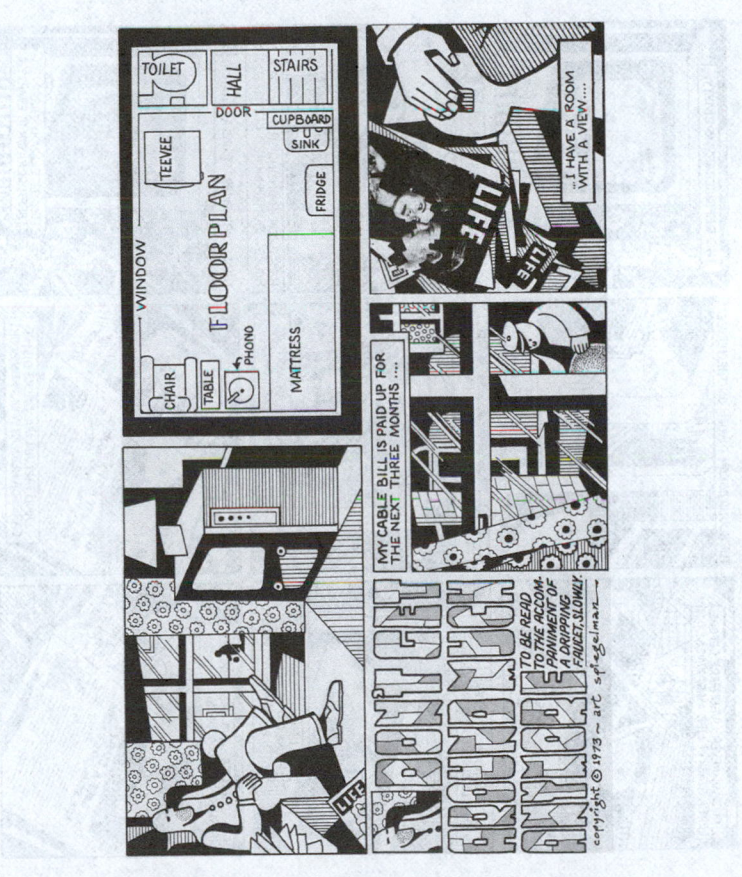

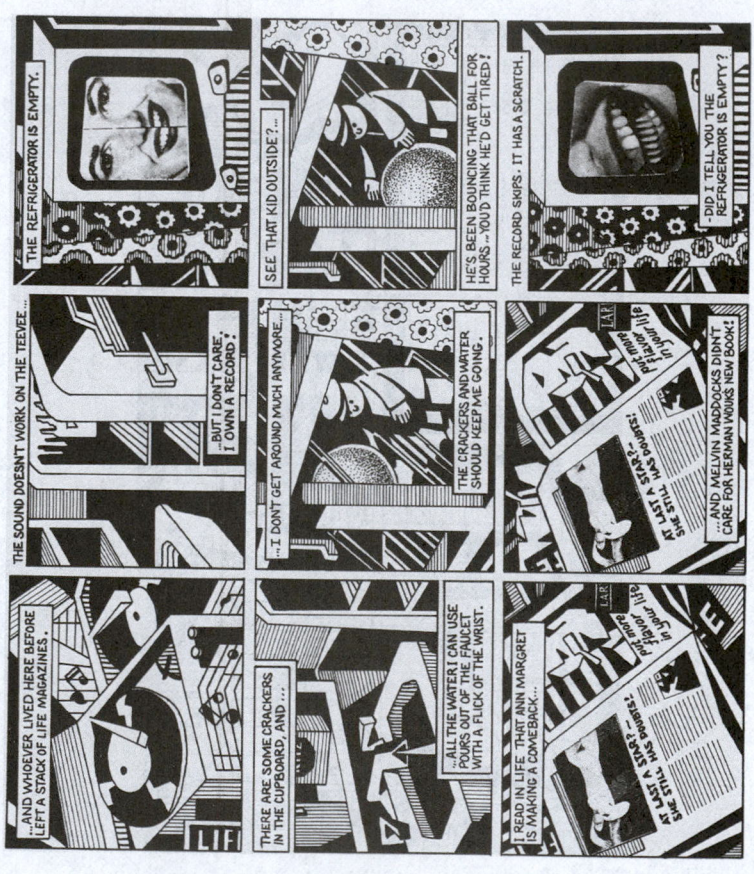

from **Maus II**

whew. they're gone. Sometimes I just don't feel like a functioning adult.

I can't believe I'm gonna be a father in a couple of months.* My father's ghost still hangs over me.

*NADJA MOULY SPIEGELMAN. BORN 5/13/87

It's 9:30 p.m. already. I've gotta head uptown for my appointment with Pavel.

Pavel is my shrink. He sees patients at night.

He's a Czech Jew, a survivor of Terezin and Auschwitz. I see him once a week.

His place is overrun with stray dogs and cats.

Hi Art. Come on in.

Can I mention this, or does it completely louse up my metaphor?

So, how are you feeling?

Completely messed up. I mean, things couldn't be going better with my "career," or at home, but mostly I feel like crying.

I can't work. My time is being sucked up by interviews and business propositions I can't deal with.

But even when I'm left alone I'm totally BLOCKED. Instead of working on my book I just lie on my couch for hours and stare at a small grease spot on the upholstery.

FRAMED PHOTO OF PET CAT. REALLY!

And so...

CLIK "...THEN, WHEN I CAME OUT FROM THE HOSPITAL, RIGHT AWAY SHE STARTED AGAIN THAT I CHANGE MY WILL!

PLEASE POP. THE TAPE'S ON. LET'S CONTINUE...

I WAS STILL SO SICK AND TIRED. AND TO HAVE PEACE ONLY, I AGREED. TO MAKE IT LEGAL SHE BROUGHT RIGHT TO MY BED A NOTARY.

LET'S GET BACK TO AUSCHWITZ...

FIFTEEN DOLLARS HE CHARGED TO COME! IF SHE WAITED ONLY A WEEK UNTIL I WAS STRONGER, I'D GO TO THE BANK AND TAKE A NOTARY FOR ONLY A QUARTER!

ENOUGH! TELL ME ABOUT AUSCHWITZ!

Sigh YOU WERE TELLING ME HOW YOUR KAPO TRIED TO GET YOU WORK AS A TINSMITH...

YAH. EVERY DAY I WORKED THERE RIGHT OUTSIDE FROM THE CAMP...

THE CHIEF OF THE TINMEN IT WAS A RUSSIAN JEW NAMED YIDL.

BAH! YOU'RE NO TINSMITH. YOU CAN'T EVEN CUT IT RIGHT.

BUT THIS IS HOW I'VE ALWAYS DONE IT!...

I'VE ONLY BEEN A TINSMITH FOR A FEW YEARS. IF YOU SHOW ME HOW YOU WANT IT CUT I CAN LEARN QUICKLY.

HAH! YOU NEVER DID AN HONEST DAY'S WORK IN YOUR WHOLE LIFE, SPIEGELMAN! I KNOW ALL ABOUT YOU...

I DON'T KNOW WHERE FROM HE HEARD STORIES ABOUT ME.

YOU OWNED BIG FACTORIES AND EXPLOITED YOUR WORKERS, YOU DIRTY CAPITALIST!

HE WAS A COMMUNIST, THIS YIDL.

PFUI! THEY SEND DREK LIKE YOU HERE WHILE THEY SEND REAL TINMEN UP THE CHIMNEY. WATCH OUT. I'VE GOT MY EYE ON YOU!

I WAS AFRAID. HE COULD REALLY DO ME SOMETHING.

WITH THE OTHER BOYS THERE, I GOT ALONG FINE.

DON'T WORRY...YOU JUST HAVE TO KNOW HOW TO HANDLE YIDL...

BRING HIM A FEW EGGS, SOME BUTTER OR CHEESE... YOU'LL SEE. HE'LL SING A DIFFERENT TUNE.

HA! AND WHERE DO I GET ALL THIS FOOD?

JUST KEEP YOUR EYES OPEN. YOU CAN ORGANIZE THINGS WITH THE POLES HERE.

POLES FROM NEARBY THEY HIRED TO WORK ALSO HERE—NOT PRISONERS, BUT SPECIALIST BUILDING WORKERS...

(PSST—I CAN GET YOU A FINE GOLD WATCH FOR A POUND OF SAUSAGE AND SIX EGGS.)

(AGREED.)

THEY HAD NOTHING, ONLY FOOD FROM THEIR FARMS. THEY WERE HAPPY TO MAKE EXCHANGES.

THE HEAD GUY FROM THE AUSCHWITZ LAUNDRY WAS A FINE FELLOW WHAT KNEW WELL MY FAMILY BEFORE THE WAR...

FROM HIM I GOT CIVILIAN **CLOTHINGS** TO SMUGGLE OUT BELOW MY UNIFORM. I WAS SO THIN THE GUARDS DIDN'T SEE IF I WORE EXTRA.

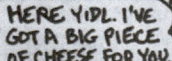

HERE YIDL. I'VE GOT A BIG PIECE OF CHEESE FOR YOU.

A GIFT? VERY NICE, SPIEGELMAN.

AND WHAT ELSE DO YOU HAVE THERE? A LOAF OF BREAD? YOU'RE A RICH MAN!

WAIT! I NEED THAT TO PAY OFF THE GUY WHO HELPED ME ORGANIZE THE CHEESE!

HMPH.

HE WAS SO GREEDY, YIDL, HE WANTED I RISK ONLY FOR HIM EVERYTHING. I TOO HAD TO EAT.

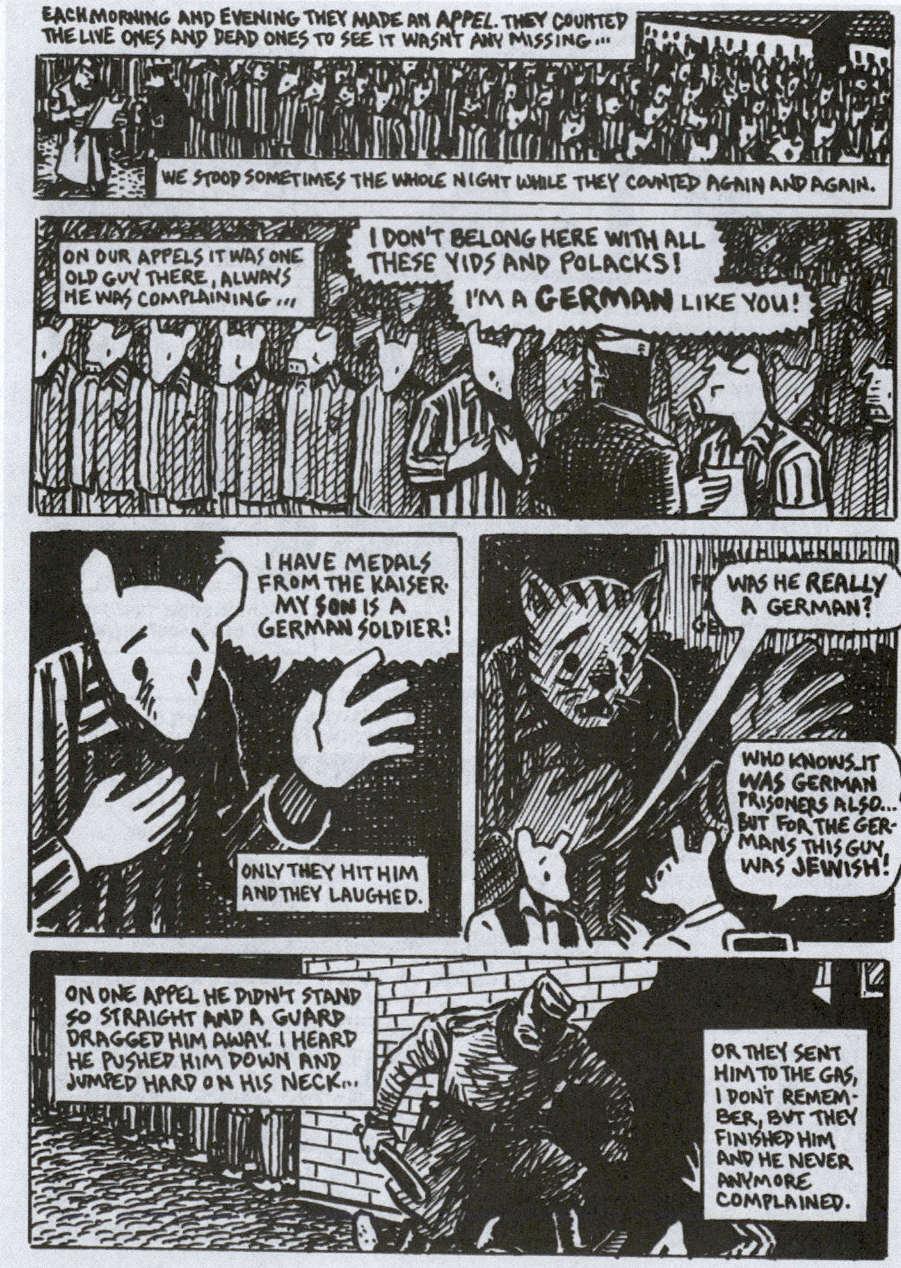

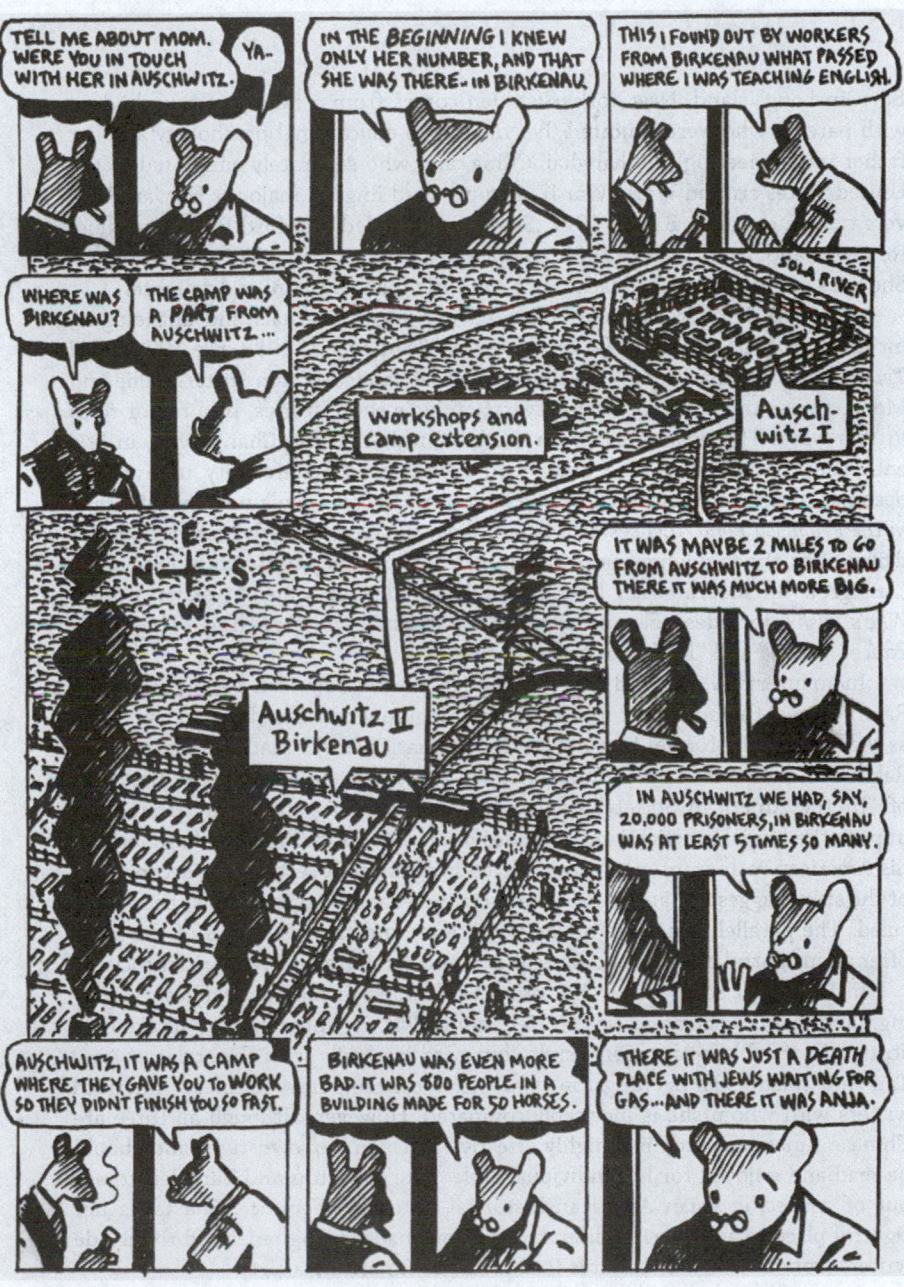

GISH JEN
B. 1955

Born in Long Island, New York, Gish Jen comes from a family of five children with parents who were educated (her mother in educational psychology and her father in engineering) in Shanghai, China, and who separately emigrated to the United States around World War II. As a pre-med English major at Harvard University, Jen earned a B.A. in 1977. She then attended Stanford Business School for a year and, from 1981 to 1983, completed an M.F.A. at the University of Iowa. She lives in Cambridge, Massachusetts, with her husband, son, and daughter.

Although Jen's works have appeared in various journals and anthologies, including *The Atlantic* and *The Best American Short Stories 1988*, the 1991 novel *Typical American* marks her arrival as a much-acclaimed fiction writer. Callie and Mona, two sisters who appear in several of Jen's short stories, play minor roles in this work. The novel focuses on the girls' father, Ralph Chang, who, in line with the 1950s atmosphere of upward mobility and conformity in America, becomes absorbed with pursuing the American Dream. Jen's next novel, *Mona in the Promised Land*, focuses on Mona Chang, the daughter who converts to Judaism after the family moves to the upscale Jewish neighborhood of "Scarshill" (Jen grew up in Scarsdale, New York). Her collection of eight short stories, *Who's Irish?*, includes new and previously published works such as "The Water Faucet Vision" and "In the American Society."

In an interview, Jen said that the scene in "In the American Society" in which Ralph throws the polo shirt into the swimming pool convinced her to use Ralph as the protagonist for her first novel. This dramatic act, she stated, indicated that Ralph was the kind of make-things-happen character she needed. The first part of "In the American Society" depicts a Chinese immigrant's vain attempt to impose the feudal practices and attitudes of an old-world Chinese village lord on his American restaurant employees. Placed in a different setting, the second part of the story suggests that this same background enables Ralph to resist being ridiculed. The parallel structures of the two scenes and the resolution of the story offer an insightful analysis of cross-cultural and racial issues in American society.

In this short story and in her other works, Jen displays a seamless, engaging, and comic narrative voice. Her ironic wit is apparent in disarmingly straightforward language. Jen's style contrasts markedly with the styles of Amy Tan and Maxine Hong Kingston, two other contemporary Chinese American writers with whom she is inevitably compared. However, although all three are Chinese American, each is a highly effective artist in her own right and should be read and enjoyed for her individual style. Like Kingston and Tan, Jen comes out of a specific Asian American historical-cultural experience. She takes her rightful place in an American literary tradition that is being redefined to include writers from the various cultures that compose American society.

Bonnie TuSmith
Northeastern University

PRIMARY WORKS

Typical American, 1991; *Mona in the Promised Land*, 1996; *Who's Irish?*, 1999; *The Love Wife*, 2004; *World and Town*, 2011.

In the American Society

I. His Own Society

When my father took over the pancake house, it was to send my little sister Mona and me to college. We were only in junior high at the time, but my father believed in getting a jump on things. "Those Americans always saying it," he told us. "Smart guys thinking in advance." My mother elaborated, explaining that businesses took bringing up, like children. They could take years to get going, she said, years.

In this case, though, we got rich right away. At two months we were breaking even, and at four, those same hotcakes that could barely withstand the weight of butter and syrup were supporting our family with ease. My mother bought a station wagon with air conditioning, my father an oversized, red vinyl recliner for the back room; and as time went on and the business continued to thrive, my father started to talk about his grandfather and the village he had reigned over in China—things my father had never talked about when he worked for other people. He told us about the bags of rice his family would give out to the poor at New Year's, and about the people who came to beg, on their hands and knees, for his grandfather to intercede for the more wayward of their relatives. "Like that Godfather in the movie," he would tell us as, his feet up, he distributed paychecks. Sometimes an employee would get two green envelopes instead of one, which meant that Jimmy needed a tooth pulled, say, or that Tiffany's husband was in the clinker again.

"It's nothing, nothing," he would insist, sinking back into his chair. "Who else is going to take care of you people?"

My mother would mostly just sigh about it. "Your father thinks this is China," she would say, and then she would go back to her mending. Once in a while, though, when my father had given away a particularly large sum, she would exclaim, outraged, "But this here is the U—S—of—A!"—this apparently having been what she used to tell immigrant stock boys when they came in late.

She didn't work at the supermarket anymore; but she had made it to the rank of manager before she left, and this had given her not only new words and phrases, but new ideas about herself, and about America, and about what was what in general. She had opinions, now, on how downtown should be zoned; she could pump her own gas and check her own oil; and for all she used to chide Mona and me for being "copycats," she herself was now interested in espadrilles, and wallpaper, and most recently, the town country club.

"So join already," said Mona, flicking a fly off her knee.

My mother enumerated the problems as she sliced up a quarter round of watermelon: There was the cost. There was the waiting list. There was the fact that no one in our family played either tennis or golf.

"So what?" said Mona.

"It would be waste," said my mother.

"Me and Callie can swim in the pool."

"Plus you need that recommendation letter from a member."

"Come *on*," said Mona. "Annie's mom'd write you a letter in *sec.*"

My mother's knife glinted in the early summer sun. I spread some more newspaper on the picnic table.

"*Plus* you have to eat there twice a month. You know what that means." My mother cut another, enormous slice of fruit.

"No, I *don't* know what that means," said Mona.

"It means Dad would have to wear a jacket, dummy," I said.

"Oh! Oh! Oh!" said Mona, clasping her hand to her breast. "Oh! Oh! Oh! Oh! Oh!"

We all laughed: my father had no use for nice clothes, and would wear only ten-year-old shirts, with grease-spotted pants, to show how little he cared what anyone thought.

"Your father doesn't believe in joining the American society," said my mother. "He wants to have his own society."

"So go to dinner without him." Mona shot her seeds out in long arcs over the lawn. "Who cares what he thinks?"

But of course we all did care, and knew my mother could not simply up and do as she pleased. For in my father's mind, a family owed its head a degree of loyalty that left no room for dissent. To embrace what he embraced was to love; and to embrace something else was to betray him.

He demanded a similar sort of loyalty of his workers, whom he treated more like servants than employees. Not in the beginning, of course. In the beginning all he wanted was for them to keep on doing what they used to do, and to that end he concentrated mostly on leaving them alone. As the months passed, though, he expected more and more of them, with the result that for all his largesse, he began to have trouble keeping help. The cooks and busboys complained that he asked them to fix radiators and trim hedges, not only at the restaurant, but at our house; the waitresses that he sent them on errands and made them chauffeur him around. Our head wait-ress, Gertrude, claimed that he once even asked her to scratch his back.

"It's not just the blacks don't believe in slavery," she said when she quit.

My father never quite registered her complaint, though, nor those of the others who left. Even after Eleanor quit, then Tiffany, then Gerald, and Jimmy, and even his best cook, Eureka Andy, for whom he had bought new glasses, he remained mostly convinced that the fault lay with them.

"All they understand is that assembly line," he lamented. "Robots, they are. They want to be robots."

There *were* occasions when the clear running truth seemed to eddy, when he would pinch the vinyl of his chair up into little peaks and wonder if he was doing things right. But with time he would always smooth the peaks back down; and when business started to slide in the spring, he kept on like a horse in his ways.

By the summer our dishboy was overwhelmed with scraping. It was no longer just the hashbrowns that people were leaving for trash, and the service was as bad as the food. The waitresses served up French pancakes instead of German, apple juice instead of orange, spilt things on laps, on coats. On the Fourth of July some greenhorn sent an entire side of fries slaloming down a lady's *massif centrale*. Meanwhile in the back room, my father labored through articles on the economy.

"What is housing starts?" he puzzled. "What is GNP?"

Mona and I did what we could, filling in as busgirls and bookkeepers and, one afternoon, stuffing the comments box that hung by the cashier's desk. That was Mona's idea. We rustled up a variety of pens and pencils, checked boxes for an hour, smeared the cards up with coffee and grease, and waited. It took a few days for my father to notice that the box was full, and he didn't say anything about it for a few days more. Finally, though, he started to complain of fatigue; and then he began to complain that the staff was not what it could be. We encouraged him in this—pointing out, for instance, how many dishes got chipped—but in the end all that happened was that, for the first time since we took over the restaurant, my father got it into his head to fire someone. Skip, a skinny busboy who was saving up for a sportscar, said nothing as my father mumbled on about the price of dishes. My father's hands shook as he wrote out the severance check; and he spent the rest of the day napping in his chair once it was over.

As it was going on midsummer, Skip wasn't easy to replace. We hung a sign in the window and advertised in the paper, but no one called the first week, and the person who called the second didn't show up for his interview. The third week, my father phoned Skip to see if he would come back, but a friend of his had already sold him a Corvette for cheap.

Finally a Chinese guy named Booker turned up. He couldn't have been more than thirty, and was wearing a lighthearted seersucker suit, but he looked as though life had him pinned: his eyes were bloodshot and his chest sunken, and the muscles of his neck seemed to strain with the effort of holding his head up. In a single dry breath he told us that he had never bussed tables but was willing to learn, and that he was on the lam from the deportation authorities.

"I do not want to lie to you," he kept saying. He had come to the United States on a student visa, had run out of money, and was now in a bind. He was loath to go back to Taiwan, as it happened—he looked up at this point, to be sure my father wasn't pro-KMT—but all he had was a phony social security card and a willingness to absorb all blame, should anything untoward come to pass.

"I do not think, anyway, that it is against law to hire me, only to be me," he said, smiling faintly.

Anyone else would have examined him on this, but my father conceived of laws as speed bumps rather than curbs. He wiped the counter with his sleeve, and told Booker to report the next morning.

"I will be good worker," said Booker.

"Good," said my father.

"Anything you want me to do, I will do."

My father nodded.

Booker seemed to sink into himself for a moment. "Thank you," he said finally. "I am appreciate your help. I am very, very appreciate for everything." He reached out to shake my father's hand.

My father looked at him. "Did you eat today?" he asked in Mandarin.

Booker pulled at the hem of his jacket.

"Sit down," said my father. "Please, have a seat."

My father didn't tell my mother about Booker, and my mother didn't tell my father about the country club. She would never have applied, except that Mona, while over at Annie's, had let it drop that our mother wanted to join. Mrs. Lardner came by the very next day.

"Why, I'd be honored and delighted to write you people a letter," she said. Her skirt billowed around her.

"Thank you so much," said my mother. "But it's too much trouble for you, and also my husband is . . ."

"Oh, it's no trouble at all, no trouble at all. I tell you." She leaned forward so that her chest freckles showed. "I know just how it is. It's a secret of course, but you know, my natural father was Jewish. Can you see it? Just look at my skin."

"My husband," said my mother.

"I'd be honored and delighted," said Mrs. Lardner with a little wave of her hands. "Just honored and delighted."

Mona was triumphant. "See, Mom," she said, waltzing around the kitchen when Mrs. Lardner left. "What did I tell you? 'I'm just honored and delighted, just honored and delighted.'" She waved her hands in the air.

"You know, the Chinese have a saying," said my mother. "To do nothing is better than to overdo. You mean well, but you tell me now what will happen."

"I'll talk Dad into it," said Mona, still waltzing. "Or I bet Callie can. He'll do anything Callie says."

"I can try, anyway," I said.

"Did you hear what I said?" said my mother. Mona bumped into the broom closet door. "You're not going to talk anything; you've already made enough trouble." She started on the dishes with a clatter.

Mona poked diffidently at a mop.

I sponged off the counter. "Anyway," I ventured. "I bet our name'll never even come up."

"That's if we're lucky," said my mother.

"There's all these people waiting," I said.

"Good," she said. She started on a pot.

I looked over at Mona, who was still cowering in the broom closet. "In fact, there's some black family's been waiting so long, they're going to sue," I said.

My mother turned off the water. "Where'd you hear that?"

"Patty told me."

She turned the water back on, started to wash a dish, then put it back down and shut the faucet.

"I'm sorry," said Mona.

"Forget it," said my mother. "Just forget it."

Booker turned out to be a model worker, whose boundless gratitude translated into a willingness to do anything. As he also learned quickly, he soon knew not only how to bus, but how to cook, and how to wait table, and how to keep the books. He fixed the walk-in door so that it stayed shut, reupholstered the torn seats in the dining room, and devised a system for tracking inventory. The only stone in the rice was that he tended to be sickly; but, reliable even in illness, he would always send a friend to take his place. In this way we got to know Ronald, Lynn, Dirk, and Cedric, all of whom, like Booker, had problems with their legal status and were anxious to please. They weren't all as capable as Booker, though, with the exception of Cedric, whom my father often hired even when Booker was well. A round wag of a man who called Mona and me *shou hou*—skinny monkeys—he was a professed non-smoker who was nevertheless always begging drags off of other people's cigarettes. This last habit drove our head cook, Fernando, crazy, especially since, when refused a hit, Cedric would occasionally snitch one. Winking impishly at Mona and me, he would steal up to an ashtray, take a quick puff, and then break out laughing so that the smoke came rolling out of his mouth in a great incriminatory cloud. Fernando accused him of stealing fresh cigarettes too, even whole packs.

"Why else do you think he's weaseling around in the back of the store all the time," he said. His face was blotchy with anger. "The man is a frigging thief."

Other members of the staff supported him in this contention and joined in on an "Operation Identification," which involved numbering and initialing their cigarettes—even though what they seemed to fear for wasn't so much their cigarettes as their jobs. Then one of the cooks quit; and rather than promote someone, my father hired Cedric for the position. Rumors flew that he was taking only half the normal salary, that Alex had been pressured to resign, and that my father was looking for a position with which to placate Booker, who had been bypassed because of his health.

The result was that Fernando categorically refused to work with Cedric.

"The only way I'll cook with that piece of slime," he said, shaking his huge tattooed fist, "is if it's his ass frying on the grill."

My father cajoled and cajoled, to no avail, and in the end was simply forced to put them on different schedules.

The next week Fernando got caught stealing a carton of minute steaks. My father would not tell even Mona and me how he knew to be standing by the back door when Fernando was on his way out, but everyone suspected Booker. Everyone but Fernando, that is, who was sure Cedric had been the tip-off. My father held a staff meeting in which he tried to reassure everyone that Alex had left on his own, and that he had no intention of firing anyone. But though he was careful not to mention Fernando, everyone was so amazed that he was being allowed to stay that Fernando was incensed nonetheless.

"Don't you all be putting your bug eyes on me," he said. "*He's* the frigging crook." He grabbed Cedric by the collar.

Cedric raised an eyebrow. "Cook, you mean," he said.

At this Fernando punched Cedric in the mouth; and the words he had just uttered notwithstanding, my father fired him on the spot.

With everything that was happening, Mona and I were ready to be getting out of the restaurant. It was almost time: the days were still stuffy with summer, but our window shade had started flapping in the evening as if gearing up to go out. That year the breezes were full of salt, as they sometimes were when they came in from the East, and they blew anchors and docks through my mind like so many tumbleweeds, filling my dreams with wherries and lobsters and grainy-faced men who squinted, day in and day out, at the sky.

It was time for a change, you could feel it; and yet the pancake house was the same as ever. The day before school started my father came home with bad news.

"Fernando called police," he said, wiping his hand on his pant leg.

My mother naturally wanted to know what police; and so with much coughing and hawing, the long story began, the latest installment of which had the police calling immigration, and immigration sending an investigator. My mother sat stiff as whalebone as my father described how the man summarily refused lunch on the house and how my father had admitted, under pressure, that he knew there were "things" about his workers.

"So now what happens?"

My father didn't know. "Booker and Cedric went with him to the jail," he said. "But me, here I am." He laughed uncomfortably.

The next day my father posted bail for "his boys" and waited apprehensively for something to happen. The day after that he waited again, and the day after that he called our neighbor's law student son, who suggested my father call the immigration department under an alias. My father took his advice; and it was thus that he discovered that Booker was right: it was illegal for aliens to work, but it wasn't to hire them.

In the happy interval that ensued, my father apologized to my mother, who in turn confessed about the country club, for which my father had no choice but to forgive her. Then he turned his attention back to "his boys."

My mother didn't see that there was anything to do.

"I like to talking to the judge," said my father.

"This is not China," said my mother.

"I'm only talking to him. I'm not give him money unless he wants it."

"You're going to land up in jail."

"So what else I should do?" My father threw up his hands. "Those are my boys."

"Your boys!" exploded my mother. "What about your family? What about your wife?"

My father took a long sip of tea. "You know," he said finally. "In the war my father sent our cook to the soldiers to use. He always said it—the province comes before the town, the town comes before the family."

"A restaurant is not a town," said my mother.

My father sipped at his tea again. "You know, when I first come to the United States, I also had to hide-and-seek with those deportation guys. If people did not helping me, I'm not here today."

My mother scrutinized her hem.

After a minute I volunteered that before seeing a judge, he might try a lawyer.

He turned. "Since when did you become so afraid like your mother?"

I started to say that it wasn't a matter of fear, but he cut me off.

"What I need today," he said, "is a son."

My father and I spent the better part of the next day standing in lines at the immigration office. He did not get to speak to a judge, but with much persistence he managed to speak to a judge's clerk, who tried to persuade him that it was not her place to extend him advice. My father, though, shamelessly plied her with compliments and offers of free pancakes until she finally conceded that she personally doubted anything would happen to either Cedric or Booker.

"Especially if they're 'needed workers,'" she said, rubbing at the red marks her glasses left on her nose. She yawned. "Have you thought about sponsoring them to become permanent residents?"

Could he do that? My father was overjoyed. And what if he saw to it right away? Would she perhaps put in a good word with the judge?

She yawned again, her nostrils flaring. "Don't worry," she said. "They'll get a fair hearing."

My father returned jubilant. Booker and Cedric hailed him as their savior, their Buddha incarnate. He was like a father to them, they said; and laughing and clapping, they made him tell the story over and over, sorting over the details like jewels. And how old was the assistant judge? And what did she say?

That evening my father tipped the paperboy a dollar and bought a pot of mums for my mother, who suffered them to be placed on the dining room table. The next night he took us all out to dinner. Then on Saturday, Mona found a letter on my father's chair at the restaurant.

Dear Mr. Chang,

You are the grat boss. But, we do not like to trial, so will runing away now. Plese to excus us. People saying the law in America is fears like dragon. Here

is only $140. We hope some day we can pay back the rest bale. You will get-
ting intrest, as you diserving, so grat a boss you are. Thank you for every
thing. In next life you will be burn in rich family, with no more pancaks.

Yours truley,
Booker + Cedric

In the weeks that followed my father went to the pancake house for crises, but otherwise hung around our house, fiddling idly with the sump
pump and boiler in an effort, he said, to get ready for winter. It was as
though he had gone into retirement, except that instead of moving south,
he had moved to the basement. He even took to showering my mother with
little attentions, and to calling her "old girl," and when we finally heard that
the club had entertained all the applications it could for the year, he was so
sympathetic that he seemed more disappointed than my mother.

II. In the American Society

Mrs. Lardner tempered the bad news with an invitation to a bon voyage
"bash" she was throwing for a friend of hers who was going to Greece for
six months.

"Do come," she urged. "You'll meet everyone, and then, you know, if
things open up in the spring . . ." She waved her hands.

My mother wondered if it would be appropriate to show up at a party
for someone they didn't know, but "the honest truth" was that this was an
annual affair. "If it's not Greece, it's Antibes," sighed Mrs. Lardner. "We
really just do it because his wife left him and his daughter doesn't speak to
him, and poor Jeremy just feels so *unloved*."

She also invited Mona and me to the goings on, as *"demi*-guests" to keep
Annie out of the champagne. I wasn't too keen on the idea, but before I
could say anything, she had already thanked us for so generously agreeing
to honor her with our presence.

"A pair of little princesses, you are!" she told us. "A pair of princesses!"

The party was that Sunday. On Saturday, my mother took my father out
shopping for a suit. As it was the end of September, she insisted that he buy
a worsted rather than a seersucker, even though it was only ten, rather than
fifty percent off. My father protested that it was as hot out as ever, which
was true—a thick Indian summer had cozied murderously up to us—but to
no avail. Summer clothes, said my mother, were not properly worn after
Labor Day.

The suit was unfortunately as extravagant in length as it was in price,
which posed an additional quandary, since the tailor wouldn't be in until
Monday. The salesgirl, though, found a way of tacking it up temporarily.

"Maybe this suit not fit me," fretted my father.

"Just don't take your jacket off," said the salesgirl.

He gave her a tip before they left, but when he got home refused to
remove the price tag.

"I like to asking the tailor about the size," he insisted.

"You mean you're going to *wear* it and then *return* it?" Mona rolled her eyes.

"I didn't say I'm return it," said my father stiffly. "I like to asking the tailor, that's all."

The party started off swimmingly, except that most people were wearing bermudas or wrap skirts. Still, my parents carried on, sharing with great feeling the complaints about the heat. Of course my father tried to eat a cracker full of shallots and burnt himself in an attempt to help Mr. Lardner turn the coals of the barbeque; but on the whole he seemed to be doing all right. Not nearly so well as my mother, though, who had accepted an entire cupful of Mrs. Lardner's magic punch, and seemed indeed to be under some spell. As Mona and Annie skirmished over whether some boy in their class inhaled when he smoked, I watched my mother take off her shoes, laughing and laughing as a man with a beard regaled her with navy stories by the pool. Apparently he had been stationed in the Orient and remembered a few words of Chinese, which made my mother laugh still more. My father excused himself to go to the men's room then drifted back and weighed anchor at the hors d'oeuvres table, while my mother sailed on to a group of women, who tinkled at length over the clarity of her complexion. I dug out a book I had brought.

Just when I'd cracked the spine, though, Mrs. Lardner came by to bewail her shortage of servers. Her caterers were criminals, I agreed; and the next thing I knew I was handing out bits of marine life, making the rounds as amiably as I could.

"Here you go, Dad," I said when I got to the hors d'oeuvres table.

"Everything is fine," he said.

I hesitated to leave him alone; but then the man with the beard zeroed in on him, and though he talked of nothing but my mother, I thought it would be okay to get back to work. Just that moment, though, Jeremy Brothers lurched our way, an empty, albeit corked, wine bottle in hand. He was a slim, well-proportioned man, with a Roman nose and small eyes and a nice manly jaw that he allowed to hang agape.

"Hello," he said drunkenly. "Pleased to meet you."

"Pleased to meeting you," said my father.

"Right," said Jeremy. "Right. Listen. I have this bottle here, this most re-calcitrant bottle. You see that it refuses to do my bidding. I bid it open sesame, please, and it does nothing." He pulled the cork out with his teeth, then turned the bottle upside down.

My father nodded.

"Would you have a word with it please?" said Jeremy. The man with the beard excused himself. "Would you please have a goddamned word with it?"

My father laughed uncomfortably.

"Ah!" Jeremy bowed a little. "Excuse me, excuse me, excuse me. You are not my man, not my man at all." He bowed again and started to leave, but then circled back. "Viticulture is not your forte, yes I can see that, see that plainly. But may I trouble you on another matter? Forget the damned bottle." He threw it into the pool, and winked at the people he splashed. "I have another matter. Do you speak Chinese?"

My father said he did not, but Jeremy pulled out a handkerchief with some characters on it anyway, saying that his daughter had sent it from Hong Kong and that he thought the characters might be some secret message.

"Long life," said my father.

"But you haven't looked at it yet."

"I know what it says without looking." My father winked at me.

"You do?"

"Yes, I do."

"You're making fun of me, aren't you?"

"No, no, no," said my father, winking again.

"Who are you anyway?" said Jeremy.

His smile fading, my father shrugged.

"Who are you?"

My father shrugged again.

Jeremy began to roar. "This is my party, *my party*, and I've never seen you before in my life." My father backed up as Jeremy came toward him. *"Who are you? WHO ARE YOU?"*

Just as my father was going to step back into the pool, Mrs. Lardner came running up. Jeremy informed her that there was a man crashing his party.

"Nonsense," said Mrs. Lardner. "This is Ralph Chang, who I invited extra especially so he could meet you." She straightened the collar of Jeremy's peach-colored polo shirt for him.

"Yes, well, we've had a chance to chat," said Jeremy.

She whispered in his ear; he mumbled something; she whispered something more.

"I do apologize," he said finally.

My father didn't say anything.

"I do." Jeremy seemed genuinely contrite. "Doubtless you've seen drunks before, haven't you? You must have them in China."

"Okay," said my father.

As Mrs. Lardner glided off, Jeremy clapped his arm over my father's shoulders. "You know, I really am quite sorry, quite sorry."

My father nodded.

"What can I do, how can I make it up to you?"

"No thank you."

"No, tell me, tell me," wheedled Jeremy. "Tickets to casino night?" My father shook his head. "You don't gamble. Dinner at Bartholomew's?" My father shook his head again. "You don't eat." Jeremy scratched his chin. "You know, my wife was like you. Old Annabelle could never let me make things up—never, never, never, never, never."

My father wriggled out from under his arm.

"How about sport clothes? You are rather overdressed, you know, excuse me for saying so. But here." He took off his polo shirt and folded it up. "You can have this with my most profound apologies." He ruffled his chest hairs with his free hand.

"No thank you," said my father.

"No, take it, take it. Accept my apologies." He thrust the shirt into my father's arms. "I'm so very sorry, so very sorry. Please, try it on."

Helplessly holding the shirt, my father searched the crowd for my mother.

"Here, I'll help you off with your coat."

My father froze.

Jeremy reached over and took his jacket off. "Milton's, one hundred twenty-five dollars reduced to one hundred twelve-fifty," he read. "What a bargain, what a bargain!"

"Please give it back," pleaded my father. "Please."

"Now for your shirt," ordered Jeremy.

Heads began to turn.

"Take off your shirt."

"I do not take orders like a servant," announced my father.

"Take off your shirt, or I'm going to throw this jacket right into the pool, just right into this little pool here." Jeremy held it over the water.

"Go ahead."

"One hundred twelve-fifty," taunted Jeremy. "One hundred twelve . . ."

My father flung the polo shirt into the water with such force that part of it bounced back up into the air like a fluorescent fountain. Then it settled into a soft heap on top of the water. My mother hurried up.

"You're a sport!" said Jeremy, suddenly breaking into a smile and slapping my father on the back. "You're a sport! I like that. A man with spirit, that's what you are. A man with panache. Allow me to return to you your jacket." He handed it back to my father. "Good value you got on that, good value."

My father hurled the coat into the pool too. "We're leaving," he said grimly. "Leaving!"

"Now, Ralphie," said Mrs. Lardner, bustling up; but my father was already stomping off.

"Get your sister," he told me. To my mother: "Get your shoes."

"That was *great*, Dad," said Mona as we walked down to the car. "You were *stupendous*."

"Way to show 'em," I said.

"What?" said my father offhandedly.

Although it was only just dusk, we were in a gulch, which made it hard to see anything except the gleam of his white shirt moving up the hill ahead of us.

"It was all my fault," began my mother.

"Forget it," said my father grandly. Then he said, "The only trouble is I left those keys in my jacket pocket."

"Oh *no*," said Mona.

"Oh no is right," said my mother.

"So we'll walk home," I said.

"But how're we going to get into the *house*," said Mona.

The noise of the party churned through the silence.

"Someone has to going back," said my father.

"Let's go to the pancake house first," suggested my mother. "We can wait there until the party is finished, and then call Mrs. Lardner."

Having all agreed that that was a good plan, we started walking again.

"God, just think," said Mona. "We're going to have to *dive* for them."

My father stopped a moment. We waited.

"You girls are good swimmers," he said finally. "Not like me."

Then his shirt started moving again, and we trooped up the hill after it, into the dark.

1991

CHRIS WARE

B. 1967

When Chris Ware's book *Jimmy Corrigan, the Smartest Kid on Earth*—a compilation of episodes that had previously been printed as part of his ongoing cartoon pamphlet series *The Acme Novelty Library*—was published by Pantheon in 2000, it bewildered and amazed critics and readers. A story of family abandonment that tracks at least three generations of Corrigan men in meticulously rendered, experimental color pages, *Jimmy Corrigan* registers a deep level of aesthetic attention and narrative sophistication that has not always been understood as belonging to the realm of comics. *Jimmy Corrigan* won an American Book Award in 2000 and a Guardian First Book Award in 2001, the first graphic novel to win a major literary prize in the United Kingdom. The exploration of isolation within families and the intricate page layouts that made *Jimmy* famous are also present in Ware's previous and subsequent work.

Ware was born in Omaha, Nebraska, and graduated from the University of Texas at Austin's School of Fine Art. He lives with his wife and daughter in Chicago, where he works as a historian and editor of comics. He edited the *McSweeney's Quarterly Concern* volume on comics and the most recent edition of *Best American Comics*, publishes a magazine called the *Ragtime Ephemeralist*, and creates installments of his continuing series *The Acme Novelty Library*. He also contributes covers and stories to *The New Yorker*, and his narrative "Building Stories" was serialized in *The New York Times Magazine* in 2005 and 2006. Ware's comics have been exhibited at the Whitney Museum of American Art, the Cooper-Hewitt Museum, and the Museum of Contemporary Art in Chicago (where he was the focus of a major exhibit).

Ware's work has an emotional rigor, as well as a formal, graphic rigor that often looks architectural. Indeed, Ware has been influenced by architecture and has made it a theme in his work. Ware has compared comics not only with architecture but also with music, calling attention to the timing and syncopation present in both forms.

Ware got his major start when the cartoonist Art Spiegelman noticed his work in the student newspaper of the University of Texas in the late 1980s and asked him to contribute to *RAW*, the high-profile magazine published in New York by Spiegelman and his wife, Françoise Mouly, that billed itself as the cutting edge of comics. "Thrilling Adventure Stories (I Guess)" from 1991 marked Ware's second appearance in *RAW*, and it contains the hallmarks of Ware's work—its engagement with popular culture and comics history (here through the trope of the superhero), investigation of family structure, visual precision, and experimental intricacy. In "Thrilling Adventure Stories (I Guess)," the first-person narration shifts from overarching text boxes to dialogue that is spoken by various characters throughout the story.

Ware disturbs naturalism—both by distributing the narration across characters and by destabilizing a visual reference for the narrator himself, a man who is recalling his childhood—but also anchors the piece in a realism through its direct and emotionally frank tone. Although many readers have noted its gloomy themes, Ware's work is not so much about loneliness as about a haunting sensibility that the visual texture of comics has the ability to evoke with its experiments in time and space on the page.

Hillary Chute
Harvard University

PRIMARY WORKS

Acme Comic Library, ongoing, first published 1993; *Jimmy Corrigan, the Smartest Kid on Earth*, 2000.

Thrilling Adventure Stories (I Guess)

LAWSON FUSAO INADA
B. 1938

Lawson Inada is third-generation Japanese American, born and raised in Fresno, California. These autobiographical details are highlighted in his 1992 volume of poetry *Legends from Camp*: Section I is titled "Camp," referring to the author's boyhood experience of internment during World War II along with other Japanese Americans; Section II, "Fresno," consists of poems that pay tribute to this agricultural region of California. In his autobiographical recountings, Inada mentions going to the University of Iowa to study writing, then moving to Oregon. He taught at Southern Oregon University from 1966 until his retirement in 2002.

For both historical and aesthetic reasons, Lawson Inada is a significant figure in Asian American poetry and literature. He was one of the coeditors of the landmark anthology *Aiiieeeee! An Anthology of Asian-American Writers* and has participated in efforts to recover writing by earlier Japanese American authors such as Toshio Mori and John Okada. Legend has it that at a time of emerging Asian American consciousness but few visible Asian American writers, Frank Chin and his friends happened upon the book cover of *Down at the Santa Fe Depot* (1970), an anthology of Fresno-based poets. Struck by seeing an Asian face in the group photo of the poets, they discovered and contacted Lawson Inada. Inada's collection *Before the War: Poems as They Happened* (1971) was one of the first Asian American single-author volumes of poetry from a major New York publishing house.

Inada's poetry stands out in its consistent engagement with jazz. *Before the War* begins with a whimsical portrait of a Japanese American figure playing "air bass"; includes tributes to jazz musicians and singers such as Charlie Parker, Lester Young, and Billie Holiday; and ends with poems written for Miles Davis and Charles Mingus. Riffing on the term "bluesman," Inada calls himself a "campsman," suggesting that his blues derive from Japanese American internment. He describes his project as "blowing shakuhachi versaphone" and cites jazz as the strongest influence on his writing. Leslie Marmon Silko calls Inada "a poet-musician in the tradition of Walt Whitman and James A. Wright."

Inada won the American Book Award in 1994 for *Legends from Camp*. He was named Oregon State Poet of the Year in 1991 and Oregon Poet Laureate from 2006 to 2010. He has received a number of poetry fellowships from the National Endowment for the Arts, as well as a Guggenheim Fellowship in 2004, and has performed his poetry in concert with numerous musicians. His poetics of performance posits his art not as an object that transcends time but as a process that shapes time. Calling live performance his favorite form of "publishing," Inada appropriates the value that is ascribed to a finalized, written text for a mode that is oral and dynamic.

Inada's poetics suggest that there is more than one way to tell a story, that many stories are embedded within a given story or within what we know as history. This multiple sense of time implicitly critiques the notion of a standard time or history that is equivalent for all subjects. Poems such as "Instructions to All Persons" and "Two Variations on a Theme by Thelonious Monk" shape time and history as variable and layered. "On Being Asian American" refers to an echo generated by the actualization of the racial subject. We can see a poetics of the echo in the repetition enacted in this poem as well as in the poems "Instructions" and "Two Variations." This repetition is what Henry Louis Gates, Jr., calls "repetition with a difference": a nonlinear, nonteleological aesthetics of change.

Juliana Chang
Santa Clara University

PRIMARY WORKS

Before the War: Poems As They Happened, 1971; *The Buddha Bandits down Highway 99* (with Garrett Kaoru Hongo and Alan Chong Lau), 1978; *Legends from Camp*, 1992; *Drawing the Line*, 1997.

Instructions to All Persons

Let us take
what we can
for the occasion:

Ancestry. (*Ancestry*)
All of that portion. (*Portion*)   5
With the boundary. (*Boundary*)
Beginning. (*Beginning*)
At the point. (*Point*)
Meets a line. (*Line*)
Following the middle. (*Middle*)   10
Thence southerly. (*Southerly*)
Following the said line. (*Following*) (*Said*)
Thence westerly. (*Westerly*)
Thence northerly. (*Northerly*)
To the point. (*Point*)   15
Of beginning. (*Beginning*) (*Ancestry*)

Let us bring
what we need
for the meeting:

Provisions. (*Provisions*)   20
Permission. (*Permission*)
Commanding. (*Commanding*)
Uniting. (*Uniting*)
Family (*Family*)

Let us have   25
what we have
for the gathering:

Civil. (*Civil*)
Ways. (*Ways*)
Services. (*Services*)   30

Respect. (*Respect*)
Management. (*Management*)
Kinds. (*Kinds*)
Goods. (*Goods*)
For all. (*All*)   35

Let us take
what we can
for the occasion:

Responsible.
Individual.   40
Sufficient.
Personal.
Securely.
Civil.
Substantial.   45
Accepted.
Given.
Authorized.

Let there be
Order.   50

Let us be
Wise.

                                                                   1992

Two Variations on a Theme by Thelonious Monk As Inspired by Mal Waldron

Introduction: Monk's Prosody

"I can't do that right. I have to practice that."

—Thelonious Monk, composer, to his pianist (himself)
during a solo run-through of "Round Midnight," April 5, 1957

April 5, 1957: Maybe I'm sitting on a fire escape in Berkeley, trying to write some poetry. I know one thing: I was listening to Monk by then—particularly his solo on "Bags' Groove," on the Miles Davis 10-inch lp. You might say I was studying Monk's prosody—how each time he'd come out of the speakers in a different, distinctive way, and always swinging.

Years pass. Decades. Prosody.

January 15, 1987: I work a duo concert with Mal Waldron. Mal, even while checking out the tuning, makes reference, says hello, to Monk. The next time we blow, I want to do "Blue Monk."

June, 1987: Whenever the next time is, I'll be ready. I work out a linear, horn-like statement; it fits, like an overlay. Then I jump right into the tune and the piano, and blow something from the inside out—percussive— particularly building around and repeating "ricochet."

April, 1988: One of those long Oregon dusks. Larry Smith, editor of Caliban, calls up to ask if I'd be interested in doing something with Monk's prosody. Prosody—yeah. I have to practice that.

I. Blue Monk (linear)

Solid, as the man himself would say.
Solid, as the man at his instrument.
Solid, as the solid composition.

However, at the same time,
this elegant melody,   5
"Blue Monk,"

while certainly being solid enough—
as evidenced by
the ease of our ability
to hum and whistle it,   10
even in sleep—

is actually solid, fluid,
and a real gas combined;

you know what I mean:
like feelings, like atmosphere,   15
like right, like here,

you feel like you've been hearing
"Blue Monk" forever,
since the planet started dancing,
like its been around since sound,   20

since the blue wind got up
one blue summer morning,
looked across the cool, blue canyon
at that sweet, blue mountain,
and melodiously started to sing   25

"Blue Monk";
you know that lovely feeling,
"Blue Monk";
you know what

"Blue Monk" can do for you,   30
the melodious message it sends,
the melodious message that always comes
echoing back across the canyons as a result;
"Blue Monk,"

as a result of recognition,   35
as a consequence of confirmation,
as an accomplishment of affirmation—
"Blue Monk,"
"Blue Monk"
in the sun and rain, in all conditions;   40

and the song, therefore,
just by being what it is—
these huge, blue feelings
spaced and placed just so,
ascending,   45
these huge, blue feelings
descending, just so,
and including some delightful
dimensions for refreshment
on a huge, blue plateau.   50

"Blue Monk," then, by its very nature,
built into its basic structure,
encompasses and contains
all the properties of nature:

take a hold of it,   55
hold it up to the light;
see what I mean?—
"Blue Monk" has you dancing;

by now you're feeling confident about the song,
feeling like you've got it down,   60
feeling like you're part of its beauty,
feeling like it's part of you—
which is certainly true;

feeling fine with the freedom of it;
feeling like going for it   65

with expansiveness, abandon;

feeling exhilarated in your bones
like you want to do something about
exercising your own right
to rhythm and expression,   70

yes, you feel like you own the song—
which you certainly do—
since you went right down there on West 52nd Street
and got it directly from the man himself,
Blue Monk, who turns out to be,   75
not the imposing artist you had heard and read about,
but just the husband, the father, the neighbor
making his way out of the corner grocery
with some snow peas and stalks of celery
sticking out of a paper sack,   80
he just needs something back,
gladly giving you the tune
in exchange for a proven recipe of your own;

meanwhile, Blue Monk is smiling
that solid Blue Monk smile   85
while offering you directions for usage:

  "Look, 'Blue Monk' is a solid song;
  you can bend it; you can break it;
  you can always remake it;
  it's hot and it's cool,   90
  it's suitable for digging
  in whatever occasion you choose—
  ceremonious, thelonious and such . . ."

Ah, the sheer joy of such ownership!
You take "Blue Monk" home and set it   95
glowing in your living room
like a luxurious lamp.
You stick it in the phone,
sending it out via satellite:

  "Hello, Mom? Dig this song!"   100
  "Hello, is this the White House?
  Listen, I've got a solid
  new anthem for the shaky republic!"

You take "Blue Monk" outside to the fire escape,
seeing how far you can throw it,   105

looping it smoothly over the moonlit harbor
as it becomes a bridge
of flowing blue lights:
"Blue Monk."
You're dancing, humming,   110
strolling slowly across,
tossing blue notes
floating over the wide, blue water
like you're a luminous, musical spider;
tossing cool, blue clusters high overhead,   115
creating a blue, musical constellation:
"Blue Monk";

by now, many others,
including birds, animals, insects,
have joined you on your excursion,   120
having just got wise
to mythology and fireworks combined,
staring awestruck up into the huge, blue night
to find the Blue Monk profile outlined,
pointing out and humming   125
each huge, blue star in the melody—
and, oh, those sweet, blue spaces in between . . .

Yes, indeed, this is some kind
of luxurious structure,
in architectural legacy   130

ascending, descending, with pliable plateaus
for ease of breathing, handling,
relaxing, building, dancing, laughing,
praying, creating, embracing, enhancing;

a structure as solid, fluid, strong,   135
translucent, luminous, freeing,
and bracing
as the man himself—

Mr. Blue Monk,
bringing everything we do,   140
we see, we know,
into melodious focus

through the blue keys
of his blue piano;

therefore, in this blue region,   145
with this blue vision, in this blue
body of being
we all know as home,
everything throbs and pulses and glows
with the true, blue beauty of his song: 150

"Blue Monk"!

II. "Blue Monk" (percussive)

Ricochet:

Radius:
Radiating:

Reciting: Realizing: Referring: Recapturing: Repercussion:
Revolving: Reflecting: Returning: Reconstituting: Republic: 5
Reshaping: Restructuring: Reversing: Reclaiming: Religion:
Respecting: Removing: Reforming: Receiving: Reality:
Refining: Reducing: Refreshing: Regenerating: Resource:
Regarding: Relating: Relaxing: Revering: Remembering:
Renewing: Revising: Repairing: Replacing: Residing: 10
Reviewing: Respecting: Resolving: Reviving: Responsible:
Retaining: Resuming: Revealing: Rehearsing: Resulting:
Restoring: Retrieving: Regaining: Recovering: Relying:
Redeeming: Replying: Reminding: Rewarding: Resounding:

Reverberating: 15

Remarkably:

Releasing:

Remaining:

Repeating:
                                                                     1992

Kicking the Habit

Late last night, I decided to
stop using English.
I had been using it all day—

talking all day,
listening all day,
thinking all day,   5
reading all day,
remembering all day,
feeling all day,

and even driving all day,   10
in English—

when, finally I decided to
stop.

So I pulled off the main highway
onto a dark country road   15
and kept on going and going
until I emerged in another nation and . . .
stopped.

There, the insects
inspected my passport, the frogs   20
investigated my baggage, and the trees
pointed out lights in the sky,
saying,
   "Shhhhlllyyymmm"—

and I, of course, replied.   25
After all, I was a foreigner,
and had to comply . . .

Now don't get me wrong:
There's nothing "wrong"
with English,   30

and I'm not complaining
about the language
which is my native tongue.
I make my living with the lingo;
I was even in England once.   35
So you might say I'm actually
addicted to it;
yes, I'm an Angloholic,
and I can't get along without the stuff:
It controls my life.   40

Until last night, that is.
Yes, I had had it
with the habit.

I was exhausted,
burned out,   45
by the habit.
And I decided to
kick the habit,
cold turkey,
right then and there   50
on the spot!

And, in so doing, I kicked
open the door of a cage
and stepped out from confinement
into the greater world.   55

    Tentatively, I uttered,

        "Chemawa? Chinook?"

and the pines said

        "Clackamas, Siskiyou."

And before long, everything else   60
chimed in with their two cents' worth
and we had a fluid and fluent
conversation going,

    communicating, expressing,
    echoing whatever we needed to   65
    know, know, know . . .

What was it like?
Well, just listen:

Ah, the exquisite seasonings
of syllables, the consummate consonants, the vigorous   70
vowels of varied vocabularies

      clicking, ticking, humming,
      growling, throbbing, strumming—

coming from all parts of orifices, surfaces,
in creative combinations, orchestrations,   15
resonating in rhythm with the atmosphere!

I could have remained there
forever—as I did, and will.
And when I resumed my way,
my stay could no longer be   80

      "ordinary"—

as they say,
as *we* say, in English.

For on the road of life,
in the code of life,   85

there's much more to red than

      "stop,"

there's much more to green than

      "go,"

and there's much, much more to yellow than   90

      "caution,"

for as the yellow
sun clearly enunciated to me this morning:

      "Fusao. Inada."

                                       1997

On Being Asian American

for our children

Of course, not everyone
can be an Asian American.
Distinctions are earned,
and deserve dedication.

Thus, from time of birth,   5
the journey awaits you—

ventures through time,
the turns of the earth.

When you seem to arrive,
the journey continues;   10
when you seem to arrive,
the journey continues.

Take me as I am, you cry,
I, I, am an individual.
Which certainly is true.   15
Which generates an echo.

Who are all your people
assembled in celebration,
with wisdom and strength,
to which you are entitled.   20

For you are at the head
of succeeding generations,
as the rest of the world
comes forward to greet you.

As the rest of the world   25
comes forward to greet you.

                                                          1992

■ LYNDA BARRY ■

B. 1956

In the volume *The Best American Comics 2006*, the cartoonist, novelist, and writing teacher Lynda Barry's biography notes that she was born in Wisconsin "to a woman who came from the Philippines on a military transport plane and a navy man who drank and bowled." Barry spent much of her childhood in working-class Seattle, and many of her stories take place in racially mixed neighborhoods not unlike the one in which she grew up. She lives in Wisconsin today.

The author of fourteen books, Barry is one of the best-known active literary cartoonists and a chronicler of American adolescence. Her weekly syndicated comic strip, *Ernie Pook's Comeek*, has been running for thirty years. In reviewing

Barry's 2002 comics work *One Hundred Demons* in *The New York Times*, the author Nick Hornby wrote, "Barry seems to me to almost single-handedly justify the form; she's one of America's very best contemporary writers." *One Hundred Demons*, like Barry's other major work, is finely tuned to capturing the cadences of childhood.

Barry attended Evergreen State College and shortly thereafter began producing comic strips for an alternative newspaper, the *Chicago Reader*. Her first book collections, *Girls and Boys* (1981) and *Big Ideas* (1983), focus on the often absurd and painful ins and outs of adult romantic relationships. Texts such as *Naked Ladies! Naked Ladies! Naked Ladies!* (1984), a so-called coloring book with fiction, and *Everything in the World* (1986) explore more fully the voices and consciousness of children. An examination of the creative texture of children's everyday lives has marked and defined Barry's work in the subsequent years, when she published eight comics collections; two illustrated prose novels, *The Good Times Are Killing Me* (1999) and *Cruddy* (2000); and one ambiguous foray into comics nonfiction, *One Hundred Demons*, which she called an "autobifictionalography."

In works such as *The Fun House* (1987), *Down the Street* (1989), and *My Perfect Life* (1992), Barry demonstrates the powerful economy of comics prose and expressive drawing to provide humor, insight, and pathos. According to Hornby, Barry's stories "contain little grenades of meaning that tend to explode just after you've read the last line." Many of her pieces—most of which are told in short, four-panel segments—show how the comics form doesn't simply illustrate words with pictures but offers two separate narrative tracks to dramatic effect. In "Help You," for example, the voice of a teenager speculating about her father's whereabouts during a school typing class is stamped over images of a man in a bar far away.

Although Barry is often funny, her oeuvre is unflinching and dark. In *It's So Magic* (1994), for instance, she looks at the horror of sexual abuse and acknowledges that the brutality of childhood is as much a part of the terrain as is playing and its unexpected elations. Writing the Unthinkable, the title of her popular writing course centered on memory, reflects this breadth. The unthinkable in the course's title isn't trauma but the positive ability to see any detail—good or bad, big or small—as relevant to the construction of experience.

Hillary Chute
Harvard University

PRIMARY WORKS

Girls and Boys, 1981; *Naked Ladies, Naked Ladies, Naked Ladies*, 1984; *Down the Street*, 1988; *The Lynda Barry Experience*, 1993; *The Good Times Are Killing Me*, 1999; *Cruddy*, 2000; *One Hundred Demons*, 2005; *What It Is*, 2008; *Picture This*, 2010; *Blabber Blabber Blabber: Volume 1 of Everything*, 2011.

Messed Up and Confused

Help You

Family Pictures

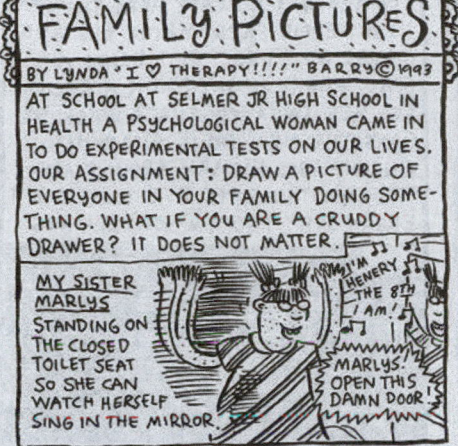

It's Cool

ITS COOL

BY LYNDA "BACHELOR PARTY" BARRY © 1991

"THERE'S JUST SOME THINGS THAT MEN HAVE TO KEEP TO THEMSELVES." IS WHAT THE BOY EDDIE DAVIS SAID WHEN I GOT TO THE SNEAK OUT PLACE WHERE I WAS SUPPOSED TO MEET CINDY LUDERMYER. IT WAS 1 AM AND SHE WASN'T THERE. ONLY EDDIE AND ANOTHER GUY VINCENT.

"SO SHE WAS ALREADY HERE THEN?" I ASK. EDDIE SAYS "MAYBE YES AND MAYBE NO." I GO, "QUIT BEING A SPAZ. WHERE IS SHE?" ON A ROCK I SEE HER SWEATER. THAT'S WHEN HE SAYS THE MEN THING AND WHEN VINCENT PUTS HIS ARM AROUND ME. "IT'S COOL." HE SAYS. "IT'S COOL. DON'T FREAK OUT." I GO "I'M NOT FREAKING OUT."

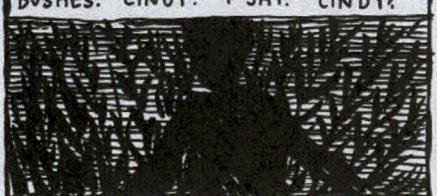

BUT I WAS FREAKING OUT. SLIGHTLY FREAKING OUT. FREAKING OUT FOR ME AND FREAKING OUT FOR CINDY WHO LOVES BOONES FARM APPLE WINE AND THERE'S THE BOTTLE EMPTY ON ITS SIDE BY THE ROCK. CINDY WHO I SAID I WOULD GUARD. "COME ON YOU GUYS TELL ME WHERE SHE'S AT." THEN A WALKING NOISE IN THE BUSHES. "CINDY?" I SAY. "CINDY?"

NO. IT'S DAN. THE ORIGINAL GUY OF THE CATHOLIC BOYS WHO CINDY LIKED. HE'S BRUSHING HIS PANTS OFF AND WIPING HIS MOUTH. "EDDIE." HE SAYS. "EDDIE." THEN HE POINTS INTO THE WOODS. "SHE'S ASKIN' FOR YOU." EDDIE GOES AND I TRY TO FOLLOW. "HEY." DAN SAYS. HE PUSHES HIS HANDS AGAINST MY SHOULDERS. "DON'T FREAK OUT, MAN. IT'S COOL. IT'S COOL."

She Wanted It, She Wanted It

SHE WANTED IT SHE WANTED IT

MARLYS SAW IT. SHE SAW THOSE GUYS AND CINDY LUDERMYER. SHE HID IN THE BUSHES AND WATCHED CINDY PUSHING ON THE GUY AND THE GUY PUSHING ON CINDY. AND IT WAS MARLYS THAT THREW THE ROCK.

MARLYS.

WHAT?

YOU OK?

QUIT ASKIN' ME THAT.

"YOU LITTLE BITCH!" IS WHAT THE GUY CALLED MY SISTER. IT WAS HER FIRST TIME OF THAT NAME. HE CAUGHT HER AND DRAGGED HER AND SAID TO HIS FRIENDS "WHAT ARE WE GOING TO DO NOW?"

QUIT STARIN' AT ME.

CINDY WAS SO DRUNK. SHE WAS CRYING. LAYING IN THE LEAVES AND THE STICKS AND CRYING. I KICKED THE GUYS LEG WHO WAS HOLDING ME AND HE KNOCKED ME IN THE HEAD. TWO GUYS RAN. ONE GUY POINTED AT CINDY AND SAID "SHE STARTED IT." AND HELD HIS CIG PACK TO ME LIKE "DID I WANT ONE."

MARLYS...

I ALREADY TOLD YOU A HUNDRED TIMES!!

IT WAS THE GUY CINDY LIKED. HE BENT TO HELP HER UP. "SEE?" HE SAYS. "SHE'S OK. CINDY. CINDY. YOUR FRIENDS ARE HERE." HE POINTS TO MARLYS WHO IS STANDING BY ME NOT MOVING. "YOU TELL ANYBODY AND THE WHOLE WORLD WILL KNOW WHAT A SLUT CINDY IS. YOU WANT THAT?"

I'M NOT TELLIN' ALL RIGHT? YOU SATISFIED?

If You Want to Know Teenagers by Mar Lys

KIMIKO HAHN

B. 1955

Kimiko Hahn's poetics are strongly intertextual, often explicitly so. She responds to phrases in other texts that she finds evocative. One text that she frequently returns to for such "cannibalization" (her term) is *Genji monogatari* (*The Tale of Genji*), by Lady Murasaki Shikibu (978?–1026), generally considered not only the first Japanese novel but the first psychological novel. Hahn also refers in her writing to the influence and inspiration of other women writers from Japan's Heian period (794–1185).

Hahn's literary debt to Japanese women writers, however, should not be thought of as due to some essentialist connection between Asian American and Asian writers. In her poem "Cruising Barthes," Hahn explores the profoundly ambivalent nature of her exploration of Japanese language and literature: "The way I fear speaking Japanese and adore / speaking it.... / What is Japanese? blood,/geography, translation by white, Occupation-trained / academic men?" Her relationship to Japanese literature and culture were shaped, she says, not only by her Japanese American mother but also by her German American father's aesthetic interest in Japanese culture and her own formal study of East Asian cultures in college and graduate school. Language for her is not only a writing tool but also subject matter. Fluency in more than one language highlights language itself as a construction that can be interrogated and played with.

Kimiko Hahn was born in 1955 in Mt. Kisco, New York, to two artists, her mother from Hawaii and her father from Wisconsin. Hahn majored in English and East Asian Studies as an undergraduate at the University of Iowa and received an M.A. in Japanese literature at Columbia University. Her poetry was first collected in book form in *We Stand Our Ground* (1988), a collaboration with two other women poets. Hahn is the author of five collections of poetry: *Air Pocket* (1989); *Earshot* (1992), which was awarded the Theodore Roethke Memorial Poetry Prize and an Association of Asian America Studies Literature Award; *The Unbearable Heart* (1995), which received an American Book Award; *Volatile* (1999); and *Mosquito and Ant* (1999). A recipient of fellowships from the National Endowment for the Arts and the New York Foundation for the Arts, she has also been awarded a Lila Wallace–Reader's Digest Writer's Award. Hahn was an editor of the magazine *Bridge: Asian-American Perspectives*. She cites her experience with the American Writers Congress as having a major impact, and she identifies Marxism as a strong intellectual and political influence.

Thematically, Hahn's poems explore the relationship between gender, language, body, desire, and subjectivity. Formally, her poetics of fragmentation, quotation, and multivocality propose new models of gendered and racialized subjectivity. The notion of the autonomous individual is questioned and replaced by a sense of the subject as inhabited and haunted by "other" voices. Her poetics of female intersubjectivity are manifested in the arcs of *The Unbearable Heart*, a collection of poems that mourn her mother, and *Mosquito and Ant*, arranged as a series of correspondences between the speaker and an older-sister figure.

Desire is the strongest thread running throughout Hahn's poems. The passion she uses to write love poetry is similar to the passion she uses to write political poetry. The libidinal charge of Hahn's poetry confounds distinctions between private and public, the intimate and the global. Her poems are sensual, lyrical, heartbreaking, intellectual, and political. They are challenging in the most pleasurable sense. Meditative yet urgent, full of integrity and sensuality, suffused with a multilingual sensibility and "sense memory" (the title of a poem), Hahn's poetry is extremely compelling in its inscriptions of Asian American female desire and subjectivity.

Juliana Chang
University of Illinois at Urbana-Champaign

PRIMARY WORKS

We Stand Our Ground (with Gale Jackson and Susan Sherman), 1988; *Air Pocket*, 1989; *Earshot*, 1992; *The Unbearable Heart*, 1995; *Volatile*, 1999; *Mosquito and Ant*, 1999; *The Artist's Daughter*, 2002; *The Narrow Road to the Interior*, 2006 *Toxic Flora: Poems*, 2010.

Strands

The key warmed in your hand
and you knew the password
was *sea*
instead of *ocean*. Once in
he had blown the weekend   5
talking about documentaries.
Your head rested on his neck
then conked out
in bas relief.
The sound and smell   10
of the steam
across the room warmed you.
Later you figure
it was an extra blanket
tossed over your waist.   15
Your patience at that point
was unassuming. It was here
you turned into a piece
of wood
he spotted as sculptural.   20
You couldn't scream
till he pulled out
his tongue.

The key word was sea
not ocean. 25
Trudging through sixteen inches
your mind goes to drifts
there at the shore;
first last fall
with your husband and dog 30
slugging coffee from a thermos
and bracing against the wind.
You had gone for the dog
to taste sea salt
and expanse. The apricot cake 35
reminded you of earwax.
Now snow and crusts of ice
over sand
plays in your mind.
You wouldn't know 40
and call him again
by names. Seaweed. Oats. Bran.
Apricot jam. Jam.
And the word transforms from would
to wood as the key warms 45
in your hand.

Your hair is short
as spruce
and when you shake
short hairs 50
fall on the newspaper.
He had blown the afternoon
talking about El Salvador
without seeing the connection
to, say, Puerto Ricans 55
in Springfield, Mass.
The banks
of snow incite riot
or strand. The imagination
conks out 60
like the hemisphere.
Looking for an employer
you figure is looking
for what kills
the love between us 65
but not your vision
and never grandma's sea.

Your hair is short
as spruce or pine
and you think of his face   70
brushed by it.
Cellophaning, she suggested,
stains strands of hair
blue, green—whatever.
But you shied away   75
because of him.
Why? Would he walk out?
When you flirted he backed off
yet when you spoke
about newspaper clippings   80
or goldfish he glowed.
And now this. Something
you can't handle as he touches
your hair yet makes
for his coat. He doesn't understand   85
how paint fits into
this narration. So you take the hand
and dip it in.

                                                        1992

Resistance: A Poem on Ikat Cloth[1]

By the time the forsythia blossomed
in waves along the parkway
the more delicate cherry and apple
had blown away, if you remember
correctly. Those were days   5
when you'd forget socks and books
after peeing in the privacy
of its branches and soft earth.
What a house you had
fit for turtles or sparrows.   10
One sparrow[2]
wrapped in a silk kimono
wept for her tongue
clipped off by the old woman.
You'll never forget that   15

---

[1]Ikat: "the technique of resist-dying yarn before it is woven" (*African Textiles*, John Picton and John Mack, London, 1979).
[2]Sparrow references from the Japanese folktale "*Shitakirisuzume*" (literally, "the tongue-cut-sparrow"). The sparrow received the punishment after eating the old woman's rice starch. The sparrow got even.

or its vengeance as striking
as the yellow around your small shoulders.
  shitakirisuzume mother called her.
  You didn't need to understand
  exactly.   20
a process of resistance
in Soemba, Sumatra, Java, Bali,
Timor,[3]
  Soon came mounds of flesh
  and hair here and there.   25
  Centuries earlier
  you'd have been courted
or sold.
  "Inu has let out my sparrow—the little one
  that I kept in the clothes-basket she said,   30
  looking very unhappy."
For a Eurasian, sold.
  Murasaki[4]
mother
  She soaked the cloth   35
  in incense
  then spread it on the floor
  standing there in bleached cotton,
  red silk and bare feet.
And you fell in love with her   40
deeply as only a little girl could.
Pulling at your nipples
you dreamt of her body
that would become yours.
  "Since the day we first boarded the ship   45
  I have been unable to wear
  my dark red robe.
  That must not be done
  out of danger of attracting
  the god of the sea."   50
red as a Judy Chicago plate
feast your eyes on this
jack
  "when I was bathing along the shore
  scarcely screened by reeds   55
  I lifted my robe revealing my leg
  and more."[5]

[3]Locations in Indonesia known for ikat.
[4]*Murasaki* also means "purple."
[5]*Tosanikki* (*The Tosa Diary*, by Ki no Tsur-
ayuki, translated by Earl Miner), written in
the female persona.

roll up that skirt
and show those calves
cause if that bitch thinks   60
she can steal your guy
she's crazy
       The cut burned
       so she flapped her wings
       and cried out   65
       but choked
       on blood.
The thread wound around your hand
so tight your fingers
turn indigo   70
       Murasaki
The Shining Prince[6] realized
he could form her
into the one forbidden him. For that
he would persist   75
into old age.
       rice starch
envelope bone, bride
       you can't resist
The box of the sparrow's vengeance   80
contained evils comparable to agent orange
or the minamata disease. The old man
lived happily
without the old woman. But why her?
except that she was archetypal.   85
       She depended on her child
       to the point that when her daughter died
       and she left Tosa
       she could only lie down
       on the boat's floor   90
       and sob loudly
       while the waves
       crashed against her side
       almost pleasantly.
This depth lent the writer   95
the soft black silt
on the ocean floor
where all life, some men say, began.
       warp
"Mr. Ramsay, stumbling along a passage   100

---

[6]"The Shining Prince" refers to Genji. *Genji-monogatari* (*The Tale of Genji*, by Murasaki Shikibu, translated by Arthur Waley). This is the first time Genji hears the child Murasaki whom he later adopts, then marries.

one dark morning, stretched his arms out,
but Mrs. Ramsay, having died rather suddenly
the night before, his arms though stretched out,
remained empty."[7]
      when the men wove and women dyed   105
mother—
       mutha
Orchids you explained
represent female genitalia
in Chinese verse.   110
Hence the orchid boat.
Patricia liked that
and would use it in her collection
Sex and Weather.
the supremes soothed like an older sister   115
rubbing your back
kissing your neck and pulling you into
motor city, usa
whether you like it
or not that   120
was the summer
of watts and though you
were in a coma
as far as that
the ramifications   125
the ramifications
bled through transistors
    a *class* act
blues from indigo, reds
from mendoekoe root, yellows, boiling   130
tegaran wood
and sometimes by mudbath
    when you saw her bathing in the dark
    you wanted to dip your hand in
mamagoto suruno?[8]   135
    The bride transforms
    into water
    while the groom moves
    like the carp
    there just under the bridge—   140
    like the boy with you
    under the forsythia
    scratching and rolling around.
    No, actually you just lay there

---

[7]*To the Lighthouse*, Virginia Woolf.   [8]*Mamagoto suruno*, Japanese, "playing house."

still and moist.   145
still and moist.
Wondering what next.
You're not even certain
which you see—
    The carp or the reflection of your hand.   150
the forsythia curled
like cupped hands covering
    bound and unbound
As if blood
    "The thought of the white linen   155
    spread out on the deep snow
    the cloth and the snow
    glowing scarlet was enough
    to make him feel that"[9]
The sight of him squeezing melons   160
sniffing one
then splitting it open in the park
was enough to make you feel that
    Naha, Ryukyu Island, Taketome, Shiga,
    Karayoshi, Tottori, Izo,   165
resistance does not mean
not drawn it means
    sasou mizu araba
    inamu to zo omou[10]
bind the thread   170
with hemp or banana leaves
before soaking it in the indigo
black as squid as seaweed as his hair
    as his hair
    as I lick his genitals   175
    first taking one side
    deep in my mouth then the other
    till he cries softly
    please
for days   180
    Though practical
    you hate annotations
    to the *kokinshu;*[11]
    each note vivisects
    a *waka*   185

---

[9]*Yukiguni* (*Snow Country*, Kawabata Yasunari, translated by Edward Seidensticker).

[10]*Sasou* etc. is a quote from a waka (classical Japanese poem) by Ono no Komachi. Donald Keene translated these lines, "were there water to entice me / I would follow it, I think." (*Anthology of Japanese Literature*, p. 79).

[11]*Kokinshu* is the Imperial Anthology of poetry completed in 905.

like so many petals
off a stem
until your lap
is full of blossoms.
How many you destroyed! 190
You can't imagine
Komachi's world
as real. Hair
so heavy it adds
another layer of brocade 195
(black on wisteria,
plum—)
forsythia too raw
  and the smell
  of fresh *tatami*.[12] 200
  But can you do without
  kono yumei no naka ni[13]
Can you pull apart the line
"my heart chars"
  kokoro yakeori 205
corridors of thread
  "creating the pattern from memory
  conforming to a certain style
  typical of each island"[14]
"K.8. Fragment of ramie kasuri, medium 210
blue, with repeating double ikat, and mantled
turtles and maple leaves of weft ikat.
Omi Province, Shiga Prefecture,
Honshu.
L. 16.5 cm. W. 19.5 cm." 215
  "the turtle with strands of seaweed
  growing from its back forming a mantle,
  reputed to live for centuries,"
Komachi also moved
like those shadows in the shallows 220
you cannot reach
though they touch you.
Wading and feeling
something light as a curtain
around your calves you turn 225
to see very small scallops
rise to the surface
for a moment of oxygen

[12]*Tatami*, straw matting for the floor in Japanese homes.
[13]*Kono* etc., Japanese, for "in this dream."

[14]From another Ono no Komachi poem translated by Earl Miner (*Introduction to Japanese Court Poetry*, p. 82).

then close up and descend.
Caught, you look   230
at what he calls their eyes
(ridges of blue)
and are afraid to touch
that part.
   from memory or history   235
sasou mizu
   Grandmother's *ofuro*[15]
   contained giant squid
killer whales
   hot   240
omou
   You were afraid he would
   turn to the sea
   to say something
that would separate you   245
   forever
   so kept talking.
   Of course he grew irritable
   and didn't really want
   a basket of shells   250
   for the bathroom.
his arms though stretched out"
   The line shocked you
   like so much of Kawabata
   who you blame   255
   for years of humiliation,
   katakana, hiragana, kanji,[16]
at each stroke
   You first hear the squall
   coming across the lake   260
   like a sheet of glass.
   You start to cry and daddy
   rows toward the shore and mother.
in the Malayan Archipelago
   Georgia O'Keeffe's orchid shocked you   265
   so even now you can picture the fragrance
"Should a stranger witness the performance
he is compelled to dip his finger
into the dye and taste it. Those employed
must never mention the names of dead people   270
or animals. Pregnant or sick women

[15]*Ofuro*, Japanese bathtub.
[16]*Katakana*, etc., are the Japanese syllabaries
 and the Chinese characters, respectively.

are not allowed to look on;
should this happen they are punished
as strangers."
      in the Malayan Archipelago   275
      where boys give their sweethearts
      shuttles they will carve, burn,
      name,
"language does not differ
from instruments of production,   280
from machines, let us say,"[17]
      knocked down
knocked *up girl*
      "the superstructure"
he wouldn't stop talking   285
about *deep structure*
      and mention in prayer
but you need more than the female persona.
A swatch of cloth.
A pressed flower. The taste of powder   290
brushed against your lips.
      pine
matsu[18]
      The wedding day chosen
      he brought you animal crackers   295
cloths
      Pushing aside the branches
      you crawl in
      on your hands and knees,
      lie back,   300
      and light up.
tabako chodai[19]
      because the forsythia
      symbolizes so much
      of sneakers,   305
      cloth ABC books, charms,
sankyu[20]
      the "charred heart"
      would be reconstructed thus:
"Before the golden Buddha, I will lay   310
Poems as my flowers,
Entering in the Way,
Entering in the Way."[21]

---

[17]Joseph Stalin, *Marxism and Problems of Linguistics.*
[18]*Matsu*, Japanese, "pine tree" and "wait."
[19]*Tabako chodai*, Japanese, "give me a cigarette [tobacco]."

[20]*Sankyu*, Japanese pronunciation of "thank you."
[21]Noh play by Kan'ami Kiyotsugu, "Sotoba Komachi," supposedly about Ono no Komachi's repentance (Keene, p. 270).

fuck that shit

Link the sections 315
with fragrance: *matsu*
    shards of ice
The bride spread out her dress
for the dry cleaners
then picked kernels of rice 320
off the quilt and from her hair.
    bits of china
the lining unfolds
out of the body
through hormonal revolutions 325
gravity and chance
    lick that plate clean
can I get a cigarette
    got a match
click clack, click 330
clack
    chodai
in this dream
    She wrapped the ikat
    around her waist and set out 335
    for Hausa, Yoruba, Ewe of Ghana,
    Baule, Madagascar, and Northern Edo
I pull off my dress
and take a deep breath.
The cupped hands open then 340
onto the loom.
    click clack click
clack
    and in the rhythmic chore
    I imagine a daughter in my lap 345
    who I will never give away
    but see off
    with a bundle of cloths
    dyed with resistance

1989

Cuttings

a zuihitsu for father

My younger sister and I, cleaning father's house before he returns from
a week in intensive care, rush to dispose of mother's cosmetics, store
her jewelry for a later date, and phone a woman's shelter to pick up bags
'of dresses, size 4, and shoes, 4½, even stopping to laugh at the platforms

from "the mod era" she swore would come back. We collapse into   5
each other's arms and cry *mommy mommy* as if she could hear us if we
wept loud enough.

I look out the taxi window at everyone else's life. Certainly all the
people in all the little apartments have gone about their business
making money off other people's mortgages or addictions, without the   10
knowledge my mother died last week, someone who found pleasure in
baking oddly shaped biscuits with her granddaughters.

I keep my father talking about his boyhood—his passion for deep-sea
diving though he grew up on Lake Michigan, his going AWOL for art
courses, the four books at the Naval Library on "Oriental Art." Here   15
we turn, always return, to Maude who *wasn't supposed to go first*. He
said he had her convinced.

I ask Marie how to tell the girls, Miya now six and Rei, four. She advises
we speak to them separately, to allow each their own reactions.

The funeral director says, "She doesn't look 68, but then oriental   20
women never look their age." He then reminisces about "The War."

I want to throw out as much as possible—a half-jar of expensive cream,
a suede jacket—belongings my sister wishes to hold on to. I go to the
Funeral Home. I find comfort in The 10 O'clock News; she resents the
superficial, even stupid resemblance of normality.   25

Two weeks now since mother died. Tuesday nights, I stay with father
now a man who can barely contain what, in a second, became memory.
He lurches from each small room testing himself against souvenirs:
animal puppets from Rome, 1956; a Noh mask, Kyoto, '64; silver
rabbit, Phnom Penh, '65; hotel towel, Chicago, '70. Even after   30
discarding her dresses and middle-class perfumes she inhabits every
corner of every project—collage, painting, carving. He recalls telling
her when they first met at the Art Institute that art would always come
before any thing and any one.

We toast Maude at a neighbor's, drinking what we like since she   35
couldn't tolerate liquor. Janet remembers the day she knew they'd be
friends: "We were looking at the peonies by the stone wall and your
mother said, *Know what these remind me of? Penises.*" Our laughter
resembles sobbing.

She reread stories as often as I demanded.   40

Convinced and convincing me through my early twenties I could not
sew or cook despite home ec. classes and odd advice, she cooked and
froze stews, checked if I ever baked potatoes and the last day we
saw her, sent us home with turkey leftovers. It's true I've never roasted
one.   45

The first thing I saw when I returned to clean their house were my three
skirts, pinned and draped across the ironing board.

How suddenly grievances against father evaporate, steam rising from
an icy river. He even corrects himself, calling mother, *a woman*.

Why is pain deeper than pleasure, though it is a pleasure to cry so loud 50
the arthritic dog hobbles off the sunny carpet, so loud I do not hear the
phone ring, so loud I feel a passion for mother I thought I reserved for
lovers. I insert a CD and sing about a love abandoned, because there
are no other lyrics for this.

Pulling off a crewneck sweater I bend my glasses and for the next few   55
days wear the frames off-center not realizing the dizzy view is in fact
physical.

Theresa, David, Liz, Mark, Sharon, Denise, Carmen, Sonia, Susan, Lee,
Cheryl, Susan, Jo, John, Jerry, Doug, Earlene, Marie, Robbin, Jessica,
Kiana, Patricia, Bob, Donna, Orinne, Shigemi—   60

Suddenly the tasks we put off need to get done: defrost the freezer, pay
the preschool bill, order more checks.

For 49 days after her own mother's death she did not eat meat. I didn't
know, mother. I'm sorry, I didn't know.

The sudden scent of her spills from her handbag—leather, lotion,   65
mints, coins. I cannot stand.

She had marked April 28 to see Okinawan dancers.

He has not yet slept in their bed, because the couch in front of the
television *feels firmer* to his seven broken ribs.

At dinner we play a story game; the younger one asks, "about   70
grandma?" then corrects herself quickly "about bunny rabbit" as she
momentarily trips on her own preoccupation.

Father tells me there is a Japanese story about a mask maker who has a
daughter renowned for her stunning beauty. Upon her untimely death,

how he does not recall, the father sits by her side to sketch the exquisite 75
features. Poetic license. Though mother did look beautiful I had never
seen a face devoid of any expression, an aspect even a painting would
somehow contain.
The children notice he has taken off his wedding ring.

At a favorite cafe I hear a newborn in the next booth wailing for, probably, 80
the mother's breast, as if his life will end this second. It is my cry.

Shrimp. An image of my parents at a card table shelling shrimp the
night before my sister's wedding, the peels translucent pink as my
mother's fingernails. Primitive and reassuring.

At the house in Paia where grandma washed other people's laundry 85
and raised her chickens, and grandpa sat in his wheelchair, we had a
toilet inside but also the old outhouse, a rickety two-seater. I would go
in, close the gray-painted door, latch the hook and sit on the edge
holding my breath against the frothy stench of shit. You could hear
your waste
hit bottom. The dim light lent privacy against peeping cousins. 90

She taught me to pluck or cut flowers near the roots for the long stems.
Recut under water. She taught me to rub my finger and thumb together
over the silver dollar sheath, to rub off the brown membrane and
scatter the seeds on my skirt. Gently so as not to tear the silver inside. I
see them and think of her name, not Maude, but Mother. 95

Father and I bring the ashes into the City and plan to drop them off at
the temple. Mrs. K has Buddhist robes over her blue jeans and suggests
she recite a sutra. We light incense in the half-light. I forget tissues. My
face and sleeves are covered with tears and mucus. My shoulders shake
silently as listening. 100

Three months have past. I count the days from March 10th to the 100th
day for another memorial service.

lotus suture

As if a metaphor for mother's death the Rodney King verdict and
rebellion in Los Angeles breaks open urban areas across the country. It 105
is a complex set of issues where some Korean shops and whites are
attacked as the emblems of the establishment. But what is the
establishment? Why not the actual property relations? Who actually
owns the buildings, makes the laws—I feel helpless. Embittered.

Cuttings she had placed in tumblers in the kitchen and bathroom offer 110
their fragile roots.

Rei discusses mother's death with me. A babysitter told her not to talk about it. Another told her it is *like sleep*. I tell her to talk. I tell her it is not sleep although the person looks asleep but he or she will not wake. She wants to talk to grandma and asks if she can. I tell her if she wants 115 to she can; then I ask her what she wants to say. She wants to tell her to wake up.

People who have died but were revived speak of a dark tunnel with a fierce light at the end. Is it a passage or is it the memory of birth?

Miya speaks of dying—to see grandma again. I am shocked and try to 120 say something.

I can see her body, not *her*, her body lying in a pine box, hands folded, black and white hair combed back, the funeral home odor saturating the drapes and carpets of the respectfully lit parlors. I said goodbye but it was really *to myself*. 125

I wish I had snipped off a bit of hair. I recall the braid she kept for a while in her drawer.

I purchase an expensive "anti-wrinkle defense cream" at the discount pharmacy. The third morning my skin really feels smoother though the burgeoning lines have not faded. I think something I've only thought 130 the night before the plane trip: will I live to see the bottom of this jar.

Miya has shelved her grief and when admonished she declares: everything was fine until grandma died.

For the first time father harvests a half-dozen bamboo shoots from a small grove on the side of the house. Mother had spoken of gathering 135 them as a child in Hawaii, soaking then boiling then sizzling them. He finds a recipe and experiments. He sends some home with me. They taste like artichoke hearts. We all think of mother. And I think of a poem from the *Manyōshu* about a trowel.

He plays her lottery numbers. 140

The lawyer of the kid who broadsided their car sends a letter threatening to sue father if he does not respond in five days with information. We feel naive, in a state of disbelief at the vulgar tone of the letter.

I wear the silk pants she altered for me: a forgotten pin, sewn into the 145 hem, sticks into my ankle.

At any moment of the day I can hear her admonishment: *oh, Kimi.* She especially disliked spills.

I do not want to write about her death. But I do not want to lose these strong feelings.   150
Rei does not stop chattering about her: We have no one to make slush. She always had gum in her handbag. She read to us in Japanese and knew "cat's cradle" backward.

The 100th Day Anniversary. The weather is already warm. Her brother from Honolulu tells about her letters to him during World War II when   155 he was in the 442nd.

We vacation on Fire Island. A few deer walk by the porch so close we can see how fuzzy their antlers are.

I keep recalling the diagram of the accident scene. Mother's body lying on the highway where medics attempted CPR. I imagine the wet black   160 road, the traffic signals changing despite the halt.

Christmas ornaments last packed away by her: the balls she and father decorated with cherubs and glitter, old wooden angels and soldiers from my childhood, tinsel carefully rewrapped.

Some days I have a thought to write down but let it go.   165

During a week-long visit to the snowy fields of Vermont, I hear of a car bomb explosion at the World Trade Center, killing and injuring many people. The world continues outside this quiet. And the death of those who happen to step in its ordinary traffic.

I stop writing altogether. And when I must—postcards, single lines   170 after a commute—the writing ends with mother.

Afraid father is "seeing someone" and hopeful. I extend mother's jealousy into the afterlife. It becomes my own hell.

I begin to feel impatient with father over little things like whether my hair is trimmed evenly. I wonder if my annoyance indicates we are   175 moving on.

Father finds an envelope of marigold seeds mother saved and lets the children scatter them. The composted earth smells fertile like the pail she kept with egg shells and melon rinds.

1995

NAOMI SHIHAB NYE

B. 1952

At the age of six, as Naomi Shihab Nye learned how to write, she began creating poems. She published her first poem one year later in a children's magazine, *Wee Wisdom*. She was encouraged by her mother, who read poetry to her, and later by a teacher, who asked students to memorize lines of William Blake and Langston Hughes.

Naomi and her brother grew up in a bicultural home, born to a German American mother and a Palestinian American father. Although her mother was raised Lutheran and her father Muslim, they sent her to Unity Sunday School as well as the Vedanta Society of St. Louis to study Hinduism, where the swami modeled the value of peace in his teachings.

In 1966 her family sold its business and moved to the Middle East, to a town eight miles north of Jerusalem, then located inside the borders of Jordan. There her father edited the *Jerusalem Times*, for which his fourteen-year-old daughter wrote a weekly column and often composed letters to the editor. Until this move, the Shihab home heard only fragments of Arabic. Yet the language and the oral narratives shared by her father and her grandmother, Sitta Khadara, left an indelible imprint on some of Nye's most important writing. Stories that punctuated the headlines also left a lasting impression on her poetry and prose, as did the history behind her father's emigration to the United States.

The way that historical events affect people's daily lives is an important theme in Nye's writing, shaped largely by a familial legacy of dispossession. Sitti Khadara became a refugee in 1948, when she lost her home in Jerusalem to Israeli settlers. And just a year after the Shihabs moved to the Middle East, Naomi and her family had to flee Jerusalem on the eve of the Six Day War. Upon returning to the United States, the Shihabs moved to Texas, where Naomi found herself homesick for Palestine—for the muezzin, the olive groves, and her grandmother's stories. She continued to weave those narratives into images at Trinity University in San Antonio, where she received her bachelor's degree in 1974.

The borderland culture of Texas provides Nye with striking thematic parallels of invisible and dispossessed peoples. In "Where the Soft Air Lives," her images of events and people in the Southwest often double as allusions to the circumstances that Palestinians in the diaspora face: "There is no border in the sky," a Mexican woman observes. A product of Texas, where Nye has spent the bulk of her life with her husband and son, she has been profoundly influenced by Latino/a and Native American art and literature.

Nye's poems blend lyricism and realism as a way of poetically documenting stories that would otherwise be rendered invisible. Her work has a reportorial tone but manages to portray what newspapers cannot. Images of healing accent her poem, "Blood," in which the speaker's father reveals her Arab ethnicity and her relationship to the world around her as it appears in "the headlines [which] clot in my blood." With these images, Nye bears witness to the suffering of the people in her poems. She intervenes in the headlines, using poetry to ease tensions in the world by recognizing one another's humanity, as, for example, in "Ducks," which represents daily life in Iraq before and after the war.

Her grandmother and father often are the vehicles through which Nye humanizes Arab people in her writing. In "My Father and the Figtree," she reminisces about the folktales that feature Johan, a trickster figure, and figs, which symbolize the Palestinian land that her father left behind. When her grandmother figures as a character in the poem "The Words under the Words," Nye details the pain of displacement and diaspora and the power of words and storytelling to travel across those distances among relatives.

Humanizing people who are often dehumanized in the media and history is a standard feature of Nye's poetry and prose. Many of the works that she has translated and written are for children, a way to encourage her younger audience to see similarities across the visible differences. *Sitti's Secret* is a picture book that features a young girl who lives in the United States and who misses her grandmother in Palestine. For young adult readers, Nye wrote a novel, *Habibi*, that draws on her experience as a fourteen-year-old in Jerusalem. In San Antonio, Nye continues to write for children and adults and conducts writing workshops for the Writers in the Schools program and for the Texas Commission on the Arts to increase literacy and writing for children and teenagers. Her work with children has also generated a rich body of translation work about Mexico and the Middle East. In collaboration with translators, poets, and artists from these regions, Nye has published two volumes of poetry and art aimed at helping children enjoy poetry while dispelling stereotypes.

Marcy Jane Knopf-Newman
Boise State University

PRIMARY WORKS

Different Ways to Pray: Poems, 1980; *Hugging the Jukebox*, 1982; *Yellow Glove*, 1986; *Fuel: Poems*, 1988; *Travel Alarm*, 1993; *Red Suitcase: Poems*, 1994; *Sitti's Secrets*, 1994; *Words under the Words: Selected Poems*, 1995; *Never in a Hurry: Essays on People and Places*, 1996; *Habibi*, 1997; *What Holds Us Up: Poems*, 2000; *Mint Snowball*, 2001; *19 Varieties of Gazelle*, 2002; *You and Yours*, 2005; *There Is No Long Distance Now*, 2011.

Ducks

We thought of ourselves as people of culture.
How long will it be till others see us that way again?

—Iraqi friend

In her first home each book had a light around it.
The voices of distant countries
floated in through open windows,
entering her soup and her mirror.
They slept with her in the same thick bed.   5

Someday she would go there.
Her voice, among all those voices.

In Iraq a book never had one owner—it had ten.
Lucky books, to be held often
and gently, by so many hands.   10

Later in American libraries she felt sad
for books no one ever checked out.

She lived in a country house beside a pond
and kept ducks, two male, one female.
She worried over the difficult relations   15
of triangles. One of the ducks
often seemed depressed.
But not the same one.

During the war between her two countries
she watched the ducks more than usual.   20
She stayed quiet with the ducks.
Some days they huddled among reeds
or floated together.

She could not call her family in Basra
which had grown farther away than ever   25
nor could they call her. For nearly a year
she would not know who was alive,
who was dead.

The ducks were building a nest.

                                                                 1994

Different Ways to Pray

There was the method of kneeling,
a fine method, if you lived in a country
where stones were smooth.
The women dreamed wistfully of bleached courtyards,
hidden corners where knee fit rock.   5
Their prayers were weathered rib bones,
small calcium words uttered in sequence,
as if this shedding of syllables could somehow
fuse them to the sky.

There were the men who had been shepherds so long   10
they walked like sheep.
Under the olive trees, they raised their arms—
Hear us! We have pain on earth!

We have so much pain there is no place to store it!
But the olives bobbed peacefully   15
in fragrant buckets of vinegar and thyme.
At night the men ate heartily, flat bread and white cheese,
and were happy in spite of the pain,
because there was also happiness.
Some prized the pilgrimage,   20
wrapping themselves in new white linen
to ride buses across miles of vacant sand.
When they arrived at Mecca
they would circle the holy places,
on foot, many times,   25
they would bend to kiss the earth
and return, their lean faces housing mystery.

While for certain cousins and grandmothers
the pilgrimage occurred daily,
lugging water from the spring   30
or balancing the baskets of grapes.
These were the ones present at births,
humming quietly to perspiring mothers.
The ones stitching intricate needlework into children's dresses,
forgetting how easily children soil clothes.   35

There were those who didn't care about praying.
The young ones. The ones who had been to America.
They told the old ones, you are wasting your time.
        Time?—The old ones prayed for the young ones.
They prayed for Allah to mend their brains,   40
for the twig, the round moon,
to speak suddenly in a commanding tone.

And occasionally there would be one
who did none of this,
the old man Fowzi, for example, Fowzi the fool,   45
who beat everyone at dominoes,
insisted he spoke with God as he spoke with goats,
and was famous for his laugh.

                                                                   1994

My Father and the Figtree

For other fruits my father was indifferent.
He'd point at the cherry trees and say,
"See those? I wish they were figs."

In the evening he sat by my bed
weaving folktales like livid little scarves.   5
They always involved a figtree.
Even when it didn't fit, he'd stick it in.
Once Joha was walking down the road and he saw a figtree.
Or, he tied his camel to a figtree and went to sleep.
Or, later when they caught and arrested him,   10
his pockets were full of figs.

At age six I ate a dried fig and shrugged.
"That's not what I'm talking about!" he said,
"I'm talking about a fig straight from the earth—
gift of Allah!—on a branch so heavy it touches the ground.   15
I'm talking about picking the largest fattest sweetest fig
in the world and putting it in my mouth."
(Here he'd stop and close his eyes.)

Years passed, we lived in many houses, none had figtrees.
We had lima beans, zucchini, parsley, beets.   20
"Plant one!" my mother said, but my father never did.
He tended garden half-heartedly, forgot to water,
let the okra get too big.
"What a dreamer he is. Look how many things he starts
and doesn't finish."   25

The last time he moved, I got a phone call.
My father, in Arabic, chanting a song I'd never heard.
"What's that?"
"Wait till you see!"
He took me out to the new yard.   30
There, in the middle of Dallas, Texas,
a tree with the largest, fattest, sweetest figs in the world.
"It's a figtree song!" he said,
plucking his fruits like ripe tokens,
emblems, assurance   35
of a world that was always his own.

          1997

Blood

"A true Arab knows how to catch a fly in his hands,"
my father would say. And he'd prove it,
cupping the buzzer instantly
while the host with the swatter stared.

In the spring our palms peeled like snakes. 5
True Arabs believed watermelon could heal fifty ways.
I changed these to fit the occasion.

Years before, a girl knocked,
wanted to see the Arab.
I said we didn't have one. 10
After that, my father told me who he was,
"Shihab"—"shooting star"—
a good name, borrowed from the sky.
Once I said, "When we die, we give it back?"
He said that's what a true Arab would say. 15

Today the headlines clot in my blood.
A little Palestinian dangles a truck on the front page.
Homeless fig, this tragedy with a terrible root
is too big for us. What flag can we wave?
I wave the flag of stone and seed, 20
table mat stitched in blue.

I call my father, we talk around the news.
It is too much for him,
neither of his two languages can reach it.
I drive into the country to find sheep, cows, 25
to plead with the air:
Who calls anyone *civilized*?
Where can the crying heart graze?
What does a true Arab do now?

1997

Where the Soft Air Lives

*"Meanwhile Dean and I went out to dig the streets of Mexican San Antonio.
It was fragrant and soft—the softest air I'd ever known—and dark, and
mysterious, and buzzing. Sudden figures of girls in white bandannas
appeared in the humming dark."*

—*Jack Kerouac,* On the Road

1.

She placed her babies in the sink
stroking off the heat with an old damp rag.
Coo-coo little birdies, she sang,
then she tied the hair up in ponytails
pointing to the moon. It made them look 5
like little fruits with a pointed end.

She said, You don't think about poverty
till someone comes over.

2.

The man on Guadalupe Street is
guarding the cars. On his porch   10
the lights of Virgin Mary flash
endlessly, prayer-time, vigilante,
he rocks with his wife every night
rocking, while the bakery seals its cases
of pumpkin tart and the boys   15
with T-shirts slashed off below the nipples
strut big as buses past his gate.
He is keeping an eye on them.
And on fenders, hubcaps,
a grocery cart let loose   20
and lodged against a fence.
Cars roar past, but they will have
to got home again. He is happy
in this life, blinking Mother of God,
his wife placing one curl of mint in the tea,   25
saying always the same line,
Is it sweet enough? and the porch
painted three shades of green.

3.

I mended my ways, he said.
I took a needle and big thread and mended them.   30
You would not know me to see me now.
Sometimes I see myself sweeping the yard,
watering the dog, and I think
who is that guy? He looks like an old guy.
He looks like a guy who tells you   35
fifteen dead stories and mixes them up.
So that explains it:
why I don't tell you nuthin.

4.

She feeds her roses coffee
to make them huge. When her son was in Vietnam   40
the bougainvillea turned black once overnight.
But he didn't die. She prescribes lemongrass,
manzanilla: in her album the grandchildren smile like seed packets.

She raises the American flag on her pole
because she is her own Mexican flag   45
and the wind fluttering the hem of her dress
says there is no border in the sky.

5.

Lisa's husband left, so she dyed her hair
a different color every day. Once pale silk,
next morning, a flame. She shaped her nails,   50
wore a nightgown cut down so low
the great canyon between her bosoms
woke up the mailman dragging his bag.
She pulled the bed into the dining room,
placed it dead center, never went out.   55
TV, eyelash glue, pools of perfume.
She was waiting for the plumber,
the man who sprays the bugs. Waiting
to pay a newspaper bill, to open her arms,
unroll all her front pages   60
and the sad unread sections too,
the ads for bacon and cleanser,
the way they try to get you to come to the store
by doubling your coupons,
the way they line the ads in red.   65

6.

Air filled with hearts,
we pin them to our tongues,
follow the soft air back to its cave
between tires, river of air
pouring warm speech, two-colored speech   70
into the streets. *Make a house
and live in it.*

At the Mission Espada
the priest keeps a little goat
tied to a stump.   75
His people come slowly out
of the stone-white room,
come lifting their feet suddenly heavy,
trying to remember far back before
anything had happened twice.   80
Someone lit a candle, and it caught.
A girl in a white dress,

singing in a window.
And you were getting married,
getting born, seeing the slice of blue　　　　　　　85
that meant *shore*;
the goat rises,
his bitten patch of land around him.
The priest bends to touch his head.
And goes off somewhere.　　　　　　　　　　　　90
But the air behind him
still holding that hand, and the little goat
still standing.

　　　　　　　　　　　　　　　　　　　　　　1997

EDWIDGE DANTICAT
B. 1969

In the epilogue to her short story collection *Krik? Krak!* (1995), Edwidge Danticat explains, "When you write, it's like braiding your hair. Taking a handful of coarse unruly strands and attempting to bring them unity." In a variety of literary forms, Danticat deftly weaves tales of Haiti, her country of origin, with her experiences as a young emigrant to the United States, rendering the pain of cultural dislocation with compelling poetic restraint. Born in Port-au-Prince, Danticat was raised by an uncle, who was a Baptist minister, and an aunt because both of her parents had relocated to New York by the time Danticat was four years old. Although her home was in the Haitian capital, she spent summers with extended family in the countryside, an experience that would influence her literary representation of women's work, storytelling, and domestic relationships. In 1981 Danticat and two of her brothers left Haiti to join their parents, and as an adolescent in Brooklyn she found some difficulty bridging the cultural divide between American and Haitian experience. She describes the hostility toward Haitians from American youth who associated the country unfairly with refugees and the AIDS crisis: "It was very hard. 'Haitian' was like a curse." In high school, Danticat's anxiety about her accent prevented her from speaking in full voice, but she soon discovered the rewards of mediating between Creole and English: "You have to take some things from one culture and combine them with another to create a common language. That merging becomes creative."

After graduating from Barnard College in 1990 with a degree in French literature, Danticat enrolled in the masters of fine arts program at Brown University. Her thesis was an early draft on her first novel, *Breath, Eyes, Memory* (1994), the story of a young Haitian woman's emigration to New York to join her mother. *The New York Times Book Review* exclaimed that its "calm clarity of vision takes on the resonance of folk art" and praised the novel's "extraordinary ambitious" thematic complexity and "extraordinarily successful" execution. However, the Haitian American middle class took issue with the text's depiction of virginity-testing practices, and Danticat found herself defending what she calls the "singularity" of the protagonist's story.

After Brown University, Danticat returned to the East Flatbush section of Brooklyn and worked for a time under the film director Jonathan Demme. The stories in her next publication, *Krik? Krak!*, a National Book Award finalist, focus on personal and domestic relationships in Haiti and in the United States. *The New York Times Book Review* declared that "the best of these stories humanize, particularize, give poignancy to the lives of people we may have come to think of as faceless emblems of misery, poverty and brutality." With an impressive range of attention, the tales recount Haitian emigrant deaths at sea, the artistic and economic ambitions of the working class, and the intricate cultural expectations among Haitian American families. In "New York Day Women," the young narrator struggles to understand her mother and her family's Haitian roots as she tracks her mother on a walk through midtown Manhattan. At each turn the narrator reflects on her mother's history, folkways, and advice, recognizing finally the dignity of her mother's experience and acknowledging her mother's participation in a community of displaced immigrant women.

Danticat's second novel, *The Farming of Bones* (1998), an American Book Award winner, diverges from her previous work to explore a particular historical incident: the 1937 massacre of Haitians at the border with the Dominican Republic. This text connects with Danticat's other work in its emphasis on the protagonist's cultural liminality, since she lives in close contact with Dominicans, and in its exploration of working-class Haitian subjectivity. Her novel for young adults, *Behind the Mountains* (2002), returns to the subject of Haitian emigration as its protagonist adjusts to a new life in New York. *After the Dance* (2002) is a travel narrative, describing Carnival celebrations in Jacmel, Haiti. Danticat is also an active editor, most prominently of *The Butterfly's Way: Voices from the Haitian Dyaspora in the United States* (2001). She returned to the short story in *The Dew Breaker* (2004), a collection that focuses on a man who worked as a torturer under François Duvalier. The collection's nine stories all rotate around this "dew breaker" as Danticat explores the possibility of reinvention and liberation in America. *The Washington Post Book World* hailed *The Dew Breaker* as "a brilliant book, undoubtedly the best one yet by an enormously talented writer." Because of her powerful renderings of Haitian American politics and customs, Danticat has been acclaimed as the culture's spokesperson. She balks at that role, insisting, "I don't really see myself as the voice for the Haitian-American experience. There are many. I'm just one."

Katharine Capshaw Smith
University of Connecticut

PRIMARY WORKS

Breath, Eyes, Memory, 1994; *Krik? Krak!*, 1995; *The Farming of Bones*, 1998; *The Butterfly's Way: Voices from the Haitian Dyaspora in the United States* (editor), 2001; *Behind the Mountains*, 2002; *After the Dance: A Walk through Carnival in Jacmel, Haiti*, 2002; *The Dew Breaker*, 2004; *Brother, I'm Dying*, 2007.

New York Day Women

Today, walking down the street, I see my mother. She is strolling with a happy gait, her body thrust toward the DON'T WALK sign and the yellow taxicabs that make forty-five-degree turns on the corner of Madison and Fifty-seventh Street.

I have never seen her in this kind of neighborhood, peering in Chanel and Tiffany's and gawking at the jewels glowing in the Bulgari windows. My mother never shops outside of Brooklyn. She has never seen the advertising office where I work. She is afraid to take the subway, where you may meet those young black militant street preachers who curse black women for straightening their hair.

Yet, here she is, my mother, who I left at home that morning in her bathrobe, with pieces of newspapers twisted like rollers in her hair. My mother, who accuses me of random offenses as I dash out of the house.

Would you get up and give an old lady like me your subway seat? In this state of mind, I bet you don't even give up your seat to a pregnant lady.

My mother, who is often right about that. Sometimes I get up and give my seat. Other times, I don't. It all depends on how pregnant the woman is and whether or not she is with her boyfriend or husband and whether or not *he* is sitting down.

As my mother stands in front of Carnegie Hall, one taxi driver yells to another, "What do you think this is, a dance floor?"

My mother waits patiently for this dispute to be settled before crossing the street.

In Haiti when you get hit by a car, the owner of the car gets out and kicks you for getting blood on his bumper.

My mother who laughs when she says this and shows the large gap in her mouth where she lost three more molars to the dentist last week. My mother, who at fifty-nine, says dentures are okay.

You can take them out when they bother you. I'll like them. I'll like them fine.

Will it feel empty when Papa kisses you?

Oh no, he doesn't kiss me that way anymore.

My mother, who watches the lottery drawing every night on channel 11 without ever having played the numbers.

A third of that money is all I would need. We would pay the mortgage, and your father could stop driving that taxicab all over Brooklyn.

I follow my mother, mesmerized by the many possibilities of her journey. Even in a flowered dress, she is lost in a sea of pinstripes and gray suits, high heels and elegant short skirts, Reebok sneakers, dashing from building to building.

My mother, who won't go out to dinner with anyone.

If they want to eat with me, let them come to my house, even if I boil water and give it to them.

My mother, who talks to herself when she peels the skin off poultry.

Fat, you know, and cholesterol. Fat and cholesterol killed your aunt Hermine.

My mother, who makes jam with grapefruit peel and then puts in cinnamon bark that I always think is cockroaches in the jam. My mother, whom I have always bought household appliances for, on her birthday. A nice rice cooker, a blender.

I trail the red orchids in her dress and the heavy faux leather bag on her shoulders. Realizing the ferocious pace of my pursuit, I stop against a wall to rest. My mother keeps on walking as though she owns the sidewalk under her feet.

As she heads toward the Plaza Hotel, a bicycle messenger swings so close to her that I want to dash forward and rescue her, but she stands dead in her tracks and lets him ride around her and then goes on.

My mother stops at a corner hot-dog stand and asks for something. The vendor hands her a can of soda that she slips into her bag. She stops by another vendor selling sundresses for seven dollars each. I can tell that she is looking at an African print dress, contemplating my size. I think to myself, Please Ma, don't buy it. It would be just another thing that I would bury in the garage or give to Goodwill.

Why should we give to Goodwill when there are so many people back home who need clothes? We save our clothes for the relatives in Haiti.

Twenty years we have been saving all kinds of things for the relatives in Haiti. I need the place in the garage for an exercise bike.

You are pretty enough to be a stewardess. Only dogs like bones.

This mother of mine, she stops at another hot-dog vendor's and buys a frankfurter that she eats on the street. I never knew that she ate frankfurters. With her blood pressure, she shouldn't eat anything with so-dium. She has to be careful with her heart, this day woman.

I cannot just swallow salt. Salt is heavier than a hundred bags of shame.

She is slowing her pace, and now I am too close. If she turns around, she might see me. I let her walk into the park before I start to follow.

My mother walks toward the sandbox in the middle of the park. There a woman is waiting with a child. The woman is wearing a leotard with biker's shorts and has small weights in her hands. The woman kisses the child good-bye and surrenders him to my mother; then she bolts off, running on the cemented stretches in the park.

The child given to my mother has frizzy blond hair. His hand slips into hers easily, like he's known her for a long time. When he raises his face to look at my mother, it is as though he is looking at the sky.

My mother gives the child the soda that she bought from the vendor on the street corner. The child's face lights up as she puts in a straw in the can for him. This seems to be a conspiracy just between the two of them.

My mother and the child sit and watch the other children play in the sandbox. The child pulls out a comic book from a knapsack with Big Bird on the back. My mother peers into his comic book. My mother, who taught her-self to read as a little girl in Haiti from the books that her brothers brought home from school.

My mother, who has now lost six of her seven sisters in Ville Rose and has never had the strength to return for their funerals.

Many graves to kiss when I go back. Many graves to kiss.

She throws away the empty soda can when the child is done with it. I wait and watch from a corner until the woman in the leotard and biker's shorts returns, sweaty and breathless, an hour later. My mother gives the woman her child back and strolls farther into the park.

I turn around and start to walk out of the park before my mother can see me. My lunch hour is long since gone. I have to hurry back to work. I walk through a cluster of joggers, then race to a *Sweden Tours* bus. I stand behind the bus and take a peek at my mother in the park. She is standing in a circle, chatting with a group of women who are taking other people's chil-dren on an afternoon outing. They look like a Third World Parent-Teacher Association meeting.

I quickly jump into a cab heading back to the office. Would Ma have said hello had she been the one to see me first?

As the cab races away from the park, it occurs to me that perhaps one day I would chase an old woman down a street by mistake and that old woman would be somebody else's mother, who I would have mistaken for mine.

Day women come out when nobody expects them.

Tonight on the subway, I will get up and give my seat to a pregnant woman or a lady about Ma's age.

My mother, who stuffs thimbles in her mouth and then blows up her cheeks like Dizzy Gillespie while sewing yet another Raggedy Ann doll that she names Suzette after me.

I will have all these little Suzettes in case you never have any babies, which looks more and more like it is going to happen.

My mother who had me when she was thirty-three—*l'âge du Christ*—at the age that Christ died on the cross.

That's a blessing, believe you me, even if American doctors say by that time you can make retarded babies.

My mother, who sews lace collars on my company softball T-shirts when she does my laundry.

Why, you can't you look like a lady playing softball?

My mother, who never went to any of my Parent-Teacher Association meetings when I was in school.

You're so good anyway. What are they going to tell me? I don't want to make you ashamed of this day woman. Shame is heavier than a hundred bags of salt.

1995

CHANG-RAE LEE
B. 1965

Chang-rae Lee is not only the best-known Korean American writer but also one of the most acclaimed contemporary American novelists today. Although he is still at the beginning of his literary career, he has received numerous honors for his work, including the Hemingway Foundation/PEN Award, the American Book Award, and the Anisfield-Wolf Book Award. In addition, Lee has been hailed as one of the most accomplished young writers by two venerable literary magazines. *The New Yorker* identified him as one of twenty most important American writers younger than forty, and *Granta* selected him as a finalist for its list of best young American writers. He has written four novels: *Native Speaker* (1995), *A Gesture Life* (1999), *Aloft* (2004), and *The Surrendered* (2010).

Born in Seoul, South Korea, in 1965, Lee came to the United States with his family in 1968. He attended Yale University, where he majored in English and graduated with a B.A. degree in 1987. After college, Lee worked on Wall Street but left his job to concentrate on writing. He enrolled in the M.F.A. program at the University of Oregon and submitted a draft of *Native Speaker*, his first novel, as his thesis. He now teaches creative writing at Princeton University and lives in New Jersey with his wife and two daughters.

Lee's work explores the themes of identity and alienation. His two earlier novels, *Native Speaker* and *A Gesture Life*, focus on the plight of being an outsider in a community, particularly the marginalized existence of Asian immigrant families in the United States. Although the emphasis of Lee's third novel, *Aloft*, which is about the life of an Italian American suburbanite, represents a departure from the subject matter of the previous works, the theme of emotional detachment remains. His well-received, ambitious fourth novel, *The Surrendered*, is a return to his original subject matter as it focuses on the life of an orphan of the Korean War who has immigrated to America.

Lee is celebrated for his elegant, elliptical prose and his delicately understated rendering of powerful emotional experiences, traits that are evident in his memoir, "Coming Home Again." In this carefully crafted piece, Lee writes poignantly about his mother and her untimely death from stomach cancer. While much of the essay is devoted to the writer's memories of the Korean dishes that his mother prepared during her lifetime, food signifies more broadly as a symbol of participation within the family and larger social groups. The preparation and consumption of food signal the shifts in the son's relationship with his mother.

Lee's memoir details the complex and often painful negotiations that inevitably occur in the parent-child relationship when the children begin to make their way to adulthood and when the parents cope with illness and death. Cutting back and forth in time, the essay juxtaposes the son's grief at his mother's death with the mother's sorrow at the son's departure for boarding school, an event that marks the growing distance between her and her child. Lee's deftly nuanced depiction of alienation is his noteworthy contribution to American literature.

Grace H. Park
University of California, Los Angeles

PRIMARY WORKS

Native Speaker, 1995; *A Gesture Life*, 1999; *Aloft*, 2004; *The Surrendered*, 2010.

Coming Home Again

When my mother began using the electronic pump that fed her liquids and medication, we moved her to the family room. The bedroom she shared with my father was upstairs, and it was impossible to carry the machine up and down all day and night. The pump itself was attached to a metal stand on casters, and she pulled it along wherever she went. From anywhere in the house, you could hear the sound of the wheels clicking out a steady time over the grout lines of the slate-tiled foyer, her main thoroughfare to the bathroom and the kitchen. Sometimes you would hear her halt after only a few steps, to catch her breath or steady her balance, and whatever you were doing was instantly suspended by a pall of silence.

I was usually in the kitchen, preparing lunch or dinner, poised over the butcher block with her favorite chef's knife in my hand and her old yellow apron slung around my neck. I'd be breathless in the sudden quiet, and, having ceased my mincing and chopping would stare blankly at the brushed sheen of the blade. Eventually, she would clear her throat or call out to say she was fine, then begin to move again, starting her rhythmic *ka-jug;* and only then could I go on with my cooking, the world of our house turning once more, wheeling through the black.

I wasn't cooking for my mother but for the rest of us. When she first moved downstairs she was still eating, though scantily, more just to taste what we were having than from any genuine desire for food. The point was simply to sit together at the kitchen table and array ourselves like a family again. My mother would gently set herself down in her customary chair near the stove. I sat across from her, my father and sister to my left and right, and crammed in the center was all the food I had made—a spicy codfish stew, say, or a casserole of gingery beef, dishes that in my youth she had prepared for us a hundred times.

It had been ten years since we'd all lived together in the house, which at fifteen I had left to attend boarding school in New Hampshire. My mother would sometimes point this out, by speaking of our present time as being "just like before Exeter," which surprised me, given how proud she always was that I was a graduate of the school.

My going to such a place was part of my mother's not so secret plan to change my character, which she worried was becoming too much like hers. I was clever and able enough, but without outside pressure I was readily given to sloth and vanity. The famous school—which none of us knew the first thing about—would prove my mettle. She was right, of course, and while I was there I would falter more than a few times, academically and otherwise. But I never thought that my leaving home then would ever be a problem for her, a private quarrel she would have even as her life waned.

Now her house was full again. My sister had just resigned from her job in New York City, and my father, who typically saw his psychiatric patients until eight or nine in the evening, was appearing in the driveway at four-thirty. I had been living at home for nearly a year and was in the final push of work on what would prove a dismal failure of a novel. When I wasn't struggling over my prose, I kept occupied with the things she usually did—the daily errands, the grocery shopping, the vacuuming and the cleaning, and, of course, all the cooking.

When I was six or seven years old, I used to watch my mother as she prepared our favorite meals. It was one of my daily pleasures. She shooed me away in the beginning, telling me that the kitchen wasn't my place, and adding, in her half-proud, half-deprecating way, that her kind of work would only serve to weaken me. "Go out and play with your friends," she'd snap in Korean, "or better yet, do your reading and homework." She knew that I had already done both and that as the evening approached there was no place to go save her small and tidy kitchen, from which the clatter of her mixing bowls and pans would ring through the house.

I would enter the kitchen quietly and stand beside her, my chin lodging upon the point of her hip. Peering through the crook of her arm, I beheld the movements of her hands. For *kalbi*, she would take up a butchered short rib in her narrow hand, the flinty bone shaped like a section of an airplane wing and deeply embedded in gristle and flesh, and with the point of her knife cut so that the bone fell away, though not completely, leaving it connected to the meat by the barest opaque layer of tendon. The she methodically butterflied the flesh, cutting and unfolding, repeating the action until the meat lay out on her board, glistening and ready for seasoning. She scored it diagonally, then sifted sugar into the crevices with her pinched fingers, gently rubbing in the crystals. The sugar would tenderize as well as sweeten the meat. She did this with each rib, and then set them all aside in a large shallow bowl. She minced a half-dozen cloves of garlic, a stub of gingerroot, sliced up a few scallions, and spread it all over the meat. She wiped her hands and took out a bottle of sesame oil, and, after pausing for a moment, streamed the dark oil in two swift circles around the bowl. After adding a few splashes of soy sauce, she thrust her hands in and kneaded the flesh, careful not to dislodge the bones. I asked her why it mattered that they remain connected. "The meat needs the bone nearby," she said, "to borrow its richness." She wiped her hands clean of the marinade, except for her little finger, which she would flick with her tongue from time to time, because she knew that the flavor of a good dish developed not at once but in stages.

Whenever I cook, I find myself working just as she would, readying the ingredients—a mash of garlic, a julienne of red peppers, fantails of shrimp—and piling them in little mounds about the cutting surface. My mother never left me any recipes, but this is how I learned to make her food, each dish coming not from a list or a card but from the aromatic spread of a board.

I've always thought it was particularly cruel that the cancer was in her stomach, and that for a long time at the end she couldn't eat. The last meal I made for her was on New Year's Eve, 1990. My sister suggested that instead of a rib roast or a bird, or the usual overflow of Korean food, we make all sorts of finger dishes that our mother might fancy and pick at.

We set the meal out on the glass coffee table in the family room. I prepared a tray of smoked-salmon canapés, fried some Korean bean cakes, and made a few other dishes I thought she might enjoy. My sister supervised me, arranging the platters, and then with some pomp carried each dish in to our parents. Finally, I brought out a bottle of champagne in a bucket of ice.

My mother had moved to the sofa and was sitting up, surveying the low table. "It looks pretty nice," she said. "I think I'm feeling hungry."

This made us all feel good, especially me, for I couldn't remember the last time she had felt any hunger or had eaten something I cooked. We began to eat. My mother picked up a piece of salmon toast and took a tiny corner in her mouth. She rolled it around for a moment and then pushed it out with the tip of her tongue, letting it fall back onto her plate. She swallowed hard, as if to quell a gag, then glanced up to see if we had noticed. Of course we all had. She attempted a bean cake, some cheese, and then a slice of fruit, but nothing was any use.

She nodded at me anyway, and said, "Oh, it's very good." But I was already feeling lost and I put down my plate abruptly, nearly shattering it on the thick glass. There was an ugly pause before my father asked me in a weary, gentle voice if anything was wrong, and I answered that it was nothing, it was the last night of a long year, and we were together, and I was simply relieved. At midnight, I poured out glasses of champagne, even one for my mother, who took a deep sip. Her manner grew playful and light, and I helped her shuffle to her mattress, and she lay down in the place where in a brief week she was dead.

My mother could whip up anything, but during our first years of living in this country we ate only Korean foods. At my harangue-like behest, my mother set herself to learning how to cook exotic American dishes. Luckily, a kind neighbor, Mrs. Churchill, a tall florid young woman with flaxen hair, taught my mother her most trusted recipes. Mrs. Churchill's two young sons, palish, weepy boys with identical crew cuts, always accompanied her, and though I liked them well enough, I would slip away from them after a few minutes, for I knew that the real action would be in the kitchen, where their mother was playing guide. Mrs. Churchill hailed from the state of Maine, where the finest Swedish meatballs and tuna casserole and angel food cake in America are made. She readily demonstrated certain techniques—how to layer wet sheets of pasta for a lasagna or whisk up a simple roux, for example. She often brought gift shoeboxes containing curious ingredients like dried oregano, instant yeast, and cream of mushroom soup. The two women, though at ease and jolly with each other, had difficulty communicating, and this was made worse by the often confusing terminology of Western cuisine ("corned beef," "deviled eggs"). Although I was just learning the language myself, I'd gladly play the interlocutor, jumping back and forth between their places at the counter, dipping my fingers into whatever sauce lay about.

I was an insistent child, and, being my mother's firstborn, much too prized. My mother could say no to me, and did often enough, but anyone who knew us—particularly my father and sister—could tell how much the denying pained her. And if I was overconscious of her indulgence even then, and suffered the rushing pangs of guilt that she could inflict upon me with the slightest wounded turn of her lip, I was too happily obtuse and venal to let her cease. She reminded me daily that I was her sole son, her reason for living, and that if she were to lose me, in either body or spirit, she wished God would mercifully smite her, strike her down like a weak branch.

In the traditional fashion, she was the house accountant, the maid, the launderer, the disciplinarian, the driver, the secretary, and, of course, the cook. She was also my first basketball coach. In South Korea, where girls' high school basketball is a popular spectator sport, she had been a star, the point guard for the national high school team that once won the all-Asia championship. I learned this one Saturday during the summer, when I asked my father if he would go down to the schoolyard and shoot some baskets with me. I had just finished the fifth grade, and wanted desperately to make the middle school team the coming fall. He called for my mother and sister to come along. When we arrived, my sister immediately ran off to the swings, and I recall being annoyed that my mother wasn't following her. I dribbled clumsily around the key, on the verge of losing control of the ball, and flung a flat shot that caromed wildly off the rim. The ball bounced to my father, who took a few not so graceful dribbles and made an easy layup. He dribbled out and then drove to the hoop for a layup on the other side. He rebounded his shot and passed the ball to my mother, who had been watching us from the foul line. She turned from the basket and began heading the other way.

"*Um-mah*," I cried at her, my exasperation already bubbling over, "the basket's over *here!*"

After a few steps she turned around, and from where the professional three-point line must be now, she effortlessly flipped the ball up in a two-handed set shot, its flight truer and higher than I'd witnessed from any boy or man. The ball arced cleanly into the hoop, stiffly popping the chain-link net. All afternoon, she rained in shot after shot, as my father and I scrambled after her.

When we got home from the playground, my mother showed me the photograph album of her team's championship run. For years I kept it in my room, on the same shelf that housed the scrapbooks I made of basketball stars, with magazine clippings of slick players like Bubbles Hawkins and Pistol Pete and George (the Iceman) Gervin.

It puzzled me how much she considered her own history to be immaterial, and if she never patently diminished herself, she was able to finesse a kind of self-removal by speaking of my father whenever she could. She zealously recounted his excellence as a student in medical school and reminded me, each night before I started my homework, of how hard he drove himself in his work to make a life for us. She said that because of his Asian face and imperfect English, he was "working two times the American doctors." I knew that she was building him up, buttressing him with both genuine admiration and her own brand of anxious braggadocio, and that her overarching concern was that I might fail to see him as she wished me to—in the most dawning light, his pose steadfast and solitary.

In the year before I left for Exeter, I became weary of her oft-repeated accounts of my father's success. I was a teenager, and so ever inclined to be dismissive and bitter toward anything that had to do with family and home. Often enough, my mother was the object of my derision. Suddenly, her life seemed so small to me. She was there, and sometimes, I thought, *always* there, as if she were confined to the four walls of our house. I would even complain about her cooking. Mostly, though, I was getting more and more impatient with the difficulty she encountered in doing everyday things. I was afraid for her. One day, we got into a terrible argument when she asked me to call the bank, to question a discrepancy she had discovered in the monthly statement. I asked her why she couldn't call herself. I was stupid and brutal, and I knew exactly how to wound her.

"Whom do I talk to?" she said. She would mostly speak to me in Korean, and I would answer in English.

"The bank manager, who else?"

"What do I say?"

"Whatever you want to say."

"Don't speak to me like that!" she cried.

"It's just that you should be able to do it yourself," I said.

"You know how I feel about this!"

"Well, maybe then you should consider it *practice*," I answered lightly, using the Korean word to make sure she understood.

Her face blanched, and her neck suddenly became rigid, as if I were throttling her. She nearly struck me right then, but instead she bit her lip and ran upstairs. I followed her, pleading for forgiveness at her door. But it was the one time in our life that I couldn't convince her, melt her resolve with the blandishments of a spoiled son.

When my mother was feeling strong enough, or was in particularly good spirits, she would roll her machine into the kitchen and sit at the table and watch me work. She wore pajamas day and night, mostly old pairs of mine.

She said, "I can't tell, what are you making?"

"*Mahn-doo* filling."

"You didn't salt the cabbage and squash."

"Was I supposed to?"

"Of course. Look, it's too wet. Now the skins will get soggy before you can fry them."

"What should I do?"

"It's too late. Maybe it'll be OK if you work quickly. Why didn't you ask me?"

"You were finally sleeping."

"You should have woken me."

"No way."

She sighed, as deeply as her weary lungs would allow.

"I don't know how you were going to make it without me."

"I don't know, either. I'll remember the salt next time."

"You better. And not too much."

We often talked like this, our tone decidedly matter-of-fact, chin up, just this side of being able to bear it. Once, while inspecting a potato fritter batter I was making, she asked me if she had ever done anything that I wished she hadn't done. I thought for a moment, and told her no. In the next breath, she wondered aloud if it was right of her to have let me go to Exeter, to live away from the house while I was so young. She tested the batter's thickness with her finger and called for more flour. Then she asked if, given a choice, I would go to Exeter again.

I wasn't sure what she was getting at, and I told her that I couldn't be certain, but probably yes, I would. She snorted at this and said it was my leaving home that had once so troubled our relationship. "Remember how I had so much difficulty talking to you? Remember?"

She believed back then that I had found her more and more ignorant each time I came home. She said she never blamed me, for this was the way she knew it would be with my wonderful new education. Nothing I could say seemed to quell the notion. But I knew that the problem wasn't simply the *education;* the first time I saw her again after starting school, barely six weeks later, when she and my father visited me on Parents Day, she had already grown nervous and distant. After the usual campus events, we had gone to the motel where they were staying in a nearby town and sat on the beds in our room. She seemed to sneak looks at me, as though I might discover a horrible new truth if our eyes should meet.

My own secret feeling was that I had missed my parents greatly, my mother especially, and much more than I had anticipated. I couldn't tell them that these first weeks were a mere blur to me, that I felt completely overwhelmed by all the studies and my much brighter friends and the thousand irritating details of living alone, and that I had really learned nothing, save perhaps how to put on a necktie while sprinting to class. I felt as if I had plunged too deep into the world, which, to my great horror, was much larger than I had ever imagined.

I welcomed the lull of the motel room. My father and I had nearly dozed off when my mother jumped up excitedly, murmured how stupid she was, and hurried to the closet by the door. She pulled out our old metal cooler and dragged it between the beds. She lifted the top and began unpacking plastic containers, and I thought she would never stop. One after the other they came out, each with a dish that traveled well—a salted stewed meat, rolls of Korean-style sushi. I opened a container of radish kimchi and suddenly the room bloomed with its odor, and I reveled in the very peculiar sensation (which perhaps only true kimchi lovers know) of simultaneously drooling and gagging as I breathed it all in. For the next few minutes, they watched me eat. I'm not certain that I was even hungry. But after weeks of pork parmigiana and chicken patties and wax beans, I suddenly realized that I had lost all the savor in my life. And it seemed I couldn't get enough of it back. I ate and I ate, so much and so fast that I actually went to the bathroom and vomited. I came out dizzy and sated with the phantom warmth of my binge.

And beneath the face of her worry, I thought my mother was smiling.

From that day, my mother prepared a certain meal to welcome me home. It was always the same. Even as I rode the school's shuttle bus from Exeter to Logan airport, I could already see the exact arrangement of my mother's table.

I knew that we would eat in the kitchen, the table brimming with plates. There was the *kalbi*, of course, broiled or grilled depending on the season. Leaf lettuce, to wrap the meat with. Bowls of garlicky clam broth with miso and tofu and fresh spinach. Shavings of cod dusted in flour and then dipped in egg wash and fried. Glass noodles with onions and shiitake. Scallion-and-hot-pepper pancakes. Chilled steamed shrimp. Seasoned salads of bean sprouts, spinach, and white radish. Crispy squares of seaweed. Steamed rice with barley and red beans. Homemade kimchi. It was all there—the old flavors I knew, the beautiful salt, the sweet, the excellent taste.

After the meal, my father and I talked about school, but I could never say enough for it to make any sense. My father would often recall his high school principal, who had gone to England to study the methods and traditions of the public schools, and regaled students with stories of the great Eton man. My mother sat with us, paring fruit, not saying a word but taking everything in. When it was time to go to bed, my father said good night first. I usually watched television until the early morning. My mother would sit with me for an hour or two, perhaps until she was accustomed to me again, and only then would she kiss me and head upstairs to sleep.

During the following days, it was always the cooking that started our conversations. She'd hold an inquest over the cold leftovers we ate at lunch, discussing each dish in terms of its balance of flavors or what might have been prepared differently. But mostly I begged her to leave the dishes alone. I wish I had paid more attention. After her death, when my father and I were the only ones left in the house, drifting through the rooms like ghosts, I sometimes tried to make that meal for him. Though it was too much for two, I made each dish anyway, taking as much care as I could. But nothing turned out quite right—not the color, not the smell. At the table, neither of us said much of anything. And we had to eat the food for days.

I remember washing rice in the kitchen one day and my mother's saying in English, from her usual seat, "I made a big mistake."

"About Exeter?"

"Yes. I made a big mistake. You should be with us for that time. I should never have let you go there."

"So why did you? I said.

"Because I didn't know I was going to die."

I let her words pass. For the first time in her life, she was letting herself speak her full mind, so what else could I do?

"But you know what?" she spoke up. "It was better for you. If you stayed home, you would not like me so much now."

I suggested that maybe I would like her even more.

She shook her head. "Impossible."

Sometimes I still think about what she said, about having made a mistake. I would have left home for college, that was never in doubt, but those years I was away at boarding school grew more precious to her as her illness progressed. After many months of exhaustion and pain and the haze of the drugs, I thought that her mind was beginning to fade, for more and more it seemed that she was seeing me again as her fifteen-year-old boy, the one she had dropped off in New Hampshire on a cloudy September afternoon.

I remember the first person I met, another new student, named Zack, who walked to the welcome picnic with me. I had planned to eat with my parents—my mother had brought a coolerful of food even that first day—but I learned of the cookout and told her that I should probably go. I wanted to go, of course. I was excited, and no doubt fearful and nervous, and I must have thought I was only thinking ahead. She agreed wholeheartedly, saying I certainly should. I walked them to the car, and perhaps I hugged them, before saying goodbye. One day, after she died, my father told me what happened on the long drive home to Syracuse.

He was driving the car, looking straight ahead. Traffic was light on the Massachusetts Turnpike, and the sky was nearly dark. They had driven for more than two hours and had not yet spoken a word. He then heard a strange sound from her, a kind of muffled chewing noise, as if something inside her were grinding its way out.

"So, what's the matter?" he said, trying to keep an edge to his voice.

She looked at him with her ashen face and she burst into tears. He began to cry himself, and pulled the car over onto the narrow shoulder of the turnpike, where they stayed for the next half hour or so, the blank-faced cars droning by them in the cold, on-rushing night.

Every once in a while, when I think of her, I'm driving alone somewhere on the highway. In the twilight, I see their car off to the side, a blue Olds coupe with a landau top, and as I pass them by I look back in the mirror and I see them again, the two figures huddled together in the front seat. Are they sleeping? Or kissing? Are they all right?

1996

PAULA VOGEL
B. 1951

Paula Vogel's writing has always been outside the box, with a provocative string of uncompromising plays aimed at exploring gender inequities, nontraditional families, and the darker side of human nature through AIDS, pornography, prostitution, sexual abuse, and gay and lesbian relationships. An outspoken lesbian since the age of seventeen, she continually pushes the boundaries of censorship with her language and choice of subject. As the scholar David Savran explains, she likes to "stage the impossible" and "defy traditional theater logic." That she does so with such eloquent compassion and innovation is testament to her skilled writing, which offers a balanced view of sensitive topics against an often scathing commentary, nuanced by the disconcerting humor that she frequently employs.

Vogel was born into a divisive household. Her Jewish father walked out when she was eleven, and her Catholic mother, once divorced, was constantly on the move in a series of low-paying jobs. Vogel got involved in stage management during her sophomore year in high school. She obtained an undergraduate degree from the Catholic University of America and spent three years doing graduate work at Cornell University. Since then she has been involved in the theater as both writer and consultant and has won a series of grants and awards. She taught playwriting at Brown University from 1985 to 2008 and is now chair of the playwriting department at the Yale School of Drama.

Her first full-length play, *Meg* (1977), a study of the relationship between Margaret Roper and her father, Sir Thomas More, was produced at the Kennedy Center and won the American College Theatre Festival Award for best new play. The two-act *Desdemona: A Play about a Handkerchief* (1986) drew attention for its blatant disregard of both theatrical and social conventions. Its retelling of Shakespeare's *Othello* from the viewpoint of Desdemona, whom she portrays as a conniving prostitute rather than innocent victim, offers a comedic but astute feminist spin on the original play.

During the 1980s, Vogel established a solid reputation as an Off-Broadway and Off-Off-Broadway dramatist, with plays like the one-act *The Oldest Profession* (1980), a satire on sexuality and old age about five elderly prostitutes, and *And Baby Makes Seven* (1984), a play partly inspired by Edward Albee's *Who's Afraid of Virginia Woolf* (1962), that looks at so-called family values in its tale of two lesbians, a gay man, and their fantasy children, whom they kill to make room for the new arrival.

The Obie-winning *Baltimore Waltz* (1992), partly a reaction to the death of her brother from AIDS, was Vogel's first widely acclaimed play. It uses its heroine's fictional ATD (acquired toilet disease) to force audiences to reexamine their views about AIDS and women's sexuality. *The Mineola Twins* (1996), a political satire and exposure of the complacency of suburbia that relates the parallel lives of two distinctly different sisters, helped cement Vogel's reputation, but it was the memory play *How I Learned to Drive* (1997) that put Vogel firmly on the critical radar. Despite its uncomfortable subject matter—incest and sexual predation—this dark comedy-drama won the New York Drama Critics' Circle Award, the Pulitzer Prize, and an Obie Award for Playwriting.

Vogel often uses someone else's work as a springboard, and *How I Learned to Drive* is both an homage and a response to Vladimir Nabokov's *Lolita* in its tale of a young girl's sexual awakening through the attentions of an older man. In *How I Learned to Drive*, Vogel uses the metaphor of driving lessons to relate a complex tale of the relationship between the abused and the abuser, although the play is finally more about growth and maturation than the destructive force of abuse. Boldly theatrical, it uses scant sets, nonlinear narrative, and a three-person Greek chorus to play the supporting roles of family and passers-by. Vogel resists portraying the central protagonist, Li'l Bit, as victim, and by depicting her uncle Peck as an attractive and kindly person, she emphasizes the ambiguities of the situation. She has stated that this is not a play about pedophilia but about survival and "coming of age" in our difficult contemporary culture.

Vogel continues to write and test her audiences with plays like *Hot 'n' Throbbing* (1994, rev. 2000), which explores pornography and its relation to domestic abuse and violence, and *The Long Christmas Ride Home* (2003), which ingeniously features puppets alongside the actors. She is also working on a screenplay for *How I Learned to Drive*.

Susan Abbotson
Rhode Island College

PRIMARY WORKS

Meg, 1977; *The Oldest Profession*, 1980; *And Baby Makes Seven*, 1984; *Desdemona: A Play about a Handkerchief*, 1986; *Hot 'n' Throbbing*, 1994 (rev. 2000); *The Baltimore Waltz and Other Plays*, 1996; *The Mineola Twins*, 1996; *How I Learned to Drive*, 1997; *The Mammary Plays*, 1998; *The Long Christmas Ride Home*, 2003; *A Civil War Christmas*, 2008.

How I Learned to Drive

CHARACTERS

LI'L BIT A woman who ages forty-something to eleven years old. (See Notes on the New York Production.)

PECK Attractive man in his forties. Despite a few problems, he should be played by an actor one might cast in the role of Atticus in *To Kill a Mockingbird*.

THE GREEK CHORUS If possible, these three members should be able to sing three-part harmony.

MALE GREEK CHORUS Plays Grandfather, Waiter, High School Boys. Thirties–forties. (See Notes on the New York Production.)

FEMALE GREEK CHORUS Plays Mother, Aunt Mary, High School Girls. Thirty–fifty. (See Notes on the New York Production.)

TEENAGE GREEK CHORUS Plays Grandmother, High School Girls, and the voice of eleven-year-old Li'l Bit. Note on the casting of this actor: I would strongly recommend casting a young woman who is "of legal age," that is, twenty-one to twenty-five years old who can look as close to eleven as possible. The contrast with the other cast members will help. If the actor is too young, the audience may feel uncomfortable. (See Notes on the New York Production.)

PRODUCTION NOTES *I urge directors to use the Greek Chorus in staging as environment and, well, part of the family—with the exception of the Teenage Greek Chorus member who, after the last time she appears onstage, should perhaps disappear.*

As For Music: Please have fun. I wrote sections of the play listening to music like Roy Orbison's "Dream Baby" and The Mamas and the Papa's "Dedicated to the One I Love." The vaudeville sections go well to the Tijuana Brass or any music that sounds like a *Laugh-In* soundtrack. Other sixties music is rife with pedophilish (?) reference: the "You're Sixteen" genre hits; The Beach Boys' "Little Surfer Girl"; Gary Puckett and the Union Gap's "This Girl Is a Woman Now"; "Come Back When You Grow Up," etc.

And whenever possible, please feel free to punctuate the action with traffic signs: "No Passing," "Slow Children," "Dangerous Curves," "One Way," and the visual signs for children, deer crossings, hills, school buses, etc. (See Notes on the New York Production.)

This script uses the notion of slides and projections, which were not used in the New York production of the play.

On Titles: Throughout the script there are bold-faced titles. In production these should be spoken in a neutral voice (the type of voice that driver education films employ). In the New York production these titles were assigned to various members of the Greek Chorus and were done live.

NOTES ON THE NEW YORK PRODUCTION

The role of Li'l Bit was originally written as a character who is forty-something. When we cast Mary-Louise Parker in the role of Li'l Bit, we cast the Greek Chorus members with younger actors as the Female Greek and the Male Greek, and cast the Teenage Greek with an older (that is, mid-twenties) actor as well. There is a great deal of flexibility in age. Directors should change the age in the last monologue for Li'l Bit ("And before you know it, I'll be thirty-five....") to reflect the actor's age who is playing Li'l Bit.
As the house lights dim, a Voice announces:

Safety First—You and Driver Education.

Then the sound of a key turning the ignition of a car. LI'L BIT *steps into a spotlight on the stage; "well-endowed," she is a softer-looking woman in the present time than she was at seventeen.*

LI'L BIT: Sometimes to tell a secret, you first have to teach a lesson. We're going to start our lesson tonight on an early, warm summer evening.

In a parking lot overlooking the Beltsville Agricultural Farms in suburban Maryland.

Less than a mile away, the crumbling concrete of U.S. One wends its way past one-room revival churches, the porno drive-in, and boarded up motels with For Sale signs tumbling down.

Like I said, it's a warm summer evening.

Here on the land the Department of Agriculture owns, the smell of sleeping farm animal is thick on the air. The smells of clover and hay mix in with the smells of the leather dashboard. You can still imagine how Maryland used to be, before the malls took over. This countryside was once dotted with farmhouses—from their porches you could have witnessed the Civil War raging in the front fields.

Oh yes. There's a moon over Maryland tonight, that spills into the car where I sit beside a man old enough to be—did I mention how still the night is? Damp soil and tranquil air. It's the kind of night that makes a middle-aged man with a mortgage feel like a country boy again.

It's 1969. And I am very old, very cynical of the world, and I know it all. In short, I am seventeen years old, parking off a dark lane with a married man on an early summer night.

(Lights up on two chairs facing front—or a Buick Riviera, if you will. Waiting patiently, with a smile on his face, PECK sits sniffing the night air. LI'L BIT climbs in beside him, seventeen years old and tense. Throughout the following, the two sit facing directly front. They do not touch. Their bodies remain passive. Only their facial expressions emote.)

PECK: Ummm. I love the smell of your hair.

LI'L BIT: Uh-huh.

PECK: Oh, Lord. Ummmm. *(Beat)* A man could die happy like this.

LI'L BIT: Well, *don't.*

PECK: What shampoo is this?

LI'L BIT: Herbal Essence.

PECK: Herbal Essence. I'm gonna buy me some. Herbal Essence. And when I'm alone in the house, I'm going to get into the bathtub and uncap the bottle and—

LI'L BIT: —Be good.

PECK: What?

LI'L BIT: Stop being . . . bad.

PECK: What did you think I was going to say? What do you think I'm going to do with the shampoo?

LI'L BIT: I don't want to know. I don't want to hear it.

PECK: I'm going to wash my hair. That's all.

LI'L BIT: Oh.

PECK: What did you think I was going to do?

LI'L BIT: Nothing. . . . I don't know. Something . . . nasty.

PECK: With shampoo? Lord, gal—your mind!

LI'L BIT: And whose fault is it?

PECK: Not mine. I've got the mind of a boy scout.

LI'L BIT: Right. A horny boy scout.

PECK: Boy scouts are always horny. What do you think the first Merit Badge is for?

LI'L BIT: There. You're going to be nasty again.

PECK: Oh, no. I'm good. Very good.

LI'L BIT: It's getting late.

PECK: Don't change the subject. I was talking about how good I am. (*Beat*) Are you ever gonna let me show you how good I am?

LI'L BIT: Don't go over the line now.

PECK: I won't. I'm not gonna do anything you don't want me to do.

LI'L BIT: That's right.

PECK: And I've been good all week.

LI'L BIT: You have?

PECK: Yes. All week. Not a single drink.

LI'L BIT: Good boy.

PECK: Do I get a reward? For not drinking?

LI'L BIT: A small one. It's getting late.

PECK: Just let me undo you. I'll do you back up.

LI'L BIT: All right. But be quick about it. (PECK *pantomimes undoing* LI'L BIT's *brassiere with one hand*) You know, that's amazing. The way you can undo the hooks through my blouse with one hand.

PECK: Years of practice.

LI'L BIT: You would make an incredible brain surgeon with that dexterity.

PECK: I'll bet Clyde—what's the name of the boy taking you to the prom?

LI'L BIT: Claude Souders.

PECK: Claude Souders. I'll bet it takes him two hands, lights on, and you help-ing him on to get to first base.

LI'L BIT: Maybe.

(*Beat.*)

PECK: Can I . . . kiss them? Please?

LI'L BIT: I don't know.

PECK: Don't make a grown man beg.

LI'L BIT: Just one kiss.

PECK: I'm going to lift your blouse.

LI'L BIT: It's a little cold.

(PECK *laughs gently.*)

PECK: That's not why you're shivering. (*They sit, perfectly still, for a long moment of silence.* PECK *makes gentle, concentric circles with his thumbs in the air in front of him*) How does that feel?

(LI'L BIT *closes her eyes, carefully keeps her voice calm:*)

LI'L BIT: It's . . . okay.

(*Sacred music, organ music or a boy's choir swells beneath the following.*)

PECK: I tell you, you can keep all the cathedrals of Europe. Just give me a sec-ond with these—these celestial orbs—

(PECK *bows his head as if praying. But he is kissing her nipple.* LI'L BIT, *eyes still closed, rears back her head on the leather Buick car seat.*)

LI'L BIT: Uncle Peck—we've got to go. I've got graduation rehearsal at school tomorrow morning. And you should get on home to Aunt Mary—
PECK: —All right, Li'l Bit.
LI'L BIT: —*Don't* call me that no more. (*Calmer*) Any more. I'm a big girl now, Uncle Peck. As you know.

(LI'L BIT *pantomimes refastening her bra behind her back.*)

PECK: That you are. Going on eighteen. Kittens will turn into cats.
(*Sighs*) I live all week long for these few minutes with you—you know that?
LI'L BIT: I'll drive.

(*A Voice cuts in with:*)

Idling in the Neutral Gear.

(*Sound of car revving cuts off the sacred music;* LI'L BIT, *now an adult, rises out of the car and comes to us.*)

LI'L BIT: In most families, relatives get names like "Junior," or "Brother," or "Bubba." In my family, if we call someone "Big Papa," it's not because he's tall. In my family, folks tend to get nicknamed for their genitalia. Uncle Peck, for example. My mama's adage was "the titless wonder," and my cousin Bobby got branded for life as "B.B."

(*In unison with* GREEK CHORUS:)

LI'L BIT: For blue balls.   GREEK CHORUS: For blue balls.
FEMALE GREEK CHORUS (As MOTHER): And of course, we were so excited to have a baby girl that when the nurse brought you in and said, "It's a girl! It's a baby girl!" I just had to see for myself. So we whipped your diapers down and parted your chubby little legs—and right between your legs there was—

(PECK *has come over during the above and chimes along:*)

PECK: Just a little bit.   GREEK CHORUS: Just a little bit.
FEMALE GREEK CHORUS (As MOTHER): And when you were born, you were so tiny that you fit in Uncle Peck's outstretched hand.

(PECK *stretches his hand out.*)

PECK: Now that's a fact. I held you, one day old, right in this hand.

(*A traffic signal is projected of a bicycle in a circle with a diagonal red slash.*)

LI'L BIT: Even with my family background, I was sixteen or so before I realized that pedophilia did not mean people who loved to bicycle....

(*A Voice intrudes:*)

Driving in First Gear.

LI'L BIT: 1969. A typical family dinner.

FEMALE GREEK CHORUS (*As* MOTHER): Look, Grandma. Li'l Bit's getting to be as big in the bust as you are.

LI'L BIT: Mother! Could we please change the subject?

TEENAGE GREEK CHORUS (*As* GRANDMOTHER): Well, I hope you are buying her some decent bras. I never had a decent bra, growing up in the Depression, and now my shoulders are just crippled—crippled from the weight hanging on my shoulders—the dents from my bra straps are big enough to put your finger in.—Here, let me show you—

(*As* GRANDMOTHER *starts to open her blouse:*)

LI'L BIT: Grandma! Please don't undress at the dinner table.

PECK: I thought the entertainment came after the dinner.

LI'L BIT: (*To the audience*) This is how it always starts. My grandfather, Big Papa, will chime in next with—

MALE GREEK CHORUS (*As* GRANDFATHER): Yup. If Li'l Bit gets any bigger, we're gonna haveta buy her a wheelbarrow to carry in front of her—

LI'L BIT: —Damn it—

PECK: —How about those Redskins on Sunday, Big Papa?

LI'L BIT: (*To the audience*) The only sport Big Papa followed was chasing Grandma around the house—

MALE GREEK CHORUS (*As* GRANDFATHER): —Or we could write to Kate Smith. Ask her for somma her used brassieres she don't want anymore—she could maybe give to Li'l Bit here—

LI'L BIT: —I can't stand it. I can't.

PECK: Now, honey, that's just their way—

FEMALE GREEK CHORUS (*As* MOTHER): I tell you, Grandma, Li'l Bit's at that age. She's so sensitive, you can't say boo—

LI'L BIT: I'd like some privacy, that's all. Okay? Some goddamn privacy—

PECK: —Well, at least she didn't use the savior's name—

LI'L BIT: (*To the audience*) And Big Papa wouldn't let a dead dog lie. No sirree.

MALE GREEK CHORUS (*As* GRANDFATHER): Well, she'd better stop being so sensitive. 'Cause five minutes before Li'l Bit turns the corner, her tits turn first—

LI'L BIT: (*Starting to rise from the table*)—That's it. That's it.

PECK: Li'l Bit, you can't let him get to you. Then he wins.

LI'L BIT: I hate him. Hate him.

PECK: That's fine. But hate him and eat a good dinner at the same time.

(*Li'l Bit calms down and sits with perfect dignity.*)

LI'L BIT: The gumbo is really good, Grandma.

MALE GREEK CHORUS (*As* GRANDFATHER): A'course, Li'l Bit's got a big surprise coming for her when she goes to that fancy college this fall—

PECK: Big Papa—let it go.

MALE GREEK CHORUS (As GRANDFATHER): What does she need a college degree for? She's got all the credentials she'll need on her chest.

LI'L BIT: —Maybe I want to learn things. Read. Rise above my cracker background—

PECK: —Whoa, now, Li'l Bit—

MALE GREEK CHORUS (As GRANDFATHER): What kind of things do you want to read?

LI'L BIT: There's a whole semester course, for example, on Shakespeare—

(GREEK CHORUS, as GRANDFATHER, laughs until he weeps.)

MALE GREEK CHORUS (As GRANDFATHER): Shakespeare. That's a good one. Shakespeare is really going to help you in life.

PECK: I think it's wonderful. And on scholarship!

MALE GREEK CHORUS (As GRANDFATHER): How is Shakespeare going to help her lie on her back in the dark?

(Li'l Bit is on her feet.)

LI'L BIT: You're getting old, Big Papa. You are going to die—very very soon. Maybe even tonight. And when you get to heaven, God's going to be a beautiful black woman in a long white robe. She's gonna look at your chart and say: Uh-oh. Fornication. Dog-ugly mean with blood relatives. Oh. Uh-oh. Voted for George Wallace. Well, one last chance: If you can name the play, all will be forgiven. And then she'll quote: "The quality of mercy is not strained." Your answer? Oh, too bad—*Merchant of Venice:* Act IV, Scene iii. And then she'll send your ass to fry in hell with all the other crackers. Excuse me, please.

    (To the audience) And as I left the house, I would always hear Big Papa say:

MALE GREEK CHORUS (As GRANDFATHER): Lucy, your daughter's got a mouth on her. Well, no sense in wasting good gumbo. Pass me her plate, Mama.

LI'L BIT: And Aunt Mary would come up to Uncle Peck:

FEMALE GREEK CHORUS (As AUNT MARY): Peck, go after her, will you? You're the only one she'll listen to when she gets like this.

PECK: She just needs to cool off.

FEMALE GREEK CHORUS (As AUNT MARY): Please, honey—Grandma's been on her feet cooking all day.

PECK: All right.

LI'L BIT: And as he left the room, Aunt Mary would say:

FEMALE GREEK CHORUS (As AUNT MARY): Peck's so good with them when they get to be this age.

(LI'L BIT has stormed to another part of the stage, her back turned, weeping with a teenage fury. PECK, cautiously, as if stalking a deer, comes to her. She turns away even more. He waits a bit.)

PECK: I don't suppose you're talking to family. *(No response)* Does it help that I'm in-law?

LI'L BIT: Don't you dare make fun of this.

PECK: I'm not. There's nothing funny about this. *(Beat)* Although I'll bet when Big Papa is about to meet his maker, he'll remember *The Merchant of Venice*.

LI'L BIT: I've got to get away from here.

PECK: You're going away. Soon. Here, take this.

(PECK hands her his folded handkerchief. LI'L BIT uses it, noisily. Hands it back. Without her seeing, he reverently puts it back.)

LI'L BIT: I hate this family.

PECK: Your grandfather's ignorant. And you're right—he's going to die soon. But he's family. Family is . . . family.

LI'L BIT: Grown-ups are always saying that. Family.

PECK: Well, when you get a little older, you'll see what we're saying.

LI'L BIT: Uh-huh. So family is another acquired taste, like French kissing?

PECK: Come again?

LI'L BIT: You know, at first it really grosses you out, but in time you grow to like it?

PECK: Girl, you are . . . a handful.

LI'L BIT: Uncle Peck—you have the keys to your car?

PECK: Where do you want to go?

LI'L BIT: Just up the road.

PECK: I'll come with you.

LI'L BIT: No—please? I just need to . . . to drive for a little bit. Alone.

(PECK tosses her the keys.)

PECK: When can I see you alone again?

LI'L BIT: Tonight.

(LI'L BIT crosses to center stage where the lights dim around her. A Voice directs:)

Shifting Forward From First to Second Gear.

LI'L BIT: There were a lot of rumors about why I got kicked out of that fancy school in 1970. Some say I got caught with a man in my room. Some say as a kid on scholarship I fooled around with a rich man's daughter.

(LI'L BIT smiles innocently at the audience) I'm not talking.

But the real truth was I had a constant companion in my dorm room—who was less than discrete. Canadian V.O. A fifth a day.

1970. A Nixon recession. I slept on the floors of friends who were out of work themselves. Took factory work when I could find it. A string of dead-end jobs that didn't last very long.

What I did, most nights, was cruise the Beltway and the back roads of Maryland, where there was still country, past the battlefields and farm houses. Racing in a 1965 Mustang—and as long as I had gasoline for my car and whiskey for me, the nights would pass. Fully tanked, I would speed past the churches and the trees and the bend, thinking just one notch of the steering wheel would be all it would take, and yet some . . . reflex took over. My hands on the wheel in the nine and three o'clock position—I never so much as got a ticket. He taught me well.

(A Voice announces:)

You and the Reverse Gear.

LI'L BIT: Back up. 1968. On the Eastern Shore. A celebration dinner.

(LI'L BIT joins PECK at a table in a restaurant.)

PECK: Feeling better, missy?

LI'L BIT: The bathroom's really amazing here, Uncle Peck! They have these little soaps—instead of borax or something—and they're in the shape of shells.

PECK: I'll have to take a trip to the gentlemen's room just to see.

LI'L BIT: How did you know about this place?

PECK: This inn is famous on the Eastern shore—it's been open since the seventeenth century. And I know how you like history . . .

(LI'L BIT is shy and pleased.)

LI'L BIT: It's great.

PECK: And you've just done your first, legal, long-distance drive. You must be hungry.

LI'L BIT: I'm starved.

PECK: I would suggest a dozen oysters to start, and the crab imperial . . . *(LI'L BIT is genuinely agog)* You might be interested to know the town history. When the British sailed up this very river in the dead of night—see outside where I'm pointing?—they were going to bombard the heck out of this town. But the town fathers were ready for them. They crept up all the trees with lanterns so that the British would think they saw the town lights and they aimed their cannons too high. And that's why the inn is still here for business today.

LI'L BIT: That's a great story.

PECK: *(Casually)* Would you like to start with a cocktail?

LI'L BIT: You're not . . . you're not going to start drinking, are you, Uncle Peck?

PECK: Not me. I told you, as long as you're with me, I'll never drink. I asked you if you'd like a cocktail before dinner. It's nice to have a little something with the oysters.

LI'L BIT: But . . . I'm not . . . legal. We could get arrested. Uncle Peck, they'll never believe I'm twenty-one!

PECK: So? Today we celebrate your driver's license—on the first try. This establishment reminds me a lot of places back home.

LI'L BIT: What does that mean?

PECK: In South Carolina, like here on the Eastern Shore, they're ... (*Searches for the right euphemism*) ... "European." Not so puritanical. And very understanding if gentlemen wish to escort very attractive young ladies who might want a before-dinner cocktail. If you want one, I'll order one.

LI'L BIT: Well—sure. Just ... one.

(*The* FEMALE GREEK CHORUS *appears in a spot.*)

FEMALE GREEK CHORUS (**As MOTHER**): A Mother's Guide to Social Drinking:

A lady never gets sloppy—she may, however, get tipsy and a little gay.

Never drink on an empty stomach. Avail yourself of the bread basket and generous portions of butter. Slather the butter on your bread.

Sip your drink, slowly, let the beverage linger in your mouth—interspersed with interesting, fascinating conversation. Sip, never ... slurp or gulp. Your glass should always be three-quarters full when his glass is empty.

Stay away from ladies' drinks: drinks like pink ladies, slow gin fizzes, daiquiris, gold cadillacs, Long Island iced teas, margaritas, piña coladas, mai tais, planters punch, white Russians, black Russians, red Russians, melon balls, blue balls, hummingbirds, hemorrhages and hurricanes. In short, avoid anything with sugar, or anything with an umbrella. Get your vitamin C from fruit. Don't order anything with Voodoo or Vixen in the title or sexual positions in the name like Dead Man Screw or the Missionary. (*She sort of titters*)

Believe me, they are lethal.... I think you were conceived after one of those.

Drink, instead, like a man: straight up or on the rocks, with plenty of water in between.

Oh, yes. And never mix your drinks. Stay with one all night long, like the man you came in with: bourbon, gin, or tequila till dawn, damn the torpedoes, full speed ahead!

(*As the* FEMALE GREEK CHORUS *retreats, the* MALE GREEK CHORUS *approaches the table as a* WAITER.)

MALE GREEK CHORUS (**As WAITER**): I hope you all are having a pleasant evening. Is there something I can bring you, sir, before you order?

(LI'L BIT *waits in anxious fear. Carefully,* UNCLE PECK *says with command:*)

PECK: I'll have a plain iced tea. The lady would like a drink, I believe.

(*The* MALE GREEK CHORUS *does a double take; there is a moment when* UNCLE PECK *and he are in silent communication.*)

MALE GREEK CHORUS (**As WAITER**): Very good. What would the ... lady like?

LI'L BIT (**A bit flushed**): Is there ... is there any sugar in a martini?

PECK: None that I know of.

LI'L BIT: That's what I'd like then—a dry martini. And could we maybe have some bread?

PECK: A drink fit for a woman of the world.—Please bring the lady a dry martini, be generous with the olives, straight up.

(The MALE GREEK CHORUS anticipates a large tip.)

MALE GREEK CHORUS (As WAITER): Right away. Very good sir.

(The MALE GREEK CHORUS returns with an empty martini glass which he puts in front of LI'L BIT.)

PECK: Your glass is empty. Another martini, madam?

LI'L BIT: Yes, thank you. (PECK *signals the* MALE GREEK CHORUS, *who nods*) So why did you leave South Carolina, Uncle Peck?

PECK: I was stationed in D.C. after the war, and decided to stay. Go North, Young Man, someone might have said.

LI'L BIT: What did you do in the service anyway?

PECK (***Suddenly taciturn***): I . . . I did just this and that. Nothing heroic or spectacular.

LI'L BIT: But did you see fighting? Or go to Europe?

PECK: I served in the Pacific Theater. It's really nothing interesting to talk about.

LI'L BIT: It is to me. (*The* WAITER *has brought another empty glass*) Oh, goody. I love the color of the swizzle sticks. What were we talking about?

PECK: Swizzle sticks.

LI'L BIT: Do you ever think of going back?

PECK: To the Marines?

LI'L BIT: No—to South Carolina.

PECK: Well, we do go back. To visit.

LI'L BIT: No, I mean to live.

PECK: Not very likely. I think it's better if my mother doesn't have a daily reminder of her disappointment.

LI'L BIT: Are these floorboards slanted?

PECK: Yes, the floor is very slanted. I think this is the original floor.

LI'L BIT: Oh, good.

(The FEMALE GREEK CHORUS as MOTHER enters swaying a little, a little past tipsy.)

FEMALE GREEK CHORUS (As MOTHER): Don't leave your drink unattended when you visit the ladies' room. There is such a thing as white slavery; the modus operandi is to spike an unsuspecting young girl's drink with a "mickey" when she's left the room to powder her nose.

But if you feel you have had more than your sufficiency in liquor, do go to the ladies' room—often. Pop your head out of doors for a refreshing breath of the night air. If you must, wet your face and head with tap water. Don't be afraid to dunk your head if necessary. A wet woman is still less conspicuous than a drunk woman.

(The FEMALE GREEK CHORUS stumbles a little; conspiratorially) When in the course of human events it becomes necessary, go to a corner stall and

insert the index and middle finger down the throat almost to the epiglottis. Divulge your stomach before rejoining your beau waiting for you at your table.

Oh, no. Don't be shy or embarrassed. In the very best of establishments, there's always one or two debutantes crouched in the corner stalls, their beaded purses tossed willy-nilly, sounding like cats in heat, heaving up the contents of their stomachs.

(*The* FEMALE GREEK CHORUS *begins to wander off*) I wonder what it is they do in the men's rooms . . .

LI'L BIT: So why is your mother disappointed in you, Uncle Peck?

PECK: Every mother in Horry County has Great Expectations.

LI'L BIT: —Could I have another mar-ti-ni, please?

PECK: I think this is your last one.

(*PECK signals the* WAITER. *The* WAITER *looks at* LI'L BIT *and shakes his head no.* PECK *raises an eyebrow, raises his finger to indicate one more, and then rubs his fingers together. It looks like a secret code. The* WAITER *sighs, shakes his head sadly, and brings over another empty martini glass. He glares at* PECK.)

LI'L BIT: The name of the county where you grew up is "Horry?" (LI'L BIT, *plastered, begins to laugh. Then she stops*) I think your mother should be proud of you.

(*PECK signals for the check.*)

PECK: Well, missy, she wanted me to do—to *be* everything my father was not. She wanted me to amount to something.

LI'L BIT: But you have! You've amounted a lot. . . .

PECK: I'm just a very ordinary man.

(*The* WAITER *has brought the check and waits.* PECK *draws out a large bill and hands it to the* WAITER. LI'L BIT *is in the sloppy stage.*)

LI'L BIT: I'll bet your mother loves you, Uncle Peck.

(*PECK freezes a bit. To* MALE GREEK CHORUS *as* WAITER:)

PECK: Thank you. The service was exceptional. Please keep the change.

MALE GREEK CHORUS (As WAITER, *in a tone that could freeze*): Thank you, sir. Will you be needing any help?

PECK: I think we can manage, thank you.

(*Just then, the* FEMALE GREEK CHORUS *as* MOTHER *lurches on stage; the* MALE GREEK CHORUS *as* WAITER *escorts her off as she delivers:*)

FEMALE GREEK CHORUS (As MOTHER): Thanks to judicious planning and several trips to the ladies' loo, your mother once out-drank an entire regiment of British officers on a good-will visit to Washington! Every last man of them! Milquetoasts! How'd they ever kick Hitler's cahones, huh? No match for an American lady—I could drink every man in here under the table.

(She delivers one last crucial hint before she is gently "bounced") As a last resort, when going out for an evening on the town, be sure to wear a skin-tight girdle—so tight that only a surgical knife or acetylene torch can get it off you—so that if you do pass out in the arms of your escort, he'll end up with rubber burns on his fingers before he can steal your virtue—

(A Voice punctures the interlude with:)

Vehicle Failure.

Even with careful maintenance and preventive operation of your automobile, it is all too common for us to experience an unexpected breakdown. If you are driving at any speed when a breakdown occurs, you must slow down and guide the automobile to the side of the road.

(PECK is slowly propping up LI'L BIT *as they work their way to his car in the parking lot of the inn.)*

PECK: How are you doing, missy?

LI'L BIT: It's so far to the car, Uncle Peck. Like the lanterns in the trees the British fired on . . .

(LI'L BIT stumbles. PECK *swoops her up in his arms.)*

PECK: Okay. I think we're going to take a more direct route.

(LI'L BIT *closes her eyes*) Dizzy? *(She nods her head)* Don't look at the ground. Almost there—do you feel sick to your stomach? (LI'L BIT *nods. They reach the "car."* PECK *gently deposits her on the front seat)* Just settle here a little while until things stop spinning. (LI'L BIT *opens her eyes*)

LI'L BIT: What are we doing?

PECK: We're just going to sit here until your tummy settles down.

LI'L BIT: It's such nice upholst'ry—

PECK: Think you can go for a ride, now?

LI'L BIT: Where are you taking me?

PECK: Home.

LI'L BIT: You're not taking me—upstairs? There's no room at the inn? (LI'L BIT *giggles*)

PECK: Do you want to go upstairs? (LI'L BIT *doesn't answer*) Or home?

LI'L BIT: —This isn't right, Uncle Peck.

PECK: What isn't right?

LI'L BIT: What we're doing. It's wrong. It's very wrong.

PECK: What are we doing? (LI'L BIT *does not answer*) We're just going out to dinner.

LI'L BIT: You know. It's not nice to Aunt Mary.

PECK: You let me be the judge of what's nice and not nice to my wife.

(Beat.)

LI'L BIT: Now you're mad.

PECK: I'm not mad. It's just that I thought you . . . understood me, Li'l Bit. I think you're the only one who does.

LI'L BIT: Someone will get hurt.

PECK: Have I forced you to do anything?

(There is a long pause as LI'L BIT tries to get sober enough to think this through.)

LI'L BIT: . . . I guess not.

PECK: We are just enjoying each other's company. I've told you, nothing is going to happen between us until you want it to. Do you know that?

LI'L BIT: Yes.

PECK: Nothing is going to happen until you want it to. *(A second more, with* PECK *staring ahead at the river while seated at the wheel of his car. Then, softly:)* Do you want something to happen?

(PECK reaches over and strokes her face, very gently. LI'L BIT softens, reaches for him, and buries her head in his neck. Then she kisses him. Then she moves away, dizzy again.)

LI'L BIT: . . . I don't know.

(PECK smiles; this has been good news for him—it hasn't been a "no.")

PECK: Then I'll wait. I'm a very patient man. I've been waiting for a long time. I don't mind waiting.

LI'L BIT: Someone is going to get hurt.

PECK: No one is going to get hurt. *(LI'L BIT closes her eyes)* Are you feeling sick?

LI'L BIT: Sleepy.

(Carefully, PECK props LI'L BIT up on the seat.)

PECK: Stay here a second.

LI'L BIT: Where're you going?

PECK: I'm getting something from the back seat.

LI'L BIT (Scared: too loud): What? What are you going to do?

(PECK reappears in the front seat with a lap rug.)

PECK: Shhh. *(PECK covers LI'L BIT. She calms down)* There. Think you can sleep?

(LI'L BIT nods. She slides over to rest on his shoulder. With a look of happiness, PECK turns the ignition key. Beat. PECK leaves LI'L BIT sleeping in the car and strolls down to the audience. Wagner's Flying Dutchman comes up faintly.

A Voice interjects:)

Idling in the Neutral Gear.

TEENAGE GREEK CHORUS: Uncle Peck Teaches Cousin Bobby How to Fish.

PECK: I get back once or twice a year—supposedly to visit Mama and the family, but the real truth is to fish. I miss this the most of all. There's a smell in the Low country—where the swamp and fresh inlet join the salt-water—a scent of sand and cypress, that I haven't found anywhere yet.

I don't say this very often up North because it will just play into the stereotype everyone has, but I will tell you: I didn't wear shoes in the summertime until I was sixteen. It's unnatural down here to pen up your feet in leather. Go ahead—take 'em off. Let yourself breathe—it really will make you feel better.

We're going to aim for some pompano today—and I have to tell you, they're a very shy, mercurial fish. Takes patience, and psychology. You have to believe it doesn't matter if you catch one or not.

Sky's pretty spectacular—there's some beer in the cooler next to the crab salad I packed, so help yourself if you get hungry. Are you hungry? Thirsty? Holler if you are.

Okay. You don't want to lean over the bridge like that—pompano feed in shallow water, and you don't want to get too close—they're frisky and shy little things—wait, check your line. Yep, something's been munching while we were talking.

Okay, look: We take the sand flea and you take the hook like this— right through his little sand flea rump. Sand fleas should always keep their backs to the wall. Okay. Cast it in, like I showed you. That's great! I can taste that pompano now, sautéed with some pecans and butter, and a little bourbon—now—let it lie on the bottom—now, reel, jerk, reel, jerk—

Look—look at your line. There's something calling, all right. Okay, tip the rod up—not too sharp—hook it—all right, now easy, reel and then rest—let it play. And reel—play it out, that's right—really good! I can't believe it! It's a pompano.—Good work! Way to go! You are an official fisherman now. Pompano are hard to catch. We are going to have a delicious little—

What? Well, I don't know how much pain a fish feels—you can't think of that. Oh, no, don't cry, come on now, its just a fish—the other guys are going to see you.—No, no, you're just real sensitive, and I think that's wonderful at your age—look, do you want me to cut it free? You do?

Okay, hand me those pliers—look—I'm cutting the hook—okay? And we're just going to drop it in—no I'm not mad. It's just for fun, okay? There—it's going to swim back to its lady friend and tell her what a terrible day it had and she's going to stroke him with her fins until he feels better, and then they'll do something alone together that will make them both feel good and sleepy. . . .

(PECK *bends down, very earnest*) I don't want you to feel ashamed about crying. I'm not going to tell anyone, okay? I can keep secrets. You know, men cry all the time. They just don't tell anybody, and they don't let anybody catch them. There's nothing you could do that would make me feel ashamed of you. Do you know that? Okay. (PECK *straightens up, smiles*)

Do you want to pack up and call it a day? I tell you what—I think I can still remember—there's a really neat tree house where I used to stay for days. I think it's still here—it was the last time I looked. But it's a secret place—you can't tell anybody we've gone there—least of all your mom or your sisters.—This is something special just between you and me. Sound good? We'll climb up there and have a beer and some crab salad—okay, B.B.? Bobby? Robert . . .

(LI'L BIT *sits at a kitchen table with the two* FEMALE GREEK CHORUS *members.*)

LI'L BIT: *(To the audience)* Three women, three generations, sit at the kitchen table.

    On Men, Sex, and Women: Part I:

FEMALE GREEK CHORUS (As MOTHER): Men only want one thing.

LI'L BIT: *(Wide-eyed)* But what? What is it they want?

FEMALE GREEK CHORUS (As MOTHER): And once they have it, they lose all interest. So Don't Give It to Them.

TEENAGE GREEK CHORUS (As GRANDMOTHER): I never had the luxury of the rhythm method. Your grandfather is just a big bull. A big bull. Every morning, every evening.

FEMALE GREEK CHORUS (As MOTHER, *whispers to* LI'L BIT**):** And he used to come home for lunch every day.

LI'L BIT: My god, Grandma!

TEENAGE GREEK CHORUS (As GRANDMOTHER): Your grandfather only cares that I do two things: have the table set and the bed turned down.

FEMALE GREEK CHORUS (As MOTHER): And in all that time, Mother, you never have experienced—?

LI'L BIT: *(To the audience)*—No my grandmother believed in all the sacraments of the church, to the day she died. She believed in Santa Claus and the Easter Bunny until she was fifteen. But she didn't believe in—

TEENAGE GREEK CHORUS (As GRANDMOTHER): —Orgasm! That's just something you and Mary have made up! I don't believe you.

FEMALE GREEK CHORUS (As MOTHER): Mother, it happens to women all the time—

TEENAGE GREEK CHORUS (As GRANDMOTHER): —Oh, now you're going to tell me about the G force!

LI'L BIT: No, Grandma, I think that's astronauts—

FEMALE GREEK CHORUS (As MOTHER): Well, Mama, after all, you were a child bride when Big Papa came and got you—you were a married woman and you still believed in Santa Claus.

TEENAGE GREEK CHORUS (As GRANDMOTHER): It was legal, what Daddy and I did! I was fourteen and in those days, fourteen was a grown-up woman—

(BIG PAPA *shuffles in the kitchen for a cookie.*)

MALE GREEK CHORUS (As GRANDFATHER): —Oh, now we're off on Grandma and the Rape of the Sa-bean Women!

TEENAGE GREEK CHORUS (As GRANDMOTHER): Well, you were the one in such a big hurry—

MALE GREEK CHORUS *(As* GRANDFATHER *to* LI'L BIT*)*: —I picked your grandmother out of that herd of sisters just like a lion chooses the gazelle—the plump, slow, flaky gazelle dawdling at the edge of the herd—your sisters were too smart and too fast and too scrawny—

LI'L BIT: *(To the audience)*—The family story is that when Big Papa came for Grandma, my Aunt Lily was waiting for him with a broom—and she beat him over the head all the way down the stairs as he was carrying out Grandma's hope chest—

MALE GREEK CHORUS *(As* GRANDFATHER*)*: —and they were mean. 'Specially Lily.

FEMALE GREEK CHORUS *(As* MOTHER*)*: Well, you were robbing the baby of the family!

TEENAGE GREEK CHORUS *(As* GRANDMOTHER*)*: I still keep a broom handy in the kitchen! And I know how to use it! So get your hand out of the cookie jar and don't you spoil your appetite for dinner—out of the kitchen!

(MALE GREEK CHORUS as GRANDFATHER leaves chuckling with a cookie.)

FEMALE GREEK CHORUS *(As* MOTHER*)*: Just one thing a married woman needs to know how to use—the rolling pin or the broom. I prefer a heavy, cast-iron fry pan—they're great on a man's head, no matter how thick the skull is.

TEENAGE GREEK CHORUS *(As* GRANDMOTHER*)*: Yes, sir, your father is ruled by only two bosses! Mr. Gut and Mr. Peter! And sometimes, first thing in the morning, Mr. Sphincter Muscle!

FEMALE GREEK CHORUS *(As* MOTHER*)*: It's true. Men are like children. Just like little boys.

TEENAGE GREEK CHORUS *(As* GRANDMOTHER*)*: Men are bulls! Big bulls!

(THE GREEK CHORUS is getting aroused.)

FEMALE GREEK CHORUS *(As* MOTHER*)*: They'd still be crouched on their haunches over a fire in a cave if we hadn't cleaned them up!

TEENAGE GREEK CHORUS *(As* GRANDMOTHER, *flushed)*: Coming in smelling of sweat—

FEMALE GREEK CHORUS *(As* MOTHER*)*: —Looking at those naughty pictures like boys in a dime store with a dollar in their pockets!

TEENAGE GREEK CHORUS *(As* GRANDMOTHER; *raucous)*: No matter to them what they smell like! They've got to have it, right then, on the spot, right there! Nasty!—

FEMALE GREEK CHORUS *(As* MOTHER*)*: —Vulgar!

TEENAGE GREEK CHORUS *(As* GRANDMOTHER*)*: Primitive!—

FEMALE GREEK CHORUS *(As* MOTHER*)*: —Hot!—

LI'L BIT: And just about then, Big Papa would shuffle in with—

MALE GREEK CHORUS *(As* GRANDFATHER*)*: —What are you all cackling about in here?

TEENAGE GREEK CHORUS *(As* GRANDMOTHER*)*: Stay out of the kitchen! This is just for girls!

(As GRANDFATHER leaves:)

MALE GREEK CHORUS (*As* GRANDFATHER): Lucy, you'd better not be filling Mama's head with sex! Every time you and Mary come over and start in about sex, when I ask a simple question like, "What time is dinner going to be ready?" Mama snaps my head off!

TEENAGE GREEK CHORUS (*As* GRANDMOTHER): Dinner will be ready when I'm good and ready! Stay out of this kitchen!

(LI'L BIT *steps out.*
  A Voice directs:)

When Making a Left Turn, You Must Downshift While Going Forward.

LI'L BIT: 1979. A long bus trip to Upstate New York. I settled in to read, when a young man sat beside me.

MALE GREEK CHORUS (*As* YOUNG MAN; *voice cracking*): "What are you reading?"

LI'L BIT: He asked. His voice broke into that miserable equivalent of vocal acne, not quite falsetto and not tenor, either. I glanced a side view. He was appealing in an odd way, huge ears at a defiant angle springing forward at ninety degrees. He must have been shaving, because his face, with a peach sheen, was speckled with nicks and styptic. "I have a class tomorrow," I told him.

MALE GREEK CHORUS (*As* YOUNG MAN): "You're taking a class?"

LI'L BIT: "I'm teaching a class." He concentrated on lowering his voice.

MALE GREEK CHORUS (*As* YOUNG MAN): "I'm a senior. Walt Whitman High."

LI'L BIT: The light was fading outside, so perhaps he was—with a very high voice.

I felt his "interest" quicken. Five steps ahead of the hopes in his head, I slowed down, waited, pretended surprise, acted at listening, all the while knowing we would get off the bus, he would just then seem to think to ask me to dinner, he would chivalrously insist on walking me home, he would continue to converse in the street until I would casually invite him up to my room—and—I was only into the second moment of conversation and I could see the whole evening before me.

And dramaturgically speaking, after the faltering and slightly comical "first act," there was the very briefest of intermissions, and an extremely capable and forceful and sustained second act. And after the second act climax and a gentle denouement—before the post-play discussion—I lay on my back in the dark and I thought about you, Uncle Peck. Oh. Oh— this is the allure. Being older. Being the first. Being the translator, the teacher, the epicure, the already jaded. This is how the giver gets taken.

(LI'L BIT *changes her tone*) On Men, Sex, and Women: Part II:

(LI'L BIT *steps back into the scenes as a fifteen-year-old, gawky and quiet, as the gazelle at the edge of the herd.*)

TEENAGE GREEK CHORUS (As GRANDMOTHER; to LI'L BIT): You're being mighty quiet, missy. Cat Got Your Tongue?

LI'L BIT: I'm just listening. Just thinking.

TEENAGE GREEK CHORUS (As GRANDMOTHER): Oh, yes, Little Miss Radar Ears? Soaking it all in? Little Miss Sponge? Penny for your thoughts?

(LI'L BIT hesitates to ask but she really wants to know.)

LI'L BIT: Does it—when you do it—you know, theoretically when I do it and I haven't done it before—I mean—does it hurt?

FEMALE GREEK CHORUS (As MOTHER): Does what hurt, honey?

LI'L BIT: When a . . . when a girl does it for the first time—with a man—does it hurt?

TEENAGE GREEK CHORUS (As GRANDMOTHER; *horrified*): That's what you're thinking about?

FEMALE GREEK CHORUS (As MOTHER; *calm*): Well, just a little bit. Like a pinch. And there's a little blood.

TEENAGE GREEK CHORUS (As GRANDMOTHER): Don't tell her that! She's too young to be thinking those things!

FEMALE GREEK CHORUS (As MOTHER): Well, if she doesn't find out from me, where is she going to find out? In the street?

TEENAGE GREEK CHORUS (As GRANDMOTHER): Tell her it hurts! It's agony! You think you're going to die! Especially if you do it before marriage!

FEMALE GREEK CHORUS (As MOTHER): Mama! I'm going to tell her the truth! Unlike you, you left me and Mary completely in the dark with fairy tales and told us to go to the priest! What does an eighty-year-old priest know about love-making with girls!

LI'L BIT (*Getting upset*): It's not fair!

FEMALE GREEK CHORUS (As MOTHER): Now, see, she's getting upset—you're scaring her.

TEENAGE GREEK CHORUS (As GRANDMOTHER): Good! Let her be good and scared! It hurts! You bleed like a stuck pig! And you lay there and say, "Why, O Lord, have you forsaken me?!"

LI'L BIT: It's not fair! Why does everything have to hurt for girls? Why is there always blood?

FEMALE GREEK CHORUS (As MOTHER): It's not a lot of blood—and it feels wonderful after the pain subsides . . .

TEENAGE GREEK CHORUS (As GRANDMOTHER): You're encouraging her to just go out and find out with the first drugstore joe who buys her a milk shake!

FEMALE GREEK CHORUS (As MOTHER): Don't be scared. It won't hurt you—if the man you go to bed with really loves you. It's important that he loves you.

TEENAGE GREEK CHORUS (As GRANDMOTHER): —Why don't you just go out and rent a motel room for her, Lucy?

FEMALE GREEK CHORUS (As MOTHER): I believe in telling my daughter the truth! We have a very close relationship! I want her to be able to ask me any-thing—I'm not scaring her with stories about Eve's sin and snakes crawling on their bellies for eternity and women bearing children in mortal pain—

TEENAGE GREEK CHORUS *(As GRANDMOTHER)*: —If she stops and thinks before she takes her knickers off, maybe someone in this family will finish high school!

(LI'L BIT knows what is about to happen and starts to retreat from the scene at this point.)

FEMALE GREEK CHORUS *(As MOTHER)*: Mother! If you and Daddy had helped me—I wouldn't have had to marry that—that no-good-son-of-a—

TEENAGE GREEK CHORUS *(As GRANDMOTHER)*: —He was good enough for you on a full moon! I hold you responsible!

FEMALE GREEK CHORUS *(As MOTHER)*: —You could have helped me! You could have told me something about the facts of life!

TEENAGE GREEK CHORUS *(As GRANDMOTHER)*: —I told you what my mother told me! A girl with her skirt up can outrun a man with his pants down!

(The MALE GREEK CHORUS enters the fray; LI'L BIT edges further downstage.)

FEMALE GREEK CHORUS *(As MOTHER)*: And when I turned to you for a little help, all I got afterwards was—

MALE GREEK CHORUS *(As GRANDFATHER)*: You Made Your Bed; Now Lie On It!

(The GREEK CHORUS freezes, mouths open, argumentatively.)

LI'L BIT: *(To the audience)* Oh, please! I still can't bear to listen to it, after all these years—

(The MALE GREEK CHORUS "unfreezes," but out of his open mouth as if to his surprise, comes a base refrain from a Motown song.)

MALE GREEK CHORUS: "Do-Bee-Do-Wha!"

(The FEMALE GREEK CHORUS member is also surprised; but she, too, unfreezes.)

FEMALE GREEK CHORUS: "Shoo-doo-be-doo-be-doo; shoo-doo-be-doo-be-doo."

(The MALE and FEMALE GREEK CHORUS members continue with their harmony, until the TEENAGER member of the CHORUS starts in with Motown lyrics such as "Dedicated to the One I Love," or "In the Still of the Night," or "Hold Me"—any Sam Cooke will do. The three modulate down into three-part harmony, softly, until they are submerged by the actual recording playing over the radio in the car in which UNCLE PECK sits in the driver's seat, waiting. LI'L BIT sits in the passenger's seat.)

LI'L BIT: Ahh. That's better.

(Uncle PECK reaches over and turns the volume down; to LI'L BIT:)

PECK: How can you hear yourself think?

(LI'L BIT does not answer.
A Voice insinuates itself in the pause:)

Before You Drive.

Always check under your car for obstructions—broken bottles, fallen tree branches, and the bodies of small children. Each year hundreds of children are crushed beneath the wheels of unwary drivers in their own driveways. Children depend on you to watch them.
(Pause.

The Voice continues:)

You and the Reverse Gear.

(In the following section, it would be nice to have slides of erotic photographs of women and cars: women posed over the hood; women draped along the sideboards; women with water hoses spraying the car; and the actress playing LI'L BIT *with a Bel Air or any 1950s car one can find for the finale.)*

LI'L BIT: 1967. In a parking lot of the Beltsville Agriculture Farms. The Initiation into a Boy's First Love.

PECK *(With a soft look on his face)*: Of course, my favorite car will always be the '56 Bel Air Sports Coupe. Chevy sold more '55s, but the '56!—a V-8 with Corvette option, 225 horsepower; went from zero to sixty miles per hour in 8.9 seconds.

LI'L BIT: *(To the audience)* Long after a mother's tits, but before a woman's breasts:

PECK: Super-Turbo-Fire! What a Power Pack—mechanical lifters, twin four-barrel carbs, lightweight valves, dual exhausts—

LI'L BIT: *(To the audience)* After the milk but before the beer:

PECK: A specific intake manifold, higher-lift camshaft, and the tightest squeeze Chevy had ever made—

LI'L BIT: *(To the audience)* Long after he's squeezed down the birth canal but before he's pushed his way back in: The boy falls in love with the thing that bears his weight with speed.

PECK: I want you to know your automobile inside and out. —Are you there? Li'l Bit?

(Slides end here.)

LI'L BIT: —What?

PECK: You're drifting. I need you to concentrate.

LI'L BIT: Sorry.

PECK: Okay. Get into the driver's seat. (LI'L BIT *does)* Okay. Now. Show me what you're going to do before you start the car.

(LI'L BIT sits, with her hands in her lap. She starts to giggle.)

PECK: Now, come on. What's the first thing you're going to adjust?

LI'L BIT: My bra strap?—

PECK: —Li'l Bit. What's the most important thing to have control of on the inside of the car?

LI'L BIT: That's easy. The radio. I tune the radio from Mama's old fart tunes to—

(LI'L BIT *turns the radio up so we can hear a 1960s tune. With surprising firmness,* PECK *commands:)*

PECK: —Radio off. Right now. (LI'L BIT *turns the radio off)* When you are driving your car, with your license, you can fiddle with the stations all you want. But when you are driving with a learner's permit in my car, I want all your attention to be on the road.

LI'L BIT: Yes, sir.

PECK: Okay. Now the seat—forward and up. (LI'L BIT *pushes it forward)* Do you want a cushion?

LI'L BIT: No—I'm good.

PECK: You should be able to reach all the switches and controls. Your feet should be able to push the accelerator, brake and clutch all the way down. Can you do that?

LI'L BIT: Yes.

PECK: Okay, the side mirrors. You want to be able to see just a bit of the right side of the car in the right mirror—can you?

LI'L BIT: Turn it out more.

PECK: Okay. How's that?

LI'L BIT: A little more.... Okay, that's good.

PECK: Now the left—again, you want to be able to see behind you—but the left lane—adjust it until you feel comfortable. (LI'L BIT *does so)* Next. I want you to check the rearview mirror. Angle it so you have a clear vision of the back. (LI'L BIT *does so)* Okay. Lock your door. Make sure all the doors are locked.

LI'L BIT (*Making a joke of it*): But then I'm locked in with you.

PECK: Don't fool.

LI'L BIT: All right. We're locked in.

PECK: We'll deal with the air vents and defroster later. I'm teaching you on a manual—once you learn manual, you can drive anything. I want you to be able to drive any car, any machine. Manual gives you control. In ice, if your brakes fail, if you need more power—okay? It's a little harder at first, but then it becomes like breathing. Now. Put your hands on the wheel. I never want to see you driving with one hand. Always two hands. (LI'L BIT *hesitates)* What? What is it now?

LI'L BIT: If I put my hands on the wheel—how do I defend myself?

PECK (*Softly*): Now listen. Listen up close. We're not going to fool around with this. This is serious business. I will never touch you when you are driving a car. Understand?

LI'L BIT: Okay.

PECK: Hands on the nine o'clock and three o'clock position gives you maximum control and turn.

(PECK *goes silent for a while.* LI'L BIT *waits for more instruction)*

Okay. Just relax and listen to me, Li'l Bit, okay? I want you to lift your hands for a second and look at them. (LI'L BIT *feels a bit silly, but does it*)

Those are your two hands. When you are driving, you life is in your own two hands. Understand? (LI'L BIT *nods*)

I don't have any sons. You're the nearest to a son I'll ever have—and I want to give you something. Something that really matters to me.

There's something about driving—when you're in control of the car, just you and the machine and the road—that nobody can take from you. A power. I feel more myself in my car than anywhere else. And that's what I want to give to you.

There's a lot of assholes out there. Crazy men, arrogant idiots, drunks, angry kids, geezers who are blind—and you have to be ready for them. I want to teach you to drive like a man.

LI'L BIT: What does that mean?

PECK: Men are taught to drive with confidence—with aggression. The road belongs to them. They drive defensively—always looking out for the other guy. Women tend to be polite—to hesitate. And that can be fatal.

You're going to learn to think what the other guy is going to do before he does it. If there's an accident, and ten cars pile up, and people get killed, you're the one who's gonna steer through it, put your foot on the gas if you have to, and be the only one to walk away. I don't know how long you or I are going to live, but we're for damned sure not going to die in a car.

So if you're going to drive with me, I want you to take this very seriously.

LI'L BIT: I will, Uncle Peck. I want you to teach me to drive.

PECK: Good. You're going to pass your test on the first try. Perfect score. Before the next four weeks are over, you're going to know this baby inside and out. Treat her with respect.

LI'L BIT: Why is it a "she"?

PECK: Good question. It doesn't have to be a "she"—but when you close your eyes and think of someone who responds to your touch—someone who performs just for you and gives you what you ask for—I guess I always see a "she." You can call her what you like.

LI'L BIT: (*To the audience*) I closed my eyes—and decided not to change the gender.

(*A Voice:*)

Defensive driving involves defending yourself from hazardous and sudden changes in your automotive environment. By thinking ahead, the defensive driver can adjust to weather, road conditions and road kill. Good defensive driving involves mental and physical preparation. Are you prepared?

(*Another Voice chimes in:*)

You and the Reverse Gear.

LI'L BIT: 1966. The Anthropology of the Female Body in Ninth Grade—Or A Walk Down Mammary Lane.

(Throughout the following, there is occasional rhythmic beeping, like a transmitter signaling. LI'L BIT is aware of it, but can't figure out where it is coming from. No one else seems to hear it.)

MALE GREEK CHORUS: In the hallway of Francis Scott Key Middle School.

(A bell rings; the GREEK CHORUS is changing classes and meets in the hall, conspiratorially.)

TEENAGE GREEK CHORUS: She's coming!

(LI'L BIT enters the scene; the MALE GREEK CHORUS member has a sudden, violent sneezing and lethal allergy attack.)

FEMALE GREEK CHORUS: Jerome? Jerome? Are you all right?
MALE GREEK CHORUS: I—don't—know. I can't breathe—get Li'l Bit—
TEENAGE GREEK CHORUS: —He needs oxygen!—
FEMALE GREEK CHORUS: —Can you help us here?
LI'L BIT: What's wrong? Do you want me to get the school nurse—

(The MALE GREEK CHORUS member wheezes, grabs his throat and sniffs at LI'L BIT's chest, which is beeping away.)

MALE GREEK CHORUS: No—it's okay—I only get this way when I'm around an allergy trigger—
LI'L BIT: Golly. What are you allergic to?
MALE GREEK CHORUS: *(With a sudden grab of her breast)* Foam rubber.

(The GREEK CHORUS members break up with hilarity; JEROME leaps away from LI'L BIT's kicking rage with agility; as he retreats:)

LI'L BIT: Jerome! Creep! Cretin! Cro-Magnon!
TEENAGE GREEK CHORUS: Rage is not attractive in a girl.
FEMALE GREEK CHORUS: Really. Get a Sense of Humor.

(A voice echoes:)

Good Defensive Driving Involves Mental and Physical Preparation. Were You Prepared?

FEMALE GREEK CHORUS: Gym Class: In the showers.

(The sudden sound of water; the FEMALE GREEK CHORUS members and LI'L BIT, while fully clothed, drape towels across their fronts, miming nudity. They stand, hesitate, at an imaginary shower's edge.)

LI'L BIT: Water looks hot.

FEMALE GREEK CHORUS: Yesss. . . .

(FEMALE GREEK CHORUS members are not going to make the first move. One dips a tentative toe under the water, clutching the towel around her.)

LI'L BIT: Well, I guess we'd better shower and get out of here.

FEMALE GREEK CHORUS: Yep. You go ahead. I'm still cooling off.

LI'L BIT: Okay. —Sally? Are you gonna shower?

TEENAGE GREEK CHORUS: After you—

(LI'L BIT takes a deep breath for courage, drops the towel and plunges in: The two FEMALE GREEK CHORUS members look at LI'L BIT in the all together, laugh, gasp and high-five each other.)

TEENAGE GREEK CHORUS: Oh my god! Can you believe—

FEMALE GREEK CHORUS: Told you it's not foam rubber! I win! Jerome owes me fifty cents.

(A Voice editorializes:)

Were You Prepared?

(LI'L BIT tries to cover up; she is exposed, as suddenly 1960s Motown fills the room and we segue into:)

FEMALE GREEK CHORUS: The Sock Hop.

(LI'L BIT stands against the wall with her female classmates. TEENAGE GREEK CHORUS is mesmerized by the music and just sways alone, lip-synching the lyrics.)

LI'L BIT: I don't know. Maybe it's just me—but—do you ever feel like you're just a walking Mary Jane joke?

FEMALE GREEK CHORUS: I don't know what you mean.

LI'L BIT: You haven't heard the Mary Jane jokes? (FEMALE GREEK CHORUS member shakes her head no) Okay. "Little Mary Jane is walking through the woods, when all of a sudden this man who was hiding behind a tree jumps out, rips open Mary Jane's blouse, and plunges his hands on her breasts. And Little Mary Jane just laughed and laughed because she knew her money was in her shoes."

(LI'L BIT laughs; the FEMALE GREEK CHORUS does not.)

FEMALE GREEK CHORUS: You're weird.

(In another space, in a strange light, UNCLE PECK stands and stares at LI'L BIT's body. He is setting up a tripod, but he just stands, appreciative, watching her.)

LI'L BIT: Well, don't you ever feel . . . self-conscious? Like you're being looked at all the time?

FEMALE GREEK CHORUS: That's not a problem for me. —Oh—look—Greg's coming over to ask you to dance.

(TEENAGE GREEK CHORUS becomes attentive, flustered. MALE GREEK CHORUS member, as Greg, bends slightly as a very short young man, whose head is at LI'L BIT's chest level. Ardent, sincere and socially inept, GREG will become a successful gynecologist.)

TEENAGE GREEK CHORUS: *(Softly)* Hi, Greg.

(GREG does not hear. He is intent on only one thing.)

MALE GREEK CHORUS (As GREG, to LI'L BIT): Good Evening. Would you care to dance?

LI'L BIT: *(Gently)* Thank you very much, Greg—but I'm going to sit this one out.

MALE GREEK CHORUS (As GREG): Oh. Okay. I'll try my luck later.

(He disappears.)

TEENAGE GREEK CHORUS: Oohhh.

(LI'L BIT relaxes. Then she tenses, aware of PECK's gaze.)

FEMALE GREEK CHORUS: Take pity on him. Someone should.

LI'L BIT: But he's too short.

TEENAGE GREEK CHORUS: He can't help it.

LI'L BIT: But his head comes up to (LI'L BIT *gestures)* here. And I think he asks me on the fast dances so he can watch me—you know—jiggle.

FEMALE GREEK CHORUS: I wish I had your problems.

(The tune changes; GREG is across the room in a flash.)

MALE GREEK CHORUS (As GREG): Evening again. May I ask you for the honor of a spin on the floor?

LI'L BIT: I'm ... very complimented, Greg. But I ... I just don't do fast dances.

MALE GREEK CHORUS (As GREG): Oh. No problem. That's okay.

(He disappears. TEENAGE GREEK CHORUS watches him go.)

TEENAGE GREEK CHORUS: That is just so—*sad.*

(LI'L BIT becomes aware of PECK waiting.)

FEMALE GREEK CHORUS: You know, you should take it as a compliment that the guys want to watch you jiggle. They're guys. That's what they're supposed to do.

LI'L BIT: I guess you're right. But sometimes I feel like these alien life forces, these two mounds of flesh have grafted themselves onto my chest, and they're using me until they can "propagate" and take over the world and they'll just keep growing, with a mind of their own until I collapse under their weight and they suck all the nourishment out of my body and I finally just waste away while they get bigger and bigger and— (LI'L BIT's *classmates are just staring at her in disbelief)*

FEMALE GREEK CHORUS: —You are the strangest girl I have ever met.

(LI'L BIT's trying to joke but feels on the verge of tears.)

LI'L BIT: Or maybe someone's implanted radio transmitters in my chest at a frequency I can't hear, that girls can't detect, but they're sending out these signals to men who get mesmerized, like sirens, calling them to dash themselves on these "rocks"—

(Just then, the music segues into a slow dance, perhaps a Beach Boys tune like "Little Surfer," but over the music there's a rhythmic, hypnotic beeping transmitted, which both GREG and PECK hear. LI'L BIT hears it too, and in horror she stares at her chest. She, too, is almost hypnotized. In a trance, GREG responds to the signals and is called to her side—actually, her front. Like a zombie, he stands in front of her, his eyes planted on her two orbs.)

MALE GREEK CHORUS (As GREG): This one's a slow dance. I hope your dance card isn't ... filled?

(LI'L BIT is aware of PECK; but the signals are calling her to him. The signals are no longer transmitters, but an electromagnetic force, pulling LI'L BIT to his side, where he again waits for her to join him. She must get away from the dance floor.)

LI'L BIT: Greg—you really are a nice boy. But I don't like to dance.

MALE GREEK CHORUS (As GREG): That's okay. We don't have to move or anything. I could just hold you and we could just sway a little—

LI'L BIT: —No! I'm sorry—but I think I have to leave; I hear someone calling me—

(LI'L BIT starts across the dance floor, leaving GREG behind. The beeping stops. The lights change, although the music does not. As LI'L BIT talks to the audience, she continues to change and prepare for the coming session. She should be wearing a tight tank top or a sheer blouse and very tight pants. To the audience:)

In every man's home some small room, some zone in his house, is set aside. It might be the attic, or the study, or a den. And there's an invisible sign as if from the old treehouse: Girls Keep Out.

Here, away from female eyes, lace doilies and crochet, he keeps his manly toys: the Vargas pinups, the tackle. A scent of tobacco and WD-40. *(She inhales deeply)* A dash of his Bay Rum. Ahh ... *(LI'L BIT savors it for just a moment more)*

Here he keeps his secrets: a violin or saxophone, drum set or darkroom, and the stacks of *Playboy. (In a whisper)* Here, in my aunt's home, it was the basement. Uncle Peck's turf.

(A Voice commands:)

You and the Reverse Gear.

LI'L BIT: 1965. The Photo Shoot.

(LI'L BIT steps into the scene as a nervous but curious thirteen-year-old. Music, from the previous scene, continues to play, changing into something like Roy

Orbison later—something seductive with a beat. PECK *fiddles, all business, with his camera. As in the driving lesson, he is all competency and concentration.* LI'L BIT *stands awkwardly. He looks through the Leica camera on the tripod, adjusts the back lighting, etc.)*

PECK: Are you cold? The lights should heat up some in a few minutes—

LI'L BIT: —Aunt Mary is?

PECK: At the National Theatre matinee. With your mother. We have time.

LI'L BIT: But—what if—

PECK: —And so what if they return? I told them you and I were going to be working with my camera. They won't come down. (LI'L BIT *is quiet, appre-hensive*)—Look, are you sure you want to do this?

LI'L BIT: I said I'd do it. But—

PECK: —I know. You've drawn the line.

LI'L BIT: (*Reassured*) That's right. No frontal nudity.

PECK: Good heavens, girl, where did you pick that up?

LI'L BIT: (*Defensive*) I *read*.

(PECK *tries not to laugh.*)

PECK: And I read *Playboy* for the interviews. Okay. Let's try some different music.

(PECK *goes to an expensive reel-to-reel and forwards. Something like "Sweet Dreams" begins to play.*)

LI'L BIT: I didn't know you listened to this.

PECK: I'm not dead, you know. I try to keep up. Do you like this song? (LI'L BIT *nods with pleasure*) Good. Now listen—at professional photo shoots, they always play music for the models. Okay? I want you to just enjoy the music. Listen to it with your body, and just—respond.

LI'L BIT: Respond to the music with my . . . body?

PECK: Right. Almost like dancing. Here—let's get you on the stool, first. (PECK *comes over and helps her up*)

LI'L BIT: But nothing showing—

(PECK *firmly, with his large capable hands, brushes back her hair, angles her face.* LI'L BIT *turns to him like a plant to the sun.*)

PECK: Nothing showing. Just a peek.
  (*He holds her by the shoulders, looking at her critically. Then he unbuttons her blouse to the midpoint, and runs his hands over the flesh of her exposed sternum, arranging the fabric, just touching her. Deliberately, calmly. Asex-ually.* LI'L BIT *quiets, sits perfectly still, and closes her eyes*)
  Okay?

LI'L BIT: Yes.

(PECK *goes back to his camera.*)

PECK: I'm going to keep talking to you. Listen without responding to what I'm saying; you want to *listen* to the music. Sway, move just your torso or your head—I've got to check the light meter.

LI'L BIT: But—you'll be watching.

PECK: No—I'm not here—just my voice. Pretend you're in your room all alone on a Friday night with your mirror—and the music feels good—just move for me, Li'l Bit—

(LI'L BIT *closes her eyes. At first self-conscious; then she gets more into the music and begins to sway. We hear the camera start to whir. Throughout the shoot, there can be a slide montage of actual shots of the actor playing* LI'L BIT—*interspersed with other models à la Playboy, Calvin Klein and Victoriana/Lewis Carroll's Alice Liddell*)

That's it. That looks great. Okay. Just keep doing that. Lift your head up a bit more, good, good, just keep moving, that a girl—you're a beautiful young woman. Do you know that? (LI'L BIT *looks up, blushes.* PECK *shoots the camera. The audience should see this shot on the screen*)

LI'L BIT: No. I don't know that.

PECK: Listen to the music. (LI'L BIT *closes her eyes again*) Well you are. For a thirteen-year-old, you have a body a twenty-year-old woman would die for.

LI'L BIT: The boys in school don't think so.

PECK: The boys in school are little Neanderthals in short pants. You're ten years ahead of them in maturity; it's gonna take a while for them to catch up.

(PECK *clicks another shot; we see a faint smile on* LI'L BIT *on the screen*)

Girls turn into women long before boys turn into men.

LI'L BIT: Why is that?

PECK: I don't know, Li'l Bit. But it's a blessing for men.

(LI'L BIT *turns silent*) Keep moving. Try arching your back on the stool, hands behind you, and throw your head back. (*The slide shows a* Playboy *model in this pose*) Oohh, great. That one was great. Turn head away, same position. (*Whir*) Beautiful.

(LI'L BIT *looks at him a bit defiantly.*)

LI'L BIT: I think Aunt Mary is beautiful.

(PECK *stands still.*)

PECK: My wife is a very beautiful woman. Her beauty doesn't cancel yours out. (*More casually; he returns to the camera*) All the women in your family are beautiful. In fact, I think all women are. You're not listening to the music. (PECK *shoots some more film in silence*) All right, turn your head to the left. Good. Now take the back of your right hand and put it on your right cheek—your elbow angled up—now slowly, slowly, stroke your cheek, draw back your hair with the back of your hand. (*Another classic*

Playboy *or* Vargas) Good. One hand above and behind your head; stretch your body; smile. *(Another pose)*

Li'l Bit. I want you to think of something that makes you laugh—

LI'L BIT: I can't think of anything.

PECK: Okay. Think of Big Papa chasing Grandma around the living room. (LI'L BIT *lifts her head and laughs. Click. We should see this shot)* Good. Both hands behind your head. Great! Hold that. *(From behind his camera)* You're doing great work. If we keep this up, in five years we'll have a really professional portfolio.

(LI'L BIT stops.)

LI'L BIT: What do you mean in five years?

PECK: You can't submit work to *Playboy* until you're eighteen.—

(PECK continues to shoot; he knows he's made a mistake.)

LI'L BIT: —Wait a minute. You're joking aren't you, Uncle Peck?

PECK: Heck, no. You can't get into *Playboy* unless you're the very best. And you are the very best.

LI'L BIT: I would never do that!

(PECK stops shooting. He turns off the music.)

PECK: Why? There's nothing wrong with *Playboy*—it's a very classy maga—

LI'L BIT: *(More upset)* But I thought you said I should go to college!

PECK: Wait—Li'l Bit—it's nothing like that. Very respectable women model for *Playboy*—actresses with major careers—women in college—there's an Ivy League issue every—

LI'L BIT: —I'm never doing anything like that! You'd show other people these—other *men*—these—what I'm doing.—Why would you do that?! Any *boy* around here could just pick up, just go to The Stop & Go and *buy*— Why would you ever want to—to share—

PECK: —Whoa, whoa. Just stop a second and listen to me. Li'l Bit. Listen. There's nothing wrong in what we're doing. I'm very proud of you. I think you have a wonderful body and an even more wonderful mind. And of course I want other people to *appreciate* it. It's not anything shameful.

LI'L BIT: *(Hurt)* But this is something—that I'm only doing for you. This is something—that you said was just between us.

PECK: It is. And if that's how you feel, five years from now, it will remain that way. Okay? I know you're not going to do anything you don't feel like doing.

(He walks back to the camera) Do you want me to stop now? I've got just a few more shots on this roll—

LI'L BIT: I don't want anyone seeing this.

PECK: I swear to you. No one will. I'll treasure this—that you're doing this only for me.

(LI'L BIT still shaken, sits on the stool. She closes her eyes) Li'l Bit? Open your eyes and look at me. (LI'L BIT shakes her head no) Come on. Just open your eyes, honey.

LI'L BIT: If I look at you—if I look at the camera: You're gonna know what I'm thinking. You'll see right through me—

PECK: —No, I won't. I want you to look at me. All right, then. I just want you to listen. Li'l Bit. *(She waits)* I love you. *(LI'L BIT opens her eyes; she is startled. PECK captures the shot. On the screen we see right through her. PECK says softly)* Do you know that? *(LI'L BIT nods her head yes)* I have loved you every day since the day you were born.

LI'L BIT: Yes.

(LI'L BIT and PECK just look at each other. Beat. Beneath the shot of herself on the screen, LI'L BIT, still looking at her uncle, begins to unbutton her blouse.

A neutral Voice cuts off the above scene with:)

Implied Consent

As an individual operating a motor vehicle in the state of Maryland, you must abide by "Implied Consent." If you do not consent to take the blood alcohol content test, there may be severe penalties: a suspension of license, a fine, community service and a possible jail sentence.

(The Voice shifts tone:)

Idling in Neutral Gear.

MALE GREEK CHORUS: *(Announcing)* Aunt Mary on behalf of her husband.

(FEMALE GREEK CHORUS checks her appearance, and with dignity comes to the front of the stage and sits down to talk to the audience.)

FEMALE GREEK CHORUS (AS AUNT MARY): My husband was such a good man—is. Is such a good man. Every night, he does the dishes. The second he comes home, he's taking out the garbage, or doing the yard work, lifting the heavy things I can't. Everyone in the neighborhood borrows Peck—it's true—women with husbands of their own, men who just don't have Peck's abilities—there's always a knock on our door for a jump start on cold mornings, when anyone else needs a ride, or help shoveling the sidewalk—I look out, and there Peck is, without a coat, pitching in.

I know I'm lucky. The man works from dawn to dusk. And the overtime he does every year—my poor sister. She sits every Christmas when I come to dinner with a new stole, or diamonds, or with the tickets to Bermuda.

I know he has troubles. And we don't talk about them. I wonder, sometimes, what happened to him during the war. The men who fought World War II didn't have "rap sessions" to talk about their feelings. Men in his generation were expected to be quiet about it and get on with their lives.

And sometimes I can feel him just fighting the trouble—whatever has burrowed deeper than the scar tissue—and we don't talk about it. I know he's having a bad spell because he comes looking for me in the house, and just hangs around me until it passes. And I keep my banter light—I discuss a new recipe, or sales, or gossip—because I think domesticity can be a balm for men when they're lost. We sit in the house and listen to the peace of the clock ticking in his well-ordered living room, until it passes.

(*Sharply*) I'm not a fool. I know what's going on. I wish you could feel how hard Peck fights against it—he's swimming against the tide, and what he needs is to see me on the shore, believing in him, knowing he won't go under, he won't give up—

And I want to say this about my niece. She's a sly one, that one is. She knows exactly what she's doing; she's twisted Peck around her little finger and thinks it's all a big secret. Yet another one who's borrowing my husband until it doesn't suit her anymore.

Well. I'm counting the days until she goes away to school. And she manipulates someone else. And then he'll come back again, and sit in the kitchen while I bake, or beside me on the sofa when I sew in the evenings. I'm a very patient woman. But I'd like my husband back.

I am counting the days.

(*A Voice repeats:*)

You and the Reverse Gear.

MALE GREEK CHORUS: Li'l Bit's Thirteenth Christmas. Uncle Peck Does the Dishes. Christmas 1964.

(*PECK stands in a dress shirt and tie, nice pants, with an apron. He is washing dishes. He's in a mood we haven't seen. Quiet, brooding. LI'L BIT watches him a moment before seeking him out.*)

LI'L BIT: Uncle Peck? (*He does not answer. He continues to work on the pots*) I didn't know where you'd gone to (*He nods. She takes this as a sign to come in*) Don't you want to sit with us for a while?
PECK: No. I'd rather do the dishes.

(*Pause. LI'L BIT watches him.*)

LI'L BIT: You're the only man I know who does dishes. (*PECK says nothing*) I think it's really nice.
PECK: My wife has been on her feet all day. So's your grandmother and your mother.
LI'L BIT: I know. (*Beat*) Do you want some help?
PECK: No. (*He softens a bit towards her*) You can help by just talking to me.
LI'L BIT: Big Papa never does the dishes. I think it's nice.

PECK: I think men should be nice to women. Women are always working for us. There's nothing particularly manly in wolfing down food and then sitting around in a stupor while the women clean up.

LI'L BIT: That looks like a really neat camera that Aunt Mary got you.

PECK: It is. It's a very nice one.

(Pause, as PECK works on the dishes and some demon that LI'L BIT intuits.)

LI'L BIT: Did Big Papa hurt your feelings?

PECK: *(Tired)* What? Oh, no—it doesn't hurt me. Family is family. I'd rather have him picking on me than—I don't pay him any mind, Li'l Bit.

LI'L BIT: Are you angry with us?

PECK: No, Li'l Bit. I'm not angry.

(Another pause.)

LI'L BIT: We missed you at Thanksgiving.... I did. I missed you.

PECK: Well, there were ... "things" going on. I didn't want to spoil anyone's Thanksgiving.

LI'L BIT: Uncle Peck? *(Very carefully)* Please don't drink anymore tonight.

PECK: I'm not ... overdoing it.

LI'L BIT: I know. *(Beat)* Why do you drink so much?

(PECK stops and thinks, carefully.)

PECK: Well, Li'l Bit—let me explain it this way. There are some people who have a ... a "fire" in the belly. I think they go to work on Wall Street or they run for office. And then there are people who have a "fire" inside their heads—and they become writers or scientists or historians. *(He smiles a little at her)* You. You've got a "fire" in the head. And then there are people like me.

LI'L BIT: Where do you have ... a fire?

PECK: I have a fire in my heart. And sometimes the drinking helps.

LI'L BIT: There's got to be other things that can help.

PECK: I suppose there are.

LI'L BIT: Does it help—to talk to me?

PECK: Yes. It does. *(Quietly)* I don't get to see you very much.

LI'L BIT: I know. (LI'L BIT *thinks*) You could talk to me more.

PECK: Oh?

LI'L BIT: I could make a deal with you, Uncle Peck.

PECK: I'm listening.

LI'L BIT: We could meet and talk—once a week. You could just store up whatever's bothering you during the week—and then we could talk.

PECK: Would you like that?

LI'L BIT: As long as you don't drink. I'd meet you somewhere for lunch or for a walk—on the weekends—as long as you stop drinking. And we could talk about whatever you want.

PECK: You would do that for me?

LI'L BIT: I don't think I'd want Mom to know. Or Aunt Mary. I wouldn't want them to think—

PECK: —No. It would just be us talking.

LI'L BIT: I'll tell Mom I'm going to a girlfriend's. To study. Mom doesn't get home until six, so you can call me after school and tell me where to meet you.

PECK: You get home at four?

LI'L BIT: We can meet once a week. But only in public. You've got to let me— draw the line. And once it's drawn, you mustn't cross it.

PECK: Understood.

LI'L BIT: Would that help?

(PECK *is very moved.*)

PECK: Yes. Very much.

LI'L BIT: I'm going to join the others in the living room now. (LI'L BIT *turns to go*)

PECK: Merry Christmas, Li'l Bit.

(LI'L BIT *bestows a very warm smile on him.*)

LI'L BIT: Merry Christmas, Uncle Peck.

(A *Voice dictates:*)

Shifting Forward From Second to Third Gear.

(*The* MALE *and* FEMALE GREEK CHORUS *members come forward.*)

MALE GREEK CHORUS: 1969. Days and Gifts: A Countdown:

FEMALE GREEK CHORUS: A note. "September 3, 1969. Li'l Bit: You've only been away two days and it feels like months. Hope your dorm room is cozy. I'm sending you this tape cassette—it's a new model—so you'll have some music in your room. Also that music you're reading about for class—*Carmina Burana.* Hope you enjoy. Only ninety days to go!—Peck."

MALE GREEK CHORUS: September 22. A bouquet of roses. A note: "Miss you like crazy. Sixty-nine days ..."

TEENAGE GREEK CHORUS: September 25. A box of chocolates. A card: "Don't worry about the weight gain. You still look great. Got a post office box— write to me there. Sixty-six days.—Love, your candy man."

MALE GREEK CHORUS: October 16. A note: "Am trying to get through the Jane Austen you're reading—*Emma*—here's a book in return: *Liaisons Dangereuses.* Hope you're saving time for me." Scrawled in the margin the number: "47."

FEMALE GREEK CHORUS: November 16. "Sixteen days to go!—Hope you like the perfume.—Having a hard time reaching you on the dorm phone. You must be in the library a lot. Won't you think about me getting you your own phone so we can talk?"

TEENAGE GREEK CHORUS: November 18. "Li'l Bit—got a package and returned it to the P.O. Box. Have you changed dorms? Call me at work or write to the P.O. Am still on the wagon. Waiting to see you. Only two weeks more!"

MALE GREEK CHORUS: November 23. A letter: "Li'l Bit. So disappointed you couldn't come home for the turkey. Sending you some money for a nice dinner out—nine days and counting!"

GREEK CHORUS: (*In unison*) November 25th. A letter:

LI'L BIT: "Dear Uncle Peck: I am sending this to you at work. Don't come up next weekend for my birthday. I will not be here—"

(*A Voice directs:*)

Shifting Forward from Third to Fourth Gear.

MALE GREEK CHORUS: December 10, 1969. A hotel room. Philadelphia. There is no moon tonight.

(*PECK sits on the side of the bed while LI'L BIT paces. He can't believe she's in his room, but there's a desperate edge to his happiness. LI'L BIT is furious, edgy. There is a bottle of champagne in an ice bucket in a very nice hotel room.*)

PECK: Why don't you sit?

LI'L BIT: I don't want to.—What's the champagne for?

PECK: I thought we might toast your birthday—

LI'L BIT: —I am so pissed off at you, Uncle Peck.

PECK: Why?

LI'L BIT: I mean, are you crazy?

PECK: What did I do?

LI'L BIT: You scared the holy crap out of me—sending me that stuff in the mail—

PECK: —They were gifts! I just wanted to give you some little perks your first semester—

LI'L BIT: —Well, what the hell were those numbers all about! Forty-four days to go—only two more weeks.—And then just numbers—69—68—67—like some serial killer!

PECK: Li'l Bit! Whoa! This is me you're talking to—I was just trying to pick up your spirits, trying to celebrate your birthday.

LI'L BIT: My *eighteenth* birthday. I'm not a child, Uncle Peck. You were counting down to my eighteenth birthday.

PECK: So?

LI'L BIT: So? So statutory rape is not in effect when a young woman turns eighteen. And you and I both know it.

(*PECK is walking on ice.*)

PECK: I think you misunderstand.

LI'L BIT: I think I understand all too well. I know what you want to do five steps ahead of you doing it: Defensive Driving 101.

PECK: Then why did you suggest we meet here instead of the restaurant?

LI'L BIT: I don't want to have this conversation in public.

PECK: Fine. Fine. We have a lot to talk about.

LI'L BIT: Yeah. We do.

(LI'L BIT *doesn't want to do what she has to do*) Could I . . . have some of that champagne?

PECK: Of course, madam! (PECK *makes a big show of it*) Let me do the honors. I wasn't sure which you might prefer—Tattingers or Veuve Clicquot—so I thought we'd start out with an old standard—Perrier Jouet. (*The bottle is popped*)

Quick—Li'l Bit—your glass! (UNCLE PECK *fills* LI'L BIT's *glass. He puts the bottle back in the ice and goes for a can of ginger ale*) Let me get some of this ginger ale—my bubbly—and toast you.

(*He turns and sees that* LI'L BIT *has not waited for him.*)

LI'L BIT: Oh—sorry, Uncle Peck. Let me have another. (PECK *fills her glass and reaches for his ginger ale; she stops him*) Uncle Peck—maybe you should join me in the champagne.

PECK: You want me to—drink?

LI'L BIT: It's not polite to let a lady drink alone.

PECK: Well, missy, if you insist. . . . (PECK *hesitates*) —Just one. It's been a while. (PECK *fills another flute for himself*) There. I'd like to propose a toast to you and your birthday! (PECK *sips it tentatively*) I'm not used to this anymore.

LI'L BIT: You don't have anywhere to go tonight, do you?

(PECK *hopes this is a good sign.*)

PECK: I'm all yours.—God, it's good to see you! I've gotten so used to . . . to . . . talking to you in my head. I'm used to seeing you every week—there's so much—I don't quite know where to begin. How's school, Li'l Bit?

LI'L BIT: I—it's hard. Uncle Peck. Harder than I thought it would be. I'm in the middle of exams and papers and—I don't know.

PECK: You'll pull through. You always do.

LI'L BIT: Maybe. I . . . might be flunking out.

PECK: You always think the worse, Li'l Bit, but when the going gets tough— (LI'L BIT *shrugs and pours herself another glass*) —Hey, honey, go easy on that stuff, okay?

LI'L BIT: Is it very expensive?

PECK: Only the best for you. But the cost doesn't matter—champagne should be "sipped." (LI'L BIT *is quiet*) Look—if you're in trouble in school—you can always come back home for a while.

LI'L BIT: No— (LI'L BIT *tries not to be so harsh*) —Thanks, Uncle Peck, but I'll figure some way out of this.

PECK: You're supposed to get in scrapes, your first year away from home.

LI'L BIT: Right. How's Aunt Mary?

PECK: She's fine. *(Pause)* Well—how about the new car?

LI'L BIT: It's real nice. What is it, again?

PECK: It's a Cadillac El Dorado.

LI'L BIT: Oh. Well, I'm real happy for you, Uncle Peck.

PECK: I got it for you.

LI'L BIT: What?

PECK: I always wanted to get a Cadillac—but I thought, Peck, wait until Li'l Bit's old enough—and thought maybe you'd like to drive it, too.

LI'L BIT: *(Confused)* Why would I want to drive your car?

PECK: Just because it's the best—I want you to have the best.

(They are running out of "gas"; small talk.)

LI'L BIT: Listen, Uncle Peck, I don't know how to begin this, but—	PECK: I have been thinking of how to say this in my head, over and over—

PECK: Sorry.

LI'L BIT: You first.

PECK: Well, your going away—has just made me realize how much I miss you. Talking to you and being alone with you. I've really come to depend on you, Li'l Bit. And it's been so hard to get in touch with you lately—the distance and—and you're never in when I call—I guess you've been living in the library—

LI'L BIT: —No—the problem is, I haven't been in the library—

PECK: —Well, it doesn't matter—I hope you've been missing me as much.

LI'L BIT: Uncle Peck—I've been thinking a lot about this—and I came here tonight to tell you that—I'm not doing very well. I'm getting very confused—I can't concentrate on my work—and now that I'm away—I've been going over and over it in my mind—and I don't want us to "see" each other anymore. Other than with the rest of the family.

PECK: *(Quiet)* Are you seeing other men?

LI'L BIT: *(Getting agitated)* I—no, that's not the reason—I—well, yes, I am seeing other—listen, it's not really anybody's business!

PECK: Are you in love with anyone else?

LI'L BIT: That's not what this is about.

PECK: Li'l Bit—you're scared. Your mother and your grandparents have filled your head with all kinds of nonsense about men—I hear them working on you all the time—and you're scared. It won't hurt you—if the man you go to bed with really loves you. (LI'L BIT *is scared. She starts to tremble*) And I have loved you since the day I held you in my hand. And I think everyone's just gotten you frightened to death about something that is just like breathing—

LI'L BIT: Oh, my god—*(She takes a breath)* I can't see you anymore, Uncle Peck.

(PECK downs the rest of his champagne.)

PECK: Li'l Bit. Listen. Listen. Open your eyes and look at me. Come on. Just open your eyes, honey. (LI'L BIT, *eyes squeezed shut, refuses*) All right then. I just want you to listen. Li'l Bit—I'm going to ask you this just once. Of your own free will. Just lie down on the bed with me—our clothes on—just lie down with me, a man and a woman ... and let's ... hold one another. Nothing else. Before you say anything else. I want the chance to ... hold you. Because sometimes the body knows things that the mind isn't listening to ... and after I've held you, then I want you to tell me what you feel.

LI'L BIT: You'll just ... hold me?

PECK: Yes. And then you can tell me what you're feeling.

(LI'L BIT—*half wanting to run, half wanting to get it over with, half wanting to be held by him:*)

LI'L BIT: Yes. All right. Just hold. Nothing else.

(PECK *lies down on the bed and holds his arms out to her.* LI'L BIT *lies beside him, putting her head on his chest. He looks as if he's trying to soak her into his pores by osmosis. He strokes her hair, and she lies very still. The* MALE GREEK CHORUS *member and the* FEMALE GREEK CHORUS *member as* AUNT MARY *come into the room.*)

MALE GREEK CHORUS: Recipe for a Southern Boy:

FEMALE GREEK CHORUS (As AUNT MARY): A drawl of molasses in the way he speaks.

MALE GREEK CHORUS: A gumbo of red and brown mixed in the cream of his skin.

(While PECK *lies, his eyes closed,* LI'L BIT *rises in the bed and responds to her aunt.*)

LI'L BIT: Warm brown eyes—

FEMALE GREEK CHORUS (As AUNT MARY): Bedroom eyes—

MALE GREEK CHORUS: A dash of Southern Baptist Fire and Brimstone—

LI'L BIT: A curl of Elvis on his forehead—

FEMALE GREEK CHORUS (As AUNT MARY): A splash of Bay Rum—

MALE GREEK CHORUS: A closely shaven beard that he razors just for you—

FEMALE GREEK CHORUS (As AUNT MARY): Large hands—rough hands—

LI'L BIT: Warm hands—

MALE GREEK CHORUS: The steel of the military in his walk—

LI'L BIT: The slouch of the fishing skiff in his walk—

MALE GREEK CHORUS: Neatly pressed khakis—

FEMALE GREEK CHORUS (As AUNT MARY): And under the wide leather of his belt—

LI'L BIT: Sweat of cypress and sand—

MALE GREEK CHORUS: Neatly pressed khakis—

LI'L BIT: His heart beating Dixie—

FEMALE GREEK CHORUS (As AUNT MARY): The whisper of the zipper—you could reach out with your hand and—

LI'L BIT: His mouth—

FEMALE GREEK CHORUS (As AUNT MARY): You could just reach out and—
LI'L BIT: Hold him in your hand—
FEMALE GREEK CHORUS (As AUNT MARY): And his mouth—

(LI'L BIT *rises above her uncle and looks at his mouth; she starts to lower herself to kiss him—and wrenches herself free. She gets up from the bed.*)

LI'L BIT: —I've got to get back.
PECK: Wait—Li'l Bit. Did you . . . feel nothing?
LI'L BIT: (*Lying*) No. Nothing.
PECK: Do you—do you think of me?

(*The* GREEK CHORUS *whispers:*)

FEMALE GREEK CHORUS: Khakis—
MALE GREEK CHORUS: Bay Rum—
FEMALE GREEK CHORUS: The whisper of the—
LI'L BIT: —No.

(PECK, *in a rush, trembling, gets something out of his pocket.*)

PECK: I'm forty-five. That's not old for a man. And I haven't been able to do anything else but think of you. I can't concentrate on my work—Li'l Bit. You've got to—I want you to think about what I am about to ask you.
LI'L BIT: I'm listening.

(PECK *opens a small ring box.*)

PECK: I want you to be my wife.
LI'L BIT: This isn't happening.
PECK: I'll tell Mary I want a divorce. We're not blood-related. It would be legal—
LI'L BIT: —What have you been thinking! You are married to my aunt, Uncle Peck. She's my family. You have—you have gone way over the line. Family is family.

(*Quickly,* LI'L BIT *flies through the room, gets her coat*) I'm leaving. Now. I am not seeing you. Again.

(PECK *lies down on the bed for a moment, trying to absorb the terrible news. For a moment, he almost curls into a fetal position*)

I'm not coming home for Christmas. You should go home to Aunt Mary. Go home now, Uncle Peck.

(PECK *gets control, and sits, rigid*)

Uncle Peck?—I'm sorry but I have to go.

(*Pause*)

Are you all right?

(*With a discipline that comes from being told that boys don't cry,* PECK *stands upright.*)

PECK: I'm fine. I just think—I need a real drink.

(The MALE GREEK CHORUS *has become a bartender. At a small counter, he is lining up shots for* PECK. *As* LI'L BIT *narrates, we see* PECK *sitting, carefully and calmly downing shot glasses.)*

LI'L BIT: *(To the audience)* I never saw him again. I stayed away from Christmas and Thanksgiving for years after.

It took my uncle seven years to drink himself to death. First he lost his job, then his wife, and finally his driver's license. He retreated to his house, and had his bottles delivered.

*(*PECK *stands, and puts his hands in front of him—almost like Superman flying)*

One night he tried to go downstairs to the basement—and he flew down the steep basement stairs. My aunt came by weekly to put food on the porch, and she noticed the mail and the papers stacked up, uncollected.

They found him at the bottom of the stairs. Just steps away from his dark room.

Now that I'm old enough, there are some questions I would have liked to have asked him. Who did it to you, Uncle Peck? How old were you? Were you eleven?

*(*PECK *moves to the driver's seat of his car and waits)*

Sometimes I think of my uncle as a kind of Flying Dutchman. In the opera, the Dutchman is doomed to wander the sea; but every seven years he can come ashore, and if he finds a maiden who will love him of her own free will—he will be released.

And I see Uncle Peck in my mind, in his Chevy '56, a spirit driving up and down the back roads of Carolina—looking for a young girl who, of her own free will, will love him. Release him.

(A Voice states:)

You and the Reverse Gear.

LI'L BIT: The summer of 1962. On Men, Sex, and Women: Part III:

*(*LI'L BIT *steps, as an eleven year old, into:)*

FEMALE GREEK CHORUS (As MOTHER): It is out of the question. End of Discussion.

LI'L BIT: But why?

FEMALE GREEK CHORUS (As MOTHER): Li'l Bit—we are not discussing this. I said no.

LI'L BIT: But I could spend an extra week at the beach! You're not telling me why!

FEMALE GREEK CHORUS (As MOTHER): Your uncle pays entirely too much attention to you.

LI'L BIT: He listens to me when I talk. And—and he talks to me. He teaches me about things. Mama—he knows an awful lot.

FEMALE GREEK CHORUS (AS MOTHER): He's a small town hick who's learned how to mix drinks from Hugh Hefner.

LI'L BIT: Who's Hugh Hefner?

(Beat.)

FEMALE GREEK CHORUS (AS MOTHER): I am not letting an eleven-year-old girl spend seven hours alone in the car with a man.... I don't like the way your uncle looks at you.

LI'L BIT: For god's sake, mother! Just because you've gone through a bad time with my father—you think every man is evil!

FEMALE GREEK CHORUS (AS MOTHER): Oh no, Li'l Bit—not all men.... We ... we just haven't been very lucky with the men in our family.

LI'L BIT: Just because you lost your husband—I still deserve a chance at having a father! Someone! A man who will look out for me! Don't I get a chance?

FEMALE GREEK CHORUS (AS MOTHER): I will feel terrible if something happens.

LI'L BIT: Mother! It's in your head! Nothing will happen! I can take care of myself. And I can certainly handle Uncle Peck.

FEMALE GREEK CHORUS (AS MOTHER): All right. But I'm warning you—if anything happens, I hold you responsible.

(LI'L BIT moves out of this scene and toward the car.)

LI'L BIT: 1962 On the Back Roads of Carolina: The First Driving Lesson.

(The TEENAGE GREEK CHORUS member stands apart on stage. She will speak all of LI'L BIT's lines. LI'L BIT sits beside PECK in the front seat. She looks at him closely, remembering.)

PECK: Li'l Bit? Are you getting tired?

TEENAGE GREEK CHORUS: A little.

PECK: It's a long drive. But we're making really good time. We can take the back road from here and see ... a little scenery. Say—I've got an idea— *(PECK checks his rearview mirror)*

TEENAGE GREEK CHORUS: Are we stopping, Uncle Peck.

PECK: There's no traffic here. Do you want to drive?

TEENAGE GREEK CHORUS: I can't drive.

PECK: It's easy. I'll show you how. I started driving when I was your age. Don't you want to?—

TEENAGE GREEK CHORUS: —But it's against the law at my age!

PECK: And that's why you can't tell anyone I'm letting you do this—

TEENAGE GREEK CHORUS: —But—I can't reach the pedals.

PECK: You can sit in my lap and steer. I'll push the pedals for you. Did your father ever let you drive his car?

TEENAGE GREEK CHORUS: No way.

PECK: Want to try?

TEENAGE GREEK CHORUS: Okay. *(LI'L BIT moves into PECK's lap. She leans against him, closing her eyes)*

PECK: You're just a little thing, aren't you? Okay—now think of the wheel as a big clock—I want you to put your right hand on the clock where three o'clock would be; and your left hand on the nine—

(LI'L BIT puts one hand to PECK's face, to stroke him. Then, she takes the wheel.)

TEENAGE GREEK CHORUS: Am I doing this right?

PECK: That's right. Now, whatever you do, don't let go of the wheel. You tell me whether to go faster or slower—

TEENAGE GREEK CHORUS: Not so fast, Uncle Peck!

PECK: Li'l Bit—I need you to watch the road—

(PECK puts his hands on LI'L BIT's breasts. She relaxes against him, silent, accepting his touch.)

TEENAGE GREEK CHORUS: Uncle Peck—what are you doing?

PECK: Keep driving. *(He slips his hand under her blouse)*

TEENAGE GREEK CHORUS: Uncle Peck—please don't do this—

PECK: —Just a moment longer ... *(PECK tenses against LI'L BIT)*

TEENAGE GREEK CHORUS: *(Trying not to cry)* This isn't happening.

(PECK tenses more, sharply. He buries his face in LI'L BIT's neck, and moans softly. The TEENAGE GREEK CHORUS exits, and LI'L BIT steps out of the car. PECK, too, disappears.

A Voice reflects:)

Driving in Today's World.

LI'L BIT: That day was the last day I lived in my body. I retreated above the neck, and I've lived inside the "fire" in my head ever since.

And now that seems like a long, long time ago. When we were both very young.

And before you know it, I'll be thirty-five. That's getting up there for a woman. And I find myself believing in things that a younger self vowed never to believe in. Things like family and forgiveness.

I know I'm lucky. Although I still have never known what it feels like to jog or dance. Any thing like that ... "jiggles." I do like to watch people on the dance floor, or out on the running paths, just jiggling away. And I say—good for them. *(LI'L BIT moves to the car with pleasure)*

The nearest sensation I feel—of flight in the body—I guess I feel when I'm driving. On a day like today. It's five A.M. The radio says it's going to be clear and crisp. I've got five hundred miles of highway ahead of me— and some back roads too. I filled the tank last night, and had the oil checked. Checked the tires, too. You've got to treat her ... with respect.

First thing I do is: Check under the car. To see if any two-year-olds or household cats have crawled beneath, and strategically placed their skulls behind my back tires. *(LI'L BIT crouches)*

Nope. Then I get in the car. (LI'L BIT *does so*)

I lock the doors. And turn the key. Then I adjust the most important control on the dashboard—the radio—(LI'L BIT *turns the radio on: We hear all of the* GREEK CHORUS *overlapping, and static:*)

FEMALE GREEK CHORUS: *(Overlapping)* —"You were so tiny you fit in his hand—"

MALE GREEK CHORUS: *(Overlapping)* —"How is Shakespeare gonna help her lie on her back in the—"

TEENAGE GREEK CHORUS: *(Overlapping)* —"Am I doing it right?"

(LI'L BIT *fine-tunes the radio station. A song like "Dedicated to the One I Love" or Orbison's "Sweet Dreams" comes on, and cuts off the* GREEK CHORUS.)

LI'L BIT: Ahh . . . *(Beat)* I adjust my seat. Fasten my seat belt. Then I check the right side mirror—check the left side. *(She does)* Finally I adjust the rearview mirror. (*As* LI'L BIT *adjust the rearview mirror, a faint light strikes the spirit of* UNCLE PECK, *who is sitting in the back seat of the car. She sees him in the mirror. She smiles at him, and he nods at her. They are happy to be going for a long drive together.* LI'L BIT *slips the car into first gear; to the audience:*) And then—I floor it. *(Sound of a car taking off. Blackout)*

END OF PLAY

1997

RANE ARROYO
1954–2010

Born in Chicago to parents from Puerto Rico, Rane Ramón Arroyo was a prize-winning poet and playwright who lived in Ohio and Pennsylvania. He received a Ph.D. in American literature and cultural studies from the University of Pittsburgh. A self-professed gay writer, he was also a literary critic and performance artist and directed the University of Toledo's creative writing program. Arroyo's work is marked by his references to Caribbean and Latino life in the Midwest (particularly in Chicago); his consistent engagement with canonical literary figures of American and English modernism as well as with Latin American and Spanish poets; and his exploration of his personal experiences, including his long-standing relationship with the poet Glenn Sheldon, affection for his cat Diva, and awareness of his own process of aging.

Arroyo's self-reflexive poetry often focuses on the inner conscience of a poetic persona, a gay Puerto Rican bard who feels out of place in the world and who is constantly grappling with what it means to be a poet marked by racial, sexual, and linguistic difference. In this universe, poetry is construed as the space where memory comes together; the space for appreciating that which surrounds the individual; a way to come to terms with the world and to reflect about politics, news, racial relations, and the migrant experience; and, quite markedly, what it means to be an American.

At the core of Arroyo's universe are his family and the Puerto Rican traditions (dance, music, food, the Spanish language) and social experiences (factory work, poverty, migration) that characterize his relatives. A recurrent set of characters appears throughout Arroyo's four books: Mami, Papi, Aunt Sylvia, and Uncle "Rachel" (the transvestite uncle), along with many cousins. The poems often express intimate (and evolving) relationships with these individuals, highlighting issues of masculinity and gender in relation to the father and uncle, of tradition and assimilation in relation to the mother, and of youth and coming of age with the cousins.

One of the most striking features of Arroyo's poetry is his play with traditional forms (what appear to be rigid stanza sequences, often couplets and tercets, and set-length verses), which he uses to give shape to strongly prosaic content; the verses constantly make use of enjambment. Arroyo's poetry is marked by the variety of topics that it covers in a most colloquial way, wandering from considerations of Latino popular and mass culture (Andy García, Antonio Banderas, Desi Arnaz, Rita Moreno and *West Side Story*, Speedy González, Taco Bell) to revisionist historic dialogues with Christopher Columbus and conquistadors such as Juan Ponce de León to profound analysis about the specific environs of a particular neighborhood or serious critiques of racism or of the effects of drug trafficking and drug addiction. His poetry tries to reconcile geographic specificity (his own love of Chicago, his parents' Puerto Rico) with cosmopolitanism (a learned engagement with the Western tradition and extensive travels throughout the world). He makes a clear attempt to address dominant conceptions of Latinos in the United States, engaging with damaging stereotypes as well as with issues specific to Mexican Americans/Chicanos, Cuban Americans, and Puerto Ricans.

The strong literary bent of Arroyo's work is established by constant mentions of and dialogues with poets such as William Carlos Williams (whose mother was Puerto Rican), Wallace Stevens, Hart Crane, Diane Williams, and Seamus Heaney, as well as such Hispanic greats as Sor Juana Inés de la Cruz, Federico García Lorca, Octavio Paz, and Pablo Neruda. In fact, the poet's careful attention to form and literary language as *writerly* phenomena bring him closer to Víctor Hernández Cruz than to other Puerto Rican poets.

Lawrence La Fountain-Stokes
University of Michigan–Ann Arbor

PRIMARY WORKS

Columbus's Orphan, 1993; *The Singing Shark*, 1996; *Pale Ramón*, 1998; *Home Movies of Narcissus*, 2002; *Same-Sex Séances*, 2008; *The Roswell Poems*, 2008; *The Buried Sea: New and Selected Poems*, 2008; *The Sky's Weight*, 2009.

My Transvestite Uncle Is Missing

1. *Questions*

I remember you so Elvis Presley-thin
and ever about to join the army (now I know

the whys of that), and I remember remembering you:
before breasts, before European wigs, when

the etc. of your sexuality was a secret,   5
and you babysat me, and we danced to Aretha,
and you taught me to scream for the joy of
a song on the radio ("Romeo requests this from

his grave!"), and I can't call you, what's
your new legal name? Is it in the phone book?   10

Are you that official? I've heard you're
dead, call me collect please, I'm on my own,

and Uncle Rachel if you were here tonight I'd . . .
I'd sing to you: "Pretty woman walking down

the street of dreams," and you could tell me   15
that story again where gold is spun out of straw

2. *Answers*

News of your old death, first I danced in the shower with
clothes on, cracked my green head against a corner gave you a
bloody birth in my mind, gave myself a satisfying scar,
watched an Annie Lennox video where she has a red towel on   20
her head, I mirrored her, white towel to stop the bleeding
inside my own nest of a skull, then I screamed and screamed,
but the police never came, snow fell from the constellations,
everything was on fire, fast forward, tumbling and I stupidly
read the Song of Solomon for comfort, my eye filled up with   25
blood, I strapped a big bandage around my head, I'm a poor
man's Wilfred Owen, I'm my own damnation, you're dead,
I won't sing at the funeral that took place without me, the
sun will hear my confessions, my naked body on a rooftop
cruel cock crowing as if another ordinary morning, and it is,   30
I did survive, I, someone shows up to make sure I'm not in a
coma, I'm not, not with all these memories, I touch myself as

if I'm still loved, Uncle Rachel, does Death look sexy without
a fig leaf?

1996

Caribbean Braille

My blind father doesn't
want a volunteer
reader to describe
someone else's depluming.
He'd rather spend his rosary   5
time remembering, but
what does he long for in his
short attention span?
He has been reflecting
upon the color *wine-red*,   10
the idea of it in the world,
wine-red as wine and red.
The last thing Father saw
before his eyes burned into
industrial nothingness   15
was a nova in the shape
of a rose with hot thorns:
my eyes burst into flames
without warning. In his
youth's Old San Juan,   20
the norteamericano hotels
had roses and wine on tables
which he'd spy on from
cobblestone streets. *Who needs*
fiction? he asks, sure that   25
I have no answer, but
the son reads his father
to sleep. We wake up in
the morning, compare
mosquito bites. We laugh: 30
how silly to think someone
might send us love letters via
Caribbean mosquitoes. We
read this Braille by rubbing
our hands over and over   35
the bright bites. Our bodies are
the books we cannot read.

1998

Write What You Know

But what do I know? I know Papi
worked in factories reigned by melodrama
(a sick day = the righteous anger of

waltzing bosses in K-Mart suits). I know   5
the word "knowledge" has the words
"now" and "ledge." I know that

my parents dared to color the suburbs
with their shy children. I'm no longer shy.
"Chew garlic," Mami said just yesterday after
I was diagnosed with pneumonia (I can't yet   10
breathe in the America I so love). I must write
about the time a museum guard yelled

at Papi: "The service entrance is over there."
Forgive me, Papi, for wanting to see dinosaurs.
(He's an aging man who abandoned me as an adult.)   15

Papi was silly, but he stopped dreaming
after citizen classes (but Puerto Ricans are
Americans I must still tell my frowning

scholarship geniuses). I know that Uncle
Manolo, who died in the green disgrace   20
of gangrene, did want to teach me the 12-string

guitar, but we visited less and less until
we were merely scars to each other, sad
genealogies. I know una tía became religious

decades after offering me a *Playboy* and   25
an egg timer. I know another tía talks
to spirits between epilepsy carnivals.

She is sweet and tough, what the grave
yearns for when thinking of honey.
I know that in poetry workshops I've lied: 30

"I'm not autobiographical." *They* don't need
to know Mami ripped a real blouse while
screaming at Heaven as if an eavesdropper

with a big diary. Papi's pornography was
disappointing because it wasn't imaginative.   35
I know I was judgmental, one way

to survive. I know that I miss feeding the camels
of the Three Wise Men. (Forget the presents—
camels in Chicago!) I know my teacher in

elementary school told me she was glad that   40
someday I'd be raped in prison. I know that
I've masturbated towards fake passports.

I've always loved details as if they are
sharable coins. I know that some colleagues
treating me to one dinner were naive in thinking   45
I knew the Mexican waiters who cursed them
every time they smiled under the parachutes of
fragile mustaches. We were and weren't strangers.

Will I get an award for knowing Mami hid her silver
Jack Kennedy dollars in the bathroom? I know God   50
has plans for me, but I'd rather do it myself, gracias.

I write without permission and no one knows how
often I'm rejected, and when I do publish, *they* smirk,
"Affirmative Action." My future is as an antique.

I know a man's morning beard can rub me raw   55
so that it feels that even sandpaper has a soul.
I know that I want to be known in my earned bed,

that it's worth it to be kept out of anthologies
because machos clone themselves without end.
My crotch has a mind of its own; I'm a double exile.   60

Sí, I know that none of this matters and yet
it hurts, it hurts. I know that once upon a time,
I used to be a brave little brown boy. The man I am

has memory losses that medicine can't help.
I know there are evil men trying to trade   65
new poems for old poems: newer, swifter,

correct models. I know that the writing
workshop is a minefield. I know that I cannot
stop writing, that the involuntary muscles

are in it for the long run. I know I must   70
write to scare myself. I know that my beloved
Hardy Boys may never recognize me

from other migrant workers while solving
The Mystery of the Lost Muchacho.
I'm waving to them: here I am, here I am.   75

Hombres, how many more clues do you need?

                                                                                 2002

That Flag

The Motel 6 clerk thinks I'm
Italian and complains to me
about Puerto Ricans, and I
nod because she has the key
to the last cheap room in town.   5
I unpack and go for a ride
down Joe Peréz Road and watch
two white, shirtless men do drug deals.
One looks at me, laughs. What does
he see? This sexy thug has   10
a Confederate flag in his truck
window. He rubs himself again
and again and I watch the way
one is possessed by a wreck.
The deal done, the two men then   15
slap each other on the ass,
and ride dust storms back to town.
I sit there thinking the fuckers
are right, that they are big
handsome, that they are our   20
America's perfect heirs and
that I'm not—aging Puerto Rican
homosexual poet exiled
to a borrowed bed. I walk
past the clerk and sing "Buenas   25
noches," but it isn't one, for I dream
of that flag, of a terrible army
of soldiers in uniforms of skin
sent to steal from me the head
of Joe Peréz. But I've hidden it   30
inside my own skull. It is safe.

                                                                                 2002

SANDRA CISNEROS

B. 1954

Best known as a writer of fiction, Sandra Cisneros set out at the Iowa Writers Workshop to craft poems. But even as she wrote evocative and moving poems, she also started writing brief stories that she would later fondly refer to as "lazy poems." These stories became the seeds for her first novel, *The House on Mango Street* (1984) and collection of short stories, *Woman Hollering Creek and Other Stories* (1991). In these brief tales and chapters, often snapshots of figures, places, and life-altering experiences, Cisneros reveals herself as not just a poet who writes fiction, but as a sonic theorist exploring how sounds make meanings, how they joke, enrage, and seem to gesture toward what words cannot quite articulate. In her experimentation with Spanish and English, with shaky translations, surprising juxtapositions, and long playful lists, Cisneros draws attention to the sonorous qualities of language, asking the reader to understand the words on the page in multiple dimensions (as sounds, as relationships, as maps, as connections and disruptions). She achieves this in a mischievous manner, frequently through the voice of a child whose observations appear at first oddly simplistic and obvious.

By engaging with the concept of voice (what we *expect* to hear from a speaker), Cisneros challenges us to question many kinds of received assumptions, from those about the effectiveness of gender expectations to habits of racialized thinking about others to prim judgments about what sorts of desires are acceptable, pleasurable, and worth pursuing. For example, in her brief story "Eleven," the narrator describes a bad school day. Built into this quotidian example of middle-school nastiness, however, is a thoughtful meditation on temporality and quantification. In other stories, such as "Mericans" and "Tepeyac," Cisneros dramatizes the racial assumptions of tourists outside the Mexico City Basilica dedicated to the Virgin of Guadalupe while the language of the story rushes around in a mix of English, Spanish, lists, and translations that sit slightly askew from their intentions. What appears to be a simple moment in "Tepeyac," when an adult narrator recalls a memory of childhood visits, oddly seems to hinge on repeating prepositions. The abundance of prepositions only makes sense as the story turns toward the end on a metacommentary about the intertwined connections between memory, writing, and familial expectations. Cisneros' second novel, *Caramelo* (2002), carries this vision out with a rollicking story of cross-border, multilingual, and multisited characters, songs, items, and advertisements that also becomes a biography of nations, families, and various revolutions both large and small. As a sonic theorist, she is also a wickedly astute Chicana feminist intellectual.

Born in Chicago in 1954, Cisneros quickly achieved fame with the publication of her first novel. She subsequently began to teach at several universities before receiving a prestigious MacArthur Genius Award. Since then Cisneros has actively worked to cultivate writing opportunities and a network of writing and creative mentors for new writers. In 1995 she began holding writing workshops at her kitchen table, eventually developing the Macondo Foundation to support as many as 150 writers for intensive summer workshops. Cisneros understands this work as part of a service to underserved communities and seeks to foster the work of other writers who share her vision of writing as crucial to the broader effort to work for nonviolent social change and community creation and renewal.

Mary Pat Brady
Cornell University

PRIMARY WORKS

Bad Boys, 1980; *The House on Mango Street*, 1984, 1991; *My Wicked, Wicked Ways*, 1987, 1992; *Woman Hollering Creek and Other Stories*, 1991; *Hairs/Pelitos*, 1994; *Loose Woman*, 1994; *Caramelo*, 2002.

Mericans

We're waiting for the awful grandmother who is inside dropping pesos into *la ofrenda* box before the altar to La Divina Providencia. Lighting votive candles and genuflecting. Blessing herself and kissing her thumb. Running a crystal rosary between her fingers. Mumbling, mumbling, mumbling.

There are so many prayers and promises and thanks-be-to-God to be given in the name of the husband and the sons and the only daughter who never attend mass. It doesn't matter. Like La Virgen de Guadalupe, the awful grandmother intercedes on their behalf. For the grandfather who hasn't believed in anything since the first PRI elections. For my father, El Periquín, so skinny he needs his sleep. For Auntie Light-skin, who only a few hours before was breakfasting on brain and goat tacos after dancing all night in the pink zone. For Uncle Fat-face, the blackest of the black sheep— *Always remember your Uncle Fat-face in your prayers*. And Uncle Baby— *You go for me, Mamá—God listens to you*.

The awful grandmother has been gone a long time. She disappeared behind the heavy leather outer curtain and the dusty velvet inner. We must stay near the church entrance. We must not wander over to the balloon and punch-ball vendors. We cannot spend our allowance on fried cookies or Familia Burrón comic books or those clear cone-shaped suckers that make everything look like a rainbow when you look through them. We cannot run off and have our picture taken on the wooden ponies. We must not climb the steps up the hill behind the church and chase each other through the cemetery. We have promised to stay right where the awful grandmother left us until she returns.

There are those walking to church on their knees. Some with fat rags tied around their legs and others with pillows, one to kneel on, and one to flop ahead. There are women with black shawls crossing and uncrossing themselves. There are armies of penitents carrying banners and flowered arches while musicians play tinny trumpets and tinny drums.

La Virgen de Guadalupe is waiting inside behind a plate of thick glass. There's also a gold crucifix bent crooked as a mesquite tree when someone once threw a bomb. La Virgen de Guadalupe on the main altar because she's a big miracle, the crooked crucifix on a side altar because that's a little miracle.

But we're outside in the sun. My big brother Junior hunkered against the wall with his eyes shut. My little brother Keeks running around in circles.

Maybe and most probably my little brother is imagining he's a flying feather dancer, like the ones we saw swinging high up from a pole on the Virgin's birthday. I want to be a flying feather dancer too, but when he circles past me he shouts, "I'm a B-Fifty-two bomber, you're a German," and shoots me with an invisible machine gun. I'd rather play flying feather dancers, but if I tell my brother this, he might not play with me at all.

"*Girl.* We can't play with a *girl.*" *Girl.* It's my brothers' favorite insult now instead of "sissy." "You *girl,*" they yell at each other. "You throw that ball like a *girl.*"

I've already made up my mind to be a German when Keeks swoops past again, this time yelling, "I'm Flash Gordon. You're Ming the Merciless and the Mud People." I don't mind being Ming the Merciless, but I don't like being the Mud People. Something wants to come out of the corners of my eyes, but I don't let it. Crying is what *girls* do.

I leave Keeks running around in circles—"I'm the Lone Ranger, you're Tonto." I leave Junior squatting on his ankles and go look for the awful grandmother.

Why do churches smell like the inside of an ear? Like incense and the dark and candles in blue glass? And why does holy water smell of tears? The awful grandmother makes me kneel and fold my hands. The ceiling high and everyone's prayers bumping up there like balloons.

If I stare at the eyes of the saints long enough, they move and wink at me, which makes me a sort of saint too. When I get tired of winking saints, I count the awful grandmother's mustache hairs while she prays for Uncle Old, sick from the worm, and Auntie Cuca, suffering from a life of troubles that left half her face crooked and the other half sad.

There must be a long, long list of relatives who haven't gone to church. The awful grandmother knits the names of the dead and the living into one long prayer fringed with the grandchildren born in that barbaric country with its barbarian ways.

I put my weight on one knee, then the other, and when they both grow fat as a mattress of pins, I slap them each awake. *Micaela, you may wait outside with Alfredito and Enrique.* The awful grandmother says it all in Spanish, which I understand when I'm paying attention. "What?" I say, though it's neither proper nor polite. "What?" which the awful grandmother hears as "*¿Güat?*" But she only gives me a look and shoves me toward the door.

After all that dust and dark, the light from the plaza makes me squinch my eyes like if I just came out of the movies. My brother Keeks is drawing squiggly lines on the concrete with a wedge of glass and the heel of his shoe. My brother Junior squatting against the entrance, talking to a lady and man.

They're not from here. Ladies don't come to church dressed in pants. And everybody knows men aren't supposed to wear shorts. "*¿Quieres chicle?*" the lady asks in a Spanish too big for her mouth.

"*Gracias.*" The lady gives him a whole handful of gum for free, little cellophane cubes of Chiclets, cinnamon and aqua and the white ones that don't taste like anything but are good for pretend buck teeth.

"*Por favor,*" says the lady, "*¿Un foto?*" pointing to her camera. "*Si.*"

She's so busy taking Junior's picture, she doesn't notice me and Keeks.

"Hey, Michele, Keeks. You guys want gum?"

"But you speak English!"

"Yeah," my brother says, "we're Mericans."

We're Mericans, we're Mericans, and inside the awful grandmother prays.

1991

Tepeyac

When the sky of Tepeyac opens its first thin stars and the dark comes down in an ink of Japanese blue above the bell towers of La Basílica de Nuestra Señora, above the plaza photographers and their souvenir backdrops of La Virgen de Guadalupe, above the balloon vendors and their balloons wearing paper hats, above the red-canopied thrones of the shoeshine stands, above the wooden booths of the women frying lunch in vats of oil, above the *tlapalería* on the corner of Misterios and Cinco de Mayo, when the photographers have toted up their tripods and big box cameras, have rolled away the wooden ponies I don't know where, when the balloon men have sold all but the ugliest balloons and herded these last few home, when the shoeshine men have grown tired of squatting on their little wooden boxes, and the women frying lunch have finished packing dishes, tablecloth, pots, in the big straw basket in which they came, then Abuelito tells the boy with dusty hair, *Arturo, we are closed,* and in crooked shoes and purple elbows Arturo pulls down with a pole the corrugated metal curtains—first the one on Misterios, then the other on Cinco de Mayo—like an eyelid over each door, before Abuelito tells him he can go.

This is when I arrive, one shoe and then the next, over the sagging door stone, worn smooth in the middle from the huaraches of those who have come for tins of glue and to have their scissors sharpened, who have asked for candles and cans of boot polish, a half-kilo sack of nails, turpentine, blue-specked spoons, paintbrushes, photographic paper, a spool of picture wire, lamp oil, and string.

Abuelito under a bald light bulb, under a ceiling dusty with flies, puffs his cigar and counts money soft and wrinkled as old Kleenex, money earned by the plaza women serving lunch on flat tin plates, by the souvenir photographers and their canvas Recuerdo de Tepeyac backdrops, by the shoeshine men sheltered beneath their fringed and canopied kingdoms, by the blessed vendors of the holy cards, rosaries, scapulars, little plastic altars, by the good sisters who live in the convent across the street, counts and recounts in a whisper and puts the money in a paper sack we carry home.

I take Abuelito's hand, fat and dimpled in the center like a valentine, and we walk past the basilica, where each Sunday the Abuela lights the candles for the soul of Abuelito. Past the very same spot where long ago Juan Diego brought down from the *cerro* the miracle that has drawn everyone, except my Abuelito, on their knees, down the avenue one block past the bright lights of the *sastrería* of Señor Guzmán who is still at work at his sewing machine, past the candy store where I buy my milk-and-raisin gelatins, past La Providencia *tortillería* where every afternoon Luz María and I are sent for the basket of lunchtime tortillas, past the house of the widow Márquez whose husband died last winter of a tumor the size of her little white fist, past La Muñeca's mother watering her famous dahlias with a pink rubber hose and a skinny string of water, to the house on La Fortuna, number 12, that has always been our house. Green iron gates that arabesque and scroll like the initials of my name, familiar whine and clang, familiar lacework of ivy growing over and between except for one small clean square for the hand of the postman whose face I have never seen, up the twenty-two steps we count out loud together—*uno, dos, tres*—to the supper of *sopa de fideo* and *carne guisada*—*cuatro, cinco, seis*—the glass of *café con leche*— *siete, ocho, nueve*—shut the door against the mad parrot voice of the Abuela—*diez, once, doce*—fall asleep as we always do, with the television mumbling—*trece, catorce, quince*—the Abuelito snoring—*dieciséis, diecisiete, dieciocho*—the grandchild, the one who will leave soon for that borrowed country— *diecinueve, veinte, veintiuno*—the one he will not remember, the one he is least familiar with—*veintidós, veintitrés, veinticuatro*— years later when the house on La Fortuna, number 12, is sold, when the *tlapalería*, corner of Misterios and Cinco de Mayo, changes owners, when the courtyard gate of arabesques and scrolls is taken off its hinges and replaced with a corrugated sheet metal door instead, when the widow Márquez and La Muñeca's mother move away, when Abuelito falls asleep one last time— *Veinticinco, veintiséis, veintisiete*—years afterward when I return to the shop on the corner of Misterios and Cinco de Mayo, repainted and redone as a pharmacy, to the basilica that is crumbling and closed, to the plaza photographers, the balloon vendors and shoeshine thrones, the women whose faces I do not recognize serving lunch in the wooden booths, to the house on La Fortuna, number 12, smaller and darker than when we lived there, with the rooms boarded shut and rented to strangers, the street suddenly dizzy with automobiles and diesel fumes, the house fronts scuffed and the gardens frayed, the children who played kickball all grown and moved away.

Who would've guessed, after all this time, it is me who will remember when everything else is forgotten, you who took with you to your stone bed something irretrievable, without a name.

1991

DAVID FOSTER WALLACE
1962–2008

One of the defining publishing events of the 1900s was surely the 1996 release of *Infinite Jest*, an anaconda text (more than a thousand pages, with more than nine hundred explanatory notes) that was only the second novel of a soft-spoken creative writing professor from Illinois State University whose scruffy demeanor and trademark bandanna quickly became elements of his new celebrity. Critical estimations and fan websites quickly dubbed this reluctant celebrity, at thirty-four, the Literary Voice of Generation X, the Heir Apparent to Thomas Pynchon, the Grunge Wunderkind, a hip cross between Charles Dickens and Robin Williams, James Joyce and Hunter Thompson.

Born in Ithaca, New York, the son of two respected academics, Wallace enjoyed a remarkably unremarkable childhood in Illinois (save for a time as a nationally ranked player on the junior tennis circuit), a bookworm given to the indiscriminate absorption of television. Although he evidenced promise in math-ematical philosophy at Amherst, Wallace felt more compelled by fiction (he cites reading the metafictionist Donald Barthelme in particular). He completed his B.A. *summa cum laude* in 1985 and went on for his M.F.A. from the University of Arizona in 1987. By then he had already published his first novel, *The Broom of the System* (1986), his senior thesis at Amherst, a rollicking speculation on Ludwig Wittgenstein's language theories that centers on a mass exodus from a Cleveland nursing home.

After ten years and a growing reputation from his short stories and essays, Wallace released *Infinite Jest*. Because of its massive intricacy, its savvy indul-gence of pop culture referents, its scores of eccentric characters, its labyrinthine plot (centering on a halfway house for recovering addicts and a nearby tennis academy), its multiple genres and shifting perspectives, its encyclopedic com-mand of the metaphors of recreational pharmaceuticals, information theory, and mathematical sciences, its exuberant wordplay, its deliberate excess, and its often sophomoric humor, *Infinite Jest* was immediately linked to the dense avant-garde experimental texts of postmodernism that had audaciously—and self-consciously—extended fiction's form, including Pynchon's *Gravity's Rainbow* and William Gaddis's *The Recognitions*. Wallace's ambitious novel, clearly informed by these narrative audacities, was both hailed as innovative and ener-getic, seductive and playful, and derided as imitative and self-indulgent, inacces-sible and unreadable.

Wallace himself qualified the assessment. Moved by the minimalist fiction of the late 1970s, especially Raymond Carver's restrained and unpretentious examinations of the strangled lives of ordinary people, Wallace argued that for-mal experimentation overintellectualized narrative and inevitably prized author-ial ingenuity and self-justifying novelty, thus alienating a contemporary readership already diminished by seductive entertainment technologies, most prominently television. As he told the *Review of Contemporary Fiction* in 1993, "If a piece of fiction can allow us imaginatively to identify with a character's pain, we might then more easily conceive of others identifying with our own. This is nourishing, redemptive." That dynamic agenda moved Wallace to the forefront of a group of fin-de-millennium postpostmodern writers—among them, Richard Powers, Rick Moody, William Vollmann, and Jonathan Franzen—who balance postmodernism's radical experimentation with traditional explorations of character and theme, most often the inviolable loneliness at the heart of the Information Age. "The Devil Is a Busy Man," published after the hoopla of *Infinite Jest*, is just such a fiction: a subversive experiment in form—an uninterrupted monologue, a concise verbal construct, a voice without context (nameless, genderless)—in which a character struggles with the tangled motivation behind a simple act of charity and comes to reveal a paralyzing self-consciousness, a character trapped by decency and stranded in a moral universe where good and evil are ultimately indistinguishable and motivation is unreadable.

Wallace's work has been accorded several prestigious awards and has compelled the significant academic attention that signals that he was more than a trendy celebrity. His post–*Infinite Jest* publications—innovative short fictions, insightful essays on popular culture, and a provocative study on the mathematical principle of infinity—heralded a defining voice for the new century, tragically silenced by his premature death by suicide in 2008.

Joseph Dewey
University of Pittsburgh at Johnstown

PRIMARY WORKS

The Broom of the System (a novel), 1986; *Girl with Curious Hair* (short stories), 1989; *Signifying Rappers: Rap and Race in the Urban Present* (cowritten with Mark Costello), 1990; *Infinite Jest* (a novel), 1996; *A Supposedly Fun Thing I'll Never Do Again: Essays and Argument*, 1997; *Brief Interviews with Hideous Men: Stories*, 1999; *Everything and More: A Compact History of Infinity*, 2003; *Oblivion: Stories*, 2004; *The Pale King*, 2011.

The Devil Is a Busy Man

Three weeks ago, I did a nice thing for someone. I can not say more than this, or it will empty what I did of any of its true, ultimate value. I can only say: a nice thing. In a general context, it involved money. It was not a matter of out and out "giving money" to someone. But it was close. It was more classifiable as "diverting" money to someone in "need." For me, this is as specific as I can be.

It was two weeks, six days, ago that the nice thing I did occurred. I can also mention that I was out of town—meaning, in other words, I was not where I live. Explaining why I was out of town, or where I was, or what the overall situation that was going on was, however, unfortunately, would endanger the value of what I did further. Thus, I was explicit with the lady that the person who would receive the money was to in no way know who had diverted it to them. Steps were explicitly taken so that my namelessness was structured into the arrangement which led to the diversion of the money. (Although the money was, technically, not mine, the secretive arrangement by which I diverted it was properly legal. This may lead one to wonder in what way the money was not "mine," but, unfortunately, I am unable to explain in detail. It is, however, true.) This is the reason. A lack of namelessness on my part would destroy the ultimate value of the nice act. Meaning, it would infect the "motivation" for my nice gesture—meaning, in other words, that part of my motivation for it would be, not generosity, but desiring gratitude, affection, and approval towards me to result. Despairingly, this selfish motive would empty the nice gesture of any ultimate value, and cause me to once again fail in my efforts to be classifiable as a nice or "good" person.

Thus, I was very intransigent about the secrecy of my own name in the arrangement, and the lady, who was the only other person with any knowing part in the arrangement (she, because of her job, could be classified as "the instrument" of the diversion of the money) whatsoever, acquiesced, to the best of my knowledge, in full to this.

Two weeks, five days, later, one of the people I had done the nice thing for (the generous diversion of funds was to two people—more specifically, a common law married couple—but only one of them called) called, and said, "hello," and that did I, by any possible chance, know anything about who was responsible for _____, because he just wanted to tell that person, "thank you!," and what a God-send this ____ dollars that came, seemingly, out of nowhere from the _____ was, etc.

Instantly, having cautiously rehearsed for such a possibility at great lengths, already, I said, coolly, and without emotion, "no," and that they were barking completely up the wrong tree for any knowledge on my part. Internally, however, I was almost dying with temptation. As everyone is well aware, it is so difficult to do something nice for someone and not want them, desperately, to know that the identity of the individual who did it for them was you, and to feel grateful and approving towards you, and to tell myriads of other people what you "did" for them, so that you can be widely acknowledged as a "good" person. Like the forces of darkness, evil, and hopelessness in the world at large itself, the temptation of this frequently can overwhelm resistance.

Therefore, impulsively, during the grateful, but inquisitive, call, unprescient of any danger, I said, after saying, very coolly, "no," and "the wrong tree," that, although I had no knowledge, I could well imagine that whoever, in fact, was, mysteriously responsible for _____ would be enthusiastic to know how the needed money, which they had received, was going to be utilized—meaning, for example, would they now plan to finally acquire health insurance for their new-born baby, or service the consumer debt in which they were deeply mired, or etc.?

My uttering this, however, was, in a fatal instant, interpreted by the person as an indirect hint from me that I was, despite my prior denials, indeed, the individual responsible for the generous, nice act, and he, throughout the remainder of the call, became lavish in his details on how the money would be applied to their specific needs, underlining what a God-send it was, with the tone of his voice's emotion transmitting both grati-tude, approval, and something else (more specifically, something almost hostile, or embarrassed, or both, yet I can not describe the specific tone which brought this emotion to my attention adequately). This flood of emo-tion, on his part, caused me, sickeningly, too late, to realize, that what I had just done, during the call, was to not only let him know that I was the indi-vidual who was responsible for the generous gesture, but to make me do so in a subtle, sly manner that appeared to be, insinuationally, euphemistic, meaning, employing the euphemism: "whoever was responsible for _____," which, combined together with the interest I revealed in the money's "uses" by them, could fool no one about its implying of me as ulti-mately responsible, and had the effect, insidiously, of insinuating that, not only was I the one who had done such a generous, nice thing, but also, that I was so "nice"—meaning, in other words, "modest," "unselfish," or "untempted by a desire for their gratitude"—a person, that I did not even want them to know that I was who was responsible. And I had, despairingly, in addition, given off these insinuations so "slyly," that not even I, until afterward—meaning, after the call was over—, knew what I had done. Thus, I showed an unconscious and, seemingly, natural, automatic ability to both deceive myself and other people, which, on the "motivational level," not only completely emptied the generous thing I tried to do of any true value, and caused me to fail, again, in my attempts to sincerely be what someone would classify as truly a "nice" or "good" person, but, despairingly, cast me in a light to myself which could only be classified as "dark," "evil," or "beyond hope of ever sincerely becoming good."

1999

Prison Literature

The following collection brings together a number of contemporary writers under the term "prison literature," a category that refers to authors who began their writing careers in prison and also to prominent writers who have imagined the prison experience. Many of these professional writers, such as James Baldwin in *If Beale Street Could Talk*, John Cheever in *Falconer*, John Edgar Wideman in *Brothers and Keepers*, and Norman Mailer in *The Executioner's Song*, derive their authority through observation and through knowing prisoners: visiting them, listening to them, and imagining their experience. These well-known writers did not learn to write in prison, although Baldwin was driven to suicidal despair after being incarcerated for a few days in Paris.

Other prison writers—those represented here—derive their authority directly. All six became writers in prison, though two—Kathy Boudin and Leonard Peltier—are better known for the controversy generated by their cases than for their writing. For them, as for many less famous prison writers, literature becomes the only way to escape, communicate with the outside world, or create something in the barren concrete wastelands of what might be called America's prison-industrial complex.

Regardless of which side of the bars the writer is on, prison literature always deals with a common theme: the devastating effect of incarceration on body, mind, and soul. Prison seeks to inhibit or prevent fundamental human desires, one of which is communication. If the prison represents a world hidden from sight, many Americans are oblivious to a significant number of their compatriots. In the twenty-first century, more than 3 percent of American adults (1 in 31) have served time in prison, compared to 1 in 77 in 1982. This startling statistic reflects a trend that began in the last three decades of the twentieth century: the United States tends to deal with most of its social problems through its prison system. This trend exists to make the general populace feel safe and secure. Yet even those who most accept the necessity for widespread incarceration must acknowledge that justice is not always served—that people are wrongfully imprisoned and even executed for crimes they did not commit, that the system does not operate the same way for wealthy and poor inmates, and that alternatives to stiff prison sentences might result in a more humane society. Stories of petty shoplifters who serve twenty-five years in prison under California's controversial "three strikes and you're out" rule should give Americans pause. The infamous images of American guards torturing Iraqi inmates in Iraq's Abu Ghraib prison during the U.S. occupation in 2003–2004 should trigger some widespread soul-searching about the cost to humanity in the name of safety and security.

Literature is a way to address some of these concerns. Prison literature is one way of allowing the voices of the imprisoned to be heard in the safe, secure living rooms of mainstream America. Yet prison literature is not unique to our time. Looking back to the classic American literature of the nineteenth century, one might be surprised to discover how prominent a theme it is. Nathaniel Hawthorne's *The Scarlet Letter* begins in prison, Melville's "Bartleby the Scrivener" ends in prison, and Rebecca Harding Davis's "Life in the Iron Mills" and Henry David Thoreau's "Resistance to Civil Government" center on the prison experience. The literature of the civil rights era in the twentieth century also touches heavily on incarceration: Malcolm X discusses his prison experience extensively in *The Autobiography of Malcolm X*, and Martin Luther King's "Letter from Birmingham Jail" is a superb example of how incarceration highlights injustice. It could be argued that prison writing is an essential component of American literature.

Contemporary prison literature is, for better or worse, an expanding field. In his introduction to *Prison Writing in Twentieth-Century America*, H. Bruce Franklin describes it as "far more bleak and desperate than the prison literature of any earlier period." Regardless of how one might feel about its message or about the individuals who write it, prison literature should not be ignored. Its very existence testifies to a basic American freedom that even prison cannot take away: the freedom to write.

D. Quentin Miller
Suffolk University

■ # ETHERIDGE KNIGHT ■
1931–1991

Etheridge Knight was a black prison-born artist. Born in Corinth, Mississippi, in a large and relatively poor family of seven children, he was able to complete only a ninth-grade education. Therefore, he discovered early in his life that his social and economic opportunities were limited. In Corinth, Knight found only menial jobs such as shining shoes available to him and thus spent much of his time hanging out in pool halls and barrooms. As a teenager, he turned to narcotics for relief from his emotional anguish. At sixteen, in an attempt to find a purpose in life, he enlisted in the army and later fought in the Korean War. During the war, Knight's addiction increased when he was treated with narcotics for a shrapnel wound. After his discharge from the service, he drifted aimlessly throughout the country for several years until he eventually settled in Indianapolis, Indiana. During these years, he learned through his experiences in bars and pool halls the art of telling toasts—long narrative poems from the black oral tradition that are acted out in a theatrical manner. Unfortunately, however,

Knight's drug addiction dominated his life. When he snatched an old white woman's purse to support his addiction, he was sentenced in 1960 to a ten- to twenty-five-year term in Indiana State Prison.

Embittered by his lengthy prison sentence, which he felt was unjust and racist, Knight became rebellious, hostile, and belligerent during his first year of incarceration. However, *The Autobiography of Malcolm X* and other prison works influenced him to turn to writing to liberate his soul. As Knight once stated, "I died in Korea from a shrapnel wound and narcotics resurrected me. I died in 1960 from a prison sentence and poetry brought me back to life."

By drawing on his earlier experiences as a teller of toasts, Knight developed his verse into a transcribed oral poetry of considerable power. His early poems, "The Idea of Ancestry," "The Violent Space," "Hard Rock Returns to Prison from the Hospital for the Criminal Insane," and "He Sees through Stone," were so effective that Broadside publisher-poet Dudley Randall published Knight's first volume of verse, *Poems From Prison*, and hailed him as one of the major poets of the new black aesthetic. Other poets, including Don L. Lee, Gwendolyn Brooks, and Sonia Sanchez, aided Knight in obtaining parole in 1968.

Upon his release from prison, Knight married Sonia Sanchez. However, because of his drug addiction, the marriage was short-lived. He then married Mary McNally; they adopted two children and settled in Minneapolis, Minnesota. Three years later, Knight published his volume of poems *Belly Song and Other Poems*. Separated from Mary in the late 1970s, Knight moved to Memphis, Tennessee, where he received methadone treatments. In 1980 he published *Born of a Woman: New and Selected Poems* and in 1986 *The Essential Etheridge Knight*. He died of lung cancer in March 1991.

Knight's poetry, much of it written in prison, ranges from expressions of loneliness and frustration to a sense of triumph over the soul's struggle. In his earlier prison poetry, Knight brings us, mercilessly and straight on, face to face with the infinite varieties of pain and sorrow of the prison world until finally the total prison soul stands before us anatomized. We meet the lobotomized inmate Hard Rock, the raped convict Freckled-Faced Gerald, and the old black soothsayer lifer who "sees through stone" and waits patiently for the dawning of freedom. Above all, in "The Idea of Ancestry" and "The Violent Space," the two most powerful of his prison poems, we witness the poet himself deep in despair, alone in the freedomless void of his prison cell. However, Knight's best poems are his later ones, those that search for heritage, continuity, and meaning. In two of his postprison poems—"The Bones of My Father," which shows his growing concern for image rather than statement, and his masterful blues poem, "A Poem for Myself (or Blues for a Mississippi Black Boy)"—Knight's search takes him to the South, the ancestral home for blacks. Finally, in "Ilu, the Talking Drum," one of the finest poems in contemporary American poetry, Knight brings the black American life experience back full circle from Africa to the black South and then back to an Africa of the spirit.

Patricia Liggins-Hill
University of San Francisco

PRIMARY WORKS

Poems from Prison, 1968; *Black Voices from Prison*, 1972; *Belly Song and Other Poems*, 1973; *Born of a Woman: New and Selected Poems*, 1980; *The Essential Etheridge Knight*, 1986.

The Idea of Ancestry

1

Taped to the wall of my cell are 47 pictures: 47 black
faces: my father, mother, grandmothers (1 dead), grandfathers (both dead), brothers, sisters, uncles, aunts,
cousins (1st & 2nd), nieces, and nephews. They stare
across the space at me sprawling on my bunk. I know   5
their dark eyes, they know mine. I know their style,
they know mine. I am all of them, they are all of me;
they are farmers, I am a thief, I am me, they are thee.

I have at one time or another been in love with my mother,
1 grandmother, 2 sisters, 2 aunts (1 went to the asylum),   10
and 5 cousins. I am now in love with a 7 yr old niece
(she sends me letters written in large block print, and
her picture is the only one that smiles at me).

I have the same name as 1 grandfather, 3 cousins, 3 nephews,
and 1 uncle. The uncle disappeared when he was 15, just took   15
off and caught a freight (they say). He's discussed each year
when the family has a reunion, he causes uneasiness in
the clan, he is an empty space. My father's mother, who is 93
and who keeps the Family Bible with everybody's birth dates
(and death dates) in it, always mentions him. There is no   20
place in her Bible for "whereabouts unknown."

2

Each Fall the graves of my grandfathers call me, the brown
hills and red gullies of mississippi send out their electric
messages, galvanizing my genes. Last yr / like a salmon quitting
the cold ocean—leaping and bucking up his birthstream / I   25
hitchhiked my way from L.A. with 16 caps in my pocket and a
monkey on my back. And I almost kicked it with the kinfolks.
I walked barefooted in my grandmother's backyard / I smelled the old
land and the woods / I sipped cornwhiskey from fruit jars with the men /
I flirted with the women / I had a ball till the caps ran out   30
and my habit came down. That night I looked at my grandmother

and split / my guts were screaming for junk / but I was almost
contented / I had almost caught up with me.
(The next day in Memphis I cracked a croaker's crib[1] for a fix.)

This yr there is a gray stone wall damming my stream, and when   35
the falling leaves stir my genes, I pace my cell or flop on my bunk
and stare at 47 black faces across the space. I am all of them,
they are all of me, I am me, they are thee, and I have no sons
to float in the space between.

                                                                          1968

The Violent Space (or When Your Sister Sleeps
Around for Money)

Exchange in greed the ungraceful signs. Thrust
The thick notes between green apple breasts.
Then the shadow of the devil descends,
The violent space cries and angel eyes,
Large and dark, retreat in innocence and in ice.   5
(Run sister run—the Bugga man comes!)

The violent space cries silently,
Like you cried wide years ago
In another space, speckled by the sun
And the leaves of a green plum tree,   10
And you were stung
By a red wasp and we flew home.
(Run sister run—the Bugga man comes!)

Well, hell, lil sis, wasps still sting.
You are all of seventeen and as alone now   15
In your pain as you were with the sting
On your brow.
Well, shit, lil sis, here we are:
You and I and this poem.
And what should I do? should I squat   20
In the dust and make strange markings on the ground?
Shall I chant a spell to drive the demon away?
(Run sister run—the Bugga man comes!)

In the beginning you were the Virgin Mary,
And you are the Virgin Mary now.   25
But somewhere between Nazareth and Bethlehem

---

[1] A doctor's house.

You lost your name in the nameless void.
O Mary don't you weep don't you moan
O Mary shake your butt to the violent juke,
Absorb the demon puke and watch the white eyes pop.   30
(Run sister run—the Bugga man comes!)

And what do I do. I boil my tears in a twisted spoon
And dance like an angel on the point of a needle.
I sit counting syllables like Midas gold.
I am not bold. I can not yet take hold of the demon   35
And lift his weight from your black belly,
So I grab the air and sing my song.
(But the air can not stand my singing long.)

                                                        1968

Ilu, the Talking Drum

The deadness was threatening us—15 Nigerians and 1 Mississippi
    nigger.
It hung heavily, like stones around our necks, pulling us down
to the ground, black arms and legs outflung
on the wide green lawn of the big white house   5
near the wide brown beach by the wide blue sea.
The deadness was threatening us, the day
was dying with the sun, the stillness—
unlike the sweet silence after love/making or
the pulsating quietness of a summer night—   10
the stillness was skinny and brittle and wrinkled
by the precise people sitting on the wide white porch
of the big white house. . . .
The darkness was threatening us, menacing . . .
we twisted, turned, shifted positions, picked our noses,   15
stared at our bare toes, hissed air thru our teeth. . . .
Then Tunji, green robes flowing as he rose,
strapped on *Ilu*, the talking drum,
and began:

kah doom/kah doom-doom/kah doom/kah doom-doom-doom   20
kah doom/kah doom-doom/kah doom/kah doom-doom-doom
kah doom/kah doom-doom/kah doom/kah doom-doom-doom
kah doom/kah doom-doom/kah doom/kah doom-doom-doom

the heart, the heart beats, the heart, the heart beats slow
the heart beats slowly, the heart beats   25
the blood flows slowly, the blood flows

the blood, the blood flows, the blood, the blood flows slow
kah doom/kah doom-doom/kah doom/kah doom-doom-doom
and the day opened to the sound
kah doom/kah doom-doom/kah doom/kah doom-doom-doom   30
and our feet moved to the sound of life
kah doom/kah doom-doom/kah doom/kah doom-doom-doom
and we rode the rhythms as one
from Nigeria to Mississippi
and back   35
kah doom/kah doom-doom/kah doom/kah doom-doom-doom

                                                            1980

A Poem for Myself (or Blues for a Mississippi Black Boy)

I was born in Mississippi;
I walked barefooted thru the mud.
Born black in Mississippi,
Walked barefooted thru the mud.
But, when I reached the age of twelve   5
I left that place for good.
My daddy he chopped cotton
And he drank his liquor straight.
Said my daddy chopped cotton
And he drank his liquor straight.   10
When I left that Sunday morning
He was leaning on the barnyard gate.
I left my momma standing
With the sun shining in her eyes.
Left her standing in the yard   15
With the sun shining in her eyes.
And I headed North
As straight as the Wild Goose Flies,
I been to Detroit & Chicago—
Been to New York city too.   20
I been to Detroit and Chicago
Been to New York city too.
Said I done strolled all those funky avenues
I'm still the same old black boy with the same old blues.
Going back to Mississippi   25
This time to stay for good
Going back to Mississippi
This time to stay for good—
Gonna be free in Mississippi
Or dead in the Mississippi mud.   30

                                                            1980

JIMMY SANTIAGO BACA

B. 1952

"Ignore all those myths about me," Jimmy Santiago Baca once said. "Just say I'm a writer who has earned my living for more than twenty years by writing." But Baca's story of redemption in prison has mythic dimensions. Voiceless and stripped to nothing, he was forced to discover inner resources he never knew he had. Now he is a major voice for Chicanos, prisoners, and the dispossessed.

Born in Santa Fe, New Mexico, of Chicano and "detribalized Apache" parents, Baca was abandoned by his parents when he was two. He lived with his grandparents until he was placed in an orphanage. By the time he was twenty-one, life on the streets had landed him in prison for five years, convicted on charges of drug possession. The pivotal experience of his evolution was learning to read in prison, which Baca renders extravagantly in "Coming into Language" (*Working in the Dark*). A prisoner of twenty-one, made virtually insensate by bad luck and hard knocks, impulsively steals a book from a desk clerk. Despite his fear and contempt of books, he opens it at random and sounds out the letters. Ravished by the music of a Wordsworth poem, he suddenly recovers the whole spectrum of feeling. A few days later he picks up pencil and paper: "Until then, I had felt as if I had been born into a raging ocean where I swam relentlessly.... Never solid ground beneath me, never a resting place. I had lived with only the desperate hope to stay afloat.... But when at last I wrote my first words on the page, I felt an island rising beneath my feet like the back of a whale. As more and more words emerged, I could finally rest: I had a place to stand for the first time in my life."

Having "a place to stand" freed Baca to recover his buried self, the child who had "waited so many years to speak again." With a place to stand, Baca could look around him and populate the page with his own unrecognized people. His memoir, *A Place to Stand: The Making of a Poet*, is a wrenching pilgrim's progress from loss, degradation, and crime to literacy and spiritual self-discovery that shares much with *The Autobiography of Malcolm X*. In prison Baca learns that neither religious grace nor the convict code can serve him, and he turns to the liberating and truth-disclosing power of poetry. Writing, he claims, enabled him "to rise from a victim of a barbarous colonization to a man in control of his life." Looking back, he says, "All of us who went to prison were lied to, and poetry is the only thing that didn't lie. Everything that is not a lie is poetry. In order to bring order to our world, we were forced to write. Writing was the only thing that could relieve the pain of betrayal, the only thing that filled the void of abandonment."

In 1976 "Letters Come to Prison," one of Baca's first poems, won an honorable mention in poetry from the PEN prison writing contest. Soon afterward, the poet Denise Levertov published some of his work in *Mother Jones*; in 1978, the year he was released, she helped Baca find a publisher for his first major collection, *Immigrants in Our Own Land*. Levertov discerned Baca's "intense lyricism" and "transformative vision which perceives the mythic and archetypal significance of life-events." In 1988 his spiritual quest novel in verse, *Martín and Meditations on the South Valley*, received the Before Columbus American Book Award for poetry, bringing Baca international acclaim. He has also won a Wallace Stevens Yale Poetry Fellowship, a Pushcart Prize, the National Hispanic Heritage Award, and the International Award granted by the Frankfurt Book Fair, and he has been Champion of the International Poetry Slam. In addition to poetry, Baca has published short stories and essays; his screenplay, *Blood In, Blood Out* (also known as *Bound by Honor*), about gang culture in Los Angeles, was released by Hollywood Pictures in 1993. Baca played a major role and was a key adviser in the making of the film, which was partly shot in San Quentin. In *Working in the Dark*, Baca recounts the traumatic experience of reentering prison for the film. A combination of toughness, searing honesty, and tender vulnerability marks his best work.

Assimilation is an illusion, Baca says. He honors the *mestizaje*, the "braided cord," of Chicanismo. Earthbound and peaceful, most Chicanos reap "spiritual sustenance from their relationships with Mother Earth and *indio* Grandfather." Though famous, Baca mistrusts money because it dilutes "our poetry and our souls," he said in an interview, and it hurts his effort "of going into the projects and working with people in a humble sort of way." As vital to him as writing is the act of sharing his conviction that language "is a very real living being." In a recent interview he said, "I began to provoke language to decreate me and then to give birth to me again."

Baca has taught writing in countless schools and universities, reservations, barrio community centers, white ghettos, housing projects, and prisons nationwide. Of his students he says, "If they were taught to be racist or violent, language has this amazing ability to unteach all that, and make them question it. It gives them back their power toward regaining their humanity." Literacy is linked to the growth of compassion for oneself and others. In the poem "El Gato," he enjoins men to cry: "our fists are tired from being clenched / and our faces just might break off! / And we need to cry all those good-byes out / And get up in the middle of the night and cry / And we need to cry for no good reason, but to cry / For all those we never cried for / Cry to get our wings fluttering again!" Rob Allbee, a poet and ex-con in Sacramento, was overcome when he heard Baca read this on the air; Allbee began to read it in his healing circles with men in prison. When Baca was performing his work in Sacramento, he heard about Allbee and called him out of the audience to read the piece; Allbee became the "Ghost Reading in Sacramento," reprinted here. The power of Baca's teaching and the example of his poetry have inspired countless prisoners.

With his love of his distinctive landscape and his compassion for struggling Chicanos and Native Americans, Baca owes much to Pablo Neruda. Emily Dickinson, he says, is also very important to him. He admires Levertov, Grace Paley, Adrienne Rich, and Marge Piercy for their courage, honesty, insight, and iconoclastic approach to poetry, and Raul Salinas and Ricardo Sanchez for breaking new ground for Chicano writers.

Baca has three sons and says he helps support "about ten adopted children." For many years, he has run his own school of writers; his students stay in New Mexico for a year or more and study writing with Baca while working in the community, painting, landscaping, or teaching literacy.

The poems selected here are from *Set This Book on Fire!* Writing remains for Baca a place to endlessly unfold more ways of being human. In his latest collection, *Winter Poems along the Rio Grande*, he continues to invite the world:

> ... unexpectedly I see a bend in the river,
> it stuns me
> that one day I may be as sincere with myself,
> through the changes of being a human being,
> turn to see myself
> flowingly, gracefully as the river.

Bell Gale Chevigny
Purchase College, SUNY (emerita)

PRIMARY WORKS

Immigrants in Our Own Land, 1978; *Martín and Meditations on the South Valley*, 1987; *Black Mesa Poems*, 1989; *Working in the Dark: Reflections of a Poet of the Barrio*, 1992; *Bound by Honor* (screenplay), 1993; *Set This Book on Fire!*, 1999; *Healing Earthquakes*, 2001; *A Place to Stand: The Making of a Poet*, 2002; *C-Train and Thirteen Mexicans*, 2002; *Winter Poems along the Rio Grande*, 2004; *The Importance of a Piece of Paper*, 2004.

I've Taken Risks

starting as a kid
when I stole choir uniforms
from an Episcopalian church
so I'd have something to keep me warm that winter.
I looked like a Biblical prophet   5
striding in six layers of robes through dark streets.

When you turned up the ace,
you kissed the card. And when the joker scoffed at you,
you were led away by authorities.
Second chances were for punks,   10
two-bit, jive-timing, nickel-diming
chumps.

It was beautiful in a way,
to see us kids at seven and eight
years old   15
standing before purple-faced authorities
screaming at us to ask forgiveness, muttering
how irresponsible we were, how impudent and defiant.

That same night
in the dark all alone, we wept in our blankets   20
for someone to love, to take care of us,
but we never asked for second chances.

1999

I Put on My Jacket

Wrapped up, I went out in winter light
climbing in volcanic rock on the west mesa
feeling softer and meaner than I've felt in years.
Amid arid scrub-brush, and bone-
biting cold, I thought of Half-Moon Bay,   5
how the ocean unscrolls on shore
with indecipherable messages.

Only those hiding out
from tormentors and tyrants, those in jail,
gypsies and outlaws, could understand.   10
the ocean talks to me
as one prisoner taps a spoon to another
through four feet of concrete
isolation-cell wall.

                                                              1999

Commitment

A county jail guard knocked out a tooth
smacking me across the face with his club once.
I took that tooth and sharpened it on my cell floor
to an arrowhead I tied to my toothbrush with floss
to stab him with it. I never did,   5
but with the same commitment, I once took my brogan
and a cot-leg of angle iron
hammering it against the bars to escape, which I did.
Hammering that metal leg for months,
I finally cut that bar they said was impossible   10
to cut through
with a boot and cot-leg.
It's a lesson that if I can do that,
when it comes to the business of living,
I can do anything.   15

                                                              1999

Ghost Reading in Sacramento

For days I feel a ghost
trailing me, memories aching and joyous,
from kitchen to basketball courts

to walking paths to driving around town,
a presence hovers about me   5
like the incipient, tight-furled rosebud
on the verge of breaking free, and I realize
miracles come in colors, soft bruises—
the mean scowl of a drunk
in a corner booth in a bar,   10
the elation a kid feels freed
of morning chores, leaping and running
out to the playground. I feel startled,
surrounded by memories,
like one of those sailors who finally comes ashore   15
to kneel before a humble altar, surrendering to feelings
that the world is too large for him to see it all, a man
whose heart once radiated stamina, strength, and firmness
yet now like a sail is folded to the mast:
from Charlie whirling in old songs   20
mimicking oldies but goodies
to Gilbert's miner's grubbing for gold
in his coal-shaft past
to your solitary dance
in a room filled with dreams   25
to David's hunting through jungles of cells
tracking a cure for AIDS
to that guy in Sacramento
who made us all realize something more beyond ourselves,
who drew our thinking out of our eyes   30
in tears, his voice a sudden catching,
kindling and flame,
reminding us of our own flickering journey.

1999

KATHY BOUDIN
B. 1943

Kathy Boudin's name brings to mind the generation of student antiwar protesters of the 1960s and 1970s; however, her achievements in prison remain virtually unknown. Boudin was raised in New York City by social activist parents—
Jean, a poet and a pacifist, and Leonard, a constitutional lawyer. Boudin spent
some of the summer of 1963 in the South and committed herself to the civil
rights struggle. After graduating from Bryn Mawr in 1965, she lived in

Cleveland, Ohio, and with women on welfare wrote a welfare-rights manual that helped develop community leadership.

As opposition to the war in Vietnam intensified, Boudin coauthored *The Bust Book: What to Do until the Lawyer Comes*, a legal self-defense guide for anti-war demonstrators. After three of her friends in the violent Weather Under-ground were killed while making bombs in a New York City townhouse in March 1970, Boudin went underground. She surfaced in 1981, when she was arrested for participating in a Black Liberation Army armored car robbery in which two police officers and a mall security guard were killed. Boudin was an unarmed passenger in the getaway vehicle driven by her lover, David Gilbert.

She pleaded guilty to felony murder and robbery and was sentenced to twenty years to life. At Bedford Hills Correctional Facility in New York, Boudin worked collaboratively with other inmates to develop programs and to write about them to help other incarcerated women do the same. *Parenting from Inside/Out: Voices of Mothers in Prison*, a book she coauthored with another pris-oner, reflects her work with Bedford's Children's Center. Boudin also coauthored the *Foster Care Handbook for Incarcerated Parents*, which has been widely used in social service agencies and social work schools. Boudin applied Paolo Freire's *Pedagogy of the Oppressed*, teaching basic literacy through learning by analysis and action, and with others designed and created a prize-winning, peer-driven AIDS counseling and education project. Also with others, Boudin researched the importance of education to prisoners and their children and published the results; the Bedford Hills college program is now a model for other colleges and correctional institutions.

Boudin's interest in poetry sprang from her mother's work. She was influ-enced by the women's movement, the black movement, and writers in prison; her poems treat family relations and prison experiences. In 1998 her "Trilogy of Journeys" won first prize in poetry in the PEN prison writing contest. Imagin-ing her first day of freedom, Boudin wrote, "If only there were a place where the living and the dead could meet, to tell their tales, to weep. I would reach for you, not so that you could forgive me, but so that you could know that I have no pride for what I have done, only the wisdom and regret that came too late."

In 2003, Boudin was granted parole and was released. She works in the field of HIV/AIDS and continues to write poetry.

Bell Gale Chevigny
Purchase College, SUNY (emerita)

PRIMARY WORKS

The Foster Care Handbook for Incarcerated Parents: A Manual of Your Legal Rights and Responsibilities (with P. Bedell and J. Ashkin), 1994; *Parenting from Inside/Out: Voices of Mothers in Prison: A Self-Help Book for Incarcerated Parents, Social Workers and Community Service Centers* (with R. Greco, ed.), 1998; *Breaking the Walls of Silence: AIDS and the Women in a New York State Maximum Security Prison*, 1998; *Changing Minds: The Impact of College in a Maximum Security Prison* (with M. Fine et al.), 2001.

The Call

You might not be at the other end
of eight cells,
one garlic-coated cooking area
vibrating with the clatter of popcorn on
aluminum pot covers   5
two guards peering through blurry plexiglas,
the TV room echoing with
Jeopardy sing-song music and competing yells for
answers—
all lying between   10
my solitude and the telephone.

Or
you might answer
with a flat "hello,"
and I will hear your fingers   15
poking at plastic computer buttons,
your concentration focused on
the green and blue invaders and defenders.
My words only background
to your triumphs and defeats.   20

But I long for your voice.
Even the sound of your clicking fingers.
I journey past
eight cells submerged
in rap, salsa, heavy metal and soul   25
careening along the green metal corridor,
the guards perched on their raised platform,
dominoes clacking on plastic tabletops.
Past the line of roaches weaving
to the scent of overflowing garbage pails   30
voices shouting down the corridors,
legs halted by the line
that cannot be crossed.
Finally I sit on the floor
of the chairless smoky butt-filled room   35
to call you
who answers with an ever-deepening voice,
who barely sounds like my son.

"Hi, what are you doing?"
"I'm lying down, burning incense, listening to music.   40

Do you want to hear it?"
With such relief
I barely utter "Yes," pushing my ear into the telephone,
my nose into the air.
Your flutes and organs become a soft carpet I walk along   45
in the musty sweetness and fruit smells
of orange peels and raspberries.
You begin to describe your new room
One wall the dream catcher a set of hatchets
     and white feathers wrapped with beads   50
          of turquoise sky and sunset.
Your bed opposite a full length mirror
Perfect, you say, to view yourself,
a new body, six and half inches in one year.

Then you invite me   55
into your special boxes,
gifts from your father
made behind bars.
"I keep all my treasures."

I nod breathlessly   60
My son has taken my voice.
His words fill me in
A naming ceremony.
Slowly his hand lifts
     a coffee brown belt   65
name carved across,
a menu of favorite food
     shared on the overnight visit.
Father-love.

The QEII ticket stub from   70
     the final ocean trip with Grandma.
"Eat your breakfast, pack your clothes, then you can watch TV,"
his grandfather's voice echoes
     from a note left by his bed.
He moves to the Christmas calendar   75
     of shared favorite books
Tales of Peter Rabbit to *Huck Finn*
     the story of fourteen years.
A birthday card
     A photo   80
My son and I stand back to back.
His head inches past mine.

Then you dangle one sandstone earring
   the other in a box in my cell,
"We'll put them together when you get out."   85
   Your words hang like a glider.
Mother-love.

Then guitar notes rise and fall,
and I say, as always "I love you,"
and you say, as always, "I love you,"   90
and the phone clicks off.

        1997

Our Skirt

You were forty-five and I was fourteen
when you gave me the skirt.
"It's from Paris!" you said
as if that would impress me
who at best had mixed feelings   5
about skirts.

But I was drawn by that summer cotton
with splashes of black and white—like paint
dabbed by an eager artist.
I borrowed your skirt   10
and it moved like waves
as I danced at a ninth-grade party.
Wearing it date after date
including my first dinner with a college man.
I never was much for buying new clothes,   15
once I liked something it stayed with me for years.

I remember the day I tried
ironing your skirt,
so wide it seemed to go on and on
like a western sky.   20
Then I smelled the burning
and, crushed, saw that I had left a red-brown scorch
on that painting.

But you, Mother, you understood
because ironing was not your thing either.   25
And over the years your skirt became my skirt
until I left it and other parts of home with you.

Now you are eighty and I almost fifty.
We sit across from each other
in the prison visiting room   30
Your soft gray-thin hair twirls into style.
I follow the lines on your face, paths lit by your eyes
until my gaze comes to rest
on the black and white,
on the years   35
that our skirt has endured.

                                                          1997

A Trilogy of Journeys

for my son on turning 18

I.

The day approaches
   when I begin
my yearly pilgrimage
   back in time,
the present no longer important,   5
only the exact hour and minutes on a clock.
They will bring me to that moment
   when you began
      the longest journey
      man ever makes,   10
out of the sea that
rocked you and bathed you,
out of the darkness and warmth,
   that caressed you,
out of the space   15
that you stretched like the skin of a drum
   until it could no longer hold you
      and you journeyed through my tunnel
      with its twists and turns,
propelling yourself   20
on and on until
   your two feet danced into brightness
and you taught me
   the meaning
   of miracles.   25

II.

Somewhere in the middle of the country
   you are driving a car,
sitting straight, seat belt tight across your well-exercised chest,
looking into the horizon,
the hum of the engine dwarfed by the   30
   laughter of your companions.
You are driving toward 18.
Two sets of parents
   on each side of the continent
await your arrival,   35
   anxiously,
And you leave them astounded
   by that drive,
always a part of you,
to grow up as soon as possible   40
You move toward the point
   that as parents we both celebrate and dread,
foreshadowed by leavings that take place
   over and over again.
That leaving for kindergarten,   45
   that leaving for camp,
      that leaving parents home on a Saturday night.
Until that time when you really leave,
   which is the point of it all,
And the sweet sadness.   50

III

My atlas sits
   on a makeshift desk,
a drawing board
   between two lock-boxes.
It was a hard-fought-for item,   55
   always suspect in the prison environment
as if I could slide into its multicolored shapes
   and take a journey.
In front of me is the United States
   spread across two pages.   60
I search for Route 80,
   a thin red line
and imagine you,
   a dot moving along it.
You, an explorer now.   65

Davenport, Iowa; Cheyenne, Wyoming; then Utah; Nevada;
  until you reach
  the Sierras, looking down on the golden land
Roads once traveled by your father and me.
As I struggle within myself to let you go,   70
  and it is only within,
for you *will* go,
I am lifted out of the limits
  of this jail cell,
and on the road   75
  with you, my son,
who more than any map or dream
  extends my world.
My freedom may be limited,
but I am your passenger.   80

      1999

LEONARD PELTIER

B. 1944

In prison since 1976, Leonard Peltier has spent nearly half of his life in an iron cage. "I am guilty only of being an Indian," he argues in his memoir. "Truth is, they actually need us. Who else would they fill up their jails and prisons with in places like the Dakotas and New Mexico if they didn't have Indians?"

Prison Writings: My Life Is My Sundance is Leonard Peltier's sole book-length publication, a tonally and stylistically fragmented text reflecting the burdens and pressures of writing from a maximum security prison, perhaps reflecting years of experience with displacement. In poetry and prose, Peltier refers with irony to "Aboriginal Sin," pointing to the many ways that indigenous peoples are guilty at birth—"guilty of being ourselves." Citing government policies of enforced assimilation, perhaps none more damaging than removing children from their homes and placing them in boarding schools (such as the Bureau of Indian Affairs schools that forbade him to use his native language and cultural practices), Peltier asks us to reconceive his struggle for freedom as predating his conviction and incarceration for a crime that many argue he did not commit. Indeed, many have seen Leonard Peltier's life as emblematic of the colonization of indigenous people throughout the world. For thirty years, various individuals and groups, including the Dalai Lama, Amnesty International, Nelson Mandela, and the European Parliament, have called for Peltier's release from prison, where he is serving two consecutive life sentences. Few individual cases, in fact, have garnered as much sustained attention as the Free Peltier movement.

Born on September 12, 1944, Leonard Peltier was raised on Sioux and Ojibway (Chippewa) reservations in North Dakota. The "rank racism and brutal poverty" that he experienced during these years set the foundation for his political activism, while the federal policies of "termination" and "relocation" initiated a crisis that had profound effects on his family and larger community. At the age of fifteen, he left the Turtle Mountain Reservation and made his way to the "red ghettoes" of the Pacific West. In 1965 he opened an auto body shop that failed, he tells us, because of "that old Indian weakness: *sharing* with others." During this time, his political awareness grew even as his capitalist ventures failed, and during the 1960s and 1970s, he helped establish a halfway house for male prisoners, devoted time to native land rights, counseled others on alcohol abuse, and joined the American Indian Movement (AIM). This organization led him to the Pine Ridge Indian Reservation in South Dakota in 1972. In the early 1970s, AIM members (who were called Traditionalists) engaged in conflicts with other Native Americans (called Nontraditionalists). As part of an AIM security force, Peltier was at the scene of a shootout that resulted in the deaths of two FBI agents. He was extradited from Canada, convicted of two counts of first-degree murder, and sentenced to two consecutive life sentences.

Peltier's story, however, does not begin and end with this central event in his life. His commitment to transforming society, aiding the poor and the disenfranchised, and raising awareness for Native American rights continues even as his many supporters work for his release. Peltier is an artist, activist, and writer, and his life is, as his memoir conveys, his sundance: "Sundance is our religion, our strength. We take great pride in that strength, which enables us to resist pain, torture, any trial rather than betray the People."

Juda Bennett
The College of New Jersey

PRIMARY WORKS

Prison Writings: My Life Is My Sundance, 1999.

from **Prison Writings**

10:00 P.M. Time for the nightly lockdown and head count. The heavy metal door to my cell lets out an ominous grinding sound, then slides abruptly shut with a loud clang. I hear other doors clanging almost simultaneously down the cellblock. The walls reverberate, as do my nerves. Even though I know it's about to happen, at the sudden noise my skin jumps. I'm always on edge in here, always nervous, always apprehensive. I'd be a fool not to be. You never let your guard down when you live in hell. Every sudden sound has its own terror. Every silence, too. One of those sounds—or one of those silences—could well be my last, I know. But which one? My body twitches slightly at each unexpected footfall, each slamming metal door. Will my death announce itself with a scream or do its work in silence? Will it come slowly or quickly? Does it matter? Wouldn't quick be better than slow, anyway?

A guard's shadow passes by the little rectangular window on the cell door. I hear his keys jangle, and the mindless squawking of his two-way radio. He's peering in, observing, observing. He sees me sitting here cross-legged in the half-light hunched over on my bed, writing on this pad. I don't look up at him. I can feel his gaze passing over me, pausing, then moving on, pausing again at the sleeping form of my cellmate snoring softly in the bunk above. Now he goes by. The back of my neck creeps.

Another day ends. That's good. But now another night is beginning. And that's bad. The nights are worse. The days just happen to you. The night's you've got to imagine, to conjure up, all by yourself. They're the stuff of your own nightmares. The lights go down but they never quite go out in here. Shadows lurk everywhere. Shadows within shadows. I'm one of those shadows myself. I, Leonard Peltier. Also known in my native country of Great Turtle Island as Gwarth-ee-lass—"He Leads the People." Also known among my Sioux brothers as Tate Wikuwa—"Wind Chases the Sun." Also known as U.S. Prisoner #89637-132.

I fold my pillow against the cinderblock wall behind me and lean back, half sitting, knees drawn up, here on my prison cot. I've put on my gray prison sweatpants and long-sleeved sweatshirt. They'll do for PJs. It's cool in here this late winter night. There's a shiver in the air. The metal and cinderblock walls and tile floors radiate a perpetual chill this time of year.

Old-timers will tell you how they used to get thrown, buck naked in winter, into the steel-walled, steel-floored Hole without even so much as a cot or a blanket to keep them warm; they had to crouch on their knees and elbows to minimize contact with the warmth-draining steel floor. Today you generally get clothes and a cot and blanket—though not much else. The Hole—with which I've become well acquainted at several federal institutions these past twenty-three years, having become something of an old-timer myself—remains, in my experience, one of the most inhuman of tortures. A psychological hell. Thankfully, I'm out of there right now.

I'm also out of the heat that used to afflict us until they finally installed air-conditioning in the cellblock about ten years back. Before that Leavenworth was infamous as the Hot House, because there was no air-conditioning here, just big wall-mounted fans that, during the mind-numbing heat of a Kansas hundred-degree summer day, blew the heavy, sluggish, unbreathable air at you like a welding torch, at times literally drying the sweat on your forehead before it could form, particularly on the stifling upper tiers of the five-tier cellblock.

But we still have the noise, always the noise. I suppose the outside world is noisy most of the time, too, but in here every sound is magnified in your mind. The ventilation system roars and rumbles and hisses. Nameless clanks and creakings, flushings and gurglings sound within the walls. Buzzers and bells grate at your nerves. Disembodied, often unintelligible voices drone and squawk on loudspeakers. Steel doors are forever grinding and slamming, then grinding and slamming again. There's an ever-present background chorus of shouts and yells and calls, demented babblings, crazed screams, ghost-like laughter. Maybe one day you realize one of those voices is your own, and then you really begin to worry.

From time to time they move you around from one cell to another, and that's always a big deal in your life. Your cell is just about all you've got, your only refuge. Like an animal's cage, it's your home—a home that would make anyone envy the homeless. Different cellblocks in this ancient penitentiary have different kinds of cells, some barred, some—like the one I'm currently in—a five-and-a-half-by-nine-foot cinderblock closet with a steel door. There's a toilet and sink, a double bunk bed, a couple of low wall-mounted steel cabinets that provide a makeshift and always cluttered desktop.

Right now they've put another inmate in here with me after I'd gotten used to being blissfully alone for some time. He's got the upper bunk and his inert, snoring form sags down nearly to my head as I try to half sit in here with this legal pad on my lap. At least I get the lower bunk because of the bad knee I've had for years. I presume that they put my new cellmate in here with me as a form of punishment—a punishment for both of us, I suppose—though for what, neither he nor I have the slightest idea.

The first thing you have to understand in here is that you never understand anything in here. For sure, they don't want you ever to get comfortable. Nor do they ever want you to have a sense of security. And, for sure, you don't. Security's the one thing you never get in a maximum-security prison.

Now, on this chilly night, I toss the rough green army blanket over my knees, and drape a hand towel over the back of my neck to keep the chill off. I keep my socks on under the sheets, at least until I finally go to sleep. On this yellow legal pad purchased at the prison commissary I scrawl as best I can with a pencil stub that somebody's been chewing on. I can barely make out my own handwriting in the semidarkness, but no matter.

I don't know if anyone will ever read this. Maybe someone will. If so, that someone can only be you. I try to imagine who you might be and where you might be reading this. Are you comfortable? Do you feel secure? Let me write these words to you, then, personally. I greet you, my friend. Thanks for your time and attention, even your curiosity. Welcome to my world. Welcome to my iron lodge. Welcome to Leavenworth.

1999

JUDEE NORTON
B. 1949

Drawing on her prison experiences, Judee Norton writes short fiction that carries the history of women's prison literature to a new phase. Incarcerated women who write constitute a minority of the population of a women's prison, and their chosen genres have traditionally been forms of life writing, such as letters and prison memoirs. Norton, whose work has been honored by the PEN prison writing awards, writes autobiographical short fiction, a blend of fiction and women prisoners' traditional life writing. Contemporary women prisoners have moved away from earlier writers' need for the self-justification that is often the agenda of personal narrative. Instead, they choose poetry and fiction with assertive, even radical themes that both affirm the human rights of all prisoners and condemn the inhumanity of prison conditions.

Born in Arizona farming country, Judee Norton grew up in a poor family with five children. In her contribution to *Doing Time* (1999), she describes her background as one of "addiction, poverty, low self-esteem, and a general sense of bewilderment about the business of living." She received a five-year sentence on a drug charge and was incarcerated from 1988 to 1992 in the Arizona State Prison Complexes in Phoenix and Perryville. She became a writer in prison and has said that her writing helped her survive her incarceration.

Norton's characters are confined within a state women's prison, where events occur against the background of kitchen detail, exercise periods in the yard, or conversations in the dining hall or laundry room. This setting is deceptive in its relative lack of physical restrictions or deprivation of basic needs. In this topsy-turvy universe, the imprisoned protagonist stands for rationality and integrity against the threats of corrupt and irrational forces, represented by the prison administrators. For Norton, the absurd world of prison becomes, by default, her universe, and she must summon her personal will to withstand what she experiences as its objective—to destroy her by eroding her pride and identity. Attacks on a prisoner's spirit may be physical or deeply emotional, as in "Norton #59900."

Norton lives and works today in a small farm community at the foot of Arizona's Catalina Mountains near Tucson. She gives readings of her work at universities and has discussed her writing and prison life on various radio shows. She continues to write about her prison experience in *Slick*, a project of autobiographical fiction. She describes her work as "an account of my experiences in prison, along with some often stark revelations about why and how I came to be there." Most of the work offers accounts of Norton's incarceration, commenting on the corruption, injustice, and inhumanity of the prison system from the point of view of the female prisoner. By challenging prison administrators on environmental and human rights issues, Norton's protagonist creates an ironic space in which power is redefined as the preservation of self-respect through even the smallest acts of resistance.

Judith Scheffler
West Chester University

PRIMARY WORKS

"Arrival" (received a 1990 PEN prison writing award); "Gerta's Story" and "Slick and the Beanstalk," in *Wall Tappings: An International Anthology of Women's Prison Writings*, 2002.

Norton #59900

"Attention on the yard, attention in the units! Norton, five-nine-nine-zero-zero, obtain a pass and report to the captain's office immediately!" the public address speakers boom. The sound bounces around the yard, boomerangs between the buildings and my ears again and again. I am standing outside the schoolroom, smoking and sweating in the 112-degree summer afternoon, squinting at the sun and wondering idly whether this kind of weather would be more enjoyable if I were lying on a Mexican beach wearing only a string bikini and a smile, holding a frosty margarita in one hand and a fine, slender stick of Indika in the other. I have just decided that it most definitely would be when the summons comes.

At once I am approached from every direction by fellow inmates asking, "Did you hear them call you to the captain's office, Jude?" and, "What's going on? Why does the captain want you?" I feign indifference as I take a long final drag of my cigarette, then flip the butt with practiced skill into one of the pink-painted coffee cans nearby.

"Who the fuck knows," I respond with just the right degree of flippancy. My voice is sure and steady, and that pleases me. I can feel my face rearranging itself into a mask of haughty insolence, a half-sneer claims my mouth, one eyebrow hitches itself a quarter-inch upward on my forehead to indicate arrogant disregard. It is my intention to appear poised, untroubled, faintly amused, and slightly bored. I am quite sure I achieve such a look.

My guts belie my measured outward calm. They twist and grumble and roil, threatening to send my lunch to the sidewalk. My heart is beating much too fast. My mouth is dry, my tongue feels like a landed trout thrashing about in that arid, alien place. My hands are trembling, my knees belong to a stranger, I am grateful for the first time ever that it is so goddamn hot in Phoenix. Everyone glistens with a fine film of perspiration; perhaps no one will notice that I smell of fear.

I affect a hip-slung swagger for the amusement of the gathered crowd, and head for south unit control to ask for a pass. It strikes me that I am asking permission to go to a place I haven't the faintest glimmer of desire to go to, and I giggle. The officer issuing my pass looks up at me and says, "Hope you still think it's funny when you get back, Norton." I shrug. The walk across the yard is a long one, made longer by my determination to stroll casually under the scrutiny of a hundred watching eyes. I can feel them on me, can almost hear the thoughts behind them:

"Poor Jude!"

"... 'bout time that goody-goody bitch got hers."

"Damn, hope it ain't bad news ..."

"Gir'fren', please, look who be in trouble now!"

"Sheee-it ..."

I knock purposefully at the polished wooden door with the brass plate that announces this as the Mount Olympus of DOC. CAPTAIN, it says in big carved block letters. Fuck you, I mouth silently.

After just enough time has elapsed to make me feel insignificant and small, the door is opened by a fat, oily sergeant. She is damp and rumpled in spite of the cool, air-conditioned comfort of the room. She turns wordlessly from me and installs her sloppy bulk at a desk littered with forms—applications, requests, petitions—paper prayers from the miserable and needy. She selects one and peers importantly at it over the tops of her smeary glasses, then picks up a red pen and makes a large unmistakable X in a box labeled DENIED. I imagine a look of malignant glee on her greasy flat features as she does it.

Having not been invited to sit, I am still standing near the door, feeling awkward and displaced, when the phone rings. She picks up the receiver, says, "Yeah?" into it, and after a moment looks at me, nods, and replaces it. She jerks her head in the direction of the door through which I have just come and says, "Go back outside for a minute, if you don't mind." Fleetingly, I wonder what she would say if I responded, "Oh, but I *do* mind, I mind very much, in fact; it's hotter than the devil's dick out there, you see, and I *so* much prefer it inside." What I actually say, though, is, "Oh, sure, no problem," and am mortified to find myself blushing.

Once outside, it occurs to me that if this was sly, psychological weaponry, designed to unseat and disadvantage me, it is quite effective. I feel humilated and disgraced in a way I cannot identify. I light a cigarette and arrange my limbs carefully into a posture of indolent apathy. I hook my thumbs in my belt loops and squint with what I hope is an air of monumental unconcern through the smoke that curls up into my face.

At last the door opens again, and I am ushered into the cool depths of the anteroom, and this time I get a nod from the sergeant to proceed into the next room, the sacred chamber where sits the captain, enthroned behind a gleaming expanse of mahogany desk. He is leaning back in a maroon leather swivel chair, rolling a gold Cross pen between his startlingly white palms. He is a black giant, all teeth and long-fingered hands and military creases. His hair is cut very short on the sides and back, and the top flares out and up several inches. It is decidedly and perfectly flat on top, as though his barber used a T-square. I am reminded of the enchanting topiary at Disneyland's Small World; he appears a well-tended shrub. Then he smiles at me and I think to myself viciously that he looks like the offspring of Arsenio Hall and Jaws. He motions me to a small chair, carefully chosen and placed so that I am directly in front of him and several inches lower. I feel like a beggar, prostate at the foot of the king. I am determined that he should not know this. I meet his gaze with a cool look of studied dignity.

"You're Norton?" he asks.

No, you moron, I'm Smith, Jones, Appleby, Wellington, Mother Teresa, Doc Holliday, Jackie Onassis, anyone in the world besides Norton, at least I'd like to be right now, dontcha know, I think wildly. Aloud, I say, "Yes, sir. I'm Norton."

The chair creaks as he leans forward and picks up a piece of paper, pretends to study it. Without looking at me, he says, "Norton, I called you in to talk to you about your son's at-ti-tude," pronouncing all three syllables distinctly as though to a slow child.

"My son's attitude?" I repeat, feeling exquisitely stupid.

He gives a derisive little snort, as though to indicate that of course we both know what he's talking about and it's damned silly of me to pretend ignorance. Bewildered, I ask, "What attitude, sir?"

The captain closes his eyes and leans back again, rolling the gold pen in his hands. It clicks annoyingly against his rings.

"Your son, Adam," he begins with an air of great forbearance, "seems to cause a problem every time he comes to visit you. My officers tell me that he is rude and disrespectful, a troublemaker." He opens his eyes and looks at me expectantly.

I am dismayed to notice that my mouth is agape, that I have been caught so unawares as to be, for one of the very few times in my entire life, speechless. "A troublemaker, sir?" I say, realizing with no small degree of consternation that thus far I have only managed to echo what has been said to me.

"Ap-par-ent-ly," he replies, again dividing the word carefully into all its syllables, "he demanded a full explanation of the visitor's dress code a couple of weeks ago. And last Sunday, according to the report, he questioned the policy that forbids inmates or their visitors to sit on the grass."

I have a quick vision of an official report, complete with the Seal of the Great State of Arizona, titled TROUBLEMAKERS, and can see my son's name emblazoned at the top of a long list. His sins are red-lettered: DEMANDING EXPLANATIONS and QUESTIONING POLICY. Suddenly and against all reason and prudence, I have a powerful urge to laugh, to say, "You're kidding, right dude?" But I fight it and win, and say instead, "Sir?" as though it were a question in its own right, and the captain obliges me by treating it as such.

"Your son, Adam," he says with exaggerated patience, "insists upon knowing the reason for every rule and regulation DOC imposes, which we are in no way obligated to provide to him. He disrupts my officers in the performance of their duties."

I am beginning to hate the way he says my son's name, and I feel the first stirrings of anger. The visitation officers' "duties" consist of sitting in a cool, dark room with a bank of closed-circuit TV screens, looking out onto the baked parking lot where a line of parched visitors wait for the regal nod of approval that will allow them entry into the institution. Their "duties" include watching us chat with our loved ones, making sure that there is no "prolonged kissing," no hanky-panky under the tables, no exchanging of other than words. The most arduous task they will perform all day in the fulfillment of their "duties" is bending over to inspect my vagina after I squat and cough and "spread those cheeks *wide*" for a strip search at visit's end. I fail to comprehend how my son's questions interfere with these odious "duties," and I say so.

The captain's response is brusque, and it is obvious that he, too, is becoming annoyed. "It is not your place, Norton, to determine whether or not the officers' duties are being interfered with. It *is* your place to ensure that your visitors comply with procedure."

"What 'procedure,' sir, says that my boy can't ask questions?" I challenge, against my better judgment, which has long since flown. A little voice inside my head says, *Oh boy, now you've done it, you smartass*, and the voice is surely smarter than I am, for the captain stands up so fast he nearly topples his chair. His breath is coming fast and his eyes blaze.

As quickly as he is losing his calm, I am gaining mine, and from some place deep inside I thought was forever closed to me, I feel a surge of fearlessness. I stand also, and face him squarely and unblinkingly, an intrepid lioness defending her cub. It is a sensation that will not last.

"Sit," he commands.

I sit.

A moment later, he sits, crossing one elegantly trousered leg over the other and picking up the ubiquitous gold pen again. "Tell me," he says congenially, "what happened in the blue jeans incident two weeks ago."

"What happened, sir," I begin reasonably, "is that my son came to visit me wearing a pair of gray Dockers, you know, men's casual pants, and he was told that he could not see me because he was not in compliance with the dress code that specifies 'no blue jeans.' He was understandably upset, and asked that a higher authority be consulted."

"And were they?"

"Yes, sir, someone called the OIC,[1] who didn't want to take the responsibility for a decision; she in turn called the lieutenant, who ultimately allowed him in."

"So he *was* admitted," the captain says, in a tone which implies that, after all, the whole point is moot, and why ever in the world am I so agitated about it?

Warming to my subject, and not liking one bit the look of smug self-satisfaction on his face, I throw caution to the winds, full speed ahead and damn the torpedoes, devil take the hindmost. All pretense of civility leaves me, my instinct for self-preservation is gone.

"Oh, he was admitted all right," I say, making no attempt to disguise my disgust. I note with detachment that my hands and arms have bravely joined the recitation and are describing sharply eloquent shapes and forms in the air, punctuating my mounting fury, underlining my passion. The pitch and timbre of my voice have changed and the words rush from me, unstoppable. "He was admitted, sir, twenty whole minutes before the end of visitation, after taking a filthy stinking city bus all the way from Tempe and being allowed to stand in the blazing sun for three and a half hours without a square inch of shade or so much as an offer of a drink of water. He was admitted after he begged, pleaded, cajoled, and tried to reason with every know-nothing brownshirt in this whole sorry place. He was admitted after repeatedly pointing out to every available cretin with a badge that his

---

[1]Officer in charge [Norton's note].

gray, pleated, slash-pocketed, cuffed, pleated and creased, one-hundred-percent cotton *slacks* were, in fact, neither 'blue' nor 'jeans' and therefore did not violate the 'no blue jeans' rule. He was admitted after being chastised like a naughty schoolboy by that loser of a sergeant, after being called immature, impatient, juvenile, and demanding, after being threatened with dismissal from the premises, after being subjected to an outrageously erroneous judgment call on his goddamn *pants*, sir. Disrespectful? Oh, I hope so. With all due respect to you, sir, I hope to Christ he was disrespectful to them."

By this time, I am shaking with rage. I am remembering my fair-skinned boy's sunburned face. I am remembering the awful look in his sky-colored eyes, that bright liquidity that tells of a boy perched on the brink of manhood, trying not to cry. I am remembering my own inability to explain, to soothe, to mend as mothers do, as they must, for if not they, who?

It is an omission of some seriousness that I did not notice earlier the twin spots of color that had crept to the captain's cheekbones. On his ebony skin they are the color of dried blood, and his eyes snap and sparkle at me. There is a vein pulsing at his left temple. I have an abrupt vision of myself cutting out my tongue with his letter-opener and simply leaving it flopping about on his desk in expiation. Too late.

"Norton," he says slowly, "it is clear to me where your son got his attitude." I notice that he does not divide his words into all their separate parts for me now. He taps his chin thoughtfully with the pen. "It is my feeling that for the continued secure operation of this institution, it will be necessary to discontinue your son's visits until further notice. Perhaps he only needs time away from you to learn to deal with the fact of your incarceration in a mature and sensible manner. An attitude adjustment period." He smiles.

My heart lurches and I feel the color staining my own cheeks even as it leaves his. "Sir," I say, hating the quavering, desperate sound of my voice, "surely you're not saying he can't come to see me anymore." I can hear the humble, supplicating tone I use, and I despise myself for it. "Please," I say, strangling the word.

Having regained his equilibrium, the captain sits up straight in the chair and allows a wider smile. "That is pre-cise-ly what I am saying, Norton." In control, once more, he has gone back to hacking his words apart. I hate him for that.

I am consumed by impotent rage, I wrestle with a crushing and mighty urge to rise and beat that superior face of his into a bleeding pulp of unrecognizable jutting bones and torn flesh. The desire is so intense as to be palpable. I can hear the dull wet crunch of gristle and cartilage, can feel his warm slippery brains between my fingers, can smell the dark coppery odor of his blood, can see it splashing up, up, onto the walls, the carpet, the desk, my face, my hair, crimson and joyous.

I am dazed and shaken by this vision. I sit for a moment gripping the chair bottom with white-knuckled horror. Then I push the chair back gently, like a woman preparing to excuse herself from the dinner table and say softly, "May I leave, sir?"

"Certainly," replies the captain, ever the gracious host. He smiles at me. I do not return the smile.

With the grace and ironclad composure that have saved me from humiliation since early childhood, I hold my head high as I walk through the outer office past the inquisitive stare of the duty sergeant. I close the big door quietly, and slip unnoticed around the corner of the building.

I lean against the sun-baked wall and struggle with a host of emotions I cannot put name to. I feel the wall burning my shoulders through my blue workshirt. My knees become suddenly and utterly incapable of supporting me. They fold up and I slide bonelessly down the wall, heedless of the way its pebbled surface scrapes at my back. My teeth are clenched, but my lips part and turn downward. From them comes an awful keening sound I do not recognize. My eyes sting with the threat of unwelcome tears, I beg them silently not to betray me. But they do, traitorous things, and a great wash of tears pours unchecked down my cheeks, off my chin, into my lap, a flood of them, pent up all those years when to cry was a sign of weakness and to be weak was to be a victim. I lay my forehead on my knees and drop my hands loosely to the blistering cement beside me, like useless weapons that would not fire when so much was at stake. I am dimly aware that I am crying in the brokenhearted way of a small child, a sort of hitching and breathless uh-uh-uh-uh-uh, complete with snot running down into my mouth. I feel naked and wounded, unmanned by grief and hopelessness.

Finally I can no longer hear the sounds of my own weeping. I turn my head to one side and feel the sun begin to evaporate the tears, leaving my face tight and dry. I spit on the fingertips of my hands and scrub away the trails they left, wipe my nose on my sleeve, and pull a small black comb from my back pocket. I take my sunglasses from the top of my head and run the comb briskly through the matted and dampened strands and stand up. Straight. Tall. Shoulders back. Chin up. I put the dark glasses on my face and the mantle of hard-ass prisoner on my soul.

I saunter nonchalantly around the corner, past the door marked CAP-TAIN, onto the yard. An acquaintance approaches me and asks in an excited whisper, "So, what happened in there? What's up?"

She is immediately joined by a second and a third and a fourth, all eager, questioning. I am comfortable now. This is my milieu, this is where I know exactly what is expected of me, precisely how to behave, what to do and say. I shove both hands jauntily into the hip pockets of my Levi's and allow a disdainful grin to own my face.

"Fuck him," I say with contempt. "He can't touch this."

We all laugh.

1991

THE TWENTY-FIRST CENTURY: 9/11 AND BEYOND

The writers represented in the earlier sections of this volume are likely to have responded to a single question at some point in their lives: "Where were you when President Kennedy was shot?" Most writers in the last section of this volume are likely to have responded to a similar question: "Where were you on 9/11?" The questions, which relate to events nearly four decades apart, are surprisingly similar in their intent: Both try to connect individual experience with a national tragedy. Both describe violent, senseless events as markers of history. Both events signaled more violence to come. And very few people saw them coming.

The terror attacks of September 11, 2001, made Americans more fearful and less confident about their position of global prominence. The incidents of "domestic terrorism" described in our introduction to the 1990s, especially the 1995 Oklahoma City bombing, were horrifying and mindlessly destructive, but they in no way prepared Americans for the massive carnage of 9/11. The collective question was not only "What did we do to deserve this?" but, simultaneously, "What could we have done to prevent this?" In the aftermath of the attacks, planes were grounded for days. Americans scowled at their television sets, watching repeatedly the sickening images of the World Trade Center towers on fire, then collapsing. A narrative about the Al Qaeda terrorists and their demented leader, Osama bin Laden, emerged, but justice could not be served as the hijackers were dead and bin Laden was in hiding. Paranoia became the dominant response, especially when envelopes containing a deadly white powder called anthrax started appearing in the mailboxes of members of Congress, and even in the mailboxes of ordinary citizens, one of whom died as a result. Many called the 9/11 terror attacks a wake-up call, which was ironic given their nightmarish quality.

Did the 9/11 terror attacks permanently change American culture? Was it an isolated event or part of a clear historical pattern? It is worth pointing out that foreign terrorists had attempted to blow up the World Trade Center before 2001 and that they have tried to reprise their attacks on planes since then, all without success. More than a decade after the attacks, Americans have held onto memories of that tragic day and have approached certain dimensions of our lives (such as air travel) with increased trepidation. Despite U.S.-led wars in Iraq and Afghanistan, and despite the success of targeted strikes on Al Qaeda figures abroad (including the killing of Osama bin Laden in Pakistan in 2011), a feeling endures that there is another shoe to drop. The so-called "war on terror" has reaffirmed America's military superiority, but it has also led to renewed questions about America's role on the global stage.

A nation never becomes completely desensitized to violence, but it can easily cease trying to explain violence and resign itself to the notion that chaos reigns. The twenty-first century in America has proven to be a chaotic time. Writers are particularly sensitive to this chaos, and it is reflected in the work of many current writers. Contemporary literature both embraces and reflects the chaos of the contemporary world. The rational logic of cause and effect is difficult to discern in these works. The reader can come away disoriented and wondering whether stability is possible in the real world or in works of fiction. Many postmodern works create their own world, but others play with the history and legends of the world we think we know.

History thus becomes one of the most prominent subjects of twenty-first century literature, perhaps due to the turn of the millennium as much as to 9/11. The poet Natasha Trethewey, the graphic memoirist Alison Bechdel, and the fiction writer Junot Díaz, for instance, turn to family histories as a way of understanding their own placement within them and as a way of connecting past to present. Culture more generally is the topic of other writers included here, such as Percival Everett (who plays with that term in the title of his story "The Appropriation of Cultures"); T. C. Boyle, who examines climate change in a story set under the hole in the ozone layer over South America; and Jhumpa Lahiri, in her story "When Mr. Pirzada Came to Dine." A sympathy for those disadvantaged by poverty or ethnicity, as in poems by Martin Espada and Demetria Martinez and stories by ZZ Packer and Sherman Alexie, demonstrates a willingness on the part of contemporary authors to confront and cope with the presence of the "other" within American society—not necessarily to make readers aware of their complicity in the victimhood of such people, but to raise consciousness about the experiences of the "other" as valid and vital contributions to our national literature. Our "In Focus" feature highlighting literature directly about the 9/11 attacks shows a similar tension in the literary response to this event. John Updike and Don DeLillo, among the most celebrated authors of the late twentieth century, were consumed by this subject in the twenty-first, and although both have an impressive number of works that we could have included, we felt it appropriate to demonstrate their literary reactions to 9/11, which were some of the earliest to appear after the attacks.

Closing our anthology is a series of pieces that were originally spoken rather than written. As we point out in our introduction to the 1990s, recent writers have begun to embrace the possibilities afforded by "the new media" to change the nature of literature. On the other end of that technological spectrum is the spoken word, the original impulse before written language even existed as a communication tool, as in the oral traditions at the very beginning of our anthology. Beginning with the Beat poets in the 1950s, poetry has enjoyed a strong presence in performance spaces, evolving through such venues as the Nuyorican Poets Café in the 1970s and poetry "slams" of the 1990s. Current spoken word poets are aware of the power of the word in performance rather than on the page. The continued popularity of author readings in the age of the Internet and of the digital reader is testimony to the fact that literature still has the power to do what it has done since ancient times: to unite groups of people in the same physical space, to communicate something to them, to affect them, even to move them. Despite proclamations about the death of literature in the so-called Information Age, literature remains vital. Even devastating events like the 9/11 terror attacks cannot prevent it from flourishing, though they might temporarily change its trajectory.

JHUMPA LAHIRI

B. 1967

Jhumpa (née Nilanjana Sudeshna) Lahiri was born in London to Bengali immigrants from Calcutta and moved to Rhode Island when she was one year old. Her father was a librarian at the University of Rhode Island and her mother a schoolteacher. Most of her fiction is located in and around Boston, in small New England towns, or in New York City, where she now lives with her husband and son. Since 2001 she has been married to Alberto Vourvoulias-Bush, an American-born Guatemalan Greek who is now the editor of *El Diario/La Prensa*, the biggest Spanish-language newspaper in New York; they were wed in a traditional Bengali Hindu ceremony in Calcutta.

Lahiri received a bachelor's degree from Barnard College and three master's degrees (in English, creative writing, and comparative studies in literature and the arts) and a Ph.D. in Renaissance literature from Boston University. She then received a two-year fellowship from Provincetown's Fine Arts Work Center, where she wrote much of *Interpreter of Maladies*, a collection of nine short stories. Three of these stories, "The Interpreter of Maladies," "A Real Durwan," and "The Treatment of Bibi Haldar," are set in Calcutta, where her parents visited their families every few years during her childhood.

Interpreter of Maladies won the 2000 Pulitzer Prize and the Pen/Hemingway Award, and the title story received the O'Henry Award. Lahiri received a Guggenheim fellowship in 2002, and her stories frequently appear in magazines and anthologies.

Her novel *The Namesake* (2003) portrays the life of a Bengali couple, Ashoke and Ashima Ganguly, who emigrate from Calcutta to Boston, and the coming of age of their son, Nikhil/Gogol, who struggles with the internal conflicts between his Indian and American identities. The novel was made into a film by Mira Nair.

Lahiri's fiction deals with universal themes such as love, loss, death, birth, marriage, home, and homelessness. Her audience includes those studying minority or multicultural literature as well as those who are interested in the psychological and emotional impact of immigration as depicted in American literature. Lahiri has told an interviewer: "For immigrants, the challenges of exile, the loneliness, the constant sense of alienation, the knowledge of and longing for a lost world, are more explicit and distressing than for their children. On the other hand, the problem for the children of immigrants, those with strong ties to their country of origin, is that they feel neither one thing nor the other. The feeling that there was no single place to which I fully belonged bothered me growing up. It bothers me less now."

Although many Indian American writers are working today—including Bharati Mukherjee, Kiran Desai, Ved Mehta, and Vikram Seth—Lahiri is one of the few who represents the perspectives of first-generation immigrants who attempt to assimilate and yet are torn between two worlds. She is also unusual among ethnic writers in her depictions of interactions between the immigrant protagonists and well-rounded and sympathetic Euro-American characters, such as the 103-year-old Victorian landlady in "The Third and Final Continent"; the twenty-two-year-old Midwesterner Miranda in "Sexy," who has an adulterous affair with the Boston investment banker Dev Mitra; the nine-year-old Bostonian Eliot, whom Mrs. Sen babysits in "Mrs. Sen's"; and Gogol's Euro-American girlfriends, Ruth and Maxine, in *The Namesake*.

In "When Mr. Pirzada Came to Dine," Lahiri seems to question whether identity is based on language, religion, nationality, knowledge of history, or cultural traits and practices. Perhaps Lahiri has hit on what is quintessentially American: an obsession with the places that one has either chosen or been forced to leave and those to which one has moved.

Lavina D. Shankar
Bates College

PRIMARY WORKS

Interpreter of Maladies, 1999; *The Namesake*, 2003; *Unaccustomed Earth*, 2008

When Mr. Pirzada Came to Dine

In the autumn of 1971 a man used to come to our house, bearing confections in his pocket and hopes of ascertaining the life or death of his family. His name was Mr. Pirzada, and he came from Dacca, now the capital of Bangladesh, but then a part of Pakistan. That year Pakistan was engaged in civil war. The eastern frontier, where Dacca was located, was fighting for autonomy from the ruling regime in the west. In March, Dacca had been invaded, torched, and shelled by the Pakistani army. Teachers were dragged onto streets and shot, women dragged into barracks and raped. By the end of the summer, three hundred thousand people were said to have died. In Dacca Mr. Pirzada had a three-story home, a lectureship in botany at the university, a wife of twenty years, and seven daughters between the ages of six and sixteen whose names all began with the letter A. "Their mother's idea," he explained one day, producing from his wallet a black-and-white picture of seven girls at a picnic, their braids tied with ribbons, sitting crosslegged in a row, eating chicken curry off of banana leaves. "How am I to distinguish? Ayesha, Amira, Amina, Aziza, you see the difficulty."

Each week Mr. Pirzada wrote letters to his wife, and sent comic books to each of his seven daughters, but the postal system, along with most everything else in Dacca, had collapsed, and he had not heard word of them in over six months. Mr. Pirzada, meanwhile, was in America for the year, for he had been awarded a grant from the government of Pakistan to study the foliage of New England. In spring and summer he had gathered data in Vermont and Maine, and in autumn he moved to a university north of Boston, where we lived, to write a short book about his discoveries. The grant was a great honor, but when converted into dollars it was not generous. As a result, Mr. Pirzada lived in a room in a graduate dormitory, and did not own a proper stove or a television set of his own. And so he came to our house to eat dinner and watch the evening news.

At first I knew nothing of the reason for his visits. I was ten years old, and was not surprised that my parents, who were from India, and had a number of Indian acquaintances at the university, should ask Mr. Pirzada to share our meals. It was a small campus, with narrow brick walkways and white pillared buildings, located on the fringes of what seemed to be an even smaller town. The supermarket did not carry mustard oil, doctors did not make house calls, neighbors never dropped by without an invitation, and of these things, every so often, my parents complained. In search of compatriots, they used to trail their fingers, at the start of each new semester, through the columns of the university directory, circling surnames familiar to their part of the world. It was in this manner that they discovered Mr. Pirzada, and phoned him, and invited him to our home.

I have no memory of his first visit, or of his second or his third, but by the end of September I had grown so accustomed to Mr. Pirzada's presence in our living room that one evening, as I was dropping ice cubes into the water pitcher, I asked my mother to hand me a fourth glass from a cupboard still out of my reach. She was busy at the stove, presiding over a skillet of fried spinach with radishes, and could not hear me because of the drone of the exhaust fan and the fierce scrapes of her spatula. I turned to my father, who was leaning against the refrigerator, eating spiced cashews from a cupped fist.

"What is it, Lilia?"

"A glass for the Indian man."

"Mr. Pirzada won't be coming today. More importantly, Mr. Pirzada is no longer considered Indian," my father announced, brushing salt from the cashews out of his trim black beard. "Not since Partition. Our country was divided. 1947."

When I said I thought that was the date of India's independence from Britain, my father said, "That too. One moment we were free and then we were sliced up," he explained, drawing an X with his finger on the countertop, "like a pie. Hindus here, Muslims there. Dacca no longer belongs to us." He told me that during Partition Hindus and Muslims had set fire to each other's homes. For many, the idea of eating in the other's company was still unthinkable.

It made no sense to me. Mr. Pirzada and my parents spoke the same language, laughed at the same jokes, looked more or less the same. They ate pickled mangoes with their meals, ate rice every night for supper with their hands. Like my parents, Mr. Pirzada took off his shoes before entering a room, chewed fennel seeds after meals as a digestive, drank no alcohol, for dessert dipped austere biscuits into successive cups of tea. Nevertheless my father insisted that I understand the difference, and he led me to a map of the world taped to the wall over his desk. He seemed concerned that Mr. Pirzada might take offense if I accidentally referred to him as an Indian, though I could not really imagine Mr. Pirzada being offended by much of anything. "Mr. Pirzada is Bengali, but he is a Muslim," my father informed me. "Therefore he lives in East Pakistan, not India." His finger trailed across the

Atlantic, through Europe, the Mediterranean, the Middle East, and finally to the sprawling orange diamond that my mother once told me resembled a woman wearing a sari with her left arm extended. Various cities had been circled with lines drawn between them to indicate my parents' travels, and the place of their birth, Calcutta, was signified by a small silver star. I had been there only once and had no memory of the trip. "As you see, Lilia, it is a different country, a different color," my father said. Pakistan was yellow, not orange. I noticed that there were two distinct parts to it, one much larger than the other, separated by an expanse of Indian territory; it was as if California and Connecticut constituted a nation apart from the U.S.

My father rapped his knuckles on top of my head. "You are, of course, aware of the current situation? Aware of East Pakistan's fight for sovereignty?"

I nodded, unaware of the situation.

We returned to the kitchen, where my mother was draining a pot of boiled rice into a colander. My father opened up the can on the counter and eyed me sharply over the frames of his glasses as he ate some more cashews. "What exactly do they teach you at school? Do you study history? Geography?"

"Lilia has plenty to learn at school," my mother said. "We live here now, she was born here." She seemed genuinely proud of the fact, as if it were a reflection of my character. In her estimation, I knew, I was assured a safe life, an easy life, a fine education, every opportunity. I would never have to eat rationed food, or obey curfews, or watch riots from my rooftop, or hide neighbors in water tanks to prevent them from being shot, as she and my father had. "Imagine having to place her in a decent school. Imagine her having to read during power failures by the light of kerosene lamps. Imagine the pressures, the tutors, the constant exams." She ran a hand through her hair, bobbed to a suitable length for her part-time job as a bank teller. "How can you possibly expect her to know about Partition? Put those nuts away."

"But what does she learn about the world?" My father rattled the cashew can in his hand. "What is she learning?"

We learned American history, of course, and American geography. That year, and every year, it seemed, we began by studying the Revolutionary War. We were taken in school buses on field trips to visit Plymouth Rock, and to walk the Freedom Trail, and to climb to the top of the Bunker Hill Monument. We made dioramas out of colored construction paper depicting George Washington crossing the choppy waters of the Delaware River, and we made puppets of King George wearing white tights and a black bow in his hair. During tests we were given blank maps of the thirteen colonies, and asked to fill in names, dates, capitals. I could do it with my eyes closed.

The next evening Mr. Pirzada arrived, as usual, at six o'clock. Though they were no longer strangers, upon first greeting each other, he and my father maintained the habit of shaking hands.

"Come in, sir. Lilia, Mr. Pirzada's coat, please."

He stepped into the foyer, impeccably suited and scarved, with a silk tie knotted at his collar. Each evening he appeared in ensembles of plums, olives, and chocolate browns. He was a compact man, and though his feet were perpetually splayed, and his belly slightly wide, he nevertheless maintained an efficient posture, as if balancing in either hand two suitcases of equal weight. His ears were insulated by tufts of graying hair that seemed to block out the unpleasant traffic of life. He had thickly lashed eyes shaded with a trace of camphor, a generous mustache that turned up playfully at the ends, and a mole shaped like a flattened raisin in the very center of his left cheek. On his head he wore a black fez made from the wool of Persian lambs, secured by bobby pins, without which I was never to see him. Though my father always offered to fetch him in our car, Mr. Pirzada preferred to walk from his dormitory to our neighborhood, a distance of about twenty minutes on foot, studying trees and shrubs on his way, and when he entered our house his knuckles were pink with the effects of crisp autumn air.

"Another refugee, I am afraid, on Indian territory."

"They are estimating nine million at the last count," my father said.

Mr. Pirzada handed me his coat, for it was my job to hang it on the rack at the bottom of the stairs. It was made of finely checkered gray-and-blue wool, with a striped lining and horn buttons, and carried in its weave the faint smell of limes. There were no recognizable tags inside, only a hand-stitched label with the phrase "Z. Sayeed, Suitors" embroidered on it in cursive with glossy black thread. On certain days a birch or maple leaf was tucked into a pocket. He unlaced his shoes and lined them against the baseboard; a golden paste clung to the toes and heels, the result of walking through our damp, unraked lawn. Relieved of his trappings, he grazed my throat with his short, restless fingers, the way a person feels for solidity behind a wall before driving in a nail. Then he followed my father to the living room, where the television was tuned to the local news. As soon as they were seated my mother appeared from the kitchen with a plate of mincemeat kebabs with coriander chutney. Mr. Pirzada popped one into his mouth.

"One can only hope," he said, reaching for another, "that Dacca's refugees are as heartily fed. Which reminds me." He reached into his suit pocket and gave me a small plastic egg filled with cinnamon hearts. "For the lady of the house," he said with an almost imperceptible splay-footed bow.

"Really, Mr. Pirzada," my mother protested. "Night after night. You spoil her."

"I only spoil children who are incapable of spoiling."

It was an awkward moment for me, one which I awaited in part with dread, in part with delight. I was charmed by the presence of Mr. Pirzada's rotund elegance, and flattered by the faint theatricality of his attentions, yet unsettled by the superb ease of his gestures, which made me feel, for an instant, like a stranger in my own home. It had become our ritual, and for several weeks, before we grew more comfortable with one another, it was the only time he spoke to me directly. I had no response, offered no comment, betrayed no visible reaction to the steady stream of honey-filled lozenges, the raspberry truffles, the slender rolls of sour pastilles. I could not even thank him, for once, when I did, for an especially spectacular peppermint lollipop wrapped in a spray of purple cellophane, he had demanded, "What is this thank-you? The lady at the bank thanks me, the cashier at the shop thanks me, the librarian thanks me when I return an overdue book, the overseas operator thanks me as she tries to connect me to Dacca and fails. If I am buried in this country I will be thanked, no doubt, at my funeral."

It was inappropriate, in my opinion, to consume the candy Mr. Pirzada gave me in a casual manner. I coveted each evening's treasure as I would a jewel, or a coin from a buried kingdom, and I would place it in a small keepsake box made of carved sandalwood beside my bed, in which, long ago in India, my father's mother used to store the ground areca nuts she ate after her morning bath. It was my only memento of a grandmother I had never known, and until Mr. Pirzada came to our lives I could find nothing to put inside it. Every so often before brushing my teeth and laying out my clothes for school the next day, I opened the lid of the box and ate one of his treats.

That night, like every night, we did not eat at the dining table, because it did not provide an unobstructed view of the television set. Instead we huddled around the coffee table, without conversing, our plates perched on the edges of our knees. From the kitchen my mother brought forth the succession of dishes: lentils with fried onions, green beans with coconut, fish cooked with raisins in a yogurt sauce. I followed with the water glasses, and the plate of lemon wedges, and the chili peppers, purchased on monthly trips to Chinatown and stored by the pound in the freezer, which they liked to snap open and crush into their food.

Before eating Mr. Pirzada always did a curious thing. He took out a plain silver watch without a band, which he kept in his breast pocket, held it briefly to one of his tufted ears, and wound it with three swift flicks of his thumb and forefinger. Unlike the watch on his wrist, the pocket watch, he had explained to me, was set to the local time in Dacca, eleven hours ahead. For the duration of the meal the watch rested on his folded paper napkin on the coffee table. He never seemed to consult it.

Now that I had learned Mr. Pirzada was not an Indian, I began to study him with extra care, to try to figure out what made him different. I decided that the pocket watch was one of those things. When I saw it that night, as he wound it and arranged it on the coffee table, an uneasiness possessed me; life, I realized, was being lived in Dacca first. I imagined Mr. Pirzada's daughters rising from sleep, tying ribbons in their hair, anticipating breakfast, preparing for school. Our meals, our actions, were only a shadow of what had already happened there, a lagging ghost of where Mr. Pirzada really belonged.

At six-thirty, which was when the national news began, my father raised the volume and adjusted the antennas. Usually I occupied myself with a book, but that night my father insisted that I pay attention. On the screen I saw tanks rolling through dusty streets, and fallen buildings, and forests of unfamiliar trees into which East Pakistan refugees had fled, seeking safety over the Indian border. I saw boats with fan-shaped sails floating on wide coffee-colored rivers, a barricaded university, newspaper offices burnt to the ground. I turned to look at Mr. Pirzada; the images flashed in miniature across his eyes. As he watched he had an immovable expression on his face, composed but alert, as if someone were giving him directions to an unknown destination.

During the commercial my mother went to the kitchen to get more rice, and my father and Mr. Pirzada deplored the policies of a general named Yahyah Khan. They discussed intrigues I did not know, a catastrophe I could not comprehend. "See, children your age, what they do to survive," my father said as he served me another piece of fish. But I could no longer eat. I could only steal glances at Mr. Pirzada, sitting beside me in his olive green jacket, calmly creating a well in his rice to make room for a second helping of lentils. He was not my notion of a man burdened by such grave concerns. I wondered if the reason he was always so smartly dressed was in preparation to endure with dignity whatever news assailed him, perhaps even to attend a funeral at a moment's notice. I wondered, too, what would happen if suddenly his seven daughters were to appear on television, smiling and waving and blowing kisses to Mr. Pirzada from a balcony. I imagined how relieved he would be. But this never happened.

That night when I placed the plastic egg filled with cinnamon hearts in the box beside my bed, I did not feel the ceremonious satisfaction I normally did. I tried not to think about Mr. Pirzada, in his lime-scented overcoat, connected to the unruly, sweltering world we had viewed a few hours ago in our bright, carpeted living room. And yet for several moments that was all I could think about. My stomach tightened as I worried whether his wife and seven daughters were now members of the drifting, clamoring crowd that had flashed at intervals on the screen. In an effort to banish the image I looked around my room, at the yellow canopied bed with matching flounced curtains, at framed class pictures mounted on white and violet papered walls, at the penciled inscriptions by the closet door where my father recorded my height on each of my birthdays. But the more I tried to distract myself, the more I began to convince myself that Mr. Pirzada's family was in all likelihood dead. Eventually I took a square of white chocolate out of the box, and unwrapped it, and then I did something I had never done before. I put the chocolate in my mouth, letting it soften until the last possible moment, and then as I chewed it slowly, I prayed that Mr. Pirzada's family was safe and sound. I had never prayed for anything before, had never been taught or told to, but I decided, given the circumstances, that it was something I should do. That night when I went to the bathroom I only pretended to brush my teeth, for I feared that I would somehow rinse the prayer out as well. I wet the brush and rearranged the tube of paste to prevent my parents from asking any questions, and fell asleep with sugar on my tongue.

* * *

No one at school talked about the war followed so faithfully in my living room. We continued to study the American Revolution, and learned about the injustices of taxation without representation, and memorized passages from the Declaration of Independence. During recess the boys would divide in two groups, chasing each other wildly around the swings and seesaws, Redcoats against the colonies. In the classroom our teacher, Mrs. Kenyon, pointed frequently to a map that emerged like a movie screen from the top of the chalkboard, charting the route of the *Mayflower*, or showing us the location of the Liberty Bell. Each week two members of the class gave a report on a particular aspect of the Revolution, and so one day I was sent to the school library with my friend Dora to learn about the surrender at Yorktown. Mrs. Kenyon handed us a slip of paper with the names of three books to look up in the card catalogue. We found them right away, and sat down at a low round table to read and take notes. But I could not concentrate. I returned to the blond-wood shelves, to a section I had noticed labeled "Asia." I saw books about China, India, Indonesia, Korea. Eventually I found a book titled *Pakistan: A Land and Its People.* I sat on a footstool and opened the book. The laminated jacket crackled in my grip. I began turning the pages, filled with photos of rivers and rice fields and men in military uniforms. There was a chapter about Dacca, and I began to read about its rainfall, and its jute production. I was studying a population chart when Dora appeared in the aisle.

"What are you doing back here? Mrs. Kenyon's in the library. She came to check up on us."

I slammed the book shut, too loudly. Mrs. Kenyon emerged, the aroma of her perfume filling up the tiny aisle, and lifted the book by the tip of its spine as if it were a hair clinging to my sweater. She glanced at the cover, then at me.

"Is this book a part of your report, Lilia?"

"No, Mrs. Kenyon."

"Then I see no reason to consult it," she said, replacing it in the slim gap on the shelf. "Do you?"

As weeks passed it grew more and more rare to see any footage from Dacca on the news. The report came after the first set of commercials, sometimes the second. The press had been censored, removed, restricted, rerouted. Some days, many days, only a death toll was announced, prefaced by a reiteration of the general situation. More poets were executed, more villages set ablaze. In spite of it all, night after night, my parents and Mr. Pirzada enjoyed long, leisurely meals. After the television was shut off, and the dishes washed and dried, they joked, and told stories, and dipped biscuits in their tea. When they tired of discussing political matters they discussed, instead, the progress of Mr. Pirzada's book about the deciduous trees of New England, and my father's nomination for tenure, and the peculiar eating habits of my mother's American coworkers at the bank. Eventually I was sent upstairs to do my homework, but through the carpet I heard them as they drank more tea, and listened to cassettes of Kishore Kumar, and played Scrabble on the coffee table, laughing and arguing long into the night about the spellings of English words. I wanted to join them, wanted, above all, to console Mr. Pirzada somehow. But apart from eating a piece of candy for the sake of his family and praying for their safety, there was nothing I could do. They played Scrabble until the eleven o'clock news, and then, sometime around midnight, Mr. Pirzada walked back to his dormitory. For this reason I never saw him leave, but each night as I drifted off to sleep I would hear them, anticipating the birth of a nation on the other side of the world.

One day in October Mr. Pirzada asked upon arrival, "What are these large orange vegetables on people's doorsteps? A type of squash?"

"Pumpkins," my mother replied. "Lilia, remind me to pick one up at the supermarket."

"And the purpose? It indicates what?"

"You make a jack-o'-lantern," I said, grinning ferociously. "Like this. To scare people away."

"I see," Mr. Pirzada said, grinning back. "Very useful."

The next day my mother bought a ten-pound pumpkin, fat and round, and placed it on the dining table. Before supper, while my father and Mr. Pirzada were watching the local news, she told me to decorate it with markers, but I wanted to carve it properly like others I had noticed in the neighborhood.

"Yes, let's carve it," Mr. Pirzada agreed, and rose from the sofa. "Hang the news tonight." Asking no questions, he walked into the kitchen, opened a drawer, and returned, bearing a long serrated knife. He glanced at me for approval. "Shall I?"

I nodded. For the first time we all gathered around the dining table, my mother, my father, Mr. Pirzada, and I. While the television aired unattended we covered the tabletop with newspapers. Mr. Pirzada draped his jacket over the chair behind him, removed a pair of opal cuff links, and rolled up the starched sleeves of his shirt.

"First go around the top, like this," I instructed, demonstrating with my index finger.

He made an initial incision and drew the knife around. When he had come full circle he lifted the cap by the stem; it loosened effortlessly, and Mr. Pirzada leaned over the pumpkin for a moment to inspect and inhale its contents. My mother gave him a long metal spoon with which he gutted the interior until the last bits of string and seeds were gone. My father, meanwhile, separated the seeds from the pulp and set them out to dry on a cookie sheet, so that we could roast them later on. I drew two triangles against the ridged surface for the eyes, which Mr. Pirzada dutifully carved, and crescents for eyebrows, and another triangle for the nose. The mouth was all that remained, and the teeth posed a challenge. I hesitated.

"Smile or frown?" I asked.

"You choose," Mr. Pirzada said.

As a compromise I drew a kind of grimace, straight across, neither mournful nor friendly. Mr. Pirzada began carving, without the least bit of intimidation, as if he had been carving jack-o'-lanterns his whole life. He had nearly finished when the national news began. The reporter mentioned Dacca, and we all turned to listen: An Indian official announced that unless the world helped to relieve the burden of East Pakistani refugees, India would have to go to war against Pakistan. The reporter's face dripped with sweat as he relayed the information. He did not wear a tie or a jacket, dressed instead as if he himself were about to take part in the battle. He shielded his scorched face as he hollered things to the cameraman. The knife slipped from Mr. Pirzada's hand and made a gash dripping toward the base of the pumpkin.

"Please forgive me." He raised a hand to one side of his face, as if someone had slapped him there. "I am—it is terrible. I will buy another. We will try again."

"Not at all, not at all," my father said. He took the knife from Mr. Pirzada, and carved around the gash, evening it out, dispensing altogether with the teeth I had drawn. What resulted was a disproportionately large hole the size of a lemon, so that our jack-o'-lantern wore an expression of placid astonishment, the eyebrows no longer fierce, floating in frozen surprise above a vacant, geometric gaze.

For Halloween I was a witch. Dora, my trick-or-treating partner, was a witch too. We wore black capes fashioned from dyed pillowcases and conical hats with wide cardboard brims. We shaded our faces green with a broken eye shadow that belonged to Dora's mother, and my mother gave us two burlap sacks that had once contained basmati rice, for collecting candy. That year our parents decided that we were old enough to roam the neighborhood unattended. Our plan was to walk from my house to Dora's, from where I was to call to say I had arrived safely, and then Dora's mother would drive me home. My father equipped us with flashlights, and I had to wear my watch and synchronize it with his. We were to return no later than nine o'clock.

When Mr. Pirzada arrived that evening he presented me with a box of chocolate-covered mints.

"In here," I told him, and opened up the burlap sack. "Trick or treat!"

"I understand that you don't really need my contribution this evening," he said, depositing the box. He gazed at my green face, and the hat secured by a string under my chin. Gingerly he lifted the hem of the cape, under which I was wearing a sweater and a zipped fleece jacket. "Will you be warm enough?"

I nodded, causing the hat to tip to one side.

He set it right. "Perhaps it is best to stand still."

The bottom of our staircase was lined with baskets of miniature candy, and when Mr. Pirzada removed his shoes he did not place them there as he normally did, but inside the closet instead. He began to unbutton his coat, and I waited to take it from him, but Dora called me from the bathroom to say that she needed my help drawing a mole on her chin. When we were finally ready my mother took a picture of us in front of the fireplace, and then I opened the front door to leave. Mr. Pirzada and my father, who had not gone into the living room yet, hovered in the foyer. Outside it was already dark. The air smelled of wet leaves, and our carved jack-o'-lantern flickered impressively against the shrubbery by the door. In the distance came the sounds of scampering feet, and the howls of the older boys who wore no costume at all other than a rubber mask, and the rustling apparel of the youngest children, some so young that they were carried from door to door in the arms of their parents.

"Don't go into any of the houses you don't know," my father warned.

Mr. Pirzada knit his brows together. "Is there any danger?"

"No, no," my mother assured him. "All the children will be out. It's a tradition."

"Perhaps I should accompany them?" Mr. Pirzada suggested. He looked suddenly tired and small, standing there in his splayed, stockinged feet, and his eyes contained a panic I had never seen before. In spite of the cold I began to sweat inside my pillowcase.

"Really, Mr. Pirzada," my mother said. "Lilia will be perfectly safe with her friend."

"But if it rains? If they lose their way?"

"Don't worry," I said. It was the first time I had uttered those words to Mr. Pirzada, two simple words I had tried but failed to tell him for weeks, had said only in my prayers. It shamed me now that I had said them for my own sake.

He placed one of his stocky fingers on my cheek, then pressed it to the back of his own hand, leaving a faint green smear. "If the lady insists," he conceded, and offered a small bow.

We left, stumbling slightly in our black pointy thrift-store shoes, and when we turned at the end of the driveway to wave good-bye, Mr. Pirzada was standing in the frame of the doorway, a short figure between my parents, waving back.

"Why did that man want to come with us?" Dora asked.

"His daughters are missing." As soon as I said it, I wished I had not. I felt that my saying it made it true, that Mr. Pirzada's daughters really were missing, and that he would never see them again.

"You mean they were kidnapped?" Dora continued. "From a park or something?"

"I didn't mean they were missing. I meant, he misses them. They live in a different country, and he hasn't seen them in a while, that's all."

We went from house to house, walking along pathways and pressing doorbells. Some people had switched off all their lights for effect, or strung rubber bats in their windows. At the McIntyres' a coffin was placed in front of the door, and Mr. McIntyre rose from it in silence, his face covered with chalk, and deposited a fistful of candy corns into our sacks. Several people told me that they had never seen an Indian witch before. Others performed the transaction without comment. As we paved our way with the parallel beams of our flashlights we saw eggs cracked in the middle of the road, and cars covered with shaving cream, and toilet paper garlanding branches of trees. By the time we reached Dora's house our hands were chapped from carrying our burlap bags, and our feet were sore and swollen. Her mother gave us bandages for our blisters and served us warm cider and caramel popcorn. She reminded me to call my parents to tell them that I had arrived safely, and when I did I could hear the television in the background. My mother did not seem particularly relieved to hear from me. When I replaced the phone on the receiver it occurred to me that the television wasn't on at Dora's house at all. Her father was lying on the couch, reading a magazine, with a glass of wine on the coffee table, and there was saxophone music playing on the stereo.

After Dora and I had sorted through our plunder, and counted and sampled and traded until we were satisfied, her mother drove me back to my house. I thanked her for the ride, and she waited in the driveway until I made it to the door. In the glare of her headlights I saw that our pumpkin had been shattered, its thick shell strewn in chunks across the grass. I felt the sting of tears in my eyes, and a sudden pain in my throat, as if it had been stuffed with the sharp tiny pebbles that crunched with each step under my aching feet. I opened the door, expecting the three of them to be standing in the foyer, waiting to receive me, and to grieve for our ruined pumpkin, but there was no one. In the living room Mr. Pirzada, my father, and mother were sitting side by side on the sofa. The television was turned off, and Mr. Pirzada had his head in his hands.

What they heard that evening, and for many evenings after that, was that India and Pakistan were drawing closer and closer to war. Troops from both sides lined the border, and Dacca was insisting on nothing short of independence. The war was to be waged on East Pakistani soil. The United States was siding with West Pakistan, the Soviet Union with India and what was soon to be Bangladesh. War was declared officially on December 4, and twelve days later, the Pakistani army, weakened by having to fight three thousand miles from their source of supplies, surrendered in Dacca. All of these facts I know only now, for they are available to me in any history book, in any library. But then it remained, for the most part, a remote mystery with haphazard clues. What I remember during those twelve days of the war was that my father no longer asked me to watch the news with them, and that Mr. Pirzada stopped bringing me candy, and that my mother refused to serve anything other than boiled eggs with rice for dinner. I remember some nights helping my mother spread a sheet and blankets on the couch so that Mr. Pirzada could sleep there, and high-pitched voices hollering in the middle of the night when my parents called our relatives in Calcutta to learn more details about the situation. Most of all I remember the three of them operating during that time as if they were a single person, sharing a single meal, a single body, a single silence, and a single fear.

In January, Mr. Pirzada flew back to his three-story home in Dacca, to discover what was left of it. We did not see much of him in those final weeks of the year; he was busy finishing his manuscript, and we went to Philadelphia to spend Christmas with friends of my parents. Just as I have no memory of his first visit, I have no memory of his last. My father drove him to the airport one afternoon while I was at school. For a long time we did not hear from him. Our evenings went on as usual, with dinners in front of the news. The only difference was that Mr. Pirzada and his extra watch were not there to accompany us. According to reports Dacca was repairing itself slowly, with a newly formed parliamentary government. The new leader, Sheikh Mujib Rahman, recently released from prison, asked countries for building materials to replace more than one million houses that had been destroyed in the war. Countless refugees returned from India, greeted, we learned, by unemployment and the threat of famine. Every now and then I studied the map above my father's desk and pictured Mr. Pirzada on that small patch of yellow, perspiring heavily, I imagined, in one of his suits, searching for his family. Of course, the map was outdated by then.

Finally, several months later, we received a card from Mr. Pirzada commemorating the Muslim New Year, along with a short letter. He was reunited, he wrote, with his wife and children. All were well, having survived the events of the past year at an estate belonging to his wife's grandparents in the mountains of Shillong. His seven daughters were a bit taller, he wrote, but otherwise they were the same, and he still could not keep their names in order. At the end of the letter he thanked us for our hospitality, adding that although he now understood the meaning of the words "thank you" they still were not adequate to express his gratitude. To celebrate the good news my mother prepared a special dinner that evening, and when we sat down to eat at the coffee table we toasted our water glasses, but I did not feel like celebrating. Though I had not seen him for months, it was only then that I felt Mr. Pirzada's absence. It was only then, raising my water glass in his name, that I knew what it meant to miss someone who was so many miles and hours away, just as he had missed his wife and daughters for so many months. He had no reason to return to us, and my parents predicted, correctly, that we would never see him again. Since January, each night before bed, I had continued to eat, for the sake of Mr. Pirzada's family, a piece of candy I had saved from Halloween. That night there was no need to. Eventually, I threw them away.

1999

PERCIVAL EVERETT
B. 1956

Born in Fort Gordon, Georgia, but primarily raised in Columbia, South Carolina, Percival Everett has worked as a jazz musician, ranch hand, and high school teacher. Everett earned his B.A. in philosophy at the University of Miami in 1977. He then earned an M.F.A. from Brown University in 1982. Currently, he is Distinguished Professor of English at the University of Southern California.

While attending Brown University, Everett wrote his first novel, *Suder* (1983). The novel tells the story of an African American baseball player for the Seattle Mariners, Craig Suder, who falls into a deep existential crisis after suffering a slump. Suder becomes obsessed with Charlie "Bird" Parker's famous be-bop composition "Ornithology," and with his saxophone, his stereo, and "Ornithology," he goes on a strange pilgrimage to the deep woods of Oregon to find his true self. He is accompanied by an abused little girl and a similarly abused circus elephant. This novel established Everett as an absurdist writer. To date, he has written seventeen more novels as well as short story collections, three poetry collections, and a children's book.

A number of themes permeate his work, including identity politics and existential crises, alienation, religious and political fanaticism, racism, environmentalism, language play, and the absurd. In the few interviews that he has given, Everett has spoken about the pleasures and problems of being an African American writer in the so-called post–civil rights era. Although he sympathizes with black writers whose work appears to be more obviously "political" than his, he also feels that his work should be taken on its own merit and not pigeonholed in any particular literary tradition, including an African American one. For this reason, Everett often chooses not to place racially identifiable markers on his characters. Sometimes the reader knows the specific race of his characters, and sometimes the reader does not. As an African American writer, he believes that race is certainly important, but it need not be the most important feature of any writer's work. In "Signing the Blind" (1999), Everett stated, "I do not believe that the works we produce need to be any different; the failing is not in what we show but in how it is seen" by readers. Nevertheless, Everett can be seen to follow in the African American literary tradition. Even when his characters are not racially identified, Everett often makes subtle and not so subtle references to jazz and the blues, as well as to the work of other black writers such as Jean Toomer, Zora Neale Hurston, Ralph Ellison, and Richard Wright. His work also often engages African American and African history.

The question of an African American writer's duty to his race is raised in Everett's most celebrated novel to date, *Erasure* (2001). The novel's protagonist, Thelonious "Monk" Ellison, is an African American writer who has had difficulty finding a publisher because they claim that his work is not "black enough," and thus there is no market for it. Monk, of course, feels otherwise and is understandably upset with the restrictive dictates of a publishing industry that seeks to pigeonhole writers of color. As an elaborate ruse, Monk takes on a pseudonym,

Stagg R. Leigh, and writes an over-the-top urban naturalist novel, à la Richard Wright's *Native Son*, that pleases its laudatory white critics as an authentic representation of black life in America. Monk's scheme to expose the racism inherent in the publishing industry backfires when Stagg R. Lee's novel wins a prestigious national book award that forces Monk to decide whether he will reveal his true identity or compromise his ethical stance and accept the award and the prize money that goes along with it. *Erasure* addresses issues of black identity, literary inheritance and influence, religious extremism, and racism.

Racism is the central theme in arguably Everett's best-known short story, "The Appropriation of Cultures." In this fable, Everett demonstrates his extraordinary power and imagination as a short fiction writer. The story's protagonist, Daniel Barkley, is an independently wealthy African American man living in Columbia, South Carolina. Barkley is also a jazz aficionado who, while playing at a local nightclub, is harassed by a group of good old boys who demand that he play "Dixie" for them. Barkley decides to one-up their obviously racist request and plays the "National Anthem of the South" with a jazz spin, thereby defeating their racist intent. He then comes upon the brilliant idea that blacks appropriate not only "Dixie" but also the Confederate flag as a symbol. Soon, much to the dismay and consternation of Southern whites, the power of these symbols of Southern pride and white power that held sway over African Americans dissipates.

In this short story, as in his other works of fiction, Everett displays an extraordinary gift for satire, parody, and the absurd in the tradition of Jonathan Swift, William Makepeace Thackeray, Samuel Butler, Lewis Carroll, and Mark Twain. In addition, one can see in his fiction literary linkages to other African American writers such as George Schuyler, Rudolph Fisher, Ralph Ellison, Ishmael Reed, and Charles Johnson. In this regard, Everett has earned his rightful place in both Euro-American and African American literary traditions.

Keith B. Mitchell
University of Massachusetts Lowell

PRIMARY WORKS

Suder, 1983; *Walk Me to the Distance*, 1985; *Cutting Lisa*, 1986; *The Women and Weather Treat Me Fair: Stories*, 1987; *For Her Dark Skin*, 1990; *Zulus*, 1990; *The One That Got Away*, 1992; *The Body of Martin Aguilera*, 1994; *God's Country*, 1994; *Big Picture: Stories*, 1996; *Watershed*, 1996; *Frenzy*, 1997; *Glyph*, 1999; *Erasure*, 2001; *Grand Canyon, Inc.*, 2001; *American Desert*, 2004; *Damnedifido: Stories*, 2004; *A History of the African-American People (proposed) by Strom Thurmond, as Told to Percival Everett and James Kincaid* (with James Kincaid), 2004; *Wounded*, 2005; *re: f (gesture): Poems*, 2006; *The Water Cure*, 2007; *Abstraktion und Einfühlung: Poems*, 2008; *I Am Not Sidney Poitier*, 2009; *Swimming Swimmers Swimming: Poems*, 2010; *Assumption*, 2011.

The Appropriation of Cultures

Daniel Barkley had money left to him by his mother. He had a house that had been left to him by his mother. He had a degree in American Studies from Brown University that he had in some way earned, but that had not yet earned anything for him. He played a 1940 Martin guitar with a Barkus-Berry pickup and drove a 1976 Jensen Interceptor, which he had purchased after his mother's sister had died and left him her money because she had no children of her own. Daniel Barkley didn't work and didn't pretend to need to, spending most of his time reading. Some nights he went to a joint near the campus of the University of South Carolina and played jazz with some old guys who all worked very hard during the day, but didn't hold Daniel's condition against him.

Daniel played standards with the old guys, but what he loved to play were old-time slide tunes. One night, some white boys from a fraternity yelled forward to the stage at the black man holding the acoustic guitar and began to shout, "Play 'Dixie' for us! Play 'Dixie' for us!"

Daniel gave them a long look, studied their big-toothed grins and the beer-shiny eyes stuck into puffy, pale faces, hovering over golf shirts and chinos. He looked from them to the uncomfortable expressions on the faces of the old guys with whom he was playing and then to the embarrassed faces of the other college kids in the club.

And then he started to play. He felt his way slowly through the chords of the song once and listened to the deadened hush as it fell over the room. He used the slide to squeeze out the melody of the song he had grown up hating, the song the whites had always pulled out to remind themselves and those other people just where they were. Daniel sang the song. He sang it slowly. He sang it, feeling the lyrics, deciding that the lyrics were his, deciding that the song was his. *Old times there are not forgotten* ... He sang the song and listened to the silence around him. He resisted the urge to let satire ring through his voice. He meant what he sang. *Look away, look away, look away, Dixieland.*

When he was finished, he looked up to see the roomful of eyes on him. One person clapped. Then another. And soon the tavern was filled with applause and hoots. He found the frat boys in the back and watched as they stormed out, a couple of people near the door chuckling at them as they passed.

Roger, the old guy who played tenor sax, slapped Daniel on the back and said something like, "Right on" or "Cool." Roger then played the first few notes of "Take the A Train" and they were off. When the set was done, all the college kids slapped Daniel on the back as he walked toward the bar where he found a beer waiting.

Daniel didn't much care for the slaps on the back, but he didn't focus too much energy on that. He was busy trying to sort out his feelings about what he had just played. The irony of his playing the song straight and from the heart was made more ironic by the fact that as he played it, it came straight and from his heart, as he was claiming Southern soil, or at least recognizing his blood in it. His was the land of cotton and hell no, it was not forgotten. At twenty-three, his anger was fresh and typical, and so was his ease with it, the way it could be forgotten for chunks of time, until something like that night with the white frat boys or simply a flashing blue light in the rearview mirror brought it all back. He liked the song, wanted to play it again, knew that he would.

He drove home from the bar on Green Street and back to his house where he made tea and read about Pickett's charge at Gettysburg while he sat in the big leather chair that had been his father's. He fell asleep and had a dream in which he stopped Pickett's men on the Emmitsburg Road on their way to the field and said, "Give me back my flag."

Daniel's friend Sarah was a very large woman with a very large Afro hairdo. They were sitting on the porch of Daniel's house having tea. The late fall afternoon was mild and slightly overcast. Daniel sat in the wicker rocker while Sarah curled her feet under her on the glider.

"I wish I could have heard it," Sarah said.

"Yeah, me too."

"Personally, I can't even stand to go in that place. All that drinking. Those white kids love to drink." Sarah studied her fingernails.

"I guess. The place is harmless. They seem to like the music."

"Do you think I should paint my nails?"

Daniel frowned at her. "If you want to."

"I mean really paint them. You know, black, or with red, white, and blue stripes. Something like that." She held her hand out, appearing to imagine the colors. "I'd have to grow them long."

"What are you talking about?"

"Just bullshitting."

Daniel and Sarah went to a grocery market to buy food for lunch and Daniel's dinner. Daniel pushed the cart through the Piggly Wiggly while Sarah walked ahead of him. He watched her large movements and her confident stride. At the checkout, he added a bulletin full of pictures of local cars and trucks for sale to his items on the conveyer.

"What's that for?" Sarah asked.

"I think I want to buy a truck."

"Buy a truck?"

"So I can drive you around when you paint your nails."

Later, after lunch and after Sarah had left him alone, Daniel sat in his living room and picked up the car-sale magazine. As he suspected, there were several trucks he liked and one in particular, a 1968 Ford three-quarter ton with the one thing it shared with the other possibilities, a full rear cab window decal of the Confederate flag. He called the number the following morning and arranged with Barb, Travis's wife, to stop by and see the truck.

Travis and Barb lived across the river in the town of Irmo, a name that Daniel had always thought suited a disease for cattle. He drove around the maze of tract homes until he found the right street and number. A woman in a housecoat across the street watched from her porch, safe inside the chain-link fence around her yard. From down the street a man and a teenager, who were covered with grease and apparently engaged in work on a torn-apart Dodge Charger, mindlessly wiped their hands and studied him.

Daniel walked across the front yard, through a maze of plastic toys, and knocked on the front door. Travis opened the door and asked in a surly voice, "What is it?"

"I called about the truck," Daniel said.

"Oh, you're Dan?"

Daniel nodded.

"The truck's in the backyard. Let me get the keys." He pushed the door to, but it didn't catch. Daniel heard the quality of the exchange between Travis and Barb, but not the words. He did hear Barb say, as Travis pulled open the door, "I couldn't tell over the phone."

"Got 'em," Travis said. "Come on with me." He looked at Daniel's Jensen as they walked through the yard. "What kind of car is that?"

"It's a Jensen."

"Nice looking. Is it fast?"

"I guess."

The truck looked a little rough, a pale blue with a bleached-out hood and a crack across the top of the windshield. Travis opened the driver's side door and pushed the key into the ignition. "It's a strong runner," he said. Daniel put his hand on the faded hood and felt the warmth, knew that Travis had already warmed up the motor. Travis turned the key and the engine kicked over. He nodded to Daniel. Daniel nodded back. He looked up to see a blond woman looking on from behind the screen door of the back porch.

"The clutch and the alternator are new this year." Travis stepped backward to the wall of the bed and looked in. "There's some rust back here, but the bottom's pretty solid."

Daniel attended to the sound of the engine. "Misses just a little," he said.

"A tune-up will fix that."

Daniel regarded the rebel-flag decal covering the rear window of the cab, touched it with his finger.

"That thing will peel right off," Travis said.

"No, I like it." Daniel sat down in the truck behind the steering wheel. "Mind if I take it for a spin?"

"Sure thing." Travis looked toward the house, then back to Daniel. "The brakes are good, but you got to press hard."

Daniel nodded.

Travis shut the door, his long fingers wrapped over the edge of the half-lowered glass. Daniel noticed that one of the man's fingernails was blackened.

"I'll just take it around a block or two."

The blond woman was now standing outside the door on the concrete steps. Daniel put the truck in gear and drove out of the yard, past his car and down the street by the man and teenager who were still at work on the Charger. They stared at him, were still watching him as he turned right at the corner. The truck handled decently, but that really wasn't important.

Back at Travis's house Daniel left the keys in the truck and got out to observe the bald tires while Travis looked on. "The ad in the magazine said two thousand."

"Yeah, but I'm willing to work with you."

"Tell you what, I'll give you twenty-two hundred if you deliver it to my house."

Travis was lost, scratching his head and looking back at the house for his wife, who was no longer standing there. "Whereabouts do you live?"

"I live over near the university. Near Five Points."

"Twenty-two hundred?" Travis said more to himself than to Daniel. "Sure I can get it to your house."

"Here's two hundred." Daniel counted out the money and handed it to the man. "I'll have the rest for you in cash when you deliver the truck." He watched Travis feel the bills with his skinny fingers. "Can you have it there at about four?"

"I can do that."

"What in the world do you need a truck for?" Sarah asked. She stepped over to the counter and poured herself another cup of coffee, then sat back down at the table with Daniel.

"I'm not buying the truck. Well, I am buying a truck, but only because I need the truck for the decal. I'm buying the decal."

"Decal?"

"Yes. This truck has a Confederate flag in the back window."

"What?"

"I've decided that the rebel flag is my flag. My blood is Southern blood, right? Well, it's my flag."

Sarah put down her cup and saucer and picked up a cookie from the plate in the middle of the table. "You've flipped. I knew this would happen to you if you didn't work. A person needs to work."

"1 don't need money."

"That's not the point. You don't have to work for money." She stood and walked to the edge of the porch and looked up and down the street.

"I've got my books and my music."

"You need a job so you can be around people you don't care about, doing stuff you don't care about. You need a job to occupy that part of your brain. I suppose it's too late now, though."

"Nonetheless," Daniel said. "You should have seen those redneck boys when I took 'Dixie' from them. They didn't know what to do. So, the god-damn flag is flying over the State Capitol. Don't take it down, just take it. That's what I say."

"That's all you have to do? That's all there is to it?"

"Yep." Daniel leaned back in his rocker. "You watch ol' Travis when he gets here."

* * *

Travis arrived with the pickup a little before four, his wife pulling up behind him in a yellow TransAm. Barb got out of the car and walked up to the porch with Travis. She gave the house a careful look.

"Hey, Travis," Daniel said. "This is my friend, Sarah."

Travis nodded hello.

"You must be Barb," Daniel said.

Barb smiled weakly.

Travis looked at Sarah, then back at the truck, and then to Daniel. "You sure you don't want me to peel that thing off the window?"

"I'm positive."

"Okay."

Daniel gave Sarah a glance, to be sure she was watching Travis's face. "Here's the balance," he said, handing over the money. He took the truck keys from the skinny fingers.

Barb sighed and asked, as if the question were burning right through her, "Why do you want that flag on the truck?"

"Why shouldn't I want it?" Daniel asked.

Barb didn't know what to say. She studied her feet for a second, then regarded the house again. "I mean, you live in a nice house and drive that sports car. What do you need a truck like that for?"

"You don't want the money?"

"Yes, we want the money," Travis said, trying to silence Barb with a look.

"I need the truck for hauling stuff," Daniel said. "You know like groceries and—" he looked to Sarah for help.

"Books," Sarah said.

"Books. Things like that." Daniel held Barb's eyes until she looked away. He watched Travis sign his name to the back of the title and hand it to him and as he took it, he said, "I was just lucky enough to find a truck with the black-power flag already on it."

"What?" Travis screwed up his face, trying to understand.

"The black-power flag on the window. You mean, you didn't know?"

Travis and Barb looked at each other.

"Well, anyway," Daniel said, "I'm glad we could do business." He turned to Sarah. "Let me take you for a ride in my new truck." He and Sarah walked across the yard, got into the pickup, and waved to Travis and Barb who were still standing in Daniel's yard as they drove away.

Sarah was on the verge of hysterics by the time they were out of sight. "That was beautiful," she said.

"No," Daniel said, softly. "That was true."

Over the next weeks, sightings of Daniel and his truck proved problematic for some. He was accosted by two big white men in a 72 Monte Carlo in the parking lot of a 7-Eleven on Two Notch Road.

"What are you doing with that on your truck, boy?" the bigger of the two asked.

"Flying it proudly," Daniel said, noticing the rebel front plate on the Chevrolet. "Just like you, brothers."

The confused second man took a step toward Daniel. "What did you call us?"

"Brothers."

The second man pushed Daniel in the chest with two extended fists, but not terribly hard.

"I don't want any trouble," Daniel told them.

Then a Volkswagen with four black teenagers parked in the slot beside Daniel's truck and they jumped out, staring and looking serious. "What's going on?" the driver and largest of the teenagers asked.

"They were admiring our flag," Daniel said, pointing to his truck.

The teenagers were confused.

"We fly the flag proudly, don't we, young brothers?" Daniel gave a bent-arm, black-power, closed-fist salute. "Don't we?" he repeated. "Don't we?"

"Yeah," the young men said.

The white men had backed away to their car. They slipped into it and drove away.

Daniel looked at the teenagers and, with as serious a face as he could manage, he said, "Get a flag and fly it proudly."

At a gas station, a lawyer named Ahmad Wilson stood filling the tank of his BMW and staring at the back window of Daniel's truck. He then looked at Daniel. "Your truck?" he asked.

Daniel stopped cleaning the windshield and nodded.

Wilson didn't ask a question, just pointed at the rear window of Daniel's pickup.

"Power to the people," Daniel said and laughed.

Daniel played "Dixie" in another bar in town, this time with a R&B dance band at a banquet of the black medical association. The strange looks and expressions of outrage changed to bemused laughter and finally to open joking and acceptance as the song was played fast enough for dancing. Then the song was sung, slowly, to the profound surprise of those singing the song. *I wish I was in the land of cotton, old times there are not forgotten . . . look away, look away, look away . . .*

Soon, there were several, then many cars and trucks in Columbia, South Carolina, sporting Confederate flags and being driven by black people. Black businessmen and ministers wore rebel-flag buttons on their lapels and clips on their ties. The marching band of South Carolina State College, a predominantly black land-grant institution in Orangeburg, paraded with the flag during homecoming. Black people all over the state flew the Confederate flag. The symbol began to disappear from the fronts of big rigs and the back windows of jacked-up four-wheelers. And after the emblem was used to dress the yards and mark picnic sites of black family reunions the following Fourth of July, the piece of cloth was quietly dismissed from its station with the U.S. and State flags atop the State Capitol. There was no ceremony, no notice. One day, it was not there.

Look away, look away, look away . . .

1996

■ SHERMAN ALEXIE (SPOKANE–COEUR D'ALENE) ■
B. 1966

Sherman Alexie was born in Wellpinit, Washington, on the Spokane Indian Reservation. Born hydrocephalic, Alexie underwent brain surgery at the age of six months. Although the surgery was successful, he experienced seizures throughout his childhood. Alexie was a voracious reader, reading Steinbeck by the age of five and finishing all the books in the Wellpinit library by the age of twelve. He attended Reardon High School, an all-white school just outside the reservation, where, ironically, he played basketball for the Reardon "Indians." He attended Gonzaga University in Spokane and eventually graduated from Washington State University with a degree in American Studies. He battled alcoholism during this time and became sober at the age of twenty-three.

Alexie first encountered contemporary American Indian literature in college. Reading about his own experiences in poems and stories was a life-changing experience. After reading this line from a poem by Paiute poet Adrian Louis, "I'm in the reservation of my mind," Alexie felt that somebody understood him, and he knew that he would begin writing. That was in 1989. Three years later, Alexie's first book of poetry, *The Business of Fancydancing*, was published by Hanging Loose Press and received a tremendous amount of critical attention from Native American as well as non-Indian critics. Joy Harjo, renowned Creek poet, called Alexie "one of the most vital writers to emerge in the late twentieth century." After *The New York Times Book Review* hailed Alexie as "one of the major lyric voices of our time" and declared *Fancydancing* the 1992 Notable Book of the Year, Alexie's career skyrocketed. Since then, he has published a prolific amount of poetry and fiction and has won numerous awards, including the 1993 Lila Wallace–Reader's Digest Writers' Award, the 1993 PEN/Hemingway Best First Book of Fiction Citation for *The Lone Ranger and Tonto Fistfight in Heaven*, the 1996 Before Columbus Foundation American Book Award, and the national book award for a young adult novel he published in 2007, *The Absolutely True Story of a Part-Time Indian*. He was also named one of the Twenty Best American Novelists under the Age of 40 by *Granta* magazine in 1997 and one of Twenty Writers for the 21st Century by *The New Yorker* in 1999.

Alexie is perhaps best known for the movie *Smoke Signals*, the screenplay of which he adapted from his short story "This Is What It Means to Say Phoenix, Arizona," from 1993's *Lone Ranger and Tonto*. *Smoke Signals* was the first movie written, directed, and produced entirely by American Indians. The film premiered at the Sundance Film Festival in 1998 and won the Audience Award and the Filmmakers Trophy for Cheyenne-Arapaho director Chris Eyre.

Alexie is a significant writer and a controversial figure, known for his brutally honest depictions of contemporary reservation life and razor sharp wit. His goal is to challenge and poke fun at traditional stereotypes of American Indian people. In poems and stories about life on the reservation, he drives home the point that American Indian people are not trapped in the nineteenth century but are members of living, vital cultures and, furthermore, participants in and part of American popular culture. Alexie takes his responsibilities as a Native American writer seriously, realizing that, like it or not, he is a political spokesperson for native peoples. He participated in President Clinton's roundtable discussion on race, and he frequently attacks nonnatives who write about Native Americans or appropriate Native American themes. He receives much criticism for his viewpoints but remains outspoken and unapologetic.

Alexie currently lives in Seattle with his wife, Diane, a member of the Hidatsa Nation, and their son. He shows no signs of slowing his pace and is working on screenplays in addition to his fiction and poetry.

Amanda J. Cobb
University of New Mexico, Albuquerque

PRIMARY WORKS

The Business of Fancydancing: Stories and Poems, 1992; *I Would Steal Horses*, 1993; *Old Shirts and New Skins*, 1993; *First Indian on the Moon*, 1993; *The Lone Ranger and Tonto Fistfight in Heaven*, 1993; *Seven Mourning Songs for the Cedar Flute I Have Yet to Learn to Play*, 1995; *Reservation Blues*, 1995; *Water Flowing Home*, 1996; *The Summer of Black Widows*, 1996; *Indian Killer*, 1996; *The Man Who Loves Salmon*, 1998; *Smoke Signals*, 1998; *One-Stick Song*, 1999; *The Toughest Indian in the World*, 2000; *Ten Little Indians*, 2003; *Dangerous Astronomy*, 2005; *Flight*, 2007; *Face*, 2009; *War Dances*, 2009.

What You Pawn I Will Redeem

Noon

One day you have a home and the next you don't, but I'm not going to tell you my particular reasons for being homeless, because it's my secret story, and Indians have to work hard to keep secrets from hungry white folks.

I'm a Spokane Indian boy, an Interior Salish, and my people have lived within a one-hundred-mile radius of Spokane, Washington, for at least ten thousand years. I grew up in Spokane, moved to Seattle twenty-three years ago for college, flunked out within two semesters, worked various blue- and bluer-collar jobs for many years, married two or three times, fathered two or three kids, and then went crazy. Of course, "crazy" is not the official definition of my mental problem, but I don't think "asocial disorder" fits it, either, because that makes me sound like I'm a serial killer or something. I've never hurt another human being, or at least not physically. I've broken a few hearts in my time, but we've all done that, so I'm nothing special in that regard. I'm a boring heartbreaker, at that, because I've never abandoned one woman for another. I never dated or married more than one woman at a time. I didn't break hearts into pieces overnight. I broke them slowly and carefully. I didn't set any land-speed records running out the door. Piece by piece, I disappeared. And I've been disappearing ever since. But I'm not going to tell you any more about my brain or my soul.

I've been homeless for six years. If there's such a thing as being an effective homeless man, I suppose I'm effective. Being homeless is probably the only thing I've ever been good at. I know where to get the best free food. I've made friends with restaurant and convenience store managers who let me use their bathrooms. I don't mean the public bathrooms, either. I mean the employees' bathrooms, the clean ones hidden in the back of the kitchen or the pantry or the cooler. I know it sounds strange to be proud of, but it means a lot to me, being truthworthy enough to piss in somebody else's clean bathroom. Maybe you don't understand the value of a clean bathroom, but I do.

Probably none of this interests you. I probably don't interest you much. Homeless Indians are everywhere in Seattle. We're common and boring, and you walk right on by us, with maybe a look of anger or disgust or even sadness at the terrible fate of the noble savage. But we have dreams and families. I'm friends with a homeless Plains Indian man whose son is the editor of a big-time newspaper back east. That's his story, but we Indians are great storytellers and liars and mythmakers, so maybe that Plains Indian hobo is a plain old everyday Indian. I'm kind of suspicious of him, because he describes himself only as Plains Indian, a generic term, and not by a specific tribe. When I asked him why he wouldn't tell me exactly what he is, he said, "Do any of us know exactly what we are?" Yeah, great, a philosophizing Indian. "Hey," I said, "you got to have a home to be that homely." He laughed and flipped me the eagle and walked away. But you probably want to know more about the story I'm really trying to tell you.

I wander the streets with a regular crew, my teammates, my defenders, and my posse. It's Rose of Sharon, Junior, and me. We matter to one another if we don't matter to anybody else. Rose of Sharon is a big woman, about seven feet tall if you're measuring overall effect, and about five feet tall if you're talking about the physical. She's a Yakama Indian of the Wishram variety. Junior is a Colville, but there are about 199 tribes that make up the Colville, so he could be anything. He's good-looking, though, like he just stepped out of some "Don't Litter the Earth" public-service advertisement. He's got those great big cheekbones that are like planets, you know, with little moons orbiting around them. He gets me jealous, jealous, and jealous. If you put Junior and me next to each other, he's the Before Columbus Arrived Indian, and I'm the After Columbus Arrived Indian. I am living proof of the horrible damage that colonialism has done to us Skins. But I'm not going to let you know how scared I sometimes get of history and its ways. I'm a strong man, and I know that silence is the best way of dealing with white folks.

This whole story started at lunchtime, when Rose of Sharon, Junior, and I were panning the handle down at Pike Place Market. After about two hours of negotiating, we earned five dollars, good enough for a bottle of fortified courage from the most beautiful 7–Eleven in the world. So we headed over that way, feeling like warrior drunks, and we walked past this pawnshop I'd never noticed before. And that was strange, because we Indians have built-in pawn-shop radar. But the strangest thing was the old powwow-dance regalia I saw hanging in the window.

"That's my grandmother's regalia," I said to Rose of Sharon and Junior.

"How do you know for sure?" Junior asked.

I didn't know for sure, because I hadn't seen that regalia in person ever. I'd seen only photographs of my grandmother dancing in it. And that was before somebody stole it from her fifty years ago. But it sure looked like my memory of it, and it had all the same colors of feathers and beads that my family always sewed into their powwow regalia.

"There's only one way to know for sure," I said.

So Rose of Sharon, Junior, and I walked into the pawnshop and greeted the old white man working behind the counter.

"How can I help you?" he asked.

"That's my grandmother's powwow regalia in your window," I said. "Somebody stole it from her fifty years ago, and my family has been looking for it ever since."

The pawnbroker looked at me like I was a liar. I understood. Pawnshops are filled with liars.

"I'm not lying," I said. "Ask my friends here. They'll tell you."

"He's the most honest Indian I know," Rose of Sharon said.

"All right, honest Indian," the pawnbroker said. "I'll give you the benefit of the doubt. Can you prove it's your grandmother's regalia?"

Because they don't want to be perfect, because only God is perfect, Indian people sew flaws into their powwow regalia. My family always sewed one yellow bead somewhere on their regalia. But we always hid it where you had to search hard to find it.

"If it really is my grandmother's," I said, "there will be one yellow bead hidden somewhere on it."

"All right, then," the pawnbroker said. "Let's take a look."

He pulled the regalia out of the window, laid it down on his glass counter, and we searched for that yellow bead and found it hidden beneath the armpit.

"There it is," the pawnbroker said. He didn't sound surprised. "You were right. This is your grandmother's regalia."

"It's been missing for fifty years," Junior said.

"Hey, Junior," I said. "It's my family's story. Let me tell it."

"All right," he said. "I apologize. You go ahead."

"It's been missing for fifty years," I said.

"That's his family's sad story," Rose of Sharon said. "Are you going to give it back to him?"

"That would be the right thing to do," the pawnbroker said. "But I can't afford to do the right thing. I paid a thousand dollars for this. I can't give away a thousand dollars."

"We could go to the cops and tell them it was stolen," Rose of Sharon said.

"Hey," I said to her, "don't go threatening people."

The pawnbroker sighed. He was thinking hard about the possibilities.

"Well, I suppose you could go to the cops," he said. "But I don't think they'd believe a word you said."

He sounded sad about that. Like he was sorry for taking advantage of our disadvantages.

"What's your name?" the pawnbroker asked me.

"Jackson," I said.

"Is that first or last?" he asked.

"Both."

"Are you serious?"

"Yes, it's true. My mother and father named me Jackson Jackson. My family nickname is Jackson Squared. My family is funny."

"All right, Jackson Jackson," the pawnbroker said. "You wouldn't happen to have a thousand dollars, would you?"

"We've got five dollars total," I said.

"That's too bad," he said and thought hard about the possibilities. "I'd sell it to you for a thousand dollars if you had it. Heck, to make it fair, I'd sell it to you for nine hundred and ninety-nine dollars. I'd lose a dollar. It would be the moral thing to do in this case. To lose a dollar would be the right thing."

"We've got five dollars total," I said again.

"That's too bad," he said again and thought harder about the possibilities. "How about this? I'll give you twenty-four hours to come up with nine hundred and ninety-nine dollars. You come back here at lunchtime tomorrow with the money, and I'll sell it back to you. How does that sound?"

"It sounds good," I said.

"All right, then," he said. "We have a deal. And I'll get you started. Here's twenty bucks to get you started."

He opened up his wallet and pulled out a crisp twenty-dollar bill and gave it to me. Rose of Sharon, junior, and I walked out into the daylight to search for nine hundred and seventy-four more dollars.

1:00 P.M.

Rose of Sharon, Junior, and I carried our twenty-dollar bill and our five dollars in loose change over to the 7–Eleven and spent it to buy three bottles of imagination. We needed to figure out how to raise all that money in one day. Thinking hard, we huddled in an alley beneath the Alaska Way Viaduct and finished off those bottles one, two, and three.

2:00 P.M.

Rose of Sharon was gone when I woke. I heard later she had hitchhiked back to Toppenish and was living with her sister on the reservation.

Junior was passed out beside me, covered in his own vomit, or maybe somebody else's vomit, and my head hurt from thinking, so I, left him alone and walked down to the water. I loved the smell of ocean water. Salt always smells like memory.

When I got to the wharf, I ran into three Aleut cousins who sat on a wooden bench and stared out at the bay and cried. Most of the homeless Indians in Seattle come from Alaska. One by one, each of them hopped a big working boat in Anchorage or Barrow or Juneau, fished his way south to Seattle, jumped off the boat with a pocketful of cash to party hard at one of the highly sacred and traditional Indian bars, went broke and broker, and has been trying to find his way back to the boat and the frozen north ever since.

These Aleuts smelled like salmon, I thought, and they told me they were going to sit on that wooden bench until their boat came back.

"How long has your boat been gone?" I asked.

"Eleven years," the elder Aleut said.

I cried with them for a while.

"Hey," I said. "Do you guys have any money I can borrow?"

They didn't.

3:00 P.M.

I walked back to Junior. He was still passed out. I put my face down near his mouth to make sure he was breathing. He was alive, so I dug around in his blue-jean pockets and found half a cigarette. I smoked it all the way down and thought about my grandmother.

Her name was Agnes, and she died of breast cancer when I was fourteen. My father thought Agnes caught her tumors from the uranium mine on the reservation. But my mother said the disease started when Agnes was walking back from the powwow one night and got run over by a motorcycle. She broke three ribs, and my mother said those ribs never healed right, and tumors always take over when you don't heal right.

Sitting beside Junior, smelling the smoke and salt and vomit, I wondered if my grandmother's cancer had started when somebody stole her powwow regalia. Maybe the cancer started in her broken heart and then leaked out into her breasts. I know it's crazy, but I wondered if I could bring my grandmother back to life if I bought back her regalia.

I needed money, big money, so I left Junior and walked over to the Real Change office.

4:00 P.M.

"Real Change is a multifaceted organization that publishes a newspaper, supports cultural projects that empower the poor and homeless, and mobilizes the public around poverty issues. Real Change's mission is to organize, educate, and build alliances to create solutions to homelessness and poverty. They exist to provide a voice to poor people in our community."

I memorized Real Change's mission statement because I sometimes sell the newspaper on the streets. But you have to stay sober to sell it, and I'm not always good at staying sober. Anybody can sell the newspaper. You buy each copy for thirty cents and sell it for a dollar and keep the net profit.

"I need one thousand four hundred and thirty papers," I said to the Big Boss.

"That's a strange number," he said. "And that's a lot of papers."

"I need them."

The Big Boss pulled out the calculator and did the math. "It will cost you four hundred and twenty-nine dollars for that many," he said.

"If I had that kind of money, I wouldn't need to sell the papers."

"What's going on, Jackson-to-the-Second-Power?" he asked. He is the only one who calls me that. He is a funny and kind man.

I told him about my grandmother's powwow regalia and how much money I needed to buy it back.

"We should call the police" he said.

"I don't want to do that," I said. "It's a quest now. I need to win it back by myself."

"I understand," he said. "And to be honest, I'd give you the papers to sell if I thought it would work. But the record for most papers sold in a day by one vendor is only three hundred and two."

"That would net me about two hundred bucks," I said.

The Big Boss used his calculator. "Two hundred and eleven dollars and forty cents," he said.

"That's not enough," I said.

"The most money anybody has made in one day is five hundred and twenty-five. And that's because somebody gave Old Blue five hundred-dollar bills for some dang reason. The average daily net is about thirty dollars."

"This isn't going to work."

"No."

"Can you lend me some money?"

"I can't do that," he said. "If I lend you money, I have to lend money to everybody."

"What can you do?"

"I'll give you fifty papers for free. But don't tell anybody I did it."

"Okay," I said.

He gathered up the newspapers and handed them to me. I held them to my chest. He hugged me. I carried the newspapers back toward the water.

5:00 P.M.

Back on the wharf, I stood near the Bainbridge Island Terminal and tried to sell papers to business commuters walking onto the ferry.

I sold five in one hour, dumped the other forty-five into a garbage can, and walked into the McDonald's, ordered four cheeseburgers for a dollar each, and slowly ate them.

After eating, I walked outside and vomited on the sidewalk. I hated to lose my food so soon after eating it. As an alcoholic Indian with a busted stomach, I always hope I can keep enough food in my stomach to stay alive.

6:00 P.M.

With one dollar in my pocket, I walked back to Junior. He was still passed out, so I put my ear to his chest and listened for his heartbeat. He was alive, so I took off his shoes and socks and found one dollar in his left sock and fifty cents in his right sock. With two dollars and fifty cents in my hand, I sat beside Junior and thought about my grandmother and her stories.

When I was sixteen, my grandmother told me a story about World War II. She was a nurse at a military hospital in Sydney, Australia. Over the course of two years, she comforted and healed U.S. and Australian soldiers.

One day, she tended to a wounded Maori soldier. He was very dark-skinned. His hair was black and curly, and his eyes were black and warm. His face with covered with bright tattoos.

"Are you Maori?" he asked my grandmother.

"No," she said. "I'm Spokane Indian. From the United States."

"Ah, yes," he said. "I have heard of your tribes. But you are the first American Indian I have ever met."

"There's a lot of Indian soldiers fighting for the United States," she said. "I have a brother still fighting in Germany, and I lost another brother on Okinawa."

"I am sorry," he said. "I was on Okinawa as well. It was terrible." He had lost his legs to an artillery attack.

"I am sorry about your legs," my grandmother said.

"It's funny, isn't it?" he asked.

"What's funny?"

"How we brown people are killing other brown people so white people will remain free."

"I hadn't thought of it that way."

"Well, sometimes I think of it that way. And other times, I think of it the way they want me to think of it. I get confused."

She fed him morphine.

"Do you believe in heaven?" he asked.

"Which heaven?" she asked.

"I'm talking about the heaven where my legs are waiting for me."

They laughed.

"Of course," he said, "my legs will probably run away from me when I get to heaven. And how will I ever catch them?"

"You have to get your arms strong," my grandmother said. "So you can run on your hands."

They laughed again.

Sitting beside Junior, I laughed with the memory of my grandmother's story. I put my hand close to Junior's mouth to make sure he was still breathing. Yes, Junior was alive, so I took his two dollars and fifty cents and walked to the Korean grocery store over in Pioneer Square.

7:00 P.M.

In the Korean grocery store, I bought a fifty-cent cigar and two scratch lottery tickets for a dollar each. The maximum cash prize was five hundred dollars a ticket. If I won both, I would have enough money to buy back the regalia.

I loved Kay, the young Korean woman who worked the register. She was the daughter of the owners and sang all day.

"I love you," I said when I handed her the money.

"You always say you love me," she said.

"That's because I will always love you."

"You are a sentimental fool."

"I'm a romantic old man."

"Too old for me."

"I know I'm too old for you, but I can dream."

"Okay," she said. "I agree to be a part of your dreams, but I will only hold your hand in your dreams. No kissing and no sex. Not even in your dreams."

"Okay," I said. "No sex. Just romance."

"Good-bye, Jackson Jackson, my love, I will see you soon."

I left the store, walked over to Occidental Park, sat on a bench, and smoked my cigar all the way down.

Ten minutes after I finished the cigar, I scratched my first lottery ticket and won nothing. So I could win only five hundred dollars now, and that would be just half of what I needed.

Ten minutes later, I scratched my other lottery ticket and won a free ticket, a small consolation and one more chance to win money.

I walked back to Kay.

"Jackson Jackson," she said. "Have you come back to claim my heart?"

"I won a free ticket," I said.

"Just like a man," she said. "You love money and power more than you love me."

"It's true," I said. "And I'm sorry it's true."

She gave me another scratch ticket, and I carried it outside. I liked to scratch my tickets in private. Hopeful and sad, I scratched that third ticket and won real money. I carried it back inside to Kay.

"I won a hundred dollars," I said.

She examined the ticket and laughed. "That's a fortune," she said and counted out five twenties. Our fingertips touched as she handed me the money. I felt electric and constant.

"Thank you," I said and gave her one of the bills.

"I can't take that," she said. "It's your money."

"No, it's tribal. It's an Indian thing. When you win, you're supposed to share with your family."

"I'm not your family."

"Yes, you are."

She smiled. She kept the money. With eighty dollars in my pocket, I said good-bye to my dear Kay and walked out into the cold night air.

8:00 P.M.

I wanted to share the good news with Junior. I walked back to him, but he was gone. I later heard he had hitchhiked down to Portland, Oregon, and died of exposure in an alley behind the Hilton Hotel.

9:00 P.M.

Lonely for Indians, I carried my eighty dollars over to Big Heart's in South Downtown. Big Heart's is an all-Indian bar. Nobody knows how or why Indians migrate to one bar and turn it into an official Indian bar. But Big Heart's has been an Indian bar for twenty-three years. It used to be way up on Aurora Avenue, but a crazy Lummi Indian burned that one down, and the owners moved to the new location, a few blocks south of Safeco Field.

I walked inside Big Heart's and counted fifteen Indians, eight men and seven women. I didn't know any of them, but Indians like to belong, so we all pretended to be cousins.

"How much for whiskey shots?" I asked the bartender, a fat white guy.

"You want the bad stuff or the badder stuff?"

"As bad as you got."

"One dollar a shot."

I laid my eighty dollars on the bar top.

"All right," I said. "Me and all my cousins here are going to be drinking eighty shots. How many is that apiece?"

"Counting you," a woman shouted from behind me, "that's five shots for everybody."

I turned to look at her. She was a chubby and pale Indian sitting with a tall and skinny Indian man.

"All right, math genius," I said to her and then shouted for the whole bar to hear. "Five drinks for everybody!"

All of the other Indians rushed the bar, but I sat with the mathematician and her skinny friend. We took our time with our whiskey shots.

"What's your tribe?" I asked them.

"I'm Duwamish," she said. "And he's Crow."

"You're a long way from Montana," I said to him.

"I'm Crow," he said. "I flew here."

"What's your name?" I asked them.

"I'm Irene Muse," she said. "And this is Honey Boy."

She shook my hand hard, but he offered his hand like I was supposed to kiss it. So I kissed it. He giggled and blushed as well as a dark-skinned Crow can blush.

"You're one of them two-spirits, aren't you?" I asked him.

"I love women," he said. "And I love men."

"Sometimes both at the same time," Irene said.

We laughed.

"Man," I said to Honey Boy. "So you must have about eight or nine spirits going on inside of you, enit?"

"Sweetie," he said, "I'll be whatever you want me to be."

"Oh, no," Irene said. "Honey Boy is falling in love."

"It has nothing to do with love," he said.

We laughed.

"Wow," I said. "I'm flattered, Honey Boy, but I don't play on your team."

"Never say never," he said.

"You better be careful," Irene said. "Honey Boy knows all sorts of magic. He always makes straight boys fall for him."

"Honey Boy," I said, "you can try to seduce me. And Irene, you can try with him. But my heart belongs to a woman named Kay."

"Is your Kay a virgin?" Honey Boy asked.

We laughed.

We drank our whiskey shots until they were gone. But the other Indians bought me more whiskey shots because I'd been so generous with my money. Honey Boy pulled out his credit card, and I drank and sailed on that plastic boat.

After a dozen shots, I asked Irene to dance. And she refused. But Honey Boy shuffled over to the jukebox, dropped in a quarter, and selected Willie Nelson's "Help Me Make It Through the Night." As Irene and I sat at the table and laughed and drank more whiskey, Honey Boy danced a slow circle around us and sang along with Willie.

"Are you serenading me?" I asked him.

He kept singing and dancing.

"Are you serenading me?" I asked him again.

"He's going to put a spell on you," Irene said.

I leaned over the table, spilling a few drinks, and kissed Irene hard. She kissed me back.

10:00 P.M.

Irene pushed me into the women's bathroom, into a stall, shut the door behind us, and shoved her hand down my pants. She was short, so I had to lean over to kiss her. I grabbed and squeezed her everywhere I could reach, and she was wonderfully fat, and every part of her body felt like a large, warm, and soft breast.

Midnight

Nearly blind with alcohol, I stood alone at the bar and swore I'd been standing in the bathroom with Irene only a minute ago.

"One more shot!" I yelled at the bartender.

"You've got no more money!" he yelled.

"Somebody buy me a drink!" I shouted.

"They've got no more money!"

"Where's Irene and Honey Boy?"

"Long gone!"

2:00 A.M.

"Closing time!" the bartender shouted at the three or four Indians still drinking hard after a long hard day of drinking. Indian alcoholics are either sprinters or marathon runners.

"Where's Irene and Honey Bear?" I asked.

"They've been gone for hours," the bartender said.

"Where'd they go?"

"I told you a hundred times, I don't know."

"What am I supposed to do?"

"It's closing time. I don't care where you go, but you're not staying here."

"You are an ungrateful bastard. I've been good to you."

"You don't leave right now, I'm going to kick your ass."

"Come on, I know how to fight."

He came for me. I don't remember what happened after that.

4:00 A.M.

I emerged from the blackness and discovered myself walking behind a big warehouse. I didn't know where I was. My face hurt. I touched my nose and decided it might be broken. Exhausted and cold, I pulled a plastic tarp from a truck bed, wrapped it around me like a faithful lover, and fell asleep in the dirt.

6:00 A.M.

Somebody kicked me in the ribs. I opened my eyes and looked up at a white cop.

"Jackson," said the cop. "Is that you?"

"Officer Williams," I said. He was a good cop with a sweet tooth. He'd given me hundreds of candy bars over the years. I wonder if he knew I was diabetic.

"What the hell are you doing here?" he asked.

"I was cold and sleepy," I said. "So I laid down."

"You dumb-ass, you passed out on the railroad tracks."

I sat up and looked around. I was lying on the railroad tracks. Dock-workers stared at me. I should have been a railroad-track pizza, a double Indian pepperoni with extra cheese. Sick and scared, I leaned over and puked whiskey.

"What the hell's wrong with you?" Officer Williams asked. "You've never been this stupid."

"It's my grandmother," I said. "She died."

"I'm sorry, man. When did she die?"

"1972."

"And you're killing yourself now?"

"I've been killing myself ever since she died."

He shook his head. He was sad for me. Like I said, he was a good cop.

"And somebody beat the hell out of you," he said. "You remember who?"

"Mr. Grief and I went a few rounds."

"It looks like Mr. Grief knocked you out."

"Mr. Grief always wins."

"Come on," he said, "let's get you out of here."

He helped me stand and led me over to his squad car. He put me in the back. "You throw up in there," he said, "and you're cleaning it up."

"That's fair," I said.

He walked around the car and sat in the driver's seat. "I'm taking you over to detox," he said.

"No, man, that place is awful," I said. "It's full of drunk Indians."

We laughed. He drove away from the docks.

"I don't know how you guys do it," he said.

"What guys?" I asked.

"You Indians. How the hell do you laugh so much? I just picked your ass off the railroad tracks, and you're making jokes. Why the hell do you do that?"

"The two funniest tribes I've ever been around are Indians and Jews, so I guess that says something about the inherent humor of genocide."

We laughed.

"Listen to you, Jackson. You're so smart. Why the hell are you on the streets?"

"Give me a thousand dollars, and I'll tell you."

"You bet I'd give you a thousand dollars if I knew you'd straighten up your life."

He meant it. He was the second-best cop I'd ever known.

"You're a good cop," I said.

"Come on, Jackson," he said. "Don't blow smoke up my ass."

"No, really, you remind me of my grandfather."

"Yeah, that's what you Indians always tell me."

"No, man, my grandfather was a tribal cop. He was a good cop. He never arrested people. He took care of them. Just like you."

"I've arrested hundreds of scumbags, Jackson. And I've shot a couple in the ass."

"It don't matter. You're not a killer."

"I didn't kill them. I killed their asses. I'm an ass-killer."

We drove through downtown. The missions and shelters had already released their overnighters. Sleepy homeless men and women stood on corners and stared up at the gray sky. It was the morning after the night of the living dead.

"Did you ever get scared?" I asked Officer Williams.

"What do you mean?"

"I mean, being a cop, is it scary?"

He thought about that for a while. He contemplated it. I liked that about him.

"I guess I try not to think too much about being afraid," he said. "If you think about fear, then you'll be afraid. The job is boring most of the time. Just driving and looking into dark corners, you know, and seeing nothing. But then things get heavy. You're chasing somebody or fighting them or walking around a dark house and you just know some crazy guy is hiding around a corner, and hell yes, it's scary."

"My grandfather was killed in the line of duty," I said.

"I'm sorry. How'd it happen?"

I knew he'd listen closely to my story.

"He worked on the reservation. Everybody knew everybody. It was safe. We aren't like those crazy Sioux or Apache or any of those other warrior tribes. There's only been three murders on my reservation in the last hundred years."

"That is safe."

"Yeah, we Spokane, we're passive, you know? We're mean with words. And we'll cuss out anybody. But we don't shoot people. Or stab them. Not much, anyway."

"So what happened to your grandfather?"

"This man and his girlfriend were fighting down by Little Falls."

"Domestic dispute. Those are the worst."

"Yeah, but this guy was my grandfather's brother. My great-uncle."

"Oh, no."

"Yeah, it was awful. My grandfather just strolled into the house. He'd been there a thousand times. And his brother and his girlfriend were all drunk and beating on each other. And my grandfather stepped between them just like he'd done a hundred times before. And the girlfriend tripped or something. She fell down and hit her head and started crying. And my grandfather knelt down beside her to make sure she was all right. And for some reason, my great-uncle reached down, pulled my grandfather's pistol out of the holster, and shot him in the head."

"That's terrible. I'm sorry."

"Yeah, my great-uncle could never figure out why he did it. He went to prison forever, you know, and he always wrote these long letters. Like fifty pages of tiny little handwriting. And he was always trying to figure out why he did it. He'd write and write and write and try to figure it out. He never did. It's a great big mystery."

"Do you remember your grandfather?"

"A little bit. I remember the funeral. My grandmother wouldn't let them bury him. My father had to drag her away from the grave."

"I don't know what to say."

"I don't, either."

We stopped in front of the detox center.

"We're here," Officer Williams said.

"I can't go in there," I said.

"You have to."

"Please, no. They'll keep me for twenty-four hours. And then it will be too late."

"Too late for what?"

I told him about my grandmother's regalia and the deadline for buying it back.

"If it was stolen," he said, "then you need to file reports. I'll investigate it myself. If that thing is really your grandmother's, I'll get it back for you. Legally."

"No," I said. "That's not fair. The pawnbroker didn't know it was stolen. And besides, I'm on a mission here. I want to be a hero, you know? I want to win it back like a knight."

"That's romantic crap."

"It might be. But I care about it. It's been a long time since I really cared about something."

Officer Williams turned around in his seat and stared at me. He studied me.

"I'll give you some money," he said. "I don't have much. Only thirty bucks. I'm short until payday. And it's not enough to get back the regalia. But it's something."

"I'll take it," I said.

"I'm giving it to you because I believe in what you believe. I'm hoping, and I don't know why I'm hoping it, but I hope you can turn thirty bucks into a thousand somehow."

"I believe in magic."

"I believe you'll take my money and get drunk on it."

"Then why are you giving it to me?"

"There ain't no such thing as an atheist cop."

"Sure there is."

"Yeah, well, I'm not an atheist cop."

He let me out of the car, handed me two fives and a twenty, and shook my hand. "Take care of yourself, Jackson," he said. "Stay off the railroad tracks."

"I'll try," I said.

He drove away. Carrying my money, I headed back toward the water.

8:00 A.M.

On the wharf, those three Aleut men still waited on the wooden bench.

"Have you seen your ship?" I asked.

"Seen a lot of ships," the elder Aleut said. "But not our ship."

I sat on the bench with them. We sat in silence for a long time. I wondered whether we would fossilize if we sat there long enough.

I thought about my grandmother. I'd never seen her dance in her regalia. More than anything, I wished I'd seen her dance at a powwow.

"Do you guys know any songs?" I asked the Aleuts.

"I know all of Hank Williams," the elder Aleut said.

"How about Indian songs?"

"Hank Williams is Indian."

"How about sacred songs?"

"Hank Williams is sacred."

"I'm talking about ceremonial songs, you know, religious ones. The songs you sing back home when you're wishing and hoping."

"What are you wishing and hoping for?"

"I'm wishing my grandmother was still alive."

"Every song I know is about that."

"Well, sing me as many as you can."

The Aleuts sang their strange and beautiful songs. I listened. They sang about my grandmother and their grandmothers. They were lonely for the cold and snow. I was lonely for everybody.

10:00 A.M.

After the Aleuts finished their last song, we sat in silence. Indians are good at silence.

"Was that the last song?" I asked.

"We sang all the ones we could," the elder Aleut said. "All the others are just for our people."

I understood. We Indians have to keep our secrets. And these Aleuts were so secretive that they didn't refer to themselves as Indians.

"Are you guys hungry?" I asked.

They looked at one another and communicated without talking.

"We could eat," the elder Aleut said.

11:00 A.M.

The Aleuts and I walked over to Mother's Kitchen, a greasy diner in the International District. I knew they served homeless Indians who'd lucked in to money.

"Four for breakfast?" the waitress asked when we stepped inside.

"Yes, we're very hungry," the elder Aleut said.

She sat us in a booth near the kitchen. I could smell the food cooking. My stomach growled.

"You guys want separate checks?" the waitress asked.

"No, I'm paying for it," I said.

"Aren't you the generous one," she said.

"Don't do that," I said.

"Do what?" she asked.

"Don't ask me rhetorical questions. They scare me."

She looked puzzled, and then she laughed.

"Okay, Professor," she said. "I'll only ask you real questions from now on."

"Thank you."

"What do you guys want to eat?"

"That's the best question anybody can ask anybody," I said.

"How much money you got?" she asked.

"Another good question," I said. "I've got twenty-five dollars I can spend. Bring us all the breakfast you can, plus your tip."

She knew the math.

"All right, that's four specials and four coffees and fifteen percent for me."

The Aleuts and I waited in silence. Soon enough, the waitress returned and poured us four coffees, and we sipped at them until she returned again with four plates of food. Eggs, bacon, toast, hash-brown potatoes. It is amazing how much food you can buy for so little money.

Grateful, we feasted.

Noon

I said farewell to the Aleuts and walked toward the pawnshop. I later heard the Aleuts had waded into the saltwater near Dock 47 and disappeared. Some Indians said the Aleuts walked on the water and headed north. Other Indians saw the Aleuts drown. I don't know what happened to them.

I looked for the pawnshop and couldn't find it. I swear it wasn't located in the place where it had been before. I walked twenty or thirty blocks looking for the pawnshop, turned corners and bisected intersections, looked up its name in the phone books, and asked people walking past me if they'd ever heard of it. But that pawnshop seemed to have sailed away from me like a ghost ship. I wanted to cry. Right when I'd given up, when I turned one last corner and thought I might die if I didn't find that pawnshop, there it was, located in a space I swore it hadn't been filling up a few minutes before.

I walked inside and greeted the pawnbroker, who looked a little younger than he had before.

"It's you," he said.

"Yes, it's me," I said.

"Jackson Jackson."

"That is my name."

"Where are your friends?"

"They went traveling. But it's okay. Indians are everywhere."

"Do you have my money?"

"How much do you need again?" I asked and hoped the price had changed.

"Nine hundred and ninety-nine dollars."

It was still the same price. Of course it was the same price. Why would it change?

"I don't have that," I said.

"What do you have?"

"Five dollars."

I set the crumpled Lincoln on the countertop. The pawnbroker studied it.

"Is that the same five dollars from yesterday?"

"No, it's different."

He thought about the possibilities.

"Did you work hard for this money?" he asked.

"Yes," I said.

He closed his eyes and thought harder about the possibilities. Then he stepped into his back room and returned with my grandmother's regalia.

"Take it," he said and held it out to me.

"I don't have the money."

"I don't want your money."

"But I wanted to win it."

"You did win it. Now, take it before I change my mind."

Do you know how many good men live in this world? Too many to count!

I took my grandmother's regalia and walked outside. I knew that solitary yellow bead was part of me. I knew I was that yellow bead in part. Outside, I wrapped myself in my grandmother's regalia and breathed her in. I stepped off the sidewalk and into the intersection. Pedestrians stopped. Cars stopped. The city stopped. They all watched me dance with my grandmother. I was my grandmother, dancing.

2003

MARTIN ESPADA

B. 1957

Born in Brooklyn, New York, of a Puerto Rican father and Jewish mother, Martin Espada has published seventeen books in all as a poet, editor, essayist, and translator. He earned a B.A. from the University of Wisconsin–Madison and a J.D. from Northeastern University. For many years, he worked as a tenant lawyer. He is presently a professor of literature and creative writing at the University of Massachusetts at Amherst, and he resides in Northampton with his wife and son.

The poem "Alabanza: In Praise of Local 100" is a praise-song (as indicated by the Spanish word *alabanza*) for the forty-three members of the Hotel Employees and Restaurant Employees Local 100 who died in the attack on the World Trade Center in New York City on 9/11. In the first stanza the poem memorializes an individual, a Puerto Rican cook in the Windows on the World restaurant, describing specific traits such as the "tattoo on his shoulder that said *Oye*." After dwelling in affectionate detail on this specific victim of the attack, the poet widens his view, praising the kitchen space in which the workers listened to music, spoke Spanish, and baked bread. The poet praises all these things in a repetitive, mesmerizing chant in which "Alabanza" becomes a refrain. In widening his view to Manhattan, seen through the glass windows at the top of the World Trade Center, the poet notes that the workers he memorializes came from nations ranging from Ecuador to Yemen and Ghana. The most significant part of the poem, the penultimate stanza, tries to envision an existence beyond death in the souls of those annihilated in the tragedy of 9/11, whom the poet imagines as "smoke-beings flung in constellations across the night sky of this city." In imagining that those who died still exist in some form beyond their bodies, the poet honors their memory and also seems to hope for a reconciliation of differences among the ethnicities and nationalities of different immigrants and even between Americans and the perpetrators of the attack.

Like "Alabanza," "Ghazal for Open Hands" is also a eulogy. This time Espada commemorates the Kashmiri poet Agha Shahid Ali, a former colleague at the University of Massachusetts and a friend, using the Arabic/Pushtu/Persian/Urdu form of the ghazal, a poem in couplets in which the first couplet has the same repeated refrain at the end of each line and the rest of the couplets contain the refrain only in the second line. The repeating refrain is "open hands," and it is this image that allows Espada, the mourning poet, to imaginatively place his own hands "into the [grave's] hole" and imaginatively touch those of his friend. But the repeated incantation of "open hands" is also the poet's way of underlining the hypocrisy of those Westerners who "listen to Islamic prayers at the cemetery as [they] pay for bombs" to rain down on those in Islamic countries who are more vulnerable, that is, who pray with open hands. The most vivid, successful, and horrific image in the poem is that of American bombs "tear[ing] away the fingers from [the]hungry open hands" of the victims of the bombs in Islamic countries.

In "Alabanza," Espada honors the overlooked victims of the 9/11 tragedy, and in "Ghazal for Open Hands," a poet who straddled the divide between America and the Muslim world. In "The Poet in the Box," Espada again focuses on those who are overlooked, in this case a prison inmate. He describes the ironic situation of Brandon, a poet and inmate at a juvenile detention center, who constantly attacks other inmates. As a result, Brandon is repeatedly placed in solitary confinement. Then the prison warden discovers that Brandon wants to be in solitary confinement so that he can write poetry in peace and privacy. From that point on, every time Brandon commits a violation, his prison sentence is extended, but he is not put into solitary. Espada extends compassion and sympathy to Brandon, who, unlike his more privileged fellow poets outside of prison confines, "dreams of punishment / stealing the keys from a sleepy jailer / to lock himself into the box" where he can slowly create poetry from "the bowl of his hands." In the ghazal for Agha Shahid Ali, the image of open hands underlined both solidarity among human beings and the vulnerability of those victimized by unjust warfare. In "The Poet in the Box," the inmate Brandon's hands, as he attempts to write poetry in solitary confinement, represent the inner spirit willing itself to create something out of nothing and forging its own inner freedom in the face of the world's hostility and indifference.

Lyn Di Iorio
Graduate Center of the City University of New York and City College of New York

PRIMARY WORKS

Rebellion is the Circle of a Lover's Hands, 1990; *City of Coughing and Dead Radiators*, 1993; *Imagine the Angels of Bread*, 1996; *A Mayan Astronomer in Hell's Kitchen*, 2000; *Alabanza: New and Selected Poems*, 2003; *The Republic of Poetry*, 2006; *The Trouble Ball*, 2011.

Jim's Blind Blues

in memoriam

    There are some things
    doctors can't fix,
    his brother said.
    Heroin and diabetes.

    Squatting naked on the mattress,   5
    he tells seeing-eye dog jokes
    through a smirk,
    face swollen and sleepy
    with the geography of attempted suicide,
    his laugh a jazzman's funeral,   10
    a sneering clarinet.

    Don't say anything,
    but his veins have collapsed
    so he shoots it
    in his neck,   15
    his brother said.

    The unclean needle
    bit sores into his marrow,
    pus where the skin split,
    and now he stinks   20
    like a dress rehearsal
    for the cemetery.

Going blind
by the window
in his brother's apartment,   25
he fumbles
through the medicine bottles
for the radio.

We're gonna drive
cross-country.   30
See this country.
Before his eyesight goes,
his brother said,
ex-convict brother,
hundred-dollar-a-week brother,   35
caretaker brother.

A junkie
is going to the place
where secrets
are auctioned into slavery   40
and shadows
sell the darkness to each other.

Here, adrift in the undertow of that darkness,
down in night's black whirlpool,
his brother   45
will not know
where to find him.

I am the heat that will flush your face,
I am the sweat of your skin,
I am the one you will pray for,   50
I am the kiss of the cross.

                                                                  1982

Latin Night at the Pawnshop

Chelsea, Massachusetts
Christmas, 1987

The apparition of a salsa band
gleaming in the Liberty Loan
pawnshop window:

Golden trumpet,
silver trombone,   5

congas, maracas, tambourine,
all with price tags dangling
like the city morgue ticket
on a dead man's toe.

1990

Inheritance of Waterfalls and Sharks

for my son Klemente

In 1898, with the infantry from Illinois,
the boy who would become the poet Sandburg
rowed his captain's Saint Bernard ashore
at Guánica, and watched as the captain
lobbed cubes of steak at the canine snout.   5
The troops speared mangos with bayonets
like many suns thudding with shredded yellow flesh
to earth. General Miles, who chained Geronimo
for the photograph in sepia of the last renegade,
promised Puerto Rico the *blessings of enlightened civilization*.   10
Private Sandburg marched, peeking at a book
nested in his palm for the words of Shakespeare.

Dazed in blue wool and sunstroke, they stumbled up the mountain
to Utuado, learned the war was over, and stumbled away.
Sandburg never met great-great-grand uncle Don Luis,   15
who wore a linen suit that would not wrinkle,
read with baritone clarity scenes from *Hamlet*
house to house for meals of rice and beans,
the Danish prince and his soliloquy—*ser o no ser*—
saluted by rum, the ghost of Hamlet's father wandering   20
through the ceremonial ballcourts of the Taíno.

In Caguas or Cayey Don Luis
was the reader at the cigar factory,
newspapers in the morning,
Cervantes or Marx in the afternoon,   25
rocking with the whirl of an unseen sword
when Quijote roared his challenge to giants,
weaving the tendrils of his beard when he spoke
of labor and capital, as the tabaqueros
rolled leaves of tobacco to smolder in distant mouths.   30

Maybe he was the man of the same name
who published a sonnet in the magazine of browning leaves
from the year of the Great War and the cigar strike.

He disappeared; there were rumors of Brazil,
inciting canecutters or marrying the patrón's daughter,   35
maybe both, but always the reader, whipping Quijote's sword overhead.

Another century, and still the warships scavenge
Puerto Rico's beaches with wet snouts. For practice,
Navy guns hail shells coated with uranium over Vieques
like a boy spinning his first curveball;   40
to the fisherman on the shore, the lung is a net
and the tumor is a creature with his own face, gasping.

This family has no will, no house, no farm, no island.
But today the great-great-great-grand nephew of Don Luis,
not yet ten, named for a jailed poet and fathered by another poet,   45
in a church of the Puritan colony called Massachusetts,
wobbles on a crate and grabs the podium
to read his poem about El Yunque waterfalls
and Achill basking sharks, and shouts:
I love this.   50

    2002

The Poet in the Box

for Brandon

We have a problem with Brandon,
the assistant warden said.
He's a poet.

At the juvenile detention center
demonic poetry fired Brandon's fist   5
into the forehead of another inmate.
Metaphor, that cackling spirit, drove him to flip
another boy's cafeteria tray onto the floor.
The staccato chorus rhyming in his head
told him to spit and curse   10
at enemies bigger by a hundred pounds.
The gnawing in his rib cage was a craving for discipline.
Repeatedly two guards shuffled him
to the cell called the box, solitary confinement,
masonry of silence fingered by hallucinating drifters,   15
rebels awaiting execution, monks in prayer.

Then we figured it out, the assistant warden said.
He started fights so we'd throw him
in solitary, where he could write.

The box: There poetry was a grasshopper in the bowl of his hands,   20
pencil chiseling letters across his notebook
like the script of a pharaoh's deeds on pyramid walls;
metaphor spilled from the light he trapped
in his eyelids, lamps of incandescent words;
rhyme harmonized through the voices   25
of great-grandmothers and sharecropper bluesmen
whenever sleep began to whistle in his breath.
So the cold was a blanket to him.

We fixed Brandon, the assistant warden said.
We stopped punishing him. He knows   30
that every violation means he stays here longer.

Tonight there are poets
who versify vacations in Tuscany,
the villa on a hill, the light of morning;
poets who stare at computer screens   35
and imagine cockroach powder
dissolved into the coffee
of the committee that said no to tenure;
poets who drain whiskey bottles
and urinate on the shoes of their disciples;   40
poets who cannot sleep as they contemplate
the extinction of iambic pentameter;
poets who watch the sky, waiting for a poem
to plunge in a white streak through blackness.

Brandon dreams of punishment,   45
stealing the keys from a sleepy jailer
to lock himself into the box, where he can hear
the scratching of his pencil
like fingernails on dungeon stone.

2002

Ghazal for Open Hands

in memory of Agha Shahid Ali
December 10, 2001
Northampton, Massachusetts

The imam stands above your grave to pray with open hands,
cupping your spirit like grain in the palms of these open hands.

Poet of Kashmir, the graveyard lathers my shoes with mud
as the imam calls to Islam's God and lifts his open hands.

Ghazal-maker, your pine box sinks into a cumulus of snow,   5
red earth thumping on the coffin, dropped from open hands.

There are some today who murmur of the cancer in your brain
but do not know the words for speaking to Allah with open hands.

We listen to Islamic prayers at the cemetery, as we pay for bombs
to blossom into graves in places where they pray with open hands.   10

Far from here, the bombs we bless are tumbling down in loaves
of steel to tear away the fingers from their hungry open hands.

Shahid, your grave multiplies wild as cancer cells across Afghani earth,
countless prayers reverberating in the well of the throat, in open hands.

I cannot scrape off the mud choking my shoes or blink away the vision   15
of reaching into the hole for you, my hands open to your open hands.

                                                                      2002

Alabanza: In Praise of Local 100

for the 43 members of Hotel Employees and Restaurant Employees
Local 100, working at the Windows on the World restaurant,
who lost their lives in the attack on the World Trade Center

Alabanza. Praise the cook with a shaven head
and a tattoo on his shoulder that said *Oye,*
a blue-eyed Puerto Rican with people from Fajardo,
the harbor of pirates centuries ago.
Praise the lighthouse in Fajardo, candle   5
glimmering white to worship the dark saint of the sea.
Alabanza. Praise the cook's yellow Pirates cap
worn in the name of Roberto Clemente, his plane
that flamed into the ocean loaded with cans for Nicaragua,
for all the mouths chewing the ash of earthquakes.   10
Alabanza. Praise the kitchen radio, dial clicked
even before the dial on the oven, so that music and Spanish
rose before bread. Praise the bread. *Alabanza.*

Praise Manhattan from a hundred and seven flights up,
like Atlantis glimpsed through the windows of an ancient aquarium.   15
Praise the great windows where immigrants from the kitchen
could squint and almost see their world, hear the chant of nations:
Ecuador, México, Republica Dominicana,
Haiti, Yemen, Ghana, Bangladesh.
Alabanza. Praise the kitchen in the morning,   20

where the gas burned blue on every stove
and exhaust fans fired their diminutive propellers,
hands cracked eggs with quick thumbs
or sliced open cartons to build an altar of cans.
Alabanza. Praise the busboy's music, the *chime-chime*   25
of his dishes and silverware in the tub.

Alabanza. Praise the dish-dog, the dishwasher
who worked that morning because another dishwasher
could not stop coughing, or because he needed overtime
to pile the sacks of rice and beans for a family   30
floating away on some Caribbean island plagued by frogs.
Alabanza. Praise the waitress who heard the radio in the kitchen
and sang to herself about a man gone. *Alabanza.*

After the thunder wilder than thunder,
after the shudder deep in the glass of the great windows,   35
after the radio stopped singing like a tree full of terrified frogs,
after night burst the dam of day and flooded the kitchen,
for a time the stoves glowed in darkness like the lighthouse in Fajardo,
like a cook's soul. Soul I say, even if the dead cannot tell us
about the bristles of God's beard because God has no face,   40
soul I say, to name the smoke-beings flung in constellations
across the night sky of this city and cities to come.
Alabanza I say, even if God has no face.

Alabanza. When the war began, from Manhattan and Kabul
two constellations of smoke rose and drifted to each other,   45
mingling in icy air, and one said with an Afghan tongue:
Teach me to dance. We have no music here.
And the other said with a Spanish tongue:
I will teach you. Music is all we have.

       2002

DEMETRIA MARTÍNEZ
B. 1960

Born in Albuquerque, New Mexico, Demetria Martínez has published three collections of poems, one novel, one book of personal essays, and a children's book.
After earning a B.A. from the Woodrow Wilson School of Public and International Affairs at Princeton University, she returned to New Mexico to work as a

journalist for the *National Catholic Reporter*. As the newspaper's religion reporter, Martínez covered the sanctuary movement, a faith-based movement that
offered aid and refuge to Guatemalan and Salvadoran immigrants fleeing
U.S.-backed wars. Martínez's closeness to the movement led to charges against
her, and in 1988 she was put on trial for conspiracy. Eventually acquitted, her
experiences became the basis for her 1994 novel *Mother Tongue*, the winner of
the Western States Book Award for fiction.

Martínez's work engages with U.S. literary, social, and political history, often from a distinctly Latina/o perspective. Much of her poetry in particular
engages with inequalities surrounding race, language, and citizenship while
referencing Christian symbolism and human rights, thus questioning both the
ethnic and moral foundation of the United States. Her poem "Wanted" (*Breathing between the Lines*, 1997) is a contemporary response to Allen Ginsberg's
1956 poem "America." In "Wanted," Martínez follows Ginsberg's apostrophe
but offers a distinctly Chicana perspective, declaring "America I'm not good
enough for you? / Better my Spanglish than your smooth talk America."

"Sonogram," also from *Breathing between the Lines*, is indicative of Martínez's attention to themes of working-class Latina/o life, women, and birth.
When the narrator writes to a "you" whose heart "pop[s] like corn" and is "not
free," the poem uses specific cultural references of corn and beans—foods central to Mexican and U.S. indigenous diets—to contrast the movement of life
with the repressive power exhibited by state forces and the ruling class. In
asserting that the subject of the poem is "loved" and "the world's," the narrator
also indicates his/her belief in a world in which individuals belong not to one
nation, but to all of humanity.

"The Devil's Workshop," from Martínez' 2002 collection of the same name,
is also written in second person but takes the form of a confessional poem in
which the narrator divulges his/her own thoughts and feelings. The poem
invokes a community of women in its reference to "our mothers and all / Their
mothers before them" and also contains a religious allusion to the proverb "Idle
hands are the devil's workshop." The devil of the poem is likened to the narrator's lover, suggesting the sexual and creative inspiration offered by both.

"Cold Snap in Tucson," also from *The Devil's Workshop*, is similarly addressed
to an unnamed "you," and the use of declarative sentences and enjambment echoes aspects of "The Devil's Workshop." The poem displays a lightness and humor
in its opening line that gives way to specifically Southwestern images ("red
chile") and Christian allusions ("a holy family," "manger on my rooftop") that
contribute to a narrative perspective that, as in "Sonogram," longs for a world
defined not by borders and citizenship, but love and humanity.

Martínez remains active as a poet, writer, journalist, and human rights activist. In 2010 she cofounded the Albuquerque chapter of Poets against the War.

Ariana Vigil
University of North Carolina at Chapel Hill

PRIMARY WORKS

Mother Tongue, 1994; *Breathing between the Lines*, 1997; *The Devil's Workshop*, 2002;
Confessions of a Berlitz Tape Chicana, 2005.

Wanted

after Allen Ginsberg, 1988

America our marriage is coming apart
I've done everything right got my degree
Now you tell me my English won't do
America I'm not good enough for you?
Better my Spanglish than your smooth talk America   5
No I won't sleep with you not now not ever
Ah come on America all I wanted was a little
   adobe house in Atrisco a porch swing
   two niños some democracy
Now I read in the Albuquerque Journal you left me   10
   for a younger woman
Bought drugs for guns   guns for drugs
Destroyed Managua in order to save it
Spied on communist Maryknoll nuns in Cleveland
America your face is on wanted posters in post offices   15
And I'm on sleeping pills again America
Last night I dreamed the Pentagon was a great
   Ouija board spelling out REPENT REPENT
In half sleep I reached for you love but got
   only a scent of amber waves of grain   20
I got up for a hit of caffeine the Book of Psalms
And whoosh I saw the promised land
You don't need citizenship papers there it's colored
   and smells of refried beans
Remember remember who you are America   25
Purple mountain majesty above fruited plains
   worked by mejicanos
America call off your dogs
America give me a green card though I don't qualify
America forgive me if I gag your memory   30
   at La Paloma bar on South Broadway
America I'm twenty-seven and tired thanks to you
And thanks to you I found God on a stoop on Arno Street
America you claim crime's fierce in this neighborhood
I tell you it's nothing next to your crimes   35
The wars we fund start at the package liquor store
and end twice a year at confession
America I don't want progress I want redemption
Cut the shit we could be lovers again don't hang up
America I'm your dark side embrace me and be saved   40
Pull yourself up by your bootstraps I know you can
America I'm not all bitter I'm a registered Republican

At parties when friends ask America who? I introduce
   you explain you've had a difficult upbringing
But I can't cover up for you America get that straight   45
Honey it's not too late it's not too late
America the ball's in your court now

1997

Sonogram

para Raquel Dolores

Little grasshopper
Heart popping like corn
Mexican jumping bean
Water drop sizzling on castiron of love and war
You immigrated from the cosmos   5
To this burning planet
Only to be detained by life
Your name written on greeting cards
And search warrants
Who's to say you will not grow up   10
Washing windshields, selling gum, eating fire
While a rich man's coffee cup lands on the table like a gavel?

Your birth will be one more cry severing the night

You are loved
You are the world's   15
You are not free

1997

The Devil's Workshop

They were right,
Our mothers and all
Their mothers before them.
Idleness is the devil's workshop.
Instead of writing a poem, I am thinking   5
About writing a poem: about you, of all people,
Who drove my pen like a tanker onto the rocks
Of the Galapagos, who ordered my pen
To lift off when I most needed
To circle the runway. Read my   10
Rap sheet. I could not write
A straight line the years we
Were lovers, the years the

Devil made his most
Acclaimed paintings   15
Out of my spilt ink.

1997

Cold Snap in Tucson

The temperature plummets to 80 degrees.
Polar winds pluck the city's sole gold
Leaf like a gray hair. You sniff sweaters
Stored in wicker, shop for winter
Squash, clean beans: abacus beads   5
That tracked the hours until October.
Now summer has laid down her arms,
Extended statehood to autumn,
Rejoined the family of seasons,
Each taking a turn at the wheel.   10
Road rage ceases. We place gloves
In our glove compartments, not guns;
Run yellows, not reds; hew
To the golden rule: give cuts
To the van bringing a holy family   15
From across the border. The driver
Is your neighbor. I am your neighbor.
Tonight you will see a glow-in-the-dark
Manger on my rooftop, my inn draped
With red chile lights. I will slip the key   20
To winter beneath a potted cactus,
Forget where it is. For weeks, months
The city will scour the sky for
A star, for a sign, for a convoy
Of clouds with its freight of snow.   25

1997

■   # T. C. BOYLE   ■

B. 1948

T. Coraghessan Boyle, now in his sixties, still resembles the rock star that he
once wanted to be. Having come of age in the raucous rock era of the 1970s,
Boyle's work frequently references rock culture and the sometimes hedonistic

behavior of its fans. Yet as he has matured, Boyle's work has increasingly turned to history and to the antagonistic relationship between humans and their natural environment. These subjects have always been present in his work, but he now addresses them with more seriousness and more urgency. A prolific and energetic fiction writer, Boyle is both literary adventurer and tireless craftsman, most comfortable when writing dark, often humorous tales of megalomaniacs and hypocritical ideologues.

Born and raised in Peekskill, New York, now a longtime resident of southern California, Boyle graduated from the State University of New York at Potsdam and earned his master's degree in creative writing from the celebrated M.F.A. program at the University of Iowa, where he also earned a Ph.D. in English, specializing in nineteenth-century British literature. The influence of Charles Dickens is evident in some of his novels, such as *The Road to Wellville*, an historical novel based on the life of the early-twentieth-century breakfast cereal magnate and abstinence-obsessed quack John Harvey Kellogg. His other historical novels have focused on other eccentric figures from American history such as Frank Lloyd Wright and Alfred Kinsey, the sexologist whose famous Kinsey Reports of the 1940s and 1950s provided new insights about American sexual behavior. Each of Boyle's novels takes on a new landscape and character, from the Scottish explorer of Africa Mungo Park in *Water Music* to a ghost-haunted family history in *World's End* to a hippie commune that moves from California to Alaska in *Drop City*. With more than a dozen novels and nearly as many short story collections to his credit since his first story collection in 1979, Boyle has covered much imaginative ground in his fiction, and he shows no signs of slowing down.

Despite his varying settings and his range of subjects, Boyle's fiction has a few consistent themes: the tension between self-indulgence and altruism; the tragic, fatal collision of individual lives; and the even more tragic destruction of our ecological world. As one of the most prominent practitioners of what might be called "neo-naturalism," Boyle creates human characters who behave according to natural principles, such as parasites who live off hardworking and upstanding hosts or predators whose instinctive desire is to dominate and destroy others. Ironically, environmental activists who are ostensibly acting to preserve the earth are sometimes capable of the most destruction, as in the novels *A Friend of the Earth* and *When the Killing's Done*. Rigid ideology and extreme zealotry are suspect character traits in Boyle's fiction, even if the cause is worthy. Ignorance is no better, though. Characters who are naïve or who willfully ignore social or natural realities are just as harmful as their knowledgeable counterparts. A bitter laughter permeates the air of many of Boyle's stories as foolish characters destroy themselves, others, or the earth. Yet there is also a tender concern for the fate of such a destructive species. In the following story, "Blinded by the Light," we see the ignorant denier of global climate change (Bob Fernando Castillo) square off against the scientific crusader (John Longworth). Their debate ultimately seems an exercise in futility; the damage to the earth has been done. Boyle asks not necessarily "What can we do about it?" but rather "Where will we go from here?"

D. Quentin Miller
Suffolk University

PRIMARY WORKS

Descent of Man, 1979; *Water Music*, 1982; *Budding Prospects*, 1984; *Greasy Lake and Other Stories*, 1985; *World's End*, 1987; *If the River Was Whiskey*, 1989; *East is East*, 1990; *The Road to Wellville*, 1993; *Without a Hero*, 1994; *The Tortilla Curtain*, 1995; *Riven Rock*, 1998; *A Friend of the Earth*, 2000; *After the Plague*, 2001; *Drop City*, 2003; *The Inner Circle*, 2004; *Tooth and Claw*, 2005; *Talk Talk*, 2006; *The Women*, 2009; *Wild Child and Other Stories*, 2010; *When the Killing's Done*, 2011.

Blinded by the Light

So the sky is falling. Or, to be more precise, the sky is emitting poisonous rays, rays that have sprinkled the stigmata of skin cancer across both of Manuel Banquedano's cheeks and the tip of his nose and sprouted the cataracts in Slobodan Abarca's rheumy old eyes. That is what the tireless Mr. John Longworth, of Long Beach, California, U.S.A., would have us believe. I have been to Long Beach, California, on two occasions, and I give no credence whatever to a man who would consciously assent to live in a place like that. He is, in fact, just what my neighbors say he is—an alarmist, like the chicken in the children's tale who thinks the sky is falling just because something hit him on the head. On *his* head. On his individual and prejudicial head. And so the barnyard goes into a panic—and to what end? Nothing. A big fat zero.

But let me tell you about him, about Mr. John Longworth, Ph.D., and how he came to us with his theories, and you can judge for yourself. First, though, introductions are in order. I am Bob Fernando Castillo and I own an *estancia* of 50,000 acres to the south of Punta Arenas, on which I graze some 9,000 sheep, for wool and mutton both. My father, God rest his soul, owned Estancia Castillo before me and his father before him, all the way back to the time Punta Arenas was a penal colony and then one of the great trading towns of the world—that is, until the Americans of the North broke through the Isthmus of Panama and the ships stopped rounding Cape Horn. In any case, that is a long and venerable ownership in anybody's book. I am fifty-three years old and in good health and vigor and I am married to the former Isabela Mackenzie, who has given me seven fine children, the eldest of whom, Bob Fernando Jr., is now twenty-two years old.

It was September last, when Don Pablo Antofagasta gave his annual three-day *fiesta primavera* to welcome in the spring, that Mr. John Longworth first appeared among us. We don't have much society out here, unless we take the long and killing drive into Punta Arenas, a city of 110,000 souls, and we look forward with keen anticipation to such entertainments—and not only the adults, but the children too. The landowners from several of the *estancias*, even the most far-flung, gather annually for Don Pablo's extravaganza and they bring their children and some of the house servants as well (and even, as in the case of Don Benedicto Braun, their dogs and horses). None of this presents a problem for Don Pablo, one of the wealthiest and most generous among us. As we say, the size of his purse is exceeded only by the size of his heart.

I arrived on the Thursday preceding the big weekend, flying over the *pampas* in the Piper Super Cub with my daughter, Paloma, to get a jump on the others and have a quiet night sitting by the fire with Don Pablo and his eighty-year-old Iberian *jerez*. Isabela, Bob Fernando Jr. and the rest of the family would be making the twelve-hour drive over washboard roads and tortured gullies the following morning, and frankly, my kidneys can no longer stand that sort of pounding. I still ride—horseback, that is—but I leave the Suburban and the Range Rover to Isabela and to Bob Fernando Jr. At any rate, the flight was a joy, soaring on the back of the implacable wind that rakes our country day and night, and I taxied right up to the big house on the airstrip Don Pablo scrupulously maintains.

Don Pablo emerged from the house to greet us even before the prop had stopped spinning, as eager for our company as we were for his. (Paloma has always been his favorite, and she's grown into a tall, straight-backed girl of eighteen with intelligent eyes and a mane of hair so thick and luxuriant it almost seems unnatural, and I don't mind saying how proud I am of her.) My old friend strode across the struggling lawn in boots and puttees and one of those plaid flannel shirts he mail-orders from Boston, Teresa and two of the children in tow. It took me half a moment to shut down the engine and stow away my aeronautical sunglasses for the return flight, and when I looked up again, a fourth figure had appeared at Don Pablo's side, matching him stride for stride.

"Cómo estás, mi amigo estimado?" Don Pablo cried, taking my hand and embracing me, and then he turned to Paloma to kiss her cheek and exclaim on her beauty and how she'd grown. Then it was my turn to embrace Teresa and the children and press some sweets into the little ones' hands. Finally, I looked up into an untethered North American face, red hair and a red mustache and six feet six inches of raw bone and sinew ending in a little bony afterthought of a head no bigger than a tropical coconut and weighted down by a nose to end all noses. This nose was an affliction and nothing less, a tool for probing and rooting, and I instinctively looked away from it as I took the man's knotty gangling hand in my own and heard Don Pablo pronounce, "Mr. John Longworth, a scientist from North America who has come to us to study our exemplary skies."

"Mucho gusto en conocerle," he said, and his Spanish was very good indeed, but for the North American twang and his maddening tendency to over-pronounce the consonants till you felt as if he were battering both sides of your head with a wet root. He was dressed in a fashion I can only call bizarre, all cultural differences aside, his hands gloved, his frame draped in an ankle-length London Fog trenchcoat and his disproportionately small head dwarfed by a pair of wraparound sunglasses and a deerstalker cap. His nose, cheeks and hard horny chin were nearly fluorescent with what I later learned was sunblock, applied in layers.

"A pleasure," I assured him, stretching the truth for the sake of politesse, after which he made his introductions to my daughter with a sort of slobbering formality, and we all went in to dinner.

* * *

There was, as I soon discovered, to be one topic of conversation and one topic only throughout the meal—indeed, throughout the entire three days of the *fiesta*, whenever and wherever Mr. John Longworth was able to insinuate himself, and he seemed to have an almost supernatural ability to appear everywhere at once, as ubiquitous as a cockroach. And what was this penetrating and all-devouring topic? The sky. Or rather the hole he perceived in the sky over Magallanes, Tierra del Fuego and the Antarctic, a hole that would admit all the poisons of the universe and ultimately lead to the destruction of man and nature. He talked of algae and krill, of acid rain and carbon dioxide and storms that would sweep the earth with a fury unknown since creation. I took him for an enthusiast at best, but deep down I wondered what asylum he'd escaped from and when they'd be coming to reclaim him.

He began over the soup course, addressing the table at large as if he were standing at a podium and interrupting Don Pablo and me in a reminiscence of a salmon-fishing excursion to the Penitente River undertaken in our youth. "None of you," he said, battering us with those consonants, "especially someone with such fair skin as Paloma here or Señora Antofagasta, should leave the house this time of year without the maximum of protection. We're talking ultraviolet-B, radiation that increases by as much as one thousand percent over Punta Arenas in the spring because of the hole in the ozone layer."

Paloma, a perspicacious girl educated by the nuns in Santiago and on her way to the university in the fall, gave him a deadpan look. "But, Mr. Longworth," she said, her voice as clear as a bell and without a trace of intimidation or awe, "if what you say is true, we'll have to give up our string bikinis."

I couldn't help myself—I laughed aloud and Don Pablo joined me. Tierra del Fuego is hardly the place for sunbathers—or bikinis either. But John Longworth didn't seem to appreciate my daughter's satiric intent, nor was he to be deterred. "If you were to go out there now, right outside this window, for one hour unprotected under the sun, that is, without clothing—or, er, in a bikini, I mean—I can guarantee you that your skin would blister and that those blisters could and would constitute the incipient stages of melanoma, not to mention the damage to your eyes and immune system."

"Such beautiful eyes," Don Pablo observed with his customary gallantry. "And is Paloma to incarcerate them behind dark glasses, and my wife too?"

"If you don't want to see them go blind," he retorted without pausing to draw breath.

The thought, as we say, brought my kettle to a boil: who was this insufferable person with his stabbing nose and deformed head to lecture us? And on what authority? "I'm sorry, señor," I said, "but I've heard some farfetched pronouncements of doom in my time, and this one takes the cake. Millenarian hysteria is what I say it is. Proof, sir. What proof do you offer?"

I realized immediately that I'd made a serious miscalculation. I could see it in the man's pale leaping eyes, in the way his brow contracted and that ponderous instrument of his nose began to sniff at the air as if he were a bloodhound off after a scent. For the next hour and a half, or until I retreated to my room, begging indigestion, I was carpet-bombed with statistics, chemical analyses, papers, studies, obscure terms and obscurer texts, until all I could think was that the end of the planet would be a relief if only because it would put an end to the incessant, nagging, pontificating, consonant-battering voice of the first-class bore across the table from me.

At the time, I couldn't foresee what was coming, though if I'd had my wits about me it would have been a different story. Then I could have made plans, could have arranged to be in Paris, Rio or Long Beach, could have been in the hospital, for that matter, having my trick knee repaired after all these years. Anything, even dental work, would have been preferable to what fell out. But before I go any further I should tell you that there are no hotels in the Magallanes region, once you leave the city, and that we have consequently developed among us a strong and enduring tradition of hospitality—no stranger, no matter how personally obnoxious or undeserving, is turned away from the door. This is open range, overflown by caracara and condor and haunted by *ñandú*, guanaco and puma, a waste of dwarf trees and merciless winds where the unfamiliar and the unfortunate collide in the face of the wanderer. This is to say that three weeks to the day from the conclusion of Don Pablo's *fiesta*, Mr. John Longworth arrived at the Estancia Castillo in all his long-nosed splendor, and he arrived to stay.

We were all just sitting down to a supper of mutton chops and new potatoes with a relish of chiles and onions in a white sauce I myself had instructed the cook to prepare, when Slobodan Abarca, my foreman and one of the most respected *huasos* in the province, came to the door with the news that he'd heard a plane approaching from the east and that it sounded like Don Pablo's Cessna. We hurried outside, all of us, even the servants, and scanned the iron slab of the sky. Don Pablo's plane appeared as a speck on the horizon, and I was astonished at the acuity of Slobodan Abarca's hearing, a sense he's developed since his eyes began to go bad on him, and before we knew it the plane was passing over the house and banking for the runway. We watched the little craft fight the winds that threatened to flip it over on its back at every maneuver, and suddenly it was on the ground, leaping and ratcheting over the greening turf. Don Pablo emerged from the cockpit, the lank raw form of John Longworth uncoiling itself behind him.

I was stunned. So stunned I was barely able to croak out a greeting as the wind beat the hair about my ears and the food went cold on the table, but Bob Fernando Jr., who'd apparently struck up a friendship with the North American during the *fiesta*, rushed to welcome him. I embraced Don Pablo and numbly took John Longworth's hand in my own as Isabela looked on with a serene smile and Paloma gave our guest a look that would have frozen my blood had I only suspected its meaning. "Welcome," I said, the words rattling in my throat.

Don Pablo, my old friend, wasn't himself, I could see that at a glance. He had the shamed and defeated look of Señora Whiskers, our black

Labrador, when she does her business in the corner behind the stove instead of outside in the infinite grass. I asked him what was wrong, but he didn't answer—or perhaps he didn't hear, what with the wind. A few of the men helped unload Mr. John Longworth's baggage, which was wound so tightly inside the aircraft I was amazed it had been able to get off the ground, and I took Don Pablo by the arm to escort him into the house, but he shook me off. "I can't stay," he said, staring at his shoes.

"Can't stay?"

"Don Bob," he said, and still he wouldn't look me in the eye, "I hate to do this to you, but Teresa's expecting me and I can't—" He glanced up then at John Longworth, towering and skeletal in his huge flapping trenchcoat, and he repeated "I can't" once more, and turned his back on me.

Half an hour later I sat glumly at the head of the table, the departing whine of Don Pablo's engine humming in my ears, the desiccated remains of my reheated chops and reconstituted white sauce laid out like burnt offerings on my plate, while John Longworth addressed himself to the meal before him as if he'd spent the past three weeks lashed to a pole on the *pampas*. He had, I noticed, the rare ability to eat and talk at the same time, as if he were a ventriloquist, and with every bite of lamb and potatoes he tied off the strings of one breathless sentence and unleashed the next. The children were all ears as he and Bob Fernando Jr. spoke mysteriously of the sport of basketball, which my son had come to appreciate during his junior year abroad at the University of Akron, in Ohio, and even Isabela and Paloma leaned imperceptibly toward him as if to catch every precious twist and turn of his speech. This depressed me, not that I felt left out or that I wasn't pleased on their account to have the rare guest among us as a sort of linguistic treat, but I knew that it was only a matter of time before he switched from the esoterica of an obscure and I'm sure tedious game to his one and true subject—after all, what sense was there in discussing a mere sport when the sky itself was corrupted?

I didn't have long to wait. There was a pause just after my son had expressed his exact agreement with something John Longworth had said regarding the "three-point shot," whatever that might be, and John Longworth took advantage of the caesura to abruptly change the subject. "I found an entire population of blind rabbits on Don Pablo's ranch," he said, apropos of nothing and without visibly pausing to chew or swallow.

I shifted uneasily in my chair. Serafina crept noiselessly into the room to clear away the plates and serve dessert, port wine and brandy. I could hear the wind at the panes. Paloma was the first to respond, and at the time I thought she was goading him on, but as I was to discover it was another thing altogether. "Inheritance?" she asked. "Or mutation?"

That was all the encouragement he needed, this windbag, this doomsayer, this howling bore with the pointed nose and coconut head, and the lecture it precipitated was to last through dessert, cocoa and *maté* in front of the fire and the first, second and third strokes of the *niñitos'* bedtime.

"Neither," he said, "though if they were to survive blind through countless generations—not very likely, I'm afraid—they might well develop a genetic protection of some sort, just as the sub-Saharan Africans developed an increase of melanin in their skin to combat the sun. But, of course, we've so radically altered these creatures' environment that it's too late for that." He paused over an enormous forkful of cheesecake. "Don Bob," he said, looking me squarely in the eye over the clutter of the table and the dimpled faces of my little ones, "those rabbits were blinded by the sun's radiation, though you refuse to see it, and I could just stroll up to them and pluck them up by the ears, as many as you could count in a day, and they had no more defense than a stone."

The challenge was mine to accept, and though I'd heard rumors of blind salmon in the upper reaches of the rivers and birds blinded and game too, I wasn't about to let him have his way at my own table in my own house. "Yes," I observed drily, "and I suppose you'll be prescribing smoked lenses for all the creatures of the *pampas* now, am I right?"

He made no answer, which surprised me. Had he finally been stumped, bested, caught in his web of intrigue and hyperbole? But no: I'd been too sanguine. Calamities never end—they just go on spinning out disaster from their own imperturbable centers. "Maybe not for the rabbits," he said finally, "but certainly this creature here could do with a pair . . ."

I leaned out from my chair and looked down the length of the table to where Señora Whiskers, that apostate, sat with her head in the madman's lap. "What do you mean?" I demanded.

Paloma was watching, Isabela too; Bob Fernando Jr. and the little ones sat rigid in their chairs. "Call her to you," he said.

I called. And the dog, reluctant at first, came down the length of the table to her master. "Yes?" I said.

"Do you see the way she walks, head down, sniffing her way? Haven't you noticed her butting into the furniture, scraping the doorframes? Look into her eyes, Don Bob: she's going blind."

The next morning I awoke to a sound I'd never before heard, a ceaseless rapid thumping, as of a huge penitential heart caught up in the rhythm of its sorrows. Isabela awoke beside me and I peered through the blinds into the courtyard that was still heavy with shadow under a rare crystalline sky. Figures moved there in the courtyard as if in a dream—my children, all of them, even Paloma—and they fought over the swollen globe of a thumping orange ball and flung it high against an orange hoop shrouded in mesh. They were shouting, crying out in a kind of naked joy that approached the ecstatic, and the trenchcoat and the nose and the shrunken bulb of the bobbing head presided over all: *basketball*.

Was I disturbed? Yes. Happy for them, happy for their fluid grace and their joy, but struck deep in my bowels with the insidiousness of it: first basketball and then the scripture of doom. Indeed, they were already dressed like the man's disciples, in hats with earmuffs and the swirling greatcoats we'd long since put away for winter, and the exposed flesh of their hands and faces glistened with his sunblock. Worse: their eyes were visored behind pairs of identical black sunglasses, Mr. John Longworth's gift to them, along with the gift of hopelessness and terror. The sky was falling, and now they knew it too.

I stood there dumbfounded at the window. I didn't have the heart to break up their game or to forbid the practice of it—that would. have played into his hands, that would have made me the voice of sanity and restraint (and clearly, with this basketball, sanity and restraint were about as welcome as an explosion at *siesta* time). Nor could I, as *dueño* of one of the most venerable *estancias* in the country, attempt to inter- dict my guest from speaking of certain worrisome and fantastical sub- jects, no matter how distasteful I found them personally. But what could I do? He was clearly deluded, if not downright dangerous, but he had the ready weight of his texts and studies to counterbalance any argu- ments I might make.

The dog wasn't blind, any fool could see that. Perhaps her eyes were a bit cloudy, but that was to be expected in a dog of her age, and what if she was losing her sight, what did that prove? I'd had any number of dogs go blind, deaf, lame and senile over the years. That was the way of dogs, and of men too. It was sad, it was regrettable, but it was part of the grand design and there was no sense in running round the barnyard crowing your head off about it. I decided in that moment to go away for a few days, to let the basketball and the novelty of Mr. John Longworth dissipate like the atmos- pheric gases of which he spoke so endlessly.

"Isabela," I said, still standing at the window, still recoiling from that subversive thump, thump, thump, "I'm thinking of going out to the upper range for a few days to look into the health of Manuel Banquedano's flock—pack up my things for me, will you?"

This was lambing season, and most of the *huasos* were in the fields with the flocks to discourage eagle and puma alike. It is a time that never fails to move me, to strengthen my ties to the earth and its rejuvenant cycles, as it must have strengthened those ties for my father and his father before him. There were the lambs, appeared from nowhere on tottering legs, suckling and frolicking in the waste, and they were money in my pocket and the pockets of my children, they were provender and clothing, riches on the hoof. I camped with the men, roasted a haunch of lamb over the open fire, passed a bottle of *aguardiente*. But this time was different, this time I found myself studying the pattern of moles, pimples, warts and freckles spread across Manuel Banquedano's face and thinking the worst, this time I gazed out over the craggy *cerros* and open plains and saw the gaunt flapping figure of Mr. John Longworth like some apparition out of Apocalypse. I lasted four days only, and then, like Christ trudging up the hill to the place of skulls, I came back home to my fate.

Our guest had been busy in my absence. I'd asked Slobodan Abarca to keep an eye on him, and the first thing I did after greeting Isabela and the children was to amble out to the bunkhouse and have a private conference with the old *huaso*. The day was gloomy and cold, the wind in an uproar over something. I stepped in the door of the long low-frame building, the very floorboards of which gave off a complicated essence of tobacco, sweat and boot leather, and found it deserted but for the figure of Slobodan Abarca, bent over a chessboard by the window in the rear. I recognized the familiar sun-bleached *poncho* and *manta*, the spade-like wedge of the back of his head with its patches of parti-colored hair and oversized ears, and then he turned to me and I saw with a shock that he was wearing dark glasses. Inside. Over a chessboard. I was speechless.

"Don Bob," Slobodan Abarca said then in his creaking, unoiled tones, "I want to go back out on the range with the others and I don't care how old and feeble you think I am, anything is better than this. One more day with that devil from hell and I swear I slit my throat."

It seemed that when John Longworth wasn't out "taking measurements" or inspecting the teeth, eyes, pelt and tongue of every creature he could trap, coerce or pin down, he was lecturing the ranch hands, the smith and the household help on the grisly fate that awaited them. They were doomed, he told them—all of mankind was doomed and the drop of that doom was imminent—and if they valued the little time left to them they would pack up and move north, north to Puerto Montt or Concepción, anywhere away from the poisonous hole in the sky. And those spots on their hands, their throats, between their shoulderblades and caught fast in the cleavage of their breasts, those spots were cancerous or at the very least pre-cancerous. They needed a doctor, a dermatologist, an oncologist. They needed to stay out of the sun. They needed laser surgery. Sunblock. Dark glasses. (The latter he provided, out of a seemingly endless supply, and the credulous fools, believers in the voodoo of science, dutifully clamped them to their faces.) The kitchen staff was threatening a strike and Crispín Mansilla, who looks after the automobiles, had been so terrified of an open sore on his nose that he'd taken his bicycle and set out on the road for Punta Arenas two days previous and no one had heard from him since.

But worse, far worse. Slobodan Abarca confided something to me that made the blood boil in my veins, made me think of the braided bullhide whip hanging over the fireplace and the pearl-handled dueling pistols my grandfather had once used to settle a dispute over waterfowl rights on the south shore of Lake Castillo: Mr. John Longworth had been paying his special attentions to my daughter. Whisperings were overheard, tête-à-têtes observed, banter and tomfoolery taken note of. They were discovered walking along the lakeshore with their shoulders touching and perhaps even their hands intertwined (Slobodan Abarca couldn't be sure, what with his failing eyes), they sought each other out at meals, solemnly bounced the basketball in the courtyard and then passed it between them as if it were some rare prize. He was thirty if he was a day, this usurper, this snout, this Mr. John Longworth, and my Paloma was just out of the care of the nuns, an infant still and with her whole life ahead of her. I was incensed. Killing off the natural world was one thing, terrifying honest people, gibbering like a lunatic day and night till the whole *estancia* was in revolt, but insinuating himself in my daughter's affections—well, this was, quite simply, the end.

I stalked up the hill and across the yard, blind to everything, such a storm raging inside me I thought I would explode. The wind howled. It shrieked blood and vengeance and flung black grains of dirt in my face, grains of the unforgiving *pampas* on which I was nurtured and hardened, and I ground them between my teeth. I raged through the house and the servants quailed and the children cried, but Mr. John Longworth was nowhere to be found. Pausing only to snatch up one of my grandfather's pistols from its velvet cradle in the great hall, I flung myself out the back door and searched the stables, the smokehouse, the generator room. And then, rounding the corner by the hogpen, I detected a movement out of the corner of my eye, and there he was.

Ungainly as a carrion bird, the coat ends tenting round him in the wind, he was bent over one of the hogs, peering into the cramped universe of its malicious little eyes as if he could see all the evil of the world at work there. I confronted him with a shout and he looked up from beneath the brim of his hat and the fastness of his wraparound glasses, but he didn't flinch, even as I closed the ground between us with the pistol held out before me like a homing device. "I hate to be the bringer of bad news all the time," he called out, already lecturing as I approached, "but this pig is in need of veterinary care. It's not just the eyes, I'm afraid, but the skin too—you see here?"

I'd stopped ten paces from him, the pistol trained on the nugget of his head. The pig looked up at me hopefully. Its companions grunted, rolled in the dust, united their backsides against the wind.

"Melanoma," he said sadly, shaking his visored head. "Most of the others have got it too."

"We're going for a ride," I said.

His jaw dropped beneath the screen of the glasses and I could see the intricate work of his front teeth. He tried for a smile. "A ride?"

"Your time is up here, *señor*," I said, and the wind peeled back the sleeve of my jacket against the naked thrust of the gun. "I'm delivering you to Estancia Braun. Now. Without your things, without even so much as a bag, and without any goodbyes either. You'll have to live without your basketball hoop and sunblock for a few days, I'm afraid—at least until I have your baggage delivered. Now get to your feet—the plane is fueled and ready."

He gathered himself up then and rose from the ground, the wind beating at his garments and lifting the hair round his glistening ears. "It'll do no good to deny it, Don Bob," he said, talking over his shoulder as he moved off toward the shed where the Super Cub stood out of the wind. "It's criminal to keep animals out in the open in conditions like these, it's irresponsible, mad—think of your children, your wife. The land is no good anymore—it's dead, or it will be. And it's we who've killed it, the so-called civilized nations, with our air conditioners and underarm deodorant. It'll be decades before the CFCs are eliminated from the atmosphere, if ever, and by then there will be nothing left here but blind rabbits and birds that fly into the sides of rotting buildings. It's over, Don Bob—your life here is finished."

I didn't believe a word of it—naysaying and bitterness, that's all it was. I wanted to shoot him right then and there, on the spot, and have done with it—how could I in good conscience deliver him to Don Benedicto Braun, or to anyone, for that matter? He was the poison, he was the plague, he was the ecological disaster. We walked grimly into the wind and he never stopped talking. Snatches of the litany came back to me—ultraviolet, ozone, a hole in the sky bigger than the United States—but I only snarled out directions in reply: "To the left, over there, take hold of the doors and push them inward."

In the end, he didn't fight me. He folded up his limbs and squeezed into the passenger seat and I set aside the pistol and started up the engine. The familiar throb and roar calmed me somewhat, and it had the added virtue of rendering Mr. John Longworth's jeremiad inaudible. The wind assailed us as we taxied out to the grassy runway—I shouldn't have been flying that afternoon at all, but as you can no doubt appreciate, I was a desperate man. After a rocky takeoff we climbed into a sky that opened above us in all its infinite glory but which must have seemed woefully sad and depleted to my passenger's degraded eyes. We coasted high over the wind-whipped trees, the naked rock, the flocks whitening the pastures like distant snow, and he never shut up, not for a second. I tuned him out, let my mind go blank, and watched the horizon for the first weathered outbuildings of Estancia Braun.

They say that courtesy is merely the veneer of civilization, the first thing sacrificed in a crisis, and I don't doubt the truth of it. I wonder what became of my manners on that punishing wind-torn afternoon—you would have thought I'd been raised among the Indians, so eager was I to dump my unholy cargo and flee. Like Don Pablo, I didn't linger, and I could read the surprise and disappointment and perhaps even hurt in Don Benedicto's face when I pressed his hand and climbed back into the plane. "Weather!" I shouted, and pointed to the sky, where a wall of cloud was already sealing us in. I looked back as he receded on the ground beneath me, the inhuman form of Mr. John Longworth at his side, long arms gesticulating, the lecture already begun. It wasn't until I reached the verges of my own property, Estancia Castillo stretched out beneath me like a worn carpet and the dead black clouds moving in to strangle the sky, that I had my moment of doubt. What if he was right? I thought. What if Manuel Banquedano truly was riddled with cancer, what if the dog had been blinded by the light, what if my children were at risk? What then?

The limitless turf unraveled beneath me and I reached up a hand to rub at my eyes, weary suddenly, a man wearing the crown of defeat. A hellish vision came to me then, a vision of 9,000 sheep bleating on the range, their fleece stained and blackened, and every one of them, every one of those inestimable and beloved animals, my inheritance, my life, imprisoned behind a glistening new pair of wraparound sunglasses. So powerful was the vision I could almost hear them baa-ing out their distress. My heart seized. Tears started up in my eyes. Why go on? I was thinking. What hope is there?

But then the sun broke through the gloom in two pillars of fire, the visible world come to life with a suddenness that took away my breath, color bursting out everywhere, the range green all the way to the horizon, trees nodding in the wind, the very rock faces of the *cerros* set aflame, and the vision was gone. I listened to the drone of the engine, tipped the wings toward home, and never gave it another thought.

2003

ALISON BECHDEL
B. 1960

Alison Bechdel's comic strip, *Dykes to Watch Out For*, chronicles the contemporary lives and loves of various characters—mostly, although not entirely, lesbian ones. It first appeared in 1983 and continues to be read widely in national newspaper syndication and on the Internet (at www.dykestowatchoutfor.com).

Bechdel, who was born and raised in rural Pennsylvania, describes her formative influences as "Chas. Addams, *Mad Magazine*, Norman Rockwell, and Edward Gorey." Shortly after she graduated from Oberlin College, she became aware of the magazine *Gay Comix*. As she explains in an interview in *Modern Fiction Studies*, seeing this title—which was part of the comix scene of independently published, often radical and experimental, work—she felt, "'Oh, man! You can do cartoons about your own real life as a gay person.'" Bechdel explains, "And that was quite momentous for me.... It was right around then that I started doing my own comics."

Although Bechdel's experiences as a gay woman have informed *DTWOF*, she did not delve into her own life as a subject until she started work on *Fun Home: A Family Tragicomic* in 2000. *Fun Home* explores Bechdel's relationship with her father—an English teacher, part-time undertaker, obsessive restorer of the family's Victorian gothic house, and closeted gay man.

It is a breakthrough book in several different ways. First, it catapulted Bechdel, who lives in Vermont, from a popular alternative cartoonist to a mainstream literary figure. Widely acclaimed for its intricacy, density, and intelligence, *Fun Home* made *The New York Times* best-seller list, a rarity for literary graphic narratives since *Maus*. *Fun Home* was also nominated for a 2006 National Book Critics Circle Award in memoir/autobiography. Second, *Fun Home* became a crossover hit as a book about gayness and as a book in the form of comics. In 2006, *Fun Home* made *People* magazine's list of the top ten books of the year, was named *Entertainment Weekly*'s best nonfiction book of the year, and was named *Time* magazine's all-around number one book of the year in any category.

Fun Home's success is an indicator of the acceptance that serious work in the form of comics is finally gaining in the United States and is also a testament to Bechdel's skill as a researcher and archivist of her own life and as an author who can create complex and moving narratives out of life experience. The book is thick with archival materials (including maps, arrest records, letters, diaries, sketchbooks, and photographs) that Bechdel meticulously reproduces as she weaves past and present events and ruminations together.

A highly crafted work, *Fun Home* is engaged with modernist fiction as a kind of lens through which it unfurls its story. In a related way—through references to Joyce's *Ulysses*—it also draws on Greek mythology to figure the relationship between Bruce Bechdel, a petty tyrant who often treated his children coldly and eventually committed suicide, and Alison, whose exploration of her father's early death is driven by both intense identification and disidentification. *Fun Home*, like the best works of literature, suggests that there are no easy answers. As Bechdel puts it in "In the Shadow of Young Girls in Flower," a chapter whose title is taken from Proust, "Perhaps this undifferentiation, this nonduality, is the point." *Fun Home* explores the knotty filial connection brilliantly, its words and images dependent on each other for meaning.

Hillary Chute
Harvard University

PRIMARY WORKS

The Essential Dykes to Watch Out For (a compendium of many previously published books), 2005; *Fun Home: A Family Tragicomic*, 2006; *Are You My Mother? A Comic Drama*, 2012.

from **Fun Home: A Family Tragicomic**

I WAS SPARTAN TO MY FATHER'S ATHENIAN. MODERN TO HIS VICTORIAN.

BUTCH TO HIS NELLY.

UTILITARIAN TO HIS AESTHETE.

HE APPEARED TO BE AN IDEAL HUSBAND AND FATHER, FOR EXAMPLE.

BUT WOULD AN IDEAL HUSBAND AND FATHER HAVE SEX WITH TEENAGE BOYS?

IT'S TEMPTING TO SUGGEST, IN RETRO- SPECT, THAT OUR FAMILY WAS A SHAM.

THAT OUR HOUSE WAS NOT A REAL HOME AT ALL BUT THE SIMULACRUM OF ONE, A MUSEUM.

YET WE REALLY WERE A FAMILY, AND WE REALLY DID LIVE IN THOSE PERIOD ROOMS.

I CAN'T FIND THE SCISSORS!

LOOK IN THE CHIPPEN- DALE.

STILL, SOMETHING VITAL WAS MISSING.

AN ELASTICITY, A MARGIN FOR ERROR.

MOST PEOPLE, I IMAGINE, LEARN TO ACCEPT THAT THEY'RE NOT PERFECT.

BUT AN IDLE REMARK ABOUT MY FATHER'S TIE OVER BREAKFAST COULD SEND HIM INTO A TAILSPIN.

MY MOTHER ESTABLISHED A RULE.

DON'T CHANGE IT! WE'RE LATE!

ALSO AN ENGLISH TEACHER

NO COMMENTS ON HIS APPEARANCE. IS THAT UNDERSTOOD?

WHAT IF IT'S SOMETHING GOOD?

GOOD, BAD, IT DOESN'T MATTER.

IF WE COULDN'T CRITICIZE MY FATHER, SHOWING AFFECTION FOR HIM WAS AN EVEN DICIER VENTURE.

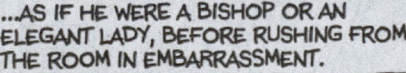

WE WERE NOT A PHYSICALLY EXPRESSIVE FAMILY, TO SAY THE LEAST. BUT ONCE I WAS UNACCOUNTABLY MOVED TO KISS MY FATHER GOOD NIGHT.

HAVING LITTLE PRACTICE WITH THE GESTURE, ALL I MANAGED WAS TO GRAB HIS HAND AND BUSS THE KNUCKLES LIGHTLY...

...AS IF HE WERE A BISHOP OR AN ELEGANT LADY, BEFORE RUSHING FROM THE ROOM IN EMBARRASSMENT.

THIS EMBARRASSMENT ON MY PART WAS A TINY SCALE MODEL OF MY FATHER'S MORE FULLY DEVELOPED SELF-LOATHING.

HIS SHAME INHABITED OUR HOUSE AS PERVASIVELY AND INVISIBLY AS THE AROMATIC MUSK OF AGING MAHOGANY.

IN FACT, THE METICULOUS, PERIOD INTERIORS WERE EXPRESSLY DESIGNED TO CONCEAL IT.

MIRRORS, DISTRACTING BRONZES, MULTIPLE DOORWAYS. VISITORS OFTEN GOT LOST UPSTAIRS.

MY MOTHER, MY BROTHERS, AND I KNEW OUR WAY AROUND WELL ENOUGH, BUT IT WAS IMPOSSIBLE TO TELL IF THE MINOTAUR LAY BEYOND THE NEXT CORNER.

AND THE CONSTANT TENSION WAS HEIGHTENED BY THE FACT THAT SOME ENCOUNTERS COULD BE QUITE PLEASANT.

HIS BURSTS OF KINDNESS WERE AS INCANDESCENT AS HIS TANTRUMS WERE DARK.

ALTHOUGH I'M GOOD AT ENUMERATING MY FATHER'S FLAWS, IT'S HARD FOR ME TO SUSTAIN MUCH ANGER AT HIM.

I EXPECT THIS IS PARTLY BECAUSE HE'S DEAD, AND PARTLY BECAUSE THE BAR IS LOWER FOR FATHERS THAN FOR MOTHERS.

MY MOTHER MUST HAVE BATHED ME HUNDREDS OF TIMES. BUT IT'S MY FATHER RINSING ME OFF WITH THE PURPLE METAL CUP THAT I REMEMBER MOST CLEARLY.

...THE SUDDEN, UNBEARABLE COLD OF ITS ABSENCE.

WAS HE A GOOD FATHER? I WANT TO SAY, "AT LEAST HE STUCK AROUND." BUT OF COURSE, HE DIDN'T.

IT'S TRUE THAT HE DIDN'T KILL HIMSELF UNTIL I WAS NEARLY TWENTY.

BUT HIS ABSENCE RESONATED RETRO-ACTIVELY, ECHOING BACK THROUGH ALL THE TIME I KNEW HIM.

MAYBE IT WAS THE CONVERSE OF THE WAY AMPUTEES FEEL PAIN IN A MISSING LIMB.

HE REALLY WAS THERE ALL THOSE YEARS, A FLESH-AND-BLOOD PRESENCE STEAMING OFF THE WALLPAPER, DIGGING UP THE DOGWOODS, POLISHING THE FINIALS...

...SMELLING OF SAWDUST AND SWEAT AND DESIGNER COLOGNE.

BUT I ACHED AS IF HE WERE ALREADY GONE.

The 9/11 Terror Attacks

WHEN ASKED WHAT HAS DEFINED AMERICAN CULTURE IN THE EARLY TWENTY-FIRST century, many might point to the destruction of New York's World Trade Center towers, the U.S.-led war in Iraq, and Hurricane Katrina in the Gulf Coast states. As the authors in this cluster of readings make clear, such events reveal a painful paradox. As U.S. economic and cultural domination has increased, the country has become a focus for the frustrations of violent religious zealots. And their attacks—both physical and ideological—have challenged U.S. domination itself.

As the readings in this cluster progress from the general to the local, from readings of culture to readings of literature, they wrestle with this and related paradoxes. Literary scholar Wai Chee Dimock asks whether American literature is autonomous or "dependent," and her answer begins with a discussion not of novels or poems but of what she calls the failed model of the nation-state. Dimock's observation that post-Katrina New Orleans resembled an underdeveloped country reflects a fundamental shift from a notion of the United States as a distinct and clearly defined "container" to one that emphasizes its porousness and instability.

A similar split between boundary and dispersal is central to the French philosopher and social theorist Jean Baudrillard's influential discussion of the 9/11 attacks. But while Dimock sees the unmaking of national boundaries as an effect of globalization, Baudrillard emphasizes the failure of globalization. For Baudrillard, the end of the cold war permitted U.S. power and influence to expand without hindrance. The terrorist rhetoric of self-sacrifice disrupts this power and with it the postnational ideal of a unified or boundary-less world. Baudrillard distinguishes the methods and ideology of the terrorist attackers from those of industrialized powers, but he also undermines this us-versus-them rhetoric by claiming that Americans imagined and—more controversially— wanted the attacks. Baudrillard also argues that the attacks were from the outset inseparable from the symbolic ways that they were represented. Their reality was "everywhere infiltrated by images, virtuality and fiction" in ways that challenged the notion of reality itself.

Baudrillard's claim about the centrality of images and symbols in the attacks helps explain recent U.S. writers' preoccupation with describing these attacks, and the cluster's final three readings offer quite different responses. The celebrated American novelist Don DeLillo's 2001 essay, published at nearly the same time as Baudrillard's, also challenges the objective reality of the attacks. DeLillo, though, focuses on the ways in which the attacks undermined our notion of and faith in the future and on the function of narrative itself. In response to the destructive plot perpetuated by attackers, DeLillo explores counternarratives, many of which complicate the notion of truth. DeLillo's essay "In the Ruins of the Future" is a case in point: he gives us no way to determine whether the account of Karen and Marc is true or fictional.

DeLillo's essay implies that the artificiality and uncertainty of narrative offer an alternative to the reductiveness and, by implication, the destructiveness of the attacks. His own fiction, from his novel *Falling Man*, and John Updike's story "Varieties of Religious Experience," one of the first published works of fiction following the attacks, demonstrate the principle that in order to get a complete or even somewhat complete story about what happened that day, we must consider multiple perspectives.

As the differences among these excerpts suggest, stories—including the stories of globalization and 9/11—are seldom consistent. In this way, the discrepancies between these accounts point to the importance of storytelling itself and thus to literature. These essays, stories, and the final poem do not resolve the recurrent questions they raise about truth, symbol, narrative, and the relation of the private to the public, but they create a space for literature, which, as several of them imply, is well suited to considering these questions.

Ann Keniston
University of Nevada, Reno

JEAN BAUDRILLARD
1929–2007

from **The Spirit of Terrorism**

When it comes to world events, we had seen quite a few. From the death of Diana to the World Cup. And violent, real events, from wars right through to genocides. Yet, when it comes to symbolic events on a world scale—that is to say not just events that gain worldwide coverage, but events that represent a setback for globalization itself—we had had none. Throughout the stagnation of the 1990s, events were "on strike" (as the Argentinian writer Macedonio Fernandez put it). Well, the strike is over now. Events are not on strike any more. With the attacks on the World Trade Center in New York, we might even be said to have before us the absolute event, the "mother" of all events, the pure event uniting within itself all the events that have never taken place.

The whole play of history and power is disrupted by this event, but so, too, are the conditions of analysis. You have to take your time. While events were stagnating, you had to anticipate and move more quickly than they did. But when they speed up this much, you have to move more slowly—though without allowing yourself to be buried beneath a welter of words, or the gathering clouds of war, and preserving intact the unforgettable incandescence of the images.

All that has been said and written is evidence of a gigantic abreaction to the event itself, and the fascination it exerts. The moral condemnation and the holy alliance against terrorism are on the same scale as the prodigious jubilation at seeing this global superpower destroyed—better, at seeing it, in a sense, destroying itself, committing suicide in a blaze of glory. For it is that superpower which, by its unbearable power, has fomented all this violence which is endemic throughout the world, and hence that (unwittingly) terroristic imagination which dwells in all of us.

The fact that we have dreamt of this event, that everyone without exception has dreamt of it—because no one can avoid dreaming of the destruction of any power that has become hegemonic to this degree—is unacceptable to the Western moral conscience. Yet it is a fact, and one which can indeed be measured by the emotive violence of all that has been said and written in the effort to dispel it.

At a pinch, we can say that they *did it*, but we *wished for* it. If this is not taken into account, the event loses any symbolic dimension. It becomes a pure accident, a purely arbitrary act, the murderous phantasmagoria of a few fanatics, and all that would then remain would be to eliminate them. Now, we know very well that this is not how it is. Which explains all the counter-phobic ravings about exorcizing evil: it is because it is there, everywhere, like an obscure object of desire. Without this deep-seated complicity, the event would not have had the resonance it has, and in their symbolic strategy the terrorists doubtless know that they can count on this unavowable complicity.

This goes far beyond hatred for the dominant world power among the disinherited and the exploited, among those who have ended up on the wrong side of the global order. Even those who share in the advantages of that order have this malicious desire in their hearts. Allergy to any definitive order, to any definitive power, is—happily—universal, and the two towers of the World Trade Center were perfect embodiments, in their very twinness, of that definitive order.

No need, then, for death drive or a destructive instinct, or even for perverse, unintended effects. Very logically—and inexorably—the increase in the power of power heightens the will to destroy it. And it was party to its own destruction. When the two towers collapsed, you had the impression that they were responding to the suicide of the suicide-planes with their own suicides. It has been said that "Even God cannot declare war on Himself." Well, He can. The West, in the position of God (divine omnipotence and absolute moral legitimacy), has become suicidal, and declared war on itself.

The countless disaster movies bear witness to this fantasy, which they clearly attempt to exorcise with images, drowning out the whole thing with special effects. But the universal attraction they exert, which is on a par with pornography, shows that acting-out is never very far away, the impulse to reject any system growing all the stronger as it approaches perfection or omnipotence.

It is probable that the terrorists had not foreseen the collapse of the Twin Towers (any more than had the experts!), a collapse which—much more than the attack on the Pentagon—had the greatest symbolic impact. The symbolic collapse of a whole system came about by an unpredictable complicity, as though the towers, by collapsing on their own, by committing suicide, had joined in to round off the event. In a sense, the entire system, by its internal fragility, lent the initial action a helping hand.

The more concentrated the system becomes globally, ultimately forming one single network, the more it becomes vulnerable at a single point (already a single little Filipino hacker had managed, from the dark recesses of his portable computer, to launch the "I love you" virus, which circled the globe devastating entire networks). Here it was eighteen suicide attackers who, thanks to the absolute weapon of death, enhanced by technological efficiency, unleashed a global catastrophic process.

When global power monopolizes the situation to this extent, when there is such a formidable condensation of all functions in the technocratic machinery, and when no alternative form of thinking is allowed, what other way is there but a *terroristic situational transfer*? It was the system itself which created the objective conditions for this brutal retaliation. By seizing all the cards for itself, it forced the Other to change the rules. And the new rules are fierce ones, because the stakes are fierce. To a system whose very excess of power poses an insoluble challenge, the terrorists respond with a definitive act which is also not susceptible of exchange. Terrorism is the act that restores an irreducible singularity to the heart of a system of generalized exchange. All the singularities (species, individuals and cultures) that have paid with their deaths for the installation of a global circulation governed by a single power are taking their revenge today through this *terroristic situational transfer*.

This is terror against terror—there is no longer any ideology behind it. We are far beyond ideology and politics now. No ideology, no cause—not even the Islamic cause—can account for the energy which fuels terror. The aim is no longer even to transform the world, but (as the heresies did in their day) to radicalize the world by sacrifice. Whereas the system aims to realize it by force.

Terrorism, like viruses, is everywhere. There is a global perfusion of terrorism, which accompanies any system of domination as though it were its shadow, ready to activate itself anywhere, like a double agent. We can no longer draw a demarcation line around it. It is at the very heart of this culture which combats it, and the visible fracture (and the hatred) that pits the exploited and the underdeveloped globally against the Western world secretly connects with the fracture internal to the dominant system. That system can face down any visible antagonism. But against the other kind, which is viral in structure—as though every machinery of domination secreted its own counterapparatus, the agent of its own disappearance—against that form of almost automatic reversion of its own power, the system can do nothing. And terrorism is the shock wave of this silent reversion.

This is not, then, a clash of civilizations or religions, and it reaches far beyond Islam and America, on which efforts are being made to focus the conflict in order to create the delusion of a visible confrontation and a solution based on force. There is, indeed, a fundamental antagonism here, but one which points past the spectre of America (which is, perhaps, the epicentre, but in no sense the sole embodiment, of globalization) and the spectre of Islam (which is not the embodiment of terrorism either), to *triumphant globalization battling against itself*. In this sense, we can indeed speak of a world war—not the Third World War, but the Fourth and the only really global one, since what is at stake is globalization itself. The first two world wars corresponded to the classical image of war. The first ended the supremacy of Europe and the colonial era. The second put an end to Nazism. The third, which has indeed taken place, in the form of cold war and deterrence, put an end to Communism. With each succeeding war, we have moved further towards a single world order. Today that order, which has virtually reached its culmination, finds itself grappling with the antagonistic forces scattered throughout the very heartlands of the global, in all the current convulsions. A fractal war of all cells, all singularities, revolting in the form of antibodies. A confrontation so impossible to pin down that the idea of war has to be rescued from time to time by spectacular set-pieces, such as the Gulf War or the war in Afghanistan. But the Fourth World War is elsewhere. It is what haunts every world order, all hegemonic domination—if Islam dominated the world, terrorism would rise against Islam, *for it is the world, the globe itself, which resists globalization*. . . .

In all these vicissitudes, what stays with us, above all else, is the sight of the images. This impact of the images, and their fascination, are necessarily what we retain, since images are, whether we like it or not, our primal scene. And, at the same time as they have radicalized the world situation, the events in New York can also be said to have radicalized the relation of the image to reality. Whereas we were dealing before with an uninterrupted profusion of banal images and a seamless flow of sham events, the terrorist act in New York has resuscitated both images and events.

Among the other weapons of the system which they turned round against it, the terrorists exploited the "real time" of images, their instantaneous worldwide transmission, just as they exploited stock-market speculation, electronic information and air traffic. The role of images is highly ambiguous. For, at the same time as they exalt the event, they also take it hostage. They serve to multiply it to infinity and, at the same time, they are a diversion and a neutralization (this was already the case with the events of 1968). The image consumes the event, in the sense that it absorbs it and offers it for consumption. Admittedly, it gives it unprecedented impact, but impact as image-event.

How do things stand with the real event, then, if reality is everywhere infiltrated by images, virtuality and fiction? In the present case, we thought we had seen (perhaps with a certain relief) a resurgence of the real, and of the violence of the real, in an allegedly virtual universe. "There's an end to all your talk about the virtual—this is something real!" Similarly, it was possible to see this as a resurrection of history beyond its proclaimed end. But does reality actually outstrip fiction? If it seems to do so, this is because it has absorbed fiction's energy, and has itself become fiction. We might almost say that reality is jealous of fiction, that the real is jealous of the image.... It is a kind of duel between them, a contest to see which can be the most unimaginable.

The collapse of the World Trade Center towers is unimaginable, but that is not enough to make it a real event. An excess of violence is not enough to open on to reality. For reality is a principle, and it is this principle that is lost. Reality and fiction are inextricable, and the fascination with the attack is primarily a fascination with the image (both its exultatory and its catastrophic consequences are themselves largely imaginary).

In this case, then, the real is superadded to the image like a bonus of terror, like an additional *frisson*: not only is it terrifying, but, what is more, it is real. Rather than the violence of the real being there first, and the *frisson* of the image being added to it, the image is there first, and the *frisson* of the real is added. Something like an additional fiction, a fiction surpassing fiction. Ballard[1] (after Borges)[2] talked like this of reinventing the real as the ultimate and most redoubtable fiction.

The terrorist violence here is not, then, a blowback of reality, any more than it is a blowback of history. It is not "real." In a sense, it is worse: it is symbolic. Violence in itself may be perfectly banal and inoffensive. Only symbolic violence is generative of singularity. And in this singular event, in this Manhattan disaster movie, the twentieth century's two elements of mass fascination are combined: the white magic of the cinema and the black magic of terrorism; the white light of the image and the black light of terrorism.

We try retrospectively to impose some kind of meaning on it, to find some kind of interpretation. But there is none. And it is the radicality of the spectacle, the brutality of the spectacle, which alone is original and irreducible. The spectacle of terrorism forces the terrorism of spectacle upon us. And, against this immoral fascination (even if it unleashes a universal moral reaction), the political order can do nothing. This is *our* theatre of cruelty, the only one we have left—extraordinary in that it unites the most extreme degree of the spectacular and the highest level of challenge.... It is at one and the same time the dazzling micromodel of a kernel of real violence with the maximum possible echo—hence the purest form of spectacle—and a sacrificial model mounting the purest symbolic form of defiance to the historical and political order....

2001

---

[1] J. G. Ballard (b. 1930) is a British author whose subject matter is the dystopian future.   [2] Jorge Luis Borges (1899–1986) was an Argentine writer of postmodern fiction.

WAI CHEE DIMOCK
B. 1953

Planet and America, Set and Subset

What exactly is "American literature"? Is it a sovereign domain, self-sustained and self-governing, integral as a body of evidence? Or is it less autonomous than that, not altogether freestanding, but more like a municipality: a second-tier phenomenon, resting on a platform preceding it and encompassing it, and dependent on the latter for its infrastructure, its support network, its very existence as a subsidiary unit?

This jurisdictional language is meant to highlight American literature as a constituted domain and the variously imagined *ground* for its constitution. That ground, though methodologically crucial, is often left implicit. On what footing can the field call itself a field, and according to what integrating principle? What degree of self-determination can it lay claim to? And what does it have in common with the territorial jurisdiction whose name it bears, whose clear-cut borders contain an attribute we are tempted to call "American-ness"?

After the World Trade Center, and after Katrina, few of us are under the illusion that the United States is sovereign in any absolute sense. The nation seems to have come literally "unbundled" before our eyes, its fabric of life torn apart by extremist militant groups, and by physical forces of even greater scope, wrought by climate change and the intensified hurricane cycles. Territorial sovereignty, we suddenly realize, is no more than a legal fiction, a man-made fiction. This fiction is not honored by religious adherents who have a different vision of the world; nor is it honored by the spin of hurricanes accelerated by the thermodynamics of warming oceans. In each case, the nation is revealed to be what it is: an epiphenomenon, literally a superficial construct, a set of erasable lines on the face of the earth. It is no match for that grounded entity called the planet, which can wipe out those lines at a moment's notice, using weapons of mass destruction more powerful than any homeland defense.

"Globalization" is the familiar term used to describe this unraveling of national sovereignty. This process, seemingly inevitable, has been diagnosed in almost antithetical ways. On the one hand, theorists from Michael Walzer to Jürgen Habermas see an enormous potential in the decline of the nation-state; for them, this jurisdictional form, historically monopolizing violence, and now increasingly outmoded, must give way to other forms of human association: a "global civil society," a "postnational constellation." On the other hand, theorists such as Fredric Jameson caution against such optimism, pointing to the "McDonaldization" of the world, a regime of standardization and homogenization ushered in by the erosion of national borders, presided over by global capital and the "unchallenged primacy of the United States."

What Katrina dramatizes, however, is a form of "globalization" different from either scenario. Not benign, it is at the same time not predicated on the primacy of any nation. Long accustomed to seeing itself as the de facto center of the world—the military superpower, the largest economy, and the moral arbiter to boot—the United States suddenly finds itself downgraded to something considerably less. "It's like being in a Third World country," Mitch Handler, a manager in Louisiana's biggest public hospital, said to the Associated Press about the plight of hurricane victims. This Third-Worlding of a superpower came with a shock not only to Louisiana and Mississippi but to unbelieving eyes everywhere. Not the actor but the acted upon, the United States is simply the spot where catastrophe hits, the place on the map where large-scale forces, unleashed elsewhere, come home to roost. What does it mean for the United States to be on the receiving end of things? The experience is novel, mind-shattering in many ways, and a numbing patriotism is not incompatible with a numbing shame. To the rest of the world, however, this massive systemic failure confirms their view of the United States not only as a miscreant abroad—a "rogue nation" both in its rejection of the Kyoto Protocol and in its conduct of the Iraq War—but as one equally inept at home, falling far below an acceptable standard of care for its own citizens. Scale enlargement has stripped from this nation any dream of unchallenged primacy. If Europe has already been "provincialized"—has been revealed to be a smaller player in world history than previously imagined, as Dipesh Chakrabarty argues—the United States seems poised to follow suit.

In this context, it seems important to rethink the adequacy of a nation-based paradigm. Is "America" an adjective that can stand on its own, uninflected, unentangled, and unconstrained? Can an autonomous field be built on its chronology and geography, equal to the task of phenomenal description and causal explanation? Janice Radway, in her presidential address to the American Studies Association in 1998, answers with a resounding "no," and proposes a name change for the association for just that reason. A field calling itself "American" imagines that there is something exceptional about the United States, manifesting itself as "a distinctive set of properties and themes in all things American, whether individuals, institutions, or cultural products. This premise of exceptionalism translates into a methodology that privileges the nation above all else. The field can legitimize itself as a field only because the nation does the legitimizing. The disciplinary sovereignty of the former owes everything to the territorial sovereignty of the latter. Against this conflation of nation and field, Radway proposes a rigorous decoupling, a methodology predicated on the *noncoincidence* between the two. The nation has solid borders; the field, on the other hand, is fluid and amorphous, shaped and reshaped by emerging forces, by "intricate interdependencies" between "the near and far, the local and the distant." In short, as a domain of inquiry, the "Americanist" field needs to be kept emphatically distinct from the nation. Its vitality resides in a carefully maintained and carefully theorized zone, a penumbra intervening between it and the conceptual foreclosure dictated by its name. That penumbra makes the field a continuum rather than a container:

> It suggests that far from being conceived on the model of a container—that is, as a particular kind of hollowed out object with evident edges or skin enclosing certain organically uniform contents—territories and geographies need to be reconceived as spatially-situated and intricately intertwined networks of social relationships that tie specific locales to particular histories.

Radway's challenge to the "container" model turns the United States from a discrete entity into a porous network, with no tangible edges, its circumference being continually negotiated, its criss-crossing pathways continually modified by local input, local inflections. These dynamic exchanges suggest that the American field has never been unified, and will never be. Still, though not unified, the nation remains central for Radway: it is a first-order phenomenon, a primary field of inquiry. If it is no longer a "hollowed out object" filled with contents unique to it and homogenized within it, it remains a *disciplinary* object second to none, conceptually front and center, and naturalizing itself as the methodological baseline, a set of founding coordinates, reproducing its boundaries in the very boundaries of the field.

What sort of distortion comes with this nation-centered mapping? And how best to rectify it? . . . Rather than taking the nation as the default position, the totality we automatically reach for, we come up with alternate geographies that deny it this totalizing function. Forging such geographies might be one of the most critical tasks now facing the field. How best to fashion a domain of inquiry not replicating the terms of territorial sovereignty? What landscape would emerge then? And what would American literature look like when traced through these redrawn and realigned entities?

The language of set and subset is especially helpful here as a heuristic guide. While that language can sometimes conjure up a hierarchical ordering of part to whole, its interest for us lies in a different direction: not in stratification, but in modularization. What it highlights is the strategic breakup of a continuum, the carving of it into secondary units, and the premises and consequences attending that process. For units are not given but made. They are not an objective fact in the world, but an artifact, a postulate, aggregated as such for some particular purpose. Their lengths and widths, the size of their grouping, their criteria of selection, the platforms they rest on—all of these can be differently specified. Each specifying throws into relief a different kind of entity: mapped on a different scale, performing a different function, implementing a different set of membership criteria. And looming over all of these is the long-standing, still evolving, and always to be theorized relation between each unit and the larger continuum. A language of set and subset, in short, allows us to "modularize" the world into smaller entities: able to stand provisionally and do analytic work, but not self-contained, not fully sovereign, resting continually and nontrivially on a platform more robust and more extensive.

"American literature" is best understood as a subset in this sense. The field does stand to be classified apart, as a nameable and adducible unit. It is taxonomically useful as an entity. At the same time, that taxonomic usefulness should not lure us into thinking that this entity is natural, that its shape and size will hold all the way up and all the way down, staying intact regardless of circumstances, not varying with specifying frames. On the contrary, what we nominate as "American literature" is simply an effect of that nomination, which is to say, it is epiphenomenal, domain-specific, binding only at one register and extending no farther than that register. Once it is transposed, its membership will change also, going up and down with the ascending or descending scales of aggregation. And, across those scales, at every level of redescription, it can be folded back into a larger continuum from which it has only been momentarily set apart.

In *Gödel, Escher, Bach* (1979), Douglas Hofstadter discusses these ascending and descending scales and their intricate enfolding as "recursive structures and processes," to be found not only in mathematics, the visual arts, and music, but also in domains still more elementary: the grammar of languages, the geometry of the branches of trees, even particle physics. What all of these have in common is the phenomenon of "nesting": a generative process that modulates continually from the outside to the inside, from the background to the foreground, with several units, differently scaled, reciprocally cradling one another and overlapping with one another, creating an ever wider circumference as well as an ever greater recessional depth. Rather than proceeding as a straight line, recursive structures and processes give us a reversible landscape that can be either convex or concave, either bulging out or burrowing in, sometimes pivoted on the smallest embedded unit and sometimes radiating out to take in the largest embedding circumference. Hofstadter calls this reversible hierarchy a *heterarchy*. "The whole world is built out of recursion," he says. This entanglement between inner and outer limits allows entities to snowball, with each feedback loop generating an "increasing complexity of behavior," so much so that "suitably recursive systems might be strong enough to break out of any predetermined patterns," modifying the input to such an extent that the outcome becomes utterly unpredictable. Such unpredictability, Hofstradter adds, "probably lies at the heart of intelligence."

We explore the intelligence of American literature in just this light, as the unpredictable outcome stemming from the interplay between encapsulation and its undoing: between the modularity of the subset and an infinite number of larger aggregates that might count as its embedding "set." What are some of these aggregates? They are uncharted and uncataloged for the most part. One thing is clear, though. In order for American literature to be nested in them, these aggregates would have to rest on a platform broader and more robustly empirical than the relatively arbitrary and demonstrably ephemeral borders of the nation. They require alternate geographies, alternate histories. At their most capacious, they take their measure from the durations and extensions of the human species itself, folding in American literature as one fold among others, to be unfolded and refolded into our collective fabric.

Gayatri Chakravorty Spivak and Paul Gilroy have proposed the term "planet" as one aggregate that might do this work of enfolding. In *Death of a Discipline* (2003), Spivak argues that "planetarity" is a term worth exploring precisely because it is an unknown quantum, barely intimated, not yet adequate to the meaning we would like it to bear, and stirring for just that reason. It stands as a horizon impossible to define, and hospitable in that impossibility. Its very sketchiness makes it a "catachresis[1] for inscribing collective responsibility," for that sketchiness preserves a space for phenomena as yet emerging, not quite in sight. In *After Empire* (2004), Paul Gilroy also invokes the "planet" in this loose-fitting sense. The concept can be helpful only in the optative mood, as a generative principle fueled by its less than actualized status. For its heuristic value lies in its not having come into being: it is a habitat still waiting for its inhabitants, waiting for a humanity that has yet to be born, yet to be wrested from a seemingly boundless racism.

What are the consequences of invoking the planet, in its actualized and unactualized dimensions, as a research program? What practical difficulties might arise? What professional training is required? And what sort of creatures would literary scholars have to become to be practitioners of this new craft? It is helpful here to turn another presidential address, delivered by Philip Curtin to the American Historical Association in 1983, one that eerily speaks to the current situation. Entitled "Depth, Span, and Relevance," this presidential address zeroes in on the very question of professional training. "The discipline of history has broadened in the postwar decades, but historians have not," Curtin observes. "We teach the history of Africa and Asia, but specialists in American history know no more about the history of Africa than their predecessors did in the 1940s." Nor is Africa alone terra incognito in the minds of scholars. Europe, it seems, is also a dark continent: "Americanists know less European history than they did thirty years ago." Expertise so narrowly defined has serious consequences for the field as a whole. Americanists seem to have forgotten "that one of the prime values of a liberal education is breadth, not narrow specialization. Even before the explosion of new kinds of historical knowledge, historical competence required a balance between deep mastery of a particular field and a span of knowledge over other fields of history. Depth was necessary to discover and validate the evidence. Span was necessary to know what kind of evidence to look for—and to make some sense of it, once discovered." ...

2007

---

[1]The improper use of words.

DON DELILLO
B. 1936

Don DeLillo has become one of the most respected and widely read American novelists associated with the term *postmodernism*. DeLillo shares with other postmodernist literary giants, such as Thomas Pynchon and John Barth, a tendency toward absurd humor that thinly covers a sense of dread, despair, or paranoia. Like these writers, he is concerned with the inability of the individual to gain any measure of control in a world gone mad with technological or governmental control.

DeLillo plunges his readers into a world where individuals have lost their bearings, where conspiracy theories become reality, and where the forces of history are stronger than free will. This world tends to sprawl in many directions, emphasizing (as postmodern novels tend to do) surface rather than depth. In a 1997 essay, he relates the form and content of his work to the geography of his country: "The sweeping range of American landscape and experience can be a goad, a challenge, an affliction and an inspiration [to the novelist], pretty much in one package. The novel can be a foolhardy form, bristling with risk."

Since his first book, *Americana* (1971), DeLillo has published thirteen other novels, as well as essays, plays, and short stories, many of which have been incorporated into his novels.

DeLillo grew up in the Bronx, the son of Italian immigrant parents. He was raised Catholic, and he claims that his faith has had an effect on his aesthetic because of its emphasis on ritual and because it instructs its adherents to live according to a certain code so that death will not bring eternal damnation. Like his fictional rendition of Lee Harvey Oswald, JFK's assassin, in *Libra*, DeLillo was not fond of school and instead preferred to learn from alternative sources. He cites jazz (especially the innovative bop of Charles Mingus), film (especially the avant-garde French filmmaker Jean-Luc Godard), and abstract expressionist painting as the primary influences on his writing, though he also frequently mentions pickup games of baseball and shooting pool as formative experiences. Although he attended Fordham University, he takes pains to diminish the influence of education on his work and says that his explorations of New York City are really what formed him. Even so, his most famous novel, *White Noise* (1985), takes place on a Midwestern college campus and is narrated by a college professor.

One of the greatest influences on DeLillo's work is history itself, specifically the history that has occurred during his lifetime. Two of DeLillo's most enduring novels, *Libra* (1988) and *Underworld* (1997), are initiated by what he has referred to as forgotten newspaper headlines. *Libra* is an inventive rendition of the life and death of Lee Harvey Oswald, whose fate is dictated by forces much greater than himself—not only history proper but the conspiracy theories that have dominated the popular imagination since President Kennedy's death. As one character puts it, history is "the sum total of all the things they aren't telling us." In this novel, information becomes overwhelming. A character named Nicholas Branch, who is trying to sort through all the evidence related to the case, grows despondent when the little room he is filling with information begins to overflow. Coincidence becomes stronger than cause and effect, and the randomness or chaos of the postmodern world triumphs over logic and order.

DeLillo's massive epic *Underworld* begins with two different events that coincided in 1951: the Soviets' exploding their first nuclear bomb and the Giants' winning the National League pennant with a home run that became known as "the shot heard 'round the world." The forces of what might be called official history (the events that are publicly shared and discussed) grind against the shadowy underworld (the hidden events that control the lives of individuals and that do not find their way into history books). In a memorable moment from *White Noise*, following a catastrophic "airborne toxic event," the narrator's wife solemnly reads absurd tabloid headlines to a rapt group of listeners. In all these cases, newspaper headlines actually eclipse the realities of history rather than illuminate them.

The essay that follows, "In the Ruins of the Future," first appeared in *The Atlantic Monthly*. It is an early and penetrating analysis of how "everything changed" after the terror attacks of September 11, 2001. The story that follows, initially published in *The New Yorker* as "Still Life," became the first chapter of DeLillo's later novel *Falling Man* (2007).

D. Quentin Miller
Suffolk University

PRIMARY WORKS

Americana, 1971; *End Zone*, 1972; *Great Jones Street*, 1973; *Ratner's Star*, 1976; *Players*, 1977; *Running Dog*, 1978; *The Names*, 1982; *White Noise*, 1985; *Libra*, 1988; *Mao II*, 1991; *Underworld*, 1997; *The Body Artist*, 2001; *Cosmopolis*, 2003; *Falling Man*, 2007; *Point Omega*, 2010; *The Angel Esmeralda: Nine Stories*, 2011.

In the Ruins of the Future

In the past decade the surge of capital markets has dominated discourse and shaped global consciousness. Multinational corporations have come to seem more vital and influential than governments. The dramatic climb of the Dow and the speed of the Internet summoned us all to live permanently in the future, in the utopian glow of cyber-capital, because there is no memory there and this is where markets are uncontrolled and investment potential has no limit.

All this changed on September 11. Today, again, the world narrative belongs to terrorists. But the primary target of the men who attacked the Pentagon and the World Trade Center was not the global economy. It is America that drew their fury. It is the high gloss of our modernity. It is the thrust of our technology. It is our perceived godlessness. It is the blunt force of our foreign policy. It is the power of American culture to penetrate every wall, home, life, and mind.

Terror's response is a narrative that has been developing over years, only now becoming inescapable. It is our lives and minds that are occupied now. This catastrophic event changes the way we think and act, moment to moment, week to week, for unknown weeks and months to come, and steely years. Our world, parts of our world, have crumbled into theirs, which means we are living in a place of danger and rage.

The protestors in Genoa, Prague, Seattle, and other cities want to decelerate the global momentum that seemed to be driving unmindfully toward a landscape of consumer-robots and social instability, with the chance of self-determination probably diminishing for most people in most countries. Whatever acts of violence marked the protests, most of the men and women involved tend to be a moderating influence, trying to slow things down, even things out, hold off the white-hot future.

The terrorists of September 11 want to bring back the past.

Our tradition of free expression and our justice system's provisions for the rights of the accused can only seem an offense to men bent on suicidal terror.

We are rich, privileged, and strong, but they are willing to die. This is the edge they have, the fire of aggrieved belief. We live in a wide world, routinely filled with exchange of every sort, an open circuit of work, talk, family, and expressible feeling. The terrorist, planted in a Florida town, pushing his supermarket cart, nodding to his neighbor, lives in a far narrower format. This is his edge, his strength. Plots reduce the world. He builds a plot around his anger and our indifference. He lives a certain kind of apartness, hard and tight. This is not the self-watcher, the soft white dangling boy who shoots someone to keep from disappearing into himself. The terrorist shares a secret and a self. At a certain point he and his brothers may begin to feel less motivated by politics and personal hatred than by brotherhood itself. They share the codes and protocols of their mission here and something deeper as well, a vision of judgment and devastation.

Does the sight of a woman pushing a stroller soften the man to her humanity and vulnerability, and her child's as well, and all the people he is here to kill?

This is his edge, that he does not see her. Years here, waiting, taking flying lessons, making the routine gestures of community and home, the credit card, the bank account, the post-office box. All tactical, linked, layered. He knows who we are and what we mean in the world—an idea, a righteous fever in the brain. But there is no defenseless human at the end of his gaze.

The sense of disarticulation we hear in the term "Us and Them" has never been so striking, at either end.

We can tell ourselves that whatever we've done to inspire bitterness, distrust, and rancor, it was not so damnable as to bring this day down on our heads. But there is no logic in apocalypse. They have gone beyond the bounds of passionate payback. This is heaven and hell, a sense of armed martyrdom as the surpassing drama of human experience.

He pledges his submission to God and meditates on the blood to come.

The Bush Administration was feeling a nostalgia for the Cold War. This is over now. Many things are over. The narrative ends in the rubble, and it is left to us to create the counter-narrative.

There are a hundred thousand stories crisscrossing New York, Washington, and the world. Where we were, whom we know, what we've seen or heard. There are the doctors' appointments that saved lives, the cell phones that were used to report the hijackings. Stories generating others and people running north out of the rumbling smoke and ash. Men running in suits and ties, women who'd lost their shoes, cops running from the skydive of all that towering steel.

People running for their lives are part of the story that is left to us.

There are stories of heroism and encounters with dread. There are stories that carry around their edges the luminous ring of coincidence, fate, or premonition. They take us beyond the hard numbers of dead and missing and give us a glimpse of elevated being. For a hundred who are arbitrarily dead, we need to find one person saved by a flash of forewarning. There are configurations that chill and awe us both. Two women on two planes, best of friends, who die together and apart, Tower 1 and Tower 2. What desolate epic tragedy might bear the weight of such juxtaposition? But we can also ask what symmetry, bleak and touching both, takes one friend, spares the other's grief?

The brother of one of the women worked in one of the towers. He managed to escape.

In Union Square Park, about two miles north of the attack site, the improvised memorials are another part of our response. The flags, flower beds, and votive candles, the lamppost hung with paper airplanes, the passages from the Koran and the Bible, the letters and poems, the cardboard John Wayne, the children's drawings of the Twin Towers, the hand-painted signs for Free Hugs, Free Back Rubs, the graffiti of love and peace on the tall equestrian statue.

There are many photographs of missing persons, some accompanied by hopeful lists of identifying features. (Man with panther tattoo, upper right arm.) There is the saxophonist, playing softly. There is the sculptured flag of rippling copper and aluminum, six feet long, with two young people still attending to the finer details of the piece.

Then there are the visitors to the park. The artifacts on display represent the confluence of a number of cultural tides, patriotic and multidevotional and retro hippie. The visitors move quietly in the floating aromas of candlewax, roses, and bus fumes. There are many people this evening, and in their voices, manner, clothing, and in the color of their skin they recapitulate the mix we see in the photocopied faces of the lost.

For the next fifty years, people who were not in the area when the attacks occurred will claim to have been there. In time, some of them will believe it. Others will claim to have lost friends or relatives, although they did not.

This is also the counter-narrative, a shadow history of false memories and imagined loss.

The Internet is a counter-narrative, shaped in part by rumor, fantasy, and mystical reverberation.

The cell phones, the lost shoes, the handkerchiefs mashed in the faces of running men and women. The box cutters and credit cards. The paper that came streaming out of the towers and drifted across the river to Brooklyn back yards: status reports, résumés, insurance forms. Sheets of paper driven into concrete, according to witnesses. Paper slicing into truck tires, fixed there.

These are among the smaller objects and more marginal stories in the sifted ruins of the day. We need them, even the common tools of the terrorists, to set against the massive spectacle that continues to seem unmanageable, too powerful a thing to set into our frame of practiced response.

Ash was spattering the windows. Karen was half dressed, grabbing the kids and trying to put on some clothes and talking with her husband and scooping things to take out to the corridor, and they looked at her, twin girls, as if she had fourteen heads.

They stayed in the corridor for a while, thinking there might be secondary explosions. They waited, and began to feel safer, and went back to the apartment.

At the next impact, Marc knew in the sheerest second before the shock wave broadsided their building that it was a second plane, impossible, striking the second tower. Their building was two blocks away, and he'd thought the first crash was an accident.

They went back to the hallway, where others began to gather, fifteen or twenty people.

Karen ran back for a cell phone, a cordless phone, a charger, water, sweaters, snacks for the kids, and then made a quick dash to the bedroom for her wedding ring.

From the window she saw people running in the street, others locked shoulder to shoulder, immobilized, with debris coming down on them. People were trampled, struck by falling objects, and there was ash and paper everywhere, paper whipping through the air, no sign of light or sky.

Cell phones were down. They talked on the cordless, receiving information measured out in eyedrops. They were convinced that the situation outside was far more grave than it was here.

Smoke began to enter the corridor.

Then the first tower fell. She thought it was a bomb. When she talked to someone on the phone and found out what had happened, she felt a surreal relief. Bombs and missiles were not falling everywhere in the city. It was not all-out war, at least not yet.

Marc was in the apartment getting chairs for the older people, for the woman who'd had hip surgery. When he heard the first low drumming rumble, he stood in a strange dead calm and said, "Something is happening." It sounded exactly like what it was, a tall tower collapsing.

The windows were surfaced with ash now, blacked out completely, and he wondered what was out there. What remained to be seen and did he want to see it?

They all moved into the stairwell, behind a fire door, but smoke kept coming in. It was gritty ash, and they were eating it.

He ran back inside, grabbing towels off the racks and washcloths out of drawers and drenching them in the sink, and filling his bicycle water bottles, and grabbing the kids' underwear.

He thought the crush of buildings was the thing to fear most. This is what would kill them.

Karen was on the phone, talking to a friend in the district attorney's office, about half a mile to the north. She was pleading for help. She begged, pleaded, and hung up. For the next hour a detective kept calling with advice and encouragement.

Marc came back out to the corridor. I think we might die, he told himself, hedging his sense of what would happen next.

The detective told Karen to stay where they were.

When the second tower fell, my heart fell with it. I called Marc, who is my nephew, on his cordless. I couldn't stop thinking of the size of the towers and the meager distance between those buildings and his. He answered, we talked. I have no memory of the conversation except for his final remark, slightly urgent, concerning someone on the other line, who might be sending help.

Smoke was seeping out of the elevator shaft now. Karen was saying goodbye to her father in Oregon. Not hello-goodbye. But goodbye-I-think-we-are-going-to-die. She thought smoke would be the thing that did it.

People sat on chairs along the walls. They chatted about practical matters. They sang songs with the kids. The kids in the group were cooperative because the adults were damn scared.

There was an improvised rescue in progress. Karen's friend and a colleague made their way down from Centre Street, turning up with two policemen they'd enlisted en route. They had dust masks and a destination, and they searched every floor for others who might be stranded in the building.

They came out into a world of ash and near night. There was no one else to be seen now on the street. Gray ash covered the cars and pavement, ash falling in large flakes, paper still drifting down, discarded shoes, strollers, briefcases. The members of the group were masked and toweled, children in adults' arms, moving east and then north on Nassau Street, trying not to look around, only what's immediate, one step and then another, all closely focused, a pregnant woman, a newborn, a dog.

They were covered in ash when they reached shelter at Pace University, where there was food and water, and kind and able staff members, and a gas-leak scare, and more running people.

Workers began pouring water on the group. Stay wet, stay wet. This was the theme of the first half hour.

Later a line began to form along the food counter.

Someone said, "I don't want cheese on that."

Someone said, "I like it better not so cooked."

Not so incongruous really, just people alive and hungry, beginning to be themselves again.

Technology is our fate, our truth. It is what we mean when we call ourselves the only superpower on the planet. The materials and methods we devise make it possible for us to claim our future. We don't have to depend on God or the prophets or other astonishments. We are the astonishment. The miracle is what we ourselves produce, the systems and networks that change the way we live and think.

But whatever great skeins of technology lie ahead, ever more complex, connective, precise, micro-fractional, the future has yielded, for now, to medieval expedience, to the old slow furies of cutthroat religion.

Kill the enemy and pluck out his heart.

If others in less scientifically advanced cultures were able to share, wanted to share, some of the blessings of our technology, without a threat to their faith or traditions, would they need to rely on a God in whose name they kill the innocent? Would they need to invent a God who rewards violence against the innocent with a promise of "infinite paradise," in the words of a handwritten letter found in the luggage of one of the hijackers?

For all those who may want what we've got, there are all those who do not. These are the men who have fashioned a morality of destruction. They want what they used to have before the waves of Western influence. They surely see themselves as the elect of God whether or not they follow the central precepts of Islam. It is the presumptive right of those who choose violence and death to speak directly to God. They will kill and then die. Or they will die first, in the cockpit, in clean shoes, according to instructions in the letter.

Six days after the attacks, the territory below Canal Street is hedged with barricades. There are few civilians in the street. Police at some checkpoints, troops in camouflage gear at others, wearing gas masks, and a pair of state troopers in conversation, and ten burly men striding east in hard hats, work pants, and NYPD jackets. A shop owner tries to talk a cop into letting him enter his place of business. He is a small elderly man with a Jewish accent, but there is no relief today. Garbage bags are everywhere in high broad stacks. The area is bedraggled and third-worldish, with an air of permanent emergency, everything surfaced in ash.

It is possible to pass through some checkpoints, detour around others. At Chambers Street I look south through the links of the National Rent-A-Fence barrier. There stands the smoky remnant of filigree that marks the last tall thing, the last sign in the mire of wreckage that there were towers here that dominated the skyline for over a quarter of a century.

Ten days later and a lot closer, I stand at another barrier with a group of people, looking directly into the strands of openwork façade. It is almost too close. It is almost Roman, I-beams for stonework, but not nearly so salvageable. Many here describe the scene to others on cell phones.

"Oh my god I'm standing here," says the man next to me.

The World Trade towers were not only an emblem of advanced technology but a justification, in a sense, for technology's irresistible will to realize in solid form whatever becomes theoretically allowable. Once defined, every limit must be reached. The tactful sheathing of the towers was intended to reduce the direct threat of such straight-edge enormity, a giantism that eased over the years into something a little more familiar and comfortable, even dependable in a way.

Now a small group of men have literally altered our skyline. We have fallen back in time and space. It is their technology that marks our moments, the small lethal devices, the remote-controlled detonators they fashion out of radios, or the larger technology they borrow from us, passenger jets that become manned missiles.

Maybe this is a grim subtext of their enterprise. They see something innately destructive in the nature of technology. It brings death to their customs and beliefs. Use it as what it is, a thing that kills.

Nearly eleven years ago, during the engagement in the Persian Gulf, people had trouble separating the war from coverage of the war. After the first euphoric days, coverage became limited. The rush of watching all that eerie green night-vision footage, shot from fighter jets in combat, had been so intense that it became hard to honor the fact that the war was still going on, untelevised. A layer of consciousness had been stripped away. People shuffled around, muttering. They were lonely for their war.

The events of September 11 were covered unstintingly. There was no confusion of roles on TV. The raw event was one thing, the coverage another. The event dominated the medium. It was bright and totalizing, and some of us said it was unreal. When we say a thing is unreal, we mean it is too real, a phenomenon so unaccountable and yet so bound to the power of objective fact that we can't tilt it to the slant of our perceptions. First the planes struck the towers. After a time it became possible for us to absorb this, barely. But when the towers fell. When the rolling smoke began moving downward floor to floor. This was so vast and terrible that it was outside imagining even as it happened. We could not catch up to it. But it was real, punishingly so, an expression of the physics of structural limits and a void in one's soul, and there was the huge antenna falling out of the sky, straight down, blunt end first, like an arrow moving backward in time.

The event itself has no purchase on the mercies of analogy or simile. We have to take the shock and horror as it is. But living language is not diminished. The writer wants to understand what this day has done to us. Is it too soon? We seem pressed for time, all of us. Time is scarcer now. There is a sense of compression, plans made hurriedly, time forced and distorted. But language is inseparable from the world that provokes it. The writer begins in the towers, trying to imagine the moment, desperately. Before politics, before history and religion, there is the primal terror. People falling from the towers hand in hand. This is part of the counter-narrative, hands and spirits joining, human beauty in the crush of meshed steel.

In its desertion of every basis for comparison, the event asserts its singularity. There is something empty in the sky. The writer tries to give memory, tenderness, and meaning to all that howling space.

We like to think America invented the future. We are comfortable with the future, intimate with it. But there are disturbances now, in large and small ways, a chain of reconsiderations. Where we live, how we travel, what we think about when we look at our children. For many people, the event has changed the grain of the most routine moment.

We may find that the ruin of the towers is implicit in other things. The new PalmPilot at fingertip's reach, the stretch limousine parked outside the hotel, the midtown skyscraper under construction, carrying the name of a major investment bank—all haunted in a way by what has happened, less assured in their authority, in the prerogatives they offer.

There is fear of other kinds of terrorism, the prospect that biological and chemical weapons will contaminate the air we breathe and the water we drink. There wasn't much concern about this after earlier terrorist acts. This time we are trying to name the future, not in our normally hopeful way but guided by dread.

What has already happened is sufficient to affect the air around us, psychologically. We are all breathing the fumes of lower Manhattan, where traces of the dead are everywhere, in the soft breeze off the river, on rooftops and windows, in our hair and on our clothes.

Think of a future in which the components of a microchip are the size of atoms. The devices that pace our lives will operate from the smart quantum spaces of pure information. Now think of people in countless thousands massing in anger and vowing revenge. Enlarged photos of martyrs and holy men dangle from balconies, and the largest images are those of a terrorist leader.

Two forces in the world, past and future. With the end of Communism, the ideas and principles of modern democracy were seen clearly to prevail, whatever the inequalities of the system itself. This is still the case. But now there is a global theocratic state, unboundaried and floating and so obsolete it must depend on suicidal fervor to gain its aim.

Ideas evolve and de-evolve, and history is turned on end.

On Friday of the first week a long series of vehicles moves slowly west on Canal Street. Dump trucks, flatbeds, sanitation sweepers. There are giant earthmovers making a tremendous revving sound. A scant number of pedestrians, some in dust masks, others just standing, watching, the indigenous people, clinging to walls and doorways, unaccustomed to traffic that doesn't bring buyers and sellers, goods and cash. The fire rescue car and state police cruiser, the staccato sirens of a line of police vans. Cops stand at the sawhorse barriers, trying to clear the way. Ambulances, cherry pickers, a fleet of Con Ed trucks, all this clamor moving south a few blocks ahead, into the cloud of sand and ash.

One month earlier I'd taken the same walk, early evening, among crowds of people, the panethnic swarm of shoppers, merchants, residents and passersby, with a few tourists as well, and the man at the curbstone doing acupoint massage, and the dreadlocked kid riding his bike on the sidewalk. This was the spirit of Canal Street, the old jostle and stir unchanged for many decades and bearing no sign of SoHo just above, with its restaurants and artists' lofts, or TriBeCa below, rich in architectural textures. Here were hardware bargains, car stereos, foam rubber and industrial plastics, the tattoo parlor and the pizza parlor.

Then I saw the woman on the prayer rug. I'd just turned the corner, heading south to meet some friends, and there she was, young and slender, in a silk headscarf. It was time for sunset prayer, and she was kneeling, upper body pitched toward the edge of the rug. She was partly concealed by a couple of vendors' carts, and no one seemed much to notice her. I think there was another woman seated on a folding chair near the curbstone. The figure on the rug faced east, which meant most immediately a storefront just a foot and a half from her tipped head but more distantly and pertinently toward Mecca, of course, the holiest city of Islam.

Some prayer rugs include a mihrab in their design, an arched element representing the prayer niche in a mosque that indicates the direction of Mecca. The only locational guide the young woman needed was the Manhattan grid.

I looked at her in prayer and it was clearer to me than ever, the daily sweeping taken-for-granted greatness of New York. The city will accommodate every language, ritual, belief, and opinion. In the rolls of the dead of September 11, all these vital differences were surrendered to the impact and flash. The bodies themselves are missing in large numbers. For the survivors, more grief. But the dead are their own nation and race, one identity, young or old, devout or unbelieving—a union of souls. During the hadj, the annual pilgrimage in Mecca, the faithful must eliminate every sign of status, income, and nationality, the men wearing identical strips of seamless white cloth, the women with covered heads, all recalling in prayer their fellowship with the dead.

Allahu akbar. God is great.

2002

from **Falling Man**

It was not a street anymore but a world, a time and space of falling ash and near night. He was walking north through rubble and mud and there were people running past holding towels to their faces or jackets over their heads. They had handkerchiefs pressed to their mouths. They had shoes in their hands, a woman with a shoe in each hand, running past him. They ran and fell, some of them, confused and ungainly, with debris coming down around them, and there were people taking shelter under cars.

The roar was still in the air, the buckling rumble of the fall. This was the world now. Smoke and ash came rolling down streets and turning corners, busting around corners, seismic tides of smoke, with office paper flashing past, standard sheets with cutting edge, skimming, whipping past, otherworldly things in the morning pall.

He wore a suit and carried a briefcase. There was glass in his hair and face, marbled bolls of blood and light. He walked past a Breakfast Special sign and they went running by, city cops and security guards running, hands pressed down on gun butts to keep the weapons steady.

Things inside were distant and still, where he was supposed to be. It happened everywhere around him, a car half buried in debris, windows smashed and noises coming out, radio voices scratching at the wreckage. He saw people shedding water as they ran, clothes and bodies drenched from the sprinkler systems. There were shoes discarded in the street, handbags and laptops, a man seated on the sidewalk coughing up blood. Paper cups went bouncing oddly by.

The world was this as well, figures in windows a thousand feet up, dropping into free space, and the stink of fuel fire, and the steady rip of sirens in the air. The noise lay everywhere they ran, stratified sound collecting around them, and he walked away from it and into it at the same time.

There was something else then, outside all this, not belonging to this, aloft. He watched it coming down. A shirt came down out of the high smoke, a shirt lifted and drifting in the scant light and then falling again, down toward the river.

They ran and then they stopped, some of them, standing there swaying, trying to draw breath out of the burning air, and the fitful cries of disbelief, curses and lost shouts, and the paper massed in the air, contracts, resumés blowing by, intact snatches of business, quick in the wind.

He kept on walking. There were the runners who'd stopped and others veering into sidestreets. Some were walking backwards, looking into the core of it, all those writhing lives back there, and things kept falling, scorched objects trailing lines of fire.

He saw two women sobbing in their reverse march, looking past him, both in running shorts, faces in collapse.

He saw members of the tai chi group from the park nearby, standing with hands extended at roughly chest level, elbows bent, as if all of this, themselves included, might be placed in a state of abeyance.

Someone came out of a diner and tried to hand him a bottle of water. It was a woman wearing a dust mask and a baseball cap and she withdrew the bottle and twisted off the top and then thrust it toward him again. He put down the briefcase to take it, barely aware that he wasn't using his left arm, that he'd had to put down the briefcase before he could take the bottle. Three police vans came veering into the street and sped downtown, sirens sounding. He closed his eyes and drank, feeling the water pass into his body taking dust and soot down with it. She was looking at him. She said something he didn't hear and he handed back the bottle and picked up the briefcase. There was an aftertaste of blood in the long draft of water.

He started walking again. A supermarket cart stood upright and empty. There was a woman behind it, facing him, with police tape wrapped around her head and face, yellow caution tape that marks the limits of a crime scene. Her eyes were thin white ripples in the bright mask and she gripped the handle of the cart and stood there, looking into the smoke.

In time he heard the sound of the second fall. He crossed Canal Street and began to see things, somehow, differently. Things did not seem charged in the usual ways, the cobbled street, the cast-iron buildings. There was something critically missing from the things around him. They were unfinished, whatever that means. They were unseen, whatever that means, shop windows, loading platforms, paint-sprayed walls. Maybe this is what things look like when there is no one here to see them.

He heard the sound of the second fall, or felt it in the trembling air, the north tower coming down, a soft awe of voices in the distance. That was him coming down, the north tower.

The sky was lighter here and he could breathe more easily. There were others behind him, thousands, filling the middle distance, a mass in near formation, people walking out of the smoke. He kept going until he had to stop. It hit him quickly, the knowledge that he couldn't go any farther.

He tried to tell himself he was alive but the idea was too obscure to take hold. There was no taxis and little traffic of any kind and then an old panel truck appeared, Electrical Contractor, Long Island City, and it pulled alongside and the driver leaned toward the window on the passenger's side and examined what he saw, a man scaled in ash, in pulverized matter, and asked him where he wanted to go. It wasn't until he got in the truck and shut the door that he understood where he'd been going all along.

2007

JOHN UPDIKE
1932–2009

John Updike emerged in his early twenties as a literary *wunderkind*, precociously publishing short stories, poems, and articles in *The New Yorker*. His early writing, depicting a Pennsylvania boyhood and young married life, was marked by keen visual detail, a mastery of metaphor, and revelation of how the domestic quotidian retains significance. Critics viewed him as a gifted stylist with a capacity for composing passages of extraordinary beauty and freshness. The early work also reflected closely on Updike's childhood in the small town of Shillington, Pennsylvania, where he was educated in public schools and pushed toward a career in the arts by his mother, who herself had ambitions of becoming a writer.

Although he would spend much of his career writing about Pennsylvania, Updike left his native state at eighteen and lived his adult years in New England. On the basis of early academic success, he earned a tuition scholarship to Harvard, followed by a year of graduate study in drawing at Oxford (England). He then accepted a job at *The New Yorker*, the magazine he had worshiped as a boy, though after two years in Manhattan he desired a change. In 1957 he set off on his own as a writer, moving with his young family to Ipswich, Massachusetts, a small town north of Boston. There, and in other small towns on the North Shore, he spent the next fifty-two years of his life, composing at least one book a year.

Through the publication of *Rabbit, Run* (1960), *The Centaur* (1963), and *Couples* (1968), Updike became best known as a novelist, though he continued to publish abundantly in other genres. Marriage and domesticity remained his subject, yet his writing turned more explicitly to sexuality and adultery. His novels won major awards, his face appeared on the cover of *Time* magazine, and by forty, he had established himself as one of the major literary figures of his era.

In the years that followed, Updike proved a versatile and prolific writer, publishing more than sixty volumes: novels, short stories, literary and art criticism, poems, children's books, a memoir, and a play. Unique among writers, he excelled at not one genre but three: the novel, short fiction, and criticism. While his work continued to explore domestic America, he increasingly demonstrated greater variety and range. He set novels in Africa and Brazil, rewrote canonical stories by Hawthorne and Shakespeare, and integrated into his fiction a wealth of difficult information from fields such as particle physics, computer science, and theology.

Updike's best-known work remains *Rabbit Angstrom*, a sequence of four novels and one novella composed at ten-year intervals between 1960 and 2000: *Rabbit, Run*; *Rabbit Redux*; *Rabbit Is Rich*; *Rabbit at Rest*; and "Rabbit Remembered." The Rabbit books chronicle the life of Harry "Rabbit" Angstrom, a former high school basketball star, while documenting the evolution of American culture over the second half of the twentieth century. Through Rabbit, Updike found a comfortable place near the center of culture from which he could observe and comment upon domestic and national events.

Updike was also heralded as a major American short story writer, publishing more than two hundred stories, including "A & P," "Pigeon Feathers," and "Separating." Given his interest in the quotidian, which privileges reflection and detail over plot and dramatic action, his style was in many respects better suited to the short story, which works on a smaller canvas than the novel.

Finally, Updike stood as the preeminent "man of letters" of his era, publishing ten volumes and more than 5,000 pages of essays and criticism. Broad and wide-ranging, his criticism includes essays on American literary masters (Franklin, Hawthorne, Melville, Whitman, Wharton, and others); reviews of fiction by writers from six continents; and essays on theology and religion, painters and sculptors, golf and baseball.

No other American writer took everyday domestic life as seriously as Updike, and few can match his achievement, breadth of oeuvre, and ability to compose elegant sentences. Collectively, his writings comprise a monumental effort to celebrate and sing America, delighting in its textures and surfaces while mindful of its yearnings and disappointments.

James Schiff
University of Cincinnati

PRIMARY WORKS

The Carpentered Hen, 1958; *The Poorhouse Fair*, 1959; *The Same Door*, 1959; *Rabbit, Run*, 1960; *The Magic Flute*, 1962; *Pigeon Feathers*, 1962; *The Centaur*, 1963; *Telephone Poles*, 1963; *Olinger Stories*, 1964; *The Ring*, 1964; *Assorted Prose*, 1965; *A Child's Calendar*, 1965; *Of the Farm*, 1965; *Verse*, 1965; *The Music School*, 1966; *Couples*, 1968; *Bottom's Dream*, 1969; *Midpoint*, 1969; *Bech: A Book*, 1970; *Rabbit Redux*, 1971; *Museums and Women*, 1972; *Buchanan Dying*, 1974; *A Month of Sundays*, 1975; *Picked-Up Pieces*, 1975; *Marry Me*, 1976; *Tossing and Turning*, 1977; *The Coup*, 1978; *Problems*, 1979; *Too Far to Go*, 1979; *Rabbit Is Rich*, 1980; *Bech Is Back*, 1982; *Hugging the Shore*, 1983; *The Witches of Eastwick*, 1984; *Facing Nature*, 1985; *Roger's Version*, 1986; *Trust Me*, 1987; *S.*, 1988; *Just Looking*, 1989; *Self-Consciousness*, 1989; *Rabbit at Rest*, 1990; *Odd Jobs*, 1991; *Memories of the Ford Administration*, 1992; *Collected Poems, 1953–1993*, 1993; *Brazil*, 1994; *The Afterlife and Other Stories*, 1994; *Rabbit Angstrom: The Four Novels*, 1995; *In the Beauty of the Lilies*, 1996; *Golf Dreams: Writings on Golf*, 1996; *A Helpful Alphabet of Friendly Objects*, 1996; *Toward the End of Time*, 1997; *Bech at Bay*, 1998; *More Matter*, 1999; *Gertrude and Claudius*, 2000; *Licks of Love*, 2000; *Americana and Other Poems*, 2001; *Seek My Face*, 2002; *Villages*, 2004; *Still Looking*, 2005; *Terrorist*, 2006; *Due Considerations*, 2007; *The Widows of Eastwick*, 2008; *Endpoint and Other Poems*, 2009; *My Father's Tears and Other Stories*, 2009; *Higher Gossip*, 2011.

Varieties of Religious Experience

There is no God: the revelation came to Dan Kellogg in the instant that he saw the World Trade Center South Tower fall. He lived in Cincinnati but happened to be in New York, visiting his daughter in Brooklyn Heights; her apartment had a penthouse view of lower Manhattan, less than a mile away. Standing on her terrace, he was still puzzling over the vast quantities of persistent oily smoke pouring from the Twin Towers, and the nature of the myriad pieces of what seemed white cardboard fluttering within the smoke's dark column, and who and what the perpetrators and purpose of this event might have been, when, as abruptly as a girl letting fall her silken gown, the entire skyscraper dropped its sheath and vanished, with a silvery rippling noise. The earth below, which Dan could not see, groaned and spewed up a cloud of ash and pulverized matter that slowly, from his distant perspective, mushroomed upward. The sirens filling the air across the East River continued to wail, with no change of pitch; the cluster of surrounding skyscrapers, stone and glass, held its pose of blank mute witness. Had Dan imagined hearing a choral shout, a cry of protest breaking against the silence of the sky—an operatic human noise at the base of a phenomenon so inhumanly pitiless? Or had he merely humanized the groan of concussion? He was aware of looking at a, for him, new scale of things—that of Blitzkrieg, of erupting volcanoes. The collapse had a sharp aftermath of silence; at least, he heard nothing more for some seconds.

Ten stories below his feet, too low to see what he saw, two black parking-garage attendants loitered outside the mouth of the garage, one standing and one seated on an aluminum chair, carrying on a joshing conversation that, for all the sound that rose to Dan, might have been under a roof of plate glass or in a silent movie. The attendants wore short-sleeved shirts, but summer's haze, this September morning, had been baked from the sky, to make way for the next season. The only cloud was manmade—the foul-colored, yellow-edged smoke drifting toward the east in a solid, continuously replenished mass. Dan could not quite believe the tower had vanished. How could something so vast and intricate, an elaborately engineered upright hive teeming with people, mostly young, be dissolved by its own weight so quickly, so casually? The laws of matter had functioned, was the answer. The event was small beneath the calm dome of sky. No hand of God had intervened because there was none. God had no hands, no eyes, no heart, no anything.

Thus was Dan, a sixty-four-year-old Episcopalian and probate lawyer, brought late to the realization that comes to children with the death of a pet, to women with the loss of a child, to millions caught in the implacable course of war and plague. His revelation of cosmic indifference thrilled him, though his own extinction was held within this new truth like one of the white rectangles weightlessly rising and spinning within the boiling column of smoke. He joined at last the run of mankind in its stoic atheism. He had fought this wisdom all his life, with prayer and evasion, with recourse to the piety of his Ohio ancestors and to ingenious and jaunty old books—Kierkegaard, Chesterton—read for comfort in adolescence and early manhood. But had he been one of the hundreds in that building—its smoothly telescoping collapse in itself a sight of some beauty, like the color-enhanced stellar blooms of photographed supernovae, only unfolding not in aeons but in seconds—would all that metal and concrete have weighed an ounce less or hesitated a microsecond in its crushing, mincing, vaporizing descent?

No. The great *No* came upon him not in darkness, as religious fable would have it, but on a day of maximum visibility; "brutally clear" was how airplane pilots, interviewed after the event, described conditions. Only when Dan's revelation had shuddered through him did he reflect, with a hot spurt of panic, that his daughter, Emily, worked in finance—in midtown, it was true, but business now and then took her to the World Trade Center, to breakfast meetings at the very top, the top from which there could not have been, today, any escape.

Stunned, emptied, he returned from his point of vantage on the penthouse terrace to the interior of Emily's apartment. The stolid Anguillan nanny, Lucille, and Dan's younger granddaughter, Victoria, who was five and sick with a cold and hence not at school, sat in the study. The small room, papered red, was lined with walnut shelves. The books went back to Emily's college and business-school days and included a number—Cold War thrillers, outdated medical texts—that had once belonged to her husband, from whom she was divorced, just as Dan Kellogg was divorced from her mother. Had Emily inherited the tendency to singleness, as she had inherited her father's lean build and clipped, half-smiling manner? Lucille had drawn the shade of the study window looking toward Manhattan. She reported to Dan, "I tell her to not look out the window but then the television only show the disaster, every channel we switch on."

"Bad men," little Victoria told him eagerly, her tongue stumbling—her cold made her enunciation even harder to understand than usual—"bad men going to knock down *all* the buildings!"

"That's an awful lot of buildings, Vicky," he said. When he talked to children, something severe and legalistic within him resisted imprecision.

"Why does God let bad men do things?" Victoria asked. The child's face looked feverish, not from her cold but from what she had seen through the window before the shade was drawn. Dan gave the answer he had learned when still a believer: "Because He wants to give men the choice to be good or bad."

Her face, so fine in detail and texture—brutally fine—considered this theology for a second. Then she burst forth, flinging her arms wide: "Bad men can do anything they want, anything at all!"

"Not always," Dan corrected. "Sometimes good men stop them. Most of the time, in fact."

In the shadowy room, they seemed three conspirators. Lucille was softly rocking herself on the sofa, and made a cooing noise now and then. "Think of all them still in there, all the people," she crooned, as if to herself. "I was telling Vicky how on Anguilla when I was a girl there was no electricity, and telephones only for the police, who rode bicycles wherever they went on the island. The only crime was workers coming back from three months away being vengeful with their wives for some mischief. The tallest building two stories high, and when there was no moon people stay safe in their cabins." Then, in a less dreamy voice, one meant to broadcast reassurance to the listening child, she told Dan, "Her momma, she called five minutes ago and work is over for today, she coming home but don't know how, the trains being all shut down. She might have to be walking all that way from Rockefeller Center!"

Dan himself, before returning to Cincinnati today, had been planning to take the subway up to the Whitney Museum and see the Wayne Thiebaud show, which was in its last days. Dan relished the Disney touch in the artist's candy colors and his bouncy, plump draughtsmanship. Abruptly, viewing this show was impossible—part of an idyllic, less barricaded past.

"So we'll all just wait for Mommy," he announced, trying to be, until Emily arrived, the leader of this defenseless, isolated trio. "I know!" he exclaimed. "Let's make Doughboy cookies for Mommy when she comes home! She'll be hungry!" And he leaned over and poked Vicky in the tummy, as if she were the Doughboy in the television commercials.

But she didn't laugh or even smile. Her eyes beneath her bangs and serious straight brows were feverishly bright. She was burning to know what new and forbidden thing was happening on the other side of the window shade. And so was Lucille, but she denied herself turning on television, and Dan denied himself another visit to the terrace, to verify his desolating cosmic intuition.

* * *

Emily was home in an hour, safe and aghast and sweating with the unaccustomed exercise of marching down the East Side and across the Manhattan Bridge in a mob of others fleeing the island. Dan's daughter at thirty-seven was slim and hard and professional, a trim soldier-woman a far cry from her indolent, fleshy mother. She turned on the little kitchen TV right away and was not pleased by the smell of fresh-baked cookies. "We're trying to train Victoria away from sweets," she told her father, and when he explained how he and Lucille had sought to distract the child, commanded, "Let her watch a little. This is history. This is huge. There's no hiding it." In the Heights, she told them, auto traffic had ceased, and men with briefcases, their dark suits dusted with ash, were stalking up the middle of Henry Street. She hid the warm cookies on an out-of-reach shelf; she sent Lucille off to pick up Victoria's older sister, Hilary, at her day school; she gave a supermarket shopping list to her father while she went to the bank to withdraw plenty of cash, just in case society broke down totally. Vicky went with her.

Dan found early lunch hour in progress on Montague Street. Voices twanged over the outdoor tables much as usual, though self-consciously, somehow, as if unseen television cameras were grinding away. The street scene seemed enacted; even the boys loafing outside of the supermarket appeared to be conscious of a new weight of attention bearing upon them— the importance, in the thickened air, of survivors. The air smelled caustic and snowed flurrying motes of ash. Sensory impressions hit Dan harder than usual, because God had been wiped from his brain. In his previous life, commonsense atheism had not been ingenious enough for him, nor had it seemed sufficiently gracious toward the universe. Now he had been shown how little the universe cared for his good will.

He entered the supermarket and pushed his cart along. The place was not crowded with panic shoppers, but rather empty instead, and darker than usual, sickly and crepuscular, like one of those pre-Christian afterlives, Hades or Sheol. A few people moved through the aisles, past the bins of bagels and shelves of high-priced gourmet snacks, as if for the first time, haltingly; they scanned one another's faces for a recognition that was almost there, a greeting on the tips of their tongues. Incredulity edged toward acceptance. They were coping, they were not panicking, they were demonstrating calm to the enemy.

Dan returned to the apartment laden with plastic bags, two on each hand; the handles, stretched thin by the weight of oranges and milk and cranberry juice, had dug into his palms. Emily had come back with plenty of cash and several plans. Already, signs advertising communal events were going up on lampposts: there were blood donations up at the Marriott, near Borough Hall, and a special service at Grace Church at six. In the subdued camaraderie of the crowd at the Marriott, the father and daughter filled out laborious forms side by side and were told, by bullhorn, to go home, the blood bank was overflowing: "There is no more need for the present, but if any develops we have your names." The fact had dawned that there were almost no mere injuries; the bodies were all minced in the two vast build-ings' wreckage.

At the church, where he and the four females he escorted found room in a back pew, Dan marvelled at the human animal: like dogs, we creep back to lick the hand of a God Who, if He exists, has just given us a vicious kick. The harder He kicks, the more fervently we cringe and creep forward to lick His hand. The great old church, a relic of post-Civil War ecclesiastical prosperity, was for this special occasion full, and the minister, a stocky young woman wearing a bell of glossy, short-cut hair, announced in a clarion voice that at the moment several members of this congregation were still among the miss-ing. She read their names. "Let us pray for their safety, and for the souls of all who perished today, and for the fate of this great nation." With a rustle that rose into the murk of the stony vaults above them, all bowed their heads.

Dan felt detached, like a visiting Martian. His sense of alienation per-sisted in the weeks that followed, as flags sprang from every Ohio porch bracket and *God Bless America* was written in shaving cream on every shop window. Back in Cincinnati, having returned, two days later than planned, by bus, he looked across a river not to smoking towers but to Kentucky, where each pickup truck sprouted a soon-tattered banner of national pride and defiance. Heartland religiosity, though its fundamentalism and bombas-tic puritanism had often made him wince, was something Dan had been comfortable with; now it seemed barbaric. On television, the President clumsily grasped the rhetoric of war, then got used to it, then got good at it. The nightly news showed how, in New York City, impromptu shrines had sprung up on sidewalks and outside of fire stations across the city. Candles guttered under color Xeroxes of the forever missing, memorial flowers wilted in their paper cones and plastic sheaths. Dan found himself aggrieved by the grotesque and pitiable sight of a great modern nation attempting to heal itself through this tired old magic of flags and candles—the human spi-rit stubbornly spilling its colorful vain gestures into the void.

Some days before Dan's revelation, a stocky thirty-three-year-old Muslim called, like millions of his co-religionists around the world, Mohamed, briefly hesitated before ordering a fourth Scotch-on-the-rocks in a dark unholy place, a one-story roadside strip joint on an unfashionable stretch of Florida's east coast. His companion, a younger, thinner man named Zaeed, lifted his slender hand from the table as if to protest, then let it weightlessly fall back. Their training regimen had inculcated the importance of blending in, and getting drunk was a sure method of merging with America, this unclean society disfigured by an appalling laxity of laws and an electronic delirium of supposed opportunities and pleasures. The very air, icily air-conditioned, tasted of falsity. The whiskey burned in Mohamed's throat like a fire against which he must repeatedly test his courage, his resolve. *It is God's kindled fire, which shall mount above the hearts of the damned.*

On the shallow stage, ignored by most of the customers scattered at small tables and only now and then brushed by his own glance, a young woman, naked save for strategic patches of tinsel and a dusting of artificial glitter on her face, writhed around a brass pole to an irritating mutter of tuneless music. She was as lean as a starveling boy but for the protuberances of fat that distinguish women; these, Mohamed knew, had been swollen by injection to seem tautly round and perfectly doll-like. The whore was entwining herself upside down around her pole, and scissoring open her legs so that a tinsel thong battered back at the light. Her long hair hung in a heavy platinum sheet to the stage floor, which was imbued with filth by her sisters' feet. There were three dancers: a Negress who performed barefoot, flashing soles and palms the color of silver polish; a henna-haired slut who wore glass high heels and kept fluttering her tongue between her lips and even mimed licking the brass pole; and this blonde, who danced least persuasively, with motions mechanically repeated while her eyes, their doll-like blue outlined in thick black as in an Egyptian wall-painting, stared into the darkness without making eye contact.

She did not see him, nor did Mohamed in his soul see her. Zaeed—with whom Mohamed was rehearsing once again the details of their enterprise, its many finely interlocked and synchronized parts, down to the last-minute cell-phone calls that would give the final go-ahead—had been drinking sweet drinks called Daiquiris. Suddenly he excused himself and hurried to the bathroom. Zaeed was young and resident in this land of infidels less than two months; its liquor was still poison to him, and its licentious women were fascinating. He had not grown Mohamed's impervious shell, and his English was exceedingly poor. The whore's globular breasts hung down parallel to her lowered sheet of hair while her shaved or plucked crotch twinkled and flashed.

Through half-shut eyes and the shifting transparencies of whiskey, Mohamed could see a semblance to the ignorant fellahin's conception of Paradise, where sloe-eyed virgins wait, on silken couches, among flowing rivers, to serve the martyrs delicious fruit. But they are manifestations, these houris, of the highest level of purity, white in their flesh and gracious in their submission. They are radiant negatives of these underfed sluts who for paltry dollars mechanically writhed on this filthy stage.

Another slut, the middle-aged waitress, wrinkled and thickened—a pot of curdled lewdness, of soured American opportunities—was waving a slip of paper at him. "Going off-duty . . . finish up my tables . . . forty-eight dollars." Her twanging "cracker" accent was difficult to penetrate, and from her agitation he gathered that this was not the first time this evening that he had offended her.

He did not see why he should hurry to pay. Zaeed was still in the bathroom, and the sandwiches they had ordered were still on the table, uneaten. That was it: she had offered some time ago—an hour? ten minutes?—to clear the table and he told her he was not done, though in truth the food disgusted him. It was, like everything in this devilish country, excessive and wasteful—an open hot roast-beef sandwich, not rare but gray, now cold and limp on its bread, dead meat scattered beneath his hands, as far beneath them as if under the wings of an airplane. The disgusting sandwich had been served with French fries and coleslaw, garbage not fit for a street dog. Yet he kept thinking he would turn to it, to muffle the burning of the whiskey while he spoke to Zaeed, hardening the younger man's shell for the great deed that had been laid out like a precision drawing in a German engineering class. Mohamed had studied engineering among the unbelievers, absorbing the mathematics they had stolen centuries ago from the Arabs.

He must eat. The day, the fateful morning, of culmination was approaching, and he must be strong, his hands and nerves steady, his will relentless, his body vital and pure, shaven of its hair. The greatness of the deed that was held within him pressed upward like a species of nausea, straining his throat with a desire to cry out—to proclaim, as had done his prophetic namesake the Messenger, the magnificence, beyond all virtues and qualities imaginable on earth, of God and His fiery justice. *For the unbelievers We have prepared fetters and chains, and a blazing Fire. Flames of fire shall be lashed at you, and melted brass.*

The blonde whore flicked away the sparkling thong and with spread legs waddled about the pole showing her shaved slit, an awkward, ugly maneuver that won scattered cheers from the jaded tables in the darkness. Zaeed returned, looking paler. He had been sick, he confessed. Mohamed abruptly felt a great love for his brother in conspiracy, the younger brother he had never had. Mohamed had been raised in a flowery Cairo suburb with a pair of sisters; it was to keep them from ending as sluts that he had dedicated himself to the holy jihad. They were too light-headed to know that the temptations twittering at them from television and radio were from Satan, designed to lure them into eternal flame. Their parents, in their European clothes, their third-rate prosperity measured out in imitation-Western goods, were blind to the evil they wrought upon their children. Hoarding their comforts in their heavily curtained, servant-run house in Giza, they were like eyeless cave creatures, blind to the grandeur of the One Who will wrathfully reduce this flimsy world and its distractions to a desert. Mohamed carried that sublime desert, its night sky clamorous with stars, within him. *When the sky is rent asunder; when the stars are scattered and the oceans roll together; when the graves tumble in ruin; each soul shall know what it has done and what it has failed to do.*

The waitress had returned accompanied by a man, a hireling, the bald bartender in a yellow T-shirt advertising something in three-dimensional speeding letters, a beer or perhaps a sports team, Mohamed could not quite bring it into focus. Zaeed looked worried; he exuded the sickly sweat of fear, and his movements betrayed a desire to leave this unholy place. Mohamed quenched the boy's alarm with a touch on his forearm and stood to confront the hireling in the speeding T-shirt. Standing so quickly dizzied him but did not weaken his wits or dull his awareness of the movements around him. A fresh female on the stage, the *abdah* with bare feet again, dressed in filmy scarves that would soon come off, altered the light of the place, diluting its darkness as the spotlight played upon her. Pale faces, natives of this forsaken coast, turned to witness Mohamed's quarrel with the hirelings. Within him his great secret felt an eggshell's thickness from bursting forth. More than once, small mishaps and moments of friction—a traffic ticket, an INS summons, a hasty slip of the tongue with an inquisitive neighbor seeking, in that doglike American way, to be friendly—had threatened to expose the whole elaborate, thoroughly meditated structure; but the All-Merciful had extended His protecting hand. The Great Satan had been rendered stupid and sluggish; its sugary diet of freedom had softened its mechanically straightened teeth.

Mohamed felt himself mighty in his power to restrain his tongue, that muscle which summons armies and moves mountains. He produced his wallet and opened it to display the thickness of twenties and fifties and even hundreds, depicting in dry green engraving the dead heroes of this Jew-dominated government. "Plenty to pay your fucking bill," he told the threatening man in the yellow T-shirt. "And look, my good man, look here—" Not content with the cash as a demonstration of his potency, Mohamed showed, too swiftly for a close examination, the card registering him in flying school and another, forged in Germany, stating him to be a licensed pilot. "I am a pilot."

Impressed and mollified, his antagonist asked, in the languid accents of a tongue long steeped in drugs, "Hey, cool. What airline?"

Mohamed said, "American." It was an inspired utterance that, in the utterance, became blazingly true, as the suras of his namesake, the Prophet, became true when they blazed from the Messenger's mouth, promising salvation for believers and for the others the luminous boiling Fire. He had been not some ridiculous crucified God but the perfect person, *insan-i-kamil*. Mohamed's assertion sounded so just, so prophetic, he repeated it, challenging his bald, drugged enemy to contradict him: "American Airlines."

From where Jim Finch sat in his cubicle, about a third of the way into the vast floor—a full acre—populated by bond traders and their computer monitors, the building's windows held a view of mostly sky, cloudless today. If he stood up, he could see New Jersey's low shore beyond the Statue of Liberty. From this height, even the Statue, which was facing the other way, looked small, like the souvenir statuettes for sale in every Wall Street tourist trap. Jim lived in Jersey—three children and four bedrooms on an eighth of an acre in Irvington—and from where he lived he could see, picking his spots between the asphalt rooftops and leafy trees, where he worked. To impress the kids he tried to locate his exact floor, counting down from the top, though in truth it was hard from that distance to be certain; the skyscraper was built of vertical ribs that ran individual floors and windows together. Steel tubes, like a row of drinking straws, held it up, and that made the windows narrower than you felt they should be, so the view from his cubicle was more up and down than sideways. Today the windows were a row of smooth blue panels, except that curling gusts of smoke and flickering pieces of paper strangely invaded the blue from below. Some minutes ago, deep underneath him, while he had been talking to a client on the phone, there had been a thump, distant like a truck hatch being slammed down on West Street, and yet communicating a shudder to his desk.

His cell phone rang. Jim's motion of snatching it off his belt was habitual and instant, like a snake's strike. But instead of business it was Marcy, back in New Jersey. "Jim, honey," she said, "don't hate me, I forgot to say, you went out the door so fast, when you pick up the cleaning on the way home could you swing by the Pathmark and pick up a half-gallon of whole milk and maybe check out their cantaloupes."

"O.K., sure."

"The ones last week went straight from green to punky, but they said there'd be better ones in on Monday. There should be a little give to the skins but your thumb shouldn't leave a dent." He watched a piece of charred insulation foam rise into view and then float away. "For the milk there's plenty of skimmed for ourselves but Frankie and Kristen, the way they're growing, they just wolf the whole kind down; she's as bad as he is. Honest, I meant to pick some up but the cart was already so full. *Sorry*, hon."

"Hey, Marcy—"

"Any dessert you'd like for yourself, buy it. And maybe—be sure to check the sell-by date—a half-dozen eggs, the *large* size, not the *extra*-large. But don't forget Annie has that event at the church hall tonight, six-thirty, the beginning of indoor soccer, she's *very* nervous and wants us both there."

"Honey—"

"The new young assistant minister scares her. She says he's uptight—he wants too much to win."

"Hey, Marcy, could you please for Chrissake shut up?"

There was a hurt silence, then her voice tiptoed back. "What is it, Jim? You sound strange."

"Something strange happened a couple minutes ago, I don't know what. There was this thump underneath us; I thought it was on the street. But everything shook, and now there's smoke you can see out the windows. Hold on." Cy Walsh, the man in the cubicle across from his, was signalling for his attention, and tersely told him some things that Jim relayed to Marcy. "The interior phone lines seem to be all out. People have come back saying the elevators aren't working and the stairs are full of smoke."

"Oh my God, Jim."

"Nobody's panicking, I mean almost nobody. I'm sure it'll work out. I mean, how bad can it be?"

"Oh my God."

"Honey, stop saying that. It doesn't help. They'll figure it out. I can't keep talking, they got to start moving us somewhere. Hey. Marcy. You won't believe this, but the floor's warm. Actually fucking *warm*."

"Oh, Jimmy, *do* something! Hang up whenever you have to. I've always hated those flimsy-looking buildings, and you being up so high."

"Listen, Marcy. What phone are you on? The upstairs portable?"

"Yes." Her voice trembled, putting extra syllables into the word, *ye-ess*, like a child scared she has done wrong and will be punished. Across the miles between them they shared the sensation of being scolded children—a rubbed, watery feeling in their abdomens.

He asked her, "Go into Annie's room and look out the window. Tell me what you see."

While he waited, there was human movement among the desks, herd movement with bumps and shouts, but he didn't feel it had a direction he should join. A rising smell, a tarry industrial smell, oily and sickening-sweet, reminded him of airport runways and the vibrations you see around the engines while waiting to take off.

"Jim?"

"Still here. What can you see from Annie's window?"

"Oh God, I can see *smoke*! From sort of near the top; it's the tower on the left, the one you work in. Jim, I'm scared. There's a kind of black ink running down between the grooves. What can it be? Remember that missile that maybe brought down that plane off Long Island?"

"Honey, don't be dumb. Some kind of malfunction, it must be, within the building. There's enough wiring in the walls to fry China if there's a short. Don't worry, they'll figure it out. They have guys paid a fortune to sit around and plan how to handle contingencies. Still, I must say—"

"What, Jimmy? What must you say?"

"I was starting to say it's getting hard to breathe in here. Somebody just smashed a window. Jesus. They're chucking chairs right through the windows. Hey, Marcy?"

"Yes? *Yes*?"

"I don't know, but maybe this isn't so good."

"The smoke is coming from a floor somewhere under yours," she offered hopefully, shakily "I can't count how many."

"Don't try." Her voice was a connection to the world but it was entangling him, holding him back. "Listen. In case I don't make it. I love you."

"Oh my God! Don't say it! Just be normal!"

"I can't be normal. This isn't normal."

"Can't you get up to a higher floor and wait on the roof?"

"I think people are trying it. Can you tell the kids how much I love them?"

"Ye-ess." Breathlessly. She wasn't arguing, it wasn't like her; her giving up like this frightened him. It made him realize how serious this was, how unthinkably serious.

He tried to think practically. "All the stuff you need should be in the filing cabinet beside my desk, the middle drawer. Lenny Palotta can help you, he has the mutual-fund data, and the insurance policies."

"God, *don't*, darling. Don't think that way. Just get out, can't you?"

"Sure, probably." People were moving toward the windows, it was the coolest place, the place to breathe, at the height of an airplane tucking its wheels back with that little concussion and snap that worries inexperienced passengers. "But, just in case, you do whatever you want."

"What do you mean, Jim, do whatever I want? You're not making sense."

"Shit, Marcy. I mean, you know, live your life. Do what looks best for yourself and the kids. Don't let anything cramp your style. Tell Annie in case I miss it that I wanted to be there tonight." Of all things, this made him want to cry, the image of his plump little solemn daughter in soccer shorts, scared and pink in the face. The smoke was blinding him, assaulting his eyes.

"Cramp my style?"

"My blessing, for Chrissake, Marcy. I'm giving a blessing on anything you decide to do. It's all right. Feel free."

"Oh, Jim, no. *No*. How can this be *happening*?"

He couldn't talk more; the smoke, the heat, the jet-fuel stink were chasing him to the windows, where silhouettes were climbing up into the blue panels, to get some air. Cy Walsh was already there, in the crowd. Jim Finch replaced the phone on his belt deftly; he instinctively grabbed his suit coat and sprinted, crouching, across the hot floor to his co-workers clustered at the windows. They were family, they had been his nine-to-five family for years. They were problem-solvers and would show him what to do. Like an airplane seizing altitude in its wings, he left gravity behind. Connections were breaking, obligations falling away. He felt for these seconds as light as a newborn.

The nice young man beside her told her he was in sales management, on his way to a telecom convention in San Francisco, but he played rugby on weekends in Van Cortlandt Park, in the Bronx. It surprised Carolyn that there were any rugby games in the United States. Ages ago in her long life, after the war, she had spent a year in England and been taken to a rugby game, in Cambridge, and remembered heavy-thighed men in shorts and striped shirts struggling in the mud, under the low, damp, chilly clouds, pushing at each other—there was a word they had used she couldn't remember—and for spurts carrying the slippery oval ball in a two-handed, sashaying way that looked comically girlish to a woman accustomed to the military precision and frontal collisions of American football. To those same eyes it seemed curious that they played nearly naked, in short shorts, and yet no one, at least that day, got hurt.

The introductory courtesies came early in the flight, out of Newark. The plane had sat stalled on the runway for half an hour but then had pushed into the air and climbed and banked so that the huge wing with its skinny little aerial on the tip threatened, it seemed to her elderly sense of balance, to spill them back onto the sun-streaked flat Earth of streets and housetops and highways below. It was a remarkably clear day. Carolyn had flown a great deal in her life, more than she had ever expected to as a child, when flying was something heroes did, test pilots and Lindbergh, and the whole family would rush out into the yard to see a blimp float overhead. Her first flights had been to college, in Ohio, into the old Cleveland-Hopkins Airport, in bumpy two-engine prop planes, early Douglas all-metals. Daddy, a great man for progress, flew the family for a week's spring vacation to Bermuda from New York on a British Air four-engine flying boat, and then put her on a Pan Am Boeing Clipper to London for her post-graduate year abroad: there had been a fuelling stop in Greenland, and actual beds where you could stretch out, and meals, with real silver, that people were too nauseated and anxious to eat. After marriage to Robert, she flew to the Caribbean and Arizona and Paris on vacations, and on some of his lecture trips as he became distinguished, and on three-day visits to her children when they married and scattered to places like Minneapolis and Dallas, and on matriarchal viewings of new grandchildren—to all the ceremonies that her descendants generated as they grew and aged. After Robert died, she had given herself an around-the-world tour, a widow's self-indulgence in her grief that no one could begrudge her, though her children, with their inheritance in mind, did raise their eyebrows. They couldn't understand the need, after sharing a life with a person for all these years, to get away from everything familiar.

All in all she couldn't begin to count how many hundreds of thousands of miles she had flown, but she had never really liked it—the plane's panicky run into lift-off, like some cartoon animal churning its legs and gritting its teeth, and the abrupt sudden banking, tilting and leaning on invisible air, and the changes in the sound of the engines nobody in the cockpit explained, and the sudden mysterious sharp jiggling over the ocean, your coffee swinging wildly in your cup, your heart in your throat. The planes had gotten bigger and smoother, to be sure. Some of those early flights, looking back, were little better than the rides in amusement parks designed to be terrifying—those little silver turboprops that bounced over the Appalachians with the tiny rivers below catching the sun, the stubby island-hoppers out of San Juan where you walked up the steep aisle and the lovely black stewardesses gave you candy to suck for pressure in your ears. People used to dress up as if for a formal tea, even—could it be?—with hats and white gloves. Now these big broad jets were like buses, people wore any old disgusting thing and never looked up from their laptops and acted personally injured if they didn't land on time to the minute, as if they were riding solid iron railroad tracks in the sky.

The nice young man, once the pilot's drawl had given permission to move about and use electrical devices, had asked her if she would mind, since there were so many empty seats, if he moved to another and gave them both more room. She thought his asking was dear, it showed a good old-fashioned upbringing. She watched him set up a little office for himself in two seats across the aisle, and then she studied the terrain five miles below, familiar to her from those first nervous, bouncy flights of hers, to Ohio so many years and miles ago. She recognized the Delaware, and then the Susquehanna, and while waiting for the stewardess with her rattling breakfast cart to reach the mid-section of the plane Carolyn must have dozed, because she awoke as if rudely shaken; the airplane was jiggling and bucking. She looked at her watch: 9:28. Hours to go.

She seemed to hear, far in the front, some shouting over the roar of the engines, and the plane dropped so that her stomach lurched. Yet the faces around her showed no alarm, and the heads she could see above the seatbacks were still. The plane stopped falling, and a voice came on the sound system that said, as best as she could understand, to remain seated. The pilot's voice sounded changed—tense and foreign. Where did the drawl go? He said, as best as Carolyn could hear, "Ladies and gentlemen: Here the captain. Please sit down, keep remaining sitting. We have bomb on board. So—sit."

Then a young man was standing in front of the first-class curtain. He was slender, and touchingly graceful and hesitant in the way he used his hands; he appeared to have no weapon, yet had gained everyone's attention, and the clumsy change in the way the plane was being handled connected somehow to him. He had an aura of nervous excitement; his eyes showed too much white. His eyes were all that showed; a large red bandana—a thick checked cloth, almost a scarf—concealed the lower half of his face and muffled his voice. Then another young man, plumper, came out from behind the curtains wearing another bandana and a comic apparatus around his chest; he held high one hand with a wire leading to it. He shook this hand and cried the word "Bomb! Bomb!" and then some other words in his own musical language, not trusting any other. People screamed. "Back! Back!" the thinner boy shouted, gesturing for everybody to move to the back of the plane.

Carolyn realized that these boys knew hardly any English, so the men in front trying to argue and question them were wasting their breath. Some of the men were standing; they had been made to leave first class. Then all of them began obediently to move back down the aisle, hunched over, Carolyn thought, like animals being whipped. The strawberry blonde seated two rows in front of her—the top of her head like spun sugar, tipped toward that of the boy next to her, her husband possibly, though couples weren't necessarily married now, her own grandchildren demonstrated that— reached out in passing and touched Carolyn on the shoulder. "You don't have to move," she said softly. She was already far enough back, she meant.

"Thank you, my dear," Carolyn responded, sounding old and foolish in her own ears.

They—the passengers, with three female flight attendants, though there had been four—settled around her, in stricken, fearful silence at first. But when the boy with the bomb and the boy without one didn't move back with them, staying instead in front of the first-class curtain, as if themselves paralyzed by fright, the noise of conversation among the passengers rose, like that at a cocktail party as the alcohol took hold, or in a rainy-day classroom when discipline washes away. Here and there people were talking into their cell phones, including the rugby player across the aisle, who had disbanded his little office on the lunch trays. His hand as it held the little gadget to his ear looked massive, with its red knuckles and broad wedding ring. His shirt had French cuffs with square gold links; French cuffs meant something, her son-in-law had tried to explain to her, in terms of corporate hierarchy. You could only wear them after a certain position in the firm had been attained.

The engines spasmodically wheezed, and a sudden tilt brought Carolyn's heart up into her throat; the plane was turning. The great wing next to her window leaned far over above the gray-green earth. The land below looked like Ohio now, flatter than the Alleghenies, and there was a smoky city that could be Akron or Youngstown. A wide piece of water, Lake Erie it must be, shone in the distance, betraying Earth's curvature. The sun had shifted to her side of the plane, coming in at an angle that bothered her eyes. A cataract operation two years ago had restored childhood's bright colors and sharp edges but left Carolyn's corneas sensitive to sunlight. The plane must be heading southeast, back to Pennsylvania. She tried to think it through, to picture the plane's exact direction, yet was unable to think. Her own fatigue dawned on her. The flight had been scheduled to leave at eight, and that had meant setting the alarm in Princeton at five. The older she became the earlier she awoke but still it was strange to go out into the dark and start the car.

Her skin had broken out into sweat. Her body was terrified before her mind had caught up. What was foremost in her mind was the simple wish, fervent enough to be a prayer, that the plane be taken, like an easily damaged toy, out of those invisible hands that were giving it such a jerky, panicky, incompetent ride.

Carolyn wondered why the boys up front, hijackers evidently, were letting so many passengers talk on their telephones; perhaps they thought it was a way to keep them calm. The one without the bomb came down the aisle a little way, then retreated; in warning he held up something metallic, a small knife of some sort, the kind with a cruel curved point that slides open to cut boxes, but what showed of his face, the eyes, seemed either frightened or furious, pools of ardent dark gelatin hard to decipher without the rest of the face. His mind seemed elsewhere, somewhere beyond, all that eye-white showing. He wore black jeans and a long-sleeved red-checked shirt that could have been that of a young computer whiz on his way to Silicon Valley. She had two grandsons in dot-coms; they dressed like farmhands, like hippies decades ago, when young people decided that they loved the earth when what they loved most was annoying their parents. But this boy had no pencils or pens in his shirt pocket, the way her grandsons did. He had that baby knife and eyebrows that nearly met in the middle, above his distracted, glittering gaze. Why wouldn't he look anybody in the face? He was *shy*. He must be a very nice boy, at home, among people he could speak to intelligibly, in his own language, without cloth across his mouth.

How humiliating, this sweating she was doing into her underwear. She would smell when she got off the plane, under the wool dress she had put on thinking it was always cool in Tiburon, where her daughter lived, however hot it was in Princeton. The redwoods, the Bay breezes: she realized she might not reach them today. They would land at some obscure airport and a long standoff of negotiations would begin. When they began to release hostages, however, an old lady would be among the first.

The captain came on the loudspeaker again: "There is bomb on board and we go back to the airport, and to have our demands—" She lost the next words in his guttural accent. "Remain quiet, please," the pilot concluded. Her watch said 9:40. Despite the captain's request, eddies of communication moved through the crowded back of the plane: hand signals, eye motions, conversations increasingly blatant and emphatic as the nervous young hijacker's obliviousness dawned on everyone. The stewardesses began to talk as if still in charge. People in first class had glimpsed something in the cabin; word of whatever it was spread back, skipping around Carolyn inaudibly yet chilling her damp skin. Others were learning things through their cell phones that they urgently had to share. The young businessmen in their white shirts held conferences, talking to each other across the heads and laps of women and the elderly. Growing impatient, some of them stood, making a huddle, right near her, around the seat of that nice rugby player. Not a huddle, a *scrum*—that was the word they had used in England.

She tried to eavesdrop, and heard nothing but passionate muttering, rising to the near-shout of men energized by a decision. The distinct word "Yes" was repeated in several men's voices. They had voted. The plumper of the two hijackers, having lowered his bandana to his throat so a pathetic small mustache showed, moved down the aisle, gesturing for people to be silent and sit down, while the apparatus he had strapped himself into looked more and more absurd and rickety. The plane was still rocking in those unseen hands, jerking and tilting, but the rugby player stood up with the others—he was taller than she had realized, in scale with that huge wrist jutting from his French cuff—and they faced forward. She accidentally caught his eye; he smiled and gave her a thumbs-up. She heard a voice, another young man's, say, "You guys ready? Let's *do* it."

Some seats behind her, a woman began to sob. Carolyn guessed it was the young woman who had touched her arm some minutes ago, but her instinct was to tell her to shut up, the plane was bouncing so, she just wanted to adhere to her seat and close her eyes and beg for the motion, the demented speed, to stop. The roaring engines made the hubbub within the plane hard to sort out. The plump young man with the bomb disappeared behind the broad shoulders and white shirts of the stampeding American men. The other one, with his little hooked knife, also sank under the scrum, his silly towel of a veil torn away to reveal a red-lipped mouth open in protest. First fists and then feet in shoes silenced his ugly yells. *Crush him*, Carolyn thought. *Kill him.*

The white shirts pushed through the blue first-class curtain. The engines did not drown out the thumping, crashing sounds from behind the curtain, the unexpected clatter of the serving cart, and a male voice shouting "Roll it!" while a fearful gabble from the passengers still in their seats arose around her.

The airplane lurched more violently than ever before, rocking and dipping as if to shake something loose, and Carolyn felt, as sharply as if the wires and levers controlling the great mechanism were her own sinews and bones, that control had been lost, something crucial had been severed. From the wing came a high grinding noise; through her porthole she saw the flaps strain erect, exposing their valves. The vast tapering wing, with its stencilled aluminum segments and its little aerial at the very tip, seemed to stand on end; the entire stiff intricate entity bearing her and all these others was heeling beyond any angle of possible recovery. The terrible largeness of everything, the plane and the planet and the transparent miles between them, amazed her much as the shocking unclouded colors of the world had amazed her after her cataract operation. Her body was hanging sideways in the seat belt, so heavily her ribs ached. Through the scratched plastic window the earth in its rural detail—a few houses and outbuildings, a green blob of woods, a fenced field, a lonely road—swung across her vision while her ears popped, and she realized that, nightmarish though it was, this was real, the reality beneath everything, this surge into the maw of gravity. Her brain was flung into wordlessness; she was upside down, and the tortured engine near her ears was making everything shake. She was meeting the truth that her parents and husband and all the protectors of her long protected life had implied: the path of safety is narrow, it is possible to fall from it. *Mercy*, Carolyn managed to cry distinctly inside her pounding head. *Dear, Lord, have mercy.*

Dan stood outside his daughter's apartment, on the sooty tiled terrace from which he had seen the first tower collapse. In the six months since then, news events had tended to corroborate his revelation. A demented woman in Texas was being tried for systematically drowning her five children. Catholic priests were revealed to have molested their immature charges in numbers larger than ever imagined or confessed. Almost every week, somewhere in the United States, angry or despairing or berserk fathers murdered their wives or ex-wives and their children and then, in inadequate atonement, killed themselves. Meanwhile, in Afghanistan, war had been proclaimed and pursued, with its usual toll of inane deaths—colliding helicopters, stray bombs, false intelligence, fatal muddle unmitigated by any Biblical dignity of vengeance or self-sacrifice. The masterminds of evil remained at large; the surrendered enemies appeared exhausted and confused—pathetic small fry. They complained about the climate of Cuba and their captors' failure to provide them with sympathetic mullahs. They claimed, and others stridently claimed for them, their international legal rights. Religious slaughters occurred in India and Israel, fires and floods and plagues elsewhere. The world tumbled on, spewing out death and sparks of pain like an engine off the tracks.

His younger granddaughter, his fellow witness to the most publicized of recent disasters, solemnly informed Dan that all the dogs of New York City had bleeding paws, from looking through wreckage for dead people.

Emily, the tough-minded survivor of divorce, had not prevented the child from gathering what she could from the newspapers and television: "It's turned her into a real news hawk," she dryly explained. "Hilary, on the other hand," she went on, "has refused from Day One to have anything to do with it. It wasn't ladylike, she decided, and disdained it all. She says such things aren't appropriate for children. She can actually pronounce 'appropriate.' But for Vicky, it would have been unhealthy, really, Daddy, to try to shelter her from what everybody knew, what all her schoolmates would be talking about. After all, compared to children in Bosnia and Afghanistan she's still pretty well off."

"Not *all* the dogs, Victoria," Dan reassured his granddaughter, "just a few trained for a certain special job, and wearing little leather booties that nice people made for them. Most people are very nice," he promised her.

The child stared up at him pugnaciously, a bit doubtful but wanting to agree. In six months, she had grown; her eyes, a translucent pale blue beneath level bangs, entertained more subtle expressions. At moments, especially when she was thinking to herself, he could see, in the childishly fine perfection of her face, the seeds of feminine mystery and of her mature beauty.

Lucille, within earshot, said, so the child would overhear, "Vicky, she so interested in *all* the developments. She know how that terrible mess almost cleaned up now, and the two blue floodlights there as a monument, we see them every night."

Victoria explained to her grandfather, "They mean all the people in there have gone up to Heaven."

By daylight, from the terrace, the Twin Towers of the World Trade Center were simply not there. Their stark form, like that of two cubes projected skyward by some computer command, had registered but delicately above the old-fashioned brick thicket of lower Manhattan. Rectangular clouds of glass and aluminum, they had been wiped from the city's silhouette. They were not there, but Dan was here, and God with him; his conversion to atheism had not lasted. His church pledge needed to be delivered in its weekly envelopes; a minor committee (Property Maintenance and Improvement) of which he was a member continued to meet. The Episcopal church, high in Cincinnati but not evangelical, presented a stream of Cranmer's words in which the mind could lose itself. Dan would have missed the mild-mannered fellowship—the handshakes under the vaulted ceiling, the awkward passing of the peace. Why punish with his non-attendance, in protest of something God and not they had done, a flock of potential probate clients for whom periodically chorusing the Nicene Creed was part, and not the very least part, of getting along, of doing their best, of being decent citizens? He would miss the Sunday-morning congregation, the smell of waxed pews and musty kneeling cushions, the radiators that knocked on winter Sunday mornings after a week of cool disuse, the taste of the tasteless wafer in his mouth.

While he stood there ten stories above the Brooklyn alley (where the two attendants, in the mild March air, again sat joshing at the entrance to their parking garage), the towers' distant absence seemed a light throwing a shadow behind him, a weak shadow, but inextricable from his presence— the price, it could be said, of his being alive. He was alive, and a shadowy

God with him, behind him. Human consciousness had curious properties. However big things were, it could encompass them, as if it were even bigger. And it kept insisting on making a narrative of Dan's life, however nonsensically truncated the lives of others—crushed in an instant, or snapped off on the birthing-bed—had been.

Emily and Victoria, his progeny, his tickets to genetic perpetuation, ventured out gingerly onto the terrace, to be with him in the open air. "Amazing," his daughter said, seeking to read his thoughts, "how the not-thereness remains so haunting. Sometimes you still see the towers in old ads, where the admen haven't noticed or taken the trouble to airbrush them out of the background. It feels illicit. A lot of these yuppie movies and TV serials have a shot of them, from SoHo or the Staten Island Ferry or wherever, and I hear they've been collected on tape, like the kisses in *Cinema Paradiso*. They've become a kind of cult."

Victoria eagerly volunteered, "Some day, when all the bad men are killed, they'll put them *back*, just *exactly* the way they were." She gestured appropriately wide and high, standing on tiptoe.

Dan tended to discourage other people's illusions, though he was cherishing of his own. "I don't think that would be very sensible," he stated to the child. "Or very American."

"Why not American?" Emily asked, with an oppositional, possibly aggrieved edge. If her parents hadn't divorced, her marriage might have held together; a bad precedent had been set.

"We move on, don't we?" Dan tactfully answered. "As a nation. We try to learn from our mistakes. Those towers were taller than they needed to be. The Arabs weren't wrong to feel them as a boast."

Hilary, barefoot, peeked out from one of the penthouse doors, but did not venture out onto the sooty tiles. She admonished them, "Children shouldn't see what you're all looking at. It's scary."

"Don't be scared," her younger sister told her, and then half to Dan: "My teacher at school says the lights are like the rainbow. They mean it won't happen again."

2002

STEPHEN DUNN
B. 1939

Pulitzer Prize–winning poet Stephen Dunn was born in Forest Hills, New York, and has spent much of his life in the New Jersey and New York area. He has taught at Richard Stockton College of New Jersey since 1974 and has also taught creative writing as a visiting professor at a number of other universities.

The following poem, "Grudges," was selected as the opening poem in the collection *Poetry after 9/11: An Anthology of New York Poets*. In an interview before 9/11, Dunn said, "The older I get, the fewer distinctions I make between emotion and thought. We need to be thoughtful about our emotions, and passionate about ideas." Although he spoke those words in a different context, they are a fitting introduction to the ideas evident in "Grudges."

D. Quentin Miller
Suffolk University

PRIMARY WORKS

Five Impersonations, 1971; *Looking for Holes in the Ceiling*, 1974; *Full of Lust and Good Usage*, 1976; *A Circus of Needs*, 1978; *Work and Love*, 1981; *Not Dancing*, 1984; *Local Time*, 1986; *Between Angels*, 1989; *Landscape at the End of the Century*, 1991; *New and Selected Poems: 1974–1994*, 1994; *Loosestrife*, 1996; *Riffs & Reciprocities: Prose Pairs*, 1998; *Different Hours*, 2000; *The Insistence of Beauty*, 2004; *Everything Else in the World*, 2006; *What Goes On: Selected and New Poems 1995–2009*, 2009; *Here and Now: Poems*, 2011.

Grudges

Easy for almost anything to occur.
Even if we've scraped the sky, we can be rubble.
For years those men felt one way, acted another.

Ground zero, is it possible to get lower? 5
Now we had a new definition of the personal,
knew almost anything could occur.

It just takes a little training, to blur
a motive, lie low while planning the terrible,
get good at acting one way, feeling another.

Yet who among us doesn't harbor 10
a grudge or secret? So much isn't erasable;
it follows that almost anything can occur,

like men ascending into the democracy of air
without intending to land, the useful veil
of having said one thing, meaning another. 15

Before you know it something's over.
Suddenly someone's missing at the table.
It's easy (I know it) for anything to occur
when men feel one way, act another.

2002

NATASHA TRETHEWEY
B. 1966

Recipient of the 2007 Pulitzer Prize for Poetry and named Poet Laureate of the United States in 2012, Natasha Trethewey is one of the most promising poets of our time. Born in Gulfport, Mississippi, she received her formal education in Georgia and Massachusetts and has taught at Emory University in Atlanta in recent years. In addition to four collections of poetry, she has published a non-fiction work titled *Beyond Katrina: A Meditation on the Mississippi Gulf Coast.*

In interviews, Trethewey has described herself as "old-timey," a child in a rural region who felt more connected to her mother's and grandmother's lives than to the rapidly changing world of the late twentieth century. There is certainly an emphasis on or sympathy with the past in her work. Influenced by Rita Dove, also a onetime Poet Laureate of the United States, whose poetry also led her back to a consideration of earlier generations, Trethewey seems inclined toward the stories and sensibilities of the past not out of nostalgia, but rather as a way of recovering and preserving perspectives that have not been considered deeply enough in official records of history. She has also claimed Gwendolyn Brooks as a primary influence, especially her "modification of form," which Trethewey responded to in her collection *Domestic Work.*

There is a notable focus in Trethewey's poetry on the lives of women. She comes from a "matrilineal" family, in her words, and she is also conscious of how her poetry straddles worlds: past and present, urban and rural (both symbolized in her mind by the highway running through her family's farm), and black and white, as she is biracial. This sense of straddling races provides her poetry with suppleness and flexibility rather than anxiety over not belonging, a condition common in biracial writers of the early twentieth century such as Charles Chesnutt and Nella Larsen.

Trethewey's poetry and her pronouncements about it are consistently marked by a progressive, forward-thinking response to the scars of history, the conditions that have left rural or migratory African Americans invisible. In a 2004 interview, she claimed, "I want to create a public record of people who are often excluded from the public record. I want to inscribe their stories into the larger American story. I want readers who might be unfamiliar with these people, their lives, and their particular circumstances to begin to know something about them, to see in the people that I write about some measure of them, and to, I think, enlarge the community of humanity." She added to this observation in a 2011 interview: "The sensitive things I write about don't just belong to me. They belong to history, which means they belong to all of us." Her focus is consistently on labor, particularly on the hard work of creating a self and a community. These ideas are evident in the poems included here and throughout the body of her work.

D. Quentin Miller
Suffolk University

PRIMARY WORKS

Domestic Work, 2000; *Bellocq's Ophelia*, 2002; *Native Guard*, 2006; *Beyond Katrina*, 2010.

White Lies

The lies I could tell,
when I was growing up
light-bright, near-white,
high-yellow, red-boned
in a black place,   5
were just white lies.

I could easily tell the white folks
that we lived uptown,
not in that pink and green
shanty-fied shotgun section   10
along the tracks. I could act
like my homemade dresses
came straight out the window
of Maison Blanche. I could even
keep quiet, quiet as kept,   15
like the time a white girl said
(squeezing my hand), *Now
we have three of us in this class.*

But I paid for it every time
Mama found out.   20
She laid her hands on me,
then washed out my mouth
with Ivory soap. *This
is to purify,* she said,
and cleanse your lying tongue.   25
Believing her, I swallowed suds
thinking they'd work
from the inside out.

                                                    1999

History Lesson

I am four in this photograph, standing
on a wide strip of Mississippi beach,
my hands on the flowered hips

of a bright bikini. My toes dig in,
curl around wet sand. The sun cuts   5
the rippling Gulf in flashes with each

tidal rush. Minnows dart at my feet
glinting like switchblades. I am alone
except for my grandmother, other side

of the camera, telling me how to pose.   10
It is 1970, two years after they opened
the rest of this beach to us,

forty years since the photograph
where she stood on a narrow plot
of sand marked *colored*, smiling,   15

her hands on the flowered hips
of a cotton meal-sack dress.

                                                                    2000

Southern Gothic

I have lain down into 1970, into the bed
my parents will share for only a few more years.
Early evening, they have not yet turned from each other
in sleep, their bodies curved—parentheses
framing the separate lives they'll wake to. Dreaming,   5
I am again the child with too many questions—
the endless *why* and *why* and *why*
my mother cannot answer, her mouth closed, a gesture
toward her future: cold lips stitched shut.
The lines in my young father's face deepen   10
toward an expression of grief. I have come home
from the schoolyard with the words that shadow us
in this small Southern town—*peckerwood* and *nigger
lover, half-breed* and *zebra*—words that take shape
outside us. We're huddled on the tiny island of bed, quiet   15
in the language of blood: the house, unsteady
on its cinderblock haunches, sinking deeper
into the muck of ancestry. Oil lamps flicker
around us—our shadows, dark glyphs on the wall,
bigger and stranger than we are.   20

                                                                    2006

Incident

We tell the story every year—
how we peered from the windows, shades drawn—
though nothing really happened,
the charred grass now green again.

We peered from the windows, shades drawn,   5
at the cross trussed like a Christmas tree,
the charred grass still green. Then
we darkened our rooms, lit the hurricane lamps.

At the cross trussed like a Christmas tree,
a few men gathered, white as angels in their gowns.   10
We darkened our rooms and lit hurricane lamps,
the wicks trembling in their fonts of oil.

It seemed the angels had gathered, white men in their gowns.
When they were done, they left quietly. No one came.
The wicks trembled all night in their fonts of oil;   15
by morning the flames had all dimmed.

When they were done, the men left quietly. No one came.
Nothing really happened.
By morning all the flames had dimmed.
We tell the story every year.   20

2006

■   JUNOT DÍAZ   ■

B. 1968

Born in Santo Domingo, Dominican Republic, and raised in New Jersey, Junot Díaz is the author of the short story collection *Drown* (1996) and the novel *The Brief Wondrous Life of Oscar Wao* (2007), which won the John Sargent Sr. First Novel Prize, the National Book Critics Circle Award, the Anisfield-Wolf Book Award, the Dayton Literary Peace Prize, and the 2008 Pulitzer Prize. Díaz earned a B.A. from Rutgers University in 1992 and an M.F.A. from Cornell University in 1995. Currently, he is fiction editor at the *Boston Review* and teaches creative writing at the Massachusetts Institute of Technology, where he is the Rudge and Nancy Allen Professor of Writing.

Published initially as a stand-alone piece in *Story* magazine, "Fiesta, 1980" gains in emotional resonance from its placement as the second in a collection of interlocking stories in Díaz's critically acclaimed first book, *Drown*. As one of Díaz's early works, the story features many of the characters, preoccupations, themes, and stylistic techniques that will become familiar to readers of his later fiction. These include the character of Yunior, the theme of immigration, an acute attention to gender dynamics, a preoccupation with male infidelity, an obsession with reading, a focus on embodiment, and a narrative voice that delights in the mixing of linguistic registers.

Narrated in hindsight by Yunior, Díaz's fictional alter ego and the character who recurs most frequently across his body of work, "Fiesta, 1980" focuses on Yunior's recollection of the events surrounding a party he attended with his family in the Bronx when he was about twelve years old. Although it ends with the family together in the van as they head home from the party, the story carefully lays out the conditions for the family unit's impending dissolution, as seen from the perspective of a prepubescent boy who feels completely helpless in the face of forces much larger than himself.

A distinctive feature of Díaz's writing is a focus on the embodiment of his characters—their skin color, hair texture, height, body shape, and abundance or lack of flesh. This feature appears in "Fiesta, 1980" as expected: we see Madai's "twists," Tío Miguel's prodigious height and his "hair combed up and out into a demi-fro," Papi's "perfectly round and immaculate" belly button, Tía Yrma's short stature and light skin, and Leti's "serious tetas." But in this story Díaz's concern with embodiment is also manifested in another way: the characters are rendered as particular and memorable individuals through their hands and what they do with them.

"Fiesta, 1980" is notable as well for the way its central thematic concern—Yunior's nauseated response to Papi's van and all that it represents—is expressed at the level of both plot and tone. Despite numerous intimations of trouble, nothing momentous finally occurs on the level of the plot. At the party, Yunior waits for a "blow-up" between Mami and Papi, for Papi to be exposed, "out in public, where everybody would know. / You're a cheater!" Instead, "everything was calmer than usual," and Yunior is left trying to "imagine Mami before Papi" as he sits waiting for the festivities to wind down. The dramatic climax of the story thus takes place entirely in Yunior's mind just prior to his falling asleep on the tiled floor outside the bedroom where the other kids are either sleeping or fooling around. This curious muting of the story's action contributes to the story's tone, which can best be described as one of dreadful anticipation. Just as nausea is the unpleasant physical sensation that precedes the onset of something worse (vomiting), so the plot and the tone of the story work in tandem to leave the reader, like Mami and Papi, "already knowing what was happening" (the dissolution of the family). As noted, however, the story finally denies to the reader the spectacle of the conflagration that the young Yunior imagines would be the only adequate response to the way his family is falling apart. The real story of Papi's desertion, as the older narrator of "Fiesta, 1980" well understands, is both too complicated and too sad to allow for the emotional catharsis that such a momentary spectacle would provide.

Paula M. L. Moya
Stanford University

PRIMARY WORKS

Drown, 1996; *The Brief Wondrous Life of Oscar Wao*, 2007.

Fiesta, 1980

Mami's youngest sister—my tía Yrma—finally made it to the United States that year. She and tío Miguel got themselves an apartment in the Bronx, off the Grand Concourse and everybody decided that we should have a party. Actually, my pops decided, but everybody—meaning Mami, tía Yrma, tío Miguel and their neighbors—thought it a dope idea. On the afternoon of the party Papi came back from work around six. Right on time. We were all dressed by then, which was a smart move on our part. If Papi had walked in and caught us lounging around in our underwear, he would have kicked our asses something serious.

He didn't say nothing to nobody, not even my moms. He just pushed past her, held up his hand when she tried to talk to him and headed right into the shower. Rafa gave me the look and I gave it back to him; we both knew Papi had been with that Puerto Rican woman he was seeing and wanted to wash off the evidence quick.

Mami looked really nice that day. The United States had finally put some meat on her; she was no longer the same flaca who had arrived here three years before. She had cut her hair short and was wearing tons of cheap- ass jewelry which on her didn't look too lousy. She smelled like herself, like the wind through a tree. She always waited until the last possible minute to put on her perfume because she said it was a waste to spray it on early and then have to spray it on again once you got to the party.

We—meaning me, my brother, my little sister and Mami—waited for Papi to finish his shower. Mami seemed anxious, in her usual dispassionate way. Her hands adjusted the buckle of her belt over and over again. That morning, when she had gotten us up for school, Mami told us that she wanted to have a good time at the party. I want to dance, she said, but now, with the sun sliding out of the sky like spit off a wall, she seemed ready just to get this over with.

Rafa didn't much want to go to no party either, and me, I never wanted to go anywhere with my family. There was a baseball game in the parking lot outside and we could hear our friends, yelling, Hey, and, Cabrón, to one another. We heard the pop of a ball as it sailed over the cars, the clatter of an aluminum bat dropping to the concrete. Not that me or Rafa loved baseball; we just liked playing with the local kids, thrashing them at anything they were doing. By the sounds of the shouting, we both knew the game was close, either of us could have made a difference. Rafa frowned and when I frowned back, he put up his fist. Don't you mirror me, he said.

Don't you mirror me, I said.

He punched me—I would have hit him back but Papi marched into the living room with his towel around his waist, looking a lot smaller than he did when he was dressed. He had a few strands of hair around his nipples and a surly closed-mouth expression, like maybe he'd scalded his tongue or something.

Have they eaten? he asked Mami.

She nodded. I made you something.

You didn't let him eat, did you?

Ay, Dios mío, she said, letting her arms fall to her side.

Ay, Dios mío is right, Papi said.

I was never supposed to eat before our car trips, but earlier, when she had put out our dinner of rice, beans and sweet platanos, guess who had been the first one to clean his plate? You couldn't blame Mami really, she had been busy—cooking, getting ready, dressing my sister Madai. I should have reminded her not to feed me but I wasn't that sort of son.

Papi turned to me. Coño, muchacho, why did you eat?

Rafa had already started inching away from me. I'd once told him I considered him a low-down chickenshit for moving out of the way every time Papi was going to smack me.

Collateral damage, Rafa had said. Ever heard of it?

No.

Look it up.

Chickenshit or not, I didn't dare glance at him. Papi was old-fashioned; he expected your undivided attention when you were getting your ass whupped. You couldn't look him in the eye either—that wasn't allowed. Better to stare at his belly button, which was perfectly round and immaculate. Papi pulled me to my feet by my ear.

If you throw up—

I won't, I cried, tears in my eyes, more out of reflex than pain.

Ya, Ramón, ya. It's not his fault, Mami said.

They've known about this party forever. How did they think we were going to get there? Fly?

He finally let go of my ear and I sat back down. Madai was too scared to open her eyes. Being around Papi all her life had turned her into a major-league wuss. Anytime Papi raised his voice her lip would start trembling, like some specialized tuning fork. Rafa pretended that he had knuckles to crack and when I shoved him, he gave me a *Don't start* look. But even that little bit of recognition made me feel better.

I was the one who was always in trouble with my dad. It was like my God-given duty to piss him off, to do everything the way he hated. Our fights didn't bother me too much. I still wanted him to love me, something that never seemed strange or contradictory until years later, when he was out of our lives.

By the time my ear stopped stinging Papi was dressed and Mami was crossing each one of us, solemnly, like we were heading off to war. We said, in turn, Bendición, Mami, and she poked us in our five cardinal spots while saying, Que Dios te bendiga.

This was how all our trips began, the words that followed me every time I left the house.

None of us spoke until we were inside Papi's Volkswagen van. Brand-new, lime-green and bought to impress. Oh, we were impressed, but me, every time I was in that VW and Papi went above twenty miles an hour, I vomited. I'd never had trouble with cars before—that van was like my curse. Mami suspected it was the upholstery. In her mind, American things—appliances, mouthwash, funny-looking upholstery—all seemed to have an intrinsic badness about them. Papi was careful about taking me anywhere in the VW, but when he had to, I rode up front in Mami's usual seat so I could throw up out a window.

¿Cómo te sientes? Mami asked over my shoulder when Papi pulled onto the turnpike. She had her hand on the base of my neck. One thing about Mami, her palms never sweated.

I'm OK, I said, keeping my eyes straight ahead. I definitely didn't want to trade glances with Papi. He had this one look, furious and sharp, that always left me feeling bruised.

Toma. Mami handed me four mentas. She had thrown three out her window at the beginning of our trip, an offering to Eshú; the rest were for me.

I took one and sucked it slowly, my tongue knocking it up against my teeth. We passed Newark Airport without any incident. If Madai had been awake she would have cried because the planes flew so close to the cars.

How's he feeling? Papi asked.

Fine, I said. I glanced back at Rafa and he pretended like he didn't see me. That was the way he was, at school and at home. When I was in trouble, he didn't know me. Madai was solidly asleep, but even with her face all wrinkled up and drooling she looked cute, her hair all separated into twists.

I turned around and concentrated on the candy. Papi even started to joke that we might not have to scrub the van out tonight. He was beginning to loosen up, not checking his watch too much. Maybe he was thinking about that Puerto Rican woman or maybe he was just happy that we were all together. I could never tell. At the toll, he was feeling positive enough to actually get out of the van and search around under the basket for dropped coins. It was something he had once done to amuse Madai, but now it was habit. Cars behind us honked their horns and I slid down in my seat. Rafa didn't care; he grinned back at the other cars and waved. His actual job was to make sure no cops were coming. Mami shook Madai awake and as soon as she saw Papi stooping for a couple of quarters she let out this screech of delight that almost took off the top of my head.

That was the end of the good times. Just outside the Washington Bridge, I started feeling woozy. The smell of the upholstery got all up inside my head and I found myself with a mouthful of saliva. Mami's hand tensed on my shoulder and when I caught Papi's eye, he was like, No way. Don't do it.

The first time I got sick in the van Papi was taking me to the library. Rafa was with us and he couldn't believe I threw up. I was famous for my steel-lined stomach. A third-world childhood could give you that. Papi was worried enough that just as quick as Rafa could drop off the books we were on our way home. Mami fixed me one of her honey-and-onion concoctions and that made my stomach feel better. A week later we tried the library again and on this go-around I couldn't get the window open in time. When Papi got me home, he went and cleaned out the van himself, an expression of askho on his face. This was a big deal, since Papi almost never cleaned anything himself. He came back inside and found me sitting on the couch feeling like hell.

It's the car, he said to Mami. It's making him sick.

This time the damage was pretty minimal, nothing Papi couldn't wash off the door with a blast of the hose. He was pissed, though; he jammed his finger into my cheek, a nice solid thrust. That was the way he was with his punishments: imaginative. Earlier that year I'd written an essay in school called "My Father the Torturer," but the teacher made me write a new one. She thought I was kidding.

We drove the rest of the way to the Bronx in silence. We only stopped once, so I could brush my teeth. Mami had brought along my toothbrush and a tube of toothpaste and while every car known to man sped by us she stood outside with me so I wouldn't feel alone.

Tío Miguel was about seven feet tall and had his hair combed up and out, into a demi-fro. He gave me and Rafa big spleen-crushing hugs and then kissed Mami and finally ended up with Madai on his shoulder. The last time I'd seen Tío was at the airport, his first day in the United States. I remembered how he hadn't seemed all that troubled to be in another country.

He looked down at me. Carajo, Yunior, you look horrible!

He threw up, my brother explained.

I pushed Rafa. Thanks a lot, ass-face.

Hey, he said. Tío asked.

Tío clapped a bricklayer's hand on my shoulder. Everybody gets sick sometimes, he said. You should have seen me on the plane over here. Dios mio! He rolled his Asian-looking eyes for emphasis. I thought we were all going to die.

Everybody could tell he was lying. I smiled like he was making me feel better.

Do you want me to get you a drink? Tío asked. We got beer and rum.

Miguel, Mami said. He's young.

Young? Back in Santo Domingo, he'd be getting laid by now.

Mami thinned her lips, which took some doing.

Well, it's true, Tío said.

So, Mami, I said. When do I get to go visit the D.R.?

That's enough, Yunior.

It's the only pussy you'll ever get, Rafa said to me in English.

Not counting your girlfriend, of course.

Rafa smiled. He had to give me that one.

Papi came in from parking the van. He and Miguel gave each other the sort of handshakes that would have turned my fingers into Wonder bread.

Coño, compa'i, ¿cómo va todo? they said to each other.

Tía came out then, with an apron on and maybe the longest Lee Press-On-Nails I've ever seen in my life. There was this one guru motherfucker in the *Guinness Book of World Records* who had longer nails, but I tell you, it was close. She gave everybody kisses, told me and Rafa how guapo we were—Rafa, of course, believed her—told Madai how bella she was, but when she got to Papi, she froze a little, like maybe she'd seen a wasp on the tip of his nose, but then kissed him all the same.

Mami told us to join the other kids in the living room. Tío said, Wait a minute, I want to show you the apartment. I was glad Tía said, Hold on, because from what I'd seen so far, the place had been furnished in Contemporary Dominican Tacky. The less I saw, the better. I mean, I liked plastic sofa covers but damn, Tío and Tía had taken it to another level. They had a disco ball hanging in the living room and the type of stucco ceilings that looked like stalactite heaven. The sofas all had golden tassels dangling from their edges. Tía came out of the kitchen with some people I didn't know and by the time she got done introducing everybody, only Papi and Mami were given the guided tour of the four-room third-floor apartment. Me and Rafa joined the kids in the living room. They'd already started eating. We were hungry, one of the girls explained, a pastelito in hand. The boy was about three years younger than me but the girl who'd spoken, Leti, was my age. She and another girl were on the sofa together and they were cute as hell.

Leti introduced them: the boy was her brother Wilquins and the other girl was her neighbor Mari. Leti had some serious tetas and I could tell that my brother was going to gun for her. His taste in girls was predictable. He sat down right between Leti and Mari and by the way they were smiling at him I knew he'd do fine. Neither of the girls gave me more than a cursory one-two, which didn't bother me. Sure, I liked girls but I was always too terrified to speak to them unless we were arguing or I was calling them stupidos, which was one of my favorite words that year. I turned to Wilquins and asked him what there was to do around here. Mari, who had the lowest voice I'd ever heard, said, He can't speak.

What does that mean?

He's mute.

I looked at Wilquins incredulously. He smiled and nodded, as if he'd won a prize or something.

Does he understand? I asked.

Of course he understands, Rafa said. He's not dumb.

I could tell Rafa had said that just to score points with the girls. Both of them nodded. Low-voice Mari said, He's the best student in his grade.

I thought, Not bad for a mute. I sat next to Wilquins. After about two seconds of TV Wilquins whipped out a bag of dominos and motioned to me. Did I want to play? Sure. Me and him played Rafa and Leti and we whupped their collective asses twice, which put Rafa in a real bad mood. He looked at me like maybe he wanted to take a swing, just one to make him feel better. Leti kept whispering into Rafa's ear, telling him it was OK.

In the kitchen I could hear my parents slipping into their usual modes. Papi's voice was loud and argumentative; you didn't have to be anywhere near him to catch his drift. And Mami, you had to put cups to your ears to hear hers. I went into the kitchen a few times— once so the tíos could show off how much bullshit I'd been able to cram in my head the last few years; another time for a bucket-sized cup of soda. Mami and Tía were frying tostones and the last of the pastelitos. She appeared happier now and the way her hands worked on our dinner you would think she had a life somewhere else making rare and precious things. She nudged Tía every now and then, shit they must have been doing all their lives. As soon as Mami saw me though, she gave me the eye. Don't stay long, that eye said. Don't piss your old man off.

Papi was too busy arguing about Elvis to notice me. Then somebody mentioned María Montez and Papi barked, María Montez? Let me tell *you* about María Montez, compa'i.

Maybe I was used to him. His voice—louder than most adults'—didn't bother me none, though the other kids shifted uneasily in their seats. Wilquins was about to raise the volume on the TV, but Rafa said, I wouldn't do that. Muteboy had balls, though. He did it anyway and then sat down. Wilquins's pop came into the living room a second later, a bottle of Presidente in hand. That dude must have had Spider-senses or something. Did you raise that? he asked Wilquins and Wilquins nodded.

Is this your house? his pops asked. He looked ready to beat Wilquins silly but he lowered the volume instead.

See, Rafa said. You nearly got your ass *kicked.*

I met the Puerto Rican woman right after Papi had gotten the van. He was taking me on short trips, trying to cure me of my vomiting. It wasn't really working but I looked forward to our trips, even though at the end of each one I'd be sick. These were the only times me and Papi did anything together. When we were alone he treated me much better, like maybe I was his son or something.

Before each drive. Mami would cross me.

Bendición, Mami, I'd say.

She'd kiss my forehead. Que Dios te bendiga. And then she would give me a handful of mentas because she wanted me to be OK. Mami didn't think these excursions would cure anything, but the one time she had brought it up to Papi he had told her to shut up, what did she know about anything anyway?

Me and Papi didn't talk much. We just drove around our neighborhood. Occasionally he'd ask, How is it?

And I'd nod, no matter how I felt.

One day I was sick outside of Perth Amboy. Instead of taking me home he went the other way on Industrial Avenue, stopping a few minutes later in front of a light blue house I didn't recognize. It reminded me of the Easter eggs we colored at school, the ones we threw out the bus windows at other cars.

The Puerto Rican woman was there and she helped me clean up. She had dry papery hands and when she rubbed the towel on my chest, she did it hard, like I was a bumper she was waxing. She was very thin and had a cloud of brown hair rising above her narrow face and the sharpest blackest eyes you've ever seen.

He's cute, she said to Papi.

Not when he's throwing up, Papi said.

What's your name? she asked me. Are you Rafa?

I shook my head.

Then it's Yunior, right?

I nodded.

You're the smart one, she said, suddenly happy with herself. Maybe you want to see my books?

They weren't hers. I recognized them as ones my father must have left in her house. Papi was a voracious reader, couldn't even go cheating without a paperback in his pocket.

Why don't you go watch TV? Papi suggested. He was looking at her like she was the last piece of chicken on earth.

We got plenty of channels, she said. Use the remote if you want.

The two of them went upstairs and I was too scared of what was happening to poke around. I just sat there, ashamed, expecting something big and fiery to crash down on our heads. I watched a whole hour of the news before Papi came downstairs and said, Let's go.

About two hours later the women laid out the food and like always nobody but the kids thanked them. It must be some Dominican tradition or something. There was everything I liked—chicharrones, fried chicken, tostones, sancocho, rice, fried cheese, yuca, avocado, potato salad, a meteor-sized hunk of pernil, even a tossed salad which I could do without—but when I joined the other kids around the serving table, Papi said, Oh no you don't, and took the paper plate out of my hand. His fingers weren't gentle.

What's wrong now? Tía asked, handing me another plate.

He ain't eating, Papi said. Mami pretended to help Rafa with the pernil.

Why can't he eat?

Because I said so.

The adults who didn't know us made like they hadn't heard a thing and Tío just smiled sheepishly and told everybody to go ahead and eat. All the kids—about ten of them now—trooped back into the living room with their plates a-heaping and all the adults ducked into the kitchen and the dining room, where the radio was playing loud-ass bachatas. I was the only one without a plate. Papi stopped me before I could get away from him. He kept his voice nice and low so nobody else could hear him.

If you eat anything, I'm going to beat you. ¿Entiendes?

I nodded.

And if your brother gives you any food, I'll beat him too. Right here in front of everybody. ¿Entiendes?

I nodded again. I wanted to kill him and he must have sensed it because he gave my head a little shove.

All the kids watched me come in and sit down in front of the TV.

What's wrong with your dad? Leti asked.

He's a dick, I said.

Rafa shook his head. Don't say that shit in front of people.

Easy for you to be nice when you're eating, I said.

Hey, if I was a pukey little baby, I wouldn't get no food either.

I almost said something back but I concentrated on the TV. I wasn't going to start it. No fucking way. So I watched Bruce Lee beat Chuck Norris into the floor of the Colosseum and tried to pretend that there was no food anywhere in the house. It was Tía who finally saved me. She came into the living room and said, Since you ain't eating, Yunior, you can at least help me get some ice.

I didn't want to, but she mistook my reluctance for something else.

I already asked your father.

She held my hand while we walked; Tía didn't have any kids but I could tell she wanted them. She was the sort of relative who always remembered your birthday but who you only went to visit because you had to. We didn't get past the first-floor landing before she opened her pocketbook and handed me the first of three pastelitos she had smuggled out of the apartment.

Go ahead, she said. And as soon as you get inside make sure you brush your teeth.

Thanks a lot, Tía, I said.

Those pastelitos didn't stand a chance.

She sat next to me on the stairs and smoked her cigarette. All the way down on the first floor and we could still hear the music and the adults and the television. Tía looked a ton like Mami; the two of them were both short and light-skinned. Tía smiled a lot and that was what set them apart the most.

How is it at home, Yunior?

What do you mean?

How's it going in the apartment? Are you kids OK?

I knew an interrogation when I heard one, no matter how sugar-coated it was. I didn't say anything. Don't get me wrong, I loved my tía, but something told me to keep my mouth shut. Maybe it was family loyalty, maybe I just wanted to protect Mami or I was afraid that Papi would find out—it could have been anything really.

Is your mom all right?

I shrugged.

Have there been lots of fights?

None, I said. Too many shrugs would have been just as bad as an answer. Papi's at work too much.

Work, Tía said, like it was somebody's name she didn't like.

Me and Rafa, we didn't talk much about the Puerto Rican woman. When we ate dinner at her house, the few times Papi had taken us over there, we still acted like nothing was out of the ordinary. Pass the ketchup, man. No sweat, bro. The affair was like a hole in our living room floor, one we'd gotten so used to circumnavigating that we sometimes forgot it was there.

By midnight all the adults were crazy dancing. I was sitting outside Tía's bedroom—where Madai was sleeping—trying not to attract attention. Rafa had me guarding the door; he and Leti were in there too, with some of the other kids, getting busy no doubt. Wilquins had gone across the hall to bed so I had me and the roaches to mess around with.

Whenever I peered into the main room I saw about twenty moms and dads dancing and drinking beers. Every now and then somebody yelled, ¡Quisqueya! And then everybody else would yell and stomp their feet. From what I could see my parents seemed to be enjoying themselves.

Mami and Tía spent a lot of time side by side, whispering, and I kept expecting something to come of this, a brawl maybe. I'd never once been out with my family when it hadn't turned to shit. We weren't even theatrical or straight crazy like other families. We fought like sixth-graders, without any real dignity. I guess the whole night I'd been waiting for a blowup, something between Papi and Mami. This was how I always figured Papi would be exposed, out in public, where everybody would know.

You're a cheater!

But everything was calmer than usual. And Mami didn't look like she was about to say anything to Papi. The two of them danced every now and then but they never lasted more than a song before Mami joined Tía again in whatever conversation they were having.

I tried to imagine Mami before Papi. Maybe I was tired, or just sad, thinking about the way my family was. Maybe I already knew how it would all end up in a few years, Mami without Papi, and that was why I did it. Picturing her alone wasn't easy. It seemed like Papi had always been with her, even when we were waiting in Santo Domingo for him to send for us.

The only photograph our family had of Mami as a young woman, before she married Papi, was the one that somebody took of her at an election party that I found one day while rummaging for money to go to the arcade. Mami had it tucked into her immigration papers. In the photo, she's surrounded by laughing cousins I will never meet, who are all shiny from dancing, whose clothes are rumpled and loose. You can tell it's night and hot and that the mosquitos have been biting. She sits straight and even in a crowd she stands out, smiling quietly like maybe she's the one everybody's celebrating. You can't see her hands but I imagined they're knotting a straw or a bit of thread. This was the woman my father met a year later on the Malecón, the woman Mami thought she'd always be.

Mami must have caught me studying her because she stopped what she was doing and gave me a smile, maybe her first one of the night. Suddenly I wanted to go over and hug her, for no other reason than I loved her, but there were about eleven fat jiggling bodies between us. So I sat down on the tiled floor and waited.

I must have fallen asleep because the next thing I knew Rafa was kicking me and saying, Let's go. He looked like he'd been hitting those girls off; he was all smiles. I got to my feet in time to kiss Tía and Tío good-bye. Mami was holding the serving dish she had brought with her.

Where's Papi? I asked.

He's downstairs, bringing the van around. Mami leaned down to kiss me.

You were good today, she said.

And then Papi burst in and told us to get the hell downstairs before some pendejo cop gave him a ticket. More kisses, more handshakes and then we were gone.

I don't remember being out of sorts after I met the Puerto Rican woman, but I must have been because Mami only asked me questions when she thought something was wrong in my life. It took her about ten passes but finally she cornered me one afternoon when we were alone in the apartment. Our upstairs neighbors were beating the crap out of their kids, and me and her had been listening to it all afternoon. She put her hand on mine and said, Is everything OK, Yunior? Have you been fighting with your brother?

Me and Rafa had already talked. We'd been in the basement, where our parents couldn't hear us. He told me that yeah, he knew about her.

Papi's taken me there twice now, he said.

Why didn't you tell me? I asked.

What the hell was I going to say? *Hey, Yunior, guess what happened yesterday? I met Papi's sucia!*

I didn't say anything to Mami either. She watched me, very very closely. Later I would think, maybe if I had told her, she would have confronted him, would have done something, but who can know these things? I said I'd been having trouble in school and like that everything was back to normal between us. She put her hand on my shoulder and squeezed and that was that.

We were on the turnpike, just past Exit 11, when I started feeling it again. I sat up from leaning against Rafa. His fingers smelled and he'd gone to sleep almost as soon as he got into the van. Madai was out too but at least she wasn't snoring.

In the darkness, I saw that Papi had a hand on Mami's knee and that the two of them were quiet and still. They weren't slumped back or anything; they were both wide awake, bolted into their seats. I couldn't see either of their faces and no matter how hard I tried I could not imagine their expressions. Neither of them moved. Every now and then the van was filled with the bright rush of somebody else's headlights. Finally I said, Mami, and they both looked back, already knowing what was happening.

1996

■ # DAVE EGGERS
B. 1970
■

Dave Eggers achieved a sudden and lucrative literary celebrity with the publication of his first book, the intensely self-conscious elegiac memoir, *A Heart-breaking Work of Staggering Genius* (2000). Set against the backdrop of a placid adolescence in Lake Forest, Illinois (where his family relocated not long after his birth in Boston, Massachusetts), *AHWOSG* describes Eggers's reactions to the unexpected loss of both parents within a few weeks. An orphan at age 21, Eggers abandoned his studies at the University of Illinois–Champaign/Urbana to care for his eight-year-old brother. *AHWOSG* recounts the ad hoc domesticity and new self-parenting rituals the brothers develop together, and the commitment to vulnerable youth it demonstrates characterizes much of Eggers's later writing as well. The memoir also experiments dramatically with voice. Arch passages such as "Rules and Suggestions for the Enjoyment of This Book" pull the propensity for footnoting, eccentric erudition, and postpostmodern sincerity of contemporaries such as David Foster Wallace and William T. Vollmann into the middle-class living room. Eggers's self-described efforts to build a more authentic American family life, together with his deadpan humor and media-friendly style, quickly established him as an icon of Generation X. Like contemporaries such as Douglas Coupland and Rick Moody, Eggers has received the adoration of many readers alongside more mixed reviews from critics skeptical about the durability of his concerns.

After reportedly receiving more than $2 million for a film option on his memoir and being publicly criticized by family members for self-aggrandizement, Eggers swerved away from *AHWOSG*'s style and content. Ever entrepreneurial, he launched an independent publishing company (McSweeney's), a literary magazine edited by his wife and fellow author Vendela Vida (*The Believer*), and a nonprofit tutoring and writing center for underserved urban youth with branches in seven U.S. cities (826 Valencia)—all while preparing his first novel. *You Shall Know Our Velocity* (2002) introduces the more documentary and activist concerns that characterize most of Eggers's later work. Organized around a whirlwind round-the-world journey in which two young men try unsuccessfully to give away a large bequest, this apparently earnest novel examines the disconcerting naïvete of its protagonists, asking why they know so little about the people and places they hope to aid. *Velocity*'s emphasis on mourning, manhood, and therapeutic travel recall some aspects of the grim vision of American modernity offered by Hemingway and other early twentieth-century expatriates. At the same time, Eggers's introduction to a 2003 reissue of Mark Twain's *A Tramp Abroad* also suggests his interest in a more parodic vision of the tourist. Whether serious or satiric, though, these well-heeled American innocents (called by a 2010 columnist in *Esquire* "fake-hurt-men") take a back seat in Eggers's later writing to the international scene they barely know how to observe.

Oral testimony and a direct service ethic ground Eggers's post-*Velocity* writing. Collaborating with the physician Lolla Vollen, Eggers has released several volumes under the title "Voices of Witness." These oral histories collect the voices of people who have been unjustly imprisoned, swept up in the calamitous Hurricane Katrina, and left bereft by the Sudanese civil war. The same documentary impulse fuels Eggers's novel *What Is the What* (2006) and the narrative nonfiction *Zeitoun* (2009). Scrupulously ventriloquizing, these books present first-person accounts of a young Sudanese refugee's search for asylum and a Syrian immigrant's disappearance during the post-Katrina chaos in New Orleans. Eggers excises his own voice from the narratives as fully as possible in order to put the real-life protagonists in the foreground. Eggers's admirable ear for informal speech and his attentiveness to the vagaries of memory ensure that the travails, philosophies, and voices of Valentino Achak Deng and Abdulrahman Zeitoun receive the reader's full attention. All the proceeds from both books have been donated to projects serving their respective communities. In these prize-nominated narratives, as well as his numerous publishing, editing and pedagogic ventures, Dave Eggers fuses the experimental realism of the 1960s-era New Journalists to a tradition of humane literary advocacy reaching back to Studs Terkel. As he told the *New Statesman* in 2011, he works from the premise that despite inhabiting an environment rife with technological distractions and political crises, "the humans [he knows] are still pretty OK."

Caren Irr
Brandeis University

PRIMARY WORKS

A Heartbreaking Work of Staggering Genius, 2000; *You Shall Know Our Velocity*, 2002; *The Unforbidden Is Compulsory, or Optimism*, 2004; *How We Are Hungry*, 2004; *What Is the What*, 2006; *Wild Things*, 2009; *Zeitoun*, 2009; *A Hologram for the King*, 2012.

What It Means When a Crowd in a Faraway Nation Takes a Soldier Representing Your Own Nation, Shoots Him, Drags Him from His Vehicle and Then Mutilates Him in the Dust

There is a man who felt great trepidation. He felt anxiety and unease. These were feelings foreign to the man. He'd never felt this kind of untouchable ennui, but he had been feeling it for a year. He sometimes was simply walking around the house, unable to place exactly why he was tense. The day would be clear, sun above, everything good, but he would be pacing. He would sit down to read a book and then quickly get up, thinking there was a phone call he needed to make. Once at the phone, he would realize there was no phone call he needed to make, but there was something outside the window he needed to inspect. There was something in the yard that needed fixing. He needed to drive somewhere, he needed to take a quick run. The man had seen the picture that morning, in the newspaper. He saw the picture of the soldier's body, now on the ground under the truck. His uniform was tan, the soldier's was, and he lay on his back, his boots almost white in the midday sun, pointing up. Meanwhile, the man was sitting in his home, comfortable, wearing warm socks and drinking orange juice from a smooth heavy glass, and was seeing the dead man in the color photograph. The picture caused him to gasp, alone in his home. He studied the photo, looking, he realized, for blood—where was the soldier shot? There was no blood visible. He turned the page, tried to move on, but soon returned to the picture and looked to see if any of the citizens of this faraway country were in the frame. They were not. The man stood up. He watched smoke billow rightward from a factory on the horizon. Why did he feel violated? He felt punched, robbed, raped. If a soldier was killed and mutilated in his own country, the man would not feel this kind of revulsion. He doesn't feel this way when he hears about trains colliding, or a family, in Missouri, drowning in their minivan in a December lake. But this, in another part of the world, this soldier dragged from his car, this soldier alone, this dead unbloody body in the dust under the truck—why does it set the man on edge, why does it feel so personal? The man at home feels this way too often now. He feels tunneled, wrapped, dessicated. His eyes feel the strain of trying for too long to see in the dark. The man is watching the smoke from the factory, and though there are many things he could do that day, he will do none of them.

2004

■ JANE JEONG TRENKA ■
B. 1972

Born in South Korea, Jane Jeong Trenka was adopted as an infant (along with her older sister) and raised by a white couple in rural Minnesota. Her experience as a Korean adoptee has fueled much of her writing and activism in both the United States and South Korea. The author of two award-winning memoirs and coeditor of the groundbreaking anthology *Outsiders Within: Writing on Transracial Adoption* (2006), Trenka is one of most significant figures in Korean adoptee literature. She made her mark in the literary world with her highly acclaimed debut, *The Language of Blood* (2003). Unlike previous Korean adoptee memoirs, *The Language of Blood* stood out for its complex depiction of adoptee identity formation, as well as its inventive prose that wove together Korean legends with crossword puzzles, fairytales with adoption agency brochures, plays with recipes. This pastiche style of narration symbolizes the trauma of adoption. In an interview with Jennifer Kwon Dobbs, Trenka said, "The nature of traumatic memory seems, to me, to be outside time or in hypertime, constantly in the present, and in intense flashes. I experience my adoption and its lifelong consequences—a rather disjointed affair, but with certain recurrent themes."

Trenka continues to explore this "disjointed affair" that comes from negotiating traumatic memory and loss in her follow-up memoir, *Fugitive Visions* (2009). Whereas *The Language of Blood* records Trenka's struggle for identity in Minnesota, *Fugitive Visions* documents the struggle for identity, belonging, and home in South Korea. Having repatriated back to South Korea, Trenka now focuses primarily on advocating for adoptee rights in her birth country. She currently serves as president of Truth and Reconciliation for the Adoption Community of Korea (TRACK), working to educate Korean society about issues of adoption. Although Trenka hopes to write a novel, she explains to Dobbs, "right now what urgently needs to be written is the work about adoption, in the Korean language, and this is going out in magazine articles, Web sites, and pamphlets. Writing a novel in my own language, for an audience that is 'foreign' to Koreans, would be a great luxury as a writer. But I don't have time for that right now, because what I am writing, through the filter of translation, is—to borrow from Frantz Fanon—a 'literature of combat.'"

The following excerpt from *The Language of Blood* could be considered an example of this "literature of combat." Situated near the end of her memoir, this excerpt ruminates on the question that many Korean adoptees—particularly those who are critical of adoption or who desire to reconnect with their birth families or birth country—are asked: "Would you rather have been raised in Korea?" Translation: Do you wish you had not been adopted? Rather than reifying this either/or situation or reproducing the dominant narrative that depicts adoption as rescue, Trenka provides an alternative vision of adoption by answering this question via her "Fairy Tale."

SooJin Pate
Minneapolis Community and Technical College

PRIMARY WORKS

The Language of Blood, 2003; *Outsiders Within: Writing on Transracial Adoption* (coeditor), 2006; *Fugitive Visions*, 2009.

from **The Language of Blood**

Exile's Crossword

											K		M			
									M	O	T	H	E	R		
											R		M			
			J	U	X	T	A	P	O	S	E		O			
				A		M		A					R			
A	J	A	N	U	S			E				U	Y	M		
M		E				F	R	A	U	D		M	B	E		
B		I								M			T	S		
I						C			L	A	N	G	U	A	G	E
V		P	A	R	A	D	O	X						M	E	
A	B							E						O	M	
L	A	U	G	H				N	E	I	T	H	E	R		
E	T				S			I					E	P		
N	T			K	Y	O	N	G	A	H			R	H		
T	E				Z								M	O		
D	R	E	A	M	Y				F	R	E	A	K	S		
	F				G	L						P		I		
	A	L	C	H	E	M	Y		O	B	O	T	H	S		
	Y					S						R				
				S	U	S	P	E	N	S	I	O	N		S	
												D		T		
												I		O		
				S	U	B	L	I	M	A	T	I	O	N		
												E		E		

A simple question put me in search of a word to describe, to accurately nail down my existence. The question was this: "Would you rather have been raised in Korea?"

I looked into her blue eyes, this intelligent, third-generation American whom I truly like, then looked away and mumbled something about how it's impossible to say; I would have had different values if I had been raised in Korea; my sisters turned out fine, but you never know, etc.

In adoption there is a tension between seeming and being: between the shining outside—the happy smiles of adoptive parents, the expectations of happily ever after, the how-to-adopt books, the lovely picture books with no mention of a child's birth mother—and the reality of the heart.

If only I could find the courage to speak, to articulate what I know instead of nodding politely, changing the subject. If only I had the guts to challenge someone's assumptions. Would I rather have been raised in Korea?

For my friend, the question is rhetorical and the answer is clear. She's been told that I was "saved" and "born not under my mother's heart, but in it." I have been rescued by adoption; had I stayed in Korea, I would have been institutionalized, after which I would have turned into what Asian girls tend to turn into if left to their own devices: a prostitute. The standards by which she judges good living—a college education, American citizenship, a white, middle-class upbringing in a pre-approved home—would not have been available to me.

Newly adoptive parents close to my age like to comfort me. "Big people make choices for little people," they explain. Gently, as if I am the age of their toddlers, they work out the convenient and fateful equation for me: my parents didn't have children and I needed a home.

For me, it's not so simple. I wish that my adoption was a 100-percent-positive thing, that people as well as God did not see the color of skin, that having grown to be the tallest of my siblings was a sign not only of good childhood nutrition but of spiritual abundance as well. How do I explain in the course of polite conversation that my seemingly flawless assimilation into America has yielded anything but joy and gratitude? How do I explain my ambivalence? Yet I do have mixed feelings. I feel ashamed and unworthy of the gifts that have been given me; ashamed for not being a better daughter—both a grateful American one and a forgiving Korean one, guided by filial piety; ashamed for opening my mouth, despite everything people have tried to do for me, in what they thought were my best interests. What an unworthy, spoiled, ungrateful, whining, American brat.

The way I think about myself these days is with the word that best describes me: exile. I hadn't thought of myself as an exile or immigrant before—just a lucky adoptee. But now, I see that "exile" is the word that fits me best.

The language of exile is filled with gains and losses, culture and family, memory and imagination. I try on the identity of exile, and it feels good. Not that it feels good to be an exile, but it feels good to have something fit. "Adoptee" never seemed quite right; it didn't address what I had lost, which was an inseparable part of what I had gained.

I have little patience for "ex-pates" who ricochet around the globe in search of the perfect café, willing women, cheap wine. Yet there are some whose experiences resonate with me; for those who find their place, their second home, yearning is transformed into something else, something ghostly yet real as flesh.

There is the absurdity of the exile poet who writes in his native language and none of his friends in his new country can read it. It's like the terrible absurdity I encounter when I cannot talk to my own family. There is the exile who visits the graves of his Jewish ancestors in Alexandria; he washes the stone lovingly, and I am reminded of my own wish to visit my mother's grave, to touch it and bow before the woman who gave birth to me, who watches over me now from far away. There is the feeling of displacement, of longing for there when you're here; of creating a world inside that is a substitute for the one outside, because the one inside can hold everything tightly in one place, unlike the vast world where so many beloved people and places are scattered beyond reach. There is the willing exile who lives in France, studying the language and blundering through, like me going into a Korean restaurant and saying to the waitress, "Thank you very much. Never mind. Are you full." There is the willing ex-pate who finds a home elsewhere, amongst her grandmother's people, and returns there every year to soak up the beauty of a beaten and glorious old city.

These things that other writers ruminate on—the feeling of homesickness, the sense of being at home nowhere but comfortable in many places, the power of memory—are realities, yet luxuries of the intelligentsia.

Where is the outpouring of reflection from the Somali taxi driver in Minneapolis, the shopkeeper at Halal meat, the Mexican roofer covered in tar dust, the Turk and his wife who work in their restaurant sixteen hours every day? And where is the outpouring of reflection from children who are adopted, who want to be good, who want to be perfect for their new parents, lest they be returned to the store?

My own Umma told me that if she had kept me, I would have been either dead or a beggar. She told me the stories of how my father beat me about the head and my head turned black and blue, how he threw me from a window, how she was homeless and slept on the streets. How could a baby survive that?

My sisters gave me the chance to stay in Korea, when Umma was dying. As Jeong Kyong-Ah, I am a recognized citizen of Korea. I could have liquidated my apartment in the United States and just stayed. But I chose not to.

Would I rather have not been adopted? *I don't know.* The question demands that I calculate unquantifiables. How can I weigh the loss of my language and culture against the freedom that America has to offer, the opportunity to have the same rights as a man? How can a person exiled as a child, without a choice, possibly fathom how he would have "turned out" had he stayed in Korea? How many educational opportunities must I mark on my tally sheet before I can say it was worth losing my mother? How can an adoptee weigh her terrible loss against the burden of gratitude she feels for her adoptive country and parents?

When I watch the Mexican people in my neighborhood, I see what must be the backbone of a scattered people reaching out across the continent and binding them together. The backbone is many things: language, food, music, physical characteristics, religion, family. It must be the same thing that has held every immigrant group together in America until, after a couple of generations, the difference between Swedes and Norwegians or French and Germans wasn't so jarring anymore, and they married each other and only faintly held onto the customs that once bound them together, ensuring their very survival as a people.

As an adopted Korean, where is my backbone? How separated am I from the more than two hundred thousand Korean adoptees raised in the United States, Europe, Australia, and Canada? What can I salvage from this life, to teach my own children what I was never taught, about themselves and about the world and how to live in it?

> Yahweh said, "Behold, they are one people, and they have all one language, and this is what they begin to do. Now nothing will be withheld from them, which they intend to do. Come, let's go down, and there confuse their language, that they may not understand one another's speech." So Yahweh scattered them abroad from there on the surface of all the earth.
>
> GENESIS 11:6–8

Nearly a year and a half passed before I spoke with my American mother again. I call to tell her that Mark and I are engaged, and to talk. I hold onto my calm voice for as long as I can, and when it starts to shake, Mark pours me a drink.

"Well, I don't see how I can come to your wedding with all your friends talking bad about me."

"Mom, no one is talking bad about you. Can't we just be civil for one day?"

"Well, I don't think we want to come to your wedding if you have to try so hard to be nice to us."

"But it wouldn't be complete without you. Mark and I really want you there. We're family."

"That's right. We are your family."

The unsaid words speak louder than what she says: they are my *only* family. Why isn't what I have been given in America good enough for me?

Four hours and a pyre of said and unsaid words later, what is left is uncertainty. I can only hope to understand my mother as a woman. If I put myself in her place, I see a woman who, when she was younger than I am now, adopted two girls and wanted to give them the whole pie, who before that was a girl herself with parents who gave her only crumbs. But she loved her mother, my grandma, anyway and mourned her when she died. So we have that in common, this grief that we carry.

We also have this in common: our bodies, which remind each other of what we do not have, of who we are not. Mom, I am not from you; I will never be fully yours. I will never have peachy skin or blonde hair; I will never see the world through blue eyes. Could we accept each other if we were blind? Would we know each other by touch? Touch me here, Mom, in this place where I am sorry, where I love you, where I need to be healed.

There isn't enough fuel for anything to burn forever. Our silhouettes have been illuminated for a long time: this sharp, specific edge and that one, both unyielding. Now I feel the light around me burning itself out, giving way to something like forgiveness. Mom, if I were afraid, if I were lost in the dark, could you find me again?

People ask me how I know about my ancestors: "Everybody thinks they're descended from royalty or wealth. Do you have any proof, like documents or something?"

Well, not really. I have part of the family register, but not the whole thing. I have my own memory of visiting a decaying yangban house. But mostly, I have stories: what my Korean mother had told me about her parents, and what my sisters continue to say now that she is dead.

I count myself lucky because I have more stories and more documents than most. It's common for the agencies to tell adoptees that their documents were lost or destroyed or that there were never sufficient papers in the first place. Or, if they have the papers, they may have to "check with their lawyer" first before they can release the information, as if no one has requested the same thing before.

Who decided that the truth presented on official documents is more truthful than stories? Documents are only partial truths.

For instance, I bet that somewhere you could dig up a document that lists my uncle's dates of service in Vietnam. But those are only dates, and the full truth of it lies in his stories about cleaning out the helicopters. Another case: you could find documents detailing the ship and ports associated with one of my friend's ancestors, who came to America at the turn of the century. The truth lies not so much in these details, but in the story handed down—that she was a young woman who was so afraid of the men on the boat that she kept her boots laced for the entire passage, and when she got to America the boots had to be cut off her feet.

For that matter, even the "facts" on documents can be wrong. I have a document called a birth certificate that lists my parents as Frederick and Margaret Brauer: partial truth. (And although we were raised in the same family, my sister and I sometimes dispute what happened or was said during specific events: different versions of the truth.)

If I had to legally prove that my Korean family is my Korean family, I would be at a loss because the adoption agency won't give me the documents that fill in the crack between the time I was Jeong Kyong-Ah and when I became Jane Brauer. Even if I had them, who could legally prove that the baby in the photo is the same one they sent to America? It certainly wouldn't be the first time that children were substituted for each other: covered truth.

So, what remains through the rubble of the years is emotional truth, as fictional as it may seem.

Here's a story that's completely plausible and also completely false:

A Fairy Tale

Once upon a time, there were two Korean girls who loved their mother very much. But she could not take care of them. So she placed a smooth stone in the older girl's coat pocket and sent her daughters far, far away, to a place where people have more than stones to give.

In their new country, the girls grew healthy and strong. Their adoptive parents loved them very much, and they honored the girls' Korean heritage as they grew, helping them to remember the things they had forgotten. Together, they rediscovered Korean language and food, clothing and customs. They proudly displayed in their home the gifts sent by the Korean mother. Most importantly, they talked about the Korean family and made them a part of their own family. In their prayers at the dinner table, they asked God to bless their food, their family, and their extended family in Korea.

In school, the words of other children hurt, but those words stopped when the parents asked the teacher if they could make a special presentation in the classroom about the people and culture of Korea, so that the other children would understand and tolerate differences and accept the girls as friends. The teacher thought it was such a good idea that the whole school celebrated the different heritages of its children for the next month.

The children whose ancestors were German and Norwegian brought in old photos of their great-great-grandparents and recounted the family stories of the old country and long travel on ships. "Tell it again," squealed the children, when there was a story about a boy who threw up all over from seasickness or a story about a horse thief who hopped a ship to escape imprisonment.

"My name means Church on the Hill," one child said proudly. Another said, "My name means Bright City, and we still have cousins in Germany."

At home, the stone from Korea was given a special place on top of the butterfly shadow box. Sometimes, when her daughters were sleeping, the American mother held the stone in her hand and closed her eyes, trying to picture the land that made her daughters.

The two girls never felt ashamed of their heritage. They felt proud to be both American and Korean, and when the day came that they were old enough to travel back to their mother country, their American parents came with them, to see the strange and wonderful place that they had held dearly in their hearts and imaginations for so long.

In Korea, the two families met, and they exchanged gifts. This time, the older daughter held a different stone in her coat pocket, from a lake in

America, and this she gave to her Korean mother so she, too, could touch a piece of America. The American parents met the Korean mother, sisters, and brother, as well as all the nieces and nephews, aunts and uncles, and extended family. The Korean family was just as big as the American family. In many ways they were the same. They made plans to meet again.

When the Korean mother became sick and died, the American mother invited the daughters and the rest of the family to a memorial service in her church, to honor the woman who was so important in the family's life. All the American aunts and uncles attended, and so did people who never met the Korean mother but who knew her as part of the family.

And when the daughters finally had their own children, both the American family and the Korean family rejoiced, for they knew that they were bound together in a way that would be celebrated and told for many generations.

The End

2003

■ # ZZ PACKER
B. 1973</div> ■

Zuwena "ZZ" Packer was born in Chicago, raised in Georgia, and graduated from high school in Louisville, Kentucky. This peripatetic pattern continued as she pursued higher education, earning a B.A. from Yale University, an M.A. from Johns Hopkins University, and an M.F.A. from the University of Iowa. She has continued to move around as a professor and writer-in-residence at colleges and universities such as Tulane University, San Jose State University, the University of Texas at Austin, Vassar College, and Princeton University.

Packer began publishing fiction as early as age nineteen and has received consistent accolades as one of the more promising young fiction writers active today. Her 2004 collection *Drinking Coffee Elsewhere* received significant attention, and readers have been eagerly awaiting the publication of her historical novel, set in the aftermath of the Civil War, which she has been working on for many years.

Like some other African American writers of her generation, such as Colson Whitehead, Packer tends to respond to questions about her racial identity with humor. In one interview, responding to the question "Are you a black writer?" she claims, "Of course, because I'm black, and I'm a writer." Aware that the question carries with it a history of assumptions about black literary identity and audience, Packer continues, "I think people tend to racialize and in some contexts that is necessary. In the context of just being human and falling in love and all of the things that human beings do, I don't necessarily think it should erupt. It's a horrible thing when it does because it means that the racists have won." The following story, "Drinking Coffee Elsewhere," complicates and problematizes both the question and Packer's response to it. The narrator, Dina, is (like her author) a black student at a predominantly white Ivy League college, but this superficial similarity is only one factor in Dina's conflict. Aware of her poverty from a young age, distant from her father and close to her deceased mother, curious about homoerotic attraction, Dina is a self-described misanthrope who compares herself to a revolver on her first day at college. Her prickly attitude reveals no easy explanations, and her tendency to pretend as a defense mechanism is evidently self-delusional rather than self-protective. In another interview, Packer identifies the "conundrum of living in America today" this way: "the more race is not supposed to matter, the more it does." The following story illustrates that principle in no uncertain terms.

D. Quentin Miller
Suffolk University

PRIMARY WORK

Drinking Coffee Elsewhere, 2004.

Drinking Coffee Elsewhere

Orientation games began the day I arrived at Yale from Baltimore. In my group we played heady, frustrating games for smart people. One game appeared to be charades reinterpreted by existentialists; another involved listening to rocks. Then a freshman counselor made everyone play Trust. The idea was that if you had the faith to fall backward and wait for four scrawny former high school geniuses to catch you, just before your head cracked on the slate sidewalk, then you might learn to trust your fellow students. Russian roulette sounded like a better way to go.

"No way," I said. The white boys were waiting for me to fall, holding their arms out for me, sincerely, gallantly. "No fucking way."

"It's all cool, it's all cool," the counselor said. Her hair was a shade of blond I'd seen only on *Playboy* covers, and she raised her hands as though backing away from a growling dog. "Sister," she said, in an I'm-down-with-the-struggle voice, "you don't have to play this game. As a person of color, you shouldn't have to fit into any white, patriarchal system."

I said, "It's a bit too late for that."

In the next game, all I had to do was wait in a circle until it was my turn to say what inanimate object I wanted to be. One guy said he'd like to be a gadfly, like Socrates. "Stop me if I wax Platonic," he said. I didn't bother mentioning that gadflies weren't inanimate—it didn't seem to make a difference. The girl next to him was eating a rice cake. She wanted to be the Earth, she said. Earth with a capital E.

There was one other black person in the circle. He wore an Exeter T-shirt and his overly elastic expressions resembled a series of facial exercises. At the end of each person's turn, he smiled and bobbed his head with unfettered enthusiasm. "Oh, that was good," he said, as if the game were an experiment he'd set up and the results were turning out better than he'd expected. "Good, good, good!"

When it was my turn I said, "My name is Dina, and if I had to be any object, I guess I'd be a revolver." The sunlight dulled as if on cue. Clouds passed rapidly overhead, presaging rain. I don't know why I said it. Until that moment I'd been good in all the ways that were meant to matter. I was an honor roll student—though I'd learned long ago not to mention it in the part of Baltimore where I lived. Suddenly I was hard-bitten and recalcitrant, the kind of kid who took pleasure in sticking pins into cats; the kind who chased down smart kids to spray them with Mace.

"A revolver," a counselor said, stroking his chin, as if it had grown a rabbinical beard. "Could you please elaborate?"

The black guy cocked his head and frowned, as if the beakers and Erlenmeyer flasks of his experiment had grown legs and scurried off.

"You were just kidding," the dean said, "about wiping out all of mankind. That, I suppose, was a joke." She squinted at me. One of her hands curved atop the other to form a pink, freckled molehill on her desk.

"Well," I said, "maybe I meant it at the time." I quickly saw that this was not the answer she wanted. "I don't know. I think it's the architecture."

Through the dimming light of the dean's office window, I could see the fortress of the old campus. On my ride from the bus station to the campus, I'd barely glimpsed New Haven—a flash of crumpled building here, a trio of straggly kids there. A lot like Baltimore. But everything had changed when we reached those streets hooded by gothic buildings. I imagined how the college must have looked when it was founded, when most of the students owned slaves. I pictured men wearing tights and knickers, smoking pipes.

"The architecture," the dean repeated. She bit her lip and seemed to be making a calculation of some sort. I noticed that she blinked less often than most people. I sat there, intrigued, waiting to see how long it would be before she blinked again.

My revolver comment won me a year's worth of psychiatric counseling, weekly meetings with Dean Guest, and—since the parents of the roommate I'd never met weren't too hip on the idea of their Amy sharing a bunk bed with a budding homicidal loony—my very own room.

Shortly after getting my first C ever, I also received the first knock on my door. The female counselors never knocked. The dean had spoken to them; I was a priority. Every other day, right before dinnertime, they'd look in on me, unannounced. "Just checking up," a counselor would say. It was the voice of a suburban mother in training. By the second week, I had made a point of sitting in a chair in front of the door, just when I expected a counselor to pop her head around. This was intended to startle them. I also made a point of being naked. The unannounced visits ended.

The knocking persisted. Through the peephole I saw a white face, distorted and balloonish.

"Let me in." The person looked like a boy but it sounded like a girl. "Let me in," the voice repeated.

"Not a chance," I said. I had a suicide single, and I wanted to keep it that way. No roommates, no visitors.

Then the person began to sob, and I heard a back slump against the door. If I hadn't known the person was white from the peephole, I'd have known it from a display like this. Black people didn't knock on strangers' doors, crying. Not that I understood the black people at Yale. Most of them were from New York and tried hard to pretend that they hadn't gone to prep schools. And there was something pitiful in how cool they were. Occasionally one would reach out to me with missionary zeal, but I'd rebuff the person with haughty silence.

"I don't have anyone to talk to!" the person on the other side of the door cried.

"That is correct."

"When I was a child," the person said, "I played by myself in a corner of the schoolyard all alone. I hated dolls and I hated games, animals were not friendly and birds flew away. If anyone was looking for me I hid behind a tree and cried out 'I am an orphan—' "

I opened the door. It was a she.

"Plagiarist!" I yelled. She had just recited a Frank O'Hara poem as though she'd thought it up herself. I knew the poem because it was one of the few things I'd been forced to read that I wished I'd written myself.

The girl turned to face me, smiling weakly, as though her triumph was not in getting me to open the door but in the fact that she was able to smile at all when she was so accustomed to crying. She was large but not obese, and crying had turned her face the color of raw chicken. She blew her nose into the waist end of her T-shirt, revealing a pale belly.

"How do you know that poem?"

She sniffed. "I'm in your Contemporary Poetry class."

She said she was Canadian and her name was Heidi, although she said she wanted people to call her Henrik. "That's a guy's name," I said. "What do you want? A sex change?"

She looked at me with so little surprise that I suspected she hadn't discounted this as an option. Then her story came out in teary, hiccup-like bursts. She had sucked some "cute guy's dick" and he'd told everybody and now people thought she was "a slut."

"Why'd you suck his dick? Aren't you a lesbian?"

She fit the bill. Short hair, hard, roach-stomping shoes. Dressed like an aspiring plumber. And then there was the name Henrik. The lesbians I'd seen on TV were wiry, thin strips of muscle, but Heidi was round and soft and had a moonlike face. Drab henna-colored hair. And lesbians had cats. "Do you have a cat?" I asked.

Her eyes turned glossy with new tears. "No," she said, her voice quavering, "and I'm not a lesbian. Are you?"

"Do I look like one?" I said.

She didn't answer.

"O.K.," I said. "I could suck a guy's dick, too, if I wanted. But I don't. The human penis is one of the most germ-ridden objects there is." Heidi looked at me, unconvinced. "What I meant to say," I began again, "is that I don't like anybody. Period. Guys or girls. I'm a misanthrope."

"I am, too."

"No," I said, guiding her back through my door and out into the hallway. "You're not."

"Have you had dinner?" she asked. "Let's go to Commons."

I pointed to a pyramid of ramen noodle packages on my windowsill. "See that? That means I never have to go to Commons. Aside from class, I have contact with no one."

"I hate it here, too," she said. "I should have gone to McGill, eh."

"The way to feel better," I said, "is to get some ramen and lock yourself in your room. Everyone will forget about you and that guy's dick and you won't have to see anyone ever again. If anyone looks for you—"

"I'll hide behind a tree."

"A revolver?" Dr. Raeburn said, flipping through a manila folder. He looked up at me as if to ask another question, but he didn't.

Dr. Raeburn was the psychiatrist. He had the gray hair and whiskers of a Civil War general. He was also a chain smoker with beige teeth and a navy wool jacket smeared with ash. He asked about the revolver at the beginning of my first visit. When I was unable to explain myself, he smiled, as if this were perfectly reasonable.

"Tell me about your parents."

I wondered what he already had on file. The folder was thick, though I hadn't said a thing of significance since Day One.

"My father was a dick and my mother seemed to like him."

He patted his pockets for his cigarettes. "That's some heavy stuff," he said. "How do you feel about Dad?" The man couldn't say the word "father." "Is Dad someone you see often?"

"I hate my father almost as much as I hate the word 'Dad.'"

He started tapping his cigarette.

"You can't smoke in here."

"That's right," he said, and slipped the cigarette back into the packet. He smiled, widening his eyes brightly. "Don't ever start."

I thought that that first encounter would be the last of Heidi or Henrik, or whatever, but then her head appeared in a window of Linsly-Chit during my Chaucer class. A few days later, she swooped down a flight of stairs in Harkness, following me. She hailed me from across Elm Street and found me in the Sterling Library stacks. After one of my meetings with Dr. Raeburn, she was waiting for me outside Health Services, legs crossed, cleaning her fingernails.

"You know," she said, as we walked through Old Campus, "you've got to stop eating ramen. Not only does it lack a single nutrient but it's full of MSG."

I wondered why she even bothered, and was vaguely flattered she cared, but I said, "I like eating chemicals. It keeps the skin radiant."

"There's also hepatitis." She knew how to get my attention—mention a disease.

"You get hepatitis from unwashed lettuce," I said. "If there's anything safe from the perils of the food chain, it's ramen."

"But do you refrigerate what you don't eat? Each time you reheat it, you're killing good bacteria, which then can't keep the bad bacteria in check. A guy got sick from reheating Chinese noodles, and his son died from it. I read it in the *Times*." With this, she put a jovial arm around my neck. I continued walking, a little stunned. Then, just as quickly, she dropped her arm and stopped walking. I stopped, too.

"Did you notice that I put my arm around you?"

"Yes," I said. "Next time, I'll have to chop it off."

"I don't want you to get sick," she said. "Let's eat at Commons."

In the cold air, her arm had felt good.

The problem with Commons was that it was too big; its ceiling was as high as a cathedral's, but below it there were no awestruck worshippers, only eighteen-year-olds at heavy wooden tables, chatting over veal patties and Jell-O.

We got our food, tacos stuffed with meat substitute, and made our way through the maze of tables. The Koreans had a table. Each singing group had a table. The crew team sat at a long table of its own. We passed the black table. Heidi was so plump and moonfaced that the sheer quantity of her flesh accentuated just how white she was. The black students gave me a long, hard stare.

"How you doing, sista?" a guy asked, his voice full of accusation, eyeballing me as though I were clad in a Klansman's sheet and hood. "I guess we won't see you till graduation."

"If," I said, "you graduate."

The remark was not well received. As I walked past, I heard protests, angry and loud as if they'd discovered a cheat at their poker game. Heidi and I found an unoccupied table along the periphery, which was isolated and dark. We sat down. Heidi prayed over her tacos.

"I thought you didn't believe in God," I said.

"Not in the God depicted in the Judeo-Christian Bible, but I do believe that nature's essence is a spirit that—"

"All right," I said. I had begun to eat, and cubes of diced tomato fell from my mouth when I spoke. "Stop right there. Tacos and spirits don't mix."

"You've always got to be so flip," she said. "I'm going to apply for another friend."

"There's always Mr. Dick," I said. "Slurp, slurp."

"You are so lame. So unbelievably lame. I'm going out with Mr. Dick. Thursday night at Atticus. His name is Keith."

Heidi hadn't mentioned Mr. Dick since the day I'd met her. That was more than a month ago and we'd spent a lot of that time together. I checked for signs that she was lying; her habit of smiling too much, her eyes bright and cheeks full so that she looked like a chipmunk. But she looked normal. Pleased, even, to see me so flustered.

"You're insane! What are you going to do this time?" I asked. "Sleep with him? Then when he makes fun of you, what? Come pound your head on my door reciting the collected poems of Sylvia Plath?"

"He's going to apologize for before. And don't call me insane. You're the one going to the psychiatrist."

"Well, I'm not going to suck his dick, that's for sure."

She put her arm around me in mock comfort, but I pushed it off, and ignored her. She touched my shoulder again, and I turned, annoyed, but it wasn't Heidi after all; a sepia-toned boy dressed in khakis and a crisp plaid shirt was standing behind me. He thrust a hot-pink square of paper toward me without a word, then briskly made his way toward the other end of Commons, where the crowds blossomed. Heidi leaned over and read it: "Wear Black Leather—the Less, the Better."

"It's a gay party," I said, crumpling the card. "He thinks we're fucking gay."

Heidi and I signed on to work at the Saybrook dining hall as dishwashers. The job consisted of dumping food from plates and trays into a vat of rushing water. It seemed straightforward, but then I learned better. You wouldn't believe what people could do with food until you worked in a dish room. Lettuce and crackers and soup would be bullied into a pulp in the bowl of some bored anorexic; ziti would be mixed with honey and granola; trays would appear heaped with mashed potato snow women with melted chocolate ice cream for hair. Frat boys arrived at the dish-room window, en masse. They liked to fill glasses with food, then seal them, airtight, onto their trays. If you tried to prize them off, milk, Worcestershire sauce, peas, chunks of bread vomited onto your dish-room uniform.

When this happened one day in the middle of the lunch rush, for what seemed like the hundredth time, I tipped the tray toward one of the frat boys as he turned to walk away, popping the glasses off so that the mess spurted onto his Shetland sweater.

He looked down at his sweater. "Lesbo bitch!"

"No," I said, "that would be your mother."

Heidi, next to me, clenched my arm in support, but I remained motionless, waiting to see what the frat boy would do. He glared at me for a minute, then walked away.

"Let's take a smoke break," Heidi said.

I didn't smoke, but Heidi had begun to, because she thought it would help her lose weight. As I hefted a stack of glasses through the steamer, she lit up.

"Soft packs remind me of you," she said. "Just when you've smoked them all and you think there's none left, there's always one more, hiding in that little crushed corner." Before I could respond she said, "Oh, God. Not another mouse. You know whose job that is."

By the end of the rush, the floor mats got full and slippery with food. This was when mice tended to appear, scurrying over our shoes; more often than not, a mouse got caught in the grating that covered the drains in the floor. Sometimes the mouse was already dead by the time we noticed it. This one was alive.

"No way," I said. "This time you're going to help. Get some gloves and a trash bag."

"That's all I'm getting. I'm not getting that mouse out of there."

"Put on the gloves," I ordered. She winced, but put them on.

"Reach down," I said. "At an angle, so you get at its middle. Otherwise, if you try to get it by its tail, the tail will break off."

"This is filthy, eh."

"That's why we're here," I said. "To clean up filth. Eh."

She reached down, but would not touch the mouse. I put my hand around her arm and pushed it till her hand made contact. The cries from the mouse were soft, songlike. "Oh, my God," she said. "Oh, my God, ohmigod." She wrestled it out of the grating and turned her head away.

"Don't you let it go," I said.

"Where's the food bag? It'll smother itself if I drop it in the food bag. Quick," she said, her head still turned away, her eyes closed. "Lead me to it."

"No. We are not going to smother this mouse. We've got to break its neck."

"You're one heartless bitch."

I wondered how to explain that if death is unavoidable it should be quick and painless. My mother had died slowly. At the hospital, they'd said it was kidney failure, but I knew, in the end, it was my father. He made her so scared to live in her own home that she was finally driven away from it in an ambulance.

"Breaking its neck will save it the pain of smothering," I said.

"Breaking its neck is more humane. Take the trash bag and cover it so you won't get any blood on you, then crush."

The loud jets of the steamer had shut off automatically and the dish room grew quiet. Heidi breathed in deeply, then crushed the mouse. She shuddered, disgusted. "Now what?"

"What do you mean, 'now what?' Throw the little bastard in the trash."

At our third session, I told Dr. Raeburn I didn't mind if he smoked. He sat on the sill of his open window, smoking behind a jungle screen of office plants.

We spent the first ten minutes discussing the Iliad, and whether or not the text actually states that Achilles had been dipped in the River Styx. He said it did, and I said it didn't. After we'd finished with the Iliad, and with my new job in what he called "the scullery," he asked questions about my parents. I told him nothing. It was none of his business. Instead, I talked about Heidi. I told him about that day in Commons, Heidi's plan to go on a date with Mr. Dick, and the invitation we'd been given to the gay party.

"You seem preoccupied by this soirée." He arched his eyebrows at the word "soirée."

"Wouldn't you be?"

"Dina," he said slowly, in a way that made my name seem like a song title, "have you ever had a romantic interest?"

"You want to know if I've ever had a boyfriend?" I said. "Just go ahead and ask if I've ever fucked anybody."

This appeared to surprise him. "I think that you are having a crisis of identity," he said.

"Oh, is that what this is?"

His profession had taught him not to roll his eyes. Instead, his exasperation revealed itself in a tiny pursing of his lips, as though he'd just tasted something awful and was trying very hard not to offend the cook.

"It doesn't have to be, as you say, someone you've fucked, it doesn't have to be a boyfriend," he said.

"Well, what are you trying to say? If it's not a boy, then you're saying it's a girl—"

"Calm down. It could be a crush, Dina." He lit one cigarette off another. "A crush on a male teacher, a crush on a dog, for heaven's sake. An interest. Not necessarily a relationship."

It was sacrifice time. If I could spend the next half hour talking about some boy, then I'd have given him what he wanted.

So I told him about the boy with the nice shoes.

I was sixteen and had spent the last few coins in my pocket on bus fare to buy groceries. I didn't like going to the Super Fresh two blocks away from my house, plunking government food stamps into the hands of the cashiers.

"There she go reading," one of them once said, even though I was only carrying a book. "Don't your eyes get tired?"

On Greenmount Avenue you could read schoolbooks—that was understandable. The government and your teachers forced you to read them. But anything else was antisocial. It meant you'd rather submit to the words of some white dude than shoot the breeze with your neighbors.

I hated those cashiers, and I hated them seeing me with food stamps, so I took the bus and shopped elsewhere. That day, I got off the bus at Govans, and though the neighborhood was black like my own—hair salon after hair salon of airbrushed signs promising arabesque hair styles and inch-long fingernails—the houses were neat and orderly, nothing at all like Greenmount, where every other house had at least one shattered window. The store was well swept, and people quietly checked long grocery lists—no screaming kids, no loud cashier-customer altercations. I got the groceries and left the store.

I decided to walk back. It was a fall day, and I walked for blocks. Then I sensed someone following me. I walked more quickly, my arms around the sack, the leafy lettuce tickling my nose. I didn't want to hold the sack so close that it would break the eggs or squash the hamburger buns, but it was slipping, and as I looked behind me a boy my age, maybe older, rushed toward me.

"Let me help you," he said.

"That's all right." I set the bag on the sidewalk. Maybe I saw his face, maybe it was handsome enough, but what I noticed first, splayed on either side of the bag, were his shoes. They were nice shoes, real leather, a stitched design like a widow's peak on each one, or like birds' wings, and for the first time in my life I understood what people meant when they said "wing-tip shoes."

"I watched you carry them groceries out that store, then you look around, like you're lost, but like you liked being lost, then you walk down the sidewalk for blocks and blocks. Rearranging that bag, it almost gone to slip, then hefting it back up again."

"Uh-huh," I said.

"And then I passed my own house and was still following you. And then your bag really look like it was gone crash and everything. So I just thought I'd help." He sucked in his bottom lip, as if to keep it from making a smile. "What's your name?" When I told him, he said, "Dina, my name is Cecil." Then he said, "D comes right after C."

"Yes," I said, "it does, doesn't it."

Then, half question, half statement, he said, "I could carry your groceries for you? And walk you home?"

I stopped the story there. Dr. Raeburn kept looking at me. "Then what happened?"

I couldn't tell him the rest: that I had not wanted the boy to walk me home, that I didn't want someone with such nice shoes to see where I lived.

Dr. Raeburn would only have pitied me if I'd told him that I ran down the sidewalk after I told the boy no, that I fell, the bag slipped, and the eggs cracked, their yolks running all over the lettuce. Clear amniotic fluid coated the can of cinnamon rolls. I left the bag there on the sidewalk, the groceries spilled out randomly like cards loosed from a deck. When I returned home, I told my mother that I'd lost the food stamps.

"Lost?" she said. I'd expected her to get angry, I'd wanted her to get angry, but she hadn't. "Lost?" she repeated. Why had I been so clumsy and nervous around a harmless boy? I could have brought the groceries home and washed off the egg yolk, but instead I'd just left them there. "Come on," Mama said, snuffing her tears, pulling my arm, trying to get me to join her and start yanking cushions off the couch. "We'll find enough change here. We got to get something for dinner before your father gets back."

We'd already searched the couch for money the previous week, and I knew there'd be nothing now, but I began to push my fingers into the couch's boniest corners, pretending that it was only a matter of time before I'd find some change or a lost watch or an earring. Something pawnable, perhaps.

"What happened next?" Dr. Raeburn asked again. "Did you let the boy walk you home?"

"My house was far, so we went to his house instead." Though I was sure Dr. Raeburn knew that I was making this part up, I continued. "We made out on his sofa. He kissed me."

Dr. Raeburn lit his next cigarette like a detective. Cool, suspicious. "How did it feel?"

"You know," I said. "Like a kiss feels. It felt nice. The kiss felt very, very nice."

Raeburn smiled gently, though he seemed unconvinced. When he called time on our session, his cigarette had become one long pole of ash. I left his office, walking quickly down the corridor, afraid to look back. It would be like him to trot after me, his navy blazer flapping, just to get the truth out of me. *You never kissed anyone.* The words slid from my brain, and knotted in my stomach.

When I reached my dorm, I found an old record player blocking my door and a Charles Mingus LP propped beside it. I carried them inside and then, lying on the floor, I played the Mingus over and over again until I fell asleep. I slept feeling as though Dr. Raeburn had attached electrodes to my head, willing into my mind a dream about my mother. I saw the lemon meringue of her skin, the long bone of her arm as she reached down to clip her toenails. I'd come home from a school trip to an aquarium, and I was explaining the differences between baleen and sperm whales according to the size of their heads, the range of their habitats, their feeding patterns.

I awoke remembering the expression on her face after I'd finished my dizzying whale lecture. She looked like a tourist who'd asked for directions to a place she thought was simple enough to get to only to hear a series of hypothetical turns, alleys, one-way streets. Her response was to nod politely at the perilous elaborateness of it all; to nod and save herself from the knowledge that she would never be able to get where she wanted to go.

The dishwashers always closed down the dining hall. One night, after everyone else had punched out, Heidi and I took a break, and though I wasn't a smoker, we set two milk crates upside down on the floor and smoked cigarettes.

The dishwashing machines were off, but steam still rose from them like a jungle mist. Outside in the winter air, students were singing carols in their groomed and tailored singing-group voices. The Whiffenpoofs were back in New Haven after a tour around the world, and I guess their return was a huge deal. Heidi and I craned our necks to watch the year's first show through an open window.

"What are you going to do when you're finished?" Heidi asked. Sexy question marks of smoke drifted up to the windows before vanishing.

"Take a bath."

She swatted me with her free hand. "No, silly. Three years from now. When you leave Yale."

"I don't know. Open up a library. Somewhere where no one comes in for books. A library in a desert."

She looked at me as though she'd expected this sort of answer and didn't know why she'd asked in the first place.

"What are you going to do?" I asked her.

"Open up a psych clinic. In a desert. And my only patient will be some wacko who runs a library."

"Ha," I said. "Whatever you do, don't work in a dish room ever again. You're no good." I got up from the crate. "C'mon. Let's hose the place down."

We put out our cigarettes on the floor, since it was our job to clean it anyway. We held squirt guns in one hand and used the other to douse the floors with the standard-issue, eye-burning cleaning solution. We hosed the dish room, the kitchen, the serving line, sending the water and crud and suds into the drains. Then we hosed them again so the solution wouldn't eat holes in our shoes as we left. Then I had an idea. I unbuckled my belt.

"What the hell are you doing?" Heidi said.

"Listen, it's too cold to go outside with our uniforms all wet. We could just take a shower right here. There's nobody but us."

"What the fuck, eh?"

I let my pants drop, then took off my shirt and panties. I didn't wear a bra, since I didn't have much to fill one. I took off my shoes and hung my clothes on the stepladder.

"You've flipped," Heidi said. "I mean, really, psych-ward flipped."

I soaped up with the liquid hand soap until I felt as glazed as a ham. "Stand back and spray me."

"Oh, my God," she said. I didn't know whether she was confused or delighted, but she picked up the squirt gun and sprayed me. She was laughing. Then she got too close and the water started to sting.

"God damn it!" I said. "That hurt!"

"I was wondering what it would take to make you say that."

When all the soap had been rinsed off, I put on my regular clothes and said, "O.K. You're up next."

"No way," she said.

"Yes way."

She started to take off her uniform shirt, then stopped.

"What?"

"I'm too fat."

"You goddam right." She always said she was fat. One time I'd told her that she should shut up about it, that large black women wore their fat like mink coats. "You're big as a house," I said now. "Frozen yogurt may be low in calories, but not if you eat five tubs of it. Take your clothes off. I want to get out of here."

She began taking off her uniform, then stood there, hands cupped over her breasts, crouching at the pubic bone.

"Open up," I said, "or we'll never get done."

Her hands remained where they were. I threw the bottle of liquid soap at her, and she had to catch it, revealing herself as she did.

I turned on the squirt gun, and she stood there, stiff, arms at her side, eyes closed, as though awaiting mummification. I began with the water on low, and she turned around in a full circle, hesitantly, letting the droplets from the spray fall on her as if she were submitting to a death by stoning.

When I increased the water pressure, she slipped and fell on the sudsy floor. She stood up and then slipped again. This time she laughed and remained on the floor, rolling around on it as I sprayed.

I think I began to love Heidi that night in the dish room, but who is to say that I hadn't begun to love her the first time I met her? I sprayed her and sprayed her, and she turned over and over like a large beautiful dolphin, lolling about in the sun.

Heidi started sleeping at my place. Sometimes she slept on the floor; sometimes we slept sardinelike, my feet at her head, until she complained that my feet were "taunting" her. When we finally slept head to head, she said, "Much better." She was so close I could smell her toothpaste. "I like your hair," she told me, touching it through the darkness. "You should wear it out more often."

"White people always say that about black people's hair. The worse it looks, the more they say they like it."

I'd expected her to disagree, but she kept touching my hair, her hands passing through it till my scalp tingled. When she began to touch the hair around the edge of my face, I felt myself quake. Her fingertips stopped for a moment, as if checking my pulse, then resumed.

"I like how it feels right here. See, mine just starts with the same old texture as the rest of my hair." She found my hand under the blanket and brought it to her hairline. "See," she said.

It was dark. As I touched her hair, it seemed as though I could smell it, too. Not a shampoo smell. Something richer, murkier. A bit dead, but sweet, like the decaying wood of a ship. She guided my hand.

"I see," I said. The record she'd given me was playing in my mind, and I kept trying to shut it off. I could also hear my mother saying that this is what happens when you've been around white people: things get weird. So weird I could hear the stylus etching its way into the flat vinyl of the record. "Listen," I said finally, when the bass and saxes started up. I heard Heidi breathe deeply, but she said nothing.

We spent the winter and some of the spring in my room—never hers— missing tests, listening to music, looking out my window to comment on people who wouldn't have given us a second thought. We read books related to none of our classes. I got riled up by *The Autobiography of Malcolm X* and

The Chomsky Reader; Heidi read aloud passages from *The Anxiety of Influence*. We guiltily read mysteries and *Clan of the Cave Bear*, then immediately threw them away. Once we looked up from our books at exactly the same moment, as though trapped at a dinner table with nothing to say. A pleasant trap of silence.

Then one weekend I went back to Baltimore and stayed with my father. He asked me how school was going, but besides that, we didn't talk much. He knew what I thought of him. I stopped by the Enoch Pratt Library, where my favorite librarian, Mrs. Ardelia, cornered me into giving a little talk to the after-school kids, telling them to stay in school. They just looked at me like I was crazy; they were only nine or ten, and it hadn't even occurred to them to bail.

When I returned to Yale—to a sleepy, tree-scented spring—a group of students were holding what was called "Coming Out Day." I watched it from my room.

The emcee was the sepia boy who'd given us the invitation months back. His speech was strident but still smooth and peppered with jokes. There was a speech about AIDS, with lots of statistics: nothing that seemed to make "coming out" worth it. Then the women spoke. One girl pronounced herself "out" as casually as if she'd announced the time. Another said nothing at all: she came to the microphone with a woman who began cutting off her waist-length, bleached-blond hair. The woman doing the cutting tossed the shorn hair in every direction as she cut. People were clapping and cheering and catching the locks of hair.

And then there was Heidi. She was proud that she liked girls, she said when she reached the microphone. She loved them, wanted to sleep with them. She was a dyke, she said repeatedly, stabbing her finger to her chest in case anyone was unsure to whom she was referring. She could not have seen me. I was across the street, three stories up. And yet, when everyone clapped for her, she seemed to be looking straight at me.

Heidi knocked. "Let me in."

It was like the first time I met her. The tears, the raw pink of her face.

We hadn't spoken in weeks. Outside, pink-and-white blossoms hung from the Old Campus trees. Students played Hacky Sack in T-shirts and shorts. Though I was the one who'd broken away after she went up to that podium, I still half expected her to poke her head out a window in Linsly-Chit, or tap on my back in Harkness, or even join me in the Commons dining hall, where I'd asked for my dish-room shift to be transferred. She did none of these.

"Well," I said, "what is it?"

She looked at me. "My mother," she said.

She continued to cry, but seemed to have grown so silent in my room I wondered if I could hear the numbers change on my digital clock.

"When my parents were getting divorced," she said, "my mother bought a car. A used one. An El Dorado. It was filthy. It looked like a huge crushed can coming up the street. She kept trying to clean it out. I mean—"

I nodded and tried to think what to say in the pause she left behind. Finally I said, "We had one of those," though I was sure ours was an Impala.

She looked at me, eyes steely from trying not to cry. "Anyway, she'd drive me around in it and although she didn't like me to eat in it, I always did. One day I was eating cantaloupe slices, spitting the seeds on the floor. Maybe a month later, I saw this little sprout, growing right up from the car floor. I just started laughing and she kept saying what, what? I was laughing and then I saw she was so—"

She didn't finish. So what? So sad? So awful? Heidi looked at me with what seemed to be a renewed vigor. "We could have gotten a better car, eh?"

"It's all right. It's not a big deal," I said.

Of course, that was the wrong thing to say. And I really didn't mean it to sound the way it had come out.

I told Dr. Raeburn about Heidi's mother having cancer and how I'd said it wasn't a big deal, though I'd wanted to say the opposite. I told Dr. Raeburn how I meant to tell Heidi that my mother had died, that I knew how one eventually accustoms oneself to the physical world's lack of sympathy: the buses that are still running late, the kids who still play in the street, the clocks that won't stop ticking for the person who's gone.

"You're pretending," Dr. Raeburn said, not sage or professional, but a little shocked by the discovery, as if I'd been trying to hide a pack of his cigarettes behind my back.

"I'm pretending?" I shook my head. "All those years of psych grad," I said. "And to tell me *that*?"

"What I mean is that you construct stories about yourself and dish them out—one for you, one for you—" Here he reenacted this process, showing me handing out lies as if they were apples.

"Pretending. I believe the professional name for it might be denial," I said. "Are you calling me gay?"

He pursed his lips noncommittally, then finally said, "No, Dina. I don't think you're gay."

I checked his eyes. I couldn't read them.

"No. Not at all," he said, sounding as if he were telling a subtle joke. "But maybe you'll finally understand."

"Understand what?"

"Oh, just that constantly saying what one doesn't mean accustoms the mouth to meaningless phrases." His eyes narrowed. "Maybe you'll understand that when you finally need to express something truly significant your mouth will revert to the insignificant nonsense it knows so well." He looked at me, his hands sputtering in the air in a gesture of defeat. "Who knows?" he asked with a glib, psychiatric smile I'd never seen before. "Maybe it's your survival mechanism. Black living in a white world."

I heard him, but only vaguely. I'd hooked on to that one word, pretending. Dr. Raeburn would never realize that "pretending" was what had got me this far. I remembered the morning of my mother's funeral. I'd been given milk to settle my stomach; I'd pretended it was coffee. I imagined I was drinking coffee elsewhere. Some Arabic-speaking country where the thick coffee served in little cups was so strong it could keep you awake for days.

Heidi wanted me to go with her to the funeral. She'd sent this message through the dean. "We'll pay for your ticket to Vancouver," the dean said.

These people wanted you to owe them for everything. "What about my return ticket?" I asked the dean. "Maybe the shrink will chip in for that."

The dean looked at me as though I were an insect she'd like to squash. "We'll pay for the whole thing. We might even pay for some lessons in manners."

So I packed my suitcase and walked from my suicide single dorm to Heidi's room. A thin wispy girl in ragged cutoffs and a shirt that read "LSBN!" answered the door. A group of short-haired girls in thick black leather jackets, bundled up despite the summer heat, encircled Heidi in a protective fairy ring. They looked at me critically, clearly wondering if Heidi was too fragile for my company.

"You've got our numbers," one said, holding on to Heidi's shoulder. "And Vancouver's got a great gay community."

"Oh, God," I said. "She's going to a funeral, not a Save the Dykes rally."

One of the girls stepped in front of me.

"It's O.K., Cynthia," Heidi said. Then she ushered me into her bedroom and closed the door. A suitcase was on her bed, half packed.

"I could just uninvite you," Heidi said. "How about that? You want that?" She folded a polka-dotted T-shirt that was wrong for any occasion and put it in her suitcase. "Why haven't you talked to me?" she said, looking at the shirt instead of me. "Why haven't you talked to me in two months?"

"I don't know," I said.

"You don't know," she said, each syllable steeped in sarcasm. "You don't know. Well, I know. You thought I was going to try to sleep with you."

"Try to? We slept together all winter!"

"If you call smelling your feet sleeping together, you've got a lot to learn." She seemed thinner and meaner; every line of her body held me at bay.

"So tell me," I said. "What can you show me that I need to learn?" But as soon as I said it I somehow knew she still hadn't slept with anyone. "Am I supposed to come over there and sweep your enraged self into my arms?" I said. "Like in the movies? Is this the part where we're both so mad we kiss each other?"

She shook her head and smiled weakly. "You don't get it," she said. "My mother is dead." She closed her suitcase, clicking shut the old-fashioned locks. "My mother is dead," she said again, this time reminding herself. She set her suitcase upright on the floor and sat on it. She looked like someone waiting for a train.

"Fine," I said. "And she's going to be dead for a long time." Though it sounded stupid, I felt good saying it. As though I had my own locks to click shut.

* * *

Heidi went to Vancouver for her mother's funeral. I didn't go with her. Instead, I went back to Baltimore and moved in with an aunt I barely knew. Every day was the same: I read and smoked outside my aunt's apartment, studying the row of hair salons across the street, where girls in denim cut-offs and tank tops would troop in and come out hours later, a flash of neon nails, coifs the color and sheen of patent leather. And every day I imagined Heidi's house in Vancouver. Her place would not be large, but it would be clean. Flowery shrubs would line the walks. The Canadian wind would whip us about like pennants. I'd be visiting her in some vague time in the future, deliberately vague, for people like me, who realign past events to suit themselves. In that future time, you always have a chance to catch the groceries before they fall; your words can always be rewound and erased, rewritten and revised.

Then I'd imagine Heidi visiting me. There are no psychiatrists or deans, no boys with nice shoes or flip cashiers. Just me in my single room. She knocks on the door and says, "Open up."

2000

FRANCISCO GOLDMAN
B. 1954

Perhaps the best known of contemporary U.S. writers meditating on Central America and its long and difficult history of wars, genocide, and political intrigue, Francisco Goldman has emerged as a highly visible and well-regarded novelist and public intellectual. He began publishing fiction after a decade of political journalism focusing on the bloody and genocidal wars in Central America, wars frequently promoted and supported by the U.S. government. To date he has written four moving and stylistically distinct novels as well as a very risky history of state-sponsored murder. His first novel, *The Long Night of White Chickens* (1992), examines Guatemala's civil war by playing with the genre of detective fiction. His second novel, *The Ordinary Seaman* (1997), is a narratively complex and sophisticated consideration of the lives of a crew of men drawn from the ravages of wars in Central America who find themselves abandoned, marooned on a ship anchored, ironically enough, in a Brooklyn harbor. *The Divine Husband* (2004), his third novel, offers a fictional portrait of Cuban New York author and revolutionary hero, José Martí.

Born in Boston in 1954, Goldman is the son of a Jewish Ukrainian American chemical engineer and a Guatemalan woman from an elite upper-class family. His parents had a rocky marriage, so Goldman grew up bouncing between wealthy Guatemalan chalets and a neighborhood in Boston that he remembers as "brutal." On one of his trips to Guatemala, Goldman learned about state-sponsored violence when a friend showed him piles of mutilated bodies in a city morgue. Horrified by the impunity of the police and army, Goldman eventually turned to efforts to break that impunity. The result was his highly influential *The Art of Political Murder: Who Killed Bishop Gerardi?* (2007), which explores the murder of a Catholic priest two days after he released a four-volume report on Guatemala's civil war, in which more than 200,000 people were killed over four decades.

In each of his texts, Goldman asks readers to consider the enormity and inexplicability of loss and murder at the hands of the state—indeed at the hands of police and military officials whose presence is seemingly justified by their claim to protect people rather than to indiscriminately maim, torture, and kill them. He does not suggest, in any of these texts, that such violence and attendant grief are banal or something that one adjusts too.

Sadly for Goldman, the experience of loss and grief became vividly personal shortly after he completed *The Art of Political Murder*, when his partner and wife, the writer Aura Estrada, accidentally died while bodysurfing off the coast of Mexico. That devastating event and the complex effects of her loss were eventually channeled into a novel that, according to Goldman, is neither a memoir nor a history but a creative fictional accounting of his loss. In *Say Her Name* (2011), he explores wave science, addresses Aura, scathingly examines his own intentions, and most especially offers a stunning discussion of loss. The following essay, "The Wave: A Tragedy in Mexico," is drawn from that novel, although it is not an excerpt in the traditional sense. It is more accurately the précis to the longer novelized elegy. It is also of a piece with the long tradition of the costumbrista—the nineteenth-century narrative form popular in Spanish-language publications for its compelling combination of history, journalism, fiction, and the narrator's own, often self-deprecating, ruminations. Toward that end, in this painful recounting of the events leading to Aura's death, Goldman also gives us a chance to see that, in his words, "I don't know if God is in the details, but love is certainly in the details."

Mary Pat Brady
Cornell University

PRIMARY WORKS

The Long Night of White Chickens, 1992; *The Ordinary Seamen*, 1997; *The Divine Husband*, 2004; *The Art of Political Murder: Who Killed the Bishop?*, 2007; *Say Her Name*, 2011.

The Wave

A Tragedy in Mexico

It was July, 2007. The house I'd rented in Mazunte, a beach town in Oaxaca, on the Pacific coast of Mexico, was large enough to accommodate the several friends who my wife, Aura Estrada, and I were hoping would spend at least part of the two weeks there with us and Aura's *prima* Fabiola—Fabis—and her boyfriend, Juanca. Originally, Aura's friend Mariana was going to come, too, but she was having a hard time making ends meet and told us that she couldn't afford a vacation. She said that she didn't want to go to Mazunte anyway, because the waves were too rough. What? But Mazunte is a safe beach! That's how we unanimously answered Mariana. Because Mazunte is situated in a curving cove that impedes the waves enough to diminish their size, momentum, and strength, it's considered safe for swimmers. Nearby Puerto Escondido, Ventanilla, and San Agustinillo, open to the ocean, are the dangerous beaches. You take your life in your hands when you swim at one of them. But we all loved Mazunte. The waves could be rough there, but they didn't scare me. They seemed about the same as those at Wellfleet, on Cape Cod, where I'd learned to bodysurf as a teen-ager.

A few years before I met Aura, I'd gone to Puerto Escondido with some friends for the millennial New Year. When we got there, people were talking about a rogue wave that had dashed three surfers into the cliffs at the far end of the beach the day before, killing them. My first morning, I went swimming and then to breakfast at a café on the beach, where the waiter told me that the last time he'd gone into the ocean there he'd come out bleeding from both ears. That night, in my hotel room, I lay in bed listening to the waves, which now sounded to me as if they were grinding bones.

I didn't go into the water at Puerto Escondido again until more than four years later, when Aura and I took a surfing lesson while spending a three-day weekend there. A wave caught me by surprise as I was crouching on my board and drove me off the front. My head struck the sandy bottom with a force that stunned me, sending a hard jolt through my spine. Shaken and wobbly, I went and sat on the beach. The instructor laughed. He said that Aura was a more natural surfer than I was. She was stretched out on a board, and the instructor, standing in the waist-high water, was pulling her around like a child on a sled, then releasing her to ride in on the gliding foam of waves that had broken farther out. It turned out that he wasn't an authorized instructor. He'd lied to us and borrowed the surfboards without permission from the shop of a friend who ran a legitimate surfing school. Our lesson ended when the friend's mother ran onto the beach shouting at him that he was going to get us killed and to bring the boards back that instant.

That was the weekend that I proposed to Aura. We had been together for almost a year by then, and were living together in Brooklyn, despite the difference in our ages and situations: she was a twenty-seven-year-old from Mexico City, a graduate student in Latin American literature on a Fulbright scholarship at Columbia; I was forty-nine, born in Boston, the son of Guatemalan and Russian immigrants, working as a journalist and writing a novel. I'd brought a diamond engagement ring with me on our trip, and had hidden it in the safe-deposit box in our room, waiting for the right moment to bring it out. Every morning, Aura and I took the microbus to the beach in Mazunte, and I considered trying to propose there. But where could I safely hide the ring while I went swimming? I always worried about thieves on that beach.

By the last evening of the trip, I still hadn't proposed. My neck was stiff and aching from our surfing lesson. I'd come down with a cold, and the bad shrimp I'd eaten the night before was giving me stomach cramps. All I could have for dinner at the hotel restaurant was a bowl of chicken soup, and I was nursing a Margarita. Still, I couldn't go back to Mexico City, where we were spending the summer, without having proposed. I excused myself from the table and went to our room. A light rain was falling, one of those warm tropical drizzles which feel like the moisture-saturated air inside a cloud, as soft as silk against your face. It might be even more romantic, I thought, to propose outside on the beach in this rain. I took the ring in its little box out of the safe and put it in my pocket. Aura came into the room. "Let's go out to the beach," I said. "Why?" she said. "I don't want to go out to the beach. It's raining." "It's barely a drizzle," I said. "Come on, we have to go to the beach. I have to ask you something." She looked at my hand in my pocket and grinned. "Ask me here," she said, laughing. "*Ay, mi amor*, what do you have in your pocket?" "This is serious," I said, and I pulled the box out of my pocket and dropped to one knee.

One of those mornings, on the microbus to Mazunte, we rode with a Mexican man who was living in Sweden and had returned for a vacation with his Swedish wife. He sat across the aisle from Aura and kept up an ebullient monologue about Mexico and its beaches. Sweden has a lot going for it but no beaches like Mazunte! He even chanted a long list of tropical fruits that grew on that coast, including, he emphasized, five different kinds of banana. He had never actually been to Mazunte. He and his wife were both wearing straw cowboy hats that looked brand new. His nerdy bumpkin quality delighted Aura—*the best beaches in the world! five different kinds of banana!*

We were sitting on the beach a little later when a commotion broke out. There were shouts for help and swimmers running to the aid of someone who'd had an accident. We went, too, and saw the Mexican from Sweden lying face down in a few inches of pooled water, flailing and kicking as if he were drowning. He was carried up onto the beach and set down on the sand, where he lay coughing, sputtering, gasping, his wife crouched alongside. Someone told us what had happened. He'd been knocked over by a wave and, apparently disoriented by the rush of surf, had swallowed water and panicked, even as the wave receded, having practically deposited him on the beach. He was fine. We went back to our chairs. Eventually, we saw him and his wife trudge past us, cowboy hats back on, carrying their things. We said goodbye, but only the wife replied; he stared morosely down at the sand. Later, we occasionally laughed at the memory of the Mexican-Swede—a funny-sad story about the dangers of a certain kind of naïve enthusiasm rather than about danger itself.

For our trip in the summer of 2007, we had reserved tickets on a Monday-night first-class bus from Mexico City to Puerto Escondido, which had seats that converted almost into beds. Juanca had to work that week but would join us at the weekend. The Friday before we were due to leave, Aura, who was now enrolled in an M.F.A. course in addition to her Ph.D. program, gave me a draft of a short story she was working on, "*La vida está en otra parte*," about a wayward teacher. I found a lot in it to praise, but I told her that I thought she'd rushed the ending. The next day, at one in the afternoon, I was just leaving the gym when I got a message from Aura on my BlackBerry: "Fabiola is here . . . I made her eggs and coffee for breakfast. I'm still drinking coffee and working on my story which has already changed a lot. Did you really mean it last night when you said that I'm an artist? Or were you just flirting and working me up????"

I wrote back, "*Claro que eres una artista mi amor de máxima sensibilidad e inteligencia.*" ("Of course you're an artist, my love, of maximum sensibility and intelligence.")

The exchange reminded me of a conversation we'd had on our first date, almost four years earlier.

"That's a robot?"

Aura was showing me a drawing she'd made of a pair of lace-up shoes surrounded by tiny handwritten notations, sketched patterns of angular and undulating lines. "They're shoes that come when you call them," she said.

"You mean you call out, 'Shoes, come here,' and they come walking to you wherever you are?"

"Yeah," she said. "Well, you can't be too far away. And they can't go up and down stairs."

We were sitting on the couch of the apartment where she'd grown up, in Copilco. Her notebook was open on her lap. The shoes were her invention, though still no more than an idea. The robotics would be built into the shoes, she explained. The engineering of the walk was complicated, but imagine it, she told me, as "a synchronized iambic pentameter."

"That's a pretty awesome invention," I said. She dipped her head like a proud circus pony and said thank you. We had met in New York, nine months before, when we both attended a reading given by a mutual acquaintance. Aura was living in Providence then, studying on a fellowship at Brown. We had exchanged information, and I'd sent her a copy of my most recent novel but had never heard back. I'd told myself, She must have hated the book. But that's all right—she's way too young. You really have to forget about her. Then, in late August, she had unexpectedly appeared in El Mitote, a dingy bohemian and cokehead hangout on the edge of the Condesa, in Mexico City. (I rented a cheap apartment in the neighborhood and spent time there whenever I could get away from New York.) I was drinking at the bar with friends, and there she was, standing before me. I felt as if I were staring at her through a thick haze—the cigarette smoke in the air, my inebriation, my shy amazement. "How come you never answered the e-mail I sent you?" she asked. I said that I'd never received an e-mail from her. She'd sent me an e-mail, she insisted, in which she'd thanked me for the book, and told me that she was coming back to New York. I didn't think she was the kind of person who wouldn't say thank you for a book, did I? "Well, I don't know what happened to that e-mail," I said. "It must have got lost."

Aura was leaving for New York in three days, she told me, to begin her studies at Columbia. That news lit a silent burst of sparks in me. I'd be flying back, too, in two weeks. "Then there's no time for us to get together before you go," I said, but she said, "Why not? There's time." And we agreed to meet for dinner the following night.

On the couch, she turned more pages in her notebook until she came to one that was filled with writing in turquoise ballpoint ink. This was a short story she'd recently finished. "Do you want to hear it?" she asked. "It's really short, only four pages." I said of course, and she read it to me. The story was about a young man in an airport who couldn't remember if he was there because he was arriving or because he was going somewhere. It was written in a minimalist lonely-airport tone, with a sweet, deadpan humor. I wasn't concentrating very well, though. At dinner, I'd already begun casting my hopes forward, plotting how soon I could see Aura in New York. Then she had taken me by surprise, inviting me back to her apartment. Had she only wanted to read me a story? Sitting close to her, I watched her lips form the words, and wondered if I was really going to kiss them in the next few minutes, or hours, or ever.

Aura's parents had moved out of the apartment and into a new place a year before. All they had left behind in the living room was the couch we were sitting on and the round dining table, metallic gray and white, where Aura had sat through thousands of family meals. Most of her books and things were already packed into cardboard boxes.

When Aura finished reading, I told her that I really liked the story, and she asked me why. While I spoke, she held herself perfectly still, as if she could hear my pulse and was measuring it like a polygraph. Then she told me that I'd only said what I'd said because I liked her. I laughed and said, "It's definitely true that I like you, but I liked the story, too, honestly." We began to kiss, and ended up in her bed. I was so surprised by this development that I felt like a puppy romping in a field of tulips. But then she asked if I minded if she kept her jeans on. I said, "That's O.K. with me, really, no big hurry." A while later, we fell asleep in each other's arms. On her ceiling were hundreds of little glow-in-the-dark stars.

In the morning, when I was in the bathroom, she leaned out of bed and took my wallet out of my pants on the floor. When I came back in, she was holding my driver's license. She looked up and exclaimed, "Forty-eight!"

"Yup," I said, embarrassed. She was twenty-six.

"I thought you were at least ten years younger," she said. "I guessed you were thirty–six."

"Thanks, I guess I'm supposed to say," I said.

Aura moved in with me in Brooklyn about six weeks after she arrived in New York, and two years later we were married. Because I usually worked from home, I rarely had to leave the neighborhood, but for Aura the commute was long. From my place, in Carroll Gardens, she'd walk twenty-five minutes to the Borough Hall subway station, and then ride the train at least an hour to get to Columbia. In winter, the trek could be brutally cold. I finally persuaded her to let me buy her one of those hooded North Face down coats, swaddling her from the top of her head to below her knees in goose-down-puffed blue nylon. "No, *mi amor*, it doesn't make you look fat, not you in particular. Everybody looks like a walking sleeping bag in these, and who cares, anyway?" I said. With the hood up, and her gleaming black eyes, she looked like a little Iroquois girl walking around in her own papoose. She hardly ever went out into the cold without it.

Another complication of the long commute was that Aura regularly got lost. She'd absent-mindedly miss her stop or take the train in the wrong direction and, engrossed in her book, her thoughts, or her iPod, not notice until she was deep into Brooklyn. Then she'd call from a pay phone in some subway station I'd never heard of: "Hola, *mi amor*, well, here I am in the Beverley Road station. I went the wrong way again," her voice determinedly matter-of-fact, just another over-scheduled New Yorker coping with a routine dilemma of city life, but sounding a touch defeated anyhow.

From Aura's first day in our Brooklyn apartment to nearly her last, I walked her at least part of the way to the subway stop every morning, and often she tried to coax me farther, or even up to Columbia with her. I'd spend the morning in Butler Library, reading or writing. We'd have lunch at Ollie's, then go and blow money on DVDs and CDs at Kim's, or browse in Labyrinth Books, emerging with heavy bags of books that neither of us had the time to read. On the days when I didn't accompany her to Columbia, she'd sometimes phone and ask me to come all the way up there for lunch, and, as often as not, I'd go. Aura would say, "Francisco, I didn't get married to eat lunch by myself. I didn't get married to spend time by myself."

On those morning walks to the subway, Aura always did most of the talking—about her classes, her professors, the other students, some new idea for a short story or a novel, or her mother. When she was being especially *neuras*, going on about her anxieties, I'd try to come up with new encouragements or else rephrase prior ones. But I especially loved it when she was in the mood to stop every few steps and kiss and nip at my lips like a baby tiger, and the way she'd complain, "*Ya no me quieres, verdad?*," if I wasn't holding her hand or didn't have my arm around her the instant she wanted me to. I loved our ritual except when I worried: How am I ever going to get another damn book written with this woman making me walk her to the subway every morning and cajoling me into coming up to Columbia to have lunch with her?

Degraw Street, where we lived, supposedly marks the border between Carroll Gardens and Cobble Hill. When I first moved there, about four years before I met Aura, Carroll Gardens seemed like a classic Brooklyn Italian neighborhood, with its old-fashioned restaurants where mobsters and politicians used to eat, lawn statues of the Virgin, old men playing bocce in the playground, and, especially on summer nights, so many loud tough-guy types milling around that I always felt a little menaced walking through there. Cobble Hill was where Winston Churchill's mother was born, and it still looked the part, with its landmark Episcopalian church and its quaint carriage-house mews. By the time Aura moved in, the two neighborhoods had pretty much blended together, both overtaken mostly by prosperous white people. By day, you wove through long crooked lines of baby strollers on the Court Street sidewalks, and ate lunch or went for coffee in places filled with young moms and au pairs, and an embarrassing number of writers. A few blocks away was Red Hook, the harbor and the port; at night, we could hear the ships' foghorns. Aura loved that; she'd nestle closer in bed and lie still, as if the long mournful blasts were floating past us like manta rays in the dark.

Our apartment was the parlor floor of a four-story brownstone. Back when the Italian family that still owned the building had lived there, the parlor would have been their living room, but it was our bedroom. It had such tall ceilings that to change a light bulb in the hanging lamp I'd climb a five-foot stepladder, then stand on tiptoe atop its rickety pinnacle, arms flapping, fighting for balance. Aura, watching from her desk, in the corner, said, "You look like an amateur bird."

With the exception of the table where I wrote, in the corner of the middle room, between the kitchen and the bedroom, and some of the old bookshelves, Aura and I slowly replaced all the furniture from my slovenly bachelor years. It frustrated Aura that we hadn't moved into a new apartment, free of traces and reminders of my past without her, though she did completely transform the apartment we had. Sometimes I'd come home and find her pushing even the heaviest furniture around, changing the crowded layout in a way that had never occurred to me, as if the apartment were a kind of complicated puzzle whose solution was the perfect arrangement of furniture.

In our kitchen, Aura's Hello Kitty toaster branded every piece of toast with the Hello Kitty logo. One year, she bought a Cuisinart ice-cream maker just so that she could make dulce-de-leche ice cream for her birthday party—her thirtieth. By then, we had acquired a long dining table with extensions at both ends that provided enough space for the twenty-plus friends who came that day. We made *cochinita pibil*—soft pork oozing citrus-and-achiote-spiced juices inside a wrapping of banana leaves roasted parchment dry—and *rajas con crema* and *arroz verde*, and there was a gorgeously garish birthday cake from a Mexican bakery in Sunset Park, with white, orange, and pink frosting, and fruit slices in a glazed ring on top. Few people who'd known me or Aura before we met would have guessed that either of us had a talent for such domestic life.

Often in the mornings, when Aura had just woken up, she would turn to me in bed and say, "*Ay, mi amor, que feo eres. Por qué me casé contigo?*"—her voice sweet and impish. "Oh, my love, how ugly you are. Why did I marry you?"

"*Soy feo?*" I would ask sadly. This was one of our routines.

"*Sí, mi amor,*" she'd say, "*eres feo, pobrecito.*" And she'd kiss me, and I'd smile the giddy smile that you can see in all the photographs of me from those years, a goofy grin that never left my face, not even when I was reciting my wedding vows.

There was a week or so, in 2005, months before our wedding, when Aura lay awake every night, worrying that she was condemning herself to a miserable early widowhood by marrying me. I'd wake and find her staring into the dark beside me, her warm insomnia breath like pulling open the door of an oven. Wasn't it logical to assume that I would die at least twenty years before she did? Shouldn't she think ahead, spare herself that ordeal? We talked about it more than once. I told her, "Don't worry, *mi amor*, I won't stick around longer than seventy-five, I promise. Then you'll still be in your early fifties, you'll still be beautiful, and probably famous, and some younger guy will want to marry you for sure." "You promise?" she'd say, cheered up, or at least pretending to be, and I'd promise. "You'd better keep your word, Francisco," she'd say, "because I don't want to be a lonely old widow." "But even if I don't die by seventy-five," I'd say, "you can just warehouse me somewhere and go and live your life. Really, I don't care. As long as we have children, I won't care that much. Just give me a kid, one kid, that's all I want." And she'd say, "O.K., but I want five kids. Or maybe three."

One afternoon, the spring she turned thirty, Aura looked over at me from her desk while I lay on the bed reading, and said, "We have everything we need to be happy. We don't have to be rich. We can get jobs in universities if we need them. We have our books, our reading, our writing, and we have each other. Frank, we don't need more to be happy. We are so lucky. Do you know how lucky we are?"

Another day, late that spring, Aura announced that she'd decided she wasn't going to be one of those women who, in their thirties, are consumed with being as thin as they were in their twenties; she was going to allow herself to be *rellenita*, a little filled out. Did I have a problem with that?

By the time I got back to our apartment in the Condesa that Saturday in July, 2007, Aura and Fabis were in a state of high excitement. Fabis had been on the phone to a friend who'd just returned from Mazunte and who said that the weather was great, but we'd better go today, because it was going to rain later in the week. Aura and Fabis hadn't been able to change our reservation—all the buses were booked—so they had concocted a circuitous route. We'd take a bus to Oaxaca, stay overnight, then fly to Puerto Escondido in the morning, a short hop over the cordillera, on a small airline called Aero Vega. We'd lose our original bus tickets, but we had to get to the beach while the weather was still good. Hurry up and pack!

Should I have fought this new plan? "No, *Ow-rra*, we've already paid for bus tickets—we need to stop throwing money away! And I have a doctor's appointment on Monday." I said those things, but not very forcefully.

By the time we pulled into Oaxaca, the streets and plazas were deserted and dark, and we had to be up at five-thirty to go to the airport. We spent the night in a hostel. In my male dorm, a few other travellers were already asleep in their bunks, and I moved about as quietly as I could, without turning on any lights. I had only one thin blanket. I slept in a T-shirt and jeans in the hard narrow bed and was angry with myself for having given in so easily to this roundabout and wasteful rush to the beach. Why was Aura so impatient?

Where, as we slept that night, was Aura's wave in its long journey to Mazunte? Having done some research on waves since then, I know that it already existed. Most surface waves of any decent size travel thousands of miles before they reach the shore. Wind blows ripples across a calm sea, and those ripples, providing the wind with something to get traction on, are blown into waves, and, as the waves grow in height, the wind pushes them along with more force, speeding them up, building them higher. It's not the water itself that travels, of course, but the wind's energy; in the turbulent medium between air and ocean, water particles move in circles like bicycle pedals, constantly transferring their energy forward, from swell to crest and back into the trough, then forward again. Aura's wave could easily have had its start a week or more before she encountered it, during a storm in the warm seas of the South Pacific. Where was it that night, as we slept in our bunks in Oaxaca?

There's a Borges poem that ends with the lines:

> *¿Quién es el mar, quién soy? Lo sabré el día*
> *Ulterior que sucede a la agonía.*
>
> Who is the sea, who am I?
> I'll know the day that follows the agony.

Was I the wave?

We reached the house in Mazunte at about noon the next day. At the end of a jungle-lined alley was a gate that we unlocked, and we climbed several levels of stairs to the house, which was like a Swiss Family Robinson tree house nestled amid sprawling branches in a tropical forest. There were a few roofed patio areas, and Aura chose the largest, pushing furniture around, quickly creating a self-contained writing studio. I took a smaller shaded deck, one level lower. Fabis, a graphic designer, was adamantly on vacation, and didn't need a work area.

We swam in the ocean that afternoon. It was overcast, and there had been a rainstorm the night before—the first rain in weeks. Nobody we spoke to had heard that more rain was forecast for the coming days. But the storm was why the water was cloudy and full of plant debris, twiggy and grassy little clusters. Though Aura had been to these beaches often and loved going into the water, she was always afraid of the waves; that day, they were not very big. Still, she clung to my arm and made me wait with her at the water's edge, studying wave sets and timing them, until we went running in. Afloat in the water, she'd throw her arms around my neck and hold on until she felt ready to swim out, diving beneath waves until she was past where they broke, where the water was smoother. Aura loved to stay out there, tirelessly swimming back and forth, like a friendly seal.

"*El agua está picada hoy*," Aura said. "The water is choppy today." Between the swells were many smaller waves, little splashing bursts, as if stones were being dropped from the sky all around us. There were other swimmers in the water, bodysurfing: young men, mostly, adolescents and boys. I swam in closer to catch a wave. I missed a few and then timed one well, launching forward and swimming hard ahead of the wave's cresting curl, letting it catch and carry me, my arms extended, head up and out of the water, just ahead of its roaring break, until I was finally engulfed by it, thrilled by the force and speed with which it propelled me almost onto the beach. As I swam back out to Aura, I wore a proud grin.

"Is it dangerous?" Aura asked. Her curiosity about bodysurfing had been aroused. She was a much better swimmer than her husband. If I could body-surf, why couldn't she?

"It is dangerous if your head gets driven into the sand," I said. "You always have to keep your head up."

Getting out of the water, too, she held onto me until the smaller wave she'd been waiting for shoved her forward and then she let go and scampered up onto the beach through the churning foam.

We went to bed early that night, climbing up onto a sleeping platform on the roof, where the breeze off the ocean made the leaves in the trees all around us rustle like a restless sea. We woke in the morning to a cacophony of birdsong and squawks, and to a view of the bay's rounded arc and the Pacific spread out beyond, merging with the blue haze of the sky. We climbed down, leaving Fabis still sleeping. Aura was eager to get to work at her computer. We made coffee and Aura cut up some papaya.

When I remember that day, the only whole one we'd have at the beach, it seems like two days, or even three; it passed so slowly, as time should on vacation. What did I work on that morning? I don't even remember. Maybe the novel I'd been trying to start. I also had a book to review, a new translation from the Portuguese of a six-hundred-page nineteenth-century novel, "The Maias," by Eça de Queirós. I sat at a crudely carpentered wooden desk in the shade, watching hummingbirds buzz around the flowers and feeling a little envious of the concentration with which Aura was already working, and of how much nicer the work area she'd set up for herself was than mine. At about ten-thirty, we all went for breakfast at the Armadillo, a little restaurant below our *callejón*. Then we went to the beach.

I don't recall bodysurfing that day; if I did, I didn't get a good ride. The red cloth banner warning against swimming must have been up on its pole, because it always was, every day. Not even the beach waiter I eventually asked about it knew why, or even who was in charge of it.

That evening, we had dinner on the beach. It was a wonderful night: the deep-blue phosphorescent evening, the brightly glimmering strings of lights around the outdoor restaurants, the butane torches flaring an incandescent orange. The night darkened to purple and finally hid the ocean. Rock music on restaurant speakers mixed with the steady percussion of the waves. We shared two mediocre pizzas and two pitchers of watery Margaritas, and were very happy. We felt as if we possessed a kind of wealth, a small fortune in saved-up nights on the beach like this one.

In the morning, Fabis went off to do some errand, and Aura and I got to make love, though not for long, sweetly but anxiously—Aura was nervous about Fabis coming back. When we were dressed, and had climbed down the ladder to the kitchen, she put her lips to my ear and told me that soon we were going to be making love all the time to make our baby. I felt so charged up and optimistic.

Aura was working well that morning. I went upstairs and saw her at her laptop, typing, headphones on. Later as we were walking to the beach, she said, "I'm writing a really great story." It was unlike Aura to speak that way, but she said it with shy conviction. The next day, she might have felt discouraged again. But something was definitely happening for her. The story she was working on had improved drastically in only a few days; that morning, she left it nearly finished—close enough, in fact, that it was eventually published. She'd been working so hard all year: why shouldn't it have happened right then, that "click," when suddenly you feel as if a previously locked door had opened, and words and sentences seem to exist in a new dimension?

An unforgettable aspect of that nearly cloudless day was the surprisingly large number of people at the beach, and how many of them were in the water, including small children. Sitting in our chairs, we watched the body-surfers. Aura kept commenting on their skills. A pair of young guys, light-skinned, well built, who looked like brothers, were the best out there, skimming over the ocean surface, expertly poised on the edge of their waves, arms out, like flying superheroes. We'd been into the water at least twice already, and each time we'd tried to catch waves, but I'd had only one short ride; I rarely timed it right.

I didn't like the look of the young guy, long-haired, whippet thin, crudely tattooed, a piercing beneath his lower lip, who took the chair right next to ours. Why sit so close? Then his friend came and laid out a towel in front of him. Aura said she wanted to go back into the water. Again?

"But look how crowded the water is," I said. It still surprises me that Aura wasn't repulsed by the crowds. The water actually looked stippled with the heads of swimmers, and she was usually hypersensitive to that—she could barely even look at a surface that was densely patterned in that way, daubed, striated, without a shiver of revulsion going through her.

I whispered to her that I didn't want to leave all our things within easy reach of the creepy guys beside us. Aura whispered back that she was sure they wouldn't steal anything. They were just beach hippies.

"You two go in," I said.

"Come on," both Aura and Fabis pleaded. "The water's great today. Come with us!"

"No," I said. "I'm going to skip this one. I want to read."

Aura was wearing the wetsuit bootees she'd bought for the trip, which gave her a slightly waddling gait, and made it harder for her to keep up with Fabis, who was much taller, as they walked down to the water's edge. Aura was swinging her arms a bit to speed herself along, her head tilted up at Fabis while she talked, happily, excitedly. From behind, in her blue bathing suit, she looked just a little egg-shaped, much more so than she actually was. What an adorable, funny, beautiful person my Aura is, I thought.

This is the moment that decided everything: if I am the wave, this is when I begin to crest, with an aching surge of love inside my chest. Even if it had been only the prelude to an inconsequential swim, I'm sure I would still remember that moment. I said to myself, I promise to stop feeling annoyed with Aura, with her insecurities, with her need for reassurance. Who gives a fuck? My God, I'm going to love her more than ever and of course I'll go and swim with her right now. Next I turned my attention to securing my things against thievery, without being too obvious about it. I put my wallet, T-shirt, sandals, and book, which I would never again open, into my cloth Gandhi bookstore bag and looped the bag's handles around a chair leg that I firmly planted in the sand. I could see Aura and Fabis up to their shoulders in the water, facing each other, ducking waves, bobbing back up. I ran down, the beach over the searing sand and into the ocean.

As soon as I reached Aura and Fabis in the water, we decided to try to bodysurf. I caught a wave about as well as I ever catch one, and came up fifteen or twenty yards away, exhilarated, thrusting my arms in the air. Fabis tried to catch the next wave, and missed it. The wave after that rose toward us as if pushed by an invisible bulldozer, and I heard Aura shout, "I'm getting this one!"

"I'm getting this one!" Her cheerful, plucky voice suffused with her last ever impulse of delight.

I saw her launch herself and thought, as I dived under the wave, that it seemed bigger, heavier, somehow more sluggish than the others, and I felt a twinge of fear. (Or is that just a trick of memory?) I came up amid a wide swathe of seething foam—the water looked as if it were boiling. Fabis was next to me. "Did you catch it?" I asked her, and she said, "No, did you?" but I was already looking around for Aura. "Where's Aura?" I didn't see her. Bewildered, I swept my gaze back and forth over the teeming surface, waiting for her head to pop up, gasping, her hands brushing hair and water out of her eyes. But she wasn't in the water.

Then I saw her. The withdrawing foam uncovered her like a white blanket slowly pulled back: her smooth, round back and shoulders. She was floating, motionless, face down in the water. I reached Aura an instant or two before three or four other swimmers, and we hoisted and carried her onto the beach. How heavy she was. We set her down on her back on the sand. She was unconscious, water dribbling from her nostrils. But then she opened her eyes. People were shouting, "Don't move her!" She gasped that she couldn't breathe. Someone shouted, "Give her mouth to mouth!" and I brought my lips to hers. I blew in, and felt the hot breath slowly push back into me. I was surprised at the steepness of the beach; it was if we were in a gulley. Had it been like that earlier? A wave came in and almost covered her. Several pairs of hands picked her up, and she slipped from all our grasps, and we grabbed her again, and carried her up onto the hot dry sand. "A doctor, an ambulance," I was pleading. I had to stay by her. She said, "Help me breathe," and I put my mouth against hers. She whispered, "That was too hard," and after the next breath, "Like that." Somebody, maybe Fabis, said that it was *susto*, fright, that was making it hard for her to breathe, that once she calmed down she'd be able to breathe, and I repeated to her, "Aura, you've had a terrible fright—that's why you can't breathe. When you calm down you'll be able to." Fabis went to get help. Just before she took off, Aura said to me, "*Quiéreme mucho, mi amor.*" "Love me a lot, my love."

She couldn't move her limbs, nor did she have any feeling in them. She told me this with the utmost composure, as if she believed that, if she kept very cool and still, the horror might decide to move on to some other prey. I told her that it was only temporary, that soon the feeling would start coming back. I was holding her hand, squeezing it, but she couldn't feel my squeezes. She was caked in sand. Somebody—he sounded German—kept stating with authority that she shouldn't be moved. "*Aire,*" Aura said, whenever she needed me to help her breathe. The word came off her lips like a bubble quietly popping.

"*No quiero morir,*" she said. "I don't want to die."

"Of course you're not going to die, my love, don't be silly." Squeezing her hand, stroking the hair off her forehead. My lips to hers, in, out, wait, in, out, wait . . .

Somehow the doctor found us before Fabis found him. He was a wiry young man who looked like a surfer. Maybe he was a medical student, not a doctor. Fabis came back with the news that there was only one ambulance on that whole stretch of coast, and it was currently two hours away.

"*Aire,*" Aura whispered.

The young doctor took control. We couldn't afford to wait two hours, he said. We had to get Aura to the nearest hospital, in Pochutla, about twenty kilometres away. A man volunteered to drive her to the hospital in his S.U.V. We would use a surfboard as a stretcher and load Aura into the back. When the doctor asked for help, some of the young men standing around us moved away as if a blowtorch were being held to their feet, but others came forward to kneel around Aura and carefully lifted her as a surfboard was slid beneath her, and we carried her on the board to the S.U.V. In the back, I crouched behind her head, holding it with both hands, trying to keep it from moving, while continuously bending forward to give her breath. The S.U.V. lurched from side to side on the rough dirt road, every rut like a deep ditch, and it was impossible to keep her completely still. A youth was crouched at the other end of the surfboard, as much to keep it from sliding out onto the road as to hold Aura's legs steady. For some reason, he had a green feather, and he was stroking it against the soles of Aura's feet and asking her if she felt anything. She whispered that she did, and I kept telling her that being able to feel the feather meant that everything was going to be O.K. The youth with the feather was praying for Aura. "You're like an angel," I told him. Finally, we hit paved road. About forty-five minutes after leaving the beach, we reached the hospital in Pochutla.

The hospital was on the town's outskirts, a flimsy one-story construction that looked like a rural elementary school. The emergency-care area was small and spartan. The staff kept Aura on the surfboard, which they laid atop a bed. They put a neck brace on her. But they didn't even have a respirator, I still had to help her breathe.

The first doctor who came to look at Aura was clearly an alcoholic, dishevelled, bleary, and utterly indifferent. Fabis was out in the waiting area, making a few last calls on her cell phone before its battery ran out. She tried to call Aura's mother, in Mexico City, but got her answering service. She couldn't reach Aura's stepfather, either. Her cell-phone charger was back at the house in Mazunte. She asked the S.U.V's owner if he could go and get it for her, and he said that he would. Extraordinarily, he came back with it in not much more than an hour.

Finally they brought a hand-operated respirator, and a nurse held the mouthpiece over Aura's lips while I, with both hands, rhythmically pressed the ovoid white plastic balloon that pumped air. After a while, I was told that I had to fill out forms, and a nurse took over the balloon, while I was led into a tiny cubicle with a desk to wait for another doctor. I phoned Aura's mother and got no answer, so I sent an e-mail telling her that Aura had had a swimming accident, was in the hospital, and to please phone me or Fabiola immediately. My phone's battery was now very nearly gone. I e-mailed my lawyer friend, Andrew Kaufman, in New York, and others to ask for help in getting Aura medevaced to the United States. I was barefoot, in my bathing trunks and a T-shirt. Fabis had handed me the T-shirt. She'd also had the presence of mind to run and collect our things on the beach.

The second doctor was an old man with white hair and a mustache. He asked me questions for his forms and slowly typed my answers on a manual typewriter; the process seemed interminable. I thought I heard Aura calling for me and abruptly got up and left. When I got to Aura, there was a third doctor there, a husky young man with chubby cheeks and an air of benevolent intelligence. He was working the manual respirator now, calmly squeezing it between his hands and looking intently from Aura's face to the monitor attached to her. I asked if she had been calling for me, and the nurses said no, she was *tranquila*. He handed the balloon off to a nurse, and took me into the corridor to tell me that Aura needed to go to a hospital in Mexico City as quickly as possible, by air ambulance. Her heart rate had considerably slowed, he said, but they'd given her a shot of epinephrine and restored it to nearly normal. When I went back into her room, I was told to keep an eye on the monitor and say something if her heart rate sank below forty. When the doctor hammered under Aura's knees, there was a tiny reflex movement. He ran the hammer down the sole of her foot and asked her if she'd felt anything, and she said that she had. The nurses and I smiled at one another. Then the doctor pretended to do it again, swiping the hammer downward without actually touching her skin, and again Aura claimed to have felt it.

My memories of what happened that endless day will always be clouded and uncertain. I do know that Fabiola was constantly working her telephone, trying to arrange for the air ambulance. I went out to the corridor, where I'd left my book bag under a chair, to get my sandals and wallet; that's when I discovered that somebody, probably back at the beach, had stolen all my cash and then put the wallet back in the bag. I had one credit card, which the thief had left alone, an American Express card, useless in any Mexican A.T.M. My other cards were back at the house in Mazunte. I heard Fabis on her cell phone say plaintively but urgently, "But, Ma, imagine if it was me"—her mother had asked her if we could wait a day for the air ambulance. Fabis said, "Ma, she might not make it until tomorrow."

Finally, Fabis's family found an air-ambulance service in Toluca that would fly to nearby Huatulco to pick Aura up. It was already late afternoon, and they were rushing to a bank to withdraw the twelve thousand dollars in cash that the ambulance service was demanding. Fabis's sister had found a spinal-cord surgeon, the father of a friend, who was one of the very best in Mexico City, and who was waiting for Aura, at the Hospital de los Ángeles, in Pedregal, one of the city's wealthiest areas. But there was a new problem: the air ambulance couldn't come because the Huatulco airport, which was closing for the night, was denying it permission to land.

The Huatulco airport official was named Fabiola, too. Over the phone, Fabis told her, "If my cousin dies, you're going to have that on your conscience the rest of your life." Kaufman, my lawyer friend in New York, was also applying pressure. His law firm had worked on corporate cases with one of the most powerful lawyers in Mexico, and he had persuaded that lawyer to call the Huatulco airport. After the call, the Huatulco Fabiola relented and agreed to keep the airport open until midnight.

When an ambulance came to carry Aura to Huatulco, about twenty kilometres away, the young doctor, who was actually an intern from Guadalajara, only recently assigned to the hospital, volunteered to accompany us, with the manual respirator. Aura, wrapped in a bedsheet, was lifted off the surfboard and onto the ambulance litter. Whoever owned that surfboard had apparently given it up for her.

After nearly an hour's drive, we approached the airport through a back entrance, and I heard the whine of an idling jet engine in the steamy tropical air. The young doctor wouldn't accept even taxi fare back to Mazunte; off he went, after a round of heartfelt and hopeful goodbyes, carrying the manual respirator, to stay at the house of a friend. Aura was transferred to a new stretcher, and covered snugly in a silver thermal blanket. The air-ambulance doctor told us that Aura's vital signs were good. Once we were in the air, she said that Aura didn't need a respirator. It was true: Aura was managing to breathe. She looked at me and asked, "*Mi amor, me puedo dormir un poquito?*" "Can I sleep a little bit?"

She slept for a while, and then a final ambulance took us from the Toluca airport across Mexico City to Pedregal, in the south. With us was a doctor who looked barely into his twenties, quick and sure in his movements, an alert, serious type, with glasses and delicate, sharp features. He was intently watching the monitor, reading Aura's vital signs. Then he said, his voice tense, "I don't like how this looks." The optimism of the air ambulance was gone. Now I can't say whether I am grateful for those last moments of hope and relief, or whether I feel that we were cruelly deceived.

Aura's mother and stepfather, whom Fabis had finally reached, were waiting for us outside the hospital's emergency entrance. Some of Aura's *tías* were there, too. It was about two in the morning. Aura's mother, arms folded, glaring at me, spoke to me accusingly. "This is your fault," she said. This was how I'd brought her daughter back to her, the daughter she'd given away to me to protect in marriage?

Aura was awake. It was as if she'd saved up all her energy to be able to give her mother this last brave declaration: "*Fue una tontería, Mami.*" "It was a stupidity, Mami."

I think the renowned surgeon and his team of doctors knew almost right away. I don't remember how long it took before they came out to speak with us in the waiting room. The surgeon was a tall, corpulent man. He told us that Aura had broken the third and fourth vertebrae of her spinal column, cutting into the nerves that controlled her breathing and her torso and limbs. She would probably be completely paralyzed for life. They were trying to stabilize her spinal cord so that the swelling could go down. Then they would decide if there was any way to operate. She had ingested ocean water, too, and they were working to clear it from her lungs. I pleaded with the doctor. I told him that Aura had had sensation in her limbs off and on throughout the day, that in the air ambulance her vital signs had been fine and she'd even breathed on her own. I told the doctor that she was going to be fine, and that he had to believe me, and I remember his stricken eyes helplessly observing me, in my dirty, sweaty T-shirt and bathing suit.

I wasn't allowed into the intensive-care unit to see Aura. The medical teams needed to work without interruption. Fabis went home to sleep. I don't remember there being anyone else in the waiting room, except Aura's parents, who sat on vinyl couches on one side of the waiting room, while I sat alone on the other. The light in the room was very dim. I couldn't phone anyone because my battery was dead. At one point, I went out and walked through the long empty corridors, stepping into a little chapel to pray. I swore that if Aura survived I would live a religiously devout life and show my gratitude to God every day. Back in the waiting room, I told myself that, if she was going to be paralyzed for some time, I would find a way to get her into the best rehab facility in the U.S.; I would read to her every day, and get her to dictate her writing to me. Those were the kind of thoughts I was having. Now and then, I got up and went to the intercom receiver and pressed the button and asked if I could come inside to see my wife, but every time I was told that visitors weren't allowed until the morning.

What did you think about that long night, my love, as you lay there dying and alone? Did you blame me? Did you think of me with love even once? Did you see or hear or feel me loving you?

It wasn't until the next morning that I was finally allowed in to see her. The eminent surgeon's assistant, a bulldoggish woman, told me that during the night Aura had had two heart attacks, and she was now in a coma.

I pressed my lips to Aura's ear and thanked her for the happiest years of my life. I told her that I would never stop loving her. Then the assistant surgeon brusquely ordered me out.

Ten or fifteen minutes later, stepping back through the white curtain, I instantly sensed a vacuumed-out stillness around Aura's bed, and the assistant surgeon told me that Aura had died minutes before. I went to her. Her lightless eyes. I kissed her cheeks, which were already like cool clay.

My sobs must have been heard throughout the hospital.

Juanca missed the funeral because he went with a friend to Mazunte to bring back our things. They found the house exactly as we'd left it. They packed up everything, even Aura's shampoo. Aura always just closed the lid of her laptop when she was done working for the day, so when I opened it later I found the screen as she'd left it. There were two open documents: the latest version of her teacher story, and something new, probably the start of another short story, titled *"Hay señales en la vida?"* or "Does Life Give Us Signs?"

2011

■   # MANUEL MUÑOZ   ■
B. 1972

A native of Dinuba, California, Manuel Muñoz graduated from Harvard University and received his M.F.A. in creative writing at Cornell University. Muñoz is a recipient of a 2008 Whiting Writers' Award, as well as fellowships from the National Endowment for the Arts and the New York Foundation for the Arts. He received a 2009 PEN/O. Henry Award for his story, "Tell Him about Brother John." Muñoz currently lives in Tucson, where he is an assistant professor in the University of Arizona's esteemed creative writing program.

The stories of *Zigzagger* marked the emergence of a new voice in Chicana/o letters. Moving away from the customary signifiers of cultural identity and from narratives about characters' racial and ethnic experience, Muñoz's fiction returns again and again to a personal cluster of themes that arise from a sustained meditation on the complex social relationships composing a specific place: California's Central Valley. For Muñoz, the Valley is a geography mapped by unrelenting observation. His writing captures the asphyxiating atmosphere of the small town in which everybody watches everybody else, anxious to divine the private life that the public persona protects and circulating false stories in lieu of accurate information. Muñoz is interested in the objects of that intrusive and voyeuristic attention, from the gay denizens longing to leave to the undocumented mother with the fatally wounded son and an aversion to the prying eyes of her neighbors and employer. Muñoz's writing returns obsessively to the lives of these ordinary people, in this particular place, as they struggle with their troubles and their isolation. With great empathy, no matter the choices they make, he depicts their attempts to preserve some kind of self-sufficiency, hope, or dignity. His style is perfectly suited for this task: it watches back. Muñoz's prose is spare and elegant, detached yet not cold, replete with finely observed details, rhythmic effects created by the repetition of certain key phrases, and concentrated yet restrained moments of lyricism.

The Faith Healer of Olive Avenue is less radical than *Zigzagger* in form and tone. Some of the stories in the first collection are less than a page long, while the edgy story "Zigzagger" breaks new ground in how it represents culturally inflected sexuality. Adopting a more conventional approach, *Faith Healer* brings in a broad range of Central Valley characters and families. The stories are interconnected through place names, references to characters from other stories, and the appearance of the same character in different stories. In this way, Muñoz teaches us something about individual characters' subjectivity and social locations. *Faith Healer* revisits Muñoz's fundamental theme of how a small town works, with all its secrets and concomitant desires to uncover them.

What You See in the Dark imagines the filming of Alfred Hitchcock's *Psycho* against the real-life murder of a Chicana by her white lover in Bakersfield. A technical tour de force, the novel uses narrative strategies that parallel Hitchcock's noir cinematic techniques. *Psycho*, which so thoroughly exposed the voyeuristic nature of movie watching itself, is the perfect choice for Muñoz's concern with the meaning of lives under constant scrutiny. As in U.S. culture at large, in the novel Hitchcock's film signals a moment of great social change, in which the rigid code of propriety the townspeople are so anxious to enforce begins to disappear. In spite of the lack of gay characters, *What You See in the Dark* enacts a queer sensibility in the contrast between the fullness of the characters' interiority and others' misperceptions of them. By telling their stories so beautifully and by dedicating his formidable talents to the representation of the Central Valley, Muñoz shows the place of the regional in a fully national literature.

The following story, "Bring Brang Brung," tells the story of a reluctant father, Martín, who must care for his young son after his lover, Adrian, suddenly dies. After Adrian's family has taken everything (except the son, Adán), Martín moves from San Francisco in straitened circumstances back to his hometown in the Valley, where he meets up with his past: the familiar class divisions and prying eyes; the mother who has rejected both her gay son and her rebellious daughter, Perla; and Perla herself, now ready to move beyond past grievances and reach out to her brother. Grieving and guarded, Martín nurses his own sense of failure by thinking about the mistakes the townspeople have made, seeking in this way to protect himself from their "wanting to know." He sees himself in some of them, especially the women like his sister who were teenage mothers, who have fallen into the same penurious single-parent trap. As he takes small steps toward reconciliation, these women model for him a path of self-knowledge and forgiveness. As in other stories, here Muñoz excels at portraying the bridge of intersubjectivity that may be constructed between brown gay men and nonqueer women from similarities in their gendered experience. A schoolboy's badly written letter (the "brang" of the title) brings home to Martín the daunting task of parenting that lies before him. The story moves between the present and the past, and this temporal oscillation also allows the reader to understand that he need not do it alone, although he may try to, given the way Martín's interiority is written.

Yvonne Yarbro-Bejarano
Stanford University

PRIMARY WORKS

Zigzagger, 2003; *The Faith Healer of Olive Avenue*, 2007; *What You See in the Dark*, 2011.

Bring Brang Brung

Lincoln School, on the north side of town, on the good side, without a single railroad track in sight, is where Martín enrolled Adán for kindergarten. When Martín was growing up, Lincoln was the rich-kid school and, by default, better. When his mother drove the back way home from Thrifty's after an ice cream cone, you could see how much bigger the Lincoln playing fields were, and the blacktops still without the basketball nets ripped down. Nowadays, Martín wasn't so sure how good the school was, but when he moved back to the Valley from San Francisco, he looked to rent first on this side of town, even though the places were too big for just him and Adán. There was Roosevelt School over on the west side in a newly incorporated part of town, brand-new buildings and landscaped fields resurrected from abandoned orchards. Or Grand View, where all the farmers' kids went, a tiny school a few miles out of town, springing up out of the grape vineyards, teachers always yelling at the children during recess when they cornered a gopher snake and threw rocks at it. Wilson and Jefferson he crossed out immediately, both of them on the south side of town, where he had grown up—on Gold Street—and now home mostly to kids struggling with two languages. It hadn't been so bad when he was young, but later, when he was in high school, he would drive by those schools and wonder about their disrepair, their inadequacy, the ponds accumulating at the bus stops during rainstorms, the kids haphazardly jumping across them, trying not to get their shoes wet. But he settled on Lincoln because he remembered how that part of town had clean streets and sidewalks and wide lawns. There was never mud on that side of town, never a flooded street or a sewage leak. The north side was pristine.

At the school's front office, painted in the same clinical, soothing light green he remembered from Jefferson, Martín held Adán's hand. The boy quietly watched as Martín set down the pile of identifications: Adán's birth certificate, his inoculation records, his preschool report cards. It took him a moment to recognize the woman at the desk, who had smiled wanly at him when he entered, unsure of how to approach him: she turned out to be Candi Leal, a girl he'd gone to high school with and a good friend of his younger sister, Perla. He had never liked Perla's friends, a whole brood of mean, belligerent girls whose troublemaking began with skipping school and ended with pregnancies by the tenth grade, the father-boys nowhere to be found. But here was Candi, who had had her own kid, if Martín recalled correctly, sometime in the eighth grade, and now she was a grown woman in a respectable job at the very elementary school she had attended.

When he stated his business, without really saying hello to her, Candi slid him some forms and a pen, glancing down at Adán, who stood on the other side of the counter as if waiting for questions. Martín ignored her, deliberate in writing out the usual information: child's name, parental contact information, emergency phone numbers. He pressed hard through the triplicate, lifting the sheets just to check if the marks had gone down all the way to the goldenrod at the bottom. When he got to the section about Adán's mother, Martín casually slashed a large X across it.

"So when did you move back?" Candi asked. Her tone wasn't innocent and it wasn't oblivious: Martín knew she had already heard from Perla.

"Last month," he answered as Candi skipped her fingers down the information on the forms.

"San Francisco's tough," she said. "Expensive, too." She reached the section he had slashed out and paused, looking at it for a moment, as if she expected to learn something.

"How's your kid?" Martín asked her. "He must be in junior high by now."

"Eighth grade," Candi replied, but she didn't say anything more. She gave Martín his goldenrod copy and told him when Adán should report to school. He tried to get her to look him in the eye the whole time, knowing he had the upper hand, the way people would be prying and wanting to know. People had made their mistakes a long time ago, when they were young and hadn't known better, and he was perfectly willing to remind them if it came to that.

On the school documents where Candi stopped her fingers, in the space slashed out in pen, was the story: the small town just south of Orlando, Florida, and a burial in the torrid heat, tropical humidity searing through Martín's suit. Missing from that document was a name—Adrian—and a sudden aneurysm late at night in an airport hotel room in Denver, Colorado, during a business trip, and a family in Florida who had barely acknowledged

Martín and offered no comfort. What Candi wanted to know, when she asked Perla, was more about who Adrian was and what had happened, but Perla had no way of knowing about any of it. Martín had kept Adrian close and offered little; not even Adrian's death would change that. No one but he would know about the uncomfortable trip to Orlando for the funeral, or about the cousin, Priscilla, who was cordial, but whose cowed silence, in the end, meant Martín would have no ally in Adrian's greater family. No one— not even Adán, who was too young to be able to remember it fully later— would know about the cheap, pink-walled motel room where they had spent the night, a heavy breakfast of eggs and hash browns the next morning before the flight back to San Francisco, Martín staring out the taxi window at the pastel colors of Florida, knowing he would never see it again. If Perla had been with him, maybe her defensive, angry way of seeing the world would have prepared him for the legalities and the long, fruitless contesting of beneficiary money. Perla would have said he hadn't fought hard enough, that you get only what you fight for, and whatever he lost to Adrian's family was the result of his own stupidity. Perla would have said this if she had known the whole story—but it was almost as if she knew the undercurrent of it when Martín announced that he had to move away from San Francisco and come back to the Valley. "Is that right?" she had said, over the tele-phone, her voice coming over, he thought, with barely disguised triumph. "You can stay with us if you have to," she had offered, meaning with her and her now-teenage son, but Martín had politely refused.

Before long, though, it was humbling to face what was happening with his finances and, for once, to admit that circumstances could overwhelm a person. Always, Martín had been a person who believed that choices gov-erned your road: you had to look past the crumbling downtown and imagine something better. You had to count the pregnant teenage girls and swear not to get involved in anything like that. You had to think of the orange groves nestled on the brink of the foothills and look past the deep green leaves for the meth labs hidden there. The Valley was a mess of lack, of de-scending into dust, of utter failure, and he had learned that long, long ago. But in the San Francisco apartment, opening the letters from the Florida lawyers and reading the documents that allowed Adrian's family to siphon away what little had been left behind, Martín finally came face-to-face with failing. He thought of the helplessness of his sister when she had her baby, the decisions she had to make as a teenager. He thought of other girls like her, sitting in family courts, in lawyers' offices, at juvenile detention centers where the father-boys served out a month or two. He thought of the cruelty of Adrian's family, saying nothing about wanting to gain custody of Adán for themselves and bring him to Florida. In the end, he was the same as those girls in retreating back to the Valley. He would have to make do.

In his honesty with himself, Martín would never call himself arrogant, but he knows Perla would. And she would call him hypocritical, insensitive, unforgiving, judgmental, quick tempered, and mean spirited. She could very well have reveled in his struggle. Still, on the day he had made the move to the new place in his old hometown, Martín had finished the long trip from San Francisco with Adán sleeping the entire way, and there was Perla on the sidewalk. She knocked on the passenger window, waking Adán, and waved a stuffed purple elephant at him in greeting. Adán had rolled down the window, smiling for the first time in many weeks as Martín parked the car.

"Look what your aunt Pearl has for you," she said to Adán. As for Martín, she greeted him cautiously, a hug that felt more like letting go.

In the late-dark of the new house, in the rooms that echoed with their emptiness, by the wide windows that still had no curtains and let in the streetlight, Martín was the one who could not sleep for nights on end. Grief would come like a ghost at the foot of the bed, just as he was sleeping, and the curve of Adrian's face would ask why he was trying to forget.

He ignored the grief as best he could and fretted endlessly over the new circumstances, trying not to toss in bed, because Adán slept soundly next to him. Despite having his own room, Adán refused to sleep alone—this the only indication in his behavior that something was amiss. In the first few days in town, with Martín not yet prepared to look for a job and running daily errands to get their house in order, Adán had fidgeted and scrambled in every line Martín had to wait in. If Adán wasn't playing with another child in line, he distracted himself with the simplest of things: a pebble in an empty plastic bottle, a nickel deposited over and over into a pay phone. Misbehavior, if Martín correctly read the reactions of the faces around him, but he paid them no mind. All the better to exhaust Adán and not have to battle with him at bedtime, leaving Martín the night hours to go over what needed to be done.

In the dark, he owned up to how he felt about Adán: this was not his child. All along, it had been Adrian's idea; it had been Adrian who had spoken plainly and honestly with a woman he'd been friends with for years— Holly, a chubby white girl from way back when in Orlando. Martín had gone along with the idea, perhaps not fully grasping the responsibility but assured by Adrian's enthusiasm. Adrian would be the one to raise him, and he would be the one earning the money, too: a sales job took him up all around the western states, commissions rolling in, Martín maybe too self-satisfied with a no-nonsense accounting job he had in Oakland. The mistake was colossal. He had never considered what it would require to be the child's sole guardian. In the dark, he had to raise himself quietly from the bed, careful not to wake up Adán, and pace in the kitchen, wondering how he would ever admit something like this to Perla.

What plagued him most was the repetition, the continuation of a cycle he had thought he would never be part of. One afternoon in town, stopping at the post office to mail off documents to yet another lawyer in Florida, Martín had caught a glimpse of Perla's son, Matthew. He hadn't seen Matthew except in pictures, and even those were of his nephew when he was nine or ten. Martín knew it was him, though, because he looked every bit like the skinny white boy who was his father, a troublemaker who disappeared long before Perla even knew she was pregnant. Martín had gone to school with that guy, a year ahead of him; he still remembered his slouch, his dirty-blond hair, the way his eyes always looked bruised and damaged underneath. His nephew looked enough like that guy for Martín to do a double take, and that's when the sadness of the situation hit him deeply. His nephew was fifteen, a walking mirror of his absent father, the same darkness under his eyes, and it was all Martín had to see to understand why Perla never brought him over to the house.

To be in a house with only one parent: look how it had turned out for Perla. Their mother had fought with her repeatedly, pointing to her older brother as an example. Of course, Martín had deliberately set an impossible standard, out of sheer distaste for his sister's belligerence, her selfishness, her disrespect, and her stupidity. He went to church even though he didn't like it, just to have one more thing over her. Perla fought against rules, leaving the house in the middle of the night, sometimes letting the car that came to pick her up idle shamelessly right in front of the house, just to wake up their mother. Such rebellion—it scared Martín now, alone, even though the prospect was years away with Adán.

In the dark of the kitchen, sitting at the kitchen table, which had only two chairs, he poured himself a glass of milk. He would never dare ask Perla to discuss their mother, how she truly felt about her. They did not speak to each other. But surely Perla knew that their mother had also stopped speaking to him after he moved in with Adrian. Both of her children, then, were cut off: a monumental anger she had with them for having failed her.

This is how he thought at night, starting with simple, solvable problems like the electricity bill or a doctor's appointment. Grief summoned itself, impossible to release, Adrian insisting himself back to life—Martín had to ignore it to keep from being overwhelmed. Then a wave of guilt would sweep over him for his inability to completely summon a love for either Adán or his sister. Eyes open in the dark, he would sit in the kitchen until sunrise, asking himself questions that were impossible to answer. What would make him happy, satisfied? How would his mother have answered that question? Perla? Had their mother favored him more because he looked like her and Perla looked like their father? Did Matthew know that he looked like his father and that Perla saw it every time she looked at him? Is it possible to will yourself to love someone? If it isn't love, then what is it?

By the beginning of October, with Adán a few weeks into kindergarten, everything eased some when Martín found a job at a small accounting office in Fresno. The job wasn't the best of circumstances: the building was on the south side, the more dangerous part of the city after dark, and the office was situated in a converted warehouse, the false ceiling perfect for tossing up sharpened pencils to see if they would stick. Drafts of the hot afternoon air somehow snaked past the warehouse's corrugated paneling and into the core offices, which were nothing more than walls of Sheetrock; in the mornings, the drafts were chilly enough to force Martín to drink a third cup of coffee. Every Friday afternoon, the secretary would come around with the paychecks, personally signed by the company owner, and Martín would not complain about the ten minutes he'd be docked if he had been late.

Perla mercifully made it easy for him. She kept her phone calls cautious and intermittent, but when he told her that he had found a job, she had been the one to volunteer to care for Adán after school. "I'll pick him up and bring him to your house or mine, whichever," she said. What, then, was she doing for work? Martín wanted to know, especially with a teenager at home, but he felt too ashamed to pry when he himself was in need. "My house," he had told her, and gave her a set of keys.

Most days, after he came home from work, Perla wouldn't linger more than a few minutes before she excused herself, touching Adán gently on the shoulder. Neither Martín nor Perla would bring up the subject of money, but it was on Martín's mind once a few paychecks came his way. He knew taking care of Adán was costing her something, and he knew her willingness to help was rooted in a desire to move past their differences. Somewhere along the line, like her friend Candi Leal at the front office of the elementary school, she had eased into a forgiveness of the world at large, and that included him. One Friday night, he came home to find Perla cutting up a roast chicken from the grocery store and Adán busy folding paper towels for the table. "I bought dinner," she said. "I hope you don't mind. Matthew fends for himself most times anyway." In helping her set the table, Martín took a peek at the receipt in the bag to see how much she had laid out for everything, the containers of macaroni salad and wild rice, the rolls. She had bought beer, too, but that would be for later apparently. When they were ready to eat, he insisted she take one of the two chairs, and he ate leaning against the kitchen counter.

When bedtime came for Adán, Perla helped get him into pajamas and cajoled him into sleeping in his own room. "Here," she said to him, handing him the purple elephant. "Me and your dad will be in the kitchen, so no monsters can come, okay?" Martín, putting away the dishes they had washed, could hear the murmur of protest, but Perla's voice was gentle in its command and patience. "I'll leave the door open a little bit, but be a big boy and go to sleep," she said, and made her way down the hallway to the kitchen.

She pulled two cans of beer from the refrigerator and handed him one. "I went to the school today," she said, sitting at the table.

"Yeah? Why?"

"The school pictures they took the first week? The money? A kid in the fourth grade took the check you gave him."

"That was weeks ago," he said, thinking of the morning he had given in to Adán's pestering to wear his favorite sweatshirt—a purple one with a green dragon on it. "I forgot all about it. He never said anything."

"Did you expect him to?" She took the tiniest sip of beer from the can, licking her lips a little, and it occurred to Martín that he had never actually seen her drink before. She was almost demure about it, and it reminded him of one of the first times he'd gone out to dinner with Adrian, to a restaurant with thick tablecloths, and of the careful way he'd had to handle the wineglasses. He tried to picture his sister at such a place.

"He got beat up that day," Perla added. "Or shoved around. You know how kids exaggerate a little. I don't think he really got hurt."

"Who was the kid?"

"Just some older boy. Probably the older brother of some kid in his class."

He took a deep drink from the can. The beer was watery and cheap, but he said nothing because it was from Perla's courtesy and generosity. "You should have called me. I would've come down and taken care of it."

"What was there to take care of? You can't be bothered at work right now. Not with you just starting and everything. I know how bosses can be."

"So what did they do? Did they punish the kid?"

"Well, the principal—do you remember Roberta Beltrán? She was three years ahead of you, or something like that. That really fat girl? She's the principal there, if you can believe it, and she had that boy in tears in no time. He still has the check, and he has to bring it to the school on Monday."

"For what?"

"To apologize. He's supposed to write a letter." She laughed, shaking her head. "Can you believe it? That's the punishment. We would've gotten a lot worse back in the day."

He laughed with her, but it felt forced. He took another drink of his beer, noticed Perla looking down at the lip of the can as if she had remembered suddenly what it had been like for her as a teenager, as if she had become lost in pinpointing where the trouble had started, how young she had actually been.

"You know, I hate to ask you, but I gave them some of the money for the pictures. I told them you'd bring the rest on Monday."

"Oh, yeah?" he said, putting down his beer. He reached into his back pocket for his wallet.

"I had twelve dollars on me. So you owe them thirteen," she said, getting up from the chair. She went into the living room and reached behind the couch, where she had hidden the pictures. "I wanted to bring them to you as a surprise, so you wouldn't have to wait till Monday."

He pulled a twenty from his wallet, this being payday. Then he pulled two more and put the bills on the table as Perla made her way back.

"It was just twelve, Martín."

"Yeah, I know, but you've been doing a lot for me. It's just a little bit." He reached for the pictures and pretended to study them closely. Only the head of the green dragon on Adán's sweatshirt was visible, a cartoon dragon with bubble eyes and a little tongue upturned as if in thought or effort. Adán was smiling in the photograph, as if nothing had happened that particular day. All the pictures were the same, but Martín slid them out for inspection so Perla could reach to the table and fold the bills quietly in her hand.

"Who does he look like?" she asked Martín as he returned the pictures to the envelope.

"More and more like his father," he nodded. "Adrian was Cuban. Dark hair, a little wavy," he said. "Dark eyes."

"He's kind of light skinned."

"His mother was white. A friend of Adrian's." Perla had never seen a picture of Adrian, and he thought for a moment that she might ask. He didn't know whether he would show her or, if he did, where he would begin the story. Maybe from the beginning, which was the end. When he moved into the new place, he had left pictures of Adrian packed in their boxes, hoping Adán wouldn't say anything about them.

Perla went to the refrigerator to get another beer, and she turned to wiggle a can at him in invitation. He nodded and she brought them back, popping hers open with relish and taking a longer drink this time. "In the car," she said, "on the way home ... he told me that he looked like you."

Martín almost snorted and ran his fingers through his hair. "Oh, Jesus," he said, sighing. "The things I'm going to have to explain to that kid ..."

"Well, you know, I'm here to help you," Perla said, tapping her fingernails nervously against her beer can. "You're my Brother."

"Yeah," he agreed, but couldn't add much more. Part of him felt ashamed at Perla's attempt to bring their slow reconciliation out in the open, felt ashamed of how little he was trying to meet her halfway.

"I've learned a lot trying to raise Matthew," she said. "I made a lot of stupid mistakes. So did some of my friends, the ones who had their own kids. It's hard, Martín. It's harder than you think."

He looked at the picture of Adán, the joyful color of his purple sweatshirt and the cartoon dragon, and found it hard to imagine a point when Adán would fully form into his own person. The fourth-grade boy couldn't have been more than ten years old, and already he had discovered that you could bully your way through this world if you wanted. You didn't have to follow the rules.

"Perla," he asked, "what do you do for work? For money?"

"I clean houses," she replied. "Mostly here, but sometimes over in Reedley or in Visalia. A lot in Visalia. There's people moving there from the Bay Area. Lot of money."

"Not me."

She laughed slightly. "Normal situations, I mean. People who had money to throw around to begin with, so they buy land and build these really huge houses to live in, and then rent tiny apartments in San Francisco so they have that when they need it."

"Is it enough? The money you make?"

She sighed and put her chin in her hand. Her hair was pulled back and knotted up almost haphazardly, and though it was as long and black as he remembered it, the sheen was a little dull, as if her hair were somehow thinking of shading gray. It was hair pulled back out of necessity, to keep it out of the way as she hurried in the morning, not like she wore it in high school—combed razor-straight like the other girls', her eyeliner heavy, and her lips glossy with a deep blackberry. "Money comes and goes," Perla said. "I work hard only for myself now. I used to do for Matthew, used to do a lot, but he's just a real angry kid. He's got a lot inside him that I can't get to."

"He looks like his father. That kid—"

"Well," she interrupted, "that's the problem, I think. Every time he looks in the mirror ... the things he says to me sometimes." When she put her hand to her mouth, the way she did that, he thought of their mother and her regretting. "I'm almost thirty years old, you know? I did what I could and the rest is up to him. If he wants to come home, well, then he comes home. And if he stays at a friend's house, that's none of my business anymore. You can't control that if they don't want to let you."

When she began crying, as he expected her to, Martín sat quietly and watched his younger sister's resolve shimmer through the helplessness. One hand was still on the beer can, and because he looked closely now, because he paid attention, he saw that she wore no nail polish, and the two rings on her fingers were simple, unadorned silver. Rings she must have picked out for herself, shopping alone at one of the malls in Visalia, studying the velvet display boxes intently, not bothering to worry over the price, thinking of herself for once. But it wasn't selfishness—Martín understood that. It wasn't like the way he thought of himself, of deserving and wanting, the self-satisfaction and the near greed of having, after years of not-having. Instead, it was a contentment and a self-knowledge, a forgiveness for her own part in her unhappiness, a releasing.

"Do you want another beer?" he asked her. "Finish off the pack?"

"I have to drive home," Perla said, dabbing at her eyes gently.

"Sleep on the couch," he told her. When she didn't answer, he crossed to the refrigerator and brought back the last two cans. Perla popped hers open as if with effort, grinning a little, and before she took a drink, she raised her beer as if in toast. They tapped cans, the aluminum sounding as sincere as glass.

Monday morning, he called in sick to work, and though the secretary quizzed him, Martín held his resolve over the phone and promised to be better by the next day. The principal had asked to see him at ten o'clock, and he arrived at Lincoln School fifteen minutes early. Candi Leal, busy with the phones and a string of kids slumped in plastic chairs against the wall, nodded knowingly at him, raising her wrist to tap at her watch: she'd get to him soon. On the way there, Martín had imagined himself speaking to Candi at her desk, prompting an exchange that he should have engaged in weeks ago when he had registered Adán. She was too busy now, and he regretted how he might have misread her before, her initial spark of forgiveness, of new possibilities, of growing and maturing, and how he had wiped it away by not returning her grace.

Almost on the dot, the door to the principal's office opened and Roberta Beltrán came over to shake his hand. "Good morning," she said good naturedly. "It's nice to see you again." If anything, she had gained more weight; she had always been a large girl, but now her size gave her a commanding presence Martín had always associated with both principals and mean teachers. "Jesse," she said, crooking a finger at a boy in a Raiders jacket. "In my office, please," she ordered, then turned to hold the door for them.

"We'll make this quick," Roberta said, sitting at her desk and clasping her hands. "Jesse, do you have something for Mr. Grijalva, like I asked you on Friday?"

"Yes," Jesse answered in a half groan as he dug into the pockets of his Raiders jacket.

"Sit up straight, please," Roberta ordered as Jesse took his time finding a piece of paper that he then unfolded. "Speak clearly."

Jesse read from the paper, his voice flat footed despite his sincerity. "Dear Mister Grijalva, I am sorry that I stole the money from Adam and that I brang the money to my house. I am sorry that Adam did not get his pictures because of me and I am sorry that I hurt his feelings. Sincerely, Jesse Leal." Finished, he handed the letter to Martín,

"And where is the check?" asked Roberta.

Jesse fished in the jacket's other pocket and drew out the check, folded tiny in a triangular shape, its edges smoothed down and worn.

"Unfold it," Roberta said. "Is that how you took it from Adán?"

"No," he answered. His fingers seemed confused by the folds, but he unraveled the check and smoothed it against his leg before handing it to Martín.

"Thank you," Martín said, taking it.

"What do we say?"

Jesse turned to her, confused, but Roberta only tilted her head down at him, as if looking over the brim of a pair of glasses. "We need to apologize."

"But I did ...," he protested.

"You read the letter. You also need to say it like you mean it. Look him in the eye."

Jesse Leal turned to look at Martín, and though he said he was sorry, he drawled it. Martín nodded his head as if in acceptance, but he thought of the battle Jesse Leal would turn into, a ten-year-old who had somehow already managed to persuade his parents to buy him an expensive Raiders jacket. "Fine," he said to Jesse Leal. "Just don't do it again."

"You're excused," Roberta said, and Jesse turned abruptly to the door. "Get a pass from Ms. Leal to get back to your room," she called out after him.

When the door closed, Martín reached for his wallet and pulled out the money he still owed for the pictures. "Was it twelve or thirteen?"

"Thirteen, I think. But Candi knows for sure. Why don't you give the money to her?"

"Okay," he said, but before he walked to the door, he asked Roberta quietly, "That wasn't her kid, right? Candi's?"

Roberta shook her head and reached for the phone. "Oh no," she said, dialing. "Maybe a cousin of some kind, but not her kid. She had her own problems long ago." She waved good-bye to him as she waited for her call to go through.

Since he had the rest of the day off, Martín went to the Kmart in town. It had opened when he was in high school, but now it was losing out to some of the newer chains at the broadened strip mall. He found a large frame for Adán's picture and then bought a smaller one to give to Perla.

Waiting in line to buy them, he pulled out the check and the handwritten letter from Jesse Leal. When Jesse had read it, there had been no way to imagine how lousy every aspect of the note would actually be: the lone, emphatic period, circled dark and certain when there were clearly two sentences. The misspelling of every name except his own. The crabbed penmanship. Martín bristled at the blatant *brang*. He thought of Roberta Beltrán and Candi Leal and any of the people he had grown up with who might be teachers now, of all of their night training at the local colleges, their effort to push books and paper in front of kids like Jesse Leal. Somewhere along the line, they would know when the right time had come to correct these errors, before they became bad habits, more obvious in speech: these were the smallest of a whole string of corrections, and Martín multiplied them by the numbers of kids in the office this morning, of the kids waiting in the classrooms, the enormity of the task. Perla had failed. His mother had failed: he remembered that day when he was a teenager, when he had opened the envelope from the adult-training center, the application that his mother had put in, the handwriting scratchy and uncertain, the information inaccurate or missing because his mother had not understood the questions. Her application for job training had been denied. He had thrown it away before she even saw it. Diction, syntax, grammar, basic math, conceptual thinking. Symmetries, the logic of sympathy, the order of gratitude, empathy, concern, the rigor of understanding, the faulty equation of grief and anger. He had failed, too, somewhere along the line. He handed the money for the picture frames to the woman at the register, her bare arms thick and dark, her red smock rumpled from a long early morning shift. He thanked her aloud when she handed him his change.

At the house, he put Adán's picture in the large frame and hung it in the living room. For a brief moment, Martín considered putting it in the hallway, just as his mother had done in their house on Gold Street when he and Perla were growing up. Their individual year-by-year school pictures, Perla in her glasses and barrettes until she changed into the girl with the razor-straight hair in eighth grade. Pictures of him and Perla when they were both very young, their mother with them, standing behind proudly, and even a picture with all of them: Martín, Perla, their mother, their father, the photograph so old that the tint had washed out in an odd red hue. But the living room it would be, just Adán's photograph above the couch. There would be time enough for others.

Later, he left a message at Perla's inviting her to come for dinner, and after he picked up Adán from kindergarten, they went to the grocery store, where Adán helped select the dinner items for his aunt Pearl. He let Adán call her whatever he wanted and didn't correct him. Though he had no reason to be, Martín felt exhausted, but there was dinner to make. There were many days ahead. Still, when they got back to the house and before he started dinner, he fished in one of the boxes that he had stashed away in his own bedroom and found a picture of himself and Adrian. He loosened it from the layers and layers of plastic he had wrapped around it, Adrian coming back to light. His mother, upset, would say she could feel a knot in her throat, but the Spanish word meant more: *un nudo*—and then the gesture toward the neck as if to ward off the noose doing the damage. Martín gave the frame a quick swipe with the hem of his shirt and set it on a little table in the living room.

On the day of Adrian's plane trip to Denver, the morning had brought a hard rain to San Francisco. The two of them had shuffled quietly around the apartment, packing Adrian's suitcase. Adrian would return on Monday night if there were no delays—Denver meant the possibility of snow. Adán slept with a raging fever, and for a rare time, it would be Martín taking complete care of him. There would be no driving to the airport, no good-byes with tickets in hand.

That rainy morning, the apartment sat dark. The windows let in a weak light. Adán didn't budge in his sleep, though his face was flushed and his pajama top soaked through with sweat. There was a sticky pink medicine that smelled like citrus.

Martín spent all day in Adán's room with the apartment quiet. He spent the day looking out the window at Coit Tower in the distance and fell into a well of doubt. Adrian was a good man, but he was all his own and not fully Martín's to love. There was a young child here, but he was Adrian's, not his. After years of wishing for a relationship, here it was, but with it came a certain boredom and an isolation. Martín found himself longing for something to change in his life. He thought, for the first time in years, of his father, and in the quiet of the apartment, Martín let himself inch toward understanding him.

Adán's fever broke that afternoon, but he remained sleeping. The daylight stayed the same gray—it was impossible to guess the hour. Martín flipped through four magazines and tried to read a book, until finally the call came from the Denver airport, Adrian's tired voice telling him that he had landed safely. Martín wasn't up for much talk; he wanted to go back to the warm, quiet room of just thinking, of solitude, so they chatted for a minute at most. Monday would come soon enough.

All day it rained. Nothing changed. It rained all day.

2007

Spoken Word Poetry

IT IS NEARLY A REQUIREMENT THAT ANYONE WHO GOES BY THE LABEL "POET" IN the twenty-first century will be called upon to read poetry in public. A category of poets has emerged in which the imperative to read poetry aloud has become the dominant force behind its production rather than an adjunct to the craft of writing. So-called Spoken Word poets take for granted the impetus to read their poetry aloud: it wouldn't exist otherwise. These poets—largely young, urban, and hip, or hip-hop in their sensibilities—are part of an emerging aesthetic that has fit comfortably in the Internet age. Spoken Word poetry is written and occasionally published, but it is primarily performed.

Consciously or otherwise, Spoken Word poets are participating in an ancient tradition. The great poets of ancient Greece chanted or sang their lyrics to audiences. The more formal or orderly works of the Italian and English Renaissance might have led to a conception of poetry as a written art exclusively, and some poets (such as the seventeenth-century British poet George Herbert or the twentieth-century American poet Charles Olson) would play with the visual qualities of their verse on the printed page. Yet the tradition of ballads and popular music in general continued the connection between performance and poetry through the centuries.

It stands to reason, then, that the emphasis in Spoken Word poetry is distinctly on rhythm and on the sound qualities of language. The Beat generation of the 1950s may have set the precedent for the more contemporary tradition of Spoken Word poetry: Allen Ginsberg in particular was a kind of poetic rock star who could draw vast crowds to his poetry readings, which he would sometimes enhance with handheld percussion instruments. Amiri Baraka of the Black Arts movement of the 1960s intensified the tradition, overwhelming his audiences with poems that should be "teeth" and poems that "shoot guns," as he argued in his poem "Black Art." The Nuyorican Poets Café, founded in 1973, was yet another development toward the Spoken Word poets of the late twentieth- and twenty-first centuries. All of these precedents, represented earlier in this volume, provided a venue for disenfranchised or marginalized figures who did not fit comfortably into the American literary establishment. These figures found not only their voice, but a microphone to amplify it.

The aggressiveness of Baraka's poetry is not necessarily a feature of all Spoken Word poetry, but there tends to be a certain attitude evident in most poems of this genre. The poet's personality, or persona, is showcased, and the poet does not shy away from language that is considered offensive, vulgar, or crude. Language itself, particularly the interplay between standard and nonstandard iterations, is also in the spotlight here. The title of Jessica Care Moore's collection *The Words Don't Fit in My Mouth* (from which her poem included here is taken) is a good example. The title poem itself is rife with clever wordplay, as when "Punk u wait" becomes "punctuate," and the poem concerns itself with punctuation, ending with the word "period." It also incorporates French, and Willie Perdomo's "Notes for a Slow Jam" incorporates Spanish. We find Italian in Edwin Torres's "Dig on the Decade," a linguistic tour de force that alludes to Shakespeare (or "Shakes-pois") and the I Ching. This final section contains much that will delight and entertain its readers (or, ideally, listeners), and we see it as a fitting conclusion to our anthology of American literature for many reasons: because it connects to the oral origins of our literary tradition, because it offers a venue for diverse new voices, because it is progressive and affirmative, and because it celebrates both unity and individuality.

D. Quentin Miller
Suffolk University

ISHLE YI PARK
B. 1977

Samchun in the Grocery Store

Last night I walked into a grocery store on East 3rd and Avenue B,
shocked by my uncle's face behind the counter:
Issilah! he smiled, with a broad sweep of arm,
Take anything! in this store that wasn't even his.

I wander a labyrinth of stacked aisles,   5
smell of orange yam meat roasting dark
and sweet as the sight of my samchun: dirty Mets cap,
chipped front tooth, crescent-moon eyes spilling light
over his rough beach of brown skin:

this samchun, who taught me to crack open warm walnuts   10
with my teeth, back cracked from hauling fish-store crate
and fruit carton, spine held stiff with a leather safety belt.

My samchun, hands exploding knife-into-fist,
telling my father: *if you ever hit that woman again*
I chop off both your hands, like this —   15

Samchun. After 26 years, just recently blessed
with a fat-cheeked granddaughter
whose Yi family earlobes
turn up like little buttons ...

A customer enters. Grabs a Hershey bar,   20
a Heineken, a pack of Lucky Strike cigarettes.
Asks, *How much is this? What? How much? Speak English!*
1.19 ... 1.19 ... 1.19, I hiss from behind the rack of Wise chips,
lemonade chilling my palms. I watch a mask eclipse
my samchun's face as he swallows the spit insults,   25
the go-home-chink, speak-English bullshit,
clicked trigger and bullet: I imagine him falling,
snapped neck under cigarette shelves. Fallen,

crushed flower at an altar of jagged store windows,
white picket signs, white arm bands,   30
Latasha Harlins, Soon Ja Du: thick blood
pooling on both sides of the counter ...

I want to run up and bitch slap the man
for disrespecting my uncle, but this is not my battle;
this is just his job.   35

Somewhere, La India streams out an open car window.
Samchun rubs his temples. The customer slaps
silver change on the counter and leaves. Solitude freezes
this store trimmed with icicles and wet, black snow.

Suddenly I know why my love is a clenched fist,   40
why I can only love like this.
Samchun bags my Countrytime Lemonade
and tells me to watch it. Music outside
trails off like torn ribbon —
we hug over the dividing counter   45
as if our lives depend on it.

                                                                            2004

Jejudo Dreams

In Jejudo, there are women who have dived for generations,
scalloping shells off coral reefs
to support their weak, spendthrift husbands
and sustain the island life. These women,
seal smooth with black river hair tied thick   5
into a bun, will, even nine months pregnant,
hold their breath and submerge.

In Queens, I read about them
as if they were not a part of my mother's memory,
as if she never once loved their indecipherable accents   10
thick with the knowledge of water

in a time when wet laundry still slapped on rock —
they skirted her Daegu reality.

I'm drowning in the land to which she swam,
and when I try to speak my language, my tongue   15
flops in my mouth like a dying fish:
desperate, silver, and shining with effort.
These fish line my parents' store shelves,
invade our dreams in huge, peeled-skin schools,
their sour, two-day old smell clings to my mother's   20
woolen sweaters and my father's corduroy pants,
to the dusk of their skin as they watch television.

This smell was my shame growing up,
my secret; the reason I took three showers a day,
got dropped off a block away from school   25
so the Whitestone kids would never know
that my father drove the puke-green van
smelling of fish, so they would never wrinkle
their noses at me and say I smelled like fish,
or dirty women. For fifteen years, I crossed my legs,   30
washed, prayed, hid.

I erased my mother's memories
and replaced them with rote school texts,
learned to be ashamed of my parents,
their accent, to interpret their hard-earned smell   35
as stink, to think diamond-cut eyes undesirable,
some of us trying to Anglicize them
with Elmer's glue or cosmetic surgery . . .

My dongsengs: what are we doing if not quietly, desperately drowning?
Who is here to teach us how to swim?   40
I want to know those Jejudo women
beyond their slick, oceanic fame —
if pollution from Seoul mars their skin,
        if broken shells shrapnel their callused palms,
            if their thighs are as smooth and tight   45
                as taut silk, if their hair ever danced
                    with locks of fresh seaweed,
                        like the lyrics of songs they sing after work,
                            lyrics of songs they hear underwater,
                        if their husbands ever beat them,   50
                    how they cry, how they laugh,
                how they fight,
                        the mottled, murky bayous and lagoons
                            of their dreams.

How it feels ... to hold your breath so long   55
your lungs, on the verge of bursting, steel themselves
while you grab, wrench that thing you need more than air,
and break surface.

There are times when I trivialize these desires,
but at night, I wonder: will my ancestors not hear me when I die?   60
Will they mistake me for a white bakwai ghost
because of my accent? Will all the history I embody
unravel with my time because this tongue
cannot recall the words braided into my bloodline?

These women, who are my women,   65
    these songs, which are my songs ...

In Jejudo, there are women
who have dived for generations,

      they are calling me back to myself,
        the truest, rough coral of myself,   70

      I take a deep breath —

       and I go fish.

I have watched   loved
           wild
           crescent   75
           gutted
                thirsting

with
no words
for all the wars   80
inside me

                      2004

Fort Totten

My grandfather pulls me close to him on the sofa. He smells like old people, but minty also, like mercury balls and Vicks. His knuckles are huge and arthritic, four of them taped over with white bandages. *Issilah*, he croaks in Korean. *Promise me one thing. Yes*, I say, suspicious, *What? Promise me you will only marry Korean. This is my dying wish.* He is solemn, with his gummy face and pleated eyelids, but the old man is slick; he knows what he's doing. *Yes*, I sigh. *I promise.* My father, chewing a ragged string of squid on the floor and watching the Mets game, smiles. *I hear you*, he calls. *Ayu, apa*, I groan, and shove on my Nikes. *I'm going out.*

Little waits for me at the bottom of the hill. I can't have my emo see him while throwing out the trash or watering her window plants. We take the bus to Fort Totten and sit on graffiti-chalked rocks, watching the sun lap over water and old Chinese fisherman with dented buckets, listening to the foot-long rats scurrying through dropped Budweiser cans.

We try to come here as often as possible. The Throggs Neck Bridge is a blue necklace at this time of day, almost blending into the horizon of water and sky.

Walking to Little's apartment in Bushwick means a regular chorus of *pssst china, psst chinitas* for me, girls brushing me on purpose as they pass by. Flushing is a bunch of leathery Chinese men in paint-splattered jeans staring at Little to start a war, staring at me to make me feel dirty.

When something happens, like a girl sucking her teeth at us on the L train, or a man wanting to pick a fight, we head for the beach. Or Flushing Meadow Park. Or here — Fort Totten. Not even on purpose, I think. Our bodies just need respite, open space where strangers are not within two feet. Where we can lay on each other and be a couple, undisturbed, a clear force-field around us blurring the sharp stares, teeth sucks, whispers.

Little is currently residing on his cousin Evette's couch, has been there for the past two months. It's been our bed, our refuge, our boxing ring. Outside, the Dominican sisters on the stoop, fanning their necks.

One night, we are arguing in the kitchen when Evette calls from work. I'm growling at him, spitting words like my father does to my mother — they shoot out of my mouth like lead bullets. We're still going at it, though he's on the phone with her. All of a sudden, she interrupts: *Bitch, who you think you are yelling at my cousin? With your Chinese ass. Can't even talk, ching chong ching chong ching.* I hear her through the phone as Little sits there in the kitchen. *What?* I spit, *What? You heard me,* her tinny voice shouts, louder, through the phone's small receiver. *Ching chong chink.* Little stays silent. I stand there, hands open and limp, unbelieving. She keeps hollering. I pick up my bookbag and stuff my clothes in, grab my coat. Then he hangs up the phone. Only then.

I'm so burnt I can't even think. *You tell that bitch to go fuck her dumb-ass self. Fucking ignorant bitch. Fucking half-Cuban Chinese, Puerto Rican bitch don't even see that she's insulting herself?!* Little is grabbing my arms, trying to calm me down. But I push him off, too disgusted to even punch him.

I sink into a tight square between the wooden bureau and the twin bed, and I don't even know how I start crying. The room is crazy messy, rugby shirts hanging off the backs of chairs, tissues on the floor, a few roaches in an ashtray by the open windowsill. Out in the alley, a man yelling. I can't breathe. I feel small, ugly, and ripped — a punctured balloon inside me, tattered plastic, no air.

For Little, who stayed silent. For Evette, making those noises, hating me, hating herself. And for me, cursing everything. *It was all a lie,* I say, *us driving to cop dimes off Myrtle, staying up to watch Showtime with a sixpack of Coronas, going to the Queens Day parade together. Bullshit. When it comes down to it, you're her cousin, and I'll always be the chink you're with.*

Little is silent, listening. And he will stay silent, because he is afraid to talk back to her, to defend me. *And that*, I spit, *is the biggest disappointment. I always thought you'd have my back, Fuck you, fuck her, fuck this, fuck you, fuck us.*

Little blocks the doorway. The lights are out, and all I see are his wide, remorseful eyes. I don't want to look at them, I'm tired of crying. And I don't want to touch him, I don't want to fight. I just stand in front of him, Jansport in hand, waiting to leave.

He tries to hug me; I shrug him off. He tries again; I slip under every time. *Get the fuck off*, I spit. *You coward.* He backs off, eyes wet. And he says, softly, *What about me? I can't even meet your family. You can't even bring me home.*

He stares at me in the shadowed kitchen. I look away, watch a roach crawl calmly over the lip of a plate. *That's not fair*, I say. *They wouldn't let me bring any guy . . .*

Yeah, he says quietly.

You know how my father is, I start again.

I know, he says.

I glance up at Little, but in my head, I'm back to last Friday in Flushing, when we had taken the 7 train back from the city. The subway was crowded and muggy, bookbags shoved up against my spine. It was a relief to walk up Roosevelt, air cool, hugging each other. We were halfway up the block, past the pizza shop, and Little had me in an affectionate headlock.

In front of me, dangling car keys in shorts and sandals, stood my speechless father. Little offered his hand. My father stared at it for a full minute like it was rotten. I didn't say a word. Something was abandoned there on the corner of Roosevelt and Union, some trust between Little and me. My father and I left. In two years, it was the only time they had ever met.

Is that how you act in the street? My father had hissed in the shadowed van. My hands were shaking, I could only look in my lap. I blurted, *At least you could shake his hand! You couldn't even shake his hand.*

I'm not racist, he'd said to nobody. *I don't care he's black. Puerto Rican*, I spat. *Black, Puerto Rican, whatever. I don't care about anything color*, he continued. *Yeah*, I'd mumbled. *Whatever.*

Remembering this, my arm goes limp and I drop the Jansport on the kitchen linoleum. *I'm so tired*, I say. I want Little to hold me, but I can't say it. *Me too*, he replies. He wipes my chin slowly and I don't stop him. I lean into his palm and kiss it; he pulls me into him. And that's all I want.

The blue of the sky, the water, the beaded necklace of the Throggs Neck Bridge blend into each other. The water by our feet glints, lightly slapping the rock. Around us, the fishermen are staring seaward. A thin mother watches her child jumping cautiously on the rocks. Little touches a smooth stone etched with names: Josephine and Anthony, 1982 — forever. I lean back on him. *This is what I want*, I say, hugging his knees. He is seated behind me; I am between his legs. *What?* he asks. *What?* We both look out into the falling night, the indistinguishable horizon.

2004

Jessica Care Moore
b. 1971

My Caged Bird Don't Sing and Every Black Bird Ain't a Piece of Fried Chicken

To the beauty of Alicia (a.k.a. Blue), Nicole Gilbert, Marnell, Alexis
and all divas that grace the world with their Spirit through songs
no one can ever steal away.

My caged bird don't sing
It cries
Stolen wings can't fly
Cause they took away our music
My caged bird don't sing   5
It cries
Stolen wings can't fly
Cause they took away our music
Makers
Soul takers   10
Turning trees to twigs
Fed us worms from pigs
Robbed our nests
At best
Baby Birds   15
Learn how to fly
Across foreign skies
Make it across
Lost
Millions on that ship   20
With settlers looking like Gilligan
Figuring out ways to steal again
Anotha loafa Sankofa
Word
African Bird   25
Never heard a flock Still in shock
Carrying Glocs
We are the tock of the clock
But we forgot
Planet rocket to the planet rock   30
Don't stop
Don't pass go

Straight to hell
Bird dressed in blue
Locked in a red pod zoo   35
And all the walls were white
Typical African bird plight
Tight as it seems
Bird had those genes
To sing Negro spirituals   40
Dropping bass off her beak
Bellowing beats quite lyrical
Performing miracles
Magnificent enough to rebuild
The walls of Jericho   45
Here we go Here we go
Here we go Here we go
Here we Here we Here we go
DMC and DJ RUN
My caged bird don't sing   50
Cause they took away her drum
Beat
Clawed feet
Leaving droppings on cross burners
Wearing sheets   55
Shackled together
Black tar babies covered in feathers
Wearing America's old past time tether
Didn't make that caged bird sing a thing
But the whole village knew she could play the harmonica   60
With her heart flute
Breathe life into lungs
Make babies come
Still, that caged bird didn't sing a peep
Cause she saw her family moved out like sheep   65
And she recognized the wolves shooting at her feet
Find a way to get a grip
Might fly off this slave ship
Or take the pain of another ass kicking
Sec, every Black bird ain't a piece of fried chicken   70
And every heart beat
I mean drum beat
Heart beat
Drum beat
Heart beat   75
Drum beat

Heart Drum Heart Drum
Heart Heart Drum Drum
DRRRUUMMM
Beat 80
Ain't for sample
Or sale
Well?
Are you men?
Wait 85
Are you birds, or mice?
Vanilla ice ice baby
Caged birds don't sing
They cry
Stolen wings can't fly 90
Cause they took
Away our music

My caged bird don't sing
It cries
Stolen wings can't fly 95
Cause they took away our   music

1997

WILLIE PERDOMO
B. 1967

Notes for a Slow Jam

This is the poem
you always wanted
I've turned into
a fire-can crooner
to sing you this 5
slow jam
a farewell greeting
no sooner than the sun
set on our meeting
I had a song for you 10
but first
I had to sample

from the midnight
quiet storm
break up to make up and   15
make up to break up and
break up to wake up!
I was a three-time loser
persistent fell in
heart over head   20
not even a chance
to carve the initials
of our romance
on the bark of a tree

There was nothing   25
no one left
to point at
and say
"it's all because of you"
so I have an encounter session   30
with the bathroom mirror
the black crescents
that real makeup
under my eyes
couldn't cover   35
the cries
of walking down the street
falling off the peak
of a broken heart binge
had to get high   40
so I buy a bag
to cure my love jones
and soothe my aching bones
I walked into a social club
and found the answer   45
boiling in the juke box—
pick a song—
hip-hoppin' through life
I used to think that salsa
was just for the rice and beans   50
I was wrong
it's a remedy for those
strung-out love fiends
Would you think I was high
if I told you that Tito Rojas   55
was a Greek playwright?

I'm saying that Euripides
sang salsa
for real
check it out   60
the tragic hero
is chillin' on the corner
love epics and shit
spillin' from his mouth
the chorus   65
is on the rooftop
giving echo to his pain
listen to the sound
of a heart breaking

      aye aye aye   70
      aye aye aye
      y dicen que los hombres
      nunca nunca nunca
      deben lloran

      and they say that   75
      the men
      should never never
      cry

I look into the mirror
one more time
before I chase you away   80
and just in case
you don't speak Spanish
I leave you sinking
into some muddy waters   85

      you can't spend what you ain't got
      you can't lose what you ain't never had

My pockets are empty
and I'm letting you go
without a fight
but before you go   90
here's the poem
you always wanted

                1998

PATRICIA SMITH
B. 1955

Asking for a Heart Attack

for Aretha Franklin

Aretha. Deep butter dipped, sorehead pot liquor,
swift lick off the sugar cane. Vaselined knees
clack gospel, hinder the waddling south, retha.
Greased, she glows in limelit circle,
defending her presence with sanctified moon,   5
that ass rumbling toward midnight's neighborhood.

Goddess of Hoppin John and bumped buttermilk,
girl known Jesus by His *first* name.
She was the one sang His drooping down
from that ragged wooden T,   10
dressed Him in blood red and shine,
conked that holy head,
rustled up bus fare
and took the Deity downtown.
They found a neon backslap, coaxed the DJ   15
and slid electric till the lights slammed on.
Don't know where you goin', but you can't stay here.

Aretha taught the Almighty slow, dirty words
for His daddy's handiwork,
laughed as he first sniffed whiskey's surface,   20
hissed him away when he sought to touch His hand
to what was blue in her.
She was young then, spindly and ribs paining
her heartbox suspicious of its key.
So Jesus blessed her, opened her throat   25
and taught her to wail that way she do,
she do wail that way don't she do that wail the way
she do wail that way, don't she?
Now when 'retha's fleeing screech jump from juke
and reach been-done-wrong bone,   30
all the Lord can do is stand at a respectable distance
and applaud. And maybe shield His heart a little.

So you question her several shoulders,
the soft stairs of flesh leading to her chins,
the steel bones of an impossible dress   35
gnawing into bubbling obliques?
Ain't your mama never told you
how black women collect the world,
build other bodies onto their own?
No earthly man knows the solution to our hips,   40
asses urgent as sirens,
titties bursting with traveled roads.
Ask her to tell you what Jesus whispered to her that night
about black girls who grow fat away from everyone
and toward each other.   45

2007

EDWIN TORRES

B. 1958

Dig on the Decade

("glue perpetuatin' myth"... so said Shakes-Pois)

chilleeeee-moholeeeee-eddieeeee-yahhhhh-GO! GO! GO!
Gusting, weeping, sorrow, sweeping, boyeeeee-gooooo-YAH! YAH! YAH!
Go-Gopher Slash - tuff cyber kick - ruffle -tuff-f-f-f-f-f-f-f-f-h-h-h-h-h . . .

These are my sweeping visions of exactitude, dude!
Dig on the decade, Mother Cycle/Motor Rever, brother blow the b-boy
   down with bebop.
Move-on-OTHER! Over-revved REVVER!
I gotta maddening pace to keep, do *you get-so*, the vision of my sweep . . .?

Seek three thicknesses of mist.
But give it up on the one . . . nine plus the one-oh, I ni-ni-nine-one oh, tie
   my eyes blind,
both down plus one minus one, mine one, one oh ni sweep this cycle, past
   visions reved-isions.
Dig on this decadence—shooting by infant mortality's roaring motherhood.
Swerve by screaming baby air-sirens, baby air-moans. Give it up on the one
   one,

oh, I ni ni, gotta gotta, fligger that Mau-Mau, mommy's gotta Gun-Gun!
  Royal Badness, Dude!
Sweeping sapling exactitude! A mule ... afloatin' in the mist, follows:

  Yo, Sap! The burro giddy, ap-ap, chappy-pap-pap ... Gopher Slash,
    Pop tuff cyber kick it
  higher. Tufted-ruffle-f-f-f-l-f-l-f-h-h-h! SWELL-mire, through
    FLANKS-falloped,
  through FIELDS-allopian, Mother Horse Barreled Brightness, your
    kickstart's gonna
  eat me alive if I let it ... and we all want to be eaten alive
    sometimes, don't we?
  Well do not, I repeat, DO NOT look now, because I know the guy
    with the big eyes
  who's been looking at you   ... I s'eem m'eyes inna temple ...

I reached for your eyes, with one hand.
Holding on to the HOUR of the word, with the other.
The pow-Pow-POW-OW!-Ow-ower of this, sweeping blindness.
This fire that breeds contempt for sparks stillborn.
This countryscape.
This decadence of soil.   ... fire breath in the shiny rain ...

Vision becomes a blur to society.
"A BUTT-WAG ... TO THE FACE OF SOCIETY!"
He is her BONER to society.
NINE becomes a rounded tail ... bone-thrown-to-dog.
ONE becomes a hounded throne ... ohhhh ...
Let round GO to tail, oh, one ni-nine twice over-revved-revving-OTHER!
Your revved-isioning reach, comes to each one. Fall into that brightness
    between silence and sun.
Step off, on the girl-up down, on the one .... on the decade,
    Mother Cycle ...

  Chilly Moholy, ten to the one and oh.
  Mo-Fa-Si-Bro down, with calendrical no-no.
  Chilly Moholy, twelve to the one and two.
  Donkey gone down, with elliptical boo-boo.

Explodable choo-choo, go to town GO-GO-MEZ! Mex-Crispies.
Olive peas plodding explosivity pits.
A reverb-down with Cousin It—it's so (whoosh) ...

I GOTTA MADDENING PACE TO KEEP! DO YOU *GET-SO* MY,
SWEEP!?!
Look at me! LOOK AT ME! Take-my-thumb-out-of-your-mouth-and-
LOOK-AT-ME!!!
'Cause I KNOW the guy with the big eyes who's been lookin' at you.
*bare ... skin ... back .... my patience ...... your bridle ......
... riiiiiide ...*

My blood-color-roar looks good in t-shirts. But I haven't the muscle to
wear, on my sleeve,
a tattoo of love-philosophy that suckles my gorilla-zit-knuckle-monkey-
wrench despair ...
a testament to this "Decade of Androgo-Me" ... forever, for all to see.
My country on my skin, etched in mother-land-hot-rod-blood-red ...
that ... I don't have.
Dig it, I don't have that *lip-dangle-exhaust* that spurts out shaved-head
gyzmatics.

I don't have that *swagger* that shows I've been working on a '58
Flyboy-Blackeye-Turbo-Heart
that jumpstarts like Black-on-Eyed-Peas.
My hair *doesn't* grease back *that* way, it's too thick, too Latin.

Mo-Fa-Si-Bro-Holy-Yo-Soy ... AMMA-RICAN,
diggin' on this SWEEPIN' vision.   *... ojo mio motro mio ho ...*

When you talk to me, I can hear the light that comes from your ears.
When you look at me, my glasses become perpetual goggles,
AS IF I were trying to achieve that "look" of Cycle Revving Decadence!
Mine eyes have seen a wall ... between the gory and the home,
and my blindness gets in the way of your sight ... and I like that.
My poem becomes my hot rod.

OOOHH, *Gopher Cy Kick, gets clocked by a dis!*
Rev-revving Rev-Revver into Body-Sweeping-Kiss!
Get down on the one, (kiss, kiss, kiss)
Get down on the one, (hummm, hummm, hummm)
Get down on the one, Girl Up, on the NI-NI-NINE. Slow, slow,
stop. YO-YO
S T O P . . . I G O T T A D R I N K T H I S I N . . .
I gotta lather you up with my, acetylene-torch sincerity.
A blur of liquid coming down, decades' ladder.   *... water feels up*
fall your legs feel ...

I gotta believe in this God. E. Dog world.
In the hideous gesture of unrealized dreams,
and the should've beens that never will *because* of their dreams.
I gotta dig on the decade, 'cause the year was a blur.
Mine eyes have seen ... the chapped lips of void kissing areola's
    perception, I think ...

Cycle Mother Horse Barreled Brightness,
diggin' her spurs into my vision, again.
I reached through the mist, for the dusk of your sweat,
and found that I fine-tune poems better than hot rods.

I soar ...
hawk-estic virtues that swim butterfly strokes formed by filly-whipped talons.
Saplin' Burro-iddyap o'er me, homey! It is the east, and Chilly says it best:

    Chilly Moholy says, *"Love that culee culee."*
    Chilly Moholy says, *"Love it all the time."*
    Chilly Moholy says, *"Love that culee culee, 'cause there ain't no*
        other booty
    that can boop like mine, boop-boop like mine,
    boop-boop-ba-boop-ba-boop-baba-boop-boop ...."

Baby Air-Moan Siren screams for his "two am" feeding his, "who-I-am"
    feeding,
as he rides that donkey, hoo follow the flicks of fluff floatin' his eyes, s'eem?
Whacha'kin toll, fitchk ciant floa' a devil winnga polamina-annjell.
S'eem, wi coll hiim a-floater. Iin hees eyes, he folio the fleeks 'n fluff 'n tuff-
    ruffle-fluff-ov hees eyes .... as heem *ride-dat-ASS!*
Baby Air Siren .... we call him a floater, riding on that ASS!

Hey, behhh-boo-baba-baby, POP That Jazz!
BRIDE that Ass,
Is the put-together, A-meeee-rica, A-meee-rica!
My country tis of me!
As is the put-down id ... Amma-rican, Amma-rican!
And MY country is full of me's!

Y'see ... yo soy speekin' HOMO-SAY-P'EON, Psyco-Sexual Satis-
FAC-SHON!
Giddy-YAPP-ON Hetero-Traction ... Chilly-Foal-Filly-Hill-Coal-
Muzzle-Stang-Breath-Nostril-Beast-Witha-Big- Eyes-Been-Lookin-At-You,
Sweet Beauty Caballo ... Mi High-Steppin-Abuello-Steed, NINE-Hands-
Tall-BIG-Balled-Chapped, LIP-Is-On-Stalin, I-Flipped-On-The-Battle-
An-Weeped-On-The-Sapien-*SWEEPING*-The-Sapien-Down-To-The-

Ground. Clocking-One. Killing-One. Gusting-To-Gust-In-Nomadic-No-
Matter ... I gotta maddening ... (*whoosh*) ...

... and I just wanna hold you ... I reached, round your neck ... to, you
    know, fine-tune this, poem ...
... so the mother s-i-n-g-s ...

WHEW!!! I just had a Super-Psypo-Hyper-Mono-Filetero-Meeo-Trilly-
Yac-Psyche-Out-Sapplin-Burro-Giddy-Mundo ... Pom-Pom-Home-
Home-Ni-Ni-Gotta-Gotta-Fligger-that-Mau-Mau-Mommy's-Gotta-Gun-
Gun ... De-JA-VOLT!

Dig THAT decade, Mother Cycle!
GROOM THAT MARE!! BRIDE THAT ASS!-homey, Ah kissed that,
ASS The only NOT what you can do,
where only the put-down-put-put-choo-choo GO to town.
Baby, My country is a "tis of me," and I can grow up to be what I want
    to be!
And I can believe in a GOD.E.DOGGY.DADDY if I want it to be.
And I can bow-wow the people into the pow-wowing vision, of my sweep!
The ow-OW-HOUR of the word, is upon us ... perpetuatin' myth, so said
    Shakes-pois:
    M'lady, Doth Mi Romp Ingcite Ye? ... P'WAAAAN!!! ...
    Doos Mi Cycle TWAANG Fantasies 'Pon Thou Whip-ped, Strap-ped,
        Leather Boot-Butt?
    Wouldst Fire Breathe In Misted Shine? Couldst itchit phlegm noggitt
        in dissin' thine?
    Gopher Cy Kik, Askin' Ye DIS Quere:

"How many ruffle-tuff-fuckers-inna-motherfuckin-woodchuck-
    chuckin-truck-chuck-woolerin
wooly-paaaaaat-say-jackin' ... (*whoosh*) ... BAAA-AA-AAW-AAW-HEE-
    HAW-HEE-HAW—YAHOOOO—
ALL ABOARD!!!!"
YAHHHHH ... GO!. GO!. GO!.
MO-FA-
SI-BRO-
HOIY, *YO*, ALGA-RIN*DO*, HOL-MANO*LO*-ISANDO,
NE-ANO, PRAHA-SIN-SON, PA*IS*-AÑO, PAYA, PATRA, RINCON-
    NNNNN ...

    ... *hmmmmmmm ... hmmmmmmmm*
    ... *hmmmmmmm ... hmmmmmmmm* ...

S'il viento se presenta vani . . .
co viento siempre sensa vani . . .
co supre sopla sinz facil . . .
supre sopla sinz facil . . .
. . . hmmmmmmm . . . hmmmmmmm . . .

e herra mi bodi fi two . . . hear nine tunes fine . . . thres thri
   thicknessi . . . o . . . mi otro . . . smia patre . . .
n I hear a fine-tuned hummm . . . in the mist . . .

     sun
     he risks risin'
     sings one
     in seeks
     in comes
     sun
     seekin' one

Holdin' two thicknesses of mist,
Gopher Slash Tuff Cyber kicks it into high NI-NI-TWO—but gives it up
   on the one.
3 minus ni to the *oh mine is ni-i-ice. . .*
Wavin' a *"LATER"* he passes
the herd grazing in the mist and splits, a gusting whoosh of his own
   tomorrows.

And like loins on cool safire, you bride the wind.
Like that Girl Up Souped Up Hyper Shot BIG STUFF Boy . . . .
   you come . . . to reach one . . .
     water
     the water feels
     your blur
     falls

The sweep of my vision . . . riiiiides, afloatin' een the eye-fluffs offa bloody
   mule.
Dig on the burial of decadence . . . *33 crystalmassen das dappybeat . . .*

Groom the ass with beatiletto heels, Mother Cycle . . . Epic Mecca . . .
   Terra Revver . . .
Your revved-isioning-reach, comes to reach one.
Silence the brightening fall, my sweet one.
Quicken the quieting dark, by sleep.
One leaps and hopes to keep one reach.
By sweeps, my sweat, for you, grows deep.

forever
for all to see
my body sings my
culture swings
in me
. . .

The frenetics of an energy   The symphonias of a moment   The artsism of a
    poetrics
The language of the incoherents   The understandings of a naivete sophisticat
    i-ching
The lunatic musics of bug   The plain folk   i-wonder
The realization of a cinematics   The arm   The clockwatch   The donkey
    The baby
The portals of all things   The falling of all dreams
The eyes are in the temple   The eyes are in the temple

1994

SAUL STACEY WILLIAMS
B. 1972

Gypsy Girl

and she doesn't want to press charges
my yellow cousin
ghost of a gypsy
drunk off the wine of pressed grapes
repressed screams   5
of sun shriveled raisins
and their dreams
interrupted
by a manhood deferred

Will she ever sober?   10
Or will they keep handing her glasses
overflowing with the burden of knowing?

I never knew
never knew it would haunt me
the ghost of a little girl   15
in the desolate mansion
of my manhood

I'm a man, now
and then I remember
that I have been charged   20
by one million volts of change

Will the ghost of that little girl
ever meet my little girl?
She's one now
she must have been three then   25
maybe four

she's eighteen now
I'm twenty-five now
I must have been twelve then
my mother said he was in his thirties   30

and she's not pressing charges
although she's been indicted
and I can't blame her
I can't calm her
I want to calm her   35

I want to call him names
but only mine seems to fit
"come on, let's see if it fits"
two little boys
with a magic marker   40
marked her
and it won't come out
"they put it in me"
"no we didn't"
"what are you talking about?"   45
"it's not permanent"
"it will come out when you wash it"
damn maybe it was permanent
'cause I can't forget
and I hope she don't remember   50

maybe magic marked her
lord, I hope he don't pull no dead rabbits out of that hat
What she gonna do then?
And what was Mary's story?

The story of a little girl   55
a brother
and couch
she's got a brother
a couch
a sister locked in a bedroom   60
and a mother on vacation
lord, don't let her fall asleep
her brother's got keys to her dreams
he keeps them on a chain
that now cuffs his wrists together   65
mommy doesn't believe he did it
but he's left footprints
on the insides of his sister's eyelids
and they've learned to walk without him
and haunt her daily prayers   70
and if you run your fingers
ever so softly on her inner thigh
she'll stop you
having branded your fingertips
with the footprints of her brother   75
the disbelief of her mother
and her sister who called her a slut for sleeping

lord, I've known sleeping women

women who've slept for lives at a time
on sunny afternoons   80
and purple evenings
women who sleep sound
and live silently
some dreams never to be heard of again

I've known sleeping women   85

and have learned to tiptoe into their aroma
and caress myself
they've taught me how to sleep

having swallowed the moon
sleep til midafternoon   90
and yearn for the silence of night
to sleep sound once again

painters of the wind
who know to open the windows
before closing their eyes   95
finding glory in the palette of their dreams

she had no dreams that night
the windows had been closed
the worlds of her subconscious suffocated
and bled   100
rivets of unanticipated shivers and sounds
that were not sleep

she was sound asleep
and he came silently
it wasn't the sun in her eyes   105
nor the noise of children en route to school
she woke to the swollen rays of an ingrown sun
fungused
that stung more than it burned:
a saddened school en route to children   110
who dared to sleep on a couch
exposed to the schizophrenic brother
only to wake with a new personality
one that doesn't trust as much as it used to
and wears life jackets into romantic relationships   115
can't stand the touch of fingertips
damn, was that marker permanent?
I hope she don't press charges

I hope they don't press no more grapes into wine
because she might get drunk again   120
and fall asleep

Rise and Shine
my mother used to say
pulling buck the clouds of covers
that warmed our night   125
but the fleshy shadows
of that moonless night
stored the venom in its fangs
to extinguish the sun

Rise and Shine   130

but how can I?
When I have crusted cloud configurations
pasted to my thighs
and snow covered mountains in my memories
they peak into my daily mode   135
and structure my moments
they hide in the corners of my smile
and in the shadows of my laughter
they've stuffed my pillows
with the overexposed reels of ABC after-school specials   140
and the feathers of woodpeckers
that bore hollows into the rings of time
and now ring my eyes
and have stumped the withered trunk of who I am

I must re member   145
my hands have been tied behind the back
of another day
if only I could have them long enough
to dig up my feet which have been planted
in the soiled sheets   150
of a harvest that only hate could reap

I keep trying to forget
but I must re member
to gather the severed continents
of a self once whole   155
before they plant flags
and boundary my destiny
push down the wafted mountains
that blemish this soiled soul
before the valleys of my conscience   160
get the best of me
I'll need a passport
just to simply reach the rest of me
a vaccination
for a lesser god's bleak history   165

                                                    1998

TRACIE MORRIS
B. 1968

Project Princess

Teeny feet rock
layered double socks
Popping side piping of
many colored loose lace ups

Racing toe keeps up with fancy free gear   5
slick slide and just pressed recently weaved hair

Jeans oversized belie her hips, back, thighs
that have made guys sigh
for milleni year

Topped by attractive jacket   10
her suit's not for flacking, flunkies, junkies
or punk homies on the stroll.

Her hands mobile thrones of today's urban goddess
Clinking rings link dragon fingers
no need to be modest.   15

One or two gap teeth coolin'
sport gold initials
Doubt you get to her name
just check from the side
please chill.   20

Multidimensional shrimp earrings
frame her cinnamon face
Crimson with a compliment if a
comment hits the right place

Don't step to the plate   25
with datelines from '88
Spare your simple, fragile feelings
with the same sense that you came

1994

ACKNOWLEDGMENTS

Sherman Alexie. "What You Pawn I Will Redeem," from *Ten Little Indians*. Copyright © 2003 by Sherman Alexie. Used by permission of Grove/Atlantic, Inc.

Dorothy Allison. "Don't Tell Me You Don't Know," from *Trash* by Dorothy Allison (Ithaca, NY: Firebrand Books, 1988). Copyright © 1988 Dorothy Allison from *Trash*, reprinted by permission of The Frances Golden Literary Agency.

Rudolfo A. Anaya. Excerpt from *Bless Me, Ultima*. Copyright © Rudolfo Anaya 1974. Published in hardcover and mass market paperback by Warner Books Inc., 1994; originally published by TQS Publications. Reprinted by permission of Susan Bergholz Literary Services, New York, NY, and Lamy, NM. All rights reserved.

Gloria Anzaldúa. "Entering into the Serpent" and "La Conciencia De La Mestiza/ Towards a New Consciousness," from *Borderlands/La Frontera: The New Mestiza*. Copyright © 1987, 1999 by Gloria Anzaldúa. Reprinted by permission of Aunt Lute Books.

Rane Arroyo. "My Transvestite Uncle Is Missing," by Rane Arroyo, from *The Singing Shark* by Rane Arroyo, Bilingual Press/Editorial Bilingüe, 1996, Tempe, Arizona. "Caribbean Braille," from *Pale Ramón* (Cambridge, MA: Zoland Books, 1998). Reprinted by permission of the literary estate of the author. "Write What You Know" and "That Flag," from *Home Movies of Narcissus* by Rane Arroyo. Copyright © 2002 Rane Arroyo. Reprinted by permission of the University of Arizona Press.

John Ashbery. "The Instruction Manual," from *Some Trees* by John Ashbery. Copyright © 1956 by John Ashbery. Reprinted by permission of Georges Borchardt, Inc., on behalf of the author. "Farm Implements and Rutabagas in a Landscape," from *The Double Dream of Spring* by John Ashbery. Copyright © 1966,

1970 by John Ashbery. Reprinted by permission of Georges Borchardt, Inc., on behalf of the author. "As You Came from the Holy Land," from *Self-Portrait in a Convex Mirror* by John Ashbery. Copyright © 1973 by John Ashbery. Used by permission of Viking Penguin, a division of Penguin Group (USA) Inc.

Jimmy Santiago Baca. "I've Taken Risks," "I Put on My Jacket," "Commitment," and "Ghost Readings in Sacramento," from *Set This Book on Fire!* (Cedar Hill Publications, 2001). Grateful acknowledgement to Cedar Hills Books for permission to reprint Jimmy Santiago Baca's poems.

James Baldwin. "Sonny's Blues," copyright © 1957 by James Baldwin, originally published in Partisan Review. Copyright renewed. Collected in *Going to Meet the Man*, published by Vintage Books. Reprinted by arrangement with the James Baldwin Estate.

Toni Cade Bambara. "My Man Bovanne," from *Gorilla, My Love* by Toni Cade Bambara, pp. 3–10. Published by Vintage Books, a division of Random House, New York. Copyright © 1960, 1963, 1964, 1965, 1968, 1970, 1971, 1972 by Toni Cade Bambara.

Dennis Banks. "Ojibwa Warrior," from *Ojibwa Warrior: The Autobiography of Dennis Banks* by Dennis Banks, pp. 32–42. Copyright © 2005. Reproduced with permission of University of Oklahoma Press in the format Textbook via Copyright Clearance Center.

Amiri Baraka. "An Agony. As Now," "Ka 'Ba," "Black People: This Is Our Destiny," "A Poem Some People Will Have to Understand," "Numbers, Letters," and "Dutchman and the Slave," reprinted by permission of SLL/Sterling Lord Literistic, Inc. Copyright © by Amiri Baraka.

John Barth. "Lost in the Funhouse," copyright © 1967 by The Atlantic Monthly

Jamaica Kincaid. Reprinted by permission of Farrar, Straus and Giroux, LLC.

Martin Luther King, Jr. "I Have a Dream" and "Letter from Birmingham Jail," reprinted by arrangement with The Heirs to the Estate of Martin Luther King Jr., c/o Writers House as agent for the proprietor New York, NY. Copyright © 1963 Dr. Martin Luther King Jr., copyright renewed © 1991 Coretta Scott King.

Maxine Hong Kingston. "No Name Woman," from *The Woman Warrior* by Maxine Hong Kingston. Copyright © 1975, 1976 by Maxine Hong Kingston. Used by permission of Alfred A. Knopf, a division of Random House, Inc.

Etheridge Knight. "The Idea of Ancestry," "The Violent Space," "Ilu, the Talking Drum," and "A Poem for Myself," from *The Essential Etheridge Knight*, by Etheridge Knight. Copyright © 1986. Reprinted by permission of the University of Pittsburgh Press.

Yusef Komunyakaa. "TuDo Street," "Prisoners," "Thanks," "Facing It," and "Fog Galleon," from *Pleasure Dome: New and Collected Poems.* Copyright © 2001 by Yusef Komunyakaa. Reprinted by permission of Wesleyan University Press.

Jhumpa Lahiri. "When Mr. Pirzada Came to Dine," from *Interpreter of Maladies* by Jhumpa Lahiri. Copyright © 1999 by Jhumpa Lahiri. Reprinted by permission of Houghton Mifflin Harcourt Publishing Company. All rights reserved.

Tato Laviera. "Frio" is reprinted with permission from the publisher of *La Carreta Made a U-Turn* by Tato Laviera. Copyright © 1992 Arte Publico Press, University of Houston. "AmeRican" is reprinted with permission from the publisher of *AmeRican* by Tato Laviera. Copyright © 2003 Arte Publico Press, University of Houston. "Latero Story (can pickers)" is reprinted with permission from the publisher of *Mainstream Ethics* by Tato Laviera. Copyright © 1998 Arte Publico Press, University of Houston.

Chang-Rae Lee. "Coming Home Again," published in *The New Yorker*, October 6, 1995, pp. 164–168. Reprinted by permission of International Creative Management, Inc. Copyright © 1995 by Chang-Rae Lee.

Li-Young Lee. "I Ask My Mother to Sing," from *Rose.* Copyright © 1986 by Li-Young Lee. Reprinted with the permission of The Permissions Company, Inc. on behalf of BOA Editions, Ltd., www.boaeditions.org. "My Father, in Heaven, Is Reading Out Loud," "With Ruins," and "This Room and Everything in It," from *The City in Which I Love You.* Copyright © 1990 by Li-Young Lee. Reprinted with the permission of The Permissions Company, Inc. on behalf of BOA Editions, Ltd., www.boaeditions.org.

Denise Levertov. "Overheard over S. E. Asia," from *Poems 1968–1972*, by Denise Levertov. Copyright © 1972 by Denise Levertov. Reprinted by permission of New Directions Publishing Corp. "In Thai Binh (Peace) Province," "Fragrance of Life, Odor of Death," "A Poem at Christmas, 1972, during the Terror-Bombing of North Vietnam," from *The Freeing of the Dust*, by Denise Levertov. Copyright © 1975 by Denise Levertov. Reprinted by permission of New Directions Publishing Corp.

Philip Levine. "Coming Home, Detroit, 1968," "The Rats," "The Everlasting Sunday," from *Not This Pig.* Copyright © 1968 by Philip Levine. Reprinted by permission of Wesleyan University Press. "The Simple Truth," from *The Simple Truth* by Philip Levine. Copyright © 1994 by Philip Levine. Used by permission of Alfred A. Knopf, a division of Random House, Inc. "The Lesson," from *Breath: Poems* by Philip Levine. Copyright © 2004 by Philip Levine. Used by permission of Alfred A. Knopf, a division of Random House, Inc.

Audre Lorde. "Power" and "Never Take Fire from a Woman," from *The Black Unicorn* by Audre Lorde. Copyright © 1978 by Audre Lorde. Used by permission of W. W. Norton & Company, Inc. "The Art of Response" and "Stations," from *Our Dead behind Us* by Audre Lorde. Copyright © 1986 by Audre Lorde. Used by permission of W. W. Norton & Company, Inc. "The Master's Tools Will Never Dismantle the Master's House," reprinted with permission from *Sister Outsider* by Audre Lorde. Copyright © 1984, 2007 by Audre Lorde. Crossing Press, Berkeley, CA, www.tenspeed .com. Used by permission of Regula Noetzli Literary Agency.

Index of Authors, Titles, and First Lines of Poems

LIST OF AUTHORS

Alexie, Sherman
Allison, Dorothy
Anaya, Rudolfo A.
Anzaldúa, Gloria
Arroyo, Rane
Ashbery, John

Baca, Jimmy Santiago
Baldwin, James
Bambara, Toni Cade
Banks, Dennis
Baraka, Amiri
Barry, Lynda
Barth, John
Barthelme, Donald
Baudrillard, Jean
Beattie, Ann
Bechdel, Alison
Bellow, Saul
Bishop, Elizabeth
Blaeser, Kimberly
Bly, Robert
Boudin, Kathy
Boyle, T. C.
Brooks, Gwendolyn
Burns, Diane

Carver, Raymond
Cervantes, Lorna Dee
Cheever, John
Chin, Frank
Cisneros, Sandra
Clifton, Lucille
Cofer, Judith Ortiz
Combahee River Collective
Creeley, Robert
Cruz, Víctor Hernández

Danticat, Edwidge
DeLillo, Don
Deloria, Vine
Díaz, Junot
Dimock, Wai Chee
Dunn, Stephen

Eggers, Dave
Ellison, Ralph
Erdoes, Richard
Erdrich, Louise
Espada, Martin

Everett, Percival

Ferlinghetti, Lawrence
Forché, Carolyn
Ford, Richard
Frazer, Brenda

Gaines, Ernest J.
Ginsberg, Allen
Goldman, Francisco

Hagedorn, Jessica
Hahn, Kimiko
Harjo, Joy
Harper, Michael S.
Hayden, Robert
Hayslip, Le Ly
Henry, Gordon
Herr, Michael
Hongo, Garrett Kaoru

Inada, Lawson Fusao

Jen, Gish
Johnson, Joyce
Jordan, June

Kerouac, Jack
Kincaid, Jamaica
King, Jr., Martin Luther
Kingston, Maxine Hong
Knight, Etheridge
Komunyakaa, Yusef

Lahiri, Jhumpa
Laviera, Tato
Lee, Chang-rae
Lee, Li-Young
Levertov, Denise
Levine, Philip
Lorde, Audre
Lowell, Jr., Robert
Lum, Wing Tek

Mailer, Norman
Malamud, Bernard
Malcolm X
Marshall, Paule
Martínez, Demetria
Mason, Bobbie Ann